THE ECONOMICS OF
JOHN MAYNARD KEYNES

The Theory of a Monetary Economy

John Maynard Keynes

(1883-1946)

THE ECONOMICS OF
JOHN MAYNARD KEYNES

The Theory of a Monetary Economy

by

DUDLEY DILLARD

PROFESSOR OF ECONOMICS
UNIVERSITY OF MARYLAND

PRENTICE-HALL, INC.
Englewood Cliffs, N. J.

PRENTICE-HALL ECONOMICS SERIES
E. A. J. JOHNSON, Editor

FIRST PRINTING .... OCTOBER 1948

SECOND PRINTING ...... FEBRUARY 1949

THIRD PRINTING .... AUGUST 1949

FOURTH PRINTING .... JUNE 1952

FIFTH PRINTING .... JUNE 1953

SIXTH PRINTING .... MAY 1955

SEVENTH PRINTING .... JUNE 1957

EIGHTH PRINTING ....APRIL 1958

NINTH PRINTING .... JANUARY 1960

PRINTED IN THE UNITED STATES OF AMERICA
23110

To

LOUISA

My wife and colleague

Preface

THIS BOOK is an exposition of the economics of John Maynard
Keynes. By any test, Keynes ranks as one of the great economists of all time and as the most influential economic thinker
the twentieth century has so far produced. His book, *The
General Theory of Employment, Interest and Money,* published in 1936, has already become one of the classics of economic thought. Unfortunately for the undergraduate and for
the general reader, the *General Theory* is addressed to professional economists and is not very intelligible to others.
However, the fundamental ideas underlying Keynes' work are
relatively simple and can be understood by anyone who is
acquainted with broad problems of economic policy such as
unemployment and inflation.

The present discussion of the economics of Keynes focuses
on the forces which determine the volume of effective demand,
an insufficiency of which leads to unemployment, and an excess of which causes inflation. The plan has been to follow the
outline of the *General Theory* and to bring in at appropriate
points the other aspects of Keynes' work which contribute to
his fundamental position. Restatements and modifications
made by Keynes in articles after 1936 have been incorporated
into his general theory, with the last statement being taken as
definitive. The chapter on war and postwar inflation is based
mainly on Keynes' *How to Pay for the War* (1940). In the
concluding chapter, an interpretation is given of the meaning
and significance of Keynes' entire contribution to economic
theory and policy.

The subject matter of this book is the economics of Keynes
rather than Keynesian economics. The distinction is important. In recent years the scientific, as well as the not-so-scien-

tific, literature in economics has been filled with books and articles refining, enlarging, criticizing, and "refuting" what is now commonly referred to as "The New Economics." The positive contributions of others in this vast literature are important, but in a book of this size and type it is not possible to encompass the field of discussion and controversy. The basic idea behind this book is the need for a simple and thorough exposition of the ideas of the one man who stands out above all others as the chief architect of "The New Economics." The extent to which Keynes dominates recent developments in economics is indicated by the fact that "The Keynesian Revolution" is a synonym for "The New Economics." Occasionally in the text and in footnotes, some of the more important extensions and refinements of Keynes' work have been introduced, but there is no systematic attempt to survey the supplementary literature or to interpret the numerous debates which have centered around Keynes. For the benefit of readers who wish to pursue these issues further, a list of suggested readings is included for each chapter, as well as a bibliography of Keynes' own writings at the end of the book.

Perhaps the chief task which confronts a writer who attempts to simplify and clarify economic theory is to discover a method which will give concrete meaning to the abstract concepts which constitute the theory. Arithmetical examples, diagrams, and summaries are all useful, but they are not enough. From a pedagogical as well as from other points of view, I am thoroughly convinced that Keynes' theories are most easily understood when they are related to the policies with which they were associated in his thinking, especially since Keynes' ideas were always oriented toward positive policy. Keynes did not forge new tools of analysis just for the love of tool-making. His ideas are operationally significant and have been translated into action by statesmen. The meaning of his abstract theory is to be discovered on the solid ground of economic policy, that is, in terms of its consequences when put into practice. Hence, if there is anything distinctive about this presentation, it is the self-conscious manner in which I have attempted to explain the somewhat complicated and, in many respects, intrinsically difficult body of theory by linking it to the policies which Keynes advocated.

Although the Keynesian tools of analysis are now being incorporated into the new principles of economics, this does not involve an acceptance of Keynes' practical policy or social philosophy. The concepts developed by Keynes are not limited to the uses to which he put them. They have proven useful tools for others with different ideas about policy. Nevertheless, it should be recognized that in the larger sense, the tools of analysis which economists use are never divorced entirely from their preferences with respect to policy. People with widely differing social philosophies make use of quite different tools. Those who believe firmly in the laissez-faire premise that the economic system of private property is self-adjusting at full employment without inflation have no positive use for most of the tools of analysis forged by Keynes. Therefore, it seems safe to conclude that the widespread acceptance of Keynes' theory is an indication of a declining faith among economists and others in the automatic, self-adjusting nature of our economic system.

Despite the widespread acceptance of his ideas, Keynes was and remains a controversial figure. In so far as matters of controversy touch the present volume, it is what would probably be called "sympathetic" to Keynes. In my judgment, a good exposition of any economist's work should be sympathetic in order to be understanding and illuminating. However, I am not unaware of Keynes' shortcomings as an expounder of the ideas of people of whom he was critical and of his impatience for detail. Keynes was an original thinker in the sense that he arrived at his ideas in his own way. The ideas he advanced were his own even though someone else may have expounded the same or similar ideas at an earlier date. For this as well as for other reasons, no attempt is made to trace the antecedents of Keynes' ideas either as they relate

to heterodox predecessors on the principle of effective demand
or to the more contemporary Anglo-Saxon and Swedish writers on monetary theory. Much more important than the influence of other people was the influence of historical circumstances in leading Keynes to his new theory. To explain this
is one of the main purposes of the final chapter. In connection
with Keynes' criticisms of what he called "classical" economics, especially the work of Professor Pigou, it should be
observed that Keynes was prone to state his case strongly in
order to lend clarity and persuasiveness to his position.

My concentrated attention was first directed to Keynes by
the late Professor Leo Rogin of the University of California,
who from the beginning recognized the revolutionary significance of the *General Theory*. Professor Rogin's untimely
death is an irreparable loss to the economics profession, which
has been deprived of one of its great minds.

The present volume was written at the suggestion of Dr.
E. A. J. Johnson of New York University and editor of the
Prentice-Hall Economics Series.

I wish to express my sincere gratitude to all who have assisted in the preparation of this book. Dr. Allan G. Gruchy
of the University of Maryland, Dr. H. Gordon Hayes of Ohio
State University, Dr. Everett E. Hagen formerly of the Bureau
of the Budget and now of the University of Illinois, and Dr.
Paul A. Samuelson of the Massachusetts Institute of Technology have read the manuscript and made valuable suggestions for its improvement. Special acknowledgment is made
to Dr. Gruchy for his keen criticisms and stimulating counsel
throughout the entire period of preparation of this book. His
generous assistance and valuable suggestions are deeply
appreciated. I am grateful to Willard O. Ash of the University
of Maryland for helpful suggestions regarding Chapter 5.
Most of all, I am indebted to my wife, Louisa Gardner Dillard, for invaluable assistance at every stage in every detail in
organizing, writing, typing, checking footnotes, preparing
bibliography, and reading proof. As a small token of my

appreciation for all she has done, this book is dedicated to her.

Harcourt, Brace and Company, the American publishers of Keynes' works, have kindly granted permission for use of quotations, especially from *The General Theory of Employment, Interest and Money*. The page numbers inserted parenthetically in the text refer to the *General Theory* unless otherwise indicated by the context. Appreciation is expressed to *The Journal of Economic History* for the use of part of my article, "The Pragmatic Bases of Keynes' Political Economy."

Dudley Dillard

Table of Contents

CONTENTS

List of Figures

List of Tables

THE ECONOMICS OF
JOHN MAYNARD KEYNES
The Theory of a Monetary Economy

CHAPTER 1

Introduction and Fundamental Ideas

> I am more attached to the comparatively simple funda-
> mental ideas which underlie my theory than to the par-
> ticular forms in which I have embodied them . . . .
>
> J. M. Keynes, *The Quarterly Journal of Economics*,
> February, 1937, page 211.

WITHIN the first dozen years following its publication, John
Maynard Keynes' *The General Theory of Employment, Interest and Money* (1936) has had more influence upon the
thinking of professional economists and public policy makers
than any other book in the whole history of economic thought
in a comparable number of years. Like Adam Smith's *Wealth
of Nations* in the eighteenth century and Karl Marx's *Capital*
in the nineteenth century, Keynes' *General Theory* has been
the center of controversy among both professional and non-
professional writers. Smith's book is a ringing challenge to
mercantilism, Marx's book is a searching criticism of capitalism, and Keynes' book is a repudiation of the foundations
of laissez-faire. Many economists who were at first highly
critical of Keynes have deserted their old position for the
Keynesian camp. In book after book, leading economists
acknowledge a heavy debt to the stimulating thought of Lord
Keynes.

If the influence of Lord Keynes were limited to the field

of technical economic doctrine, it would be of little interest
to the world at large. However, practical economic policy
bears even more deeply than economic theory the imprint of
Keynes' thought. A few examples of the wide and growing
acceptance of Keynes' philosophy of governmental intervention, public investment, and other forms of economic policy
designed to fill the gaps in the private enterprise economy
are: the economic policies of the New Deal, the special economic message of President Truman to Congress at the close
of the second world war, the English, Canadian, and Aus-
tralian "White Papers" on unemployment policy, the Murray Full Employment Bill of 1945 and the Employment Act
of 1946 in the United States, the provision in the new French
Constitution which requires an annual employment budget,
the newer thinking in the field of fiscal policy, the International Monetary Fund, and the International Bank for Reconstruction and Development. It appears that the trend in economic policy in those countries where private enterprise is
still vigorous will be in the direction which Lord Keynes
charted. Many of his ideas and most of his theoretical apparatus can be useful in socialist economies even though his
fundamental social philosophy is anti-Marxian.

During his lifetime Keynes wrote numerous books, many
of which are outstanding contributions to special fields of
economics. Clearly, however, *The General Theory of Employment, Interest and Money* contains the essence of his
contribution to general economic theory. This work, published
when he was fifty-two years of age (he lived to be sixty-two),
is a product of his mature thought. It seems appropriate that
a book on the economics of Keynes should begin with a discussion of the fundamentals of his thinking as outlined in
the *General Theory*. The fundamental ideas are to be distinguished from the form in which these ideas are expressed.
In the first restatement of his position after publication of the
General Theory, Keynes wrote: "I am more attached to the
comparatively simple fundamental ideas which underlie my
theory than to the particular forms in which I have embodied

them . . ."[1] The theory stands or falls on these basic ideas. The forms in which the ideas are presented, on the other hand, allow for compromise. It is mainly these forms which have been the subject of debate subsequent to the publication of the *General Theory*. Once the fundamental ideas are clear, the rest falls easily into place. A full statement of the underlying ideas involves, of course, an explanation of the framework upon which they are built, but for the purpose of a general introduction the framework can be temporarily neglected. These fundamental ideas center around the following: (1) the *general* nature of Keynes' theory, (2) the role of money, (3) the relation of interest to money, (4) investment, and (5) uncertainty about the future.

(1) *A General Theory:* In the title of his book *The General Theory of Employment, Interest and Money*,[2] Keynes' emphasis is on the word *general*. His theory deals with *all* levels of employment in contrast with what he calls "classical" economics, which is concerned with the special case of full employment. The purpose of Keynes' general theory is to explain what determines the volume of employment at any given time, whether it happens to be full employment, widespread unemployment, or some intermediate level. For reasons to be explained in the following chapter, the classical school assumes there is a tendency for the economic system based on private property in the means of production to be self-adjusting at full employment. Keynes challenges this assumption and calls the classical theory which is based on it a *special* theory, applicable only to one of the limiting cases of his *general* theory. Keynes attempts to show that the normal situation under laissez-faire capitalism in its present stage of development is a fluctuating state of economic activity which may range all the way from full employment to widespread unemployment, with the characteristic level far

---

1. "The General Theory of Employment," *The Quarterly Journal of Economics*, February, 1937, Vol. LI, No. 2, page 211.

2. Keynes, J. M., *The General Theory of Employment, Interest and Money.* New York: Harcourt, Brace and Co., Inc., 1936.

short of full employment. Although unemployment is characteristic, it is by no means inevitable. Another "general" aspect of the general theory is that it explains inflation as readily as it does unemployment since both are primarily a matter of the volume of effective demand. When demand is deficient, unemployment results, and when demand is excessive, inflation results. If Keynes' more general theory is correct, then the special theory is at fault not only in being the theory of a limiting case, but also in being largely irrelevant to the actual world in which unemployment is obviously one of the gravest problems. Most of the significant differences between the classical theory and Keynes' theory stem from the difference between the assumption that full employment is normal and the assumption that less than full employment is normal. The one is a theory of a stationary equilibrium and the other a theory of a shifting equilibrium.

There is another equally important meaning associated with the term "general" as it appears in the title of Keynes' book. His theory relates to changes in employment and output in the *economic system as a whole* in contrast with traditional theory which relates primarily, but not entirely, to the economics of the individual business firm and the individual industry. The basic concepts of Keynes' over-all theory are the aggregates of employment, national income, national output, aggregate supply, aggregate demand, total social consumption, total social investment, and total social savings. The relationships between individual commodities expressed in terms of individual prices and values, which constitute the chief subject matter of traditional economics, are important in Keynes' general theory, but they are subsidiary to the aggregate or over-all concepts of employment, income, et cetera. A little reflection will reveal that conclusions which are valid for the individual unit may not be valid when applied to the economic system as a whole. For example, some people may get rich by stealing from others, but obviously a whole community cannot enrich itself merely by its members plundering each other.

(2) *The Theory of a Monetary Economy:* During his early career, Keynes was primarily a specialist in monetary theory and monetary policy. His greatest work prior to his *General Theory* was a two volume *Treatise on Money.* When he moved from the narrower field of monetary theory to the broader field of general economic theory, Keynes took money along with him and gave it a place of tremendous importance in the determination of employment and production in the economic system as a whole. He refers to his analysis as "the theory of a monetary economy." (pp. vii, 239, 293) Money serves three functions: as a medium of exchange, as a unit of account, and as a store of value. Of these three, the store-of-value function is most important in defining Keynes' "monetary economy." People with more income and wealth than they currently consume may store the surplus in several forms, including hoarding money, lending money, and investing in some type of capital asset. If they choose to store their wealth in the form of money, they receive no income; if they lend their money, they receive interest; and if they purchase an investment asset, they expect to receive profits. Since money as a store of wealth is barren and other forms of wealth yield returns in the form of interest or profit, there must be a special explanation why people sometimes prefer to store wealth in the barren money form. Keynes gives as an answer the fact that money may be the safest form in which to store wealth. In lending money and in buying income property, there are uncertainties which do not exist as long as one's wealth is kept in the money form. Owners of money have a type of security which owners of other kinds of wealth do not enjoy.

When wealth-holders generally express a preference for hoarding money rather than lending or investing it, the production of real social wealth is handicapped. This preference for owning money rather than owning income-yielding wealth exists to a significant degree only in a world in which the economic future is uncertain. If the world were one in which the economic future could be predicted with mathematical certainty, there would be no sense in storing wealth in the barren money form. Only the highly uncertain nature of the economic future explains why there is a preference for storing wealth in the form of non-income-yielding money. As Keynes says, the desire to store wealth in the form of money is "a barometer of the degree of our distrust of our own calculations and conventions concerning the future. . . . The possession of actual money lulls our disquietude; and the premium which we require to make us part with money is the measure of the degree of our disquietude."[3]

(3) *Interest a Premium for Not-hoarding Money:* The desire of wealth-holders to store wealth in the form of money against the risks of lending is not an absolute desire. It may be overcome by paying a premium in the form of interest. Interest is the reward for parting with control over wealth in its liquid form. The *rate* of interest depends on the intensity of the desire to hoard, or on what Keynes calls "liquidity preference," for speculative purposes. The stronger the liquidity preference, the higher the rate of interest which must be paid. An increase in the desire of the public to hold money increases the rate of interest, although it is possible for the banking and monetary authorities to meet this increased desire by increasing the quantity of money. Keynes' emphasis is not on the actual hoarding of money but on the *desire* to hoard. "Hoarding" is one of those phenomena which appear quite different when looked at from the individual, as compared with the economy-wide, point of view. An individual wealth-holder can increase the amount of money he holds only at the expense of someone else as long as the total supply of money does not increase. Therefore when the public as a whole wants more money, it cannot get it, and the increased desire for money results in the necessity of paying a higher premium to those who do part with their money. But when the price that must be paid for money increases, many types of new business activity that might be

---

3. "The General Theory of Employment," *op. cit.,* page 216.

carried out at lower rates of interest will not be carried out at all. Therefore, an increase in interest rates tends to reduce effective demand and, in normal times, to cause unemployment.

Although the notion that interest is a reward for not-hoarding money may seem very ordinary from the layman's point of view, it is most unusual from the point of view of traditional economic theory. Interest has been looked upon by economists as a reward for saving, that is, a reward for postponing consumption rather than as a premium for surrendering liquidity. The importance of interest and money in Keynes' theory is indicated by their inclusion in the title *The General Theory of Employment, Interest and Money.* As further discussion will indicate, the ultimate theoretical explanation of unemployment in Keynes' theory is found in the peculiar properties of money and interest. In the absence of money or of any form of wealth with the properties of conventional money, Keynes contends the economic system would tend to be self-adjusting at the point of full employment (p. 235). Although the title indicates a theoretical emphasis on money and interest as the basis of the ultimate explanation of unemployment, from the point of view of practical policy Keynes places even greater stress on the instability of demand for capital assets arising from the irrationality of the private investment market.

(4) *Investment the Important Determinant of Employment:* In a society characterized by great inequality of wealth and income, the economic ability of the community to consume is limited. The rich have more income than they wish to consume currently and the poor have so little income that their ability to consume is narrowly restricted. As a consequence, there is a sizable potential surplus of resources in excess of what is needed to produce consumers goods. This surplus, if it is to be used at all, must be devoted to producing things that are not to be currently consumed. This production in excess of what is currently consumed is called investment. Investment includes such activity as building new

factories, new houses, new railroads, and all other types of goods which are not to be consumed as fast as they are produced. The distinction between consumption and investment is fundamental to Keynes' entire analysis. His theory reduced to its simplest terms states that employment depends upon the amount of investment, or that unemployment is caused by an insufficiency of investment. This, of course, is a great simplification. Nevertheless, it indicates the emphasis on investment. Not only do some workers receive employment directly in building new factories, houses, railroads, et cetera, but the workers so employed spend their money for the products of factories already built, pay rent on houses already built, ride railroads already built, et cetera. In brief, employment in investment activity helps to maintain demand for the consumption output of existing facilities. In order to make full use of the factories already in existence, we must always be building new factories. Otherwise, in our society with its characteristic widespread inequality of income, there will not be enough money spent to keep the old factories going. If investment falls off, unemployment results. Clearly, it is very important to understand what determines the amount of investment that actually takes place. The most important section of Keynes' *General Theory* is Book IV entitled, "The Inducement to Invest." If we mean by a "cause" that factor in a complex combination of factors which fluctuates most widely and suddenly, we may say that investment is the determinant of employment. Employment fluctuates primarily because investment fluctuates. Unemployment results primarily from an inadequacy of investment. If investment can be controlled, total employment can be controlled. A high level of employment depends upon a high level of investment. The clue to understanding the general theory of employment is found in the answer to the question: What causes investment to fluctuate and characteristically to be less than the amount required for full employment?

(5) *Psychological Irrationality a Cause of Instability:* Investment fluctuates because present knowledge about the

future rests on a precarious basis and therefore decisions which relate to the uncertain future also are precarious and subject to sudden and sweeping revision. Since investment is production other than for present consumption, it is connected with the future in a direct manner. Although investment may take the form of producing more consumers goods than are currently consumed, the more important form is investment in durable producers goods, like factories, houses, railroads, apartment houses, et cetera.[4] A decision to build a factory depends on what is expected to happen in the future. However, the outstanding fact about the future, so far as economic life is concerned at least, is that we know very little about it. The potential investor must be guided by his *expectations* in reaching his decision to build or not to build a new factory. The vague and uncertain state of our knowledge rules out the possibility that these expectations can be reduced to a rational, scientific basis. Yet as practical people living in a society whose productivity depends upon large-scale investment in durable assets, we must make and do make decisions concerning the long-term future, even though they rest on a foundation of shifting sand. Since those who make these dollars-and-cents decisions have very little confidence in the correctness of the judgment which leads to any particular investment, the prevailing attitudes which affect investment and employment so seriously are easily provoked to sudden change. If wealth-accumulation were a matter of secondary importance, the vague and uncertain state of our knowledge of the future would not matter so greatly. But under modern industrial capitalism, wealth-accumulation (investment) is the basis of the successful functioning of the entire economic system.

In the market place, entrepreneurs and other prospective investors shelter themselves from the turbulent stream of

---

4. Houses might be included in durable consumers goods, but income statistics classify them under investment. They are of such obvious importance that they have been used for illustrative purposes here, even though they are not strictly a producers good.

coming events that flows out of a dimly lit future by adopting protective attitudes that give the appearance of rational conduct. These attitudes include the assumption that the present is a much better guide to the future than a candid examination of the past would warrant. There is, in other words, a tendency to abstract from the fact that we know very little about the long-term future. The further assumption is made that existing opinions as reflected in the stock market, bond market, and other organized markets are based on a correct summing up of future prospects. Finally, because investors have so little confidence in their own opinions, they tend to rely upon the judgment of the majority or average. What Keynes calls "conventional judgments" become the basis of market-place behavior. They are conventional because they involve a general concurrence of opinion or the acceptance of a convention as a substitute for genuine knowledge which does not exist. Although investors have grave doubts concerning the soundness of action based on mass psychology, they accept it as correct behavior in the absence of any positive evidence that it is incorrect. When something new does turn up to indicate that past behavior has been incorrect, a violent shift takes place. Conventional judgments lend some stability as long as the convention is accepted, but when the convention breaks down, instability becomes the order of the day. Thus the state of expectations rests on a razor's edge and investment markets are charged with potential panic. When one conventional judgment gives way to another, all new judgments tend to move in the same direction. The sweeping nature of changes in conventional judgments stands in contrast with the classical theory of the market which assumes that the pessimistic decisions of some strong-minded individuals will offset the optimistic decisions of other strong-minded individuals.

By assuming that investors possess present knowledge about the future quite different from that which they actually possess, the classical theory underestimates "the concealed factors of utter doubt, precariousness, hope and fear."[5] The over-rationalistic psychology of the classical economists leads to a misinterpretation of behavior in the investment market, and to a neglect of the strategic role of money as a protective link between the present and the uncertain future. For as we have seen, the uncertain future which makes real investment hazardous also lends enchantment to money as a store of value.

Despite these important differences between the psychological assumptions of Keynes and those of the classical school, there is one respect in which their psychological theory is similar. The classicists assume rational behavior on the part of individuals. The individual behavior posited by Keynes is also rational, within the limitations of the given situation. It is quite rational for a bewildered investor to want to hold money during a depression-created crisis, even though this behavior brings results that are highly irrational from the point of view of the economic system as a whole. Whereas the classical economists are concerned with rational behavior in a rational world, Keynes is concerned with rational behavior in an irrational world.

Under five separate headings we have outlined the fundamental ideas of Keynes' *General Theory*. It is a general theory that pertains to all levels of employment for the economic system as a whole. It is a theory of a monetary economy in the sense that money is an important form in which to store wealth, and interest is the premium paid for not-hoarding wealth in this form. It is a theory in which fluctuations in the volume of investment account for fluctuations in employment. Fluctuations in the volume of investment are largely accounted for by the fluctuating and uncertain nature of expectations regarding the future returns from capital assets and the future terms on which money may be lent at interest. From the presentation of these basic ideas, it is apparent that they are closely related to each other. One idea cannot be discussed without

---

5. "The General Theory of Employment," *op. cit.*, page 222.

bringing in the others. The theory of interest and money is really one theory. Investment involves consideration of money as an alternative form of storing wealth. Investment in real capital assets occurs only if the expectations of profits are in excess of the premium that must be paid for borrowing money. The uncertain nature of knowledge about the future accounts both for the existence of money as a store of value and the precariousness of investment in real capital assets. These related ideas are all brought together into one theory of employment, which is the essence of the *General Theory*, and may be stated as follows: In a world in which the economic future is highly uncertain and in which money is an important form for storing wealth, the general level of employment depends upon the relation between the expected profits from investment in capital assets and the interest premium which must be paid to induce wealth-holders to surrender control of their money. If there is confidence in the future, real investment will occur and employment will be at a high level. Although interest will continue to be paid for not-hoarding, this premium can be paid and still enable entrepreneurs to carry out real investment on terms which they expect to be profitable. When confidence in the future is lacking and the expectations for profits are dim, the premium required to get wealth-holders to part with their money will exceed the expected rate of return. Investment and employment will fall to a low level. A depression is a period in which the premium that must be paid for not-hoarding money exceeds the rate of return expected from building new capital assets of almost every type. Therefore, men are not employed to build new factories, and lacking income, they have little money with which to buy the output of existing factories. While the economic storm is raging, no one is able to pay the premium necessary to lure away from wealth-holders their highly preferred cash. Wealth-accumulation dwindles, workers lose their jobs, and the storm grows worse.

References for Further Reading
See references at end of Chapter 3.

CHAPTER 2

The Classical Background

> I shall argue that the postulates of the classical theory are
> applicable to a special case only and not to the general
> case . . . Moreover, the characteristics of the special case
> assumed by the classical theory happen not to be those of
> the economic society in which we actually live, with the
> result that its teaching is misleading and disastrous if
> we attempt to apply it to the facts of experience.
>
> J. M. Keynes, *The General Theory of Employment, Interest
> and Money*.*

To UNDERSTAND the nature and novelty of Keynes' ideas, it is
useful to know their setting. The fundamental ideas sketched
in the preceding chapter represent a reaction to what seemed
to him the unsatisfactory character of the prevailing principles of economics. On the first page of the text of the *General
Theory*, Keynes says, ". . . the classical theory . . . is misleading and disastrous if we attempt to apply it to the facts of
experience." Classical economics bears to Keynes' *General
Theory* much the same relation that mercantilism bears to
Adam Smith's *Wealth of Nations*. Just as it would be difficult,
if not impossible, to understand Smith without knowing something about mercantilist theory and practice, so it is difficult
to understand Keynes without knowing something about
classical theory and practice. An insistence upon practice as
well as principles is important because the ultimate meaning

* Harcourt, Brace and Co., Inc., 1936, page 3.

of the principles is to be discovered only when they are put into practice.

The term "classical economics" as used by Keynes refers to the traditional or orthodox principles of economics which have been handed down and generally accepted by academic economists since the time of David Ricardo, the famous English economist of the early nineteenth century.[1] Although these principles have been refined and elaborated by many writers of varying shades of opinion, they comprise a well-established body of doctrine which forms the core of analytical material presented in principles of economics textbooks which appeared before 1947. This set of principles has become so widely accepted over a period of more than a century that it merits the label "classical." Keynes has been criticized for viewing the classical theory as a single body of unified thought. Undoubtedly he was guilty of oversimplifying a vast body of doctrine contributed to by many able scholars. Whether his oversimplification is in general unfair to the classical position is an issue on which there is likely to be disagreement. However, the present chapter is concerned with the classical theory as background and not with what Keynes said it was. So far as possible, polemics have been dispensed with in the following discussion of the classical background.[2]

1. As Keynes points out, he uses the term "classical economics" and "classical economists" in a rather unusual sense. He means by "classical economists" the *followers* of Ricardo, including John Stuart Mill, Alfred Marshall, and A. C. Pigou. The term "classical economists" was invented by Karl Marx to refer to Ricardo and his *predecessors*, including Adam Smith. Throughout this book the term "classical" is used in the sense in which Keynes employs it, to refer to the orthodox economics of the past century and a quarter. The writings of Professor Pigou are the special target of many of Keynes' criticisms of "classical" economics because Professor Pigou is the latest of the great representatives of this body of doctrine. However, Professor Pigou, along with many other economists, has modified his position as a result of Keynes' influence. Nevertheless, he has accepted the mantle of classicism and continues to write in its defense.

2. A full understanding of Keynes' attack on classical economics presupposes a knowledge of Keynes' own theory. His more detailed criticism of the classical position will be found in the *General Theory*, Chapter 2, "The Postulates of Classical Economics." In this chapter his criticisms are specifically directed at Professor Pigou's *The Theory of Unemployment*. Keynes recognized

Whatever may be said about the fairness of Keynes' criticisms, he was not an uninitiated outsider when he launched his attack on the citadel of classicism. He was brought up on and for many years adhered to the Cambridge version of the classical theory. His father, John Neville Keynes, was a distinguished lecturer at Cambridge University and a close friend of Alfred Marshall, the greatest of all the Cambridge classical economists, whose *Principles of Economics,* first published in 1890, still stands as the landmark of classical achievement. John Maynard Keynes was a student and disciple of Marshall. During most of his career, he accepted and taught the classical principles in the form in which they emanated from Marshall. There is much in the classical principles which Keynes continued to accept as valid and useful. In his last article, which appeared posthumously in 1946, he wrote: "I find myself moved, not for the first time, to remind contemporary economists that the classical teaching embodied some permanent truths of great significance, which we are liable to-day to overlook because we associate them with other doctrines which we cannot now accept without much qualification . . . It shows how much modernist stuff, gone wrong and turned sour and silly, is circulating in our system . . ."[3] By 1946 Keynes probably felt his triumph over the classical theory was secure enough to justify this warning to the younger "revolutionaries," some of whom he felt had gone too far in throwing overboard the classical tradition. In his *General Theory,* Keynes emphasized the differences rather than the similarities between his and the classical theory in order better to drive home his main points.

It would, however, be a mistake to underestimate the fundamental significance of Keynes' attack on classical eco-

---

the shortcomings of this chapter and stated it was the part of his *General Theory* most in need of revision. Some of the changes are to be found in Keynes' article, "Relative Movements of Real Wages and Output," *The Economic Journal,* March, 1939, Vol. XLIX, No. 193, pages 34-51. His fundamental argument remains unaffected by these amendments.

3. "The Balance of Payments of the United States," *The Economic Journal,* June, 1946, Vol. LVI, No. 222, pages 185-186.

nomics. In an age in which laissez-faire is dead, it is important to divorce economic theory from laissez-faire, even though that marriage, which was performed so well by Adam Smith, has been losing ground at least since the time of John Stuart Mill. Viewing classical theory as a whole, its practical meaning is still to be found in the presumption in favor of laissez-faire. Viewing Keynes' theory as a whole, its revolutionary nature lies in the repudiation of any presumption in favor of laissez-faire. In this sense, Keynes' challenge strikes at the heart of classical theory and ramifies especially into the fields of unemployment theory, monetary theory, interest theory, price theory, inflation, business cycles, fiscal policy, international trade, foreign exchange, and other major fields of economics.

The Content of Classical Economics

Classical economic theory rests on the assumption of full employment of labor and other resources. There may be lapses from full employment, but these are regarded as abnormal and their explanation does not constitute a basic part of the subject matter of classical economics. If at any time there is not actually full employment, the classical theory asserts there is always a *tendency* toward full employment.[4] The normal situation is stable equilibrium at full employment. If disturbance does persist, it is attributed by the classical school to interference by government or private monopoly with the free play of market forces. As a general rule to which there are minor exceptions, the social policy which guarantees normal full employment is laissez-faire, the absence of government control of private enterprise. In contrast with this, Keynes takes the normal condition of laissez-faire capitalism to be a fluctuating level of employment. The primary purpose of Keynes' theory is to explain what determines the volume of employment at any time.

---

4. Pigou, A. C., *Equilibrium and Employment,* page 78. London: Macmillan and Co., Ltd., 1941. See also, *Lapses from Full Employment,* Chapter V. London: Macmillan and Co., Ltd., 1945.

Instead of attempting to explain what determines the volume of employment, the classical theory assumes full employment and goes on to explain how a *given* total volume of resources is allocated in production and how the income derived from production is distributed to the different types of resources participating in production. The market forces which allocate resources in production and determine the rewards in distribution are supply and demand. The general relations of supply and demand determine the relative values of individual resources and commodities. Expressed in terms of money, these values are prices, and the pricing system is the unconscious "planning" mechanism which guides private individuals, in pursuit of maximum individual rewards, to allocate economically and fully the total resources of the economic system. This, in brief outline, is the well-known theory of value, distribution, and production, which forms the core of classical economic theory.

Classical theory focuses on the use of a given quantity of resources by individual firms and individual industries within the economic system as a whole. If more resources are employed in one industry, they are assumed to be drawn away from other industries. If more resources are employed by one firm, they are assumed to be drawn away from other firms. Thus the choice is between employment here and employment there, and not between employment and unemployment. Additions to total output in one direction are at the expense of deductions from total output somewhere else in the economic system and are not additions to total output resulting from putting to work previously unemployed resources. Thus classical economics is a study of the alternative uses of a given quantity of employed resources. When resources are ideally allocated, there is no way by which total output can be increased by reallocation. In the long run, of course, increases in population and productivity and the discovery of new resources result in increases in total employment and output. In contrast with the emphasis upon the use of a given total quantity of resources by individual firms and industries,

Keynes' general theory of employment deals with changes in output and employment in the economic system as a whole as a result of fluctuations in the quantity of employed resources.

Acceptance of full employment as the normal condition of an exchange economy is justified in classical economics by the assumption that supply creates its own demand. This assumption or "principle" is called Say's law of markets, after J. B. Say, an early nineteenth-century French economist who was one of the first to state the "law" in a dogmatic form. By supply creating its own demand is meant that every producer who brings goods to market does so only in order to exchange them for other goods. Say assumed that the only reason people work and produce is in order to enjoy the satisfaction of consuming. In an exchange economy, therefore, whatever is produced represents the demand for another product. Additional supply is additional demand. The analysis is carried on in terms of barter, but the fact that sales and purchases are made with money is assumed not to affect the process, except that exchange based on money is more efficient than exchange based on barter. When a resource is put to work a product (output) is produced and income is paid to those who contribute to its production. The sales receipts or proceeds which an employer can expect to receive from the output produced is assumed to cover the cost of the output for all levels of employment in the economic system, provided the contributors of resources are willing to accept rewards commensurate with their productivity. This does not mean that each additional worker need purchase exactly the same product which he himself produces. It signifies merely that the new income from his employment will create a sufficient demand to take off the market an amount of output equivalent to that produced by virtue of his employment. As long as production is directed into proper channels, whatever is produced can be sold. Misdirected production may result in temporary oversupply of some particular items but there can be no general overproduction as long as supply creates its own demand. If errors result in excess production of some particular items of output, this will be corrected when entrepreneurs shift from the production of things they cannot sell (at a profit) to the production of things they can sell (at a profit). In brief, Say's law of markets is a denial of the possibility of general over-production, that is, a denial of the possibility of a deficiency of aggregate demand. Therefore, the employment of more resources will always be profitable and will take place up to the point of full employment, subject to the limitation that the contributors of resources are willing to accept rewards no greater than their physical productivity justifies. There can be no general unemployment, according to this view, if workers will accept what they are "worth."

In an exchange economy, Say's law means there will always be a sufficient rate of spending to maintain full employment. The classical justification of full employment as "normal" rests on the assumption that income is spent automatically at a rate which will keep all resources employed. Although most people spend most of their income fairly "automatically" for things they need or want to consume, there is also in any community a certain proportion of income that is saved. This, however, is no obstacle to spending or employment in the classical analysis because what each individual saves is assumed nevertheless to be spent. Saving is spending for producers goods (investment). Since saving is just another form of spending, according to the classical theory, all income is spent, partly for consumption and partly for investment (producers goods). There is no reason to expect a break in the flow of the income stream and therefore supply creates its own demand.

Flexibility in the rate of interest is the mechanism which is supposed to maintain equality of community saving and community investment in the classical scheme. If the amount of saving *tends* to become excessive, forces operating through the rate of interest are set in motion to reduce saving and to increase investment until they are brought to equality with each other. In the first place, the higher rate of saving will tend to lower the rate of interest, and a lower rate of interest will lessen the incentive to save. Since interest is viewed as the reward for saving, an increase in interest rates will increase saving and a decrease in interest rates will decrease saving. In the second place, the lower rate of interest will increase the incentive to invest to an extent which will absorb the additional savings which remain after the rate of interest has declined. Other influences also enter the picture to maintain the equality of saving and investment at full employment. An increase in saving represents a decrease in the demand for consumption goods and causes their prices to fall. Lower prices mean lower profits, which cause resources to shift out of the consumers goods industries into investment goods industries, where the demand has increased. It should be observed that saving is linked to investment by a delicate mechanism, yet one which bears a heavy burden in making the adjustments that preserve full employment. If it seems strange that investment should increase at the very time consumption is decreasing, this is explained in the classical theory in terms of the presupposition that a decision to consume less today is linked directly with a decision to consume more at a later date. The classical theory does not acknowledge that a fall in consumption, instead of leading to an increase in investment, may lead to a fall in total demand and thereby to unemployment. Nor does the classical theory recognize as a significant motive for saving the desire for wealth as such.

The Meaning of Full Employment and Unemployment: The assertion that classical economic theory rests on the assumption of full employment calls for definitions of "full employment" and "unemployment." It is more accurate to say that the classical position assumes there is no involuntary unemployment, as distinguished from voluntary and frictional unemployment. Voluntary unemployment exists when potential workers are unwilling to accept the going wage or wages slightly less than the going wage. Workers on strike for higher wages are an example of voluntary unemployment. They are voluntarily unemployed in the sense that by taking a lower wage than they are asking they could be employed.

There are other forms of voluntary idleness on the part of potential workers which hardly justify being classed as unemployment at all. Some wealthy persons, the "idle rich," and some habitually lazy people, the "idle poor," are of this type. When people refuse of their own volition to work, they should not be classified as unemployed, and therefore full employment can exist even though some people are voluntarily idle.

Frictional unemployment exists when men are temporarily out of work because of imperfections in the labor market. Many factors may account for frictional unemployment: the immobility of labor, the seasonal nature of some work, shortages of materials, breakdowns in machinery and equipment, ignorance of job opportunities, et cetera. In a dynamic society in which some industries are declining and others are rising and in which people are free to work wherever they wish (providing they can find a job), the volume of frictional unemployment may be fairly large at any time. In the United States, where the total labor force is approximately sixty millions, it is estimated that frictional unemployment averages at least two millions, or about three per cent, at all times. Frictional unemployment is undesirable and every possible step should be taken to minimize it within the limits of freedom of occupational choice, but it is not a major problem because employable persons seeking work will not, as a rule, remain unemployed for frictional reasons more than a few weeks or months.

"Full employment" as thus defined is consistent with voluntary unemployment and allows for a certain amount of frictional unemployment. Full employment exists in the absence of involuntary unemployment. In the classical theory, this type of unemployment does not exist.[5] While there is

---

5. Keynes cites the following passage from Professor Pigou's major work, the *Economics of Welfare*, to illustrate how the classical economists ignored the problem of involuntary unemployment: "Throughout this discussion, except when the contrary is expressly stated, the fact that some resources are generally unemployed against the will of the owners is ignored. *This does not affect the substance of the argument*, while it simplifies its exposition." Pigou, *Economics of Welfare*, 4th edition, page 127. Cited in Keynes' *General Theory*, page 5. The italics are supplied by Keynes.

more involved in the issue between Keynes and the classicists than mere facts, the latter cannot be ignored since, after all, issues like this must ultimately be resolved by an appeal to common sense and the hard facts of experience. In the United States at the bottom of the depression in 1932, there were approximately 15,000,000 unemployed workers, and at the top of the business cycle in 1937 there remained more than 7,500,000 unemployed. Allowing for as many as 3,000,000 frictionally unemployed, it hardly seems plausible that the remaining millions were in any significant sense voluntarily unemployed. Millions tramped the streets looking for work at almost any price and found only "No Help Wanted" signs. The same conclusion seems justified for the United Kingdom, where between the first and second world wars the percentage of workers out of employment seldom fell below 10 per cent, and ranged upward to 22 per cent of the registered workers. Since 2 or 3 per cent is considered normal frictional unemployment, is it any wonder that Keynes and others found unsatisfactory a theory which appeared to do such violence to the facts of experience?

How do the representatives of the classical school reconcile their denial of involuntary unemployment with the undeniable fact that there do exist large numbers of idle men and women who want work but cannot find it? The crux of the answer to this important question seems to be that collective action as taken by labor unions and in the form of governmental intervention creates an imperfect labor market in which wage rates are not free to fall to their competitive levels. Monopolistic behavior on the part of labor and labor's friends is responsible for unemployment. Under perfectly free competition, or what Professor Pigou calls "thorough-going competition," among wage earners, wage rates fall under the pressure of unemployment until all who are willing to work can find employment. As long as there is anybody unemployed, he will, under thorough-going competition, offer himself for employment and beat down wage rates until it is profitable for employers to hire everyone who wants to work.

Professor Pigou contends that these conditions substantially obtained prior to the first world war when unemployment, apart from cyclical manifestations, remained at a low level. Since that time and to some extent even in the earlier period, certain new phenomena have arisen to weaken greatly the competitive forces in the labor market. Chief among these are collective bargaining by trade unions, minimum-wage laws, unemployment insurance, increased work relief payments, and tacit agreement among workers generally not to accept lower wages than what they and the community consider a reasonable living wage. The group pressures exerted by labor unions and government intervention in the labor market have tended to maintain wage rates above the level at which the demand for work is satisfied before everyone willing to work at prevailing wage rates can find employment. Much of this unemployment is not strictly voluntary on the part of the individual unemployed worker since there is relatively little he can do about the closed shop, minimum-wage laws, or the more-than-competitive wages being received by the employed. In fact, relatively high unemployment insurance payments and poor relief remove the incentive for wage earners to work for the low wage rates which many of them must accept if they want employment. Some individuals can, of course, find employment by accepting wage reductions which other workers refuse to accept. However, many prefer to remain idle rather than be subjected to the humiliating taunts that they are despicable "scabs" who lower the standards of fellow workers. Where the union contract or the law does not restrain, the forces of class pressure may work with great effectiveness to maintain wage rates above the competitive ideal which would permit full employment. The conclusion drawn by the classical school from these considerations is that in spite of strong group pressure this type of unemployment is nevertheless voluntary in the sense that acceptance of lower wage rates would create a demand for more employment. If wage rates were lowered sufficiently, all non-frictional unemployment would disappear. Thus, according

to the classical theory, labor is guilty of a type of group behavior in the form of collective bargaining and otherwise
which causes many fellow-workers to suffer unemployment.
The responsibility for unemployment is placed at the door of
labor itself. The practical lesson is clear: Since unemployment, apart from the frictional type, is caused by wages being
too high, the cure is lower wages.[6]

Keynes' Objections to Classical Theory

What Keynes objected to most strongly in the classical reasoning is the notion that unemployment will disappear if
workers will just accept sufficiently low wage rates. He repudiates the assumption that the labor market is always a seller's
market in which labor can be sold if workers will just be willing to accept wage cuts. There are two aspects of Keynes'
objection to Pigou's view that flexible wage rates will cure
unemployment. The first may be called the practical and the
second the theoretical aspect.

In a practical sense labor unions are an integral part of
modern democratic economics, and welfare legislation such

6. While it would be unfair to attribute the position stated in the above
paragraph to many of the so-called classical economists, it is, I believe, a correct paraphrase of the meaning of Professor Pigou's *Theory of Unemployment*,
upon which Keynes bases his statement of the classical theory of unemployment. In his *Lapses from Full Employment*, published in 1945, Professor Pigou
says he is in favor of attacking the problem of unemployment by manipulating
demand rather than by manipulating wages. This involves a major departure
from the classical position and a major triumph for Keynes. Despite his position on policy, which clearly differs from that taken in his *Theory of Unemployment* (1933), Professor Pigou continues to defend the classical position,
although he acknowledges some oversights in formulation. In *Lapses from Full
Employment* Pigou concludes a chapter, "The Classical View," with this
statement: "The final result of this discussion is to suggest that, though there
are subtleties of theory which the classicists did not envisage, for broad *practical* purposes their conclusion was correct. In stable conditions, apart from
frictions, immobility and so on, thorough-going competition among wage-
earners would ensure the establishment and maintenance of full employment
except in circumstances which we are very unlikely to meet with in fact."
(page 25). It is left for the reader to try to reconcile this statement with that
in the Preface, where he states: "Professor Dennis Robertson . . . has warned
me that the form of the book may suggest that I am in favour of attacking the
problem of unemployment by manipulating wages rather than by manipulating
demand. I wish, therefore, to say clearly that this is not so." (page v).

as minimum-wage laws and unemployment insurance are probably here to stay. Therefore, it is bad politics even if it should be considered good economics to object to labor unions and to liberal labor legislation. Pigou's solution of lower wage rates could only be realized in a freely competitive labor market or in a completely authoritarian economy. In democratic societies, which both Keynes and Pigou presuppose, labor unions are not likely to be eliminated, minimum-wage laws are not likely to be repealed, unemployment compensation is not likely to be lowered, and public opinion as to what constitutes a reasonable living wage is not likely to be revised downwards in the light of the tremendous productivity of modern technology. A minimum charge against Pigou's theory of unemployment is its irrelevance as a guide to policy under conditions as they have come to exist in the actual world of the past several decades and as they will probably continue to exist in the foreseeable future.

However, even if all the conditions necessary to restore perfectly free or thorough-going competition among wage earners might, by some miracle, be realized, this would not meet Keynes' fundamental challenge to the classical school. His theory of employment and unemployment does not rest on the premise of rigid wage rates. He contends that the volume of employment is determined by effective demand and not by the wage bargains between workers and employers. Keynes' ultimate theoretical explanation of unemployment rests, as was hinted in the preceding chapter and as will be developed more fully subsequently, on the stickiness of interest rates taken in conjunction with the irrationality of business men's expectations about investment in durable capital assets. In Keynes' view, the peculiar characteristics of a developed monetary economy account for unemployment. Even if wage rates were perfectly flexible and commodity prices perfectly competitive, unemployment could still exist. His explanation of unemployment does not depend on the decline of competition of recent decades.

While the above discussion does not do justice to the relations between Keynes and the classical theory,[7] perhaps enough has been said to indicate the circumstances which provoked him to advance *The General Theory of Employment, Interest and Money* in 1936. The great depression of the 1930's, like all depressions, involved tremendous loss of human and material values. Mass unemployment is second, perhaps, only to war in the magnitude of its human degradation and physical wastefulness. The world was poor not because it lacked material resources, technical skill, or the will to work, or even because it misallocated its employed resources; it was poor because something was radically wrong with the way men thought and conducted their economic affairs. The practical advice which came implicitly if not always explicitly from the classical theory seemed misleading and disastrous. Cutting wages and salaries seemed to Keynes both demoralizing and unsound. He sought a means to prosperity through monetary expansion, public investment, and other forms of governmental action. This represented a departure from traditional laissez-faire, but Keynes had no illusions about the invisible hand that is supposed to guide men in the right paths if they will just pursue their own self-interest. He had long since written off laissez-faire. Keynes disagreed with those who seemed to say we cannot do what we must do because if we do we shall lose our freedom. Such a view seemed to indicate a lack of faith in freedom and representative government rather than their defense. Keynes wanted governmental action because he saw the need for rules of the road from which all will benefit but without which people get in each other's way and no one gets anywhere. As one writer has aptly stated, Keynes was the first academic economist of high professional repute since Malthus to attack the doctrine that the economic forces of a private-property economy tend to bring about the employment of all who wish to work at the prevailing wage rates.[8]

---

7. This is discussed more fully in the final chapter.

8. Hayes, H. Gordon, *Spending, Saving, and Employment*, page 133. New York: Alfred A. Knopf, Inc., 1945.

The great fault of the classical theory is its irrelevance to conditions in the contemporary capitalist world. In many significant respects, the classical theory, as summed up by Alfred Marshall, is more useful in a socialist economy, which may be assumed to conform closely to the ideal of full employment. In capitalist economies where widespread unemployment, business cycles, inflation, and other forms of instability constitute the chief problems of public policy, the basic need is for a theory which will diagnose these ills in a manner which will furnish a guide to action for their solution or alleviation. Such a new and more relevant theory has emerged in Keynes' general theory of employment, interest and money.

References for Further Reading

See references at end of Chapter 3.

CHAPTER 3

A Preliminary Summary of the General Theory of Employment

This analysis supplies us with an explanation of the paradox of poverty in the midst of plenty. For the mere existence of an insufficiency of effective demand may, and often will, bring the increase of employment to a standstill *before* a level of full employment has been reached . . . Moreover the richer the community, the wider will tend to be the gap between its actual and its potential production; and therefore the more obvious and outrageous the defects of the economic system.

J. M. Keynes, *The General Theory of Employment, Interest and Money.**

A SUMMARY of Keynes' general theory of employment naturally focuses on the principle of effective demand, which embodies in a systematic manner the fundamental ideas discussed in Chapter 1 above. The purpose of this summary is to give the reader a bird's eye view of the whole theory before presenting a detailed account of its individual parts. Subsequent discussion of the individual parts will have more meaning if their relations to the rest of the theory are already understood. This appears to be the best way to resolve the dilemma which inevitably arises in explaining a systematic

* Harcourt, Brace and Co., Inc., 1936, pages 30-31.

28

body of thought: The parts have meaning only in relation to the whole, yet the whole is made up of individual parts which must be appreciated before the whole can be explained. In our preliminary survey it will be necessary to use some special terms whose full meaning must await more detailed explanation in subsequent chapters.

The Principle of Effective Demand

The logical starting point of Keynes' theory of employment is the principle of effective demand.[1] Total employment depends on total demand, and unemployment results from a deficiency of total demand. Effective demand manifests itself in the spending of income. As employment increases, income increases. A fundamental principle is that as the real income of a community increases, consumption will also increase but by less than income. Therefore, in order to have sufficient demand to sustain an increase in employment there must be an increase in real investment equal to the gap between income and the consumption demand out of that income. In other words, employment cannot increase unless investment increases. This is the core of the principle of effective demand. Since it is fundamental to the general theory of employment, it will be restated on an expanded basis in the following paragraphs.

Aggregate demand and aggregate supply

The term "demand" as used by Keynes refers to aggregate demand of the whole economic system. Aggregate demand must be clearly distinguished from the demand for the products of individual firms and individual industries which is the usual type represented in supply and demand diagrams. The demand for a firm or industry means a schedule of vari-

---

1. As explained below, the adjective "effective" is used to designate the point on the aggregate demand curve where it is intersected by the aggregate supply curve. There are other points on the aggregate demand curve but these are not effective in determining the actual volume of employment. "Effective" is also helpful in emphasizing the distinction between mere desire to buy and desire plus ability to buy. Only the latter has economic significance.

ous amounts of a commodity which will be purchased at a series of prices. Price means the amount of money received from the sale of a given physical quantity of output, such as a bushel of wheat or a ton of steel. Since the output of the entire economic system cannot be measured in any simple physical unit like a bushel or ton, Keynes uses the amount of labor employed as the measure of output as a whole. The aggregate demand "price" for the output of any given amount of employment is the total sum of money, or proceeds, which is expected from the sale of the output produced when that amount of labor is employed. The aggregate demand curve,

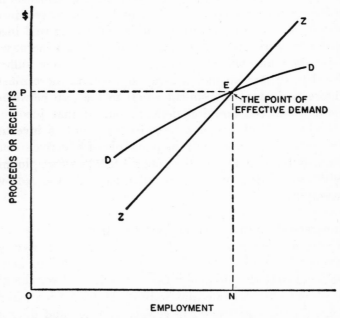

DD —The Aggregate Demand Schedule: The proceeds or receipts (P) *expected* to be forthcoming for output produced by varying amounts of employment (N).

ZZ —The Aggregate Supply Schedule: The proceeds or receipts (P) which will *just induce* given amounts of employment (N).

Figure 1. Aggregate Demand and Aggregate Supply.

or "aggregate demand function" as Keynes calls it (represented by DD in Figure 1), is a schedule of the proceeds expected from the sale of the output resulting from varying amounts of employment. As more labor is employed, more output is produced, and the total proceeds are greater. In other words, aggregate demand price increases as the amount of employment increases, and decreases as the amount of employment decreases.

In Figure 1 the aggregate demand price or proceeds is represented along the vertical axis, and the quantity of employment (N) along the horizontal axis. The aggregate demand schedule slants up toward the right, indicating that demand increases with employment. This contrasts with an industry demand curve which slants down toward the right, indicating that the quantity sold will increase as the price falls.

In a business-enterprise economy in which production is motivated by profit, each business man will employ that number of workers which will yield him the greatest profit. The total number of men employed in the whole economy is the total or aggregate of those employed by all entrepreneurs. A certain minimum amount of proceeds will be necessary to induce employers as a whole to offer any given aggregate amount of employment. This minimum price or proceeds which will just induce employment on a given scale is called the aggregate supply price of that amount of employment. The aggregate supply function is a schedule of the minimum amounts of proceeds required to induce varying quantities of employment. As the amount of proceeds increases, a greater amount of employment will be offered to workers by employers. Therefore, the aggregate supply schedule (ZZ in Figure 1), like the aggregate demand schedule, slants up toward the right as the amount of employment (N) increases. It will not, however, follow the same course. There will be some amounts of employment for which the proceeds expected will exceed the proceeds necessary to induce a given volume of employment and there will be some amounts of employment for which the proceeds expected will not be sufficient to in-

duce that amount of employment. In between there will be
some amount of employment for which the expected proceeds
will just equal the necessary proceeds to make the employment profitable to entrepreneurs. At this point the aggregate
demand function intersects the aggregate supply function, and
the point of intersection determines the actual amount of employment at any time. This is the crux of Keynes' theory of
employment. The aggregate demand schedule (DD) and the
aggregate supply schedule (ZZ), as represented in Figure 1,
intersect at the point E, corresponding to the amount of employment N. E at the point of intersection represents *the effective demand.* At this point, entrepreneurs maximize their
expected profits. If either more or less employment were
offered, profits would be less. Thus at any one time, there is,
according to Keynes' theory, a uniquely determined amount
of employment which will be most profitable for entrepreneurs to offer to workers. There is no reason to assume this
point will correspond to full employment. The labor market
is not, as a rule, a seller's market. Aggregate demand and
aggregate supply might be equal at full employment, but
this will occur only if investment demand happens to equal
the gap between the aggregate supply price corresponding to
full employment and the amount which consumers in the aggregate choose to spend for consumption out of income at full
employment. According to Keynes, the typical investment
demand will be inadequate to fill the gap between the amount
of income corresponding to full employment and the consumption demand out of that income. Therefore, the aggregate demand schedule and the aggregate supply schedule will
intersect at a point of less than full employment. This estab-
lishes an equilibrium from which there will be no tendency to
depart in the absence of some external change. In the absence
of a large volume of expected proceeds from the sale of investment goods, the total proceeds expected by employers
will be less than is necessary to induce them to offer employment to all who are willing to work. Full employment is im-

portant only as a limiting case. It may be defined as an amount of employment beyond which further increases in effective demand do not increase output and employment (p. 26).

The maxim that "supply creates its own demand" means that *any* increase in employment will lead to an additional amount of proceeds sufficient to induce entrepreneurs to offer the increased employment. If this maxim were valid, aggregate demand and aggregate supply would be equal for all amounts of employment (N). On a diagram similar to Figure 1, the classical theory would represent DD and ZZ as equal for all amounts of employment (N). Since the expected proceeds would always be adequate to induce more employment, competition among entrepreneurs for workers and among workers for jobs would lead to an expansion of employment as long as anyone is involuntarily unemployed. The classical theory breaks down in attempting to apply Say's law to the demand for investment. For while it is true that more employment will create more income of which some will be spent for consumers goods, all of it will not be spent in this way and there is no reason to assume that the difference will be devoted to investment expenditure. If investment does not increase when employment increases, the sum of consumption demand and investment demand will be less than the aggregate supply price for the higher level of employment. Entrepreneurs will reduce employment to a level at which the aggregate supply price exceeds the consumption demand by the actual amount of investment.

Further statement of the principle of effective demand

Since there is little that is novel about the aggregate supply function, the essence of Keynes' theory is found in his analysis of the aggregate demand function. Since employment depends on demand and total demand is equal to total income, the general theory of employment is also a theory of aggregate demand or of aggregate income. Since the value of total output is equal to total income, Keynes' theory may also be

called a theory of aggregate output. Employment results in
the production of output on the one hand and in the creation
of income on the other. Total output will have a value equal
to total income. Total output consists of the production of consumers goods and the production of investment goods.[2] Total

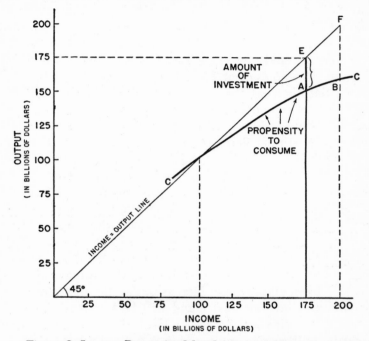

**Figure 2. Income Determined by the Propensity to Consume
and the Amount of Investment.**

---

2. Any number of divisions of total output could be made. For some purposes it is convenient to make a three-fold division of total national product
by setting the contribution of government apart in a separate category. For
other problems a four-fold division into consumption, private investment, government investment, and foreign investment (net exports) is used. In the
General Theory Keynes uses only the two-fold division into consumption and
investment. At this point in our discussion it would complicate the analysis
and add little to the essential meaning of Keynes' theory to depart from his
simple classification of output as consumption and investment. This two-fold
division is not arbitrary. It is based on the empirical premise that the behavior
that determines consumption and that which determines investment are different
in a way which has great practical significance. One is stable in relation to
income and the other is highly unstable and largely autonomous.

income is earned from the production of consumers goods and the production of investment. If we start from less than full employment, any *increase* in employment must be divided between consumption output and investment output in a manner which corresponds to the way in which income receivers choose to divide their *increase* in income between consumption expenditure and saving.

Assuming as Keynes does the aggregate supply function to be given, the thesis of his *General Theory* is that employment is determined by aggregate demand, which in turn depends on the propensity to consume and the amount of investment at a given time.

Since employment is assumed to be uniquely correlated with income, we may show income along the horizontal axis in place of employment, which was represented there in Figure 1. The value of total output is shown along the vertical axis. Since total income is equal to the value of total output, the equilibrium adjustment must lie along the 45° line indicated in Figure 2.[3] The point of effective demand (E) will be on the 45° line at the point at which the volume of investment is equal to the distance between this line and the consumption schedule, CC.

The consumption schedule (propensity to consume) will be discussed in detail later. This schedule represents the stable relationship which Keynes assumes to exist between the size of the national income and the amount which will be spent by

---

3. The 45° line in Figure 2 is not the same as the aggregate supply schedule in Figure 1. The 45° line is merely a line along which income equals output for any value of output. Keynes did not use a diagram to explain his theory of effective demand, but geometrical drawings have been widely used for this purpose. Figure 2 differs from most of the diagrams of this type in that it shows "output" along the vertical axis. It would perhaps be more appropriate to call this the "demand for output." If Figure 2 were to be broken down into more detail, it would show income, which is along the horizontal axis, divided into two parts, consumption expenditure and saving; and output, which is along the vertical axis, divided into consumption output (or consumption demand) and investment demand. This presentation has pedagogical advantages over diagrams which show consumption, investment and saving along the vertical axis. The proportionality of the two parts of these two lines is an essential condition of an equilibrium position. It also can be used to show the meaning of the equality of saving to investment.

the public for consumption. In Figure 2 the consumption schedule is drawn to represent the following assumed relations between income and consumption, in billions of dollars:

Income	100	125	150	175	200
Consumption	100	120	137.5	150	160

This schedule follows the fundamental maxim that when income rises, consumption also rises, but less than income. The difference between income and consumption increases from zero at $100 billion of income, to $5 billion at $125 billion, to $12.5 billion at $150 billion, to $25 billion at $175 billion, and finally to $40 billion at the assumed full employment income of $200 billion.

If AE ($25 billion) is the amount of investment at a given time, the total output most profitable for entrepreneurs to pro duce will be $175 billion. This total output will consist of two parts, $150 billion worth of consumption output in addition to $25 billion worth of investment output. Total income, which is equal to total output will also be $175 billion. If the amount of investment becomes less than AE, income must fall below $175 billion. When investment is zero, income will be $100 billion, and all output will be consumption output. The distance FB ($40 billion) represents the amount of investment that would be necessary to raise income to the full employment level of $200 billion.

Since consumption expenditure increases by less than income when income increases, there can be no increase in employment unless there is an increase in investment. This means that investment must increase to fill the gap between income and consumption. Less than 100 per cent of any increase in aggregate income will be spent for consumption goods and consequently less than 100 per cent of output must be in the form of consumption goods. Otherwise what is produced will not correspond to what is demanded out of the higher income. In the absence of an increase in the demand for investment, business men who employ additional workers to produce more output will be unable in the aggregate to sell what they produce except at losses. If newly employed work-

ers are set to producing all consumers goods, there will be
an insufficient demand to buy these goods at prices profitable
to entrepreneurs because only a part of the newly created
income will be spent to buy consumers goods. In the circumstances illustrated in Figure 2, let us suppose entrepreneurs
were to hire the unemployed workers to produce an additional
$25 billion worth of consumers goods. This would make a
total output of $175 billion of consumption output and $25
billion of investment output, and a total income of $200
billion. Since out of this income only $160 billion will be
spent for consumption, there will be $15 billion worth of
unsold consumption output. Losses will result because all the
additional workers have been employed to produce consumers goods and only part of the additional demand will be
for consumers goods. But if newly employed workers are set
to producing less than 100 per cent of consumers goods, there
will be no market for the non-consumer (investment) goods
in the absence of an increase in the demand for investment.
Losses will result in either case because the proceeds received
by entrepreneurs will be less than sufficient to cover the total
costs (aggregate supply price) of the higher level of employment. Consequently output and employment will reach an
equilibrium only at the point where income exceeds consumption by the actual amount of investment. This illustrates again
the principle that employment cannot increase unless investment increases. This principle rests on the assumption that the
propensity to consume (consumption function) remains
unchanged.

The Propensity to Consume

Consumption demand depends on the size of income and
the share that is spent for consumers goods. We have already
observed that for any level of national income there is a fairly
stable proportion which will be spent for consumption by the
public. If the American public chooses to spend $160 billion
for consumption when the national income is $200 billion, the
average propensity to consume at this point is 80 per cent.

Some income recipients will spend more than 80 per cent and others will spend less than 80 per cent of their incomes for consumption, but the average (arithmetic mean) will be 80 per cent. At different levels of national income the amount of consumption will change, and the proportion which total consumption is of total income will also change. The absolute amount of consumption will increase as income increases, and will decrease as income decreases. A schedule showing the various amounts of consumption which correspond to different levels of income is the "schedule of the propensity to consume," which for the sake of brevity is referred to simply as the propensity to consume." It is a functional relationship indicating how consumption varies when income varies. Such a relationship may be shown for an individual or family consumption unit, but in Keynes' theory it is the relationship between aggregate community consumption and aggregate community income that is important.

  Keynes' assumption that the propensity to consume is relatively stable in the short run is a generalization about actual experience and is an essential part of the structure of his theory. If this assumption is valid, the amount of community consumption varies in a regular manner with aggregate income. What the actual schedule of the propensity to consume will be at any time depends on the established customs of the community, the distribution of income, the tax system, and other factors, which will be discussed in Chapter 5. A high propensity to consume is favorable to employment because it leaves relatively small gaps between income and the consumption out of income corresponding to different levels of employment. If the schedule of the propensity to consume is relatively low, the gaps between income and consumption will be greater and, in order to maintain high levels of employment, the amount of investment must be relatively great. If the average propensity to consume were 100 per cent for all levels of income, full employment would be assured because no investment would be required. As income was received, it would all be spent for consumers goods. Supply would create its own demand. However, it is a characteristic of the actual world that the average propensity to consume is less than 100 per cent for all high levels of employment. Only if employment falls low enough, will a point be reached where consumption is equal to income. This is a lower limit below which employment will not fall, except perhaps temporarily. In wealthy industrial societies this level of employment is so low that it would provoke revolutionary action if long maintained. Investment is required to maintain employment above a relatively low and socially intolerable level.

The Inducement to Invest

Effective demand for investment is more complex and more unstable than effective demand for consumption. As previously indicated, investment means producing more than is currently consumed, and takes the form of adding to the accumulated wealth of society. Although investment sometimes takes the form of additions to the stocks of finished goods in the hands of retailers and wholesalers, its most important form is in expenditures by business men for factories, machinery, and other forms of producers goods. The inducement to business men to build factories and to invest in other ways arises from the expectation that such investment will prove profitable. Since these expectations are often based on precarious estimates of the future, the volume of investment is subject to wide fluctuations. Business men will borrow to invest up to the point at which the expected return from new investment is equal to the cost of borrowing funds with which to carry out the investment. The inducement to invest is determined in Keynes' analysis by the business men's estimates of the profitability of investment in relation to the rate of interest on money for investment. The expected profitability of new investment is called the marginal efficiency of capital.

The marginal efficiency of capital

The marginal efficiency of a capital asset is the highest *rate* of return over cost expected from producing one more unit (a marginal unit) of a particular type of capital asset. In the language of the man in the street, it may be thought of as the expected rate of percentage profit per year on real investments of the most efficient type. Assume that in a growing community a store building that can be built for $20,000 will yield $1200 per year in rental and has depreciation and maintenance of $200 per year, giving a net return of $1000 per year. If the rate of interest is 4 per cent, this building is worth $25,000 ($1000 divided by .04). A building of this type already constructed should be worth $25,000. However, it will be preferable to borrow $20,000 at 4 per cent to build a new building, and receive a net return of $1000 or 5 per cent. The efficiency of this type of capital asset is 5 per cent, which is higher than the rate of interest of 4 per cent. If 5 per cent is the highest rate of return which can be secured from any type of real investment, the marginal efficiency of capital *in general* is 5 per cent. Investment continues as long as the expected rate of return exceeds the rate of interest. If the cost of construction of a new asset is less than the purchase price of the old asset of the same type, it will be profitable to build a new one rather than to buy the old one. This explains what is meant by the expected rate of profit being in excess of the rate of interest.

Keynes uses the term marginal efficiency of capital rather than expected rate of profit or some other conventional term like the marginal productivity of capital because he wishes to emphasize the dynamic setting in which the present and future are linked by the expectations of investors. In the example of the store building referred to above, the fact that the current yield from such assets is $1000 per year does not justify the assumption that the yield will continue at this level in the future. It may rise above $1000 in some years, fall below $1000 in other years, or behave in almost any other way depending on the future course of events, some of which may be foreseen clearly but not with certainty, others which may be only dimly anticipated, and still others which are completely unforeseen at the time the investment is made. In this dynamic setting, the investor is extremely cautious about investments that will realize their value, if at all, only over many years to come. The longer the period involved, the greater the chance that unforeseen events will intervene to disappoint today's investors. The role of capital assets as a link by which wealth-holders bridge the gap between the present and the future is one of the fundamental ideas underlying Keynes' entire analysis.

The marginal efficiency of capital is characterized by short-term instability and a tendency toward long-term decline. Fluctuations in the marginal efficiency of capital are the fundamental cause of the business cycle. Feverish building activity in the capital goods industries that marks the later phase of the expansion stage of the cycle results from the optimistic expectations of investors. For some time the increased activity brings larger profits and adds fuel to prevailing optimism. Meanwhile, however, great additions to the existing supply of capital goods force down the expected rate of return below the rate of interest. The cessation in capital accumulation (investment) which follows leads inevitably to collapse and depression. This transition from expansion to contraction is frequently highlighted by the gyration of the stock exchange, whose violent fluctuations are an objectification of the instability of the marginal efficiency of capital. The speculation and financial manipulation that characterize stock market activities are among the chief manifestations of the instability of capitalist economies.

Since every new investment competes with every old investment, there is a tendency in the secular long run for the growing abundance of capital assets to cause a decline in the rate of return. This tendency may be offset by unusual circumstances like those which characterized the western world during the nineteenth century when rapid growth in population, the existence of great undeveloped geographical frontiers, and great technological innovations like the railroad provided unprecedented demands for new capital, and forestalled the fall in the rate of return to capital. Geographical expansion has come to a close with the end of the frontiers in America and elsewhere, population growth has slowed down, and inventions are more of the labor-saving than of the capital-absorbing type. These underlying structural changes of recent decades provide a plausible explanation for the mass unemployment which struck capitalist economies in the 1930's. However, the unemployment trends set up by a falling marginal efficiency of capital can be offset, at least temporarily, by a corresponding fall in the rate of interest.

The rate of interest

The rate of interest, the other factor which determines the volume of investment, depends upon two things: (a) the state of liquidity preference and (b) the quantity of money. The former is the demand aspect and the latter the supply aspect of the price of money, that is, the rate of interest. Liquidity preference refers to the desire of people to hold some of their assets in the form of money. The quantity of money refers to the amount of funds in the form of coins, paper currency, and bank deposits outstanding in the hands of the public.

There are several reasons why people may wish to hold wealth in the form of money. Classified according to motive, these include the transactions motive, the precautionary motive, and the speculative motive (p. 170). The demand for money for the transactions motive refers to the use of money as a medium of exchange for ordinary transactions such as buying raw materials, paying rent, paying wages, paying dividends, et cetera. For any given level of employment, output, and prices, there is a relatively definite and stable quantity of money needed for this purpose. As the level of employment and output rises, the number of transactions will, of course, increase and thus increase the demand for money for transactions. Likewise, a general rise in prices or wages will increase the amount of money needed for transactions. The precautionary motive for holding money arises from the need for meeting unforeseen emergencies which will involve outlays greater than those involved in the usual anticipated transactions. Here again the amount of money needed to satisfy this demand is relatively stable and predictable.

The type of liquidity preference which is important in relation to the rate of interest is that arising in connection with the speculative motive. Keynes defines the speculative motive as "the object of securing profit from knowing better than the market what the future will bring forth" (p. 170). Quite apart from needs for money as a medium of exchange, people hold money as a store of wealth. They hold their assets in this form because they prefer it to any other means of storing wealth. This is a type of speculation because in holding their wealth in the barren money form, people are speculating on the chances that conditions will change so they will be able to convert their money into earning assets on better terms at a later date, and on terms which will be enough better to offset any earnings that might be made by parting with liquidity now. Chiefly responsible for this type of preference for money is uncertainty concerning the future rate of interest. If it is thought that the interest rate may rise in the future, there will be an incentive to hold money and avoid buying income-yielding securities such as bonds. A future rise in the rate of interest may wipe out an amount of the capitalized value of purchased assets to an extent that will more than offset any temporary returns in the form of interest or dividends. The lower the interest rate goes, the stronger becomes the incentive to hold wealth in the form of money. There is an increasing danger of capital loss arising from a slight rise in the interest rate. The long-term rate of interest will be especially sensitive to liquidity preference because over a long period the uncertainty of events increases in a sort of geometric proportion.

In the light of these circumstances, the demand for money to satisfy the speculative motive is subject to erratic fluctuations, in contrast with the relatively stable demand for the transactions and precautionary motives. When liquidity preference for the speculative motive weakens, the interest

rate will fall, and when liquidity preference for the speculative motive strengthens, the rate of interest will rise. Liquidity preference rises and falls according to the changing attitudes of the public toward the economic and political future.
Thus the level of the interest rate depends upon factors which
are highly psychological in nature. The so-called psychological factors are themselves conditioned by more objective
events in the economic and political arena.

A rise in the interest rate resulting from increased liquidity preference indicates that the desire to store wealth in the
form of money is not an absolute desire, but one which is
relative to the desire for rewards offered by other alternatives.
If the reward for surrendering liquidity is high enough—
that is, if the interest rate is high enough—illiquidity will
be risked. The interest rate is a price which fluctuates according to the supply and demand for money. The supply is fixed
by the banking system and the demand is determined by
the preference for holding cash. As long as the supply remains fixed, the price, or rate, varies with the demand. The
rate of interest is the price which "equilibrates the desire to
hold wealth in the form of cash with the available quantity
of cash" (p. 167). If the rate of interest were lower at any
particular time the public would want to hold more cash
than is available, and if the rate of interest were higher at
any time, the public would not wish to hold all the cash that
is available.[4] Interest is the reward paid for the use of money,
and the reward, like any price, must be neither too high nor
too low in relation to the supply.

Although the public does not control the quantity of
money, the banking system does. All the public can do when
it wants to hold more money and there is no more money is
to bid up the price, the rate of interest. But the banking
authorities are in a position to answer the demand for more
money by increasing the supply, and thus preventing the rate
of interest from rising. Consequently, the position of the

4. The word "cash" as used here is equivalent to "money" including demand
deposits.

banking and monetary authorities is strategic in relation to the rate of interest. By pursuing a policy of a flexible money supply, the banking system can, within limits, control the rate of interest. If the banking authorities cannot control the psychological ups and downs of the public in its attitude toward liquidity preference, they can at least offset the effects of these changes on the interest rate by letting a public which desires to hold more cash actually hold more cash. It is crucial to Keynes' position that the monetary authorities should be strong and during depressions should pursue an easy money policy which will lower interest rates and permit them to remain low.

In the transition from depression to recovery, the demand for money for transactions will be increasing. If this increased demand must be met by drawing upon money used to satisfy the speculative motive, the rate of interest will rise, and recovery will be impeded. Therefore, unless the banks are ready to lend more cash, or unless the liquidity preference of the public for the speculative motive decreases considerably, the volume of investment will fall off and recovery may be nipped before it has really begun. This shortage of money would retard investment and recovery no matter how much the desire of the public to save might increase.

The Relation of Investment to Consumption

There exists a definite relation between the amount of consumption output and the amount of investment output which it will be profitable for entrepreneurs to produce. Given the propensity to consume, the amount of consumption demand depends on the size of national income. National income is created partly from the output of consumption and partly from the output of investment. The volume of investment depends on the inducement to invest as determined by the principles discussed in the preceding section. Hence, the amount of consumption goods that it will be profitable for entrepreneurs to produce depends partly on the amount of investment output that is being produced. If the inducement to invest is such that entrepreneurs in the United States are producing $40 billion worth of investment goods, and if the propensity to consume is four-fifths, it will pay to produce $160 billion worth of consumption output in addition to the $40 billion worth of investment output. The output is divided four-fifths to consumption and one-fifth to investment because demand is in the ratio of four to one. If output is to be sold without losses, it must be proportioned between consumption goods and investment goods in the ratio which corresponds to the ratio in which income receivers choose to divide their incomes between consumption expenditure and saving. The *amount* of total output it will pay to produce in this ratio depends on the amount of investment demand.

In the arithmetical example cited in the preceding paragraph, the $160 billion of effective demand for consumption comes from the income, some of which is earned in investment activity. For example, men working on the construction of a factory (investment goods) spend part of their incomes for groceries and clothes (consumption goods) just as do men who work in factories turning out consumers goods. Thus if the number employed in building factories decreases, so will the demand for consumption goods decrease. Using the above figures, suppose investment falls from $40 to $39 billion. If the ratio of consumption to investment remains 4 to 1, there will have to be a fall in consumption to a level of 4 times $39 billion or $156 billion. From a fall of $1 billion in investment there results a fall of $4 billion in consumption, making a total fall of $5 billion. National income decreases from $200 to $195 billion ($156 plus $39 equals $195). While the ratio may not remain exactly 4 to 1, it will not change very much as long as total income remains in the neighborhood of $200 billion.

Ratio 4:1   What would happen if entrepreneurs did not reduce their output of consumption goods by $4 billion when investment falls from $40 billion to $39 billion? Suppose they continued to produce the same amount of consumers goods as before, $160 billion worth. They would be unable to sell all the consumers goods produced, because the workers who lost their jobs in investment activity and other income recipients whose incomes had been lowered as a result of the falling off of investment would not spend as much for consumers goods as before. When incomes are less, consumption expenditure will be less, given the propensity to consume. The original impact of the $1 billion fall in investment is to lower income from $200 billion to $199 billion. But this is not the end of the process. Retailers and others whose sales are reduced will suffer reduced income, wholesalers who sell to retailers will also suffer reduced income, and the manufacturers who sell to wholesalers will suffer likewise. This process of cumulative income reduction will go on until the total fall in income resulting from a decline in consumption demand is 4 times the fall in investment demand. The over-all ratio of 4 to 1 between consumption and investment will be reestablished at 156 to 39, or at a total income of $195 billion. These relations between investment and consumption will be explored more fully in the discussion of the multiplier in Chapter 5.

What would be the result of applying the classical theory to the above situation? Under conditions of full employment assumed by the classical theory, income and total effective demand remain constant in the short period. Effective demand will always be sufficient to lead to full employment. Starting with an income of $200 billion, divided $160 billion to consumption and $40 billion to investment, a fall in investment of $1 billion would have to result in an *increase* in consumption from $160 billion to $161 billion. This would change the ratio of consumption to investment in a way inconsistent with Keynes' principle of effective demand. It would also seem to violate common sense because it assumes consumption will increase at the very time when men are losing jobs and spending less for consumers goods than before. Although the classical analysis may seem to violate common sense, it is not without an answer as to why decreases in investment lead to increases in consumption. The answer relates to the classical theory of the rate of interest, which brings the volume of investment to equality with the volume of saving, a subject which will be explored further in Chapter 8.

Summary of the General Theory of Employment

From the foregoing discussion and from Figure 3 it may be seen that there are several alternative ways of expressing the essence of the general theory of employment. An over-all summary may be stated in the form of the following propositions:

1. Total income depends on the volume of total employment.
2. According to the propensity to consume, the amount of expenditure for consumption depends on the level of income, and therefore on total employment (from No. 1 above).
3. Total employment depends on total effective demand (D), which is made up of two parts: (a) consumption expenditure (D_1) and (b) investment expenditure (D_2).
   $(D = D_1 + D_2)$
4. In equilibrium, the aggregate demand (D) is equal to the aggregate supply (Z). Therefore, aggregate supply exceeds the effective demand for consumption by the amount of the effective demand for investment.
   $(D = D_1 + D_2$, or $D_2 = D - D_1$. Since $D = Z$, therefore $D_2 = Z - D_1$.)
5. In equilibrium, aggregate supply is equal to aggregate demand, and aggregate demand is determined by the propensity to consume and the volume of investment. Therefore, the volume of employment depends on (a) the aggregate supply function, (b) the propensity to consume, and (c) the volume of investment.
6. Both the aggregate supply function, which depends mainly on physical conditions of supply, and the propensity to consume are relatively stable, and therefore fluctuations in employment depend mainly on the volume of investment.
7. The volume of investment depends on (a) the marginal

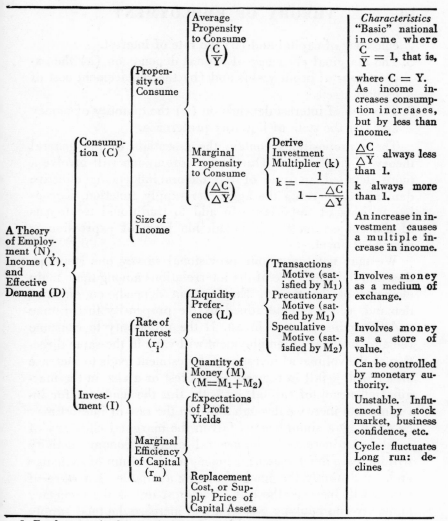

1. Employment (and income) depend on effective demand.
2. Effective demand is determined by the propensity to consume and the volume of investment.
3. The propensity to consume is relatively stable.
4. Employment depends on the volume of investment if the propensity to consume is unchanged.
5. Investment depends on the rate of interest and the marginal efficiency of capital.
6. The rate of interest depends on the quantity of money and liquidity preference.
7. The marginal efficiency of capital depends on the expectations of profit yields and the replacement cost of capital assets.

Figure 3. An Outline of the General Theory of Employment

efficiency of capital and (b) the rate of interest.

8. The marginal efficiency of capital depend on (a) the expectations of profit yields and (b) the replacement cost of capital assets.

9. The rate of interest depends on (a) the quantity of money and (b) the state of liquidity preference.

These propositions contain the essentials of the general theory of employment. Our further discussion will involve a more detailed analysis of the factors influencing effective demand. Concerning the aggregate supply function, Keynes has nothing of importance to add to traditional treatments of the subject matter, although his form of expression is somewhat novel.

We may now carry our provisional survey one step further and indicate some of the interrelations among these main elements of the theory. Employment depends on effective demand, which is determined by the propensity to consume and the inducement to invest. If the propensity to consume remains unchanged, employment will vary in the same direction as the volume af investment. Investment tends to increase either with a fall in the rate of interest or a rise in the marginal efficiency of capital, or both. But the tendency for investment to increase through a fall in the rate of interest may be offset by a simultaneous fall in the marginal efficiency of capital. An increase in the general level of economic activity will increase the demand for money as a medium of exchange and, by draining the fund of money available as a store of value, will increase the rate of interest unless the monetary authority and banking system act to increase the total supply of money. And even though the quantity of money may be increasing, the rate of interest may nevertheless rise as a result of an unfavorable shift in the attitude of wealth-holders toward liquidity. Expectations of rising future yields from capital assets will tend to raise the marginal efficiency of capital and thus raise investment and employment. This favorable effect may be offset by a simultaneous rise in the current supply price (cost of production) of capital assets.

Although rising investment will usually be accompanied by rising employment, this need not happen if the propensity to consume is falling. On the other hand, employment can rise without a rise in investment if the propensity to consume is rising. As a rule, however, the propensity to consume, or consumption function, is stable in the short run.

Finally, increases in investment bring about increases in income, and out of larger income there arises a greater demand for consumption which leads to still further increases in income. Taken in reverse, this process means that a fall in investment will decrease income and out of the decreased income there will be less demand for consumption, which leads to still further decreases in income. Once set in motion, movements of income and employment tend to be cumulative. These cumulative movements account for the fluctuating nature of employment. Limits to amplitude of fluctuation are set in the downward direction at the level at which income falls to equality with consumption, and in the upward direction at full employment. Actual fluctuations will not, as a rule, range all the way from one extreme to the other. An upward movement will characteristically stop short of full employment and a downward movement will usually stop short of the point at which income has fallen to equality with consumption. What the actual range will be depends upon the strength or weakness of the propensity to consume and the inducement to invest under the prevailing circumstances.

Practical Meaning of the Main Concepts

Among all the terms and concepts used by Keynes in *The General Theory of Employment, Interest and Money*, the three which stand out above all the rest as the strategic, independent variables are the propensity to consume (consumption schedule), the marginal efficiency of capital (investment-demand schedule), and the rate of interest (liquidity-preference schedule). The choice of these three independent variables or strategic factors arises from the nature of Keynes' interest in practical policy. The ultimate purpose of his

theory is to explain what determines the volume of employment, or in terms of the practical problems involved, what
causes unemployment. To explain the cause means, in a
significant sense, to point to those factors or to a course of
action which, if changed or followed, will remedy the malady.
Thus when we say a common cold is caused by sitting in a
draft, we usually mean that by not sitting in a draft a cold
will not occur or is less likely to occur. To explain unemployment means to indicate those aspects of the economic system
which need to be changed or subjected to social control in
order to assure a high level of employment. Keynes says:
"Our final task might be to select those variables which can
be deliberately controlled or managed by central authority
in the kind of system in which we actually live."[5]

Realistic theory is necessarily conditioned by the theorist's
sense of values and by his ideas as to what is practicable
policy. The realistic nature of Keynes' theory may be attributed largely to his vital concern with a specific type of economic program. This does not mean that Keynes' theoretical
concepts are worthless in relation to policies other than those
advocated by him, nor does it mean that his policies or any
other policies necessarily follow from his abstract, theoretical
concepts. However, a recognition of the social values and
practical aims of a pioneering theorist like Keynes gives a
richer insight into the meaning of his abstract theoretical
concepts and propositions. A concept like the propensity to
consume, or consumption function, is a formal, mathematical
relationship between amounts of consumption corresponding
to amounts of income for the community as a whole. But this
is only the bare bones. The full meaning of this formal concept as used by Keynes emerges in terms of the use to which
he puts it. He uses it to show the necessity of a high rate of
consumer expenditure, which, perhaps, can be obtained by
a more equal distribution of income and wealth. He uses it
to indicate the desirability of steeply progressive taxation

5. Keynes, *The General Theory of Employment, Interest and Money*. New
York: Harcourt, Brace and Co., Inc., 1936, page 247.

and large government outlays for social services. The propensity to consume is further refined in the form of the marginal propensity to consume, which is used to derive the concept of the investment multiplier. The common-sense meaning of the investment multiplier is that in times of depression when private investment lags, government investment in public works will increase the national income not only by the amount of the public outlay but by some multiple of it.

In these terms Keynes makes a case for public works and becomes an advocate of public spending. His theory is referred to as a "spending" theory. To call a theory a spending theory has no meaning except in relation to some fairly specific steps or policies that may be followed to increase aggregate demand above what it would be in the absence of such policies. When we trace the concepts to their practical consequences, the lifeless forms of abstraction begin to take on definite shape and meaning. We see them emerging as plans of action, altered behavior, policies. The theory is put into practice. Only when theory is put into practice—that is, only when we trace the theory to its practical consequences—can we hope to test its validity by an appeal to facts and thus arrive at an evaluation of its probable workability in the actual world.

The operational or practical meaning of Keynes' theory will be referred to often in this book in the belief that this method will facilitate the understanding of what is likely to appear to be an intrinsically difficult body of doctrine. At this juncture we allude briefly to the operational significance of Keynes' theories of the rate of interest and the marginal efficiency of capital, the two independent variables which, along with the propensity to consume referred to in the preceding paragraph, determine the level of employment. The uniqueness of Keynes' theory of the rate of interest runs in terms of the importance of controlling the quantity of money. The novel concept is liquidity preference for the speculative motive. Wealth-holders have a preference for keeping their assets in a liquid form, the form of money, and it is this desire to hoard which determines the level of interest rates. An easy money policy under a strong monetary authority can keep down the interest rates and thus stimulate investment and employment. However, Keynes' practical sense is too strong to lead him to attach sole importance to interest rates and so we find a parallel stress on the marginal efficiency of capital. The chief characteristic of the marginal efficiency of capital is its great instability. It may fall so low in depression that no reduction in interest rates will induce private investment. To alleviate the consequences of instability in the marginal efficiency of private capital, Keynes advocates government direction of total investment, including public investment, to compensate for the inevitable fluctuations in private investment. A low rate of interest and a high marginal efficiency of capital are the conditions favorable to investment and employment. Since the natural tendency is for the rate of interest to stay up and the marginal efficiency of capital to come down, laissez-faire policies will leave the volume of investment short of what is necessary for full employment. Both of these determinates of investment involve psychological attitudes toward the future which cause investment to be much less stable than the volume of consumption. The instability of these factors determining investment leads Keynes to say that employment is determined by investment.

The Paradox of Poverty and Potential Plenty

Keynes' principle of effective demand furnishes an explanation of the paradox of poverty in the midst of potential plenty, one of the grave contradictions of modern capitalism. A poor community will have little difficulty employing all its resources because it will tend to spend on consumption a large proportion of its total income. Only a small gap needs to be filled by investment, and since the stock of accumulated capital assets will be slight in the poor community, the demand for investment will be brisk. A wealthy community, on the contrary, will have great difficulty maintaining full employment because the gap between income and consumption will be large. Its investment outlets must be great if there are to be enough jobs for all. Failing to find these outlets, the potentially wealthy community will be forced to reduce its actual output until it becomes so poor that the excess of output over consumption will be reduced to the actual amount of investment. To make matters worse, the very fact that a community is rich in accumulated capital assets weakens the inducement to invest because every new investment must compete with an already large supply of old investments. The inadequacy of demand for investment reacts in a cumulative fashion on the demand for consumption. The factories that are already built cannot be used because more factories are not being built. Unemployment on a mass scale exists in the midst of potential plenty. Thus as Keynes says, "the richer the community . . . the more obvious and outrageous the defects of the economic system." Keynes finds no reason to assume that the growing gap between income and consumption at high levels of employment will be filled automatically, that is, without conscious social action, except under special historical circumstances like those existing in the nineteenth century or in time of war. War has a distinct if ironical advantage over peaceful industry in that it calls for the production of things which are to be exploded and shot away and do not remain to compete with more production of the same type at a later date. If war and threat of war are banished from the world, the capitalist countries will once more be confronted with the tasks of finding sufficient outlets for new investment to provide employment for all of its millions of workers who cannot be employed in consumption industries.

References for Further Reading

Keynes, J. M., *The General Theory of Employment, Interest and Money*. Chapters 1, 2, 3, and 18. New York: Harcourt, Brace and Company, 1936.

———, "The General Theory of Employment," *The Quarterly Jour-*

nal of Economics, February, 1937, Vol. LI, pages 209-223. Reprinted in *The New Economics,* edited by S. E. Harris. New York: Alfred A. Knopf, 1947. (This is the best statement of the essence of *The General Theory of Employment, Interest and Money* made by the author himself.)

Cassel, Gustav, "Mr. Keynes' 'General Theory,' " *International Labour Review,* October, 1937, Vol. XXVI, pages 437-445. (A critical review)

Darrell, John (Pseudonym), "Economic Consequences of Mr. Keynes," *Science and Society,* Winter, 1937, Vol. I, pages 194-211. (A Marxist review)

Haberler, Gottfried, "The Place of the General Theory of Employment, Interest and Money in the History of Economic Thought," *The Review of Economic Statistics,* November, 1946, Vol. XXVIII, pages 187-194. Reprinted in *The New Economics,* edited by S. E. Harris. New York: Alfred A. Knopf, 1947.

Hansen, A. H., "Mr. Keynes on Underemployment Equilibrium," *The Journal of Political Economy,* October, 1936, Vol. XLIV, pages 667-686. (A sympathetic review)

————, "Keynes and the General Theory," *The Review of Economic Statistics,* November, 1946, Vol. XXVIII, pages 182-187. Reprinted in *The New Economics,* edited by S. E. Harris. New York: Alfred A. Knopf, 1947. (This 1946 review is more favorable to Keynes than the one which Professor Hansen wrote in 1936.)

Harris, S. E., *The New Economics,* edited by S. E. Harris, Part I. New York: Alfred A. Knopf, 1947.

Harrod, R. F., "Mr. Keynes and Traditional Theory," *Econometrica,* January, 1937, Vol. V, pages 74-86. (A sympathetic review by one of Keynes' leading disciples)

Hawtrey, R. G., *Capital and Employment,* Chapter VII. New York: Longmans, Green, 1937. (A critical but helpful review)

Hicks, J. R., "Mr. Keynes' Theory of Employment," *The Economic Journal,* June, 1936, Vol. XLVI, pages 238-253. (A sympathetic review)

————, "Mr. Keynes and the Classics: A Suggested Interpretation," *Econometrica,* April, 1937, Vol. V, pages 147-159. (A statement of the *General Theory* in mathematical terms)

Klein, L. R., *The Keynesian Revolution,* esp. Chapter III. New York: The Macmillan Company, 1947.

Knight, F. H., "Unemployment: And Mr. Keynes's Revolution in Economic Thought," *The Canadian Journal of Economics and Po-*

litical Science, February, 1937, Vol. III, pages 100-123. (A very critical review)

Lange, Oscar, "The Rate of Interest and the Optimum Propensity to Consume," *Economica*, February, 1938, Vol. V (new series), pages 12-32.

Lederer, Emil, "Commentary on Keynes," *Social Research*, November, 1936, Vol. III, pages 478-487.

Leontief, Wassily, "The Fundamental Assumption of Mr. Keynes' Monetary Theory of Unemployment," *The Quarterly Journal of Economics*, November, 1936, Vol. LI, pages 192-197.

———, "Postulates: Keynes' *General Theory* and the Classicists," in *The New Economics*, edited by S. E. Harris, Chapter XIX. New York: Alfred A. Knopf, 1947.

Lerner, A. P., "Mr. Keynes' 'General Theory of Employment, Interest and Money,'" *International Labour Review*, October, 1936, Vol. XXXIV, pages 435-454. (An important review which was approved by Keynes)

Mount, Edward, "The Equilibrists and Mr. Keynes," *The New Masses*, September 1 and 8, 1936, Vol. XX, pages 18-19 and 17-18. (A Marxist review)

Neisser, Hans, "Commentary on Keynes," *Social Research*, November, 1936, Vol. III, pages 459-478.

Pigou, A. C., "Mr. J. M. Keynes' General Theory of Employment, Interest and Money," *Economica*, May, 1936, Vol. III (new series), pages 115-132.

Reddaway, W. B., "The General Theory of Employment, Interest and Money," *Economic Record*, June, 1936, Vol. XII, pages 28-36. (An excellent and sympathetic review)

Robertson, D. H., "Some Notes on Mr. Keynes' General Theory of Employment," *The Quarterly Journal of Economics*, November, 1936, Vol. LI, pages 168-191. (An excellent review which is critical of Keynes' theory of interest and his terminology, especially saving and investment)

Rueff, Jacques, "The Fallacies of Lord Keynes' General Theory," *The Quarterly Journal of Economics*, May, 1947, Vol. LXI, pages 343-367.

Schumpeter, J. A., "Keynes' General Theory of Employment, Interest and Money," *Journal of the American Statistical Association*, December, 1936, Vol. XXXI (new series), pages 791-795. (A brief, critical and significant review)

Shibata, Kei, "Some Questions on Mr. Keynes' General Theory of Employment, Interest and Money," *Kyoto Economic Review*, July, 1937, Vol. XII, pages 83-96.

Shibata, Kei, "Further Comments on Mr. Keynes' General Theory," *Kyoto Economic Review*, July 1939, Vol. XIV, pages 45-72. (Both of Shibata's articles are excellent.)

Takata, Yasuma, "Unemployment and Wages: A Critical Review of Mr. Keynes' Theory of Employment," *Kyoto Economic Review*, December, 1937, Vol. XII, pages 1-18.

Tarshis, Lorie, "An Exposition of Keynesian Economics," *The American Economic Review, Papers and Proceedings*, May, 1948, Vol. XXXVIII, pages 261-272.

Viner, Jacob, "Mr. Keynes on the Causes of Unemployment," *The Quarterly Journal of Economics*, November, 1936, Vol. LI, pages 147-167.

Williams, J. H., "An Appraisal of Keynesian Economics," *The American Economic Review, Papers and Proceedings*, May, 1948, Vol. XXXVIII, pages 273-290.

CHAPTER 4

Investment, Saving, Income, and the Wage–Unit

It is true, that, when an individual saves he increases his own wealth. But the conclusion that he also increases aggregate wealth fails to allow for the possibility that an act of individual saving may react on someone else's savings and hence on someone else's wealth.

J. M. Keynes, *The General Theory of Employment, Interest and Money.*[*]

IN KEYNES' *General Theory* aggregate investment always equals aggregate saving. This equality is a condition of equilibrium regardless of what the level of employment happens to be. Equality between investment and saving is a consequence of changes in the level of income. If investment increases, then income will increase until the saving out of the higher income is equal to the increased investment; and if investment falls, income will fall until the saving out of the lower income is equal to the reduced investment. Hence, these concepts are geared to the fundamental idea of a shifting equilibrium as distinguished from a special, full-employment equilibrium in which investment equals saving only at full employment. Investment, saving, and income are key terms which must be defined more fully. Like any set of con-

---

[*] Harcourt, Brace and Co., Inc., 1936, pages 83-84.

cepts, they take on their full meaning only in relation to the whole theory of which they are a part. It is not the individual definitions in isolation that are important but the concepts in relation to each other and to the rest of the theory. If we bear in mind that Keynes' method is one which investigates the problem of unemployment in terms of an equilibrium system in which the equality of aggregate demand and aggregate supply is the fundamental condition, we may avoid the confusion that has characterized many discussions of saving and investment.

Since Keynes' theory deals with the economic system as a whole, the terms investment, saving, and income mean aggregate or total national or social investment, saving, and income. Investment is the addition to the existing stock of *real* capital assets, such as the construction of new factories, new office buildings, transportation facilities, and additions to inventories. This use of the term is to be carefully distinguished from purely financial investment such as the purchase of a stock or bond in the securities market. In the latter case, one party exchanges money for securities and another party exchanges securities for money. The additional financial investment of the party who purchases securities is just offset by the financial disinvestment of the party who sells securities. Hence, if we look at both sides of a financial investment it is consistent with Keynes' definition of (aggregate) investment because in the economic system as a whole financial investments cancel each other. No addition is made to real capital as a result of such a transaction and therefore no real investment occurs. When new securities are issued to finance plant expansion, et cetera, and labor and materials are purchased to build real capital assets, it is the latter and not the purchase of the securities as such that constitute the real investment.

The exact line of demarcation between investment and consumption is not a matter of great importance so long as it is consistently maintained. Some expenditures such as those for food and clothing are clearly consumption. Others such as the building of factories and railroads clearly represent investment. Some items such as consumers durable goods are not so easily classified. It is customary, for example, to regard outlays on housing construction as investment and outlays for automobiles as consumption, but this distinction is clearly one which might be, and has been, a subject of debate. The fact that there are no hard and fast rules for classifying some items as investment and others as consumption does not raise any important theoretical question. In statistical tabulations of the division of total output, it is, of course, important to indicate what items are placed in each category.

Investment includes additions to inventories as well as to fixed capital. These additions may be either intentional or unintentional. Intended increases are motivated by larger volume of sales or by anticipation of price changes or by other related factors which are part of the ordinary planning activities of business enterprise. Unintended investment is the accumulation of unsold finished goods (liquid capital in Keynes' terminology) arising from unforeseen changes in the market. Some writers view the distinction between intended and unintended accumulations of inventories as of prime significance but for Keynes' general theory the difference is not important (p. 76).

Saving is defined as the excess of income over consumption expenditure. This definition applies to individual saving and to aggregate saving of the economic system. An individual who has a yearly income of $2000, taxes being disregarded, and spends $1800 for consumption, saves $200. An economy which has a national income of $200 billion per year and spends $180 billion for consumption, saves $20 billion. In both cases, saving is equal to income minus consumption. However, in dealing with the over-all behavior of the economic system, account must frequently be taken of factors which may be ignored when we are concerned only with the behavior of the individual units in isolation. Saving is behavior of this type. Although individual saving and community saving are both defined in the same terms, and although community saving is the net resultant of the saving of all individual units within the community, individual saving does not always result in community saving. Individual saving is not-spending for consumption, and a failure to spend by one individual may reduce the income of others and hence impair their ability to save. Unless it is clearly understood that the kind of saving Keynes is talking about in the *General Theory* is aggregate or collective saving, the equality between investment and saving will be difficult to grasp.

The fundamental fact about saving is that its volume depends upon income. At varying levels of national income, the community will want to save amounts which are more or less stable and predictable at any given time. In other words, the propensity to save is stable. Investment, on the other hand, does not depend to any significant degree upon the size of the national income. Investment depends mainly on dynamic factors like growth of population, geographical expansion, and technological progress as these growth factors affect the profit expectations of entrepreneurs. Individuals save without any thought of building factories or otherwise making real investment. Entrepreneurs invest without ascertaining whether or not there has been an equivalent amount of saving. Despite the fact that investors and savers are, as a rule, two separate sets of persons who make their decisions freely and independently of one another, the net result of their collective behavior is to invest and to save in the aggregate identical amounts during any given period. The clue to this equality is found in fluctuations in income. Whereas experience indicates that saving is stable, more or less predictable, and induced, investment is unstable, unpredictable, and autonomous. Hence, in terms of the facts of experience, the behavior of investors is a more dynamic factor than is the behavior of savers. Investment rules the roost.

Varying levels of income cannot be sustained unless the amounts of saving at these levels of income are offset by an equivalent volume of investment. If potential savings are not offset, the potential income corresponding to these savings cannot be realized. The equilibrium level of income is realized where saving out of income is just equal to the actual amount of investment.

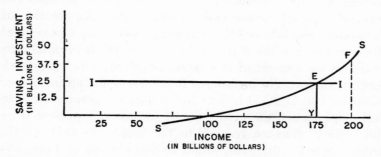

Figure 4. Saving Schedule and Investment Schedule Determine Income.

The relations between income, investment, and saving are indicated in Figure 4.[1] Income is shown along the horizontal axis and saving and investment along the vertical axis. SS is the saving schedule showing how the amount of saving increases with income. At very low levels of income, saving will be negative, meaning that consumption will exceed income. If investment is completely autonomous, in the sense that it does not vary with income, the investment schedule may be represented by the horizontal straight line II. This means that changes in investment take the form of spontaneous shifts in the entire schedule. The facts seem to be that while investment is not completely autonomous, it will not increase

---

1. Diagrams similar to Figure 4 have appeared frequently in the economics literature to explain Keynes' theory, although Keynes himself did not use such a diagram. See, for example, P. A. Samuelson, *Economics, An Introductory Analysis*, page 259. New York: McGraw-Hill Book Company, Inc., 1948; L. R. Klein, *The Keynesian Revolution*, page 76. New York: The Macmillan Company, 1947. Numerous attempts have been made to derive statistically the schedules for saving and investment. On the American data see, for example, M. Ezekiel, in *The American Economic Review*, March and June, 1942, Vol. XXXII, Nos. 1 and 2, pages 22-49 and 272-307.

as rapidly as saving when income rises. This is, of course, fundamental to Keynes' entire theory. Figure 4 concerns the simplest case in which investment remains constant for all levels of income. When investment is $25 billion, the equilibrium level of income will be $175 billion because only at this income will the amount of saving also be $25 billion. The level of national income is determined by the intersection of the saving schedule and the investment schedule. The vertical distance between the saving schedule and the horizontal axis indicates the amount of investment required to maintain each level of income. No investment is necessary for an income of $100 billion. If $200 billion is the income corresponding to full employment, the saving out of income is represented by the vertical distance from F to the horizontal axis, which, according to the diagram, would be $40 billion. Full employment can be achieved only if there is enough investment to offset this amount of saving.

There is a close relationship between Figure 4 and Figure 2. The data used in Figure 2 were, in billions of dollars:

Income	100	125	150	175	200
Consumption	100	120	137.5	150	160

The data used in Figure 4 to show the relation between income and saving are, in terms of billions of dollars:

Income	100	125	150	175	200
Saving	0	5	12.5	25	40

Thus the saving schedule, or the schedule of the propensity to save, may be found by subtracting the amounts of consumption from the corresponding amounts of income. Saving is the excess of income over consumption. The propensity to consume and the propensity to save are the same thing looked at in different ways. Figure 2 illustrates the important principle that income is determined by the propensity to consume and the amount of investment. Figure 4 illustrates the same principle in slightly different terms, namely, that income is determined by the propensity to save and the amount of investment.

Having shown that the equality of the volume of investment and the volume of saving is a condition of equilibrium, we may now restate the relations which lead to this equality. Employment results in the production of output on the one hand and the creation of income on the other. The value of total output is equal to total income. Total income (Y) is equal to the sum of the income created by the production of consumers output plus the income created by the production of investment output, $(Y = C + I)$. Investment is that part of current output which is in excess of the value of consumption goods. Saving is the excess of income over expenditure for consumption. Therefore investment must be equal to saving since they are both equal to the excess of equal values (output and income) over consumption.

Thus:

$Y = C + I$ ... Income = Consumption + Investment
$S = Y - C$ ... Saving = Income — Consumption

Transposing:

$Y = C + S$ ... Income = Consumption + Saving

Therefore,

$I = S$ ... Investment = Saving

The novelty of Keynes' treatment of saving and investment lies not in the fact that they are equal but that they can be and normally are equal at less than full employment. Whereas the classical school associates the equality between investment and saving with automatic changes in the rate of interest, Keynes associates it with changes in the level of income. The fault which Keynes finds with the classical theory is the inference that every act of not-spending (saving) by an individual will increase aggregate investment by the same amount. If this were true, any failure to spend for consumption would be offset by a corresponding increase in investment, and unemployment would not exist.

There appears to be a tendency to think of depression as a

situation in which saving is in excess of investment. Most people are so accustomed to viewing saving from their own individual point of view that it is difficult for them to think of saving from the social or community point of view. Saving is to most people putting money in the bank, or into securities, or into the mattress or an old sock. It is only by an act of conscious intellectual effort that we think far enough into the economic process of society to realize that saving is a two-sided affair. Attempts to save, which are successful so far as the individual is concerned since he adds to his individual wealth, may be self-defeating and even positively harmful so far as society at large is concerned. We plan to save for society as well as for ourselves, but in the absence of co-operation from entrepreneurs we do not assist society even when we attain our personal objectives. Putting part of a monthly salary into a savings account means only that an individual has not spent all his income. The effect of not-spending as such is to reduce the demand for consumption below what it would have been if the money which is saved had been spent. In the absence of some entrepreneur's action to invest, an act of individual saving will prove abortive for the community. It will merely reduce effective demand for consumption without any, compensating increase in the demand for investment. The decrease in effective demand for consumption reduces employment and income. One of the important lessons of the *General Theory* is that spending rather than individual saving is the essential condition of production and prosperity in an exchange economy where one man's spending is another man's income.

A further difficulty in reconciling the equality of saving to investment when there is unemployment arises from ancient mores which condition us to see in personal frugality a virtue applicable equally to society and to ourselves. That a private virtue like saving may be a public vice (unemployment) is almost as foreign to our thinking today as it was in the eighteenth century when Bernard Mandeville's *Fable of the Bees*, an allegorical poem which portrays the sad plight of a once prosperous community in which spending had been cut down in the interest of frugality and virtue, was convicted as a nuisance by a grand jury in England. Individual saving is a mere residual and is no part of effective demand. Individual saving *per se* is a withdrawal of potential effective demand. In the absence of adequate offsets to saving, thrift produces poverty and not wealth. A reluctance to spend takes on a different social significance when it is regarded not as a factor which tends to increase investment but as a factor which tends to cause unemployment (p. 185).

Income

The aggregate income of an entire economic system can be defined in any one of several different ways. Two of the figures most commonly used to refer to the over-all performance of any economy are the gross national product and the net national product. The gross national product is the money value of all the *final* goods and services produced during a given period, and the net national product is equal to the gross national product minus depreciation and obsolescence of capital assets. Final goods are finished articles which are the end products of production. They include final consumer goods like bread and automobiles and final investment goods like factories and locomotives and increases in inventory. They do not include raw materials and intermediate products like iron ore and steel which are sold, say, to automobile manufacturers. The reason for counting only final goods and not raw materials or intermediate goods in the national product is obvious. To do otherwise would involve counting the same products more than once. For example, if the value of steel sold to automobile manufacturers were added to the total market value of the automobile, which includes the cost of the steel purchased from the manufacturer, there would be double counting. This does not mean the whole contribution to national output is made at the final stage of production.

The total value of the product is the sum of the values added at each stage and is embodied in the final product.

As Keynes defines it, aggregate or national income is an amount which lies between the value of the gross national and the net national product as these terms are usually defined. He subtracts some but not all depreciation and obsolescence from the gross national product (which equals the gross national income) to arrive at his concept of "income." He chooses this definition of income because it is the concept which he believes is causally significant in the decisions that determine the amount of employment. Entrepreneurs will offer the amount of employment which maximizes their expected profits. Some depreciation on equipment inherited from the previous period will occur whether or not it is used for production during the current period. For the current period this is an involuntary expense over which the entrepreneur has no control. The entrepreneur does have voluntary control over the extra depreciation and extra maintenance which will occur as a result of the equipment being used rather than not being used. What he controls from now on governs his behavior in determining what scale of output will maximize his profits and what amount of employment will be needed to produce that output. The loss of value resulting from using equipment rather than not using it is called the *user cost* (p. 70). User cost is one of the expenses of production voluntarily undertaken when entrepreneurs decide how many workers to employ. For example, if a machine which is worth $1000 at the beginning of the year is used in production during the year and has a value of $750 at the end of the year, the user cost is not the full $250 decline in value. If the machine had not been used at all during the year it would have declined in value as a result of obsolescence and some forms of depreciation. Suppose its value could have been maintained at $900 at the end of the year by a small maintenance expenditure of $10 when it is not used in production. The user cost for the year is $140 ($900 — $10 — $750), or the difference between the decline in value of

$250 when used and the decline in value of $110 when not used, with allowance for the optimum amount of maintenance involved even when not used.[2]

The income of an individual business firm is therefore defined as that sum which it attempts to maximize and in terms of which it decides how much employment to offer. To arrive at this sum, the firm must subtract from its total proceeds the user cost plus the amounts paid out to other factors of production in the form of wages, interest, and rent (factor cost). Since these latter costs (wages, interest, and rent) represent the income of the rest of the community, the total national income is equal to the aggregate proceeds of all business firms less the aggregate user cost. If gross national income is represented by A and the aggregate user cost by U, the income of the economic system is A — U.

Although income as just defined is the important concept in determining how much employment entrepreneurs will offer, *net income* is the important concept in relation to the amount which will be spent for consumption. Since expenditure for consumption is an important element of effective demand, net income as well as income has a significant place in Keynes' general theory of employment. Net income, either for the firm or the whole economy, is equal to income minus the rest of the expected depreciation and obsolescence which is not included in user cost. This extra depreciation and obsolescence is called the *supplementary cost*. Since supplementary cost is a loss in value which is beyond the control of entrepreneurs, it occurs without regard to decisions whether or not to use equipment and on what scale to employ labor. For the individual business enterprise, net income is the figure which remains after all expenses, including *all* depreciation and obsolescence, have been deducted from proceeds. For the economic system, net income is the aggregate net income (net profits) of all business enterprises plus the payments to

---

2. The total user cost of non-integrated firms also makes allowance for the purchases of the firm from other firms. For the economic system as a whole these interfirm purchases cancel out and do not affect the aggregate user cost.

all other factors of production in the form of wages, interest, and rent. If supplementary cost is represented by V, the aggregate or national *net* income is equal to A — U — V, as compared with the national income, which is equal to A — U.[3]

The importance of net income rather than income in determining how much will be spent on consumption should be obvious. An individual entrepreneur who does not allow for full depreciation before deciding the scale of his consumption is prodigal indeed, even though he would be unwise to determine the scale of his output and employment on this basis. In corporate enterprises, the payment of dividends is limited by law to the amount of net income (net profits), either current or past. Any enterprise which consumed up to the full extent of its income, as defined by Keynes, would not be able to replace its full capital equipment. On the other hand, any practice which understates the amount of net income will tend to retard the amount of consumption and thereby to retard employment. Excessive allowances for depreciation, which are sanctioned and generally practiced by "conservative" accountants, result in an understatement of net income and thereby may contribute to a restriction of consumption and employment (pp. 98-104).

Although the definitions of investment and saving and the equality between them are unaffected by the manner in which income is defined, the magnitudes of saving and investment do depend on the definition of income. Since income is defined as a form of gross income and output as a form of gross output, saving and investment represent a form of gross saving

---

3. If we use lower case letters for individual firms to correspond to upper case letters for the whole economy, the income and *net* income for individual business enterprises are, respectively, a – u – f, and a – u – f – v. An advantage of Keynes' terms is that the firm and national incomes and net incomes are represented by the same symbols except for the obvious fact that the factor cost (f) of the entrepreneur represents the income of the rest of the community and therefore is not to be deducted in arriving at the national income. Wages, for example, are a factor cost to the firm, to be deducted from gross income before arriving at income (profits) or net income (net profits), but to the economic system, wages are a part of the national income.

and gross investment. The excess of gross income over consumption is gross saving and the excess of gross output over consumption is gross investment. Similarly net saving is equal to the excess of net income over consumption and net investment is the excess of net output over consumption. Used without modification, saving means gross saving and investment means gross investment. As with income and net income, Keynes' distinction is between saving and net saving and between investment and net investment. Following his procedure, we shall not use the modifier "gross" when we speak of income, saving, and investment, but it is well to keep in mind how these three important terms are defined.

The Wage-Unit

In order to measure the quantities of output, income, investment, saving, consumption, and demand for the economic system as a whole, Keynes uses two basic units, money and labor. Money is, of course, a basic unit of measurement in any type of economic analysis. Money alone, however, is not enough to enable us to describe the workings of the economic system. In addition to money, there is need for some type of physical unit of production or output. As long as we are dealing with the output of a single enterprise or of a single industry producing a uniform type of product, we may use the physical unit appropriate to each industry. Thus we speak of an individual refinery producing so many million gallons of gasoline, and all the refiners in the petroleum industry producing so many billion gallons of gasoline. The output of every industry can be determined by adding together the appropriate physical units of production of all the firms in the industry. However, if we attempt to add together the output of different industries to arrive at a total output for the entire economic system, we are confronted with an embarrassing situation. The output of the economic system is a combination of gallons of gasoline, tons of coal, pairs of shoes, numbers of automobiles, et cetera. If the number of automobiles produced increases and the number of pairs of shoes decreases, we cannot say whether total output has risen or fallen. Obviously, these non-homogeneous units cannot be added together.

In his *General Theory*, Keynes uses quantities of employment as the index for measuring changes in output of the economic system as a whole. Fluctuations in real output and real income are assumed to correspond to changes in the volume of employment of labor applied to the existing stock of capital equipment. The unit of employment is an hour of labor of ordinary skill, or what is referred to as common labor. One hour of employment of common labor is one labor-unit. The money-unit and the labor-unit are combined to form the wage-unit. The wage-unit is the amount of money received by labor of ordinary skill in one hour of working time. Labor of superior skill is equated to labor of ordinary skill in proportion to its remuneration.[4] For example, if the rate of remuneration of labor of ordinary skill is one dollar per hour, the wage-unit is one dollar. If a bricklayer receives three dollars per hour, then one hour of a bricklayer's labor represents three labor-units and his compensation per hour represents three wage-units.

At any time, total output or total income and other aggregate magnitudes will have a certain value in terms of wage-units. One of the arguments in favor of the wage-unit is the relative stability of the rate of pay to labor of ordinary skill. As long as the hourly money wage of common labor remains unchanged, the wage-unit is constant, and changes in output, measured in terms of wage-units, vary with changes in the amount of labor employed. Keynes does not attempt to use the wage-unit to make comparisons of output over historical time or between different countries or between the output resulting from different quantities of capital equipment. Most of the analysis in the *General Theory* assumes the wage-unit to be constant. Some parts of the analysis,

---

4. For Keynes' defense of this point, see the *General Theory*, pages 41-43.

however, explicitly take into account the influence of changes in the size of the wage-unit. In the theory of prices and inflation, for example, an increase in the hourly wage rate which occurs as employment rises is the basic factor to which a rise in prices is attributed. When hourly wages rise, the wage-unit increases, and when hourly wages fall, the wage-unit decreases. While the wage-unit is not an entirely satisfactory concept, it is important to understand that it is used (1) because changes in output are measured by changes in the amount of employment and (2) because Keynes' general theory of employment deals with the economic system as a whole rather than with individual firms and industries.

References for Further Reading

Keynes, J. M., *The General Theory of Employment, Interest and Money*, Chapters 4, 6, 7, and 8. New York: Harcourt, Brace and Company, 1936.

——, "The Process of Capital Formation," *The Economic Journal*, September, 1939, Vol. XLIX, pages 569-574.

Altman, O. L., *Saving, Investment, and National Income*, Temporary National Economic Committee, Monograph No. 37. Washington: U. S. Government Printing Office, 1941.

Curtis, Myra, "Is Money Saving Equal to Investment?" *The Quarterly Journal of Economics*, August, 1937, Vol. LI, pages 604-625.

Ezekiel, Mordecai, "Saving, Consumption, and Investment," *The American Economic Review*, March and June, 1942, Vol. XXXII, pages 22-49, 272-307.

Gilbert, Milton, and Jaszi, George, "National Product and Income Statistics as an Aid in Economic Problems," *Readings in the Theory of Income Distribution*, selected by a Committee of the American Economic Association. Philadelphia: The Blakiston Company, 1946.

Hansen, A. H., "A Note on Savings and Investment," *The Review of Economic Statistics*, February, 1948, Vol. XXX, pages 30-33.

——, "National Income and Gross National Product," Chapter III in *Economic Policy and Full Employment*. New York: McGraw-Hill Book Company, Inc., 1947.

Hayes, H. Gordon, *Spending, Saving, and Employment*. New York: Alfred A. Knopf, 1945.

Kuznets, Simon, *National Income: A Summary of Findings*. New York: National Bureau of Economic Research, 1946. (Professor Kuznets has done the pioneer work in national income studies of the United States.)

Lerner, A. P., "Saving Equals Investment," *The Quarterly Journal of Economics*, February, 1938, Vol. LII, pages 297-309. Reprinted in *The New Economics*, edited by S. E. Harris. New York: Alfred A. Knopf, 1947.

———, "Saving and Investment: Definitions, Assumptions, Objectives," *The Quarterly Journal of Economics*, August, 1939, Vol. LIII, pages 611-619. Reprinted in *Readings in Business Cycle Theory*, selected by a Committee of the American Economic Association. Philadelphia: The Blakiston Company, 1944; and in *The New Economics*, edited by S. E. Harris. New York: Alfred A. Knopf, 1947.

———, "User Cost and Prime User Cost," *The American Economic Review*, March, 1943, Vol. XXXIII, pages 131-132.

Lutz, F. A., "Outcome of the Saving-Investment Discussion," *The Quarterly Journal of Economics*, August, 1938, Vol. LII, pages 588-614. Reprinted in *Readings in Business Cycle Theory*, selected by a Committee of the American Economic Association. Philadelphia: The Blakiston Company, 1944.

Morgan, Theodore, *Income and Employment*. New York: Prentice, Hall, Inc., 1947.

Ohlin, Bertil, "Some Notes on the Stockholm Theory of Savings and Investment," *The Economic Journal*, March and June, 1937, Vol. XLVII, pages 53-69, 221-240.

Robertson, D. H., "Saving and Hoarding," *The Economic Journal*, September, 1933, Vol. XLIII, pages 399-413. Reprinted in Robertson, D. H., *Essays in Monetary Theory*. London: P. S. King and Son, Ltd., 1940.

Shoup, Carl S., *Principles of National Income Analysis*. Boston: Houghton Mifflin Company, 1947.

U. S. Department of Commerce, *Survey of Current Business, Supplement* on "National Income," July, 1947, Vol. 27. (A valuable statement of the revised basis for computing national income in the United States.)

CHAPTER 5

The Propensity to Consume and the Investment Multiplier

The psychology of the community is such that when aggregate real income is increased aggregate consumption is increased, but not by so much as income . . . Unless the psychological propensities of the public are different from what we are supposing, we have here established the law that increased employment for investment must necessarily stimulate the industries producing for consumption and thus lead to a total increase of employment which is a multiple of the primary employment required by the investment itself.

J. M. Keynes, *The General Theory of Employment, Interest and Money.**

THE ULTIMATE purpose of Keynes' theory is to explain what determines the volume of employment. The starting point is the principle of effective demand, which states that employment depends on the sum of consumption expenditures and investment expenditures. Consumption depends on the size of consumers' net income and the propensity to consume, and investment depends on the marginal efficiency of capital taken in conjunction with the rate of interest. A high propensity to consume is favorable to employment, and one of

* Harcourt, Brace and Co., Inc., 1936, pages 27 and 118.

the remedies for unemployment is to be found in measures designed to increase the propensity to consume. When investment increases and causes income to rise, the resulting additions to income are expended largely for consumption. The relationship between increases in investment and increases in consumption, which was discussed in a preliminary fashion in Chapter 3, is explored more fully in the present chapter in terms of the investment multiplier, which is the ratio of an increase of income to a given increase in new investment. In common-sense terms, the investment multiplier means that when investment increases, national income will increase not only by the amount of investment but by some multiple of it. The great practical significance of the multiplier arises in relation to Keynes' advocacy of public investment and other forms of governmental expenditure as a source of effective demand in periods in which private enterprise does not furnish adequate investment to provide full employment of labor and other resources.

The Concept of the Propensity to Consume

The propensity to consume, which is simply the relationship between income and consumption, may be represented by means of a diagram. If values for income (Y) are plotted along the horizontal axis and consumption (C) along the vertical axis, the line which relates these two variables represents the schedule of the propensity to consume, or what is called for the sake of brevity, the propensity to consume. This schedule of the propensity to consume may also be referred to as the "consumption function" because it shows the functional relationship between the two variables, income and consumption. "Propensity to consume" does not mean a mere desire to consume, but the actual consumption that takes place, or is expected to take place, out of varying amounts of income. In this respect it is similar to a demand schedule, which refers not to mere desire to buy but to willingness plus ability to buy. The data on income and consumption in a schedule of the propensity to consume may be either for the community as a whole or for an individual consuming unit. In Keynes' analysis of aggregates, as previously indicated, it is the national income and national consumption that are significant. When used without qualification, "propensity to consume" or "consumption function" will mean the community or aggregate concept, and in other cases the adjective "family" or "individual" will be used.

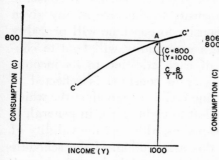

Figure 5a. The Average Propensity to Consume.

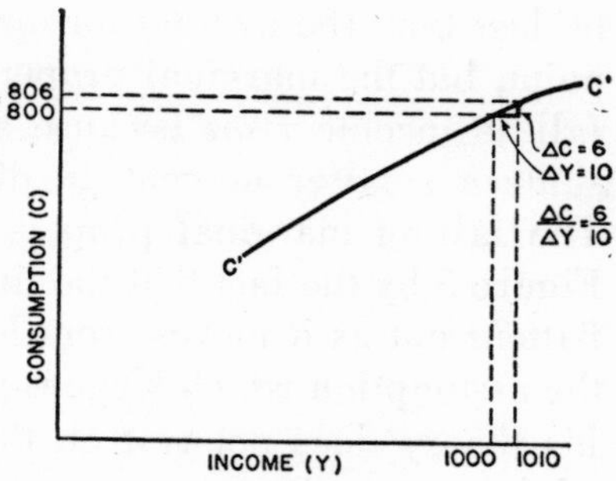

Figure 5b. The Marginal Propensity to Consume.

In Figure 5a the *average* propensity to consume at any level of income is represented by the distance along the vertical axis divided by the corresponding distance along the horizontal axis, that is, by $\frac{C}{Y}$. From the line C'C', which represents the schedule of the propensity to consume, the average propensity to consume at any point is easily ascertained. For example, at the point A, consumption is 800 and income is 1000, and the average propensity to consume is thus 800 divided by 1000, or $\frac{8}{10}$. This means that $\frac{8}{10}$, or 80 per cent, of an income of 1000 will be spent for consumption.

The marginal propensity to consume, represented in Figure 5b, is the ratio of a small change in consumption to a small change in income. It may be designated by $\frac{\Delta C}{\Delta Y}$, where the symbol $\triangle$ (delta) stands for a small increment.[1] Keynes' fundamental principle that consumption increases less than income when income increases means that the ratio of the increase in consumption to the increase in income is always less than one, that is, $\triangle Y$ is always greater than $\triangle C$. In Figure 5b, if consumption increases by 6 (from 800 to 806) when income increases by 10 (from 1000 to 1010), the marginal propensity to consume is $\%_{10}$, or 60 per cent. This is less than the average propensity to consume, which is 80 per cent. Not only will the marginal propensity to consume be less than the average propensity to consume at any given point, but the marginal propensity to consume will probably fall as income rises because a community will tend to consume a smaller percentage of each addition to its income. The falling marginal propensity to consume is reflected in Figure 5 by the fact that the line $C'C'$ is a smooth curve which flattens out as it moves from left to right. This, in general, is the assumption which Keynes makes, although the validity of his theory does not rest on this assumption. If the schedule of the propensity to consume were a straight line, the marginal propensity to consume would be the same at all points because the ratio of increases in consumption to increases in income would always be the same. The only assumption which is vital to Keynes' theory is that the absolute amount of consumption increases less than the absolute amount of income whenever income increases. This may be expressed

---

1. Although Keynes defines the marginal propensity to consume as $\dfrac{dC}{dY}$ (p. 115), the concept he makes use of is $\dfrac{\triangle C}{\triangle Y}$. In practical application, the distinction is relatively unimportant. $\dfrac{dC}{dY}$ measures the slope of the line $C'C'$ at any point, whereas $\dfrac{\triangle C}{\triangle Y}$ measures the average slope over a small range of the line $C'C'$. In a strict sense $\dfrac{\triangle C}{\triangle Y}$ is really an average of the marginal propensities to consume over a finite range of the line $C'C'$. In the following discussion we shall use the average marginal propensity to consume, but shall refer to it without the qualifying adjective "average." The *average marginal* propensity to consume is not to be confused with the *average* propensity to consume as explained in the text above.

by saying the slope of the line $C'C'$ must be positive and less than one, which merely means that the marginal propensity to consume must be positive and less than one.

Stability of the Propensity to Consume

Let us look more closely at the factors which determine how much will be spent for consumption in a given community at any time. As already indicated, the factor of overwhelming importance is the size of the community's income. As community income rises, consumption also rises; and as community income falls, consumption also falls. The justification for the concept, the propensity to consume, a concept of great practical significance as well as a great simplifier of economic analysis, is the premise that the amounts by which consumption rises and falls as income rises and falls will follow a fairly regular pattern. Only if this is true can the propensity to consume be stable, as Keynes assumes it to be.

We must distinguish clearly between two questions: How much will be spent for consumption, given the propensity to consume? and, How much will be spent for consumption out of a given income? These questions involve a distinction between the amount of consumption and the propensity to consume, that is, between an *amount* and a *schedule*. The amount of consumption is not stable because it depends on income, which in turn is not stable because the inducement to invest is not stable. The (schedule of the) propensity to consume is stable because it is determined by psychological characteristics of human nature and by the general social structure and practices of society, and these do not change readily except under unusual conditions such as social revolution, drastic inflation, or some other abnormal circumstance. In a given community over a short period of time, the subjective and objective factors determining the propensity to consume and to save are relatively fixed. In different communities and over long periods of time, the subjective motives of individuals to refrain from spending will vary with social institutions,

education, convention, religion, morals, et cetera. Although
the propensity to consume is stable in the short period, it is
not absolutely rigid. Changes in government fiscal policy
(taxing and spending), substantial changes in the rate of interest, and rapid changes in capital values such as occur
during a stock market boom or crash may have some effect on
the over-all propensity to consume. Apart from fiscal policy
of an unconventional type, however, even these factors are
not likely to be very important.

Figure 6 illustrates the distinction between changes in
consumption caused by an increase in income (with no change
in the propensity to consume) and changes in consumption
caused by a change in the propensity to consume (with no
change in income).

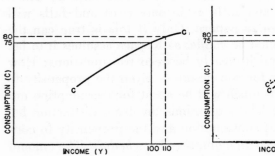 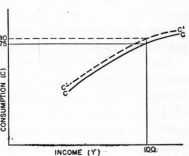

Figure 6a. An Increase in Consumption Caused by an In-
crease in Income (No Change
in the Propensity to Consume).

Figure 6b. An Increase in Consumption Caused by an In-
crease in the Propensity to Consume (No Change in Income).

In Figure 6a, consumption increases from 75 to 80 as a
result of an increase in income from 100 to 110. The propensity to consume, represented by the line CC, does not
change. In Figure 6b, consumption increases from 75 to 80
as a result of an increase in the propensity to consume from
CC to $C'C'$. The average propensity to consume at an income
of 100 rises from 75 to 80 per cent. Most short-run changes
in consumption are of the type represented in 6a, that is,

changes in consumption caused by changes in income with the propensity to consume remaining the same. The type represented in 6b is less likely to occur because of the stability of the propensity to consume in the short run. In the simple situation depicted in 6b, there is no change in income. This means that if the average propensity to consume does rise, say from 75 to 80 per cent, the same amount of income can be produced with less investment. However, if investment remains unchanged or increases when the propensity to consume rises, total income and employment will rise.

An important factor determining how much will be spent for consumption out of a given size of community income is the distribution of income. Since individual saving (not-consuming) represents surplus income which is not used for current consumption, saving depends on the presence of people with incomes in excess of their current consumption needs. It is easy for the rich to save but difficult for the poor. One of the chief characteristics of modern capitalistic countries is great inequality in the distribution of income, which results from concentration of the ownership of income-yielding property in the hands of a small fraction of the total population. For the very wealthy, saving is more or less automatic. They may buy everything they need or want and still have income left over for saving. All statistical studies of saving show that a large proportion of total saving is done by a relatively few high-income recipients and that a small part of total saving is done by the great mass of low-income recipients. If total income were more evenly distributed, the total saving out of a given size of community income would tend to be less. Thus widespread inequality of income and wealth tend to lower the propensity to consume. The lower the propensity to consume, the greater the dependence of the economy on investment for maintaining a high level of employment and income. Hence, the fundamental proposition that a high level of employment depends on a large amount of investment is true partly because the inequality of incomes greatly restricts the amount of consumption that will take place at high levels of income. If we were looking at the problem of unemployment from the point of view of social structure, we could truthfully say that one of its causes is inequality in the distribution of income. Keynes' theory and policy stress the importance of investment, i.e., of the necessity of having to produce much in excess of current consumption, because he accepts for purposes of most of the analysis of the *General Theory* the existing social structure, including the distribution of income and wealth. Except for occasional digressions with regard to certain long-term secular changes, Keynes' theory is not oriented to changes in the social structure, but is primarily concerned with how to make capitalism work, given the existing social structure. The distribution of income can be changed materially only by far-reaching alterations in the basic fabric of society. To deal adequately with changes of this type would require a different kind of theory from that offered by Keynes. It should, however, be added that his theory, though not oriented to changes in underlying social institutions, throws much light on the consequences of these institutions, including private property in the means of production and the resulting pattern of income distribution.

In an age of progressive taxation, the distinction between the distribution of income before taxation and the distribution of income after taxation is of great significance. Progressive taxation reduces inequalities of income because it takes a relatively larger part of the incomes of the wealthy than it does of the poor, and thereby provides some relief from the inadequate demand for consumption in capitalist economies. Keynes advocates progressive taxation as one of the important measures for alleviating unemployment. Without doubt, it is one of the powerful weapons in this connection. Progressive taxation is not, however, a panacea for unemployment. There are distinct limitations to the extent to which progressive taxes are used and can be used to promote high levels of economic activity. The whole tax *system* must be progressive for effective results. While the United States has some highly progressive individual taxes, like the federal income tax and

death duties, there are a great number of regressive taxes such
as the general sales tax in many states and excise taxes levied
by the federal government. An inevitable limitation on the
extent to which progressive taxes can be used arises from
the fact that the money which is taxed away from the rich can
hardly be given directly to the poor, although to some extent
this is possible in the form of pensions, relief payments,
et cetera. Therefore, the government which collects taxes for
purposes of redistribution must either pay subsidies to private citizens or expand the scope of its activities in order to
provide social services for lower-income groups. Services like
education, medical care, and public recreational facilities
are illustrations of such social services. Although services of
this type are of great social significance, they do not enable
the low-income groups to increase the money income out of
which they must feed, clothe, and house themselves. Subsidies for housing, or low-cost government housing, are, of
course, possible but tend to be strongly opposed by private
interest groups. A further limitation to redistributing income
by means of progressive taxation is the danger that high rates
on large incomes may discourage private investment, upon
which the private capitalist economy primarily depends for
filling the gap between income and consumption at high levels
of employment. If progressive taxation increases the community's propensity to consume at the expense of weakening the
inducement to invest, the losses in employment from the latter may more than cancel the gains from the former. Despite
limitations to the use of taxation as a fundamental approach
to problems associated with the unequal distribution of income, a fiscal policy in which the amount of money collected
and spent by government is highly flexible offers a significant
weapon against short-term fluctuations in economic activity.
These will be discussed in more detail in the next chapter.

Other factors which make for a low propensity to consume
or a high propensity to save in modern communities like the
United States are the great magnitudes of life insurance and
social insurance and the financial prudence of business cor-

porations in regard to dividend payments and depreciation allowances. The desirability of life insurance and the various forms of social insurance is not to be questioned from the standpoint of the individual or family unit. Nevertheless, it must be recognized that such insurance involves large withdrawals from the income stream which might otherwise be spent for current consumption. The burden on investment for maintaining high levels of employment is increased to the degree to which consumption is restrained. If the amounts paid out in life insurance and social insurance benefits are equal to the premiums paid in (by different sets of persons), there is, of course, no net saving. As long as the total amount of insurance is increasing, however, there is a net withdrawal from consumption demand. The financial prudence that provokes corporation managers to be cautious in paying cash dividends to the full extent of current net profits can hardly be questioned on a business basis, but it is nevertheless a drag on the propensity to consume. Corporations "force" many shareholders to save by withholding from the latter's control income which they would otherwise be free to spend or save as they saw fit. Prudent dividend policy, taken in conjunction with the over-cautious depreciation policy typically followed by American business enterprise, is a major factor tending to lower the propensity to consume.

Over the long run, from decade to decade, we cannot assume that the propensity to consume will remain unchanged. Statistical studies indicate that historically there is a tendency in progressive communities for the consumption function to shift upward in the sense that more is spent for consumption out of incomes of a given size. The upward secular drift of the consumption schedule is reflected in a steady rise in the standard of living of progressive economies like the United States. But in the short run, with which Keynes is primarily concerned, changes in the amount of consumption depend mainly on changes in the amount of income and not on changes in the propensity to consume out of a given income

(p. 110). To repeat for emphasis, this conclusion makes investment the strategic variable in the general theory of employment. The important proposition that employment can increase only if investment increases presupposes a stable propensity to consume. Moreover, the strategic nature of investment is reinforced by the fact that the schedule of the propensity to consume is stable at a relatively low level.

The Marginal Propensity to Consume and the Multiplier

The propensity to consume tells us that there is a fairly definite relationship between consumption and income at all levels of employment. As a further development of this relation, a definite ratio may be established between investment and income. From the marginal propensity to consume, we can tell *how much* income and employment will increase as a result of a given increase in investment. If the propensity to consume is given, a definite ratio will exist between any increase in income ($\triangle Y$) and any given increase in investment ($\triangle I$). This ratio is called the investment multiplier (k) and is equal, subject to certain assumptions, to the employment multiplier (k'). The relation between the marginal propensity to consume $\left(\frac{\triangle C}{\triangle Y}\right)$ and the investment multiplier $\left(\frac{\triangle Y}{\triangle I}\right)$ may be illustrated by a simple arithmetical example. Assume a $100 increment in income is derived $90 from consumption and $10 from investment:

$$\triangle Y = \triangle C + \triangle I$$
$$\$100 = \$90 + \$10$$

The marginal propensity to consume, $\frac{\triangle C}{\triangle Y}$, is $90/100$. The multiplier, $\frac{\triangle Y}{\triangle I}$, is $100/10$ or 10. We may generalize and say the multiplier is equal to the reciprocal of one minus the marginal propensity to consume; and the marginal propensity to consume is equal to one minus the reciprocal of the multiplier.[2] In the above illustration, the marginal propensity to consume is $\frac{9}{10}$, one minus $\frac{9}{10}$ is $\frac{1}{10}$, and the multiplier is the reciprocal of $\frac{1}{10}$ or 10.

The arithmetical relation of the marginal propensity to consume to the investment multiplier may be thought of even more simply: The multiplier is the reciprocal of the marginal propensity to save, which is always equal to one minus the marginal propensity to consume. Thus, if the marginal propensity to consume is $\frac{9}{10}$, the marginal propensity to save is $\frac{1}{10}$, and the multiplier is 10. If the marginal propensity to consume is $\frac{4}{5}$, the marginal propensity to save is $\frac{1}{5}$, and the multiplier is 5. If the marginal propensity to consume is $\frac{2}{3}$, the marginal propensity to save is $\frac{1}{3}$, and the multiplier is 3. The following table lists the values of the multiplier which correspond to certain values of the marginal propensity to consume.

The size of the multiplier varies directly with the size of the marginal propensity to consume. When the latter is high the multiplier is high, and when the marginal propensity to consume is low the multiplier is also low. Theoretically the values of the multiplier can range all the way from one to infinity. However, it can never fall to one if consumption

---

2. The investment multiplier may be derived from the marginal propensity to consume in the following manner. Starting with the "fundamental psychological law" that $\triangle Y$ and $\triangle C$ have the same sign but $\triangle Y$ exceeds $\triangle C$, it follows that the marginal propensity to consume is positive and always less than 1. Let us assume it is less than 1 by a fraction $\frac{1}{k}$, where k stands for the multiplier. We then have given:

(1) $\dfrac{\triangle C}{\triangle Y} = 1 - \dfrac{1}{k}$, where k is equal to or greater than 1; and

(2) $\triangle Y = \triangle C + \triangle I$. Transposing and dividing through by $\triangle Y$, we get

(3) $\dfrac{\triangle C}{\triangle Y} = 1 - \dfrac{\triangle I}{\triangle Y}$. From (1) and (3), it follows that

(4) $\dfrac{1}{k} = \dfrac{\triangle I}{\triangle Y}$, or (5) $k = \dfrac{\triangle Y}{\triangle I}$, which may also be written (6) $\triangle Y = k(\triangle I)$. By transposing (1) we get (7) $\dfrac{1}{k} = 1 - \dfrac{\triangle C}{\triangle Y}$, or (8) $k = \dfrac{1}{1 - \frac{\triangle C}{\triangle Y}}$, which may also be written (9) $k = \dfrac{\triangle Y}{\triangle Y - \triangle C}$. $1 - \dfrac{\triangle C}{\triangle Y}$ in (8) is, of course, the marginal propensity to save.

TABLE 1

CORRESPONDING VALUES FOR THE
MARGINAL PROPENSITY TO CONSUME AND THE MULTIPLIER

Marginal Propensity to Consume $\left(\dfrac{\Delta C}{\Delta Y}\right)$	Multiplier (k)
0	1
1/3	1 1/2
3/8	1 3/5
2/5	1 2/3
1/2	2
3/5	2 1/2
5/8	2 2/3
7/10	3 1/3
3/4	4
4/5	5
9/10	10
99/100	100
1	Infinity

always increases when income increases because this means the marginal propensity to consume is never zero. At the same time, the multiplier can never be equal to infinity if Keynes' assumption that the marginal propensity to consume is always less than one is valid. The actual value of the marginal propensity to consume is not likely to fall outside the range from ⅓ to 9/10, and therefore the multiplier will lie somewhere between 1.5 and 10. Keynes estimates the actual value of the multiplier to be about 3, with variations in different phases of the business cycle. Since the multiplier is more than unity but not very great, any new investment will increase income by more than the amount of the investment, but a small increase in investment will not be sufficient to lift the economy from a low level of employment to full employment.

The process whereby new investment brings a multiple increase in income by increasing consumption may be illustrated by an arithmetical example. Assume the marginal propensity to consume is ⅘. The multiplier will then be 5. One million dollars of new investment will lead to a total increase in income of $5,000,000. The initial $1,000,000 outlay for investment increases the incomes of the recipients by $1,000,-000. Since the marginal propensity to consume is ⅘, only 80 per cent of this initial increase in income will be spent for consumption. The $800,000 which is spent for consumption will add, at the second round, to the community's income by that amount, one person's expenditure being another's income. Of the $800,000 addition to income, 80 per cent will again be spent on consumer outlays, and in turn the community's income will increase by $640,000. Out of the further increase in income of $640,000, 80 per cent will go into consumption and income will increase by an additional $512,000. This process whereby consumption increases to the extent of 80 per cent of each addition to income will continue through successive stages toward a definite limit until the aggregate increase in community income is equal to 5 times the original investment. The various stages of expansion or income turnovers are not to be thought of in terms of a series of time periods, but as cumulative increases that occur simultaneously.

Does this mean that Keynes' theory is invalid since, obviously, the spending and respending of income for consumption cannot possibly take place simultaneously with the new investment? No, it is an assumption which simplifies the exposition and, at the same time, illustrates Keynes' basic contention that in every interval of time the increase in income is equal to the increase in investment multiplied by the multiplier (p. 123). In the first place, investment does not occur simultaneously, but over time. If the consumption industries anticipate the expansion of income that will be available to buy consumers goods, the time lag is greatly reduced. However, the increased demand for consumption may not be foreseen, so that investment will create new income for which no new consumption goods have been produced. In these circumstances, the new demand may be met partly by depletion of stocks (disinvestment) and partly postponed because of resistance to higher prices and also because the type of goods demanded is not available. To the extent that consumption is postponed, the marginal propensity to consume and the multiplier will fall temporarily below their normal size. Later when the goods become available, the marginal propensity to consume may rise above its normal level and "eventu• ally returns to its normal level." (p. 124)

The temporary departure of the marginal propensity to consume from normal is important in explaining how the equality of investment and saving is maintained throughout the expansionary process. If there are no new consumers goods at all to meet the additional demand arising from the income distributed by the new investment, there can be no increase in real consumption, so that, momentarily, income would increase but consumption would not. Hence, added saving (the excess of income over consumption), which is equal to added income, would be equal to added investment. Total saving and total investment are equal, and would remain equal regardless of the time lag. Momentarily, the marginal propensity to consume would be zero and the multiplier equal to one. They would rise gradually and return to normal after an interval of time. The emphasis in Keynes' analysis at this point is as follows: The efforts of consumers to spend their additional income according to their normal marginal propensity to consume will result in more consumption, which in turn will lead to the creation of more income, and out of the larger income more will be saved. When the normal marginal propensity to consume is functioning, the total addition to national income will be equal to the investment multiplied by the normal multiplier. Table 2 shows how the expansion of income takes place when the marginal propensity to consume is at its assumed normal level of 80 per cent. It would be a misrepresentation of Keynes' position to assume that investment originally exceeds saving, and becomes equal to it only after all the stages have been completed, which might be a very long time indeed. Keynes is not unaware of time lags, but for the pure theory of the multiplier, which we are discussing in this chapter, the introduction of time lags would greatly complicate the analysis. In the next chapter, which deals with the application of the multiplier principle, account will be taken of time lags.[3]

The following table presents the first 10 stages of this multiplying process whereby an original investment of $1,000,000 raises total income by $5,000,000 when the marginal propensity to consume is $\frac{8}{10}$, and therefore the multiplier is 5. The data in this table indicate that the formula for the multiplier, the reciprocal of the marginal propensity to

TABLE 2

EFFECT OF INCREASED INVESTMENT ON
INCOME, CONSUMPTION, AND SAVING

Original Increase in Investment $\triangle I$	Induced Increase in Income $\triangle Y$	Additional Consumption from Increased Income ($\frac{8}{10}$ of $\triangle Y$)	Saving out of Income
$1,000,000	$1,000,000	$800,000	$200,000
	800,000	640,000	160,000
	640,000	512,000	128,000
	512,000	409,600	102,400
	409,600	327,680	81,920
	327,680	262,144	65,536
	262,144	209,715	52,429
	209,715	167,772	41,943
	167,772	134,218	33,554
	134,218	107,375	26,843
	107,375		
	etc.	etc.	etc.
Totals $1,000,000 Investment	$5,000,000 Income	$4,000,000 Consumption	$1,000,000 Saving

3. The above paragraph is based on Keynes' discussion in the *General Theory*, pages 117, 122-125, and upon the clarification of this aspect of Keynes by Professor Alvin Hansen in "A Note on Savings and Investment," *The Review of Economic Statistics*, February, 1948, Vol. XXX, No. 1, pages 30-33. The adaptation of the multiplier to take account of time lags has been worked out by a number of writers, including Professor Hansen, Professor Fritz Machlup, and others.

save, is just a shorthand method for simplifying the arithmetical calculations involved in the table. If the successive additions were made in the table, the total in the income column would be $5,000,000, or 5 times the original investment, and 5 is the value for k, which is the reciprocal of ⅕, the marginal propensity to save.

The sum of the consumption column at its mathematical limit is $4,000,000. The increase in investment of $1,000,000 plus the $4,000,000 increase in consumption equals the total increase in income of $5,000,000. Thus given the marginal propensity to consume and the amount of the increment in investment, we can determine the total resulting increase in income by finding k and substituting in the equation $\triangle Y = k \cdot \triangle I$. Thus, $5,000,000 = 5 \cdot \$1,000,000$.

That part of newly created income which is not re-spent is, of course, saved. In Table 2 total saving is equal to the investment of $1,000,000, which is as it should be. This amount of saving results from the propensity of the community to save 20 per cent of the $5,000,000 addition to its income. Income which is not spent for consumption (shown in the last column in Table 2) is sometimes spoken of as a "leakage" in the cumulative income stream. It is this leakage which limits the extent of the total increase in national income. If there were no leakage, that is, if the marginal propensity to consume were 100 per cent, full employment would result, and beyond full employment, inflation would set in, from any small increase in investment because, under the ideal conditions assumed in Table 2, the second column would show an infinite number of constant additions to income. Since these successive additions diminish at each stage, the total increase in income is a finite amount.

The form which leakages take is determined by what happens to the money received as income but not spent for consumption. It may be used to pay off debts, to add to idle cash balances, or to purchase bonds, stocks, mortgages, insurance policies, and similar financial investments. The particular form of leakage is of no direct consequence as long as we hold to the assumption that the marginal propensity to consume is 80 per cent, and that total new investment is $1,000,000. These two factors together determine the total effect of new investment on income and employment. Leakages which tend to reduce the size of new, net investment (the multiplicand), rather than the size of the multiplier, will be considered in the chapter on fiscal policy in depression. Foreign trade and corporate saving will also be discussed in this connection.

To take two more very simple cases showing the relation of the marginal propensity to consume to the multiplier: If the marginal propensity to consume is ½, the multiplier is 2 because 1 plus ½ plus ¼ plus ⅛ plus ⅟₁₆ etc. add up to 2. With a multiplier of 2, each $1 of additional investment will result in a $2 increase in income. Or if the marginal propensity to consume is ⅔, the multiplier is 3 because 1 plus ⅔ plus ⁴⁄₉ plus ⁸⁄₂₇ etc. add up to 3. In this case each $1 of investment will result in a $3 increase in income.

The multiplier concept is concerned only with original investment as a stimulus to consumption and thereby to income. It is not intended to deal with the question whether additional consumption will induce further investment. The effect of added consumption upon the demand for investment involves the so-called "acceleration" principle, which is not an important part of Keynes' theory.[4]

Amount of investment needed to sustain various levels of income and employment

Keynes' fundamental position is that income and employment can rise only if investment increases, subject to qualifi-

4. For studies which integrate the principle of acceleration with Keynes' multiplier analysis, see R. F. Harrod, *The Trade Cycle*. London: Oxford University Press, 1936; A. H. Hansen, *Fiscal Policy and Business Cycles*. New York: W. W. Norton and Company, Inc., 1941, Chapter 12; Paul A. Samuelson, "Interactions between the Multiplier Analysis and the Principle of Acceleration," reprinted from *The Review of Economic Statistics*, 1939, in *Readings in Business Cycle Theory*. Philadelphia: The Blakiston Company, 1944, Chapter 12, and "A Synthesis of the Principle of Acceleration and the Multiplier," *The Journal of Political Economy*, December, 1939, Vol. XLVII, No. 6, pages 786-797.

cations that may be ruled out as of no great practical significance in the short run. The reason why income can increase
only if investment increases is that as income rises, consumption will rise but by less than income, and so a gap is left to
be filled by investment. Consequently, increases in output
above a low level at which aggregate income is equal to
aggregate consumption will have to be divided partly to
consumption goods and partly to investment goods. If the
marginal propensity to consume is $\frac{8}{10}$, for example, an addition to output of a million dollars must be divided $\frac{8}{10}$ to
consumption goods and $\frac{2}{10}$ to investment goods. This means
the multiplier is 5 because an addition to investment of, say,
$2,000,000 will be accompanied by an increase in consump-
tion of $8,000,000 and a total increase in income of
$10,000,000.

In order to ascertain how much investment is necessary to
give full employment, or any other level of employment for
that matter, we may set up a table of income, consumption,
and investment. From this table it is easy to calculate the
amount of investment required to boost income and employment to higher levels. Following is such a table with hypo-
thetical figures. In addition to figures on income, consumption, and investment, data are also given for employment, the
marginal propensity to consume, the multiplier, and the
average propensity to consume.

The range of national income shown in the table is from
$100 billion to $200 billion. The higher figure is assumed to
represent full employment and maximum attainable real
income. At the lower level of $100 billion, consumption is
equal to income, and the average propensity to consume $\left(\frac{C}{Y}\right)$
is unity. No net investment is necessary to maintain a $100
billion flow of income. Supply tends to create its own demand
up to this level, and if income falls below consumption, as it
may temporarily do, there will be a tendency for income to
rise to the level at which it equals consumption because the
effective demand for consumption will call forth an output

TABLE 3

AMOUNT OF INVESTMENT NEEDED TO SUSTAIN VARIOUS LEVELS OF INCOME AND EMPLOYMENT

Employ-ment (millions of workers) N	Income (billions of dollars) Y	*Consumption (billions of dollars) C	**Investment (billions of dollars) I	Marg. Prop. to Consume $\frac{\triangle C}{\triangle Y}$	Multiplier (k)	Average Prop. to Consume $\frac{C}{Y}$
30	100	100	0			1.00
33	110	109	1	.90	10	.99
36	120	117	3	.80	5	.98
39	130	124.5	5.5	.75	4	.96
42	140	131.5	8.5	.70	3 ⅓	.94
45	150	138	12	.65	2 6/7	.92
48	160	144	16	.60	2 ½	.90
51	170	149.5	20.5	.55	2 2/9	.88
54	180	154.5	25.5	.50	2	.86
57	190	159	31	.45	1 9/11	.84
60	200	163	37	.40	1 ⅔	.82

* Including tax-financed government expenditures.
** Including loan-financed government expenditures.

equal to the entire value of consumption. At income levels below $100 billion there is no gap that needs to be filled by investment. This basic national income, as Professor Hansen aptly calls it, is self-perpetuating. Above the basic income is the dynamic income, which is not self-perpetuating because it depends on investment to maintain itself and there is nothing automatic about investment. At $100 billion the gap begins to develop and income can rise above this level only as a result of deliberate calculations on the part of private businessmen to invest in new capital assets or on the part of governmental authorities to promote public investment. If the margin between basic national income and income at full employment is to be filled at all, it will be filled by investment plus the consumption induced by that investment under the multiplier principle. The concepts of the multiplier and the marginal propensity to consume become of practical significance in the range of incomes, in our example, above $100 billion.

Thus for all levels of income above $100 billion, consumption is less than income, and each addition to new investment will boost the national income by more than the amount of the investment because consumption will rise from the stimulus furnished by investment. The first billion-dollar increase in investment raises the national income by $10 billion, which means that the (average) multiplier between incomes of $100 and.$110 billion is 10, or the average marginal propensity to consume is .9, and this first $10 billion rise in output is divided $9 billion to consumption and $1 billion to investment. The next $10 billion rise in income requires a $2 billion outlay on investment, or twice as much as the first $10 billion rise, because the (average) multiplier has fallen from 10 to 5, or the marginal propensity to consume from .9 to .8. And the third $10 billion rise, from $120 billion to $130 billion, is divided $7.5 billion to consumption and $2.5 billion to investment because the average multiplier is 4 and the average marginal propensity to consume is .75 in this range of income. Finally, the last $10 billion rise to the full-employment income of $200 billion is divided $4 billion to consumption and $6 billion to investment, which means that the multiplier has fallen to 1⅔ and the marginal propensity to consume to .4. These figures show how the marginal propensity to consume indicates the division of additions to output between consumption and investment, and they also indicate that the investment multiplier is just another way of talking about the marginal propensity to consume.[5]

In Table 3 both the marginal and average propensities to consume fall as income rises, and rise as income falls. Over a broad range of the schedule, the decline in the average propensity to consume is a necessary condition of Keynes' analy-

---

5. We have been dealing with the average marginal propensity to consume and the average multiplier. "Marginal" is a mathematical concept which involves small, incremental changes. Obviously, $10 billion in $100 billion or in $200 billion does violence to the concept of small variations. But for the purposes at hand, it is perfectly legitimate to speak of the average marginal propensity to consume and the average value of the multiplier over a given range. See note 1 above. See also *General Theory*, page 121.

sis, and the decline in the marginal propensity to consume is a probable condition of actual experience. At the bottom of a very bad depression the average propensity to consume may be greater than one because consumption may exceed income while the community is depleting stocks of goods and large numbers of people are living off their past savings. However, any fall in income below consumption will tend to be restored by the self-sustaining nature of basic national income. Above the point at which income equals consumption ($100 billion in Table 3), aggregate consumption is less than aggregate income. The average propensity to consume has obviously fallen to less than one.

Keynes accounts for the relative stability of the economic system by this characteristic of a community to increase consumption by a lesser *absolute* amount than income when income rises, and to decrease consumption by less than income when income decreases (pp. 97, 251). Although there is great instability in economic life, it is not so great as to cause fluctuation all the way from zero employment to full employment. Movements upward and movements downward both encounter self-limiting forces. Changes upward are limited by the increasing difficulty of finding investment to fill the widening gap between income and consumption. Changes downward are limited because income falls more rapidly than consumption and therefore catches up with falling consumption long before a point of zero employment is reached. At the point on the downswing where consumption is equal to income—where the average propensity to consume is unity— economic activity reaches its self-sustaining basis. If Keynes' fundamental psychological law did not hold at all, any small increment in investment would set up a cumulative increase in effective demand which would go unchecked until full employment was reached; and any decrease in investment, however small, would set in motion a cumulative decrease in effective demand until everyone was out of a job. However unstable we may think economic life actually is, as compared with what it ought to be or might be, it is not nearly as unstable as it would be if the so-called fundamental psychological law did not obtain.

The actual arithmetical values of the multiplier in experience help to account for the relative stability of our economic system. The multiplier is neither extremely large nor is it so small as unity. If the multiplier were very large, small additions to investment would result in a great cumulative rise in effective demand, income, and employment. But Keynes estimates the actual multiplier to be somewhere between 2½ and 3 in the United States and England, varying, of course, at different levels of employment in different phases of the business cycle. Thus the multiplier is not so large as to lead to wild fluctuations in employment as a result of small changes in the volume of investment, yet it is small enough to require huge amounts of investment to sustain economic activity at high levels of employment in wealthy communities.

Since the marginal propensity to consume and the multiplier will be higher in a poor community than in a wealthy community, it might appear that the poor community would be subject to more violent fluctuations in employment as a result of changes in investment. This, however, is not the case. The degree of instability depends on the average as well as the marginal propensity to consume. While a high marginal propensity to consume makes for large relative changes in income from a given amount of investment, a high average propensity to consume reduces the absolute amount of investment needed to sustain full employment. A poor community which produces little more than enough to sustain itself will have a high average as well as a high marginal propensity to consume. Therefore, its absolute dependence on investment will not be great, even though changes in its small amount of investment may cause large relative fluctuations. A wealthy community, on the other hand, will have a low average as well as a low marginal propensity to consume. There will be a large absolute gap between income and consumption at all high levels of employment, and therefore large absolute amounts of investment are required to fill this gap. While the relative fluctuation in income from a given amount of investment will not be great because of the low value of the marginal propensity to consume and the multiplier, the absolute amount of fluctuation will be great because the low average propensity to consume makes the wealthy community dependent on a large volume of investment, the demand for which is unstable. Instability in the wealthy community is accentuated by the weak inducement to invest that is associated with a large previous accumulation of capital assets.

The Employment Multiplier: Attention is now directed to the first column in Table 3. This column shows the volume of employment which corresponds to various levels of income ranging from the low of 30 million workers to the full-employment level of 60 million. It is assumed that increases in employment are directly proportional to increases in income, so that, for example, a doubling of employment from 30 million to 60 million men is accompanied by a doubling of national income from $100 billion to $200 billion. Obviously this exact relationship will not hold in any rigid fashion, but as a first approximation it may be accepted as valid. Under this assumption, the employment multiplier (k') will be equal to the investment multiplier (k). Since Keynes' work is primarily concerned with the volume of employment, it is important to discuss the multiplier in terms of employment as well as in terms of income and investment. The employment multiplier is the ratio of increase in total employment (N) to the increase in primary employment (N_2), in the same way in which the investment multiplier is the ratio of increase in income to the increase in (primary) investment. Thus the expression for increases in employment, $\triangle N = k' \cdot \triangle N_2$, is analogous to the expression for increases in income, $\triangle Y = k \cdot \triangle I$. The simplifying assumption that the employment multiplier is equal to the investment multiplier does no violence to the general theory of employment. Most of Keynes' analysis is stated in terms of the investment multiplier because of greater convenience of expression, but the employment multiplier is useful for showing the relation of the foregoing discussion to the problem of primary and secondary employment from public works.

All discussions of public works recognize that in addition to the original or "primary" employment directly relating to the public works there will be a further or "secondary" employment resulting from the public works. The total benefit of public works as a remedy for unemployment is greater than the immediate or primary employment. "Secondary" employment is that which occurs in consumption goods industries as a result of the primary employment in investment industries. The employment multiplier tells us the number of men who will be added to employment for every one that is directly employed. When the multiplier is 5, for example, every man newly employed in investment goods production will cause four other men to be newly employed in consumption goods industries, for a total new employment of five men.

From Table 3, we can ascertain what income and employment will be if we know the volume of investment. If we are able to control the volume of investment, we can make real income what we want it to be, up to the point of full employment. Above full employment, true inflation sets in and further increases in income will be purely monetary, i.e., inflationary. From earlier discussion, it is clear that the volume of private investment is highly variable, largely because of the inherently unstable nature of the marginal efficiency of private capital. The first object of public policy designed to work within the private-enterprise economy is to maintain a high level of private investment. But since this is at best precarious, governmental authorities should be prepared to offset the effects of variations in the volume of private investment by effecting counter-variations in public investment. The objective is to maintain total investment, private and public, at a level which will fill the gap between the desired level of income and consumption out of that income. If the volume of private investment is chronically deficient, the maintenance of a high level of employment calls for permanent supplementary investment in public projects. According to the figures in Table 3, if at a certain time investment is taking place at a rate of $12 billion per year, there will be 45 million people employed and income creation will be at a rate of $150 billion per year. In order to raise employment to 48 million workers and national income to $160 billion, investment must be increased by $4 billion to a total of $16 billion. In order to reach full employment, total investment must be raised to $37 billion. Any other level of activity may be attained by variations in the amount of investment. This illustrates the meaning of Keynes' important proposition·that changes in employment depend upon changes in investment, given the propensity to consume.

References for Further Reading

Keynes, J. M., *The General Theory of Employment, Interest and Money.* Chapters 8, 9, and 10. New York: Harcourt, Brace and Company, 1936.

———, *The Means to Prosperity.* New York: Harcourt, Brace and Company, 1933.

———, "Fluctuations in Net Investment in the United States," *The Economic Journal,* September, 1936, Vol. XLVI, pages 540-547.

———, "Mr. Keynes' Consumption Function: Reply," *The Quarterly Journal of Economics,* August, 1938, Vol. LII, pages 708-709. (A reply to an article by G. R. Holden in the same volume, pages 281-296. See a further brief comment by Keynes in the same Journal, November, 1938, Vol. LIII, page 160.)

———, "The Income and Fiscal Potential of Great Britain," *The Economic Journal,* December, 1939, Vol. XLIX, pages 626-635.

———, "The Concept of National Income, A Supplementary Note," *The Economic Journal,* March, 1940, Vol. L, pages 60-65, also page 341.

———, "Mr. Keynes on the Distribution of Incomes and 'Propensity to Consume,' A Reply," *The Review of Economic Statistics,* August, 1939, Vol. XXI, page 129.

Gilboy, E. W., "The Propensity to Consume," *The Quarterly Journal of Economics,* November, 1938, and August, 1939, Vol. LIII, pages 120-140, 633-638. (Pages 633-636 contain an important letter from Keynes to Dr. Gilboy on the propensity to consume.)

Goodwin, R. M., "The Multiplier," *The New Economics,* edited by S. E. Harris, Chapter XXXVI, pages 482-499. New York: Alfred A. Knopf, 1947.

Hansen, A. H., *Fiscal Policy and Business Cycles,* Chapters XI and XII. New York: W. W. Norton and Co., 1941.

Kahn, R. F., "The Relation of Home Investment to Unemployment," *The Economic Journal,* June, 1931, Vol. XLI, pages 173-198. (Keynes credits Mr. Kahn with introducing the conception of the multiplier into economic theory in this well-known article.)

Lange, Oscar, "The Theory of the Multiplier," *Econometrica,* July-October, 1943, Vol. II, pages 227-245. (A mathematical treatment)

Machlup, Fritz, "Period Analysis and Multiplier Theory," *The Quarterly Journal of Economics,* November, 1939, Vol. LIV, pages 1-27. Reprinted in *Readings in Business Cycle Theory,* selected by a Committee of the American Economic Association. Philadelphia: The Blakiston Company, 1944.

Salant, W. S., "The Demand for Money and the Concept of Income Velocity," *The Journal of Political Economy,* June, 1941, Vol. XLIX, pages 395-421.

Samuelson, P. A., "Interactions Between the Multiplier Analysis and the Principle of Acceleration," *The Review of Economic Statistics,* May, 1939, Vol. XXXI, pages 75-78. Reprinted in *Readings in Business Cycle Theory,* selected by a Committee of the American Economic Association. Philadelphia: The Blakiston Co., 1944.

————, "A Synthesis of the Principle of Acceleration and the Multiplier," *The Journal of Political Economy,* December, 1939, Vol. XLVII, pages 786-797.

(See also the items listed for Chapter 6.)

CHAPTER 6

Fiscal Policy in Depression

> Thus we are so sensible, have schooled ourselves to so
> close a semblance of prudent financiers, taking careful
> thought before we add to the "financial" burdens of pos-
> terity by building them houses to live in, that we have no
> such easy escape from the sufferings of unemployment.
>
> J. M. Keynes, *The General Theory of Employment, Interest
> and Money.**

KEYNES viewed fiscal policy, that is, government spending,
taxing, and borrowing, as the most important weapon against
unemployment. His general explanation of the need for
positive fiscal policy runs as follows: At a level of income
corresponding to full employment, the gap between total income and total consumption is so great in advanced industrial
economies that private investment is inadequate to fill it. If
unemployment is to be avoided, the gap must be bridged
either by filling in with government expenditure or by reducing the size of the gap by increasing the propensity to consume. The problem has both its cyclical and its secular
aspects. If the average propensity to consume can be raised
through such measures as progressive taxation, the magnitude
of cyclical fluctuations can be reduced. Although Keynes has
made suggestions in this connection, he emphasizes that in a

* Harcourt, Brace and Co., Inc., 1936, page 131.

capitalist economy, characterized by wide inequalities in the distribution of income and other institutional factors which make for a high propensity to save, the propensity to consume cannot easily be raised enough to have a significant effect upon employment. Therefore, the chief burden for maintenance of high levels of employment falls on public expenditures designed to fill in the existing gap between income and consumption at full employment.

Public expenditure for the purpose of relieving unemployment raises two main questions: Is it justified in terms of good economy? and, How effective is it in creating and stimulating employment? The investment multiplier is important in relation to the second issue. The basic case for public works, when there are unemployed resources, does not rest on the validity of the multiplier theory. In the language of common sense, the case for public works, or more generally public investment, rests on the notion that, from the point of view of the whole economic system, it pays to employ workers as long as they produce anything more than nothing. Since unemployed workers contribute nothing to the national income, whatever they produce when employed represents a net gain to society. This idea may be expressed by saying that the marginal cost to society of employing labor which otherwise would be idle is zero or virtually zero. Slight additional social cost may arise, for example, if men eat more, or otherwise consume more, when they work than when they do not. It is better for a man to produce something, however little, while working and maintaining his self-respect, than to remain idle and produce nothing at all. As Keynes says, it is obvious that 100,000 new homes are a national asset and that 1,000,000 unemployed men are a public liability.[1]

As the representative of the entire nation, a national government has the duty to behave in a manner which will increase the national income. The individual, as the representative of his own interests, is expected to behave in a manner

---

1. *The Means to Prosperity*, page 22. London: Macmillan and Company, Ltd., 1933.

which will increase his individual income. Since individual and social costs and revenues do not always correspond, the government may take action which will benefit the whole economy when no individual is in a position to do so. The theory that government should not participate in economic life rests on the assumption that the national income will be maximized when business profits are maximized. National income must always be the criterion of social welfare. Business profits are only one part, and a relatively small part, of total national income, and cannot provide an adequate criterion of social welfare. Yet the motivation to production derives from the expectation of profit. Business men have the power, the legal right, and often the incentive to withhold from use the means of production to which the labor of the community must be applied in order to produce the goods and services that provide the basis of community welfare. Without equipment, labor cannot produce. When business men decide to let their factories remain idle, they serve their own interest but they do not serve the interest of the community. This is perfectly "natural." It is not in the nature of business accounting to be directly concerned with what happens to the national income when wages and salaries fall because of unemployment. Workers employed by a single business enterprise usually purchase only a relatively small part of the output of the enterprise for which they work, whereas their wages as a rule constitute a major portion of the expenses of their firm. Hence, any firm is in a position to lower its costs more than its returns by reducing its payroll at any time, even though this may prove disastrous to all firms if all act in the same way. To the individual business enterprise, labor is a variable cost that ceases when employment ceases. But to the economy as a whole, labor is an overhead or fixed cost which goes on whether the worker is employed or unemployed. Workers must eat whether or not they have jobs. There is the alternative of letting the unemployed starve, but this is more callous than the proponents of "sound" finance would tolerate, so they advocate supporting the unemployed on relief where they produce nothing rather than giving them useful employment where they will add directly to the national income. It is the divergence between the principles of social and private accounting which holds the clue to the inconsistencies of so-called "sound" finance.

Obviously, it is not very convincing to tell an unemployed man that society cannot afford to burden his future by building him a house in which to live, even though he and his fellow-workers are doing nothing with their time and skill. The staunch advocates of annually balanced budgets are perhaps so accustomed to thinking in terms of the financial principles appropriate to an economy of full employment that they do not see the implications for public finance of an economy with widespread unemployment. When there is full employment, the real cost of hiring a man is what he produced in the job he gives up in order to accept a new position. When there is unemployment, the real cost of hiring an unemployed person is nothing because nothing is sacrificed by the employment of his labor. This fundamental principle is not altered when money is brought into the picture in order to finance the employment.

Having in mind that the basic case for public works and other forms of income-creating expenditures in time of depression does not rest on the multiplier effect but is merely reinforced by this effect, it will be understood that the limitations and qualifications to the multiplier in practice do not invalidate the case for public investment. Even if the multiplier effect were lacking altogether, public works might be desirable as a means for employing otherwise idle resources.

The Multiplier and Public Investment

The present section is concerned with the practical application of the multiplier as contrasted with the "pure" or "logical" theory of the multiplier discussed in the preceding chapter. It is one thing to accept the logical conversion of the marginal propensity to consume into the investment multiplier and quite another to accept the hypothesis that each dollar of public spending in depression will add several dollars to the national income. Responsible statesman called upon to vote large sums of money for public works on the assumption that this will bring recovery will want to know more than that the investment multiplier is equal to the reciprocal of the marginal propensity to save. While support for public expenditure might be secured just because it is better to have men producing something rather than nothing, the possible repercussions of public spending on private spending should be explored. If it can be demonstrated that an increase in government spending will increase national income by more than the original outlay, the case for such expansionary policies will be much more convincing than if there is no multiplying effect. After all, the idea of public works as a remedy for unemployment is very old. The multiplier aspect of it is the modern innovation.

Two preliminary points need to be made. The first concerns the relation of the multiplier to pump-priming, and the second the meaning of the term "public investment" in reference to the multiplier effects of public spending. The multiplier theory is not pump-priming. The latter rests on the assumption that a *temporary* new expenditure will have a lasting tendency to raise the level of economic activity, whereas the multiplier theory assumes that the income-generating effects of new expenditure will continue only as long as the expenditure is present, working with some time lag. Although Keynes did at one time believe in the pump-priming hypothesis, he had passed beyond that stage when he wrote his *General Theory*. Pump-priming implies that the economic system has been in *unstable* equilibrium before the injection of new spending pushes it back on the track from which it has been derailed by some fortuitous event.[2] Keynes' theory is that the economic system is characteristically in stable under-employment equilibrium from which there is no tendency to depart.

2. See Paul A. Samuelson, "The Theory of Pump-Priming Reëxamined," *The American Economic Review*, September, 1940, Vol. XXX, No. 3, page 502.

Therefore, repeated shoves and not just a single shove are required to move the economic machine up the high road to prosperity. In this sense, Keynes' theory is really a repudiation of the pump-priming thesis. Furthermore, the multiplier theory does not imply that public spending will stimulate private investment as a result of the stimulus it gives to private consumption. This may happen, but it is not part of the multiplier doctrine.

The term "public investment," in the sense in which it is relevant to cumulative increases in private consumption under the multiplier influence, means any autonomous increase in net government outlays. Hence, it includes new consumption expenditures as well as public works of the durable type. Consumption expenditures such as relief payments and subsidies to education may be viewed as investments in human beings, which no government can afford to neglect even though private enterprise may do so. More important, however, is the fact that government expenditure, even for consumption, does not depend on the size of the consumers' income in the way that private consumption expenditure does. Private consumption varies in a regular manner with income, but government expenditure, like private investment, results from autonomous decisions. Saving rises automatically with income and requires offsets, which may be in the form of public expenditure just as well as private investment. In Keynes' theory, investment is important because it distributes demand for consumption output without adding immediately to the supply of consumption output that must be sold. Not only is government expenditure capable of acting as an offset to saving, but it has the further, ironical advantage that often it is of such a nature as not to bring forth future consumption output.

With these preliminaries in mind, the following discussion of the effects of government investment may be summarized as follows: (1) If the government spends money that would not otherwise be spent, either because it would not have been in existence or because it would have remained idle, (2) if this spending has no repercussions on existing spending, and (3) if leakages and the multiplier remain unchanged long enough for the effects of successive respendings of the funds to work themselves out, then repeated government expenditures will permanently raise the national income by the multiplier times the expenditure in question.

Method of financing

The increase in income that results from new investment is equal to the multiplier times the new investment (the multiplicand). The increase in income may be affected either by changes in the size of the multiplier or in the amount of investment. Since any government spending will replace some amount of private spending, we cannot assume, for example, that an expenditure of one million dollars when the multiplier is 5 will increase income by $5 million. Keynes estimates that in a community like the United States in depression the marginal propensity to consume is about 80 per cent, indicating a multiplier of 5, but that the actual increase in income will be more nearly 2 or 3 times the amount of government expenditure. We may refer to the latter as the government expenditure multiplier, in contrast with the full value of the multiplier of 5 when the marginal propensity to consume is 80 per cent. Among the factors accounting for this difference is the method of financing public expenditure. If outlays are to be income-generating, they must represent "new" expenditure, and not just a substitution of one expenditure for another. Workers who receive $100 per month on public works and who previously received $40 per month on relief have a net increase in income of $60 and not of $100. Furthermore, the over-all economic effect depends upon how the former relief was financed as compared with how the present public works are financed. The greatest stimulation to employment will result when a public construction program financed by borrowing replaces a public relief program which was paid for out of taxation. Less stimulation is felt when both the former relief and the new public works are financed by loans. Least stimulating would be the case in which both the former relief and the new public works were financed from taxation. The expenditure of funds raised by taxation represents mainly a substitution of one form of expenditure for another, that is, a reduction in private spending and an increase in government spending. The expenditure of funds raised by borrowing represents mainly new expenditure and therefore an addition to total effective demand. In order to have significant expansionary effects, therefore, a program of public investment should be financed by borrowing rather than by taxation. This kind of borrowing or loan expenditure is popularly called "deficit financing," although the term "income-creating finance" is a more appropriate designation. The term "deficit financing" means, of course, simply that the government spends more than it collects in taxes, leaving the budget unbalanced. The belief that deficit financing will bankrupt the government or the economic system arises from a false analogy between the economic system as a whole and the individual business enterprise. An individual who keeps on spending more than he takes in will go bankrupt and, so the argument runs, the same will happen to a government that spends more than it collects in taxes. However, the same tests of "soundness" do not apply to the economy and to the parts which make up the economy. An individual, a business enterprise, or a government can spend more than it receives, but the economic system as a whole cannot spend more than it receives (ignoring for the time being international economic relations or considering the whole world as the economic unit). Therefore, if the government pays out (spends) more money than it takes away from the public in the form of taxes, there must be a net addition to the money income available for spending by the public. This represents a net addition to effective demand. When there is unemployment, this increase in effective demand results in more employment and the creation of a larger real national income. The amount of the increase in effective demand will be at least equal to the amount of the new or additional spending, which is equal to the excess of the amount of money the government spends over the amount which it takes away from the taxpayers in the form of taxes. The deficit results on the books of the government if the government borrows from its citizens in order to get the money to spend. When a government, or anyone else, borrows, it goes into debt. Since the government is a representative of its citizens, this means some people will owe money to others. Taxpayers will owe money to bondholders. However, the government may, if it wishes, issue new money rather than borrow it, in which case there is no loan-deficit. Hence, deficit financing is a consequence of a particular manner of financing income-creating expenditures. The important thing is that the spending should represent new expenditures. New expenditures will increase the national income, and out of the enlarged income saving will increase by an amount equal to the deficit.[3]

In addition to the distinction between loans and taxes, there are significant differences between various types of loans and taxes. Loans from banks are more expansionary than loans from the public because bank loans result in the creation of new deposit money, whereas loans made by the public result merely in the transfer of part of the existing money supply from the public to the government. In the former case, no one need restrict either his consumption or his investment. The bond is purchased with new money created within the banking system in the form of new checkbook money. The total quantity of money is increased by the lending activities of the banking system. There is no transfer or giving up of means of purchase by one party for expenditure by the government; there is merely the creation of additional means of purchase. Selling bonds to banks is not, as a rule, difficult because in depression banks have excess reserves

---

3. The expression saving = investment may be phrased: saving = private investment + the government deficit. Expressed in terms of total government expenditure and taxes, this means that saving + taxes = private investment + government expenditure.

which they are willing to make use of by investing in government bonds, even though the rate of interest paid on government bonds may be quite low. The eagerness of the banks to purchase bonds is subject to the qualification that they feel the rate of interest will not rise in the calculable future to cause a fall in the market value of the bonds they purchased when interest rates were low.

Loan expenditures which are financed by selling government bonds to individuals (the public) are stimulating, but to a lesser extent than expenditures from funds raised by selling bonds to the banking system. When an individual as distinct from a bank buys a bond, a transfer rather than a new creation of means of purchase occurs. The individual buyer transfers his command over purchasing power to the government. No new money is created as a result of this form of borrowing. Such borrowing is a stimulus to economic activity, however, to the extent to which the government spends more readily than did the individual who formerly commanded the funds. Borrowing of this type is sometimes referred to as "tapping the savings stream." Individual savings which might otherwise have found no outlet in investment find an outlet in the form of governmental expenditure. Individual saving which otherwise would have forced a reduction in income to the point where social income exceeds aggregate consumption by the amount of actual investment is offset by public investment. Of course, if the individual who buys a government bond would otherwise have spent his money on either consumption or investment, there will be no net stimulus when he transfers his money to the government for spending. As a rule, however, a considerable proportion of the money used to buy government bonds would not otherwise have been spent, so the effect is generally stimulating. Nevertheless, borrowing from the public, especially on a large scale, is likely to restrict consumption or private investment to some degree, and is therefore less desirable in a deep depression than borrowing from banks. As over-all economic activity expands in a business recovery and the savings stream rises, borrowing from the public becomes both more feasible and more desirable. Once full employment has been attained, inflation will be forestalled by borrowing from the public or by taxation rather than by borrowing from the banks.

Among the different types of taxes, those which are progressive tend to restrict consumption less than those which are regressive. All taxes tend to be deflationary in the sense that money turned over to the government in the form of taxes would have been spent, in some part at least, had it been left in the control of the taxpayer. If public works are financed by funds raised by progressive income taxes or death duties which fall mainly on the wealthy, total consumption from private expenditure probably will not be much reduced because the consumption of wealthy persons tends to be about the same regardless of the amount of taxes they pay. In the case of very high tax rates, this would not be true. To the extent that taxes are paid from funds which would not otherwise be spent during the current period, idle money has been tapped and put to work by government spending. A further disadvantage of steeply progressive taxation is the danger that it may react adversely on the inducement to private investment. Private investment is a process which often does not lend itself to rational calculation. It depends to an important degree upon the state of confidence and spontaneous optimism of the business community. Highly progressive taxation is an element that tends to depress business confidence and inhibit spontaneous optimism.

Least desirable of all methods of financing public expenditure in depression is that by which taxes fall largely upon funds which would have been spent if left in the hands of taxpayers. Consumer sales taxes illustrate this least desirable way of raising funds to finance public investment in periods of depression. Consumer sales taxes reduce expenditure on consumption by nearly the full amount of the tax. Hence, government expenditures financed by regressive taxes are much less effective against unemployment than expenditures financed by progressive taxes, which in turn are less effective than expenditures financed by borrowing.

It is quite consistent for those who advocate loan expenditure, or deficit financing, in depression to advocate balanced budgets in boom periods. The purpose of deficit financing is to create full utilization of resources. Beyond the point of full employment, there is no need for further deficit financing. Keynes' program is one which calls for full employment without inflation or deflation. Monetary expansion through income-creating expenditure which is designed to increase both investment and consumption is the appropriate policy in depression years. High taxes and debt reduction are the fiscal tools for preventing inflation in boom years like those which usually characterize postwar periods.

Interest-free financing

An aspect of fiscal policy which Keynes does not discuss but which naturally arises in view of his position on the nature of interest is the question of interest-free financing of public expenditures which are designed to put idle resources to work. Loan expenditure involves an increase in the public debt and in annual interest payments on the public debt. The nature and significance of the public debt is one of the least understood issues in public life, but the common misconceptions cannot be examined here. However, if a major objection to loan financing is the increase in the principal and in the service charge on the public debt, the question arises as to why society should have to pay interest to banks and others in order to get the money needed to mobilize idle resources. Is there any necessity for subsidizing the commercial banks by paying them huge amounts of interest to create the new money which is required for economic expansion? Is not the creation of new money properly a government function, and if so, what is there to prevent the government from issuing new money directly, without paying interest on bonds to commercial banks?

The answer, in terms of Keynes' theory of interest which

will be discussed more fully later, is that there is no necessity for paying interest under these circumstances. Interest payments are not needed to induce people to save nor to reward them for saving. The banks, which receive most of the interest, create new balances on a basis of excess reserves to pay for the bonds they buy, and, therefore, interest payments to them are in no sense an inducement to curb consumption. The interest income received by commercial banks, except for the amount used to defray cost of performing a few clerical services, is a monopoly payment which rewards no genuine sacrifice or function. The risk is very slight on government bonds, which are considered to be the nearest possible approach to a riskless investment. Consequently, there appears to be no valid economic reason why the government should not by-pass the commercial banks and increase the money supply directly without resort to the sale of interest-bearing bonds. The particular technique employed to carry out the increase in money supply would depend on the nature of the central monetary authority. In the United States, the Treasury could issue non-interest bearing notes to the Federal Reserve banks with instructions to increase the government deposits to the extent of the value of the notes. The government could then spend its balances in the usual fashion for public works and other expenditures.

The objection that a policy of interest-free financing is certain to be inflationary is easily answered in terms of the general theory of employment. As long as there are unemployed resources, the increase in money expenditure will increase employment rather than prices.[4] Beyond the point of full employment there is no necessity for further monetary expansion. If monetary expansion continues after full employment is attained, inflation will result. This, however, is a consequence of monetary expansion *per se* and not of the manner of its execution. For example, selling interest-bearing bonds to commercial banks can cause inflation if carried to excess. In

---

4. See Chapter 9, section on the theory of prices, for a fuller statement of what happens to prices as employment and output increase.

fact, any mismanagement of the money supply will cause either inflation or deflation. Objections of this type are not objections to interest-free financing as such but to any type of managed currency. They are objections which indicate a lack of trust in the competence of government monetary authorities to act with wisdom and restraint. For better or for worse, any type of managed currency implies a faith in the wisdom and restraint of the monetary authorities. Since the abandonment of metallic standards, the money systems of the world are almost exclusively managed systems.

Leakages

Foreign Trade: The multiplying force of new expenditures is reduced by leakages which take the form of spending for imported goods and services. If the marginal propensity to consume is $8/10$ of which $2/10$ is for imports, the effective domestic marginal propensity to consume is lowered to $6/10$. A reduction in the marginal propensity to consume from $8/10$ to $6/10$ will cause the multiplier to fall from 5 to $2\frac{1}{2}$. In a nation like Great Britain, where imports are estimated to constitute 20 per cent of consumption, the foreign trade leakage alone is sufficient to explain the discrepancy between a potential multiplier of 5, based on a marginal propensity to consume of 80 per cent, and the empirical estimates of a multiplier of approximately $2\frac{1}{2}$ to 3. In the United States, where the proportion of imports is only about 5 per cent, the effect of foreign trade on the multiplier is much less than in Britain. A fall in the marginal propensity to consume from 80 per cent to 75 per cent will lower the multiplier from 5 to 4. The foreign trade figure which is relevant in these estimates is the proportion of *additional* or new expenditure which is made abroad and not the average proportion of *all* expenditures which are made abroad. In other words, the distinction between the marginal and the average propensity to consume is to be borne in mind.

The foreign trade leakage means that employment at home increases less than it would if all spending were for products produced within the domestic economy. The loss is only a national and not a world loss because benefits will accrue to foreign countries to the extent to which they are lost to the domestic economy. Improved economic conditions in foreign countries will, as a rule, react favorably upon the domestic economy in the form of increased exports. If we reduce the multiplier to allow for imports, any increase in exports should be included as new investment and hence as one of the favorable repercussions. There is no reason to assume, however, that what is lost by way of spending on imports will be gained back in the form of increased exports, especially in the short run. Since there is in any national economy some foreign spending for imports, the world multiplier is always larger than the domestic multiplier for any given primary expenditure. This strengthens the case for world economic co-operation in the form of simultaneous expansionary policies in all national economies.

Taxes and Corporation Saving: The marginal propensity to consume out of national income depends on taxation and corporation dividend policies. When the national income in the United States is at $200 billion, more than $50 billion is collected in taxes (federal, state and local at 1948 tax rates) and the proportion of increases in income taken by taxes is much more than 25 per cent because of the progressive nature of federal income taxes. Hence, the size of the marginal propensity to consume calculated in terms of the total national income is much lower than if calculated in terms of net disposable income (roughly equivalent to "take home" pay). At each stage in the income-generating process, consumption is reduced by the drain of taxation. Of course, not all income paid in taxes would otherwise be spent, but probably a very large part of it would be if the taxpayer were free to dispose of it as he wished.

The national income includes corporation earnings which are not paid out in dividends as well as those which are paid out in dividends. Undistributed profits are not available for consumption spending and represent a factor tending to reduce the propensity to consume out of total national income. When corporate saving is added to taxes, there is a large difference between the total national income and the net disposable income available for consumer spending. Hence, it is not surprising that the marginal propensity to consume calculated on a basis of the total national income is smaller than it might appear to be if the only leakages taken into account were the savings of individual consumers out of their disposable income. Any change in tax rates or dividend policies will affect the size of the marginal propensity to consume and hence the size of the government expenditure multiplier.

Neutralizing factors

Public works in time of depression have as their fundamental purpose an increase in aggregate employment in the economy as a whole, including the private and the public sectors. Any decrease in private investment which results from increases in public investment tends to neutralize the employment- and income-creating effects of public investment. Any increase in private investment that may be induced by the greater amount of consumption tends to increase employment and the income-creating effects of public investment. In accordance with Keynes' theory of the inducement to private investment, any repercussion of public spending can be traced to a change either in the rate of interest or in the marginal efficiency of capital, or both.

The Rate of Interest: In the absence of positive action on the part of the monetary authority to make available a larger supply of money for transactions, the rate of interest will tend to rise as a result of an expansionary program. Any rise in the rate of interest will tend to discourage private investment. There is no necessary reason, however, why a program of large-scale public investment should cause the rate of interest to rise. If the quantity of money is increased sufficiently to prevent a drain on the balances held to satisfy the speculative motive, the interest rate will not rise. The mone-

tary authority may exercise policies which will induce the
banks to expand their deposits and to buy large issues of government securities so there will be no necessity to borrow
from the public. The state of liquidity preference for the
speculative motive, which together with the quantity of
money determines the rate of interest, is less manageable and
less predictable than the quantity of money itself. If the situation which accompanies a large-scale program of public
works is confused and confusing, liquidity preference may
rise and cause the rate of interest to increase. Above all, the
monetary authority should appear firm in its determination to
prevent the long-term rate of interest from rising.

The Marginal Efficiency of Capital: The beneficial effects
of public investment financed by loan expenditure may be
neutralized by a fall in the marginal efficiency of private
capital. These neutralizing effects may work either through
an increase in the costs of producing capital goods or through
unfavorable expectations of entrepreneurs. Some increase in
the costs of capital assets must inevitably occur during the
transition from low levels to high levels of investment and
employment. In a large-scale public works program, increases
in demand are concentrated on building materials and construction workers. Since private and public investment are
dependent upon the same type of factors of production, increases in the cost for one represent increases in the cost for
the other. As costs of production rise under the impact of increasing demand, the marginal efficiency of private capital
tends to fall and this in turn tends to lessen the volume of
private investment.

Private investment may also be deterred if public investment creates an unfavorable psychological attitude on the part
of business entrepreneurs toward the prospective yields of
private investment. In their political outlook, businessmen are
characteristically conservative to a degree that renders them
highly sensitive to unbalanced budgets and government spending. Fortunately business "confidence" is not so sensitive as to

be completely overruled by the political prejudices of the business community. Public investment on a sufficient scale must inevitably increase the sales of business firms and bring dollars rolling into their cash registers and bank accounts. Dr. A. P. Lerner optimistically suggests that "Their pockets will ultimately overcome their prejudices" even though they continue to grumble that the prosperity which is enriching them is "artificial," "illusory," and "unsound."[5]

In so far as large-scale government investment involves the expansion of public enterprise into fields previously restricted to private enterprise, further private investment in these fields may be discouraged by the fear that profits will be lowered by the competition of public enterprise. Such fear on the part of private investors can be offset only partly by limiting public investment to strictly government activity like road-building, reclamation, flood control, and public buildings. Projects like the Tennessee Valley Authority compete with private power companies, and government housing competes with private housing. Under capitalism, private investment is normally much greater than public investment. As long as chief reliance is upon private investment to fill the gap between income and consumption at full employment, it is important to avoid weakening the incentives to private investment.

When there is involuntary unemployment, even wasteful expenditure may enrich the community if the multiplier is greater than one. Let us suppose a million dollars is paid out to men for some activity like leaf-raking which we may assume adds nothing to the real income or real wealth of society. If the multiplier is three, the total addition to money income is three million dollars. Subtracting the one million dollars of money payment for which no corresponding value of output has been produced, the addition to real income and wealth is two million dollars. The original outlay to leaf-rakers results merely in a redistribution of existing real wealth, with the rest of the community losing what the leaf-rakers gain. But when

5. Lerner, A. P., *The Economics of Control*, page 321. New York: The Macmillan Company, 1944.

the two-thirds of a million dollars of effective demand is spent for consumption, it calls forth the production of an equivalent amount of real income and real output. The total indirect effect of the original outlay for a worthless project is to add two million dollars to real income and to real output. Of course, it is better to have useful expenditure, but if this is politically objectionable, wasteful expenditure is better than nothing. Thus, says Keynes, "Pyramid-building, earthquakes, even wars may serve to increase wealth, if the education of our statesmen on the principles of the classical economics stands in the way of anything better." (p. 129) Lest there be any misunderstanding, this statement does not mean that Keynes recommended pyramid-building, earthquakes, and wars.

Even though there may be no actual encroachment by public enterprise into the fields previously limited to private enterprise, the existence of large-scale public works may create the fear of encroachment in the future. Such fear will tend to dampen the expectations of private entrepreneurs. What the actual effect of planned public investment upon the "confidence" of business men will be, and how it will be manifested in their economic behavior with regard to investment decisions, is one of the enigmas of public policy. It is not the kind of issue that can be demonstrated definitively one way or the other. No economic theory is capable of assigning quantitative values to all the variables in such situations.

In concluding the discussion of neutralizing effects of public spending, it is to be noted that the cumulative increase in effective demand stemming from primary public expenditure may induce new private investment. As the demand for consumers goods rises, existing plant capacities in some fields may prove inadequate. Plant expansion in these fields will then be in order. Likewise, investments in inventories are likely to be induced by any cumulative rise in demand even though there is no increase in the demand for new investment in durable plant and equipment. Keynes excludes these considerations from the multiplier theory by the assumption that creases in economic activity at nearly every turn between 1933 and 1940 seems to be more than a mere coincidence. Experience of this period seems to verify the thesis that economic expansion can be promoted by government expenditures, and that the total increase in income will exceed the amount of primary expenditure (the multiplier effect). Certainly Keynes thought there was verification of his loan expenditure and his multiplier theories in this experience. The failure of private investment to regain the level of the 'twenties gives some plausibility to the thesis that public spending and unbalanced budgets tend to discourage new private investment in durable capital assets. The failure to achieve full recovery and full employment throughout the decade of the 'thirties clearly indicates the inadequacies, if not the inherent weaknesses, of New Deal spending policies. Keynes' chief criticisms of the New Deal loan-expenditure program were that it was on too small a scale to achieve full recovery and that it was inadequately planned and poorly executed. At the end of the 'thirties, there had been no test of how large the loan expenditure would have to be to lift the economy to full employment.

In 1940, at the beginning of the American defense program, Keynes expressed the hope that at last a situation had arisen which would prove his case and make the "grand experiment" that would demonstrate "what level of total output accompanied by what level of consumption is needed to bring a free, modern community having the intense development of the United States within sight of the optimum employment of its resources."[11] In summarizing the experience of the 'thirties, Keynes wrote: "The conclusion is that at all recent times investment expenditure has been on a scale which was hopelessly inadequate to the problem. . . . It appears to be politically impossible for a capitalistic democracy to organize expenditure on a scale necessary to make the grand experiment

---

11. "The United States and the Keynes Plan," *The New Republic,* July 29, 1940, Vol. CIII, No. 3—Part 2, page 159.

between 1933 and 1945 seems to (1) repudiate the pump-priming thesis, (2) verify the multiplier theory, (3) indicate that a very great volume of loan expenditure is necessary to bring a modern industrial economy to full employment, and (4) demonstrate conclusively that public spending on a sufficient scale will raise output and income quickly to a level corresponding to full employment. The pump-priming thesis that a temporary priming of the economic system by government expenditure will set the private enterprise system going on its own power proved illusory during the 'thirties. Total economic activity suffered a relapse at each withdrawal of government loan expenditure. As long as loan expenditure continued, however, it appears to have acted as a quick stimulant to total economic activity. National income increased not only by the amount of government spending but by several times that amount, the amount of this multiple being the (empirical) multiplier. Failure of the economic system to attain a high level of employment at any time during the 'thirties despite the multiplying effect of government loan expenditure indicates that full employment can be attained only with a much larger volume of loan expenditure than was forthcoming under the New Deal program of that period. When the amount of federal loan expenditure skyrocketed in the defense and war periods beginning in 1940, unemployment disappeared rapidly. Full employment became merely a question of how long a time was required to remedy technological obstacles to expanded output. We shall have more to say about the inflation of the war and postwar periods in Chapters 9 and 10.

References for Further Reading

Keynes, J. M., *The General Theory of Employment, Interest and Money*, Chapter 10. New York: Harcourt, Brace and Company, 1936.

Clark, Colin, "Determination of the Multiplier from National Income Statistics," *The Economic Journal*, September, 1938, Vol. XLVIII, pages 435-448.

Clark, J. M., *Economics of Planning Public Works*. Washington: U. S. Government Printing Office, 1935.

————, "An Appraisal of the Workability of Compensatory Devices," *The American Economic Review, Papers and Proceedings*, March, 1939, Vol. XXIX, pages 194-208. Reprinted in *Readings in Business Cycle Theory*, selected by a Committee of the American Economic Association. Philadelphia: The Blakiston Company, 1944.

Colm, Gerhard, "Fiscal Policy," *The New Economics*, edited by S. E. Harris. Chapter XXXIV, pages 450-467. New York: Alfred A. Knopf, 1947.

Fine, S. M., *Public Spending and Postwar Economic Policy*. New York: Columbia Univ. Press, 1944.

Hagen, E. E., "The Problem of Timing Fiscal Policy," *The American Economic Review, Papers and Proceedings*, May, 1948, Vol. XXXVIII, pages 417-429.

Hansen, A. H., *Fiscal Policy and Business Cycles*, especially Chapters I, IV, VI, IX, XI, XII, XIII, XVII, and XX. New York: W. W. Norton and Co., 1941.

Harris, S. E., *The National Debt and the New Economics*. New York: McGraw-Hill Book Company, Inc., 1947.

Higgins, Benjamin, *Public Investment and Full Employment*. Montreal: International Labour Office, 1946.

————, "Keynesian Economics and Public Investment Policy," *The New Economics*, edited by S. E. Harris, Chapter XXXV, pages 468-481. New York: Alfred A. Knopf, 1947.

Machlup, Fritz, *International Trade and the National Income Multiplier*. Philadelphia: The Blakiston Company, 1943.

Samuelson, Paul A., "The Theory of Pump-Priming Reëxamined," *The American Economic Review*, September, 1940, Vol. XXX, pages 492-506.

————, "Fiscal Policy and Income Determination," *The Quarterly Journal of Economics*, August, 1942, Vol. LVI, pages 575-605.

Smithies, Arthur, "The Multiplier," *The American Economic Review, Papers and Proceedings*, May, 1948, Vol. XXXVIII, pages 299-305.

Somers, H. M., "The Impact of Fiscal Policy on National Income," *The Canadian Journal of Economics and Political Science*, August, 1942, Vol. VIII, pages 364-385.

Stone, R. and Stone, W. M., "The Marginal Propensity to Consume and the Multiplier, A Statistical Investigation," *The Review of Economic Studies*, October, 1938, Vol. VI, pages 1-21.

Villard, H. H., *Deficit Spending and the National Income.* New York: Farrar and Rinehart, 1941.

Wallich, H. C., "Income-Generating Effects of a Balanced Budget," *The Quarterly Journal of Economics,* November, 1944, Vol. LIX, pages 78-91.

CHAPTER 7

The Marginal Efficiency of Capital

> Speculators may do no harm as bubbles on a steady
> stream of enterprise. But the position is serious when
> enterprise becomes the bubble on a whirlpool of specula-
> tion. When the capital development of a country becomes
> a by-product of the activities of a casino, the job is likely
> to be ill-done.
>
> J. M. Keynes, *The General Theory of Employment, Interest
> and Money.**

THE MARGINAL efficiency of capital in conjunction with the
rate of interest determines the amount of new investment,
which in turn determines the volume of employment, given
the propensity to consume. In this chapter the marginal efficiency of capital is discussed, with special attention to the
prospective yields of capital assets, and in the next chapter
the rate of interest is considered.

As indicated in Chapter 3, the marginal efficiency of capital
is equivalent to what is ordinarily called the rate of profit, or
better, the *expected* rate of profit. The word "efficiency" as
used in the term "marginal efficiency of capital" refers to
the effectiveness, or rate of return over cost, or profitability,
of a capital asset. The efficiency or earning power of any capital asset is its rate of return over cost. The *marginal* effi-

---

* Harcourt, Brace and Co., Inc., 1936, page 159.

ciency of a particular type of capital asset is the highest rate of return over cost expected from an additional, or marginal, unit of that type of asset. The marginal efficiency of capital *in general* is the highest rate of return over cost expected from producing an additional, or marginal, unit of the most profitable of *all* types of capital assets.[1]

Any investment opportunity which is as yet unutilized will be carried out as long as the expected rate of return over cost exceeds the rate of interest. This fundamental principle that new investment will be carried to the point at which the marginal efficiency of capital is equal to the rate of interest (on money) rests on the assumption that business men and other wealth-holders will attempt to maximize the returns from their investments. People with money in excess of that which is used for current consumption, will invest it, lend it, or hoard it, according to the relative advantages offered by these various alternatives. The advantages of storing wealth in the form of money, that is, of hoarding, are discussed in the following chapter. Here we may approach the concept of the marginal efficiency of capital in terms of the advantages of constructing a new capital asset rather than buying an old one or of lending money at interest.

The Concept

The marginal efficiency of capital is a rate or ratio of two elements, (1) the expected yields or returns from an income-yielding asset, and (2) the supply price or replacement cost of the asset which is the source of the prospective yields. Prospective yield is what a business firm expects to obtain from selling the output of its capital assets. These yields take the form of a flow of money income over a period of time. For example, when a factory is built and equipped, the investor

1. Keynes says that the concept "marginal efficiency of capital" was first introduced into economic theory by Irving Fisher under the name of "rate of return over cost" in his *Theory of Interest* (1930). See *The Lessons of Monetary Experience—Essays in Honor of Irving Fisher*, edited by A. D. Gayer, page 145. New York: Farrar and Rinehart, Inc., 1937. See also *General Theory*, pages 140, 141.

136   MARGINAL EFFICIENCY OF CAPITAL

expects to get back his original investment plus a surplus in the form of a continuing series of receipts from sales of the output of the factory. If we divide the total expected life of the factory into a series of periods, say years, we may refer to the annual returns as a series of annuities represented by $Q_1, Q_2, Q_3, \ldots Q_n$, the subscripts referring to the years of the respective annuities. If we estimate the values of the Q's and if we know what it will cost to produce the necessary capital assets which will be the source of these yields, then a comparison of the expected returns with the cost gives the rate or ratio known as the marginal efficiency of capital. Keynes defines the marginal efficiency of capital in this manner: "More precisely, I define the marginal efficiency of capital as being equal to that rate of discount which would make the present value of the series of annuities given by the returns expected from the capital-asset during its life just equal to its supply price." (p. 135) [2] This definition may be expressed in the following terms:

Supply Price _Demand Price_ = Discounted Prospective Yields

or,   Supply Price = $\dfrac{Q_1}{(1+r_m)} + \dfrac{Q_2}{(1+r_m)^2} + \dfrac{Q_3}{(1+r_m)^3} + \cdots \dfrac{Q_n}{(1+r_m)^n}$

The Q's are the prospective yields in the various years 1, 2, 3, and n; and r_m is the marginal efficiency of capital, or the rate of discount. The values of the Q's are not necessarily the same for each year, and the presumption in a dynamic world is that only by the rarest accident would any of them turn out to be identical. There will be some unique value of the marginal efficiency of this particular investment which will bring the two sides of the equation into equality. The term $\dfrac{Q_1}{(1+r_m)}$ represents the present value of the yield or annuity to be received at the end of the first year discounted at the rate r_m. If the rate of discount is 10 per cent, each dollar due or expected one year hence is worth 90.91 cents ($1.00 divided by

---

2. *The General Theory of Employment, Interest and Money.* New York: Harcourt, Brace and Co., Inc., 1936.

1.10). This means each 90.91 cents invested at 10 per cent will grow to $1.00 in one year. The term $\frac{Q_2}{(1+r_m)^2}$ represents the present value of the expected yield at the end of the second year discounted also at the rate r_m. At 10 per cent, each dollar due or expected two years hence is worth 82.65 cents ($1.00 divided by $(1.10)^2$, or $1.00 divided by 1.21), which means that 82.65 cents invested now at 10 per cent will grow to $1.00 in two years. Regardless of the number of annuities, the present value of each would be discounted in the same way to bring the aggregate of all the annuities into equality with the current supply price or replacement cost of their source.

A simple arithmetical example will illustrate the meaning of the efficiency of capital as a rate of discount. Suppose we are contemplating the construction of an asset which is expected to yield $1100 at the end of one year and $2420 at the end of two years, after which time it will cease to have any economic value. If the supply price, or cost of constructing this capital asset is $3000, its efficiency is 10 per cent, because this is the rate of discount which will equate the value of the future yields to the current supply price. At 10 per cent, the present value of $1100 discounted for one year plus $2420 discounted for two years gives a total sum of $3000, the current supply price.

Supply Price $=$ Discounted Prospective Yields

$$\$3000 \quad = \quad \frac{\$1100}{1.10} \quad + \quad \frac{\$2420}{(1.10)^2}$$

$$\$3000 \quad = \quad \$1000 \quad + \quad \$2000$$

If the yields were less than those used in the above calculation, the rate of discount which would equate the two sides of the equation would be lower than 10 per cent. Naturally, a fall in the amount of expected yield will lower the rate of expected yield. Likewise, if the supply price were more than $3000, the rate of discount would be lower. The more costly the construction of a capital asset, the lower will be its rate of return if the amounts of the yields remain the same. The rate of return over cost may change either because the cost changes or because the amount of return changes.

If 10 per cent is the highest rate of return that can be secured from any capital asset newly produced, it is the *marginal* efficiency of capital in general. Since the marginal efficiency is expressed as a per cent per year, it can be compared directly with the rate of interest. In the above example, if the rate of interest on money is less than 10 per cent, the construction of a new capital asset of the type in question would be worthwhile. People with money to invest can get more by building the new capital asset than by lending their money at interest, or by buying an old capital asset of the type in question. People who have access to money at less than 10 per cent will profit by borrowing in order to build this capital asset. The market value of an asset which promises to yield $1100 at the end of one year and $2420 at the end of two years will be greater than $3000 when the interest rate is less than 10 per cent. For example, if the market rate of interest is 5 per cent, the capital asset will have a present value of:

$$\frac{\$1100}{1.05} + \frac{\$2420}{(1.05)^2} = \$1047.62 + \$2195.01 = \$3242.63$$

This is what Keynes calls the demand price, in contrast with the supply price, of a capital asset. The demand price of any asset is defined as the sum of the expected future yields discounted at the *current rate of interest*. Thus defined, the demand price of an asset is its true present value, what it is worth in the market. The demand price and the supply price are determined respectively:

> Demand Price = Sum of prospective yields discounted at the *rate of interest*.
>
> Supply Price = Sum of prospective yields discounted by the *marginal efficiency of capital*.

The demand price is greater the lower the rate of interest at which it is discounted. Hence, the lower the rate of interest, the greater will be the number of capital assets for which the demand price will exceed the supply price, and the greater the pace of investment in new capital assets. The marginal efficiency of capital will exceed the rate of interest, and therefore new investment in capital assets will prove profitable as long as the supply price or cost of production remains less than the demand price.

Since investors in income-yielding wealth desire to maximize their prospective yields, they will naturally buy the source of these prospective yields as cheaply as possible. When it is cheaper to create a new source of prospective yields than to buy an already existing source, the former course of action will be followed. If, and only if, these conditions prevail, will new capital assets be produced by private investors. The existence of such circumstances is the essential condition for the successful functioning of an economic system in which private profit is the stimulus to enterprise.

It is to be noted that the market value of an asset, whether it be a capital asset or a claim upon capital assets in the form of marketable securities, cannot be determined from a knowledge of the marginal efficiency of capital. Nor can the rate of interest be deduced from the prospective yields or the marginal efficiency of capital. Before the present market value of an asset can be ascertained, the rate of interest must be determined independently from a knowledge of the quantity of money and the state of liquidity preference. The rate of interest as well as the marginal efficiency of capital must be known before the volume of investment is determined. These two rates are determined independently of one another, the marginal efficiency being the resultant of the supply price and the prospective yields of assets, and the rate of interest the resultant of the schedule of liquidity preference and the quantity of money. The fact that investment will be carried to the point at which the marginal efficiency of capital is reduced to equality with the rate of interest does not mean that these two rates depend upon the same things or that they depend upon each other. They are independent variables, and investment is dependent upon them. There is a sense, however, in which the marginal efficiency adjusts to the rate of interest rather than the other way around. For changes in the volume of investment directly influence the marginal efficiency of capital but not the rate of interest, and it is changes in the volume of investment which bring the two rates to equality. As long as the marginal efficiency of capital exceeds the rate of interest, investment will continue, and when there are no more investments for which the marginal efficiency exceeds the rate of interest, investment will come to a halt. When it is recalled that employment cannot increase without an increase in investment, the propensity to consume being unchanged, the importance of the relationship of the marginal efficiency to the rate of interest for the problem of employment will be appreciated as being of the most fundamental significance.

The marginal efficiencies of all types of capital assets which may be made during a given period of time represent the *schedule* of the marginal efficiency of capital, or the investment-demand schedule. A diagram representing the schedule of the marginal efficiency of capital of all types would take the general shape of an ordinary demand curve, slanting down toward the right as the quantity of investment for the period increases. It will show how much investment can be carried out in a given period of time at 10 per cent, at 8 per cent, at 7½, at 7, 6½, 6, 5½, 5 per cent, etc. The larger the amount of investment per unit of time, the lower the marginal efficiency of capital will fall.

The position and shape of this investment-demand schedule is of great significance in determining the volume of employment because it will indicate the extent to which the amount of investment will change in response to changes in the rate of interest. The more elastic the schedule of the marginal efficiency of capital, the greater will be the increase in investment in response to a given fall in the rate of interest. The more inelastic the schedule of the marginal efficiency of capital, the less will be the increase in investment in response to a given fall in the rate of interest. Figures 7a and 7b contrast a relatively elastic and a relatively inelastic schedule of the marginal efficiency of capital.

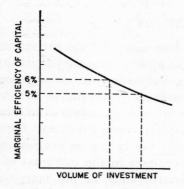

Figure 7a. A Relatively Elastic Schedule of the Marginal Efficiency of Capital, or Investment Demand Schedule.

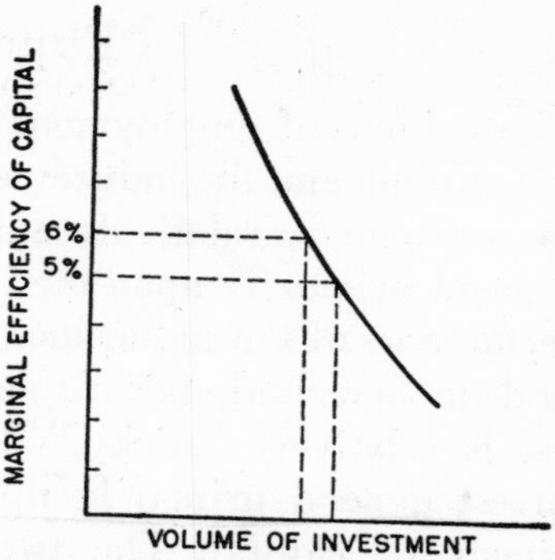

Figure 7b. A Relatively Inelastic Schedule of the Marginal Efficiency of Capital, or Investment Demand Schedule.

In 7a the schedule is relatively elastic so that a fall of one per cent in the rate of interest will result in a relatively large increase in the volume of investment, whereas in 7b a fall of one per cent in the rate of interest will result in a much smaller increase in the volume of investment. What the actual position and shape of this curve will be depends upon many complex factors which are subject to different estimation by each entrepreneur and to frequent revision, but it is not impossible to draw an approximate schedule of the marginal efficiency for particular industries and for the economy as a whole at any given time. Experience indicates that the schedule of the marginal efficiency of capital tends to be inelastic (7b) rather than elastic (7a). Therefore, changes in the rate of interest only slightly influence the flow of new investment. More important than decreases in the rate of interest are the dynamic forces of growth and technological progress which are constantly lifting the schedule of the marginal efficiency of capital. When these dynamic forces weaken, the rate of investment per period of time decreases causing unemployment, and in the absence of such growth factors, opportunities for profitable new investment would soon disappear altogether.

Expectations

The volume of employment is determined by the propensity to consume and the inducement to invest. Since the propensity to consume is relatively stable, fluctuations in employment depend primarily upon the inducement to invest. The two determinants of the inducement to invest are the rate of interest and the marginal efficiency of capital. Since the rate of interest is relatively "sticky," fluctuations in the inducement to invest depend primarily upon changes in the marginal efficiency of capital. The two determinants of the marginal efficiency of capital are the supply price or cost and the prospective yield or return. It is the prospective yield which gives the marginal efficiency of capital its most important characteristic, its instability. Hence, a great part of the instability of economic life under capitalism is attributable to the unstable character of prospective yields from capital assets. Since it is important to account for instability of employment, and because of the role played by prospective yields in this connection, it becomes important to explore the nature of the forces which determine prospective yields.

These yields which figure so prominently in determining the volume of employment are *prospective* yields because at the time an investment is made they are nothing but expectations on the part of the investor. The expectations may never be realized at all, and an entrepreneur does not really believe that everything will turn out just as he predicts when the investment is made. In other words, the investor expects to be "surprised," either favorably or unfavorably, because he cannot honestly hope that events will actually unfold in exactly the way he foresees as most probable. Thus investment decisions are governed by expectations of yield and not by actual yields. Because of the nature of capital assets, especially those of a durable type, large immediate outlays are required before any actual returns can begin to flow back to the investor. Capital assets are a link between the present and the uncertain future.

A prospective yield is what an entrepreneur expects to obtain from selling the output of his capital assets. There are two types of expectations regarding the yields of assets: (1) short-term expectations and (2) long-term expectations. Short-term expectations concern the sales proceeds from the output of existing plant. Long-term expectations concern the sales proceeds which an entrepreneur can hope to earn with variations in the size of his plant or from the building of entirely new plant. In short-term expectations, the plant is assumed to be of a fixed size; only the output from that given sized plant is variable. In long-term expectations, the size of the plant as well as the amount of output from plant is variable.

Short-term Expectations: Short-term expectations are more stable than long-term expectations because the *realized* results of the recent past are a relatively safe guide to what will happen in the near future, whereas there exists no past experience which will serve as a comparably safe guide to what will happen in the distant future. Realized results of past activity are important only in so far as they influence current expectations about the future. It is always the current expectations concerning prospective future yields that are relevant to current investment and therefore to current employment. In the case of short-term expectations, most of the circumstances which influence current output remain substantially the same from day to day or from week to week or month to month. In economic life, as in other areas of experience, there is a high degree of continuity over short periods. In the absence of definite evidence for expecting a change, the most recent events may be expected to continue in the near future. By their very nature, short-term expectations are subject to frequent check in the light of realized results. Since realized results are a satisfactory guide to the near future, it is relatively safe to substitute these realized results for expectations relating to the near future. Short-term expectations are relatively stable. Hence, it may be concluded that short-term expectations are less important than they would be if realized results of the recent past were not a relatively safe guide to what to expect in the near future. It is not necessary to try to predict the future when only short-term plans are in question. It is safe to rely upon past results.

Long-term Expectations: In contrast with short-term expectations, long-term expectations regarding the probable yields of new investments in durable plant and equipment are highly unstable and therefore more important in explaining the fluctuations in aggregate investment and aggregate employment in the economic system. While we may safely assume that economic activity next week will be approximately what it was during the past week, experience tells us that we cannot safely assume the next five years will be approximately like the past five years as concerns events which will determine the yields to be received from current investments. Realized results of past years are not a trustworthy guide to future years. It is not possible in the case of durable assets to check expectations against realized results at short intervals as can be done in the case of short-term expectations.

There are some considerations affecting long-term expectations which do not rest upon the shifting sands of a precarious future. Decisions to invest are partly based upon facts regarding the existing stock of capital assets. Especially relevant are the types of assets which will be available to compete with the projected new investment. For example, a decision to build a new steel plant depends partly upon the amount of existing steel capacity. Steel capacity is a fact that can be ascertained with more or less certainty. Likewise, the ability of the existing capacity to meet the existing demand at the prices being paid for current output are data of a more or less definite nature. But as we begin to look ahead, the horizon becomes more clouded. The probable life and maintenance of the plant the construction of which is being contemplated cannot be accurately predicted. Still less predictable are such considerations as possible changes in technology in the steel industry which would influence the rate of obsolescence of the projected plant. In the precarious zone are considerations of the general level of effective demand 10 or 20 years hence, the amount of new competition, the prices which can be realized from year to year, the prospect of war, the size of the export market, changes in tax burdens, conditions in the labor market including the level of wages and freedom from strikes, and finally, the political climate of future decades which will influence the extent of social control over industry. Concerning these latter events, there is no probability calculus upon which to base scientific judgments.

Our general ignorance of the future and the precariousness of the basis of what we think we do know about the future stand out above all other aspects of long-term expectations in an unplanned economy. The distant future is never clearly foreseen and this is especially true when entrepreneurial decisions are made by a large number of private entrepreneurs whose decisions are uncoordinated. Nevertheless, mere social survival, not to speak of economic progress, requires that decisions be made no matter how precarious the basis upon which they rest. The upshot of the extreme precariousness of the circumstances in which long-term expectations are formed is the great instability which characterizes these expectations and the consequent instability of economic life in general. Long-term expectations are subject to sudden revisions. Periods of feverish investment activity tend to be followed by periods of extreme pessimism and depression in which investment in durable capital assets falls to an extremely low level.

In making a most probable forecast as to what will happen to a long-term investment, not much weight is or can be attached to matters which are very uncertain. We cannot act in any positive fashion upon what we do not know. Hence, there is a tendency for long-term expectations to be influenced to a disproportionate degree by the ascertainable facts of the current situation and to assume that the existing summing up of the future is correct and that things will continue as they are in the absence of specific reasons for changing our expectations. Nevertheless, the things we do not know exert a powerful influence upon investment activity. For the degree of confidence with which most probable forecasts are made is affected by what we do not know. It is lack of confidence in the most probable forecasts which renders investment decisions so subject to sudden shifts. Furthermore, when there is great uncertainty about which of several alternative investment opportunities offers the highest return, there is a tendency to postpone a positive decision in the hope that the view of the future will become clearer at a later date. Thus, even when there is confidence that profitable investment opportunities do exist, the lack of confidence in ability to determine which is most profitable will tend to depress the marginal efficiency of capital and reduce the volume of investment and employment. Investors with limited resources cannot exploit all investment opportunities they believe will turn out to be profitable, and therefore they will try to make certain that their limited resources are placed where the returns are maximized. The belief that knowledge will improve is a cause of apathy in the investment market. If for some reason the vista seems to become clearer to a significant degree, apathy will give way to a wave of new investment. This bunching of positive decisions to invest following a period of apathy is one of the causes of fluctuations in employment.[3]

Influence of the Stock Market Upon Prospective Yields: The prevailing state of long-term expectations in modern capitalistic societies is reflected in the activities of the stock exchange. When prospective yields are viewed favorably, stock prices tend to be high; and when prospective yields are viewed unfavorably, stock prices tend to be depressed. A purchase of securities does not, of course, represent real invest-

---

3. G. L. S. Shackle, "Expectations and Employment," *The Economic Journal,* September, 1939, Vol. XLIX, No. 195, pages 442-452.

ment. It is purely a financial transaction involving the transfer of titles to existing wealth and does not involve the production of new wealth or of social income. Securities traded on the stock exchange are "old stocks" already outstanding in the hands of the public. When one party purchases such stocks, representing claims to existing capital assets, he increases his individual investment. But at the same time someone else disinvests to the same extent when he sells the securities. The sale is equal to the purchase and the disinvestment is equal to the investment. Aggregate social investment, as well as aggregate financial investment, remains unchanged as a result of stock exchange transactions. What matters for employment is the use of men and materials to build new factories and other forms of capital assets. When real investments of this type are made, new securities may be floated through investment banking channels and thereafter the securities may be traded on the stock exchange.

How then does stock market activity affect real investment and employment? The prices of "old" securities traded on the stock exchange influence the prices at which "new" securities can be floated in the new investment market. When the price of old securities is high, the price of new securities will tend to be high also. Ability to float new securities at high prices will encourage investment in new projects on a scale which might seem extravagant in other circumstances. High quotations for existing stocks mean that the marginal efficiency of capital for this type of enterprise is high in relation to the rate of interest and consequently the inducement to invest is strong. It is cheaper to build new capital assets of a given variety than to buy the claims to existing capital assets of the same variety. On the other hand, when the prices of securities on the stock exchange are low, it will be cheaper to buy claims to existing enterprises than to build new capital assets; the supply price (cost of building new capital assets) exceeds the demand price (present value of existing capital assets discounted at the current rate of interest); or, to express the same idea in still another way, the marginal efficiency of capital is below the rate of interest. This condition is unfavorable to the inducement to invest. In general, new investment in many types of capital assets is governed by quotations in the stock market.

In highly organized markets like the stock exchange, existing investments are revalued daily, even hourly. The chief basis for changes in valuations are changes in current expectations concerning future events which will influence future yields. Such markets are links between the present and the future. Any event that is expected to happen in the future is taken into account ("discounted") in the present prices of securities. When an event actually occurs, it will influence the prices of securities only in so far as it is "unexpected" in the sense that it has not been foreseen, or has been "uncertain" in the sense that the event confirms views previously held with less than complete confidence. For example, several commercial airplane crashes occurring over a week-end are likely to depress the prices of commercial airline stocks when the exchange opens on Monday morning because these crashes will not have been foreseen. Presidential veto of a bill to reduce business taxes, which veto has been generally expected but concerning which there has been some doubt, may tend to depress the prices of securities because what was previously uncertain becomes certain. However, in the latter case the effect will probably not be great since the veto will have been largely discounted in advance.

Speculative activity in the stock exchange contributes to the instability of the marginal efficiency of capital. If "speculation" is defined as the attempt to forecast the psychology of the market, and "enterprise" as the attempt to forecast the yield of assets over their entire life, Keynes concludes that the state of long-term expectations which governs the quotations of securities in the stock exchange is more the result of speculation than of enterprise. The tendency for speculation to outrun enterprise arises from various psychological and institutional factors connected with the precarious basis of knowledge regarding the future. Investors are aware that their individual judgments about the long-term future are practically worthless and they tend to rely upon the judgment of others who may be better informed. This is especially true of the mass of amateur investors who do not possess even the technical and business knowledge which is utilized by professionals. The main concern is what other people think. It is assumed that existing quotations accurately reflect the future, so that in the absence of specific reasons for expecting a change it is further assumed that there will be no major shifts in the market in the near future. Therefore, the only major risk lies in a change of news and views in the near future. Even the amateur may feel capable of judging the significance of new knowledge in relation to changes in stock prices. Since the market is "liquid," i.e., since anyone can sell out on a moment's notice if something drastic should happen, the investor need not worry about the long-term prospects of the enterprise in which he invests because there is no need to continue to hold these securities for a long time. Thus, in practice, long-term expectations rest upon the acceptance of a conventional judgment, i.e., the acceptance of the unique correctness of the existing estimate of the future and the assumption that only genuine new knowledge will cause a significant change. The widespread acceptance of this convention gives a certain stability to the market *so long as the convention is maintained.*

The separation of ownership from management in modern corporate business enterprise has fostered reliance upon conventional judgments. The ignorance of most shareholders in regard to the organization and functioning of the business enterprise of which they are part owners diminishes the profitability of professional attempts to judge long-term prospective yields. Instead of trying to estimate the probable yields of capital assets over their entire life, investors are guided under modern institutional arrangements by forecasts of the psychology of the market over the relatively short run. The quotations which will exist at any time reflect the dominant opinion of the mass of participants. If the dominant opinion three months hence is optimistic, the market will be good; and if dominant opinion three months hence is pessimistic, the market will be bad. One who wishes to make money in the stock market should then try to forecast what the predominant opinion will be three months hence. Since the dominant opinion is largely a conventional matter, those who make the most money in the stock market will be those who are most successful in forecasting what average opinion thinks average opinion will be three months from now. Investment becomes a psychological game which can be played by amateur and professional alike.

The investor who wishes to base his behavior upon more genuine and scientific forecasts of long-term yields is confronted with at least two major obstacles. First, the intrinsic difficulty of accurately judging the long-term future makes all such forecasts extremely precarious. There exists hardly any basis for being "scientific" in judging the prospects of a transoceanic steamship line 20 years hence. Think of the great French liner, *Normandie*, in the year 1935. Within less than ten years she had been the victim of war, fire, and scrapping. Second, the long-term yield is largely irrelevant in relation to what the price of an asset will be next week or next month. If a security now selling at 100 is expected to be down to 50 ten years hence but up to 120 next month, it is more profitable to buy the security now and sell it next month than to sell now merely because the long-term future is gloomy. The most profitable occupation for even the skilled forecaster is to anticipate market psychology, to rationalize the irrational activities of the mob of less skilled participants in the market. Hence "speculation" tends to dominate "enterprise" in the stock market.

A conventional judgment which rests on the mass psychology of a group of investors who are without knowledge or conviction about real market forces affecting long-term yields is a highly unstable basis upon which to build the capital development of a country. Resting as it does upon the assumption that things will continue as they now are unless there is reason to expect a change, the conventional judgment is stable only as long as the convention holds, i.e., as long as there is no reason to expect things to change. Ignorant investors are in no position to judge what kind of factors will make a real difference and so they may be provoked into a chain reaction of pessimism or optimism by superficial events which bear no relation to the actual long-term yield of an enterprise. Doubt as to the significance of some new event may lead to further doubt as to whether the present state of the market does sum up accurately the future. In the event of a con-sensus that present security prices do not accurately reflect the future, stability, based on a convention that no longer holds, gives way to erratic fluctuations. Like all speculation based on ignorance, the market is subject to unreasonable spurts and irrational collapses. "Speculators may do no harm as bubbles on a steady stream of enterprise. But the position is serious when enterprise becomes the bubble on a whirlpool of speculation. When the capital development of a country becomes a by-product of the activities of a casino, the job is likely to be ill-done."[4]

New investment is facilitated on the one hand and impeded on the other by markets organized with a view to individual liquidity. In highly organized markets like the stock ex-change, the individual wealth-owner holds his assets in a form which can readily be converted into cash. Investment is facilitated because the stock exchange enables the investor, as an individual, to liquidate his holdings at any time. This encourages individual investors to contribute to the risk-taking involved in new enterprises. On the other hand, the separation of ownership from control, the general ignorance of the majority of investors, the mass psychology which dominates the market, and the undue weight given to super-ficial occurrences, render the market supersensitive to slight disturbances and make the individual prone to convert his holdings into money upon relatively slight provocation, lead-

---

4. Keynes, *The General Theory of Employment, Interest and Money.* New York: Harcourt, Brace and Co., Inc., 1936, page 159.

ing to easy breakdown and to a dampening of prospective yields which weaken the inducement to invest. Liquidity exists for the individual investor but not for the community as a whole. Individuals may dispose of their holdings in enterprises with specialized plant and equipment, but there is no way by which the community as a whole can liquidate these fixed assets. But in their desire to liquidate, individuals who make up the community depress the marginal efficiency of capital, weakening the inducement to invest and increasing unemployment for the community as a whole. Prior to the separation of ownership from management and the emergence of organized stock exchanges, decisions to invest in enterprise were irrevocable for the individual as well as for the community as a whole. A major contribution of the stock market is the ease with which capital can be mobilized for the development of new productive wealth, but a great disadvantage is the associated instability arising from a speculative liquidity which can lead to a paralyzing collapse of the existing productive capacity of society.

It would be misleading to suppose that instability of investment decisions is entirely the outcome of rational calculations and speculative conventions within the framework of an irrational institutional setting. The non-rational aspect of human behavior finds an outlet in the investment market. In fact, much long-term investment would never occur if investors depended upon mathematical calculation or even psychological convention. In a practical sense, the basis for scientific calculation often does not exist. The propensity of human nature toward spontaneous optimism, the human urge to action rather than inaction, the tendency for positive activity to depend upon a sort of animal spirit or *élan vital*—all these are nurtured by and at the same time contribute to the extreme uncertainty of long-term expectations. Even in the market place, human behavior is not always guided by an "irrational passion for dispassionate rationality." Even in the money market, "the heart knows reasons that reason cannot know."

The foregoing discussion indicates clearly that instability is the outstanding short-run characteristic of the marginal efficiency of capital. Over historical time, there are upward and downward movements in the expected rates of return from new investment. Since the rate of interest does not fluctuate in a comparable manner, the rate of investment, which is determined by these two forces, must also fluctuate and in turn cause the total volume of employment and output to fluctuate. These variations in over-all economic activity follow a cyclical pattern familiarly known as the business cycle. In a later discussion we shall see that the essence of the business cycle is to be found in the more or less rhythmic fluctuations in the marginal efficiency of capital.

Secular Decline in the Marginal Efficiency of Capital

In the secular long run, the significant characteristic of the marginal efficiency of capital is its tendency to fall. The diminishing marginal efficiency of capital is a new name for the old idea of the falling rate of profit. Many of the great economists, including Adam Smith, David Ricardo, Karl Marx, and John Stuart Mill, accepted the tendency for the rate of profit to fall as one of the basic phenomena of long-term development of the capitalistic economy. Despite wide acceptance of the tendency of the rate of profit to fall, there has been scant agreement as to why it falls. Adam Smith attributed the falling rate of profit to the mere fact that capital becomes more abundant in a progressive society. Ricardo and Mill saw the basic cause for falling profits in the niggardliness of nature in the sense that the food supply for an increasing population had to be grown from land of ever-diminishing productivity. Marx's theory of the falling tendency of the rate of profit is associated with the nature of capital itself rather than with the niggardliness of nature. Keynes' theory of the declining marginal efficiency of capital differs from all of these others but has most in common with Smith's explanation. Keynes' theory has something in common with that of Marx and is most unlike that of Ricardo and Mill.

Keynes' explanation of the decline of the marginal efficiency of capital, like other secular aspects of his theory, is not fully developed. The general idea is that diminution results in the long run from decreased prospective yields associated with a growing stock of capital assets. The marginal efficiency of capital is determined by the supply price or cost of production and the prospective yields. It may fall either from a rise in the supply price or from a decrease in prospective yields. In the short run, the more important factor is the increase in supply price. The longer the period becomes, the less important is the increase in supply price and the more important the diminution in prospective yields. Thus the secular decline in the marginal efficiency of capital is almost entirely the result of a fall in prospective yields.

Prospective yields fall because capital assets become more abundant. The returns from capital assets over their life exceed their cost only because they are scarce. Every increase in investment brings an increase in output which competes with the output of existing capital. The greater abundance of output tends to lower prices and hence to lower also the expected yields from further plant capacity. The process of creating more capital assets to compete with existing capital assets continues as long as the marginal efficiency exceeds the rate of interest. If the rate of interest were permitted to fall to zero, the unimpeded accumulation of real capital would lower the prospective yields to the point where there would be no return in excess of cost. Capital assets would cease to be scarce; they would yield a return just equal to their cost of production; the marginal efficiency of capital would be zero. With uninterrupted production, Keynes suggests that capital assets might cease to be scarce within one or two generations.

The decline in the marginal efficiency of capital arising from the fall in prospective yields is a tendency which may be offset by dynamic growth factors such as increase of population, territorial expansion, and certain types of technological change. During the nineteenth century, these growth factors and the frequency of war were sufficient to forestall the *tendency* from becoming an actuality. Even though the rate of interest did not decline, the marginal efficiency of capital was maintained at a level sufficiently high to prevent chronic unemployment of an amount so intolerable as to provoke revolutionary changes in the economic system. Unemployment in the nineteenth century manifested itself primarily in the form of periodic depressions sandwiched between spurts of feverish investment activity. In the twentieth century, the rate of growth of population has slowed down and territorial expansion has virtually ceased. Changes in technology have been increasingly of the capital-saving type, which means there has been no marked rise in the ratio of capital assets to output. Under these circumstances, brief periods of capital accumulation like that between 1922 and 1929 in the United States are sufficient to lower the marginal efficiency of capital to equality with the rate of interest. Hence, the inducement to invest is weakened, and with capital accumulation at a virtual standstill, chronic mass unemployment like that of the 1930's results. Secular stagnation is the end result of the slowing down in the dynamic growth factors. Although Keynes makes no dogmatic assertions concerning the inevitability of secular stagnation, his hypothesis that wealthy capitalist economies cannot hope to maintain full employment without social control of investment rests on the view that investment opportunities in the present stage of capitalist development are less than they were in the earlier centuries of capitalism. The concept of secular stagnation, which pervades Keynes' *General Theory*, has been more fully developed by Professor Alvin Hansen.[5]

---

5. See especially Alvin H. Hansen, *Full Recovery or Stagnation?* New York: W. W. Norton and Company, Inc., 1938, and *Fiscal Policy and Business Cycles*, New York: W. W. Norton and Company, Inc., 1941.

Some Practical Conclusions

Keynes' analysis of the characteristics of the marginal efficiency of capital leads him to the practical conclusion that the control of investment in capital assets cannot safely be left in private hands (p. 164). The precarious nature of long-term expectations which finds its objectification in the violent fluctuations of the stock market leads to an instability in the marginal efficiency of capital so great that it cannot be offset by any practicable changes in the rate of interest. The secular decline caused by uninterrupted production of new capital assets would soon (within one or two decades) push the rate of return down so low that a securities market organized according to the principles of private profit could not provide adequately for the development of society's future productive power. The state, which is in a better position than private enterprise to calculate long-run needs in terms of general social advantage, should assume greater responsibility for directly organizing investment. The practical counterpart, or the operational meaning, of the theoretical concept of the marginal efficiency of capital is referred to by Keynes as the "socialisation of investment."

Although the *General Theory* contains numerous references to the socialization of investment, it is nowhere elaborated. In the broadest sense, it may be taken to include a policy of investment control to offset cyclical fluctuations in private investment, and to overcome the obstacles in the way of, and the difficulties arising in connection with, the secular decline in the marginal efficiency of capital. In regard to cyclical control, Keynes' ideas about public works and other forms of public investment have been referred to in connection with the multiplier. Keynes first advocated public investment as a recovery measure in the British election campaign of 1929, and he became during the 'thirties the leading scientific authority for this type of "spending" policy. When little came of public works in Great Britain, Keynes turned his attention to the New Deal in the United States, where he praised the principle of the public-works program of President Roosevelt. However, he was critical of the lack of planning in American public works, and used the shortcomings of the New Deal policy to reinforce his demands for a well-ordered public-expenditures program. In 1938 Keynes recommended that the British government set up a Board of Public Investment, whose function would be to make plans for increases in public investment to supplement private investment whenever an economic recession threatened. To critics of this plan, Keynes replied that such a program had never been given a fair trial. President Roosevelt's program, although useful in saving the United States from a more complete economic collapse, was largely improvised as a system of work relief. Plans for increased public investment on housing, public utilities, and railroads, to mention a few of the potential outlets, were still in a stage of preparation when the 1937 recession wiped out most of the recovery gains made in the United States up to that time. Keynes saw in this lack of preparedness for public investment the main cause of the recession of 1937 and 1938.[6] The Board of Public Investment was to be organized as a permanent agency of the government, although Keynes did not believe it necessary to carry out new projects continuously at that juncture of his country's economic development. The Board should, however, stand in readiness with plans to be executed at the first sign of a slump.

Keynes' suggestions for implementing the long-term secular aspects of the socialization of investment are less satisfactorily discussed by him than the short-term, public works phase. The secular policy involves government control over the entire investment process, private as well as public. Keynes held some such idea for state control over aggregate investment and saving at least as early as 1926, when he questioned the desirability of leaving to private judgment and private profit the allocation of resources going into investment.[7] This idea becomes more prominent in the *General*

6. *The Times*, London, January 3, 1938, page 13.
7. *Laissez-faire and Communism*, page 69. New York: New Republic, 1926.

Theory, but even here it is left undeveloped. Presumably this long-range control over investment would be placed in the hands of a governmental agency resembling the Board of Public Investment suggested for Great Britain in 1937. Through the appropriate agency, the government would determine the total volume of resources to be allocated to investment. The basis for deciding what proportion this should be would, of course, have to be related to total consumption as determined by the propensity to consume at full employment. State authority would also determine the basic rate of return to the owners of the instruments of production, as long as such rewards were paid. Even after the average rate of return on capital assets has fallen to zero, and mere ownership ceases to be a basis for income, there will remain functional capitalists who can make income from superior skill in calculating risks on alternative forms of investment. Keynes apparently did not intend that state authority should control the allocation of resources among various forms of investment even though state authority did determine the total quantity of investment. He states explicitly that socialized investment does not mean that the instruments of production would be owned or operated by the government, although, of course, there would be some expansion of the amount of actual public investment as a result of an enlarged public-works program.

Beyond these few principles, Keynes does not set forth the principles and procedures for allocating investment funds. This failure may be attributed to the undeveloped nature of his secular analysis. Just how investment could be "socialized" while management and ownership remained in private hands requires explanation that Keynes fails to supply. The suggestion may be ventured, however, that if Keynes had followed out his secular analysis for the elimination of rewards for ownership in a private-property economy, his proposal for socializing investment might have led to the necessity for over-all economic planning, and this in turn to the fundamental question whether over-all planning is possible under private ownership of the means of production. Keynes advocated neither general planning nor the nationalization of industry.

Some further implications of Keynes' social philosophy will be considered in the concluding chapter. It should be clear from what has already been said that the fulfillment of his program, involving as it does the elimination of income from mere ownership of property, would constitute a minor revolution in the social structure of the traditional private-enterprise system. Yet this "euthanasia of the rentier," as Keynes calls it, would be achieved peacefully and gradually as a result of the accumulation of so much productive wealth that capital assets would cease to be scarce. Before the marginal efficiency of capital could fall so low, however, the rate of interest would have to be correspondingly reduced. Otherwise, wealth-holders would universally prefer to own "debts" or money rather than productive assets. Real investment occurs only as long as the marginal efficiency of capital exceeds the rate of interest. The nature of the problem of reducing the rate of interest in order to stimulate the inducement to invest requires further investigation of interest and money.

References for Further Reading

Keynes, J. M., *The General Theory of Employment, Interest and Money*, Chapters 11, 12, and 5. New York: Harcourt, Brace and Co., 1936.

———, "Some Consequences of a Declining Population," *Eugenics Review*, April, 1937, Vol. XXIX, pages 13-17.

Fisher, Irving, *The Theory of Interest*, Chapter VII, pages 150-177. New York: The Macmillan Company, 1930. (Fisher discusses the "rate of return over cost" and the "marginal rate of return over cost.")

Hansen, A. H., "Economic Progress and Declining Population Growth," *The American Economic Review*, March, 1939, Vol. XXIX, pages 1-15. Reprinted in *Readings in Business Cycle Theory*, selected by a Committee of the American Economic Association. Philadelphia: The Blakiston Company, 1944.

———, *Full Recovery or Stagnation?* especially Chapter XIX,

"Investment Outlets and Secular Stagnation." New York: W. W. Norton and Co., 1938.

Hart, A. G., "Keynes' Analysis of Expectations and Uncertainty," in *The New Economics,* edited by S. E. Harris, Chapter XXXI, pages 415-424. New York: Alfred A. Knopf, 1947.

———, *Anticipations, Uncertainty and Dynamic Planning.* Chicago: University of Chicago Press, 1940.

———, "Uncertainty and Inducements to Invest," *The Review of Economic Studies,* October, 1940, Vol. VIII, pages 49-53.

Kaldor, Nicholas, "Speculation and Economic Stability," *The Review of Economic Studies,* October, 1939, Vol. VII, pages 1-27.

Shackle, G. L. S., *Expectations, Investment, and Income.* London: Oxford, 1938.

———, "Expectations and Employment," *The Economic Journal,* September, 1939, Vol. XLIX, pages 442-452.

———, "The Nature of the Inducement to Invest," *The Review of Economic Studies,* October, 1940, Vol. VIII, pages 44-48, 54-57.

Strachey, John, "Mr. J. M. Keynes and the Falling Rate of Profit," *The Modern Quarterly,* October, 1938, Vol. I, pages 337-347. (A Marxist interpretation of Keynes' declining marginal efficiency of capital)

Swanson, E. W., and Schmidt, E. P., *Economic Stagnation or Progress.* New York: The McGraw-Hill Book Company, 1946. (Severely critical of the "Keynes-Hansen School")

Sweezy, A. R., "Population Growth and Investment Opportunities," *The Quarterly Journal of Economics,* November, 1940, Vol. LV, pages 64-79.

———, "Secular Stagnation?" in *Postwar Economic Problems,* edited by S. E. Harris, Chapter IV, pages 67-82. New York: McGraw-Hill Book Company, Inc., 1943.

———, "Declining Investment Opportunity," *The New Economics,* edited by S. E. Harris, Chapter XXXII, pages 425-435. New York: Alfred A. Knopf, 1947.

Terborgh, George W., *The Bogy of Economic Maturity.* Chicago, Illinois: Machinery and Allied Products Institute, 1945. (Severely critical of Keynes and Hansen)

CHAPTER 8

Interest and Money

For the importance of money essentially flows from its being a link between the present and the future.

J. M. Keynes, *The General Theory of Employment, Interest and Money*, page 293.*

The possession of actual money lulls our disquietude; and the premium which we require to make us part with money is the measure of the degree of our disquietude.

J. M. Keynes, *The Quarterly Journal of Economics*, February, 1937, page 216.

INTEREST is a payment for the use of money. Since this is just what the arithmetic books say it is, it would be unnecessary to make much of the point if traditional economic theory had not viewed interest as something quite different, as a payment for "waiting," for "saving," for "abstinence," or for "time preference."

The difference between the traditional theory of interest and Keynes' money theory of interest is a fundamental aspect of the difference between the economics of full employment and the economics of less than full employment. By the economics of full employment is meant an economic analysis which assumes that no resources are involuntarily unem-

---
* Harcourt, Brace and Co., Inc., 1936.

161

ployed so that an increase in the production of one thing necessarily involves the withdrawal of resources from some other employment. If investment is to be increased, for example, this can only be done if resources are withdrawn from employment in the consumers goods industries. If people can be induced to wait a while for some of their consumption, resources can be shifted out of consumers-goods production into investment-goods production to an extent corresponding to the reduction in spending for consumers goods. The inducement which is paid to get people to forego present consumption is interest, the payment for waiting. Within the framework of a system of theory built on the assumption of full employment, the notion of interest as a reward for waiting or abstinence is highly plausible. It is the premise that resources are typically fully employed that lacks plausibility in the contemporary world.

If unemployed resources are present on a large scale, there is no obvious necessity for paying people to abstain from consumption, i.e., to wait, in order that more resources may be devoted to the production of capital goods (investment). The obvious way to produce more capital goods is to put the idle resources to work and not to withdraw resources already employed from the production of consumers goods. Up to the point where full or approximately full employment is reached, it would be foolish to try to force or even to try to induce people to forego consuming in order to free resources so that more capital assets could be produced. In fact, a reduction in the demand for consumers goods is likely to lessen the incentive to produce capital goods if the reduction in consumer demand represents a permanent change of habit on the part of the consuming public. Something other than a theory of "waiting" or "time preference" is needed to explain why interest is paid.

Keynes' explanation is that interest is a purely monetary phenomenon, a payment for the use of money. This view of interest gives at the same time an explanation of the role of money in the economic system. The main tradition in economic theory since the time of eighteenth century mercantilism has banished money as a significant factor in the main body of principles of economics, but Keynes' monetary theory of interest reintegrates money into the theory of output and employment for the economy as a whole. While technical monetary theory falls into the background, the essential role of money is explained in relation to the theory of interest. The rate of interest is vital in relation to investment, and investment is the strategic determinant of the volume of employment since, according to the principle of effective demand, employment cannot increase unless there is an increase in investment. Thus monetary theory becomes an essential part of general economic theory through its relation to the theory of interest, and monetary policy becomes a vital part of general economic policy.

At every step in the following discussion of the theory of interest, it is helpful to bear in mind the close connection between Keynes' theory and the policy which he advocates. The theory of interest is at the same time part of the theory of money, and control of the rate of interest is to be attained through control of the supply of money. Control of the supply of money is one of the most effective and least objectionable methods of controlling output and employment. This is the operational meaning of Keynes' theory of interest and money referred to in Chapter 3. The agency of control of the money supply is the monetary authority, in particular the central banking system.

Banking policy in the past has all too frequently resulted in a shortage of money when more money was needed and an oversupply when less money was needed. The former contributes to unemployment and the latter to inflation. Since the long-term trend under private capitalism in its present stage of development is probably toward unemployment rather than inflation, Keynes gives special attention to the necessity of an "easy money" policy. He recognizes at the same time the dangers of inflation in war and postwar periods and has made outstanding proposals for coping with such situations. Keynes' theory of interest and money has its operational or practical meaning in the thesis that the banking system holds the key to the expansion of employment. With this in mind, the meaning and significance of interest rates will easily be understood. In a period of expanding output, a bank policy which does not permit a sufficient increase in the supply of money will cause a rise in the rate of interest and in this manner choke off the incipient expansion. An energetic policy by the monetary authority can do much to lower the long-term rate of interest to a level which will stimulate enough investment to fill the ever-threatening gap between income and consumption.

Statement of the Theory of Interest

The proposition that interest is a monetary phenomenon does not, of course, in itself constitute a theory of money or of interest. However, it does provide a point of departure for a theory of interest which differs fundamentally from the traditional view of interest as a reward for "waiting." Interest is a monetary phenomenon in the sense that the rate of interest is determined by the demand for and the supply of money. Money is demanded because it is the only perfectly liquid asset. People who need money for personal and business reasons and do not possess it are willing to pay a price for its use. Before a holder of money will surrender the advantages that attach to the ownership of the only perfectly liquid asset, he must be paid a reward. Interest is the reward paid for parting with liquidity, or in slightly different terms, the reward for not-hoarding. The rate at which interest will be paid depends on the strength of the preference for liquidity in relation to the total quantity of money available to satisfy the desire for liquidity. The stronger the liquidity preference, the higher is the rate of interest; and the greater the quantity of money, the lower is the rate of interest. A decrease in liquidity preference will tend to lower the rate of interest and a decrease in the quantity of money will tend to raise the rate of interest. The rate of interest, like any price in a free market, is established at a level at which the demand will be equilibrated with the supply available to meet the demand. At any time, an increase in the desire of the public to hold cash—that is, an increase in its liquidity preference—may be met either by an increase in the price paid (interest) or by an increase in the quantity available. Since money cannot be produced by the public, the direct result of an increase in its desire for money will not be to increase the quantity available but to increase the premium paid to those who give up their cash holdings. An increase in the rate of interest means a larger reward is paid for not-hoarding, and people who otherwise would not be satisfied except to increase their cash holdings will be satisfied as a result of the higher premium they receive for not holding cash. If the rate of interest did not rise when liquidity preference increased, the total amount of cash the public would wish to hold at the existing rate of interest would exceed the available supply. If the rate of interest did not fall when liquidity preference decreased, there would be a surplus of cash which no one would be willing to hold. Thus, if the rate of interest tends to be too high or too low, an adjustment takes place whereby the demand is equated to the available supply.

Since the quantity of money is the other factor which, along with the state of liquidity preference, determines the rate of interest, it is possible for the monetary authority to meet an increase in the desire on the part of the public to hold money with an actual increase in the supply of money. If people want to hold more money, the monetary authority, and only the monetary authority, can give them what they want. If the quantity of money is increased in proportion to the increase in liquidity preference, the rate of interest will not rise as it does when the quantity of money remains unchanged and liquidity preference increases. Since the rate of interest is one of the co-determinants of investment, and investment is the main determinant of employment, the importance of monetary policy in determining the volume of employment is easily seen.

The relationship between the rate of interest, the quantity of money, and liquidity preference may be represented by means of a diagram. In Figure 8, the quantity of money is shown along the horizontal axis and the rate of interest along the vertical axis. The liquidity-preference schedule will then appear as a smooth curve which decreases toward the right as the quantity of money increases. It is obvious from the

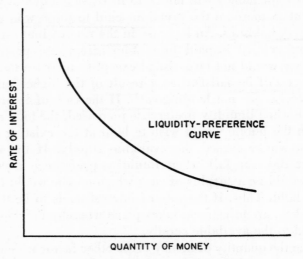

Figure 8. Liquidity-Preference Schedule.

diagram that larger quantities of money will be associated with lower rates of interest as long as the liquidity-preference schedule remains unchanged.

Interest appears in the market in the form of a reward paid to a wealth-holder who parts with control of money in exchange for a debt, e.g., for a bond or note or mortgage, for a stated period of time. The *rate* of reward per unit of time differs for debts of varying lengths. Thus there will be one rate of interest on call loans, another rate on three-day loans, and still other rates on six-month, one-year, five-year, ten-year and longer loans. While these rates differ in amount, they are all of the same specie. It is convenient in discussions of the theory of interest to speak of *the* rate of interest without reference to debts of any particular maturity. This simplification should not cover the fact that what really exists in the money market is a complex of rates of interest. Sometimes it is convenient to distinguish the short-term rate of interest paid on commercial bank loans from the long-term rate paid on bonds. In Keynes' general theory of employment, the important role played by real investment in durable capital assets makes the long-term rate of interest on loans used to finance such investments of prime significance. Fluctuations in the long-term rate of interest are reflected in changes in the price of bonds in the securities markets. As the price of bonds already outstanding in the market rises, the effective rate of interest falls; and as the price of bonds falls, the rate of interest rises. Thus, if a bond paying $50 per year sells at $1000 in the market, the prevailing rate of interest on that type of security is 5 per cent. If the price of the bond in the market rises above $1000, this means the effective rate of interest falls below 5 per cent because more than $1000 is now required to purchase an annual income of $50. Thus, references to changes in the rate of interest arising from changes in the state of liquidity preference or from changes in the supply of money may be visualized as taking the form of fluctuations in the price of bonds in the organized securities markets. A decrease in liquidity preference is reflected in an eagerness on the part of the public to purchase bonds at current prices, thus pushing up the prices of bonds and lowering the rate of interest. An increase in liquidity preference is reflected in an eagerness by the public to sell bonds in order to get cash. On a seller's market, the price of bonds falls and the rate of interest rises. The monetary authority may increase the supply of money and thus prevent the rise in the rate of interest by purchasing securities which the public wishes to sell at the current market price. When the monetary authority pays for its purchases with "new" money, it increases the supply of money and forestalls a rise in the rate of interest.

Liquidity Preference

The demand for money is a demand for liquidity. Liquidity may be analyzed in more detail by distinguishing three separate motives which lead to liquidity preference: (1) the transactions motive, (2) the precautionary motive, and (3) the speculative motive. Although interest is peculiarly related to the speculative motive, the other two motives cannot be ignored because money held for one purpose is a perfect substitute for money held for other purposes. A cash balance is, as a rule, held in a single pool the size of which is determined by a combination of the motives for liquidity preference. Part of the total may be held primarily for one purpose and secondarily for another purpose so that even the possessor does not have clearly in mind how much he holds for each separate motive (p. 195). In the total economy, an increase in the demand for money, e.g., for transactions, may be met by drawing upon the amount held for the speculative motive, in which case the rate of interest would tend to rise even though there were no change in the strength of the speculative motive and no change in the aggregate supply of money. Therefore, consideration is given to the transactions and the precautionary as well as to the speculative motive. But it is the last named which calls for the most attention in connection with the theory of interest.

Transactions motive

The quantity of money required to satisfy liquidity preference for the transactions motive is closely related to the volume of income and employment, that is, to the general level of business activity. As total output and employment rise and as prices and wages rise, the transactions demand for money also rises. A cash balance is required to bridge the interval between the receipt of income and its outlay for expenditures. The size of the cash balance will be related to the size of the income received and also to the frequency of income payment and the frequency of expenditure. If everyone received income in cash and simultaneously paid their expenses in cash, there would be little necessity for holding money balances for transactions purposes. There would be no interval to bridge. In the case of personal accounts, the cash balance actually held will be greater in proportion to the length of interval between paydays. A person who is paid monthly will have need for a larger average cash balance than an individual who is paid daily, assuming that there is some similarity in their expenditure habits. For example, a man who receives his entire income of $300 per month in a single payment and spends it in constant outlays of $10 per day will have a $300 balance the first day and a balance which decreases by $10 per day until at the end of the month he has a zero balance. The average cash balance for the month would be $150. But if this same individual were to be paid weekly, he would require an average balance of only $37.50, or one-half of his weekly $75 pay check.

Business firms, like individuals, find it necessary to hold bank balances to bridge the gap between outlays for expenses and the receipt of cash from sales of finished products. Again as with individuals, the size of the balance will vary directly with the length of the interval. The business motive for holding cash will rise as business activity increases. Payments from one entrepreneur to another will vary with the number of stages through which goods pass on their way to final completion, that is, with the degree of integration in the economy as a whole. Increasing integration will, other things being equal, diminish the demand for money. However, factors like the degree of business integration change relatively slowly, and, except for fluctuations in the level of business activity, there is no major factor causing changes in the demand for cash for transactions in the short run.

Precautionary motive

The second motive for liquidity preference—the precautionary motive—arises because individuals and business firms find it good practice to hold a reserve of cash in addition to what is needed for transactions. An individual who goes shopping will normally take more money than just the amount he thinks he will need for planned purchases. Plans may change, or opportunities may arise to make especially advantageous purchases if they are transacted on the spot without delay. In business the need for immediate cash may arise in order to meet contingent liabilities or unforeseen opportunities to make advantageous purchases. The quantity of money held to satisfy the precautionary motive will vary widely with individuals and businesses, according to their degree of financial conservatism, the nature of their enterprise, their access to the credit market, and the stage of development of organized markets for quick conversion of earning assets such as stocks and bonds into cash. Danger of being cut off from the credit market, say as a result of business losses, will be an especially important factor tending to increase the size of precautionary holdings by business firms. As long as individuals and businesses feel assured of ready access to extra cash by temporary borrowing, the precautionary motive to hold money will be relatively weak.

Although organized markets in which securities can be converted quickly and cheaply into cash tend to reduce the size of precautionary holdings, the possibility of forced liquidation under highly unfavorable conditions serves as a precautionary basis for preferring cash to securities. Precautionary balances may be held in savings deposits, where they will earn a low rate of return but where there is no danger, apart from failure of the bank, that the money value of the investment will depreciate. If, however, a notice of thirty days or so is required before funds may be withdrawn, the savings account lacks the advantage of perfect liquidity. Savings deposits are useful as a form of asset with a value fixed in terms of money which can be used to meet a subsequent liability fixed in terms of money. The cash reserves of a bank are themselves money held by the bank to protect itself against outstanding liabilities, the payment date of which cannot be predicted with certainty.

Speculative motive

Despite some important differences between the demand for money for transactions and that for precautionary motives, Keynes lumps these two together in discussing the relation of money to the rate of interest. While cash for transactions will be kept to a minimum, there is an obvious point where the convenience of holding cash to pay for regular expenditures will not be much affected by changes in the rate of interest. Likewise precautionary holdings, which depend mainly on the nature of the contingencies that are envisaged, are unlikely to be much affected by small changes in the rate of interest. Thus the significant type of liquidity preference in relation to the rate of interest is that arising from the so-called speculative motive, because speculative holdings are especially sensitive to changes in the rate of interest. If the total supply of money is designated by M, we may refer to that part of M held for transactions and precautionary motives as M_1, and to that part held for the speculative motive as M_2. Thus $M = M_1 + M_2$. The rate of interest is primarily determined by the propensity of the public to hold money for the speculative motive in relation to the quantity of money available for that purpose, i.e., M_2. The quantity of money which will be held to satisfy the speculative (M_2) is a function (L_2) of the rate of interest (r), or reward paid for giving up temporary control over money. A convenient shorthand expression for this relationship between money held for the speculative motive and the rate of interest is $M_2 = L_2(r)$. Since the amount of money held for the transactions and precautionary motive (M_1) depends primarily upon the general level of business activity, which may be measured by income (Y), the shorthand for this is $M_1 = L_1(Y)$. Then the equation $M = M_1 + M_2$ may be expressed, $M = L_1(Y) + L_2(r)$.

In connection with liquidity preference for the speculative motive (the desire for money as a store of wealth), the fundamental issues of modern monetary theory are raised. Why should anyone with a surplus of wealth choose to store it in the form of money and thus sacrifice the interest income which could be earned by exchanging money for a debt in the form of a bond or mortgage, et cetera? According to Keynes, the one essential condition in the absence of which liquidity preference for money as a store of value could not exist is the *uncertainty as to the future of the rate of interest,* by which is meant uncertainty as to the future of the complex of interest rates on debts of varying lengths which will prevail in the future. A wealth-holder who does not know on what terms he may be able to convert debts into money in the future has reason to believe that a postponed purchase may be preferable to a present purchase of a debt. For example, a man who contemplates paying $1000 for a bond yielding $30 per year when the rate of interest on this type of bond is 3 per cent will hesitate to do so if he thinks the rate of interest on this same type of security may later rise, say to 4 per cent. At 4 per cent it is necessary to invest only $750 to get a return of $30 per year. Therefore, the price of the security will fall to approximately $750, which will mean a virtual loss of $250, less whatever interest is received in the interval, to anyone who paid $1000 for such a bond.

At any moment of time, the *current* rates of interest on debts of different maturities are known with certainty because there are actual quotations in the market. The rates of interest that will prevail in the future are not known with certainty. The current rates of interest do, however, take into account estimates or guesses concerning what the future rates will be. Market quotations represent the predominant, but not the universal, opinion as to what the future rates of interest will be. An individual who thinks he knows better than the market, i.e., better than the predominant opinion, what the future will bring, is in a position to profit if his guesses actually turn out to be better than the predominant opinion. In the absence of uncertainty about the future rates of interest, the rates at which debts of varying maturities could be converted into money at any future date would also be known with certainty now because present rates would be perfectly adjusted to future prices. Under these circumstances, which would exist if there were no uncertainty, there would always be clear economic advantage in owning interest-bearing securities as compared with holding non-income-earning cash. There would exist no basis for liquidity preference for the speculative motive. This helps to explain why in the classical theory, which rests upon generally static assumptions, no significance is attached to the speculative motive and therefore M_2 is equal to zero. Under static theory there may be change, but since the direction and extent of the change is assumed to be known now, the future changes are subject to rational discounting which incorporates them into current calculations. Hence, uncertainty in any significant sense is ruled out of the theory. It is precisely at this point that Keynes' theory differs fundamentally from the classical theory of interest. Wealth-holders lull their disquietude about the future by storing wealth in the form of money just because the actual world is highly dynamic and the future is above all uncertain. The degree of disquietude is measured by the rate of interest. Of course the nature of the real world is not changed by making assumptions which differ from reality. The upshot of oversimplified assumptions is to render theory irrelevant for many types of problems. By assuming a kind of knowledge about the future which we do not and cannot possess, the classical theory rules out liquidity preference for the speculative motive, and with this, out goes the basis for a theory of interest. " 'Interest' has really no business to turn up at all in Marshall's *Principles of Economics*,—" says Keynes, "it belongs to another branch of the subject." (p. 189)

The speculative motive for liquidity preference is thus defined as attempting to secure a profit from knowing better than the market what the future will bring (p. 170). Purchases of bonds will be postponed if the rate of interest is expected to rise.[1] If and when the rate of interest does rise, the price of bonds will fall. The person who has speculated by holding money can now buy at the lower price and realize a profit. An individual who expects the price of bonds to rise (the rate of interest to fall) more than predominant opinion, as expressed in market quotations, expects them to rise, is in a position to profit by borrowing money on short term in order to buy securities now and then sell them at a profit later when and if the price does in fact rise. In the language of the market, a "bear" position leads to a holding of cash in anticipation of a fall in the price of bonds (a rise in interest rates) and a "bull" position leads to the purchase of securities in anticipation of a rise in bond prices (a fall in interest rates). As either the "bear" or the "bull" position predominates in the market, there is an alternate rise and fall in the desire to hold cash. In the absence of changes in the total quantity of money (M), these speculative fluctuations impinge on output and employment by changing the rate of interest and thus reacting upon the volume of current real investment.

The difference of opinion among "bears" and "bulls" is in itself a stabilizing influence and contributes to the feasibility of monetary control of the economic system. Differences of opinion prevent, or at least reduce, the extent of shifts in the rate of interest. An increase in the desire on the part of some wealth-holders to hold money is offset by a decrease in the desires of others so that changing events often result in a redistribution of cash holdings rather than a mass rush into cash or out of cash. If the banking authority, through open market operations, is able to purchase bonds by bidding up the price by slight amounts, it does so by causing some "bull" (a person holding securities) to exchange his bonds for the new cash and thus become a "bear." The rise in the price of bonds represents a fall in the rate of interest which, other things being the same, stimulates real investment and em-

---

1. The word "bond" is used as representative of debts of all types. "Debts" would be technically more accurate.

ployment. If everyone reacted in the same way to changing events, the fluctuations in the rate of interest would be much more violent and the stability of the system would be lessened. As Keynes says: "It is interesting that the stability of the system and its sensitiveness to changes in the quantity of money should be so dependent on the existence of a *variety* of opinion about what is uncertain. Best of all that we should know the future. But if not, then, if we are to control the activity of the economic system by changing the quantity of money, it is important that opinions should differ." (p. 172)[2] Since the transactions and the precautionary motives are both relatively insensitive to changes in the rate of interest, the effect of changes in the quantity of money upon the speculative motive is the substantial basis upon which monetary management rests its case for control of interest rates.

Although monetary management by the central monetary authority offers distinct possibilities for social control of employment, it is subject to important limitations which arise from the nature of the speculative motive. For while an increase in the quantity of money will, other things remaining unchanged, lower the rate of interest, it will not do so if liquidity preference is increasing more than the quantity of money (p. 173). In this connection, it is important to distinguish between two points on the same liquidity-preference curve and two different liquidity-preference curves. Figures 9a and 9b are similar to Figure 8 except that the horizontal axis measures only the quantity of money available to satisfy the speculative motive. This is represented by M_2. Corresponding to M_2, the liquidity function for the speculative motive is L_2. As already noted, this function may be written $M_2 = L_2(r)$, meaning the quantity of money held for the speculative motive is a function of the rate of interest. In Figure 9a, A and B represent two points on the same liquidity-preference curve, and in 9b, A and C represent points on two different liquidity-preference curves. This distinction is analo-

---

2. *The General Theory of Employment, Interest and Money.* New York: Harcourt, Brace and Co., Inc., 1936.

gous to that between two points on the same demand curve and
a shift in an entire demand curve.

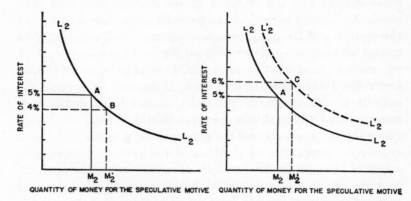

Figure 9a. Two Points on the Same Liquidity-Preference Schedule.

Figure 9b. A Change in Liquidity Preference.

In Figure 9a an increase in the quantity of money from
M_2 to M_2' is accompanied by a fall in the interest rate from
5 per cent to 4 per cent. The assumption behind this lowering
of the interest rate is that the action of the monetary authority in increasing the supply of money did not affect the expectations of wealth-holders. The additional supply of money
was absorbed by the sale of securities to the banking authority with a resultant rise in security prices and a fall in
the interest rate.

In Figure 9b the increase in the quantity of money from
M_2 to M_2' is accompanied by a revision of expectations in
the market such that the entire liquidity-preference schedule
shifts upward to an extent that more than offsets the effect of
the increase in the quantity of money for satisfying the
speculative motive. Hence, instead of falling as in 9a, the
interest rate rises from 5 per cent to 6 per cent. This means
that central bank policy or some event accompanying it has
led wealth-holders to increase their preference for holding
money. Such an upward shift could be caused by many fac-

tors and might take place independently of a change in bank policy. When such shifts in liquidity preference occur, a considerable fluctuation in the rate of interest, i.e., in the prices of bonds, may take place with very little activity in the bond market. Shifts in the liquidity function may be either downward or upward depending on the way in which the public interprets a change in events. In so far as different individuals react differently to the new situation, movements will be less marked. On the other hand, if everyone interprets the new situation in the same way, the change in interest rate may take place without any buying or selling of bonds and therefore without any redistribution of cash holdings.

As previously indicated, the total quantity of money (M) consists of two parts, money held to satisfy the transactions and precautionary motives (M_1) and money held to satisfy the speculative motive (M_2). Demand for the former varies primarily with changes in income (Y), or in terms of the equation $M_1 = L_1(Y)$. Demand for the latter (M_2) varies primarily with changes in the rate of interest, such that $M_2 = L_2(r)$. However, income (Y) depends partly on the rate of interest (r) and therefore changes in either r or M_1 will affect the other indirectly. This relationship becomes important for monetary policy in periods of expanding output. If income (Y) is rising, the demand for M_1 is also rising. If there is no increase in the total quantity of money (M), the increase in M_1 will take place by a transfer of funds from M_2. The decrease in funds available to satisfy the speculative motive will tend to increase the rate of interest, which in turn will react adversely on investment, and hence upon income. This rise in the rate of interest, which will tend to place a brake on expansion, can be offset by increasing the total quantity of money (M) so that the increase in funds needed to satisfy the growing transactions demand will not be met at the expense of money needed to satisfy the speculative motive (M_2). Here the banking authority is called upon to act in a way which will not allow a shortage of money to lead to a premature brake on expanding output and employment.

We are now in a position to see the practical implications of Keynes' theory of money and interest. The banking authority may be called upon to stimulate employment by increasing the supply of money. The theory behind the idea that an easy-money policy can stimulate expansion is as follows: An increase in the total supply of money (M) operates by increasing the amount of money available for the speculative motive (M_2), which will cause the rate of interest to fall. A fall in the rate of interest will increase investment, and an increase in investment will lead to a multiple increase in income. As income rises, the amount of money required for transactions (M_1) will increase so that the total increase in money (M) will be divided in some fashion between M_1 and M_2. How effective monetary stimulation will be depends on how much the rate of interest falls in response to an increase in M_2 (upon the elasticity of the L_2 function); how responsive investment is to a fall in the rate of interest (the elasticity of the schedule of the marginal efficiency of capital); and how much a given increase in investment will increase income (the size of the investment multiplier).

The pitfalls which may beset monetary policy will be recognized as very great. We have already noted that an increase in the quantity of money will not lower the rate of interest if liquidity preference is increasing more than the quantity of money. Although a fall in the rate of interest will, other things being equal, increase investment and employment, it will not do so if the marginal efficiency of capital is falling more rapidly than the rate of interest. In a bad depression when the preference for liquidity is high and the expectations of entrepreneurs for profitable investment are low, monetary policy may be helpless to break the economic deadlock.

It is much easier to bring down short-term than long-term interest rates. The reason for this is obvious. The chief barrier to a fall in interest rates is the expectation that they may rise later to an extent that makes it worth while to hold cash in anticipation of buying on better terms at a later date. If the banking authority launches a large-scale open-market policy to lower the interest rates, it is logical to assume that this policy will probably be pursued for some time. There will be little reason to expect a rise in the rate of interest in the near future and therefore little incentive to remain liquid in order to buy on better terms later. Furthermore, commitments to debts on short-term cannot involve very great losses even if expectations prove wrong. Securities may be held a short while until maturity when they will be redeemed at face value. It is well known that short-term interest rates have been extremely low in the United States and Britain in recent years.

The long-term rate of interest is more difficult to lower and it becomes increasingly resistant to further reductions at every step on its downward path; at some level, say about 2 per cent, no further reductions may be attainable. To illustrate, let us compare the consequences of a rise from 5 to 6 per cent with the consequences of a rise of from 2 to 3 per cent. To simplify the example, let us assume that the securities bought are perpetual bonds, that is, have no maturity date, like British consols or French rentes. When the rate of interest is 5 per cent, a bond paying $50 per year is purchased at $1000. Three years later the rate of interest on this type of security rises to 6 per cent as a result of which the price of the bond falls to $833 (at 6 per cent $833 will purchase an income of $50 per year). The capital loss is $167 but, during the three-year period, interest income amounting to $150 has been collected. Hence the net loss is negligible. In contrast, when the rate of interest is 2 per cent, a bond paying $20 can be purchased for $1000. Three years later the rate of interest rises to 3 per cent, as a result of which the price of the bond falls to $667 (at 3 per cent $667 will purchase an income of $20 per year). The capital loss of $333 is offset only to the extent of $60 in interest income received in the three-year period. Thus the loss from a rise in the interest rate from 2 to 3 per cent is much greater than from 5 to 6 per cent, first, because the loss in capital value is greater and, second, because the interest income is less at the lower level.

The increasing risk of loss at lower rates of interest will be reflected in the liquidity-preference schedule by a flattening out of the liquidity curve. This flattening of the curve indicates a growing elasticity of the liquidity-preference function. Translated into monetary policy, this means a point will be reached below which it is extremely difficult to lower the interest rate any further. At about 2 per cent, Keynes suggests the liquidity curve may become horizontal, indicating perfect elasticity, and meaning that no further reduction in the rate can be attained merely by increasing the quantity of money. When this point is reached, the demand for money has become absolute in the sense that everyone prefers to hold money rather than long-term securities yielding a return of 2 per cent or less.

When Keynes wrote the *General Theory*, he no longer believed in the adequacy of mere monetary policy, but nevertheless he thought the full possibilities of interest rate control had never been tested. Central bank purchases in the open market had been too limited in amount and confined mainly to short-term securities to the neglect of long-term securities bearing directly upon the much more important long-term rate of interest. The interest rate is a highly psychological or conventional phenomenon and investors who have become accustomed to high rates as "normal" will continue to harbor the hope of a return to "normalcy" unless and until bold monetary policy by the banking authorities breaks through conventional beliefs to convince the public that low long-term rates are both sound and certain to continue. Any monetary policy that appears experimental is self-defeating. The chief hope of lowering the long-term interest rate to a point consistent with full employment rests upon the ability of the monetary authority to convince the community that it should accept as a permanent fact lower rates of return on long-term debts. Such a policy should not be neglected just because it will ultimately reach a limit where it will no longer be effective because of the flattening out of the liquidity curve.

Hoarding and liquidity preference

There is a relationship but not an identity between Keynes' concept of liquidity preference for the speculative motive and the common-sense notion of hoarding. Unemployment and depression are sometimes attributed to "hoarding" although the exact meaning of this term is usually not clear. "Hoarding" in the sense of an actual increase in cash balances in the hands of the public is an incomplete and misleading notion. Since the total quantity of money cannot be altered by the public, but only by the banking system, the public can merely *try* to hold more money. It may increase its liquidity *preference*. At any given time, the total supply of money (M) is, by definition, held by someone. If one individual comes into possession of more money as a result of his increased desire for liquidity, someone else in the economy must decrease his cash holdings, as long as there is no change in the total supply of money as determined by the banking system. The distribution of cash holdings among the public may be changed but no alteration in the aggregate holdings can occur as a result of initiative taken by the public.

Nevertheless, the anxiety on the part of the public to hoard more money has very important consequences for the economic system, since, as will be evident, it is nothing more than an expression of increased liquidity preference. Liquidity preference may be defined as the propensity to hoard. When liquidity preference or the propensity to hoard rises, the rate of interest will also rise, unless the banking system meets the increase in liquidity preference by enlarging the quantity of money available to wealth-holders. An increase in the desire to hoard money can be overcome by paying higher interest to potential hoarders. A rise in the rate of interest chokes off investment and leads to a decrease in income and employment. Thus the notion of "hoarding," rightly viewed, is the heart of Keynes' analysis of unemployment. Unemployment may be caused by "hoarding," in this sense, even if no actual wealth is transferred into money, because hoarding money and not-hoarding it are not simple alternatives. Liquidity preference is always liquidity at a price. The price is the rate of interest. The rate of interest will always be high enough to overcome the liquidity preference of all those who want cash somewhat less intensely than those who actually hold the limited supply available. The rate of interest will be determined immediately by the liquidity preferences of those who are marginal between holding money and purchasing an interest-bearing security. An increase in the desire to shift wealth from securities into money is what causes a rise in the price that must be paid to marginal hoarders to induce them not to hoard. Only those most insistent on having cash will be able to get it. The doubts and fears of others will be lulled by interest payments. This view of the economic process has led Keynes to a sympathetic understanding with those reformers who have suggested that a special levy be placed upon money in order to make it "unhoardable." He praises the proposal of Silvio Gesell, the stamped-money reformer, who wanted to impose a tax upon money to encourage people to spend it before the tax came due. Money held in an inactive balance for an extended period of time would, under Gesell's plan, gradually lose its entire value.

Changes in the Quantity of Money

The rate of interest depends upon the state of liquidity preference taken in conjunction with the quantity of money. If liquidity preference remains unchanged, increases in the quantity of money will lower the rate of interest, and decreases in the quantity of money will raise the rate of interest. It is important to say something more about how changes in the quantity of money occur in modern economic societies.

The total supply of money consists of bank deposits, paper money, and metallic coins. In highly developed capitalistic economies like the United States, the supply of money con-

sists overwhelmingly of bank deposits, which represent liabilities of banks to pay money to depositors. No matter of
principle is involved in determining whether savings deposits
should be included under the category of money. If money is
defined as the perfectly liquid asset, the presumption is
against including savings deposits because banks have the
right to require a certain number of days' notice before they
will convert a savings or time deposit into legal money. On
the other hand, savings accounts differ from debts in that their
value in terms of money is not subject to change. In some
countries the statistical data do not permit a breakdown of
total deposits between demand and time deposits. Even
though a bank has the legal right to require, say, thirty days'
notice on savings accounts, this requirement is not always
strictly followed. Keynes does, in general, include as money
time deposits in banks. What matters most for the present
discussion, however, is not what makes up the total quantity
of money (M), but how changes in this total come about.
These changes arise mainly from the lending and borrowing
activities of the banking system. Therefore demand deposits,
or what may be called check-book money, are the significant
element of the money supply so far as the interest rate and
Keynes' theory of money are concerned.

Banks add to the total supply of money by the creation of
bank credit, that is, by increasing the liquid claims against
themselves in favor of their customers whose additional
money takes the form of increased balances. Balances which
add to the total quantity of money arise when loans are made
or when a security, like a bond, is purchased by a bank as an
investment. For example, when a bank advances a loan to a
business man for $1000, the total supply of money (M) is
increased by $1000. The only physical evidence of this trans-
action is a bookkeeping entry in the accounts of the bank,
debiting "Loans and Discounts" and crediting "Deposits."
Loans and discounts represent an asset of the bank because
they are rights or claims of the bank against its borrowers
to be collected at some specific date in the future, the date

depending upon the length of the loan. "Deposits" are a liability of the bank, representing its obligation to pay money
on demand to the borrower-depositor. What matters from
the money side is that an increase in total bank loans represents an increase in liquid claims, that is, in bank credit,
which is just as good as money for most types of transactions
and therefore is part of the supply of money.

When a bank loan is repaid, the quantity of money is reduced, unless of course a new loan of corresponding amount
is made at the same time. The physical evidence of this destruction of money is again merely a bookkeeping entry in
the accounting records of the bank. The "Loans and Discounts" account is credited to indicate a decrease in this
asset, and the "Deposits" account is debited to indicate a
decrease in the liability to pay money. If the loan is repaid
in cash, the "Cash" account will be debited. As a result of
the loan, the bank will have added to its income in the form
of interest charged the borrower.

These deposits which result directly from the lending and
investing activities of individual banks with individuals,
firms, and the government, are called "derivative" deposits,
as distinguished from "primary" deposits which result from
the actual deposit of cash or its equivalent.[3] Derivative deposits create additional bank credit whereas primary deposits do not. Since bank credit is included in our definition of
money, derivative deposits increase the total supply of
money outstanding in the economic system. In contrast, if a
man deposits metallic or paper money, he exchanges one
type of money for another. The structure of the money supply
outside the banking system is changed; bank deposits have
increased and the metallic or paper money in the hands of
the public has decreased, but the total quantity of money (M)
is not altered. Likewise, a man who deposits his pay check or
any other check with his bank does not increase the total

---

3. See Keynes, *Treatise on Money*, Vol. I, Chapter 2. New York: Harcourt,
Brace and Company, Inc., 1930, also C. A. Phillips, *Bank Credit*, page 40. New
York: The Macmillan Company, 1921.

supply of money, but merely increases his claims against the bank at the expense of someone else whose claims are decreased. Hence, changes in the total supply of money come about primarily as a result of the lending and investing activities of the banking system associated with derivative deposits. If the public desires to become more liquid, only the banking system can permit it to do so.

There are, of course, limits to the extent to which the banking system is able to increase the liquid claims against itself. In any nation the power of the banking system to alter the quantity of deposit money is limited by legal requirements or business customs. In the United States the central monetary authority, the Board of Governors of the Federal Reserve System, is authorized under law to control the quantity of liquid claims which member banks are permitted to have outstanding by (1) varying the reserve requirements of the member banks, (2) altering the rediscount rate at which member banks may borrow from the Federal Reserve Banks, and (3) engaging in open market operations in order to make rediscount rates effective and in order to influence directly the prices of securities and thereby the rate of interest. When the central banking authority lowers the ratio of legal reserves to deposits which the member banks must hold, it gives the member banks an incentive to increase the claims outstanding since cash for a bank, as for any wealth-holder, is not an earning asset and excess cash reserves represent a basis for potential earning power that is not being utilized. More loans will tend to increase bank profits. Whether the member banks will actually lend more as a result of lowered reserve requirements depends partly on their willingness to lower the rate of interest which they charge and partly on the rate which business men and other borrowers are willing to pay. In any event, it may be supposed that more will be borrowed at lower than at higher interest rates, other things remaining the same. The extent of demand for bank loans will depend upon profit expectations, that is, upon the marginal efficiency of capital. If the marginal efficiency of capital is

very low, as it is in time of depression, no fall in the interest
rate will have much effect upon the quantity of borrowing. In
this respect the initiative for expansion must come from outside the banking system.

When the central banking authorities lower the rediscount
rate, they make it cheaper for member banks to add to their
cash reserves by selling (rediscounting) commercial paper
to the Federal Reserve Banks. In the United States it is customary for member banks to borrow from the Federal Reserve Banks because the rediscount rate is lower than the
discount rate charged by the member banks. This means that
member banks may be able to add to their reserves at, say, 2
per cent and advance loans to business men at 4 per cent. It
will therefore be more profitable to borrow from the central
banks when the rediscount rate charged by the central bank
is lowered. Here again there are barriers to increasing the
quantity of money or liquid claims against member banks.
If the member banks already have excess reserves, there will
be no incentive which did not already exist to lower their
interest rates nor for them to add still more to excess reserves
by borrowing from the central bank. Again, the initiative
must come from outside the banking system if the quantity of
liquid claims is to be increased.

A more positive weapon of monetary control in the hands
of the central banking authority is open-market operations.
Here the central authority can take the initiative to change the
quantity of liquid claims outstanding against the banking
system. Open-market operations represent the purchase and
sale of securities by the central banks in the open market.
"Open market" refers to transactions which are not exclusively with banks and includes especially the bond markets
of great financial centers like New York City. The purchase
and sale of securities by banks differ from those between
two private persons in that the quantity of money in the
economy is changed when a bank buys or sells. The purchase
of a bond by one person from another person involves only
a *transfer* of money and no change in the total quantity of

money and also no change in the money-creating capacity of the banking system as represented by the extent of its reserves. When a central bank buys a bond, it pays with funds which it creates for the purpose. If, for example, an individual sells a bond to the central bank, the individual receives in payment from the central bank a check which, when deposited with the individual's (member) bank, represents a net increase in the supply of money in the economy outside the banking system. What is potentially more important for monetary expansion arises when the member bank presents the check for payment from the central bank. The central bank makes payment to the member bank by increasing the balance of the member bank. Since balances held by member banks with central banks represent reserves, the capacity of the member bank to expand its loans is increased by an amount which depends upon the reserve ratio. If the ratio is $1 of reserve for each $5 of deposits, an increase in reserves of $1000 means that total deposits in the banking system may be increased by $5000. Open-market operations thus bring about changes in the reserves of member banks. Frequently, open-market operations are used to bring pressure upon the member banks to change their discount rates in accordance with changes in the central bank rediscount rates. In depression a lowering of the rediscount rate coupled with an increase in member bank reserves resulting from open-market purchases by the central bank will presumably give the member banks incentive to expand their loans to customers. In expansion, an increase in the rediscount rate may be ineffective if the member banks have excess reserves, but if these reserves are reduced through open-market sales by the central bank, the member banks will be forced either to replenish their reserves by rediscounting commercial paper at the higher rediscount rates or to restrict the volume of, their loans to customers, which is the objective of the central bank policy.

Open-market operations affect not only the short-term rate of interest on bank loans but also the long-term rate of interest through the prices of securities. Even the purchase of short-term securities will react upon the longer-term rates of interest, but a more direct effect on long-term rates of interest results from dealings in long-term securities. Keynes criticizes the Federal Reserve authorities for confining their open-market purchases during 1933 and 1934 to very short-dated securities with the result that the effect was confined mainly, though not exclusively, to the very short-term rate of interest. Keynes suggests the most important practical improvement which can be made in the technique of monetary management would be "a complex offer by the central bank to buy and sell at stated prices gilt-edged bonds of all maturities." (p. 206)

Some limitations to monetary control have already been indicated. In general, the limitations of monetary management in controlling the level of employment are limitations of interest rate control. Although proper management of the supply of money is a necessary condition for a stable economy, it is not a sufficient condition. Mismanagement of money may in itself be sufficiently disturbing to lead to economic breakdown. But the best monetary policy in the world can do little to lift an economy out of the depths of a secondary deflation like that experienced in the United States in the early 1930's. What this means in terms of Keynes' principal variables is that if the marginal efficiency of capital has fallen to a very low or even negative position, there is nothing the central banking authority can do to bring about revival through lowering the rate of interest. There might be no demand for investment loans even if the rate of interest were reduced to zero. As long as loans have to be repaid and are not automatically renewable, any borrower runs the risk of being unable to repay his loans. Where the private marginal efficiency of capital has collapsed to a point where no one wants to borrow even at a zero rate of interest, it becomes necessary for a government which wishes to stimulate economic activity to take more direct action to increase the volume of investment and thus to lift the level of income and employment.

The Classical Theory of Interest

The contrast between Keynes' *general* theory of interest and the special theory of interest of the classical school is analogous to the contrast between his general theory of employment and the special theory of employment of the classical school. Both distinctions between the general theory and a special theory arise from the difference between fluctuating levels of employment and income in contrast with the fixed level of full employment and a corresponding fixed level of income. By neglecting the all-important changes in the level of income, the classical school is led into the error of viewing the rate of interest as the factor which brings about the equality of saving and investment, that is, the equality of demand for investible funds and the supply of funds provided by saving. This may be represented by a diagram showing the rate of interest along the vertical axis and saving and investment along the horizontal axis. The rate of interest is thus

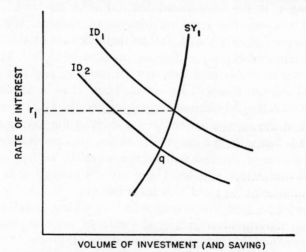

Figure 10. The Classical Theory of the Rate of Interest.

determined by the point of intersection of the investment-demand schedule, ID_1, and the supply of saving line, SY_1. The investment-demand schedule is Keynes' schedule of the marginal efficiency of capital. The line SY_1 represents the amount of saving out of a level of income Y_1 which, under classical assumptions, presumably would be the level of income corresponding to full employment.

Keynes accepts the classical position of equality of saving and investment but attributes this equality to changes in the level of income rather than to the rate of interest. Keynes also would agree with the classical theory that *if the level of income is assumed to be given,* the current rate of interest lies at the point of intersection of the investment-demand schedule and the schedule of saving which will be made at varying rates of interest out of that level of income. Keynes parts company with the classicists when they go a step further and assume that if the investment-demand schedule shifts to the position ID_2, the intersection of this new investment-demand schedule and the old SY_1 at the point q in Figure 10 will determine the new rate of interest. The classical error lies in assuming that the investment-demand schedule can change without causing the level of income to change. We know from Keynes' theory that a fall in the schedule of the marginal efficiency of capital will cause investment to fall. The fall in investment leads to a decrease in income, and out of the reduced income less will be saved. Thus, it is inconsistent to assume that the investment-demand schedule (ID) can shift without at the same time causing a shift in the saving schedule (SY). Since the SY curve also shifts, we cannot determine what the rate of interest will be nor what the volume of saving and investment will be. There are not enough data in the classical scheme to yield this information.

In order to find the saving schedule which is relevant to the new investment schedule, the rate of interest must first be determined by introducing the state of liquidity preference and the quantity of money. The appropriate SY curve will be that which intersects ID_2 immediately opposite the

new rate of interest, whatever it may be. If the new rate of
interest is r_2, the relevant saving schedule is SY_2 in Figure
11. The amount of investment (and saving) is now determined on the horizontal axis immediately below the point of
intersection of the ID_2 line and the SY_2 line. If the rate of
interest remains unchanged at r_1—because the state of
liquidity preference and the quantity of money for the speculative motive remain the same—the relevant saving-out-of-
income schedule will be SY_2', and the point at which this line
intersects the ID_2 line will indicate the amount of saving and
investment. The point q in Figure 11 corresponds to the same
point in Figure 10. It indicates the solution given by the
classical theory, which assumes that income and saving-out-
of-income remain unchanged when the rate of investment
changes, and on a basis of this special assumption, views the
rate of interest as the balancing factor which equates the
volume of saving to the volume of investment.

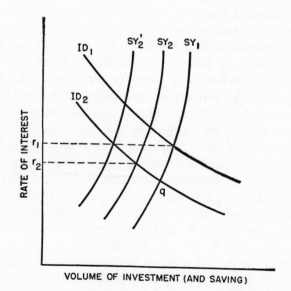

VOLUME OF INVESTMENT (AND SAVING)

Figure 11. The Rate of Interest and Changing Levels of Income.

The distinctive aspect of Keynes' theory is represented in the diagram by the SY curves. There is a different SY curve for each level of income. In assuming continuous full employment, the classical theory deals only with the SY_1 curve, and in this manner escapes the necessity of having to discover a general explanation for interest. By assuming that the investment-demand schedule (ID) can shift without affecting the level of income, and therefore the schedule of saving out of income (SY), the classical school is led to view interest as the "price" which equates the demand for investment to the supply of saving. This, however, is not an explanation of interest, but a special condition which follows from the special assumption of full employment and a fixed level of income. Nevertheless, the classical school goes on to work out a view of the interest rate as an automatic, self-regulating mechanism for equating saving to investment. When the demand for investment falls, the rate of interest is supposed to fall and lessen the supply of saving to correspond to the reduced demand for investment. Or, if the public decides to save more, the rate of interest is supposed to fall to a point where investment will increase to take care of the increase in saving. Thus, a decrease in the demand for consumption (increase in the desire to save) is supposed to be compensated for by an increase in investment through the mechanism of the rate of interest. This is just another way of saying that there will be no changes in aggregate income or aggregate employment when the demand for consumption declines. A fall in the demand for consumers goods is more likely to diminish than to increase the demand for investment. Empirical verification for this may be gleaned from the statistical fact that, except in war and other rare periods of strained resources, consumption and investment move in the same direction and not in opposite directions.

A glance at the SY curves in Diagrams 10 and 11 indicates that Keynes is willing to accept the view that more will be saved at a higher rate of interest than at a lower rate of interest out of a given income, although saving is not very sensitive to changes in the rate of interest (the SY curves are steep, or interest-inelastic). This is not to be interpreted to mean that more will be saved at a higher rate of interest than at a lower rate of interest when changes in income related to changes in the rate of interest are brought into the picture, as Keynes insists they must be. A rise in the rate of interest will actually lead to a decrease in the amount of saving. For when the interest rate rises, investment falls, and a fall in investment causes a decline in income, and out of a smaller income less will be saved. The fall in saving will be just equal to the fall in investment since the two were equal before income fell and must be equal after income falls. Just as surely as a rise in the rate of interest leads to a decrease in investment so must it also lead to a decrease in saving. This divergence of views between Keynes and the classical school boils down once again to the differences between the logic of an economics of full employment and the logic of an economics of less than full employment.

Observations on the Nature of Capital and Interest

Interest is so universally linked to capital in discussions of economic science that it is useful to ask the question: What view of capital is associated with Keynes' theory of interest? Capital is not an unambiguous concept, but probably it is most commonly defined as produced means of production, in contrast with natural means of production, referred to as "land," and meaning all natural resources used in production. Capital is man-made and land is nature-given. Keynes does not quarrel with this definition of real capital nor with the distinction between land and capital. But the rate or ratio which relates the income yields from real capital to its total value is called by Keynes the (marginal) efficiency of capital, which is quite separate and distinct from the rate of interest as a payment for the use of money. Traditional theory does not distinguish clearly, and from Keynes' point of view confuses, the marginal efficiency of capital as a reward or income derived from the ownership of scarce capital assets and interest as a reward or income for not-hoarding money. The arithmetical equality of the rate of interest and the marginal efficiency of capital in equilibrium has probably been a major cause of the failure to distinguish between the two phenomena.

The size of the reward paid as interest is traditionally viewed as a matter of the (marginal) *productivity of capital.* Interest is said to be the reward for saving, or for waiting until a later date for consumption which could be enjoyed now but which is foregone, as a result of which resources can be diverted from consumption to investment activity with a consequent increase in the total productiveness of capital. However, if interest, like the rent of land, is a scarcity payment which rewards no genuine sacrifice, there is little point in speaking of capital as "productive." Capital assets yield over their life a return in excess of their original cost only because they are scarce. As the scarcity of capital diminishes, the rate of return to owners will fall "without its having become less productive—at least in the physical sense." (p. 213) The main reason capital assets are kept scarce is because the rate of interest on money offers an alternative to wealth-holders which is more remunerative than the prospective yield (expressed as a rate) from newly-created capital assets. The rate of interest on money is a kind of institutional monopoly which leads to an artificial scarcity of capital assets.

In rejecting the idea that capital is productive, Keynes sympathizes with the labor theory of value that everything is produced by labor. Labor, working in an environment of technology, natural resources, and the assets produced by past labor, is capable of making capital assets less scarce. Capital is the product of past labor embodied in assets. Labor, of course, is used in a broad sense to include mental as well as manual labor, and the services of entrepreneurs as well as the services of those who work for wages. Labor working with machines is more productive than labor working without machines, just as labor working on fertile land is more productive than labor working on infertile land. Acceptance of the human agent as the sole creative force in production does not involve belittling the importance of machinery for increasing productivity. But it does involve an unorthodox way of looking at the economic process. One might view it as a revolutionary doctrine were it not for the fact that Adam Smith and Ricardo and practically all their contemporaries looked at the economic process in much the same manner. Only after the socialists took over the labor theory of value did it lose its respectability among academic economists. The labor theory of value is after all a very humanistic doctrine, which attributes production and productivity only to persons and never to things. It views machines as a mere extension of man's power over his economic environment rather than as co-ordinate partners that labor along with man. It imputes the added productivity that manifests itself in machinery back to the human agent which created the machinery. There is no really serious issue here, however, because it is largely a matter of terminology. Nevertheless, it is important to explain Keynes' departure from the classical (post-Ricardian) terminology and his preference for this way of speaking about the nature of interest and money.

There is implicit in Keynes' views of capital and interest a fundamental criticism of the existing social order. If interest is a payment for money and as such rewards no genuine sacrifice, it is unearned income. It is a form of income that would not need to be paid, at least not for long, under different institutional arrangements. Yet interest is, in a sense, inevitable under laissez-faire capitalism. The implication of Keynes' theory is that income received from not-hoarding money represents an institutional monopoly whereby the possessors of money enjoy the fruits of an unearned income snatched from an economic community so arranged that those who hold surplus money must be bribed before they will surrender it to those who will put it to a socially beneficial use, that is, will use the money as a device for mobilizing labor, material, and machines for the production of goods and services. Those who receive interest income are performing no socially necessary function. The propensity to hoard money impedes full employment and prevents greater production of capital and consumers goods, and denies to the public the full enjoyment of potential consumption. It creates an unnecessary and anti-social scarcity of productive equipment. Operationally, this is an appeal for an easy-money policy as a means to fuller and more abundant production.

Relation of the Marginal Efficiency of Capital to the Rate of Interest

In this chapter and the preceding one, the two basic determinants of the inducement to invest, the marginal efficiency of capital and the rate of interest, have been examined independently of each other. Since each concept is an independent variable and quite distinct, this procedure of separate discussion is justified. The analysis would be incomplete, however, without an examination of the way in which the two variables are related to each other. Traditional economics does not follow Keynes in his clear-cut distinction between the rate of interest and the marginal efficiency of capital. Interest has frequently been viewed as the reward for capital assets and the *rate* of interest as the measure of the marginal productivity of capital assets. Obviously, economists are aware that interest is paid on money borrowed from banks and from other sources. But the classical tradition has been to view the bank rate as the "money side" of the "real rate" of interest. In this strictly classical theory, the real and money rates of interest cannot get out of line because automatic market forces are always at work to prevent any divergence.

Some economists have developed the idea of interest somewhat further by distinguishing between the "market" or "money" rate and the "natural" rate, and have recognized that a divergence between the two might have important consequences. In this setting, economists like Wicksell, Hayek, and Keynes in his *Treatise on Money*, begin to give money a significant role in economic theory. We may identify this as the neo-classical theory of interest. When the market rate set by the banking system is equal to the natural rate, the economic system is in equilibrium according to this neo-classical version. If the banking system permits the market rate to diverge from the natural rate, a disequilibrium of some sort will result. Keynes' distinction between the rate of interest on money and the marginal efficiency of real capital is a further development of the neo-classical distinction between the market rate and the natural rate of interest. However, there is a fundamental difference between Keynes' earlier and later views. First, the natural rate of interest as used, for example, in Keynes' *Treatise,* although cognate with the marginal efficiency of capital, differs in that the natural rate is a unique rate which will prevail under conditions of full employment. The equilibrium which is attained when the market rate of interest is equal to the natural rate of interest is a full-employment equilibrium. But in the perspective of the *General Theory,* there is a different natural rate (or marginal efficiency of capital) for every level of employment. The earlier theory does not allow for the possibility of equilibrium at less than full employment. In brief, it is not a general theory. Second, in the classical and neo-classical views, the money rate of interest adjusts to the real or natural rate and in this sense the real or natural rate determines the money rate of interest or at least determines what it should be. But in Keynes' *General Theory* it is the marginal efficiency of capital that adjusts to the money rate of interest rather than the other way around. It is more correct to say that the rate of interest on money determines the marginal efficiency of (real) capital than it is to say that the marginal efficiency of capital determines the money rate of interest.[4]

---

4. On this very important point Keynes' words are: "Thus, instead of the marginal efficiency of capital determining the rate of interest, it is true (though not a full statement of the case) to say that it is the rate of interest which determines the marginal efficiency of capital." *Quarterly Journal of Economics,* February, 1937, Vol. LI, No. 2, page 223.

In equilibrium, the marginal efficiency of capital is equal to the rate of interest on money. These two rates are brought to equality by the efforts of wealth-holders to maximize the advantages of owning various forms of wealth. Persons who decide to give up immediate command over money still have the alternatives of owning debts (like bonds) or owning capital assets (which may be in the form of equity claims, i.e., stocks). The significant thing here, so far as employment is concerned, is that capital assets are capable of being newly produced. Producing new capital assets is another expression for investment. Preference will be given to building new capital assets rather than buying claims to old ones when it is cheaper to build than to buy, that is, when the supply price or replacement cost is less than the demand price or present value, which is found by discounting the prospective yields by the current rate of interest (see above p. 138). If the prospective yields discounted at the current rate of interest place the demand price or present value of capital assets above their replacement cost or supply price, new capital assets will be produced, i.e., investment will occur. New capital assets will continue to be produced until the marginal efficiency of capital falls to a level at which there is no longer any advantage in building more capital assets as compared with buying old ones or buying debts (bonds).

The marginal efficiency of capital is flexible and will fall under the impact of new investment. Since the marginal efficiency of capital varies with the volume of investment, and since income changes as investment changes, the marginal efficiency is not determined unless the level of income is also determined. Unless the level of income is assumed to be given or unless the rate of interest is determined independently of both the marginal efficiency of capital and the level of income, we do not know at what level the marginal efficiency will be equal to the rate of interest, as it must be in equilibrium. In an economy of fluctuating income, the marginal efficiency of capital is indeterminate as long as the rate of interest is not determined. Keynes solves the equilibrium by determining the rate of interest independently of the level of income.[5] The rate of interest depends upon the quantity of money and the state of liquidity preference. In this sense, the rate of interest sets the pace by fixing the level to which the marginal efficiency will fall. Between them, these two determine the volume of investment, and income falls into line as a truly dependent variable.

The classical theory in which the marginal efficiency of capital sets the pace to which the rate of interest is supposed to adjust is determinate only if the level of income is assumed to be given in order that the marginal efficiency can be found independently of the rate of interest. The classical theory assumes that income is given at the point corresponding to full employment. In a world characterized by wide and almost continuous fluctuations in income below the level of full employment, such a special theory is not very relevant. Thus the fatal flaw in classical economics is the lack of an adequate theory of interest. There are not enough data in the classical scheme to make the system solvable except under special, limiting assumptions. In mathematical language, the

5. This statement that the rate of interest is determined independently of income is subject to the following qualification. The rate of interest depends on the quantity of money available for satisfying the speculative motive (M_2) and this is related to the quantity of money available for the transactions motive (M_1), the demand for which depends on income. Therefore, indirectly the rate of interest depends on income. This is the main reference to "a full statement of the case" in the quotation from Keynes given in the preceding note. If Keynes' recommendation that the total quantity of money be increased to meet the rising transactions demand were followed, the rate of interest would not rise. In this practical sense then, if not in a strict theoretical sense, the rate of interest is determined by bank policy independently of income. Default in banking policy is of course always possible. The purpose of this section on the relation of the rate of interest to the marginal efficiency of capital is to indicate why Keynes thought his theory of interest and money was the distinctive contribution of the *General Theory*. Lest there be some doubt of this, the title of his book is the best *prima facie* evidence. This is not the same thing as saying that the rate of interest is most important in the policy sense, although Keynes seems never to have completely escaped this idea. What it probably does indicate, on a fundamental philosophical level, is an inconsistency between Keynes' theoretical and practical emphasis. However, since the purpose of this book is to give an exposition and not a critique of Keynes, this issue would carry us far afield. See, however, the last chapter below.

classical theory is one equation short of a determinate solution. This is the equation which gives a general theory of interest in which the rate of interest is fixed by the quantity of money and the state of liquidity preference. In Keynes' general theory of employment and income, the money theory of the rate of interest is the linchpin of the system, lacking which no determinate solution can be reached. In contrast, in the classical theory the rate of interest is subsidiary to the marginal efficiency (productivity) of capital, and money has no independent significance in relation to output and employment. It is money's function as a store of value which sets Keynes' theory apart from the classical theory because the holding of money is a crucial alternative both to the ownership of debts and the ownership of durable capital assets. Classical theory is led into a mistaken theory of investment by a false rationalization concerning the type of knowledge which we have about the future. In a world of a calculable future, there is no place for money as a store of value. It would always be preferable to own a debt rather than to hold money. Under these conditions, the rate of interest would fall and investment would increase until all resources were employed. The chief fault of the classical theory lies in its assumptions rather than in its logic.

The preceding analysis shows that the marginal efficiency of capital is more flexible than the rate of interest on money. The former changes fairly readily in response to changes in the quantity of capital assets, whereas the rate of interest is "sticky." The level at which the two rates are equal is dependent more upon the rate of interest than upon the marginal efficiency of capital in the sense that new capital assets are built until their marginal efficiency is reduced to the level of the rate of interest on money. Investment stops and unemployment exists because of the barrier set by the money rate of interest. In the absence of money, or any commodity with the characteristics of money, the marginal efficiency of capital would fall under the impact of increasing investment until full employment were reached.

What are the peculiar characteristics of money that prevent its rate of interest from falling in a manner similar to the fall of the marginal efficiency of all other types of assets? The answer to this important question involves a subtle analysis of the properties of money and interest which may, however, be summarized in fairly simple terms. The properties of money which make the rate of interest "sticky" are found in (1) the zero or negligible elasticity of production of money, (2) the zero or negligible elasticity of substitution of other factors for money, and (3) the high elasticity of demand for money as a store of value.

(1) *Negligible elasticity of production:* Unlike most other commodities, the output of money cannot be increased readily by private enterprise, as distinct from the monetary authority. When the demand for money increases relative to the demand for other things, labor cannot be employed by private enterprise to increase the production of money. If this were the case, the courses of depressions would be different, as indeed they are to some extent in gold-producing countries. With a fall in the demand for things other than money and a rise in the demand for money, men who lost their jobs in producing the former could be put to work in the latter, and unemployment would be avoided or at least mitigated. Modern money, however, is predominantly bank money, and is not produced according to the principles which govern the employment of labor by private enterprise for the production of real goods and services. In so far as gold is still a part of the money supply, there is some mitigation of unemployment. In depression when prices fall and the value of money, including gold, rises, gold mining tends to employ more labor than in prosperity. In gold-mining countries, this may be of some practical significance in offsetting unemployment in other industries, but for the world as a whole it is of minor significance.

Since money cannot be produced by labor, the rate of interest does not decline in the way that the prices of other commodities fall as a result of the increase in their output.

Here the monetary authority can play a part by increasing the quantity of money in an attempt to lower the rate of interest. While this does not result in any increase in employment to produce money, it may lower the rate of interest and permit more labor to be employed in producing other forms of (real) wealth which are now relatively more desirable because the value of money has fallen.

(2) *Negligible elasticity of substitution:* There is no efficient substitute for money as a medium of exchange. When the demand for money increases relative to other things, there is no tendency to substitute other things for money as in the case of other commodities. In the case of land, for example, the elasticity of production is negligible, which means that no more land can be produced as demand for it increases, but nevertheless other factors of production will be substituted for land as its price rises. More machinery and more labor may be used in place of land to produce more output when the price (rent) of land rises. But since there is no other factor capable of performing money's function nearly as efficiently as does money, no substitution of other factors for money takes place.

(3) *High elasticity of demand for money as a store of value:* Even when the quantity of money is made elastic by action of the banking authority, or when the quantity of money available as a store of value (M_2) is increased by virtue of a release from the quantity used for transactions (M_1), the demand for money as a store of wealth is such as to be unresponsive to changes in the proportion which money bears to other forms of wealth. In other words, when M_2 is increased, the rate of interest will not fall readily, and below a certain level of, say, 2 per cent, the rate of interest will not fall at all because the preference for holding wealth in the form of money rather than in the form of debts (like bonds) becomes relatively absolute. (See above p. 180.) This means that the rate of interest does not fall in response to an increase in the quantity of money in the same manner that

the marginal efficiency of capital assets falls in response to increases in their quantity. If the number of houses were to be greatly increased, the marginal efficiency of houses would fall quite rapidly; but great increases in the quantity of money do not lead to marked decreases in the rate of interest, especially after the latter has fallen to a certain level. The demand for money as a store of wealth is relatively insatiable (so long as there is no flight from the currency), whereas the demand for other forms of wealth is quite satiable. One important reason for the willingness to increase ownership of wealth in the money form is the low or negligible carrying cost of money.

Keynes' basic contention is that these properties of money are responsible for unemployment in the sense that in the absence of a form of wealth with the characteristics of money, the ordinary forces of the market would cause the economic system to be self-adjusting at full employment. In the absence of the barrier set by the money rate of interest, the marginal efficiencies of all types of capital assets would be free to fall to a level at which the amount of investment would be sufficient to result in full employment. Actually, however, the level of the money rate of interest sets a limit below which the marginal efficiency of capital cannot fall. Production of new wealth stops at this point because further increases would reduce the marginal efficiency to a level at which the return from new investment would be less than the return from buying existing assets or from buying debts (like bonds). In this explanation of why the special properties of money set the limits to the fall in the rate of interest, we gain insight into why, after all, Keynes' work is called a general theory of employment, *interest and money*. The equilibrium level of employment is reached when the advantages of holding money, owning debts, buying capital assets, and building new assets are equalized. The form of wealth ownership is a matter of indifference to marginal investors. But to the economy as a whole, a preponderant desire to store wealth in the form of money means unemployment and depression which, far from being a matter of indifference, may point the way to revolution.

References for Further Reading

Keynes, J. M., *The General Theory of Employment, Interest and Money*, Chapters 13, 14, 15, 16 and 17. New York: Harcourt, Brace and Company, 1936.

——, *Monetary Reform*. New York: Harcourt, Brace and Company, 1924.

——, *A Treatise on Money*. New York: Harcourt, Brace and Company, 1930.

——, "The Theory of the Rate of Interest," in *The Lessons of Monetary Experience*, edited by A. D. Gayer, pages 145-152. New York: Farrar and Rinehart, Inc., 1937. Reprinted in *Readings in the Theory of Income Distribution*, selected by a Committee of the American Economic Association. Philadelphia: The Blakiston Company, 1946.

——, "Alternative Theories of the Rate of Interest," *The Economic Journal*, June, 1937, Vol. XLVII, pages 241-252.

——, "The 'Ex-Ante' Theory of the Rate of Interest," *The Economic Journal*, December, 1937, Vol. XLVII, pages 663-669.

——, "Mr. Keynes and 'Finance,'" *The Economic Journal*, June, 1938, Vol. XLVIII, pages 318-322.

Ellsworth, P. T., "Mr. Keynes on the Rate of Interest and the Marginal Efficiency of Capital," *The Journal of Political Economy*, December, 1936, Vol. XLIV, pages 767-790.

Hawtrey, R. G., "Alternative Theories of the Rate of Interest," *The Economic Journal*, September, 1937, Vol. XLVII, pages 436-443.

Lerner, A. P., "Alternative Formulations of the Theory of Interest," *The Economic Journal*, June, 1938, Vol. XLVIII, pages 211-230.

Lusher, D. W., "The Structure of Interest Rates and the Keynesian Theory of Interest," *The Journal of Political Economy*, April, 1942, Vol. L, pages 272-279.

Ohlin, Bertil, "Alternative Theories of the Rate of Interest," *The Economic Journal*, September, 1937, Vol. XLVII, pages 423-427.

Phillips, C. A., *Bank Credit*, especially Chapter III, "The Philosophy of Bank Credit." New York: The Macmillan Company, 1921.

Robertson, D. H., "Mr. Keynes and the Rate of Interest," *Essays in Monetary Theory*, Chapter I, pages 1-38. London: P. S. King and Son, Ltd., 1940. Reprinted in *Readings in the Theory of*

Income Distribution, selected by a Committee of the American Economic Association. Philadelphia: The Blakiston Company, 1946.

——, "Alternative Theories of the Rate of Interest," *The Economic Journal,* September, 1937, Vol. XLVII, pages 428-436.

Robinson, Joan, "The Concept of Hoarding," *The Economic Journal,* June, 1938, Vol. XLVIII, pages 231-236.

Smithies, Arthur, "The Quantity of Money and the Rate of Interest," *The Review of Economic Statistics,* February, 1943, Vol. XXV, pages 69-76.

Somers, H. M., "Monetary Policy and the Theory of Interest," *The Quarterly Journal of Economics,* May, 1941, Vol. LV, pages 488-507. Reprinted in the *Theory of Income Distribution,* selected by a Committee of the American Economic Association. Philadelphia: The Blakiston Company, 1946.

Wallich, H. C., "The Current Significance of Liquidity Preference," *The Quarterly Journal of Economics,* August, 1947, Vol. LXI pages 490-512.

CHAPTER 9

Money Wages and Prices

There is, perhaps, something a little perplexing in the apparent asymmetry between Inflation and Deflation. For whilst a deflation of effective demand below the level required for full employment will diminish employment as well as prices, an inflation of it above this level will merely affect prices.

J. M. Keynes, *The General Theory of Employment, Interest and Money*, page 291.

Introduction

In the first four books of the *General Theory*, Keynes states the essence of his theory of employment in terms of the assumption that money wages and prices are constant, i.e., that they do not change as employment and output rise and fall. In contending that employment as a whole is not determined by the wage bargains between workers and employers, Keynes argues that employment depends on effective demand rather than upon the level of money wages. However, all increases in effective demand are not consistent with further increases in employment. Above a certain level, further additions to aggregate effective demand will result in inflation. This point where aggregate employment becomes inelastic in response to further increases in effective demand is the point of full employment. Prices and money wages rise sharply without increasing output and employment. In contrast to Keynes' position is the classical theory that employment depends upon the level of wages, both money and real wages, arrived at through bargaining between workers and employers. If there is unemployment, it is because wages are too high; unemployment can be eliminated if wage earners are willing to accept lower money wages and, in the classical view, lower real wages. In the absence of rigidities, workers will prefer to accept lower wages rather than remain unemployed.

In Book V on "Money Wages and Prices," Keynes drops the simplifying assumption of constant money wages in order to take account of the influence of wage rates on employment. For while wage rates are not a central consideration in Keynes' analysis, they can hardly be ignored in a complete theory of employment. Changes in money wages are capable of influencing employment and output through the repercussions which they exert on the principal determinants of employment—the rate of interest, the marginal efficiency of capital, and the propensity to consume. Since changes in money wages do react upon employment in a roundabout manner involving the principal determinants, it has been necessary to postpone a full discussion of the repercussions until after the main body of the general theory has been presented.

In the following discussion, the term "wages" or "wage rates," used without a qualifying adjective, refers to basic hourly wages. The term "real wages" refers to hourly money wages adjusted for a cost of living index. Where reference is made to the amount of wages received per week, or for any other period longer than an hour, the appropriate modifiers will be used, as "weekly wages," "annual wages," et cetera.

Money Wages and Employment

The classical argument

Although there is no doubt about the conclusion reached by the classical theory of the relation of wage-rate reductions to employment, there is some doubt as to the reasoning by which the classical economists arrive at their conclusion, which is, of course, that wage cuts will reduce unemployment and if pursued with vigor, will restore full employment. In its crudest form, the argument that wage cuts can eliminate unemployment runs as follows: In a competitive system, lower wages mean lower prices and lower prices result in an increase in sales. As more is sold, more will have to be produced and more workers employed. This increase in employment is assumed to be worthwhile because lower money wages are supposed to result in lower real wages, which in turn mean increased profits to entrepreneurs. Profits increase because the fall in wages is assumed to be greater than the drop in prices. This process of falling wages and prices accompanied by rising profits and employment continues until equilibrium is reached at full employment. Thus the classical equilibrium is a full employment equilibrium.

The main flaw in this argument that unemployment can be remedied by cutting wages arises from neglect of effective demand. It assumes that money wages can be reduced and leave aggregate effective demand unchanged. While it is almost certain that a reduction in the money wages of workers in a single industry, say the shoe industry, will increase employment in the shoe industry if there is no fall in the demand for shoes, it cannot safely be assumed that the demand for shoes will remain unaffected by a reduction in the wages of all workers throughout the economy. If the wages of shoe workers only are reduced, the costs of production of shoes will be reduced much more than the demand for shoes will decrease. For while workers in the shoe industry will have less money to spend for things in general, including shoes, workers in all other industries will be able to spend just as much for shoes as before, and if the price of shoes is reduced to correspond to the diminution in their costs of production, there will be a greater quantity of sales than before. Therefore, more employment will be needed to produce the added output of shoes. At the same time, the real income of shoe workers will be lowered as a result of the lessened money wage and the unchanged prices which shoe workers must pay for the things they buy (except for the negligible element of shoes).

So far we have dealt with a wage cut in a single industry only. The demand for shoes has not fallen because wages have been cut only in the shoe industry. However, the wage cut which is proposed by the classical analysis is a general wage cut affecting all workers. If all wages are reduced in the same proportion, the demand for shoes will be affected materially because a lesser volume of effective demand will be forthcoming out of the lowered money incomes. The demand curve for any one commodity like shoes depends upon the incomes received by workers in all industries, e.g., textiles, steel, automobiles, et cetera. Thus, the reasoning which is valid with respect to a single industry cannot be applied to the economy as a whole. Although a reduction of wages in a single industry will not materially reduce the demand for the product of that industry, neither will the increased employment in that industry do much toward relieving unemployment. In fact, increased employment in the shoe industry, for example, will tend to be offset, or may be more than offset, by decreased employment in all other industries resulting from less demand from shoe workers for all the things that shoe workers buy. Any benefits to employment that might result from lowered costs will be offset by reduced effective demand. Since one man's expenditure is another man's income, money incomes fall to the extent of the decrease in expenditure resulting from the economy-wide reduction in money wages. Costs may fall but so does effective demand. Money wages have fallen but there is no assurance that real wages have fallen since the general fall in prices resulting from the general cut in wages may be just sufficient for the two to offset each other. Real wages are left then about as they were before. Keynes does assume that prices fall in the same proportion as wage rates. On this assumption real wage rates will not fall, and if real wages do not fall, profits cannot rise. Unless profits rise there is no incentive for entrepreneurs to increase output. We are brought back once again to the conclusion that the classical analysis suffers from the lack of a theory of effective demand. This lack is revealed here in an attempt to apply to the economy as a whole the logic of a theory designed to apply to a particular industry.

Another version or aspect of the classical theory of the relation between wage cuts and employment rests upon the belief that the demand for labor is elastic. Although each worker previously employed will receive less per hour, the total amount of wages paid will increase because the added quantity of employment will more than offset the reduction in hourly wage rates. As a result, total demand will be greater, and more employment can be sustained at lower than at higher wage rates. Even if profit per unit of output does not increase, the total amount of profit is believed to increase. This version of the wage-cut argument suffers from the same basic weakness as all the other versions. It assumes that supply creates its own demand for both consumption and investment output. But if Keynes' rejection of Say's law is valid, the wage-cut theory cannot be valid. While it is true that the extra workers and others who share in the newly-created income will bring extra buying power into the market for consumption output, they will not bring enough extra demand to absorb all the output. Some of the extra income earned will be saved because consumption demand will not increase as much as income. If investment does not increase, employment cannot increase. There is nothing automatic about increases in investment. This is the simple and essential point of Keynes' rejection of the wage-cut argument.

Whether or not the above analysis gives an accurate picture of the classical reasoning is not the main issue. The ultimate difference between Keynes and the classical school on the effects of wage cuts on employment resolves itself into a practical matter. Keynes denies and the classical school asserts that wage cuts can be a significant factor in restoring full employment when there is widespread unemployment. Although Keynes assumes for the purpose of analysis that prices fall in proportion to the fall in money wages, leaving real wage rates unchanged, his argument does not hinge on the validity of this assumption. He never denies the possibility of some decline in real wages as a consequence of money-wage cuts. He does not even say that wage cuts can never result in some increase in employment. What he does deny most emphatically is that wage cuts are of practical significance in restoring higher levels of employment. The chief weakness which he finds in the theories of those who differ on this important practical matter is their lack of a theory of effective demand.

Let us examine the classical argument for wage cuts in terms most favorable for its success. Suppose employers *believe* they can make higher profits by an all-around wage cut. If they believe they can make larger profits, they will be willing to expand their output and increase employment. Only if the expectations of higher profits prove illusory will they reduce output and employment to the former level. Business men might expect to make larger profits and be able to employ more workers after a general all-around wage cut because they are accustomed to looking at the economic process from the viewpoint of their own individual businesses. It is obvious to the business man that a wage cut will lower his costs. It is not so obvious that the wage cut, even though economy-wide in scope, will reduce the demand for his product. He may expect to sell a larger output at a greater net profit just because his own costs are lower.

Let us assume that entrepreneurs, in view of their expectations of larger profits, hire more workers and expand their output after cutting the wage rates paid to their workers. Will they realize the larger profits which they expect? As we have seen from the principle of effective demand, profits can increase only if:

(1) The marginal propensity to consume is equal to unity so that the increased income will go entirely into consump-

tion demand, thereby clearing the market of the increased supply of goods produced as a result of increased employment. Say's law that supply creates its own demand comes into its own when there is no gap between the increment of income and the increment of consumption. Hence, no investment is necessary to keep the process of production going at its existing level. However, this cannot happen because employment will not fall, except possibly temporarily, below the point where the marginal propensity to consume is unity. This assumption is contrary to the fundamental principle that as income increases, consumption increases by less than income. Some of the increased output of goods could be sold to consumers but there would remain an unsold quantity of goods equivalent to the gap between the increase in income and the increase in consumption.

(2) There is an increase in investment demand equal to the gap between the increased income and the increased consumption. Such an increase in investment demand will occur only if there is an increase in the marginal efficiency of capital relative to the rate of interest since these two factors are the determinants of the inducement to invest. There is nothing in the nature of a wage cut that will lead *directly* either to a rise in the marginal efficiency of capital or to a fall in the rate of interest. Therefore, the producers who have added to their output will be unable to sell what they have produced except at losses. The losses may be concentrated in a few firms producing investment goods or they may be scattered among all types of firms. In any event, the business losses will result in a contraction of output. As workers are laid off, their incomes fall and the initial increase in demand for consumers goods begins to contract. This process continues until output and employment are lowered to the former level at which profits are maximized (or losses minimized). The practical refutation of the classical logic reveals itself in the form of business losses. The proceeds from the added output have fallen short of the cost of producing that added output. There is no sustaining basis for the employment of a greater number of

workers as a consequence of the economy-wide cut in money wages.

Classical economic theory is primarily the theory of a particular industry and as such is not designed to answer the important question of the effects of wage cuts on employment because it lacks a theory of effective demand. Keynes' *general* theory, on the other hand, is specifically designed to come to grips with this problem. The answer arrived at thus far is that there is clearly no *direct* tendency for a cut in money-wage rates to increase employment. Employment can increase only if there is an increase in the propensity to consume, or an increase in the marginal efficiency of capital, or a fall in the rate of interest. Any validity in the classical position must come about through indirect effects of wage cuts upon one or more of these three independent variables. There are many repercussions of a general cut in money wages upon these three variables, but we shall confine our discussion to the most obvious and important ones.

(1) *Propensity to Consume:* The effect of wage cuts on the propensity to consume is more likely to be unfavorable than favorable. In so far as the distribution of income is affected, there will be a redistribution from wage earners to other income recipients, especially entrepreneurs and rentiers. This represents a shift from a high-consuming to a high-savings group and will tend to lower rather than raise the consumption function. A stimulating influence, however, will be the price reductions that accompany wage cuts. The fall in prices will increase the real purchasing power of people's fixed money *wealth* and thereby tend to increase the consumption function.

(2) *The Marginal Efficiency of Capital:* The repercussion of wage cuts upon the marginal efficiency of capital which offers the best chance of increasing employment will be the reaction on the expectations of entrepreneurs. If the reduction in wages is a once-and-for-all wage cut, that is, a reduction not expected to be followed by further reductions, the marginal efficiency of capital will be favorably affected.

Entrepreneurs will be stimulated to make alterations and additions to plant and equipment and to build new plant while wage rates are at a minimum level. If a reduction in wages is expected to be followed by further wage cuts at a later date, the marginal efficiency of capital will be lowered because entrepreneurs, in anticipation of further cuts, will tend to postpone investment until wage rates have fallen to still lower levels.

The conditions which would give practical importance to this repercussion in its favorable aspect are extremely difficult to attain, except in an authoritarian economy. Under any system of relatively free labor and management, there can be no guarantee that once wage cuts have begun they will not be followed by further wage cuts. Labor as a whole and management as a whole seldom if ever act together in such a policy, and if labor were organized in strong unions, strikes would undoubtedly mar attempts to increase employment by lowering wage rates. In the probable event that labor would not act on a common front in permitting wage reductions, the weakest unions would probably be cut first, and having revealed their weakness would be vulnerable to further cuts. A slowly sagging wage level will have a highly unfavorable effect on the marginal efficiency of capital. This is acknowledged even by those economists whose theoretical models are designed to demonstrate that employment can be increased by lowering money wages.[1] A rigid money-wage policy would probably have a more favorable influence upon the marginal efficiency of capital than a policy in which wages sag slowly to lower and lower levels. If it is true that, as a matter of practical policy, a once-and-for-all wage cut is difficult to attain, especially under non-authoritarian conditions, it follows that the effect of lower money wages on the marginal efficiency of capital does not appear to offer much hope as a means for decreasing unemployment in a depression in democratic economies.

1. See A. C. Pigou, "Real and Money Wage Rates in Relation to Unemployment," *The Economic Journal*, September, 1937, Vol. XLVII, No. 187, page 405.

(3) *The Rate of Interest:* The most favorable repercussion of a general wage cut upon employment arises in connection with its possible influence in lowering the rate of interest. A fall in wages will normally be accompanied by a fall in prices. Lower wages and lower prices reduce the amount of money needed to carry on transactions (M_1). Assuming the total supply of money (M) remains constant, a lessening of the demand for transactions (M_1) will increase the amount of money available to satisfy the speculative motive (M_2), and this, as the preceding analysis of interest and money indicates, will tend to lower the rate of interest. The greater the fall in wages and prices, the greater the quantity of money released from active balances to inactive balances and, therefore, the greater the fall in the interest rate. The extent of the fall in the interest rate will depend not only upon the increase in money available to satisfy the liquidity preference for the speculative motive but also upon the shape of the liquidity function. If the liquidity function is elastic, the fall in interest rates will be less than if it is inelastic. Analytically, the process whereby lower wage rates lead to lower interest rates is no different from that whereby the total quantity of money (M) is increased in order to increase the amount of money available for inactive balances (M_2).

Although a flexible wage policy is *analytically* an alternative to a flexible money policy, there are important practical difficulties with the former which do not apply to monetary policy. To be successful as a check to unemployment, the reduction in wages in time of depression must be general, all-around, and simultaneous, and since labor as a whole does not bargain with employers as a whole, it is virtually impossible to execute such a policy in a democratic society with strong, independent, labor unions. Consequently, even though workers knew that wage cuts would mean more jobs for labor in general, in the absence of over-all collective bargaining, self-interest would lead any one sector of the labor supply to resist reductions in money wages. Those who accepted wage cuts first and in the greatest amount would suffer relative to other groups who resisted longer and finally acceded to lesser cuts.

Even if all wage earners could be persuaded to accept a policy of equal, all-around, money-wage reductions, they would be acting contrary to their own best interest unless all non-labor incomes were also reduced in the same proportion. Rentiers receiving income from bonds and other forms of contractual securities containing promises to pay fixed in terms of money would gain a real advantage at the expense of the working class if the latter accepted wage reductions while contractual incomes remained inviolable. Since sanctity of contract is one of the foundations of a business civilization, it is highly improbable that this condition essential to justice and to voluntary acceptance on the part of wage earners would be realized. Thus even the working class as a whole— at least the employed part of it—would be acting contrary to its best interests if it agreed to accept money-wage reductions of the type suggested by the classical theory. Keynes pointed to all these difficulties at the time of Britain's return to the gold standard under Chancellor of the Exchequer Winston Churchill in 1925.

Another strong objection to money-wage cuts arises because a lower price level increases the real burden of debt, both private and public. Entrepreneurs who are heavily in debt will find themselves saddled with still heavier real charges when prices fall and the money size of their obligations does not fall. A lower price level will increase the real burden of taxation required to service and repay the public debt. If the public debt is large, this becomes a major objection to any deflationary policy like wage and price reductions. The adverse effect of the increase in the real burden of debt will be somewhat offset by the favorable influence on the propensity to consume arising from the tendency for a fall in prices to stimulate spending out of fixed money wealth.

Should wages be increased in depression?

So far we have examined the effects of wage cuts on employment in depression. At the opposite pole is what may be called the "trade unionist argument" that the way out of depression is to raise money wages. Higher wages, it is argued, will increase purchasing power and employment. So far as the *direct* effects upon employment are concerned, this argument suffers from the same faults as the one for wage cuts. Higher wages will increase costs and prices by an amount that will offset the nominal increase in purchasing power. Real wages will remain at the same level. There will be an increase in nominal effective demand but no increase in real effective demand and therefore no increase in employment on a continuing basis. There is nothing in the nature of a wage increase to stimulate more demand for investment, and, as Keynes' theory of effective demand tells us, there can be no increase in employment unless there is an increase in the demand for investment sufficient to fill the gap between increased income and increased consumption.

The *indirect* repercussions of a rise in wage rates will probably be even less favorable to employment than wage cuts. While the effect may be to increase the propensity to consume through a favorable influence upon the distribution of income, both the marginal efficiency of capital and the rate of interest will tend to be influenced in a manner unfavorable to employment. An increase in wages in the depths of a depression when business is suffering losses from costs in excess of revenues is hardly likely to restore the confidence of the business community in the prospects for profitable operations. Of course, the announcement that higher wage rates are to go into effect at a specific future date may temporarily stimulate entrepreneurs to complete their investments before the higher wage rates become effective. After the higher rates go into effect, however, investment will fall back to less than its previous level to the extent that improvements that might have been spread evenly over time have been bunched in order to beat the higher cost period.

With regard to the rate of interest, the effect of higher wage rates will be unfavorable. Higher wages and higher prices will increase the requirements for money for transactions and, in the absence of an expansion in the total quantity of money, will drain the quantity available as a store of value. The interest rate will tend to rise with the consequent unfavorable reaction upon investment, income, and employment.

Conclusions on a flexible wage policy in relation to a flexible money policy

The foregoing examination of a flexible wage policy leads to the conclusion that neither wage cuts nor wage boosts are effective measures for increasing employment in depression. At best, a flexible wage policy is no better than a flexible monetary policy. In the most likely circumstances under which a flexible wage policy would have to be carried out in a non-authoritarian society, a flexible wage policy would be much less satisfactory than a flexible monetary policy.

It is important to view Keynes' conclusions on wage policy in the broad perspective of his position as a theorist and as an advocate of monetary policy. What his analysis amounts to, after all is said and done, is simply that a flexible monetary policy is an alternative to and on both economic and political grounds is preferable to a flexible wage policy. He acknowledges that money-wage cuts may increase employment slightly, but his main contention is that anything which might be accomplished by cutting wages can, as a matter of practical policy, be accomplished better by monetary policy.

Although Keynes' theory opposes the idea that labor is to blame for unemployment, his views do not constitute a defense of organized labor in any positive or partisan sense. This is evidenced by his rejection of money-wage increases as well as money-wage decreases. It is further evidenced by his acceptance in the *General Theory* of the classical view that an increase in employment will be accompanied by a fall in *real* wage rates, a conclusion which follows from his assumption of the principle of diminishing returns in the short run. When statistical investigations indicated that real wages did not in fact fall as employment rose, Keynes acknowledged he had accepted too readily the classical assumption in regard to falling real wages. However, if in fact real wages did not decline, he said his practical conclusions would be strengthened and his theory simplified.[2]

Although real wages may not rise in the short run, they will rise in the long run as a consequence of the increase in output per man hour which results from the greater amount of equipment per worker. Higher real wages may take the form either of rising money wages with stable prices, or of stable money wages with gradually falling prices. Keynes prefers the former of these two alternatives because a policy of rising money wages combined with a stable price level will (a) have a favorable influence upon the expectations of investors and hence upon the inducement to invest, (b) diminish the real burden of debt without inequities to the lending classes, who will receive in payment of their loans money of the same value as that which they gave up on advancing the loans, (c) give greater psychological encouragement to the active, producing, working class than will real wages in the form of constant money wages and falling prices, and (d) facilitate the transfer of resources out of declining industries into growing industries by raising money wages in the latter without having to lower them in the former (p. 271).

Nature of the issue between Keynes' theory and the classical theory

The foregoing discussion has referred to some points of disagreement between Keynes and the classical economists. In addition to the technical points already discussed, these issues raise the important question of the nature of controversies in economic theory. The reader should be warned that economic theory is a subtle discipline full of pitfalls for the unwary. When economists disagree in a fundamental way,

---

2. See "Relative Movements of Real Wages and Output," *The Economic Journal*, March, 1939, Vol. XLIX, No. 193, pages 40-41. In this article, Keynes states that Chapter 2 of the *General Theory* "is the portion of my book which most needs to be revised." *Ibid.*, page 40 n.

they seldom are able to settle their differences in a mutually satisfactory manner. Between the classical theory and Keynes' theory there are fundamental differences in the explanation of unemployment. The classical theory attributes unemployment to wages being too high (i.e., higher than they would be under thorough-going competition among wage earners), and Keynes attributes unemployment to an insufficiency of effective demand. What these two different positions mean in objective, operational terms is that the classical school sees the cure for unemployment in reductions in wage rates whereas Keynes sees the cure in an expansionary monetary and fiscal program designed to increase the volume of effective demand. This controversy concerning the theory of unemployment between Keynes and Professor Pigou, the chief representative of the classical school on this issue, has never been settled in any satisfactory manner despite long and drawn-out discussion.[3] However, when Professor Pigou finally conceded that he favors attacking the problem of unemployment by manipulating demand rather than by manipulating wages, the controversy for all practical purposes was settled in favor of Keynes.[4] The real issue between Keynes and Professor Pigou has always been one of intuition about the relative importance of things in the actual world. Keynes has triumphed because he possessed a superior insight into practical affairs combined with a remarkable ability to develop his insights into a systematic body of economic theory.

The way in which intuition or insight into practical affairs

---

3. In addition to the several books by Professor Pigou already referred to and Keynes' *General Theory*, especially chapters 2 and 19, see Pigou, "Real and Money Wage Rates in Relation to Unemployment," *The Economic Journal*, September, 1937, Vol. XLVII, No. 187, pages 405-422; Keynes, "Professor Pigou on Money Wages in Relation to Unemployment," *Ibid.*, pages 743-745; N. Kaldor, "Professor Pigou on Money Wages in Relation to Unemployment," *Ibid.*, pages 745-753; Pigou, "Money Wages in Relation to Unemployment," *The Economic Journal*, March, 1938, Vol. XLVIII, No. 189, pages 134-138; and Keynes, "Relative Movements of Real Wages and Output," *The Economic Journal*, March, 1939, Vol. XLIX, No. 193, pages 34-51.

4. See Pigou. *Lapses from Full Employment*, page v.

influences the formulation of economic theory may be further illustrated. A theory is an attempt to give a simplified explanation of some relatively complex area of experience. The process of simplification involves the selection of those aspects of experience which are regarded as most important in relation to the problem at hand, in this case unemployment. The theories which emerge are not and cannot be complete pictures of the actual world. They are simplified pictures, or models, of the economist's idea of what are the most important and relevant considerations. As Professor Pigou himself points out, the question whether the elements in the model are those which are most important in the actual world is a matter of intuition.[5] Quite naturally, each economist builds a model of the elements which his intuition evaluates as most important, although in model building some individuals are more heavily influenced by traditional approaches than others. The relative merits of the two theoretical explanations, or models, will depend to a large extent upon the relative acuteness of the intuition of the two economists in question. The logic of both models may be impeccable but their relevance may be worlds apart. Here the all-important point is that Keynes was endowed with a remarkably keen intuition or insight into problems of actual experience. This fact more than anything else appears to explain the great acclaim that his *General Theory* has received. Keynes' theory is not necessarily more logical nor otherwise more nearly perfect in terms of internal consistency than Professor Pigou's theory. It is just more relevant. Professor Pigou, on the other hand, feels, or at least used to feel, that his model contains those elements which are most important in the actual world. Professional and popular opinion does not appear to agree with him in this belief. Keynes' theory is considered of revolutionary significance because it stands for a course of action which is practicable in the modern world. It accepts collective bar-

5. "Real and Money Wage Rates in Relation to Unemployment," *The Economic Journal*, September, 1937, Vol. XLVII, No. 187, page 422.

gaining, minimum-wage legislation, and unemployment insurance, and points to a way of escape from unemployment through increasing effective demand.

The Theory of Prices

Integration of monetary theory with the theory of value and output

The theory of prices, as this phrase is used in economic analysis, is a study of the way in which changes in the quantity of money react upon the price level. Individual prices are individual values expressed in terms of money, and the level of prices in general is related in some systematic manner to the total quantity of money in the economic system. In general, this relationship is such that an increase in the quantity of money is associated with a rise in the level of prices, and a reduction in the quantity of money with a fall in the level of prices. The details of this relationship between the quantity of money and the level of prices are studied in connection with what economists call the quantity theory of money.

Keynes' theory of prices, like the rest of his theory, is of a more general nature than is the traditional doctrine.[6] He accepts the traditional conclusion that increases in the quantity of money will be associated with increases in the level of prices, but differs fundamentally from the traditional analysis of the causal process by which changes in the quantity of money react upon the level of prices. From the foregoing chapters, it is clear that the initial impact of an increase in the quantity of money is to lower the rate of interest by in-

6. Keynes' purpose in referring to the traditional theory of prices is to contrast his own position with the generally accepted theory laid down in treatises on the principles of economics. He does not attempt to assess the theory of money and prices contained in the work of specialists in monetary and business cycle theory. Typical of the type of theory against which Keynes directs his criticism is the work of Professor Taussig, who says, "We may brush aside not only the notion that interest arises from the use of money but that the rate of interest depends on the quantity of money. More money makes higher prices, not lower interest." *Principles of Economics*, Fourth Edition, Vol. II, page 8. New York: The Macmillan Company, 1939.

creasing the amount of money available to satisfy liquidity preference for the speculative motive. A lowering of the rate of interest tends to increase effective demand for investment, which in turn is associated with rising income, employment, and output. As income, employment, and output begin to rise, prices also begin to rise because of increasing labor costs resulting from the enhanced bargaining position of labor, diminishing returns in the short run, bottlenecks, and other reasons to be examined in this chapter. Employment and prices both rise, with the emphasis at first almost exclusively on increases in employment but shifting more and more to prices as the point of full employment is approached. Once full employment has been attained, no further increases in employment are possible, by definition, and further increases in effective demand become truly inflationary in the sense that they spend themselves entirely in rising prices.

Prices of individual commodities as well as the general price level of output as a whole correspond closely to costs of production, which change with variations in the volume of output. The general level of prices multiplied by output at any time determines the quantity of money absorbed in the active balances or active circulation (M_1). The rest of the total supply of money spills over into inactive balances (M_2), where, in conjunction with the state of liquidity preference, it determines the rate of interest. M_2 is a residual quantity which, with given prices and output, absorbs the increases and decreases in the total supply of money. Changes in the quantity of money do not affect prices directly, because prices are determined primarily by costs of production. The initial impact of changes in the total quantity of money falls on the rate of interest rather than on prices. The level of prices is affected indirectly through the effect of changes in the quantity of money upon the rate of interest acting as one of the three main determinants of the volume of output and employment (the other two main determinants being the marginal efficiency of capital and the propensity to consume). As output changes, costs of production change, and prices adjust to changing costs of production. The demand for money for transactions increases *because* prices and output rise. Prices do not rise directly in response to increases in the quantity of money, although they are indirectly influenced by such increases. Keynes' analysis is sometimes spoken of as the "contra-quantity theory of causation" because it treats rises in prices as a cause of the increase in the quantity of money for transactions instead of treating the increases in the quantity of money (for transactions) as a cause of the rise in prices. Of course, the distinction between money for transactions and money as a store of value is absolutely essential to this contra-quantity causation.

The great merit of Keynes' theory of prices is that it integrates monetary theory with the theory of value, which means that it integrates monetary theory with what has been regarded as the main body of the principles of economics. The theory of value teaches us that price, which is value expressed in terms of money, is governed by the conditions of supply and demand. In connection with supply and demand, the most important concepts are marginal cost and marginal revenue (which determine the extent to which output will be carried since their equality designates the point of maximum profit), and elasticity of short-period supply and elasticity of demand (which determine the relative changes in output which correspond to relative changes in price of the commodity in question). When Keynes comes to the theory of prices in general (price levels), he still emphasizes cost of production, elasticity of supply, demand, and the other concepts which are important in the theory of value or individual price. Prices rise as costs of production rise; costs of production rise partly because of the inelasticity of short-period supply of output and employment; and the theory of demand is all-important in calling forth the increased output and employment.

In addition to integrating the theory of value with the theory of money, Keynes also integrates the theory of output with the theory of money. In fact, it is through the theory of output that value theory and monetary theory are brought into juxtaposition with each other. For changes in the quantity of money are capable of changing the level of output. As the level of output varies, costs change, and as costs vary, values (prices) are affected. Since the theory of money is part and parcel of the theory of interest, and interest is intimately related to expectations concerning the future, it follows that discussions of the effects of changing expectations about the future must be stated in monetary terms. The emphasis shifts to money as a store of value, as a link between the present and the future. This emphasis is lacking in the traditional presentations of the general economic theory of value and output and monetary theory, and accounts to no small degree for the lack of integration of monetary theory with general economic theory in classical economics. The traditional statement of the theory of prices overlooks the influence of the quantity of money in the determination of the rate of interest, and thereby upon output, and goes directly from increases in the quantity of money to increases in the level of prices. This important omission in traditional economic theory arises from its assumption of full employment of resources. If full employment is assumed from the beginning, there is no possibility that an increase in the quantity of money, or anything else for that matter, can increase employment and output (in the short run). In ruling out by assumption changes in output, there is no need in the theory of price levels for the concepts that figure so prominently in the theory of value, such as marginal cost, elasticity of supply, and the theory of demand. In a sense, there is no occasion for integrating the theory of value with the theory of money. Since money cannot affect employment, it can influence only prices. This leads to the conclusion that *all* increases in the quantity of money tend to be inflationary, a conclusion quite valid under the assumption that resources are fully employed, but a nonsense conclusion when this special assumption is dropped. The theory of prices becomes nothing more than a theory of price levels, that is, of the value of money. Money is essentially a lubricant which is useful because it is more efficient than barter. The extremely important relations between changes in the quantity of money and changes in employment are ignored. The theory of the value of individual commodities is divorced from the theory of prices of commodities in general. Monetary theory remains outside the main body of economic theory, which is concerned with value and output.

It is to be recognized that there were some economists before Keynes who were not guilty of separating the theory of money from the theory of value and output, but this characterization holds true of the presentations found in treatises on the principles of economics. Perhaps it is best to make as few representations as possible as to just what the traditional position regarding the theory of prices and money has been because any positive assertion may be challenged on some plausible grounds. Whatever the traditional presentation may have been, it is clear that a theory based upon the assumption that unemployment is the normal circumstance and full employment the exception offers an opportunity for bringing together the theory of money and prices with the theory of value and output.

The reformulated quantity theory of money

It is possible by introducing a sufficient number of qualifications to formulate a simplified version of what may be called the reformed quantity theory of money. If there is perfectly elastic supply of productive factors when there is unemployment and perfectly inelastic supply when there is full employment, and if the increase in effective demand is proportional to the increase in the quantity of money, then the reformed quantity theory which takes into account the condition of unemployment as well as the special case of full employment may be stated as follows: "So long as there is unemployment, *employment* will change in the same proportion as the quantity of money; and when there is full employment, *prices* will change in the same proportion as the quantity of

money." (p. 296) [7] Before introducing the necessary qualifications to this reformulation of the quantity theory, let us
state the practical implication of this proposition in its barest,
unqualified form. It tells us when to fear and when not to
fear inflation. It tells us that, subject to the qualifying assumptions, inflation is not to be feared when there is large-
scale unemployment; and it tells us that once full employment has been attained, inflation does become a threat. Thus
it relieves us of the dread of inflation when we are plagued
with mass unemployment, and it warns us that once we have
conquered unemployment we must be on guard against inflation. Those who cry "inflation" in criticizing policies of
monetary expansion during the depths of depression like that
of the 1930's are either guilty of political propaganda or
lack understanding of the most elementary truths of monetary
theory and policy. For what is needed in depression is expansion of output, and the way to expand output is to increase
effective demand. Hence, monetary expansion by means of
public investment, low interest rates, and the encouragement
of spending rather than not-spending are all part of economic
policy designed to increase output and employment in a
period of depression.

The proposition that changes in the quantity of money will
affect employment when there is unemployment and will affect prices when there is full employment is no more than a
rough approximation to the truth. It is a generalized statement subject to so many qualifications that there is reasonable
doubt as to its usefulness as a leading proposition of monetary theory. Prices may rise substantially before full employment is reached, especially in the later stages of expansion.
These are not mere chance increases arising from fortuitous
circumstances. The increases in prices that occur as output
expands are more or less inevitably associated with expanding output and can be explained in terms of well-established
principles of economic analysis. The most important reasons

7. Keynes, *The General Theory of Employment, Interest and Money.* New
York: Harcourt, Brace and Co., Inc., 1936.

why costs and prices rise as employment increases are (1)
the enhanced bargaining position of workers, (2) diminishing returns in the short run, and (3) bottlenecks in production.

(1) *Enhanced Bargaining Position of Workers as Unemployment Declines:* An increase in the demand for labor will
tend to increase the money wages of workers. Both organized
and unorganized workers, and especially the former, find
themselves in a better bargaining position when employment
is rising. The extent to which money-wage rates will rise depends, of course, upon the relative bargaining strengths of
employers and wage earners, but regardless of their relative
positions, a growing scarcity of labor will tend to enhance
the position of wage earners and to weaken that of the employer, just as growing unemployment tends to have the
opposite effect in periods of contraction. Entrepreneurs will
be more willing to meet the demands of workers when business is improving because it is feasible to pass on increased
costs by raising prices. This is true not only of competitive
but also of various forms of monopolistic pricing. Monopo-
lists and oligopolists may even welcome wage increases because they can use them as an excuse for price gouging which
would otherwise be inexpedient because public opinion,
which will tolerate higher prices when wages rise, will not
tolerate unprovoked price increases. It is always easy to con-
fuse the public on the question of how much a given wage
boost will increase unit costs of production. The steel industry seems to have used the wage increase granted coal miners
in 1947 to increase steel prices several times more than was
justified on a basis of increases in the cost of coal.

Even though money-wage rates will rise, real-wage rates
for workers in general will not rise because the increase in
prices will be more than sufficient to offset higher money-
wage rates. However, any particular group of workers which
can push up its money-wage rates more rapidly than workers
in general will gain at the expense of other workers and may
be able to increase their money-wage rates more rapidly than

the cost-of-living and thereby increase their real-wage rates. Because of this possibility, there is pressure on trade-union leaders to gain increases larger than the average granted to labor in general. To a considerable extent, the success of labor leaders will be measured in terms of their ability to gain larger concessions than other labor leaders. As full employment is approached, the inflationary dangers from competing labor groups increase. As a result there is a strong case for a unified labor movement rather than many different labor organizations, each of which competes with the other to secure better bargains. Sir William Beveridge has proposed a single national labor organization as a prerequisite for a guaranteed full employment program which is to avoid the danger of inflation.

Organized workers as a whole will probably gain larger concessions than unorganized workers as a whole. In the United States, where scarcely one third of the total number of wage and salary earners are members of organized labor groups, the opportunity for organized labor to get more than a proportionate share of the total increases in money wages is especially good. Of course, unorganized workers are also in a better bargaining position in an expanding labor market, but in relation to union labor they will probably find themselves falling behind. The distinction between wage rates and amounts of wages is also to be noted. Even though real-wage rates go down, workers who are employed more hours per week or more weeks per year may receive a larger annual real income. Workers who were previously unemployed will benefit from new-found employment, and previously employed workers whose real wage per hour may be going down because prices are rising more rapidly than money-wage rates, may work enough additional hours to gain a larger real wage per week or per year.

Increases in wage rates which occur during a period of expanding output will not be continuous but periodic, depending on the duration of trade-union contracts, and on the political strategy of trade-union leaders and employers. Increases in wages and prices will tend to be greatest in the sectors of the economy where expansion is most rapid. For example, if expansion begins in the construction industry, building trades-men and those working for firms which supply construction materials will be in a more strategic bargaining position than workers in other industries.

(2) *Diminishing Returns in the Short Run:* Prices will rise before full employment is attained also because of the tendency toward diminishing returns in the short run. Dimin-ishing return means that cost per unit of output rises as the volume of output increases. The short run is a period in which the amount of equipment is assumed to be given. When more men are employed to operate the existing equipment, there will tend to be a less than proportionate increase in output. If to start with, there is a large amount of idle equipment of the best quality as well as large numbers of idle workers, the tendency toward diminishing return will develop slowly. This will be especially characteristic of large-scale industries which operate on a mass-production basis. There may be a range, in fact, over which unit variable costs will decline. But neither men nor machines are of equal efficiency, and if it is assumed that the more efficient men and equipment are the first to be employed, then those subsequently employed will add a less than proportionate return. If the newly employed workers are less efficient than those previously employed and if the less efficient are paid the same time-wage as the more effi-cient, then the prime cost per unit of output must rise even though the equipment is of equal efficiency. If workers are re-warded in strict proportion to their efficiency, there will be con-stant unit cost rather than increasing unit cost. If the additional machinery put into use is less efficient than that already in service, increasing costs per unit of output will result even if the workers are rewarded in strict proportion to their effi-ciency. A machine with a greater spoilage of raw material fed into it is a typical illustration of an increasing cost situation caused by the employment of less efficient equipment; or a

machine which operates more slowly than other machines will not permit a worker to produce as much output as an equally efficient worker using more efficient machines. What is called "stand-by equipment" is less efficient, as a rule, and is placed in use only in emergencies when no other equipment is at hand and there is no time to procure more efficient machinery or when the demand for the particular output is not expected to continue long enough to justify the procurement of new equipment. Thus the lack of uniformity or homogeneity of resources is one important reason why the cost of production and the price based upon cost of production will rise as employment increases.

(3) *"Bottlenecks" in Production:* Even if all resources were perfectly homogeneous, increasing costs from diminishing returns would set in prior to full employment because all types of resources would not reach a point of full employment simultaneously. Skilled laborers may be fully employed when there still remain many unskilled workers in the ranks of the unemployed. Steelworkers may be out of work because of a temporary shortage of coal arising perhaps from the reluctance of workers to become coal miners; building may be held up because of a scarcity of plumbing materials; automobiles because of a shortage of rubber for tires, et cetera. Full employment of all resources requires that resources be available in certain proportions, which can be varied within limits, but beyond these limits real bottlenecks exist because the substitution of one resource for another is beyond the limits of technical feasibility. This disproportionality of available resources is especially serious in a recovery that follows a prolonged and severe depression like that of the 1930's. During that depression, there was a great decline in the number of skilled laborers because of death, retirement, loss of skill through idleness, and the small number of new apprentices coming into the skilled trades during the depressed years. In the upswing of the business cycle in the spring of 1937, an acute shortage of skilled workmen developed at a time when there were millions of unemployed

among the unskilled workers of the nation. Bottlenecks are accentuated by a rapid increase in output. In the great defense and war expansion from 1940 to 1943, shortages developed in many types of labor, materials, and equipment. Serious bottlenecks were experienced in aluminum, magnesium, steel, rubber, and in many other commodities. When a bottleneck is reached in one line of production, the price of the item in question tends to rise sharply, in the absence of price control, even though other prices are rising only gently. In the short run, supply is inelastic in the sense that output does not respond immediately to increases in prices. The increase in demand is diverted into a rise in price until the output has time to expand to meet the demand. Increases in prices of this sort are referred to as "bottleneck inflation."

"Bottleneck inflation" differs in a fundamental way from the general inflation that accompanies full employment of all other resources. For given sufficient time, bottlenecks can be broken by an increase in the output of the item in question. If there are no more workers available of a certain skill, more can be trained given sufficient time. If there is insufficient aluminum capacity, more can be built. If there is not enough rubber, more can be produced. The length of time that must elapse before the bottleneck is broken will, of course, depend upon technical considerations. Wartime shortages of skilled labor were met rather quickly in the United States because they were attacked with vigor and intelligence. The rubber shortage dragged on for years while various interest groups fought over who should supply the synthetic raw materials to replace the unavailable supplies of natural rubber. The increases in prices which result from particular shortages as compared with general shortages occur because resources are not perfectly interchangeable.

These are the chief factors which account for rising costs and rising prices in the phase of expansion short of full employment. Generally speaking, in contemporary industrial economies the rise in money wages resulting from the enhanced demand for labor is probably a more important factor contributing to higher prices than the tendency toward diminishing return.[8] The quantitative importance of the two factors will vary, however, with the scale of production, and the relation between costs and prices will vary with the degree of competition and monopoly, which in turn is likely to be related to the scale of production. Throughout the *General Theory*, Keynes takes as "given" the degree of monopoly and competition (p. 245). For the purposes of his analysis, competition and monopoly are not strategic factors. His theory of unemployment and of prices does not depend in any way on the presence or absence of either monopoly or competition. If the theory of effective demand is valid, unemployment would exist even though there were pure competition or absolute monopoly. Keynes' assumption that prices will rise when costs of production rise does not require the further premise that prices are equal to costs of production. Under competitive conditions prices will tend to equal total unit cost, and under monopolistic conditions prices will tend to exceed total unit cost. A monopolist will increase his prices when costs rise almost as readily as a competitive firm. The quantitative relation of costs to prices does depend, however, on the scale of production and the degree of monopoly. Under large-scale enterprise, the economies of full utilization which accompany expanding output may offset the increases in wage rates over a wide range of output. The tendency for prices not to rise because the two component parts of price tend to offset each other is reinforced if industrial producers are content with a smaller profit per unit of output as output increases. Where there is imperfection of competition, producers tend to maintain prices when output is falling and to increase prices by less than the full amount of the increases in unit cost when output is rising.[9] Hence, under monopolistic

---

8. See Keynes' post-*General Theory* article, "Relative Movements of Real Wages and Output," *The Economic Journal*, March, 1939, Vol XLIX, No. 193, page 46.

9. *Loc. cit.*

conditions prices will tend to move with costs, but they tend to move by lesser amounts, and if total costs do not vary because higher wage costs are offset by lower non-wage costs, there may be a considerable stability of unit costs and a still greater stability of prices over a wide range of output. Exceptions occur in boom periods when producers are overwhelmed with orders they cannot fill. In these exceptional periods, wage boosts may be used as an excuse for price gouging, that is, for increasing prices much more than costs have increased. Wage increases become the occasion rather than the cause of unreasonable price increases.

In small-scale enterprise, diminishing return tends to act more strongly and competition is more effective. Costs move up and down with increases and decreases in output, and prices tend to be even more flexible than costs. Only in the long run does the equality of prices to total unit cost tend to prevail.

The two preceding paragraphs are in the nature of elaborations of the general thesis that in the early stages of expansion when there are abundant supplies of efficient resources, the general level of prices will probably not rise very much. As full employment is approached, the pressure for costs and prices to rise increases progressively because the bargaining strength of labor is greatly enhanced and the remaining unemployed resources become less and less efficient as the "bottom of the barrel" is scraped. The number of bottlenecks multiplies rapidly. Shortages are more and more difficult to overcome as substitutes are more difficult to find because the most satisfactory substitutes have already been fully employed, or nearly so. But as long as there is unemployment, increases in effective demand will increase employment. When full employment is at last attained, further increases in effective demand no longer increase employment. They spend themselves entirely on increases in prices. A condition of true inflation sets in as soon as full employment is reached. One of Keynes' definitions of full employment is the point beyond which output proves inelastic in response to further increases in effective demand.

As Keynes points out, there is a lack of symmetry on the two sides of the level at which true inflation sets in. A reduction in effective demand below this critical level reduces both prices and output, but above this point only prices (not output) increase. This lack of symmetry is explained by the resistance which workers and other factors of production offer to reductions in their money rewards. Money wages do not fall without limit as soon as unemployment appears. The resistance of wage earners to reductions in wages in conditions of unemployment gives a degree of stability to wages and prices which would not otherwise exist (p. 304). This does not mean, however, that unemployment could be cured if wages were flexible in a downward direction. Unemployment arises from a deficiency of effective demand which does not depend on the flexibility of wages and prices.

Long-term price movements

Even if full employment without inflation can be achieved, there remains the important question whether, with rising productivity per man hour and falling unit costs of production, prices in the long run should fall as costs fall or remain constant as money (and real) wages rise. Keynes recommends as the desirable policy a stabilization of prices, within limits, and rising money wages. The reasons for this preference have already been indicated in connection with the discussion of money wages.

References for Further Reading

Keynes, J. M., *The General Theory of Employment, Interest and Money*, Chapters 2, 19, and 21. New York: Harcourt, Brace and Company, 1936.

———, "Relative Movements of Real Wages and Output," *The Economic Journal*, March, 1939, Vol. XLIX, pages 34-51.

———, "Professor Pigou on Money Wages in Relation to Unemployment," *The Economic Journal*, December, 1937, Vol. XLVII, pages 743-745.

Bangs, R. B., "Wage Reductions and Employment," *The Jou nal of Political Economy*, April, 1942, Vol. L, pages 251-271.

Dunlop, J. T., "The Movement of Real and Money Wage Rates," *The Economic Journal*, September, 1938, Vol. XLVIII, pages 413-434.

———, "The Supply and Demand Functions for Labor," *The American Economic Review, Papers and Proceedings*, May, 1948, Vol. XXXVIII, pages 340-350.

Ellis, Howard S., "Some Fundamentals in the Theory of Velocity," *The Quarterly Journal of Economics*, May, 1938, Vol. LII, pages 431-472.

Hansen, A. H., "Cost Functions and Full Employment," *The American Economic Review*, September, 1947, Vol. XXXVII, pages 552-565.

Lerner, A. P., "The Relation of Wage Policies and Price Policies," *The American Economic Review, Papers and Proceedings*, March, 1939, Vol. XXIX, pages 158-169.

Marget, Arthur W., *The Theory of Prices*, 2 volumes. New York: Prentice-Hall, Inc., 1938 and 1942.

Pigou, A. C., "Real and Money Wages in Relation to Unemployment," *The Economic Journal*, September, 1937, Vol. XLVII, pages 405-422.

———, "Money Wages in Relation to Unemployment," *The Economic Journal*, March, 1938, Vol. XLVIII, pages 134-138.

———, *The Theory of Unemployment*, especially Part V, Chapter III,"Wage Policy as a Determinant of Unemployment." London: Macmillan and Co., Ltd., 1933.

———, *Employment and Equilibrium*. London: Macmillan and Co., Ltd., 1941.

———, *Lapses from Full Employment*. London: Macmillan and Co., Ltd., 1945.

Rosenstein-Rodan, P. N., "The Coordination of the General Theories of Money and Price," *Economica*, August, 1936, Vol. III (new series), pages 257-280.

Tobin, James, "Money Wage Rates and Employment," in *The New Economics*, edited by S. E. Harris, Chapter XL, pages 572-587. New York: Alfred A. Knopf, 1947.

Sweezy, Alan R., "Wages and Investment," *The Journal of Political Economy*, February, 1942, Vol. L, pages 117-129.

CHAPTER 10

War and Postwar Inflation

> An individual cannot by saving more protect himself
> from the consequences of inflation if others do not follow
> his example; just as he cannot protect himself from acci-
> dents by obeying the rule of the road if others disregard
> it. We have here the perfect opportunity for social action,
> where everyone can be protected by making a certain rule
> of behaviour universal.
>
> J. M. Keynes, *How to Pay for the War*, page 70.

THUS FAR the theory of prices has been discussed only in relation to circumstances of less than full employment. In this
connection, Keynes makes his most important contribution
to the theory of prices by integrating the theory of value
(individual prices) with the theory of money (price levels)
and output. Prices are assumed to correspond closely to costs
of production. Prior to full employment, prices rise because
of increasing costs which are associated with higher money
wages and with diminishing returns as the scale of output increases in the short run. After full employment is attained,
further increases in effective demand spend themselves entirely in raising prices. Thus full employment is the point
at which true inflation sets in and inflation is in this sense a
phenomenon of full employment. True inflation occurs when
prices rise without being accompanied by a rise in employ-

ment and output. Inflation is caused by further increases in effective demand after full employment is attained.

Although Keynes' most important contribution to the theory of prices is in relation to circumstances of less than full employment, he also has made important contributions to the theory of prices under full employment, that is, to the theory of inflation. Monetary changes which do not increase total production are significant in themselves in so far as they affect different people and classes in different ways and to different degrees. If inflation were to affect everyone in exactly the same way and in the same degree, it would have no importance whatsoever. Its tremendous social significance arises from the fact that it always does affect people and classes differently. Inflation takes wealth away from some people and hands it over to others in a manner which disregards the maxims of social equity. Yet this subtle thievery is perfectly legal. The inequity of inflation is an economic problem hardly less important than the vast waste associated with mass unemployment. One of Keynes' foremost preoccupations as an economist has been the process of inflation and means of minimizing its evil consequences. He has sometimes been called an "inflationist," but such a label is misleading. If he has shown a preference for inflation over deflation, it is purely a matter of the lesser of two evils. For deflation is a double evil—it redistributes wealth in an arbitrary manner and also impedes the creation of new wealth by causing unemployment. Inflation, except when it approaches breakdown proportions, errs only in the arbitrary redistribution of wealth. It does not, except indirectly, cause unemployment. Stability of the value of money has always been one of the goals of Keynes' analytical and programmatic skill. The brilliant suggestions put forth near the end of his life for financing the second world war with a minimum of inflation marks a worthy conclusion to this lifelong preoccupation.

Keynes applies the same concepts to the special case of full employment that he uses where unemployment prevails. No new techniques are required to explain the mechanism of inflation. Inflation merely represents the special case in which output ceases to be responsive to further increases in effective demand and as a result prices only, and not output, rise. Increases in the quantity of money still work their way into the economic system through liquidity preference, the rate of interest, the inducement to invest, the multiplier, and income. An increase in the total quantity of money goes first into idle balances (M_2), where it lowers the rate of interest. The lower rate of interest increases the inducement to invest, which is already adequate for full employment. The increase in investment causes income in money units to increase by more than the increase in investment, according to the principle of the investment multiplier. The increase in money income must be sufficient to cause an amount of saving out of that income to equal the increase in investment. Since income cannot increase in real terms (wage units), it increases in money terms by means of a rise in prices (a rise in the wage unit). This is a state of true inflation because prices are rising when employment and output are constant.

The gap between income and consumption, which holds the clue to the explanation of unemployment when there is an inadequacy of effective demand, is also the clue to inflation when there is an excess of effective demand. Unemployment exists when the amount of investment is insufficient to fill the gap between income and consumption corresponding to full employment. Inflation arises because investment is more than adequate to fill the gap between income and consumption at the level corresponding to full employment *at existing prices*. The sum of the effective demand for consumption and the effective demand for investment exceeds the aggregate income expressed in current prices. The adjustment which makes $Y = C + I$ and $I = S$ comes about through an increase in prices, money income, and money savings, until money savings are equal to the total amount of investment, also expressed in terms of a new level of prices. The equality between investment and saving is brought about by changes in the level of income when there is full employment as well as when there is less than full employment. The inflationary potential or inflationary gap is measured by the excess of consumption demand (D_1) plus investment demand (D_2) over income (Y) at full employment expressed in current prices. Potential inflation becomes actual inflation unless measures are taken to suppress it.

Measures to suppress an inflationary potential involve a reduction of total effective demand below its potential level. Suppression may take the form of a decrease in the propensity to consume or in the inducement to invest. The propensity to consume may be reduced by higher taxation or by an increase in the desire to save, which may be induced by appeals to buy bonds and other saving media, or, to some extent, by an increase in the rate of interest. Taxation intended to reduce aggregate consumption will be effective to the extent that it falls upon income which would otherwise be spent for consumption. A regressive tax will be a more effective curb to inflation than a progressive tax since the propensity to consume is proportionately higher for lower-income groups than for higher-income groups. The inducement to invest can be lowered by a rise in the rate of interest or by a fall in the marginal efficiency of capital. Since the private marginal efficiency of capital is largely beyond the reach of government control, restraints upon the volume of private investment must work mainly through the rate of interest by means of a restriction in the quantity of money. Reductions in government spending will also tend to suppress the inflationary pressures. To sum up, inflation arises because too much money is spent by individuals, businesses, and governments. The obvious way to prevent inflation is to reduce the total volume of spending. In so far as individuals and businesses tend to spend too much money, the government may take the excess away from them in the form of increased taxation or by inducing a higher ratio of saving to income. If full employment exists and government feels the need to spend more, as in time of war, inflation can only be avoided by withdrawing some of the potential private expenditures.

Wartime Inflation

Inflation is by no means unknown as a peacetime phenomenon, but it is an almost universal and inevitable accompaniment of war and postwar economic conditions. Perhaps it is not an exaggeration to say that inflation and full employment are the normal conditions of a wartime economy and that deflation and unemployment are the normal conditions of a peacetime economy in the present stage of capitalist development. After the primary postwar depression of 1920-21, the commodity price levels in the United States and other capitalistic countries of the western world showed a remarkable stability until the collapse of 1929. Even in the boom years of 1928 and 1929, commodity price inflation was not typical. The most important forms of inflation in the United States between 1922 and 1929 were in the prices of securities sold on the stock exchanges and in the amounts of profits earned by industrial enterprises.[1] On the other hand, commodity price inflation was an outstanding characteristic of the first and second world wars and their aftermaths. Hence any discussion of inflation in commodity prices which is to be close to actual experience must be concerned primarily with war and postwar conditions.

The social framework of Keynes' general theory of employment, interest, and money is that of a peacetime capitalist economy rather than of a wartime economy. Although Keynes envisages a large amount of governmental control in peacetime, the extent of regulation is small in comparison with that required by the exigencies of modern warfare. Consequently, Keynes' general theory is most useful as an instrument of analysis within the premises of peacetime capitalism. Yet the war experience is significant in relation to Keynes' theory in at least two important respects. First, war experience indicates clearly that a sufficient rate of governmental

1. "Profit inflation" is a special term coined by Keynes in his *Treatise on Money* to describe the condition when prices increase more than business costs or prices fall less than costs. See *Treatise on Money*, Vol. 1, page 155.

expenditure can soon bring even the wealthiest of the modern
industrial economies to full employment, at which point the
drag of unemployment is replaced by the threat of inflation.
Second, Keynes' suggestion of how to pay for the war, a plan
offered in Great Britain in 1939, shows the flexibility and the
fruitfulness for practical action of the kind of thinking that
went into the general theory of employment, interest, and
money.[2] There is nothing in Keynes' plan for preventing inflation in war that contradicts his explanation of unemployment in peace. The plan for war finance suggests the
need for compulsory saving whereas the emphasis in the
General Theory is upon the social disadvantages of thrift.
The reversal of circumstances from peace to war calls for a
reversal of emphasis. The plan for compulsory saving is an
extension of Keynes' basic theory to wartime conditions. The
change from peace to war calls for a shift in emphasis but
involves no change in the framework of the analysis.

Wartime inflation is not basically different from peacetime
inflation except in the greater pressures that exist in war and
the more drastic remedies required to cope with these pressures. The fundamental principle is, to repeat, that the total
effective demand for consumers goods (D_1) plus the effective
demand for investment goods (D_2) exceeds the total value of
output at full employment in terms of existing prices. In the
absence of measures to suppress excessive demand, prices
must rise until income is sufficient to permit saving to equal
investment. Investment in a war economy is best thought of
as all goods and services which are not for private consumption. Investment then includes all government outlays plus
private capital accumulation.

In terms of the three independent variables which determine the volume of effective demand—the propensity to consume, the rate of interest, and the marginal efficiency of
capital—it is the last which provides the stimulus to effective
demand which in turn gives rise to inflation or the threat of

---

2. *How to Pay for the War.* New York: Harcourt, Brace and Co., Inc., 1940.

inflation in war. Wartime "investment" is not influenced to any important extent by changes in the rate of interest. War expenditures are largely a function of military requirements, taken in conjunction with estimates of the quantity of consumers goods, with a tendency to maximize war production and to minimize consumption output. War may be viewed as a great new industry whose colossal demands stimulate economic activity in every nook and cranny of the economic system. The expected yields which raise the marginal efficiency of government investment are mainly in terms of social and military advantages rather than pecuniary profits. In so far as wartime plant and equipment is furnished by private capital, the investments are made in the expectation that high yields will bring returns at least equal to the supply price within a fairly short period. Thus it is a sharp rise in the marginal efficiency of capital that increases effective demand and sets up the inflationary potential in a war economy.

Since the exigencies of war do not permit consumers goods to increase in response to effective demand from consumer spending, plans for preventing wartime inflation must focus upon suppressing current consumer demand. The fundamental problem is how to prevent consumption expenditure from increasing when income is increasing. "The fiscal problem," said Keynes with reference to British conditions in 1939, "is how to permit an increase of incomes by 15 to 20 per cent. without any of this increase being spent on increased real consumption."[3] Modern warfare requires more guns and less butter without regard for the fundamental psychological principle that as income rises consumption also rises. Belts must be tightened in war. And even if a nation is so fortunate as to be able to afford as much consumption as before the war, it certainly cannot permit consumption to rise according to the peacetime schedule of the propensity to consume. To hold the *amount* of consumption constant when income rises means to lower the schedule of the propensity to consume.

---

3. "The Income and Fiscal Potential of Great Britain," *The Economic Journal*, December, 1939, Vol. XLIX, No. 196, page 629.

Since the production of consumers goods cannot be adjusted upwards to correspond to normal consumer demand, the amount of consumer demand must be adjusted downward to correspond to the output of consumers goods. In other words, the schedule of the *propensity* to consume must be lowered so that the *amount* of consumption will not rise as income rises. If the propensity to consume is not lowered, a sharp rise in the prices of consumers goods is unavoidable. In war it is hardly possible by normal means to adjust the division of consumer output and non-consumer output to the proportions which income recipients will voluntarily choose to spend and not to spend. In the absence of unusual measures, the increasing money expenditure coming into the consumer market for a fixed or declining volume of consumers goods and services will cause a sharp increase in the prices of consumers goods. Price fixing and rationing are subsidiary measures for depressing the propensity to consume special commodities. They are incapable of suppressing effectively and efficiently the general flow of consumer demand.

Alternatives in war finance

Bearing in mind that the primary problem of war finance is to restrict consumption expenditure when income is rising, the alternative policies for attaining this objective are relatively few in number. The problem is less that of lowering the absolute level of consumption than of preventing consumption from rising when income is rising rapidly. The alternative means of lowering the general propensity to private consumption are: (1) to increase taxation on consumption expenditure, (2) to rely upon voluntary saving plus increases in normal taxation, (3) to institute a system of compulsory saving aimed primarily at consumption expenditure.

(1) *Increase Taxation:* Since it is the potential expenditures of the lower income groups which must be suppressed, increases in taxes which would provide any solution to the inflation problem must fall most heavily upon these groups. Heavy taxation upon the rich will do little to lessen aggregate

expenditure for consumption because a very large part of the incomes of the wealthy is either taxed or saved. While the rich consume more than the poor in proportion to their number, the rich do not consume enough in the aggregate, especially in time of war when extravagances are unpatriotic and many types of luxury goods and services are not produced at all, to make any practicable reduction in their consumption of consequence. Keynes found in 1939 in Great Britain, that the income group with five pounds (about $20) per week constituted about 88 per cent of the population, received 60 per cent of the total personal income, and accounted for two-thirds of the total consumption of the country. In this low-income group, incomes had risen on an average of 15 per cent in the first year of the war and there were not enough consumer goods available to permit them to consume anything like 15 per cent more than before the war. At best the absolute level of consumption of those whose incomes remained below five pounds might have been maintained at the prewar level.

About the only taxes which would drain off a sufficient amount of the increase in consumer demand of the low-income classes to serve as an effective check to the inflation of prices of consumers goods would be a stiff wage tax or a retail sales tax. Such taxes are highly regressive and therefore violate a cardinal principle of justice in taxation. Special taxes on wages meet very strong political opposition from the ranks of labor, especially if they are severe enough to be effective. Keynes estimated the necessary rate to be 20 per cent on wages, in addition to the income tax with lowered exemptions. He estimated that a retail sales tax which would be adequate would be too high to be borne by the very lowest income groups and therefore would need to be levied on nonessentials at a rate of about 50 per cent. Only the financial purists, he said, would insist that it is possible for a country with the income structure of the United Kingdom to finance a war effort of the size needed in 1940 out of current taxation. Such taxation was, Keynes contended, both socially un-

just and politically impracticable. No modern government of
a capitalistic nation has ever financed war expenditures out
of taxation to a sufficient degree to avoid inflation.[4]

(2) *Voluntary Saving:* Governments usually rely upon
voluntary saving to fill the gap between total war expenditure
and receipts from taxation. The only fault of voluntary saving as a preventive of war inflation is its inadequacy. The
inadequacy arises because the income groups which account
for the bulk of increased consumer spending in wartime are
not the groups which are likely to save voluntarily enough
of their incomes to reduce consumer demand to equality with
the amount of consumer goods available in terms of prewar
prices. No amount of saving by the rich nor any amount of
taxes levied upon the rich will suffice to reduce the spending
of the poor out of their enhanced incomes. It is not reasonable that the lower income groups will suddenly develop
habits of saving which will render reliance on voluntary saving a satisfactory anti-inflation policy. Peacetime quiescence
in the injustices of economic inequality cannot be perpetuated in wartime by mere appeals to the patriotism of the
poor. A family which has not been able to afford roast beef
before the war because of inadequate income is not likely
to refrain voluntarily from indulging a little during the war
when its income has risen sufficiently to bring roast beef
within its economic grasp. Patriotic appeals to forestall inflation which rest upon the assumption that those who ate
roast beef before the war may do so during the war, while
those who were unable to afford roast beef before the war shall
refrain from eating it during the war must surely fall upon
deaf ears as well as outrage our sense of social justice. This
is the essential nature of the problem. Although roast beef
and some other commodities may be rationed, consumption

---

4. Professor William J. Fellner has contended that a proportionate income tax
of 10 per cent applied to all income without exception and superimposed upon
the income tax structure that actually prevailed would have prevented inflation
in the United States during the second world war. See "Postscript on War
Inflation: A Lesson from World War II," *American Economic Review*, March,
1947, Vol. XXXVII, No. 1, page 47.

demand in general can be restrained efficiently only by some stronger means than an appeal to voluntary saving on the part of the lower income groups. There is no evidence from experience to indicate that voluntary saving has ever been adequate to prevent inflation in time of war, no matter how intense and how widespread the appeals to save.

There is an element of subtle deception in the belief that war finance can be adequately taken care of by "normal" methods, that is, by increasing the rates of existing taxes and by voluntary saving stimulated by propaganda. When voluntary saving is inadequate without inflation, it increases with inflation. For a sufficient degree of inflation will always occur to raise the yield of taxes and voluntary saving to the necessary level. This method whereby so-called voluntary saving is increased through inflation is typically followed by governments in wartime. Governments do not employ it willingly. It is not usually a conscious policy but what Keynes calls "Nature's remedy," the consequence which follows by default, in the absence of an adequate, positive program against inflation. It is all the more dangerous because governments slip into it unconsciously and perhaps under the delusion that it "works." It does "work" in the sense that a government which follows it will always find the cash to pay for its purchases of home-produced goods, but it does not work in the sense that it can prevent inflation. It works only because of inflation. Keynes seems to have been the first to articulate explicitly the essential nature of this inflationary process. In his *Treatise on Money* (II, pp. 173-176) he characterized British financing of the first world war as one of increasing voluntary saving and taxation through inflation. A similar description could be applied to war finance in the United States in the first and second world wars and to Britain in the second world war, although in the latter case the process was modified by a belated adoption of Keynes' plan for compulsory saving. In fact voluntary saving through inflation involves a mechanism which characterizes all inflations and has a significance which transcends the wartime

cases. The essence of the process is that price inflation raises
the level of money income until saving out of income is equal
to investment, or in the case of a wartime governmental
budget, price inflation raises national income to the point
where taxes and voluntary saving are adequate to finance
government expenditures. "Nature's remedy . . . is a rise of
prices sufficient to divert real resources out of the pockets of
the main body of consumers into the pockets of the entrepreneurs and thence to the Treasury, partly in the shape of
a higher yield from existing taxes, particularly Excess Profits
Tax, and partly in contributions to loans out of the increased
savings and reserves of the entrepreneurs."[5]

The process is perhaps best explained with reference to
an arithmetical example reduced to the simplest possible
assumptions. Suppose the national income and the national
output are $160 billion at the beginning of a war before any
inflation has taken place; that the war effort requires an
expenditure of $85 billion on the part of the government; that
private investment is zero; that taxes amount to $45 billion
and voluntary saving to $25 billion out of the $160 billion
income. A total of $70 billion comes into the government
coffers from taxes and loans and leaves the receipts short of
expenditures by $15 billion. Now this sum of $15 billion
needed to balance the government's expenditures is exactly
equal to what remains in the hands of the public in the form
of voluntary savings. This is inevitable by the rules of arithmetic. For the government has taken $85 billion out of the
total national output of $160 billion (in prewar prices) and
there are no goods left over for which the extra income in the
hands of the public can be spent. If prices do not rise, people
will find themselves with $15 billion left after buying all the
goods available in the market. If prices rise, as they undoubtedly will when $90 billion are available for $75 billion
worth of goods (in prewar prices), the higher prices will
swell the national income by $15 billion so there is just as

5. Keynes, "The Income and Fiscal Potential of Great Britain," *The Economic Journal*, December, 1939, Vol. XLIX. No. 196, pages 630-631.

much left over as before. Prices will rise by 20 per cent to bring the supply of goods into equality with the money demand. Those who sell goods worth $75 billion for $90 billion will have extra income of $15 billion.[6]

If this extra income is not captured in loans and taxes, there will be a further rise in prices when the additional $15 billion comes into the market in the second round of the inflationary process. If this happens, the volume of money income coming into the market for a constant supply of consumer goods will increase cumulatively. The prices paid by the government for war goods will also increase as other prices and costs rise. The net outcome, if this happens, is a progressive inflation without limit.

Fortunately, this is not what actually happens. The initial rise in prices transfers real income from the main body of consumers to entrepreneurs because prices rise faster than wage and salary rates. Real-wage rates are diminished and real profits are inflated. This represents a shift in real income from the lower to the higher income classes of society. The increase in aggregate national income is concentrated in the hands of a limited number of business entrepreneurs, a group which Keynes refers to as the "profiteers." The personal incomes of the profiteers are subject to very high marginal rates of taxation under the personal income tax, and their extra business profits are subject to almost confiscatory rates under the wartime excess-profits tax. As a result, the extra income which arises from the initial rise in prices, of 20 per

---

6. We may express the quantitative relations as follows: Consumption expenditure (C) + Saving (S) + Taxes (T) = Consumption output (C') + Private Investment (I) + Government Expenditure (E).

$$C + S + T = C' + I + E$$
$$90 + 25 + 45 = 75 + 0 + 85$$

But C' must equal C, and S + T must equal I + E,

$$90 + 30 + 55 = 90 + 0 + 85$$

Thus saving plus taxes are brought to equality with private investment plus government expenditure as a result of a rise in money income of $15 billion, of which $10 billion are taxed and $5 billion are voluntarily saved. The rise in income is a purely monetary one which results from an expenditure of $90 billion for consumers goods previously worth $75 billion. An inflation of 20 per cent has taken place in the prices of consumers goods.

cent in our example, is almost entirely taxed away. Most of what is not taxed may be voluntarily saved because it is in the hands of one of the saving classes of society. Most of the excess demand will be mopped up. Instead of a 20 per cent increase in the money demand for consumers goods at the second round, there may be, for example, only a 2 or 3 percent increase. Voluntary saving will have increased as a result of the rise in prices and income to the extent necessary to fill the gap between the government's total expenditure and what it collects in taxes.

This is an expedient way for a government which quails at bolder programs to meet its war expenditures. It permits real resources to be taken away from the mass of consumers by letting prices increase faster than wages. The resources taken from consumers are handed over to profiteers. Then most of the extra profits of the profiteers are taken away in the form of taxes or of loans to which they voluntarily subscribe. The profiteers are in effect tax collectors for the government. The process is not intolerable as long as the profiteers remain merely the agents and do not become the principals in taking resources away from the mass of consumers. It works with more social justice if the excess "booty" which has accrued to the profiteers is taxed away and not merely borrowed by the government. If it is merely borrowed, the profiteers retain a claim on the future although they have done nothing to deserve such claims. In order to assure more equity and avoid unjustified gains remaining in the hands of the profiteers, a capital levy should be assessed on war-won wealth quickly at the conclusion of hostilities.

Even though the excess purchasing power arising from the initial increase in prices is entirely mopped up by taxes and voluntary saving, the inflationary process is not permanently stopped. Workers whose cost of living has risen by 20 per cent will demand higher wages to compensate for the higher cost of living. In the absence of controls over wage bargaining, the increased demands of workers may be met by employers with relatively little resistance, both because they

wish to retain their workers and because there is not much
incentive to keep down business costs when tax rates are at
confiscatory levels. Fortunately, some costs are fixed and do
not increase even if wages rise. Wage increases take time to
negotiate and wars do not last forever. England got through
four years of the first world war with something less than a
doubling of prices. Voluntary saving was always adequate
to meet the necessary expenditures above taxation with the
help of a sufficient amount of inflation. The limited meaning
of the term "voluntary" should be borne in mind. Keynes
points out that this so-called voluntary saving method "is a
method of *compulsorily* converting the appropriate part of
the earnings of the worker which *he* does not save voluntarily
into the voluntary savings (and taxation) of the entrepreneur."[7] So the method of voluntary saving merely limits the
amount of inflation. It does not prevent inflation. The effect
of inflation is similar to a regressive tax. It leaves the working
class with no claim against the future and with no more consumption goods than they would have enjoyed in the aggregate if there had been no inflation. In the second world war,
Keynes suggested a plan whereby inflation could be avoided
and the working class would have a share in the claims on
the future.

(3) *Compulsory Saving:* The Keynes plan to pay for the
second world war is known as the "deferred-pay" or "com-
pulsory-saving" plan. Its provisions, which were for the purpose of preventing inflation, were: (a) A deduction from current wages and salaries to be credited to a savings account
which would remain blocked for the duration of the war. This
savings deduction is in addition to the income tax withholding. The very lowest incomes would be exempt from both tax
and savings deductions, and those just above the lowest level
would be subject to a savings but not a tax deduction. The
proportion of the total deduction which represented taxes
would increase as income increased. Interest would be paid

---

7. *How to Pay for the War,* page 69. Italics in the original.

on savings at 2½ per cent per annum. (b) At the appropriate time after the war, the savings accounts would be unblocked and become available for spending. The propitious time for unblocking this purchasing power would be when a deficiency of effective demand threatened to lead the economy into a postwar depression. (c) Other provisions included the payment of cash allowances to all families with children, an iron ration at fixed prices supported by governmental subsidies, permission to unblock some savings for exceptional and unavoidable emergencies such as illness and hospitalization, credits for prewar commitments to mortgage payments and life insurance premiums, and a capital levy for raising funds with which to make payment of the deferred incomes.

In wartime, the budget problem of how to pay for the war and the inflation problem of how to keep prices down should be approached from the consumption end. The borrowing problem then becomes "child's play."[8] The aggregate amount of wartime consumption for all classes in Britain was assumed to be fixed, regardless of the method used to finance the war. The problem of consumption was therefore one of equitable distribution of a fixed amount of goods and services. This amount was less than the aggregate prewar consumption. Keynes offered his plan of deferred pay as the only means whereby war sacrifices could be in proportion to ability to bear them. Taxation alone was not a practicable means, and voluntary saving could be made adequate only if assisted by inflation. The Keynes plan was intended to permit some increase above the prewar level in the consumption of those with incomes below 75 shillings ($15) per week, no change in the aggregate consumption of all those with incomes below 5 pounds ($20) per week, and a reduction on the average of about one-third in the consumption of those with incomes above 5 pounds ($20) per week. The progressive incidence of the plan accorded with the well-established principles of

8. Keynes, "The Income and Fiscal Potential of Great Britain," *The Economic Journal*, December, 1939, Vol. XLIX, No. 196, page 633.

social justice which a democracy should extend rather than abandon in time of war.

The low-income groups (below $20 per week) would be able in the aggregate to buy just as much as they enjoyed before the war and just as much, if not more, than they would be able to enjoy during the war under any alternate plan, and at the same time they would have savings left over with which to buy things after the war. The extra rewards for some of the extra effort expended during the war would be merely deferred and not taken away for good. Under Keynes' plan, the working class as well as the capitalist class would share in the ownership of the national debt, a privilege usually enjoyed by the capitalist class alone. Under the probable alternative of price inflation, the working class would spend all its money during the war, get no more for it, and sacrifice the privilege of spending after the war some of the money earned during the war. "Inflation . . . allows them to spend and deprives them of the fruit of spending."[9]

The deferred-pay plan is consistent with a maximum freedom of choice on the part of consumers in deciding what to consume. In contrast, a system of universal rationing presupposes that all consumers have approximately the same tastes, an assumption obviously far from valid. A few commodities like sugar, bread, and salt may be rationed in equal allotments without interfering with consumer preference, but for most items entering into consumption, tastes of individuals differ so widely that it is far better to limit the total amount of spending and let the individuals decide for themselves what they will buy. This does not mean that rationing and price control can be dispensed with altogether. It does mean that direct controls over consumption are not the most suitable method for controlling the over-all distribution of consumers goods. If, in addition to rationing, all prices are fixed and there is an excess of purchasing power, people find themselves with money in their pockets when there is nothing to

---

9. *How to Pay for the War*, page 49.

buy. If the prices of essentials only are controlled, the excess buying power is diverted to the uncontrolled items whose prices tend to skyrocket. There then develops great pressure to divert materials into those activities where prices and profits are high. Hence, it becomes necessary to control the flow of materials into channels where they are most essential rather than where they are most profitable. Such controls necessarily involve extensive interference with personal and business affairs and unavoidably degenerate into widespread "black market" operations.

Since the problem of avoiding inflation is to be attacked from the consumption end, it is misleading to suppose that the issue is primarily one of borrowing directly from the public rather than from the banking system. The amount of money that can be borrowed from the banks without setting up inflationary pressures depends on the liquidity preference of the business community and of investors for the transactions, precautionary, and speculative motives. In wartime, when investment is strictly controlled, the rate of interest is not of direct consequence in relation to the volume of investment. However, the limits to the ability of the economic system to absorb new money will be indicated by a sharp rise in the prices of securities (an undue fall in the rate of interest). In the expansion of economic activity in the early phases of war, the volume of money needed for transactions will increase because of larger output, higher prices (caused by increasing costs and profits), and higher wages. There is also need for more money to satisfy the precautionary holdings arising from large tax liabilities and other contingencies. Keynes estimated that war activity in Britain required an increase in cash holdings of from 20 to 25 per cent over prewar needs. Therefore, in the early stages of war it is desirable for the Treasury to sell bonds to the banking system. Borrowing from the banking system should not, however, be continued beyond the expansion stage. It is a once-and-for-all source of financing the governmental budget. After the supply of money has been adjusted to maximum activity, the total quantity of money should be kept approximately constant for the duration. Borrowing thereafter should come directly from the public rather than from the banking system.[10]

Financing the war and preventing inflation in Britain in the early 'forties offered a perfect opportunity for social action of the type represented in the deferred-pay plan because it was one of those situations in which each benefits by a rule that applies to all. Compulsory saving was a social guarantee that each would be protected in doing for his own good what was also good for others providing all behaved in the same way. A single individual cannot protect himself against inflation by saving when others are not saving. Therefore, in the absence of assurance that others will save, the individual has less incentive to do so, even though he would prefer to save if he knew that everybody else would do likewise. Under war conditions, if all save, all will be benefitted by lower prices now and by having something left over to spend in the future. But if some save while others do not, all will pay higher prices for a fixed amount of goods; the spenders will have nothing left over and the value of the savers' money will diminish in value as a result of the spending of the nonsavers. Authorities who appeal to individuals to save under these circumstances but do not take steps to protect the value of the savings are guilty of half-way measures. The desirable policy is to make the rules for saving the same for all. That is what Keynes' plan of deferred pay was intended to do.

Postwar Inflation

The foregoing analysis which has related the principle of effective demand to the problem of wartime inflation may be applied with only minor modifications to postwar or peacetime inflation. Inflation is always caused by an excess of effective demand above the level needed for full employment, just as unemployment is always caused by a deficiency of ef-

---

10. Keynes, "The Income and Fiscal Potential of Great Britain," *The Economic Journal*, December, 1939, Vol. XLIX, No. 196, page 635.

fective demand below the level required for full employment. Inflation and unemployment are the twin evils of the failure to harmonize the volume of effective demand with the basic aims of full employment and stable prices. If the volume of investment exceeds the size of the gap between income and consumption at full employment, prices rise until the size of the gap is accommodated to the amount of investment. In war, when government expenditures are fixed by military necessity, steps to avoid price inflation are confined to lower-' ing the current private propensity to consume, that is, to reducing private consumption until the gap between income and consumption is large enough to accommodate government expenditure plus private capital formation. In wartime the latter is of minor significance. In peacetime, price inflation may be attacked either by widening the size of the full employment gap between income and consumption until it is accommodated to the volume of investment, or by reducing the amount of investment to fit the size of the gap between income and consumption in terms of existing prices. This is merely to say the exigencies of peace are less than those of war. The effective demand for either consumption or investment, or both, may be adjusted to make the aggregate demand equal the level required for full employment without inflation.

Consumption

The means whereby the propensity to consume may be lowered are the same in peace as in war, that is, taxation, voluntary saving and compulsory saving, supplemented by price control and rationing. However, the political and social atmosphere for executing these measures is much less favorable in peace than in war. Much of the voluntary abstinence exercised by consumers during war is purely a temporary phenomenon induced by the psychological satisfaction of submitting to patriotic sacrifices. Government bonds are more readily purchased in war than in peace by the great mass of consumers. With the cessation of war there is a strong psychological release from the self-imposed sacrifices of war in favor of a propensity to spend the savings which have accumulated during the war. This psychological impatience reflects itself in free spending and in political pressure for a quick end to price controls, rationing, high taxes, and bond purchases. A compulsory-savings plan which might be politically acceptable in war, as it was to some extent in England but not in the United States during the second world war, is not likely to be tolerated in peace, although an increase in social security deductions might be used for this end to the mutual benefit of workers and non-workers alike. There may be irony but there is no paradox in the circumstance that the more successfully inflation is staved off during war, the less likely it is to be staved off after war. The bigger the dam, the bigger the deluge when the dam gives way, and analogously, the greater the success attained in restraining consumer spending in war, the greater will be the difficulty of holding back the flood of potential effective demand which the public is impatient to release as soon as the war is over. If political and personal impatience gains the upper hand before the conversion from military to civilian production is completed, the increase in prices is likely to be very great indeed. Hence, it is not so strange that inflation is often more severe in a postwar than in a war period.

Postwar inflation is not inevitable. The controls which work in war will work in peace if they are given a chance. There is no necessary reason why the purchasing power that has been dammed up in war need be permitted to break loose when the war is over. Reductions in military demands that follow the end of war ease the pressures that tend to raise prices. The inflation that struck the United States after the second world war was a consequence of the political immaturity of the general public in relation to the purpose and functions of such controls. A public steeped in the tradition that "free" competition is the cure-all for economic ills, fell easy prey to those who, whether out of self-delusion or self-interest, proclaimed that the end of price control and a return to competition would bring down prices. Urged on by a flood of propaganda, there was a headlong rush to end all controls. Without public support to continue controls, the fight against inflation was lost because no system of controls can work effectively unless it has the co-operation of the general public. Administrative rationing, which is never justified except for its greater equity as compared with the "natural" rationing of higher prices, was scrapped. This undermined price control which was quickly beaten down to a skeleton and finally placed on the ash pile in the middle of 1946. In the first six months following the end of price control in June of 1946, wholesale prices rose 25 per cent as compared with a rise of only 10 per cent in the four years from mid-1942 to mid-1946. Retail prices and the cost of living were held down quite successfully during the war but surged wildly upward following the removal of OPA controls. In some instances people with low incomes were forced to eat less because their pocketbooks were exhausted by high prices. After a Congressional investigation of prices, Senator Flanders reported in September of 1947 that many white collar workers in New York were undernourished because they were unable to afford the food required for a balanced diet. This is the manner in which the "law of supply and demand" redistributes real income in periods of inflation. It takes away from some and gives to others in ways which bear no necessary relation to what social consensus would regard as equitable. An advantage of positive social action is, of course, that equity may be consciously taken into account.

The three elements of effective demand in war are government expenditure, private consumption, and private capital formation. At the conclusion of a great war, the first element falls precipitously while the second and third rise sharply. Postwar inflation is partly a question of whether the decrease in the first element exceeds or falls short of the increase in the other two. In the United States from 1945 to 1946, government purchases fell by $52 billion, while private consumption expenditure rose $22 billion and total investment (gross domestic plus net foreign) rose by $21 billion. Meanwhile, with price controls still in effect, the cost of living index rose only 4 points, from 129 in June, 1945, to 133 in June, 1946 (1935-1939 = 100). From 1946 to 1947 government purchases fell by only $2 billion, private consumption expenditure rose by $21 billion, and total investment (gross domestic plus net foreign) rose by $7 billion. With government purchases leveling off, and consumption and investment expenditure continuing to rise, and in the absence of price controls, the cost-of-living index soared from 133 in June, 1946, to 157 in June, 1947, and reached 172 in June, 1948.[11]

Although the magnitudes of government expenditure, private consumption, and investment are the most important considerations in relation to price movements, there are other important factors bearing on price movements in immediate postwar periods. On the output side there is the major problem of converting from military to civilian production. Contemporary industrial society is characterized by an extremely complicated technology which is not easily converted from one line of production to another. There must elapse at the end of any major war a critical period during which final output falls below the potential maximum because of the change in the direction of production. Industrial disputes between labor and management also tend to delay the return to a full level of peacetime production. If during this critical conversion period, pent up demands from the war are permitted to surge into the market for whatever is available, the inevitable consequence is a sharp rise in prices. Price inflation occurs when a surplus of effective demand comes into the market to purchase the available supply of goods. Inflation can be attacked either by reducing the quantity of effective demand or by increasing the quantity of goods. In the short run, it may be necessary to suppress the effective demand. In the long run, the prodigious productive capacity of modern technology is the surest guarantee against inflation.

11. The cost-of-living data are those of the U.S. Bureau of Labor Statistics, and the national income and product data those of the U.S. Department of Commerce.

At the close of the second world war there existed an immense backlog of unsatisfied demand for consumers goods of all types. By the end of 1946 the supply of many non-durable goods had caught up with demand, and there was concern over the growing size of inventories. A longer period is required to meet the backlog of demand for durable consumers goods than for non-durables. However, by the fourth quarter of 1947 nearly all consumer durables were being produced in sufficient volume to meet an unprecedented current demand and, in addition, to cut into the backlog from the war. Radios, vacuum cleaners, washing machines, refrigerators, and automobiles were being turned out more rapidly than in the previous peak year of 1941. Only in the case of automobiles was current output failing to gain rapidly on demand. It was predicted in the spring of 1948 that any serious weakening in aggregate demand was likely to originate in the consumers durable goods sector of the economy.[12]

Investment

Private Capital Formation: In the short run, under conditions of full employment, investment is always carried on at the expense of consumption. Postwar conditions usually favor a strong inducement to invest as well as a strong propensity to consume, to cause a two-fold pressure toward an inflationary rise in prices. The inducement to invest is determined by the rate of interest and the marginal efficiency of capital. The fiscal and monetary policy followed in the United States during the second world war tended to accentuate the downward trend of interest rates. During recent years the long-term rate of interest has been reduced to about three per cent on gilt-edged corporate bonds and to less than three per cent on long-term government bonds. Short-term interest rates are even lower than long-term rates. These low interest rates, taken along with the high marginal efficiency of capital which follows the destruction of capital assets in war areas and the

---

12. See L. J. Atkinson, "Backlog Demand for Consumers' Durable Goods," *Survey of Current Business,* April, 1948, Vol. XXVIII, No. 4, pages 15-21.

war-enforced cessation of investment in many types of capital assets even in non-war areas, leads to a high level of private investment in the years following a major war. In addition to the task of restocking inventories to normal levels, there exists a heavy demand for durable producers goods. Plant and equipment which has worn out or become obsolete during the war will require replacement, and the business community will be eager to get on with its war-deferred programs for plant expansion. During 1946 gross private domestic investment (including housing) in the United States rose to $25 billion, and in 1947 to $28 billion, as compared with only $9 billion in the prewar year 1939. That part of domestic investment consisting of plant and equipment expenditures, especially in manufacturing, showed signs of leveling off in 1948, but nevertheless it continued to exert a major inflationary pressure. The great postwar housing boom is an inflationary factor, and many years will be required to fill the postwar demand. Inflationary pressures on rents and building materials promise to continue for an extended period. The longer period of time which must elapse before the demand for housing can be met is the justification for retaining rent controls after other forms of price control have been eliminated.

Exports: From the point of view of any national economy, net exports—that is, exports in excess of imports—represent a form of investment. Net exports are production in excess of current consumption, which is the fundamental meaning of investment. The huge demand from Europe and other foreign areas for American goods for rehabilitation and reconstruction is one of the great and continuing sources of inflationary pressure which has followed the second world war. Millions of tons of food, locomotives, coal, steel, clothing, and almost every conceivable type of item are being shipped abroad in response to desperate needs of these areas for the goods that will enable the people to survive and to rebuild on the rubble heaps left by the most destructive conflagration in the history of the world. At one point during 1947, the net exports from the United States rose to a rate of nearly one billion dollars per month. This means that from this source alone incomes were being earned by workers and owners in the United States to the extent of nearly a billion dollars a month in excess of the value of the goods available for purchase. The removal of goods from the domestic economy naturally leaves less to buy and creates relative shortages which, taken in conjunction with other conditions of the postwar period, tends to drive up prices. These pressures are temporary because they are peculiar to the aftermath of a great war. They will not continue indefinitely both because of the inability of foreigners to pay dollars and because the foreigners will not wish to continue to buy American goods on so vast a scale when their own domestic productive capacity is restored. But as long as these demands for exports continue and as long as dollars are available in the hands of foreigners to pay for them, net exports will contribute to higher prices for goods sold within the United States.

The rate of net exports fell off rather sharply toward the end of 1947 and in the early months of 1948, but passage of the Foreign Assistance Act in the spring of 1948 gave assurance that they would continue at a high level until 1952 or 1953. During 1948 the foreign aid program contributed to aggregate demand and thus to domestic inflation. In later years it may provide some protection against large-scale domestic unemployment. In the long run, repayment of foreign loans will depend on the willingness of the United States to accept large imports of goods. During the 1920's the United States played the comic role of insisting that debts from the first world war be paid while making repayment virtually impossible by raising tariff walls to an all-time high. If the American economy continues to operate as it did during the 1920's and 1930's, it may be better off if the postwar loans of the second world war are never repaid because a net import of goods, representing negative investment, working through the multiplier principle, might be a major factor contributing to unemployment and depression. One of the ironies of our economic system is that foreign demand, which in later years would provide a bulwark against unemployment in the United States, is concentrated in a period in which it contributes to inflation.

Large Government Expenditures: Government expenditures constitute part of aggregate effective demand. At the conclusion of the second world war the total outlays of the federal government declined sharply from the wartime levels, but remained very high in comparsion with about $8.5 billion in the late 'thirties and less than $4 billion in the 'twenties. In the first three years after the war, annual outlays had not fallen below $35 billion and appeared destined to increase rather than decrease. In combination with a high private propensity to consume and a strong private inducement to invest, large government expenditures are a major force contributing to rising prices.

Fiscal policy is the best weapon against inflation in peace as well as in war. Since inflation is caused by too much spending, its cure lies in curtailing spending. Reductions in government expenditure is one method and higher taxes is another method for lessening demand. Strangely, it is sometimes argued that the best way to combat inflation is to reduce taxes because they discourage investment, which will increase the supply of goods. This is a dangerous contention from the point of view of an effective anti-inflationary program. Where there is already full employment, additional investment reduces the flow of current consumer output and increases the flow of current consumer demand. Consumers goods which will come onto the market in the future after new factories have been built will not help to avoid inflation now. Timing fiscal policy in order to regularize the flow of effective demand is the core of the problem. Too much demand at one time, followed by too little demand at another time, has been responsible for the boom-and-bust pattern which has characterized the free enterprise economies since the Napoleonic Wars. If an economy is already in the throes of inflation, it will only intensify its malady by lowering taxes. Reduction of the federal income tax in the spring of 1948 illustrates how economic wisdom is often sacrificed to political expediency. With full employment and with prices already rising, the public was given more money to spend at the very time Congress was voting to spend billions for the Foreign Assistance Act and was preparing to increase by more billions the outlay for armaments. Under such circumstances, more money left in the pay check means more money taken out at the grocery store. In peace as in war, when the public spends more money for a fixed quantity of goods it is rewarded only with higher prices. Unfortunately, the money illusion is strong enough to protect the political profiteers. Higher rather than lower taxes are appropriate to a period of inflation.[13]

While government is not a net contributor to inflation as long as it takes more money away from people than it pays out to them, it can always suppress inflationary tendencies by increasing the amount of money it takes away or by reducing the amount it pays out. A budget surplus is in the nature of a negative investment, just as a government deficit is in the nature of a positive investment. By increasing the size of the surplus in its cash budget, the government may provide an offset to the large positive investment for private capital formation and for net exports, and help to reduce the gap between income and current consumption to a size consistent with full employment without inflation.

References for Further Reading

Keynes, J. M., *The General Theory of Employment, Interest and Money,* Chapter 21. See Index for other references. New York: Harcourt, Brace and Company, 1936.

———, *How to Pay for the War,* especially Chapter 9. New York: Harcourt, Brace and Company, 1940.

---

13. An alternative to higher taxation is greater saving. It is interesting that one of the foremost American economists, Professor Sumner Slichter, recommended in early 1948 a plan for compulsory saving similar to that recommended by Keynes during the second world war. See Sumner Slichter, "The Problem of Inflation," *The Review of Economic Statistics,* February, 1948, Vol. XXX, No. 1, page 5.

———, *Monetary Reform*. New York: Harcourt, Brace and Company, 1924.

———, *A Treatise on Money*. 2 volumes. New York: Harcourt, Brace and Company, 1930.

Fellner, William, *A Treatise on War Inflation*. Berkeley: University of California Press, 1942.

———, *Monetary Policies and Full Employment*. Berkeley: University of California Press, 1946.

Hansen, A. H., *Economic Policy and Full Employment*, Chapters I, XX, and Appendix D. New York: McGraw-Hill Book Company, Inc., 1947.

Harris, S. E., *Inflation and the American Economy*. New York: McGraw-Hill Book Company, Inc., 1945.

———, *Prices and Related Controls in the United States*. New York: McGraw-Hill Book Company, Inc., 1945.

Klein, L. R., *The Keynesian Revolution*, Chapter VI. New York: The Macmillan Co., 1947.

Salant, W. A., "The Inflationary Gap," *The American Economic Review*, June, 1942, Vol. XXXII, pages 308-314.

"Ten Economists on Inflation," *The Review of Economic Statistics*, February, 1948, Vol. XXX, pages 1-29.

(See also the items listed for Chapter 9.)

CHAPTER 11

Further Applications of Keynes' General Theory of Employment

With Keynes, practical advice was the goal and beacon-light of analysis . . .

Joseph A. Schumpeter, *The American Economic Review,*
September, 1946, page 504.

THIS CHAPTER illustrates a few of the uses that have been made of Keynes' *The General Theory of Employment, Interest and Money* in some of the more important fields of economic policy. Previous chapters have indicated the relation of the *General Theory* to monetary policy, fiscal policy, public works, and inflation. In this chapter the fruitfulness of Keynes' work is further illustrated with reference to business cycles, international trade, and international finance.

Business Cycles

In offering an explanation of what determines at any time the prevailing level of employment and income, Keynes' *General Theory* provides also an explanation of the business cycle since the business cycle is nothing more than a rhythmic fluctuation in the over-all level of employment, income, and output. During the past decade, Keynes' general theory has become the focal point of discussion in the field of business-cycle analysis. It should be clear, however, that his work is not a theory of the business cycle as such. It is much more and also much less than that. It is more than a theory of the business cycle in the sense that it offers a general explanation for the level of employment, quite independently of the cyclical nature of changes in employment. It is less than a complete theory of the business cycle because it makes no attempt to give a detailed account of the various phases of the cycle, and does not examine closely the empirical data of cyclical fluctuations, something which any complete study of the business cycle would presumably attempt to do. Keynes' Chapter 22 entitled "Notes on the Trade Cycle" serves as a link between his general theory of employment and the conventional subject matter of business-cycle theory.

Keynes finds the essence of the business cycle in variations in the rate of investment caused by cyclical fluctuations in the marginal efficiency of capital. The rate of interest, which along with the marginal efficiency of capital determines the rate of investment, is relatively "sticky" or stable and is not a motivating force in cyclical fluctuations, although it does act as a reinforcing factor, especially in the financial crisis which often marks the early stage of depression. Likewise, the propensity to consume is relatively stable and is not an important factor accounting for cyclical fluctuations. Thus, of the three independent variables determining the volume of employment (the marginal efficiency of capital, the rate of interest, and the propensity to consume), it is the marginal efficiency of capital which plays the all-important role in business cycles. When it is recalled that the marginal efficiency of capital is nothing but another name for the expected rate of profit on new investment, we arrive at the very common-sense observation that business cycles in a profit economy result from variations in the rate of profit, or more specifically, from fluctuations in expectations as to what the rates of profit on varying types of investment will be in the future. In Chapter 7, it was noted that instability is the leading characteristic of the marginal efficiency of capital in the short run, as distinct from the secular tendency to decline in the long run under the impact of an increasing abundance of capital assets. The "marginal efficiency of capital" differs from the more conventional "rate of profit" primarily in the emphasis in the former upon the *expected* as contrasted with the realized rate of return on capital assets. Our earlier discussion of expectations, including the place of the stock exchange in their determination, indicates the precarious nature of knowledge upon which expectations are based and explains why the marginal efficiency of capital is subject to sudden and violent changes. The multiplier, resting upon the fundamental principle that as income increases (decreases), consumption also increases (decreases), but by less than income, explains the cumulative nature of expansion and contraction. Once started in a given direction, activity in the whole economic system continues in that direction until checked by the exhaustion of the forces which push it upward and downward. These upswings and downswings move erratically rather than smoothly. Although there is great instability in economic life, there are limits to the degree of instability. The range within which cyclical fluctuations occur is explained by the principle that when income changes, consumption changes, but by lesser amounts.

The concept of the business cycle implies, in addition to the cumulative nature of economic forces that gradually exhaust themselves, some degree of regularity in the timing and duration of these alternate expansions and contractions. Therefore, a theory of the business cycle must explain the *cyclical* nature of economic fluctuations. Some types of economic fluctuations are not of a cyclical nature, but there are economic movements which are sufficiently regular in their recurrence to justify the concept of the business "cycle." Keynes suggests that these movements were more characteristic of the nineteenth century than they are of the twentieth. In the nineteenth century, the tremendous forces of economic growth and expansion maintained the marginal efficiency of capital at a level which, taken in relation to the rate of interest, was high enough to permit variations between full employment and less than full employment, i.e., between good times and bad times. In the twentieth century, the slowing down of factors like population growth and geographical expansion and the great increase in the accumulation of capital assets have, except in time of war and for a few years thereafter, rendered full employment virtually unattainable in an economy following the traditional policies of laissez-faire capitalism. The threat of secular stagnation has replaced the business cycle as the major problem of economic policy. But even within the framework of secular stagnation, cyclical movements persist. There are still business cycles even though they are fluctuations between bad and worse times rather than between good and bad times.

Very optimistic

Course and phases of the business cycle

If we begin our sketch of the business cycle with the period of expansion that leads into the boom, we find investment going on at a rapid pace. The outlook is optimistic, confidence in the future is firm, the marginal efficiency of capital is high, and employment is rising. The prevailing opinion is that business activity will continue to improve for an indefinite period. Through the multiplier effect, each increment of new investment stimulates consumption to cause a multiple increase in income. As expansion enters the boom stage, the economic forces which tend to lower the marginal efficiency of capital begin to assert themselves. The high marginal efficiency of capital is subjected to pressure from two directions —from increasing costs of production of new capital assets as shortages and bottlenecks of materials and labor develop, and from the increasing abundance of output from recently completed capital assets which tends to lower some yields below expectations. The marginal efficiency of capital remains high only as long as optimism prevails and confidence in the future remains. Ultimately, the belief that high rates of return from new capital assets can continue indefinitely will reveal itself as an illusion. Costs of production continue to rise and output from competing investments continues to flow into the market.

The realities of costs and competition finally triumph over psychological optimism. When this occurs, as it inevitably must, optimism gives way to skepticism and then to pessimism. At this point, the marginal efficiency of capital collapses with a suddenness that may be catastrophic. All of the psychological forces which are so important in the erratic behavior of the stock exchange play a leading role in explaining the fall in the marginal efficiency of capital. As Keynes says, "It is of the nature of organized investment markets . . . that, when disillusion falls upon an over-optimistic and over-bought market, it should fall with sudden and even catastrophic force." (p. 316) [1] Investments which were made in anticipation of six per cent may, as a result of rising costs and falling yields, fall to only two per cent in conditions of high employment. But when over-optimism is replaced by over-pessimism, unemployment spreads, and the investment which would yield two per cent under high employment conditions may yield nothing at all under conditions of widespread unemployment.

The turning point from expansion to contraction is thus explained by a collapse in the marginal efficiency of capital. The change from an upward to a downward tendency takes place suddenly, and in this respect differs from the turning point from contraction to expansion, which occurs more gradually and often imperceptibly. The contraction which follows the collapse of the marginal efficiency of capital is likely to proceed at a rapid pace both because of the multiplier effect and because of a rise in the rate of interest. When investment begins to fall, the multiplier works in reverse. Each dollar of decreased investment multiplies itself into several dollars of decreased income. Employment goes tumbling down as investment falls off. The rate of interest rises because liquidity preference rises. The desire to liquidate inventories as well as securities before prices fall far, the reluctance to buy while prices are falling, and the need for money to meet contractual obligations at a time when sales are falling, all tend to

---

1. *The General Theory of Employment, Interest and Money.* New York, Harcourt, Brace and Co., Inc., 1936.

increase the strength of liquidity preference. The rise in the
rate of interest is reflected in a fall in the prices of securities,
especially bonds, whose yields are fixed in money. When a
long-term bond paying $40 a year, previously selling at
$1000, falls in the market to $800, the market rate of interest
on this type of security has risen from 4 to approximately
5 per cent. Once the rate of interest begins to rise, the expectations of further rises tend to increase still further liquidity
preference for the speculative motive. With everyone wishing
to sell and no one wishing to buy, and with the prices of securities and goods tending to fall precipitously in a beggar-thy-
neighbor fashion, money becomes the safest form of asset in
which to store wealth during the economic crisis.

The collapse of the marginal efficiency of capital is the predominant cause of the crisis. Although many of the same
forces which precipitate the collapse of the marginal efficiency
of capital also raise the rate of interest through their influence upon expectations affecting liquidity preference, the
sharp rise in liquidity preference occurs *after* the marginal
efficiency of capital has collapsed. The rise in liquidity preference leading to a sharp increase in the rate of interest contributes to a further decline in investment and renders the
slump intractable. This increase in the interest rate which
occurs after the onset of the crisis is to be distinguished from
smaller increases which usually take place during the boom
as a result of increases in the demand for money to facilitate
a larger volume of transactions.

The drastic fall in security prices on the stock exchange
which accompanies the collapse of the marginal efficiency of
capital tends to lower the propensity to consume. Equity
holders are less prone to spend on consumption when the
value of their investments is going down than when the value
of their investments is going up. Although the propensity to
consume depends primarily on current income, it is also
influenced by capital gains and capital losses, even though
these may be purely "paper" gains and losses and do not
affect realized income. A man is more likely to feel he can

afford a new automobile each year when his stocks are high and going higher than when his stocks are low and going lower. Keynes suggests that a rising stock market may be essential to a satisfactory propensity to consume in a "stock-minded" country like the United States (p. 319).

Just as the collapse of the marginal efficiency of capital is the predominant cause of contraction in business activity, so its revival is the chief requisite of recovery. Restoration of business confidence is the most important yet the most diffi-cult factor to achieve. After contraction has been under way for a time, it may be possible through proper monetary man-agement to lower the rate of interest, but in the absence of a return of confidence, the marginal efficiency of capital may remain so low that no practicable reduction in the rate of interest can stimulate substantial investment. Even if the rate of interest were to be lowered to zero, business men would not borrow if they had no expectation of making profits.[2]

The interval which must elapse before recovery will set in is conditioned by (1) the time necessary for the wearing out and obsolescence of durable capital, and (2) the time that elapses before excess stocks, which accumulate toward the end of the boom, can be absorbed. Just as the marginal effi-ciency of capital, or rate of profit, is pushed down during expansion by a growing abundance of capital goods, so it will be pushed up during contraction by a growing scarcity of capital goods as a consequence of depreciation and obsoles-cence. Although the length of time is not rigidly determined, it will be related to the average durability of capital assets at the particular stage of economic development of the business cycle in question. Average durability of capital assets will

---

2. It is often argued that a zero rate of interest would lead to an infinite amount of borrowing and by this route to inflation. This conclusion does not follow. If loans are for a finite period and if there is no guarantee that they will be renewed, as is the case in the banking world, there is no reason to assume that a zero rate of interest would have any great stimulating effect in the depths of a severe depression. Investment would not increase as long as the marginal efficiency of capital were less than zero, as it may well be for some time after its collapse. See William J. Fellner, *Monetary Policies and Full Employment,* page 169. Berkeley: University of California Press, 1946.

change over time, and as it changes the length of the period of contraction will tend to change in a corresponding direction.

The length of the contraction period is also conditioned by the time required to absorb excess stocks of goods left over from the boom. When the slump sets in and demand falls, entrepreneurs must choose between selling currently at losses or storing their goods until prices rise again to profitable levels. The latter alternative is conditioned by the carrying costs of stocks of goods. The costs of storage set a limit to the number of months or years over which stocks can profitably be carried. This time interval differs for different types of goods and with the storage facilities of different firms. For the economy as a whole, however, there will be a fairly definite period beyond which the carrying costs of stocks become prohibitive.

During the time that stocks are being depleted, total production may be less than total consumption. The absorption of excess stocks *per se* represents disinvestment or negative investment, which has a depressing effect on employment, just as positive investment has a stimulating effect on employment. If disinvestment through stock absorption is sufficiently widespread and sufficiently rapid, total income may temporarily fall below consumption. Such a situation can be only temporary because effective demand is self-perpetuating at a level where income is equal to consumption, that is, where there is no gap between income and consumption so that no investment is required to fill the gap. When consumption exceeds income, the average propensity to consume is greater than unity. According to the principle of effective demand, income will tend to rise at least to the level at which the average propensity to consume is unity. At any rate, when the absorption process is complete and disinvestment ceases, some improvement in employment will be experienced even though there is no increase in consumption and no positive investment.

The pattern of the cycle is also influenced by changes in the volume of working capital, or goods in process, as distinct from stocks of finished goods. Disinvestment in working capital begins earlier, and reinvestment also begins earlier, than in the case of stocks of finished goods. So far as stocks and their carrying costs are causal influences, Keynes estimates the period of contraction should not as a rule exceed three to five years in a modern industrial economy. Thus, the time required for durable assets to wear out and the time required to absorb surplus stocks together explain the approximate length of time before the marginal efficiency of capital will recover from the collapse it suffers at the end of the boom.

The rate of interest plays a part in the transition from contraction to expansion, although, as in the transition from expansion to contraction, it is secondary in importance to the marginal efficiency of capital. During the period of contraction which prepares the way for the recovery of investment, the rate of interest has a "natural" tendency to fall as a result of the decrease in the quantity of money required for business and income transactions. Even in the absence of a deliberate monetary policy aimed at lowering the rate of interest, the decline in prices and in the number of transactions will make additional funds available to satisfy the demand for money as a store of value. Although liquidity preference for the speculative motive may remain high, the increased quantity of money available to satisfy this motive may be sufficient to lower the rate of interest to a significant extent. The lower rate of interest, combined with a gradual recovery of the marginal efficiency of capital, will in time increase the inducement to invest and cause the expansion phase of the business cycle to set in once again. The length of the boom will be determined, roughly, by the time necessary to produce a sufficient increase in capital assets to cause a break in the marginal efficiency of capital, which leads once again into depression.

The investment multiplier and the trade cycle

A factor in Keynes' theory of the business cycle which is of significance, even though he does not develop it in his chapter on "Notes on the Trade Cycle," is the investment multiplier. As a rule, the investment multiplier falls in the expansion phase of the cycle and rises in the contraction phase. This cyclical change, or perhaps it might more appropriately be called an anti-cyclical change since it moves against the cycle, means that the multiplying power of equal amounts of investment becomes less and less with each further increase in employment and income. Each addition to income and employment becomes more costly in terms of investment. Each higher level of economic activity becomes more difficult to attain than the preceding level in terms of investment. As a multiplier of income, investment gradually weakens until at the peak of the boom it is at its lowest point of efficiency. In contraction, the decline in income and employment is accompanied by a rising multiplier. At each lower level a fall of one dollar in investment will result in a relatively greater fall in income, so that contraction is speeded up in depression by a rising multiplier just as expansion is slowed down in the boom by a falling multiplier. Of course, the multiplier principle works in both directions with equal force at any point in the cycle. In the boom, when the multiplier has a low value, say, of 2, an additional dollar of investment will increase income by only $2, but by the same token, a decrease of $1 in investment will lower income by only $2. In deep depression when the multiplier has a high value, say of 5, a further fall in investment of $1 results in a fall in income of $5; but by the same token, an increase in investment of $1 will lift income by $5. The violence of contraction after the collapse of the marginal efficiency of capital is to be explained by the large absolute amount of fall in investment rather than by a high multiplier value. As business activity dwindles to lower levels, the absolute amount of the fall in investment declines but this tends to be offset by a rising multiplier.

The fall of the multiplier in expansion and its rise in contraction is explained by changes in the propensity to consume. The principle that short-run or cyclical changes in income are

MPS ↑ during a boom
Mult. ↓ during a boom
276   FURTHER APPLICATIONS

accompanied by smaller changes in consumption in the same direction means that as income rises, the absolute size of the gap between income and consumption increases, and as income falls, the absolute size of the gap between income and consumption diminishes. A rise in community income will result in a smaller *proportion* of income being spent for consumption, and a fall in community income will result in a larger *proportion* of income being spent for consumption. As a rule to which there may be exceptions, when community income is high a smaller proportion of *additions* to income will be spent for consumption than when community income is low. When income is high, the community will spend a lesser proportion of its total income and also a lesser proportion of additions to its income than when income is at a low level. This indicates a declining average and a declining marginal propensity to consume. In terms of saving, in contrast to consumption, the rule is that the community will save a larger proportion of its income and a larger proportion of additions to income in a boom than in a depression. The multiplier, being equal to the reciprocal of the marginal propensity to save, will therefore tend to be lower in a boom when income is high, than in a depression when income is low. If, for example, the marginal propensity to save is ½ in the boom, the multiplier will be only 2, whereas if in the bottom of a depression the marginal propensity to save is only ⅕, the multiplier will be 5. Therefore, in the boom an additional dollar of investment will increase income by only $2, whereas in the depths of depression a dollar of investment will increase income by $5. In the boom, the amount of investment necessary to maintain a high level of employment will be large both in the absolute sense and also in the relative sense that an additional dollar of investment will support only $2 of increased income. In depression, a relatively small amount of investment may be capable of keeping income at a level considerably above consumption, because each dollar of additional investment will stimulate a $5 increase in income.

Although in depression a relatively small investment is capable of keeping income at a level considerably above consumption, it is also true that a small fall in investment leads to a relatively large fall in income—in the above example a fall of $1 in investment leads to a $5 fall in income. Once contraction begins and investment continues to fall, perhaps until it reaches zero or even less, and the multiplier increases in size, what is there to prevent employment from falling until no one is employed? The answer, of course, is the principle of effective demand. Although the multiplier grows in size, the total or absolute dependence of employment upon investment becomes less and less as income falls. Since income falls faster than consumption, the absolute size of the gap between them becomes smaller and smaller until at some point considerably below full employment but also considerably above zero employment, the gap disappears entirely. Income falls to equality with consumption, and may temporarily fall below consumption. At or below the point where income equals consumption, no investment is required to stabilize the level of income. This is the level of basic national income at which supply does create its own demand and which is self-sustaining without investment. Here employment is stabilized and will rest indefinitely until investment revives and begins to lift it upward once again. Hence Keynes' theory of effective demand and the multiplier principle derived from it explain both the instability which characterizes the business cycle and also the limits of the instability.

Keynes' theory vs. overinvestment and underconsumption theories of the cycle

In a strict sense Keynes' theory of the business cycle is neither an overinvestment nor an underconsumption theory, although it has much more in common with the latter than with the former. Most underconsumption theories of the cycle explain underconsumption in terms of previous overinvestment which releases a flood of goods so great than consumer demand is incapable of absorbing them. As long as the point of reference is full employment, overinvestment and underconsumption amount to the same thing. Strange as it may seem, the starting point of many explanations of the business cycle is full employment so that many underconsumption theories are also overinvestment theories. If overinvestment were the true cause of the business cycle, the remedy for a slump would be to raise the rate of interest in order to check excessive investment during the boom. Keynes, however, is opposed to raising the rate of interest for the purpose of checking investment during expansion. He suggests a depression can best be avoided if the boom is perpetuated by creating conditions which will maintain a high rate of investment. During booms there develop maladjustments which should not be perpetuated, but, broadly speaking, the fault of the economic system is not too much investment but too little. Investment can be increased by lowering and not by raising the rate of interest. Investment of the right type should continue without interruption until capital assets cease to be scarce and their rate of return is reduced to zero. Keynes calls this the point of "full investment." Only beyond the point of full investment would "overinvestment" have any definite meaning. It would mean that additional investment would lower the marginal efficiency of capital to a negative rate. Since there would be no incentive to invest at losses, net investment would cease at the point of "full investment."

Keynes agrees with the underconsumptionists that an unequal distribution of income contributes to an inadequate demand for consumption goods and services, but he disagrees with their view that depression is caused by an oversupply of consumer goods flowing from previous overinvestment. The fault of most underconsumption theories lies in placing the blame for depression and unemployment on savings which are invested, whereas stress should be placed on potential savings which are not realized because of lack of investment. The fault is more one of underinvestment than of overinvestment. Keynes recommends attacking unemployment along two fronts—by increasing consumption and investment simultaneously.

Keynes' stress on underinvestment rather than underconsumption is associated with his conservative attitude toward economic reform He recognizes that the need for more investment grows out of the limited ability to consume which, in part at least, grows out of the concentration of income in capitalistic society. Socialistically inclined underconsumption theorists like John A. Hobson believe the remedy for unemployment lies in increasing the propensity to consume through a reconstruction of the economic system, whereas Keynes accepts the existing social structure and the accompanying distribution of income and advocates making up for the deficiency in consumer demand by increasing investment demand. Keynes apparently feels that when the point of "full investment" in his sense is reached, the redistribution of income will have automatically been taken care of because the reward for owning as such will have disappeared in a process he calls the "euthanasia of the rentier." Keynes recognizes there is a strong case for redistributing income in a manner which will increase the propensity to consume before the point of "full investment" is reached, but this suggestion is incidental rather than central and is not implemented in his theoretical apparatus.

International Economic Relations

Long before Keynes wrote *The General Theory of Employment, Interest and Money,* he was one of the leading critics of conventional views on monetary problems in the international as well as in the domestic field. Nearly all of Keynes' writings are filled with direct and indirect applications of his theories to international economic relations. The *General Theory* is more concerned with domestic than with international economics, but even this work has significant applications to international economic theory and policy. A few of these applications are developed in Chapter 23 of the *General*

Theory and others are elaborated elsewhere in his writings, especially in connection with his participation in the formation of the International Monetary Fund and the International Bank for Reconstruction and Development. Keynes was the chief author of the British plan for an International Clearing Union, which was later integrated with the American plan at Bretton Woods to form the Fund and the Bank.

The favorable balance of trade as investment

Since the time of Adam Smith, nearly all academic economists have been severe critics of what they regard as the "fallacies" of mercantilism. Keynes' criticisms of the classical theory lead quite naturally to a sympathetic attitude toward many mercantilistic ideas which economists have regarded as long since dead and buried. Although it would be misleading to call Keynes a "mercantilist," his position on some important issues is much nearer the mercantilist than the classical position.

A cardinal principle of mercantilism was high esteem for a "favorable balance of trade," by which was meant an excess of exports of goods and services over imports of goods and services. To the mercantilists, a favorable balance of trade was a technique whereby an individual nation sold more than it purchased abroad in order that it might collect the difference, or "balance," in gold and silver. Precious metals were regarded as a particularly desirable form of wealth. For nations which did not mine gold and silver within their borders, the businesslike method of acquiring them was to sell more goods than were bought in order that the balance could be collected in money, that is, in gold and silver. Classical economics teaches that the idea of a favorable balance of trade and the desire for large stores of precious metals are irrational and illusory. According to classical doctrine, gold and silver are not true wealth and it is irrational to attempt to accumulate large supplies of them. It is also irrational to want to send more goods out of the country than are brought into the country, since this leaves the nation poorer in real wealth. The so-called favorable balance of trade is an illusory technique for obtaining gold and silver except for a brief period, because the importation of precious metals increases the quantity of money within the domestic economy and, by causing prices to rise, renders the domestic economy a less favorable market in which to buy. With prices at a higher level as a result of the increase in the quantity of money, foreigners will buy less and some domestic buyers who previously purchased at home will be driven to purchase abroad because of higher domestic prices and lower foreign prices. The lower foreign prices result from the unfavorable balance of trade of countries sending gold and silver to the home country. The precious metals, which for a time flow into the domestic economy, will set in motion price movements that will cause them to flow out of the country again.

Keynes finds considerable merit in the mercantilist theory of the favorable balance of trade and points out important fallacies in the classical argument. The favorable balance of trade is desirable from the view of maintaining employment because to the domestic economy it represents a form of investment. As the *General Theory* shows, domestic employment can be maintained by a high rate of investment, which may be either domestic or foreign. The current rate of foreign investment is determined by the excess of exports over imports, that is, by the size of the favorable balance of trade. An increase in the favorable balance, either in the form of increased exports or of decreased imports, increases employment in the same way domestic investment increases employment. The multiplier effect and all the rest work in the same manner for foreign as for domestic investment. The total investment of a nation is the excess of its production over current domestic consumption. So far as the employment-creating effects are concerned, it does not matter what form the exports take. They may all be goods for current consumption by foreigners, or they may be capital goods which will be used for building up the productive capacity of the foreign

nation. The excess of exports over imports, which is investment from the domestic point of view regardless of their
form, may represent from the world point of view either consumption or investment. The foregoing chapters have emphasized repeatedly that, given the propensity to consume, the
maintenance of employment depends upon the volume of investment. Employment can increase only if there is an increase in investment. If there is unemployment at home, an
increase in the size of the favorable balance of trade represents new investment to the nation in question and will, like
domestic investment, increase income not only by the amount
of investment but by some multiple of it, depending upon
the size of the multiplier. A high rate of investment has always been a necessary condition for the successful functioning of capitalist economies. Hence, any policy which tends
to promote investment is desirable in capitalistic economies.
The mercantilists, who wrote during the period of early capitalism, were therefore fundamentally correct in their insight
which led them to advocate a favorable balance of trade.

A favorable balance of trade works in yet another way to
promote domestic employment. The importation of precious
metals resulting from the favorable balance increases the
domestic quantity of money, lowers the rate of interest at
home, and stimulates a larger volume of domestic investment.
During early capitalism when the money supply was more
closely tied to gold and silver, the importation of precious
metals had a greater influence upon the rate of interest than
would be true under the managed currencies of contemporary
capitalism. In so far as unemployment was a threat during
early capitalism—which it was to some extent—and in the
absence of positive measures to prevent it, there was merit in
the mercantilistic desire to attain a favorable balance of
trade.

Keynes' sympathetic treatment of mercantilist theories does
not mean he advocates a return to the policies historically
associated with these ideas. He does show, however, that the
practical statesmanship of the mercantilists did not rest on

fallacious reasoning but upon shrewd insights into the functioning of the economic system which they sought to guide. In order to promote the favorable balance of trade, they resorted to export restrictions and, more important, to import restrictions like protective tariffs. In the mercantilist period these trade restrictions may have been the most effective means for realizing a favorable balance, but Keynes points out that export and import controls are not necessarily the best means for achieving a large favorable balance of trade and a high level of domestic employment. During the nineteenth century, for example, he suggests that complete freedom of trade was the policy best designed to promote a maximum balance of trade for England. Thus, the British advocates of free trade in the nineteenth century were not necessarily less nationalistic in their outlook than the mercantilists. Nevertheless, the mercantilist perspective was such as to overlook many of the advantages of an international division of labor. Protectionism may yield advantages to some nations, but it is much less likely to benefit the world as a whole than free trade.

Free trade vs. protectionism

New light is shed upon the controversy of free trade versus protectionism by Keynes' *General Theory*. The traditional case for free trade proves too much because it ignores unemployment. If it is true that employment depends on effective demand, as Keynes contends, and that effective demand may be inadequate to provide full employment, then it is quite possible for a single nation to increase its employment through a system of protective tariffs, and in this manner to increase the demand for domestic labor at the expense of foreign labor. Only if full employment is assumed, does the conclusion necessarily follow that a country will be better off if it buys abroad whatever it can purchase more cheaply than it can produce at home. Then real wages and other forms of income will be maximized because incomes are proportional to productivity and productivity is maximized when each country produces those items in which it enjoys the

greatest comparative advantage, exchanging surpluses of
these commodities to other countries for the things in which
other countries have the greatest comparative advantage. Like
all classical theory, this argument for free trade is based on
the assumption of full employment. Where full and continuous employment prevails, there is little doubt concerning the
validity of the free trade argument. Under full employment,
real national income is maximized when unit costs of production are minimized, as they are under free trade. An industry
requires protection only if it is less efficient than the same
industry in some other country. Hence, protection interferes
with the most economical use of national and world resources.
Protection causes productivity to be less and real income to
be less than they would be if each nation produced those
things for which its resources are best suited under conditions of free world trade. Under protectionism, the national
income may be greater than under free trade because of a
higher level of employment resulting from a higher level of
effective demand. The wastes of unemployment may out-
weigh the wastes of a poor allocation of resources. The alternative to employing workmen less .efficiently under protectionism may be no employment at all. Of course, the higher
unit costs of production are in themselves a national disadvantage to be weighed against the advantages of greater employment. From the viewpoint of a single country, the question of tariffs is simply which of these two counteracting tendencies will yield the larger real national income. Protection
is more likely to increase real national income in periods of
large-scale unemployment than in periods of small-scale unemployment. As in all cases where Keynes' theory challenges
the conclusions of classical theory, the key to the whole matter is his assumption of less than full employment. There is
no inconsistency, except in the different assumptions, between
the theory which justifies free trade under conditions of full
employment, on the one hand, and on the other hand the
theory which justifies, under conditions of less than full employment, protective tariffs as a means to increasing national

welfare by raising employment and real national income.

The strongest case against protective tariffs in a world of unemployment is that they, like mercantilistic policies in general, are nationalistic. Benefits to one nation are gained at the expense of other nations. If protective tariffs increase employment in one country, they do so at the price of increased unemployment in other countries. Although a favorable balance of trade is equivalent to investment for the nation which exports more than it imports, for the world as a whole, it does not represent investment. World exports must equal world imports, which means that the excess of exports from some nations is offset by an excess of imports to the rest of the nations of the world. All nations cannot export more than they import and thus all cannot enjoy the benefits of a favorable balance of trade. Increases in employment which result from the favorable balance in one nation may be matched by decreases in employment in other nations of the world.

Foreign Exchange Stabilization

The international gold standard, which was closely associated with classical economic theory and its general laissez-faire attitude toward economic policy, was one of the earliest objects of criticism by Keynes. In his first book, *Indian Currency and Finance* (1913), he compared the conventional gold standard unfavorably with the gold exchange standard. In the *Tract on Monetary Reform* (1923), Keynes advocated a managed currency which he thought would permit a greater stability of the domestic price level than could be achieved under the gold standard, combined with short-term stability and long-run flexibility of foreign exchange rates. Keynes remained a relentless critic of orthodoxy in foreign exchange policy, and finally toward the end of his career, when his views on gold became generally accepted, he saw the objective outlined in his *Tract* realized in the International Monetary Fund set up at Bretton Woods.

Criticism of the international gold standard

The great fault of the international gold standard, as it operated after the first world war, was that it tended to cause deflation and unemployment in countries with an excess of imports over exports. During the 1920's England returned to the gold standard at a subsequent cost that was to prove more than she could bear, and in 1931 gold was abandoned after doing great harm to the world and to the British economy. A gold standard requires that a nation, usually through its monetary authority, stand ready to buy and to sell gold at a price fixed in terms of its domestic currency. When a nation is importing more goods than it is exporting, gold tends to go abroad to offset the unfavorable balance of trade. If the deficit in exports continues for a time, a wholesale loss of gold can be prevented only if the monetary authority takes positive steps to protect the national stock of gold. The theory of the gold standard is that the drain on gold will cause prices to fall in the deficit nation, and the influx of gold will cause prices to rise in the country with a surplus of exports. By virtue of flexible domestic prices, the country exporting gold becomes a better place in which to buy and the country importing gold a less favorable place in which to buy. The result, according to theory, is a reversal of the flow of goods and the flow of gold.

In the 1920's, when gold was flowing into the United States and out of Britain at an unprecedented rate, American prices did not rise as they should have for the automatic gold standard adjustments to take place. The failure of American prices to rise was partly because the American monetary authority, the Federal Reserve System, was fearful of the effects of rising prices and so did not allow imported gold to be used as a basis for credit expansion, and partly because there was a lesser connection between gold stocks and domestic prices than the gold standard theory takes for granted. Probably the latter was much the more important reason. In Britain, domestic prices did not fall according to the postulates of the gold standard, partly because of inflexible wages and prices, and partly because of a decreasing connection between gold stocks and domestic prices. Hence, the "automatic" adjustments presupposed in the traditional theory of the gold standard were missing. Instead of lower prices, Britain got unemployment. In order to protect the nation's declining gold stocks, the British bank rate was raised to attract foreign lending to London and to discourage foreign lending by Englishmen. An increase in the bank rate meant an increase in the domestic rate of interest, which in turn led to a fall in domestic investment, income, and employment. As domestic incomes fell, the demand for imports fell because people at home had less money to spend abroad. As a result, the unfavorable balance of trade was reduced. In England, as imports fell in relation to exports, the foreign exchange rate rose because the demand for foreign currencies (dollars) in relation to the home currency (pounds) was reduced. Less foreign currency was needed to settle the fewer purchases being made abroad.

To rescue the gold standard in a deficit nation under modern conditions means to sacrifice control of the domestic rate of interest; it means a reduction in investment, employment, and income via high interest rates; it means deflation at home, which, among other things, involves an attempt to lower costs in home industries to the point where they will be able to compete on favorable terms in foreign markets; it means pressure to reduce wage rates as a means for getting lower costs of production, and lower wage rates are resisted by organized labor; it probably means industrial strife, strikes, and interrupted production. After all these painful adjustments, the gold standard may be saved but at a price which no nation can afford to pay. Keynes concluded early in the 'twenties that unemployment and deflation, the inevitable consequences of the gold standard in a nation in Britain's position at that time, were evils which far outweighed the advantages of the gold standard.

Proposal for exchange stability
without the gold standard

Nevertheless, an undeniable advantage of the gold standard is the stability of exchange rates among gold standard countries. Stable foreign exchange rates encourage international trade by enabling those who buy from foreigners and those who sell to foreigners to know how much they will have to pay and how much they will receive in terms of their own domestic currency. Imports must be paid for in money acceptable to foreign sellers, and exports are sold to foreigners whose foreign currency must be converted into currency acceptable to the domestic sellers. Unstable exchange rates add unnecessarily to the risks of international trading. The leading problem of international finance is how to preserve the stability of foreign exchange rates, which the international gold standard did provide, without subjecting domestic economies, especially those which are importing more than they are exporting, to the ravages of unemployment and deflation which result from the high interest rate required to make the gold standard work. During the inter-war years after the breakdown of the gold standard throughout the world, there developed a hodge-podge of exchange controls, quota systems, blocked currencies, and barter agreements. These stop-gap measures are clearly unsatisfactory in a well-ordered world economy. They sacrifice many of the economic gains from an international division of labor because nations which sell under bilateral agreements are unable to buy except from the country to which they sell, and often what they might want from these countries is not available to them. To escape from these evils as well as from the ill effects of the gold standard on domestic stability, yet to gain short-term stability and long-term flexibility of foreign exchange rates, was the purpose of Keynes' proposal for an International Clearing Union. This proposal was made by the British Government in 1943 while Keynes was serving as a special adviser to the British Treasury.

In describing to the House of Lords the official British

proposal for the International Clearing Union, a plan of which he was the chief but not the exclusive author, Keynes summarized the main purpose as follows: "The principal object can be explained in a single sentence: To provide that money earned by selling goods to one country can be spent on purchasing the products of any other country. In jargon, a system of multilateral clearing. In English, a universal currency valid for trade transactions in all the world. Everything else in the plan is ancillary to that."[3] When a British textile manufacturer pays for cotton purchased in the United States, the American seller does not necessarily wish to use the proceeds of his sale to buy things from England. Nor does any other American necessarily wish to buy British goods. In so far as Americans wish to buy abroad at all, they may wish to offset the sale of cotton to Britain by the purchase of coffee from Brazil or natural rubber from the Netherlands Indies or by some combination of such purchases of imports. It is prerequisite to the widest international division of labor that Americans be able to use their foreign exchange secured from cotton sales to Britain to purchase wherever and whatever they wish. Under the International Clearing Union, the pounds paid by British buyers of American cotton would be converted into an international form of money known as "bancor" and credited to the account of the United States, which could then spend it for goods and services anywhere in the world. Every nation would have an account in "bancor" which would be debited or credited whenever purchases or sales were made in international trade. Individual countries' accounts would be cancelled against each other and the remaining balances cleared through the International Clearing Union. The clearing technique which has so long been part of domestic banking facilities was to be carried over into the field of international financial relations.

The Keynes plan for an International Clearing Union was, like all of Keynes' peacetime programs, expansionist in na-

---

3. *Parliamentary Debates on an International Clearing Union,* House of Lords, page 76. May 18, 1943, British Information Service.

ture. It provided for the establishment of large initial credits of the new international money, "bancor," which credits were in the nature of overdraft facilities so familiar in British banking. The amount of the initial credit alloted to each nation was based on the volume of foreign trade before the war. In contrast with the American or White Plan, the plan actually adopted at Bretton Woods, the Keynes plan called for no contribution of gold to the International Fund. However, gold was not completely ignored in the Keynes plan because the new international money, "bancor," could be purchased with gold even though it could not be converted into gold. Thus, countries with large stocks of gold or countries which mine large quantities of gold would not suffer from its demonitization.

One of the merits claimed by Keynes for the International Clearing Union was that it would get around the difficulty caused when some nations export without importing to an equal extent. Under the gold standard, gold flowed to the nations with a favorable balance of trade and thereafter the gold was removed from circulation so far as world trade was concerned. Between the two world wars, most of the world's monetary gold came into the possession of the United States, only to be buried under the ground at Fort Knox, Kentucky. This represented a form of international hoarding which did not decrease the total amount of money actually held but did reduce the amount in active circulation and reduced the effective demand for goods and services.

The failure of a strong exporting nation, e.g., the United States, to make use of its balance represents a fall in effective demand in world trade. It represents sales which are not followed by purchases. Under the Clearing Union, a nation exporting more goods and services than it imports could use its balance only to purchase goods from some other countries. Its balance could not be converted into gold for hoarding. Keynes believed one of the novel features of his plan was its attempt to mitigate international hoarding, to free in the international field the effective demand which tended to get locked up in buried gold. However, his plan was only a beginning and the measures in this respect were relatively mild. Nations which sold and refused to buy would find themselves with growing idle balances of "bancor" which they could not withdraw or convert into gold. They would be exposed to the world and to themselves as guilty of anti-social behavior. Keynes felt that moral pressures as well as enlightened self-interest would lead the offending creditor nations to take corrective steps to increase their international purchases and thereby reduce their unused balances. He said to the House of Lords: "We have lately come to understand more clearly than before how employment and the creation of new incomes out of new production can only be maintained through the expenditure on goods and services of the income previously earned. This is equally true of home trade and of foreign trade."[4] Keynes was striving to carry over into international economics the principles of effective demand outlined in his *General Theory* for domestic economics.

The International Clearing Union was more than an attempt to extend the principles of the general theory of employment to the field of international economic relations. It represents a natural and necessary complement to the closed-economy economics of the *General Theory*. The International Clearing Union, as well as the International Monetary Fund which was actually established, was intended to integrate domestic economic systems into the international economy without sacrificing domestic stability. The traditional gold standard integrated domestic economic systems into the international economy at the price of domestic stability, caused by high interest rates, depressed investment, unstable prices, and unemployment. The International Clearing Union retained the one chief virtue of the gold standard—short-term stability of foreign exchange rates—in a manner consistent with the domestic stabilization of employment at a high level by means of low interest rates, stable domestic price levels, and such other measures as public investment, et cetera

4. *Ibid.*, page 77.

Plan had short-term stability and long-term flexibility.

which may be required for the purpose. In the long run, the Keynes plan allowed for flexibility in foreign exchange rates to the degree necessary to adjust to long-term changes in the relation of the domestic to the international economy. This adjustment was to be one of changing the external value of the domestic currency to coincide with its domestic value, rather than making the adjustment the other way around, as required under the international gold standard.

References for Further Reading

Keynes, J. M., *The General Theory of Employment, Interest and Money*, Chapters 22 and 23. Also Chapters 11 and 12. New York: Harcourt, Brace and Company, 1936.

———, *Monetary Reform*, especially Chapter III on "The Theory of Money and of the Foreign Exchanges." New York: Harcourt, Brace and Company, 1924.

———, *A Treatise on Money*, especially Books IV, VI, and VII. New York: Harcourt, Brace and Company, 1930.

———, "The Balance of Payments of the United States," *The Economic Journal*, June, 1946, Vol. LVI, pages 172-187.

———, "The Objective of International Price Stability," *The Economic Journal*, June-September, 1943, Vol. LIII, pages 185-187.

———, "The International Clearing Union," A speech delivered by Keynes before the House of Lords, May 23, 1944. Reprinted in *The New Economics*, edited by S. E. Harris, pages 359-368. New York: Alfred A. Knopf, 1947.

———, "The International Monetary Fund," A speech delivered by Keynes before the House of Lords, May 23, 1944. Reprinted in *The New Economics*, edited by S. E. Harris, pages 369-379. New York: Alfred A. Knopf, 1947.

Angell, J. W., *Investment and Business Cycles*. New York: McGraw-Hill Book Company, Inc., 1941.

Harrod, R. F., *The Trade Cycle*. London: Oxford Press, 1936.

Kaldor, Nicholas, "A Model of the Trade Cycle," *The Economic Journal*, March, 1940, Vol. L, pages 78-92.

Kalecki, Michal, *Essays in the Theory of Economic Fluctuations*. New York: Farrar and Rinehart, Inc., 1939.

Lerner, A. P., *The Economics of Control*, Chapter 23 on business cycles and Chapters 26, 27, and 28 on foreign trade. New York: The Macmillan Company, 1944.

Metzler, L. A., "Keynes and the Theory of Business Cycles," in *The New Economics*, edited by S. E. Harris, Chapter XXXIII, pages 436-449. New York: Alfred A. Knopf, 1947.

Robinson, Joan, "The International Currency Proposals," *The Economic Journal,* June-September, 1943, Vol. LIII, pages 161-175.

Williams, John H., *Postwar Monetary Plans and Other Essays.* Third Edition. New York: Alfred A. Knopf, 1947.

CHAPTER 12

The Development of Keynes' Thought and the Social Philosophy Toward Which It Leads

> Whilst, therefore, the enlargement of the functions of government, involved in the task of adjusting to one another the propensity to consume and the inducement to invest, would seem to a nineteenth-century publicist or to a contemporary American financier to be a terrific encroachment on individualism, I defend it, on the contrary, both as the only practicable means of avoiding the destruction of existing economic forms in their entirety and as the condition of the successful functioning of individual initiative.
>
> J. M. Keynes, *The General Theory of Employment, Interest and Money*, page 380.*

THE FOREGOING chapters have dealt almost exclusively with Keynes' *The General Theory of Employment, Interest and Money*. This work, which was published in 1936 when Keynes was fifty-two years of age, marks the breaking point with the classical school and the working out of a system of economic theory along anti-classical lines. Preceding this event, Keynes had been an adherent of the general classical tradition. While his break with the classical school may appear to have been

---

* Harcourt, Brace and Co., Inc., 1936.

quite sudden, his earlier writing and thinking contain many elements of his later position. In the present chapter an attempt is made to trace the gradual development of Keynes' thought during the period in which he accepted the classical theory and to show why, after so many years, he changed to the unorthodox position which is presented in the *General Theory* and outlined in the preceding chapters.

There was nothing capricious or fortuitous about Keynes' break with the classical tradition. It grew out of long experience from which there developed gradually the conviction that classical economics is inadequate to deal with the pressing problems of contemporary economic society. The practical implications of classical economics are essentially laissez-faire, and laissez-faire was dying during the first world war and the years which followed. Keynes wrote a tract called *The End of Laissez-Faire* in 1926. Since his theory was always geared to policy, the logical outcome of the conviction that laissez-faire was dead must have led rather surely in time to the further conviction that classical economics as an adequate system of thought was also dead. To develop a systematic body of theory to replace the classical principles required time. The formative period of the *General Theory* was the decade or more prior to its publication, when it became apparent that England would not make a full recovery from the primary postwar depression. The *Treatise on Money* (1930) is in this sense a transitional work, but the real break with the classical theory came after the *Treatise* and culminates in the *General Theory*. Yet, in a broader sense, Keynes' formative period begins with his very first writing, which contains criticisms of orthodox economics. The main question to be answered is why such a book as the *General Theory* came to be written. This involves the forces at work in the environment, and the reaction of Keynes to these forces. If the *General Theory* is a great work, as surely it is, the answer to this question of why it was written must enrich our appreciation of its meaning and influence. This task might have been performed before the general theory itself was explained, but it was felt that the story of its development would have greater significance if the reader first knew what the final outcome of this process of development was to be. While this procedure would not be desirable in mystery thrillers, it seems the best approach to a solid body of economic thought.

A word should be inserted concerning the nature of Keynes' challenge to traditional economics. He has not questioned the method or the scope of classical Anglo-Saxon economics. His challenge is rather to the content, that is, the assumptions, of the classical doctrine. As previously indicated, Keynes contends that his theory is a *general* theory of employment of resources, whereas the classical theory pertains only to a special case, the case of full employment. Critics of the classical conception of the appropriate method and scope of economics will not find Keynes' general theory satisfactory, even though they may feel it is an improvement over the classical position. However, if the matter is viewed pragmatically, in a manner which takes as fundamental the relation between theory and policy, Keynes' new departure has been quite as useful in challenging the old tenets of economic policy as a challenge directed at method and scope could have been. It seems clear that the greatness of Keynes' work lies in its impact on economic policy.

Development Prior to the Great Depression

The general thesis of the following discussion is that Keynes changed from a classical to an anti-classical economic theorist because of a change in his ideas about economic policy. His anti-classical economic theory is derived from his practical position, which may be characterized as an attack on financial capitalism and a defense of industrial capitalism.

The framework of interpretation for this thesis attributes to Keynes a dualism between the financial and the industrial aspects of modern capitalism. The terms "financial" and "industrial" capitalism are not used by Keynes, but they may be approximately identified with his distinction between "finance" and "industry" or between "financial circulation" and "industrial circulation," as he employs these categories in his *Treatise on Money*. Keynes defines "finance" as "the business of holding and exchanging existing titles to wealth, . . . including Stock Exchange and Money Market transactions, speculation and the process of conveying current savings and profits into the hands of entrepreneurs." He defines "industry" as "the business of maintaining the normal process of current output, distribution and exchange and paying the factors of production their incomes for the various duties which they perform from the first beginning of production to the final satisfaction of the consumer."[1] In the *General Theory*, the dichotomy between "industry" and "finance" reappears in the form of the distinction between M_1, or money held to satisfy the transactions and precautionary motives (industry), and M_2, or money held to satisfy the speculative motive (finance).

As long as Keynes remained an adherent of the general classical tradition and was preoccupied with short-run monetary problems, he had no occasion to develop a theory of capitalism. In his later thinking, however, he began to question aspects of the fundamental structure of capitalism, even to the point of foreseeing as a condition of its survival the disappearance of all rentier capitalism. In these later writings, especially the *General Theory*, the ever-present distinction between "finance" and "industry" became the framework for his fragmentary theory of capitalism. Even in these later stages of his thought, Keynes did not develop a theory of capitalism in the self-conscious sense in which Werner Sombart, or Karl Marx, or Thorstein Veblen developed theories of capitalism. The chief task of the present section is to trace the development of Keynes' early thinking in terms of the distinction between "finance" and "industry."

Keynes was not the cloistered scholar that many, if not most, of his fellow economists have been. In his preoccupa-

---

1. *Treatise on Money*, Vol. I, Chap. XV, "The Industrial Circulation and the Financial Circulation," page 243. New York: Harcourt, Brace and Company, Inc., 1930.

tion with the world of affairs as well as with the world of theory, he found it necessary to divorce himself from the orthodox tradition and, in the process of estrangement, was led to a position which has long and interesting antecedents. This is, as Keynes partly recognized, the tradition of the monetary heretics such as Silvio Gesell, Proudhon, the Ricardian socialists, the mercantilists, and even of the canonists, with their strictures against taking interest.[2]

Keynes' early opposition to orthodox *monetary* theory is evident in his first important publication, *Indian Currency and Finance* (1913).[3] This work was essentially an attack on the report of the British Fowler Committee of 1898, which had recommended the adoption of the gold standard for India.[4] Though *Indian Currency and Finance* is for the most part a technical treatment of a special problem, Keynes draws certain conclusions which have terms of reference much broader than the problem of Indian currency and finance. He was impressed by the uneconomic consequences to India of her propensity to hoard great stores of gold and silver. At the time (1913), the price levels of western Europe were being prevented from a rapid increase only because India—the "sink of precious metals"—was absorbing large amounts of gold which were flowing in great quantities from newly opened mines, especially those of South Africa, where production had just reached its zenith. Consequently, the gold standard was not working so badly in Europe. However, Keynes warned Europe not to continue to leave "the most intimate adjustments of our economic organism at the mercy of a lucky prospector, a new chemical process, or a change of ideas in Asia."[5] These ideas regarding Indian currency and finance foreshadow Keynes' later stress on hoarding as a

2. "A Self-Adjusting Economic System?" *The New Republic*, February 20, 1935, Vol. LXXXII, No. 1055, page 35.

3. London: Macmillan and Company, Ltd., 1913. See especially page 99.

4. See *Report of the Royal Commission on Indian Currency and Finance*, Vol. I. London: His Majesty's Stationery Office, 1926.

5. *Indian Currency and Finance*, page 101.

brake on economic progress and on his preference for a managed currency instead of the "automatic" gold standard.

In *The Economic Consequences of the Peace* (1920), Keynes' chapter on "Europe Before the War" has particular significance for any study of his subsequent economic writings because here he sketches his long-view perspective of the capitalist process. His emphasis is upon the underlying instability of the outwardly placid currents of European capitalism before the war, a war which "had so shaken this system as to endanger the life of Europe altogether."[6] In numerous passages, Keynes expresses a skepticism which suggests a starting point for the rather far-reaching changes in social relations called for by the program of the *General Theory*. The relations between the laboring and capitalist classes are portrayed as a game of deception and of double bluff, designed to attain the maximum accumulation of capital, but resting on a psychological base so unstable that it might crumble if either the laboring class or the capitalist class should cease to be satisfied with a rate of consumption very small in comparison with the creation of wealth:

It was not natural for a population, of whom so few enjoyed the comforts of life, to accumulate so hugely. The war has disclosed the possibility of consumption to all and the vanity of abstinence to many. Thus the bluff is discovered; the laboring classes may be no longer willing to forego so largely, and the capitalist classes, no longer confident of the future, may seek to enjoy more fully their liberties of consumption so long as they last, and thus precipitate the hour of their confiscation.[7]

The laboring class did not consume more because its members received rights to only a small share of the national dividend. The capitalist class preferred the enjoyment of the power of accumulated wealth to the enjoyment of consumption on a large scale. "It was precisely the *inequality* of the distribution of wealth," Keynes wrote, "which made possible those vast accumulations of fixed wealth and of capital im-

---

6. Page 25. New York: Harcourt, Brace and Howe, 1920.
7. *Economic Consequences of the Peace*, page 22.

provements which distinguished that age from all others. Herein lay, in fact, the main justification of the Capitalist System."[8] Whether the laboring class would be satisfied with its lot and whether, in the light of uncertainty, the capitalist class would continue to venture its capital were crucial issues. Keynes never embraced capitalism wholeheartedly. He favored it because "Capitalism, wisely managed, can probably be made more efficient than any alternative system." But capitalism "in itself is in many ways extremely objectionable."[9]

Whereas exercise of the duty of "saving" by the capitalist class, coupled with inequality of wealth and income, yielded maximum accumulation in pre-1914 Europe, such saving was, on the whole, irrational:

> The duty of "saving" became nine-tenths of virtue and the growth of the cake the object of true religion . . . the cake increased; but to what end was not clearly contemplated. . . . Saving was for old age or for your children; but this was only in theory,—the virtue of the cake was that it was never to be consumed, neither by you nor by your children after you.[10]

This passage is interesting because, like the *General Theory,* it attacks thrift as an irrational type of behavior. It also stresses the importance of habit in influencing the propensity to save, and thus contrasts with the view that interest is the reward for saving. Keynes' subsequent refutation of the classical theory of interest rests on his repudiation of the idea that interest is a reward for saving, or for waiting, or for abstinence.

Following publication of *Economic Consequences of the Peace,* Keynes plunged into some of the most important postwar European controversies on economic policy. During the decade of the 'twenties he was concerned primarily with three problems: an appeal for reduction of war debts, reparations, and debt service; opposition to postwar deflationary tenden-

---

8. *Ibid.,* page 19.

9. *Laissez-faire and Communism,* pages 76-77. New York: New Republic, 1926.

10. *Economic Consequences of the Peace,* page 20.

cies in Britain; and opposition to the return to the gold standard. In the Preface to a collection of his more important miscellaneous writings of the 1920's, Keynes characterized his general attitude toward these, and all other similar issues, as "the profound conviction that the Economic Problem of want and poverty and the economic struggle between classes and nations is nothing but a frightful muddle, a transitory and an *unnecessary* muddle."[11] Here we see the liberal mind at work attempting to reconcile the grave issues of the day. Liberalism as a habit of mind tends to impute evil to wrong thinking rather than to irreconcilable conflicts embedded in the structure of society. This thesis that ideas are more powerful than vested interests and that by changing our minds we can change the world recurs frequently in Keynes' writings, for example, in the closing paragraph of the *General Theory*. So we find Keynes always ready with a plan, a compromise, or an amendment for resolving the problem at hand.

In the huge war debts, Keynes saw a menace to stability everywhere. As remedies, he suggested that the German cash reparations be reduced to a low figure ($10 billion) and that the interallied war debts and interest thereon be cancelled.[12] If carried out, his recommendations would have involved immediate recognition of a large national "sacrifice" by the United States and to a lesser extent by Great Britain. However, he believed the reparations and war debts among nations could not and would not be paid under any circumstances likely to exist, and therefore it was better to recognize this in advance than to suffer political and economic instability only to come out with the same result on debts in the end, default and *de facto* cancellation. The artificial financial transactions arising from war debts and reparations would, he predicted in 1920, react adversely upon the prosperity of industry.

By 1930, Keynes saw his 1920 predictions concerning war debts verified. The huge international transfers arising from

---

11. *Essays in Persuasion*, page vii. New York: Harcourt, Brace and Company, Inc., 1932.

12. *Economic Consequences of the Peace*, pages 256-282.

war debts, in conjunction with the international gold standard (after 1925), were responsible for the failure of interest rates in Britain to fall to a level compatible with full employment, according to Keynes. In 1930, Keynes maintained that the current long-term interest rates were 50 per cent above the prewar level. During the middle 'twenties, these rates started to decline and would have continued to decline, in Keynes' opinion, except for the gold standard and the war-debts-reparations muddle. The high market rate of interest led to an inadequate volume of investment, which in turn was the primary factor leading to depression in British industry at a time when most of the great capitalist countries were enjoying a considerable degree of prosperity. Keynes estimated that his country's deflationary postwar policy, associated with high interest rates, war debts, and the gold standard, decreased the production of wealth during the decade of the 'twenties by more than one billion pounds.[13]

In order to reduce the huge internal British debt arising from the war, Keynes advocated a capital levy in 1920.[14] As the next best alternative at that time, two years after the close of the war, he favored a reduction in the stipulated interest rate on the public debt. However, Keynes deemed this proposal as well as the capital levy impracticable, on equity grounds, except in the first few years after the close of the war. As a third choice immediately following the war and as first choice after the lapse of several years, he advocated a long-term rise in the internal price level as the best method for reducing the burden of the war debt. The significant point about these three proposals, however, lies in their similarities rather than in their differences. Each is a variation on the common theme that, in the interest of the economy as a whole, the "real" burden of rentier capitalist claims against the active, producing classes should be lightened. In France, Keynes said, the value of the franc would be determined in

---

13. *Treatise on Money*, Vol. II, page 181.

14. See Keynes' testimony on the capital levy before the Committee on National Debt and Taxation, *Minutes of Evidence* (1927), Vol. II, pages 534-540.

the long run by the proportion of earned income that the French taxpayer would permit to be taken from him to pay claims of the rentier.[15]

Keynes' bias against financial capital is indicated by the underlying theme of the *Tract on Monetary Reform* (1923). In the first paragraph of the Preface, he attributes all the major ills of capitalism to monetary instability.[16] Unemployment, insecurity, business losses, uncertainty, profiteering, and speculation "all proceed, in large measure, from the instability of the standard of value." Keynes argued for a managed currency, in place of the traditional gold standard to which most economists and statesmen were then assuming Britain would return at an early date. The managed currency should be directed toward stabilization of the internal price level, thus avoiding the speculative dangers of excessive inflation as well as the retarding forces of deflation.

Although he objected to both inflation and deflation, Keynes viewed moderate inflation as the lesser evil because "it is worse, in an impoverished world, to provoke unemployment than to disappoint the *rentier*."[17] In the past there had always been a tendency toward a secular rise in prices (inflation), and this had been to the good because "depreciated money assisted the new men and emancipated them from the dead hand; benefited new wealth at the expense of old, and armed enterprise against accumulation. . . . It has been a loosening influence against the rigid distribution of old-won wealth. . . . By this means each generation can disinherit in part its predecessors' heirs."[18] On the other hand, deflation permits the "dead hand of the past" to retard the wealth-producing entrepreneur. If Britain continued to foster a deflationary policy, said Keynes, an increasingly large share of the na-

---

15. "The French Franc," *The New Republic*, January 27, 1926, Vol. XLV, No. 582, page 266.

16. The American edition is called *Monetary Reform*. New York: Harcourt, Brace and Company, Inc., 1924. The following references are to the American edition.

17. *Ibid.*, pages 44-45.

18. *Ibid.*, pages 12-13.

tional income would accrue to the rentier class. An intolerable burden would fall on the productive classes, and the consequences would be inimical to the welfare of the community as a whole.

In his fight against deflation, Keynes collided head on with the policy of the conservative British government. In his budget message of 1924, Winston Churchill, then Chancellor of the Exchequer, announced that the United Kingdom would return to the international gold standard at the prewar parity by removing the embargo on gold exports. The gold standard was restored in April, 1925. Shortly after Mr. Churchill's message appeared, Keynes issued a pamphlet entitled *The Economic Consequences of Mr. Churchill*,[19] in which he predicted many dire results from the government's policy. At the time Churchill announced this policy, the pound was approximately 10 per cent below the prewar value in terms of gold. Prewar parity meant a pound worth $4.86, whereas the prevailing rate of exchange valued the pound in terms of dollars at $4.40. The return to gold at prewar parity amounted to a 10 per cent reduction in the prices of British export goods, without compensating decreases in costs of production at home. Keynes labeled the government's policy a "cold-blooded Income Deflation."[20] Automatically pressure was placed on industries producing for export—very important industries in the British economy—to reduce their costs, especially wages, in order to offset the reduction in prices.

Great Britain alone among the great powers had not recovered from the first postwar depression. Industry generally and export industries in particular were already (1925) in a distressed condition, and unemployment was at an all-time high.[21] Keynes said the Churchill policy would result in more

---

19. The American edition is entitled *The Economic Consequences of Sterling Parity*. New York: Harcourt, Brace and Company, Inc., 1925. The following quotations are from the American edition.

20. *Treatise on Money*, Vol. II, page 182.

21. See John H. Clapham, *An Economic History of Modern Britain*, Vol. III, pages 542-545. New York: The Macmillan Company, 1938.

distress to industry, more unemployment, and strikes against those firms and industries which attempted to cut wages.

In this pamphlet, *The Economic Consequences of Mr. Churchill*, Keynes devoted one chapter to an analysis of the coal industry, the leading export industry, pointing out that Churchill's policy would lead to a coal strike and perhaps to something much worse:

> The working classes . . . attacked first are faced with a depression of their standard of life, because the cost of living will not fall until all the others have been successfully attacked too; and, therefore, they are justified in defending themselves. . . . They are bound to resist so long as they can; and it must be war, until those who are economically weakest are beaten to the ground. . . . The plight of the coal miners is the first, but not—unless we are very lucky—the last. of the Economic Consequences of Sterling Parity.[22]

The validity of Keynes' prophecy was verified in 1926 when resistance by the coal miners to lower wages precipitated the general strike, which in almost any other country might have developed into revolution. The general strike was surely the greatest single catastrophe in the interwar crisis of British capitalism.

How did Keynes' opponents in this controversy view the return to gold at prewar parity? How did they justify this policy and what did they expect to gain thereby? Chancellor Churchill maintained that the return to gold was "no more responsible for the condition of affairs in the coal industry than is the Gulf Stream."[23] Churchill reported in his budget message that the return to gold was dictated by the absence of any alternative if England was to bring her financial system into agreement "with reality."

The "compelling reality" which dictated England's return to the gold standard seems to have been the shift of international financial transactions from London to New York. International banking and associated services had been one of England's largest sources of income. If the return to gold was

---

22. *Economic Consequences of Sterling Parity*, pages 9, 23.

23. *Ibid.*, page 8; also pages 20, 21, 28.

to be made at all, there was "compulsion" that it be made at prewar parity because, in the words of the Macmillan Committee (1930), the international financial world would have been immensely shocked if the world's greatest prewar creditor nation were deliberately by a positive act to reduce the value of its currency below par.[24] Any other policy would have meant a further loss of confidence in the London money market and an accentuation of such trends as the tendency of the Dominions to base their financial transactions on the dollar rather than on the pound. The government's policy was designed to restore position and prosperity to bankers, rentiers, and other financial interests without much conscious regard for the effects of such a policy upon British industrial entrepreneurs. Keynes, the champion of industrial capital and the antagonist of financial capital whenever these two interests clashed, denounced the government's policy with all the logic and rhetoric at his command.

The unfortunate consequences of Mr. Churchill's policy were not confined to the coal, textile, machine, iron and steel, and other industries producing for export markets. All industries, and especially those requiring new investment for expansion or rationalization, suffered because, in order to attract and protect a gold balance adequate to maintain the gold standard, the Bank of England's discount rate and consequently all interest rates in Britain had to be maintained at an abnormally high level. Shortly after Churchill's announcement that England would return to the gold standard, the Bank of England advanced its discount rate to a high level in order to assure sufficient gold to prepare for removal of the embargo on the export of gold during 1925. This policy led to a restriction of credit to industry and was accompanied by an increase in unemployment.

The government's policy found support among those who gave first emphasis to London's monetary and financial power and those who were naïvely unaware how much the world

---

24. Great Britain, Committee on Finance and Industry, *Report*, page 109. London: His Majesty's Stationery Office, 1931.

economy had changed from the prewar era when the gold standard had not been incompatible with domestic prosperity in industry. *The Times* of London pointed out that the higher discount rate was necessary to attract funds which were then going to New York because the United States had remained on the gold standard. "Once back on the gold standard we should find that foreign balances which have been kept in New York should return to us and our financial and monetary power would be greatly increased."[25] In contrast with the optimistic tone of *The Times,* Keynes took the gloomy view that a return to the gold standard would compel the Bank of England to act in a manner inimical to industrial prosperity. The rules of the gold standard under the circumstances then existing in Great Britain necessitated a high bank rate and a consequent restriction of credit to business. The inevitable result, Keynes predicted, would be discouragement of industrial enterprise and intensification of unemployment.[26]

Keynes did not deny *The Times'* assertion that this policy might greatly increase his country's financial and monetary power. His statement does represent, however, a strenuous objection to a policy that attempted to gain a large share of international banking business at the expense of domestic industry and employment.

Another objection made by Keynes to the Churchill policy also represents a criticism of financial capital. This refers to the windfall gains accruing to rentiers or functionless investors as a result of the deflation policy: "When we raise the value of sterling by 10 per cent, we transfer about $5,000,-000,000 into the pockets of the *rentiers* out of the pockets of the rest of us, and we increase the real burden of the National Debt by some $3,750,000,000. This . . . is inevitable."[27]

The "dead hand of the past," which Keynes deprecated in his *Tract,* again stood as one of the chief barriers to a rational program. As a firm believer in the power of persuasion

25. *The Times,* London, March 5, 1925, page 15.
26. *Economic Consequences of Sterling Parity,* pages 18-19.
27. *Ibid.,* page 11.

to reconcile group conflict, Keynes thought it possible that the trade unionists might be willing to accept a reduction in money-wage rates were it not for the automatic transfer of wealth to the rentier class. But, in the light of this transfer, he thought it both unjust and inconceivable that the representatives of labor could be reconciled to reductions in money wages. Prime Minister Stanley Baldwin in an interview with the coal miners' representatives stated: "All the workers in this country have got to face a reduction of wages . . . to help put industry on its feet."[28] Keynes predicted that the laboring classes would resist the Churchill-Baldwin policy until they were "beaten to the ground." His prediction proved literally true.

In Britain's gold-standard controversy of the 1920's, industrial interests clearly stood opposed to the interests of English international finance and of the rentier. Here, as always, Keynes stood for and advocated a course of action that placed him in the position of a defender of industrial capital and a critic of financial capital. He was not acting as a champion of the working class. Here as elsewhere Keynes did not object in principle to reductions in money-wage and real-wage rates. His position was that, as a matter of practical policy, it was impossible to secure the necessary reductions in money-wage rates without causing strikes and increasing unemployment, which would interfere with the continuity of industrial production.

When the Macmillan Committee was seeking an explanation for Britain's depressed economic condition of the 1920's, Keynes, who was a member of the committee, maneuvered Bank of England officials like Montagu Norman and Sir Ernest Harvey into positions in which they were compelled to confess a disregard for the welfare of home industry. By implicitly placing the blame for Britain's industrial depression on the banking policy of the nation, Keynes expressed his ever present criticism of finance capital.

28. See Allen Hutt, *The Post-War History of the British Working Class*, page 89. New York: Coward-McCann, 1938.

Before the Great Depression, Keynes believed that monetary reforms were adequate for attaining whatever social reforms were necessary. He had said in 1925, "Mr. Churchill's Budget is the real source of our industrial troubles."[29] His optimism concerning the possibilities of monetary reform is indicated by the following statement:

The supporters of Monetary Reform, of which I, after further study and reflection, am a more convinced adherent than before, as the most important and significant measure Great Britain can take to increase economic welfare, must expound their arguments more fully, more clearly, and more simply, before they can overwhelm the forces of old custom and general ignorance . . . . [It is] my belief that fluctations of trade and employment are . . . the greatest and the most remediable of the economic diseases of modern society, that they are mainly diseases of our credit and banking system . . . .[30]

The British election of 1929 was the occasion for a new development in Keynes' practical outlook. His position as a purely monetary reformer was qualified by the addition of public works and government loans to the agenda of social control. Unemployment was the leading issue in the campaign in which Lloyd George was the leader of the Liberal party and Stanley Baldwin and Ramsay MacDonald the leaders of the Conservative and Labour parties, respectively. Lloyd George offered a public works program as the remedy for unemployment. In support of the Liberal party program, Keynes, in collaboration with Mr. H. D. Henderson, issued a pamphlet entitled *Can Lloyd George Do it? An Examination of the Liberal Pledge.*[31] Keynes supported Lloyd George's promise that his proposed public works program would involve no rise in taxation, since the increased primary and secondary employment would augment the taxable national income while decreasing expenditures for unemployment relief in amounts sufficient to offset the additional outlays for public works. In attempting to establish the validity of these

29. *Economic Consequences of Sterling Parity,* page 25.

30. "The Return Towards Gold," *The New Republic,* March 18, 1925, Vol. XLII, No. 537, pages 92, 93.

31. London: The Nation and Athenaeum, 1929.

promises, Keynes and Henderson tried to make quantitative estimates of the relation between initial outlay in public works and the final increase in national income. This, so far as Keynes is concerned, marks the genesis of the so-called "theory of the multiplier," which is a refinement of the common-sense insight that, in an environment of unused resources, an expenditure for public works will increase the national income not only by the amount of the direct government outlay but by some multiple of it.[32]

Here we see public works emerging in a liberal democracy during the interwar period as a program designed to place new purchasing power in circulation after it was found virtually impossible to force funds into circulation in times of depression merely by manipulation of the banking mechanism.[33] The extension of government activity in the form of public works was in no sense intended to be an entering wedge for socialism. On the contrary, public works as well as monetary control were part of the liberal program for avoiding socialism.

The Break With the Classical Theory

Keynes changed from an orthodox to an unorthodox general economist in the period between his *Treatise on Money* (1930) and his *General Theory* (1936). His transition to a distinctly anti-classical position was precipitated at that time by the incompatibility between the policy Keynes advocated and the practical implication of classical principles of economics. In its theoretical aspect, the *Treatise* makes no attack on the main body of traditional economic principles but is confined to a pretentious monetary theory of the trade cycle.

32. Keynes and others have credited R. F. Kahn with the invention of the multiplier theory. This is true only in the sense that Kahn first gave it a refined technical formulation. The basic insight and a clear explanation of its practical significance is clearly expressed in the Keynes-Henderson pamphlet of 1929, whereas Kahn's article in *The Economic Journal* did not appear until 1931.

33. For a standard textbook view of the relation between monetary control and public works, see James Arthur Estey, *Business Cycles; Their Nature, Cause, and Control*, page 405. New York: Prentice-Hall, 1941.

The practical problem envisaged is control of the trade cycle. The general tone is optimistic. There is no hint in Keynes' writings and speeches during 1929 that he foresaw the stock market crash, nor, in 1930, that he realized its severity. Public works were viewed as a temporary expedient, as indicated by a statement made in May, 1929: "In three to five years we should be able to employ every one without the aid of special schemes. . . . We must lift ourselves out of the rut. Once we have succeeded in doing that, our business men will be able to run things for themselves."[34]

This optimistic tone is replaced in the *General Theory* by doubts concerning the survival powers of capitalism. Rather than mitigation or elimination of the trade cycle, the problem in the *General Theory* is one of implementing a declining capitalism against the loss of the self-recuperative powers that characterized it during the nineteenth century. The uniqueness and objectives of the *General Theory*, both as a proposal for practical action and as an attack on the old principles of economics, can be appreciated only by understanding Keynes' shift in viewpoint.

The most important event influencing Keynes during this transition period seems to have been the financial crisis of 1931. The economic depression that began in 1929 appeared to him as a recurrence of earlier trade cycles until it developed into a severe crisis two years later. Whereas in his *Treatise* Keynes refers to the "slump of 1930," in 1931 we find him asking, "Can we prevent an almost complete collapse of the financial structure of modern capitalism? One begins to wonder and to doubt."[35] On another occasion, in June, 1931, he said, "We are today in the middle of the greatest economic catastrophe . . . of the modern world."[36]

In this pessimistic frame of mind, Keynes collided head on

34. *The Times*, London, May 29, 1929, page 9.

35. *The World's Economic Crisis and the Way of Escape*, page 57. New York: Century Company, 1932.

36. Quincy Wright, ed., *Unemployment as a World-Problem*, page 3. Chicago: The University of Chicago Press, 1931.

with the classical view that personal thrift and reduced government spending are desirable because individual saving and a balanced budget facilitate recovery from depression. According to the traditional view, accumulating savings would lower interest rates and thus encourage investment. What the traditional view called "savings," Keynes saw as "hoarding," which resulted not in increased investment but in decreased employment. He protested against the competitive struggle for liquidity, and labeled acts of curtailed expenditure for useful things "anti-social acts."[37] His insight that a preference for liquidity may have far-reaching anti-social consequences is developed in the *General Theory* as the basis for the liquidity-preference theory of interest, which from an anti-classical point of view is the most important theoretical concept in the *General Theory*. Although the preference for owning money rather than other forms of wealth is a common type of social behavior, which becomes accentuated in crises, it became all-important in the Keynesian model as a result of a historical impression on the part of one who by training, experience, and traditional anti-rentier bias was sensitive to its consequences for industrial production.

Keynes' thought was crystallized into an anti-classical mold during the financial crisis of 1931 by the tenacity with which the British government stuck to principles of orthodox finance, and the strong opposition that most of his fellow economists offered to Keynes' policy suggestions. In the face of shrinking effective demand, Parliament passed the Budget and Economy Act in August, 1931. This measure supposedly followed the rules of "sound" finance, since it was directed toward a balanced budget. A policy of cutting wages, reducing relief payments, and retrenching on housing and road building followed the Economy Act. Keynes characterized this triumph of the "Treasury view" in its most extreme form as a curtailment of purchasing power, whereby "if the theory which underlies all this is to be accepted, the end will be that

---

37. *The World's Economic Crisis and the Way of Escape*, page 61.

no one can be employed except those happy few who grow their own potatoes."[38]

An aspect of the financial crisis of 1931 was England's effort to remain on the gold standard. Events at this time were a sequel to the return to gold in the middle 'twenties and, when England was forced to abandon the gold standard in September, 1931, represented a partial fulfillment of Keynes' prophetic statement of 1925: "The British Public will submit their necks once more to the Golden Yoke, as a prelude, perhaps, to throwing it off forever at a not distant date."[39] The return to gold had restored to some extent the international financial prestige of London, but it also reacted, as Keynes said it would, to the distress of industry in Britain. In 1931, the demand for a balanced budget was in part motivated by a desire to bolster confidence in the pound in order to prevent a drain of English gold reserves. It appeared that events had justified Keynes' prognostications of 1925. He predicted strikes and strikes had resulted; he said the gold standard was unworkable and so it had proved to be; he said industry would suffer under the gold standard and suffered it had. In 1931 we find Keynes mournfully picturing himself as a Cassandra whose predictions were prophetic but whose prophecies were never heeded. This whole unhappy episode of the return to gold seems destined to live in British opinion as the "straitjacket of 1925-1931."

A considerable portion of the *General Theory* is devoted to a polemic against the so-called classical political economy. In offering advice on matters of policy, Keynes found his efforts frustrated because of the conflicting practical advice given by his fellow economists. We may refer briefly to controversies with Professors Pigou and Robbins and Sir William Beveridge during the years preceding publication of the *General Theory*.

38. "The Budget," *The New Statesman and Nation*, September 19, 1931, New Series, Vol. II, No. 30, page 329.

39. "Is the Pound Overvalued?" *The New Republic*, May 6, 1925, Vol. LXII, No. 544, page 287.

Professor Pigou, in testimony before the Macmillan Committee, attributed unemployment to interferences with the "free working of economic forces," and to wage rates "out of adjustment with the general conditions of demand."[40] Pigou insisted that his analysis was on the "real" and not the "money" level. Keynes, as a member of the questioning committee, tried to get Pigou to shift from the "real" to a "money" analysis, but without success.

In *The Theory of Unemployment* (1933) and in *Economics in Practice* (1935), Pigou continued to emphasize the "real" as against the "monetary" analysis. From his theoretical analysis he concluded that unemployment is caused primarily by wage rates which are too high, and that money and interest are unimportant both in explaining unemployment and in finding ways of eliminating it. Speaking of a policy of lower wage rates, Pigou says, "This policy, if it could be practically carried out, would in my view, be a true antidote, within its limits, to slump conditions. It would not abolish, but it would effectively lessen the waste of unemployment."[41] Pigou's theoretical position, combined with the advice that he gave on practical affairs, is of special interest in explaining the sharp anti-classical position taken by Keynes in the *General Theory*.

In 1931, Sir William Beveridge denounced Keynes' proposal to levy a general protective tariff, with rebates on all imported materials entering into exports. Beveridge criticized the proposal in typical classical fashion when he asserted a protective tariff could do only harm, because the reduction in imports that would follow would result in a reduction of exports. Keynes replied that, contrary to the classical assumption implied in Beveridge's argument, "There is . . . no simple and direct relationship between the volume of exports and the volume of imports."[42]

---

40. Committee on Finance and Industry, *Minutes of Evidence*, Vol. II, page 78.

41. A. C. Pigou, *Economics in Practice*, page 51. See also page 70. London: Macmillan and Company, Ltd., 1935.

42. *The Times*, London, April 2, 1931, page 6.

Lionel Robbins, like Beveridge, invoked traditional free-trade arguments to ridicule Keynes' suggestions for protective tariffs and referred to his proposals as "petty devices of economic nationalism." True to the classical tradition, Robbins attributed the current economic distress to economic frictions, and in particular to wage rates that were too high to permit full employment. Robbins accused Keynes of being so muddled over the wage question that he was blinded to the obvious need for a downward readjustment in wage rates. "If he had not been so anxious to discredit his late associates and to destroy that which he once adored," said Robbins, "he might have chosen terms less glaringly inconsistent with his own earlier pronouncements."[43]

Undoubtedly Keynes' new position on the relation of protectionism to unemployment was, to orthodox economists, one of the most distressing changes in his thinking because free trade was one of the cornerstones of classical economics, and repudiation of free trade was in direct contradiction to the position Keynes had previously taken. For example, in 1923 he had written, "The claim to cure unemployment involves the Protectionist fallacy in its grossest and also in its crudest form."[44] In the *General Theory*, Keynes explicitly repudiates this earlier position and maintains that protectionism may be an aid to national employment. As previously indicated, the free-trade argument, which is valid under conditions of full employment, requires qualification for all types of duties and bounties when the assumption of full employment is dropped and maximum national income rather than minimum unit cost of production is taken as the criterion for judging desirable policy. Keynes never became a true advocate of protectionism, but on occasions such as the crisis of 1931, when international economic co-operation seemed hopeless, he viewed tariffs as a lesser evil than unemployment. His critical

---

43. Lionel Robbins, "A Reply to Mr. Keynes," *The New Statesman and Nation*, March 14, 1931, New Series, Vol. I, No. 3, page 100.

44. "Free Trade for England," *The New Republic*, December 19, 1923, Vol. XXXVII, No. 472, page 87.

attitude toward free trade was but one specific illustration of the change that had taken place in his thinking. The correspondence between controversy in theory and controversy in policy suggests that Keynes' transition to a distinctly anticlassical position was greatly influenced by his conviction that classical theory is vicious in its practical implications.

Thus Keynes' break with his past in economic theory was more abrupt than the accompanying change in his practical point of view. There had been important and fundamental changes in his views on policy, but they were in nearly all cases nascent in his earlier writings. His strong predisposition to be critical of certain social classes and institutions crystallized in the *General Theory* into a theory of the capitalist process and found expression in a program more sweeping than anything he had previously proposed. For example, while Keynes was always antipathetic toward rentiers, it was not until the *General Theory* that his program envisaged complete disappearance of the rentier class. To take another example, the significance of inequality of income distribution for the instability of capitalism was clearly stated in the *Economic Consequences of the Peace,* but Keynes had never, prior to the *General Theory,* advocated a program that took the broader implications of this inequality and instability into account. During the years that intervened between *Economic Consequences* and the *General Theory,* inequality of income and wealth was viewed by Keynes as a condition favorable to economic progress, albeit a capricious one, but in the *General Theory* inequality is in a very fundamental sense the root cause of unemployment and the greatest barrier to economic progress, "progress" being defined in the classical sense of capital accumulation.

By 1935, Keynes had become a self-acknowledged heretic from the general body of classical doctrine. In an article provoked by a discussion among English economists on the problem of poverty and potential plenty, Keynes maintains, contrary to the classical theory, that the capitalist economic system is not self-adjusting. Chiefly responsible for the lack of automatic adjustment to an equilibrium at full employment was the special nature of the rate of interest.[45] He refers to the traditional theory of interest as the "fatal flaw" in the whole of orthodox thinking of the past century. By repudiating the classical theory of interest and substituting a monetary theory of interest, Keynes believed he was on the way (in 1935) to a general theory of what determines the level of effective demand and the volume of aggregate employment, and therefore to a theoretical explanation of poverty in the midst of potential plenty.

The foregoing discussion has shown that Keynes was predisposed to be critical of orthodox economic policy and theory from the beginning of his career. The evolution of his position as a practical reformer went on more or less continuously from the time of his first important publication on *Indian Currency and Finance*. Although Keynes was critical of monetary and trade cycle theory early in his career, the change in his position as a general economic theorist came rather abruptly in the period between his *Treatise on Money* in 1930 and his *General Theory* in 1936. After accepting, or at least tolerating, the orthodox principles of economics for fully twenty of his mature years, Keynes found himself during the financial crisis of 1931 in a position where the breach between the policies he was advocating and the principles upon which he had been nurtured became too great to tolerate longer. The old principles, particularly as they related to the theories of interest, money and employment, were cast aside for a new set of doctrines in his *General Theory*.

---

45. "Now I range myself with the heretics. I believe their flair and their instinct move them towards the right conclusion . . . . There is, I am convinced, a fatal flaw in that part of the orthodox reasoning . . . due to the failure of the classical doctrine to develop a satisfactory and realistic theory of the rate of interest." "A Self-Adjusting Economic System?" *The New Republic*, February 20, 1935, Vol. LXXXII, No. 1055, page 36.

Political Liberalism, Class Loyalties, and Anti-Marxism

Keynes' major purpose may be characterized as an attempt to buttress political liberalism with a new economic program and to fortify this economic program with a new political economy. In this sense, Keynes follows in the tradition of the great British economists since Adam Smith, all of whom were liberals, with the possible exception of Malthus, and none of whom questioned the fundamental efficacy of private property. Smith and Ricardo were the champions of a new liberalism, which in their time was founded on laissez-faire. Beginning with John Stuart Mill, the advice given by classical economists on matters of practical policy became increasingly interventionist.[46] Keynes differs from his liberal predecessors in the extent of intervention which his program entails and in his willingness to lop off the dead wood of rentierism, of which all the classical economists, again with the exception of Malthus, were critical. Keynes is the first great British economist in this tradition explicitly to repudiate laissez-faire. The spirit of individualism still pervades his thinking quite as intensely as it did that of nineteenth-century British economists. Of government participation in economic life, Keynes says: "I defend it . . . both as the only practicable means of avoiding the destruction of existing economic forms in their entirety and as the condition of the successful functioning of individual initiative." (p. 380)[47]

In politics, Keynes was always a self-avowed, self-styled liberal. As a member of the British Liberal party, he consistently rejected the political philosophies of both the Conservative and Labour parties. The Conservatives were to him the "Die Hards," the representatives of the "Do-Nothing Party," led by men "incapable of distinguishing novel mea-

---

46. Jacob Viner, "Marshall's Economics, The Man and His Times," *The American Economic Review*, June, 1941, Vol. XXXI, No. 2, page 225.

47. *The General Theory of Employment, Interest and Money*. New York: Harcourt, Brace and Company, Inc., 1936.

sures for safeguarding Capitalism from what they call Bolshevism."[48] Keynes rejected the notion of class struggle, as seen both from the conservative and from the labor side. When Winston Churchill quit the Liberal party to join the Conservatives, Keynes said it would be fortunate for the Liberal party if all those who believed like Churchill "that the coming political struggle is best described as Capitalism *versus* Socialism, and, thinking in these terms, mean to die in the last ditch for Capitalism," were to do the same.[49]

Keynes rejected membership in the Labour party primarily because it is a class party, and if there is to be a class struggle in politics Keynes wished to be associated with the bourgeoisie and not the "boorish proletariat." In listing his objections to joining the Labour party, Keynes wrote in 1925:

To begin with, it is a *class* party, and the class is not my class. If I am going to pursue sectional interests at all, I shall pursue my own. When it comes to the class struggle as such, my local and personal patriotisms, . . . are attached to my own surroundings. I can be influenced by what seems to me to be Justice and good sense; but the *Class* war will find me on the side of the educated *bourgeoisie*.[50]

Keynes' criticisms of the Labour party referred to the inherent difficulties of securing leadership capable of acting in the interests of the community as a whole. The class character of the party requires its leaders to depend upon an appeal to "widespread passions and jealousies" against those who have wealth and power, rather than upon an appeal to reason and to justice. There is danger that an autocratic inner ring will seize control of labor and make decisions in the interest of that element within the Labour party which "hates and despises existing institutions and believes that great good will result merely from overthrowing them—or at least that to

---

48. *Essays in Persuasion,* page 327.

49. *Ibid.,* page 343.

50. *Ibid.,* page 324. The British election of 1945 seems to indicate that many of the "educated bourgeoisie" disagree with Keynes regarding membership in the Labour party. Approximately one-half of the Labour Members of Parliament elected in the overwhelming Labour victory are from middle-class professions and trades.

overthrow them is the necessary preliminary to any great good." The progressive Liberal has the advantage over the most admirable Labour representative because "He can work out his policies without having to do lip-service to Trade-Unionist tyrannies, to the beauties of the class war, or to doctrinaire State Socialism."[51] Although Keynes acknowledges elements of potential good in the Labour party, the class character of the party itself imposes limitations on its capacity for dealing appropriately with social and economic issues.

The economic counterpart of Keynes' political bias against the Labour party is reflected in his preference for social services instead of higher money wages as the best means of bettering the standard of life of the wage-earning class. Speaking with reference to England, Keynes maintained in 1930 in the midst of depression that a rise in wage rates would increase costs to an internationally uneconomic level. These higher costs, he said, would tend to drive British capital abroad, whereas the benefits of higher wages could be secured through social services paid for out of taxes which would not have the disadvantages of higher wages.[52] During 1939 and 1940, when Britain was threatened by dangerous inflation, Keynes appealed to the working class to accept his liberal plan of "forced savings" as the only method by which the long-run interests of wage earners could be safeguarded.

Keynes always dealt with the wage problem indirectly and never developed anything that could properly be called a theory of wages. He strenuously objected to reductions in money-wage rates during depression periods, but on the other hand he did not advocate higher wage rates. The direct problem to him was one of interest rates, profit expectations, distribution of income, effective demand, money supply, money standards, and stock market speculation, but never wages as such. In *How to Pay for the War* is a typical statement: "I

51. *Ibid.*, page 342.

52. "The Question of High Wages," *The Political Quarterly*, January, 1930, Vol. I, No. 1, pages 110-124.

have not attempted to deal directly with the problem of wages. It is wiser, I expect, to deal with it indirectly."[53]

Although Keynes frequently addressed his proposals to the working class, the latter never received them with much enthusiasm. Keynes' plan in *How to Pay for the War* provoked from a British labor group a critical reply in the form of a pamphlet entitled, *The Keynes Plan—Its Dangers to Workers.*[54] Keynes was accused of fighting the battle of the capitalists, however well meaning he may have been, and his plan was characterized as a subtle argument for reducing real wages. The idea of postwar payment of wages earned during the war was scornfully labeled "pie in the sky." Among the important reasons why Keynes' plan was not acceptable to these labor critics were: (1) The funds for payment of deferred wages were to be raised by a levy on capital after the war at a time when there was danger of a depression. That funds could be raised in this manner at such a time was considered highly doubtful. (2) There was a long tradition of broken promises of the government to labor, the most prominent case cited being the Sankey Commission case of 1919. (3) Inflation of prices might reduce to practically nothing the real value of wages to be paid in the future. The pamphlet denied Keynes' basic premise that the total quantity of consumers goods going to labor during the war was fixed, and therefore denied also that labor had nothing to lose under the plan. As an alternative to Keynes' plan, it was proposed that labor should increase its real wages now at the expense of profits. If necessary this should be done by government operation of vital industries on a non-profit-making basis, without compensation being paid to the owners for "being deprived of the opportunity for profiteering." The tone of the argument shows clearly that Keynes' plan struck an unsympathetic chord with these socialistically inclined Labourites.

Keynes' repudiation of the classical position with respect to the self-adjusting nature of the modern economy and his

---

53. *How to Pay for the War*, page 55.
54. London: Farleigh Press, 1940.

proposals for government control of investment did not lead him to advocate collectivism. In fact, he is much further from the socialist position than that archclassicist, Professor Pigou, who in his *Socialism versus Capitalism* (1937)[55] becomes virtually a socialist. For the most part, Keynes ignores the socialist argument that social ownership of the means of production is essential, but his occasional references indicate a strong opposition to collectivism. This is illustrated in a negative way by the foregoing discussion of Keynes' political and class biases. It is illustrated in a positive fashion by his lack of regard for the work of Marx, his opposition to socialization of the instruments of production, and his attitude toward Soviet Russia.

Apart from a bare recognition that Marx had something to say about effective demand, Keynes was always scornful of the work of Marx. "Marxian Socialism," he wrote in 1925, "must always remain a portent to the historians of Opinion —how a doctrine so illogical and so dull can have exercised so powerful and enduring an influence over the minds of men, and, through them, the events of history."[56] Discussing the Soviet Union after his visit there in 1925, Keynes wrote, "How can I accept a doctrine which sets up as its bible, above and beyond criticism, an obsolete economic textbook which I know to be not only scientifically erroneous but without interest or application for the modern world?"[57] Keynes' praise of what he calls the "anti-Marxian socialism" of Silvio Gesell, the stamped-money reformer, illustrates his own anti-Marxian bias. Gesell was just such a critic of financial capital and staunch defender of private industrial capitalism as we have indicated Keynes to be. Keynes' judgment of the relative merits of Marx and Gesell, so apparently false in the light of history, would seem to reveal much more about Keynes

55. London: Macmillan and Company, Ltd., 1937.

56. *Laissez-faire and Communism*, pages 47-48.

57. *Ibid.*, page 99.

than it does about either Marx or Gesell.[58]

In a manner characteristic of the outlook of a financial reformer, Keynes has viewed social ownership of the means of production as an unimportant issue. He wrote in 1926 that large-scale enterprise tends to socialize itself because the shareholders become dissociated from the management. The direct personal interest of management under these conditions is in the general stability and reputation of the enterprise, and the making of large profits becomes secondary to management. This optimistic acceptance by Keynes of the separation of ownership from control in modern corporate enterprise stands in sharp contrast to the alarm expressed by many economists.[59] Keynes' attitude toward nationalization of railroads also minimizes the importance of socialization of the means of production. "There is . . . no so-called important political question so really unimportant, so irrelevant to the re-organization of the economic life of Great Britain, as the Nationalisation of the Railways."[60] On another occasion Keynes speaks of "the falsity of the supposed historic antithesis between socialism and individualism."[61] These and similar views, expressed before he departed from the classical position, are reasserted in the *General Theory*, where he states, "It is not the ownership of the instruments of production which it is important for the State to assume," (p. 378) and also in his references to the "anti-Marxian socialism" of Gesell. In spite of the high degree of government intervention involved in Keynes' program, it is clear that he remained

---

58. "I am no Marxian. Yet I sufficiently recognize the greatness of Marx to be offended at seeing him classed with Silvio Gesell and Major Douglas."— J. A. Schumpeter, in his reveiw of Keynes' *General Theory* in the *Journal of the American Statistical Association*, December, 1936, New Series, Vol. XXXI, No. 196, page 793n.

59. For example, by Thorstein Veblen in *Absentee Ownership and Business Enterprise in Recent Times; the Case of America.* New York: B. W. Huebsch, 1923; and by Adolf A. Berle and G. C. Means in *The Modern Corporation and Private Property.* New York and Chicago: Commerce Clearing House, 1932.

60. *Laissez-faire and Communism,* page 64.

61. *The Times,* London, August 1, 1927, page 7.

fundamentally an individualist in his economic and social philosophy.

Keynes' perspective on social and economic issues is also revealed by his attitude toward Soviet Russia. Following his visit there in the 'twenties, Keynes concluded that, if communism had a future, it was as a new religion and not as a more efficient form of economic organization. He appears to have been tremendously impressed with Soviet economic inefficiency:

On the economic side I cannot perceive that Russian Communism has made any contribution to our economic problems of intellectual interest or scientific value. I do not think that it contains, or is likely to contain, any piece of useful economic technique which we could not apply, if we chose, with equal or greater success in a society which retained all the marks . . . of British bourgeois ideals.[62]

Nevertheless, Keynes thought that what was happening in Soviet Russia was important, much more important, for example, than anything happening in the United States during the 1920's. Communism, he thought, would survive in spite of its economic inefficiency because, unlike capitalism, it does not place economics and religion in separate compartments. Capitalism, wrote Keynes, "is absolutely irreligious, without internal union, without much public spirit, often, though not always, a mere congeries of possessors and pursuers. Such a system has to be immensely, not merely moderately, successful to survive."[63] While expressing the belief that capitalism, rightly organized, is probably more efficient than any other form of economic organization, capitalism is in itself highly objectionable on moral grounds. The business man motivated by the "love of money" is tolerable as a means but not as an end. This feeling that contemporary capitalism is

---

62. *Laissez-faire and Communism*, page 130. There is no evidence from Keynes' published writings that his fundamental skepticism of and dislike for the economic structure of Soviet Russia ever changed in any important respect. On the contrary, such positive evidence as exists in occasional references in his later writings indicates a continuation of his earlier bias. See *General Theory*, pages 380, 381; *How to Pay for the War*, pages 7, 53, 55.

63. *Laissez-faire and Communism*, page 131.

spiritually and morally bankrupt probably explains, at least in part, the psychological basis for Keynes' consistent attacks upon the financial abuses and speculative orgies of this system.

Here one finds in Keynes something of the medieval schoolman, to whom avarice was a deadly sin. But as the later canonists found, there is a dilemma where private property renders indistinguishable the motives of speculation (finance) and enterprise (industry). The solution is a compromise which in the ideal society reduces all income to the reward for labor, including profit as a special type of wage, but eliminates "usury," that is, income from lending money.[64] Neither with the canonists nor with Keynes does the criticism extend to the institution of private property in the means of production.

The historic significance of Keynes' new political economy is that it furnishes the theoretical basis for a new liberalism, which, unlike classical liberalism, rejects laissez-faire. The concept of a pre-established harmony of economic forces, which Eli Heckscher has described as the fundamental preconception of laissez-faire, is absent from Keynes' thinking. In this sense Keynes fits into the mercantilist tradition, which likewise uniformly lacked the postulate of pre-established harmony.[65]

Because a private property economy lacks pre-established harmony, social controls are needed to prevent it from plunging to its own destruction. The greatest disharmony of laissez-faire capitalism is that full employment becomes increasingly difficult to attain with the progressive accumulation of wealth. The dilemma of poverty in the midst of potential plenty arises because the increase of wealth necessitates a

64. See R. H. Tawney, *Religion and the Rise of Capitalism*, pages 48-49. Hammondsworth, Middlesex, England: Pelican Books, 1938. For Keynes' strictures on usury, see his *General Theory*, pages 241, 340, 351, 353. For Keynes' acceptance of the labor theory of value, see the *General Theory*, pages 213, 214.

65. Eli F. Heckscher, *Mercantilism*, Vol. II, especially pages 316-324. London: G. Allen and Unwin, 1935.

greater quantity of investment, while at the same time accumulation weakens the inducement to invest. The dilemma is heightened because the power to consume is limited by the unequal distribution of wealth which is characteristic of laissez-faire capitalism. The general perspective from which Keynes projected both his earlier and his later theory and practice was that of liberalism. The essence of his liberalism is a criticism of financial capitalism, combined with a strong desire to establish an environment in which industrial capitalism, the system of private enterprise, can function. His work in this sense is essentially conservative and oriented toward a preservation of the status quo.

The General Theory as a Program of Action

Thus far the present chapter has traced the development of Keynes' thought and has indicated the general point of view within which this development took place. The ultimate significance of the theory which emerged from this process of development resides in the program of action with which it is associated. Being critical of the status quo, Keynes calls for a program of social reform, but, not being revolutionary, he envisions the execution of his program within the framework of the existing social order. There is no plea in Keynes' work for a total reconstruction of economic society along socialistic lines. At the same time, however, the explicit and inferential changes called for are hardly of a mild variety. They are severely liberal. Above all, they are dedicated to a preservation of civil rights and liberties and to the creation of an economic environment which will allow the individual to realize his full potentialities. Any society which tolerates mass unemployment not only fails to produce the goods and services of which it is capable, but denies to millions of individuals the dignity of creative labor and the possibility of self-realization of personality. Therefore, the first prerequisite of a better society is the abolition of unemployment. The second prerequisite is a more equitable and less arbitrary distribution of wealth and income (p. 372).

The immediate steps

The immediate proposals suggested by Keynes for promoting a high level of employment have been indicated in connection with the discussion of various parts of his theory and need only be summarized here before passing to his long-range view of social change. Fortunately, the steps which will promote a higher level of employment will also result in a more equal distribution of income and wealth. The most important proposals in Keynes' program for increasing employment are the following: (1) Progressive taxation to raise the community propensity to consume; (2) Public investment and public control of private investment to compensate for and to reduce the magnitude of fluctuations in the marginal efficiency of private investment; (3) Strong monetary authority to control the supply of money and lower the rate of interest.

(1) Since unemployment develops because our society as organized must produce much more than we have the economic ability to consume at full employment, the two approaches to full or nearly full employment are to increase the ability to consume and to raise the volume of investment to a level at which it will fill the gap between total income and consumption at full employment. Increasing the ability to consume means increasing the propensity to consume so more will be consumed at given levels of a national income. Keynes' main suggestion in this connection is to use progressive taxation to redistribute the social income from individuals with a low propensity to consume (the rich) to those with a high propensity to consume (the poor) and thus raise the community's average propensity to consume.

(2) Investment may be increased either by raising the marginal efficiency of capital or by lowering the rate of interest. The marginal efficiency of capital has its operational or practical meaning in what Keynes calls the "socialisation

of investment." As indicated in Chapter 7, Keynes does not say precisely what he means by the socialization of investment, but the proposal seems to suggest control of private investment of a rather far-reaching nature as well as public investment on an expanded scale. Private investment should be encouraged in every possible manner. However, private investors are very sensitive to government controls and there is danger that attempts to foster private investment may react unfavorably on the marginal efficiency of capital. This means there is not a great deal that can be done in a positive way to increase private investment through the marginal efficiency of capital. Some good may be achieved by a heavy transfer tax on all stock-market transactions. Such a tax would discourage buying and selling of stocks merely for the capital appreciation and might mitigate the dominance of speculation over enterprise in the securities market. Legislation like the American Securities and Exchange Act is in line with Keynes' desire to eliminate the worst faults of financial capital. Generally speaking, however, not much can be done to stabilize private investment at a high level. Therefore, a public investment authority like the Board of Public Investment suggested by Keynes in 1938 (see Chapter 7) should stand prepared to compensate for the fluctuations and inadequacies of private investment with public investment projects. The Council of Economic Advisers established under the Employment Act of 1946 is the type of government agency which might perform a similar function in the United States. Although the Employment Act of 1946 hardly goes beyond the advisory stage, its preamble represents a step in the direction of Keynes' philosophy of the role of government in maintaining high levels of employment. In the preamble Congress declares, "It is the continuing policy and responsibility of the Federal Government to use all practicable means consistent with its needs and obligations and other essential considerations of national policy, and with the assistance and cooperation of industry, agriculture, labor and state and local governments, to coordinate and utilize all its plans, functions and resources for the purpose of creating and maintaining, in a manner calculated to foster and promote free competitive enterprise and the general welfare, conditions under which there will be afforded useful employment opportunities, including self-employment, for those able, willing, and seeking to work, and to promote maximum employment, production, and purchasing power."

(3) The third of the fundamental determinants of employment, the rate of interest, finds its operational meaning in the proposal for a strong monetary authority with rigorous control over the total quantity of money as a means of lowering the rate of interest in order to stimulate private investment. In this suggestion for a strong central banking authority Keynes gives practical expression to the liquidity-preference theory of the rate of interest. In a series of articles on "How to Avoid a Slump," appearing in *The Times* of London in January, 1937, Keynes affirmed his faith in the ability of the central monetary authority to push down and keep down the long-term rate of interest to a level compatible with a flow of investment that would insure against an economic slump. He was aware that once a boom collapsed into a slump, the profit expectations of potential investors would probably fall so low that no reduction in interest rates could stimulate recovery from depression. As noted in the chapter on interest, it is important not only to push down the interest rate, but to give assurance that it will stay down in the future, since one of the great obstacles to a low long-term rate is the anticipation that the rate may rise in the future.

The long view

Even if these immediate proposals were put into effect and worked successfully, they would prove inadequate in the long run because the marginal efficiency of capital would continue to decline whereas the rate of interest could not be lowered by ordinary means below a level of, say, two per cent. Investment would therefore cease, and widespread unemployment would return to plague the economic system. Consequently, some means other than conventional bank control over the quantity of money must be found to lower the long-term interest rate from two per cent down to zero. Keynes makes no specific proposal for accomplishing this necessary step. He praises the principle behind the stamped-money plan of Silvio Gesell, who suggested that money, like other commodities, should be made to incur carrying costs in order to discourage storing wealth in the form of money.[66] Gesell suggested that this could be done by requiring that currency notes be stamped periodically as a condition of retaining their value. According to Keynes, the stamped-money idea is theoretically sound and may contain "the essence of what is needed," but it is not workable in the form proposed by Gesell. Nevertheless, Keynes felt that we should look to Gesell's work rather than to that of Marx for the ultimate solution of the economic problem. Beyond these hints, Keynes makes no attempt to point out what steps might be taken to reduce the rate of interest to zero in order to make it possible for investment to advance unimpeded to the point at which the marginal efficiency of capital would also be lowered to zero.

Although the concrete proposals for the long-run solution of the economic problem are not given by Keynes, his preference for Gesell rather than Marx, plus other aspects of his social philosophy, indicates the general nature of his solution. His goal is an alternative to socialism in the Marxian sense of government ownership of the means of production. His criticisms are directed toward the financial, rentier and speculative features of capitalism. In the long run the answer to the capitalist dilemma is to be discovered in the elimination of these faults rather than in the elimination of private ownership of the means of production.

The analyses of the capitalist process given by Keynes and Marx have a good deal in common. It is the operational meanings of their analyses as reflected in what to do about the situation that indicate the fundamental difference between

---

66. See Silvio Gesell, *The Natural Economic Order.* San Antonio: Free Economy Publishing Company, 1936.

the two systems of thought. In both theories, the successful functioning of the capitalist system depends on a high rate of capital accumulation because the unequal distribution of income and wealth leads to great potential savings which must be realized in the form of new capital assets if they are to be realized at all. The alternative is mass unemployment. These potential savings cannot be realized in the form of consumers goods and services because the unequal distribution of income is associated with a low propensity to consume. In its historical development, capitalism shows a tendency for the capacity to produce to outrun the capacity to consume. This means the gap between income and consumption at full employment is growing constantly larger. The capacity to consume refers, of course, to economic capacity and not physical capacity for consumption. As long as this inequality persists, there remains the necessity of capitalizing, in the form of capital assets, the surplus portion of large incomes, or suffering the only alternative of mass unemployment. Inequality arises primarily from the concentration of income from property as contrasted with income from labor. The social and economic problem cannot be solved as long as inequality exists.

Keynes' view that inequality of income is a barrier to the creation of new wealth reverses the traditional notion that the accumulation of wealth depends on the savings of the rich out of their superfluity. The old idea that equality and progress are incompatible is transformed by Keynes' theory into the revolutionary doctrine that greater equality is one of the essential conditions of progress. As he says, "One of the chief social justifications of great inequality is, therefore, removed." (p. 373) Keynes is not an equalitarian in the sense that he believes everyone should be rewarded equally. He saw social and psychological justification for "significant inequalities." However, the disparities are much greater than can be justified on social and psychological grounds, and also much greater than is compatible with a high level of aggregate demand.

Society cannot go on forever widening the gap between what it currently produces and what it currently consumes at full employment. Sooner or later the capacity to consume must be brought into harmony with the capacity to produce. This is not possible, however, in a society in which a relatively few owners receive nearly all the income from property and the great mass of non-owners receive only labor income. Getting rid of the deficiency of consumption means ultimately getting rid of gross inequality in the distribution of income. Up to this point, Keynes and Marx could agree. Beyond this point, however, there are two fundamental directions which economic evolution might follow. It is here that Keynes and Marx part company. Marx sees the only realistic solution of the contradiction between the capacity to produce and the capacity to consume in the socialization of the means of production. This will automatically socialize surplus incomes. Inequality will not disappear completely, but it will be greatly reduced and will cease to be a barrier to full employment. Investment will become a collective activity of society based on social need, rather than the consequence of private profit calculation.

The second road, the one which Keynes takes, regards the socialization of income-yielding property as unnecessary and undesirable. According to Keynes, capital assets yield income because they are scarce. When they cease to be scarce, they will cease to be a source of income to their owners. When property ceases to yield income, only labor, both mental and physical, will constitute a basis for receiving income. Therefore, if capital assets can be made sufficiently abundant, property income will disappear and with it the inequality of income distribution which is the great barrier to a high level of consumption and employment. However, the elimination of income from mere ownership would probably not eliminate the desire to save out of income at full employment. Presumably, the "socialisation of investment" would take care of the task of finding offsets to saving. Here is the perspective from which Keynes views the solution of the social and economic problems of unemployment and inequality. This perspective leads quite logically to the view that labor is the sole factor of production and to a sympathy with the labor theory of value.[67] Even in accepting the labor theory of value, which was a fundamental part of Marx's theory, Keynes differs from Marx. Keynes is careful to include as functional labor the full services of entrepreneurs, whereas Marx excluded from functional labor a large part of the activities of entrepreneurs because he thought they were devoted to the exploitation of wage earners under a system of private ownership of the means of production and were unnecessary in a rationally organized society.

If these inferences of the long view seem to raise more questions than they answer, we can only express sympathy with the reader and add that it is unfortunate Lord Keynes did not live to grapple with the secular problem. If it seems utopian to suppose that private enterprise can continue to function after the rewards of ownership have ceased, we can merely offer the observation that "socialists" of this variety have been labeled "utopian" for the past hundred years. At this point a warning is in order. We should not belittle the value of Keynes' short-run analysis, which is all he intended to give, just because the secular aspects of his theory are left undeveloped. The *General Theory* may have great merit in relation to problems of unemployment and inflation and not be very useful as a tool of secular analysis.

The fulfillment of Keynes' long-term goal would indeed constitute a minor revolution in class relations. The rentier capitalist, the functionless investor, would disappear as a class. Ownership would no longer constitute a basis for the receipt of income. The process would take place gradually, however, as the continuation of what has been going on in Great Britain for several decades, and would require no violent break with the past for its completion. To Keynes this minor revolution is desirable not only because it would

---

67. See pages 194-195.

produce a more just society, but, more important, because it is the necessary price that must be paid in order to avert in the long run a major revolution of the Marxian variety. It represents the alternative to Marxism. Its basic purpose is to preserve private industrial capitalism, and in no sense does Keynes view it as the entering wedge for a gradual transition to collectivism. Financial capital, speculation, and rentierism, with all their abuses, are a cancerous growth on the body of private enterprise and are not an organic part of the system. Nevertheless, saving the patient requires a serious operation. In brief, Keynes believes the preservation of private capitalism requires the elimination of its worst faults. He also believes these faults can be abolished without at the same time destroying the foundations of private industrial capitalism.

References for Further Reading

Keynes, J. M., *The General Theory of Employment, Interest and Money*, Chapter 24. New York: Harcourt, Brace and Co., 1936.
———, *Essays in Persuasion*, especially Part IV. New York: Harcourt, Brace and Co., 1932.
———, *Laissez-faire and Communism*. New York: The New Republic, Inc., 1926.

Alexander, S. S., "Mr. Keynes and Mr. Marx," *The Review of Economic Studies*, February, 1940, Vol. VII, pages 123-135.
Ayres, C. E., "The Impact of the Great Depression on Economic Thinking," *The American Economic Review, Papers and Proceedings*, May, 1946, Vol. XXXVI, pages 112-125.
Clark, J. M., *Alternative to Serfdom*, Chapter IV, "Revolution in Economics," pages 91-117. New York: Alfred A. Knopf, 1948.
Dillard, Dudley, "Keynes and Proudhon," *The Journal of Economic History*, May, 1942, Vol. II, pages 63-76.
———, "Gesell's Monetary Theory of Social Reform," *The American Economic Review*, June, 1942, Vol. XXXII, pages 348-352.
Fan-Hung, "Keynes and Marx on the Theory of Capital Accumulation, Money and Interest," *The Review of Economic Studies*, October, 1939, Vol. VII, pages 28-41.
Gruchy, Allan G., "The Philosophical Basis of the New Keynesian Economics," *Ethics*, July, 1948, Vol. LVIII, pages 235-244.

Harrod, R. F., "John Maynard Keynes," *The Review of Economic Statistics*, November, 1946, Vol. XXVIII, pages 178-182. Reprinted in *The New Economics*, edited by S. E. Harris. New York: Alfred A. Knopf, 1947.

Klein, L. R., *The Keynesian Revolution*, Chapter VII on "Keynes and Social Reform." New York: The Macmillan Company, 1947.

Neisser, H. P., "Keynes as an Economist," *Social Research*, June, 1946, Vol. XIII, pages 225-235.

Robinson, E. A. G., "John Maynard Keynes, 1883-1946," *The Economic Journal*, March, 1947, Vol. LVII, pages 1-68.

Robinson, Joan, *An Essay on Marxian Economics*. London: Macmillan and Co., 1942.

Schumpeter, J. A., "John Maynard Keynes, 1883-1946," *The American Economic Review*, September, 1946, Vol. XXXVI, pages 495-518. Reprinted in *The New Economics*, edited by S. E. Harris. New York: Alfred A. Knopf, 1947.

Somerville, H., "Mr. Keynes and the Canonists," *Commonweal*, June 12, 1936, Vol. XXIV, pages 177-179.

Sweezy, Paul M., "John Maynard Keynes," *Science and Society*, Fall, 1946, Vol. X, pages 398-405. Reprinted in *The New Economics*, edited by S. E. Harris. New York: Alfred A. Knopf, 1947.

Trachtenberg, I., "Soviet Comment on Keynesian Theories of Full Employment," *Science and Society*, Fall, 1946, Vol. X, pages 405-409.

Wright, D. McC., "Future of Keynesian Economics," *The American Economic Review*, June, 1945, Vol. XXXV, pages 284-307.

Bibliography of John Maynard Keynes' Writings

Keynes was a prolific writer as the following bibliography attests. As editor of *The Economic Journal*, the quarterly journal of the Royal Economic Society, for more than thirty years, he undoubtedly wrote many unsigned notes and notices. As editor of the liberal British weekly, *The Nation and the Athenaeum*, he contributed numerous unsigned articles and editorials. As a member of several government commissions and committees (the Royal Commission on Indian Currency and Finance, 1914; the Macmillan Committee on Finance and Industry, 1931; and the Treasury group that drew up the *Plan for an International Clearing Union*, 1943), Keynes made further, important contributions. Since individual authorship cannot be clearly attributed in most of these cases, I have not listed them in the bibliography of Keynes' writings. Apart from these items and certain brief bits of correspondence and duplicate articles, I have included practically all of Keynes' publications. A bibliography that lists some anonymous articles believed to have been written by or discussed with Keynes before publication will be found in *The New Economics*, edited by Seymour E. Harris (New York: Alfred A. Knopf, 1947), pages 665-686.

Classified Bibliography
(arranged chronologically by each classification)

I.   Books and Pamphlets
II. Articles

A. Money, Interest, Prices, and Inflation
B. International Economics, including Foreign Exchange and Gold
C. Unemployment, Employment, and Wages
D. Consumption, Saving, Investment, and Income
E. War and Peace, including War Debts and Reparations
F. Politics and Social Philosophy
G. Biographical
H. Miscellaneous
III. Book Reviews

I. Books and Pamphlets

Indian Currency and Finance. London: Macmillan and Co., Ltd., 1913. 263 pages.

The Economic Consequences of the Peace. New York: Harcourt, Brace and Howe, 1920. 298 pages.

A Treatise on Probability. London: Macmillan and Co., Ltd., 1921. 466 pages.

A Revision of the Treaty. New York: Harcourt, Brace and Co., 1922. 242 pages.

Monetary Reform. New York: Harcourt, Brace and Co., 1924. 227 pages. (The English edition is entitled *A Tract on Monetary Reform.*)

The Economic Consequences of Sterling Parity. New York: Harcourt, Brace and Co., 1925. 32 pages. (The English edition is entitled *The Economic Consequences of Mr. Churchill.*)

A Short View of Russia. London: Woolf, 1925. 27 pages. (Reprinted in *Laissez-Faire and Communism.*)

The End of Laissez-Faire. London: Woolf, 1926. 54 pages. (Reprinted in *Laissez-Faire and Communism.*)

Laissez-Faire and Communism. New York: New Republic, Inc., 1926. 144 pages. I. *The End of Laissez-Faire;* II. *A Short View of Russia.*

Réflexions sur le franc et sur quelques autres sujets. Paris: Simon Kra, 1928. 182 pages. (A collection of articles from *l'Information, l'Europe Nouvelle, The Economic Journal,* and *The Nation and the Athenaeum.*)

(with H. D. Henderson) *Can Lloyd George Do It? An Examination of the Liberal Pledge.* London: The Nation and the Athenaeum, 1929. 44 pages.

A Treatise on Money. London: Macmillan and Co., Ltd., 1930. Vol. I The Pure Theory of Money, 363 pages; Vol. II The Applied Theory of Money, 424 pages.

Essays in Persuasion. New York: Harcourt, Brace and Co., 1932. 376 pages.

Essays in Biography. London: Macmillan and Co., Ltd., 1933. 318 pages.

The Means to Prosperity. New York: Harcourt, Brace and Co., 1933. 37 pages.

The General Theory of Employment, Interest and Money. New York: Harcourt, Brace and Co., 1936. 403 pages.

How to Pay for the War. New York: Harcourt, Brace and Co., 1940. 88 pages.

II. Articles

A. Money, interest, prices, and inflation

"The Recent Economic Events in India," *The Economic Journal,* March, 1909, Vol. XIX, pages 51-67.

"Report of the National Monetary Commission of the United States," *The Economic Journal,* March, 1912, Vol. XXII, pages 150-151.

"Report of the Mint," *The Economic Journal,* December, 1912, Vol. XXII, pages 633-634.

"Currency in 1912," *The Economic Journal,* March, 1914, Vol. XXIV, pages 152-157. (Review of the *Forty-third Annual Report of the Deputy Master of the Mint.*)

"The City of London and the Bank of England, August, 1914," *The Quarterly Journal of Economics,* November, 1914, Vol. XXIX, pages 48-71.

"The Prospects of Money, November, 1914," *The Economic Journal,* December, 1914, Vol. XXIV, pages 610-634.

"Inflation as a Method of Taxation," *Manchester Guardian Commercial, Reconstruction in Europe,* July 27, 1922, Fifth Section, pages 268-269.

"The Consequences to Society of Changes in the Value of Money," *Manchester Guardian Commercial, Reconstruction in Europe,* July 27, 1922, Fifth Section, pages 321-328.

"Is Credit Abundant?—The Grand Trunk Railway," *The Nation and the Athenaeum,* July 7, 1923, Vol. XXXIII, page 470.

"Bank Rate at Four Per Cent," *The Nation and the Athenaeum,* July 14, 1923, Vol. XXXIII, page 502.

"Bank Rate and Stability of Prices—A Reply to Critics," *The Nation and the Athenaeum,* July 21, 1923, Vol. XXXIII, pages 511-512.

"A Comment on Professor Cannan's Article ('Limitation of Currency or Limitation of Credit?')," *The Economic Journal,* March, 1924, Vol. XXXIV, pages 65-68.

"Monetary Reform," *The Economic Journal,* June, 1924, Vol. XXXIV, pages 169-176.

"The Policy of the Bank of England," *The Nation and the Athenaeum,* July 19, 1924, Vol. XXXV, pages 500-501.

"The Bank Rate," *The Nation and the Athenaeum,* March 7, 1925, Vol. XXXVI, pages 790-792.

"The Amalgamation of the British Note Issues," *The Economic Journal,* June, 1928, Vol. XXXVIII, pages 321-328.

"The Bank Rate, Five-and-a-half Per Cent," *The Nation and the Athenaeum,* February 16, 1929, Vol. XLIV, pages 679-680.

"Mr. Keynes' Theory of Money: A Rejoinder" (to D. H. Robertson), *The Economic Journal,* September, 1931, Vol. XLI, pages 412-423.

"The Pure Theory of Money: A Reply to Dr. Hayek," *Economica,* November, 1931, Vol. XI, pages 387-397.

"Banks and the Collapse of Money Values," *Vanity Fair,* January, 1932, pages 21-23.

"Member Bank Reserves in the United States," *The Economic Journal,* March, 1932, Vol. XLII, pages 27-31.

"A Note on the Long-term Rate of Interest in Relation to the Conversion Scheme," *The Economic Journal,* September, 1932, Vol. XLII, pages 415-423.

"The Monetary Policy of the Labour Party," *The New Statesman and Nation,* September 17 and 24, 1932, Vol. IV, pages 306-307 and 338-339.

"Mr. Keynes's Control Scheme," *The American Economic Review,* December, 1933, Vol. XXIII, page 675.

"Report of the Monetary Committee, 1934, New Zealand," *The Economic Journal,* March, 1935, Vol. XLV, pages 192-196.

"Future of the Interest Rates," *The Times* (London), February 20, 1936, page 21.

"The Theory of the Rate of Interest," *Lessons of Monetary Experience, Essays in Honor of Irving Fisher,* edited by A. D. Gayer, pages 145-152. New York: Farrar and Rinehart, 1937.

"Alternative Theories of the Rate of Interest," *The Economic Journal*, June, 1937, Vol. XLVII, pages 241-252.

"The 'Ex-Ante' Theory of the Rate of Interest," *The Economic Journal*, December, 1937, Vol. XLVII, pages 663-669.

"Mr. Keynes and 'Finance,'" *The Economic Journal*, June, 1938, Vol. XLVIII, pages 318-322.

"The United States and the Keynes Plan," *The New Republic*, July 29, 1940, Vol. CIII, pages 156-159.

B. International economics, including foreign exchange and gold

"Return of Estimated Value of Foreign Trade of the United Kingdom at Prices of 1900," *The Economic Journal*, December, 1912, Vol. XXII, pages 630-631.

"The Stabilization of the European Exchanges," I and II, *The Manchester Guardian Commercial, Reconstruction in Europe*, April 20, 1922, Number One, pages 3-5; and December 7, 1922, Eleventh Number, pages 658-661.

"The Theory of the Exchanges and 'Purchasing Power Parity,'" *The Manchester Guardian Commercial, Reconstruction in Europe*, April 20, 1922, Number One, pages 6-8.

"The Forward Market in Foreign Exchange," *Manchester Guardian Commercial, Reconstruction in Europe*, April 20, 1922, Number One, pages 11-15.

"Professor Jevons on the Indian Exchange," *The Economic Journal*, March, 1923, Vol. XXXIII, pages 60-65.

"Trustee Investments—Home, Colonial, and Indian," *The Nation and the Athenaeum*, June 2, 1923, Vol. XXXIII, page 318.

"Free Trade for England," *The New Republic*, December 19, 1923, Vol. XXXVII, pages 86-87.

"Gold in 1923," *The New Republic*, February 27, 1924, Vol. XXXVIII, pages 10-11.

"The Prospects of Gold," *The New Republic*, March 12, 1924, Vol. XXXVIII, pages 66-67.

"The Franc," *The New Republic*, March 26, 1924, Vol. XXXVIII, pages 120-121.

"The Return Towards Gold," *The New Republic*, March 18, 1925, Vol. XLII, pages 92-94.

"The Problem of the Gold Standard," *The Nation and the Athenaeum*, March 21, 1925, Vol XXXVI, pages 866-870.

"The Gold Standard," *The Nation and the Athenaeum*, May 2, 1925, Vol. XXXVII, pages 129-130.

"Is the Pound Overvalued?" *The New Republic,* May 6, 1925, Vol. XLII, pages 286-287.

"The Gold Standard—A Correction," *The Nation and the Athenaeum,* May 9, 1925, Vol. XXXVII, pages 169-170.

"England's Gold Standard," *The New Republic,* May 20, 1925, Vol. XLII, pages 339-340.

"The Gold Standard Act," *The Economic Journal,* June, 1925, Vol. XXXV, pages 312-313.

"The Arithmetic of the Sterling Exchange," *The Nation and the Athenaeum,* June 13, 1925, Vol. XXXVII, page 338.

"Great Britain's Cross of Gold," *The New Republic,* September 16, 1925, Vol. XLIV, pages 88-90.

"The French Franc," *The New Republic,* January 27, 1926, Vol. XLV, pages 266-268.

"The First Fruits of the British Gold Standard," *The New Republic,* June 2, 1926, Vol. XLVII, pages 54-55.

"The Future of the Franc," *The New Republic,* August 11, 1926, Vol. XLVII, pages 328-329.

"Will England Restrict Foreign Investments?" *The New Republic,* December 1, 1926, Vol. XLIX, pages 34-36.

"A Model Form for Statements of International Balances," *The Economic Journal,* September, 1927, Vol. XXXVII, pages 472-476.

"The British Balance of Trade, 1925-27," *The Economic Journal,* December, 1927, Vol. XXXVII, pages 551-565.

"Note on the British Balance of Trade," *The Economic Journal,* March, 1928, Vol. XXXVIII, pages 146-147.

"The United States' Balance of Trade in 1927," *The Economic Journal,* September, 1928, Vol. XXXVIII, pages 487-489.

"Is There Enough Gold?" *The Nation and the Athenaeum,* January 19, 1929, Vol. XLIV, pages 545-546.

"Proposal for a Revenue Tariff," *The New Statesman and Nation,* March 7, 1931, Vol. I, pages 53-54.

"Revenue Tariff for Great Britain," *The New Republic,* April 8, 1931, Vol. LXVI, pages 196-197.

"Paradox of British Economic Policy: Will England Introduce a Revenue Tariff?" *Journal of the Institute of Bankers in South Africa,* May, 1931, Vol. XXVIII, pages 72-76.

"The Prospects of the Sterling Exchange," *Yale Review,* March, 1932, Vol. XXI, pages 433-447.

"Reflections on the Sterling Exchange," *Lloyds Bank Limited Monthly Review,* April, 1932, Vol. III, pages 143-160.

"The World's Economic Outlook," *Atlantic Monthly*, May, 1932, Vol. CXLIX, pages 521-526.

"The World Economic Conference, 1933," *The New Statesman and Nation*, December 24, 1932, Vol. IV, pages 825-826.

"National Self-Sufficiency," *Yale Review*, Summer, 1933, Vol. XXII, pages 755-769.

"The Solid Business of the Conference: A Plan to End the Chaos of the Exchanges," *Journal of the Institute of Bankers in South Africa*, July, 1933, Vol. XXX, pages 226-230.

"President Roosevelt's Gold Policy," *The New Statesman and Nation*, January 20, 1934, Vol. VII, pages 76-77.

"The Bank for International Settlements, Fourth Annual Report (1933-4)," *The Economic Journal*, September, 1934, Vol. XLIV, pages 514-518.

"The Bank for International Settlements, Fifth Annual Report (1934-5)," *The Economic Journal*, September, 1935, Vol. XLV, pages 594-597.

"The Future of the Foreign Exchanges," *Lloyds Bank Limited Monthly Review*, October, 1935, Vol. VI, pages 527-535.

"The Supply of Gold," *The Economic Journal*, September, 1936, Vol. XLVI, pages 412-418.

"International Clearing Union," (Speech before the House of Lords), May 18, 1943, *Hansard Lords*, Vol. CXXVII, pages 527-537. (Reprinted in *The New Economics*, edited by S. E. Harris. New York: Alfred A. Knopf, 1947.)

"The Objective of International Price Stability," *The Economic Journal*, June-September, 1943, Vol. LIII, pages 185-187.

"International Monetary Fund," (Speech before the House of Lords), May 23, 1944, *Hansard Lords*, Vol. CXXXI, pages 838-849. (Reprinted, in *The New Economics*, edited by S. E. Harris. New York: Alfred A. Knopf, 1947.)

"The Bank for Reconstruction and Development," (Speech delivered as Chairman of the Second Commission of the Bank, July 3, 1944). (Published in *The New Economics*, edited by S. E. Harris, Chapter XXIX, pages 396-400. New York: Alfred A. Knopf, 1947.)

"A Rejoinder to Professor Graham," (On the Objective of International Price Stability), *The Economic Journal*, December, 1944, Vol. LIV, pages 429-430.

"Anglo-American Financial Arrangements," (Speech before the House of Lords), December 18, 1945, *Hansard Lords*, Vol. CXXXVIII, pages 777-794. (Reprinted in *The New Economics*,

edited by S. E. Harris. New York: Alfred A. Knopf, 1947.)
"The Balance of Payments of the United States," *The Economic Journal*, June, 1946, Vol. LVI, pages 172-187.

C. Unemployment, employment, and wages

"Currency Policy and Unemployment," *The Nation and the Athenaeum*, August 11, 1923, Vol. XXXIII, pages 611-612.

"Does Unemployment Need a Drastic Remedy?" *The Nation and the Athenaeum*, May 24, 1924, Vol. XXXV, pages 235-236.

"A Drastic Remedy for Unemployment: Reply to Critics," *The Nation and the Athenaeum*, June 7, 1924, Vol. XXXV, pages 311-312.

"Back to the Coal Problem," *The Nation and the Athenaeum*, May 15, 1926, Vol. XXXIX, page 159.

"The Question of High Wages," *Political Quarterly*, January, 1930, Vol. I, pages 110-124.

"British Industry, Unemployment, and High Wages," *Barrons*, March 24, 1930, Vol. X, pages 22-23.

"The Industrial Crisis," *The Nation and the Athenaeum*, May 10, 1930, Vol. XLVII, pages 163-164.

"The Great Slump of 1930," *The Nation and the Athenaeum*, December 20 and 27, 1930, Vol. XLVIII, pages 402, 427-428.

"An Economic Analysis of Unemployment," in *Unemployment as a World-Problem*, edited by Quincy Wright, Chapter I, pages 3-42. Chicago: University of Chicago Press, 1931.

"Causes of World Depression," *The Forum and Century*, January, 1931, Vol. LXXXV, pages 21-25.

"Some Consequences of the Economy Report," *The New Statesman and Nation*, August 15, 1931, Vol. II, pages 189-190.

"The World's Economic Crisis and the Way of Escape," Halley Stewart Lecture, 1931, Chapter III, pages 57-75, in *The World's Economic Crisis and the Way of Escape*. New York: The Century Co., 1932.

"A Plan to Save the World," *Journal of the Institute of Bankers in South Africa*, February, 1933, Vol. XXIX, pages 735-741.

"A Programme for Unemployment," *The New Statesman and Nation*, February 4, 1933, Vol. V, pages 121-122.

"The Multiplier," *The New Statesman and Nation*, April 1, 1933, Vol. V, pages 405-407.

"Economic Revival," *The New York Times*, April 2, 1933, Section VIII, page 3.

"Public Works: Earnings, Direct and Indirect," *The Times* (London), July 28, 1933, page 10.

"From Keynes to Roosevelt: Our Recovery Plan Assayed," (An open letter to President Roosevelt), *The New York Times,* December 31, 1933, Section VIII, page 2.

"Mr. Roosevelt's Experiments," *The Times* (London), January 2, 1934, pages 11-12.

"U. S. Recovery Needs," *The New York Times,* June 10, 1934, Section IV, page 1E.

"A Self-adjusting Economic System?" *The New Republic,* February 20, 1935, Vol. LXXXII, pages 35-37.

"How to Avoid a Slump," *The Times* (London), January 12, 13, 14, 1937, pages 13f, 13f, 13f.

"The General Theory of Employment," *The Quarterly Journal of Economics,* February, 1937, Vol. LI, pages 209-223.

"Professor Pigou on Money Wages in Relation to Unemployment," *The Economic Journal,* December, 1937, Vol. XLVII, pages 743-745.

"Public Works, Improvisation or Planning?" *The Times* (London), January 3, 1938, page 13.

"Relative Movements of Real Wages and Output," *The Economic Journal,* March, 1939, Vol. XLIX, pages 34-51.

D. Consumption, saving, investment, and income

"Saving and Usury," *The Economic Journal,* March, 1932, Vol. XLII, pages 135-137.

"Mr. Robertson on 'Saving' and 'Hoarding'," *The Economic Journal,* December, 1933, Vol. XLIII, pages 699-701.

"Fluctuations in Net Investment in the United States," *The Economic Journal,* September, 1936, Vol. XLVI, pages 540-547.

"Mr. Keynes' Consumption Function: Reply," *The Quarterly Journal of Economics,* August, 1938, Vol. LII, pages 708-709. (A reply to an article by G. R. Holden, in the same volume, pages 281-296. See a further brief comment by Keynes in the same journal, November, 1938, Vol. LIII, page 160.)

"Mr. Keynes on the Distribution of Incomes and 'Propensity to Consume': A Reply," *The Review of Economic Statistics,* August, 1939, Vol. XXI, page 129. (See Hans Staehle, in the same journal, August, 1938, Vol. XX, pages 128-141; and August, 1939, Vol. XXI, pages 129-130.)

"The Process of Capital Formation," *The Economic Journal,* September, 1939, Vol. XLIX, pages 569-574.

"Professor Tinbergen's Method: The Statistical Testing of Business-Cycle Theories," *The Economic Journal,* September, 1939, Vol.

XLIX, pages 558-568. (See "Comment" by Keynes in response to a reply by Tinbergen, *The Economic Journal,* March, 1940, Vol. L, pages 154-156.)
"The Concept of National Income: A Supplementary Note," *The Economic Journal,* March, 1940, Vol. L, pages 60-65.

E. War and peace, including war debts and reparations

"War and the Financial System, August, 1914," *The Economic Journal,* September, 1914, Vol. XXIV, pages 460-486.

"The Economics of War in Germany," *The Economic Journal,* September, 1915, Vol. XXV, pages 443-452.

"Editorial Foreword," to European Reconstruction, *Manchester Guardian Commercial, Reconstruction in Europe,* April 20, 1922, Number One, page 2. (Keynes was general editor of this special publication of the *Manchester Guardian Commercial.*)

"The Reconstruction of Europe: A General Introduction," *The Manchester Guardian Commercial, Reconstruction in Europe,* May 18, 1922, Second Number, pages 66-67.

"The Genoa Conference," *The Manchester Guardian Commercial, Reconstruction in Europe,* June 15, 1922, Third Number, pages 132-133.

"Is a Settlement of the Reparation Question Possible Now?" *The Manchester Guardian Commercial, Reconstruction in Europe,* September 28, 1922, Eighth Number, pages 462-464.

"Speculation in the Mark and Germany's Balances Abroad," *The Manchester Guardian Commercial, Reconstruction in Europe,* September 28, 1922, Eighth Number, pages 480-482.

"The Underlying Principles," *The Manchester Guardian Commercial, Reconstruction in Europe,* January 4, 1923, Twelfth Number, pages 717-718.

"British Policy in Europe," *The Nation and the Athenaeum,* May 5, 1923, Vol. XXXIII, pages 148-150.

"The German Offer and the French Reply," *The Nation and the Athenaeum,* May 12, 1923, Vol. XXXIII, pages 188-189.

"The German Loan Delusion," *The New Republic,* June 13, 1923, Vol. XXXV, pages 62-64.

"A Reparations Plan," *The New Republic,* August 8, 1923, Vol. XXXV, pages 280-281.

"The Experts' Reports. I. The Dawes Report," and "II. The McKenna Report," *The Nation and the Athenaeum,* April 12, 1924, and April 19, 1924, Vol. XXXV, pages 40-41 and 76-77.

"How Can the Dawes Plan Work?" *The New Republic*, April 23, 1924, Vol. XXXVIII, pages 224-226.

"The American Debt," *The Nation and the Athenaeum*, August 4, 1924, Vol. XXXV, pages 584-587.

"What the Dawes Plan Will Do," *The New Republic*, October 22, 1924, Vol. XL, pages 195-196.

"The Interallied Debts," *The New Republic*, January 21, 1925, Vol. XLI, pages 221-222.

"Germany's Coming Problem," *The New Republic*, February 17, 1926, Vol. XLV, pages 348-349.

"Mr. Churchill on the Peace," *The Nation and the Athenaeum*, March 9, 1929, Vol. XLIV, pages 782-783.

"The German Transfer Problem," *The Economic Journal*, March, 1929, Vol. XXXIX, pages 1-7.

"The Reparations Problem: A Discussion: II. A Rejoinder," *The Economic Journal*, June, 1929, Vol. XXXIX, pages 179-182.

"Views on the Transfer Problem: III. A Reply," *The Economic Journal*, September, 1929, Vol. XXXIX, pages 404-408.

"The Reparations Crisis," *The New Republic*, May 1, 1929, Vol. LVIII, pages 296-297.

"The Report of the Young Committee," *The Nation and the Athenaeum*, June 15, 1929, Vol. XLIV, pages 359-361.

"Reaping the Whirlwind of the Peace Treaty," *The Golden Book Magazine*, January, 1932, Vol. XV, pages 31-32.

"An End of Reparations?" *The New Statesman and Nation*, January 16, 1932, Vol. III, pages 57-58.

"Britain for Cancellation," *The New Republic*, January 27, 1932, Vol. LXIX, pages 284-285.

"A Policy for Lausanne," *The Times* (London), June 15, 1932, page 15.

"A Positive Peace Programme," *The New Statesman and Nation*, March 26 and April 9, 1938, Vol. XV, pages 509-510, and 605.

"A British Peace Program," *The New Republic*, April 13, 1938, Vol. XCIV, pages 295-296.

"The Policy of Government Storage of Foodstuffs and Raw Materials," *The Economic Journal*, September, 1938, Vol. XLVIII, pages 449-460.

"Crisis Finance," *The Times* (London), April 17 and 18, 1939, pages 13-14 and 15-16.

"The Income and Fiscal Potential of Great Britain," *The Economic Journal*, December, 1939, Vol. XLIX, pages 626-635.

F. Politics and social philosophy

"Russia," *Manchester Guardian Commercial, Reconstruction in Europe,* July 6, 1922, Fourth Number, pages 200-201.

"Mr. Baldwin's Task," *The New Republic,* August 1, 1923, Vol. XXXV, pages 252-253.

"Public and Private Enterprise," *The Nation and the Athenaeum,* June 21, 1924, Vol. XXXV, pages 374-375.

"The Balance of Political Power in Great Britain," *The New Republic,* November 26, 1924, Vol. XLI, pages 18-19.

"Mr. Churchill on Rates and the Liberal Industrial Inquiry," *The Nation and the Athenaeum,* April 28, 1928, Vol. XLIII, pages 99-100.

"Soviet Russia," *The New Republic,* October 28, November 4, and November 11, 1925, Vol. XLIV, pages 246-248, 275-277, and 301-303.

"Liberalism and Labor in England," *The New Republic,* March 3, 1926, Vol. XLVI, pages 38-39.

"The Treasury Contribution to the White Paper," *The Nation and the Athenaeum,* May 18, 1929, Vol. XLV, pages 227-228.

"Sir Oswald Moseley's Manifesto," *The Nation and the Athenaeum,* December 13, 1930, Vol. XLVIII, page 367.

"A Criticism of Mr. Snowden's Budget," *Journal of the Institute of Bankers in South Africa,* June, 1931, Vol. XXXVIII, pages 106-107.

"The Budget," *The New Statesman and Nation,* September 19, 1931, Vol. II, page 329.

"Enjoying Russia" (review of Low's drawings), *The New Statesman and Nation,* December 10, 1932, Vol. IV, page 770.

"Shaw on Wells on Stalin," *The New Statesman and Nation,* November 10, 1934, Vol. VIII, pages 653-654.

"British Foreign Policy," *The New Statesman and Nation,* July 10, 1937, Vol. XIV, pages 61-62. (In the same journal see also Keynes' correspondence on British foreign policy, July 18, August 8, August 15, August 29, and September 12, 1936, Vol. XII, pages 82-83, 188, 219, 284, and 348.)

"Mr. Chamberlain's Foreign Policy," *The New Statesman and Nation,* October 8, 1938, Vol. XVI, pages 518-519.

"Democracy and Efficiency" (discussion with Kingsley Martin), *The New Statesman and Nation,* January 28, 1939, Vol. XVII, pages 121-122.

G. Biographical

"Frederic Hillersdon Keeling," *The Economic Journal,* September, 1916, Vol. XXVI, pages 403-404.

"Alfred Marshall, 1842-1924," *The Economic Journal,* September, 1924, Vol. XXXIV, pages 311-372.

"Bibliographical List of the Writings of Alfred Marshall," *The Economic Journal,* December, 1924, Vol. XXXIV, pages 627-637. (Reprinted in *Memorials of Alfred Marshall.*)

"Francis Ysidro Edgeworth, 1845-1926," *The Economic Journal,* March, 1926, Vol. XXXVI, pages 140-150. (Reprinted in *Essays in Biography.*)

"F. P. Ramsey," *The Economic Journal,* March, 1930, Vol. XL, pages 153-154.

"C. P. Sanger," *The Economic Journal,* March, 1930, Vol. XL, pages 154-155.

"The Earl of Balfour," *The Economic Journal,* June, 1930, Vol. XL, pages 336-338.

"Commemoration of T. R. Malthus," *The Economic Journal,* June, 1935, Vol. XLV, pages 230-234.

"Sir Henry Cunynghame," *The Economic Journal,* June, 1935, Vol. XLV, pages 398-406.

"Andrew Andreades (1876-1935)," *The Economic Journal,* September, 1935, Vol. XLV, pages 597-599.

"William Stanley Jevons, 1835-1882," *Journal of the Royal Statistical Society,* 1936, Vol. XCIX, Part III, pages 516-548, 554-555.

"Herbert Somerton Foxwell," *The Economic Journal,* December, 1936, Vol. XLVI, pages 589-614.

"Adam Smith as Student and Professor," *Economic History (Economic Journal Supplement),* February, 1938, Vols. III-IV, pages 33-46.

"George Broomhall, 1857-1938," *The Economic Journal,* September, 1938, Vol. XLVIII, pages 576-578.

"Alfred Hoare, 1850-1938," *The Economic Journal,* December, 1938, Vol. XLVIII, pages 753-756.

(with Clara Collet) "Henry Higgs," *The Economic Journal,* December, 1940, Vol. L, pages 546-558.

"Mary Paley Marshall," *The Economic Journal,* June-September, 1944, Vol. LIV, pages 268-284.

H. Miscellaneous

"The Principal Averages, and the Laws of Error Which Lead to Them," *Journal of the Royal Statistical Society,* February, 1911, Vol. LXXIV, pages 322-331.

"The Influence of Parental Alcoholism," *Journal of the Royal Statistical Society*, February, 1911, Vol. LXXIV, pages 339-345.

"Report of the Commissioners of Inland Revenue for the Year Ended 31st March, 1912," *The Economic Journal*, December, 1912, Vol. XXII, pages 632-633.

"Report of the Committee on Irish Finance," "Government of Ireland Bill: Outline of Financial Provisions," and "Return Showing the Debt Incurred for Purely Irish Purposes," (reviews of official documents), *The Economic Journal*, September, 1912, Vol. XXII, pages 498-502.

"An Economist's View of Population," *Manchester Guardian Commercial, Reconstruction in Europe*, August 17, 1922, Sixth Number, pages 340-341.

(assisted by R. B. Lewis) "Stocks of Staple Commodities," *London and Cambridge Economic Service*, Special Memorandum No. 1, April, 1923, pages 2-20.

"Is Britain Overpopulated?" *The New Republic*, October 31, 1923, Vol. XXXVI, pages 247-248.

"A Reply to Sir William Beveridge's 'Population and Unemployment'," *The Economic Journal*, December, 1923, Vol. XXXIII, pages 476-486. (See Sir William Beveridge, *ibid.*, pages 447-475.)

"Investment Policy for Insurance Companies," *The Nation and the Athenaeum*, May 17, 1924, Vol. XXXV, page 226.

"Stocks of Staple Commodities," *London and Cambridge Economic Service*, Special Memorandum No. 6, June, 1924, pages 2-18.

(with J. W. F. Rowe) "Stocks of Staple Commodities," *London and Cambridge Economic Service*, Special Memorandum No. 12, July, 1925, pages 2-18; Special Memorandum No. 16, February, 1926, pages 2-18; Special Memorandum No. 22, March, 1927, pages 2-23; and Special Memorandum No. 29, August, 1929, pages 2-25.

"Coal: A Suggestion," *The Nation and the Athenaeum*, April 24, 1926, Vol. XXXIX, pages 91-92.

"The Colwyn Report on National Debt and Taxation," *The Economic Journal*, June, 1927, Vol. XXXVII, pages 198-212.

(with J. W. F. Rowe and G. L. Schwartz) "Stocks of Staple Commodities," *London and Cambridge Economic Service*, Special Memorandum No. 32, September, 1930, pages 2-30.

"Professor Laski and the Issue of Freedom," *The New Statesman and Nation*, July 21, 1934, Vol. VIII, pages 86-87.

"Some Economic Consequences of a Declining Population," *Eugenics Review*, April, 1937, Vol. XXIX, pages 13-17.

(with Piero Sraffa) "Introduction" to an *Abstract of a Treatise of Human Nature*, by David Hume, pages v-xxxii. Cambridge: University Press, 1938.

III. Book Reviews

The Rupee Problem, by Montagu de Pomeroy Webb. *The Economic Journal*, September, 1910, Vol. XX, pages 438-440.

The Purchasing Power of Money, by Irving Fisher. *The Economic Journal*, September, 1911, Vol. XXI, pages 393-398.

The Economic Transition in India, by T. Morrison. *The Economic Journal*, September, 1911, Vol. XXI, pages 426-431.

Theory of Political Economy, Fourth Edition, by W. Stanley Jevons. *The Economic Journal*, March, 1912, Vol. XXII, pages 78-80.

The Economic Principles of Confucius and His School, by Chen Huan-Chang. *The Economic Journal*, December, 1912, Vol. XXII, pages 584-588.

The Course of Prices in New Zealand, by James W. McIlbraith, and *Report of Commission on the Cost of Living in New Zealand. The Economic Journal*, December, 1912, Vol. XXII, pages 595-598.

The Standard of Value, by Sir David M. Barbour. *The Economic Journal*, June, 1913, Vol. XXIII, pages 390-393.

Gold, Prices, and Wages, by John A. Hobson. *The Economic Journal*, June, 1913, Vol. XXIII, pages 393-398.

Le Thaler de Marie Thérèse, by Marcel-Maurice Fischel. *The Economic Journal*, June, 1914, Vol. XXIV, pages 257-260.

Theorie des Geldes und der Umlaufsmittel, by Ludwig von Mises, and *Geld und Kapital*, by Friedrich Bendixen. *The Economic Journal*, September, 1914, Vol. XXIV, pages 417-419.

What is Money? by Mitchell Innes. *The Economic Journal*, September, 1914, Vol. XXIV, pages 419-421.

The Works and Life of Walter Bagehot, by Mrs. Russell Barrington. *The Economic Journal*, September, 1915, Vol. XXV, pages 369-375.

Currency and Credit, by R. G. Hawtrey. *The Economic Journal*, September, 1920, Vol. XXX, pages 362-365.

Indian Finance and Banking, by G. Findlay Shirras. *The Economic Journal*, September, 1920, Vol. XXX, pages 396-397.

The Future of Exchange and the Indian Currency, by H. Stanley Jevons. *The Economic Journal,* March, 1923, Vol. XXXIII, pages 60-65.

The Behavior of Prices: A Report of an Investigation, by F. C. Mills. *The Economic Journal,* December, 1928, Vol. XXXVIII, pages 606-608.

Inter-relationships of Supply and Price, by G. F. Warren and F. A. Pearson. *The Economic Journal,* March, 1929, Vol. XXXIX, pages 92-95.

Unemployment and Inflation, by Alfred Hoare. *The Economic Journal,* September, 1933, Vol. XLIII, pages 474-475.

Consumers' Credits and Unemployment, by J. E. Meade. *The Economic Journal,* March, 1938, Vol. XLVIII, pages 67-71.

English Economic History, Mainly Since 1700, by C. R. Fay. *The Economic Journal,* June-September, 1940, Vol. L, pages 259-261.

INDEX

Demand *(Cont.)* :
function, aggregate, 31-33
investment *(see* Investment)
meaning in Keynes' theory, 29-31
schedule, aggregate (diagram), 30
Demand price of capital assets, 138-139, 147
Deposits:
derivative, 184, 185
primary, 184
Depreciation:
excessive, 70
user cost and, 68-69
Depression *(see* Business cycle, Fiscal policy, Multiplier, Public investment, and Unemployment)
Dillard, Dudley, 334
Diminishing returns, 218, 223, 230-231
Disinvestment, 88, 264, 273
Distribution of income and wealth, 7, 81-83, 217, 238, 244-245, 246; 299-300, 316, 327, 331
effect of inflation on, 238
inequality of, and unemployment, 7, 81-83
progressive taxation and, 82-83, 327
saving and, 81
Douglas, Major, 323n
Dunlop, J. T., 236

E

Economic Consequences of Mr. Churchill, The (1925), 304, 305, 307
Economic Consequences of the Peace, The (1919), 299-300, 316
Economic planning, 17, 158-159
Economics, classical *(see* Classical economics)
Economics of full employment *vs.* economics of less than full employment, 3, 161-162, 189, 193, 197, 226
Effective demand:
business cycle and, 277
defined, 32
employment and, 25, 28-51, 75, 235, 237
increases beyond full employment, 226-227, 239-240, 255-256
prices and, 223-235, 237
principle of, 29-37

Effective Demand *(Cont.)* :
quantity of money and, 226, 239
summary of theory of, 48-50
wage costs and, 209
wartime, 242, 243
Elasticity of demand for labor, 210
Elasticity of demand for money, 180, 202-203
Elasticity of production of money, 200-201
Elasticity of substitution of money, 202
Elasticity of supply, 224, 225, 232
Ellis, Howard S., 236
Ellsworth, P. T., 204
Employment:
full *(see* Full employment)
investment and, 7-8, 36, 37, 39-45, 76, 92-100, 156-158, 217
lower limit of, 39, 51, 93-94, 96, 277
real wages and, 218-219
theory of:
fundamental ideas, 3-12
general nature of, 3-4
practical meaning of, 13-14, 25-26, 51-55, 76, 105-106, 156-157, 163, 178-179, 218-219, 220, 227, 255, 266-267, 279-280, 283-284, 285, 291-292, 296, 303, 309-310, 317, 323, 326-334
summarized, 48-51, 75-76
Employment Act of 1946, 2, 328-329
End of Laissez-faire, The (1926), 295 *(see also* Laissez-faire and Communism)
England *(see* Great Britain)
Enterprise *vs.* speculation in the stock market, 148-150
Equilibrium:
full-employment, 16, 33, 59, 189, 199
shifting, 4, 59, 189
unstable, 106
Estey, J. A., 310n
Euthanasia of the rentier 159, 279
Excess bank reserves, 187
Exchange rates, 285, 286, 287, 288-292
Expectations, 142-153
interest rate and, 176-177
long-term, 9, 144-146
short-term, 143-144, 154
stock market influence on, 146-152

Colección
DOCUMENTOS

Negar la evidencia

Negar la evidencia

Bush en la guerra, parte III

Bob Woodward

BELACQVA

Woodward, Bob, 1944-
    Negar la evidencia / Bob Woodward ; traductores
    Santiago Ochoa ... [et al.]. -- Bogotá : Editorial Belacqva, 2006.
    522 p. ; 23 cm. -- (Colección documentos)
    Título original. State of Denial.
    ISBN 978-958-04-9857-5
    1. Bush, George Walker, 1946- 2. Seguridad nacional -
Estados Unidos - Toma de decisiones 3. Guerra de Irak, 2003
4. Estados Unidos - Política militar - Toma de decisiones
5. Estados Unidos - Funcionarios y empleados I. Ochoa,
Santiago, tr. II. Tít. II. Serie.
973.931 cd 21 ed.
A1102840

    CEP-Banco de la República-Biblioteca Luis Ángel Arango

Título original: *State of Denial. Bush at War part III*
© 2006, Bob Woodward.
© Primera edición: Simon&Schuster, 2006.
© De la presente edición en español: Belacqva de Ediciones y Publicaciones S.L.
Ronda de Sant Pere, 5, 4a planta, Barcelona.

Primera edición: diciembre de 2006.

Edición: Luis Fernando Páez
Traducción: Santiago Ochoa, Yasmín López, Ángela García, Andrea Moure
Revisión de textos: Álvaro Sánchez
Imagen de cubierta: Agencia Cover
Diseño de cubierta: María Clara Salazar
Armada: Luz Jazmine Güechá
Impreso por: Imprelibros S.A.
Impreso en Colombia - *Printed in Colombia*

ISBN 978-958-04-9857-5
CC. 32917

Para Mary Walsh

NOTA DEL AUTOR

Dos PERSONAS me ayudaron en todas las etapas de este libro, trabajando en unas oficinas habilitadas en el tercer piso de mi casa, en Washington, D. C.

Bill Murphy, antiguo reportero y abogado que sirvió en el Cuerpo de abogados defensores del Ejército y en el Departamento de Justicia, concluyó que yo necesitaba escribir un tercer libro sobre el presidente Bush, cuyo tema principal fuera la guerra en Irak. Honesto, directo y preocupado por la justicia y la verdad, Murphy es un reportero natural que se ha ganado la confianza de varias fuentes clave. Centrado e increíblemente recursivo, Bill se convirtió en mi socio. Rara vez los escritores contamos con socios que tengan semejante madurez y destreza y nos ofrezcan consejos tan sabios. Sin él, nunca hubiera podido terminar este libro, que es tanto suyo como mío.

Christine Parthemore, una estudiante graduada con honores en ciencia política en Ohio State University, en 2003, es una especie de *mujer maravilla* de la era informática; es capaz de encontrar todo tipo de información. Nunca me ha decepcionado; es meticulosa y diligente en cada labor, desde la trascripción de cientos de horas de entrevistas grabadas hasta la edición del manuscrito. Es una mujer culta, franca e inteligente. Editora innata, sabe cómo llegar a la esencia de las cosas. Tal como lo demostró todos y cada uno de los días, Christine tiene la energía de seis personas y una capacidad de trabajo infinita.

PRÓLOGO

A FINALES DE DICIEMBRE DEL 2000, menos de un mes antes de su posesión, el presidente electo George W. Bush aún estaba pensando quién podría ser su secretario de Defensa. El ex senador Dan Coats, un partido republicano de Indiana que había trabajado en el Comité de Servicios Armados, ocupaba el primer lugar en la lista de Bush y tenía el respaldo de su base conservadora. Pero durante su entrevista, Coats no impresionó favorablemente a Bush ni a Dick Cheney, el vicepresidente electo que estaba a cargo del equipo de transición del nuevo gobierno. Coats conocía poco a los generales de más alto rango y no tenía muchos conocimientos acerca del sistema nacional de defensa y misiles que Bush había prometido durante su campaña. Además, Coats nunca había dirigido ninguna organización grande. Bush comprendió que necesitaría un subsecretario fuerte y experimentado en el Pentágono. Coats no era el hombre que estaba buscando; Bush necesitaba a alguien que no sólo batallara con los generales, sino que tuviera también tanto peso como el resto de su nuevo equipo de seguridad nacional. Cheney había sido secretario de Defensa de Bush padre; Colin Powell, a quien Bush había nombrado como secretario de Estado, había sido presidente del Estado Mayor Conjunto y asesor de seguridad nacional de Reagan. Bush necesitaba un secretario de Defensa de mayor envergadura, firmeza y experiencia.

¿Qué tal Donald Rumsfeld? Con 68 años de edad, antiguo jefe y mentor de Cheney, Rumsfeld tenía una hoja de vida de ensueño. Había sido secretario de Defensa del presidente Ford de 1975 a 1977, piloto de la Marina en los años cincuenta, congresista electo durante cuatro períodos, jefe de gabinete de la Casa Blanca en la administración de Ford, y presidente de dos compañías "Fortune 500". El presidente y el vicepresidente habían discutido la posibilidad de nombrar a Rumsfeld como director de la CIA, pero tal vez no sería una decisión acertada. Probablemente lo necesitaban de nuevo en el Departamento de Defensa.

Tres días antes de Navidad, Bush, Cheney y Rumsfeld sostuvieron una larga reunión y almorzaron juntos. Áspero, engreído, seguro de sí mismo y con una intensidad casi infantil, este hombre parecía tener la mitad de su edad. Pareció un verdadero tornado durante la entrevista, completamente emotivo y visionario. Conocía el Pentágono y, recientemente, había dirigido comisiones sobre la utilización espacial y la amenaza de misiles balísticos. Parecía saberlo todo.

Bush se sorprendió de la fuerte impresión que le causó; después de la reunión, habló con Andrew H. Card Jr., el nuevo jefe de gabinete de la Casa Blanca.

Bush había nombrado a este hombre de 53 años porque su padre le había dicho que no existía otra persona que fuera más leal. En 1988, Card había desempeñado un papel fundamental en la victoria de Bush padre en las importantísimas primarias de New Hampshire. Más tarde, se había desempeñado como jefe de gabinete de la Casa Blanca y como secretario de Transporte.

Card creyó que el presidente le pediría que dirigiera el equipo de transición después de las elecciones del 2000. "No; no me refiero a ese cargo", le dijo Bush, "sino al más importante". Card insistió en que si Bush quería que fuera el jefe de gabinete, tendrían que entablar una relación cercana y completamente abierta, y que él debía tener libertad para imponer sus propias condiciones. Debería tener acceso a todas las personas, reuniones e información. "Y no puedo a la vez ser un amigo", dijo Card.

"Por supuesto", respondió Bush.

En noviembre, semanas antes de que la Corte Suprema decidiera las elecciones a su favor, Bush anunció el nombramiento de Card, enviando un mensaje fuerte e intencional: exceptuando al vicepresidente, Andy Card sería el hombre más importante en la Casa Blanca de Bush, en todos los asuntos y a todas horas.

BUSH LE DIJO A CARD que Coats le parecía un hombre bueno, pero que la diferencia con Rumsfeld era enorme. Este último entendía el significado de la transformación militar: hacer que las tropas y las armas fueran más rápidas, tuvieran mayor movilidad y tecnología y fueran más letales. También señaló que Rumsfeld era un ser admirable. *Esto es lo que tiene que hacerse. Ésta es la forma de hacerlo. Éste es el tipo de personas que se necesita.* Era como si ya tuviera todo un programa. Rumsfeld tenía 43 años cuando había desempeñado el mismo cargo un cuarto de siglo atrás. Era como si ahora estuviera diciendo: "creo que tengo algunas cosas que me gustaría terminar".

Bush y Card conversaron sobre otro aspecto. Rumsfeld y Bush padre no se soportaban. Ambos había sido jóvenes estrellas del partido republicano en los años 70, y existía una fuerte rivalidad entre ellos. Bush padre pensaba que Rumsfeld era arrogante, ególatra, demasiado seguro de sí mismo y maquiavélico. Opinaba que Rumsfeld había manipulado al presidente Ford en

1975 para que lo nombrara como director de la CIA, agencia que en aquella época se encontraba quizás en su peor momento, a tal punto que se pensaba que ser su director era un camino sin salida. Aunque las cosas resultaron ser diferentes, Bush padre no confiaba en Rumsfeld. Éste también había expresado comentarios desagradables a nivel privado; había dicho que Bush no tenía el peso suficiente, que había sido débil como director de la CIA durante la Guerra Fría, que no había dimensionado la amenaza soviética y había sido manipulado por Henry Kissinger, el secretario de Estado.

Card comprendió que el nuevo presidente estaba dispuesto a superar su escepticismo acerca de Rumsfeld; era una oportunidad para demostrar que su padre se había equivocado. Además, Rumsfeld encajaba en el modelo propuesto por Cheney.

Cheney había sido encargado de encontrar al compañero de fórmula presidencial de Bush, y había dicho que quería a una persona con mucha experiencia. El candidato ideal tendría que conocer la Casa Blanca y el Congreso, haber desempeñado un cargo por elección popular y una agencia federal grande. También debía ser alguien que no fuera tan sólo un producto de Washington; debía tener experiencia en el mundo real, quizás en el mundo corporativo, haber sido presidente de una compañía o algo similar. Tal vez no era sorprendente que Cheney, quien había sido congresista, jefe de gabinete de la Casa Blanca, secretario de Defensa y presidente de una compañía que estaba en la lista Fortune 500, valorara su propia experiencia y moldeara al candidato ideal según su propia imagen. Bush entendió el mensaje y eligió a Cheney como candidato a la vicepresidencia. Parecía que Cheney lo había logrado de nuevo. Había creado un modelo para el secretario de Defensa que reflejaba su hoja de vida. Cheney pensaba que Bush necesitaba un Cheney en el Pentágono, y nadie se asemejaba más a él que Rumsfeld. Por lo menos en el papel, ambos parecían casi perfectos.

Bush le dijo a Card que nominaría a Rumsfeld. Había elegido a Cheney por sus credenciales en materia de seguridad nacional; era todo un experto y esta era una decisión que requería mucha pericia. Sin embargo, Bush le manifestó en privado a Card su preocupación por posibles dificultades que pudieran presentarse, es decir, si acaso había algo que él no había visto; después de todo, su padre había tenido presentimientos muy fuertes.

¿Se trataría de una especie de trampilla?, preguntó.

Un mes más tarde podía haber comenzado el rodaje una película sobre la presidencia de George W. Bush en el Salón Oval, el 26 de enero de 2001, seis días después de la inauguración, cuando Rumsfeld juró como secretario de Defensa. Un fotógrafo de la Casa Blanca capturó la escena. Rumsfeld viste un traje a rayas y posa su mano izquierda sobre una Biblia que sostiene Joyce, con quien lleva 46 años de casado; levanta su mano derecha. Bush presta tanta atención que casi se pone de pie; inclina su cabeza hacia adelante, sus ojos giran rápidamente a la izquierda y mira fijamente a Rumsfeld. Cheney está a un lado, ligeramente detrás, exhibiendo su típica sonrisa. El hombre que viste una túnica negra y que imparte el juramento es el juez Laurence H. Silberman, amigo cercano de Rumsfeld y de Cheney, amistad que se remonta a los días de Ford, cuando el juez era diputado y se desempeñaba como procurador general. Es un día frío y seco, y las ramas desnudas de los árboles que hay afuera pueden verse a través de las ventanas del Salón Oval.

El fotógrafo de la Casa Blanca capta un momento que enlaza al pasado con el futuro. En los días de la presidencia de Ford, después de Watergate –el perdón de Nixon, la caída de Saigón– Cheney y Rumsfeld habían trabajado casi todos los días en el mismo Salón Oval donde ahora se encuentran de nuevo. El otro hombre que aparece en la foto es Bush, quien estudió en la escuela de negocios de Harvard, es cinco años menor que Cheney y casi 14 años más joven que Rumsfeld. Bush llega a la presidencia con menos tiempo y experiencia en cargos gubernamentales que cualquier otro presidente desde Woodrow Wilson en 1913.

La mayoría de los compañeros y amigos de Rumsfeld ya se han jubilado, pues todos tienen más de 70 años, pero ahora él está en la cúspide, listo para participar de nuevo en la competencia. Se parece a George Smiley, el personaje ficticio de John le Carré, que se desempeña como jefe de la inteligencia británica durante la Guerra Fría, un hombre que "a su avanzada edad, se había dado la oportunidad de regresar de nuevo a las competencias interrumpidas de su vida y participar en ellas".

"Esta vez hazlo bien", le dijo Cheney a Rumsfeld.

1

EN EL OTOÑO DE 1997, el ex presidente George H. W. Bush, que en ese entonces tenía 74 años y llevaba cinco por fuera de la Casa Blanca, llamó al príncipe Bandar bin Sultan, uno de sus amigos más cercanos y embajador de Arabia Saudita en los Estados Unidos desde mucho tiempo atrás.

"Bandar" le dijo Bush. "W. quisiera hablar contigo cuando tengas tiempo. ¿Podrías venir a hablar con él?". George W. Bush, su hijo mayor y quien tenía su mismo nombre, llevaba casi tres años como gobernador de Texas; estaba consultando con un grupo de personas sobre una decisión importante y quería conversar en privado con él.

La vida de Bandar giraba alrededor de ese tipo de conversaciones privadas. No preguntó qué quería hablar con él, aunque los medios ya habían sugerido ampliamente que W. estaba pensando en lanzarse como candidato a la presidencia. Bandar, de 49 años, llevaba 15 como embajador de Arabia Saudita, y tenía una posición extraordinaria en Washington. Su influencia y sus conexiones probablemente sólo eran comparables con las del ex presidente Bush.

La relación que tenían databa de los años 80. Bush, el vicepresidente que vivía a la sombra del presidente Ronald Reagan, era ampliamente considerado como un débil y un pelele, pero Bandar lo trataba con el respeto, la atención y la seriedad debidos a un futuro presidente. Ofreció una gran fiesta en honor de Bush en su propiedad palaciega con vista al río Potomac, en la que cantó Roberta Flack, y fue a pescar con él en la casa de vacaciones de Bush, localizada en Kennebunkport, Maine. Era una actividad que poco le agradaba a Bandar, pero que Bush disfrutaba considerablemente. Su relación se basaba en el contacto continuo, tanto por teléfono como personalmente.

Como buenos agentes de inteligencia –Bush había sido director de la CIA y Bandar tenía relaciones cercanas con importantes servicios de inteligencia en todo el mundo–, se habían reclutado mutuamente. Su amistad era tan útil como genuina, y la utilidad y la autenticidad se reforzaban entre ellas. Durante la Guerra del Golfo adelantada en 1991 por Bush para expulsar a Saddam Hussein de Kuwait y evitar que invadiera a Arabia Saudita, Bandar había sido prácticamente un miembro del gabinete de guerra de Bush.

Alrededor de las cuatro de la mañana del día de las elecciones de 1992, cuando parecía que Bush iba a fracasar en su aspiración para un segundo período presidencial, Bandar le había enviado una carta privada en la que le decía: "Usted es mi amigo por el resto de la vida. Usted salvó a nuestro país. Me siento como uno de su familia, y lo considero como uno de la mía. ¿Y sabe otra cosa, señor presidente? Usted va a ganar, no importa lo que pase; debería ganar, se lo merece. Pero si pierde, estará en la agradable compañía de Winston Churchill, quien ganó la guerra y perdió las elecciones".

Bush llamó a Bandar alrededor de la una de la tarde y le dijo, "Amigo, tu carta ha sido la única buena noticia que he recibido en todo el día". Unas 12 horas más tarde, en la mañana del día posterior a las elecciones, Bush lo llamó de nuevo y le dijo: "Todo ha terminado".

Bandar fue la persona que más lo ayudó, rescatándolo de un aislamiento que rayaba en la depresión. Fue la primera persona en visitar a Bush en Kennebunkport en calidad de huésped, una vez que el mandatario abandonó la Casa Blanca, y posteriormente lo visitó en otras dos ocasiones. Envió a varios amigos desde Inglaterra a Houston para que visitaran a Bush. En enero de 1993, invitó al ex presidente a su mansión de 32 habitaciones en Aspen, Colorado. Cuando Bush cruzó la puerta, se encontró ante un "rincón de la Tormenta del Desierto", llamado así en honor a la operación militar adelantada por los Estados Unidos en la Guerra del Golfo; su retrato estaba en el centro. Bandar jugó tenis y otros deportes con él, todo ello para mantenerlo entretenido.

Irreverente, implacable y suave, Bandar era prácticamente el quinto poder en Washington, y trabajaba de manera atenta y obsesiva con los medios de comunicación y las esferas políticas. Pero, en calidad de embajador, le interesaba principalmente la presidencia norteamericana, sin importar quién la ocupara, y asegurarse de que siempre hubiera una puerta abierta para Arabia Saudita, nación que tenía las reservas de petróleo más grandes del mundo, pero que no contaba con un aparato militar poderoso en la volátil zona del Medio Oriente. Cuando Michael Deaver, uno de los principales asesores del presidente Reagan, salió de la Casa Blanca para desempeñarse como abogado, Nancy Reagan, otra amiga cercana de Bandar, lo llamó y le pidió que ayudara a Deaver. Bandar le otorgó un contrato de consultoría por 500.000 dólares y nunca más volvió a verlo.

Bandar estuvo presente en la noche de las elecciones de 1994, cuando dos de los hijos de Bush, George W. y Jeb, se presentaban como candidatos para las gobernaciones de Texas y Florida. Bush y Bárbara, la ex primera dama, creían que Jeb ganaría en Florida y que George W. perdería en Texas. A medida que entregaban los resultados de las elecciones durante la noche,

Bandar se sorprendió al ver a Bush con cuatro páginas de nombres y números telefónicos: dos eran de Texas, y dos de la Florida.

Como si fuera un experimentado corredor de apuestas de Las Vegas, Bush permaneció toda la noche hablando por teléfono, haciendo preguntas y agradeciéndole a todo el mundo. Dedicó el mismo tiempo y atención a quienes apoyaron al nuevo gobernador de Texas y al candidato derrotado en Florida.

Bandar observó que Bush sabía que podía contar con todos sus amigos. Lo hizo con tanta suavidad y humanidad que no pareció un gesto oportunista ni rapaz. Fred Dutton, un antiguo colaborador de Kennedy en los años 60 y abogado y cabildero de Bandar en Washington, señaló que era así como había operado el viejo Kennedy, en referencia al embajador Joseph P. Kennedy, aunque su estilo fue cualquier cosa menos sutil.

BANDAR PROGRAMÓ SU VISITA al gobernador de Texas en 1997 aprovechando un partido de fútbol de los Dallas Cowboys, su equipo favorito. Según declaró, este pretexto les ofrecería "discreción". Quería que el encuentro fuera muy prudente, y dio órdenes para que su avión privado aterrizara en Austin.

Cuando aterrizaron, el jefe del estado mayor de Bandar llegó corriendo para avisarle que el gobernador se encontraba afuera del avión. Bandar se dispuso a abandonar la nave.

"Hola, ¿cómo estás?", lo saludó George W. Bush, quien ya había cruzado la puerta de la nave antes de que Bandar pudiera salir. Bush estaba ansioso por hablar.

"¿Aquí?", le preguntó Bandar, pensando que conversarían en la oficina o en la mansión del gobernador.

"Sí. Prefiero que conversemos aquí".

Bandar había sido piloto de combate en su país durante 17 años y era un favorito del rey Fahd. Su padre era el príncipe Sultan, ministro de Defensa de Arabia Saudita. Bush había sido piloto en la Guardia Nacional Aérea de Texas. Aunque ya se conocían, George W. Bush era para Bandar tan sólo uno de los cuatro hijos del ex presidente, y no el más brillante.

"Estoy pensando en lanzarme a la presidencia" le dijo Bush, que en ese entonces tenía 52 años. Escasamente había comenzado su campaña para la reelección como gobernador de Texas. Llevaba varios meses actuando con mucha cautela, esforzándose para no estropear su imagen como posible candidato presidencial, a la vez que procuraba no dar señales prematuras ni ofrecerles a los sufragantes de Texas la sensación de que los estaba abandonando.

Bush le dijo a Bandar que tenía ideas muy claras sobre lo que necesitaba hacerse con respeto a la política doméstica nacional. Pero, agregó, "no tengo la menor idea acerca de política internacional".

"Mi papá me dijo que hablara contigo antes de decidirlo. Me dijo que, primero, tú eres nuestro amigo. *Nuestro* quiere decir de los Estados Unidos, no sólo de la familia Bush. Segundo, que tú conocías a todos los personajes importantes en el mundo y, tercero, que me ofrecerías tu visión sobre los sucesos mundiales y podrías conseguirme reuniones con personalidades de todo el mundo".

"Gobernador", le dijo Bandar, "primero, me siento honrado de que me haga esta pregunta". Era muy difícil. "Segundo", continuó Bandar, "¿está seguro de que quiere hacerlo?". Una cosa había sido la victoria de su padre, quien en aquel entonces era el vicepresidente que sucedería al popular Reagan en 1988, pero otra cosa muy diferente era llegar a la Casa Blanca después del presidente Bill Clinton y de los demócratas, quienes probablemente nominarían al vicepresidente Al Gore. En referencia a Clinton, Bandar señaló, "el presidente de teflón no es Reagan; es él".

A Bush le brillaron los ojos. Era como si el hijo del ex presidente quisiera vengar la derrota que Clinton le había propinado a su padre. Fue un momento singular. Bandar pensó que era como si el hijo estuviera diciendo, "voy a demostrarle a este tipo quién es el mejor".

"Está bien", dijo Bandar luego de entender el mensaje. Bush hijo quería dar la pelea. "¿Qué quieres saber?".

Bush le pidió que le hablara sobre aquello que considerara de importancia, así que Bandar le dio una visión global del mundo. Como era el embajador en los Estados Unidos de un país tan rico en petróleo, Bandar tenía contacto con muchos líderes mundiales, y el rey Fahd lo enviaba con frecuencia en misiones secretas. Bandar era una especie de mago que muchas veces encontraba una solución mágica, aunque en otras ocasiones se resultaba enfrascado en misiones imposibles. Tenía relaciones personales con los líderes de Rusia, China, Siria, Gran Bretaña e, incluso, de Israel. Bandar le habló con franqueza sobre los líderes del Medio Oriente, del Lejano Oriente, de Rusia, China y Europa. Le describió algunas de las reuniones personales que había tenido; su contacto con Mijaíl Gorbachov cuando estaba planeando el retiro de las tropas soviéticas de Afganistán. Le habló de Margaret Thatcher y de Tony Blair, el primer ministro británico; del papel desempeñado por Arabia Saudita cuando trabajaron con el Papa y con Reagan para contener al comunismo. Con frecuencia, la diplomacia hacía extraños compañeros de cama.

"En este país hay personas que son tus enemigos" le dijo Bush, "y que piensan también que mi papá es amigo tuyo".

"¿Y eso qué?", replicó Bandar, sin preguntar quiénes eran, aunque era evidente que se refería, entre otros, a quienes respaldaban a Israel.

Bush le dijo que las personas que se opusieron al triunfo de su padre en 1992 también estarían en contra suya si se lanzaba como candidato presidencial. Eran las mismas personas que no simpatizaban con Bandar.

"¿Puedo darle un consejo?", le preguntó Bandar.

"¿Cuál?"

"Señor gobernador, dígame que usted realmente quiere ser presidente de los Estados Unidos".

Bush le dijo que sí.

"Si usted me dice eso, quiero decirle algo: al diablo con Arabia Saudita, con quienes estén a favor o en contra de mi país, y con quienes simpaticen conmigo o no. Si usted cree que alguien odia a su papá o a un amigo suyo, pero puede ser importante para marcar la diferencia en su victoria, es mejor que se trague el orgullo y se haga amigo de él. Yo podría ayudarle, quejarme de usted y asegurarme de que entiendan y que le ayudarán a usted".

Bush entendió el mensaje del *Padrino*: mantén cerca a tus amigos, y aun más cerca a tus enemigos. Sin embargo, se sintió incómodo y señaló que esa actitud no era muy honesta.

"No importa si realmente quiere ser honesto", respondió Bandar. "No estamos en un confesionario. Si quiere ser fiel a sus principios, disfrute de este período presidencial y haga algo divertido. Los juegos de las personas influyentes son letales, sangrientos y desagradables".

Bandar cambió de tema. "Quería decirle algo que no tiene nada que ver con asuntos internacionales. Cuando yo piloteaba aviones F-102 en Perrin, la base de la Fuerza Aérea en Sherman, Texas, usted estaba volando los mismos aviones en otra base aérea del mismo Estado. Nuestros destinos nos unieron hace mucho tiempo por el hecho de ser pilotos, así no nos conociéramos". Luego le dijo que quería sugerirle otra cosa.

"¿Qué?", preguntó George W.

"Si todavía recuerda lo que nos enseñaron en la Fuerza Aérea –yo lo recuerdo porque pasé 17 años allí, y usted sólo estuvo pocos años–, la lección es: hay que mantener los ojos abiertos. Si estoy piloteando un avión y le doy alcance a la nave enemiga, sé que mi vida está en juego y no me importa lo que suceda con todo lo demás. Mantengo mis ojos en ese avión y hago lo que tenga que hacer. *No quitaré mis ojos de encima por nada del mundo*".

EL EX PRESIDENTE BUSH siguió esforzándose en ampliar la visión de su hijo y tal vez en reclutarle futuro personal.

"Como usted lo sabe, George W. Bush está pensando en lo que quiere hacer" le dijo a Condoleezza Rice, la decana académica de la Universidad de Stanford de 43 años y uno de los miembros juveniles preferidos del Consejo Nacional de Seguridad durante su presidencia. "Estará en Kennebunkport. ¿Quieres ir este fin de semana?".

Era agosto de 1998. El ex presidente estaba organizando un seminario de política para su hijo.

Rice había sido una de las principales expertas en Rusia en el Consejo Nacional de Seguridad (en adelante CNS). Había conocido a George W. en una recepción en la Casa Blanca. Luego lo vio en 1995, mientras estaba en Houston, durante una reunión de la junta directiva de la petrolera Chevron, de la cual ella hacía parte. Bush padre la invitó a Austin, donde W. había jurado recientemente como gobernador. Ella habló de temas familiares y deportivos con el gobernador por una hora, y luego disfrutó de la compañía del ex presidente durante un almuerzo de su hijo con el representante a la cámara por Texas y con el lugarteniente del gobernador.

Ese fin de semana en Kennebunkport fue una de sus varias estadías de jueves a domingo durante el mes de agosto en el campamento Bush, donde había desayuno, almuerzo, cena, pesca, juegos de herradura y otras competencias.

"No tengo la menor idea en materia asuntos exteriores" le dijo el gobernador Bush a Rice. "No es mi campo".

Rice concluyó que el gobernador se estaba preguntando, "¿debería hacerlo?". O, probablemente, "¿seré capaz de hacerlo?". Mientras padre e hijo pescaban en el bote, W. le pidió a Rice que le hablara sobre China y Rusia, y le hizo preguntas todo el fin de semana: qué pasaba con este país, con este líder, con este asunto, qué significado podría tener y cuáles eran las implicaciones para la política de los Estados Unidos.

Rice fue invitada de nuevo a Austin a comienzos del año siguiente, cuando Bush fue reelegido como gobernador de Texas y antes de que anunciara formalmente su candidatura a la presidencia. Ella estaba dispuesta a renunciar a su cargo de decana académica de la Universidad de Stanford y pensaba tomarse un año sabático o trabajar un par de años en la banca de inversión.

"Quiero que dirijas mi política exterior", le dijo Bush. Ella se encargaría de reclutar a un grupo de expertos.

"Eso suena interesante", respondió Rice, y aceptó. Era una elección bastante acertada en política exterior, si él conseguía ganar las elecciones.

BUSH LE CONFIÓ un asunto importante a Karen Hughes, su asesora cercana, que en ese entonces tenía 43 años y había sido reportera de televisión, y que llevaba cinco años trabajando como su directora de comunicaciones en Texas.

Él le dijo que necesitaba definir por qué quería ser presidente. "Ya sabes, tiene que haber una razón" dijo. "Tiene que existir una verdadera razón para lanzarse como candidato".

Hughes se concentró en encontrar un tema central para su campaña. Sabía que Bush tenía tres pasiones en materia de política. En primer lugar estaban las iniciativas basadas en la fe, unos planes para otorgar más dinero público a programas sociales relacionados con grupos religiosos. A Bush le entusiasmaba eso, pero era un tema que no podía ser la columna vertebral de una campaña presidencial.

La segunda era que Bush estaba interesado en la educación. Sin embargo, las escuelas norteamericanas funcionaban local y estatalmente. Sería difícil lanzarse como candidato a la presidencia basándose en una plataforma de educación nacional.

La tercera idea de Bush, la reducción de impuestos, era promisoria; podía ofrecer una base real. *A charge to keep,* la autobiografía que Hughes escribió con Bush para la campaña y que fue publicada en noviembre de 1999, incluía 19 alusiones a la "educación" y 17 entradas de la palabra "impuestos". Las "organizaciones basadas en la fe" fueron mencionadas tres veces y el término "política exterior" aparecía dos veces, ambas en el contexto del comercio libre. Había una sola referencia a Irak, y no se mencionaba a Saddam Hussein, a los terroristas, ni al terrorismo.

Durante una de las primarias del 2000, Bush llamó a Al Hubbard, quien se había desempeñado como subdirector de personal del vicepresidente J. Danforth Quayle. Era uno de los consejeros reclutados por Bush padre para enseñarle temas económicos a su hijo.

"Hubbard", exclamó Bush. "¿Puedes creer que me voy a lanzar proponiendo una reducción de impuestos?".

BUSH INVITÓ A RICHARD L. ARMITAGE, un ex asistente del secretario de Estado en la administración de Reagan, para que se uniera a su equipo de asesores en política exterior. Armitage, de 54 años, era el mejor amigo de Colin Powell. De pecho musculoso y cabeza afeitada, Armitage era un fanático del levantamiento de pesas, y podía levantar 330 libras. Se había graduado de la Academia Naval en 1967, y aceptó la invitación de Bush porque pensaba que la administración de Clinton no tenía un marco teórico ni un principio de fondo en materia de defensa ni de política exterior, como si se tratara de un asunto honorario. Los republicanos tenían la oportunidad de enmendar esto. Armitage admiraba a Bush padre, pues pensaba que entendía la necesidad de una posición fuerte en materia de política exterior que se caracterizara por la contención.

Armitage pensaba que el aparato militar norteamericano ocupaba un lugar privilegiado en el mundo y podía dominar o controlar cualquier tipo de situación. Clinton y su equipo habían fracasado en desarrollar estrategias acertadas para salir de conflictos foráneos como los de Bosnia o Kosovo.

También creía que un trabajo importante para el próximo presidente era nada menos que definir el objetivo de la política exterior norteamericana. El equipo de Rice se autodenominaba como los Vulcanos. El término había comenzado en broma, pues Birmingham, Alabama, la ciudad natal de Rice, era conocida por sus acerías y poseía una estatua gigantesca de Vulcano, el dios romano del fuego y el metal. Al grupo, en el que también estaba Paul Wolfowitz, el subsecretario de política de Cheney en el Pentágono, le gustaba la imagen de dureza, y muy pronto los Vulcanos se convirtieron en su propia descripción.

En 1999, Armitage asistió a cinco reuniones con Bush y con varios Vulcanos. Se encontró con noticias buenas y noticias malas. La mejor noticia era que Bush quería que Powell fuera su secretario de Estado.

Durante la primera reunión de los Vulcanos, en febrero de 1999, Bush había preguntado, "¿la defensa será un tema importante en las elecciones del 2000?". Sus consejeros opinaron que no. Bush dijo que quería hacer de la defensa un tema importante, que quería transformar el aparato militar y dejarlo en capacidad de enfrentar amenazas nuevas y emergentes.

Sus consejeros dijeron que, para lograr aquello, el aparato militar necesitaría nuevos equipos, para ser más moderno y tener mayor movilidad y entrenamiento, así como una recolección de inteligencia más sofisticada. Eso podría tomar entre 15 y 20 años para alcanzar resultados reales. En otras palabras, era algo que se daría mucho después de la presidencia de Bush, tal vez ni siquiera durante sus vidas.

Bush señaló que estaba dispuesto a emprender esa tarea. Armitage y otras personas elaboraron un discurso que Bush pronunció el 23 de septiembre de 1999 en La Citadela, la Universidad Militar Pública de Carolina del Sur.

"Defenderé a los norteamericanos de los misiles y del terror", dijo Bush, "y comenzaré a crear el aparato militar del próximo siglo... La defensa de nuestro continente se ha convertido en un deber urgente". Bush citó la posibilidad de "terrorismo biológico, químico y nuclear... Todas las sociedades y naciones deben saber que si apoyan dichos ataques, nuestra respuesta será devastadora.

"No dirigiré el nuevo aparato militar que crearemos aunque sea elegido presidente. Esto le corresponderá al presidente que me suceda. Los resultados de nuestros esfuerzos se verán dentro de muchos años".

A Armitage le gustó ver esa dosis de realismo en la campaña presidencial. Pensaba que el terrorismo y los posibles actos perpetrados por Estados renegados como Irak, Irán y Corea del Norte podrían causar problemas, aunque no serían letales. Los temas más importantes en materia de política de defensa eran las relaciones con Rusia, China e India.

No obstante, también había malas noticias con respecto a Bush, "Por alguna razón, cree que va a ser presidente", le dijo Armitage a Powell. Era como si tuviera algún presentimiento sobre el futuro. Bush hablaba como si existiera una certeza, pues decía "cuando sea presidente...". Aunque no era inusual que los candidatos hablaran de esta forma durante sus discursos, Bush hablaba así en las conversaciones privadas con sus asesores. Era como si estuviera tratando de convencerse a sí mismo.

Bush también tenía una sonrisa presumida, señaló Armitage, quien pensaba, además, que el gran problema era que no creía que Bush tuviera talla presidencial. Su inexperiencia era descomunal. Armitage le dijo a su esposa y a Powell que no estaba seguro de que Bush entendiera el papel que tenían los Estados Unidos como potencia mundial.

2

Uno de los integrantes de los Vulcanos era Stephen J. Hadley, un veterano que había trabajado para Cheney en el Pentágono y se había desempeñado como asistente del secretario de Defensa para políticas de seguridad internacional. Era el cargo que Armitage había ocupado en la administración de Reagan, una especie de Departamento de Estado dentro del Pentágono, orientado a las relaciones exteriores. Hadley, de 52 años, era tan suave y silencioso como Armitage podía ser duro y hablador. Hadley creció en Ohio, se graduó con honores en la Universidad de Cornell y obtuvo un título en derecho en la Universidad de Yale. Era un estudioso de la seguridad nacional y había trabajado en el Consejo Nacional de Seguridad durante la administración Ford.

Adicionalmente, había ayudado a preparar el discurso pronunciado por Bush en La Citadela. Cuando Bush dijo que quería un programa de reforma o transformación para el Pentágono, varios Vulcanos demostraron su conocimiento del armamento pesado del Ejército, y citaron de memoria los nombres de algunos de los vehículos más livianos que podrían ser utilizados para remplazar a los pesados tanques. Bush comenzó haciendo preguntas sobre los diferentes vehículos livianos y sus ventajas.

"No le aconsejo que se meta en eso", le dijo Hadley a Bush, "porque si propone una alternativa para los tanques, en Washington hay 200 especialistas listos para objetar lo que usted diga, y señalar que 'este tipo no sabe de lo que está hablando'. Le recomiendo que no se meta en eso".

"Le diré lo que pienso acerca de las elecciones", replicó Bush. "Quiero reformar el Departamento de Defensa. Ahora, cuando sea elegido y les diga a los miembros de la jefatura conjunta del Estado Mayor: 'A propósito, quiero reformar el Departamento de Defensa', ellos me responderán: '¿Quién eres? Te irás en cuatro años y nosotros nos quedaremos aquí. Muchas gracias, pero no'".

"Si me dirijo a los norteamericanos y les digo: 'Reformaré el Departamento de Defensa; les diré por qué y esto es lo que haré', y cuando sea elegido, me reúno con la jefatura conjunta del Estado Mayor y les digo que 'el pueblo norteamericano acaba de elegirme para reformar el Departamento de Defensa', ¿en qué quedamos entonces? Eso marca una gran diferencia". Aparentemente,

Bush no sabía que los jefes del Estado Mayor se desempeñan por un período de cuatro años; Bush pensaba que eran figuras inamovibles.

En otra reunión celebrada en la fase inicial de la candidatura de Bush, los Vulcanos estaban discutiendo el control del armamento. Bush hacía muchas preguntas y recibía muchas respuestas. Hadley le dijo a Bush: "Ellos dominan este campo a la perfección. Usted no necesita toda esta información técnica. Usted tiene un gran instinto. Si pudiera darle un consejo, sería: 'confíe en sus instintos'".

Bush no tenía ningún problema para confiar en sus instintos. Era casi como su segunda religión. En una entrevista que le hice varios años después, el 20 de agosto de 2002, se refirió una docena de veces a sus "instintos" o a sus reacciones "instintivas" como una guía para tomar decisiones. Durante el transcurso de la entrevista, me dijo, "no soy un intérprete de libros, soy un intérprete de instintos".

ADEMÁS DE BUSCAR TUTORES de política exterior para su hijo, el ex presidente pasó los años posteriores a su presidencia defendiendo sus políticas de la Guerra del Golfo Pérsico de 1991. Las Naciones Unidas habían autorizado el uso de la fuerza para expulsar a las tropas de Saddam Hussein de Kuwait, nación que este dictador había invadido el verano anterior. Era una misión definida y respaldada por casi todos los países del mundo. Las tropas de Saddam fueron expulsadas de Kuwait, pero como aquél había sobrevivido a la guerra y permanecido en el poder, varios críticos, muchos de ellos republicanos conservadores, dijeron que Bush se había equivocado y que debió haber insistido para derrocar al dictador iraquí.

El 28 de febrero de 1999, el ex presidente fue el invitado de honor en una reunión de unos 200 veteranos de la Guerra del Golfo, en la base del Ejército de Fort Myer, a orillas del río Potomac.

Bush se exasperaba cuando decían que él no había concluido la misión, y argüía: "Hubiéramos podido entrar a Bagdad. Ustedes hubieran podido hacerlo; podrían haber estado allí en 48 horas. ¿Y luego qué? Los sargentos y soldados habrían arriesgado sus vidas en una cacería infructuosa, enfrascados en una guerra de guerrillas urbana para tratar de encontrar al dictador más seguro del mundo. Las vidas de todas estas personas estarían en mis manos en calidad de comandante en jefe, porque yo, de manera unilateral, hubiera violado las leyes internacionales, hubiera transgredido los límites de la misión establecida y hubiera dicho que íbamos a demostrar nuestro machismo. Vamos a Bagdad; seremos una fuerza invasora: Norteamérica entrará a un territorio árabe, todo esto sin tener ningún aliado de parte nuestra. Hubiera sido desastroso".

EL PRÍNCIPE BANDAR se mantuvo en contacto con George W. Bush cuando éste obtuvo la nominación presidencial por el partido republicano. El fin de semana del 10 de junio de 2000, Bandar asistió a una fiesta sorpresa para celebrar el cumpleaños número 75 de Bárbara Bush en la casa que tenían en Kennebunkport. A Bandar le pareció una fiesta pintoresca y anticuada; todos los miembros de la familia Bush ofrecieron un espectáculo de variedades con sátiras cómicas que duró 45 minutos. Le sorprendió el esfuerzo de los Bush para hacer estas parodias y el espectáculo le pareció muy divertido.

George W. Bush llamó a Bandar a un lado.

"Bandar, creo que eres el tipo que más sabe sobre el mundo. Explícame una cosa".

"Dígame, señor gobernador".

"¿Por qué debería preocuparme por Corea del Norte?".

Bandar le dijo que realmente no lo sabía. Era uno de los pocos países sobre los cuales no había trabajado para el rey Fahd.

"Recibo informes de todas las partes del mundo", dijo Bush, "y todos me advierten sobre Corea del Norte".

"Le diré algo, gobernador", dijo Bandar. "Le daré una razón por la que debería tener cuidado con ese país".

"Está bien, sabelotodo", dijo Bush. "Dime cuál es".

"Los 38.000 militares estadounidenses que se hallan en la frontera". Casi toda la Segunda División de infantería norteamericana estaba estacionada allí, al igual que miles de integrantes del Ejército, la Marina y la Fuerza Aérea. "Es probable que lo demás no importe, pero esto sí. Un disparo en la frontera y usted perderá inmediatamente a la mitad de estas personas. Perderá quince mil norteamericanos en un ataque químico, biológico o, incluso, regular. Los Estados Unidos de América entrarán en guerra de inmediato".

"¡Mmm!", murmuró Bush. "Me gustaría que esos imbéciles fueran directos con nosotros. Entiendo la mitad de lo que leo sobre la historia de Corea del Norte".

"Le daré otra respuesta. ¿No quiere preocuparse más por Corea del Norte?", le preguntó Bandar. Los saudíes querían que Norteamérica se concentrara en el Medio Oriente y que no se dejara arrastrar a un conflicto en el Este de Asia.

"No dije eso", respondió Bush.

"Pero si no lo hace, usted retirará de nuevo las tropas y estallará un conflicto local. Luego, tendrá todo el tiempo para pensar: '¿debería involucrarme en el conflicto? ¿Sería mejor no hacerlo?', etcétera".

Colin Powell se acercó en ese momento.

"Colin", dijo Bush, "ven acá. Bandar y yo estábamos hablando tonterías. Dos pilotos de combate hablando tonterías", dijo sin mencionar el tema.

"Señor gobernador", dijo Bandar, "el general Powell es casi un piloto de combate. Puede hacerlo casi tan bien como nosotros".

BANDAR SIGUIÓ la primera campaña presidencial de W. como lo haría un periodista político de tiempo completo o un adicto a las noticias. Valoró el esfuerzo y la estrategia del candidato. Bush padre prometió ir después de las elecciones a la propiedad que Bandar tenía en las afueras de Londres para cazar faisanes. Le dijo a Bandar: "Cuando vaya a cazar contigo, estaremos celebrando que mi hijo esté en la Casa Blanca, o nos estaremos lamentando porque perdió".

Bandar, quien tenía sus adicciones y obsesiones, dedicaba una gran parte de su tiempo a estudiar la psicología de los seres humanos, y elaboró una teoría acerca de lo que movía la ambición de George W. Bush. Primero, W. había rechazado a James A. Baker III, la figura más importante en el ascenso de su padre a la presidencia, y quien fue su secretario de Estado y principal director político. En opinión de W., Baker no había hecho lo suficiente en la campaña de reelección de 1992 y había abandonado a su padre. Bárbara Bush pensaba que a Baker sólo le importaba su carrera personal.

Sin embargo, W. tuvo que enfrentarse a la batalla por el recuento de votos en la Florida en el año 2000. Se tragó el orgullo y nombró a Baker para le dirigiera el recuento de los votos. ¿Había alguien que jugara mejor al juego sangriento y despiadado de los personajes importantes, que Baker?

"Creo que Bush llegó a la presidencia con una misión", dijo Bandar. "Muchas personas la confunden con su fe religiosa. Creo que él tiene una misión agnóstica, que está convencido de que la misión tiene que realizarse y que él es el único que puede realizarla. La misión es la siguiente: se ha cometido una injusticia con George Herbert Bush, un hombre bueno, que fue un héroe, que sirvió a su país, que todo lo hizo bien". Bush padre había sido un piloto condecorado en la Segunda Guerra Mundial, congresista, embajador en las Naciones Unidas, presidente del Comité Nacional Republicano, enviado oficial a China, director de la CIA, y vicepresidente; había sido todo lo que no había sido su hijo. Y cuando llegó a la presidencia, entabló una guerra, en 1991, para expulsar a Saddam Hussein de Kuwait. "Y la ganó", continuó Bandar; "sin embargo, lo derrotó un charlatán, un remiso, etcétera (según él). Fue una injusticia".

La victoria de Clinton en 1992 fue catalizadora. "Así que desde 1992, este hombre joven, que llevó una vida turbulenta en su juventud, maduró y se concentró en una misión: 'hay una injusticia, hay algo que no está bien y yo voy a corregir esto'".

Después de las elecciones del 2000, Bandar visitó con frecuencia al presidente Bush en la Casa Blanca y mantuvo contacto permanente con su padre. En una ocasión, vio juntos a padre e hijo. Había un vínculo, una conexión emocional aparente y, sin embargo, había una actitud distante, una distancia inexplicable. En muchas ocasiones, Bush padre le habló a Bandar sobre ciertas políticas que su hijo quería adoptar.

"¿Por qué no lo llamas?", le preguntó Bandar.

"Ya tuve mi oportunidad", replicó Bush padre. "Ahora es la suya. Tengo que permanecer alejado del escenario. No hice un solo comentario sobre Clinton en ocho años, y no haré ningún comentario con respecto a mi hijo, no sólo por principio, sino también para dejar que actúe por sí mismo".

EN SU PEQUEÑA OFICINA de consultoría internacional, localizada en un rincón de un quinto piso, tres cuadras al norte de la Casa Blanca, Brent Scowcroft, uno de los pocos hombres tan cercanos al ex presidente Bush como Bandar, presenció el primer término presidencial de Bush hijo con emociones mezcladas. Mormón, de contextura menuda, con un doctorado en relaciones internacionales, 29 años de servicio militar y general de tres estrellas en la Fuerza Aérea, Scowcroft se había desempeñado también como asesor nacional de seguridad de Gerald Ford y George H. W. Bush.

Él y Bush padre eran contemporáneos; sólo se llevaban nueve meses. No sólo eran compañeros del alma; eran tan cercanos en términos políticos que, en vez de escribir unas memorias presidenciales, Bush llamó a Scowcroft en 1998 para que escribieran entre los dos un libro de 566 páginas, titulado *A World Transformed*. Era una especie de semimemorias, uno de los libros más inusuales escritos por presidente alguno del siglo veinte. Bush y Scowcroft escribieron capítulos alternados con fragmentos narrativos. El libro demostraba su participación en los acontecimientos que ocurrieron durante la presidencia de Bush, desde 1989 hasta 1992, incluida la revelación (aunque cuidadosamente maquillada) del colapso de la Unión Soviética y la Guerra del Golfo.

Scowcroft se comunicaba tanto con Bush padre como Bandar. Sabía que el ex presidente no quería dar la impresión de que estaba mirando por encima del hombro de su hijo. Scowcroft creía que si se llegaba siquiera a sugerir que Bush padre tenía el menor rastro de presencia oculta en la administración de su hijo, esto degradaría a Bush hijo, disminuiría el respeto y el apoyo a su presidencia, y la socavaría, incluso.

Pero Scowcroft también sabía que era algo muy personal, una historia clásica que comprendía más de medio siglo de tensiones sutiles y no sutiles entre padre e hijo; amor, alegría, rivalidades y decepciones. Después de todo, Scowcroft sabía que allí estaba el padre que lo había hecho todo, y bastante bien, según su opinión.

Hasta donde Scowcroft podía calcular, George W. Bush sólo supo quién era él mismo después de cumplir 45 años. ¿Y ahora era presidente? Era realmente sorprendente. Scowcroft también sabía que el padre no había lastimado la autoconfianza de su hijo. Él y Bárbara le habían dado al mundo no sólo un hijo sino también un presidente de los Estados Unidos. Bush padre quería que triunfara a toda costa. Y la mejor forma de ayudarlo era permanecer alejado de su camino.

"TAN PRONTO RETIRE MI MANO de la Biblia, quiero un plan de acción", le dijo George W. Bush a Karl Rove, su principal estratega político, el 12 de diciembre del 2000, inmediatamente después de que la Corte Suprema lo declarara ganador de las elecciones. "Vi lo que le pasó a mi padre, a quien amo más que a la vida misma. Llegó a la presidencia sin ningún plan". También dijo que había visto a Clinton sumergirse rápidamente en controversias pasajeras sobre los homosexuales en el Ejército y sobre los nombramientos para su gabinete. Bush dijo que quería concentrarse en temas importantes.

"El tiempo es nuestro aliado al comienzo de la administración", le dijo a Rove. "En algún momento se volverá en mi contra". Bush quería aprovechar el impulso, y quería que su agenda se centrara en el país y en el debate político del Congreso. "Así que quiero un plan".

Bush conocía a Rove desde hacía 28 años. Como explicó uno de sus socios políticos más importantes en Texas, "Karl tiene una especie de personalidad dividida: puede ser tu amigo querido y leal, o cortarte la garganta al día siguiente si cree que eres una amenaza para él". Rove podía volverse paranoico, dijo su socio, y nunca pudo deshacerse de su paranoia. Pero Bush sabía que la paranoia —especialmente en la versión de Rove— era útil en la política.

Cuando Bush decidió lanzarse a la presidencia, le pidió a Rove que se retirara de la Karl Rove & Company, su firma de consultoría política, donde recibía su correspondencia. "Si vas a ser mi socio, tienes que vender tu negocio y trabajar tiempo completo para mí. Si vas a ser mi socio, vas a ser *mi* socio". Rove era un hombre de opiniones fuertes y le gustaba tener mucho control, así que, en muchas ocasiones, Bush tenía que frenarlo en seco, a veces con amabilidad, y a veces con rudeza.

Ahora, Bush quería asegurarse de que *mi hombre* estuviera a su lado en la Casa Blanca. A Rove no se le asignaron responsabilidades definidas sino más bien una licencia amplia y abierta para encargarse de diversos asuntos. El primero era la salud política de Bush durante ese día, esa semana y ese mes.

El segundo era la salud política de Bush a largo plazo, a fin de posicionarlo para la reelección en el 2004.

Rove, de 50 años, se estableció en una oficina del segundo piso del ala oeste de la Casa Blanca, la cual había sido ocupada anteriormente por Hillary Clinton. Él creía que el prospecto de la reelección de Bush descansaba en un primer gobierno exitoso y en los primeros meses de su presidencia, lo cual significaba una sola cosa: la reducción de impuestos como tema central de la agenda doméstica de Bush. En un debate efectuado durante las primarias republicanas, Bush había dicho: "esto no sólo es 'no más impuestos nuevos'", citando el lema de la campaña de su padre, que luego había violado. "Esto es 'reducción de impuestos', así que, válgame Dios".

Rove se concentró en la reducción de impuestos, pues pensaba que eso definiría la presidencia de Bush. En contraste, y a pesar de toda la instrucción recibida, Bush no tenía ningún programa en materia de asuntos exteriores. No tenía convicciones del tipo de "así que, válgame Dios".

3

Durante su primer servicio en el Pentágono, Donald Rumsfeld había sentido un fuerte desprecio por grandes sectores del mismo sistema que iba a liderar de nuevo. Le había parecido que el Pentágono y el complejo militar de los Estados Unidos eran inmanejables. Una noche, durante una cena en mi casa, doce años después de abandonar el Pentágono por primera vez, Rumsfeld dijo que ser secretario era "como tener una electrodoméstico en una mano y el enchufe en la otra, mientras corres para tratar de conectarlo en algún lugar". Fue una imagen que se grabó en mi mente: Rumsfeld corriendo por los pasillos del Pentágono, el *hombre con el electrodoméstico* buscando una toma eléctrica escurridiza, procurando que las cosas funcionaran y sintiendo que los generales y los almirantes lo desconectaban.

Esta vez iba a asumir el control; no se dejaría distraer por asuntos ajenos. Los servicios militares —el Ejército, la Marina, los *marines* y la Fuerza Aérea— eran particularmente serviles y de mentalidad estrecha. Aunque Rumsfeld había sido congresista, pensaba que el Congreso también era limitado, inútil y sujeto a las costumbres y al protocolo. Los visitantes y oficiales extranjeros consumían mucho tiempo, y la rutina, las ceremonias y las reuniones eran un verdadero dolor de cabeza. No, él tenía cosas más importantes por hacer. Eso significaba concentrarse: iba a cambiar todo el aparato militar norteamericano, y lo iba a transformar en una máquina de guerra más esbelta, eficiente, ágil y letal. Creía que esto no sólo era importante para los estamentos militares, sino también para la credibilidad de los Estados Unidos.

Poco después de que Rumsfeld se instalara en su oficina, el presidente de la jefatura del Estado Mayor Conjunto, el general del Ejército Henry H. *Hugh* Shelton, quien había sido nombrado por el presidente Clinton como el militar más importante de la nación, solicitó una reunión privada.

"Cuando el presidente Bush juró como primer mandatario, mi lealtad se dirigió de inmediato hacia él en su calidad de comandante en jefe", dijo Shelton. "Quiero que me considere un miembro de su equipo".

Shelton, de 59 años, era un paracaidista de 37 años de vida militar, incluidas dos temporadas en Vietnam. Alto y amigable, era un hombre directo; nunca fue considerado un intelectual del Ejército. Conocía el valor de la lealtad política y sabía que las elecciones habían sido muy polémicas. Estaba haciéndole un ofrecimiento de paz al nuevo régimen.

Durante los últimos quince años, el presidente de la jefatura del Estado Mayor había sido el enlace y el canal de comunicaciones entre el secretario de Defensa y los comandantes de guerra. El modelo que seguían era el de la Guerra del Golfo de 1991, cuando Colin Powell, presidente de la jefatura del Estado Mayor Conjunto, había sido el principal canal de información y órdenes entre el secretario de Defensa Cheney y el general H. Norman Schwarzkopf, el comandante de la Operación Tormenta del Desierto.

El presidente de la jefatura tenía poder e influencia como enlace y consejero, pero no estaba en la cadena de mando.

"¿Cuáles son exactamente sus deberes?", le preguntó Rumsfeld a Shelton. Desde su primera vez como secretario de Defensa, en la administración Ford, la reforma legislativa Goldwater-Nichols de 1986 había aumentado los poderes del presidente de la jefatura del Estado Mayor, al menos en el papel.

"Soy el principal asesor militar de presidente, de usted y del Consejo Nacional de Seguridad", respondió Shelton, refiriéndose a la autoridad conferida por la mencionada ley en el Libro X del Código de los Estados Unidos, la cual tenía quince años de antigüedad.

"No", dijo Rumsfeld, "del Consejo Nacional de Seguridad, no".

"Sí, señor", repitió serenamente Shelton. La ley era clara.

"No del Consejo Nacional de Seguridad", insistió Rumsfeld. Los miembros de este organismo que trabajaron en la administración de Ford le habían parecido problemáticos y arrogantes, como si estuvieran hablando en nombre del presidente.

Shelton aceptó que no sería asesor del Consejo Nacional de Seguridad. Sin embargo, era el principal asesor militar de este organismo y se relacionaba con sus miembros más importantes: con el presidente, el vicepresidente, el secretario de Estado, el secretario de Defensa, el asesor de Seguridad Nacional del presidente y el director de la CIA. Aunque la ley decía que el papel del director del CNS se limitaba a la asesoría, a las comunicaciones y a la supervisión, él tenía una silla en la Sala de Situaciones de la Casa Blanca, donde se discutía asuntos políticos y de guerra.

A Rumsfeld le incomodaba ese sistema que interfería con la estricta cadena de mando, que iba desde el presidente, como comandante en jefe, hasta él, como secretario de Defensa, y luego pasaba a los comandantes de guerra alrededor del mundo, desde el Océano Pacífico hasta el Medio Oriente.

Una semana después, Rumsfeld le dijo a Shelton que tenía una idea para reducir el personal. Colin Powell había hecho de la jefatura conjunta del Estado Mayor una poderosa dependencia que contaba con cientos de ambiciosos oficiales de nivel medio y de alto rango. Powell la definió como "equipo de acción", organizado y dedicado a que las cosas se hicieran. Esta dependencia era considerada la más poderosa de Washington, y los cargos directivos eran ocupados por generales y almirantes de dos y tres estrellas.

"Es demasiado grande", dijo Rumsfeld. Quería que Shelton la redujera y que despidiera a quienes habían manejado las relaciones públicas, los contactos legislativos y los asuntos legales del presidente de esta dependencia. Si era necesario, Shelton podría utilizar a los empleados civiles de Rumsfeld para dichas labores.

"Señor, se supone que yo debo ofrecer una asesoría militar independiente", respondió Shelton. Señaló que él tenía unos 30 empleados, mientras que Rumsfeld tenía más de 200. También sugirió que el recorte debía practicarse entre el personal civil.

Rumsfeld abandonó el tema momentáneamente.

SHELTON ESTABA PREOCUPADO por la confianza que pudiera existir entre el nuevo secretario y él, y había recibido una advertencia preocupante antes de que Rumsfeld fuera confirmado en su nuevo cargo. Un capitán retirado de la Marina que había trabajado para George S. Brown, general de la Fuerza Aérea y presidente de la Jefatura Conjunta durante el primer período de Rumsfeld como secretario de Defensa, le había enviado una carta en la que criticaba duramente a éste y decía que no se podía confiar en Rumsfeld, quien, entre otras cosas, despreciaba a los militares uniformados.

"No vas a disfrutar nada esta relación", le escribió. "Intentará tener un control absoluto". Shelton les mostró la carta a varios generales y almirantes importantes.

"Cielos, espero que no sea cierto", dijo Shelton, advirtiendo que sólo le faltaban nueve meses para dejar su cargo. "No quiero pasar mi último año en esa clase de ambiente".

Otros oficiales militares de alto rango contaban historias preocupantes sobre las reprimendas que les había propinado Rumsfeld. El almirante James L. Holloway, jefe de operaciones navales de 1974 a 1978, dijo que Rumsfeld lo había puesto en ridículo frente a 40 civiles y militares de alto rango. Rumsfeld estaba preocupado por un testimonio ante el Congreso y Holloway había intentado explicarle.

"Cállate", recordó Holloway que le había dicho Rumsfeld, "no quiero disculpas. Quedarás despedido y no tendrás tiempo de recoger tus cosas si no te encargas de esto" .

A Shelton le preocupaba que Rumsfeld estuviera armando una camarilla de asistentes y consejeros especiales en la secretaría de Defensa, la cual se estaba convirtiendo en una fortaleza ocupada por viejos amigos y oficiales militares retirados. El primero fue Stephen Cambone, un intelectual de defensa que medía 1,90 metros de estatura y había trabajado de cerca con Rumsfeld en comisiones de defensa espacial y de misiles en los años 90. Cambone fue nombrado como principal asistente civil de Rumsfeld; el segundo era Martin Hoffman, quien había sido compañero de cuarto de Rumsfeld, integrante de la promoción de 1954 de la Universidad de Princeton y secretario del Ejército durante la primera estadía de Rumsfeld en el Pentágono. Tenían una amistad cercana que se remontaba casi 50 años atrás. El tercero era M. Staser Holcomb, un vicealmirante retirado de la Marina, que había sido asistente militar de Rumsfeld en los años 70.

El cuarto, y quizás el miembro más importante de la camarilla, era Steve Herbits, abogado de 59 años y amigo de Rumsfeld desde 1967. Herbits había sido uno de los asistentes civiles especiales de Rumsfeld cuando éste se desempeñó por primera vez como secretario de Defensa, y dirigió también la transición en esta secretaría y el reclutamiento de personal para Caspar Weinberger en 1981, así como para Cheney en 1989, cuando asumieron respectivamente como secretarios de Defensa. Herbits también fue un alto ejecutivo de la Seagram Company, el gigante de la industria de licores. Probablemente, no había nadie que tuviera mayor credibilidad ni vigencia con Rumsfeld en temas administrativos y militares. El secretario hizo de Herbits un asesor que tenía licencia para analizar los problemas actuales, a la vez que funcionaba como un hombre que solucionaba todo lo referente a la administración, algo así como lo que hizo Karl Rove para el presidente Bush.

Herbits, que también era un activista por los derechos de los homosexuales, había contribuido ocasionalmente a campañas de candidatos demócratas, motivo por el cual muchos expertos republicanos en defensa lo consideraban extraño; también era conocido por los comentarios incisivos, provocadores y devastadores que hacía sobre funcionarios e instituciones. Rumsfeld admiraba su estilo y capacidad para contrarrestar las dificultades propias de la burocracia del Pentágono y el análisis del mínimo común denominador.

Rumsfeld y Cambone estaban buscando un asistente militar de alto rango, cargo muy importante en el equipo del secretario. Anteriormente, este cargo había sido desempeñado por un general o almirante de tres estrellas. Rumsfeld dijo que ya era suficiente; quería demostrar en qué consistía la reducción. La burocracia del Pentágono estaba en su apogeo y los militares seguían colocando a oficiales de un rango cada vez más alto en puestos clave, como si se tratara de una inflación de rangos militares. Rumsfeld iba a descender dos rangos, pues no quería contratar a un oficial de dos estrellas, sino de una: a un oficial subalterno.

Ellos pensaban en J. J. Quinn, contralmirante de la Marina que había dirigido el Comando Naval Espacial y que el año anterior había ofrecido un testimonio sincero ante la comisión espacial de Rumsfeld. Quinn, graduado en la Academia Naval en 1974, había testificado en secreto que el pequeño programa espacial de la Marina debería incrementarse para ayudar a los comandos de guerra. Si el programa no era aumentado, tal vez sería mejor que la Marina se retirara del programa espacial. Era casi insólito que un comandante militar sugiriera que su comando fuera eliminado.

Rumsfeld y Hoffman llamaron a Quinn para una entrevista. Quinn, de 48 años y 1,88 de estatura, había sido capitán del equipo de béisbol de la Academia Naval. Rumsfeld, ex piloto de la Marina, indagó sobre la carrera de Quinn.

Era un aviador naval, aunque no un piloto. Había volado a bordo de un avión de combate F-14 como oficial de intercepciones por radar y, más tarde, como instructor de la Academia de Armamento de la Marina. Había sido edecán militar del presidente Reagan durante 19 meses, y de Bush padre durante cinco; había estado a cargo del llamado *balón de fútbol*, es decir, de los códigos para la guerra nuclear.

Rumsfeld le preguntó a Quinn sobre su servicio como comandante de un escuadrón F-14 en el USS *Ranger* durante la Guerra del Golfo. Quinn le dijo que había participado en 51 vuelos como escolta de ataque y en misiones de reconocimiento fotográfico durante 43 días. Después de la guerra había estudiado 20 meses en la Escuela de Energía Nuclear fundada por el difunto almirante Hyman Rickover, a fin de prepararse para el comando de un portaaviones nuclear.

Rumsfeld le preguntó sobre su servicio como comandante oficial del USS *Abraham Lincoln*.

"Fue la mejor época de mi vida", dijo Quinn, quien había dirigido una tripulación de 5.000 hombres, así como un portaviones y un equipo naval que costaban 12.000 millones de dólares. Rumsfeld sabía que el mando en alta mar era el clímax emocional para un oficial de la Marina. "Para eso vivimos", dijo Quinn.

Marty Hoffman tomó una hoja en blanco y le pidió a Quinn que escribiera algo para ver si Rumsfeld podía entender su escritura.

Quinn escribió: "Señor secretario, realmente quiero este trabajo".

"Puedo leerlo", dijo Rumsfeld sonriendo. En menos de dos semanas, Quinn estaba sentado en el escritorio de una pequeña oficina adyacente a la de Rumsfeld, en la que había un cuadro donde aparecían varios ayudantes de los generales de la Guerra Civil sosteniendo las riendas de los caballos. El cuadro, titulado *Los que llevan las riendas,* había sido firmado por anteriores asistentes militares de los secretarios de Defensa. Entre las firmas figuraba la de Colin Powell, quien había desempeñado ese cargo para el secretario de Defensa Weinberger y actualmente era el secretario de Estado de Bush.

EL VIERNES 16 DE FEBRERO, cuando Rumsfeld llevaba 21 días en su cargo, 24 aviones norteamericanos y británicos bombardearon 20 estaciones de radar y centros de comando en Irak, imponiendo así las zonas de exclusión de vuelos decretadas por las Naciones Unidas luego de la Guerra del Golfo de 1991. Eran los ataques más fuertes en dos años. Un general del Estado Mayor Conjunto informó a la Casa Blanca sobre el bombardeo, pero Rumsfeld estaba descompuesto, pues creía que no le habían informado con la rapidez necesaria. La información de los comandantes de campo le llegaba a través de Shelton. Podían pasar de 6 a 10 horas antes de que él supiera lo que había sucedido.

"Yo soy el secretario de Defensa", dijo. "Yo estoy en la cima de la cadena de mando". Él —no los generales ni la Jefatura Conjunta— trabajaría con la Casa Blanca y con el presidente en materia de operaciones.

Rumsfeld le exigió a Shelton que le hiciera una reconstrucción detallada del proceso. ¿Cuáles objetivos se había elegido? ¿Quién los había aprobado? ¿Quién había informado? ¿Quién lo sabía? ¿Quién había planeado los ataques? Estos habían sido dirigidos contra los radares de largo alcance localizados en las afueras de Bagdad; las explosiones se escucharon en la capital iraquí, así que CNN cubrió la noticia. Parecía tratarse de un ataque aéreo sobre Bagdad, y esto llamó la atención internacional. Por un momento breve, pareció como si la nueva administración de Bush hubiera lanzado una guerra contra Saddam Hussein en su primer mes.

Rumsfeld sintió que lo habían engañado, que no le habían avisado ni le habían informado en detalle con antelación.

El vicealmirante Scott A. Fry, jefe del Estado Mayor Conjunto y mano derecha del general Shelton, creía que a Rumsfeld no le faltaba razón; todo debió haber sido más claro. Habían fallado al no avisarle y habían violado la ley de no sorprender, de no sorprender al jefe.

Fry, de 51 años y graduado en la Academia Naval en 1971, era uno de los oficiales más promisorios de la Marina. Había leído las carreras de muchos de los almirantes más relevantes cuando era oficial subalterno, y había soñado con ser jefe del Estado Mayor Conjunto. Pensaba que era el mejor cargo que un oficial de tres estrellas podía tener en los Estados Unidos. Se había desempeñado anteriormente como asistente ejecutivo del jefe de operaciones navales, había sido subdirector de programas y de la dirección de políticas (J-5) del Estado Mayor Conjunto. Además, había comandado un grupo de portaviones de combate conformado por el USS *Eisenhower*, dos cruceros, cuatro destructores y dos submarinos, es decir, la columna vertebral de la Marina. Luego fue promovido a director de operaciones (J-3), y, finalmente, obtuvo el cargo más deseado: el de jefe del Estado Mayor.

Fry concluyó que la actitud de Rumsfeld era de una profunda desconfianza, lo cual significaba que tenían que demostrarle lo contrario. Un día, llevó dos informes confidenciales sobre una operación menor a la oficina de Rumsfeld. Iba a examinarlos con Cambone cuando Rumsfeld entró.

"¿Por qué están clasificadas como confidenciales?", preguntó Rumsfeld.

Fry no lo sabía con seguridad. Era el nivel más bajo de clasificación. La mayoría de los asuntos que recibía el secretario tenían una clasificación mucho más alta: SECRETA, ALTO SECRETO, programas de acceso restringido con palabras codificadas, compartimientos especiales para limitar la distribución de información sensible. Rumsfeld, Cambone y Fry no tardaron en enfrascarse en una discusión sobre la clasificación. Fry admitió que los dos informes no necesitaban clasificación y quería examinar su contenido.

"No", dijo Rumsfeld. "Anda, consigue nuevos informes, y tráelos debidamente marcados como no clasificados".

Fry habló con Shelton, quien se desahogó luego de la avalancha de preguntas formuladas por Rumsfeld: ¿Por qué el presidente tenía un asistente especial que viajaba al exterior con Powell? ¿Qué significaba esto? Rumsfeld quería saberlo. ¿A quién le informaba? ¿Cuál era el flujo de información? ¿Cuándo se enteraría Rumsfeld de lo que hacía Powell? Dime por qué tienes un abogado.

Rumsfeld repartía *copos de nieve* por todo el edificio; eran unas notas breves en las que hacía preguntas o pedía detalles y reconstrucciones de los hechos cuando lo que había sucedido no le parecía claro. Había instaurado este sistema durante la administración de Nixon mientras dirigía la Oficina de Oportunidades Económicas. Aunque no las firmaba, todos sabían que eran órdenes o preguntas del jefe. Y si alguna llegaba filtrarse, era posible negarla, pues no estaba firmada ni tenía huellas dactilares. Rumsfeld se sentía orgulloso de su nueva herramienta administrativa. Cuando se desempeñó como embajador en la OTAN, de 1973 a 1974, sus comunicados eran escritos en papel amarillo, y eran llamados *peligros amarillos*. Ahora estaban escritos en papel blanco; los *copos de nieve* habían cobrado vida.

Rumsfeld los escribía a mano o los dictaba, y Delonie Henry, su asistente confidencial, los pasaba en computador. El contralmirante J. J. Quinn, el nuevo asistente militar, se encargó de la custodia de los *copos de nieve*, los cuales eran de tres tipos diferentes: administrativos ("llama y organiza un almuerzo con Alan Greenspan, el director de la Reserva Federal", viejo amigo de Rumsfeld desde los días de Ford); simples pensamientos o reflexiones personales, y comunicados solicitando información o acción. Algunos eran considerablemente extensos y exigentes, y Quinn los distribuía personalmente si eran importantes y urgentes. Rumsfeld guardaba copias en archivadores que mantenía en su escritorio. Tenía un archivo para Shelton, otro para Quinn, uno para Cambone y otros para sus ayudantes principales.

En una entrevista posterior, Quinn dijo: "Era un método simple y efectivo que le permitía llevar la cuenta de lo que había pedido y de lo que quería que se hiciera. Era un recurso que le permitía abarcar a este monstruo descomunal que es el aparato militar de los Estados Unidos".

Rumsfeld se metía en las narices de todos. Nadie estaba a salvo. Muchos funcionarios del Pentágono consideraban que los *copos de nieve* eran toda una molestia. A otros les parecían indiscretos y a veces, incluso, mezquinos. Algunos pensaban que no había forma de cumplir con ellos.

El vicealmirante Fry le dijo al Estado Mayor Conjunto que esta era una oportunidad para examinar lo que estaban haciendo y el porqué. Indagar a fondo y de manera introspectiva era provechoso, sobre todo para el Estado Mayor Conjunto. "Necesitamos hacerlo", dijo. "Lo haremos. Nos ganaremos su confianza y Rumsfeld se sentirá cómodo con nosotros".

EN EL ANTIGUO SISTEMA instaurado por el secretario de Defensa William S. Cohen y el general Shelton, cuando sucedía un incidente significativo —el choque de un barco, la violación a las zonas de exclusión aéreas en Irak o, en el peor de los casos, el estallido de una guerra— el general o almirante de servicio en el Comando Central Militar Nacional (CCMN), que hacía parte del Estado Mayor Conjunto y funcionaba las 24 horas del día, llamaba a Shelton. Rumsfeld preguntó a Shelton por qué no lo habían llamado a él, pues a fin de cuentas el primero en la cadena de mando no era Shelton, sino él, Rumsfeld, quien reportaba al presidente. Shelton respondió que muchas veces tenía que recibir respuestas del general o el almirante de servicio, y que tenía que anticiparse a las preguntas del secretario de Defensa, para tener respuestas cuando éste lo llamara.

"No", dijo Rumsfeld. Él quería ser el primero en enterarse. ¿Y qué, si se trataba de algo serio y tenía que llamar al presidente? El centro de comando monitorea a todo el mundo y el oficial de servicio llama con frecuencia a Shelton. Rumsfeld exigió una reconstrucción completa de la secuencia de los acontecimientos siempre que esto sucediera; cuándo llamaban a Shelton, cuándo lo llamaban a él, qué información recibía cada uno, así como explicaciones por los retrasos y discrepancias en los informes, algo que sucedía casi todos los días. Rumsfeld contrató a otro almirante retirado para que realizara un estudio sobre el CCMN. Como supervisor de este organismo y de los oficiales de servicio, Fry estaba en el medio.

EL JUEVES 15 DE MARZO DE 2001, cuando Bush llevaba 53 días en la presidencia, el príncipe Bandar fue al Salón Oval con Rihab Massoud, su fiel edecán. Condoleezza Rice, quien ya era la asesora nacional de seguridad de Bush, estuvo presente en la reunión. Era bastante inusual que un embajador tuviera un acceso tan directo a un presidente.

Bandar se quejó de un pronunciamiento expresado una semana atrás por el secretario de Estado Powell en un testimonio ante el Congreso. Los Estados Unidos pensaban trasladar su embajada de Tel Aviv a "Jerusalén, la capital de Israel", según palabras de Powell. Era una declaración descabellada, pues los árabes reclamaban que una parte de Jerusalén era palestina.

Bush dijo que sabía que Jerusalén era un punto sensible para los saudíes, y que probablemente Powell se había equivocado.

A partir de un mensaje del príncipe de la corona, el líder *de facto* de Arabia Saudita, Bandar dijo que avanzar en el proceso de paz entre los palestinos e Israel, nación que acababa de elegir a Ariel Sharon como su nuevo líder, era crucial para poder consolidar una coalición de árabes moderados y presionar a Saddam Hussein. Luego preguntó por cuánto tiempo más se extendería la ley de exclusión de vuelos en Irak decretada por las Naciones Unidas. ¿Cinco años? ¿Diez años? "Esto nos está costando en términos militares, económicos y, más importante aun, en términos políticos", dijo el embajador. "Y no está afectando a Saddam Hussein".

Bush pareció estar de acuerdo con él. "Si se emprende una acción militar, tendrá que ser decisiva y acabar con el problema", dijo el presidente. "La oposición iraquí es inútil e incapaz". Discutieron la dificultad de realizar acciones encubiertas para derrocar a Saddam; el presidente expresó su preocupación por el aumento de los precios del petróleo, asunto en el que los saudíes tenían una fuerte influencia. Le dijo a Bandar que quería que se vieran por lo menos una vez al mes, pues quería hablar detenidamente con él.

Bandar se alegró profundamente y le envió un mensaje secreto al príncipe de la corona: "Muchas señales positivas en lo referente a las relaciones y asuntos que atañen a ambas naciones. La lealtad y la honestidad son temas sensibles para este presidente. Es importante que invirtamos de manera muy positiva en este hombre".

RUMSFELD ESTABA INTENTANDO definir sus deberes y anotarlos en papel. Sus dictados, comunicados, borradores corregidos y *copos de nieve* revelaban su convicción de que se enfrentaba a obstáculos enormes. El 20 de marzo, dictó un comunicado de cuatro páginas. "Asunto: el desafío, la importancia de triunfar".

"Después de dos meses en este cargo, me parece evidente que el aparato de defensa está atado a la cadena del ancla" dictó. El Congreso solicitaba cientos de informes; el Pentágono no podía construir un edificio de 500.000 dólares sin recibir la aprobación del Congreso. Había demasiados auditores, investigadores, fiscalizadores y monitores que observaban todo lo que sucedía en el Pentágono; estos funcionarios eran más numerosos quizás "que los 24.000 hombres armados que podía desplegar el Ejército norteamericano en zonas de guerra en un día cualquiera". Las políticas para el personal militar "estaban diseñadas para manejar una fuerza de soldados reclutados" y no habían sido modificadas para desplegar "fuerzas voluntarias que tuvieran familia". Muchos oficiales militares eran transferidos "de una misión a otra aproximadamente cada 20 o 25 meses, de tal forma que los oficiales exitosos pasaban de una misión a otra con tal rapidez que ni siquiera podían aprender de sus propios errores". Los incentivos militares "utilizaban de manera inconsciente sistemas semejantes al fracasado modelo centralizado soviético para asuntos como vivienda, comisariatos, salud y educación, en lugar de utilizar los modelos competitivos del sector privado, que son la envidia de todo el mundo".

Señaló también que "la desconfianza entre el Congreso y el Departamento de Estado era tan grande que, desde un punto de vista práctico, este departamento ya no tiene autoridad para encargarse de sus propios asuntos".

"Las numerosas limitaciones obligan al departamento a funcionar de una manera tan lenta, pesada e ineficiente, que todo lo que se haga tendrá inevitablemente una década de retraso".

Rumsfeld concluyó que si no se cambiaban y mejoraban las relaciones con el Congreso, "no será posible la transformación de nuestras Fuerzas Armadas".

Seis días después, le envió un *copo de nieve* a Wolfowitz, a Cambone y a dos personas más, pidiéndoles una corrección del texto e ideas adicionales. Este comunicado, denominado *la cadena del ancla,* adquirió renombre entre el personal de Rumsfeld, a medida que observaban y le ayudaban a definir la magnitud de sus problemas. El 10 de abril dictó una versión de 10 páginas, la cual aumentó a 12 el primero de mayo. Para ese entonces, Rumsfeld había descubierto que el Congreso pedía 905 informes al año. La Ley de Autorización de Defensa de 1962 tenía una sola página, y en 1975, cuando él había sido secretario, había aumentado a 75 páginas. "Actualmente, la Ley se ha inflado a 988 páginas".

Parecía como si él hubiera renunciado a reformar el Pentágono durante la presidencia de George W. Bush. La misión era tan ardua y tomaría tanto tiempo, dictó él, que "por lo tanto, nuestra labor es trabajar juntos para afilar la espada que empuñará el próximo presidente".

"Tengo cuatro borradores", le dije a Rumsfeld en una entrevista que le hice en el 2006.

"¿De veras?".

"Sí, señor", respondí, entregándole las copias. "Quería entregárselas".

"Las cosas han mejorado", señaló.

"Así es", coincidí. "Parece que usted realmente se está esforzando, si he de ser sincero".

"Este es un trabajo difícil", dijo. "Este no es un departamento fácil. Recuerdo que, cuando llevaba un mes o dos en este cargo, estaba sentado en mi escritorio en horas de la noche, reflexionando sobre todo esto, y me dije: "Está bien, me pidieron que hiciera este trabajo y acepté. ¿En qué consiste? ¿Cómo defines el trabajo, cuáles son los problemas que estás enfrentando, y cuáles son los obstáculos para su realización? ¿Qué se puede hacer y qué no se puede hacer?".

Cité una frase del último borrador del comunicado: "Tendremos que hacerlo para el próximo presidente".

"Ya sabes", dijo, "en un lugar tan grande como este, eso es válido para casi todas las cosas". Señaló que en 1975, cuando asumió por primera vez como secretario de Defensa, aprobó el tanque M1, que fue utilizado inicialmente en la Guerra del Golfo y luego en la reciente invasión a Irak. También había aprobado el F-16, que aún era utilizado en operaciones aéreas sobre Irak. Habló casi con nostalgia: "Las decisiones que tomas se desarrollan en un lapso prolongado, bien sea para beneficio del país o, por el contrario, para su detrimento, si no logras hacer algo".

4

El primero de abril, China obligó a aterrizar a un avión espía EP-3E de la Marina norteamericana y retuvo a sus 24 tripulantes; fue la primera gran crisis en materia de política exterior de la nueva administración Bush. La Casa Blanca estaba determinada a mantener al presidente Bush por fuera de la delicada situación de los rehenes. Los presidentes Jimmy Carter y Ronald Reagan les habían concedido mucha importancia a los captores de los rehenes; se habían involucrado emocionalmente intentando rescatar a los norteamericanos cautivos en Irán y el Líbano. En el caso de Carter, esto había conducido a una sensación generalizada de impotencia y temor en el país, tanto así que el noticiero de la cadena televisiva ABC presentaba todas las noches un programa llamado *Norteamérica en cautiverio,* que todos los días les recordaba a los televidentes cuánto tiempo llevaban los norteamericanos prisioneros. Bajo Reagan, la crisis de rehenes desencadenó las ventas secretas de armas a Irán, así como el caso *Irán-contras,* el mayor escándalo de su presidencia. No se permitiría que la imagen de impotencia que habían sufrido sus predecesores afectara a la administración de George W. Bush.

El secretario de Estado Powell recibió instrucciones para negociar un acuerdo con los chinos. Powell reclutó al príncipe Bandar, quien tenía relaciones especiales con ellos, gracias a varios negocios relacionados con compras de armas y de misiles. Adicionalmente, China estaba comenzando a depender del petróleo saudí.

Eventualmente, Bandar logró que los chinos liberaran a los veinticuatro rehenes. Este embajador, que no era nada modesto acerca de su influencia, consideró la devolución como un favor personal. Los chinos querían que los Estados Unidos les enviaran una carta en la que pidieran disculpas, y este tipo de jerigonza diplomática era la especialidad de Bandar. Tal como los chinos deseaban, los Estados Unidos dirían que "lamentaban profundamente" que el avión espía hubiera ingresado al espacio aéreo chino para realizar un aterrizaje de emergencia, pero no pedían disculpas por lo que, consideraban, era una misión legítima de recolección de inteligencia. La Agencia Nacional de Seguridad monitoreó las conversaciones telefónicas entre Bandar y los chinos, y le envió informes a Powell sobre las negociaciones, incluyendo el acuerdo final logrado por Bandar. Powell lo llamó para felicitarlo.

"¡Es fantástico!", le dijo Powell.

"¿Cómo diablos te enteraste?", le preguntó Bandar.

Powell se sintió avergonzado por su comentario inoportuno e intentó explicarle. Bandar sabía que sus llamadas eran monitoreadas, pero él y Powell realmente no podían hablar sobre una de las operaciones más secretas y delicadas del gobierno norteamericano en materia de recolección de información de los gobiernos extranjeros. Así que, por espacio de un año, Powell y Bandar se rieron y bromearon sobre esto, sin llegar realmente a llamarlo por su nombre.

Rumsfeld exigió una reconstrucción completa de la secuencia desde el momento inicial del vuelo del EP-3. No le gustó nada de lo que escuchó. El EP-3 fue seguido de cerca y hostigado por un caza chino, y los dos aviones se rozaron. Una de las preguntas era si el piloto norteamericano había tomado la decisión acertada al aterrizar en China. Rumsfeld investigó más a fondo y preguntó cuál era el objetivo de estas misiones de inteligencia. ¿Quién las autorizaba? ¿Quién evaluaba el valor de la inteligencia recolectada? ¿Qué pasaba con los riesgos comparados con las recompensas? Esto originó otras preguntas, así como una evaluación exhaustiva de las misiones de recolección de inteligencia ejecutadas por todas las tropas aerotransportadas de los Estados Unidos.

"Es algo doloroso pero importante", le dijo Fry al Estado Mayor Conjunto y a los expertos en inteligencia. Estas misiones de alto riesgo se habían cumplido durante muchos años de manera casi automática. Fry creía que tenían que evaluarse de nuevo, pero a medida que Rumsfeld removía piedras, Fry encontraba demasiados gusanos.

La cuestión era cuándo reanudar las misiones del EP-3 por fuera del territorio chino. Pocos días después, Rumsfeld convocó a una conferencia de seguridad con el vicepresidente del Estado Mayor Conjunto Richard B. Myers y el almirante Dennis Blair, comandante en jefe del Comando Pacífico y comandante de guerra en la región. Myers asistió en representación del Estado Mayor Conjunto, pues el general Shelton estaba de viaje. Este hombre caballeroso que medía más de 1,90 de estatura había sido suplente de Shelton por poco más de un año. Fue piloto de combate en la guerra de Vietnam, donde piloteó aviones de combate Phantom F-4. También había servido como comandante en jefe del Comando Espacial norteamericano antes de asumir la subjefatura de esta dependencia en marzo del 2000.

El contralmirante Quinn tomó notas mientras Rumsfeld, el almirante Blair y el general Myers conversaban.

Blair recomendó que las misiones de espionaje se reanudaran con prontitud. Los chinos sostuvieron que los vuelos violaban su espacio aéreo, pero los Estados Unidos reconocían un límite de 12 millas náuticas y no querían hacer ninguna concesión ni sucumbir a las intimidaciones chinas. Blair elaboró un calendario aleatorio para la reanudación de los vuelos.

"Denny", le dijo Rumsfeld, "parece un buen plan. Envíame un mensaje de una página con los detalles exactos para mostrárselo a Condi Rice y a Colin Powell mañana por la mañana". Rumsfeld hablaba sobre asuntos de seguridad con estos dos funcionarios todos los días de la semana a las 7:15 de la mañana.

"¡Sí, señor!", exclamó Blair.

A las seis de la mañana del día siguiente, Quinn ya estaba buscando el mensaje de Blair cuando Rumsfeld lo llamó.

"No veo el mensaje de Denny Blair", dijo.

"Señor secretario, yo también lo estoy buscando y no puedo encontrarlo".

Quinn entró a la oficina de Fry antes de las siete de la mañana. Fry estaba en una reunión. Su asistente ejecutivo, un capitán de la Marina y firme creyente en la cadena de mando, lo miró desconcertado cuando Quinn le preguntó por el mensaje del almirante Blair. Aparentemente, Blair había enviado el mensaje siguiendo la vieja costumbre: se lo había enviado a Shelton y al Estado Mayor Conjunto, pero no a Rumsfeld.

El asistente ejecutivo de Fry dijo que sólo estaba dirigido al Estado Mayor Conjunto y que en ese sentido no podía hacer nada. "No puedo dártelo".

Cuando Fry regresó, su asistente ejecutivo tenía una copia del mensaje de Blair. "Ah, y a propósito", dijo el capitán, "le diré a J. J. Quinn que el secretario no podrá verlo sino hasta cuando el presidente del Estado Mayor Conjunto lo haya visto".

Quinn recordó que también le había preguntado a Fry por el mensaje, y sostuvo que éste se negó a entregarle una copia. Fry le atribuyó la responsabilidad a su asistente ejecutivo.

Sea como fuesen las cosas, Quinn regresó a la oficina de Rumsfeld para informarle: "Señor secretario, el mensaje está en la oficina del jefe del Estado Mayor Conjunto y se niegan a entregármelo".

Rumsfeld cogió el teléfono. Shelton seguía de viaje, así que el secretario llamó a Myers.

Myers corrió a la oficina de Rumsfeld. "¿Sucede algún problema, señor secretario?".

"¿Qué demonios están pensando ustedes?", explotó Rumsfeld. "No puedo creer esto".

Quinn estaba en el otro extremo de la oficina. Rumsfeld estaba más furioso que nunca.

"¿Dónde está la lealtad aquí?", gritó Rumsfeld, y acto seguido la emprendió contra Myers. Llevaba meses atado a la cadena del ancla, y se desbordó luego de tanta frustración. Quinn estaba atónito, pues nunca antes había visto algo así en más de 25 años que llevaba en la Marina.

Myers insistió en que ellos no estaban intentando ocultarle nada al secretario; eso sería absurdo. Ambos habían estado en la teleconferencia con Blair. Obviamente, se habían presentado errores en la forma de comunicación. Sí, estaba claro que Rumsfeld era el jefe, pero Myers también intentó defender al Estado Mayor Conjunto.

Rumsfeld no estaba dispuesto a escucharlo y siguió despotricando de Myers. Quinn miró el reloj y vio que marcaba las 7:02 de la mañana. La conferencia entre Powell, Rumsfeld y Rice comenzaría en trece minutos.

Cuando terminaron, Myers salió y le preguntó a Quinn: "¿Qué diablos está pasando?".

Quinn lo puso al tanto, y Myers corrió para obtener una copia del mensaje, la cual dejó en la oficina de Rumsfeld antes de que la conferencia empezara.

Una vez concluyó esta, Rumsfeld llamó al citófono de la oficina de Quinn y le preguntó: "¿Puedes venir?".

Quinn lo visitó y Rumsfeld le pidió su opinión sobre lo sucedido.

"Señor secretario, la próxima vez que usted la emprenda contra un oficial de cuatro estrellas, pediré que me trague la tierra".

"No. Quiero que seas un testigo". Luego le pidió que hablara con el asesor general del Pentágono, pues quería saber qué autoridad legal tenía sobre el Estado Mayor Conjunto, y qué poder tenía para despedir empleados.

Rumsfeld estaba fuera de sí. La mayoría de los empleados civiles más importantes que había nombrado no habían sido confirmados, así que todavía no contaba con su equipo. "Estoy aquí y nadie trabaja para mí", dijo. Llamó a Steve Herbits; estaba alterado y exasperado porque llevaba varias semanas en su cargo y la cadena de mando aún no funcionaba.

"Quiero hablar con los comandantes de guerra", le dijo Rumsfeld. "Que se reporten conmigo. Es lo que ordena la ley". Se quejó de que siempre recibía la información del Estado Mayor Conjunto con mucho retraso. Estaba furioso con Shelton y con Fry.

"Tiene que despedir a alguien", le propuso Herbits. "Tiene que hacerles saber a todos quién es el jefe. Este es el momento ideal". Fry parecía incompetente. "Despida a Fry".

Shelton ya había regresado y no tardó en enterarse de que Rumsfeld estaba pensando hacer precisamente eso. Shelton y Myers creían que habían explicado el error cometido con el mensaje del almirante Blair, y habían prometido que no volvería a suceder. Shelton no sabía si se trataba de esto o de un nuevo problema; se dirigió a la oficina de Fry para ver si Rumsfeld había enviado un *copo de nieve*.

Steve Cambone había expedido una orden, la cual estipulaba que todos los *copos de nieve* debían ser respondidos a más tardar en 24 horas, y Fry explicó que intentaba mantenerse al día. A veces pensaba que le estaba tocando responder casi todos los cuestionarios que Rumsfeld le enviaba al Estado Mayor Conjunto. "No hay suficiente personal en el Pentágono para responder a todos los *copos de nieve* que llegan del tercer muelle", dijo, refiriéndose al tercer piso, donde estaba la oficina de Rumsfeld.

Shelton advirtió que Fry, un trabajador incansable que tenía un gran futuro, estaba agotado, pues trabajaba los fines de semana y permanecía respondiendo los *copos de nieve* hasta la medianoche.

Se dirigió a la oficina de Rumsfeld, entró apresuradamente y lo confrontó.

"Si usted no está contento con Scott Fry", le dijo, "él trabaja para mí, y si no está contento con él, quiere decir que está descontento conmigo. Puede despedirnos a los dos", le dijo Shelton.

Rumsfeld pareció retroceder y negó con energía haber considerado plan alguno contra Fry.

Shelton fue a hablar con Fry.

"Nunca has tomado una licencia", le dijo Shelton. "Nunca has tenido un día libre. Has permanecido acá todos los días desde que estoy en mi cargo. ¿Por qué no te tomas un par de días libres?.

"No es necesario", respondió Fry. "Así estamos bien".

"Tómate un par de días", le ordenó Shelton. "Nos veremos el jueves".

Fry comenzaba a trabajar alrededor de las seis de la mañana, hora en que iba al Centro del Comando Nacional Militar para recibir información sobre lo sucedido en la noche, revisar mensajes y hacer llamadas internacionales para actualizarse. Le informaba a Shelton a las siete, antes de su reunión con Rumsfeld de las 8:30. Después de esto, Fry asistió en representación del Estado Mayor Conjunto a una reunión dispuesta por Rumsfeld unas horas más tarde. Durante esta reunión, Rumsfeld recorrió la mesa y preguntó si alguien tenía información. "Hoy no hay nada, señor secretario", fue la respuesta acostumbrada de Fry, pues toda la información valiosa se la había entregado a Shelton, quien a su vez se la había suministrado a Rumsfeld.

"Fry viene a mis reuniones", les dijo Rumsfeld a sus subalternos, "y nunca tiene nada qué decir".

El 25 de abril de 2001, la cadena de televisión ABC presentó una entrevista con Bush sobre sus primeros cien días en la presidencia. Charles Gibson, el entrevistador, le preguntó al presidente si los Estados Unidos tenían la obligación de defender a Taiwán.

"Claro que sí. Y los chinos deben entender esto", respondió Bush.

"¿Y usted lo haría?".

"Sí. Lo haría".

"¿Con el apoyo de todas las fuerzas militares norteamericanas?".

"Con todo que sea necesario para defender a Taiwán".

Esta fue una de las declaraciones más contundentes pronunciadas por los Estados Unidos sobre el delicado tema de Taiwán. Los chinos se molestaron bastante.

Condoleezza Rice llamó a Brent Scowcroft, quien había desempeñado su mismo cargo durante la administración de Bush padre, y le pidió que hablara con el presidente. Scowcroft se reunió en privado con Bush y Rice.

"¿Qué hago para salir de esto?", fue básicamente lo que preguntó Bush.

Después de escuchar a Scowcroft, Bush le pidió que hiciera un viaje en secreto a China, hablara con el presidente Jiang Zemin, y le explicara la política norteamericana. Scowcroft, quien iría a la China en un viaje privado de negocios, aceptó hablar con Jiang en nombre de Bush. Le dijo al líder chino que la política de Bush era defender a Taiwán si la isla era atacada injustamente, pero que si los taiwaneses hacían algo para alterar el *statu quo*, los Estados Unidos no los defenderían. Jiang y Bush parecieron quedar satisfechos, y la misión secreta de Scowcroft nunca se divulgó.

A Scowcroft le complació ver que la administración hubiera superado este *impasse*. Tanto él como Bush padre creían que el ingrediente principal para una política exterior sólida y razonable era lograr una posición equilibrada y moderada. Esta fue una buena noticia.

LAS CONVERSACIONES TELEFÓNICAS que Rumsfeld sostenía diariamente con Powell y Rice a las 7:15 de la mañana no estaban exentas de dificultades. Gracias a los contactos que había establecido durante sus 35 años de servicio militar, posteriormente como asesor de Seguridad Nacional de Reagan, y ahora, cuando dirigía la diplomacia de Bush, Powell tenía quizás mayor acceso a información de inteligencia que cualquier otro funcionario del gobierno norteamericano. Richard Armitage, su mejor amigo, era el subsecretario de Estado y ejecutaba una agresiva recolección de información durante sus reuniones y llamadas telefónicas. "Alimenten a la bestia", decía, pues quería pasarle información valiosa a Powell. "Vamos", insistía.

Cuando Rumsfeld, Rice y Powell hablaban por teléfono, éste ya había recibido información reciente del exterior o de sus contactos en Washington. Le complacía suministrar información militar desconocida para Rumsfeld. En la reunión que sostenía horas más tarde con Shelton, Rumsfeld preguntaba con frecuencia: "¿Por qué Powell sabía esto y yo no?". Esto solía conducir a una reconstrucción del flujo de información. ¿Cómo era posible que alguien perteneciente al extenso aparato militar norteamericano supiera algo tan importante y no se lo comunicara al secretario de Defensa? Una las preguntas que más le gustaba hacerle a Shelton era la siguiente: "¿Por qué los comandantes de guerra hablan contigo sabiendo que trabajan para mí?".

Los *copos de nieve* circulaban sin descanso. En un momento, Fry comprendió que no sería capaz de crear un sistema de rastreo que pudiera monitorear adecuadamente todo lo que fuera importante para los miembros del Estado Mayor y para esta dependencia. Esto se debía a que Rumsfeld les enviaba *copos de nieve* a casi todos los funcionarios del Pentágono, sin que importara su rango o posición. Los *copos de nieve* enviados a otras personas muchas veces llegaban a manos de Fry, ya fuera total o parcialmente, y de un momento a otro había una gran cantidad de preguntas que había que responder en muy pocas horas. Sin embargo, Rumsfeld tenía su propio sistema de rastreo, lo que conducía a más preguntas y *copos de nieve* indagando qué había sucedido con aquellos que no habían sido respondidos.

Un día, Cambone fue a quejarse a la oficina de Quinn, luego de ser reprendido por Rumsfeld. "¿Lo estoy haciendo tan mal?", preguntó.

Otro día, Quinn le pidió un consejo al vicepresidente Cheney, durante una recepción en el Pentágono. "Esto es lo que puedo decirte sobre Donald Rumsfeld", dijo Cheney. "Nunca te felicitará, y sólo sabrás que estás haciendo bien tu trabajo si te da más. Si así sucede, es porque lo estás haciendo bien".

Quinn comprendió que Rumsfeld tenía una misión noble y necesaria. El jefe del Estado Mayor Conjunto y el jefe del gabinete habían asumido el control del Pentágono durante los ocho años de la presidencia de Clinton, y Rumsfeld estaba intentando arrebatarles el poder para dejarlo en manos civiles. Las relaciones que Quinn tenía con Fry y los oficiales superiores de la Marina integrantes del Estado Mayor Conjunto eran desastrosas. Estos hacían gala de su rango superior, y Quinn concluyó que no estaba trasmitiendo las peticiones y órdenes de Rumsfeld con la autoridad y urgencia con que habían sido emitidas. Un día, Fry le dijo a Quinn que Rumsfeld y sus subalternos civiles no estaban cooperando con *ellos* "con el Estado Mayor Conjunto" como si fueran ellos los que mandaran.

La esposa y las dos pequeñas hijas de Quinn vivían a una hora y media de Maryland, donde estaba localizado el comando naval espacial, así que Quinn sólo realizaba una breve visita a su casa en los fines de semana. Intentó conseguir una vivienda para ellas en una de las bases más cercanas al Pentágono, pero esto le causó fuertes disputas con el Ejército. Cambone intervino, pero parecía tratarse de una campaña de hostigamiento, y Quinn nunca pudo conseguir vivienda en ninguna base local. Fry pensaba que esto desgastaba emocionalmente a Quinn y le quitaba mucho tiempo, así que comenzó a decir que no estaba cumpliendo con su trabajo.

El problema de vivienda era incidental para Quinn. Sentía que no podía hacer su trabajo, así que fue a hablar con Rumsfeld.

"Usted tiene que hacer un cambio con respecto a su asistente militar", le dijo. "Yo sólo tengo una estrella, y los generales de tres y cuatro estrellas no me hacen caso. Se andan con rodeos y pasan por encima de mí. La cultura militar no me permite transmitir órdenes".

"No. Tenemos buena química; superaremos este inconveniente".

Sin embargo, Rumsfeld se quejó ante Herbits por el desorden que había en su oficina. Todo funcionaba con mucha lentitud y no le gustaba la forma en que los militares uniformados le estaban respondiendo. Herbits decidió abandonar su oficina de transición del primer piso y trasladarse al despacho de Rumsfeld para vigilar personalmente el tráfico de personas y de información. Se ubicó entre el almirante Quinn y Steve Cambone, el asistente civil de Rumsfeld.

Herbits fue a la oficina de Rumsfeld después de haber observado el trabajo de Quinn durante algunas semanas.

"Esto no va a funcionar", dijo, reflejando la autoevaluación hecha por el mismo Quinn.

"¿Por qué?", preguntó Rumsfeld.

Quinn era un oficial honesto y competente, pero su estrella no le daba suficiente poder en la jerarquía propia del aparato militar. Sólo estaba un peldaño por encima de un capitán de la Marina o de un coronel del Ejército, y realmente no podía dar órdenes ni hablar de igual a igual con los generales de tres estrellas que hacían parte del Estado Mayor Conjunto y de otros departamentos. Fry y los demás lo estaban ignorando. El enlace entre el asistente militar de Rumsfeld y el jefe del Estado Mayor Conjunto era vital para el funcionamiento del Pentágono, señaló Herbits. Era una las relaciones más importantes de esta institución. En algunos aspectos era, incluso, el más importante; sin embargo, no estaba funcionando.

Aquella primavera, la Marina anunció que iba a reanudar las pruebas de bombardeo en Vieques, una pequeña isla de Puerto Rico sobre la cual había una antigua controversia. Dos años atrás, un guardia civil había muerto durante una prueba de bombardeo; quienes protestaban ocuparon el campo y la candidata que ganó las elecciones para la gobernación de Puerto Rico en el 2000 había propuesto como tema central de su campaña que la Marina se retirara de Vieques.

"Necesito tomar una decisión sobre Vieques", le dijo Rumsfeld a Quinn. "Llama a la Marina. Diles que quiero un informe que no contenga más de cinco o diez diapositivas". Detestaba cuando exponían 60, así como las presentaciones en Power Point elaboradas a última hora y que eran famosas en el Pentágono. "Un informe de diez minutos y luego 20 para discutir", ordenó.

Quinn les transmitió las instrucciones a los principales almirantes de operaciones de la Marina del Pentágono y al almirante de cuatro estrellas encargado de la flota del Atlántico. Rumsfeld había sido muy explícito: no más de cinco o diez cuadros, seguidos de una discusión de 20 minutos. A Rumsfeld, que tenía una mente activa, le gustaban estas discusiones.

El almirante a cargo de la flota del Atlántico no tardó en ir a la oficina de Rumsfeld con ocho personas y 60 diapositivas, y presentó quince en media hora. Rumsfeld estaba exasperado y saltaba literalmente en su silla.

"Tendré que suspender esta reunión", dijo; recurrió a un pretexto y los sacó a todos.

"¿No les dijiste lo que yo quería?", le preguntó a Quinn, quien respondió que se lo había dicho una y otra vez.

"No hacen caso, ¿verdad?", comentó Rumsfeld.

"Las costumbres impiden que un oficial de una estrella pueda hacerlo", repitió Quinn.

Con respecto al problema de Vieques, Rumsfeld le dijo a Quinn: "Les devolveremos la isla y compraremos otra. Es una pesadilla política y de medios". No obstante, Rumsfeld estaba muy preocupado por la Marina, su antigua institución. Durante sus primeros días en el Pentágono, un submarino de la Marina, el USS *Greeneville*, estaba ensayando una rutina de emergencia; salió a flote en la costa de Hawai y derribó un barco pesquero japonés, matando a nueve personas, entre ellas algunos estudiantes japoneses. Luego ocurrió el incidente con el avión espía EP-3, y ahora había sucedido lo de Vieques.

A las 7:51 de la mañana del 27 de abril, Rumsfeld dictó un *copo de nieve* en el que resumía sus sentimientos y pensamientos.

"Asunto: la Marina... Los problemas en la Marina pueden ser sistemáticos. Una cosa es cometer errores cuando sobrepasas los límites, y otra muy diferente cometer errores mientras trabajas".

5

SHELTON SE SENTÍA cada vez más pesimista. Rumsfeld le había sugerido que le prestara sus servicios de asesoría militar al presidente a través de él. Shelton reiteró que no veía cómo podía funcionar este sistema, pues el Libro X lo consideraba el "principal asesor militar" del presidente, de tal forma que tenía que ofrecerle asesoría de manera directa.

"Ustedes no están ofreciendo ningún valor agregado", dijo Rumsfeld durante una visita al *Tanque*, la sala de conferencias del Estado Mayor Conjunto.

El almirante Vern Clark, jefe de operaciones navales de 56 años, de lentes y estudioso, retrocedió. "Ni siquiera podemos obtener copias de todos los estudios que están haciendo sus consultores", respondió. Había un documento en particular que no se le había permitido ver. "¿Cómo puede pedirnos un comentario cuando ni siquiera hemos visto el documento?".

Rumsfeld lo contradijo acaloradamente. "Eso no es cierto. El documento está disponible para todos ustedes".

"Señor secretario", dijo Clark, "llamé personalmente a su oficina hace 30 minutos para obtener una copia de ese documento, y me dijeron que yo no estaba autorizado para verlo".

Rumsfeld dijo que había ordenado los estudios porque el Estado Mayor Conjunto era básicamente una dependencia inútil. Se especializaba en voluminosos estudios que tardaban meses o más, no abordaban los asuntos esenciales y eran prácticamente ilegibles. "No he recibido un sólo producto de esos tipos", dijo.

Clark estaba en desacuerdo. A comienzos de su carrera había sido director de esa dependencia, y señaló que ellos realizaban una gran labor. Añadió que Rumsfeld debería valorarla y que, si no lo había hecho aún, aprendería a hacerlo.

Rumsfeld se burló. Luego regresó a su oficina con Quinn.

"¿Viste al jefe de operaciones navales?", preguntó Rumsfeld.

"Sí, señor" respondió Quinn. "Es la primera vez que veo que un militar de cuatro estrellas le echa el agua sucia a usted".

Quinn ventiló sus pensamientos: "Señor secretario, usted necesita buscar al militar de tres estrellas más duro e importante que haya en este edificio y nombrarlo su asistente militar. Y tiene que encontrar la forma de dejar claro que él es su carta, y que será el próximo jefe del Estado Mayor Conjunto. Es lo único que puede servir para que los almirantes y generales le hagan caso".

Todo lo que hizo Rumsfeld fue sonreír.

En entrevistas posteriores, Quinn señaló que los militares creían que Rumsfeld quería arrebatarles el poder de una manera hostil. "Fui considerado un traidor", dijo Quinn.

Herbits concluyó que el mejor candidato para reemplazar a Quinn probablemente era el subdirector de las operaciones navales para recursos, requerimientos y evaluaciones de guerra: el vicealmirante Edmund P. Giambastiani, especialista en submarinos nucleares. Este hombre, conocido como *el almirante G* porque muchas personas tenían dificultades para pronunciar su apellido, se había graduado en 1970 en la Academia Naval. Había sido el capitán del NR-1, el único submarino nuclear de la Marina que practicaba exploraciones en aguas profundas, y posteriormente había comandado el USS *Russell*, un submarino nuclear de ataque rápido que había ejecutado algunas de las misiones encubiertas más importantes y riesgosas durante la Guerra Fría, mientras espiaba en la Unión Soviética. Había sido asistente especial del subdirector de la CIA en los años 80, y recientemente había comandado toda la flota de submarinos del Atlántico.

Poco después, Vern Clark, el jefe de operaciones navales, estaba en el tercer hoyo de un campo de golf, en Nags Head, Carolina del Norte, cuando recibió una llamada; le dijeron que se comunicara con Rumsfeld cuando terminara los primeros nueve hoyos. Clark era uno de los hombres que tenían menores probabilidades de dirigir la Marina; a diferencia de 25 de sus 26 predecesores, no había estudiado en la Academia Naval de Anápolis, Maryland. Clark, quien era profundamente cristiano, se había graduado en el Evangel College, una institución de Missouri afiliada a una pequeña iglesia. Había asistido a una escuela para aspirantes a oficiales en 1968, durante el apogeo de la guerra de Vietnam. Se retiró en 1972, después de su primera ronda de servicio, porque no sentía mucho respeto por la mayoría de los oficiales que querían hacer carrera en la Marina, pero se enlistó al año siguiente, pues pensaba que la Marina era algo que debería hacer por un tiempo.

Clark había sido comandante en alta mar y ocupado los cargos más importantes del Estado Mayor Conjunto bajo el general Shelton: director de operaciones o J-3, supervisando todas las operaciones militares en curso, y, posteriormente, director de esta dependencia. Clark había sido el comandante oficial de la lancha cañonera USS *Grand Rapids* (PG-98) unos 25 años atrás, cuando era comandante de la Marina. El subcomandante había sido un teniente de navío llamado Scott Fry, el actual jefe del Estado Mayor.

Aunque Rumsfeld albergaba profundas dudas sobre la Marina y sobre Fry, creía que el almirante Clark iba a reformar la Marina.

"Pasa algo con mi asistente militar", dijo Rumsfeld cuando habló con el almirante Clark. "Ya sabes, no está funcionando".

"Entiendo", respondió Clark, quien sabía de las vicisitudes del contralmirante Quinn. "Haremos lo que sea necesario. Usted necesita el mayor respaldo posible".

"Pero yo no quiero herirlo", señaló Rumsfeld.

"Señor secretario, yo puedo hacer algo al respecto", le dijo Clark. "Le ordenaré que asuma el mando de un barco transportador de tropas; es la primera labor que debe desempeñar un militar de su rango. No será un trabajo pesado ni degradante; lo que quiera hacer con su futuro depende de él. Yo puedo hacer esto en cuestión de minutos. Así que hagámoslo; tenemos que protegerlo a usted y a su despacho, y es obvio que quienes trabajen allí deben realizar una buena labor. Así que cuente con eso".

"De acuerdo, Vern. Muchas gracias".

Clark ya iba a colgar.

"Espera un momento, Vern. Tengo que hacer un reemplazo".

"Sí".

"Me han hablado del almirante G; trabaja para ti".

"¿No estará bromeando, señor secretario?".

"¿Es bueno?"

"Claro que sí; dirigió mi equipo de transición. Es una persona increíble".

Clark señaló que Rumsfeld no tenía un asistente militar de tres estrellas, pero que eso podría arreglarse. "Se aplican las mismas reglas" dijo. "Tenemos que cuidarte".

El almirante G. estaba su oficina cuando recibió la llamada.

"¿El secretario de qué?" preguntó.

"El secretario de Defensa".

"No lo conozco".

"Quiere hablar contigo".

"Escribí estas dos cosas", le dijo Rumsfeld a Giambastiani. ¿Podrías leerlas y hacer una crítica?".

El primer documento tenía sólo una página, pero el otro tenía cinco y señalaba las diferencias que Rumsfeld había detectado entre el Pentágono como era durante su primer período, de 1975 a 1977, y el que encontró en 2001; era la última versión del informe denominado *La cadena del ancla*. Hacer críticas de este tipo de documentos era algo que le encantaba a Giambastiani, un hombre meticuloso y experto en asuntos nucleares. Intentó dilucidar el significado exacto, descubrir qué se había omitido y cuáles preguntas no se había formulado. Tardó 45 minutos en leer los documentos y hacer la crítica. Rumsfeld lo invitó a almorzar, y al día siguiente le pidió que fuera su asistente militar.

A comienzos de mayo, el contralmirante Quinn dejó su cargo para comandar el USS *Truman,* un barco transportador de tropas, y el almirante G, quien tenía tres estrellas, comenzó a trabajar como asistente militar en el despacho de Rumsfeld. Giambastiani tenía una gran ventaja: cuando se graduó en la Academia Naval en 1970, obtuvo un rango superior al alcanzado por Scott Fry en 1971.

EL MES ANTERIOR, Rumsfeld le había enviado un *copo de nieve* de dos frases a Paul Wolfowitz, el subsecretario de Defensa. "Una persona de Illinois me envió esta entrevista hecha 22 años atrás, en la que yo hablaba del gobierno. Es probable que quieras leerla". Rumsfeld adjuntó una fotocopia de un artículo publicado en 1979 por la revista *Fortune*, en el cual opinaba qué significaba ser un importante ex funcionario gubernamental que se desempeñaba en el mundo de los negocios. Habló sobre los grupos de trabajo, la eliminación de negocios de bajo rendimiento y el estilo administrativo.

"Fui instructor de vuelo en la Marina", había dicho Rumsfeld. "Lo primero que hace generalmente un piloto novato, cuando se sube al avión, es sujetar la palanca y apretarla tan duro que le queda doliendo el brazo. Como ha apretado tan fuerte, todos sus movimientos serán bruscos. Cuando los funcionarios gubernamentales se encuentran en una situación difícil, tienden a hacer lo mismo: se vuelven bruscos, controlan excesivamente y microgestionan".

Algunos de los funcionarios civiles nombrados por Rumsfeld se sorprendieron y alarmaron por la dureza con que el secretario estaba apretando los controles del Pentágono. Todos los días microgestionaba la vida del Pentágono y pasaba por encima de todos. Rumsfeld había escogido a Powell A. Moore, de 63 años, oriundo de Georgia y quien llevaba más de cuatro décadas en Washington, como su asistente para asuntos legislativos, el enlace clave entre el Pentágono y el Congreso. Moore tenía un largo y pintoresco historial en Washington, entre el que figuraba haber sido uno de los voceros del comité para la reelección de Nixon, donde había tenido a su cargo la poco envidiable labor de negar de manera categórica los rumores sobre el Watergate. Moore sabía trabajar para personas difíciles y aceptó su cargo como enlace con el Congreso, acordando previamente que tendría acceso directo a Rumsfeld. Discutieron largamente acerca de cómo cuidar y *alimentar* a los representantes electos.

Pocas personas entendían como él al Congreso o la forma en que debía aceitarse la máquina para que funcionara. Sin embargo, esto no le interesaba a Rumsfeld, a pesar de haber sido congresista. A Moore le sorprendió el desprecio que su jefe sentía por el Congreso, y que no se molestara, además, en ocultar sus sentimientos al respecto.

En una confrontación pública durante una audiencia con la senadora Susan Collins, una honesta representante republicana por el estado de Maine, Rumsfeld la humilló de un modo que le sorprendió incluso a él mismo. Por un momento, a ella le tembló la voz. Poco después, Moore le aconsejó que la llamara para limar asperezas.

"¡Olvídalo!", replicó Rumsfeld. "Es ella la que tiene que pedirme disculpas".

En otra ocasión, Moore vio el borrador de una dura carta que Rumsfeld había dictado para Ike Skelton, representante demócrata por Missouri, y quien desde decía mucho tiempo era miembro del Comité de Servicios Armados de la Cámara de Representantes. "Suavice un poco el tono", le recomendó Moore.

"Si permites que las personas te maltraten", le replicó Rumsfeld, "volverán a hacerlo una y otra vez".

La microgestión de Rumsfeld era casi cómica. En una ocasión, comandó una delegación del Congreso a Columbia, Carolina del Sur, donde se llevaban a cabo las exequias de Floyd Spence, un representante republicano que había sido un *halcón* defensor del Pentágono durante tres décadas. Moore organizó la ubicación de los pasajeros en el avión de Rumsfeld por orden de antigüedad, tal como se hacía en el Congreso.

"Así no", dijo Rumsfeld, y dispuso personalmente la ubicación de los pasajeros. Envió a la parte trasera del avión a Duncan Hunter, representante republicano por California, quien pronto sería el presidente del comité de la Cámara de Representantes para servicios armados.

En mayo, Trent Lott, senador por Mississippi y líder de la mayoría, quería que uno de sus antiguos colaboradores fuera nombrado como subsecretario del departamento de adquisiciones de la Marina. En Pascagoula, Mississippi, había un gran complejo astillero, así que para él esto era simple política estatal.

Steve Herbits tenía otro candidato y estaba cabildeando a su favor, pues pensaba que tenía más experiencia. Herbits había planeado dejar el Pentágono a mediados de mayo y regresar a la Florida, su Estado natal. Según algunas de las normas que el Gobierno tenía para sus contratistas, no estaba claro que pudiera permanecer legalmente en el Pentágono después del 15 de mayo.

Aparentemente, Lott no sabía que Herbits se retiraría tan pronto, y suspendió temporalmente varias confirmaciones de cargos hechas por el Departamento de Defensa.

"Si quiere que las personas que usted nombró sean confirmadas, envíe a Herbits a la Florida", le dijo Lott a Rumsfeld.

El secretario estaba maniatado. "Si cedo a ese chantaje, me seguirán chantajeando siempre", le dijo a Moore. Luego llamó a Herbits.

"No puedes retirarte", le dijo.

"¿Por qué no?".

"Porque no puedo parecer como si me estuviera agachando ante Lott".

Eventualmente, el período de Herbits llegó a su fin, y él se fue a la Florida. Los funcionarios civiles de alto rango del Pentágono pronto serían confirmados por el Senado.

Rumsfeld había sido campeón de lucha en la categoría de 154 libras en la Universidad de Princeton, y Moore concluyó que casi todas las conversaciones con él eran semejantes a una pelea de lucha ¿Quién dominará a quién? ¿Quién derribará a quién? En una ocasión, Moore le preguntó a Rumsfeld por su juego de golf. "Juego como lucho". Moore dedujo que Rumsfeld apretaba demasiado el palo y le daba muy duro a la bola, dos errores clásicos en golf.

EL SECRETARIO NO ESTABA SATISFECHO con ningún aspecto de su departamento, así que le envió a Kenneth Adelman, uno de sus mejores amigos, el borrador de una nueva estrategia de defensa que presentaría ante el Congreso.

Adelman había trabajado para Rumsfeld cuando éste dirigía la Oficina de Oportunidades Económicas, una agencia federal para la erradicación de la pobreza, durante la administración de Richard Nixon, en la que también había trabajado Dick Cheney. Adelman se había desempeñado como asistente especial civil de Rumsfeld durante su primer período como secretario de Defensa, y más tarde había sido el director de la Agencia para el Desarme y Control de Armas, durante la administración de Reagan. Tenía un doctorado en teoría política, y era un halcón y militarista declarado.

Antes de cada posesión considerada *buena* —es decir, de un presidente republicano— Adelman y su esposa ofrecían cenas de gala en su casa, a las que asistían Rumsfeld y Cheney. Rumsfeld ofreció un *brunch* en el Jockey Club en 1981, antes de la posesión de Ronald Reagan y le dijo a Adelman: "Invita a alguien desconocido, y asegúrate de que sea interesante". Adelman invitó a un profesor de la Universidad Johns Hopkins; se llamaba Paul Wolfowitz, tenía 38 años y había sido asistente auxiliar del secretario de Defensa en la administración de Carter. Después del *brunch*, Cheney y Rumsfeld dijeron que habían quedado muy impresionados con Wolfowitz. Se preguntaron de dónde había salido y por qué sabía tantas cosas.

Posteriormente, los Rumsfeld y los Adelman pasaron juntos muchas vacaciones en las casas que Rumsfeld tenía en Taos y en Santa Fe, y en su apartamento de Chicago. En 1986, Rumsfeld visitó a los Adelman en su casa de vacaciones de República Dominicana.

"Me voy a lanzar a la presidencia", le dijo Rumsfeld a Adelman. "Quiero que dirijas mi campaña".

"Es un campo especializado", respondió Adelman, quien no tenía la menor idea acerca de dirigir una campaña presidencial.

"Aprenderás", le dijo Rumsfeld.

Era inútil; Rumsfeld no necesitaba un amateur.

"Puedes hacer las cosas importantes".

Adelman se rió. "No. Ya sabes que tú mismo las harás".

"Podrías escribirme los discursos".

"No, ya hice eso". Era evidente que él apoyaría la candidatura de su viejo amigo y que le ayudaría, pero que no estaba dispuesto a dirigir su campaña.

Las ambiciones presidenciales de Rumsfeld fracasaron a comienzos del año siguiente, pues no pudo recaudar fondos. Sin embargo, continuaron siendo tan buenos amigos como siempre.

Adelman, quien ahora tenía 54 años, leyó el documento que Rumsfeld pensaba presentar como testimonio sobre la nueva estrategia nacional de defensa. "El testimonio está quedando bien", le escribió en un *copo de nieve* de tres páginas que le envió a Rumsfeld, "pero la nueva estrategia del secretario aún necesita títulos", y propuso "UN MARGEN DE SEGURIDAD PARA NORTEAMÉRICA".

También enunció dos advertencias: "Una vez que nuestras democracias derrotaron a los monstruos totalitarios del nazismo y el comunismo", los norteamericanos anhelaron una época de paz. "No tan rápido", dijo Adelman, y señaló que en 1914 había reinado la misma esperanza. Citó al "joven y sabio Winston Churchill", quien había resumido dicho optimismo en términos sarcásticos: "La guerra es demasiado estúpida y demasiado fantástica como para pensar en ella en el siglo veinte... la civilización ha superado semejantes peligros... la interdependencia de las naciones... el sentido de la ley pública... han hecho que tales pesadillas sean imposibles". Adelman señaló que era "una lástima que la Primera Guerra Mundial hubiera estallado ese mismo año, sólo para ser seguida por una segunda guerra aun más desastrosa. Las guerras inesperadas se convertían en tragedias inimaginables. Alrededor de 60 millones de muertos demuestran que fue una verdadera lástima estar tan equivocados".

Rumsfeld escribió "utilizar" en el margen de la cita de Churchill.

El último párrafo del memorando de Adelman decía: "INCLUIR EN AL-GUNA PARTE: el elemento sorpresa es no saber de dónde vendrá el peligro. Cuando Dick Cheney, mi sucesor y antiguo predecesor, asumió el cargo, no pudo imaginar que su principal confrontación militar sería con Irak, nación que había sido amiga de nuestro país, que nunca fue mencionada en el testimonio de confirmación de Cheney, en el que a ningún senador se le ocurrió hacerle preguntas sobre Irak".

El *copo de nieve* escrito por Rumsfeld el 16 de mayo sobre los comentarios de Adelman, señalaba que eran de "primera categoría" y que debía incorporarlos. "Creo que, definitivamente, debería utilizarlos".

Doce días después, en un discurso pronunciado en el cementerio nacional de Arlington con ocasión del Día de los Caídos, fecha en que se recuerda a los norteamericanos muertos en las guerras, Rumsfeld utilizó la cita de Churchill y agregó que esperar el fin de las guerras en el siglo veintiuno "sería mucho más que una lástima".

Diez días después, Rumsfeld utilizó la cita de Churchill en una reunión de la OTAN en Bruselas. En el testimonio que presentó ante el Senado sobre la estrategia del Departamento de Defensa, señaló que Cheney no había mencionado a Irak en su testimonio de confirmación en 1989, y utilizó la expresión "margen de seguridad", sugerida por Adelman, para definir su estrategia.

En mayo, el príncipe Abdullah de Arabia Saudita rechazó una invitación a la Casa Blanca, arguyendo que los Estados Unidos estaban ciegos ante la grave situación de los palestinos. "¿No ven lo que les está sucediendo a los niños, mujeres y ancianos palestinos? ¿No ven la humillación ni el hambre?", reclamó el príncipe.

El primero de junio, un suicida detonó una bomba en un bar de Tel Aviv, que dejó 21 personas muertas. Era el mayor ataque en nueve meses. "Condeno en los términos más fuertes el horrible ataque terrorista perpetrado esta noche de Sabbath en Tel Aviv", señaló Bush. "No existe ninguna justificación para estos absurdos ataques contra los civiles inocentes". Dos días después, el príncipe Bandar y Rihab Massoud cenaron en la Casa Blanca con Bush, Powell y Rice.

Bandar llevó un extenso borrador con la percepción que tenía el mundo árabe sobre los Estados Unidos. Bush organizaba este tipo de eventos para enterarse de las costumbres mundiales, vistas a través de la perspectiva saudí. Fue una velada notable que duró cinco horas; comenzó a las siete de la noche, y Bush permaneció despierto hasta más tarde de lo acostumbrado.

La situación en el Medio Oriente estaba empeorando, dijo Bandar. "Este deterioro progresivo les dará a los extremistas de ambos bandos la oportunidad de prosperar, y sólo ellos triunfarán. Los Estados Unidos y los *mutethila* árabes (los moderados) pagarán un precio muy alto. No hay duda alguna de que tanto los países árabes moderados como los Estados Unidos han perdido la guerra mediática y fracasado ante la opinión pública del mundo árabe. Lo que ven los ciudadanos árabes corrientes es doloroso y muy perturbador: mujeres, niños y ancianos que son asesinados y torturados por los israelíes".

Las unidades militares israelíes, muchas veces equipadas con armamento fabricado en los Estados Unidos, estaban realizando incursiones en territorio palestino, en represalia por los ataques recibidos. Un año atrás, las tropas israelíes habían asesinado a un niño palestino mientras su padre intentaba protegerlo. Fue una imagen difundida una y otra vez por la televisión árabe.

Bandar dijo que la percepción era que los Estados Unidos respaldaban a los israelíes en su propósito de destruir a la Autoridad Palestina y a la economía de este territorio. "El empleo sistemático de armamento norteamericano contra la población civil, contra las instituciones y entidades palestinas, confirman la opinión pública de que resistir la ocupación israelí por todos los medios posibles es considerado como legítimo en la mentalidad de la población civil".

Bush, Powell y Rice intentaron rebatirlo, pero Bandar continuó hablando. No se refería necesariamente a los hechos sino a las percepciones reinantes: "Estas percepciones se convierten en realidades en la mentalidad de los árabes", dijo Bandar, "y esto tendrá un impacto devastador y extremadamente peligroso para los intereses norteamericanos en la región. Y, desgraciadamente, la percepción que tiene el mundo árabe de los Estados Unidos, la única potencia mundial, no es la de un país justo y amable, sino la de una nación que está completamente del lado israelí".

Bandar recordó varias ocasiones en que los Estados Unidos habían condenado la violencia cuando las víctimas eran israelíes "tal como lo había hecho Bush dos días atrás", mientras guardaba "un silencio total cuando sucede algo similar y las víctimas son palestinas". Esto pone en riesgo la "labor de los países muy cercanos a los Estados Unidos, como Arabia Saudita, Egipto y Jordania".

Bandar dijo que estos países comprendían la relación especial que había entre los Estados Unidos e Israel, pero que esta era demasiado unilateral. "Los Estados Unidos tienen que encontrar la forma de separar los actos del gobierno israelí de sus intereses en la región".

También señaló que el deterioro en esta región "ha amenazado, incluso, la situación interna de Jordania, y la posición del rey Abdullah ha sido puesta en entredicho". En una admisión bastante inusual, aunque cuidadosa, señaló que, incluso, en Arabia Saudita, "por primera vez en 30 años estamos enfrentando una situación interna muy discutible".

Bandar sabía cuáles botones debía oprimir. "El deterioro progresivo le está ofreciendo dos oportunidades inmejorables a Saddam Hussein: la primera, para crear una crisis artificial de petróleo y perturbar el mercado". La segunda, dijo, tiene que ver con que "los constantes llamados de Saddam para que la *jihad* ataque al enemigo sionista y al imperialismo norteamericano tendrán un terreno muy abonado". Los árabes actuarán, dijo él, particularmente debido "a la ausencia de una participación real y genuina, y de una política equilibrada por parte de los Estados Unidos".

También señaló que el colapso de la Autoridad Palestina, "así como la pérdida de toda esperanza entre los palestinos, crearán una situación muy peligrosa, la cual no sólo será difícil para los Estados Unidos y para los países árabes moderados, sino, *incluso, para Israel*".

Bandar lanzó fuertes críticas a la política israelí de destruir los hogares de cualquier persona que estuviera involucrada en actos de terrorismo contra Israel. "¿Cómo cree usted, señor presidente, que reaccionaría el pueblo norteamericano si usted destruye las casas de todos los familiares de McVeigh, el responsable de las bombas en Oklahoma City?".

Bandar estaba implorando: "Señor presidente, usted tiene que hacer algo. En otras palabras, básicamente nos están matando; estamos siendo asesinados a mansalva y usted no está haciendo nada".

Bush lanzó fuertes críticas contra el líder palestino Yasser Arafat y su decisión de abandonar en el último minuto un acuerdo con Israel al final de la administración de Clinton. "Arafat es un mentiroso", dijo Bush, quien señaló además que era imposible confiar o trabajar con él, con quien no negociaría.

"Está bien", dijo Bandar. "Es un mentiroso. Ya lo sabemos; usted lo sabe. Es un imbécil; pero es el único imbécil con el que podemos negociar". El problema no se limitaba a una sola persona; era mucho más amplio.

El mensaje final de Bandar fue: "El Medio Oriente está hirviendo cada vez más y más".

EL 16 DE JUNIO, Bush se encontraba en Eslovenia para reunirse con el presidente ruso Vladimir Putin; era uno de los eventos de su primera gira internacional como presidente. Bush estaba esperando de pie la llegada de Putin. A su lado estaba Donald B. Ensenat, un antiguo compañero universitario que había sido nombrado diez días antes jefe de protocolo del Departamento de Estado. Ambos se habían graduado en 1968 y habían sido miembros de la Delta Kappa Epsilon, una asociación universitaria también conocida como *Deke*. La primera declaración que concedió Bush al *New York Times* fue en noviembre de 1967, cuando, en calidad de ex presidente de *Deke*, justificó la práctica de marcar con un gancho caliente a los nuevos miembros de la asociación.

En una entrevista concedida en 2002, Bush me hizo un recuento de su conversación con Ensenat mientras esperaban al mandatario ruso en el castillo esloveno.

"Es sorprendente, ¿verdad, Enzo?", le dijo Bush, llamando a Ensenat por el sobrenombre que tenía en la asociación estudiantil.

"Sí, señor presidente".

"Realmente estamos muy lejos de *Deke*".

"Sí, señor presidente".

6

El 10 de julio de 2001, George Tenet, director de la CIA, se reunió en el cuartel general de la agencia con el jefe de contraterrorismo Cofer Black, para analizar la última información recibida sobre Osama bin Laden y su organización terrorista de al Qaeda. Black suministró toda la información, que consistía en la intercepción de comunicaciones e inteligencia de ALTO SECRETO, la cual mostraba que había una probabilidad cada vez mayor de que al Qaeda atacara muy pronto a los Estados Unidos. Era un compendio de información aislada, que ofrecía, sin embargo, un caso sólido, tanto así que Tenet decidió que debería dirigirse en ese instante a la Casa Blanca en compañía de Black. Llamó a Condoleezza Rice desde su auto y le dijo que necesitaba hablar con ella de inmediato. No era posible que ella pudiera rechazar semejante petición por parte del director de la CIA.

Tenet llevaba varios meses presionando a Rice para que estableciera una fuerte política de contraterrorismo, que constara de órdenes presidenciales concretas de búsqueda que le darían a la CIA una mayor autoridad para realizar operaciones encubiertas contra bin Laden. Era probable que una visita súbita –Black la denominó una sesión "fuera de ciclo", diferente de la reunión habitual que sostenía semanalmente con Rice–, captara la atención de la funcionaria.

Tenet estaba sumamente preocupado por los recientes informes de inteligencia que había recibido. No había nada concluyente ni particularmente alarmante, pero el volumen de información era tan grande que los instintos de un oficial de inteligencia no vacilarían en sugerirle que algo se estaba cocinando. Tenet y Black esperaban transmitirle su preocupación a Rice e instarla a que el gobierno tomara medidas inmediatas.

Tenet, de 48 años, un fornido y sociable hijo de inmigrantes griegos, llevaba cuatro años como director de la CIA. Era el único funcionario de la administración de Clinton que tenía una silla en el Consejo Nacional de Seguridad de George W. Bush, y, por lo tanto, el único miembro de esta dependencia que había trabajado en noviembre y diciembre de 1999, justo antes del nuevo milenio, cuando se había desmantelado una serie de atentados terroristas planeados por al Qaeda en todo el mundo. Esto le recordó a Tenet la situación actual.

En 1999, la Agencia Nacional de Seguridad había interceptado una llamada telefónica de un compañero de bin Laden en la que decía: "El tiempo de entrenamiento ha terminado", y que precedió al estallido de ataques en Jordania e Israel. Ahmed Ressam, un argelino de 32 años y miembro de la *jihad*, había sido arrestado poco antes de la Navidad de 1999, cuando viajó con explosivos desde Canadá a los Estados Unidos, con el objetivo de realizar un atentado en el aeropuerto internacional de Los Ángeles. Tenet les había ordenado a los agentes de la CIA que ocuparan los puestos de batalla. "El pueblo norteamericano espera que ustedes y yo tomemos todas las medidas necesarias para protegerlo durante este período", dijo en un cable antes del nuevo milenio. Le advirtió al presidente Clinton que podrían presentarse entre 15 y 20 ataques; habló con los jefes de los servicios de inteligencia de 20 países aliados de los Estados Unidos, condujo operaciones antiterroristas y ejecutó arrestos en ocho países.

Tenet creía que ahora estaba sucediendo algo similar, aunque probablemente mucho peor. La Agencia Nacional de Seguridad había interceptado llamadas amenazantes entre los secuaces de bin Laden –más de 34 en total– en las que hacían declaraciones premonitorias sobre una "hora cero" inminente, y el pronunciamiento de que "sucederá algo espectacular". Diez días antes, el 30 de junio, Tenet les había ordenado a todos los jefes de estaciones que compartieran la información sobre al Qaeda con gobiernos amigos de los Estados Unidos, y que los servicios de inteligencia deberían desmantelar las células sospechosas de terrorismo en sus países. Tal como lo había hecho en 1999, Tenet hizo llamadas personales y se comunicó con los jefes de los servicios de inteligencia de estas 20 naciones el 3 de julio; les pidió que detuvieran a los integrantes de al Qaeda en sus países y que hostigaran a los miembros de todas las células terroristas afiliadas a al Qaeda.

Tenet no sabía cuándo, dónde, ni cómo sería el ataque, pero pensaba que había demasiado ruido en los sistemas de inteligencia. Dos semanas antes le había dicho a Richard A. Clark, director de contraterrorismo del Consejo Nacional de Seguridad: "Mi sexto sentido me dice que algo va a suceder, y que será un golpe muy fuerte".

Sin embargo, Tenet tenía dificultades para adelantar una operación inmediata contra bin Laden, debido parcialmente a que Rumsfeld había cuestionado toda la información interceptada por la Agencia Nacional de Seguridad. "¿Se trataría de un gran engaño?", preguntó Rumsfeld. Probablemente sólo se trataba de un plan para medir la defensa y reacción de los Estados Unidos. Tenet hizo que la Agencia Nacional de Seguridad revisara toda la información interceptada, y se concluyó que todas estas comunicaciones realmente pertenecían a al Qaeda. El 30 de junio, se presentó un informe de inteligencia de ALTO SECRETO que contenía un artículo titulado "Las amenazas de bin Laden son reales".

Tenet esperaba que Rice reaccionara luego de su intempestivo encuentro. Él y Black, un veterano agente encubierto, calvo, de voz demasiado delgada y modales delicados que le hacían parecer una versión más alta de Karl Rove, le transmitieron todos los mensajes importantes cuando se reunieron con ella. El primero se refería a que al Qaeda iba a atacar intereses estadounidenses, probablemente en territorio norteamericano. Black señaló que esto equivalía a una advertencia estratégica, y que el problema era tan serio que requería un plan y una estrategia integrales. El segundo afirmaba que se trataba de un grave problema de política exterior que necesitaba resolverse de inmediato. Necesitaban actuar en ese instante y emprender algún tipo de acción –encubierta, militar o de cualquier otro tipo– para neutralizar a bin Laden.

Los dos agentes le dijeron a Rice que los Estados Unidos contaban con recursos técnicos y humanos, y que la información obtenida era confiable. Black reconoció que una parte de esta era *vudú*, es decir, incierta, pero que en muchas ocasiones ese tipo de información era la señal más efectiva.

Ambos advirtieron que no lograron conmover a Rice. Ella fue amable, pero no les hizo mucho caso. El mismo Bush ya había dicho que no quería matar moscas. Todos los altos funcionarios sabían que ya se estaba fraguando un plan coherente para poner en práctica operaciones encubiertas contra bin Laden, pero esto tomaría algún tiempo. En una reunión a puerta cerrada que se había efectuado recientemente, todos los estamentos del Consejo Nacional de Seguridad había considerado la posibilidad de emprender acciones contra bin Laden, incluido el uso de una nueva arma secreta, el *predator*, una nave aérea a control remoto, también llamada *zángano*, que lanzaba misiles Hellfire, con la cual podrían matarlo a él o a sus lugartenientes. Parecía una solución posible, pero hubo una ardua disputa entre la CIA y el Pentágono para decidir quién financiaría el desarrollo de esta arma y tendría la autoridad para dispararla. Adicionalmente, Rice parecía haberse concentrado en otras prioridades de la administración, especialmente en el sistema defensivo de misiles balísticos que Bush había promovido en su campaña. Ella estaba en otro mundo.

Tenet salió frustrado de la reunión. Aunque Rice lo escuchó, el hecho de que no se tomara medidas inmediatas implicaba un alto riesgo. Black pensó que la decisión de limitarse a seguir haciendo planes era una política fallida. Rice y el equipo de Bush habían estado hibernando demasiado tiempo. "Los adultos no deberían tener un sistema como este", señaló Black posteriormente.

Black calculó que si le hubieran dado 500 millones de dólares para un fondo de acciones encubiertas en ese momento, así como una autorización razonable por parte del presidente para matar a bin Laden, hubiera podido causarle grandes estragos e, incluso, liquidarlo. Bin Laden operaba desde un remoto santuario en Afganistán, país gobernado por los extremistas talibanes. Una posible acción encubierta no era ninguna idea abstracta. Durante los dos años anteriores –y hasta marzo de 2001– la CIA había desplegado en cinco ocasiones grupos paramilitares en Afganistán, para que trabajaran con la Alianza del Norte, un conjunto de milicias y tribus de ese país que se oponían a los talibanes. La CIA tenía aproximadamente cien fuentes e informantes operando en Afganistán. Si le hubieran dado el dinero y la autorización, Black podría haber entregado la cabeza de bin Laden dentro de una caja.

LA REUNIÓN QUE SOSTUVIERON Tenet, Black y Rice el 10 de julio de 2001 no se mencionó en los diversos informes de investigaciones referentes a los ataques terroristas que ocurrieron el 11 de septiembre del 2001 en los Estados Unidos. Sin embargo, tanto Tenet como Black creyeron que era la advertencia más fuerte que le habían dado a la Casa Blanca sobre bin Laden y al Qaeda. Aunque los investigadores tenían acceso a todos los documentos sobre esta reunión, Black creía que había cosas que las comisiones querían saber y cosas que no querían saber. Esto solía suceder en las investigaciones; había preguntas que les gustaba hacer, y otras que no.

Philip Zelikow, el agresivo director ejecutivo de la comisión sobre el 9/11, quien había investigado los ataques terroristas, era también profesor de la Universidad de Virginia y había escrito un libro sobre Alemania en compañía de Rice, obtuvo alguna información sobre la reunión del 10 de julio. De hecho, Tenet y Black habían exigido ese día que se tomaran medidas inmediatas, pero Zelikow no sabía con claridad en qué consistían. La advertencia estratégica pronunciada por Tenet y Black carecía de ciertos detalles ¿Cuándo, dónde y cómo sería el ataque?

Además, concluyó Zelikow, el plan para emprender una acción encubierta con el fin de perseguir a bin Laden en su santuario de Afganistán se esbozó realmente con mucha rapidez, tal vez demasiado rápido para la burocracia de Seguridad Nacional, creyó él, aunque el plan no fuera aprobado antes de los ataques del 11 de septiembre. De hecho, Rice le ordenó a la Directiva Presidencial de Seguridad Nacional que pusiera en marcha un plan para una nueva ofensiva encubierta contra bin Laden, el cual le sería enviado a Bush el 10 de septiembre de 2001. Era el NSPD-9, es decir que otros ocho asuntos de política exterior habían sido formalmente debatidos, acordados y firmados por el presidente como políticas de la administración antes de adelantar la campaña para localizar a bin Laden.

RUMSFELD TRABAJABA todos los fines de semana. Un sábado, a comienzos de agosto de 2001, llamó a Shelton y a todos los jefes de las divisiones que participaron en los 68 planes de guerra que fueron archivados, entre los que figuraban planes contra Irak y Corea del Norte; fue una jornada agotadora. Rumsfeld quería evaluar las suposiciones. "Yo estaba sentado allí y ellos no podían creerlo", me dijo en una entrevista. "Nos tomó casi todo el día; luego un coronel se puso de pie, habló de las especulaciones, y yo expresé mis opiniones. Y después, otro tipo se puso de pie y discutimos cada una de las especulaciones". Los lineamientos formales de estos planes trazados por el presidente y la secretaría de Defensa tenían en algunos casos cuatro o cinco años antigüedad. "Sin embargo, nunca fueron siquiera discutidos aquí, en mi oficina", señaló Rumsfeld con desdén.

"Si seguimos así, permaneceremos una semana aquí", le dijo el almirante Giambastiani a Rumsfeld ese día.

Rumsfeld no iba a claudicar; los planes se habían frustrado por el problema técnico que suponía combinar los objetivos con los niveles de fuerza. El secretario opinaba que esta era una labor desagradable que los coroneles creían solucionar simplemente agregando más y más tropas a los planes de guerra. Sentían aversión por los riesgos, pero él no. Rumsfeld estaba dispuesto, incluso, deseoso de asumir el riesgo.

SHELTON HABÍA SIDO JEFE del Estado Mayor desde 1997. Su período de cuatro años terminaría en otoño. Rumsfeld le asignó a Staser Holcomb la delicada tarea de ayudarle a buscar un reemplazo de Shelton. Holcomb era asesor de camarilla y vicealmirante retirado, y había sido su asistente militar 25 años atrás; ahora comenzó con una enorme lista de 150 oficiales, entrevistó personalmente a la mitad e hizo consultas sobre 40 civiles y militares, activos o retirados, a quienes se refería como "amigos viejos y confiables". La lista incluía algunos oficiales retirados y generales de tres estrellas que técnicamente no eran elegibles. Enumeró una docena de características que debería tener el nuevo director: "Candor y franqueza, disposición para disentir y luego respaldar de manera efectiva las decisiones tomadas".

El prospecto de que un oficial de tres estrellas o retirado pudiera asumir este cargo conmocionó a los militares activos de cuatro estrellas.

Holcomb había solicitado una entrevista con el general James L. Jones, comandante de la Marina, un hombre fuerte y cosmopolita que medía 1,92 metros. Jones se había criado en París, hablaba francés y en 1966 había obtenido un título en relaciones internacionales de la Universidad de Georgetown. Se había unido a los *marines,* gracias a la escuela de aspirantes a oficiales, el año siguiente, y había servido como líder de pelotón de combate en Vietnam. Había desempeñado todos los cargos importantes: jefe de edecanes del comandante de la Marina, comandante de división de la Marina, y edecán militar del secretario de Defensa William Cohen en 1997. Cohen y Jones eran amigos cercanos desde hacía casi dos décadas, cuando Cohen era senador por Maine, y Jones, quien en ese entonces tenía rango de mayor, era el enlace de la Marina en el Senado. Cohen sabía que Jones había sido nombrado comandante, que era el *marine* de mayor rango y miembro del Estado Mayor Conjunto. Jones sabía que su conexión con Cohen lo hacía sospechoso ante el Pentágono de Rumsfeld.

Cuando Holcomb habló con Jones, le dijo que una de las labores que debía hacer para Rumsfeld consistía en identificar generales brillantes de dos y tres estrellas que tuvieran una opinión similar sobre la transformación. Holcomb dijo que sólo le restaban seis semanas.

"Almirante", le dijo Jones, "todos los que han estado aquí han dicho lo mismo".

Jones opinaba que este era uno de los problemas que tenía el modelo de Rumsfeld. El aparato militar estadounidense no era un comité asesor en el que los asesores que entraban y salían con ideas buenas, nuevas y atrevidas, realmente pudieran ser de ayuda.

Sin embargo, Jones figuraba en la lista de Holcomb como el futuro jefe del Estado Mayor. Lo llamaron sin previo aviso a una entrevista con Rumsfeld el día sábado, para hablar sobre el cargo. Jones no sabía muy bien qué estaba haciendo Rumsfeld en el Pentágono durante sus primeros meses. Lo cierto es que era el *marine* de mayor rango –la contraparte de Vern Clark en la Marina– pero tampoco podía obtener copias de algunos de los estudios que Rumsfeld les asignaba a sus consultores y empleados civiles.

Jones era respetuoso, siempre tenía tiempo para los demás, sin que importara su origen y posición, y se sorprendió por la forma tan caballerosa como se comportó Rumsfeld, pues muchas veces ni siquiera saludaba. Jones creía que, básicamente, a Rumsfeld sólo le importaban sus propias ideas. Dio la impresión de ser prudente y atento, pero al mismo tiempo parecía no tener pelos en la lengua. La arrogancia de Rumsfeld y la importancia que se daba a sí mismo terminaban por infectarlo todo, concluyó Jones. ¿Quién quería ser jefe de Estado Mayor y asesor militar de cabecera del secretario, cuando todo parecía indicar que Rumsfeld realmente no quería asesoría militar? Lo único que quería era que sus subalternos le pasaran una información voluminosa y detallada, y siempre actuaba obedeciendo a sus propias ideas.

Jones tomó la decisión inusual de declinar la entrevista, arguyendo que quería seguir desempeñándose como comandante de la Marina.

SHELTON, UN MILITAR DEL EJÉRCITO, concluyó que el mejor candidato para sucederlo era el almirante Clark, jefe de operaciones navales. Aunque sólo llevaba cerca de un año en este cargo, su desempeño demostraba que conocía el sistema. En opinión de Shelton, Clark era un hombre inusual: le gustaba trabajar en equipo pero era bastante independiente. Si estaba en desacuerdo con algo, lo manifestaba; su estilo era directo y nada amenazante. Clark era el único que podría sobrevivir a Rumsfeld y conservar una dosis de dignidad e independencia con respecto a los militares uniformados. Tenían que nombrarlo en ese cargo antes de que Rumsfeld cambiara el sistema para siempre.

Clark, quien tenía una maestría de la Universidad de Arkansas, era muy aficionado a leer *best-sellers* sobre negocios. Uno de sus favoritos era *Empresas que sobresalen,* escrito por Jim Collins, que versaba sobre negocios que daban un rendimiento normal y experimentaban un crecimiento considerable y repentino. Este libro resaltaba la importancia de la humildad y la disciplina, y la forma en que las creencias fundamentales de un individuo contribuían a definir la cultura corporativa. Esta obra le produjo un fuerte impacto.

"¿En qué crees realmente?", era una de sus preguntas favoritas cuando entrevistaba a oficiales de alto rango de la Marina. Cuando las creencias de un individuo no se alineaban con la cultura y valores de una organización, comenzaban a surgir problemas.

En el verano de 2001, cuando empezó la competencia para reemplazar a Shelton, Clark recibió un mensaje que lo citaba a una reunión con Bush dentro de varios días.

Clark llamó al almirante G., su antiguo suplente, a la oficina de Rumsfeld. "¿De qué se trata?".

"Te van a entrevistar para ser el nuevo jefe del Estado Mayor", le dijo Giambastiani.

"Al diablo con eso. No aceptaré una entrevista para asumir la jefatura a menos que haya hablado previamente con Don Rumsfeld. Nadie me ha dicho nada al respecto".

"¡Debe estar bromeando, señor!", replicó Giambastiani. Rumsfeld y Clark se habían reunido recientemente. "¿De qué hablaron en la reunión?".

"Sobre los candidatos; quiénes eran, qué líderes había en los diferentes departamentos y cuáles eran sus cualidades".

"¿Y nunca propusiste tu nombre?".

"No".

"Tú también estás en la lista", le dijo Giambastiani.

Clark pensaba que, en términos ideales, el próximo jefe del Estado Mayor no debería pertenecer a la jefatura de ninguna de las cuatro ramas del aparato militar. Debería ser elegido más bien entre los comandantes de guerra –CEJ, abreviatura de comandantes en jefe– que controlaban las fuerzas operativas, como, por ejemplo, el almirante Blair en el Pacífico o Tommy Franks, general del Ejército en el Medio Oriente.

Según la legislación Goldwater-Nichols, el poder había sido transferido de los jefes de servicio a los CEJ. Los jefes de servicio, incluido él mismo, eran demasiado parroquianos y, simplemente, reclutaban, equipaban y entrenaban a sus servicios individuales. Por otra parte, los CEJ utilizaban las fuerzas y participaban en las guerras. Estos eran los comandantes adjuntos –un almirante de la Marina o un general de la Fuerza Aérea podían liderar las tropas terrestres del Ejército y los *marines*– y el futuro del aparato militar estaba en la unión de las fuerzas, en que trabajaran mancomunadamente. Clark opinaba que necesitaban como director a un CEJ que hubiera trabajado en esa línea. Clark había sido un CEJ –jefe del comando del Atlántico– aunque sólo por seis meses, antes de ser el jefe de operaciones navales, cargo que no le otorgaba ninguna función real en términos operativos, aunque cumplía un papel importante como el almirante más importante de la Marina. Y Clark creía que iba a mejorar a esta institución.

"No me reuniré con el presidente", le dijo a Giambastiani, "mientras no haya hablado con Don Rumsfeld sobre esto.

7

El almirante Giambastiani organizó un encuentro entre Clark y Rumsfeld un viernes a las 6:45 de la tarde. Rumsfeld tenía prisa ese día, y decidieron hablar el domingo después de misa.

Clark fue muy enfático: "No iré a conversar acerca de esto. Usted y yo nunca hemos hablado sobre esto". Clark le dijo a Rumsfeld que necesitaba discutir todos los aspectos para ver cuáles eran sus prioridades, metas y creencias. ¿Tendrían las mismas? ¿Qué quería Rumsfeld? Ellos dos necesitaban entenderse. Había mucha confusión sobre el papel del jefe del Estado Mayor. Clark creía en el establecimiento de prioridades; él se había concentrado en cinco prioridades importantes en la Marina. Si se tiene cien prioridades, nunca se hará nada. ¿Cuáles eran las prioridades de Rumsfeld para el aparato militar estadounidense?

Rumsfeld anduvo con rodeos.

"Usted no confía nosotros", dijo Clark, aludiendo al problema más espinoso. Era la primera vez que tenía la oportunidad de desahogarse y expresar lo que pensaba de Rumsfeld.

"Por supuesto que confío en ti", le dijo Rumsfeld tan amablemente como pudo. "Tú eres el jefe de la Marina de los Estados Unidos". Sin embargo, el secretario dio un giro abrupto: "¿Cómo puedes decir eso?", preguntó con tono agresivo; parecía herido. Luego recobró la calma y dijo en un tono alto: "Tengo una gran confianza".

Clark comprendió que el elogio efusivo era una manera sorprendentemente efectiva de dejar a un lado el tema de la confianza. No quería detenerse en minucias y rebajarse con Rumsfeld, pero le reclamó que no les permitía ver muchos estudios e informes a los jefes del Estado Mayor Conjunto. "Señor secretario", dijo, usted nos ha dejado por fuera de este proceso. He leído todo lo que se me permite ver, y este es el día en que aún no se nos permite tener acceso a cierta información.

"Señor secretario, hasta donde yo sé, no creo que usted y yo estemos del mismo lado para liderar el aparato militar de los Estados Unidos ni para que yo sea su asesor militar de cabecera. Si voy a ocupar ese cargo, usted tiene que saber lo que yo pienso, y yo tengo que saber lo que usted piensa".

Rumsfeld señaló que Clark estaba enfrascado en detalles. "Ya tendremos tiempo para hablar de esto", le aseguró a Clark.

"Señor secretario, no quiero ir mañana a la Casa Blanca, pues sé que la primera pregunta que me hará el presidente Bush será: "Vern, ¿quieres ser el director?". No estamos listos para ese tipo de conversación".

"Está bien, no hay ningún problema", respondió Rumsfeld. "El presidente no te ofrecerá el cargo mañana. El procedimiento no es así. Se trata de una entrevista preliminar".

Clark aceptó, pues creyó que las cosas eran de ese modo. "Asistiré mañana, señor".

ANTES DE SU REUNIÓN con Bush, el almirante Clark sacó una copia del Libro X del Acta Goldwater-Nichols, sobre los jefes del Estado Mayor y el director de esta dependencia. Además de designar a dicho director como "principal asesor militar" del presidente, del secretario de Defensa y del Consejo Nacional de Seguridad, la ley decía que los otros jefes en servicio también eran asesores militares, y que debían expresar también sus puntos de vista aunque no estuvieran de acuerdo con el director. Mientras se dirigía la Casa Blanca, Clark se recordó a sí mismo insistir en que los jefes del Estado Mayor no eran un grupo unánime.

El único contacto real que había tenido Clark con Bush había sido seis meses atrás, el 20 de enero de 2001, durante el desfile inaugural de Bush. Mientras un gran contingente de la Marina desfilaba frente al estrado presidencial en la Casa Blanca, Clark, como almirante de mayor rango, subió para escoltar al presidente. Saludó a Bush, se hizo al lado suyo y le describió las diferentes unidades de la Marina. Cuando pasó la última, Clark chocó sus talones y lo saludó nuevo.

"Señor presidente", le dijo, "es un placer estar hoy aquí y participar en este evento tan importante. Los hombres y las mujeres de la Marina de los Estados Unidos están preparados para servir bajo su liderazgo. Y a nivel personal, quiero que sepa que estaré rezando por usted".

Bush se puso pálido.

CLARK FUE RECIBIDO en el Salón Oval por Bush, Cheney y Rumsfeld. Después de hablar brevemente sobre asuntos informales, el presidente dijo: "Bien, Vern, ¿qué piensas acerca de ser el presidente de la jefatura del Estado Mayor?".

Clark le lanzó una mirada a Rumsfeld; comprendió que tendría que salvar su pellejo e intentó dar respuestas evasivas. Dijo que se sentía muy honrado de ser el jefe de la Marina, y que el futuro estaba en que las fuerzas operaran de manera conjunta.

Bush le hizo algunas preguntas generales sobre la Marina.

Clark tenía preparado su discurso y mencionó sus cinco prioridades para transformar a la Marina, las cuales se concentraban en el aspecto humano, la rapidez y la construcción de nuevos astilleros.

Soltó su discurso de siempre, esperando que le agradara a Bush, y dijo que los Estados Unidos habían dejado de hablar sobre el servicio, incluido el militar, en los años 90. "La Marina es parte de él", señaló. "Sólo se hablaba de 'yo, yo; mi, mi; no tengo esto, no tengo aquello'; es una posición lastimosa con respecto a la vida", continuó Clark. "Usted sabe, señor presidente, que yo soy una persona de fe".

El presidente se limitó a asentir.

"Mi padre era predicador", continuó Clark. Antes de su primer encuentro, como jefe de operaciones navales, con todos sus almirantes subalternos, Clark señaló que un edecán le había dicho: "Necesitamos una sesión de reavivamiento". Clark relató que habló con los almirantes y les dijo: "Prestamos un servicio, y la calidad del servicio no sólo significa calidad de vida, es decir, atención médica, condiciones de vivienda y otros beneficios adicionales. El servicio significa lo siguiente: comenzaremos a hablar sobre la calidad del trabajo. El servicio significa comprometernos con un propósito más elevado".

"Las misiones también tienen un lugar prioritario", dijo Clark. El Congreso continental no creó a la Marina para que ofreciera una vista agradable en alta mar. Nuestra labor es alcanzar al enemigo".

Clark mencionó que a Rumsfeld le gustaba hablar sobre la "transformación", es decir, sobre la modernización y el cambio en los estamentos militares. Clark también dijo que él había practicado la "transformación" antes de que esta palabra fuera utilizada, ciertamente antes de que Bush fuera elegido presidente y Rumsfeld asumiera como secretario de Defensa.

Cheney escasamente habló. Después de la reunión, Rumsfeld no le dijo nada a Clark, quien opinó que el encuentro había sido irrelevante y que nadie había aprendido gran cosa.

Varias semanas después, Clark supo que Cheney quería hablar a solas con él. El encuentro estaba programado para durar 20 minutos, lo que mostraba un esfuerzo real por parte del gobierno. La Casa Blanca estaba investigando exhaustivamente, y Clark creyó que no tenía muchas posibilidades como candidato. Sin embargo, tenía tiempo para prepararse.

"No sé si lo recuerda, pero combatí a su lado en la Guerra del Golfo", dijo Clark. "Yo le pasaba las órdenes para el despliegue de tropas".

Cheney pretendió no recordar. En ese entonces, Clark era capitán de la Marina.

Clark señaló que ya era hora de hacer un fuerte ajuste al aparato militar, pero que creía que los principios de transformación que Rumsfeld proponía eran correctos.

Cheney quería saber cómo había ascendido Clark hasta ser el jefe de la Marina.

Clark dijo que, en el año 2000, el jefe del estado mayor del secretario de Defensa William Cohen le había preguntado: "Vern, ¿cómo pudimos caer tan bajo?", refiriéndose al estado actual de la Marina. La respuesta de Clark había sido: "Porque escogieron al personal equivocado". Sólo uno de los cinco almirantes principales de la Marina había comandado una nave con tropas de combate. Había muchos almirantes de escritorio, y era fundamental elegir a los líderes que tuvieran una experiencia operativa adecuada. "No importa lo que usted haga, pero no permita que las cosas sean así de nuevo", le aconsejó al vicepresidente.

Clark dijo que había instaurado el "estudio estúpido" o "escuela estúpida" para los nuevos almirantes. En vez de la antigua instrucción que se les ofrecía a los oficiales superiores de la Marina, la cual giraba en torno a la etiqueta y les enseñaban cómo sostener el cuchillo y el tenedor en embajadas extranjeras o en la Casa Blanca, ahora recibían un curso de dos semanas sobre temas importantes. "Los almirantes no sabían nada de finanzas", dijo. Sólo sabían gastar dinero, pero no cómo administrar presupuestos, así que recibieron clases de finanzas. Clark había hecho investigaciones sobre cómo ser un gerente general, y no escatimó esfuerzos para que los almirantes distribuyeran su tiempo según el modelo contemporáneo de los negocios: dedicar una tercera parte del tiempo a las principales prioridades, otra tercera parte al desarrollo y a la práctica, y la tercera restante a evaluar el producto o los resultados.

"Usted sabe", agregó Clark, "que aquí no hacemos esta última parte. Sólo elaboramos un nuevo presupuesto, y eso está mal. Tenemos que encontrar la forma de hacerlo mejor. Yo les estoy enseñando a mis hombres a que lo hagan; es parte de mi agenda, y no de la agenda de Donald Rumsfeld. Para eso estamos aquí".

Cheney se mostró receptivo, y Clark le relató algunas experiencias que vivió durante la administración de Clinton. Todo indicaba que al vicepresidente le gustaba escuchar ese tipo de historias.

"Asegúrese de rodearse de personas que le digan al presidente cuál es la realidad exacta, y que no se repita lo que hicimos en Kosovo", le sugirió Clark. Luego le dijo que cuando era el director de operaciones del Estado Mayor Conjunto, había asistido a los encuentros efectuados en la Casa Blanca en 1999, cuando Clinton decidió enfrentar la limpieza étnica emprendida por el líder yugoslavo Slobodan Milosevic. Bien sea que se hubiera tratado de un error de cálculo o, simplemente, de un maquillaje de la realidad, los asesores le dijeron al presidente Clinton que Milosevic cedería a las amenazas; cuando estas fueron infructuosas, conceptuaron ante el presidente que un bombardeo surtiría efecto.

"Se suponía que todo iba a terminar en 48 horas, y luego en 72", comentó Clark. En lugar de esto se necesitaron 78 días de bombardeos para disuadir a Milosevic. "Se necesitaron decenas de psiquiatras para aconsejar a todos los miembros del gabinete, y vigilarlos para que no se cortaran las venas, porque se habían equivocado terriblemente acerca de lo que iba a suceder y de la forma en que se lo presentaron al presidente". Algunos de los miembros del equipo nacional de seguridad de Clinton se habían dedicado a vender esperanzas y habían perdido el sentido de la realidad, comentó Clark.

"Y usted debe asegurarse de que nunca se vea enfrascado en esa situación", le dijo.

El optimismo era tan grande con respecto a Kosovo, señaló Clark, que tenían un plan de ataque que duraría 72 horas, pero no tenían ningún plan para lo que sucedería después. "Absolutamente ninguno", agregó. No tenían ningún plan en caso de que el optimismo no funcionara, de tal suerte que tuvieron que apresurarse. "Con la experiencia que usted tiene" le dijo al ex secretario de Defensa, "podrá desarrollar una labor diferente de lo que ha sucedido durante mucho tiempo. Y por el amor de Dios, nombren un director que no permita que esto pase de nuevo".

Cheney era todo sonrisas; parecía hacer caso y estar dispuesto a escuchar, así que Clark continuó hablando; dijo que el general Shelton había insistido en que los directores del Estado Mayor Conjunto leyeran *Negligencia: Lyndon Johnson, Robert McNamara, los jefes del Estado Mayor Conjunto y las mentiras que condujeron a Vietnam*, libro publicado en 1997 por H. R. McMaster, quien se había graduado en 1984 en la academia militar de West Point. Durante la guerra de Vietnam, los líderes militares fueron débiles y no ofrecieron las mejores sugerencias a nivel militar, dijo Clark. Los jefes no habían trabajado en grupo y no tenían buenas relaciones con los líderes civiles.

Clark señaló que los líderes militares de la era de Vietnam habían perdido la capacidad para influir en el proceso, de tal forma que el presidente hizo cosas que contribuyeron al detrimento de la nación. Perdieron su influencia, no hablaron claramente, y McNamara manipuló el sistema. El país y el aparato militar pagaron un alto precio por ello. "Señor vicepresidente, sea lo que sea que usted haga, tiene que asegurarse de escoger a un líder militar que nunca permita que esto vuelva a suceder".

Clark volvió a hablar sobre la época en que había sido capitán de la Marina durante la Guerra del Golfo. Había observado la relación entre Cheney, como secretario de Defensa, y Powell, como jefe del Estado Mayor Conjunto. Hasta donde él sabía, dijo Clark, era el modelo ideal; se trataba de un hombre de mentalidad independiente que era, sin embargo, cercano al secretario de Defensa. Clark señaló que había cierta tensión entre Rumsfeld y Shelton. "Esta conexión es muy importante, y será un gran desafío ahora que Rumsfeld está a cargo". Luego agregó: "Tengo un trabajo fabuloso; quiero que lo entienda. Me divierto mucho en la Marina". Y esto era algo que Cheney, Rumsfeld y el presidente deberían tener en cuenta para elegir al candidato.

"Bueno", dijo Cheney, "me parece que usted sería muy valioso en este cargo".

La reunión duró una hora y 20 minutos, una hora más de lo estipulado. Clark pensó: "¿Qué irá a pasar?". Había andado con rodeos, pero concluyó que había sido un encuentro muy cálido. Creía que había hecho buenas migas con Cheney y que todo iba a jugar a su favor.

Clark fue citado sin aviso previo a la Casa Blanca para una entrevista de 30 minutos con Bush y Cheney.

"Señor presidente", dijo Clark, "usted sabe que tengo un trabajo maravilloso. Realmente no estoy persiguiendo el trabajo que me ofrecen".

"Sí", dijo Bush, "eso me han dicho. No te importa si no te damos ese puesto, ¿verdad? Dime por qué".

"Señor presidente", respondió el almirante. "En primer lugar, es para mí un honor inmenso poder servirle a la patria". Agregó que un comandante militar dedicado a los programas y problemas propios de su labor tendría dificultades al asumir el cargo propuesto, pues era algo que exigía una integración total. "También existe otra razón significativa. Es importante que las personas sean ambiciosas, aunque creo que el exceso de ambición en los líderes militares de más alto rango es algo peligroso".

Clark dejó que su observación flotara en el aire, y concluyó que debía tener cuidado con su teoría sobre la ambición; a fin de cuentas, nadie podría ser presidente si no era demasiado ambicioso. "Por supuesto", agregó Clark intentando rectificar su posición, "que hay posiciones a las que no se puede aspirar a menos que uno tenga ambición. Pero los cargos militares son ante todo una labor de servicio. Y creo que es peligroso cuando la ambición se mezcla con el servicio".

"Vern y yo tuvimos una reunión maravillosa hace un par de días", dijo Cheney. "Está haciendo muchas cosas en la Marina, y creo que es importante que las comparta con usted. ¿Por qué no le cuentas en detalle lo que estás haciendo allí?".

Clark hizo un recuento de sus cinco prioridades y enfatizó en la importancia que tenían las personas, así como la necesidad de una nueva definición del servicio. Dijo que la permanencia de oficiales y de hombres reclutados por la Marina estaba aumentando gracias a los programas para mejorar no sólo la calidad de vida sino también la calidad del servicio. La permanencia era tan alta que pronto tendría que crear un nuevo programa que obligara a las personas a retirarse de la Marina.

Antes de la reunión, Clark había sido conducido al Salón Roosevelt y no al *lobby* del ala oeste, donde habitualmente esperaban los visitantes. Clark vio que el vicepresidente de la jefatura del Estado Mayor Richard Myers había hablado con Bush y con Cheney poco antes de su cita. Quería demostrar que sabía cómo eran las cosas, y le dijo al presidente que entendía que probablemente el cargo estaba entre Myers y él. "Quiero decirle a usted que Dick Myers será un buen director", dijo Clark. Eligió la palabra "buen" de manera intencional; no dijo "gran", ni "ideal"; sólo "buen".

Clark señaló que era vital que Bush eligiera a una persona cuyo nombramiento hiciera que todos los estamentos militares se alegraran. Era muy importante que los hombres y mujeres militares "desde los soldados rasos hasta los comandantes de mayor rango" tuvieran confianza en sus líderes. Este era un aspecto clave no sólo en el reclutamiento y en la permanencia, sino también en el rendimiento. "Un militar que no respete a sus propios líderes, no prosperará", dijo.

El presidente le preguntó a Clark qué pensaba del papel del jefe del Estado Mayor Conjunto.

Clark dijo que era el principal asesor militar del presidente, del secretario de Defensa, y del Consejo Nacional de Seguridad, señalando, además, que él había sido presidente de la jefatura conjunta y que conocía la legislatura. Aclaró también que "ante todo y en primera instancia, trabaja para el secretario de Defensa" y que la legislación Goldwater-Nichols estipulaba que este funcionario debía representar los puntos de vista y opiniones de los otros jefes.

"Háblale de tu experiencia en Kosovo", le dijo Cheney a Clark. Cuéntale lo que me dijiste".

"Yo no tenía cuatro estrellas; sólo tres", le dijo Clark al presidente. "Trabajaba para el jefe del Estado Mayor; pude conocerlo personalmente y de cerca". Clark contó que llegó a la Casa Blanca en 1999 en compañía de Shelton, para lo que llamó "conversaciones para prepararse a disparar", y que a veces se sentaba detrás de su jefe cuando iban al salón del gabinete o a la Sala de Situaciones. Dijo que era importante que el presidente Clinton recibiera información sobre los hechos, así como análisis realistas. "Cuando estás listo para apretar el gatillo", dijo Clark, "debes tener un jefe, en el que confías plenamente, que te suministrará toda la información".

Clark señaló que crear falsas tentativas era un problema muy grave; luego hizo un recuento del bombardeo a Kosovo y dijo que el gabinete de Clinton tendría que haber sido más pequeño.

Bush sonrió.

"La relación entre el presidente y el jefe del Estado Mayor es importante. Pero más importante aun es la relación entre el secretario y el jefe: lo he visto con claridad a lo largo de mi carrera. Y el modelo que usted debería emular es el que había cuando él –dijo señalando a Cheney–, era el secretario de Defensa y Colin Powell era el jefe del Estado Mayor".

Cheney no dijo nada, aunque sabía que su relación con Powell no había sido tan perfecta ni intachable como se creía.

"Es un honor hablar con ustedes, aunque lo que yo diga no sea tan importante como lo que pudiera decir el secretario de Defensa. Esa es la persona con quien ustedes tendrán que hablar".

Clark continuó: "Esta entrevista es muy interesante", y miró a Bush. "Y la conexión entre usted y yo, en caso de que fuera elegido como jefe, es importante, aunque no tanto como la conexión entre el jefe del Estado Mayor y el secretario de Defensa. Así que lo más importante es que usted elija a alguien que tenga una gran conexión con el secretario de Defensa".

"¿Tienes ese tipo de relación con Donald Rumsfeld?", le preguntó Bush.

"Todavía no", respondió Clark.

"Hmm. Está bien", dijo Bush.

CLARK CREÍA en la intervención divina. Salió de la entrevista esperando que le dieran el cargo, pero también agradeció la oportunidad de comunicarle al presidente las verdaderas necesidades de los militares, lo que necesitaba hacer el mandatario y cómo debía abordar los asuntos militares; muchos de sus colegas hubieran dado la vida por semejante oportunidad.

Adicionalmente, Clark creía que se había despojado del boato de muchos de sus compañeros, especialmente de los de las academias de servicio. Clark creía que no había tenido que arrodillase ante nadie para llegar hasta allí.

SHELTON HABÍA HABLADO frecuentemente con Rumsfeld, procurando tener voz y voto en el proceso de selección de su sucesor. Y como el cargo iba a quedar entre Clark y Myers, Shelton creyó que le debía su recomendación a Rumsfeld.

"Vern es, obviamente, el mejor de los dos", dijo. Clark no vacilaría en enfrentarse a Rumsfeld, algo que no le vendría mal al secretario. Myers era todo lo contrario; expresaría sus opiniones, pero si Rumsfeld no estaba de acuerdo, desistiría de ellas y se doblegaría ante él. Shelton ya había visto eso.

Rumsfeld sonrió y simplemente dijo: "Está bien".

Shelton no le comentó a Clark ni a Myers a quién había recomendado; no sabía a quién nombrarían, y no quería tener roces con ellos.

POR LA MISMA ÉPOCA, Steve Herbits almorzó en privado con Rumsfeld, quien le dijo que decidirían entre Clark y Myers.

"Si quieres que haya una transformación en este departamento", le dijo Herbits, "Clark es el hombre; es analítico, brillante, un verdadero líder del cambio, y sabe cómo hacer trabajar a los demás". Clark estaba completamente permeado por la Marina, la rama más tradicional y conservadora del estamento militar. "Sabe cómo elegir los agentes del cambio; transformó la Marina. Ha ejecutado una labor increíble".

Herbits señaló que Myers tenía una gran cualidad. "Si usted cree que existe la posibilidad de ir a la guerra, harían mejor en nombrarlo a él.

"¿Por qué?".

"Porque él tiene más experiencia en materia de guerra", respondió Herbits. Myers había volado 600 horas en misiones de combate en Vietnam. Aunque aquello había sucedido tres décadas atrás, podría tener una importancia simbólica. "Y los militares que se enfrenten a una situación militar confiarán más en él que en Clark, que tiene todas las credenciales, pero no tiene experiencia en materia de guerra".

8

Clark fue citado por Rumsfeld dos días después de la entrevista. Clark quería confirmar que era el favorito de Rumsfeld pero, cuando entró a la oficina, sintió el ambiente completamente tenso. No era que él y el secretario no tuvieran una relación laboral amable o que no se llevaran bien, sino que la conversación se centró inmediatamente en el escollo principal.

"Bien", dijo Rumsfeld, "hablaste con el presidente".

Clark señaló que había sido una conversación provechosa y saludable, pero que había confirmado sus preocupaciones. "Mis reservas siguen siendo las mismas", dijo Clark. "Le dije al presidente que el aspecto más importante sobre esta elección no era la relación entre el militar y el presidente, sino la relación entre el militar y el secretario de Defensa. Y cité como ejemplo el modelo que vi entre Colin Powell y Dick Cheney. El presidente me preguntó si mi relación con usted era semejante, y yo le respondí que aún no".

Rumsfeld parecía estar menos impaciente de lo habitual, y Clark le preguntó sobre sus creencias. ¿En qué creía realmente Rumsfeld? "No podré ser su jefe del Estado Mayor y presentarme ante el mundo abrazado con usted como su asesor militar de cabecera mientras yo no sepa en qué cree usted".

Rumsfeld había comisionado una gran cantidad de estudios: sistemas y estrategias armamentísticas, planes de guerra y de personal; de todo lo imaginable. Había 18 destacamentos especiales haciendo estudios, algunos de los cuales le parecían casi ridículos a Clark. Sin embargo, le preguntó con delicadeza sobre ellos, particularmente sobre un estudio que sugería que se podía ganar todas las guerras desde la base de la Fuerza Aérea de Whiteman, en Missouri, sede de los bombarderos B-2, los cuales podrían ejecutar misiones de bombardeo en cualquier lugar del mundo por espacio de 50 horas seguidas, gracias a su sistema de reabastecimiento de combustible. Otro estudio de Rumsfeld sugería igualmente que se podría entablar guerras a cientos e, incluso, miles de kilómetros de distancia, sin necesidad de desplegar tropas. El despliegue de tropas era una función esencial de la Marina, pues tenía portaviones y flotas estacionadas en zonas de conflicto o cerca de estas. ¿El secretario creía que todo podía solucionarse seleccionando objetivos que estaban a gran distancia?

Rumsfeld no respondió; parecía estar mudo de asombro. Clark pensaba que todos estos estudios –la colmena de actividad, la tiranía de la urgencia– habían abrumado a Rumsfeld. No conocía los detalles o no tenía la suficiente comprensión estratégica para abordar cómodamente una discusión sobre la formación del aparato militar.

"¿Usted cree que va a cambiar la historia y enfrentar a todos los enemigos potenciales que tenga nuestro país sin ensuciarse las manos? Si eso es lo que usted cree", lo retó Clark, "usted y yo no podemos trabajar juntos, porque no creemos en las mismas cosas".

"Todavía no hemos hecho nada de eso", se limitó a responder Rumsfeld, que estaba completamente sumergido en sus planes y estudios. La transformación significaba una nueva forma de pensar, y él quería asegurarse de conformar una red que fuera amplia, profundizar en los asuntos y tener injerencia en todo.

Clark le preguntó sobre la función que tenían los jefes, particularmente la que tenía el jefe del Estado Mayor Conjunto. Clark dijo que esta dependencia era un tesoro nacional, y que el secretario tendía a subestimarla y hasta a menospreciarla, y que él creía que Rumsfeld estaba completamente equivocado en ese aspecto.

Rumsfeld se burló de nuevo; dijo que la información que ofrecían no valía el papel en que estaba escrita, y que no era oportuna ni útil. ¿Para qué necesita el jefe del Estado Mayor un director de política, un vocero, un enlace con el Congreso o a un abogado?, preguntó Rumsfeld, repitiendo los comentarios que le había hecho a Shelton. "¿Por qué, mejor, no utiliza a mi abogado?".

Clark dijo que el jefe interactuaba con los líderes militares de todo el mundo, y que la ley estipulaba que era miembro del Consejo Nacional de Seguridad. "Él debe expresar sus opiniones en materia de política cada vez que ustedes se reúnan", dijo Clark, aludiendo a las reuniones que realizaba la plana mayor del Consejo Nacional de Seguridad sin dicho jefe.

Rumsfeld entró en cólera.

"Si me eligen para este cargo", dijo Clark, "no vacilaré en cumplir con mi responsabilidad como asesor militar del presidente". Una de las funciones de este cargo era ofrecer una asesoría independiente. "Haré que se conozca mi posición aunque estemos en desacuerdo, porque así lo estipula la ley".

Rumsfeld no estaba ofreciendo respuestas directas, y era claro que no quería este tipo de discusión. Clark corrió su silla hacia atrás.

"Bueno, tendría que desempeñarme durante cuatro años como secretario de Defensa y escribir un libro", replicó Rumsfeld en tono sarcástico, "antes de saber las respuestas a todas tus preguntas".

"Usted y yo sabemos que yo no estoy hablando de eso", señaló Clark y se puso de pie.

"Creo que no tiene sentido seguir hablando de esto", dijo Rumsfeld.

"Estoy de acuerdo", respondió Clark, se dio vuelta y salió de la oficina. Fue a hablar con Shelton de inmediato.

"Acabo de estropear todas mis probabilidades", dijo Clark, haciendo un recuento detallado de su entrevista con Rumsfeld. "Nunca seré jefe del Estado Mayor".

"Así es", comentó Shelton con una risa sofocada, "creo que no lo serás".

POSTERIORMENTE le pregunté a Rumsfeld qué pensaba de Clark. "Es un tipo increíble", dijo. Pero la posibilidad de que Clark fuera nombrado para este cargo parecía ser un tema sensible, pues cuando dije que entendía que el general Shelton había recomendado a Clark, Rumsfeld respondió: "No lo sé".

Luego nos enfrascamos en una verdadera disputa verbal.

"¿Usted no cree que lo hizo?", comencé.

"Yo no dije que creía o no creía", respondió Rumsfeld. "Dije que no lo sabía. Soy muy preciso. Si usted dice algo que yo no recuerdo, yo no diría que es falso ni que es cierto; diría que no lo sé".

"Está bien".

"Y yo no lo sé", dijo.

"Usted no lo recuerda, y entonces…"

"No lo recuerdo", admitió finalmente, respondiendo así a mi pregunta. Con respecto a Clark, señaló: "No parecía querer el cargo. Estaba muy comprometido con la Marina; estaba haciendo una gran labor y no sentí que estuviera deseando el cargo ni que tuviera ansiedad por ocuparlo". Dijo que Clark ocupaba un lugar prominente en su lista de candidatos y que el presidente lo sabía, "pero a mí me gusta alguien que quiera hacer algo, porque estos son trabajos difíciles y uno tiene que hacer muchas cosas. Me parece que la persona necesita tomar la iniciativa y debe querer hacerlo. Y yo sentí que Vern quizás no quería hacerlo".

Le pregunté si Clark había dicho que debía ofrecerle una asesoría militar independiente al presidente si era nombrado en el cargo, pues así lo estipulaba la ley.

"Por supuesto", señaló Rumsfeld. "Así ha sido siempre y, obviamente, estoy de acuerdo. A eso se refiere la ley; no hay duda alguna. No sólo debe ofrecérsela al presidente, sino también al Consejo Nacional de Seguridad.

"¿Usted recuerda haber tenido una verdadera confrontación con él?".

"No; eso no".

Unos cuatro días después del acalorado encuentro que sostuvieron Clark y Rumsfeld, *The Washington Times,* el diario conservador de la capital del país, publicó el sábado 11 de agosto un artículo en primera página titulado "Almirante toma la delantera para la jefatura del Estado Mayor. Se dice que Clark ha impresionado a Bush".

El artículo, escrito por Rowan Scarborough, quien tenía buenos contactos con la administración de Bush, afirmó: "Una fuente de alta credibilidad señaló anoche que el presidente Bush se inclinaba por el almirante Clark". El periodista también afirmó que Clark era un hombre "profundamente religioso", y citó otra fuente que señalaba que Clark recordaba al vicepresidente Cheney "en su apariencia y en su actitud ejecutiva".

Esa mañana, Clark estaba jugando golf en la base aérea de Andrews. Estaba en el noveno hoyo y uno bajo par, uno de los mejores juegos de toda su vida, cuando su esposa lo llamó al teléfono móvil. "Salí a comprar el periódico y el titular dice que tienes la mayor opción para el cargo", le dijo, y añadió que el teléfono de la casa no dejaba de sonar.

Clark sacó la bola del campo, hizo otro lanzamiento, sacó la bola de nuevo y terminó con un *triple-bogey*.

El 24 de agosto de 2001, en la parte exterior de su rancho de Crawford, Texas, el presidente anunció su elección para el nuevo cargo y se refirió a aspectos como el entrenamiento, equipamiento, manejo y transformación del aparato militar. "El secretario Rumsfeld y yo hemos meditado, intensamente y durante mucho tiempo, sobre esta importante elección, y coincidimos de manera unánime". El nuevo jefe del Estado Mayor era Richard B. Myers, general de la Fuerza Aérea. Bush prometió que trabajaría de cerca con Myers, "quien se asegurará de que la opinión de los militares siempre sea escuchada en la Casa Blanca".

Rumsfeld les había dicho a Bush y a Cheney que Clark quería seguir como jefe de operaciones navales de la Marina, así que escogieron a Myers.

Clark estaba viajando con su esposa cuando escucharon el anuncio de Bush en vivo. Rumsfeld lo llamó para darle personalmente la noticia y agradecerle por haber cumplido todo el proceso. La conversación había sido muy cordial.

"Fue muy amable", le dijo Clark a su esposa.

Myers, de 59 años, un hombre apuesto que parecía presidente de un consejo estudiantil, era caballeroso y moderado. Se había criado en Kansas y había obtenido una licenciatura en ingeniería mecánica en la Universidad Estatal de Kansas antes de ingresar a la Fuerza Aérea en 1965, cuando se estaba intensificando la guerra de Vietnam. Había piloteado aviones de combate Phantom F-4 en peligrosas misiones sobre Vietnam del Norte, atacando objetivos terrestres. Luego había ejecutado varias misiones contra los sistemas de misiles tierra-aire norvietnamitas, conocidos como *comadrejas salvajes*. Había sido director del comando espacial por cuatro años, y vicepresidente de la jefatura conjunta durante un año y medio. Myers reconoció ante sus amigos que quería el cargo.

Shelton se decepcionó. Tal como lo había sospechado, parecía que Rumsfeld sólo quería un jefe en el papel. La elección significaba que cuando se tuviera que tomar las decisiones más difíciles, no habría ningún militar uniformado nombrado y apoyado por la ley que pudiera darle consejos diferentes al presidente y confrontar a Rumsfeld. Debido a todos los debates ocurridos durante los primeros meses de la nueva administración, parecía que los temas de mayor importancia eran el desarrollo de un sistema de defensa con misiles, la adquisición de equipos militares, y la reorganización y modernización de las fuerzas. Casi todo el tiempo y las energías estaban dirigidos a estos problemas, los cuales habían sido también el tema central de las declaraciones pronunciadas por Bush cuando anunció el nombramiento de Myers.

Shelton tenía una opinión diferente. Había combatido en Vietnam y había sido asistente de comandante de división para las operaciones del Airborne 101 durante la Guerra del Golfo. Las decisiones realmente difíciles hacían referencia al uso de la fuerza militar: qué tipo de estrategia y de plan, qué tipo de fuerza, cuándo, cuánto, contra cuáles enemigos o amenazas. La decisión de declarar la guerra definía a una nación no sólo ante el mundo sino también ante ella misma. La guerra era la razón fundamental de la existencia del aparato militar. Las decisiones podrían significar la muerte de miles de personas. Los hombres y mujeres de las fuerzas armadas de los Estados Unidos, que ascendían a 1,4 millones, contaban con el jefe del Estado Mayor Conjunto, quien los representaría cuando el presidente y el Consejo Nacional de Seguridad sopesaran y debatieran dichos asuntos. Shelton temía que con Myers en el cargo, esa voz sería apagada y silenciada.

El general John P. Jumper, un piloto de combate que había sido asistente militar de dos secretarios de Defensa, juró el 6 de septiembre de 2001 como jefe del Estado Mayor de la Fuerza Aérea, cargo equivalente al que tenía el almirante Clark en la Marina, y al del general Jones en los *marines*.

"Bienvenido al grupo más decepcionante con el que te habrás de asociar", le dijo Jones a Jumper cuando asumió el cargo. "Las opiniones de los militares no nacen: están comprometidas por el liderazgo político".

EL ANUNCIO DE MYERS ocurrió 18 días antes del 11 de septiembre de 2001, y él se sorprendió bastante de haber sido nombrado. Se había reunido varias veces con Bush y con Cheney durante 15 o 20 minutos; habían discutido la transformación y la posibilidad de que pudiera trabajar con Rumsfeld. Bush y Cheney le hicieron preguntas para asegurarse de que dejara atrás su uniforme de la Fuerza Aérea. Hasta donde él recordaba, no hablaron de asuntos bélicos, ni de los posibles errores cometidos en Kosovo o Vietnam.

Myers tenía una buena relación con Rumsfeld, aunque también habían tenido varias disputas acaloradas. Creía que el secretario expresaba sus posiciones de una manera exagerada. Un día, Rumsfeld revisó el sistema de aprovisionamiento del Pentágono. No dejó de despotricar: "Tenemos que reformar esto; es sencillamente horrible", dijo.

"Ya basta", lo interrumpió Myers. "Eso no es cierto. Usted está equivocado". Pero Myers tendía a suavizar sus opiniones: "Está bien, señor secretario, puede que sea cierto, y está claro que nuestro sistema no es muy bueno. Hay muchos aspectos que necesitan reformarse", dijo para congraciarse con el secretario. Luego mencionó un aspecto positivo del sistema: "Por otra parte, fabricamos el mejor equipo militar que hay en el mundo. Todos quieren nuestras armas, así que nuestra forma de hacer las cosas y el sistema que tenemos para desarrollar armas, partiendo de conceptos y requerimientos operativos, hasta el momento en que salen por la puerta del hangar o de la fábrica, debe tener algo positivo".

La elección de Myers se había filtrado a las noticias de televisión por cable, pero él se resistía a creerlo y les preguntó a los reporteros: "¿Qué saben ustedes?". Rumsfeld lo llamó algunas horas después y le dijo: "Te hemos elegido para el cargo. El presidente te escogió como nuevo jefe del Estado Mayor Conjunto". Rumsfeld no le dijo la razón por la cual lo habían elegido, e inmediatamente especuló sobre quién debería ser el nuevo subdirector. No tardaron en decidirse por Peter Pace, general de la Marina de bajo perfil, graduado en la Academia Naval y veterano de Vietnam y Somalia.

Myers concluyó que Rumsfeld acomodaba tanto las cosas, que le confesó a unos de sus asistentes que a veces se preguntaba qué estaba haciendo allí. Ensayaban todo antes de ir a la Casa Blanca. Hacían lo que Myers llamaba "licuefacción mental", es decir que él adaptaba su mentalidad a la de Rumsfeld. Muchos oficiales importantes, entre ellos algunos jefes de servicio, observaron la relación que había entre Myers y Rumsfeld.

Andy Card, quien asistía a todas las reuniones del Consejo Nacional de Seguridad y de los secretarios, se sorprendió de que Rumsfeld y Myers tendieran a opinar lo mismo. Era como un eco, y no recordaba ninguna ocasión en que la opinión de Myers desafiara a la de Rumsfeld. A veces llegó, incluso, a pensar que era muy particular que el jefe del Estado Mayor Conjunto no dijera nada. Su silencio podría significar que no estaba de acuerdo, pero era imposible saberlo.

Al final de una larga entrevista que le hice a Myers en su oficina del Pentágono el 9 de enero de 2002, cuatro meses después de los ataques terroristas del 9/11, le pedí que me ayudara a decodificar a Rumsfeld.

"Si pudiera hacerlo, tendría la presión sanguínea mucho más baja", dijo. Es probable que hubiera sido un día particularmente difícil para él, pero lo cierto fue que Myers puso sus brazos en la pequeña mesa y recostó su cabeza sobre ellos. No pude saber si era señal de molestia, desespero o algo intermedio. Yo nunca había visto una escena semejante: un oficial de alto rango ocultando la cabeza entre sus brazos.

Myers se puso rápidamente de pie. La tormenta, sin importar su causa o intensidad, había pasado. Sin embargo, fue una escena que yo recordaré, una instantánea de la vida como realmente sucedía en el Pentágono de Rumsfeld.

Escribí un libro sobre la guerra de Afganistán y la respuesta al 9/11, y otro sobre la decisión de invadir a Irak. Durante el transcurso de la investigación entrevisté a decenas de protagonistas, incluido el presidente, y examiné la información de muchas de las deliberaciones internas y reuniones del Consejo Nacional de Seguridad de más alto nivel. Myers aparece allí, expresando un comentario ocasional, a veces presentando, incluso, un informe, y todas sus declaraciones son embarazosamente repetidas por Rumsfeld. Es como si el secretario no hubiera escuchado lo que había dicho su asesor.

En algunas ocasiones, Myers les preguntó a sus ayudantes cercanos si creían que era posible que Rumsfeld abandonara su cargo. La respuesta siempre fue negativa. Myers se limitaba a sacudir su cabeza o a agacharla.

Rumsfeld estaba completamente dedicado a llenar las vacantes clave en el Estado Mayor Conjunto. Si Rumsfeld quería nombrar a alguien y Myers no estaba de acuerdo, el secretario se olvidaba generalmente de su candidato y proponía a otra persona. Sin embargo, el secretario insistía en imponer un veto sobre los asuntos primordiales. En una ocasión, Myers tenía un candidato para un cargo en el Estado Mayor Conjunto y Rumsfeld tenía el suyo. Myers sintió una gran frustración, pues sus posiciones eran diametralmente opuestas y tuvieron un pequeño roce.

La disputa permaneció irresuelta por unas tres semanas, y en una ocasión, mientras estaban en el ascensor del Pentágono, Rumsfeld trajo el tema a colación.

"Te agradecería si cedes en esto", le dijo Rumsfeld.

Myers comprendió que Rumsfeld le estaba diciendo: "No voy a ceder; yo soy el jefe". Obviamente, Rumsfeld se salió con la suya. Myers declaró posteriormente: "Nosotros servimos a los amos civiles y a la cadena de mando. Lo haces a menos que sea ilegal, inmoral o poco ético. Si no puedes tolerarlo, tienes otras opciones: puedes retirarte".

Durante el primer año en su cargo, Rumsfeld le pasó a Myers una copia de un artículo sobre la administración de Nixon. El representante ante el Consejo Nacional de Seguridad del almirante Thomas H. Moorer y jefe del Estado Mayor, había sido sorprendido espiando en la Casa Blanca y pasando documentos secretos al Pentágono.

"Oye", le dijo Rumsfeld a Myers, "esto puede parecerte interesante".

Myers no pudo creerlo; se sintió atrapado en los procedimientos, discusiones y reuniones interminables de Rumsfeld. Una vez asistió a una reunión con los jefes de Estado Mayor; parecía completamente desmoronado.

"Tuve que permanecer dos horas allí", dijo Myers rayando en el desespero, "y escuchar toda esa basura una y otra vez. Y luego tuve que regresar de nuevo. Lo siento, pero tengo que volver en cinco minutos".

Myers se desabrochó los puños de la camisa y se rascó los brazos de manera compulsiva; su comportamiento era tan inconsciente que algunos de los jefes creyeron que no sabía lo que hacía. A veces miraba hacia un rincón de la oficina, como si no estuviera allí ni le importara lo que estaban diciendo y haciendo.

Cuando Myers perdía la paciencia, se refería a Rumsfeld como "hijo de perra" o "idiota". Varias personas lo vieron ocultar su cabeza entre sus brazos en la mesa de la sala de conferencias, así como yo lo vi en su oficina.

Era irónico que Rumsfeld hubiera establecido un sistema que no le garantizara que los militares uniformados le hicieran advertencias sobre situaciones comprometedoras como las ocurridas desde Vietnam a Kosovo. Los reparos fuertes y energéticos de los militares uniformados eran suprimidos de su sistema; ellos sólo eran empleados, y su voz era un susurro amable. Rumsfeld creyó que había ganado; tenía el control.

9

En el verano de 2001, los israelíes y los palestinos habían declarado y violado varios cese al fuego. En agosto, el príncipe de la corona saudita vio por televisión a un soldado israelí que empujaba y pisoteaba a una anciana palestina. De acuerdo con la versión saudí de este incidente, el príncipe comisionó a Bandar para que llevara un mensaje a la Casa Blanca. El embajador visitó a Bush el 27 de agosto.

"Señor presidente", comenzó Bandar, "este es el mensaje más difícil que he tenido que transmitir entre los dos gobiernos desde que llegué a trabajar a Washington, en 1982". Bandar relató detalladamente los numerosos encuentros que Bush, Cheney y Powell habían sostenido con el príncipe de la corona.

"Señor presidente", dijo Bandar con una expresión seria, "el liderazgo en Arabia Saudita siempre ha sentido el pulso del pueblo, y también ha reflejado en sus políticas los sentimientos del pueblo".

Arabia Saudita era una de las últimas monarquías del mundo. Los líderes —el rey y el príncipe de la corona— hacían lo que querían.

Bandar se refirió a la sociedad entre Arabia Saudita y Bush padre en la Guerra del Golfo, y a la ocasión en que el ex presidente suspendió las garantías de préstamos cuando los israelíes violaron su promesa sobre los asentamientos. La política norteamericana había sido más equilibrada en el pasado. "El príncipe de la corona ha tratado de encontrar muchas excusas para esta administración y no ha podido hacerlo". El presidente Bush le había permitido al primer ministro israelí Ariel Sharon "determinarlo todo en el Medio Oriente". La política israelí de ocupación y asesinatos era semejante a la que había tenido Inglaterra con las colonias americanas en el siglo XVIII, era como la de Francia con Argelia, la de Norteamérica con Vietnam, y la de la Unión Soviética con Afganistán; sin embargo, todas habían fracasado.

"Lo que más le duele al príncipe de la corona es que los Estados Unidos sigan ignorando las políticas adoptadas por Israel, como si una gota de sangre judía fuera igual a las vidas de miles de palestinos".

Luego expuso la decisión adoptada por el príncipe: "Por lo tanto, el príncipe de la corona no tendrá ningún tipo de comunicación con usted, y Arabia

Saudita tomará todas sus decisiones políticas, económicas y de seguridad de acuerdo con sus propios intereses en la región y sin tener en cuenta los intereses de los Estados Unidos, ya que es obvio que esta nación ha tomado la decisión estratégica de respaldar las políticas de Sharon".

Bush pareció sorprendido. "Quiero asegurarle que los Estados Unidos no han determinado ninguna decisión estratégica", le dijo a Bandar.

Poco después, Powell reprendió a Bandar. "¿Qué carajos estás haciendo? Has asustado terriblemente a todo el mundo aquí.

"Me importa un comino lo que puedas sentir", le contestó Bandar. "Nosotros también estamos asustados".

Bien sea que esto hubiera sido un cuidadoso acto de histrionismo, una preocupación genuina o una combinación de espectáculo y sinceridad, la amenaza saudí funcionó. Dos días después, el 29 de agosto, Bush le envió una carta de dos páginas al príncipe de la corona: "Ante todo quiero aclarar una cosa: nada deberá estropear las relaciones entre nosotros. No ha habido ningún cambio en la ecuación estratégica".

"Creo firmemente que el pueblo palestino tiene derecho a la autodeterminación y a vivir en paz y seguridad en su propio Estado y en su propia tierra, así como los israelíes tienen el derecho a vivir en paz y seguridad en su propio Estado". Era un paso más grande que el dado por el presidente Clinton, quien, incluso, aunque quería dejar los acuerdos de paz en el Medio Oriente como su principal legado, nunca había respaldado directamente un Estado autónomo palestino.

Bandar voló de inmediato a Arabia Saudita con la carta. El príncipe de la corona le respondió a Bush el 6 de septiembre: "Señor presidente, fue un gran alivio para mí encontrar en su carta un compromiso claro, confirmando así el principio bajo el cual se estableció el proceso de paz. Me complació particularmente su compromiso con el derecho que tienen los palestinos a la autodeterminación, así como el derecho a vivir en paz y sin humillaciones en su Estado independiente". La respuesta formal agregaba: "Primero, es esencial que usted manifieste públicamente la opinión expresada en su carta. Dicha declaración descartará la impresión prevaleciente en la región en el sentido que los Estados Unidos están a favor de Israel".

Bush aceptó declarar en público su aprobación de un Estado palestino, y se programó un anuncio muy significativo para la semana del 10 de septiembre de 2001.

CASI TRES MIL PERSONAS MURIERON en los ataques terroristas perpetrados por al Qaeda en los Estados Unidos el 11 de septiembre de 2001. Los detalles de los ataques y la reacción de Bush son bien conocidos. El presidente se encontraba en una escuela de primaria en Florida cuando los dos aviones impactaron las torres gemelas. Pocas horas después de los ataques, mientras volaba por el sur de los Estados Unidos en el avión presidencial, manteniéndose alejado de Washington para evitar posibles ataques, Bush llamó a Rumsfeld. "Es un día de tragedia nacional", le dijo Bush, "limpiaremos los escombros; luego el juego estará en tus manos y en las de Dick Myers".

Sin embargo, Rumsfeld y el Pentágono estaban con las manos vacías. Sus esfuerzos de transformación no habían surtido efecto. El general Tommy Franks, jefe del Comando Central (CENTCOM), que incluía al Medio Oriente, no tenía planes de atacar a Afganistán, donde se habían refugiado bin Laden y sus secuaces, y le dijo a Rumsfeld que tardarían varios meses en desplegar tropas en ese país. Durante una reunión del Consejo Nacional de Seguridad, celebrada un día después de los ataques terroristas, Bush preguntó qué podían hacer los militares en ese instante. Rumsfeld respondió: "La verdad, muy poco".

Horas más tarde, en otra reunión del Consejo Nacional de Seguridad, Rumsfeld le preguntó a Bush: "¿Por qué no atacamos no sólo a al Qaeda sino también a Irak?" Rumsfeld era una de las personas que sostenían que Bush padre había fallado al no derrocar a Saddam. Una noche de 1995, mientras se encontraba en Vietnam con Ken Adelman, el secretario lo mantuvo despierto hasta las tres de la mañana y lanzó una perorata acerca del error garrafal cometido por el ex presidente. Nunca debería haber aceptado un cese al fuego que le permitiera a Saddam seguir en el poder, dijo Rumsfeld, y debería haber causado una mayor destrucción al ejército iraquí mientras estaban en guerra.

El presidente disuadió a Rumsfeld, pues quería concentrarse en Afganistán, en al Qaeda, y en Osama bin Laden.

La CIA APARECIÓ para llenar el vacío dejado por el secretario de Defensa y los militares uniformados. Tenet y Cofer Black le entregaron su plan a Bush en menos de 48 horas. Podían recolectar todos los recursos de inteligencia, recurrir al poderío militar de los Estados Unidos y de las Fuerzas Especiales, trabajar conjuntamente con la facción opositora conocida como Alianza del Norte, derrocar a los talibanes y clausurar el santuario de al Qaeda. Mientras que la admisión de Rumsfeld sobre la impotencia de Pentágono era preocupante, la propuesta de Black fue muy tranquilizadora: "Señor presidente, podemos hacerlo", dijo, "no tengo la menor duda".

Quince días después de los ataques terroristas, Tenet envió un equipo paramilitar encubierto de la CIA, cuyo nombre codificado era *Jawbreaker*, al interior de Afganistán. Once días después, el 7 de octubre de 2001, comenzó la ofensiva aérea. La campaña supuso uno de los mejores momentos de la agencia después del 9/11, y una época frustrante para Rumsfeld. Para el primer día de los bombardeos, el general Franks sólo había definido 31 objetivos talibanes y de al Qaeda, mientras que Rumsfeld quería dispararle a todo, insistiendo en que deberían destruir unos 60 aviones talibanes.

El capitán de la Fuerza Aérea Charles F. Wald, comandante de la división aérea del CENTCOM en Arabia Saudita, le dijo a su jefe, el general Franks, que habían bombardeado y destruido las pistas aéreas. Los aviones talibanes no eran una amenaza porque no tenían cómo despegar.

"¡Me van a despedir!", le dijo Franks. El primer día de los bombardeos, Franks y su equipo aparecieron en la videoconferencia de seguridad desde el cuartel general del CENTCOM en Tampa, Florida, con camisas de golf. Franks profirió un torrente de vulgaridades, insistiendo en que bombardearan los "malditos aviones".

Wald ordenó los ataques. Sin embargo, los procedimientos militares no les permitían confirmar, en nombre de Franks, que los ataques habían sido exitosos y que los aviones habían sido destruidos, mientras no tuvieran imágenes satelitales de los objetivos. Rumsfeld estalló en cólera cuando tardaron en hacerlo. Franks le insistió a Wald que lo iban a relevar del cargo. Finalmente, Wald recibió la convalidación de la Agencia de Inteligencia de Defensa.

El *Jawbreaker* y otros destacamentos paramilitares de la CIA estaban haciendo lo que había prometido Tenet: despejar el camino para expulsar a los talibanes del poder, privar a bin Laden de su santuario y obligarlo a esconderse. Con un pequeño equipo integrado aproximadamente por 110 agentes de la CIA y 316 hombres de las Fuerzas Especiales, las que en muchos aspectos eran semejantes a las fuerzas militares con mayor movilidad que proponía Rumsfeld, y en alianza con una fuerte ofensiva aérea, estaban logrando su propósito.

No obstante, Rumsfeld estaba muy molesto. Su frustración se hizo palpable durante una reunión del Consejo Nacional de Seguridad celebrada el 16 de octubre. "Esta es la estrategia de la CIA", declaró. "Ellos desarrollaron la estrategia, pero nosotros la estamos ejecutando".

John McLaughlin, subdirector de la CIA y quien había asistido a la reunión en representación de Tenet, insistió en que la agencia sólo estaba apoyando a Franks.

"No", replicó Rumsfeld, "ustedes son los que mandan".

Armitage, quien estaba en representación de Powell, le dijo a Rumsfeld: "Hasta donde yo sé, lo único que estamos haciendo es cagándonos en todo". ¿Cómo podían entablar una guerra si no se ponían de acuerdo sobre quién la iba a dirigir?

El presidente le ordenó a Rice: "Aclara este enredo".

Después de la reunión, Rice habló a solas con Rumsfeld: "Don, esta es una operación militar y tú tienes que dirigirla".

Steve Hadley, el subsecretario de Rice, también opinó; le dijo a Rumsfeld que necesitaba planear una estrategia. "Está en tus manos".

Posteriormente, Powell también le dijo a Rumsfeld que era él quién mandaba, sin que importara si quería hacerlo o no.

Rumsfeld fue humillado por McLaughlin, Armitage, el presidente, Rice, Hadley y Powell.

Esto nunca volvería a suceder. Al mes siguiente, cuando el presidente le ordenó analizar detenidamente el plan de guerra contra Irak, Rumsfeld se apropió del proyecto: él se encargaría de ejecutarlo.

POSTERIORMENTE, TENET DECLARÓ que en la reunión que sostuvo el 10 de julio de 2001 con Rice, dos meses antes del 9/11, se había perdido una gran oportunidad de prevenir o desmantelar los ataques del 9/11. Describió las relaciones que tenían él y la CIA con Rice y con el Consejo Nacional de Seguridad. En teoría, Tenet le informaba a Bush, pero en términos prácticos, el director de la CIA trabajaba todos los días para el asesor de Seguridad Nacional.

Tenet se había reportado frecuentemente a Bush durante los seis primeros meses de su presidencia, y estaba construyendo una relación personal con el mandatario. Sin embargo, era muy diferente de la que Bush tenía con Rice, quien vivía sola, pasaba muchos fines de semana con el presidente y su esposa en Camp David, y lo visitaba con frecuencia en su rancho de Texas; ella era casi parte de la familia.

Tenet creía que Rice podía haber convencido a Bush de que la amenaza de bin Laden era real, pero ella no lo entendió oportunamente. Tenet creía que él había hecho su trabajo, que había informado sobre la amenaza con mucha claridad, pero que Rice no había reaccionado con rapidez. Pensaba que ella no era una persona organizada y que no había presionado a los funcionarios como él lo hacía con el personal de la CIA.

Cuando se develaron las múltiples investigaciones sobre el 9/11, toda la culpabilidad cayó sobre la CIA: fallaron al hacer esto, fallaron al hacer aquello, fallaron al conectar este punto con este otro. Tenet creía que la CIA había trabajado a toda máquina y que, en cierto modo, el FBI había sido exonerado injustamente. Si esta agencia sólo hubiera examinado las tarjetas de crédito de Nawaf al-Hazmi y de Khalid al-Mihdhar, dos de los secuestradores del 9/11 que habían sido identificados en los Estados Unidos antes de esta fecha, habrían visto que ellos habían comprado 10 tiquetes aéreos a nombre de otras personas del Medio Oriente para la mañana del 11 de septiembre de 2001. Los ataques se habrían podido desmantelar simplemente con esa información.

Un mes después de la reunión de julio de 2001, en un Informe Diario de ALTO SECRETO dirigido al presidente y que más tarde alcanzó notoriedad, la CIA advirtió de nuevo: "Bin Laden decidido a perpetrar ataque en los Estados Unidos". Tenet se referiría posteriormente a dichos acontecimientos: "Todas las alarmas estaban encendidas". Pero el punto de quiebre, cuando pudieron haber pasado de las palabras de alarma a la acción directa, fue el 10 de julio. Rice rechazó, quizás, la mejor oportunidad. Los servicios de inteligencia estadounidenses habían recolectado información suficiente y estaban a un paso de lograr un avance importante o, incluso, crucial. La angustia que le causó Rice a Tenet en la reunión del julio de 2001 se transformó en dolor y luego en desdén. Si la Casa Blanca, Bush, la CIA y todos los altos funcionarios, incluyendo a Tenet —como él mismo lo reconoció— hubieran reaccionado con rapidez, probablemente no se habrían presentado problemas en los años subsiguientes.

Todo agente de inteligencia, desde los rangos inferiores hasta el director de la CIA, quiere ser un oráculo, ver el futuro con claridad, recolectar la más ardua información de inteligencia, mezclarla con el *vudú* y predecir lo que sucederá. Tenet creía que había hecho esto. Su deber más importante era prevenir una catástrofe, un problema o un ataque inesperado. Creyó haberlo visto, y pensó que había advertido de la manera más contundente posible. Sin embargo, no le habían hecho caso; la reunión con Rice había sido el punto culminante. Como señaló posteriormente Cofer Black, "Lo único que nos faltó fue apretar el gatillo de la pistola que le pusimos en la cabeza a Rice".

BUSH PADRE SE PREOCUPÓ por su hijo después del 9/11 y llamó al príncipe Bandar. "Está en un momento difícil", le dijo. "Por favor, ayúdale".

El 13 de septiembre, dos días después de los ataques, Bandar se reunió de nuevo con el presidente en la Casa Blanca. Cheney, Rice y Rihab Massoud, el asistente de Bandar, acompañaban al embajador y al presidente de los Estados Unidos en el Balcón Truman, situado en el segundo piso. En una fotografía del encuentro, Bush y Bandar aparecen con cigarros.

Los saudíes habían capturado a algunos sospechosos de al Qaeda justo antes y después del 9/11. El presidente le dijo a Bandar: "Si capturamos a alguien y no logramos que coopere, se lo entregaremos a ustedes".

Con estas palabras, el presidente expresó de manera casual lo que terminó siendo la política de sometimiento practicada por el gobierno norteamericano: llevar a los sospechosos del terrorismo de un país a otro para que fueran interrogados. La Constitución de los Estados Unidos contiene derechos y protecciones que prohíben interrogatorios sin restricciones a sus ciudadanos. Pero en países como Arabia Saudita no había nada que se pareciera a la Constitución norteamericana; los sospechosos de terrorismo tenían muy pocos derechos. Aunque los saudíes lo negaron, la CIA creía que allí torturaban a los sospechosos para hacerlos confesar. Y luego de los atentados del 9/11, Bush quería que los detenidos hablaran.

DESPUÉS DEL 9/11, el índice de popularidad de Bush subió del 55% al 90%, un aumento sin precedentes. El presidente fingió desinterés cuando Rove le mostró las estadísticas, aunque se suponía que el trabajo de este funcionario era asegurarse de que el amplio respaldo fuera utilizado de manera efectiva. Rove calculó que anteriormente, cuando la opinión pública respaldaba a los presidentes en tiempos de crisis, el aumento de la popularidad duraba de 7 a 10 meses.

Bush dejó en claro que su presidencia no giraría en torno al 9/11. Así como la generación de mi padre fue llamada a combatir en la Segunda Guerra Mundial, nuestra generación está siendo llamada, le dijo a Rove. Bush padre se había enlistado en la Marina en 1942, cuando cumplió 18 años, y piloteó aviones en el Pacífico. Lo habían derribado y había visto morir a varios amigos; había sido una experiencia formadora.

Bush hijo y Rove nunca habían combatido en una guerra, pero ahora, cuando tenían más de 50 años, sentían que estaban siendo llamados.

"Estoy aquí por una razón", le dijo Bush a Rove, "y nos juzgarán por esto". Ese era su nuevo plan.

El 21 de noviembre, un día antes del Día de Acción de Gracias y 71 días después de los ataques del 9/11, Bush le pidió a Rumsfeld que comenzara a actualizar el plan de guerra contra Irak.

"Comencemos de una vez", recordó Bush haber dicho ese día, "y asegúrate de que Tommy Franks haga lo que sea necesario para proteger al país y derrocar a Saddam Hussein si es necesario". El presidente se preguntó si este plan podría ser realizado y mantenido en secreto. Russell dijo que era posible, puesto que él estaba "refrescando" todos los planes de guerra de los Estados Unidos.

Ese día, Bush dio inicio formal a la cadena de eventos que 16 meses después conducirían a la invasión de Irak. El plan de guerra contra esta nación sufrió numerosos cambios luego de decenas de reuniones, muchas de ellas con el presidente y el gabinete de guerra, las cuales describí en mi libro *Plan de ataque*.

El plan de guerra contra Irak era el tablero de ajedrez en el que Rumsfeld ensayaría, desarrollaría, expandiría y modificaría sus ideas sobre la transformación militar. El concepto predominante era "menos es más". Era una nueva concepción sobre una fuerza más liviana, pequeña, rápida y efectiva. La guerra relámpago de Russell reivindicaría su liderazgo en el Pentágono.

El secretario era su principal arquitecto, así que dirigía las reuniones y los cambios. Su ejecutor de cabecera era el general Franks. Cuando más, el general Myers operaba al margen. Aunque este creía que lo mantenían informado y al tanto de todas las decisiones, no era un verdadero participante. En *Soldado americano,* las memorias escritas por Franks, Myers sólo aparece asistiendo o tomando notas en las sesiones para planear la guerra contra Irak. Franks, de 58 años, un tejano de temperamento irascible que tenía fama de gritarle a sus subalternos cuando estaba impaciente, se refería abiertamente a los jefes del Estado Mayor como los "cabrones del Libro X", pues creía que Myers y sus colegas eran básicamente irrelevantes en el proceso.

Un contraste importante con este proceso puede encontrarse en los documentos de la planeación de la Guerra del Golfo de 1991. Mi libro *Los comandantes,* así como las memorias de Powell, quien era el jefe del Estado Mayor, y H. Norman Schwarzkopf, quien era el comandante del CENTCOM en esa guerra, ilustran la diferencia.

Schwarzkopf declara que cuando Powell se desempeñaba en ese cargo, era su intermediario, consejero, contacto frecuente, asesor y siquiatra. Cuando Saddam invadió a Kuwait en 1990, el presidente Bush padre ordenó la Operación Tormenta del Desierto, que incluía el despliegue de unos 250.000 soldados en el Medio Oriente para defender a Arabia Saudita. A finales de octubre de 1990, Bush y su secretario de Defensa Cheney querían saber cuántas tropas se necesitaban para ofrecer una opción ofensiva, es decir, para expulsar al ejército de Saddam de Kuwait. No se lo preguntaron a Schwarzkopf sino a Powell, quien voló a Arabia Saudita, donde Schwarzkopf se encontraba estacionado; éste dijo que necesitaba dos divisiones adicionales. Powell le envió cuatro en lugar de dos. Colin relató en sus memorias la conversación que tuvieron. "¿Portaviones? "Enviemos seis". La idea era "hacerlo en grande y terminar rápido. No podíamos enfrascar a los Estados Unidos en otro Vietnam". El plan para utilizar una fuerza abrumadora y garantizar así la victoria se conoció como la Doctrina Powell.

Powell le había dicho a Bush y a Cheney que necesitaban 200.000 hombres adicionales, lo que equivalía a duplicar las fuerzas que defendían a Arabia Saudita. El presidente Bush padre dijo: "Si eso es lo que necesitas, lo haremos".

Sin embargo, la situación era muy diferente en el 2001. El presidente Bush hijo quería una opción para invadir a Irak y derrocar a Saddam, aunque había prometido una transformación militar durante su campaña presidencial. Él y Rumsfeld querían una nueva modalidad para combatir las guerras. La Doctrina Powell había quedado atrás. Durante el año siguiente, convergieron dos ideas importantes en el Pentágono: un plan de guerra nuevo y "refrescado" contra Irak, como lo llamó Rumsfeld, y la transformación militar.

DESPUÉS DE LA CAMPAÑA de bombardeos contra Afganistán, el subsecretario de Defensa Paul Wolfowitz llamó a Christopher DeMuth, un viejo amigo suyo que durante mucho tiempo había sido presidente del American Enterprise Institute (AEI), el *think tank* conservador de Washington. Antes de trabajar en el Pentágono, Wolfowitz era decano de la Escuela Paul H. Nitze de Estudios Internacionales Avanzados de la Universidad Johns Hopkins de Washington, también conocida como SAIS. El AEI y la SAIS, localizados a pocas cuadras entre sí, eran el foro para la interpolinización de muchos intelectuales.

El gobierno norteamericano, especialmente el Pentágono, era incapaz de generar el tipo de ideas y estrategias que se necesitaban para enfrentar una crisis de la magnitud del 9/11, le dijo Wolfowitz a DeMuth. Necesitaban ampliar su espectro para abordar las preguntas más importantes. ¿Quiénes son los terroristas? ¿De dónde salieron? ¿Qué relación tiene esto con la historia islámica, con la historia del Medio Oriente y con las tensiones contemporáneas de esa región? ¿Contra qué nos estamos enfrentando?

Wolfowitz dijo que sus ideas eran semejantes a las del Bletchley Park, el grupo de matemáticos y criptógrafos conformado por los británicos durante la Segunda Guerra Mundial para identificar el código de comunicaciones alemán conocido como ULTRA. ¿Podría DeMuth conformar rápidamente un talentoso grupo que redactara un informe que recibirían Bush, Cheney, Powell, Rumsfeld, Rice y Tenet?

Preguntarle a un *think tank* si estaba dispuesto a planear una estrategia para los políticos más importantes durante una crisis extraordinaria era como preguntarle a la General Motors si estaba dispuesta a vender otro millón de autos. DeMuth, un abogado suave y cortés que había estudiado en la Escuela de Derecho de la Universidad de Chicago y era experto en regulaciones gubernamentales, aceptó con entusiasmo. El AEI era prácticamente la granja experimental de los intelectuales y la casa de retiro de los conservadores de Washington. Algunos de sus socios y académicos eran Newt Gingrich, antiguo presidente de la Cámara, y Lynne Cheney, la esposa del vicepresidente. A su vez, Dick Cheney también había sido socio del AEI entre sus temporadas como secretario de Defensa y como presidente de Halliburton, el gigante contratista de defensa.

DeMuth reclutó a 12 personas y posteriormente declaró que habían aceptado trabajar sólo "si yo les prometía que todo se mantenía en secreto".

Algunos de los miembros de este grupo eran Bernard Lewis, favorito de Cheney y experto en el Islam, quien había escrito ampliamente sobre las tensiones entre el Medio Oriente y Occidente; Mark Palmer, ex embajador norteamericano en Hungría y especialista en dictaduras; Fareed Zakaria, editor de la revista *Newsweek International* y columnista de *Newsweek;* Fouad Ajami, director del programa de estudios sobre el Medio Oriente en el SAIS; James Q. Wilson, profesor y especialista en moral humana y criminalística, y Reuel Marc Gerecht, un antiguo experto de la CIA en el Medio Oriente. Rumsfeld envió a Steve Herbits, su asesor y solucionador de problemas generales, para que participara. Herbits, quien había concebido la idea original y había invitado a Wolfowitz a desarrollarla, bautizó al grupo "Bletchley II".

La noche del jueves 29 de noviembre de 2001, DeMuth se reunió con el grupo en un lugar seguro de Virginia durante el fin de semana, y los participantes compartieron sus escritos. A DeMuth le sorprendió el consenso que había entre el grupo. Permaneció despierto hasta altas horas de la noche del domingo, reflejando sus pensamientos en un documento de siete páginas a un solo espacio, titulado "Delta del terrorismo". La palabra "delta" se utilizaba en el sentido geográfico, para representar la boca de un río desde la que todo fluye.

En una entrevista, DeMuth se negó a suministrar una copia de su documento, pero aceptó enumerar sus conclusiones.

"Lo que vimos en los ataques del 9/11 y en otros sucedidos en los años 90, como el efectuado contra el USS *Cole,* –en el cual murieron 17 integrantes de la Marina– demuestra que había una guerra en el interior del Islam y en toda la región. Era un problema profundo, y el 9/11 no fue un acto aislado que requería el establecimiento de políticas y el combate al crimen".

Era un terrorismo diferente de la versión de los años 70, donde había facciones locales como las Brigadas Rojas de Italia. En términos generales, el informe concluía que los Estados Unidos probablemente se enfrascarían en una batalla con el Islam radical, que se prolongaría por dos generaciones.

"La conclusión general era que Egipto y Arabia Saudita, de donde provenían la mayoría de los secuestradores, eran la clave, pero que los problemas que había allí eran insolubles. Irán era un caso diferente, ya que mostraba una tendencia más definida y había establecido un gobierno radical". Sin embargo, la manera como debían enfrentar a este país era igualmente difícil, declaró.

Saddam Hussein era distinto, más débil y vulnerable. DeMuth dijo que habían concluido que el "baathismo era una modalidad árabe del fascismo trasplantada a Irak". El Partido Baath, controlado por Saddam Hussein, había gobernado a Irak desde 1968.

"Concluimos que la confrontación con Saddam era inevitable. Él era una amenaza creciente, la más peligrosa, activa e inevitable. Coincidimos en que Saddam tendría que desaparecer del panorama antes de enfrentarnos al problema". Era la única manera de reformar la región.

Las copias del informe, salido directamente del ensayo de estrategias neoconservadoras, fueron entregadas personalmente a los miembros del gabinete de guerra. En algunas instancias se otorgó al informe la clasificación SECRETA. A Cheney le gustó el documento, el cual le produjo un fuerte impacto al presidente Bush y lo obligó a concentrarse en la "malignidad" del Medio Oriente. A Rice le pareció "bastante persuasivo".

Rumsfeld dijo posteriormente que recordaba el plan general, pero no los detalles del informe. Su intención era, dijo él, "reunir algunas mentes privilegiadas en un entorno significativamente confidencial que le ofreciera un contenido intelectual" a la era posterior al 9/11.

Herbits estaba muy satisfecho con los resultados del grupo Bletchley II, pero Rumsfeld no le otorgó carácter permanente al grupo. Resumiendo sus conclusiones, Herbits dijo: "Estamos enfrentados a una guerra de dos generaciones. Y comenzaremos con Irak".

10

El 18 de enero de 2002, Bush decidió que las protecciones de la Convención de Ginebra no se aplicarían a los miembros de los talibanes y de al Qaeda detenidos como posibles terroristas, quienes serían declarados "combatientes ilegales" sin derecho a las protecciones conferidas por dicha convención a los prisioneros de guerra.

El general Myers no había participado en esta decisión. Disentía de ella porque abría la puerta para el maltrato de personal estadounidense tomado como prisionero de guerra. Le expresó su opinión a Rumsfeld, pero no logró que estuviera de acuerdo con él. Peor aun, no sabía cuál era la posición del secretario en este sentido.

Powell le pidió al presidente que recapacitara sobre su decisión. Poco después, Myers y Rumsfeld estuvieron en desacuerdo durante una reunión del Consejo Nacional de Seguridad a la que también asistieron Bush y Cheney. Fue una de las pocas ocasiones en que no habían coordinado de antemano la alineación de la posición de Myers con la de Rumsfeld.

"Señor presidente", dijo Myers, "creo que usted ve que soy el único que no cuenta con ningún respaldo. No tengo un abogado". Los otros miembros del Consejo Nacional de Seguridad habían asistido con sus asesores legales. "No creo que esto sea un asunto legal, y entiendo por qué la Convención de Ginebra no se aplica técnicamente a estos combatientes". Ellos no combatían en ejércitos nacionales organizados ni vestían uniformes, como lo exigía la Convención. "Entiendo eso, pero creo que hay otro asunto sobre el cual necesitamos reflexionar, y que no ha sido debidamente aclarado".

Myers dijo que le preocupaba el impacto que esto pudiera tener sobre los prisioneros de guerra estadounidenses. "Usted debe recordar que así como los tratemos, probablemente, seremos tratados". Ese era el panorama posible y esperado. "Podrían tratarnos, incluso, peor, pero no deberíamos darles la oportunidad". Los terroristas u otros futuros enemigos podrían utilizar fácilmente la política norteamericana contra los talibanes como un pretexto para ignorar a su vez la Convención de Ginebra.

En febrero, el presidente ya había decidido rectificar su posición. Los talibanes estarían cubiertos por la Convención de Ginebra, pero no serían clasificados como prisioneros de guerra, quienes tenían los más altos niveles de protección y no podían ser sometidos, por ejemplo, a castigos físicos durante los interrogatorios. La administración no les otorgaría este *status* a los terroristas de al Qaeda, aunque les daría un tratamiento humanitario.

Se suponía que el secretario de prensa Ari Fleischer transmitiría esta decisión a los medios de comunicación el 7 de febrero, pero Steve Hadley, el subsecretario de Rice, le había enviado una copia a Rumsfeld, en la cual lo alertaba. Rumsfeld –como sucedía a menudo– arguyó una objeción de último minuto, y Hadley le ordenó a Fleischer que no leyera el comunicado.

Ese día, Bush estaba mirando un resumen del comunicado ofrecido por Fleischer. Cuando terminó a la 1:28 de la tarde, el presidente se sorprendió de que el secretario no hubiera anunciado la decisión.

Bush lo llamó. "Yo autoricé la declaración", le dijo el presidente, y le dio instrucciones al secretario de prensa para que la leyera. A la 1:40 de la tarde, –sólo doce minutos después de haber abandonado el podio– Fleischer apareció de nuevo en la sala de conferencias para emitir un segundo informe inesperado e inusual.

"La Convención de Ginebra se aplicará a los detenidos talibanes, pero no a los terroristas internacionales de al Qaeda", anunció Fleischer, y expuso la distinción significativa de que "los talibanes detenidos no tienen derecho a ser considerados como prisioneros de guerra".

"El presidente ha honrado el compromiso de los Estados Unidos con los principios de la Convención de Ginebra, al mismo tiempo que reconoce que esta no se aplica para todas las situaciones en que las fuerzas militares puedan capturar o detener personas, tal como sucede actualmente en Afganistán".

EL PRESIDENTE BUSH había pasado las vacaciones en su rancho de Crawford, Texas, durante casi todo el mes de agosto. Bandar lo visitó el martes 27 de agosto de 2002, un año después del día en que le había entregado el mensaje del príncipe de la corona y lo había presionado exitosamente para que Bush declarara el apoyo explícito de los Estados Unidos a la existencia de un Estado palestino soberano e independiente. Hablaron durante horas aquella mañana. Bandar había visto personalmente a Saddam en cuatro ocasiones, entre 1985 y 1990, y ventiló sus propias opiniones, así como las del rey Fahd, quien se había reunido muchas veces con Saddam.

Bandar le relató a Bush una conversación que el rey Fahd había tenido con Saddam después de la toma de la Gran Mezquita de la Meca, ocurrida el 20 de noviembre 1979, por parte de centenares de militantes que reclamaban que el gobierno saudí estaba siendo demasiado liberal y amigo de Occidente. Anteriormente, Saddam había sido vicepresidente y presidente encargado durante algún tiempo, pero acababa de asumir como presidente y asistía por primera vez a la cumbre de los países árabes.

"Mata a esa gente", le sugirió Saddam a Fahd.

Fahd le dijo que, cuando arrestaran a los militantes, los líderes serían ejecutados y los demás serían encarcelados.

"Estoy preocupado", dijo Saddam. "Tus comentarios me hacen sentir incómodo".

El rey Fahd le preguntó qué quería decir con eso.

"Pienso que no hay ninguna duda de que debes matarlos a todos; eso es un hecho. Escúchame atentamente; mata a todos los hombres de este grupo que tengan un hermano o un padre. Si tienen un primo que tú crees que tiene el valor para buscar venganza, mátalos. Debes propagar el temor de Dios en todo lo que pertenezca a ellos; sólo así podrás dormir de noche".

Según Bandar, Saddam les exigía a sus guardias personales que hicieran dos cosas para probarse a sí mismos: matar a alguien de su propia tribu y matar a alguien de otra tribu; así habría una doble venganza.

Bandar explicó: "Es una maldad inteligente, porque si le quitas la maldad, es algo que tiene mucho sentido. Si quiero confiarle mi vida a usted, quiero asegurarme de que usted sólo pueda estar seguro conmigo".

Después, Saddam señaló a unos hombres que estaban a su alrededor y le dijo a Fahd: "Son muy leales a mí".

"Es bueno rodearse de las personas más leales", replicó Fahd.

"No, Su Majestad. No dije eso", corrigió Saddam. "Dije que son muy leales a mí porque todos tienen las manos untadas de sangre. Cada uno de ellos sabe que cuando yo muera, no encontrarán ni un pedacito así de mi cuerpo". Saddam señaló un pequeño fragmento de piel entre sus dedos. "Me cortarán en pedazos, y si eso me sucede, será el fin de ellos".

Con respecto a sus encuentros personales con el dictador iraquí, Bandar dijo "Lo más sorprendente de Saddam es que al mismo tiempo es seguro, relajado, amable y peligroso. Y todos estos atributos son claros y se presentan de manera simultánea".

Saddam podía hacer temblar a sus generales más importantes, dijo Bandar. En una ocasión, cuando Bandar se reunió con Saddam en los años 80 para buscar el fin de la guerra entre Irán e Irak, Saddam le dijo: "Bandar, todos estos hombres son leales a mí. Conozco a un hombre cuando lo miro a los ojos. Puedo decirte si es leal o no. Si comienza a entrecerrar los ojos, sé qué es un traidor, y lo extermino".

Bandar dijo que a Saddam le emocionaba hacer alarde de su poder, y que lo había hecho con una voz tan suave y con unos modales tan amables, que él tardó cinco segundos en comprender que hablaba en serio.

"Eres un hombre con presencia", le dijo Bandar al dictador iraquí. "No me sorprendería que algunos de tus oficiales o ministros más jóvenes puedan sentir pánico, cosa que sería natural. ¿Me vas a decir, entonces, que matarías a alguien que sintió pánico sólo porque siente un temor reverencial por ti?".

"Ja, ja, ja, ja", respondió Saddam con la risa más macabra. Luego tocó a Bandar en el hombro. "Prefiero matar a alguien sin estar seguro de que es un traidor, que dejar que un traidor se salga con la suya".

En el otoño de 2002, Tenet y Bush tuvieron una conversación de 30 segundos en la que el presidente aclaró que la guerra con Irak era necesaria e inevitable. Tenet se sorprendió demasiado, pero el presidente expresó su comentario con tal convicción que Tenet comprendió que iban camino a la guerra. Hubo algo en la actitud decidida del lenguaje corporal de Bush que hizo que Tenet comprendiera que todas las conversaciones y planes de guerra de ALTO SECRETO tenían un propósito específico. Bush dijo que las amenazas presentadas por Saddam aumentarían con el tiempo.

"No vamos a esperar", dijo.

El 4 de noviembre de 2002, Rob Richer, un veterano agente encubierto y antiguo jefe de la oficina de la CIA en Amán, Jordania, asumió como jefe de la dirección de operaciones de la CIA para el Cercano Oriente y el Sudeste asiático. Tenía todo el Medio Oriente a su cargo y era el principal centro de operaciones que administraba directamente el trabajo clandestino adelantado en la región. En menos de un mes, mientras su grupo de operaciones en Irak infiltraba secretamente dos equipos paramilitares de la CIA en el norte de Irak, Richard tuvo su primera reunión sobre Irak y le preguntó a Tenet si creía que habría una guerra.

"Tenlo por seguro", le dijo abiertamente Tenet. "No se trata de si habrá guerra o no, sino de cuándo será. Este presidente declarará la guerra. Haz los preparativos. Estaremos en guerra".

Tenet ventiló algunos de sus pensamientos en las discusiones que sostuvo con John O. Brennan, uno de sus confidentes más cercanos. Brennan, un veterano que llevaba 22 años en la agencia, había suministrado los informes diarios a la Casa Blanca durante dos años en la administración de Clinton. Posteriormente había servido como jefe de la oficina de la CIA en Arabia Saudita, y como el jefe del estado mayor de Tenet por dos años. Actualmente se desempeñaba como subdirector ejecutivo de la CIA.

Tenet le dijo a Brennan que la guerra se aproximaba y que Bush estaba decidido. Le dijo que era probable que Bush aún no lo estuviera pensando, pero que otros miembros de su equipo como Cheney y Wolfowitz estaban absolutamente decididos a declarar la guerra.

Tenet le explicó a Brennan que sus instintos le decían que invadir a Irak no era lo correcto. Bush y su equipo eran realmente ingenuos, pues pensaban que serían capaces de invadir a Irak y derrocar al gobierno.

"Es un error", le dijo Tenet.

Sin embargo, el director de la CIA nunca le manifestó sus opiniones al presidente. Bush nunca le había pedido su verdadera opinión al respecto, aunque Tenet creía que durante sus conversaciones el presidente había abierto la puerta para que él hubiera podido decir: "No, esto es absurdo. No debería hacerlo; no funcionará". Pero Tenet nunca dijo nada de esto.

Lo que le impidió hacerlo era un asunto complejo. A pesar de sus dudas, Tenet le aseguró el 21 de diciembre de 2002 a Bush que el hecho de que Saddam tuviera armas de destrucción masiva (ADM), la principal razón para la invasión inminente, era "fabricada". Para Tenet, la tentación de invadir a Irak era real porque no había duda de que los Estados Unidos podían derrocar a Saddam y propinarle una derrota contundente al ejército iraquí sin mayores problemas. Adicionalmente, había un gran impulso; se trataba de todos los planes realizados por la CIA y el aparato militar, entre los que figuraban haber logrado que otros países como Inglaterra se hubieran comprometido a participar. Era difícil dar un paso atrás. Como dijo Tenet posteriormente, "Si das el primer paso, ya no podrás retirarte. Reclutamos a todos los aliados —saudíes, jordanos—, así que no podíamos abandonarlos. Nos habían ofrecido su apoyo confidencial".

Y, en última instancia, estaba Cheney. ¿Estaría el vicepresidente, con toda su experiencia y aparente serenidad, detrás de una fuerte ofensiva? ¿Le habría dicho a Bush: "Sí, tienes que hacerlo"? Tenet no estaba en el salón cuando esto sucedió, pero creía que Cheney había presionado a Bush en privado y recomendado enfáticamente la guerra como única solución al problema de Saddam Hussein.

A FINALES DE SEPTIEMBRE DE 2002, Rumsfeld se reunió con el general Franks, su director operativo, con el teniente general Victor E. *Gene* Renuart Jr. de la Fuerza Aérea, y con Douglas J. Feith, el subsecretario de políticas del Pentágono. Feith, de 49 años, era protegido de Richard Perle, secretario de Defensa de Reagan, y uno de los halcones más partidarios de una guerra contra Irak.

Rumsfeld dijo que el Departamento de Defensa estaba en mejores condiciones para administrar a Irak después de la guerra que el Departamento de Estado, y que creía que aquel departamento debía asumir el mando.

Feith coincidió con él y señaló que quería que sus políticas operativas lideraran los esfuerzos posteriores a la guerra. Durante los meses anteriores, él había asistido a unos almuerzos secretos entre los subdirectores de las diferentes agencias, coordinados por Steve Hadley. Habían discutido todos los aspectos de manera exhaustiva, y Feith sacó un cuaderno de catorce centímetros de grosor, donde describía los planes y temas principales.

"Envíale una copia a Condoleezza", le dijo Rumsfeld, quien pareció quedar favorablemente impresionado con el cuaderno. Señaló que, si había una guerra con Irak, se aseguraría de que no se repitiera lo de Bosnia; quería que los planes de reconstrucción y los asuntos políticos se definieran de antemano. "No quiero verme en una posición en que, si alguien falla en hacer algo, arrastre consigo y de manera indefinida a todas nuestras fuerzas de la manera como parecieron hacerlo indefinidamente en Bosnia". Rumsfeld había presionado para reducir las tropas de la OTAN que aún seguían estacionadas en Bosnia, y que recientemente habían llegado a 18.000 hombres.

El secretario dijo que Feith se encargaría de ese trabajo para el Departamento de Defensa. Su objetivo era muy preciso: "Unidad de esfuerzo y unidad de liderazgo para todas las actividades de reconstrucción que se necesita realizar a fin de declarar que la misión ha terminado y que las tropas pueden regresar a casa".

"Jefe, ¿escuchó lo que creo haber escuchado?", le preguntó Renuart a Franks cuando salieron de la reunión.

"¿Qué es lo que crees haber escuchado?".

"Bueno", dijo Renuart, un piloto de combate que tomaba notas en un libro llamado *el libro negro de la muerte*, "me parece que se trata de una política de la Oficina de la Secretaría de Defensa". La oficina de Feith "tiene la responsabilidad de planear el posconflicto, y nuestra responsabilidad es la seguridad. Además, la reconstrucción no nos corresponde a nosotros".

"Yo también veo las cosas del mismo modo", anotó el jefe del Comando Central.

"Creo que acabamos de esquivar una bala", dijo Renuart.

"Quizás tengas razón", comentó Franks. "Yo tengo que cumplir órdenes. El secretario quiere que nos concentremos en la seguridad".

Feith y sus subalternos comenzaron a esbozar la orientación de políticas, establecieron grupos de trabajo y crearon células específicas para analizar temas como la energía, la estabilidad y la soberanía. Rumsfeld aceptó crear una nueva oficina dedicada específicamente a la reconstrucción y a la ayuda humanitaria.

"Usted será el responsable de esto", le dijo Feith a Rumsfeld. "Creemos la oficina".

"Sí", coincidió Rumsfeld, "creemos la oficina". Luego dijo que no, después que sí, y otra vez que no; discutieron este asunto en repetidas ocasiones. Feith habló con Hadley, quien le expresó que un acuerdo diplomático con Saddam todavía era una opción, razón por la cual no querían crear una oficina para atender asuntos posteriores al conflicto.

A FINALES DE SEPTIEMBRE, el teniente general del Ejército James *Spider* Marks, de 49 años, se estaba preparando para la misión de su vida: sería el oficial de inteligencia número uno de las fuerzas de los Estados Unidos que planeaban invadir a Irak. Ésta era la culminación de sus 27 años en el Ejército. Apodado *Spider* desde que era estudiante de secundaria, cuando era un futbolista de 1,85 metros de estatura y 60 kilos de peso, Marks pertenecía a la tercera generación de West Point. Se había graduado en 1975, un mes después de la caída de Saigón, probablemente el punto más bajo de la moral militar norteamericana. Marks era uno de los siete militares, entre los 875 de su promoción, que obtuvieron un rango de dos estrellas, y estaba decidido a no estropear su importante misión.

De figura esbelta, apuesto y juvenil, elegante y completamente entusiasta, Marks serviría directamente bajo el comandante terrestre, el teniente general David D. McKiernan. Ellos dos sabían que una inteligencia precisa y oportuna sería crucial, y que tal vez definiría el éxito o el fracaso de la invasión.

El 26 de agosto, el vicepresidente Cheney había pronunciado un discurso que Marks creía que *debía* haber sido confirmado por la inteligencia estadounidense. "En términos claros, no hay duda de que Saddam Hussein tiene actualmente armas de destrucción masivas", dijo Cheney. "Es indudable que está acumulándolas para utilizarlas contra nuestros amigos, nuestros aliados, y contra nosotros". Su retórica era muy fuerte; Marks lo tomó como una prueba de que las pruebas eran igualmente sólidas: Saddam tenía ADM.

Marks comprendió de inmediato que las fuerzas de invasión terrestres probablemente saldrían de Kuwait, el país desértico, petrolero y rico que compartía una frontera de 170 kilómetros con Irak, país que bloqueaba casi todo su acceso al Golfo Pérsico. Esto significaba que a él lo enviarían allí probablemente varios meses antes de la guerra; sería un blanco fácil junto con los demás generales de las fuerzas terrestres. ¿Había otro objetivo más fácil para Saddam que efectuar un ataque preventivo con armas químicas o biológicas? Eso sería muy arriesgado, pensó, pero también era bastante probable. Era muy posible que no regresara con vida. Marks, que era católico, no compartió sus conclusiones fatalistas con su esposa e hijas, pero se confesó y dejó todos sus asuntos en orden.

Durante los 11 años que habían transcurrido desde la Guerra del Golfo de 1991, los Estados Unidos se habían enfrascado en lo que equivalía a una guerra no declarada de bajo nivel para mantener a Saddam en su sitio. Los aviones de guerra norteamericanos vigilaban dos zonas de exclusión de vuelos en Irak en las que no podía circular ningún avión iraquí. Los pilotos norteamericanos habían ingresado 150.000 veces al espacio aéreo iraquí durante la última década gracias a una resolución de las Naciones Unidas. Los iraquíes habían lanzado cientos de ataques, pero no había muerto un solo piloto norteamericano, especialmente porque los Estados Unidos tenían una inteligencia técnica insuperable. Las fotos satelitales y otras imágenes y operaciones de intercepción de comunicaciones adelantadas por la Agencia Nacional de Seguridad les daban una ventaja ideal. Si los pilotos iraquíes o la defensa aérea se comunicaban por radio, la ANS lo escuchaba todo. El cielo iraquí era un libro abierto, un "teatro con cúpula de cristal", como se decía en la jerga militar y de inteligencia. La inteligencia norteamericana calificaba su desempeño según su capacidad para penetrar en Irak en apoyo de las operaciones de vigilancia del Norte y del Sur, y se puso a sí misma la máxima calificación.

Pero, luego de estudiar la inteligencia iraquí, Marks descubrió que esta superioridad técnica se había convertido en un comodín, en una especie de actitud de *dejemos que pase el próximo satélite*. Esto podría ofrecer una ayuda invaluable para establecer la localización, disposición, capacidad y movimiento de las fuerzas de Saddam durante una invasión. La desventaja era que se trataba de una recolección de información a distancia. Casi no contaban con inteligencia terrestre, algo que necesitaban para encontrar las ADM que, se aseguraba, Saddam estaba escondiendo.

Marks concertó un encuentro con los principales expertos en Irak y en ADM de la Agencia de Inteligencia de Defensa. Creía que estos expertos de la DIA –creada por el secretario de Defensa Robert S. McNamara durante los períodos de Kennedy y Johnson, que era un servicio de inteligencia de primera magnitud– eran los *sabios*.

El 4 de octubre de 2002, se reunió en una sala de conferencias del Pentágono con aproximadamente una docena de *sabios* de la DIA. Estaba el experto en satélites, los expertos en armas químicas biológicas y nucleares, los expertos en asuntos regionales del Medio Oriente y los expertos en sistemas de recolección de inteligencia general.

"¿Qué sabemos sobre las armas de destrucción masivas de Saddam?", les preguntó.

Ellos le presentaron una base de datos de clasificación alta sobre ADM en Irak, llamada Lista Maestra de Sitios con Armas de Destrucción Masiva (LMSADM). Era un listado de 946 sitios donde la inteligencia indicaba que había plantas de producción o bodegas de almacenamiento de material químico, biológico o nuclear en Irak.

El primer asunto, escribió Marks en sus notas, sería la ESS (Exploración de Sitios Sensibles). ¿Qué harían las fuerzas terrestres invasoras norteamericanas con cada uno de los sitios que albergaban ADM? ¿Destruirlas? ¿Examinarlas? ¿Almacenarlas? ¿Desactivarlas?

"¿Quiénes harán esto en términos físicos?", preguntó Marks.

"Bueno, aún no tenemos los nombres", respondió uno de ellos.

"¿Por qué no?", preguntó Marks. "¿Qué unidades lo harán?".

"Tenemos unidades que lo hagan".

"¿Ya les han notificado?".

"Todavía no".

"¿Y cómo se va a definir esto, entonces?", preguntó Marks. "No quiero parecer estúpido, pero yo –y otros 400 o 500 tipos– seremos los que cargaremos con el muerto. ¿Me podrían dar alguna pista?".

Los detalles exactos sobre cada uno de los 946 sitios sospechosos (localización, tipos de ADM, condiciones de seguridad) eran más importantes para los integrantes de las fuerzas terrestres que para cualquier otra persona, incluido el presidente. Bush podía jugarse su capital político, pero las tropas se estaban jugando la vida.

Lo cierto era que los expertos civiles del Pentágono, con sus trajes, camisas y corbatas, no tenían mucha información para Marks sobre estos asuntos. "No hemos hecho nada", dijo uno de ellos. Eran consideraciones operativas que serían decididas por los comandantes militares y no por ellos, indicaron varios expertos.

La brecha entre la inteligencia y los operativos no existe en el frente de combate, señaló Marks. "El personal operativo y el de inteligencia están tan íntimamente ligados como gemelos siameses. Están unidos", dijo. Dependían unos de otros, y tendrían que trabajar juntos cuando estallara la guerra porque todo sucedía de manera instantánea y en tiempo real. De ello dependía que sobrevivieran y tuvieran éxito.

Por ejemplo, cuando las unidades de exploración de ADM llegaran a los sitios sospechosos en Irak, tendrían que establecer prioridades y atenderlas según la inminencia y la amenaza. No habría una línea claramente trazada entre la inteligencia –lo que necesitaban saber– y las operaciones –lo que necesitaban hacer–.

Sería un asunto de experiencia y equipamiento, explicó. ¿Tendrían que llevar muestras de las ADM a los laboratorios para examinarlas? ¿Sería posible obtener muestras? ¿Sería un método seguro? ¿Podrían almacenar y marcar las muestras para examinarlas después?

Los rostros de los miembros de inteligencia parecían decir "ese no es problema nuestro".

Marks examinó la copia de la LMSADM. "¿Se ha establecido prioridades?", preguntó. "¿El sitio número 1 es más importante que el 946?".

"Por supuesto, general", se limitó a decir uno de ellos. "¿Por qué no habría de serlo?".

"No, lo que quiero decir es, ¿dónde está exactamente el 946?", preguntó Marks. "¿La lista de prioridades se ha elaborado según la posibilidad de que se encuentren ADM allí?". ¿Era seguro que hubiera ADM allí? ¿Había más seguridad en unos sitios que en otros?

Nadie tenía una respuesta.

Marks indagó más a fondo; quería saber por qué el sitio número 946 era menos importante que el número 1.

De nuevo, nadie tenía una respuesta real.

¿El sitio número 1 era el primero en el listado porque pensaban que tenía la mayor cantidad de ADM? ¿O era acaso por el tipo de ADM: químicas, biológicas, nucleares, misiles o armamento de otro tipo? ¿El orden de la lista obedecía a la magnitud de la amenaza que suponía el sitio? ¿O se debía más bien a la facilidad o rapidez con que Saddam podría utilizar las ADM? "¿Cómo están dispuestas y almacenadas?", preguntó Marks.

Los expertos señalaron que, relativamente, el número 1 era el más importante.

Está bien. Intentemos definir el significado de "importante", dijo Marks.

Los expertos dijeron que 120 de los 946 sitios eran de "alta prioridad"; Marks tomó nota.

"En términos operativos", comenzó Marks, y se detuvo un segundo para mirar a su alrededor; la falta de interés de los asistentes parecía ir en aumento. Marks dedujo que la mayoría de ellos nunca se habían puesto un uniforme. Dibujó un mapa en una hoja.

"Irak es más o menos así. Seguramente estaremos aquí, en Kuwait", dijo Marks. "Los soldados a bordo de tanques y vehículos de combate Bradley serán los primeros en llegar a estos sitios localizados a lo largo del país". Cuando cruzaran la frontera, dijo Marks, tendrían muchas misiones por delante. "Tienen que matar a los enemigos, tienen que protegerse a sí mismos, tienen que proteger a sus compañeros, tienen que manejar su equipamiento". Y ahora les darían otra misión: custodiar cerca de mil sitios donde se cree que hay ADM.

Marks percibió que muchos de los expertos estaban poniendo sus ojos en blanco. Eran demasiados detalles, demasiadas preguntas y aspectos prácticos y operativos.

"El primer sitio podría estar aquí, justo a un lado de la frontera", dijo Marks, "pero podría ser el sitio 833. ¿Qué deberían hacer? ¿Deberían entrar?

¿Es importante? Es decir, existe un requerimiento operativo y yo necesito que ustedes me ofrezcan un panorama más razonable". Agregó que no les estaba pidiendo que le dijeran lo que deberían hacer las fuerzas terrestres, pues no era asunto de ellos. "Pero tengo que darles a las fuerzas operativas una idea razonable de la importancia y prioridad de ese sitio; catalogarlo como el número 833 de la lista es algo que no me dice nada".

Marks salió muy preocupado de la reunión. "Me sorprendió la falta de detalles", dijo posteriormente. Se suponía que eran algunas de las personas más inteligentes y preparadas que estaban investigando las ADM en Irak. Marks comprendió que el Pentágono no iba a ser de gran ayuda en este asunto tan importante.

Examinó a fondo las evidencias que sugerían que cada uno de los 946 sitios de la Lista Maestra de Armas de Destrucción Masiva realmente contenía este tipo de armas. Las pruebas eran muy débiles; se limitaban a imágenes satelitales muy antiguas, que en algunos casos tenían cuatro o cinco años, o a fragmentos de conversaciones interceptadas, pero no había nada concluyente relacionado con un sitio específico o con una ADM en concreto. Aun más, no había ninguna grabación donde un oficial iraquí dijera: "El gas nervioso VX está almacenado en el primer piso del edificio 1600 de la Avenida Saddam". La lista de ADM figuraba en la red de computadores, pero si imprimía toda la información obtendría un máximo de 15 a 20 páginas, muchas de las cuales tenían un valor cuestionable.

El aislamiento entre los Estados Unidos e Irak desde la Guerra del Golfo era casi total; no había existido comercio, intercambio ni diálogo político; por lo tanto, tampoco había una inteligencia terrestre real. La inteligencia técnica había sido muy eficaz para hacer cumplir las zonas de exclusión de vuelos, pero era casi inútil para encontrar, neutralizar o destruir ADM en los casi mil sitios desperdigados alrededor del país, antes de que pudieran ser utilizadas.

Marks se estaba enfrentando a una década de ceguera por parte de la inteligencia. De hecho, concluyó que, de los 946 sitios que figuraban en la lista de ADM, no podría asegurar que hubiera armas de destrucción masiva o reservas en un solo sitio. Ni siquiera en uno.

"Vamos de culo" se convirtió en frase emblema de Marks, pues se la decía al personal de la DIA (Agencia de Inteligencia de Defensa) y a sus subalternos, reunión tras reunión. Tenía que hacer que los demás reaccionaran, mientras seguía preguntándose: "¿Por qué somos los únicos en hacer esto? No lo entiendo".

11

EL 7 DE OCTUBRE, Bush pronunciaría un discurso en Cincinnati, en horario de máxima audiencia, en el cual describiría las pruebas contra Saddam. La CIA seguía de cerca lo que Bush iba a decir, y en una ocasión advirtió que el presidente pensaba expresar un comentario alarmante sobre un posible programa nuclear de Saddam, indicando que se había descubierto que Irak pretendía comprar óxido de uranio en África.

"Hay que eliminar esta maldita frase porque no creemos en ella", le dijo Tenet a Hadley cuando leyó el borrador. Hadley la eliminó. En cambio, Bush dijo: "Muchas personas han preguntado qué tan cerca está Saddam Hussein de desarrollar un arma nuclear. No lo sabemos con exactitud, y ese es el problema". Era una declaración modesta que reproducía con fidelidad la Evaluación Nacional de Inteligencia (ENI), es decir, la valoración colectiva de todas las agencias de inteligencia norteamericanas, la cual había sido expedida cinco días atrás. La ENI de MÁXIMO SECRETO señalaba con una "seguridad moderada" que "Irak no tiene un arma nuclear ni suficiente material para fabricarla, aunque es probable que la desarrolle entre el 2007 y el 2009".

Pero en vez de decir que faltaban cinco años para que Irak tuviera un arma nuclear, el presidente encendió las alarmas. "Ante una clara evidencia de peligro", advirtió, "no podemos esperar que la prueba final aparezca en una nube con forma de hongo".

EN UNA VIDEOCONFERENCIA realizada el 9 de octubre, el general Franks explicó que el presidente Bush, el gabinete de guerra y él mismo, todavía estaban concentrados en un plan de guerra para invadir a Irak.

"El presidente no está satisfecho con el plan que tenemos", señaló Franks. A Bush le preocupaba que Saddam y sus fuerzas se replegaran en la capital y convirtieran a Bagdad en una especie de fortín, lo cual conduciría a una prolongada guerra de guerrillas urbana. Rice y Card habían expresado este mismo temor durante varios meses, mientras adelantaban reuniones secretas para planear la guerra. La prioridad número uno era encontrar una estrategia para contrarrestar esta situación.

Franks dijo que la segunda prioridad del presidente era "el problema de las ADM".

Ese problema también le correspondía a Marks.

Marks recurrió a todas las personas posibles, revisó las listas de promoción del Ejército y buscó entre el personal que trabajaba para él. Reclutó un total de 400 oficiales militares y miembros de las agencias civiles de inteligencia. Eligió como subdirector al coronel Steve Rotkoff, de 47 años, un alto oficial de inteligencia que llevaba 25 años en el Ejército y que se había graduado de West Point dos años después de él. Marks pensaba que Rotkoff era uno de los oficiales más talentosos del Ejército, y era su carta segura como oficial número dos en el personal de inteligencia.

Rotkoff era un oficial atípico en algunos aspectos; era un intelectual judío, un neoyorquino irreverente y un ratón de biblioteca de cejas gruesas y pobladas. También era un trabajador incansable que sabía cómo obtener resultados. Marks sabía que Rotkoff iba a retirarse del Ejército, y esto le pareció una ventaja; podía hacer las cosas de un modo diferente y que funcionaran. Su primera orden al nuevo subdirector fue: "Tienes autoridad total para ser contestatario, incisivo e insubordinado".

Rotkoff decidió llevar un diario de guerra, y en seis meses completó seis volúmenes. En muchas ocasiones se sentía presionado por el tiempo, y resumía sus pensamientos y sentimientos en *haikus* de tres renglones.

Uno de los primeros fue:

> *Rumsfeld es un tonto*
> *No enviará las fuerzas que necesitamos*
> *Seremos demasiado vulnerables.*

Entre octubre y noviembre de 2002, cuando el general McKiernan trasladó su cuartel a Kuwait con el objeto de prepararse para la guerra, Rotkoff advirtió que los altos oficiales y estrategas no estaban muy concentrados en las ADM. Sin embargo, Marks, Rotkoff y su personal les dedicaron mucho tiempo. Un ejemplo práctico era que si Saddam lanzaba un pequeño ataque con armas químicas o biológicas sobre las tropas norteamericanas mientras entraban a Irak desde Kuwait, podría retrasar o, incluso, detener el avance.

Marks y Rotkoff dirigieron personalmente a sus hombres. Trabajaron de manera incansable; elaboraron una carpeta individual para cada uno de los 946 sitios, e intentaron mejorar y actualizar la información que existía sobre los sitios principales. Marks solicitó nuevas imágenes satelitales y aéreas.

Michael V. Hayden, teniente general de la Fuerza Aérea y director de la Agencia Nacional de Seguridad (ANS), había ordenado que entre 300 y 400 millones de dólares pertenecientes a la agencia fueran transferidos a operaciones y objetivos dirigidos "exclusivamente a Irak". La mayoría de este presupuesto estaría destinado a obtener información sobre campos de batalla, pero la ANS estaba interceptando información sobre las ADM. Hayden opinaba que estaban consiguiendo pruebas sólidas y circunstanciales sobre este tipo de armas. Marks no consideraba que fueran "sólidas"; sólo eran un cúmulo de fragmentos, circunstanciales, por cierto.

A finales de noviembre de 2002, cuando Saddam permitió que el equipo de inspección de armas de las Naciones Unidas, dirigido por el abogado sueco Hans Blix, entrara a territorio iraquí, Marks advirtió una actividad sospechosa en las fotos satelitales más recientes, las cuales mostraban a los inspectores de la ONU entrando por la puerta de un sitio que supuestamente contenía ADM, mientras los iraquíes llevaban algún tipo de material a la parte posterior del edificio y lo cargaban en camiones.

¿Estarían adelantándose? ¿Cómo habían hecho para saber que los inspectores visitarían ese sitio? Le ordenó a su personal que intentaran rastrear los camiones hasta la frontera con Siria.

No obstante, el mayor problema era que nadie estaba seguro que se tratara de ADM; sólo podían adivinar o suponerlo.

"No sé si se trata de bicicletas fabricadas en los Estados Unidos", comentó Marks después de observar el recorrido de un camión hasta la frontera Siria, y recurrió a una antigua expresión militar que se utilizaba cuando no se podía descifrar el verdadero significado: "un cerdo mirando un reloj".

La situación era paradójica. Por una parte, le perturbaba que aún no estuviera en condiciones de asegurar que en algún sitio había ADM. Por otra, estaba convencido de que las armas estaban en algún lugar; la información obtenida lo había acondicionado a pensar que así era.

Marks ignoraba que Rumsfeld tenía las mismas preocupaciones referentes a los informes sobre ADM. En un informe clasificado de tres páginas y expedido el 15 de octubre de 2002, Rumsfeld enunciaba 29 aspectos que podrían salir mal en la guerra de Irak; las examinó con el presidente y con el CNS. El ítem número tres decía: "Es probable que los Estados Unidos no puedan encontrar ADM en suelo iraquí".

Era obvio que él tenía muchas dudas al respecto, y le pregunté por esto en el 2006.

"Estaba muy preocupado por eso", me dijo. "Me preocupa la información; tengo que hacerlo".

Le pregunté a Rumsfeld si conocía a un general de dos estrellas llamado *Spider* Marks, quien estaba al frente de las labores de inteligencia terrestre y tenía dudas sobre la existencia de ADM.

"No", dijo Rumsfeld. "Es decir, nos hemos entendido con el personal del comandante de guerra. Es probable que lo haya visto, pero no lo conozco".

EN OCTUBRE, EL CONGRESO APROBÓ por mayoría abrumadora la guerra contra Irak. Tres semanas después, en las elecciones legislativas de mitad del período presidencial, los republicanos retuvieron el control de la Cámara y asumieron el control del Senado; ganaron dos sillas en el Senado y ocho en la Cámara. Era sumamente extraño que el partido del presidente lograra avances en estas elecciones. "Cómo lograron el triunfo (y ahora vienen los grandes desafíos)", fue el titular de portada en la revista *Time*, acompañado de una foto, en la que aparecen George W. Bush y Karl Rove, abrazados y sonrientes en el Salón Oval.

En el Departamento de Estado, Armitage concluyó que el plan de invadir a Irak había recibido un gran respaldo. Dijo que Bush "realmente piensa que su papel es transformar el mundo y el ataque del 9/11 se lo permitió; combinado con las elecciones de 2002, en las que emergió como el presidente poderoso de todo el pueblo, éste es el efecto de la victoria; finalmente se convirtió en el presidente elegido popularmente".

Armitage y Powell recibieron informes de líderes extranjeros que se habían reunido con Bush, en los que se señalaba que el presidente estaba actuando como si hubiera recibido una validación y una reivindicación. El mandatario decía: "Tenemos que aprovechar el momento. Nos han dado una oportunidad". Armitage pensaba que Rice respaldaba cada vez más al presidente. "En mi opinión, siempre que alguien no estaba inmediatamente dispuesto a hacer exactamente lo que el presidente quería, Condoleezza pensaba que era casi desleal".

"NADIE SABE CUÁNTO los presionaré para que entren a Bagdad. Ustedes asumirán el riesgo", les dijo Tommy Franks a sus generales el 7 de diciembre, frase que *Spider* Marks escribió en su diario. Ése era el objetivo del plan: entrar rápidamente a Bagdad. Por otra parte, reflejaba los deseos de Rumsfeld: "asumir riesgos". La Doctrina Powell, que trataba de asegurar el éxito, había quedado atrás. Ahora se trataba de una guerra rápida y decisiva.

Marks seguían pidiendo ayuda sobre los sitios y las listas de ADM; los miembros de las unidades creían que esto estaba relacionado con las armas durante y después de la guerra. Marks cuestionaba repetidamente la validez de utilizar sólo métodos técnicos para los sitios sospechosos de almacenar ADM. Quería aumentar lo que él llamaba el *Fingerspitzengefühl* –palabra alemana que significaba sentido y comprensión instintivos– de Irak, por medio de recursos humanos. Sin embargo, ya era demasiado tarde para desarrollar dichos recursos, y tanto la CIA como la DIA prácticamente no tenían personal en Irak.

Marks intentó alertar a la DIA en Washington, pero no tuvo mayor éxito.

"No pude hacer que la DIA reaccionara", le dijo un día al general McKiernan. "Deberían despedirme".

McKiernan no le hizo caso, y Marks fue más enfático.

"Señor, no he podido confirmar lo que hay en ninguno de estos sitios", le dijo. Explicó su reserva sobre un sitio particular de la lista, una supuesta planta de producción química. "No hay informes que confirmen que eso es lo que se hace allí. Está clasificada así, está marcada con varios signos que se puede ver en imágenes aéreas. Tenemos algunos planes arquitectónicos y está diseñada para tal fin. Pero no puedo confirmar que eso es lo que se esté haciendo hoy, en el año 2002 de Nuestro Señor".

"Entiendo", replicó McKiernan. "Continúa".

Marks dedujo que esto demostraba que era él quien tendría que resolver el problema. Los oficiales militares de alto rango como Marks habían sido entrenados para hacer cosas. "No puedo" era una expresión prohibida; él vivía en el mundo de las soluciones, no en de las quejas o las disculpas. Su jefe estaba ocupado y tenía sus propios problemas. Era casi un principio de liderazgo del Ejército, y Marks lo convirtió en un lema: "No le pases tu infierno personal a tu jefe". Su subdirector, el coronel Rotkoff, escuchaba esta frase con tanta frecuencia que la anotó en su diario como la típica frase de Marks. "No compartas tu infierno personal".

En Kuwait, el lunes era el día más temible de la semana para el coronel Rotkoff. Al igual que el resto del personal norteamericano, muchos días se ponía su traje de protección contra armas químicas; se trataba de una bolsa de nylon que contenía una máscara de gas y una capucha atada a la cintura. Incluso el J-LIST, una versión más moderna y liviana de ese traje, era pesado e incómodo. No obstante, sentía pavor cuando se lo quitaba.

Rotkoff podía sacar 15 minutos de su horario para ducharse los lunes. Cada vez que lo hacía, pensaba que Saddam lanzaría un ataque con armas químicas o biológicas en ese mismo instante. El dictador iraquí había lanzado 88 misiles Scud en un rango de varios cientos de kilómetros a la redonda contra las tropas norteamericanas en la primera Guerra del Golfo, y otros 39 hacia Israel, en un intento para hacer que esta nación entrara en guerra, y fracturar así la coalición existente entre Estados Unidos y los árabes. Actualmente, todos esperaban que Saddam atacara de nuevo, sólo que esta vez reforzaría los misiles con cabezas químicas o biológicas. Todos estaban absolutamente *seguros* de que esto iba a suceder.

Día tras día, el temor a las ADM le ofreció inspiración a Rotkoff para escribir haikus en su diario:

> *Ántrax+viruela*
> *Máscaras de gas, J-Lists a toda hora*
> *Escalofriante estar aquí.*

> *Ah-ejercicios de SCUDS*
> *Máscaras durante horas evitando trabajar*
> *El sudor resbalando por mi cara*

> *No es un simulacro*
> *Máscara y traje químicos con rapidez*
> *Procura no angustiarte*

Esta era la reacción visceral, pero el problema era que había una ausencia real de informes convincentes.

"Todos los días se levantaban y se ponían los trajes protectores", recordó posteriormente Rumsfeld. "No porque sí, sino porque temían que las armas químicas acabaran con ellos. Ninguno de nosotros pensó que ellos tuvieran armas nucleares; la única preocupación real era que tuvieran armas químicas".

LA VERSIÓN ESCRITA y completa del plan de guerra contra Irak, llamado Plan Op 1003 V, contenía un anexo dedicado a la labor de búsqueda de ADM. Esta era la buena noticia, pensó Marks. La mala era que jamás se había destinado ninguna unidad militar a esta labor; ese era el problema operativo con el que había estado luchando Marks durante varios meses, desde su primer encuentro con los expertos de la DIA, celebrado en octubre en el Pentágono.

Después de muchas discusiones, el Comando Central de Franks aceptó asignarle una misión al batallón, denominada "Destacamento especial para la búsqueda de sitios sensibles". Sin embargo, un batallón era una fuerza pequeña, de varios cientos de hombres, y el teniente coronel al mando era una oficial de rango relativamente bajo como para comandar la misión, habida cuenta de que las armas de destrucción masiva eran el motivo principal para declarar la guerra. Esto le parecía extraño a Marks, e, incluso, negligente. "No hay una misión más importante o crítica para la nación", escribió en su diario, "pero el Departamento de Defensa continúa evadiéndonos y rechazando nuestras peticiones. ¡Es increíble!".

Acudió a una unidad más grande, y en diciembre de 2002 llegó a una solución con el general del Tercer Cuerpo del Ejército en Fort Sill, Oklahoma.

"Vendrá una brigada de artillería", dijo Marks. "Les hemos recomendado que dejen el armamento grande y que más bien se ocupen de las ADM". La brigada, conformada por unos 400 hombres y comandada por un corpulento coronel llamado Richard McPhee, fue rebautizada como el 75° Destacamento Especial de Búsqueda, al cual se le encomendó la tarea de encontrar las ADM cuando las fuerzas norteamericanas ingresaran a Irak. Era lo que en términos militares se llamaba una "solución oportuna y de campo", es decir, arreglárselas con lo que había. Por fin se le había encomendado el trabajo de las ADM a alguien.

EL JUEVES 5 DE DICIEMBRE DE 2002, en medio de los planes más intensos para la invasión a Irak, Steve Herbits entró a la oficina de Rumsfeld.

"No te gustará lo que voy a decirte," advirtió, "pero estás en la delicada posición de ser la única persona responsable de que el presidente no sea reelegido, si no solucionas algo".

Rumsfeld se sonrojó.

Herbits continuó. "Ahora que he captado tu atención, tienes que concentrarte en planear lo que sucederá después de Irak. La situación está bastante deteriorada. No podremos conseguir la paz".

Posteriormente le pregunté a Rumsfeld si recordaba la conversación con Herbits. "No", dijo él, "pero no significa que no haya tenido lugar".

Rumsfeld había recibido instrucciones del presidente Bush para supervisar el despliegue masivo de cientos de miles de tropas norteamericanas en Irak sin informarle al mundo ni a Saddam Hussein que la guerra era inevitable. El presidente aún estaba inmerso en la diplomacia de las Naciones Unidas, de tal suerte que Rumsfeld supervisó personalmente el sistema de movilización y despliegue, denominado TPFDD[1] (Despliegue Progresivo de Fuerzas e Información). El secretario creía haber levantado una roca y encontrado un sistema completamente deteriorado, y no tardó en decidir personalmente cuáles unidades serían trasladadas y cuándo. Esto supuso un enorme grado de microgestión que frustró y enfureció a los militares.

Herbits le advirtió a Rumsfeld que la política del subsecretario Feith estaba fracasando. La disputa entre los departamentos de Estado y de Defensa era tan intensa que las reuniones entre las agencias eran a veces poco más que competencias de gritos. Los planes para el Irak de posguerra eran tan desatinados que el secretario tuvo que intervenir personalmente.

Rumsfeld no habló mucho, pero pronto convocó a uno de sus encuentros relámpago de los sábados, con Feith y otros participantes.

---

1. Sigla que en inglés quiere decir *Time-Phased Force and Deployment Data*. (N. de E.)

"¿Qué es lo que está sucediendo?", preguntó. "Tenemos que rectificar el rumbo".

A COMIENZOS DE ENERO de 2003, Jones, comandante general de la Marina, fue a hablar con Rumsfeld; sólo estaban ellos dos. Jones había declinado una entrevista para la jefatura del Estado Mayor Conjunto 18 meses atrás, pero Rumsfeld quería asignarle un cargo de primera magnitud: ser al mismo tiempo el comandante supremo en la OTAN y el comandante de guerra en Europa.

Las disquisiciones de Rumsfeld cobraron vida en Irak después de la batalla. Saddam Hussein había acordonado el país de manera efectiva y brutal. ¿Que estaría sucediendo en Irak? ¿Qué estaría haciendo y pensando la gente? Era difícil, le confesó Rumsfeld a Jones, encontrar a alguien que realmente supiera algo sobre Irak, y que conociera la situación real.

"Trabajé para alguien que es considerado un héroe en Kurdistán", dijo Jones, refiriéndose a la región septentrional iraquí. "Es Jay Garner".

"¡Yo lo conozco!", exclamó Rumsfeld cuando escuchó el nombre. Garner había trabajado en la comisión espacial de Rumsfeld durante la administración de Clinton.

Garner, un general de tres estrellas retirado del Ejército, había conducido la Operación *Provide Comfort*[2] después de la Guerra del Golfo de 1991, cuando rescataron a miles de kurdos en el norte de Irak. A través del tiempo, esta operación se había convertido en la regla de oro de las misiones humanitarias militares.

Jones explicó que, cuando era coronel, había comandado un contingente de 2.200 *marines* asignadas a esta operación. Dijo que Garner merecía mucha parte del crédito por el éxito de la operación, pues había instalado sistemas de purificación de agua y ofrecido ayuda humanitaria. En términos generales, Garner había comandado una fuerza norteamericana de 20.000 hombres, que expulsó a las tropas de Saddam del norte de Irak. Finalmente, un domingo por la mañana de 1991, Colin Powell, que era el jefe del Estado Mayor Conjunto, había trazado una línea en un mapa, y establecido así la frontera sur de Kurdistán. Después de la Operación *Provide Comfort*, los kurdos establecieron un enclave autónomo en el norte de Irak. Saddam los hostigaba continuamente, pero también eran una verdadera espina en su talón y una excepción notable a su mano de hierro.

---

2. Suministro de Bienestar (N. del E.).

La Operación *Provide Comfort* fue considerada un gran éxito por otra razón importante: Garner y las fuerzas estadounidenses había cumplido su labor y regresado a casa en pocos meses.

EL NOMBRE DE GARNER quedó grabado en la mente de Rumsfeld. Mientras más pensaba en él, más razonable le parecía su nombramiento. Le dijo a Feith que había decidido que Garner liderara la oficina para asuntos de posguerra.

El jueves 9 de enero, Garner, que en ese entonces era el jefe de una división del L-3, un multimillonario contratista de defensa especializado en vigilancia, inteligencia y equipo de reconocimiento de alta tecnología, se encontraba en Nueva York para asistir a una reunión de su compañía. Recibió una llamada en su teléfono móvil, de la oficina de Feith.

"Queremos hablar contigo. ¿Podrías venir?", le preguntó Ron Yaggi, asistente militar de Feith y general de una estrella de la Fuerza Aérea.

"¿De qué quieren hablar conmigo?" preguntó Garner.

"Es un poco delicado para decirlo por teléfono", replicó Yaggi.

"Mire, general", dijo Garner ligeramente irritado. "Esta es la única forma en que podemos hablar". Garner, explosivo hombre de 64 años que medía 1,73 metros de estatura, se había retirado del Ejército doce años atrás, después de 23 años de servicio, incluidas dos campañas en Vietnam.

"Estamos conformando una organización para adelantar un trabajo de posguerra. Estoy seguro que usted sabe dónde", le explicó Yaggi, intentando hablar con hermetismo por una línea telefónica que no era muy segura. "Nos gustaría que usted la dirigiera, o por lo menos que la organizara".

Yaggi le explicó que Garner conformaría la organización, pero que no tendría que ir a Irak después de las operaciones de combate. Garner pensó que no podía permanecer en su cargo actual si aceptaba la misión.

"Creo que no puedo hacerlo", dijo. "Estoy dirigiendo una compañía que tiene más de mil empleados que dependen de mí, y no puedo retirarme de un momento a otro".

FEITH LLAMÓ A GARNER el lunes siguiente, un 13 de enero. "El secretario de Defensa dijo que si usted rechaza este trabajo tendrá que venir y explicárselo personalmente".

Ninguno de los dos dijo lo que era obvio: que sería casi impensable que alguien de la posición ejecutiva de Garner, que dependía de los contratos con el Pentágono, se negara a hablar con el secretario de Defensa. Los oficiales retirados que eran contratistas importantes del Departamento de Defensa estaban en una especie de reserva no oficial para labores especiales. Por lo tanto, no fue sorprendente que el director ejecutivo de la L-3 tomara una licencia laboral.

"Estaré en casa a finales de junio", le prometió Garner a Connie, con quien llevaba más de 40 años de casado. "Estaré en casa para el asado del 4 de julio"[3].

Ese mismo día, el presidente Bush citó a Colin Powell a una reunión de dos minutos en el Salón Oval, para informarle que había decidido declararle la guerra a Irak.

"¿Está seguro?", le preguntó Powell.

Bush respondió que sí.

"Usted entiende las consecuencias", señaló Powell en una pregunta a medias. El secretario llevaba unos seis meses meditando sobre la complejidad de gobernar a Irak después de la guerra. "¿Sabe que ese país será prácticamente suyo?".

Bush dijo que así lo entendía.

"¿Estás conmigo en esto?", le preguntó el presidente a su secretario de Estado. "Creo que tengo que hacerlo, y quiero que estés conmigo".

"Estoy con usted, señor presidente", señaló Powell.

En caso de que tuviera alguna duda –y Powell no podía tener ninguna, pues era un soldado bueno y obediente–, el presidente le dijo explícitamente al antiguo jefe del Estado Mayor Conjunto: "Es hora de ponerte tu uniforme de guerra".

El presidente me confirmó de manera muy reticente que le había pedido a Powell que lo apoyara, pero mencionó un tanto irritado algo que era más bien obvio: "Yo no necesitaba su permiso".

Elliot Abrams, director de asuntos para el Medio Oriente del Consejo Nacional de Seguridad, era uno de los conservadores más recalcitrantes, agresivos y controvertidos. Había sido subsecretario de Estado en la administración de Reagan, y había apoyado incondicionalmente la guerra encubierta de la CIA en Nicaragua. Se declaró culpable de ocultar información al Congreso en el escándalo *Irán-contras*, pero Bush padre lo perdonó en 1992.

---

3. Gracias a documentos, conversaciones, cronologías, cartas, transcripciones, notas personales y las de su asistente ejecutivo, el papel de Garner es presentado extensivamente y en detalle porque fue la primera persona a la cual se le adjudicó total responsabilidad por el Irak de posguerra. Este es el recuento más completo y documentado que existe sobre su experiencia, ya que decidió no escribir un libro ni hablar en público de manera extensiva. Garner concedió largas entrevistas el 19 de septiembre 2005, el 16 de octubre de 2005, el 13 de diciembre 2005 y el 22 de abril de 2006. Los miembros de su oficina de planeación para el Irak de posguerra también fueron entrevistados y algunos suministraron notas y documentos adicionales.

Rice había llevado a Abrams al CNS, donde trabajó como una bestia de carga; se le asignó la misión humanitaria en Irak. Abrams había trabajado con el Comando Central del general Franks, redactando listas para prohibir huelgas y evitar que bombardearan los hospitales, las plantas de agua y las redes eléctricas iraquíes cuando comenzara la guerra.

El 15 de enero, dos días después de que Bush le informara a Powell que declararía la guerra, el presidente se reunió con el CNS para que Abrams presentara en secreto los planes para la ayuda humanitaria. Dos meses antes del comienzo de la guerra, el presidente recibió el primer informe importante sobre los planes de posguerra.

Abrams dijo que la guerra podría dejar a más de 2 millones de iraquíes desplazados. Los Estados Unidos estaban almacenando alimentos, carpas y agua. Adicionalmente, tendrían que enviar dinero de manera discreta a las agencias de las Naciones Unidas y a otras organizaciones no gubernamentales (ONG) para que estuvieran preparadas.

Abrams señaló que la cifra exacta de refugiados y desplazados sería determinada por las tensiones étnicas entre kurdos, chiítas y sunitas, por el nivel de violencia, las repatriaciones, y por las armas de destrucción masiva, independientemente de que fueran utilizadas o no. Una presentación en PowerPoint mostró cómo Saddam Hussein podría destruir represas e inundar varias zonas del país. No era un panorama muy agradable; al contrario, era un augurio perturbador de lo que podía ser una de las peores crisis humanitarias en épocas recientes.

"Esta es una oportunidad para cambiar la imagen de los Estados Unidos", le dijo Bush al gabinete de guerra. El presidente vio una oportunidad en materia de relaciones públicas. "Necesitamos sacar el mayor provecho posible de esta ayuda humanitaria, por medio de nuestra diplomacia pública. Quiero que tengamos capacidad de reconstrucción", y comenzó a dar órdenes, "quiero barcos que estén listos para entregar alimentos y suplementos de ayuda, y para que podamos entrar rápidamente". Luego añadió: "Hay muchas cosas que podrían salir mal, pero no por falta de planeación".

GARNER, QUIEN PRÓXIMAMENTE asumiría la misión humanitaria de posguerra, no fue invitado a la presentación de Abrams. Al día siguiente, se sentó con Rumsfeld y Feith en la oficina del secretario.

"Jay", comenzó Rumsfeld, "no hagas caso a lo que te digan; el Gobierno ha hecho innumerables planes para esto". Sin embargo, todo se había hecho en la "estufa vertical" de cada una de las agencias federales, incluido el Departamento de Defensa. "Yo recomendé que intentaras conectar horizontalmente los planes, que detectaras los problemas y los solucionaras, al igual que otras fallas que percibieras".

Feith estaba muy molesto con las secuelas de la guerra de Afganistán del 2001-2002. Creía que el Departamento de Estado –al que a veces llamaba "Departamento de los bondadosos"–, había cometido muchos errores, pues no había estabilizado a este país con la rapidez suficiente. Feith también quería que el Pentágono asumiera el control de Irak después de la guerra, hasta que el Departamento de Estado pudiera consolidarse como una especie de embajada. Hasta tanto, este departamento estaría subordinado al de Defensa.

A Garner le preocupaba la falta de tiempo. Le dijo a Rumsfeld que, durante la Segunda Guerra Mundial, los Estados Unidos habían comenzado a planear la Europa de posguerra antes de que terminara el conflicto. "Usted está pensando que este problema tomará de cinco a diez semanas para solucionarse".

"Lo sé", replicó Rumsfeld. "Haremos algo. Mientras tanto, optimiza el tiempo disponible".

FRANK MILLER, UN ANTIGUO BURÓCRATA que llevaba 22 años en el Pentágono y había servido en siete secretarías de Defensa, en algunos de los cargos civiles más delicados e importantes, se desempeñaba actualmente como director de Defensa del CNS para Rice. Había dirigido el Grupo Ejecutivo de Gobierno, encargado de coordinar los asuntos iraquíes entre las diferentes agencias federales. Miller, que utilizaba lentes gruesos, era el tipo de mando medio serio e invisible que hace que una organización funcione, el equivalente del distribuidor de encendido de un auto: vital, pero casi imperceptible hasta que deja de funcionar.

A comienzos de 2003, Miller sintió que Rumsfeld le estaba haciendo la vida casi imposible. Había una tensión constante entre el CNS y el Pentágono de Rumsfeld, y el secretario no ahorraba esfuerzos para controlar la información. Con mucha frecuencia, Rumsfeld asistía a la Casa Blanca en compañía del general Franks para informarle al presidente, al CNS y algunos funcionarios sobre los planes de la invasión a Irak. El secretario se aseguraba de que las presentaciones y los folletos fueran distribuidos justo antes de la reunión, y de que se recogieran al término de ésta. Algunas veces, los folletos que le entregaba al presidente tenían 140 páginas, pero los funcionarios de rangos menores como Miller sólo recibían 40. En una ocasión, Rumsfeld no llevó ejemplares suficientes para todos los principales, y Rice tuvo que ver el de la persona que estaba a su lado. Era un procedimiento mezquino; Miller y otros intentaban anotar los puntos más importantes.

Algunas veces, Rumsfeld decía en medio de un informe: "No deben tomar notas". Los reprendía: "No deben tomar notas aquí".

Miller pensaba que esto era completamente descabellado. ¿Cómo podía asesorar a Rice, a Hadley o al presidente si no tenía acceso a la información del Pentágono? Miller le había dirigido los temas más sensibles relacionados con planes de guerra a Cheney cuando era secretario de Defensa, y en cinco oportunidades había recibido la Medalla de Defensa al Servicio Civil Distinguido, la condecoración más alta concedida a un funcionario civil. Rumsfeld lo trataba a él, así como a otros miembros del CNS, como funcionarios poco leales, de tercera categoría, y a veces ni siquiera advertía su presencia; esto le molestó profundamente a Miller, quien pensó que era una conducta contraproducente. ¿Acaso no estaban todos del mismo lado?

Cuando los generales iban a la Casa Blanca con Rumsfeld, el secretario era el primero en hablar, presentaba a los asistentes y explicaba de qué hablarían. Miller pensaba que Rumsfeld estaba completamente absorto en sí mismo, como si fuera el director de una orquesta. La situación de Myers era más degradante aun; él y Miller eran viejos amigos, y éste último veía que Myers estaba sufriendo.

Miller era también el jefe del estado mayor *de facto* del comité de diputados del CNS, entre quienes figuraban subsecretarios como Wolfowitz, Armitage y McLaughlin, pero el caos era tal que todas las semanas debía sostener reuniones informales con Card, Rice, Hadley y con I. Lewis *Scooter* Libby, el jefe de gabinete del vicepresidente Cheney, para alertar al Pentágono y hacer que Rumsfeld reaccionara. En respuesta a la dificultad para obtener información, Rice le sugería a Miller que intentara otras estrategias; que si no podía obtener la información por los canales directos, llamara a algún conocido y la obtuviera por otros medios. Miller tenía muchos contactos en el Pentágono y en las tropas desplegadas. Había conocido y era amigo de muchos oficiales en el Pentágono que ahora tenían tres o cuatro estrellas.

Rice le ordenaba con frecuencia que consiguiera la información por cualquier vía. "Solucionálo", le decía.

A Rice le parecía insólito que Rumsfeld no le devolviera algunas llamadas, cuando quería preguntarle sobre planes de guerra o transporte de tropas. Se quejó ante Rumsfeld, quien le recordó que la asesora de seguridad nacional no figuraba en la cadena de mando.

Rice se quejó ante el presidente.

La respuesta de Bush fue bromear con Rumsfeld.

"Sé qué no te gusta hablar con Condi", le dijo en una ocasión al secretario, "pero tienes que hablar con ella".

Card estaba asombrado.

La escena hubiera sido cómica, pensó Miller, si no se tratara de la guerra, de la vida y de la muerte.

12

HADLEY LLEVABA varios meses trabajando en la transición del poder después del derrocamiento de Saddam. Se había especulado bastante sobre la posibilidad de nombrar al general Franks como procónsul de Irak, quien tendría amplios poderes. La desventaja era que, de ser así, la presencia norteamericana en ese país parecería una ocupación. No necesitaban otro general MacArthur; necesitaban a una figura civil que asumiera el liderazgo. A Rice le horrorizaba el prospecto de decirles a los iraquíes que Tommy Franks sería su nuevo presidente. "¿Crear otro MacArthur?", preguntó. Sabía que Bush ni los iraquíes permitirían esto.

¿Cuál era, entonces, la solución? Hadley sabía que Rumsfeld y Feith pensaban que la situación de posguerra en Afganistán había sido un fracaso. El secretario reclamaría que los Estados Unidos habían fallado al dividir las labores entre varios países. Se suponía que Alemania entrenaría al cuerpo de policía e Italia haría lo propio con la rama judicial. El mismo gobierno norteamericano había fragmentado las tareas: el Departamento de Estado tenía unas, el del Tesoro tenía otras, y el resultado fue que Afganistán terminó siendo una prioridad de nadie.

Hadley creía que la idea del equipo de Garner se había inspirado en esa experiencia. El término militar para las operaciones de posguerra era Fase IV –"operaciones de estabilización"–, pero el presidente quería algo más que estabilidad en el Irak de posguerra; quería democracia, así que Hadley propuso un plan incluyente de posguerra que lo abarcara todo.

El Departamento de Estado había trabajado por espacio de un año en lo que se conocía como el "Futuro de Irak", proyecto de miles de páginas que contenía informes y recomendaciones sobre el gobierno, el petróleo, la justicia y la agricultura. A pesar de este esfuerzo, y en contradicción con sus declaraciones posteriores, Powell admitió que era apenas lógico transferirle al Departamento de Defensa las responsabilidades propias de la posguerra. Rumsfeld tendría decenas de miles de militares en tierra, todo el dinero y los recursos. Powell, un hombre militar, se inclinaba instintivamente por un plan que respetara el principio de la unidad de mando. Tenía que haber alguien –una persona– que estuviera al mando, y el Departamento de Defensa tenía que asumir esta tarea. Esto no le parecía nada extraño a Powell; era lo mismo que se había hecho en Alemania y Japón después de la Segunda Guerra Mundial.

Hadley, Feith y los miembros del CNS tenían aproximadamente una semana para preparar un documento legal que establecía la autoridad del Departamento de Defensa.

El 20 de enero de 2003, el presidente Bush firmó la NSPD-24, una Directiva Presidencial Nacional de Seguridad secreta. El tema principal era establecer una "Oficina de Planeación para el Irak de Posguerra" en el interior del Departamento de Defensa.

Garner no recibió ninguna información al respecto. Pocos días después, cuando comenzó a trabajar en una oficina cercana a la de Rumsfeld, leyó el documento de cuatro páginas que estaba clasificado como SECRETO. Quedó perplejo.

"Si fuera necesario que una coalición militar liderada por los Estados Unidos liberara a Irak", comenzaba la directiva, "los Estados Unidos quisieran estar en una posición que les permitiera atender los desafíos administrativos, humanitarios y de reconstrucción que enfrentará el país después de las operaciones de combate. La responsabilidad inmediata recaerá en el Comando Central de los Estados Unidos. No obstante, el éxito general requerirá un esfuerzo nacional".

La nueva oficina de posguerra de Garner sería responsable de "planear en detalle todo el espectro de asuntos que el gobierno de los Estados Unidos abordaría con respecto a la administración de Irak durante la posguerra". Entre éstos figuraban todos los asuntos políticos, económicos y de seguridad[4]. El general Garner creía que lo habían llamado para desempeñar la honorable función de jefe de estado, pero la directiva presidencial le asignaba la responsabilidad de todas las labores conducidas normalmente por gobiernos nacionales, estatales y locales, en el Irak posterior a Saddam.

La directiva ordenaba que diez agencias federales –desde la CIA y el Departamento de Estado, hasta los departamentos de Agricultura y Educación– comenzaran a contratar expertos de alto rango –coroneles, generales de

---

4. La lista incluía: a. Suministrar ayuda humanitaria; b. Desmantelar las armas de destrucción masivas; c. Derrotar y desarticular las redes terroristas; d. Proteger los recursos naturales y la infraestructura; e. Facilitar la reconstrucción del país y la protección de su infraestructura y economía; f. Ayudar al restablecimiento de los principales servicios civiles como el suministro de alimentos, el agua, la electricidad y la atención médica; g. Reformar el aparato militar iraquí; h. Reformar los organismos de seguridad interna; i. Respaldar la transición del poder a los iraquíes a su debido tiempo.

una estrella y civiles del más alto nivel– que tuvieran el peso necesario para "coordinar los asuntos de las agencias cuando fuera necesario".

La directiva señalaba que, en caso de guerra, "la Oficina de Planeación deberá trasladarse a Irak para conformar el núcleo del aparato administrativo que ayudará a administrar a Irak por un período limitado de tiempo".

Garner habló con Rumsfeld después de haber digerido la directiva presidencial.

"Esto es lo que creo que debemos hacer", dijo. Necesitaban funcionarios que pudieran coordinar los esfuerzos en tres áreas principales: la reconstrucción, la administración civil y los temas humanitarios. Luego necesitarían un grupo operativo –casi exclusivamente militar– que estuviera encargado de la logística: alimentos, vivienda, seguridad física y transporte. Finalmente, debían dividir el país en tres zonas: la del Norte, la del Sur y la región central que incluyera a Bagdad y zonas aledañas.

"¿Le parece bien?", preguntó Garner. Rumsfeld dijo que sí, pero Garner percibió que el secretario tenía la mente ocupada en la invasión y no en lo que sucediera después.

Garner se despertaba a las dos de la mañana para redactar listas de tareas. Comprendió que le habían asignado una labor imposible, pero su actitud ejecutiva, la del militar que era, prevaleció sobre sus dudas. "Creí que iba hacer algo extremadamente difícil", me dijo algún tiempo después. Y agregó: "Nunca fracasé en nada".

La noche del sábado 25 de enero de 2003, el presidente Bush asistió a la 90ª cena anual del Club Alfalfa, que había tomado su nombre de un alimento vegetal poco apetecido. La cena, de corte europeo y traje de etiqueta, tuvo lugar en el hotel Capital Hilton, a tres cuadras de la Casa Blanca, y reunió a los principales personajes de la política y los negocios, entre quienes estaban el padre y la madre del presidente.

El presidente Bush hizo comentarios breves y le dijo a la audiencia que su madre le había aconsejado que no hiciera bromas sobre los inspectores de armas de las Naciones Unidas en Irak, y que no hablara de Corea del Norte.

"Entonces, le dije: '¿Por qué, más bien, no te encargas del discurso?'. Así que, damas y caballeros, aquí está mi madre".

Bárbara Bush, la *Zorra de Plata,* como la llamaba su esposo, subió al estrado. "La gente nunca me cree, pero era un niño modelo", dijo. "Se ponía su ropa de *cowboy* y jugaba varias horas combatiendo a los tipos malos o, como decía él, *al eje del mal*". Bush hijo había hecho célebre esta expresión al referirse así a Irán, Irak y Corea del Norte en su discurso del Estado de la unión de 2002.

"Nunca olvidaré el ensayo que escribió cuando estaba en cuarto grado, en el que explicó que, en 1519, Fernando Magallanes salió a '*circuncidar* el mundo'". Bárbara recibió una estruendosa ovación.

Poco después, la ex primera dama se acercó a David L. Boren, un viejo amigo y antiguo senador demócrata de centro por Oklahoma, que había sido director del comité selecto para asuntos de inteligencia durante la presidencia de George H. W. Bush. Boren era presidente de la Universidad de Oklahoma, pero aún tenía contactos con Washington, especialmente a través de George Tenet, quien había integrado el comité de inteligencia comandado por Boren. Tenet le había causado muy buena impresión; Boren se convirtió en su mentor y lo recomendó al presidente Clinton en 1992, y a George W. Bush a comienzos de 2001.

Boren y Bush padre se conocían desde hacía varias décadas y eran amigos cercanos.

"Sí, señora", le dijo Boren.

"¿Me dirás la verdad?".

"Por supuesto".

"¿Deberíamos preocuparnos por Irak?".

"Sí; estoy muy preocupado".

"¿Crees que sería un error?".

"Sí, señora", replicó Boren. "Creo que será un gran error entrar allí ahora y de esta manera".

"Mi esposo está tan preocupado que no puede dormir. Pasa las noches en vela".

"¿Y por qué no habla con el presidente?".

"Cree que no es apropiado, a menos que él se lo pida", señaló Bárbara Bush. Se trataba de la distancia propia entre padre e hijo, dijo ella, y su esposo no estaba dispuesto a tomar la iniciativa.

"Bien", respondió Boren, "entiendo lo que pueda sentir un padre, pero él fue presidente de los Estados Unidos y es un experto en este tema".

Bárbara Bush sacudió su cabeza de manera solemne, casi con tristeza.

Luego, Boren saludó a Bush padre.

"¿Te ves con nuestro amigo Colin?", le preguntó el ex presidente.

"Ocasionalmente".

"Asegúrate de decirle que creo que está haciendo una buena labor".

Ambos sabían que Powell era el guerrero renuente que intentaba solucionar el problema Irak por la vía diplomática.

"Sí, señor presidente", dijo Boren. "Por supuesto que lo haré; tengo la misma opinión suya".

EL TENIENTE GENERAL JOHN ABIZAID, lugarteniente del general Franks, era un antiguo experto militar sobre el Medio Oriente. Se había graduado en 1973 en la academia de West Point, poco después de Vietnam, y su participación en la invasión a Granada fue dramatizada en la película *El sargento de hierro*, filmada en 1986 y protagonizada por Clint Eastwood. Abizaid había hecho estudios de postgrado en Harvard y en la Universidad de Jordania. Hablaba árabe. Visitó por primera vez a Irak a finales de los años 70.

En su calidad de presidente del Estado Mayor Conjunto –había sucedido al vicealmirante Fry en 2001-2002–, Abizaid sintió todo el peso de la impaciencia de Rumsfeld, quien lo reprendía con frecuencia. "A veces era amable; otras veces no", le dijo a un colega. "Lo admiro mucho aunque, necesariamente, no me agrade… tiene una debilidad: es que quiere meter las manos en todo".

A comienzos de 2003, Abizaid estaba charlando con *Spider* Marks en la base del Ejército norteamericano en Kuwait. Hablaron de la Lista Maestra de Sitios con Armas de Destrucción Masiva.

"¿Qué crees, *Spider*?", le preguntó Abizaid. Puso sus brazos en los hombros del jefe de las fuerzas de inteligencia. "¿Qué piensas realmente sobre estos sitios con armas de destrucción masiva?".

"Me importa un carajo", dijo Marks. Fue una respuesta frívola para un general de alto rango, pero Marks conocía a Abizaid desde que ambos eran cadetes en West Point, y sabía que él quería una opinión sincera.

"Aunque las haya o no –y tengo que decirte que no puedo asegurarlo–, de todos modos tendré que hacer algo al respecto. Tendré que arriesgarme a que hombres y mujeres norteamericanos vayan y hagan algo".

Era una cruda reflexión sobre este problema. Aunque Marks no tenía el tiempo ni los recursos para saber con seguridad si realmente había ADM en los 946 sitios de la lista, tenía que proceder bajo la presunción de que sí las había. Para los generales pragmáticos que habían entablado una guerra debido a las supuestas ADM, la prueba supuestamente irrefutable de que Irak tenía este tipo de armas era cada vez menos relevante.

EN 1991, cuando era teniente coronel, Abizaid había comandado un batallón de infantería, al servicio de Garner, durante la Operación Provide Comfort. Garner opinaba que Abizaid conocía tan bien la mentalidad de los árabes y su actitud militar, que no tardó en pedirle consejos, y tomó nota de lo que dijo su antiguo subordinado. "Lo que tenemos que hacer es ofrecer una oportunidad para que el ejército iraquí salga de esto con alguna dosis de honor". El ejército iraquí estaba conformado mayoritariamente por sunitas, quienes se resistían a creer que lo estaban perdiendo todo.

En una entrevista posterior, Rumsfeld dijo que estaba de acuerdo con la visión de Abizaid. "Él pensaba eso de los sunitas; que estaban perdiendo el control del país, y procuraba que las decisiones fueran justas y representativas para ellos".

Garner coincidió en esto. La idea era derrotar al ejército iraquí y ocuparlo en labores de reconstrucción; hacer que reconstruyeran puentes, que manejaran la seguridad fronteriza y de todas las edificaciones. Había que mantenerlos ocupados, pues un ejército desocupado causaría problemas.

Abizaid le advirtió que la parte más difícil sería cuando derrotaran al ejército iraquí. Después de esto, señaló Abizaid, "habrá una gran cantidad de actividades terroristas. Tendremos que lidiar con muchas cosas: con una población civil molesta, con focos de resistencia y actividad guerrillera".

CASI A FINALES DE ENERO, Garner y su jefe de estado mayor, Jared Bates, un general de tres estrellas retirado del Ejército, se reunieron con el general Franks en el Pentágono. Los tres eran contemporáneos y habían sido comandantes de batallón en Alemania en los años 80. Estuvieron de acuerdo en que tenía mucho sentido que Garner y Franks se reportaran directamente a Rumsfeld.

"Tú y yo trabajamos para el mismo jefe", le dijo Franks a Garner, y añadió que le preocupaba el proceso del CNS, donde varios departamentos y agencias intentaban llegar a un consenso. "Lo que tienes que hacer es mantenerme alejado un tiempo de la pugna entre las agencias", dijo Franks, "pero haz que trabajen juntos y que no se hagan daño". Prometió que enviaría a Garner y a su equipo a Irak tan pronto terminaran los combates más cruentos. Luego hizo un comentario que dejó preocupados a los otros dos: "no creo que ustedes viajen antes de 60 o 90 días". Garner y Bates pensaron que sería una espera muy prolongada, pero ninguno de los dos dijo nada.

El 28 de enero, Garner se reunió con Zalmay M. Khalilzad, director del CNS para la región del Golfo, en el Edificio Eisenhower, a un lado de la Casa Blanca. Khalilzad había nacido y crecido en Afganistán y tenía un Ph.D. de la Universidad de Chicago. Era considerado neoconservador y había trabajado con Wolfowitz en las administraciones de Reagan y de Bush padre.

"Necesitamos conformar un grupo de asesores expertos que nos digan qué es lo que necesitamos hacer para transferirles el gobierno a los iraquíes", le dijo Khalilzad. Gracias a todas las conversaciones que había tenido con muchas personas, Garner había concluido que el plan norteamericano era instaurar un gobierno provisional. Khalilzad fue el primer funcionario de la administración en decirle básicamente: "No debemos hacer eso. Lo que necesitamos es hacer que los iraquíes se gobiernen a sí mismos tan rápido como sea posible.

"Estoy de acuerdo contigo", dijo Garner. Le había complacido la conversación, pues confirmó su idea de que tenía que transferir rápidamente el poder a los iraquíes. Había encontrado un aliado.

LA PRIMERA SEMANA de febrero de 2003, Garner y Bates volaron al cuartel general del Comando Central, localizado en Doha, Qatar, con el objeto de hablar detenidamente con Franks y Abizaid. Era como si estuvieran reviviendo viejos tiempos en el Ejército. Bates era muy cercano a Abizaid; había sido su superior en el 75º Regimiento Ranger, cuando era el segundo al mando de ese batallón. Abizaid era un teniente relativamente joven de la misma división. Los coroneles y los mayores son los mentores de los capitanes y comandantes del Ejército, y los oficiales de alto rango tienen una influencia perdurable en los estamentos militares.

Franks decía constantemente que Dough Feith era el "cabrón más imbécil, el hijo de puta más grande que hay sobre la tierra". Les dijo a Garner y a Bates: "Me siento muy cómodo al saber que ustedes dos están al mando". Les reiteró que no quería que le hablaran de Washington. "Concentrémonos en los camiones y en las ROWPU", dijo, refiriéndose a las Unidades de Purificación Acuática con Ósmosis Inversa[5], que extraían agua contaminada de los ríos y la purificaban. Franks estaba concentrado en los asuntos humanitarios.

Bates advirtió que Abizaid entendía muy bien cuál era la tarea más urgente. El especialista del Ejército en asuntos árabes estaba concentrado en el Irak después de la guerra, en lo que necesitaba hacerse y en la rapidez con que se hiciera.

Abizaid dijo que habría que instaurar un gobierno. "Tenemos que darle un aspecto iraquí; tiene que ser un gobierno multiétnico". El nuevo gobierno debería estar conformado por todos los iraquíes, no sólo por los sunitas, chiítas y kurdos, sino también por las diversas tribus y facciones, explicó. Los iraquíes no nos quieren, dijo, y no les gustará que estemos en su país. A Bates le agradó que Abizaid no quisiera reducir el problema a una simple etiqueta.

Sin embargo, Abizaid se mostró descontento con la forma en que Washington estaba planeando el período de posguerra. A cada rato escuchaba que al Pentágono le disgustaba profundamente el partido Baath de Saddam.

---

5. *Reverse Osmosis Water Purification Units*, según las siglas en inglés. (N. del E.)

De acuerdo; pero sí un iraquí quería un trabajo decente, especialmente en el gobierno, tenía que ser prácticamente miembro de ese partido. Abizaid dijo que los Estados Unidos iban a necesitar que algunos integrantes del partido Baath participaran en el nuevo gobierno.

Durante una reunión con Abizaid y varios funcionarios importantes que se encontraban esa semana en el cuartel general del Comando Central, Garner explicó que pensaba ir detrás de las unidades de combate cuando entraran a Irak.

"¿En serio?", preguntó la coronel Carol Stewart, directora de la división para asuntos de inteligencia del Comando Central. Ella se preguntó si Garner entendía que el plan de guerra no contemplaba la toma y ocupación de ciudades. No estamos pensando en tomar a Basora y a Nasiriyah; iremos directo a Bagdad.

"¿Quién se encargará de la seguridad de Irak?", preguntó Stewart. Garner dijo que esperaba que la policía iraquí lo hiciera. Stewart no estuvo de acuerdo pero no dijo nada, pues había muchos oficiales de rangos mayores del suyo.

Durante el mes anterior, la división de Stewart había intentado calcular cuántas tropas se necesitarían para el mantenimiento de la paz en Irak, teniendo como marco de referencia la experiencia norteamericana en Bosnia y Kosovo. Calcularon que la cifra ascendía a 450.000. Sin embargo, ningún oficial del Ejército estaba pensando en cifras tan altas, así que discutieron otras opciones. ¿Qué tal si en vez de ocupar todo el país se concentraban en las principales ciudades? Concluyeron que en el mejor de los casos, si las fuerzas americanas encontraban un ambiente de paz en Irak y los iraquíes respaldaban de manera irrestricta la ocupación norteamericana, necesitarían al menos 60.000 hombres; en caso contrario, si encontraban una fuerte oposición y eran atacados por los principales grupos étnicos iraquíes, calcularon que necesitarían de 180.000 a 200.000 para asegurar tan sólo las 26 o 27 ciudades más importantes.

Ese mismo día, en otra reunión que Garner sostuvo con otros altos oficiales, Stewart se expresó con mayor libertad, y declaró que todos los cálculos del Comando Central señalaban que no habría policía iraquí cuando invadieran a Irak.

"¿Qué quieres decir con que no habrá policía?", le preguntó un general.

"Sucederá lo mismo que en Panamá", respondió ella, refiriéndose a la invasión efectuada en 1989 por Estados Unidos con unos 24.000 militares. Cuando los norteamericanos derrocaron al gobierno y al ejército, la fuerza policial ya había dejado de existir. Lo mismo podía suceder en Irak.

Ella se dirigió a Garner: "Dijiste que irías detrás de las tropas de combate, y esa no es una buena idea".

Había más noticias desagradables. Un oficial señaló que si querían que la policía y otros cuerpos civiles hicieran su trabajo después de la invasión, alguien tendría que pagarles. Garner le dijo a Bates: "Tendremos que regresar a Washington y conseguir una chequera", dijo.

BATES SIGUIÓ MANTENIENDO contacto frecuente con Abizaid en los meses siguientes. Abizaid seguía expresando su preocupación por Washington; era algo más que los típicos comentarios de un militar estacionado quejándose de las altas esferas. Al término de una reunión formal, Bates y Abizaid hablaron como amigos. "Ya sabes", dijo Abizaid, "esos cabrones de Washington no tienen idea de lo que hacen; creo que voy a retirarme. No quiero seguir siendo parte de esto".

13

El vicepresidente Cheney creía firmemente que había una conexión entre Saddam y al Qaeda, pero la CIA no estaba de acuerdo. Tenet y sus hombres habían examinado la información tan exhaustivamente como era posible. Tenet dijo que, simplemente, no existía ninguna prueba. Era cierto que un jordano llamado Abu Musab al-Zarqawi, quien tenía fuertes vínculos con al Qaeda, había participado en varios atentados terroristas en Irak, y que el régimen de Saddam le había ofrecido asilo. Sin embargo, no existían evidencias que indicaran que Saddam, alguien en su nombre o algún miembro de los servicios de seguridad o inteligencia iraquíes tuvieran relación con Zarqawi.

"No puedo clasificarlo como autoridad, dirección y control", señaló Tenet, refiriéndose al alto estándar que debía tener dicha información como para establecer una conexión entre Saddam Hussein y al Qaeda.

Powell iba a pronunciar un discurso en las Naciones Unidas el 5 de febrero de 2003, para anunciar la guerra contra Irak por la existencia de ADM en ese país, y Cheney quería que el secretario de Estado incluyera el señalamiento expresado por *Scooter* Libby, su jefe de estado mayor, quien decía haber encontrado un vínculo entre Saddam y al Qaeda. El cargo presentado por Libby sostenía que Mohammed Atta, el líder de los ataques del 9/11, se había reunido cuatro veces con un oficial de la inteligencia iraquí en la ciudad de Praga. La CIA había revisado informaciones que hablaban de uno o dos encuentros, pero no había podido confirmar nada, y terminó por concluir que no existían evidencias de un solo encuentro.

Powell creía que el vínculo de Atta no existía y se negó a incluirlo en su discurso. También suavizó las declaraciones que haría sobre Zarqawi en su discurso ante la ONU. Pensaba referirse exclusivamente al potencial de un vínculo entre Irak y al Qaeda.

Desde el desierto de Kuwait, el coronel Rotkoff, lugarteniente de *Spider* Marks, vio por televisión el discurso pronunciado por Powell ante la ONU el 5 de febrero. A pesar de conocer personalmente la información existente sobre la LMSADM, Rotkoff no tenía la menor duda de que Saddam tenía este tipo de armas. Ver a Powell, un general retirado de cuatro estrellas muy respetado en los círculos militares, arriesgando su credibilidad al formular esta denuncia, contribuyó a afirmar la convicción de Rotkoff. Sólo les faltaba la prueba reina.

Todos los domingos, mientras esperaban el comienzo de la guerra, Rotkoff organizaba encuentros informales con los oficiales más destacados del equipo de *Spider* Marks. Estos encuentros, que muy pronto serían conocidos como las "sesiones vespertinas dominicales de oración", eran reuniones donde trabajaban un poco, comían *pizza*, bebían cerveza y sostenían discusiones informales en las cuales las ideas novedosas e innovadoras eran bienvenidas. Nunca invitaron a *Spider* Marks ni a otros generales, así que los oficiales no temían manifestar comentarios arriesgados, expresar sus verdaderos pensamientos o decir en voz alta algo estúpido frente a sus jefes.

Un domingo de comienzos de 2003, el coronel Steve Peterson, inteligente oficial del Ejército conocido por su pensamiento creativo, le preguntó a Rotkoff si podía liderar una de las sesiones.

Peterson hizo una presentación en Power Point que tenía el título de "La estrategia de Saddam Hussein para derribar helicópteros Black Hawk". Era una referencia a *El derribamiento del Black Hawk,* un renombrado libro escrito por Mark Bowden sobre la debacle acaecida en 1993, cuando 18 soldados norteamericanos murieron en un enfrentamiento urbano en Somalia, hecho que obligó al presidente Clinton a retirar las tropas norteamericanas de ese país. Somalia se había erigido como símbolo de la renuncia norteamericana a sufrir bajas en el futuro.

Peterson propuso que la premisa sobre la estrategia de Saddam para replegarse en Bagdad podría ser completamente errada. ¿Qué tal si Saddam desmantelaba sus tropas y practicaba ataques periódicos y sorpresivos a las fuerzas norteamericanas, creando así una insurgencia a largo plazo? Saddam debía saber que las fuerzas norteamericanas tenían un armamento, un sistema táctico y un ejército muy superiores a los suyos. Peterson se refirió a la suposición de que las fuerzas norteamericanas rompieran el cerco de Bagdad. Pero, ¿y qué si Saddam pensaba que la mejor estrategia era que los iraquíes ejecutaran una campaña de ataques pequeños pero efectivos, una especie de terrorismo urbano constante y a mansalva? En ese caso, las fuerzas norteamericanas se enfrentarían a una violencia interminable, sin saber quién perpetraría el ataque, dónde ni cuándo.

Peterson dijo que su teoría se derivaba de lo siguiente:

Primero, algunos informes de inteligencia norteamericanos señalaban que Saddam había ordenado la traducción del libro, y que les entregó copias a sus oficiales más importantes. Siempre hemos creído que su objetivo era levantar la moral de sus subalternos, dijo Peterson, y demostrarles que si mataban a unos pocos americanos, los Estados Unidos se retirarían. Pero,

¿y qué, si la verdadera lección que había aprendido Saddam de este libro era que los insurgentes podían adoptar tácticas exitosas contra una fuerza militar muy superior?

Segundo, Saddam había abierto las prisiones de Irak en octubre de 2002 y liberado a decenas de miles de prisioneros, tanto políticos como delincuentes comunes. ¿Y qué, si la idea era que formaran bandas de hostigamiento o fueran agentes individuales de la alteración del orden?

Tercero, había evidencias de varios depósitos de armas convencionales en Irak, armas de fuego y explosivos, que son particularmente útiles a los insurgentes.

Cuarto, la organización del partido Baath de Saddam en las diferentes ciudades se asemejaba de alguna manera a la estructura celular del comunismo, que funcionaba basada en relaciones informales y personales que eran muy eficientes para la comunicación entre los guerrilleros.

Sumen todo esto, dijo Peterson, y la estrategia de Saddam podría ser huir y esconderse, y utilizar células del partido Baath para organizar un ejército insurgente que contaría con armas y explosivos para entablar una guerra prolongada, hasta que los norteamericanos se cansaran y perdieran su voluntad política.

Su teoría era radical y echaba por el suelo todos los planes de guerra que predicaban una rápida derrota del ejército de Saddam. Rotkoff reconoció que se necesitaba estar muy seguro para inclinarse por una teoría diferente, especialmente ahora, cuando el momento se acercaba. Sin embargo, los demás asistentes parecían pensar que aquello no era factible; la teoría del "derribamiento del Black Hawk" era tan sólo una más.

EL 14 DE FEBRERO, el presidente se reunió con Franks y el CNS. Surgió una pregunta acerca de la protección de los campos petrolíferos iraquíes durante y después de la invasión.

"¿Cómo haremos para determinar si mantenemos a la policía local?", preguntó el presidente.

Franks le ofreció una respuesta esperanzadora. Según las notas de uno de los asistentes, el general le dijo a Bush: "Tengo alcaldes para todas las ciudades iraquíes y tengo fuerzas destacadas para hacerlo mañana mismo". Franks sugirió que ya había conseguido iraquíes dispuestos a comandar la policía.

GARNER HABLÓ con el teniente general George Casey, presidente del Estado Mayor Conjunto, y le solicitó 94 personas para las operaciones de posguerra. Casey, general de cuatro estrellas, sería el comandante de las fuerzas norteamericanas en Irak entre 2004 y 2006.

"Es mucha gente", le dijo Casey. "Déjame pensarlo".

Garner y Bates, su jefe de estado mayor, lo presionaron.

"Mira, George", le dijo Bates, "el tiempo se está acabando. Necesitamos a estas personas. ¿Has hecho un pedido formal?".

"No", respondió Casey, "no lo he hecho porque ustedes están tratando de convencerme de que ésta será una operación de 24 horas al día y siete días a la semana, y no creo que lo sea".

"George", dijo Garner, "estás desvariando. ¿No crees que trabajaremos tiempo completo?".

"No", respondió Casey.

Garner llamó de nuevo a Casey. "George, se trata de algo urgente". Propuso que se reunieran a las cinco de la tarde en la oficina de Rumsfeld. "Lo discutiremos frente a él, porque yo necesito esas 94 personas".

Casi una hora después, el jefe del Estado Mayor Conjunto llamó a Garner. "¿Cuántas personas necesitas?".

Garner, quien tenía sobre sus hombros toda la responsabilidad por el Irak de posguerra, el asunto más importante asumido por el gobierno norteamericano, estaba siendo prácticamente obligado a organizar un equipo de varios centenares de hombres, pero tenía que rogar, disuadir y amenazar para poder hacerlo.

En el 2006, le dije a Rumsfeld que yo creía que "por alguna razón, el gobierno le asignó la misión más importante a un equipo escogido 'a dedo'", y le pregunté: "¿Cree que es razonable?".

"Yo no lo pensaría en esos términos". Y señaló que muchas personas talentosas habían ido a Irak en calidad de voluntarios y habían efectuado las labores más difíciles. "Usted puede ser peyorativo y decir que fue un equipo escogido a dedo. Pero, realmente, no fue así". Luego sugirió que yo cometería un error histórico si hiciera semejante comparación. "Como dice tu viejo amigo", agregó, procurando imitar a Nixon: "eso estaría mal".

Garner también reclutó a Gordon Rudd, coronel retirado del Ejército que había sido el historiador militar oficial de la Operación *Provide Comfort* de 1991. Rudd tenía un Ph. D. en historia y vivía cerca de la base de los *marines* en Quantico, Virginia, donde era profesor de las directivas de la universidad. Rudd salía de su casa a las cinco de la mañana para evitar el tráfico pesado, trabajaba 14 horas al día; prácticamente dedicó su vida a este trabajo.

"Gordon", le dijo Garner en un corredor del Pentágono, "escríbeme un artículo explicando qué deberíamos hacer con el ejército iraquí".

Rudd se tomó un día, fue a la biblioteca y leyó todo lo que encontró sobre lo que había hecho Estados Unidos con los ejércitos de Alemania y Japón al final de la Segunda Guerra Mundial. También investigó cómo habían utilizado los Estados Unidos su propio aparato militar durante el *New Deal*[6], cuando desarrollaron organizaciones como los Cuerpos Civiles de Conservación. Escribió un artículo en el que decía que, si el ejército iraquí tenía divisiones acorazadas y de artillería, también debía tener unidades de ingeniería y mantenimiento. Esto significaba que también debía tener escuelas militares: una escuela de ingeniería, otra de transporte y, quizás, una escuela médica.

Propuso que lo que se debía hacer era controlar las unidades de infantería iraquíes valiéndose de las escuelas existentes, y capacitarlas en labores específicas de reconstrucción: una escuela para el desmantelamiento de minas, otra para la recolección y destrucción de explosivos, etcétera.

Sin embargo, Rudd no tardó en descubrir que nadie sabía dónde estaban las escuelas iraquíes, lo que significaba que era casi imposible conformar un plan pragmático. Consultó con un coronel de la inteligencia del Ejército y solicitó más información a la DIA y a la CIA, pero la respuesta que recibía era simplemente: "No sabemos".

LOS FUNCIONARIOS de diversos departamentos y agencias federales comenzaron a llegar a las oficinas de Garner. Parecía una de esas escenas de las viejas películas sobre la Segunda Guerra Mundial, en las que todos se preparaban apresuradamente, se movían de un lado a otro y parecían saber lo que hacían. Pero Garner vio que el panorama era caótico; pocos sabían quién estaba trabajando en qué. Todos deambulaban pero no estaba claro hacia dónde se dirigían.

"Regresaremos al adiestramiento con piedras", dijo Garner, retomando una antigua expresión militar que aludía a la costumbre castrense de que los comandantes de campo trazaban un plan militar en el suelo, utilizando piedras para representar las diferentes unidades.

El fin de semana del 21 al 22 de febrero, Garner reunió a unas 200 personas en la Universidad Nacional de Defensa de Fort McNair, en el suroeste de Washington, con el propósito de ensayo masivo y una conferencia sobre los planes de guerra.

Durante ese fin de semana, hubo dos preguntas que no fueron respondidas en conferencia, presentación de PowerPoint o discusión alguna: ¿Quién

---

6. Política económica aplicada entre 1933 y 1940 por la administración del presidente Roosevelt.

iba a gobernar a Irak el día que terminaran los combates fuertes? ¿Existía un proceso político en Irak que hiciera posible la contratación de personal que prestara los servicios básicos de seguridad, agua y electricidad, aspectos que normalmente eran responsabilidad de los alcaldes en las ciudades norteamericanas?

Poco después, uno de los participantes, que había hablado con Garner y otros funcionarios de alto nivel, analizó la conferencia en un informe de 20 páginas, el cual identificaba muchos problemas de planeación que aún había un mes antes de la guerra. En términos retrospectivos, este informe plantea advertencias claras y vigentes:

- Los actuales contingentes de fuerzas son inadecuados para el primer paso, consistente en asegurar todas las grandes zonas urbanas, y aun más para prestar servicios policiales interinos… Existe un gran riesgo de insurgencia popular y caos civil, cuya magnitud podría dar al traste con nuestra estrategia para la estabilización de Irak. En términos más inmediatos, si nuestras tropas se enfrascaran en una guerra total, correrán el peligro de ser más vulnerables.
- Parece bastante probable que emprenderemos acciones militares antes de saber si contaremos o no con fondos suficientes para la Fase IV. Si los fondos son insuficientes, corremos el riesgo de producir una situación caótica e inestable, que tiene todo el potencial de convertirse en un caldo de cultivo para los terroristas.
- Las diversas ideas presentadas sugieren una fuerte invasión imperial. ¡Peligro, peligro!
- La conferencia no ha respondido la pregunta principal: ¿Qué clase de gobierno tenemos en mente para Irak, y cómo pensamos instaurarlo?
- ¿Qué sucederá con la ley y el orden, si las tropas norteamericanas no tienen un plan coherente para la policía ni para el gobierno civil de Irak?

Asimismo, el informe explicaba que Garner había introducido en el adiestramiento con piedras la noción de que "había que identificar los obstáculos, pues si los problemas no se solucionan, las misiones correrán riesgos".

Este informe identificaba a varios de ellos.

"La seguridad", era uno. "Este es, de lejos, el desafío más grande y nuestra mayor falencia. Si no lo hacemos bien, es probable que cambiemos el régimen, pero la estrategia nacional podría venirse abajo y nuestras tropas terrestres estarán en peligro.

"Esta escasez absoluta de las fuerzas necesarias, complementada por los desafíos que enfrentaremos en materia de seguridad, ofrecen un panorama muy perturbador. Afortunadamente, el general Garner es totalmente consciente de la importancia y urgencia de este asunto. El general ha manifestado claramente que este aspecto es fundamental y que nuestras fuerzas son insuficientes; añadió que discutiría este problema con el secretario de Defensa y con la doctora Rice... esto podría ser de ayuda, siempre y cuando ella decida discutir con el presidente de los Estados Unidos los temas más importantes: la seguridad y los costos".

Garner y su equipo salieron muy preocupados. El segundo al mando del grupo de planeación de posguerra era Ron Adams, otro general de tres estrellas retirado del Ejército, quien escribió en sus apuntes: "Suposiciones erróneas. Excesivamente optimistas. Ausencia de realismo". Posteriormente, Adams recordó: "Personalmente, salí más perturbado después del adiestramiento con piedras que cuando entré; me sentí incómodo desde el comienzo".

DURANTE EL PRIMER adiestramiento con piedras, Garner había observado a una persona que formulaba reparos a todo. El general pensó que era un verdadero "resorte", alguien que saltaba a toda hora de su asiento para cuestionar todos los asuntos. Garner habló con él durante el descanso.

"Quisiera hablar contigo", le dijo.

"Me llamo Tom Warrick", dijo. Era un funcionario civil del Departamento de Estado, de 48 años.

"¿Por qué sabes tanto?".

"He estado estudiando este tema desde hace un año y medio", señaló Warrick.

"¿Para quién has estudiado?".

"Para el Departamento de Estado", replicó Warrick. Dijo que había escrito un extenso informe sobre el Irak de posguerra. "Se llama 'El futuro de Irak'".

A Garner le pareció muy interesante; había oído hablar vagamente del estudio.

"¿Y por qué no trabajas para mí?".

"Me encantaría hacerlo", respondió Warrick.

"Quedas contratado", le dijo Garner. "Preséntate el lunes por la mañana con todas tus cosas".

Warrick llegó al Pentágono el lunes siguiente. Al mediodía, Garner vio que la mitad de las personas que estaban trabajando con Warrick estaban enfadadas con éste. Garner se alegró; necesitaban a alguien como él, a una persona que los desafiara, los pusiera en su sitio y los provocara. "Habla con todos y los hace reaccionar", señaló posteriormente Garner, quien había leído casi todo el estudio. No estaba de acuerdo con todo lo que decía, pero le parecía suficientemente útil y provocador.

Pocos días después, Garner fue citado a la oficina de Rumsfeld para una importante reunión con Wolfowitz, el general Myers y con el general Pete Pace, vicepresidente del Estado Mayor.

"Jay", dijo Rumsfeld en un momento dado, "¿por qué no te quedas cuando terminemos? Necesito que miremos un par de cosas".

Cuando todos los asistentes salieron, el secretario de Defensa se dirigió a su escritorio y comenzó a hurgar entre sus papeles; comenzó a exasperarse, pues no podía encontrar lo que estaba buscando. Finalmente sacó una pequeña hoja.

"Jay", le dijo mirándolo. "¿Hay dos personas en tu equipo de apellidos Warrick y O'Sullivan?

"Sí", respondió Garner. "Tengo uno que se llama Tom Warrick; escribió un estudio titulado 'El futuro de Irak', y tengo una chica que se llama Meghan O'Sullivan; es muy talentosa".

O'Sullivan, que también trabajaba en el Departamento de Estado, se había incorporado recientemente al equipo de Garner. Tenía 33 años, era muy inteligente, tenía un doctorado en ciencias políticas de la Universidad de Oxford y había escrito ampliamente sobre Irak y otros Estados rebeldes.

"Tengo que pedirte que los saques de tu equipo", dijo Rumsfeld.

"No puedo hacerlo. Son demasiado valiosos".

Rumsfeld miró un momento a Garner. "Mira, Jay. He recibido esta petición desde una esfera tan alta que no puedo rechazarla. Así que tengo que pedirte que los saques de tu equipo".

"¿No podemos llegar a un acuerdo en esto?", preguntó Garner.

"Lo siento, pero no", respondió Rumsfeld.

¿La petición venía desde tan arriba que el secretario de Defensa no podía rechazarla? Garner pensó que sólo podía tratarse de Bush o de Cheney.

Cuando regresó a su oficina, Garner no pudo localizar a Warrick ni a O'Sullivan. Le comentó lo sucedido a Tom Baltazar, un coronel del Ejército que se desempeñaba como su oficial de operaciones. "Eso está muy raro", dijo Baltazar.

"Búscalos", le dijo Garner. "Diles que regresen a sus empleos anteriores; que yo los llamaré de nuevo. Diles que se trata de algo temporal".

Garner habló con Steve Hadley, el asesor auxiliar de seguridad nacional.

"Realmente quiero que ellos dos regresen a mi equipo", le dijo a Hadley.

"No creo que podamos ayudarte en eso".

Garner siguió insistiendo. Warrick y O'Sullivan sabían muy bien de qué hablaban. Faltaba poco tiempo para viajar al Medio Oriente, y Garner los necesitaba.

"El caso del hombre es sumamente difícil", dijo Hadley. Sería imposible reintegrar a Warrick, aunque pareció sugerir que había una posibilidad para O'Sullivan.

Esa noche, Baltazar llamó a Garner para informarle que ya los había despedido.

"Tom", le dijo Garner, "¿de dónde diablos crees que vino la orden?".

"No sé, pero tengo un amigo que trabaja en la Casa Blanca. Lo llamaré más tarde a su teléfono privado; no quiero llamarlo a su línea oficial".

Baltazar llamó a P. J. Dermer, un coronel del Ejército que trabajaba para *Scooter* Libby, el jefe de gabinete del vicepresidente; su línea privada era segura. En última instancia, dijo Dermer, todo tenía que ver con Ahmed Chalabi, un expatriado iraquí que era director del Congreso Nacional iraquí, grupo radicado en Londres y apoyado por los Estados Unidos. Cheney estaba promoviendo la idea de que Chalabi era la respuesta a todos los problemas, y Warrick no tenía una buena opinión de él. Dermer explicó que la oposición a Warrick provenía de "un grupo de unas cinco personas" de la oficina de Cheney. Dijo que se trataba de un "conciliábulo".

El día siguiente por la mañana, Baltazar le dijo a Garner: "Fue el vicepresidente; no soporta a ninguno de los dos".

Warrick había trabajado en la administración de Clinton, y era un firme partidario de que Saddam Hussein fuera enjuiciado como criminal de guerra; había trabajado en el Departamento de Estado planeando eventuales cambios en el régimen. Se había reunido con muchos exiliados iraquíes, y había descubierto que muchos de ellos no estaban exactamente enamorados de Chalabi. De hecho, Warrick había asistido en 2002 a una conferencia organizada por los líderes de la oposición iraquí, en la que muchos manifestaron que no regresarían a su país si Chalabi y su Congreso Nacional iraquí asumían el poder.

O'Sullivan había trabajado en la Brookings Institution, un *think tank* de centro izquierda, y era considerada como una protegida de Richard N. Haass, el director de planeación de políticas del Departamento de Estado durante el secretariado de Powell. Ella y Haass habían escrito un documento en el cual recomendaban la utilización de incentivos económicos, políticos o culturales en países como Irak, en lugar de recurrir a acciones militares o a operaciones encubiertas. O'Sullivan había escrito otro documento en el que cuestionaba el apoyo ofrecido por los Estados Unidos a los exiliados iraquíes.

Garner creía que ese ardid era una mala señal. Le disgustó que las personalidades y la ideología influyeran en un asunto tan crucial como la planeación de posguerra. Haber perdido a Warrick, un gran experto en dichos asuntos, fue un fuerte golpe. Sin embargo, el equipo de Garner retomó varias ideas de "El futuro de Irak", y muchos de los iraquíes que habían trabajado en este documento terminaron incorporándose al equipo de Garner. Este incidente demostró las profundas disputas que existían entre los departamentos de Defensa y de Estado.

Powell se enteró de lo que había hecho Rumsfeld. "¿Qué diablos está sucediendo?", le preguntó por teléfono a Rumsfeld.

Éste respondió que necesitaban personas que estuvieran realmente comprometidas y que no hubieran dicho o escrito cosas que no sirvieran de apoyo.

Powell lo tomó como si los funcionarios del Departamento de Estado no respaldaran a exiliados como Chalabi. El secretario de Estado y el secretario de Defensa no tardaron en enfrascarse en una disputa acalorada. "Yo también puedo tomar prisioneros", le dijo Powell.

GARNER HABLÓ de nuevo con Rumsfeld: "Déjeme reintegrar a estas dos personas", le dijo.

"No puedo hacerlo", respondió Rumsfeld. "Te dije que de esferas muy altas me ordenaron que retirara a estas personas. Te pedí que lo hicieras y así lo hiciste. Ya no puedo volver atrás". Finalmente, Rumsfeld dijo: "Está bien, llama a la mujer". Garner podía contar con O'Sullivan. "Nadie lo sabrá".

Powell se enteró de la decisión de Rumsfeld, y se preguntó si las cosas podrían ser más extrañas. Consiguió a siete funcionarios del Departamento de Estado, pues pensaba que podían serle útiles a Garner, pero Dough Feith no quería trabajar con funcionarios de ese departamento. Powell reclamó que eso era absurdo y se enfrascó de nuevo en una disputa con Rumsfeld. Sin embargo, y luego de una semana de arduas disputas, Powell consiguió que cinco de sus siete candidatos fueran incorporados al equipo de Garner.

EL PROBLEMA DE FONDO era que no había siquiera un solo plan, pensó Paul Hughes, un coronel del Ejército que estaba en el equipo de Garner. No había ningún documento que señalara: *Estos son los objetivos. Esta es la persona que estará al mando. Estas son las tareas prioritarias. Estas son las medidas que adoptaremos para restaurar el orden.* Garner había intentado armar el rompecabezas con el adiestramiento con piedras, pero estaba muy lejos de lograrlo.

Hughes, oficial de 50 años alto y elegante que había prestado servicio activo durante 28 años, había sido director de los estudios de seguridad nacional en la Universidad de Defensa Nacional antes de incorporarse al equipo de Garner. Él y Thomas Gross, coronel y miembro del equipo, eran conocidos como "La firma legal", y tenían considerable influencia. Incluso, en algunos de los listados oficiales de teléfonos, donde sus colegas eran identificados por la división en la que trabajaban, Hughes y Gross aparecían simplemente como, "Firma legal".

Hughes llevaba unos seis meses trabajando en el Irak de posguerra, y en noviembre de 2002 había organizado un encuentro de dos días sobre este tema. La Universidad Nacional de Defensa había publicado un informe de 41 páginas con sus conclusiones, que llegó a manos de Jim Thomas, asistente especial de Paul Wolfowitz.

Hughes proponía un plan colectivo, pero la oficina de Feith le respondió con un simple "no". Hughes veía que un documento semejante requeriría de manera casi inevitable un trabajo conjunto entre las diferentes agencias que, incluyera al Departamento de Estado y a la CIA. Sin embargo, este plan no podría efectuarse, pues la NSPD-24 había creado la oficina de Garner y le había conferido expresamente al Departamento de Estado la autoridad y responsabilidad por los planes de posguerra en Irak.

RUMSFELD INVITÓ a un grupo de expertos al Pentágono para discutir la situación del Irak de posguerra. Uno de ellos era James F. Dobbins, probablemente la persona con mayor experiencia en la dirección de situaciones posteriores a conflictos. Dobbins, veterano y elegante diplomático de 60 años, era todo un experto en estos asuntos; había sido el enviado norteamericano a Kosovo, Bosnia, Haití y Somalia, donde había supervisado las famosas y controvertidas misiones de reconstrucción y estabilización en los años 90. Actualmente trabajaba en la Rand Corporation, un *think tank*, como director de política internacional y de seguridad.

En el 2001, Powell lo había comisionado para que coordinara las negociaciones entre los grupos opositores afganos, y encontrara un líder después de la caída del régimen talibán. Era una típica labor de mediación, que requería, tanto negociar con las diversas agencias y departamentos norteamericanos, como con gobiernos extranjeros. Varios oficiales de la CIA propusieron a Hamid Karzai, un líder moderado que había ocupado un cargo secundario en un ministerio afgano cuando los talibanes estaban en el poder, aunque luego desertó y se unió a las filas de la oposición. El general Franks, varios funcionarios de la CIA y de los departamentos de Defensa y Estado, dieron su consentimiento. Una vez logrado el consenso dentro de la burocracia estadounidense, Dobbins encabezó una conferencia en las Naciones Unidas, en Bonn, Alemania, en la que las facciones afganas efectuaron encuentros que se prolongaron toda la noche, con el fin de elegir un líder. Dobbins convenció a los principales actores regionales –rusos, los paquistaníes e, incluso, iraníes–, para que respaldaran a Karzai, quien juró como presidente de Afganistán el 22 de diciembre de 2001, tan sólo 102 días después del 9/11.

En el Pentágono, uno de los subalternos de Feith les entregó a Dobbins y a otros expertos independientes un plan de posguerra que parecía contemplar una ocupación completa de Irak. A Dobbins le pareció que ése era el plan que ellos querían adoptar: un procónsul con poderes casi absolutos, tal como sucedió con el general Douglas MacArthur después de la Segunda Guerra Mundial. Los Estados Unidos prepararían a Irak para que celebraran elecciones, y la soberanía les sería devuelta a los iraquíes.

Poco después, Rumsfeld se reunió con Dobbins y los demás expertos.

"Creo que desarrollamos una buena labor en Afganistán", dijo el secretario, reconociendo los buenos oficios de Dobbins, "y espero que podamos hacer lo mismo en Irak, es decir que reunamos a un grupo representativo de iraquíes y encontremos al Hamid Karzai iraquí".

Rumsfeld declararía posteriormente: "Me incliné por esta opción, una transferencia rápida del poder, y el presidente lo hizo... Es obvio que se necesitaba una figura a la que el pueblo considerara con capacidad de ejercer liderazgo en ese país. Yo siempre he creído que las tropas extranjeras son una anomalía y que, eventualmente, la situación se torna artificial; realmente, no son bienvenidas. También hay que tener en cuenta el concepto del rechazo al consentimiento".

A Dobbins le alegró que hubiera un plan B, la conferencia de Bonn que proponía una transferencia rápida del poder y la formación de un gobierno iraquí. Se preguntó cuál modelo implementarían, si el de MacArthur o el de Karzai. Parecía que no había un plan bien definido para ninguno de los dos, y tampoco había consenso dentro de la administración. Dobbins veía con mucha claridad que la administración no entendía la gran dimensión de la labor que tenían por delante, no sólo en materia de seguridad, economía y gobernabilidad, sino también en el sentido de restañar las viejas heridas causadas por la dictadura y por el odio entre los sunitas, que controlaron a Irak bajo Saddam, y los chiítas, quienes constituían la mayoría de la población.

Bush había menospreciado la reconstrucción nacional en la campaña presidencial del 2000, pero ahora esta administración iba tener que sumergirse de lleno en esta empresa tan crucial.

GARNER LLEVABA SEIS SEMANAS en su cargo cuando fue a la Casa Blanca la mañana del viernes 28 de febrero de 2003, para hablar por primera vez con el presidente Bush e informarle lo que estaba haciendo su equipo. Mientras esperaba afuera de la Sala de Situaciones, donde estaban reunidos el presidente y el gabinete de guerra, Garner reconoció a John Ashcroft, el procurador general.

"Parece que los dos estamos desinformados", dijo Garner con nerviosismo, intentando romper el hielo.

Ashcroft respondió con una mirada que a Garner le pareció que quería decir "vete al infierno".

Garner se sentó en un extremo de una mesa reluciente que había en la Sala de Situaciones. El presidente estaba en el otro extremo, y los más altos funcionarios, Powell, Rumsfeld, Rice y Tenet, estaban a ambos lados. El general Franks también se encontraba allí, y Cheney estaba en la pantalla de la teleconferencia. Frank Miller, director del CNS para asuntos de defensa, estaba presentando un informe. Garner se sentía nervioso, pues notaba que presidente no tenía la menor idea acerca de quién era él.

Mientras Miller presentaba su informe, Bush alternó su atención entre Miller y Garner; miró intensamente al primero y luego le lanzó una mirada rápida a Garner, antes de concentrar de nuevo su atención en Miller. Los miró alternativamente dos veces más.

"Será un largo día", pensó Garner. Bush levantó súbitamente su dedo pulgar en dirección a Garner, quien inmediatamente se sintió mejor; creyó que el presidente percibía su incomodidad y le estaba dando ánimos.

"Está bien, ¿quién sigue?", preguntó el presidente cuando Miller terminó.

"El general Garner está en el grupo de planeación de la posguerra", dijo Rice, "y él le hablará sobre esto".

"Antes de que lo hagas", le dijo el presidente, "háblame de un poco de ti".

"No, yo le hablaré de él", lo interrumpió Rumsfeld, y acto seguido hizo un recuento de la trayectoria de Garner en el Ejército, de su éxito en la Operación *Provide Comfort*, y de su desempeño en la comisión espacial de Rumsfeld.

"Eso está bien", dijo Bush. Luego se dirigió a Garner: "Adelante".

Garner distribuyó copias de su presentación, que constaba de 11 puntos, y comenzó a hablar. Abordó las nueve tareas que le había comisionado la NSPD-24, y dijo que cuatro de ellas no deberían ser responsabilidad suya, pues desbordaban claramente las capacidades de su pequeño equipo. Esas cuatro tareas eran: desmantelar las ADM, derrotar a los terroristas, reformar el aparato militar iraquí y reestructurar otras instituciones de seguridad interna.

En otras palabras, eran cuatro tareas realmente difíciles. Garner señaló que deberían ser responsabilidad de los militares.

El presidente asintió. Nadie intervino, a pesar de que Garner les había dicho que no podían responsabilizarlo de unas tareas de posguerra tan importantes —que eran precisamente las que tenían mayor relación con la razón esgrimida para declarar la guerra— porque su equipo no podía realizarlas.

Nadie preguntó quién se encargaría de esto si Garner no iba a hacerlo. ¿Permitirían que estos aspectos permanecieran flotando en el aire? ¿Serían importantes para ellos? Quizás Garner estuviera equivocado, quizás él pudiera o debiera encargarse de esos asuntos. La trascendencia de lo que había dicho pareció ser ajena a los pensamientos de todos los asistentes.

A continuación, Garner explicó que pretendía dividir a Irak en varias zonas, y luego se refirió a los planes entre las diferentes agencias.

"Un minuto", lo interrumpió el presidente, "¿de dónde eres?".

"De Florida, señor presidente".

"¿Por qué hablas así?", le preguntó Bush, como si estuviera tratando de identificar su acento".

"Porque nací y crecí en un rancho de la Florida. Mi papá era ranchero".

"Bienvenido al equipo", le dijo el *ranchero mayor* en señal de aprobación. Su hermano Jeb era gobernador de ese Estado, y el presidente lo visitaba con frecuencia.

Garner siguió explicando que todos los departamentos y agencias tenían que "hacer operativos" sus planes y tener una "visión" sobre los resultados finales, particularmente desde los primeros 30 días hasta un año después.

El general expuso su noción de los obstáculos, es decir, los problemas que podían poner en peligro la misión en Irak o, incluso, frenarla por completo. También necesitaba dinero, agregó.

El presidente lo escuchó.

Garner se refirió al *adiestramiento con piedras* y explicó cómo pensaban mantener la estabilidad en Irak después de los combates.

El general se refirió a "la utilización del ejército regular iraquí en la era de posguerra". Dijo: "Vamos a utilizar al Ejército; necesitamos hacerlo. Ellos tienen la formación necesaria".

"¿Cuántos crees que son?", preguntó uno de los asistentes.

"Daré un estimado amplio", respondió Garner. "Creo que entre 200.000 y 300.000".

El general miró a su alrededor. Todos parecían embelesados; nadie lo contradijo. Nadie formuló una sola pregunta sobre su plan.

Luego, Garner dijo que quería internacionalizar las labores de posguerra e inmediatamente notó cierto malestar en la sala. No por parte de Powell, pero sí de casi todos los demás. Concluyó que había muchas disputas y dedujo que la mayoría de los asistentes debían estar pensando: "¿Es que no entiendes? No queremos internacionalizar esto. Es una operación norteamericana".

Garner dijo que enviaría el primer contingente en unos diez días, y el resto diez días después. El presidente no dijo nada. Nadie dijo cuándo podría comenzar la guerra, pero era obvio que sería muy pronto.

"Muchas gracias", le dijo Bush cuando Garner terminó. Rice comenzó a hablar de otro tema. Garner supuso que lo darían de baja. El presidente lo miró cuando se iba a retirar de la sala.

"Dales duro en el trasero, Jay", le dijo Bush.

Garner esperó afuera a Rumsfeld. Bush y Rice salieron, y cuando estaban tres o cuatro pasos adelante de él, Bush se dio vuelta y le dijo:

"Oye, si tienes algún problema con ese gobernador de Florida, me lo dejas saber".

14

DESPUÉS DE QUE POWELL había atenuado la teoría de una conexión entre Hussein y al Qaeda en su discurso del 5 de febrero ante las Naciones Unidas, Cheney quiso incluir esta acusación en su discurso. Tenet se molestó; era una mentira. Consultó con su amigo John Brennan si haría bien en renunciar a su cargo. Sin embargo, Tenet no quería ser el director de inteligencia desleal que desertaba durante una crisis nacional o ante la inminencia de una guerra.

Habló con el presidente y le dijo que la inteligencia de la CIA no apoyaba la acusación que Cheney iba a formular en su discurso. Señaló que no existían pruebas de que Saddam tuviera "autoridad, dirección y control" sobre ninguna ayuda iraquí a la organización de al Qaeda. También le dijo al presidente que si Cheney mencionaba esto en su discurso, la CIA no podía ni iba a apoyarlo.

Bush respaldó a Tenet y le dijo a Cheney que no pronunciara su discurso.

GARNER FUE EL 3 DE MARZO a la sede de las Naciones Unidas en la ciudad de Nueva York sin informarle a nadie de la Casa Blanca o del Pentágono. Él y Ron Adams, su lugarteniente, creían firmemente que la mejor opción era que la guerra fuera el producto de una coalición. Garner decidió tratar de obtener personalmente la aprobación de las Naciones Unidas en tantas actividades de posguerra como fuera posible.

Este contacto era peligroso porque la Casa Blanca y el Pentágono tenían muy poco interés en las Naciones Unidas. El comentario de Garner acerca de "internacionalizar" los operativos no había tenido una buena acogida en la reunión con el CNS.

Louise Fréchette, subsecretaria general de la ONU, presidió el encuentro.

"La ONU está trabajando intensamente a fin de ofrecer una ayuda humanitaria inmediata, y no está interesada en otras labores", dijo Fréchette.

Garner le preguntó si la ONU podía al menos asignarle un enlace oficial. No, le dijo Fréchette.

Garner comprendió que no podía contar con el apoyo de esta organización. Luego se reunió con Jeremy Greenstock, el embajador británico ante la ONU, quien tenía un aspecto que denotaba profundo cansancio y agotamiento físico. La tensión que le había producido su campaña para que la ONU expidiera una segunda resolución para la inspección de armas en Irak –un esfuerzo que no tardaría en fracasar–, le estaba cobrando un alto precio.

"Estamos contigo en este aspecto", le dijo Greenstock. "Estamos juntos en esto, pero si logramos internacionalizar este esfuerzo, las cosas serán mucho más fáciles para todos nosotros". Él se refería especialmente al primer ministro Blair, quien le había prometido a su partido Laborista que buscaría una segunda resolución de la ONU. Tradicionalmente, el partido laborista le rendía homenaje a las Naciones Unidas.

Luego llegó John D. Negroponte, embajador norteamericano ante la ONU. "Mucha suerte", le dijo a Garner, y se marchó. El general advirtió que Negroponte tenía un aspecto mucho más descansado que Greenstock; a fin de cuentas, no tenía que dedicar su tiempo a rendirle homenaje a la ONU.

El día siguiente, cuatro de marzo, Doug Feith le presentó un informe secreto al presidente y al CNS, incluida una presentación en PowerPoint, sobre los "objetivos norteamericanos y de la coalición" para la guerra contra Irak. Era un compendio de ciencia política demasiado prometedor, que iba desde mejorar notablemente la calidad de vida de los iraquíes hasta moverse en dirección a la democracia y obtener "participación internacional en la reconstrucción".

Era una lista de deseos llena de esperanzas, pero sin los procedimientos necesarios para realizarlas.

Garner ignoraba que Feith se había reunido con el presidente. Un día después habló con Rice en su acogedora oficina del ala Oeste, la cual tenía techos altos, paredes pintadas de azul y una puerta sumamente gruesa; había sido la oficina del asesor de seguridad nacional durante varias décadas.

Garner le informó que había ido el lunes a las Naciones Unidas, que había solicitado un enlace oficial y que su petición había sido rechazada.

Rice permaneció en silencio.

"No quieren trabajar en tareas adicionales", continuó Garner. "Están dispuestos a ayudar pero necesitan entender nuestro concepto. Es por eso que nos han repetido varias veces, 'No entendemos su concepto. ¿Por qué van a hacerlo solos?'".

Rice continuó sin decir nada.

Garner consultó lo escrito en su agenda y señaló que necesitaba "fondos para comenzar" a trabajar en asuntos básicos como suministro de alimentos, la energía, y el cumplimiento de la ley.

"Está bien", dijo Rice, mirando a Hadley y a Frank Miller. "Comencemos a trabajar en esto. Tengámoslo listo para cuando lo necesiten".

Hadley y Miller parecían estar tomando notas, pero a Garner le dio la impresión de que las palabras de Rice se habían quedado flotando en el aire. Le pareció que no había ningún sistema de seguimiento.

Necesitamos dinero para pagarles a los servidores públicos, a la policía y a los militares iraquíes, le dijo Garner a Rice. "Pienso pagarles tan pronto llegue a Irak".

Garner supo que los Estados Unidos habían congelado fondos iraquíes por un valor de 1.600 millones de dólares, y calculó que, si tenía acceso a ese dinero, podría pagarles durante 90 días a los empleados civiles, especialmente a la policía y a unos 200.000 militares iraquíes.

Rice pareció estar de acuerdo con él.

El próximo tema de su agenda eran los ministerios. ¿Quién sería el funcionario americano designado para dirigir el Ministerio de Agricultura de Irak? ¿Quién sería el del Interior? Garner dijo que necesitaba conseguir personas que desempeñaran estos cargos, pero que aún muchos estaban vacantes.

Garner pasó a un tema crucial: todos sabían que no tenían fuerzas suficientes y que necesitaban mayor seguridad.

"¿Qué piensas al respecto?", le preguntó Rice.

Ambos sabían que parte de la respuesta era que Rumsfeld y Franks todavía estaban trabajando en el plan de guerra final. Garner creía que el último plan de Franks contemplaba un pie de fuerza muy inferior a los 500.000 hombres estipulados en el plan inicial de guerra contra Irak; tal vez fueran apenas unos 160.000. Pero si se incorporaban otros 100.000 al pie de fuerza norteamericano cuando comenzaran los combates, y si lograban que los entre 200.000 y 300.000 miembros del ejército iraquí cooperaran con las fuerzas norteamericanas, era posible lograr alguna dosis de seguridad y estabilidad.

En lo referente a los contratos para la reconstrucción y el desarrollo económico, Garner dijo que probablemente sería necesario que todos los contratistas tuvieran uno o varios subcontratistas iraquíes; sería una especie de reserva monetaria que permitiría que el dinero llegara a manos de iraquíes comunes y corrientes.

¿Y qué del número de policías y de otros oficiales representantes de la ley? Garner quería mucho dinero, pero Frank Miller sólo estaba dispuesto a suministrar 70 millones de dólares. Garner creía que esto valdría cientos de millones, pero propuso que esperaran. "No nos decidamos por un número reducido ni alto; dejemos esto abierto, de tal suerte que si yo tengo la razón, ustedes puedan ayudarme tan rápido como sea posible; y si es él quien tiene la razón, no habremos perdido nada. Sin embargo, no creo que él tenga la razón".

El próximo tema fue el dinero. "Quien tenga el dinero, tendrá el control", dijo Garner. "¿Dónde está el dinero? Lo necesito".

Rice parecía apoyarlo; sin embargo, Garner no había recibido una confirmación real sobre el dinero. Comprendió que al presidente, a Rice y a los demás les habían dicho que la guerra sería muy fácil, quizás, incluso, "un paseo", para utilizar un término expresado en *The Washington Post* por el halcón Ken Adelman, viejo amigo de Cheney y de Rumsfeld. Al igual que la mayoría de los temas, el del dinero quedó sin respuesta.

El último tema era la "gobernabilidad" ¿Cómo iban a conformar un gobierno de posguerra en Irak?, preguntó Garner. Esta era la pregunta primordial en términos de poder político. ¿Quién lo detentaría después de la guerra? Seguramente alguien; pero, ¿quién?

Rice nunca ofreció una respuesta.

El viernes 7 de mayo, Garner y Ron Adams se reunieron con Wolfowitz. Se sentían frustrados y se quejaron de que ni siquiera sabían cuándo viajarían a Kuwait. Escasamente sabían cómo llegarían allá, o dónde esperarían el comienzo de la guerra. Nadie les había dicho para cuándo estaba programado el estallido de la guerra.

"Ya deberían estar allá", les dijo Wolfowitz, quien probablemente tenía una idea de la fecha, pues era el segundo funcionario más importante del Pentágono.

SPIDER MARKS ESTABA ESTACIONADO en el desierto de Kuwait. Desconfiaba y renegaba de lo que llamaba su cadena de mando "técnica" entre los oficiales de inteligencia, incluido el brigadier general Jeff Kimmons, oficial de inteligencia de cabecera de Franks. La información que tenían sobre la LMSADM no era suficientemente confiable.

"Es completamente insatisfactoria", le dijo a Kimmons. "Jeff, tienes que rodar la bola. Yo no voy a llamar a la oficina de Rumsfeld ni a Cambone", el subsecretario de inteligencia del Departamento de Defensa. "No sabe quién soy yo. Lo cierto es que esto no está funcionando".

Esta era una ilustración vívida de la crisis. El general, cuya labor era descubrir y desmantelar las ADM que tenía Saddam Hussein, había mirado los frutos de más de una década de trabajo de inteligencia y concluyó que tenía muchas falencias. Bush y otros altos funcionarios de la administración habían subido el tono de la retórica. Ari Fleischer, el portavoz de la Casa Blanca, declaró el 5 de diciembre de 2002: "El presidente de los Estados Unidos y el secretario de Defensa no hubieran asegurado con total certeza, así como lo hicieron, que Irak tiene armas de destrucción masiva, si esto no fuera cierto, y si no tuvieran bases sólidas para afirmarlo". Fleischer anunció de nuevo el 9 de enero de 2003: "Sabemos a ciencia cierta que las armas están allí". En su alocución radial semanal, Bush declaró el 8 de febrero: "Nuestras fuentes nos han informado que Saddam Hussein autorizó recientemente a los comandantes de campo iraquíes para que utilizaran armas químicas, las mismas que el dictador niega tener".

Marks comprendió el aprieto por el que pasaba Kimmons; era semejante al suyo. Sólo eran un par de generales subalternos observando la misma maraña de información insatisfactoria. Kimmons estaba confrontando su propio infierno personal; Marks creyó que no había acudido a Franks por temor a desencadenar las explosiones notorias y profanas de este general. Kimmons podía terminar con un agujero en el pecho y, peor aún, estar tan lejos como siempre de una solución.

Pero la inteligencia no estaba logrando ningún progreso. Si Cambone y Rumsfeld no tenían la menor idea de quién era Marks, tal vez eso fuera un problema. Marks le había comentado sus preocupaciones a McKiernan, a Abizaid y a Kimmons, pero ¿podría acaso hacer algo desde el desierto de Kuwait para encender las alarmas en la cadena de mando y hacer que lo escucharan? En ese caso, ¿no deberían Rumsfeld, Franks –o, incluso, Bush– descender un peldaño o dos en la cadena de mando, buscar a un general que se encargara de la inteligencia para encontrar las ADM y preguntarle qué pensaba de todo esto? La respuesta era demasiado ambigua.

"Siguen las confusiones", escribió Marks en su diario. "¿Aseguraremos las zonas cuando pasemos por ellas, o las consideramos como obstáculos, las señalamos, las cubrimos y seguimos?". Marks continuaba esperando una respuesta coherente a una de las preguntas que había lanzado el 4 de octubre, durante el encuentro con los "sabios" de la DIA: ¿Cómo establecemos una prioridad entre los 946 sitios sospechosos de almacenar ADM en Irak?

LA GUERRA ERA A TODAS LUCES INMINENTE, pero Garner seguía en el Pentágono. Creía que la pregunta recurrente acerca de la gobernabilidad tenía que ser resuelta, pues quería conformar los ministerios iraquíes de inmediato. Sin embargo, la pregunta seguía irresuelta: ¿Quién estaría al mando? En una ocasión, Rumsfeld le había hecho una pregunta muy a su manera. "A propósito, ¿qué vas a hacer con respecto a la *desbaathización*? ¿Ya tienes un proceso de *desbaathización*?". Garner iba a tener que olvidarse de los miembros del partido Baath de Saddam, así como ocurrió durante la *desnazificación* de Alemania al término de la Segunda Guerra Mundial.

"Los ministerios no pueden ser *desbaathizados*", respondió Garner. "No quedaría nadie". La mayoría de los cargos estaban ocupados por miembros del partido. "Lo mejor será sacar a los jefes". Quizás a unos pocos más. "Permitiremos que los demás regresen, y en poco tiempo comenzarán a señalar a los malos".

"Eso me parece razonable", comentó Rumsfeld.

GARNER FUE A HABLAR de nuevo con Wolfowitz.

"Creo que no hemos pensado en la función más importante que debemos realizar", dijo Garner.

"¿Cuál es?"

"La gobernabilidad. Debemos contar con un equipo que conforme el gobierno". Necesitaban un rostro iraquí. "Lo que le estoy pidiendo que hagamos", continuó Garner, "es que busquemos a las personas más inteligentes de Norteamérica, ya sea en Harvard o en cualquier otro lugar, y conformemos un equipo de gobierno de talla mundial que podamos enviar y que comience a conformar un gobierno de inmediato".

"Déjame pensarlo", le dijo Wolfowitz.

Horas más tarde, el subsecretario llamó a Garner.

"He estado pensando en tu propuesta. ¿Qué piensas de Liz Cheney?".

"No sé quién es", replicó Garner.

"Es la hija del vicepresidente".

Liz, abogada de 36 años y madre de tres hijos, había desempeñado varios cargos en el Departamento de Estado y actualmente trabajaba como subsecretaria auxiliar de la secretaría de Estado para asuntos del Cercano Oriente. Era conservadora desde su niñez y había trabajado en la campaña de Bush y Cheney en el 2000.

"No me importa, siempre y cuando yo esté seguro de que es alguien que sabe lo que hacen sus compañeros y cómo abordan este problema".

"Vendrá mañana a primera hora; podrás explicarle qué es lo que quieres", le dijo Wolfowitz.

Al día siguiente, Garner habló con Liz Cheney en la oficina de Wolfowitz.

"Necesitamos ofrecerle al pueblo iraquí un liderazgo iraquí", le dijo Garner. "Creo que necesitamos organizar un grupo que sea capaz de lograr la gobernabilidad. Y también necesitamos comenzar a redactar una Constitución de inmediato. Debemos celebrar elecciones. Necesitamos hacer elecciones en las provincias. También necesitamos comenzar a trabajar en esto de inmediato y dejar que los iraquíes participen en todo.

Líderes, una Constitución, elecciones… eso era pedir mucho.

"Trabajaré en ello", dijo Liz Cheney. Ni ella ni Wolfowitz hicieron ningún comentario. Liz regresó al Pentágono en la tarde con algunos funcionarios del Departamento de Estado. Uno de ellos era Scout Carpenter, asistente adjunto del secretario de Estado, calvo y de aspecto juvenil, que había trabajado en el estudio "El futuro de Irak".

Garner describió su ambicioso plan de gobierno. Carpenter tomó notas y dijo: "Está bien; comenzaré a concretar esto. ¿Cuándo viajaremos?".

Garner no lo sabía. "Lo que deben hacer es permanecer aquí y armar el equipo. Luego nos veremos en Bagdad.

"Eso haré".

Liz y Carpenter se fueron, y Garner habló en privado con Wolfowitz.

"Parece un buen tipo", dijo Garner, refiriéndose a Carpenter. "Es un poco joven; no sé qué experiencia tenga. Creo que ella está bien".

"Sí, pero no podemos enviarla a Irak. Es la hija del vicepresidente y correría un gran riesgo.

"Eso tiene sentido", respondió Garner.

En la oficina 666 del prestigioso anillo E del Pentágono, en el tercer piso y a poca distancia de la oficina de Rumsfeld, el general John M. Keane, jefe auxiliar de personal del Ejército, se enteró de la nueva misión de Garner. Es extraña, pensó.

Keane, un corpulento hombre que llevaba 37 años en el Ejército, se había sorprendido por la desconfianza que sentía Rumsfeld por los líderes militares durante los primeros años. El secretario era cortante, brusco, y mostraba poco interés por las ideas y pensamientos de las demás personas. Sin embargo, a Keane le pareció que Rumsfeld tenía una gran dosis de razón en lo referente al cambio en el aparato militar, especialmente en el Ejército.

Dejando a un lado las emociones y la personalidad, Keane se había convertido en un favorito del secretario, y estaba dirigiendo prácticamente al Ejército, pues Rumsfeld había peleado con el jefe de Keane, el general Eric K. Shinseki, quien era el jefe del estado mayor del Ejército. A finales del año 2000 y a comienzos del 2001, se había armado un gran lío a raíz de la decisión de Shinseki de suministrarles boinas negras a todos los soldados del Ejército. Durante mucho tiempo, las boinas negras habían sido un símbolo de los *rangers*, el cuerpo elite del Ejército. *Rangers*, ex *rangers* y algunos miembros del Congreso se ofendieron. Un par de ex *rangers* emprendieron una marcha desde Fort Benning, Georgia, hasta Washington para protestar por el cambio. Sin embargo, Shinseki se mantuvo firme en su decisión. Bush habló en dos ocasiones con Rumsfeld sobre esta controversia, la cual se prolongó durante varios meses. Y Rumsfeld, que había regresado al Pentágono con el propósito de concentrarse en las principales prioridades, tuvo que enfrascarse en una disputa sobre el tipo y el color de la gorra que debían llevar los soldados.

En abril de 2002, Rumsfeld había propuesto que Keane fuera el comandante del Ejército. Keane había aceptado inicialmente, pero luego había cambiado de opinión; dijo que se retiraría del Ejército pues su esposa estaba gravemente enferma. Le comentó a Rumsfeld que su esposa se había sacrificado 37 años por él y que ahora él tenía que sacrificarse por ella. Entre todos los funcionarios importantes del Pentágono, a Keane le parecía que Rumsfeld era, de lejos, el más comprensivo y compasivo.

Keane le dijo a Garner que quería hablar con él, pues creía que era inteligente y estaba lleno de ideas. Garner estaba pintando en el más grande de los lienzos desde agua, alimentos y electricidad, hasta un nuevo gobierno, una Constitución y elecciones, tratando de hacer con rapidez lo mismo que los empresarios y los padres de la patria tardaron décadas en lograr.

"¿Para quien estás trabajando?", le preguntó Keane.

"Para el secretario de Defensa", respondió Garner.

"Dios mío, Jay, esa no es la respuesta correcta; tienes que estar trabajando para el general Franks, y *de facto* para el general McKiernan. No puedes estar trabajando para el secretario porque habrá un canal separado. Es decir que los mandos militares no querrán saber nada de tus hombres; trabajarán por separado. Ya lo veo: no querrán entenderse contigo. No vas a…"

"No", protestó Garner, "haremos que funcione".

Keane le recordó a Garner el principio de la unidad de mando. Una persona estaba al mando en cada frente o misión. Franks debía comandar la Fase IV y encargarse de la estabilización. Sin embargo, los militares no tardarían en asumir el control. "Jay, si algo hemos aprendido en los últimos 15 años, es precisamente eso. Piénsalo. Cada vez que hemos fracasado es porque hemos tenido problema con esto, y no queremos aprender de nuevo la lección".

"Haré que las cosas funcionen", dijo Garner, y le recordó a Keane que él era un militar y una persona muy sensible a este problema. Adicionalmente, agregó, ya había tomado decisiones.

Keane lo sabía, pero las decisiones que no se había tomado eran más preocupantes aun. Keane no tardó en saber que Abizaid también estaba presionando a Rumsfeld sobre lo referente a la gobernabilidad.

"Señor secretario", dijo Abizaid, "me preocupa saber quién va a estar al mando cuando derroquemos al régimen de Saddam. ¿Cómo será el sistema político?". Abizaid tenía cuatro o cinco variaciones de la misma pregunta. "¿Quién va a gobernar a Irak?", le preguntó en otra ocasión.

"Doug está trabajando en ello", dijo Rumsfeld en una ocasión. Keane creía que Feith era un enlace muy débil en la cadena de Rumsfeld, y no era lo suficientemente calificado para su cargo. Feith tenía muchos informes y documentos con planes elaborados. Garner, por ejemplo, era técnicamente un subalterno del general Franks, pero se estaba reportando directamente a Rumsfeld, a quien no solamente le gustaba esto, sino que insistía en ello.

Varios días antes del despliegue, Garner y Bates fueron al Departamento de Estado para hablar con Powell y Armitage. Powell y Bates se abrazaron, pues no sólo los unía un largo vínculo en el Ejército; en septiembre de 1994, Bates y Powell habían sido parte de un pequeño equipo que Clinton envió a Haití a fin de evitar una invasión norteamericana. El ex presidente Carter, Powell y el senador Sam Nunn, quien había sido director del Comité de Servicios Armados desde 1987 hasta 1995, habían sido los tres hombres encargados de la misión. Bates había sido el representante militar del Estado Mayor Conjunto.

"Señor, usted sabe", le dijo Bates a Powell, "que podríamos solucionar esto si viajáramos con el presidente Carter y con Sam Nunn". Powell se rió y lanzó algunos comentarios sobre la larga y creciente disputa que había entre los departamentos de Estado y de Defensa. Era extraordinariamente disfuncional, coincidieron los cuatro ex militares.

"¿Saben algo?", dijo Powell, "el problema es que nunca han peleado siquiera en un bar". Se refería a Bush, Cheney, Rice y Rumsfeld, y a otros funcionarios de la administración, que nunca habían servido en el Ejército ni habían participado en ningún combate. Entre los cuatro militares, incluidos los seis años que Armitage sirvió en la Marina, sumaban una experiencia de más de cien años en los estamentos militares. Ellos tenían la sensación de ser veteranos que sabían cómo eran las cosas.

"Les daré todo lo que ustedes necesiten, mientras pueda hacerlo", les dijo Powell. "Ustedes lo saben".

"Realmente me molestó que Rumsfeld te ordenara que despidieras a Warrick y a O'Sullivan", dijo Powell.

"No creo que haya sido una decisión suya. Creo que sólo estaba obedeciendo órdenes", comentó Garner.

"Te diré algo. Lo llamé por teléfono y le dije: 'Yo también puedo tomar prisioneros'. Comencé a tratar de retirar a todos los funcionarios del Departamento de Estado de tu equipo, pero luego lo pensé mejor y concluí que eso no le haría bien a nadie. Al contrario, te perjudicaría y estropearía lo que estás haciendo; menoscabaría lo que la nación está intentando hacer. Alguien tiene que asumir esto, y yo he tratado de hacerlo".

Cuando se estaban poniendo de pie para marcharse, Armitage se aproximó a Garner.

"Oye, Jay, quiero decirte algo; en tu equipo hay varios espías; están hablando de ti. Cuídate la espalda porque están pasando información".

"De acuerdo", replicó Garner. "Lo haré. Pero a ti también te están espiando".

"Sabemos quiénes son", dijo Armitage. "Les decimos murciélagos".

"¿Murciélagos?".

"Sí, porque esos hijos de perra se la pasan cubriéndose los ojos con sus alas, y tan pronto cerramos la puerta, al final de la tarde, mueven las alas, miran alrededor, revolotean toda la noche y llaman a todo el mundo".

A Bates y Garner les gustó el sobrenombre, y lo utilizaron para referirse a las personas que creían que Feith había infiltrado en su equipo para vigilarlos. Uno de los murciélagos del Pentágono tenía cuatro teléfonos móviles, lo que posteriormente fue confirmado por las cuentas. Cuando viajaron a Kuwait, había una persona que siempre estaba hablando por teléfono. Un día estaba completamente absorto en la conversación y se cayó a la piscina. "Fue el suceso del día", recordó Bates posteriormente. "Nos reímos en grande".

POR ESTA MISMA ÉPOCA, Powell sostuvo un encuentro medianamente privado con el presidente. Como ya era costumbre, Rice también estaba presente.

Powell se refirió al tema de la unidad de mando. Le dijo al presidente que había dos cadenas de mando: Garner se reportaba a Rumsfeld y Franks se reportaba a Rumsfeld.

El presidente pareció sorprendido.

"Eso no está bien", dijo Rice. "No está bien".

Powell pensaba que Rice podía ser muy segura de sí misma en algunas ocasiones, pero sabía que esta vez él tenía la razón. "Sí está bien" insistió Powell.

"Un momento", lo interrumpió Bush, tomando partido por Rice. "Eso no me parece bien".

Rice se dirigió a su oficina para comprobar, y regresó con un aspecto sumiso. "Sí, está bien", dijo ella.

"Sí", añadió Powell, consciente de su pequeño triunfo. Luego le dijo al presidente: "Usted tiene una cadena de mando que llega al secretario de Defensa y luego a usted. Pero usted también ha creado esta alternativa, que pasa por Garner o por cualquier empleado civil, y que también llega al secretario de Defensa".

Powell continuó con su pequeña lección: "Esto no tiene nada de malo siempre y cuando usted entienda lo que ha hecho. Pero también tiene que entender que, si tiene dos cadenas de mando y no cuenta con un funcionario superior común, cada disputa que tengan y que no puedan resolver irá a un lugar donde será resuelta. Y ese lugar es el Pentágono; no es el CNS ni el Departamento de Estado, sino el Pentágono".

Lo que Powell no dijo fue que él creía que el Pentágono no podía resolver los conflictos porque Wolfowitz y Feith estaban ocupados en sus asuntos y tenían su agenda propia para promover a Chalabi.

Rice pensó que era una discusión más bien teórica; si ponían a Garner por debajo de Franks, significaría que Franks sería el *virrey*, y ella sabía que Bush nunca permitiría esto.

Sin embargo, Rumsfeld quería que la cadena de mando funcionara de ese modo; que Franks y Garner se reportaran a él, para tener así todo el control: esa era su meta.

El tema del dinero siempre estaba presente. Garner pensaba que casi ningún funcionario de la administración de Bush creía que la situación de posguerra fuera a demandar mucho dinero. Un documento sobre el presupuesto, preparado por Garner el 27 de febrero de 2003, indicaba que él contaría con poco más de 27 millones de dólares para su equipo. Sin embargo, la cifra requerida para el funcionamiento básico del país era enorme. Garner calculaba que la ayuda humanitaria ascendía a más de mil millones de dólares, incluidos 800 millones para la reconstrucción, y que el funcionamiento del gobierno demandaría 10 mil millones, lo que sumaba una cifra que oscilaba entre 10 mil y 12 mil millones de dólares.

Garner estaba buscando algún tipo de orientación. "Señor secretario", recordó haberle dicho a Rumsfeld un día antes del despliegue, "tenemos tres opciones: ¿Qué queremos hacer con la reconstrucción? ¿Usted quiere que todo sea como era antes de la primera Guerra del Golfo? ¿Quiere que sea como era antes de esta guerra? ¿O usted quiere construir de ceros?". El documento sobre el presupuesto también contemplaba propuestas para emprender una reconstrucción parcial o total. Sin embargo, aún no se había propuesto cifras —lo más importante, con el signo de dólares al lado izquierdo—.

"¿Cuánto crees que costará?", preguntó Rumsfeld.

"Miles de millones de dólares", respondió Garner. "Sin que importe por cuál alternativa optemos".

"Si estás pensando que vamos a gastar nuestro dinero en eso, estás equivocado", dijo Rumsfeld de un modo completamente firme y contundente. "No vamos a hacer eso. Ellos tendrán que gastar su dinero en la reconstrucción de su país".

15

La brigada de artillería que buscaría los 946 sitios de la Lista Maestra de Sitios con ADM empezó a conformarse en Kuwait. Llegaron expertos de la Agencia de Inteligencia de Defensa y de otras agencias del Pentágono, pero el Destacamento Especial de Exploración (XTF) no tenía personal, equipamiento ni vehículos para transportar a todas las unidades que practicarían las inspecciones, así que hicieron recortes y repartieron el personal y los camiones lo mejor que pudieron.

El 10 de marzo, Rotkoff supo que tendría que llevar a un reportero del *New York Times* con los cazadores de ADM. Le dijeron que era una orden de arriba. No reconoció el nombre del periodista, pero lo anotó en su diario con las abreviaciones y la escritura descuidada propias de un militar apurado: "Judith Miller. Escribe sob quím y biol. Secdefen la quiere con XTF. Llega el miércoles".

Incluir formalmente reporteros en las unidades militares era una idea relativamente novedosa del Pentágono, y las tropas en el campo de batalla apenas se estaban acostumbrando a ello. La guerra era ahora un asunto de 24 horas, y Rotkoff sabía muy bien de qué manera los oficiales militares podían gastar medio día, gracias a las transmisiones de video mundiales, instantáneas y seguras, reuniendo información y realizando informes para los jefes en Washington.

Rotkoff obedecería la orden. Sin embargo, sentía cierta aversión por los reporteros del *New York Times* después de la experiencia que tuvo con Michael Gordon, otro periodista de ese periódico que había estado en el cuartel general de las fuerzas terrestres. Gordon era un reportero hábil y experimentado en asuntos militares, pero tenía fama de ser frío y arrogante. Rotkoff escribió un haiku sobre él:

> *Gordon N.Y. Times*
> *Demuestra la ética de los medios*
> *Toda en torno a él*

EL MARTES 11 DE MARZO, Garner ofreció un comunicado de prensa en el Pentágono. Se situó en la parte posterior para que lo tomaran por un simple "oficial de defensa".

En caso de que existieran dudas sobre su plan, les dijo a los reporteros: "Lo que necesitamos hacer inmediatamente es pagarles a los funcionarios de los ministerios, pagarle al ejército, al sistema penal y a los departamentos encargados del cumplimiento de la ley". Garner declaró que esperaba permanecer sólo unos meses en Irak, pues ese país estaba en mejores condiciones que Afganistán. "Irak es un país un poco más sofisticado y estructurado que Afganistán... Tiene infraestructura y mecanismos para funcionar de una manera eficiente".

Un reportero le preguntó sobre el CNI, el Congreso Nacional Iraquí, dirigido por Ahmed Chalabi.

"No estamos pensando en trabajar con ninguno de ellos", dijo Garner. Luego agregó: "No hemos tenido contacto con ellos".

Esa noche, Feith llamó a Garner; estaba disgustado. Has estropeado la credibilidad de Chalabi y del CNI, dijo.

"Dough: número uno, yo no tengo un candidato para gobernar a Irak después de la invasión", le respondió Garner, "y, a propósito, tu jefe tampoco tiene a nadie. He escuchado a Rumsfeld decir en dos o tres oportunidades: 'no tengo un candidato; ya aparecerá el mejor'".

Feith no cedió. A Garner le pareció que era un funcionario inteligente pero sumamente desorganizado, y parecía estar muy preocupado, casi en estado de *shock*. Feith prácticamente le dijo que había cometido un gran error. Nos has causado muchos problemas, y todos en el Pentágono están realmente molestos contigo.

"Mira, Dough, la respuesta a tu problema es fácil: despídeme. Mañana mismo puedo regresar a mi compañía. No tienes que depender de mí. Ve y busca a otra persona".

"No podemos hacerlo ahora", le dijo Feith.

Wolfowitz también llamó a Garner. A diferencia de Feith, el subsecretario de Defensa estaba calmado, pero, de todos modos, Garner sintió que lo estaba reprendiendo.

"Tenemos que ser realmente cuidadosos", le dijo Wolfowitz, "porque existen muchos compromisos con Chalabi y con el CNI; así que tenemos que ser muy cuidadosos con la forma en que expresamos nuestros comentarios".

Esa noche, Garner se enteró que no debía hablar con la prensa antes de que viajara. Un par de días más tarde, un capitán de reserva de la Marina que trabajaba como su oficial para asuntos públicos se enteró de otra orden oficial: Garner no hablaría con la prensa, ni aun después de llegar a Kuwait.

Posteriormente, la trascripción oficial del comunicado de Garner elaborada por el Departamento de Defensa fue enmendada; le fueron añadidas tres "aclaraciones" considerablemente inusuales, que elogiaban al CNI y contradecían lo expresado por Garner.

"El CNI ha desempeñado un papel importante, ya que a través del tiempo ha hecho posible que los diferentes grupos de oposición iraquíes cooperen entre sí". Esta aclaración estaba entre paréntesis. "El gobierno de los Estados Unidos admira el éxito que ha tenido el CNI en conseguir un respaldo basado en los principios que el Gobierno de los Estados Unidos favorece para la creación de un nuevo gobierno democrático en Irak".

Larry DiRita, ex oficial de la Marina que había trabajado en el Estado Mayor Conjunto y que actualmente era asistente especial y mano derecha de Rumsfeld, llamó a Garner el 13 de marzo.

"El secretario de Defensa quiere que te reportes antes de viajar", le dijo.

Al día siguiente por la mañana, Garner y su equipo se reunieron con Rumsfeld, Wolfowitz, Feith y los principales oficiales del Estado Mayor Conjunto: su jefe Myers, el subjefe Pace, el general Case y otros diez altos funcionarios.

Rumsfeld parecía un poco rígido y distraído. Garner no sabía que Bush iba a darle un ultimátum a Saddam: le declararía la guerra si no se iba de Irak. Rumsfeld era firme partidario de que le dieran un plazo de 48 horas.

"Soy la alcaldesa de Bagdad", dijo Bárbara Bodine, una controvertida ex embajadora que estaba en el equipo de Garner.

"¡Qué interesante!", comentó Rumsfeld con sarcasmo.

A Garner le pareció que el comentario de Bodine había sido estúpido y desatinado, pero no dijo nada.

Esa noche, Larry DiRita llamó a Garner. "El secretario de Defensa quiere reunirse contigo a las ocho de la mañana".

Al día siguiente, Rumsfeld y Garner hablaron en privado.

"Mira, Jay", comenzó Rumsfeld, "acepto la responsabilidad por todo esto, pues no te he dado el tiempo que debería haberte dado". Esta era una admisión inusual por parte de Rumsfeld. "Realmente he estado tan inmerso en los planes de guerra que no he tenido tiempo para concentrarme en todo lo que has estado haciendo. Intenté mantenerme al tanto, pero no pude sacar el tiempo necesario".

"Me siento realmente incómodo con todas esas personas que has comisionado para dirigir los ministerios", dijo. En Irak había 23 ministerios; la mayoría eran similares a los departamentos del gabinete del gobierno de los Estados Unidos: Agricultura, Trabajo, Salud, Educación, Justicia, Relaciones exteriores y Defensa. Los otros ministerios iraquíes reflejaban los problemas o la economía de ese país: Electricidad, Irrigación, Cultura y asuntos religiosos. Menos de la mitad de los funcionarios nombrados para dirigir los ministerios provenían del Departamento de Defensa. "Creo que todos deberían ser de mi departamento" señaló Rumsfeld.

"Señor secretario", respondió Garner, "no podemos hacer eso. Es evidente que hay funciones que son más propias de otras agencias que del Departamento de Defensa". La directiva NSPD-24 de Bush había estipulado que la oficina de planeación estuviera conformada por diversas agencias.

"No", insistió Rumsfeld, "creo que todos deberían pertenecer al Departamento de Defensa". La directiva le había conferido el mando a este departamento.

"Creo que no podemos ponernos de acuerdo en esto", dijo Garner.

Continuaron discutiendo, pero Rumsfeld tenía todo a su favor; a fin de cuentas, era el jefe. Fue amable, pero insistente.

"Está bien", dijo Garner, intentando otra estrategia. "¿Quién es tu nominado para el Ministerio de Agricultura?". Garner había reclutado a Henry Lee Schatz, del servicio exterior agrícola del Departamento de Agricultura. Schatz había trabajado casi tres décadas en el ámbito internacional con este departamento.

"Encontraremos a los funcionarios apropiados", le dijo Rumsfeld. "Te armaré un buen equipo".

"No quiero eso", respondió Garner. "Miremos el Ministerio de Salud". El general había designado al doctor Frederick *Skip* Burkle, otro antiguo funcionario de la Operación *Provide Comfort*. "Ha estado en todo este tipo de operaciones, ha manejado la salud desde 1986, y nunca ha fallado. Sabe muy bien lo que hace".

"Nosotros también tenemos gente competente", reclamó Rumsfeld.

"Usted no tiene a nadie tan competente como Burkle", dijo Garner. "No hay otro como él. Tenemos que conseguir a los mejores, y no todos están en el Departamento de Defensa".

"Yo me decidiría por alguien como Robin Raphel, porque la conozco, la respeto mucho y sé que es una gran trabajadora". Raphel, que había sido embajadora en Túnez, estaría a cargo del Ministerio de Comercio iraquí. Ella había trabajado con Rumsfeld cuando éste había sido enviado especial al Medio Oriente en 1983 y 1984. "No me siento cómodo con los demás funcionarios", agregó Rumsfeld. Era evidente que el secretario no tenía alternativas, y propuso una especie de compromiso, o por lo menos un aplazamiento. "Piénsalo bien durante el viaje, y me llamas tan pronto llegues a Kuwait".

"Así lo haré", le dijo Garner.

El general no podía creerlo; lo único que tenía que hacer era asegurarse de traer a las personas que había nombrado y comisionado.

TRES DÍAS ANTES DEL COMIENZO de la guerra, el domingo 16 de marzo, el vicepresidente Cheney apareció en el programa *Encuentro con la prensa,* de la cadena NBC. "Creo que, de hecho, seremos recibidos como libertadores", predijo.

El presentador Tim Russert señaló que el general Shinseki había testificado ante el Congreso que probablemente se necesitarían centenares de miles de hombres de tropa para el período de posguerra en Irak.

"No creo que sea acertado sugerir que necesitamos varios centenares de miles de hombres al término de las operaciones militares, una vez termine el conflicto; eso no es exacto. Creo que es una exageración", comentó Cheney.

Por esta misma época, Garner y los casi 150 hombres de su equipo se reunieron en una zona de estacionamiento afuera del Pentágono. Rumsfeld fue a despedirse de ellos. Era la primera vez que la mayoría del equipo veía al secretario en persona. Volaron a la base Andrews de la Fuerza Aérea, en Maryland, y de allí salieron hacia Kuwait en un vuelo fletado de la US Airways.

El ambiente estaba cargado de emotividad. "Todo el tiempo pensaba: espero lograrlo", recordó Garner. "Sólo necesito un poco más de tiempo. Tan sólo un poco más de tiempo".

Pocas horas después de aterrizar en Kuwait el 17 de marzo, el teniente general McKiernan, comandante de las fuerzas terrestres, citó a Garner y a Bates a un encuentro con sus oficiales de cabecera.

"Estos son los dos nuevos miembros del equipo", les dijo McKiernan a los oficiales, abrazando a Garner y a Bates. "Háganlos sentir cómodos".

McKiernan había dicho que en la base militar no había espacio disponible para el equipo de Garner, así que se alojaron en un Hotel Hilton recién construido en los suburbios de la ciudad de Kuwait. El complejo había sido alquilado por Kellog, Brown and Root, compañía contratista de defensa subsidiaria de Halliburton, la antigua empresa de Cheney, en previsión de la guerra. El complejo estaba a una hora de la ciudad.

Ese mismo día, Garner y Ron Adams llamaron a Rumsfeld para revisar la lista de los ministerios. Rumsfeld los presionó de nuevo para que nombraran a funcionarios del Departamento de Defensa.

"Está bien, tal vez podamos contratar a una persona de ese departamento", le dijo Garner en un momento dado, y luego agregó: "Tal vez podamos colocar a alguien de allí". Parecía como si Rumsfeld estuviera consiguiendo que sus hombres fueran nombrados hasta que fueran mayoría.

"Confía en mí", le dijo Rumsfeld. "Te armaré un buen equipo. Será un equipo excelente".

"Señor secretario, no podrá enviarlos a tiempo", replicó Garner. La guerra comenzaría en cualquier momento.

"Jay, te daremos un equipo mucho mejor que el que tienes actualmente", le prometió Rumsfeld.

"De acuerdo. Está bien", dijo Garner.

Cuando colgó, le dijo a Adams: "No haremos nada. Tendremos que trabajar con lo que tenemos. No le digas una sola palabra a nadie; nunca lo sabrán".

LA GUERRA COMENZÓ el 19 de marzo con una ofensiva aérea contra Dora Farm, un complejo al sureste de Bagdad, a orillas del río Tigris, donde habían supuesto erróneamente que se ocultaba Saddam.

La invasión estaba saliendo sorprendentemente bien como operación militar. El tercer día, la 3ª División de Infantería avanzó 250 kilómetros en territorio iraquí, y el ejército de Saddam sufría fuertes derrotas o se estaba disolviendo. Sin embargo, algunos de los soldados iraquíes aparecían vestidos de civiles o con el atuendo negro y blanco de los *fedayines* de Saddam, una milicia comandada por Uday, el hijo del dictador iraquí. Estos combatientes civiles se lanzaban sin ninguna protección contra las formaciones armadas; casi todos morían irremediablemente. Intentaban tácticas suicidas, imposibles y descabelladas; atacaban tanques a pie, o trataban de emboscar a los vehículos Bradley con armas pequeñas.

Rotkoff escribió un haiku:

Fedayines de Saddam
¿De dónde diablos salieron?
Nadie los vio

Spider Marks concluyó que los hombres leales a Saddam estaban amenazando a la población civil: la ponían a elegir entre atacar a los norteamericanos o morir de inmediato. La población iraquí estaba considerablemente atemorizada. Pocos días después de la invasión, Marks, McKiernan y otro par de oficiales comentaron la situación con Tenet.

"¿Qué crees?", le preguntó Marks al director de la CIA. "Ellos están combatiendo; nos están atacando".

"No tengo la menor idea", señaló Tenet.

El 21 de marzo de 2003 –el segundo día de la guerra– Rice y Hadley le presentaron a Bush y al CNS un informe formal sobre los nueve objetivos de guerra estadounidenses y de la coalición. El objetivo era asegurarse de que todos estuvieran de acuerdo con los planes trazados para Irak cuando terminaran los enfrentamientos. Uno de los objetivos fue enunciado de la siguiente manera: "Se observa que Irak se está moviendo en dirección a las instituciones democráticas y que sirve de modelo para la región". Adicionalmente, tenían que "designar a muchos iraquíes en posiciones visibles de autoridad con la mayor rapidez posible... lo anterior tiene que cumplirse con urgencia".

Esto concordaba con lo que Garner le había dicho al presidente la única vez que se reunieron. Sus esfuerzos habían sido aprobados por los funcionarios de mayor rango, incluido Rumsfeld.

Garner hablaba con Rumsfeld por teleconferencia desde Kuwait casi todos los días. Generalmente, había muchas personas en ambas salas. El 22 de marzo volvieron a discutir sobre quiénes dirigirían los ministerios. Rumsfeld aún quería escogerlos personalmente a todos; Garner intentó apelar a la realidad y le dijo que sería imposible que dichos funcionarios llegaran a tiempo.

De acuerdo con alguien que estaba tomando notas, Rumsfeld le dijo: "¿Sabes algo? Parece que no estás en nuestro equipo".

"Está bien. Dejémoslo así", respondió Garner, y la teleconferencia terminó. Garner le envió por fax una larga nota escrita a mano, en la que declaraba que tenían las mismas metas. "Yo sí estoy en el equipo", le escribió. Garner estaba profundamente ofendido, pues era la peor táctica de chantaje: si no estás de acuerdo conmigo, entonces eres desleal.

Ninguna ADM fue utilizada o descubierta en los primeros días de la invasión. El intenso ritmo con que trabajaba el equipo de inteligencia de Marks se hizo aún más frenético. La calidad de la inteligencia sobre los cientos de sitios restantes que figuraban en la lista de ADM seguía siendo insatisfactoria, y la inesperada oposición iraquí comenzaba a ser desafiante. Prever este tipo de situaciones era una tarea que le correspondía a la inteligencia, y, sin embargo, no lo habían hecho.

En un momento dado, Marks tuvo que animarse a sí mismo. El 29 de marzo escribió que uno de los jefes de la CIA con los que estaba trabajando le dijo: "ha estado analizando esta región durante toda su vida profesional y no entiende el profundo desespero de la gente. No te deprimas, Marks". Todos estaban rendidos. "Este es el trabajo que más me ha llenado, pero también ha sido el más difícil y frustrante que he tenido que hacer", escribió Marks en su diario. "La magnitud de las responsabilidades, los plazos cortos para su ejecución, el poco tiempo para cualquier otra cosa que no sea la ejecución; no dejan tiempo para pensar. La esencia es importante, pero el proceso me está matando. El simple acto de mantener el motor encendido es una tarea monumental".

Rotkoff lo describió de una manera sucinta, dejando al desnudo su agotamiento, frustración y dudas:

> *Mente y huesos cansados*
> *Difícil permanecer indeseado*
> *No puedo descansar - hombres morirán*

"MILES DE SOLDADOS están dejando el uniforme y regresando a casa", le dijo Bush al primer ministro Blair en una conversación telefónica.

"Sí, se están esfumando".

"Exactamente, se están esfumando", repitió Bush.

Bush, realmente, no tuvo que trabajar mucho una vez comenzó la guerra. Las notas de sus conversaciones y reuniones muestran que siempre hablaba de la victoria, pero también revelan a un presidente preocupado porque los Estados Unidos pudieran ganar los combates terrestres y perder, sin embargo, la guerra de propaganda.

"Necesitamos recordarle a la gente por qué estamos aquí", afirmó el mandatario en una reunión celebrada en el Pentágono el 25 de marzo. Le dijo a Rumsfeld: "Tienes que recordarle al mundo a quién estamos combatiendo".

La Fuerza Aérea tenía tres enormes aviones Comando de cuatro motores volando con estaciones de radio y televisión que trasmitían la guerra de Irak.

"¿Qué piensa de esto un iraquí promedio?", preguntó Bush en una reunión con el CNS el 28 de marzo. La respuesta fue que las transmisiones eran difundidas en Bagdad cinco horas al día, de las 6 a las 11:00 de la noche. No estaban difundiendo videos, sólo fotografías.

Bush comentó que eso no era suficiente. "Hay que calibrarlo. Hay que promocionar los programas. La gente no enciende la televisión si no hay nada para ver".

Tres días después, el presidente se comunicó con el general Franks por teleconferencia. "¿Estás satisfecho con nuestra campaña informativa?", le preguntó. "¿Puedes transmitir nuestro mensaje en Bagdad?".

Franks le dijo que no le gustaba que la televisión iraquí todavía estuviera al aire, y que necesitaba más traductores para "subir la calidad y el volumen de las transmisiones en lengua árabe".

Bush dijo: "Si necesitas ayuda de los Estados Unidos, te la daremos".

El 4 de abril, hacia el final de otra reunión del CNS, alguien mencionó que Bagdad estaba sin luz; las fuerzas norteamericanas aún no habían llegado allí.

"¿Quién apagó las luces de Bagdad?", preguntó Bush.

"Probablemente lo hizo el régimen, para reponer sus fuerzas", le dijo Franks a través de la pantalla. "Pero no lo sabemos con seguridad".

"Si fue el régimen, aclara que no lo hicimos nosotros", dijo Bush.

Sin embargo, el presidente parecía estar optimista. "Sólo importa una cosa: ganar", dijo en una reunión con el CNS, a la vez que descartó "dudas sobre el mundo después de Irak". Hadley le preguntó en privado cómo se sentía.

"Tomé la decisión", dijo Bush. "Estoy durmiendo bien".

16

"No sé cuánto tiempo tomará ni cuanto costará", repetía con frecuencia Rumsfeld a sus subalternos. El 2 de abril, el secretario de Defensa envió un memorando de una página a los secretarios del servicio, al jefe del Estado Mayor Conjunto, a Feith, a Franks y a otras personas clave del Pentágono. En él daba instrucciones de apoyar a Garner "en lo que necesite", y decía que la misión del general era "ayudar a crear en Irak las condiciones para hacer la transición a un gobierno local autónomo, así como retirar las fuerzas de la coalición después de alcanzar los objetivos militares". En Kuwait, el coronel Tom Baltazar, quien hacía parte del equipo de Garner, recibió una copia de la comunicación. El memorando había sido escrito porque el grupo de Garner, sencillamente, no lograba la cooperación de los mandos militares. Es increíble, pensó. Para estos tipos no es suficiente con la firma del presidente en la Directiva Presidencial para la Seguridad Nacional del 20 de enero, que decía: "apóyenlos". Tenemos que conseguir la firma de Rumsfeld, también.

Aparte de ser el líder del Congreso Nacional Iraquí, Ahmed Chalabi era la cabeza de un grupo de iraquíes exilados que habían recibido algún entrenamiento militar financiado por los Estados Unidos. Pero todo lo relacionado con este grupo había sido un fiasco. No solamente había sido entrenada una pequeñísima fracción del número de iraquíes que supuestamente debían estar armados y preparados, sino que, además, se había presentado una disputa sobre el nombre que debía recibir la agrupación. Finalmente, el grupo de Chalabi recibió el aliterado pero redundante nombre de Combatientes Libres por la Liberación de Irak.

A principios de abril, Chalabi pedía a gritos entrar a Irak. A pesar del apoyo que recibía de sus benefactores en el Pentágono y en Washington, los generales norteamericanos en el Medio Oriente le veían poca utilidad. Lo último que querían era poner a Chalabi y a su pequeño ejército en plena zona de guerra, aunque recibían presiones para hacer precisamente eso.

Finalmente, Abizaid accedió. "Muy bien, llevemos al hijo de puta allá y veamos si puede hacer todo lo que ellos piensan que puede hacer", le dijo a Garner. "Y yo le aseguro que no podrá".

Los Estados Unidos llevaron a Chalabi, a sus Combatientes Libres por la Liberación de Irak y a otros de sus socios a Nasiriyah a bordo de un Hércules C-130, uno de esos resistentes aviones de carga que pueden despegar y aterrizar en cualquier parte. *Spider* Marks estaba allí cuando Chalabi aterrizó. Pensó que el líder del CNI estaba tratando de emular el regreso de MacArthur a las Filipinas. Chalabi llevaba una camisa deportiva negra con un gorra de campaña y dirigía uno de sus grupos. Así que estos son los Combatientes Libres por la Liberación de Irak, pensó Marks. "Estén atentos a sus bolsillos muchachos; es un grupo de cuidado".

Empezaron a llegar reportes de que los Combatientes Libres por la Liberación de Irak estaban tomando represalias, robando y saqueando.

Una noche, Marks y otro oficial de inteligencia, el coronel Jon *Jake* Jones, iban en un Humvee descapotado, apuntando sus armas hacia afuera y preguntándose si tendrían que enfrentarse con algún enemigo desconocido.

"Baja la velocidad", dijo Jones, señalando a cuatro o cinco iraquíes barbados reunidos alrededor de una fogata al borde de la carretera. Estaban asando alguna clase de animal –una oveja, tal vez un perro– y bailaban alrededor de él. Los oficiales pensaron que estaban fumando marihuana. La escena parecía salida de *El señor de los anillos*.

Jones y Marks se miraron y llegaron a la misma conclusión. "Combatientes Libres por la Liberación de Irak", dijeron los dos al unísono, antes de hundir el acelerador.

CHRISTOPHER *RYAN* HENRY había empezado a trabajar en febrero como subsecretario principal del Departamento de Defensa para asuntos políticos, convirtiéndose en el segundo al mando de más alto rango de Dough Feith. Henry, quien era capitán retirado de la Marina y había sido un alto funcionario de SAIC –una empresa contratista del Departamento de Defensa–, tenía una conexión única con el secretario de Defensa. Su esposa, Delonnie Henry, era la secretaria jefe y asistente privada de Rumsfeld, además de ser quien digitaba sus *copos de nieve* y llevaba sus archivos. Rumsfeld seguía presionando para ganar el control de los ministerios iraquíes; el 6 de abril, Henry llamó a Garner con la nueva lista de personas de Defensa.

"Ryan, eso es magnífico", dijo Garner. "¿Cuándo llegarán?"

"Bueno, no sabemos. Algunos de ellos ni siquiera han sido notificados todavía".

"Ryan, seamos razonables. No logrará que lleguen a tiempo". Las operaciones principales de combate terminarían pronto. Las tropas de Estados Unidos se estaban acercando a Bagdad.

"No", dijo Henry, "vamos a trabajar duro en esto".

Garner y Bates sabían que el problema iba a estar pronto en Bagdad, tal y como lo habían estado diciendo por meses; la pregunta era quién iba a estar a cargo. Garner tuvo una idea: "Esto es lo que tiene que hacer para tener éxito", le aseguró a Rumsfeld. "Traiga a John Abizaid al país y lo asciende". Como segundo al mando de Franks, Abizaid estaba demasiado alejado de la verdadera acción. "Nómbrelo comandante unificado subordinado, porque necesita a alguien de cuatro estrellas. Y me pone a mí a cargo de toda la reconstrucción, de la administración civil. Asigne a McKiernan la administración de toda la seguridad y las operaciones militares".

Rumsfeld se rehusó pero sin explicar por qué no le parecía una buena idea. Garner insistió. Creía que era la solución, que su propuesta aseguraba la unidad de mando porque tanto McKiernan como él se reportarían a Abizaid.

"No voy a hablar más del asunto", dijo Rumsfeld en otra conversación telefónica.

La tercera o cuarta vez que Garner hizo su sugerencia, Rumsfeld dijo, "Mira, Jay, ya hemos discutido esto antes y conoces mi posición". Le tiró el teléfono. Bush y Rice habían sido muy claros en que ningún militar iba a obtener ese cargo. Imagínese, pensó Rice: "presidente John Abizaid".

RICE PENSABA QUE GARNER había estaba demasiado tiempo en Kuwait. No se estaba haciendo nada de lo que debía hacerse –dirigir el gobierno, poner a funcionar los ministerios–. Según sabía, Irak tenía muy buen servicio civil, y asumió que éste continuaba allí. Pero, algunos días después del inicio de la guerra, recibió reportes de que los trabajadores del gobierno, incluidos los trabajadores petroleros, habían desaparecido.

"¿Qué quiere decir con que han desaparecido?", preguntó.

La estructura del país estaba debilitada, fue su conclusión. Siendo, como era, una experta en la Unión Soviética, había estudiado lo que sucede en los sistemas totalitarios cuando colapsan. Recordó haber leído sobre 1953, año en que murió Stalin. Durante cinco semanas, la Unión Soviética dejó de funcionar. Nadie podía hacer nada porque todos dependían de las órdenes de la jerarquía más elevada. Irak parecía haberse agrietado de la misma manera o peor. Pero, a juzgar por lo que la historia predecía, esto sería algo pasajero. Al final, confiaba ella, el orden se afirmaría, como había pasado en la antigua Rusia.

FUE NECESARIO REDUCIR la XTF –la brigada de artillería se convirtió en la unidad de búsqueda de ADM–. El plan había sido enviar cinco equipos para que acompañaran a las fuerzas de combate y catalogaran o se encargasen rápidamente de cualquier ADM con la que se toparan, y enviar al campo de acción tres equipos adicionales con mayor experiencia para visitar sistemáticamente los sitios indicados en la lista maestra de búsqueda de ADM. Por la limitación de personal y vehículos, fue necesario disminuir a cuatro el número de equipos que irían con las unidades de invasión, y formar dos equipos de entre 12 y 25 personas, denominados equipos de explotación móvil (MET, por sus iniciales en inglés) para hacer más intensivas las inspecciones.

El 18 de abril, el coronel Richard McPhee, comandante de la XTF, llegó a Irak con una de las dos unidades MET. Iba camino a su primera inspección en un pequeño pueblo al sur de Bagdad, donde la inteligencia de búsqueda de ADM había sugerido que encontrarían armas químicas. No había nada. Enterrados donde ellos pensaban que debían buscar, solamente encontraron 55 galones de gasolina empacados en tambores.

Parte del equipo se apresuró hacia otro emplazamiento sospechoso en Karbala, a unos 96 kilómetros al suroeste de Bagdad. Allí oyeron un rumor sobre un hombre iraquí que había pasado una nota a las fuerzas estadounidenses diciendo que era un científico que había trabajado con ADM, que tenía información para la coalición y que quería entregarse. Después de buscar durante 24 horas por el desierto iraquí, la unidad logró rastrear a los soldados que tenían la nota, y encontrar al científico.

El coronel McPhee abandonó el equipo y regresó rápidamente a Kuwait en helicóptero para reunirse con Marks. Había una tensión creciente acerca de si los equipos debían continuar inspeccionando los emplazamientos sospechosos de la lista maestra, o si era mejor seguir las nuevas pistas que el científico había sugerido.

"Lo digo en serio; esto es de suma importancia", dijo McPhee a Marks, y describió al científico iraquí, quien no pedía nada de los estadounidenses. McPhee quería obtener permiso para concentrarse en esta asignación.

"Rich, no es necesario que hagas eso", respondió Marks, queriendo decir que McPhee no tenía que volver a Kuwait a pedir permiso para hacer su trabajo. "Por supuesto que no. Tienes que ir y hacerlo".

Marks escribió en su diario un breve comentario sobre la reunión. "Pruebas de ADM… mantener bajas las expectativas". Incluso, a pesar de estar descontento con la calidad del servicio de inteligencia, Marks había estado pensando: ¡946 sitios! Es imposible que estén equivocados con todos, ¿verdad? Aunque sólo tuvieran razón en un 30% de los lugares, seguirían siendo muchas malditas ADM. Batear 300 era suficiente para que un beisbolista ingresara al salón de la fama. "Nos vamos todos para Cooperstone",[7] pensó

---

7. Ciudad del estado de Nueva York que alberga el Salón Nacional de la Fama del Béisbol.

Marks. No obstante, la noticia del científico iraquí seguía siendo un alivio muy bien recibido.

McPhee volvió a Irak y la unidad MET estuvo casi un día y medio con el científico. Buscaron primero exactamente donde él pensaba que habían sido enterrados los materiales de ADM, luego ampliaron el área y buscaron en los demás puntos posibles.

McPhee contactó a Marks por la radio de seguridad y el correo electrónico clasificado. "Sin buenas nuevas", reportó.

Era un momento crítico para Marks. "Sin buenas noticias" lo decía todo.

EL 9 DE ABRIL, el general Franks estaba conectado, por medio de una línea de video de seguridad, a la reunión del Consejo Nacional de Seguridad en la Casa Blanca. Según su reporte, la guerra iba bien: "En el Sur todas la formaciones enemigas están destruidas. Hay pequeños grupos activos, pero no representan ninguna amenaza. Los *marines* y los británicos están acabando con las divisiones iraquíes".

En la región de Bagdad, habían destruido el 90 por ciento de los equipos de las fuerzas iraquíes, reportó Franks.

"¿Estamos atrapando a los chicos malos?", preguntó Bush.
"Hemos distribuido fotografías de los 55 más buscados. Todavía no hay muchos refugiados. Algunos chicos malos se escabullirán pero estamos haciendo todo lo que podemos para cerrarles las vías principales".

Franks reportó que no se había presentado crisis humanitaria, ni quema de campos de petróleo, ni ataques con ADM. 900, de los 1.000 pozos de petróleo del sur, estaban bajo control, y los últimos 100 lo estarían en las siguientes 48 horas. "La población de Umm Qasr" —el puerto de aguas profundas más grande de Irak, justo al lado de la frontera con Kuwait— ha pasado, en una semana, de 15.000 a 40.00 habitantes. El agua es mejor que antes de la guerra; se ha reanudado el servicio eléctrico; se consigue comida", dijo Franks. Había algunos problemas en otras ciudades, pero la mayoría estaban bajo control.

Bush le pidió que se asegurara de que alguien estuviera recogiendo estadísticas sobre la vida en Irak antes de la guerra, cuando el país estaba bajo las órdenes de Saddam.

"No podemos permitir que venga gente a una de estas ciudades, la compare con una ciudad norteamericana y diga que las condiciones son atroces. Es necesario compararla con las condiciones de vida de esa misma ciudad antes de la guerra", dijo Bush. "Este tipo tardó de veinte a treinta años para arruinar este país. Va a tomar algún tiempo reconstruirlo".

Vamos a trasladar la base de operaciones de McKiernan a Bagdad, anunció Franks. Eventualmente seguiría el equipo de Garner. "La exploración de emplazamientos sospechosos seguirá". Hasta ese momento no habían encontrado depósitos de ADM.

En unos días, informó Franks, habrá una conferencia de representantes de Irak en Tallil, en las afueras de Nasiriyah, unos 161 kilómetros al sur de Bagdad. "Será una reunión logística sin compromisos", lo que significaba que era preliminar.

"Bien pensado", comentó Bush. "Será un centro de atención para que el mundo vea que no estamos simplemente imponiendo nuestra elección allí. ¿Que si creemos en la democracia? Sí. Estamos organizando a esta gente".

"Tenemos que ganar la historia en la era de la paz", le dijo Bush al primer ministro de Inglaterra, Blair. "Hemos ganado la guerra. No podemos dejar que la gente defina el tiempo de paz por nosotros".

RUMSFELD DESPACHÓ A LARRY DIRITA, su asistente especial, para Irak. DiRita estaba en Qatar ese mismo día, el 9 de abril, esperando tomar un avión para Kuwait, donde se reuniría con Garner.

En el aeropuerto, DiRita vio por televisión cómo se desarrollaba una sorprendente escena en el centro de Bagdad, emitida en vivo a todo el mundo. Un grupo de *marines* que habían entrado a la ciudad estaban ayudando a un grupo de iraquíes a derribar una escultura de Saddam, de 6 metros de altura, usando un vehículo blindado y una cadena. Aquello marcaba el final simbólico del régimen de Saddam.

Esa noche, después de que DiRita aterrizó en Kuwait, la gente de Garner preparó para él una serie de sesiones informativas en un pequeño comedor de una de los *chalets* del Kuwait City Hilton. Una de las discusiones se concentró en los beneficios que los iraquíes disfrutarían como resultado de los planes de reconstrucción de los estadounidenses.

Según recuerda el coronel Paul Hughes, DiRita dio un puñetazo a una mesa de roble macizo y exclamó: "¡No les debemos nada a los iraquíes! Les estamos dando la libertad. Eso es todo lo que debemos darles. No les debemos ningún otro beneficio".

DiRita no recuerda los comentarios, pero dice que lo que trataba de decir era que Estados Unidos tenía que ayudar a los iraquíes a hacer las cosas por sí mismos. Si Estados Unidos aportaba grandes cantidades de efectivo que salían de los bolsillos de toda la gente, eso haría que los iraquíes se retrajeran. Rumsfeld quería que se levantaran.

Unos días después, DiRita se reunió con los miembros de más alto rango de Garner en el Kuwait City Hilton.

"Nos metimos en los Balcanes y en Bosnia y en Kosovo, y allí seguimos", recuerda Hughes que dijo DiRita. "Probablemente vamos a estar en Afganistán por mucho tiempo, porque el Departamento de Estado no es capaz de hacer bien su trabajo; porque siguen echando a perder las cosas. El Departamento de Defensa termina atascado en esos lugares. No vamos a dejar que esto pase en Irak".

La reacción general fue de admiración: "¿Se da cuenta este tipo de que la mitad de la gente que hay en la habitación es del Departamento de Estado?".

DiRita continuó, según recuerda Hughes: "Para finales de agosto vamos a tener de 25.000 a 30.000 soldados en Irak".

DiRita había oído a Rumsfeld hablar en privado muchas veces sobre las ocupaciones extranjeras. "Es como un hueso roto", decía Rumsfeld. "Si no lo arreglas desde el principio, siempre va a estar, de alguna manera, roto". Más tarde Rumsfeld comentó: "Creo que usé la caracterización de un brazo roto. Si no se arregla, todo crece alrededor de la fractura y uno termina con esa anormalidad ahí, para siempre". Demasiadas ocupaciones, como la de Kosovo y la de Bosnia, habían sido manejadas como si tuvieran la intención de ser permanentes, y habían terminado por convertirse en eso.

Otras personas presentes en la habitación ese día no recuerdan que las palabras de DiRita fueran tan duras, pero la mayoría de los integrantes del Departamento de Estado que estaban allí presentían que no había manera de gobernar Irak del modo que Defensa visualizaba. Invadir y luego salir rápidamente parecía, además de imposible desde un punto de vista físico, moralmente dudoso. Robin Raphel miraba al techo, mientras pensaba para sus adentros: "¿Qué está fumando Larry DiRita? Pobre chico. No entiende nada de nada".

EL DÍA SIGUIENTE, 10 de abril, *Ryan* Henry llamó de nuevo a Garner.

"Tenemos, un gran problema en los ministerios", dijo Henry.

"¿Qué pasa?".

Pues, explicó Henry, la Casa Blanca se había enterado de la lista del Departamento de Defensa para los ministerios iraquíes. "Y quieren saber por qué ellos no están nombrando la gente y por qué lo estamos haciendo nosotros. Así que tenemos que enviar la lista a la Casa Blanca, y creemos que la van a rehacer, de modo que nos tomará un poco más de tiempo".

"No hay problema", dijo Garner con sarcasmo. "Cuando los reúnan y los entrenen y los manden acá, los recibiremos con los brazos abiertos".

Rumsfeld no creía que el grupo de Garner tuviera la talla necesaria. Aunque esto poco importaba. Según Garner, ni Rumsfeld ni Henry tenían idea de lo que estaba pasando.

Algunos días después del derribamiento de la escultura de Saddam, el Príncipe Bandar fue a ver al presidente a la Casa Blanca. Rumsfeld estaba saliendo cuando él llegó.

"Aceleraremos la retirada", le aseguró a Bandar. "No se preocupe".

Bandar le expresó a Bush su preocupación por la estabilidad de Irak. El ejército de los Estados Unidos había ocupado el país, pero Rumsfeld estaba hablando de una retirada rápida. Bandar repitió lo que le había dicho a Bush antes de la guerra. Era seguro que habría un vacío de poder en Irak. El partido Baath, el ejército, la inteligencia y los servicios de seguridad iraquíes habían manejado el país hasta entonces.

"Eliminen el escalón más alto por haber participado en el régimen y por tener las manos manchadas de sangre", recomendó Bandar. "Pero conserven la integridad de las instituciones. Lo que deberían hacer es avisar a todos los militares que se reporten de nuevo en sus barracas, y conservar los cargos de los coroneles y sus subordinados. Alguien tiene que dirigir las cosas". Y hagan lo mismo con la inteligencia iraquí y los servicios de seguridad. "Miren, el servicio de inteligencia era el más eficiente. Destituyan el nivel más alto, conserven la segunda línea y dejen que ellos encuentren a los chicos malos, porque éstos sabrán como encontrar a los otros". Tal vez podrían encontrar a Saddam.

"Eso es demasiado maquiavélico", comentó alguien. Las notas de la reunión en lengua árabe indican que fue Bush o Rice.

"Dejen que los malos encuentren a los malos y después se deshacen de ellos", sugirió Bandar. "¿Cuál es el lío? Traiciónenlos. ¡Por todos los cielos!, ¿quién dijo que les debemos algo?".

Nadie respondió.

Arabia Saudita compartía una frontera de 804 kilómetros con Irak, y después de la guerra la estabilidad del país se había convertido en una preocupación fundamental. El caos o la implantación de un régimen extremista favorable al régimen chiíta iraní sería una pesadilla para los saudíes, posiblemente peor que la relativa estabilidad que brindaba Saddam.

Los saudíes estimaban que había unos 3 millones de jubilados en Irak, sentados en casa, ganando el equivalente de 6 dólares al mes. "Páguenles durante seis meses, por Dios santo", aconsejó Bandar. "Dense cuenta de que cada uno de ellos sostiene una familia. Así que con 3 millones de personas podrían obtener el apoyo de, literalmente, 10 millones. Y, como por arte de magia, tienen una electorado a su favor, porque les han pagado".

Era la manera saudita. Pagar a tres millones de jubilados costaría aproximadamente 100 millones de dólares. Bandar propuso hacer lo mismo con el ejército iraquí. Descabezar el escalón más alto y luego pagar al resto entre tres y seis meses. Eso podría representar otros 100 millones de dólares. Después de la liberación, los iraquíes tendrían grandes expectativas, dijo Bandar. "No los decepcionen; tienen que hacerles sentir que sus vidas van a mejorar".

El partido y el ejército de Saddam –los instrumentos de la represión– podrían ser instrumentos de estabilización. El costo total del programa de compra sería de alrededor de 200 millones de dólares. Podrían ser los 200 millones de dólares mejor gastados por los Estados Unidos, dijo.

Bush indicó que la decisión dependía de Rumsfeld.

EN MEDIO DEL JÚBILO por la rápida victoria militar, las noticias en Estados Unidos mostraban cada vez más imágenes de saqueos y caos. Robin Raphel, quien tenía 28 años de experiencia diplomática, principalmente en Asia del Sur y el Medio Oriente, era la funcionaria del Departamento de Estado de más alto rango entre los consejeros del ministerio. Mientras esperaban su oportunidad para ir a Irak, ella y otros veían televisión en Kuwait; su preocupación por el estado de las cosas iba en aumento. ¿Se suponía que el equipo de Garner, con apenas unos 200 hombres, iba a manejar todo el país? Era ciencia ficción.

"No se preocupen", dijo Raphel a algunos de los miembros de menor rango del equipo de Garner. "En realidad, no podemos hacer eso. Así que no se preocupen. Lo que realmente tenemos que hacer es poner nuestro dedo en el dique, ir allá, y en algunas semanas vamos a estar de rodillas ante la ONU y la comunidad internacional". Su intención era tranquilizarlos.

"HOY ABRÍ UN PERIÓDICO y, no podía creerlo", exclamó Rumsfeld durante una conferencia de prensa en el Pentágono el 11 de abril. "Leí ocho titulares que hablaban de caos, violencia y malestar. Todos armaban una tormenta en un vaso de agua. ¡Nunca había visto nada así! Tenemos un país que está siendo liberado y gente que está pasando de la represión y el yugo de un dictador despiadado a la libertad".

Los comentarios de Rumsfeld eran subrayados por una presentación de Power Point con fotografías. Las imágenes tenían anotaciones o nombres de archivo como "Iraquíes comparten una carcajada con un soldado del ejército estadounidense"; "Iraquíes jubilosos animan a soldados del ejército estadounidense"; "Iraquíes felices posan con un soldado del ejército de los Estados Unidos", y "Dos jóvenes iraquíes hacen un gesto de aprobación con los pulgares a los soldados de la coalición".

"Permítanme decir algo más", continuó Rumsfeld. "Las imágenes que están viendo por televisión, las están viendo una y otra y otra y otra vez, y se trata de la imagen de la misma persona saliendo de algún edificio con un jarrón, y la ven veinte veces, y uno piensa: 'Dios mío, ¿había tantos jarrones?'".

Tanto Rumsfeld como el grupo de periodistas soltaron una carcajada. "¿Es posible que hubiera tantos jarrones en todo el país?", preguntó.

Bush hizo eco del comentario en una conferencia de prensa dos días después. "¿Saben?, es sorprendente", dijo. "La escultura es derribada el miércoles y los titulares empiezan a decir: 'Hay desorden'. ¡Obviamente! Es una situación caótica porque Saddam Hussein creó condiciones para el caos".

"VIERNES, 11 DE ABRIL, DÍA 23" *Spider* Marks escribió en su diario de guerra: "Nada de ADM".

Al día siguiente viajó a Bagdad con McKiernan. A pesar de la euforia que le producía poner pie, por primera vez, en Irak y no obstante los cientos de cosas que tenía en la cabeza, las armas de destrucción masiva seguían siendo su prioridad. No se trataba simplemente de la incapacidad para encontrarlas; era la preocupación de que pudieran caer en manos de alguien más. "Piensen en lo peor que podría pasar", escribió Marks el 13 de abril, después de una sesión con el general Franks. Su anotación comprimida fue: "*jihadistas* extranjeros c CBW", que significa armas químicas y biológicas.

El 19 de abril, "D+31", después de una reunión con el general McKiernan, Marks anotó los dos objetivos principales de la coalición: "mantener la integridad de las fronteras de Irak" e "ident/eliminar ADM".

Pero no lograban encontrar nada. De acuerdo con un reporte escrito más tarde por el suboficial mayor, Richard *Monty* Gonzales, funcionario a cargo de una de las unidades MET del coronel McPhee, parte del problema parecían ser los intensos saqueos y "el número limitado de fuerzas disponibles para ofrecer seguridad en los sitios sospechosos".

"La destrucción de objetivos específicos era evidente en prácticamente todos los sitios", continuaba el reporte. "En cierta ocasión, en una de las bases de operación de los servicios de inteligencia en Bagdad, el equipo se sorprendió al encontrar iraquíes empeñados en la destrucción de materiales, incluso mientras las fuerzas estadounidenses registraban el área. En un ambiente urbano –sin la seguridad adecuada–, eliminar a los saqueadores, frenar los esfuerzos deliberados de destrucción y salvaguardar el equipo se volvían tareas casi imposibles".

17

Sin mencionárselo a Garner, Rumsfeld estaba trabajando en un plan para reemplazarlo por un nuevo delegado presidencial en Irak, un cargo muy por encima del que ocupaba el general. El nuevo emisario sería más un superadministrador o, incluso, un representante presidencial. El 8 de abril Rumsfeld reunió a un grupo en su oficina del Pentágono para informarles, por boca de *Ryan* Henry, sobre una lista de potenciales candidatos. A la reunión asistió Steve Herbits, quien había diseñado para Rumsfeld un sistema estructurado para la toma de decisiones importantes relacionadas con el manejo de personal, incluida la definición precisa de cargos y objetivos. "Al final de esta reunión", anunció Rumsfeld, "quiero que Herbits tome esta presentación y la vuelva hacer".

La lista de Henry, con los posibles delegados, incluía 100 nombres. En ella se mencionaba al antiguo senador de Tennessee y jefe del Gabinete de la Casa Blanca en el gobierno de Reagan, Howard Baker, a los antiguos secretarios de defensa James Schlesinger y Harold Brown, al ex gobernador de California Pete Wilson, al ex gobernador de Oklahoma Frank Keating y al ex presidente de la reserva federal, Paul Volcker. Había también algunos nombres británicos —el ex secretario de Asuntos Exteriores del Reino Unido lord Carrington era uno de ellos—, así como un par de demócratas —los secretarios de Hacienda de Clinton Robert Rubin y Larry Summers—. Herbits sabía que los demócratas no eran una opción para considerar con seriedad. En la lista no estaban personas que tenían experiencia en operaciones de estabilización en períodos de posguerra, como Richard Holbrooke, embajador de Clinton ante la ONU, quien en 1996 había negociado un acuerdo de paz entre las facciones en conflicto en Bosnia, y James Dobbins, el *señor Posguerra*, antiguo funcionario del Departamento de Estado, el más experimentado en situaciones posconflicto. Sus nombres fueron descartados por estar asociados con la reconstrucción nacional de Clinton.

Después de escuchar durante casi una hora, Rumsfeld le dijo a Herbits en privado: "Quiero que hagas esto, pero entiende que es para el presidente".

En las siguientes 48 horas, Herbits escribió de nuevo las funciones del cargo. Estas quedaron reducidas a las áreas de seguridad, reconstrucción y política. Y redujo la lista de candidatos a los 10 mejores.

En su reporte consideraba que el mejor candidato era el ex secretario de estado, George Schultz, quien alguna vez había dirigido la Corporación Bechtel, importante proveedor del gobierno. Schultz, de 83 años, tenía la reputación de ser uno de los estadistas más respetados del mundo. Herbits lo llamó "un adulto internacional". Entre las ventajas que representaba se mencionaba que era "capaz de mantenerse firme ante la prensa y los negociadores", y que "evitaba que el Departamento de Defensa fuera culpado por acción u omisión".

Las desventajas incluían: "No es conocido por ser bueno para seguir instrucciones. Es algo mayor; puede desequilibrarse cuando está sometido a estrés por demasiado tiempo… Puede ser más tolerante con los puntos de vista del Estado que alguien del Departamento de Defensa… Podría acusársele de extralimitarse en sus deberes para favorecer los intereses de Bechtel.

Pero Herbits tenía un candidato inesperado para el trabajo. En su opinión, la persona más idónea para gobernar a Irak era Paul Wolfowitz. Redactó un memorando de cuatro páginas que eventualmente sería enviado al presidente Bush y llegaría a manos del vicepresidente Cheney.

"Cómo MANEJAR BIEN la posguerra en Irak", era el título de la comunicación de Herbits del 10 de abril del 2003. "Debido a que la primera fase diplomática ha mostrado deficiencias para lograr un consenso general para la acción", escribió lanzando un dardo al Departamento de Estado, era fundamental implementar bien la fase posterior a la acción militar. Herbits, que 16 meses antes había sido miembro del grupo Bletchley II y quien había concluido que los Estados Unidos se aproximaban a una guerra de dos generaciones con los extremistas islámicos, empezando con Irak, escribió que el éxito podría indicar que Bush tenía "un modelo para la creación de un estado palestino" e, incluso, un eventual "derrocamiento iraní".

Bajo el título "Estándares para medir el éxito", Herbits escribió: "En los meses posteriores al cese de los bombardeos, es esencial que no haya guerra civil. Las guerras civiles, justificadas o injustificadas, recuerdan a Vietnam. La estrategia del presidente se iría al piso si se llegara a hacer tal comparación.

"Es necesario establecer pronto un sistema de vida ordenada y saludable que se sostenga de manera autónoma". El gobierno interino local tenía que convertirse en "un modelo valioso para el resto de los pueblos y los gobiernos que anhelan la libertad".

El emisario presidencial debía tener absoluta autoridad "sobre todos los asuntos iraquíes por fuera de la actividad militar… reportarse al presidente si fuese posible y al secretario de Defensa como única opción alternativa".

"Por qué el delegado presidencial debe ser el subsecretario de Defensa Wolfowitz", escribió Herbits al comienzo de una nueva sección. El nombramiento de Wolfowitz proporcionaría "claridad al mundo" en cuanto al enfoque libertario del presidente y evitaría "la resistencia tradicional del Departamento de Estado a buscar el cambio en la región".

En vista de que Wolfowitz ya era subsecretario de Defensa, "tiene toda la autoridad necesaria en su cargo actual. Pero tal vez lo más importante y particular sobre Paul sea el hecho de que disfruta del más amplio respaldo entre los iraquíes". En este contexto, por supuesto, "iraquíes" significaba "exiliados iraquíes", especialmente Chalabi. "Decir que *él* no es esencial podría ser como decir que *ellos* no son importantes". Su elección "demostraría sin ambages que la importancia de la diáspora iraquí es realmente primordial. Él es el mejor símbolo a largo plazo de la estrategia global".

Luego Herbits añadió, "Su origen judío es una ventaja: es una señal de que esta no es una guerra contra la religión; es una clara señal de que el cargo es temporal, de que el antiguo embajador en la más grande nación musulmana del mundo durante tres años –Wolfowitz había sido embajador en Indonesia de 1986 a 1989– "tiene experiencia en el manejo de las diferencias culturales".

La tarde siguiente, Herbits llevó el memorando a Rumsfeld. La propuesta seguía la línea de ese tipo de pensamiento súbito y poco ortodoxo que tanto atraía al secretario. Éste llamó a Delonnie Henry.

"Suprima el nombre de Herbits", le ordenó Rumsfeld. "Ponga la siguiente portada y envíela al fax privado del presidente". Escribió una corta nota diciendo que un buen amigo y asociado había escrito ese excelente texto, y agregó: "Estoy disponible todo el fin de semana por si desea discutirlo".

El fin de semana, Herbits estuvo almorzando en casa de Cheney y le informó sobre una conferencia en el American Enterprise Institute. Llevó una copia del documento sobre Wolfowitz.

"Me gustaría que viera esto", le dijo Herbits al vicepresidente al entregarle la copia, "porque podría llegar a sus manos".

Cheney miró el papel: "Ya lo he visto".

"¡Oh!".

"Fui a comer a casa de Rumsfeld anoche y no me dejó comer antes de leerlo". Hizo una pausa. "Es un buen escrito", agregó Cheney, ofreciéndole una de sus sonrisas a medias.

Steve Hadley leyó el memorando de Herbits y estuvo de acuerdo con él. Wolfowitz era su candidato. Pero Rumsfeld estaba enviando avalanchas de memorandos, cubriendo de *copos de nieve* a todos, incluido el presidente. La elección de Wolfowitz sería vista como un espaldarazo a Chalabi, y el presidente era inflexible en cuanto a no dar la impresión de que Estados Unidos ponía el dedo en un lado de la balanza. Además, el presidente sabía que Wolfowitz no tenía muy buena reputación como administrador. El subsecretario de Defensa era un pensador, pero a duras penas dirigía su propia oficina.

Tanto Herbits como Rumsfeld le comunicaron a Wolfowitz que lo estaban proponiendo como delegado para Irak.

"Si eso es lo que quieren", le comentó Wolfowitz a Rumsfeld, "estaré complacido de hacerlo".

Rumsfeld recuerda algo distinto. "Paul vino a mí diciendo que le gustaría que se tuviera en cuenta su nombre. Me pidió que lo propusiera, y lo hice".

Pese a la anotación de Herbits sobre la ventaja que significaba el origen judío de Wolfowitz, tanto a Rumsfeld como a la Casa Blanca les preocupaba poner a un administrador judío en medio del mundo árabe.

Rumsfeld nunca le explicó a Wolfowitz por qué no había sido elegido. "Probablemente el origen judío pesó mucho en su decisión", confió después Wolfowitz a un amigo iraquí-americano.

Garner estaba ansioso por llegar a Bagdad. Pensaba que la única manera de reconstruir el país era usar contratistas. Tenían que nombrar a los civiles norteamericanos e iraquíes que se encargarían de la reconstrucción, para que empezaran a trabajar inmediatamente. Pero tan sólo habían firmado tres de los trece contratos más importantes. Según el plan de Franks, Garner y su equipo no deberían ir a Irak hasta que la invasión finalizara y empezaran las operaciones de estabilización de la fase IV.

Garner fue hasta la base de operaciones del Comando Central, en Qatar, para hacerle una petición personal a Franks. Su misión estaba en peligro. El caos era el más grande de todos los espectáculos:

"Tienes que llevarme", le imploró Garner a su viejo amigo.

"Jay", dijo Franks, "todavía hay combates en la zona". Bagdad seguía siendo zona de combate. En enero, Franks le prometió llevarlo solamente después de finalizados los combates principales. "Piensa esto. A ninguno de nosotros le va a favorecer que asesinen un grupo de civiles en Bagdad".

"Mira, Tommy. Bagdad tiene vacíos que están siendo llenados con cosas que ni tú ni yo queremos, y no vamos a poder deshacernos de esas cosas a menos que lleguemos allá ahora". La violencia y los saqueos eran más graves de lo que todos esperaban. "Si no me llevas, vamos a tener más problemas que sólo unos cuantos civiles asesinados".

"Está bien, ¡maldita sea!", cedió finalmente Franks. "Llamaré a McKiernan y veré si te puede apoyar en esto". Ambos sabían que en medio de una guerra lo que menos necesita el comandante de tierra era un puñado de civiles. "Jay, McKiernan tiene muchas cosas que hacer en este momento".

"Lo sé", dijo Garner comprensivo, "y voy a intentar facilitárselas tanto como pueda, pero tienes que llevarme allá".

Franks llamó a Garner esa noche. "Tienes luz verde. Hablé con McKiernan. Dice que va a ser muy difícil darte apoyo, pero está dispuesto a intentarlo. Que Dios te bendiga. Ten cuidado".

El 21 de abril, Garner y ocho de sus hombres llegaron a Bagdad. Todo era un desastre. Las provisiones básicas escaseaban. En un momento había electricidad y al siguiente no. Garner fue a la planta de tratamiento de aguas negras y descubrió que no estaba funcionando. El calor era insoportable. Su jefe de Estado Mayor, Bates, salió con el resto del equipo en una caravana de aproximadamente 150 Chevrolet Suburbanos, en un viaje de 644 kilómetros desde Kuwait hasta Bagdad. Garner y su equipo de camionetas tomó control de un antiguo edificio de gobierno, de 258 habitaciones y apariencia de palacio, ubicado cerca del centro de la ciudad.

AL PRESIDENTE le seguía preocupando que los Estados Unidos estuvieran perdiendo la guerra en los medios. No importa cómo la nombraran –asuntos públicos, alcance mundial, diplomacia pública, comunicaciones estratégicas– la estaban perdiendo.

Uno de los miembros del personal del Consejo Nacional de Seguridad, Jeffrey Jones, coronel retirado del ejército, había presentado un informe SECRETO a los directivos del CNS titulado "Estrategia de información para Irak, Fase IV". El reporte abundaba en gráficas, tareas, organigramas, objetivos y temas. Y, no obstante, no iba a ninguna parte. Karen Hughes, zarina de la información de Bush y consejera de la Casa Blanca, creía que el Departamento de Estado no se mostraba lo suficientemente activo para explicar la política exterior de Bush. Persuadió a Margaret Tutwiler, la gran dama de la estrategia de comunicación republicana durante las administraciones de Reagan y Bush padre, para que aceptara un alto cargo en el Departamento de Estado, el de subsecretaria de diplomacia pública.

Tutwiler, de 52 años y un marcado y confiado acento sureño, descrita en un artículo de The Washington Post como "todo un equipo de operaciones psicológicas conformado por una sola mujer", nació y fue criada en Birmingham, Alabama. Durante 12 años, había trabajado sin parar como consejera política y de comunicaciones para Jim Baker, mientras este se desempeñaba en la Casa Blanca como jefe de gabinete y secretario de Hacienda para Reagan, y luego como secretario de Estado para George H. W. Bush. Concentraba en un solo objetivo su atención e interés: la imagen y el éxito de Baker.

Tutwiler se desempeñaba como embajadora de los Estados Unidos en Marruecos cuando recibió su tarea para Irak: haga por Garner lo que hizo por Baker.

Cuando Tutwiler llegó a Bagdad, se sintió abrumada por el estado de disolución gubernamental y social —no había duchas y el servicio de electricidad no era confiable—. Los mosquitos se la estaban comiendo viva. Garner personalmente le enseñó a cocinar raciones militares de campaña listas para consumir. El *tortellini* de pollo número 19 resultó ser su favorito. Había desorden, basura y sustancias pegajosas por todos lados. No había privacidad en las habitaciones, si es que se podía llamarlas de esa manera, pues ni siquiera tenían puertas o ventanas. Dormir era casi imposible.

"Hace un maldito calor insoportable", se quejó ante Garner. "Me estoy cocinando".

"Esto, Margaret", le respondió Garner, proponiendo una antigua solución de soldado, "es lo que tiene que hacer. Quítese la ropa. Solamente quédese con la que se sienta cómoda. Si tiene suficiente agua embotellada, distribúyala por todo el lugar, mójese el cuerpo y luego recuéstese en la cama bajo el mosquitero. El agua se evaporará y se sentirá más fresca".

A la mañana siguiente Garner le preguntó si aquello había funcionado.

"Me empapé", relató Tutwiler, "me metí en el mosquitero, estaba completamente mojada, cerré los ojos y me dispuse a dormir. Cuando desperté me estaba asfixiando y no pude soportarlo. Tuvimos una terrible tormenta de arena. Parecía una bola de barro".

Era tan desastroso el estado de Irak, concluyó Tutwiler, que ni siquiera Jim Baker habría podido poner las cosas en orden. Ni el gobierno ni la sociedad del país funcionaban como debían. Pero Tutwiler sabía por experiencia que el gobierno estadounidense de turno siempre buscaba control absoluto y resultados inmediatos. Muy pronto, empezó a recibir llamadas de funcionarios de la Casa Blanca y el Pentágono que se quejaban por las fotografías de saqueos y caos que mostraban la televisión y los periódicos. Ponga esas fotografías fuera de circulación, le ordenaron.

Tutwiler reportó a todos en Washington que los vacíos de poder político e infraestructura eran de una magnitud inimaginable. Sobrepasaban cualquier cosa que ella hubiera visto.

A Tutwiler le agradaba Garner. Pensaba que era un verdadero patriota, sin agenda personal. Pero no era un Jim Baker. Garner no sabía cómo alinear a todos los jugadores en el juego de Washington, es decir, el proceso interinstitucional. No tenía idea de cómo dejar felices al Pentágono, el Departamento de Estado, la CIA, la Casa Blanca y el Ministerio de Hacienda. Garner parecía tener las ideas adecuadas, pero no los contactos, ni la influencia necesaria en Washington, y tampoco contaba con el elemento humano que necesitaba en Bagdad.

Garner se quejó con Tutwiler de que había recibido órdenes de no hablar con la prensa desde que había salido de Washington, cuando, en una conferencia de prensa, se había mostrado indiferente hacia Chalabi y el Congreso Nacional Iraquí. Era ridículo. Comunicar y dar explicaciones era parte de su trabajo. La prensa sospechaba y estaba furiosa por su silencio.

Tutwiler intentó inútilmente levantar la prohibición. Habló con sus contactos personales en la Casa Blanca, el Pentágono y el Departamento de Estado. Nadie quería que Garner hablara con la prensa. No querían que hiciera declaraciones políticas. Al parecer sus reacciones eran muy impulsivas. Tutwiler recibió, incluso, quejas de que Garner iba por todo el país sin saco y corbata, mostrando una falta de respeto hacia los iraquíes.

Finalmente, Garner llamó a Rumsfeld para protestar.

"No hay tal prohibición", le aseguró Rumsfeld, "usted puede hablar con quien tenga que hacerlo".

Tutwiler organizó inmediatamente una conferencia de prensa, pero 45 minutos después le anunció a Garner: "De nuevo le han prohibido hablar".

"Llamaré a Rumsfeld", dijo Garner.

"No servirá de nada", respondió ella. "La orden viene de la Casa Blanca". Eso significaba que provenía de Karen Hughes.

Tutwiler halló, entonces, una solución a medias. Alertaría a los reporteros cuando Garner se estuviera desplazando de un sitio a otro, de modo que una que otra agencia de noticias pudiera "emboscarlo" y así él pudiera hacer breves comentarios. Luego se las arreglaría con Washington diciéndoles: "Lo acorralaron y tenía que decir algo. Las cámaras estaban encendidas. Habría sido peor no decir nada".

Pero aquellos fragmentos de noticias o comentarios breves resultaban sumamente insatisfactorios tanto para Garner como para los medios.

Tutwiler entabló amistad con Hero Talabani, esposa del líder kurdo Jalal Talabani. En medio de una discusión, Hero se volvió hacia ella y dijo algo que Tutwiler recordaría durante años: "Esperábamos más de ustedes, los americanos".

SEMANAS DESPUÉS del inicio de la guerra, en la oficina de Rumsfeld y en el Pentágono proliferaban documentos sobre cómo manejar bien el período de posguerra. Uno de los borradores de un organigrama clasificado llevaba el encabezado "La restauración: prioridad civil". La gráfica mostraba al secretario de Defensa en el nivel jerárquico más alto y en ella todo apuntaba al Comandante Central, el general Franks. Otra tenía al presidente a la cabeza, luego estaba Rumsfeld y luego un nuevo "Administrador de la coalición". Garner aparecía en la lista como subdirector de asuntos civiles, y el general Abizaid fue propuesto como subdirector de seguridad y apoyo. Ambos se reportarían al nuevo "Administrador de la coalición". Otra gráfica mencionaba a un subdirector de seguridad y apoyo, pero no incluía a Abizaid.

HERBITS SEGUÍA BUSCANDO el emisario perfecto. El 22 de abril, más de un mes después de la invasión, ya tenía una lista con las características que debía tener el candidato: compromiso con la misión del presidente, receptividad a la dirección del presidente y de Rumsfeld, buen juicio, prestigio, presencia y capacidad para comunicarse, empatía, habilidad para entablar negociaciones políticas, buena aceptación en los dos partidos, capacidad para trabajar con altos mandos militares, habilidad para operar con las distintas agencias, disponibilidad y temple. El organigrama mostraba a Garner separado de la cadena militar, reportándose al nuevo y desconocido emisario especial.

En la sección de tareas clave para lograr la transición a un gobierno local interino, todos los asuntos económicos y políticos estaban bajo el encabezado "Pendientes". La lista iba desde la deuda del país, los créditos y la política petrolera hasta las tareas de reforma, el Estado de derecho y el proceso político para formar el nuevo gobierno. Todo esto sucedía dos semanas después de la caída de Bagdad.

Puesto que cualquier funcionario relacionado con la administración Clinton era automáticamente descartado, un nombre seguía apareciendo en la corta lista de Herbits: L. Paul *Jerry* Bremer, experto en terrorismo de 61 años que había estado durante 23 años en el servicio diplomático. Bremer, protegido de Henry Kissinger, había sido embajador de los Estados Unidos en Holanda desde 1983 hasta 1986, y luego se había desempeñado como embajador viajero de contraterrorismo para el Departamento de Estado. Habiéndose retirado del servicio diplomático, su nombre no estaba mancillado por haber servido en el gobierno de Clinton. Antes de dirigir la Comisión Nacional sobre el Terrorismo en el 2000, Bremer fue director administrativo de Kissinger Associates, la firma consultora del antiguo secretario de Estado, durante más de una década. Antes de los ataques del 9/11 predijo públicamente que el suelo estadounidense sería fuertemente golpeado. Con aire infantil y tupida cabellera, Bremer proyectaba una profunda confianza en sí mismo y una fuerza que rozaba la pedantería.

El 24 de abril Rumsfeld llamó a Powell para postular a Bremer. Powell respondió que tendría que pensarlo. Él y Armitage examinaron los 23 años de carrera de Bremer en el servicio diplomático y su estrecha relación con Kissinger y el Departamento de Estado. "¡Sí!", aclamó Armitage. Bremer era un aliado seguro. Pero no querían mostrar demasiado entusiasmo porque eso echaría a perder el nombramiento.

Cuando entrevisté a Rumsfeld en 2006, estaba un poco a la defensiva en cuanto al papel que había jugado en la selección de Bremer.

"Obviamente, Jerrry Bremer era un emisario presidencial, y como tal se reportaba al presidente, a Condi y a los miembros del CNS", aclaró Rumsfeld.

"Usted lo escogió", recalqué.

"Espere un momento", dijo Rumsfeld. "Todos estábamos de acuerdo en que era él, que ése era el hombre. Creo que olvidé de dónde salió su nombre, pero tal vez haya sido George Shultz quien lo recomendó".

"Eso no es cierto", replicó Shultz luego, cuando le mencioné lo que Rumsfeld recordaba. "Don me llamó y dijo que tenía una lista". Shultz dijo que le había dicho a Rumsfeld que tenía un buen concepto de Bremer. "Pero también tenía en su lista a Howard Baker, y él sería la persona ideal porque era un político y podía llegar a los demás".

Le mencioné a Shultz que inicialmente él era la primera opción en la lista de candidatos del Pentágono.

"¡Es la primera vez que escucho eso!", dijo Shultz, casi agitado. Según sus palabras, ni Rumsfeld ni ninguna otra persona le planteó esa posibilidad.

Al parecer, el Pentágono sentía que él podría inclinarse demasiado hacia el Departamento de Estado y sería difícil controlarlo, le mencioné.

"Nunca me pudieron controlar", anotó Shultz.

Los dos líderes kurdos, Massoud Barzani y Jalal Talabani, viejos rivales y líderes de la región semiautónoma kurda, al norte de Irak, habían dejado a un lado sus diferencias, en un esfuerzo pragmático por favorecer el futuro de los kurdos iraquíes. En abril de 2003 los dos hombres declararon públicamente que querían formar un gobierno interino en Bagdad.

Garner estaba alarmado. Desde luego, hacía parte de la estrategia estadounidense poner una facción iraquí en el gobierno interino, pero Irak era, en su mayoría, chiíta. Los kurdos eran minoría, al igual que los sunitas. El nuevo gobierno debería tener más de una facción chiíta. El 22 de abril, justo después de llegar a Bagdad, Garner y Larry DiRita viajaron al norte a entrevistarse con Barzani y Talabani. Ambos hombres conocían a Garner desde la *Operación*

Provide Comfort, aunque no se habían visto en más de una década. "Hoy me siento como si volviera a casa", exclamó Garner ante una multitud de kurdos iraquíes que le daban la bienvenida. Barzani y Talabani lo recibieron con besos y abrazos, y Garner llevó a los dos líderes a un lado. "Una de las razones por las que vine es, en primer lugar, es porque quería verlos", dijo Garner afectuosamente. "Pero, en segundo lugar, entiendo que planean formar un gobierno en Bagdad, y tengo algunas objeciones al respecto".

"No vamos a formar un gobierno", replicó Talabani.

"Eso fue lo que escuché", respondió Garner.

"No. Vamos a formar un grupo asesor, una facción de líderes para ustedes. ¿No cree que lo necesitan?"

"Por supuesto", dijo Garner. "Quiero hacerlo. ¿Quién será?"

"Bueno", dijo Talabani, "seremos todos nosotros, los que trabajamos con Zal". Zalmay Khalilzad del CNS había estado trabajando con ellos durante casi año y medio, y había sido designado "embajador viajero de los iraquíes libres". Talabani mencionó tres de los iraquíes que él pensaba que debían participar. Entre ellos se encontraba Adnan Pachachi, un octogenario sunita que había sido ministro de relaciones exteriores de Irak y embajador ante la ONU antes de que Saddam Hussein asumiera el poder. Luego, estaba Ayad Allawi, el líder chiíta de un grupo de oposición con sede en Londres, llamado la Alianza Nacional Iraquí. Finalmente, por supuesto, estaba Ahmed Chalabi.

"Miren el problema que veo en todo esto", explicó Garner. "Todos esos hombres, excepto ustedes dos, son expatriados, y ustedes dos son kurdos. ¿Qué les parece alguien de adentro del país que haya estado aquí, que sea árabe?".

"Vamos a traer a Hakim", dijo Talabi, refiriéndose a Mohammed Bakir Hakim, el líder espiritual del partido chiíta más grande de Irak, el Consejo Supremo para la Revolución Islámica en Irak. "Pensamos traer a Jafari –Ibrahim al-Jafari, un exilado chiíta e iracundo oponente de Saddam– y traeremos a un cristiano".

"Está bien, eso funcionará", dijo Garner, pero agregó: "Con el único que no me siento cómodo es con Hakim. Es demasiado iraní".

"Jay", dijo Talabani, apoyando su mano en la pierna de Garner, "es mejor tener a Hakim dentro de la carpa que fuera de ella".

"Es un consejo condenadamente bueno", dijo Garner. "Procedamos. Los quiero en Bagdad en una semana, a todos ustedes. Quiero traer a sus delegados. Quiero formar un comité de adjuntos". El comité trabajaría directamente con el equipo de Garner.

"Eso haremos", confirmó Talabani.

"Miren, si esto funciona, los convertiré en un gobierno provisional", aseguró Garner a los dos líderes. "Seguirán trabajando para mí, pero los convertiré en un gobierno provisional".

El siguiente tema fueron algunas consideraciones prácticas: "Qué vamos a hacer con la constitución, porque tenemos que hacer participar a la gente", preguntó Garner.

"Ya pensamos en eso", respondió Talabani. "Tendremos una reunión de grandes proporciones convocando a unas 200 o 300 personas. Jay, esto va a ser un mosaico de Irak. Estarán todos los grupos étnicos, todas las religiones, las profesiones y los géneros. Escribiremos la Constitución. Le daremos la lista de personas y usted puede remover y agregar a quien quiera".

"¿Qué tan rápido podemos hacerlo?", preguntó Garner, recordando que le había prometido a su esposa estar en casa para el cuatro de julio.

"Lo pondremos en marcha el primero de julio", prometió Talabani.

Inmediatamente después de la reunión, Garner llamó al general Abizaid para explicarle el plan. Éste dudaba que funcionara.

"No creo que tengamos opción", repuso Garner.

"Yo tampoco. Prosigamos y hagámoslo".

"Quiero que consigas un salvoconducto para Talabani y Barzani desde el norte hasta Bagdad", le pidió Garner.

Garner le ordenó a DiRita llamar al Pentágono e informarles lo que estaba pasando. Él mismo llamó a Powell.

"¿Qué está haciendo allá?", preguntó el secretario de Estado.

Garner describió el plan del gobierno provisional que incluiría a todos bajo una gran y única carpa.

"Interesante", dijo Powell. Sonaba como una de esas maratones de ventas de autos en carpas, que promocionaban por televisión los grandes concesionarios de vehículos. Sabía que el asunto era muchísimo más complicado. Había muchas fuerzas encontradas. Era obvio que el Pentágono y Cheney estaban apoyando a Chalabi. En una ocasión, Khalilzad presentó el *Megabrief Two*, un plan secreto sobre el proceso político en Irak, a los directores –Powell, Rumsfeld, Rice, Cheney, Myers y Tenet–. Era un esquema que mostraba cómo organizar a los iraquíes en el ámbito local, lograr un consenso, empezar la construcción de partidos políticos, establecer luego gobiernos locales y trabajar a partir de allí en el ámbito nacional.

Hacer algo así tomaría años de trabajo. Así que los directores pronto dejaron de lado la idea y el reporte. Decidieron no presentarlo al presidente.

BUSH HABÍA ACEPTADO PONER a un superadministrador a cargo de Garner. Pero el presidente quería ver el organigrama del lado de los Estados Unidos y también la forma como se unificaría el gobierno en Irak.

Hadley convocó a una reunión de adjuntos, pero no lograron proponer el organigrama final. Hadley les indicó que el presidente estaba ansioso y que quería que personas clave de todos los departamentos y agencias se quedaran trabajando: Frank Miller, Elliott Abrams, alguien del Departamento de Estado y un representante de la CIA. En tono burlón anunció que los encerraría en la Sala de Situaciones hasta que terminaran el trabajo.

Dough Feith, quien representaba a Defensa, se levantó dispuesto a marcharse. El segundo al mando de Dough, William Luti, capitán retirado de la Marina que había sido asistente de Newt Gingrich y de Cheney, también se incorporó. "Bien", dijo Luti, "tengo que irme con Dough. Me dará un aventón".

"Ya oíste lo que dijo Steve", interrumpió Frank Miller. "Nos vamos a sentar aquí a trabajar".

"Trataremos de enviar a alguien", respondió Luti y se marchó, pero no apareció ningún representante del Pentágono.

Durante casi dos horas, el grupo trabajó fuertemente para diseñar un organigrama que tuviera el administrador de los Estados Unidos a la cabeza. Un consejo iraquí de mayores y un representante de las Naciones Unidas consultarían al administrador, pero la cadena de mando iba desde el administrador estadounidense hasta los ministros iraquíes, quienes inicialmente serían dirigidos por un funcionario de los Estados Unidos y contarían con consultores iraquíes. Con el tiempo los iraquíes tomarían el control y los representantes de Estados Unidos se convertirían en consultores. Algunos de los ministerios menos importantes pasarían rápidamente al mando de Irak, pero los más importantes, como los de Defensa y del Interior, permanecerían bajo el control de Estados Unidos por más tiempo.

En el esquema se vislumbraba una ocupación prolongada.

Al día siguiente se presentó la gráfica y el diagrama ante una reunión de directores. Rumsfeld entró atacando. "Este no es el resultado de un trabajo mancomunado entre agencias", dijo. "Mi gente no participó".

"Señor secretario", replicó Miller, "Hadley les ordenó que lo hicieran, su gente se marchó; dijeron que tal vez enviarían a alguien. No había otra opción. Su gente abandonó el juego".

Rumsfeld no respondió, pero las gráficas y los diagramas eran una simple abstracción. Según la directiva presidencial NSP-24, él estaba a cargo.

18

Aunque técnicamente había estado por fuera del gobierno desde 1999, el antiguo presidente de la Cámara de Representantes, Newt Gingrich, se lanzó al ruedo culpando públicamente al Departamento de Estado por el fracaso diplomático y por las riñas ideológicas que se presentaban al interior de la administración. "El Departamento de Estado vuelve a insistir en políticas que, sin duda, echarán a perder los frutos de una victoria lograda con esfuerzo", declaró el 24 de abril durante un discurso en el American Enterprise Institute.

Armitage respondió por Powell: "Es evidente que el señor Gingrich ha suspendido sus medicinas y su terapia".

Unos días después, los empleados de Armitage organizaron una pequeña fiesta en su oficina del séptimo piso para celebrar su cumpleaños número 58. Tenet envió un gran afiche con una caricatura de Armitage levantando pesas, haciendo un visible esfuerzo físico y empapado en sudor. La leyenda decía: "Suspendió sus medicinas y su terapia. Feliz cumpleaños".

Garner poco sabía de las reuniones y trifulcas de Washington. En lo que a él concernía, estaba a cargo de todas las responsabilidades de la posguerra. Cuando llegó a Bagdad, un reportero le preguntó cuánto tiempo estarían los Estados Unidos en Irak y si él era el nuevo gobernante del país.

"No puedo asegurarle que nos habremos marchado en noventa días, pero estaremos sólo el tiempo que sea necesario. Nos iremos razonablemente rápido, respondió Garner, y añadió: "El nuevo gobernante de Irak va a ser un iraquí. Yo no soy gobernante de nada".

Resultaba evidente que la situación en Irak era distinta de lo que habían anticipado. No había sucedido lo peor que pudieran haber imaginado: incendio de pozos petroleros, gente desplazada, refugiados, epidemias, bajas masivas por arsenal químico. Pero por estar muy extendidos y arraigados, los problemas eran, en muchos aspectos, más graves. El 23 de abril, Garner redactó una lista de nueve objetivos que quería lograr antes del primero de julio, día de la "reunión de la gran carpa", y de su partida. Básicamente se trataba de una ambigua agenda de buen gobierno, que abarcaba todos los aspectos, desde la policía hasta el alcantarillado[8].

En Bagdad, el 24 de abril, Garner se reunió con el general McKiernan para examinar los nueve objetivos.

Hay un décimo punto que debes añadir a la lista, señaló McKiernan: la seguridad. Todavía se presentaban peleas, si bien ningún estallido de violencia importante. Garner accedió y agregó la seguridad como décimo objetivo. Ninguno de los dos observó que McKiernan, quien estaba al mando de aproximadamente 150.000 soldados estadounidenses y británicos, estaba pasando, sutilmente, la responsabilidad de la seguridad a Garner, cuya organización sólo contaba con unos 200 hombres.

Los saqueos no daban tregua. El coronel Tom Baltazar, del equipo de Garner, recordaría luego haber visto un "maldito bote, de casi ocho metros, arrastrado por un carro en medio de una calle principal de Bagdad. No en un remolque". Algún tipo lo había encadenado a la parte trasera del carro y lo arrastraba, destrozando completamente el casco del bote. Otro carro que pasaba remolcaba un cañón antiguo, uno de los dos que los británicos habían dejado afuera de una academia militar iraquí en 1924.

Baltazar le imploró a McKiernan, "Tienes que detener esto. Nuestra misión es restablecer el gobierno, y no podemos hacerlo si están destruyendo todo".

"Tom, no quiero volver a escuchar eso de tu boca", recuerda haberle escuchado Baltazar a McKiernan. "Ese no es mi trabajo".

Aun así, Garner sentía que hacía una labor excepcionalmente buena en equipo con McKiernan. El grupo de este último era el mejor que había visto Garner. Tenía generales de una y dos estrellas al mando de secciones que podrían haber sido dirigidas sólo por un coronel. Ambos acordaron poner un oficial general –por lo menos un general de una estrella o un almirante– al frente de cada uno de los diez objetivos de Garner, mientras que éste, a su vez,

---

8. La lista de Garner de cosas por hacer antes del 1 de julio incluía: 1. Instaurar nuevamente a los ministerios iraquíes en sus funciones. 2. Pagar los salarios de todos los servidores públicos del país, incluyendo al ejército y a la policía. 3. Reestablecer la policía, las cortes y las prisiones. 4. Asegurar los servicios básicos en Bagdad (agua, alcantarillado, electricidad, etc.) Esto traería un beneficio adicional, pensaba Garner, porque la mayoría de reporteros que cubrían la guerra estaban en Bagdad. Estarían contentos -y tal vez escribirían mejores historias- si tenían aire acondicionado y duchas calientes. 5. Finalizar la crisis de combustible en Irak. 6. Comprar las cosechas iraquíes (toneladas de trigo y cebada). 7. Reestablecer el sistema de distribución de alimentos. 8. Reestablecer la gobernabilidad local interina, planeando las elecciones de los consejos de cada una de las 26 ciudades iraquíes de 100.000 o más habitantes. 9. Asegurar que el sistema local de salud estuviera funcionando y mantener los programas para evitar epidemias.

asignaría cada uno de ellos a un alto mando civil, creando un equipo civil y militar. Los oficiales subalternos hacían las cosas, en parte, porque querían convertirse en oficiales superiores. No había mejor modelo de energía y vigor que un general de una estrella con una misión.

En Bagdad, Garner se dio cuenta de que las fuerzas estadounidenses se movilizaban en tanques y vehículos militares blindados y quiso hacerlas menos visibles. Apodó a los tanques "trituradoras de aceras", y en una ocasión interpeló a una unidad: "Salgan de sus malditos camiones y dejen de hacer pedazos las aceras y los bordillos de las calles". Hasta habló con uno de los asistentes de McKiernan y le dijo que debían hacer más patrullas a pie, quitarse el chaleco antibala y los cascos de *kevlar*. Garner se negaba a usar chaleco antibalas o a viajar en vehículos blindados. Eso enviaría un mensaje equivocado.

No obstante, el ambiente en la ciudad era tenso y las fuerzas estadounidenses estaban preparadas para la acción. Generalmente iban protegidos de pies a cabeza y estaban listos para el combate.

EL 24 DE ABRIL, alrededor de las 6 de la tarde, el coronel de la Fuerza Aérea, Kim Olson, asistente ejecutivo de Garner le anunció: "Tiene una llamada del secretario de Defensa".

"Mira, Jay, lo estás haciendo magníficamente", dijo Rumsfeld cuando estuvo en el teléfono. "Estamos orgullosos de lo que estás haciendo". También mencionó que había recibido información de que el equipo de Garner llegaría en pleno y que, por lo que él veía, las cosas iban muy bien.

"Sí, señor", respondió Garner.

"A propósito", dijo Rumsfeld, "una de las razones por las que te llamo es para avisarte que el presidente ha elegido a Jerry Bremer como emisario presidencial". No sabía cuándo anunciarían la noticia, pero quería asegurarse de que Garner lo supiera antes.

"Bien", dijo Garner, a quien la noticia había tomado por sorpresa, "si el presidente ya eligió a alguien, entonces me iré a casa".

"No", objetó Rumsfeld. "No quiero que vayas a casa".

"Así no funcionan las cosas", replicó Garner. "No es posible tener al mismo tiempo al hombre que estaba a cargo y al nuevo encargado, porque se dividen las lealtades de la gente. Así que lo mejor será irme de aquí".

"No hagas nada hasta que yo llegue a Irak. Ya hablaremos tú y yo", le pidió Rumsfeld, quien planeaba llegar en unos días. "Jay, este siempre ha sido el plan. Tú lo sabes. Siempre fue el plan".

"Eso es cierto. Tengo que reconocerle eso", dijo Garner. Sin embargo, todo estaba sucediendo antes de lo que él esperaba.

"Quiero que llames a Jerry Bremer", añadió Rumsfeld y le dio el número telefónico.

"Lo haré".

Después de colgar, recordaría Garner en una entrevista, se sintió traicionado. "Pensé: Esos hijos de puta. Me rompí el trasero. Dejé todo lo que tenía. Abandoné todo lo que estaba haciendo. En ese momento pensé que había hecho un trabajo excepcionalmente bueno. Muy dentro de mí, pensaba que así era". En su declaración expresó que se había sentido engañado. "Fui muy inocente al pensar que podía poner todo a marchar y que habría un gran clamor popular entre los iraquíes... Pensé: 'He puesto todo en marcha'. Y todo lo que iban a tener que hacer era esperar y ver los frutos, y eso no iba a tardar mucho en suceder".

"Lo que más me enfureció fue que, realmente, nunca anunciaron lo que estaban haciendo. De un momento a otro, Bremer viene, y parece como si me hubieran despedido; tal vez eso fue lo que hicieron.

"Creo que para el resto del mundo yo era el emisario presidencial en Irak, o como quieran llamarlo, el primer gobernante o algo así. Para la administración, para el Departamento de Defensa, yo era un mecánico. 'Contratamos a este tipo'. Es obvio que para ellos nunca tuve la posición que tenía para el resto del mundo".

ALGUNAS HORAS DESPUÉS de haberse comunicado con Garner, Rumsfeld hizo otra llamada. El presidente había viajado ese día a Lima, Ohio, para hacer una aparición como de campaña electoral en una planta de fabricación de tanques M1 Abrams Main Battle Tank. Allí, Bush destacó y elogió la labor de Jay Garner: "Nos hemos apoyado en un equipo dirigido por este hombre, que tiene un objetivo de la más alta importancia, dejar una nación libre en manos de un pueblo libre". También alabó las bondades del tanque, de 4,3 millones de dólares y 70 toneladas de peso, diciendo que era "el vehículo más seguro para nuestro personal de combate, con la precisión que se necesita para proteger vidas inocentes". El mes anterior, durante la invasión, novecientos tanques M1 habían cruzado las fronteras de Irak.

Rumsfeld llamó a Andy Card para protestar porque habían escogido la planta de fabricación del tanque Abrams para una visita presidencial. El tanque Abrams era cosa del pasado, ya no era el arma liviana, rápida y cambiante del futuro. El presidente estaba enviando el mensaje equivocado. Debían hablar el mismo idioma: ¡transformación! Eso no habría pasado en su época de jefe del Estado Mayor, sentenció.

Es increíble, pensó Card. Rumsfeld estaba fuera de control. No solamente era, por ley, el secretario en la cadena militar de mando, sino que quería figurar hasta en las decisiones más insignificantes.

Card sentía que podía llamar a los otros secretarios del gabinete –Powell, por ejemplo– y hacerlos cooperar y cumplir las órdenes y peticiones del presidente. Pero no a Rumsfeld.

BREMER HABÍA APOYADO firmemente la decisión de invadir a Irak. Creía que era el único curso moralmente posible y que las ADM, que supuestamente existían, eran una amenaza incontestable e inminente. En abril, según escribió tiempo después, Wolfowitz y *Scooter* Libby lo habían contactado y le habían preguntado si le interesaría hacerse cargo de la etapa de posguerra en Irak. Le revelaron que nunca habían tenido la intención de dejar a Garner como cabeza permanente de los esfuerzos de reconstrucción. Necesitaban a alguien que supiera de diplomacia y política.

Luego de recibir la bendición de su esposa, Bremer fue a ver a Rumsfeld, a quien conocía desde que trabajaron juntos en la administración Ford. Poco después se reunió con el presidente.

"¿Por qué quiere un trabajo tan espinoso?", le preguntó Bush, de acuerdo con el recuento de Bremer.

"Porque creo que Estados Unidos ha hecho algo maravilloso al liberar a Irak, señor. Y porque pienso que puedo ayudar".

EN BAGDAD, la inminente llegada de Bremer era recibida con estupefacción.

"¿Por qué diablos están haciendo eso?", dijo Abizaid cuando Garner le contó.

"John, no lo sé".

McKiernan estaba sorprendido. Tutwiler dijo estar estupefacta. "¿Puedes creerlo?", exclamó Robin Raphel.

"¡Por favor! Tienes que estar bromeando", dijo DiRita cuando Garner se lo contó. Le preocupaba, no tanto la decisión de nombrar a un diplomático más experimentado, sino la manera poco ortodoxa como estaban manejando el asunto. "¡Eso no puede ser algo bueno!".

"Paul, esto no está bien", le dijo DiRita a Wolfowitz. El mensaje que estaban enviando era que Garner había fracasado. "Esto es un problema serio. Alguien tiene que salir hoy y explicar qué diablos está pasando".

Pero la decisión ya estaba tomada y nadie daba un paso al frente para dar explicaciones.

Garner se encontró con Khalilzad. "Bremer viene para acá y yo me voy", dijo.

"¿Quién?"

"Jerry Bremer".

"¿Qué quiere decir con que viene para acá?".

"Viene como emisario presidencial".

"Entonces renuncio".

"No creo que debas renunciar, Zal", respondió Garner. "Has invertido demasiado en esto. Eres un tipo muy importante. No puedes renunciar".

Khalilzad simplemente se marchó. Dos años más tarde regresaría como embajador de Estados Unidos en Irak.

Garner llamó a Rumsfeld para ver si podían retrasar algunos meses la llegada de Bremer.

"Tengo muchas cosas cocinándose y creo que puedo tenerlas todas listas para el 1 de julio", explicó Garner.

"No puedo hacer eso", sentenció Rumsfeld. "No depende de mí".

CUANDO GARNER LLEGÓ a su oficina la mañana siguiente para llamar a Bremer, el teléfono estaba sonando.

"Usted está haciendo un excelente trabajo allá", exclamó Bremer, haciendo eco de las palabras de Rumsfeld y demostrando con lujo sus habilidades de diplomático.

"Las cosas se ven muy mal desde aquí, en los periódicos", dijo Bremer en una llamada posterior. La televisión y los diarios estaban llenos de imágenes de saqueos y caos.

"Jerry", respondió Garner, "si usted va a intentar gobernar a Irak basándose en lo que sale en *The Washington Post*, prepárese para esperar un rato muy largo". Agregó que no sabía lo que publicaban los periódicos. En ese momento, dijo, ni siquiera tenía electricidad.

"Sí, pero tiene que prestar atención a la manera como se ven las cosas desde aquí", repitió Bremer. "De todos modos debe estar atento a lo que están diciendo sobre usted".

"Cuando llegue aquí usted puede hacer eso", repuso Garner.

El equipo de Garner estaba tratando de trabajar en edificios destrozados. Diecisiete de las veintitrés construcciones de los ministerios estaban prácticamente arrasadas. Las puertas, los batientes de las puertas, las ventanas, los alféizares, las tuberías y el cableado eléctrico habían sido dañados. En algunos casos, los saqueadores habían prendido fuego a los cascos vacíos de los edificios. El hollín, la suciedad, la inmundicia y los desperdicios humanos cubrían los pisos de las edificaciones. Los empleados de los ministerios habían huido. Algunos miembros del equipo de Garner fueron a Bagdad a buscarlos, preguntando casi al azar: "¿Conoce a alguien que trabajara en el Ministerio de Transporte?" o "¿Conoce a alguien del Ministerio de Salud?".

A FINALES DE ABRIL, un traductor libanés que había estado trabajando para la CIA se acercó al coronel Paul Hughes, su "socio".

"¿Ya vio esto?", preguntó.

Le mostró a Hughes un documento de una página, una traducción al inglés de una directiva que había sido emitida por la oficina central del Mukhabarat, el servicio de inteligencia de Saddam.

En el memorando se enumeraban 11 cosas que el Mukhabarat haría "en caso de que, Dios no lo permita, nuestro amado líder fuera derrocado". Cada una de las células del Baath, cada escuadrón del *fedayines* y cada agente del Mukhabarat se encargarían de asesinar a los colaboradores del derrocamiento, quemar los edificios de los ministerios, saquear, prender fuego a documentos públicos, en resumidas cuentas, de emprender acciones para provocar el caos. No decía nada de violencia sectaria, nada de hacer explotar las divisiones de los chiítas, los kurdos y los sunitas. Decía que todos los agentes independientes del partido Baath debían pensar en la manera de desencadenar un infierno si el gobierno de Saddam caía.

Hughes estaba perplejo, pues comprendió que los Estados Unidos y las fuerzas de la coalición se enfrentaban a mucho más de lo que habían imaginado.

En su libro, Bremer recuerda haber visto un documento similar, pero sólo tres meses después, a finales de julio o principios de agosto. El memorando del Mukhabarat que Bremer había visto, con fecha 23 de enero del 2003, estaba dirigido a "todas las oficinas y departamentos", y ofrecía un plan de contingencia en caso de que el país fuera invadido. "Quemen esta oficina", empezaba el memorando, y a continuación describía una estrategia de "sabotaje y saqueo" y ordenaba a los subordinados "enviar agentes a todos los pueblos. Destruir las plantas de energía y los acueductos. Infiltrar las mezquitas, los lugares chiítas sagrados".

"NO PUEDO CREER lo que ha hecho ese hijo de puta", dijo el general Myers en el *Tanque* del Pentágono. Myers no logró que el general Franks respondiera a sus preguntas, ni siquiera que pasara al teléfono. Ahora, según había escuchado, Franks quería abandonar la zona de combate y venir a Washington para la cena anual de los corresponsales en la Casa Blanca, el 26 de abril. ¿Dejar una zona de combate por una fiesta? Myers estaba perplejo. Rumsfeld debía decirle a Franks que no asistiera a la recepción.

AHORA, *SPIDER* MARKS estaba viviendo el desafío que seis meses antes él mismo había descrito para los chicos listos de la Agencia de Inteligencia del Ministerio de Defensa (AID) en el Pentágono. Ya no importaba si los intentos fallidos de encontrar ADM eran un problema de inteligencia o de logística. El hecho era que no habían hallado nada. En un momento de frustración, depositó toda la responsabilidad en los hombros del Comando Central del general Franks. Si no podía compartir con su jefe el infierno que estaba viviendo, tenía que expresarlo en algún otro lado.

"Están completamente dormidos en los laureles. Nadie anticipó o procesó el requerimiento de investigar detalles sobre las ADM", escribió Marks en su diario de guerra el 28 de abril, abreviando "requerimientos" como "req." "¡Estos tipos son unos idiotas! Es increíble".

Ese mismo día, se enteró de que la AID asumiría la búsqueda de ADM. El Grupo de Inspección para Irak, como se denominaría el destacamento, sería comandado por un general de dos estrellas llamado Keith Dayton, jefe de la sección de inteligencia humana de la AID.

Marks se puso en contacto con Dayton. "Usted va a tener una enorme tarea de coordinación, pero, tal vez, si cuenta con el respaldo de la autoridad del secretario de Defensa, pueda encontrar algunas ADM. "Cuando llegue, haga llover mierda".

Dayton mencionó que estaba retrasando su llegada a Irak para poder asistir a la graduación de su hijo. Eso quería decir que Marks y Dayton difícilmente coincidirían.

RUMSFELD VIAJÓ A IRAK el 30 de abril. En tierra, reinaba la ambigüedad. Todo había terminado pero, al mismo tiempo, nada había terminado. Se dirigió a 1.000 soldados de la Tercera División de Infantería en un inmenso hangar del aeropuerto.

"Ustedes han rescatado una nación", les dijo. "Han liberado un pueblo. Han derrocado un cruel dictador y han terminado con una amenaza para las naciones libres. Se han enfrentado a los escuadrones de la muerte y a las tormentas de arena, cruzando cientos de kilómetros para llegar a Bagdad en menos de un mes". No contuvo los deseos de dirigir una flecha de sarcasmo a quienes escribieron o dijeron que la guerra se había movido más lentamente de lo que había anticipado la administración. "Algunas personas llamaron a eso un pantanal".

Tradicionalmente en una guerra, ocupar la capital del enemigo marca el fin del conflicto. De modo que Rumsfeld y los otros —incluso Garner— se sentían victoriosos. Garner hizo unos comentarios completamente irreales a los periodistas. "Aquí no hay tantos problemas de infraestructura", dijo, "a no ser por la reconexión pendiente de algunos cables".

Rumsfeld grabó, desde uno de los Commando Solo, las naves utilizadas para las operaciones de guerra psicológica, un mensaje alentador que debía transmitirse al pueblo iraquí: "Permítanme aclarar algo: Irak les pertenece. Nosotros no queremos quedarnos con él ni gobernarlo", enfatizó Rumsfeld, intentando, tal vez, refutar la advertencia de Powell de que los Estados Unidos se quedarían con Irak. Y agregó: "Nos quedaremos el tiempo que sea necesario para ayudarlos a hacer precisamente eso… y ni un día más".

En una entrevista posterior, Rumsfeld dijo que se había dado cuenta de que "la infraestructura de Irak había estado desatendida durante décadas. Recuerdo que fui a ver una planta eléctrica. Las mantenían en pie con goma de mascar, pinzas para el pelo y alambre de embalaje. Vi esto con mis propios ojos y me dije, Dios mío, esto es el resultado de 30 años de abandono". Saddam había gobernado durante más de 30 años. "Van a necesitar otros 30 para salir de este estado, –no nosotros– ellos, si quieren volver a verse como Kuwait o Jordania o Arabia Saudita o Turquía o sus vecinos. Y pensé, Dios mío, ese va a ser el trabajo que tendrán que hacer durante mucho tiempo, porque va a ser muy largo. Y tienen riquezas. Tienen agua. Tienen petróleo. Tienen gente trabajadora. No hay duda de que son ellos quienes van a tener que hacerlo".

Rumsfeld también se reunió en privado con Garner para hablar sobre la inminente llegada de Bremer.

"Quiero que te quedes aquí y continúes trabajando", dijo. "Estás haciendo un magnífico trabajo y quiero que ayudes a Jerry a empalmarse en todo eso".

"Me quedaré", prometió Garner, "pero no por mucho tiempo".

BUSH Y SU EQUIPO experimentaban un optimismo que rayaba en lo frívolo. Los redactores de discursos del presidente, incluido Michael Gerson, presentaron el borrador de una comunicación que recordaba la rendición formal de Japón en la cubierta del buque de guerra, USS *Missouri,* al final de la Segunda Guerra Mundial. Tomaba prestadas las memorables palabras del General McArthur –"las armas han enmudecido"– y, según Rumsfeld, incluía la expresión "misión cumplida".

El *Missouri* ya no existía –no era más que un monumento conmemorativo en Pearl Harbour, en Hawai– pero el portaaviones *Abraham Lincoln* estaba en las costas de San Diego.

"Suprimí la expresión 'misión cumplida'", recuerda Rumsfeld. "Estaba en Bagdad cuando me dieron un borrador de esa cosa y sentí deseos de morirme.

Y pensé que era demasiado general. Lo corregí y lo envié de nuevo. Arreglaron el discurso pero no la pancarta.

El primero de mayo, Bush, el antiguo piloto de la Guardia Nacional de Texas, aterrizó con gran despliegue en el *Lincoln*, sentado en un avión de combate antisubmarinos de la Marina. Más tarde, después de cambiarse el traje de vuelo por uno de saco y corbata, se dirigió a la nación y al mundo. Dio su discurso frente a 5.000 miembros de la tripulación bajo una enorme pancarta que decía "Misión cumplida". Se había dicho a la tripulación del *Lincoln* que después de que el presidente abordara oficialmente el buque podrían celebrar con tanto alboroto "como fuera posible", y se les animó a mostrar todo su afecto. La Casa Blanca sostuvo luego que la pancarta con la frase "Misión cumplida" había sido idea de la Marina. Rumsfeld es el primero en decir que la expresión estaba en el borrador del discurso de la Casa Blanca.

Luego de pronunciar el discurso, previamente revisado y aprobado por Rumsfeld, Bush declaró: "Las operaciones principales de combate en Irak han finalizado". Se abstuvo de declarar la victoria formal en Irak, no solamente por la objeción de Rumsfeld, sino también, en parte, por las implicaciones que esa declaración habría tenido a la luz de la legislación internacional. "En la batalla de Irak, los Estados Unidos y nuestros aliados han prevalecido", dijo. "Y ahora nuestra coalición se propone reconstruir el país y brindarle seguridad".

El presidente señaló que estaba empezando una nueva fase de operaciones. "Tenemos trabajo duro que hacer en Irak. Estamos llevando el orden a partes de ese país que siguen siendo peligrosas. Estamos persiguiendo y encontrando líderes del antiguo régimen, quienes serán llamados a rendir cuentas por sus crímenes. Hemos empezado a buscar armas químicas y biológicas ocultas, y ya tenemos cientos de emplazamientos para inspeccionar. Estamos ayudando a reconstruir Irak, ese país donde el dictador construyó palacios para sí mismo, en vez de hospitales y escuelas para el pueblo. Y acompañaremos a los nuevos líderes de Irak mientras establecen un gobierno, de los iraquíes, con ellos y para ellos. El paso de la dictadura a la democracia tomará tiempo, pero cualquier esfuerzo vale la pena. Nuestra coalición se quedará hasta que nuestro trabajo esté listo. Luego nos iremos y atrás dejaremos a un Irak liberado".

En Bagdad, una de las impresoras del equipo de Garner no paraba de zumbar, expulsando multitud de copias de un nuevo Boletín de los Equipos del Ministerio, con fecha 2 de mayo. Era un informativo de circulación interna sobre los ministerios.

Un proyecto importante era "pedir y conseguir plásticos y cinta para cubrir las ventanas rotas y los orificios de los edificios". El Ministerio del Interior –la organización encargada de la inteligencia, la seguridad y las fuerzas de policía– estaba completamente fuera de control. "El edificio del cuartel general ha sido ocupado por una 'familia' o 'tribu'", anunciaba el boletín. "Es necesario expulsar a los ocupantes y devolver el control a la policía". El Ministerio de Agricultura no contaba con ningún tipo de seguridad y no se podía abrir hasta que alguien asignara guardias. "Hay una facción islamista en el edificio, que es necesario desalojar; los trabajadores no regresarán hasta que el edificio esté despejado y tenga guardias". Incluso, la Biblioteca Nacional fue "ocupada por un grupo religioso; los funcionarios del ministerio piden que se expulse al grupo y se asigne seguridad".

Un reporte entregado a Garner el 4 de mayo empieza: "La seguridad sigue siendo la principal preocupación de todo el ministerio y de los altos consejeros… Se siguen cancelando viajes programados con anterioridad a los ministerios, debido al número insuficiente de escoltas de la policía; los consejeros han recalcado que dichas cancelaciones afectan su credibilidad ante los empleados del ministerio, particularmente porque rara vez pueden contactar a los empleados para informarles sobre el cambio de planes". Los consejeros estadounidenses llegaron por primera vez al edificio del Ministerio de Defensa casi un mes después del colapso del gobierno de Saddam, sólo para encontrar que había sido gravemente saqueado. Había tiroteos en las calles cuando llegaron. El reporte decía que el equipo había incautado miles de documentos altamente clasificados, pero que habían quedado muchos más sin recoger y desprotegidos.

"Memorando para el director", empieza otro documento, con fecha 6 de mayo, escrito por el coronel Paul Hughes con el estilo formal de la correspondencia militar oficial. "Referencia: Reunión con oficiales militares de Irak. MEMORANDO INFORMATIVO".

El día anterior, Hughes se había reunido con un grupo de altos oficiales de Irak, quienes decían representar a cerca de 30.000 oficiales, soldados y civiles iraquíes del Ministerio de Defensa. Un coronel que acompañaba al grupo, llamado Mirjan Dhiya, sirvió de traductor.

"Antes y durante la guerra", escribió Hughes, estos oficiales y otros "sacaron computadores y archivos del Ministerio de Defensa y los llevaron a sus casas". Ahora escucharon que la coalición iba a dar un pago de emergencia de 20 dólares a cada empleado de los otros ministerios, y ellos esperaban poder lograr el mismo acuerdo para los soldados. Entre los oficiales se encontraba un brigadier que había sido el interventor del ejército de Irak. Tenían todos los registros de pagos, y el grupo estaba "dispuesto a entregar toda esta información a la coalición".

Hughes escribió que le había explicado al grupo que no les podían pagar salarios, pero que el pago de emergencia de 20 dólares era posible. "También les informé que este dinero era originalmente dinero iraquí, que se les estaba devolviendo; esto los conmovió a todos y los llevó a mostrar un profundo agradecimiento".

Dos días después, Hughes se reunió nuevamente con los oficiales iraquíes; el número de soldados que ellos sostenían que podían organizar había crecido a 137.000. El 8 de mayo se preparó un nuevo documento que debía ser firmado por otro miembro del equipo de Garner, el general Carl A. Strock, quien se desempeñaba como alto consejero interino del Ministerio de Defensa; allí se autorizaba a los generales para iraquíes trabajar con la coalición en el edificio de Bagdad donde tenía su base de operaciones el equipo de Garner. Inmediatamente se empezaron a imprimir los registros de los soldados iraquíes. Hughes estaba muy emocionado, pues pensaba que se había topado con la oportunidad de poner al antiguo ejército de Irak del lado de la coalición y, de paso, ayudarles a conservar algo de honor. Era lo que el general Grant había hecho en la Guerra Civil después de la rendición de Lee en Appomattox, pensó. Por tan sólo 20 dólares por cabeza, es decir, menos de tres millones de dólares por todos los 137.000 soldados de las listas, podrían ofrecer la libertad bajo palabra a una parte del ejército iraquí, y ponerlo a trabajar en pro de la sociedad posterior a Saddam.

Lo único que necesitaba era el dinero.

19

Desde que Jerry Bremer se reunió por primera vez con Bush en el Salón Oval hasta cuando viajó a Irak, sólo habían transcurrido dos semanas. Él, a pesar de tener una larga carrera en política internacional y contraterrorismo, no era un experto en el Medio Oriente. En esencia, lo que estaba haciendo era improvisar un nuevo equipo para reemplazar al de Garner, que a su vez había sido improvisado. El asunto en cuya definición debía estar más segura la administración de Bush estaba siendo manejado por una sucesión de equipos improvisados.

En una ocasión, James Dobbins, experto en posconflicto y ex funcionario del Departamento de Estado que trabajó para RAND Corporation, le entregó a Bremer un borrador de un estudio según el cual se requería 500.000 hombres en la etapa posterior a la guerra de Irak, tres veces el número de soldados actualmente desplegados.

Bremer envió un resumen del borrador a Rumsfeld con un memorando en la portada que decía: "Creo que deberíamos considerar esto". Pero nunca volvió a oír hablar del asunto y no reiteró su sugerencia.

El 6 de mayo en el Salón Oval, después de la 1 de la tarde y con Bremer a su lado, Bush anunció formalmente su nombramiento como emisario presidencial para Irak. "Es el tipo de persona que se le mide a todo", dijo Bush, concediéndole uno de sus mejores cumplidos. "El embajador parte con todas las bendiciones de esta administración y la absoluta confianza de todos nosotros en que puede hacer el trabajo". La prensa en general describía a Bremer como un hombre conservador, de saco y corbata, que contrastaba con el estilo informal de Garner.

Cuatro días antes de su partida, Bremer almorzó en privado con Bush en la Casa Blanca. Durante el encuentro mencionó el tema de la "unidad de mando", pero no en cuanto al ejército, como Powell y otros lo habían hecho. "No podía tener éxito si había otros en Irak diciendo que ellos también representaban al presidente", escribiría más tarde Bremer –refiriéndose especialmente a Zalmay Khalilzad, el miembro del Consejo Nacional de Seguridad que aún detentaba el título de "emisario presidencial".

Bush dijo que lo entendía y que estaba de acuerdo. Según la versión de Bremer, también mencionó el estudio de RAND que planteaba la necesidad de 500.000 hombres, pero no obtuvo respuesta y no volvió a insistir con el presidente.

Después de su almuerzo, Bush condujo a Bremer al Salón Oval para una reunión con Rumsfeld, Powell, Rice y Card. Según los registros, "Bush hizo señas de que me sentara a su lado y dijo bromeando 'No sé siquiera si necesitamos tener esta reunión. Jerry y yo ya la tuvimos'".

"Su mensaje era claro", escribió Bremer. "Yo no era ni el hombre de Rumsfeld ni el de Powell. Era el hombre del presidente".

El 9 de mayo, Bush lo puso por escrito, en el nombramiento de Bremer como su emisario "que se reportará a través del secretario de Defensa". Ahora estaba a cargo de todos, excepto de Rumsfeld y del general Franks.

Ese día Bremer se reunió con Feith y su segundo al mando, William Luti, capitán de la Marina retirado y veterano de la oficina de Cheney.

"Tengo mi carta", dijo Bremer, refiriéndose a su carta de nombramiento, palmoteando con orgullo el bolsillo de su saco.

Feith tenía en su poder el borrador de la orden de *desbaathificación*, y Bremer recuerda que Feith le iba a pedir a Garner que la emitiera.

Según Bremer, él respondió: "Espera un momento. Estoy de acuerdo en que es un paso muy importante, tan importante que pienso que debería esperar hasta que llegue allí". Bremer recordó más tarde que Feith estuvo de acuerdo y dijo que debería llevarse a cabo "incluso si la implementación de la medida causa inconvenientes administrativos". Por su parte, Feith recuerda que fue Bremer quien presionó para hacer cumplir la orden de *desbaathificación* y otra de disolución del ejército iraquí.

A PRINCIPIOS DE ABRIL, el segundo al mando de Garner, Ron Adams, se vio afectado por una neumonía severa y fue evacuado a los Estados Unidos para su recuperación. Mientras su salud se restablecía, Adams retomó el trabajo en el Pentágono como enlace de Garner.

"Todo ha cambiado por aquí", le dijo a Garner en una de sus conversaciones telefónicas diarias. "No les agradamos".

Luego de un mes, Adams finalmente recibió permiso para regresar al Medio Oriente, y el 6 de mayo llegó a Kuwait. El retirado general de tres estrellas, subdirector de la organización, quien seguía siendo el responsable oficial de la posguerra en Irak, tardó cuatro frustrantes días en conseguir un asiento en un avión militar para viajar los casi 563 kilómetros que separan a Kuwait de Bagdad.

"Domingo, 11 de mayo D+53". Así comienza otra entrada en el diario de guerra de *Spider* Marks. "No ADM", escribió de nuevo.

Era casi demasiado tarde para preocuparse por ello, porque no había posibilidad de deshacer la invasión de Irak. Tenían que seguir visitando y examinando cada uno de los 946 emplazamientos de la lista, incluso si ahora estaba casi tan seguro de que no había nada que encontrar, como lo estuvo antes en el sentido de que sí había armas.

El coronel Rotkoff resumió la situación:

> ¿Dónde están las ADM?
> Qué metida de pata si él no tiene ninguna
> Lo siento mucho

El 11 de mayo, Garner se desplazó a Qatar para reunirse con Bremer en el centro de operaciones de Franks. Los dos se estrecharon la mano por un momento, y luego de un informe militar de rutina, Garner le entregó a Bremer una copia de su lista de los diez principales objetivos que se había propuesto lograr antes del 1 de julio.

"Está bien", dijo Bremer. "Gracias".

El General Myers había viajado con Bremer a Qatar. No había tenido acceso privilegiado a la información sobre el nombramiento de aquél, y pensaba que Garner debería haberse quedado como una especie de funcionario civil, un apoyo para el general Franks.

Myers y Garner hablaron luego en privado. Garner propuso su idea de nombrar a Abizaid comandante militar de Bagdad, pero otorgándole una cuarta estrella para que tuviera más autoridad.

"Designe a Abizaid como comandante unificado subordinado", propuso Garner. "Deje que Bremer se encargue de los asuntos civiles. Mantenga a McKiernan aquí. Tiene un magnífico equipo". De esa manera, Abizaid podría mediar en las inevitables disputas que surgieran entre Bremer y McKiernan. El retiro de Franks del ejército se acercaba, y ya se había marchado de Irak. Abizaid era el hombre ideal para el trabajo.

"Estoy de acuerdo con usted, pero no logro hacer avanzar ese tema", le confesó Myers a Garner. Le había hecho la misma propuesta a Rumsfeld. El organigrama del Pentágono que mostraba la transición del control militar al civil no tenía una línea cronológica, y eso tenía razón de ser. Myers opinaba que esta nueva idea de ceder el control de la situación en Irak a Bremer estaba sucediendo de un modo demasiado abrupto. "Ya hemos tenido esa discusión", agregó Myers con señales evidentes de frustración. Rumsfeld "no va a escuchar razones".

Antes de viajar a Bagdad, Bremer y Garner pasaron un día en Basora. Más tarde, Bremer recordaría su sensación al llegar a la capital de Irak. "Iba conduciendo por la carretera destapada, envuelto en una nube de polvo, a 160 kilómetros por hora". Esa noche, él y Garner se reunieron con cerca de 30 funcionarios de alto rango en una pequeña sala de conferencias del que llamaban "palacio". Bremer se mostró cortés y agradeció a Garner y a su equipo haciendo énfasis en que ellos conocían los desafíos mejor que él.

"La cobertura que hacen los medios de comunicación de los saqueos incontrolados nos hace parecer débiles", señaló Bremer. "Cuando las fuerzas dirigidas por Estados Unidos ocuparon Haití en 1994, nuestras tropas abrieron fuego contra seis saqueadores que incumplieron el toque de queda y los saqueos cesaron. Creo que deberíamos hacer lo mismo aquí, incluso si eso implica cambiar las reglas de combate". Pero nunca hizo cambiar las reglas para permitir ese tipo de tiroteos.

EL 14 DE MAYO, aproximadamente a las 7 de la mañana, el primer día completo que Bremer pasaba en Bagdad, Robin Raphel corrió donde Garner.

"¿Ya leyó esto?", preguntó.

"No", respondió Garner. "No sé que diablos es".

"Es una política de *desbaathificación*", dijo, entregándole un documento de dos páginas.

Garner leyó rápidamente: "Orden número 1 Provisional de la Coalición. Desbaathificación de la sociedad iraquí". El partido Baath estaba organizado por rangos y la orden decía que todos los "miembros plenarios", es decir, aquellos que ocupaban los cuatro rangos más altos, serían removidos inmediatamente de sus posiciones y se les prohibiría emplearse en el futuro gobierno. Adicionalmente, los tres niveles administrativos más altos de los ministerios serían investigados por crímenes y serían considerados como posibles amenazas a la seguridad".

"No podemos hacer eso", replicó Garner. Todavía tenía en mente lo que le había dicho a Rumsfeld de que sería una "*desbaathificación* gradual", eliminar solamente al número uno del partido y a los jefes de cada ministerio. "Es demasiado drástico", agregó.

"Por eso, precisamente, no te puedes ir a casa", dijo Raphel.

Garner se encontró con Charlie, el jefe de la estación de la CIA.

"¿Ya leíste esto?", le preguntó Garner.

"Por eso estoy aquí", respondió Charlie.

"Vamos a ver a Bremer". Cerca de la 1 de la tarde los dos hombres fueron a ver al nuevo administrador de Irak. "Jerry, esto es demasiado drástico", dijo

Garner. "Danos una hora. Nos sentaremos a analizar los pro y los contra y luego hablaremos con Rumsfeld y lo suavizaremos un poco".

"De ninguna manera", dijo Bremer. "Esas son mis instrucciones y pienso cumplirlas".

"¡Diablos!", exclamó Garner, "no vas a ser capaz de dirigir nada si te pones así de radical".

Garner se volvió a Charlie. El experimentado hombre de la CIA había sido jefe de estación en otros países del Medio Oriente.

"Charlie, ¿qué va a suceder?"

"Si publica esto, va a empujar a la clandestinidad cerca de 30.000 o 50.000 baathistas antes del anochecer", le respondió Charlie, según las notas que tomó Kim Olson, asistente de Garner. Charlie sostenía que la cifra estaba más cerca de 50.000 que de 30.000. "Va a poner a 50.000 personas en las calles, en la clandestinidad y furiosos con los norteamericanos". Estas 50.000 personas eran las elites más poderosas y con mejores conexiones de la faz de la tierra.

"Ya les dije", dijo Bremer, mirando a Charlie, "que tengo instrucciones y debo aplicar esto".

Garner llamó a Rumsfeld e intentó hacerlo reconsiderar la severidad de la medida y suavizar el tono de la orden.

"Esto no viene de este edificio", respondió. "Vino de algún otro lado".

Garner supuso que se refería a la Casa Blanca, el CNS o Cheney. Sin embargo, de acuerdo con otras personas, la orden de *desbaathificación* había sido creación exclusiva del Pentágono. Como fuese, decirle a Garner que provenía de otra instancia, le daba a Rumsfeld la ventaja de poner punto final a la discusión.

Al día siguiente, el 15 de mayo, Robin Raphel le llevó a Garner un borrador de otra orden. Esta era la orden número 2 y mandaba disolver los ministerios iraquíes de Defensa y del Interior, todo el ejército y todo el cuerpo de seguridad de Saddam, así como las organizaciones paramilitares.

Garner estaba perplejo. La orden de *desbaathificación* era estúpida, pero esto era un desastre. Él le había dicho explícitamente al presidente y a todo el Consejo Nacional de Seguridad que ellos planeaban usar el ejército de Irak –por lo menos 200.000 o 300.000 efectivos– como columna vertebral de un cuerpo para reconstruir el país y brindar seguridad. Y había estado entregando reportes de seguridad sobre el plan a Rumsfeld y a Washington.

Además, el coronel Hughes había tenido varias reuniones con los antiguos generales iraquíes y sus listas de 137.000 hombres que querían volver a hacer parte de sus unidades o firmar con nuevas unidades, si cada uno recibía un pago de emergencia de 20 dólares. La CIA también había recopilado listas y se estaba reuniendo con los generales y organizando una reconstitución del ejército iraquí. El antiguo ejército iraquí estaba haciendo cada vez más ofertas, esperando tan sólo regresar de alguna manera.

Por segundo día consecutivo Garner fue a ver a Bremer. "Siempre hemos tenido planes de volver a traer al ejército", insistió. Este nuevo plan salía de la nada, echando por tierra meses de trabajo.

"Bueno, los planes han cambiado", respondió Bremer. "El concepto ahora es que no queremos las sobras del ejército viejo. Queremos un ejército nuevo y fresco".

"Jerry, es posible deshacerse de un ejército en un día, pero toma años construirlo". Garner trató de explicar que no se trataba simplemente de un soldado en el campo, o de conseguir un puñado de escopeteros. "Cualquier ejército es la suma de todos los procesos que toma equiparlo, entrenarlo, sostenerlo y hacerlo perdurar". Bremer movió la cabeza en señal de desaprobación.

"No puedes deshacerte del Ministerio del Interior", dijo Garner.

"¿Por qué no?".

"Tan sólo ayer diste un discurso y le dijiste a todo el mundo lo importante que es la fuerza policial".

"Es importante".

"Toda la policía está en el Ministerio del Interior", dijo Garner. "Si implementas esto, se irán a casa hoy".

Bremer, quien se veía sorprendido, le pidió a Garner que fuera a ver a Walter B. Slocombe, director de defensa y de seguridad nacional de Bremer. Slocombe, de 62 años, había sido subsecretario del Departamento de Defensa para Asuntos Políticos durante la mayor parte de la administración Clinton, y predecesor de Feith. Beneficiario de una beca Rhodes, ex actuario de la Corte Suprema de Justicia de Abe Fortas y reconocido abogado tributario, Slocombe sintió que en lo que concernía a la legislación internacional, la invasión de Estados Unidos significaba que Irak estaba bajo ocupación militar. No era una condición optativa, y los Estados Unidos no debían ser tímidos para ejercer autoridad. El sistema de gobierno se había desplomado y el ejército de Irak se había disuelto, creía él. Todos –el pueblo iraquí y los Estados Unidos– necesitaban la creación de un nuevo gobierno y un nuevo ejército en Irak. El ejército de Saddam había sido el principal instrumento de represión; en opinión de Slocombe, difícilmente podría utilizarse como escudo de una nueva democracia.

Pero Slocombe estaba de acuerdo en suprimir el Ministerio del Interior del borrador, de modo que pudiera quedarse la policía. Bremer firmó pronto la orden que cancelaba todo "rango, título o condición" militar. En su libro, publicado en 2006, Bremer no habla sobre sus discusiones con Garner acerca de la disolución del ejército iraquí, pero deja en claro su creencia de que cuando llegó a Irak, ya no había ejército en el país: se había "autodesmovilizado". Firmar la orden que abolía los servicios militares del antiguo régimen "no enviaba a casa un solo hombre ni disolvía una sola unidad", escribió. "Todo eso había pasado semanas antes". También estaba convencido de que los kurdos, quienes odiaban y temían al antiguo ejército, se separarían de la alianza si éste era traído de nuevo".

No obstante, al año siguiente, cada uno de los oficiales y sargentos que conformaban el nuevo ejército iraquí venían del antiguo ejército.

BREMER SE APIÑÓ en una estrecha oficina del Palacio Republicano con cuatro de sus colaboradores: Scout Carpenter, del Departamento de Estado, a quien Liz Cheney había puesto a cargo de la administración de Irak; Meghan O'Sullivan, la funcionaria del Departamento de Estado que había llegado al equipo de Garner con Tom Carric, solamente para ser ahuyentada por la oficina de Cheney y pasar de nuevo a hurtadillas con la aprobación tácita de Rumsfeld y Hadley; Ryan Crocker del Departamento de Estado, y Roman Martínez, un egresado de Harvard que había trabajado para Feith en el Pentágono. Los cinco tenían una copia de la orden de *desbaathificación*.

"La Casa Blanca, el Departamento de Defensa y el de Estado, todos firmaron esto", dijo Bremer. "Así que démosle una lectura final y, a menos que haya algún error grande en la redacción, lo firmaré".

A LA MAÑANA SIGUIENTE, el 16 de mayo, Bremer firmó la orden de *desbaathificación*. Ese mismo día, más tarde, narraría luego en su libro, le escribió un correo a su esposa, a su casa, en los Estados Unidos, como trataba de hacerlo todos los días, contándole sobre la respuesta que había oído de los norteamericanos que estaban en la zona: "Hubo un mar de gruñidos y refunfuños y muchos de ellos comentaban lo difícil que iba a ser la situación. Les recordé que la directiva del presidente era clara: la *desbaathificación* se llevaría a cabo, incluso a costa de la eficiencia administrativa. Todos la pasaron muy mal".

A ESO DE LAS 4 DE LA TARDE, ese mismo día, Abizaid, el más seguro sucesor del general Franks como encargado del Comando Central, viajó a Bagdad para reunirse con Garner. Ambos hombres estaban preocupados porque los combates continuaban en el norte de Bagdad. Algunos iraquíes no se estaban rindiendo, pero estaban tan mal equipados para el combate que los estaban masacrando. Garner y Abizaid estuvieron de acuerdo en que una manera de poner fin a la inútil resistencia y a la carnicería era mostrar a los iraquíes, de manera convincente, que habría un nuevo gobierno, y que el régimen de Saddam había terminado.

Pasaron a las políticas sobre la *desbaathificación* y la disolución del ejército.

Garner le dijo a Abizaid, "John, te lo digo. Si haces esto las cosas se van a poner feas. Van a ser necesarios 10 años para arreglar esta país, y durante tres años vas a estar enviando muchachos a sus casas envueltos en bolsas plásticas".

Abizaid no lo contradijo. "Te escucho, te escucho", dijo. Le pidió a Garner que se quedara en Irak.

"No me puedo quedar", dijo Garner.

EL VIERNES 16 DE MAYO, Bremer y John Sawers, embajador británico en Egipto, quien había sido enviado a Irak como representante del Reino Unido en la organización de Bremer, convocó oficialmente a la Autoridad Provisional de la Coalición (APC) y organizó una cena de trabajo con los líderes del grupo iraquí que Garner había reunido. A principios de la semana, Bremer se había resistido a hablar con los líderes del grupo, según recordaba, en parte porque "quería mostrarles a todos que era yo, y no Jay, quien estaba ahora a cargo".

Bremer explicó que estaba dedicado a combatir el terrorismo. Desbordante de confianza en sí mismo, proyectaba la sensación de que los iraquíes eran casi superfluos. Luego, lo dijo explícitamente: "Es necesario que se den cuenta de una cosa; ustedes no son el gobierno. Nosotros lo somos. Y estamos a cargo".

Por lo menos eran ínfulas cándidas y no estaba jugando al gato y al ratón. Pero Garner se dio cuenta de que se estaba dando el control imperial, sobre el que lo habían prevenido y que le preocupaba tres meses antes en sus adiestramientos con piedras.

Al día siguiente el equipo de gobierno interino de Garner volvió a casa. El grupo de liderazgo iraquí era ahora una habitación vacía[9].

HADLEY SE ENTERÓ de las órdenes de *desbaathificación* y disolución del ejército cuando Bremer las anunció a Irak y al mundo. No habían pasado por el proceso formal entre las agencias y, hasta donde Hadley sabía, tampoco había

---

9. Con el pasar de los meses, Bremer organizó su propio consejo de gobierno interino, conformado por casi la misma gente que Garner tenía en su grupo. Los dos primeros ministros interinos de Irak, Allawi y Jafari, venían de la iniciativa inicial de Garner de poner una cara iraquí en el gobierno, tal y como el presidente Bush había aprobado dos días después de que estallara la guerra.

imprimátur de la Casa Blanca. Rice tampoco fue consultada. Las órdenes no volvieron a manos de Washington o del CNS para que ellos tomaran una decisión. Pero a Rice no le sorprendió la medida. Después de todo, el ejército iraquí, de alguna manera, se había disipado.

A un abogado del CNS le mostraron los borradores de las políticas de *desbaathificación* de Irak y de disolución del ejército, pero solamente para tener una opinión legal. Los legisladores nunca vieron los borradores, nunca tuvieron la oportunidad de decir si pensaban que era buena idea o, incluso, de señalar que estas decisiones se alejaban radicalmente de lo planeado inicialmente y de informar al presidente al respecto.

En cambio, desde abril, los constantes toques de tambor que Hadley escuchaba en el Pentágono eran: "Esto es cosa de Don Rumsfeld, y vamos hacer el proceso entre agencias en Bagdad. Deje que Jerry lo maneje".

Ni siquiera el General Myers, principal consejero militar de Bush, de Rumsfeld y del CNS, fue consultado sobre la disolución del ejército iraquí. La decisión se presentó como un hecho consumado.

"No vamos a sentarnos a reflexionar sobre todo lo que él está haciendo", le dijo Rumsfeld a Myers en una ocasión, refiriéndose a las decisiones de Bremer.

"No tuve ningún voto en eso", le comentó Myers a un colega, "pero entiendo por qué el embajador Bremer pudo haber pensado que esto era razonable".

Tiempo después, Rumsfeld mencionó que le sorprendería que Bremer hubiera recibido de Wolfowitz y Feith las órdenes de *desbaathificación* y de disolución del ejército. Mencionó que no recordaba haber tenido una reunión con el CNS sobre el tema. Sobre Bremer, Rumsfeld recordó: "Rara vez hablé con él. Y su enfoque era distinto al de Jay. Sin duda".

BREMER ESTABA DESBORDADO de trabajo. Según sus notas, la *desbaathificación* y la disolución del ejército eran solamente parte de los deberes que había tenido que asumir en sus primeros cinco días. Pocas horas después de aterrizar en la capital iraquí, alguien quería saber si debían dejar que la Universidad de Bagdad llevara a cabo sus elecciones de funcionarios universitarios. Bremer dio luz verde. Revocó una de las leyes de Saddam que prohibía a los profesores viajar al extranjero. Instaló una estación de televisión y un periódico. Estaban intentando hacer los arreglos necesarios para instalar el servicio de teléfonos celulares. Bremer visitó el hospital infantil de Bagdad y ordenó plantas eléctricas para todos los hospitales de la ciudad. Organizó entregas de emergencia de gasolina y gas propano a Bagdad. Ninguno de los funcionarios civiles de Irak había recibido pago desde antes de la guerra, que ahora duraba tres meses. "Nos tomará tres meses diseñar un sistema de pago por niveles", exclamó uno de sus consejeros.

"Tiene tres días para hacerlo", respondió Bremer. Diseñaron una estructura salarial extremadamente simplificada, con cuatro niveles de pago, que llegaba a 200 millones de dólares mensuales.

Era una vertiginosa lista de cosas por hacer y se debía tomar decisiones en los lapsos más apretados. No había tiempo para diseñar un sistema, para consultar con los Estados Unidos o para delegar. Además, pensó Bremer, nadie en sus cabales y con alguna experiencia en la burocracia estadounidense remitiría decisiones cruciales a Washington.

Robin Raphel, contemporánea de Bremer en el Departamento de Estado y quien lo conocía desde hacía años, explicó que necesitaban reunir 150 millones de dólares para comprar el trigo y la cebada de los campesinos iraquíes "Tenemos que hacer algo ahora mismo, porque ya están recogiendo la cosecha". Ella y Bremer fueron a ver a los funcionarios de la ONU en Bagdad, quienes estaban en capacidad de desembolsar dinero del programa *Petróleo por alimentos* de la ONU –conocido como PPA– para comprar la cosecha nacional de granos.

"Señor embajador", manifestó el funcionario de la ONU, "el dinero del PPA pertenece al gobierno de Irak, y no puedo desembolsarlo sin la aprobación de dicho gobierno".

"Por ahora yo soy el gobierno iraquí", respondió Bremer. "Y en nombre del gobierno, le estoy pidiendo a las Naciones Unidas liberar estos fondos inmediatamente". Finalmente obtuvo el dinero.

Había problemas por doquier. "Díos mío", se dijo a sí mismo, "este lugar necesita arreglo. ¡Manos a la obra!".

La energía eléctrica era fluctuante. "Arregle la electricidad", ordenó Bremer a Clay McManaway, uno de sus asistentes de más confianza. "Averigüe por qué no podemos restablecerla".

McManaway, de 70 años, era una de las primeras personas que Bremer había persuadido para que trabajaran con él. Lo había traído precisamente para este tipo de misión. McManaway había estado 30 años en el servicio diplomático y, además, había trabajado algún tiempo en el Departamento de Defensa y en la CIA. Había viajado por todo el mundo, incluida una estadía de cinco años en Vietnam. Sabía cómo trabajar en lugares disfuncionales.

Las cosas eran aun peores en el sistema de aguas residuales de Bagdad, otra misión que Bremer le asignó a McManaway. Las aguas negras obstruían todo el lugar. Se podía verlas y olerlas por todas partes. Al bajar al sistema de alcantarillas, McManaway encontró que todo era un completo desastre. Bajo las calles de Bagdad había dos o tres sistemas de aguas residuales separados. No estaban conectados y ninguno de ellos funcionaba. Solamente había un norteamericano tratando de arreglar el problema, un ingeniero sanitario de Pensilvania.

"¡Ay, mierda!", exclamó McManaway.

GARNER DESPERTÓ el sábado 17 de mayo pensando en Sun Tzu, el antiguo general y estratega militar chino. En *El arte de la guerra*, Sun Tzu advertía que no es bueno irse a la cama, en la noche, con más enemigos de los que uno tenía en la mañana. Según los cálculos de Garner, ahora los Estados Unidos tenía por lo menos 350.000 enemigos más que el día anterior: los 50.000 baathistas, los 300.000 soldados oficialmente desempleados del ejército y un puñado del ahora desaparecido grupo líder de Irak.

Ese día organizó una reunión importante con Abizaid, McKiernan y los equipos de oficiales generales encargados de los diez puntos más importantes. Hacía calor y la habitación estaba repleta; había muchas personas apiñadas alrededor de una gran mesa. Una de las entradas daba directamente a la parte exterior de un patio; al frente del patio estaban las oficinas de Bremer.

El primero de los generales del equipo estaba empezando a dar su reporte cuando McManaway entró por la puerta desde el patio.

"Bremer quiere verlo", dijo éste señalando a Abizaid.

"Tan pronto como terminemos esta reunión", le respondió Abizaid.

McManaway ordenó: "¡Ahora!".

Abizaid miró a Garner como preguntando ¿qué hago?

"Ve", le dijo Garner. "Oye, él te mandó llamar".

Varios minutos después McManaway entró y dijo que Bremer quería ver a McKiernan.

"¿Quiere que vaya?", preguntó McKiernan a Garner.

"Sí".

"Bien", preguntó otro general, "¿les parece que debemos continuar esta reunión, o se acabó?".

"Sigamos adelante y terminémosla porque todo el mundo ha trabajado mucho en ella", dijo Garner. Después de todo, se dio cuenta, los asuntos por discutir eran solamente los ministerios, los pagos de salario pendientes, la policía, el agua, la electricidad, las aguas negras, el combustible, la comida, la administración, la salud y la seguridad. Nada más y nada menos que la base del futuro de Irak. ¿A quién le podría importar un bledo?

"Estaba molesto", recordó Ron Adams. "Nos estaban marginando".

Cuando la reunión acabó, Garner se dirigió a la oficina de Bremer. Cerró la puerta tras de sí con una delicadeza y un control que en ese momento no sentía.

"Nunca más me vuelvas a hacer eso".

"¿Qué quieres decir?", preguntó Bremer.

"Me viste en una reunión y empezaste a sacar a las personas", empezó Garner. Calló por un momento y luego agregó: "Tienes que respetarme. Te diré algo, Jerry, voy a facilitarte las cosas; me voy a casa".

Bremer se levantó de un salto. "No te puedes ir a casa".

"No puedo trabajar contigo, y me voy. Lo que acabas de hacer ahí adentro… nunca nadie antes me había hecho algo así, y no permitiré que me lo hagas de nuevo".

"No sabía lo que estaba pasando", se excusó.

"Mentira. Sabías exactamente lo que estaba sucediendo".

Durante uno o dos minutos estuvieron enganchados en un tire y afloje.

"Mira, Jay", dijo Bremer. "Es posible que tú y yo no estemos de acuerdo en nada, pero los dos tenemos el mismo objetivo".

"No lo creo", interrumpió Garner.

"Sí lo tenemos. Nuestro objetivo es hacer que nuestra nación tenga éxito en esta misión".

"Tienes razón", estuvo de acuerdo Garner. "Tienes razón en eso".

"Bien, si crees firmemente, igual que yo, entonces tienes que quedarte por un tiempo. Tienes que ayudarme a lograrlo".

"Te diré lo que haré, Jerry. Trabajaré con un contrato diario. La próxima vez que me hagas enojar, me voy. Hay un par de cosas que quisiera terminar y no creo que me tomen mucho tiempo. Y una vez termine esas cosas te estrecharé la mano y me iré".

"Está bien, tratemos de trabajar de esa manera", estuvo de acuerdo Bremer.

"Tienes que dejarme el personal disponible", demandó Garner.

Bremer pensó por un momento y finalmente dijo, "No creo que pueda hacer eso".

"¿Por qué?".

Bremer pensaba que, si hacía eso, él y Garner darían órdenes contrapuestas, pero aseguró que lo pensaría.

"No creo que pueda lograr nada si no tengo colaboradores", dijo Garner.

"Déjame pensarlo".

"Esto es lo que haré. Lo único urgente es pagarle a los servidores públicos y a la policía. Es un proceso muy complicado y difícil. Me voy a quedar hasta asegurarme de que ese proceso esté marchando. Y cuando esté seguro de eso, entonces tomaré la decisión, ya sea de quedarme un poco más o de irme".

"Está bien", dijo Bremer. "Ya te comunicaré algo sobre el equipo de trabajo".

Más tarde, Bremer declaró que aunque reconocía que necesitaba una transición sin sobresaltos del grupo de Garner al suyo, estaba empezando a enfurecerse con las personas –asumía que eran gente de Garner– que habían suministrado detalles de sus planes y reuniones a los medios de comunicación. Una de esas infidencias había generado la historia de la prensa sobre la idea de Bremer de que el ejército empezara a disparar a los saqueadores. "Yo quería la experiencia de Jay en la parte logística", escribió Bremer, "pero no lamentaba la salida de los infidentes".

Horas después de la confrontación, Garner y su asistente ejecutiva, la coronel Olson, se marcharon de Bagdad y se dirigieron al sur de la ciudad de Hillah. Olson pensaba que si Bremer le daba a Garner algunas asignaciones, especialmente lejos de Bagdad, él se quedaría a ayudar. Pero sentía que Bremer estaba cometiendo un típico error de dirección: no saber cómo usar el talento que tenía a su disposición.

Robin Raphel quería que Garner se quedara. Pensaba que él tenía mejor juicio sobre lo que había que hacer. Garner y su grupo de trabajo se habían esforzado para tener un punto de apoyo en Irak, pero en lo político se habían quedado cortos. En una de las pocas críticas que le hizo, estuvo de acuerdo con la Casa Blanca sobre el hábito de Garner de no usar saco y corbata. Parecía no entender que a los iraquíes les gusta la formalidad.

Bremer estaba a tono. Se vestía todos los días de traje, camisa blanca y corbata. Las botas Timberland marrón que usaba con su traje oscuro ya eran marca registrada. El séquito que lo rodeaba estaba conformado por una veintena de personas dinámicas. Algunos de ellos ridiculizaban a Garner por no tener una programación oficial diaria. El grupo de Garner se autoapodaba *Los vaqueros del espacio*, por la película de Clint Eastwood en la que un grupo de astronautas retirados se reúnen para una última misión. Al joven equipo de Bremer lo llamaban *Brigada de los niños neconservadores* o, incluso, de modo más sarcástico, jugando con las siglas de la Autoridad Provisional de la Colisión (en inglés CPA), algunos oficiales del ejército los llamaban *Los niños que juegan a ser adultos* (Children Playing as Adults).

Bremer reconocía que los desafíos eran inmensos. "Me conformaría con los problemas de McArthur", recordó haber dicho más tarde. "Las condiciones no eran así de complicadas para él". Pero, aun así, parecía muy confiado en tener éxito. ¿Era ésa su naturaleza, se preguntaba Raphel, o esa sensación provenía de la fe religiosa que compartía con el presidente?

A FINALES DE MAYO, un día antes de que Larry DiRita regresara a Washington, llegó el reporte de una explosión en la vía al aeropuerto de Bagdad –la denominada autopista BIAP– al paso de un Humvee. Nadie había muerto, pero DiRita pensó para sí: "Es curioso. Me pregunto qué hay detrás de todo esto". Parecía algo fuera de lo normal, porque la vía al aeropuerto era casi como una superautopista norteamericana, por donde nadie viajaba sin seguridad, blindaje o convoy.

Era su último día en Bagdad, y esa noche, a eso de las 11, él y varios miembros del equipo de Bremer se apilaron en un carro y viajaron atravesando medio Bagdad para cenar en un atiborrado restaurante. Todos allí parecían ser iraquíes, y el grupo de DiRita cenó y bebió algunas cervezas. Un par de soldados venían caminando por la calle y las personas del restaurante salieron a recibirlos y a agradecerles. Fue una noche memorable, muy placentera, casi una escena del París liberado después de la Segunda Guerra Mundial.

Cuando DiRita regresó al Pentágono dio un reporte a Rumsfeld de cómo se sentían los iraquíes, y describió su salida a comer durante su última noche en Bagdad.

Esto, concluyó Rumsfeld, va por buen camino.

20

A PRINCIPIOS DE MAYO DE 2003, varios ataques terroristas, dirigidos a negocios que mantenían relaciones con Estados Unidos y a tres complejos residenciales usados principalmente por occidentales, sacudieron a Riyadh, Arabia Saudita. Los atentados dejaron un centenar de heridos y 34 muertos, entre los cuales se contaban ocho estadounidenses. Fue uno de los peores ataques terroristas desde el 11 de septiembre de 2001. Bush envió a Tenet a advertir al príncipe heredero.

Al Qaeda está aquí en el reino, le aseguró Tenet al príncipe Abdullah en Arabia Saudita. Lo matarán. Están usando su país como base de lanzamiento para ataques a los Estados Unidos. Si eso pasa, se acaban las relaciones entre Arabia Saudita y Estados Unidos en la región.

Abdullah accedió a conformar un equipo conjunto de inteligencia y a ejecutar operaciones policiales dentro del reino. Pronto, la CIA estaba dando acceso a los saudíes a cada vez más información de inteligencia de Estados Unidos, incluidas transcripciones de conversaciones interceptadas por la Agencia de Seguridad Nacional (ANS) en Arabia Saudita y la región.

Para la inteligencia saudí eso no era suficiente. Los saudíes no confiaban en las traducciones norteamericanas. Alegaban que el árabe que se habla en Arabia Saudita, Marruecos, Túnez y Yemen era muy distinto. Eventualmente, la ANS empezó a entregar fragmentos de audio, con algunas de las conversaciones interceptadas, para que las fuerzas de seguridad saudíes, los informantes o los detenidos pudieran hacer traducciones más precisas y fuera posible rastrear o reconocer algunas de las voces.

DESPUÉS DEL ALTERCADO, Garner permanecía la mayor parte del tiempo por fuera de Bagdad y lejos de Bremer. En una ocasión se encontró con un teniente británico en el sur de Irak, quien le contó que disponía de cerca de un millón de dólares en sus fondos discrecionales para gastarlos en actividades de su sector. En cambio, Garner no podía mover un céntimo por cuenta propia. Fue a Babilonia, la antigua ciudad que una vez fuera conocida por su riqueza y extravagancia, a unos 13 kilómetros de Hillah, en la parte baja del río Éufrates.

"Nunca vamos a hacer esto como se debe", exclamó, según las notas de Kim Olson.

BREMER LE ESCRIBIÓ un memorando al presidente Bush y lo envió a través de Rumsfeld, una semana después de llegar al país. Haciendo gala de su nueva línea dura, Bremer insistía: "Debemos dejarles claro a todos que estamos hablando en serio: que Saddam y los baathistas están acabados". Sostenía que "la disolución de su elemento elegido para la dominación política, el partido Baath, ha sido muy bien recibida". Esto, junto con "la medida aun más contundente de disolver las estructuras militares y de inteligencia de Saddam, para enfatizar que no estamos bromeando".

Por otro lado, escribió Bremer, "debemos mostrarle al iraquí común y corriente que su vida mejorará. Nos enfrentamos a una serie de asuntos urgentes relacionados con la satisfacción de las necesidades básicas. Hemos hecho un gran progreso bajo la dirección de Jay Garner. Hemos encontrado expresiones de agradecimiento casi generalizadas hacia los Estados Unidos y hacia usted en particular, por liberar a Irak de la tiranía de Saddam. Ayer en Mosul, un pueblo del norte, un anciano, creyendo que yo era el presidente Bush (al parecer tenía muy mala señal de televisión), vino hacia mí corriendo y plantó dos besos velludos y húmedos en mis mejillas".

"¿POR QUÉ QUERRÍAMOS pagarle a un ejército al que acabamos de vencer?", interpeló Walt Slocombe a Jerry Bates, jefe de Estado Mayor de Garner.

"Porque no queremos que, de repente, se pasen al otro bando", respondió Bates. "Necesitamos tener control sobre ellos".

Slocombe y Bates habían trabajado juntos en el Pentágono durante el gobierno de Clinton. A Bates le agradaba Slocombe y pensaba que este era inteligente, pero respecto a este asunto se oponían radicalmente, y era obvio que Bremer era de la misma opinión de Slocombe. El ejército se había desintegrado, sostenía Bremer. "No existen, así que no vamos a pagarles".

El 19 de mayo de 2003, Bremer envió a Rumsfeld un memorando de dos páginas informándole que emitiría la orden de disolución del ejército iraquí. En realidad no estaba haciendo una recomendación o pidiendo autorización: "En los próximos días le sugiero que divulgue la orden adjunta".

LOS DÍAS SIGUIENTES a la orden de disolución del ejército, los vehículos que viajaban por la carretera entre Bagdad y el aeropuerto comenzaron a ser víctimas de ataques terroristas más frecuentes. Se empezaron a reunir multitudes para protestar contra la orden, aunque los reportes diferían mucho en cuanto al número de personas congregadas. El 19 de mayo, aproximadamente 500 personas protestaron afuera de las puertas de la Autoridad Provisional de la Coalición. Una semana después, el 26 de mayo, una multitud más numerosa se reunió para reclamar contra la medida. Algunos reportes de los medios de comunicación árabes, posteriormente traducidos y entregados al equipo de Bremer, hablaban de 5.000 manifestantes.

"Exigimos la formación inmediata de un gobierno, la restauración de la seguridad, el restablecimiento de las instituciones públicas y el pago de los salarios al personal militar", demandó uno de los líderes de la protesta, un general iraquí llamado Sabih al-Musawi. Su discurso fue transmitido por la cadena de televisión árabe Al Jazeera, y luego traducido para la APC. "Si nuestras exigencias no son satisfechas el próximo lunes, marcaremos el inicio de una ruptura entre el ejército y la gente de Irak, por un lado, y los ocupantes, por el otro".

PAUL HUGHES tenía ahora que vérselas con los antiguos oficiales iraquíes que pedían para sus soldados el pago de emergencia de 20 dólares, del que ahora, con la orden de Bremer, estaban excluidos. Hughes evitó por un tiempo el encuentro, pero finalmente habló con ellos.

"Coronel Paul, ¿Qué pasó?", preguntó Mirjan Dhiya, el vocero de los oficiales que hablaba inglés.

"No lo sé", dijo Hughes. "No puedo decirle lo que pasó. Estoy tan sorprendido como usted".

"Coronel Paul, nuestros hombres tienen familias. No tienen comida. Se están quedando sin nada. Debemos hacer algo".

Finalmente Hughes logró que el jefe de Estado Mayor de Slocombe se reuniera con el representante del antiguo ejército iraquí. Aún había una posibilidad de conseguir los 20 dólares para cada uno, pero las cosas marchaban muy lentamente.

GARNER FUE AL AEROPUERTO Internacional de Bagdad para reunirse con una delegación visitante del Congreso, el 26 de mayo. De regreso, condujo por la autopista BIAP en su Chevy Suburban sin blindaje hacia el "palacio" donde su equipo estaba trabajado, el cual había preparado una pequeña fiesta de despedida en su honor. Algunos de los colaboradores se preguntaban en broma si Bremer se presentaría, y sí, estuvo allí haciendo despliegue de todo su encanto.

Ese mismo día, tres exploradores de caballería, cuya tarea era brindar protección a las caravanas de suministros, también iban por la autopista BIAP, a bordo de uno de los dos Humvee blindados que viajaban en la caravana militar. Los vehículos pasaron por encima de lo que parecía un simple bolso en mitad de la carretera.

El bolso explotó, destrozó la Humvee y expulsó del vehículo a uno de los soldados. Las municiones empezaron a prenderse, causando más explosiones.

Los soldados del segundo Humvee frenaron bruscamente, alistaron sus metralletas y buscaron desesperadamente al enemigo. Un soldado salió corriendo hacia uno de los hombres caídos, Jeremiah D. Smith, un soldado raso de 25 años, de Missouri, uno de los primeros soldados americanos asesinados por fuego hostil en Irak.

Paul Hughes estaba en el "*palacio*", en la fiesta de despedida de Garner, cuando escuchó el reporte: "Acabamos de perder dos Humvee en la autopista BIAP".

"Estaba furioso", recordaría más tarde. Suponía que había soldados iraquíes detrás del ataque y estaba seguro de que los Estados Unidos habían perdido su mejor oportunidad para mantener al ejército bajo control, trabajando con los generales y coroneles iraquíes. "Los tenía agarrados por las pelotas. Se habrían parado de cabezas en el río Tigris por mí, si hubiéramos sido justos los unos con los otros. Era absolutamente trágico, ¡tan innecesario!".

Al día siguiente, uno de los agentes de inteligencia estadounidenses del "*palacio*" hizo una valoración brutal y objetiva del hecho: "Estos tipos tienen municiones en sus garajes y están furiosos. Esto es apenas el comienzo".

El 27 DE MAYO, Garner le escribió un memorando formal al presidente. Apareció luego una copia con un sello en la primera página que decía "SECDEF LEÍDO".

"En tanto se acerca el final de mi servicio", decía, "quiero agradecerle por permitirme servir al país y a usted en esta importante misión. Siento que hemos creado las condiciones para la estabilización de Irak, aunque seguramente habrá altibajos en el período por venir. Hemos reunido un maravilloso grupo de profesionales y Jerry Bremer es una excelente elección para llevar al equipo al siguiente nivel y ayudar a sentar las bases de una verdadera reforma política y económica en Irak".

Enumeró algunas de las principales tareas que había por hacer —desde las provisiones hasta la seguridad— haciendo el énfasis más optimista posible en los logros. Garner no mencionó ni dejó entrever en su comunicación que había llegado a la conclusión de que Bremer ya había cometido tres errores garrafales: ampliar la *desbaathificación*, disolver el ejército y rechazar el consejo iraquí que Garner había formado. En lugar de ello, el ex general simplemente cerró su comunicación agradeciendo nuevamente al presidente por la oportunidad de prestar sus servicios. "Fue una experiencia desafiante, regocijante y gratificante. Gracias, también a usted por su inspirador liderazgo en tiempos de guerra".

Era irónico, pensó Garner; a pesar del empeño de Rumsfeld por que el Departamento de Defensa controlara las operaciones de posguerra en Irak, casi todos los que ocupaban una posición de poder en el nuevo APC de Bremer provenían del Departamento de Estado. Y Bremer mismo, quien fuera embajador pero que jamás había manejado una organización de gran envergadura, le había arrebatado el control a Rumsfeld.

EL CONSULTOR Y EXPERTO en personal al servicio de Rumsfeld, Steve Herbits, le escribió un duro memorando confidencial de cuatro páginas sobre el desempeño de Doug Feith como subsecretario de asuntos políticos.

"Después de casi dos años, la dirección de Doug no ha mejorado; su estilo y enfoque hacia el trabajo siguen provocando una ineficiencia significativa en su equipo. Sus negativas siguen acumulándose. Seis meses de planeación de las acciones de la posguerra ahora se consideran como una seria falla, tanto en lo esencial, es decir, en la selección de personal y la cooperación con el Departamento de Defensa, como en las relaciones interinstitucionales".

En las agencias que participan en el Consejo Nacional de Seguridad, seguía Herbits, el sobrenombre de la política es "El lunático Feith y su engendro diabólico". El reporte de Herbits sugería que, en opinión de Victoria A. *Torie* Clarke, vocera del Pentágono, Feith no contaba con el respeto ni la confianza de sus subalternos y colegas.

Herbits aseguró que Wolfowitz, Pace y otros consultores podían confirmar estas apreciaciones[10].

En el CNS, Hadley sabía que Feith era muy criticado, pero pensaba que tenía algunas cosas a su favor. Era uno de los pocos hombres de confianza de Rumsfeld y uno de los pocos que podía lograr una decisión suya y hacerla cumplir. Se le ocurrían muchas buenas ideas; proporcionaba liderazgo intelectual al proceso interinstitucional y podía preparar informes y memorandos

---

10. En una entrevista concedida en el 2006, Pace afirmó que no estaba de acuerdo con la valoración de Herbits y que él pensaba que Feith era "extremadamente inteligente" y que había hecho un buen trabajo. Más tarde, Feith me envió una carta diciendo que Rumsfeld y Wolfowitz también desaprobaban la evaluación de Herbits, a la que Feith llamó "una sarta de insultos de mal gusto" que no deberían estar en mi libro. "Su memorando es sólo un cúmulo de divagaciones difamatorias de una figura marginal", escribió Feith. "Me hace daño y no arroja ninguna luz sobre nada".

en una forma que lograba la aprobación de Rumsfeld, y no eran devueltos 10 o 15 minutos después. Y, finalmente, le era leal.

Cuando Feith se metía en aprietos públicamente, Hadley concluyó, siempre lo hacía por implementar las políticas de Rumsfeld. Hadley tenía la fuerte impresión de que Feith estaba desprotegido y solo ante el peligro. El problema no era Feith, era Rumsfeld.

Según lo veía Frank Miller, del equipo del CNS, Feith estaba desesperado. Bremer no hablaba con él y ponía a sus asistentes a responder los memorandos que le enviaba. Su mensaje era muy claro: "Yo trabajo para el presidente de los Estados Unidos", pasando por encima de Feith y, por lo tanto, de Rumsfeld.

A Miller le pareció que la decisión de disolver el ejército iraquí era exasperante. Durante meses le habían informado a Bush sobre el plan para usar 300.000 soldados iraquíes en la reconstrucción del país. Miller contaba con Walt Slocombe, hombre clave de Bremer en asuntos militares, entre sus amigos cercanos, pero pensaba que era estúpido que él y otros justificaran la decisión diciendo que el ejército iraquí se había desintegrado por sí mismo. Eso fue precisamente lo que les dijimos que hicieran, pensó: la CIA lanzó panfletos en posiciones iraquíes, que decían "Váyanse a casa. Depongan sus armas y váyanse a casa".

Pero con Bremer en escena, el grupo interinstitucional que trabajaba en los planes de posguerra, es decir, el Grupo Ejecutivo de Dirección, se había desintegrado. La sensación en la Casa Blanca era la misma que en el Pentágono: Bremer no quería que ellos espiaran por encima de su hombro. En el CNS circulaban reportes de los británicos, de los medios de comunicación y de los contactos militares de Frank Miller, pero no del propio Bremer. Los saqueos continuaban; los servidores civiles iraquíes no estaban recibiendo pago, y según un reporte, 40.000 profesores habían sido despedidos por ser baathistas.

Bremer estaba haciendo declaraciones y organizando conferencias de prensa en las que sugería que esperaba estar en Bagdad por mucho tiempo.

"Ocupación es una palabra fea, con la que los norteamericanos no se sienten cómodos, pero es un hecho", le reveló Bremer a un reportero de *The Washington Post*, durante un viaje en un avión de carga C-130 de Bagdad a la ciudad de Umm Qasr, el 28 de mayo. "El presidente Bush siempre ha dicho que estaremos aquí el tiempo necesario para hacer el trabajo, y ni un día más. A la vez, debemos asegurarnos de no salir ni un día antes".

"ENCONTRAMOS LAS ARMAS de destrucción masiva", declaró el presidente Bush en una entrevista concedida a un reportero de televisión polaco, el 29 de mayo. "Encontramos laboratorios de armas biológicas. Recuerde cuando

Colin Powell se paró frente al mundo y dijo: 'Irak tiene laboratorios, laboratorios móviles para fabricar armas biológicas'. Son ilegales. Van en contra de las resoluciones de las Naciones Unidas, y hasta ahora hemos encontrado dos. Y a medida que pase el tiempo encontraremos más. Aquellos que dicen que no hemos encontrado los dispositivos de fabricación de armas prohibidas o las armas en sí, se equivocan. Las encontramos".

Bush estaba en un viaje relámpago de siete días por Europa y el Medio Oriente e hizo comentarios similares sobre el hallazgo de ADM en una entrevista en Francia. El único problema era que, en realidad, no habían encontrado las armas. El 75° Destacamento Especial de Búsqueda se estaba metiendo en graves problemas con la *gran búsqueda* de las ADM de Saddam, el menor de los cuales no era una serie de falsos positivos muy publicitados. Cada vez que parecían haber encontrado algo que podían describir como un arma —un supuesto arsenal, un depósito o hasta un pequeño frasco de armas biológicas— el hallazgo no tardaba en ser desacreditado.

El presidente no sabía que cuatro días antes de su entrevista en televisión, la AID había enviado un equipo de sus nueve expertos civiles a Irak a inspeccionar los dos laboratorios móviles que habían encontrado. El día anterior a la declaración de Bush, el equipo mandó un reporte de campo de tres páginas, donde concluía que los laboratorios no estaban destinados a la fabricación de armas biológicas. El reporte secreto de 122 páginas, terminado en su totalidad al mes siguiente, decía que los laboratorios no tenían nada que ver con ADM. Toda la evidencia indicaba que muy probablemente se dedicaban a fabricar hidrógeno para globos meteorológicos.

Un día después de las declaraciones de Bush, durante una conferencia de prensa en el Pentágono, el subsecretario de Defensa para inteligencia, de Rumsfeld, Steve Cambone, y Keith Dayton, general de división del ejército y director del servicio de inteligencia humana de la AID, anunciaron oficialmente la creación del nuevo Grupo de Inspección de Irak. Ahora, declaró Dayton, su nuevo grupo de 1.400 miembros emprenderían la búsqueda, pero tendrían otras tareas, como la recolección de información de inteligencia sobre terrorismo y crímenes de guerra. Su unidad tendría a Qatar como base, a unos 644 kilómetros al sur de Irak, al otro lado del Golfo Pérsico, donde el Comando Central del Ejército tenía establecidos sofisticados sistemas de comunicaciones para enviar información a los Estados Unidos.

SPIDER MARKS ESTABA LISTO para regresar a Estados Unidos. El Coronel Rotkoff se sentía exhausto. Se preparaba para retirarse del ejército y había hecho los arreglos necesarios para tener un trabajo de oficina en Washington por algunos meses, mientras pensaba a qué dedicarse en la vida civil. Justo antes de abandonar el Medio Oriente, resumió, en uno de los haikus finales de su diario, sus pensamientos sobre la guerra, el miedo, la impactante victoria militar, la incapacidad de encontrar las armas de destrucción masiva y sus caóticas repercusiones.

Sabíamos cómo combatir
No es cierto; construyendo una NACIÓN
Podemos perder la PAZ

EL 2 DE JUNIO, cerca de 1.000 ex soldados se reunieron en Bagdad, a las puertas de las oficinas centrales de la APC para protestar contra la disolución del ejército. Un memorando interno de la agencia narró el hecho, centrándose en la amplia cobertura que tuvo en medios árabes como Al Jazeera y Al Arabiya, y en el servicio de noticias Reuters.

"Algunos antiguos miembros del Ministerio de Defensa han hecho declaraciones públicas en las que aseguran que están dispuestos a lanzar ataques suicidas si no se atienden sus exigencias", decía el memorando. "Otros manifestantes siguen declarando que organizarán unidades armadas para luchar contra la APC y la ocupación".

"Todo el pueblo iraquí es una bomba de tiempo que le estallará en la cara a los norteamericanos si no ponen fin a la ocupación", aseguró un manifestante a los reporteros, después de reunirse con un oficial de la APC.

"Todos nosotros nos convertiremos en bombas suicidas", aseguró otro manifestante, un antiguo oficial militar. "Transformaré a mis seis hijas en bombas para matar a los norteamericanos".

"No vamos a permitir que nos chantajeen con amenazas de terrorismo, para desarrollar programas", fue la respuesta de Bremer. Además, concluyó, las manifestaciones constituían la primera vez en décadas que alguien se atrevía a protestar afuera del palacio presidencial de Saddam. ¿No era eso un avance?

BUSH VIAJÓ A QATAR para hacer una escala en medio de su viaje al pasar por Medio Oriente, y Bremer vino desde Bagdad para reunirse con él. Los dos hombres hablaron en la parte trasera de la limosina de Bush mientras se dirigían desde el cuartel general del Comando Central, cerca del aeropuerto, al hotel Ritz-Carlton.

"¿Cómo está la situación, en general?", preguntó Bush, según recuerda Bremer en su libro.

"Estoy optimista por dos razones, señor presidente", empezó Bremer, y a continuación ofreció una explicación que parecía salida de la Enciclopedia

Británica. "En primer lugar, Irak tiene excelentes recursos, gran cantidad de agua, y es fértil, además de las enormes reservas de petróleo. Y los iraquíes son gente activa y recursiva".

Al mismo tiempo, agregó Bremer, los iraquíes estaban "psicológicamente devastados" después de vivir tanto tiempo bajo el régimen de Saddam.

Sin decir una sola palabra sobre la política de *desbaathificación* o la disolución del ejército, que había dejado sin trabajo a cientos de miles de iraquíes, Bremer le explicó al presidente: "Nuestro problema más urgente es el desempleo. Pensamos que es alrededor del 50%, pero, ¿quién lo sabe realmente? Así mismo, Irak tiene una población joven, y cerca de la mitad de ella es menor de diecinueve años. Esa es una combinación explosiva".

DURANTE UNA DISCUSIÓN con Rumsfeld y Bremer, Bush les preguntó a quemarropa quién de ellos era el encargado de encontrar las ADM. ¿Quién tenía la búsqueda como su misión primordial y exclusiva? Dado que esa era una de las principales justificaciones de la guerra, muchísimas cosas dependían de los resultados de la búsqueda.

Bremer indicó que era responsabilidad de Rumsfeld.

Rumsfeld dijo que Bremer estaba a cargo.

Bush estaba a punto de explotar. Decidió que la tarea pasaría a manos de alguien más. Quería a una persona a cargo, alguien para quien esa fuera su única misión en la vida. Y puesto que la CIA había insistido en que Irak tenía ADM, la agencia podría encargarse de encontrar las armas. Así que, después dos meses y medio de guerra, la administración iba, por fin, a centrarse en ello.

Aunque técnicamente Bremer debía reportarse a Bush a través de Rumsfeld, Rice sabía que el Pentágono no tenía gran influencia sobre Bremer, mucho menos control.

"Esto no va bien", le dijo a Frank Miller, quien con su Grupo Ejecutivo de Dirección (GED) había sido el hombre clave del CNS en el período previo a la invasión. Ahora, Rice quería que Miller retomara su rol en la etapa de posguerra. "Vuelva a conformar el GED", ordenó Rice.

21

La tarde del 5 de junio, David Kay, uno de los más destacados expertos del mundo en inspecciones de armas nucleares, estaba en las oficinas principales de la CIA, en Langley, Virginia. Kay era un tejano de 64 años, de baja estatura, vehemente y conversador, doctor en ciencias políticas. Había sido jefe inspector de armas nucleares de la ONU en Irak, después de la Guerra del Golfo de 1991, y dirigido la misión que logró poner al descubierto el programa nuclear de Saddam, a 18 meses de la fabricación de una bomba. Ese había sido uno de los golpes de inteligencia más importantes de los años noventa.

Como miembro del denominado panel de expertos "barba gris", Kay estaba ahora en Langley para revisar un reporte altamente clasificado sobre los intentos clandestinos de Corea del Norte de reprocesar plutonio para la construcción de armas nucleares. Según Kay, el informe inicial no tenía gran valor, ya que los vuelos de vigilancia de Estados Unidos cerca de Corea del Norte habían sido interrumpidos por temor a perder alguna nave. Kay había recomendado que el reporte de la CIA fuera honesto y dijera que los datos no eran confiables. Tan sólo digan que no saben, recomendó, porque los datos técnicos quedan abiertos a cualquier interpretación.

Tiempo después, John McLaughlin, el segundo al mando de Tenet en la CIA, le pidió a Kay que se pasara por su oficina. "George quiere verlo", dijo McLaughlin.

Kay acababa de regresar de Irak, donde había estado durante un mes trabajando como analista experto para *NBC News*, haciendo seguimiento del trabajo del destacamento especial de búsqueda de ADM del ejército. Incluso, se había colado en algunas de sus inspecciones. Una vez había ido con ellos a inspeccionar una granja de cría de gallinas donde, según la Lista Maestra de sitios con ADM, podían hallarse sustancias prohibidas. El sitio no resultó ser más que una granja de cría de gallinas.

"¿Qué opina?", preguntó Tenet. "¿Por qué no encuentran nada?".

"Estos tipos probablemente no encontrarían nada ni aunque lo tuvieran al frente", aseguró Kay sin ambages. "No están organizados ni equipados ni orientados a ello".

"Está bien. Si fueras el rey, ¿qué harías?".

"En primer lugar, es necesario que el grupo dedicado a la tarea tenga la experiencia necesaria", dijo. El Destacamento Especial no tiene idea de lo que está haciendo. "No van a llegar a donde deben, con la orientación de los militares, porque han mostrado un enorme desinterés en el asunto. Ellos estaban interesados en impedir el uso de las armas y no consideraban que la búsqueda de ADM fuera una labor suya".

En segundo lugar, era un error empezar la búsqueda basándose en la Lista Maestra y sus 946 emplazamientos, algunos de los cuales habían sido rotulados como sospechosos desde hacía más de una década. Era un catálogo general de posibilidades. En Mayo, Kay había visto la lista en Bagdad... Un gran número de emplazamientos eran lugares que él mismo había inspeccionado en 1991 y 1992, donde no había encontrado nada.

"Es imposible encontrar armas de destrucción masiva usando una lista", dijo. "Es necesario tratar el asunto como una operación de inteligencia. Hay que ir tras las personas, no tras las cosas. No tenemos suficiente gente en el país. Es un país demasiado grande. No se puede hacer hoyos en todo el país. Así que se debe ir tras la experiencia, los guardias de seguridad que estuvieron allí, los encargados del transporte, los generales que las vieron, la Guardia Republicana Especial".

En vez de buscar arsenales u ojivas, era más importante y fácil buscar las habilidades: encontrar a los científicos que hicieron las armas, a quienes trabajaron en las instalaciones de producción, a los guardias encargados de la seguridad, a los conductores de los camiones que transportaron las armas. Si Irak tenía ADM, entonces tenía que haberlas producido o comprado en algún lugar.

"Sí, eso tiene sentido", admitió Tenet.

Kay conocía nombres y recitó una lista de iraquíes clave, explicando la manera en que creía que debían encontrarlos e interrogarlos. Pensaba que *Spider* Marks había estado exprimiendo la Lista Maestra, creyendo que encontrarían algo si simplemente iban a cada sitio de los enumerados. A Kay le habían dicho que, cuando el jefe de la estación de la CIA en Bagdad había intentado concertar una reunión para que Kay hablara con el general McKiernan, éste se había negado diciendo: "No tengo ningún interés en las ADM. ¿Por qué debería hablar con Kay?".

Según dijo Kay, las fallas que había visto en el 75° Destacamento no parecían haber mejorado con el nuevo grupo del general Dayton, el Grupo de Inspección de Irak. Ya habían empezado mal. ¿Qué estaban haciendo en Doha, Qatar, a cientos de kilómetros de Irak? ¿Por qué estaban hablando de otras misiones, diferentes a las ADM?

"No deben empezar por Doha. Hay que poner gente en la zona. Si no están ahí, hay que llevarlos. Es necesario concentrarse en una sola misión", señaló Kay.

"Los malditos militares nunca pueden organizar nada", se lamentó Tenet. "Tenemos que hablar con ellos. Nosotros no queremos este trabajo. Los militares debieron haberlo hecho. Pero ahora nosotros nos vamos a meter en aprietos con esto. Estoy seguro de que nos traerá problemas. El presidente no está nada satisfecho con lo que está pasando". Tenet añadió: "Los militares lo han echado a perder todo. Ahora no lo quiero". En la reunión no se mencionó que la mayor parte de la inteligencia y de las conclusiones sobre la "irrefutable" información de inteligencia que sugería la existencia de ADM había provenido de la CIA o llegado a través de la misma, que estaba a cargo de Tenet.

Ese fin de semana, Kay y su esposa estaban de viaje en Virginia, cuando él recibió una llamada en su teléfono móvil, de Stu Cohen, el veterano analista de la CIA, de 30 años de experiencia, quien se había desempeñado como presidente del Consejo Nacional de Inteligencia cuando fue aprobado el Estimado Nacional de Inteligencia de ADM de octubre del 2002.

"La Casa Blanca ha decidido poner a George a cargo", dijo Cohen. "Y él quiere que usted lo haga. George quiere saber si usted tomará este trabajo".

Kay estaba sorprendido de que la CIA buscara a alguien distinto de sus funcionarios para dirigir la búsqueda de ADM, pero quería hacerlo.

"Sí", dijo Kay, pero advirtió "si todas las condiciones de las que hablé con George se cumplen".

Kay estaba convencido de que Saddam tenía depósitos de ADM. Su experiencia en la Guerra del Golfo se le había quedado grabada en la memoria. Cuando fue a Irak para la ONU, después de la Guerra del Golfo de 1991, no esperaba encontrar un programa nuclear. La inteligencia de Israel, por ejemplo, estaba convencida de que el descubrimiento, en 1981, del reactor nuclear Osirak, a unas 10 millas de Bagdad, había terminado con el programa de Saddam. En cambio, Kay había rastreado unos fondos encubiertos para un programa nuclear que respondía al nombre en clave de "PC3" e involucraba a 5.000 personas en la realización de pruebas y fabricación de ingredientes para una bomba nuclear (*calutrons*, centrifugadoras, iniciadores de neutrones, lentes altamente explosivas y núcleos de bombas de uranio enriquecido). Saddam planeaba construir y detonar un arma nuclear en el desierto como un modo de decirle al mundo: "Ahora, nosotros tenemos una".

Kay recordaba con total claridad el impacto que ello había causado en Cheney, en ese entonces secretario de Defensa, y en Wolfowitz, subsecretario para Asuntos Políticos. "No sé qué habríamos hecho, de haberlo sabido", había asegurado Wolfowitz. Tal vez no habríamos tenido Guerra del Golfo para expulsar a Saddam de Kuwait. Es probable que los saudíes hubieran intentado comprar su salida del problema, como era su costumbre. En 1991, los inspectores colegas de Kay de la ONU también habían descubierto cientos de galones de gas nervioso VX, el agente nervioso más letal que se conoce, y armas biológicas, incluidos centenares de litros de ántrax y de toxina botulínica.

Dirigir las nuevas tareas de inspección en 2003 significaba que Kay tendría que convertirse en empleado oficial de la CIA. El lunes 10 de junio, le hicieron la prueba de detección de mentiras y una prueba psicológica. "Es obvio que cualquiera que sea capaz de aceptar este trabajo no pasará la prueba psicológica", dijo Kay. "Así que, simplemente, repruébenme".

Pasó la prueba y, en vista de que contaba con los certificados de seguridad de su trabajo anterior, esa misma tarde prestó su juramento ante Tenet y asumió como consejero especial del director para ADM y como director del Grupo de Inspección de Irak. Tenet hacía alarde de haber conseguido a alguien, a través del personal de la CIA, en doce horas –un récord notable para la agencia–, y afirmó que el plan era que Kay viajara a Bagdad esa noche o a más tardar al día siguiente.

"George, no puedo hacer eso", objetó Kay. "No he leído toda la evidencia que tienen ustedes. Tengo que hablar con los analistas. Tengo que hablar con la gente que está haciendo la recolección. Necesito hablar con Defensa. No puedo simplemente montarme en un avión y llegar a hacerlo".

A la siguiente semana, Kay se embarcó en un curso relámpago de inteligencia sobre ADM. En vista de que no había trabajado en el caso de las ADM de Irak desde los años 90, esperaba encontrar, luego de 15 a 18 horas diarias de lectura y revisión completa de los reportes de la CIA y el Departamento de Defensa, algún tesoro escondido. Le impactó no encontrar nada.

"No había nada nuevo", recordó. Nada con un fundamento firme o razonablemente apoyado en hechos provenía del período posterior a 1998, año en que los inspectores de la ONU habían abandonado el país. "Todo lo que había después de esa fecha o bien provenía de un disidente o llegaba a través de un servicio de inteligencia extranjero de manera confusa".

Por ejemplo, Kay encontró que toda la inteligencia de la preguerra sobre los laboratorios móviles de armas biológicas que Powell había descrito a la ONU en febrero y que, de acuerdo con la declaración del presidente, habían descubierto el 29 de mayo, provenía de una sola fuente, un disidente iraquí empleado por la inteligencia alemana que respondía al nombre en clave de Curveball.

Powell le había asegurado a la ONU y al mundo que había cuatro fuentes que apoyaban la acusación, basadas en la información de la CIA. En realidad, tres de las cuatro fuentes sólo ofrecían información sobre la carrera de Curveball o sobre un supuesto laboratorio móvil de algún tipo. "No tenían conocimiento del programa biológico", concluiría Kay, más tarde.

Las sorpresas siguieron llegando. Kay estaba perplejo al enterarse de que la CIA ni siquiera había entrevistado directamente a Curveball, sino que había confiado en los reportes que los alemanes hicieron de 112 interrogatorios que ellos habían llevado a cabo. Y lo peor, al parecer los alemanes habían advertido que Curveball era alcohólico y en los archivos estadounidenses se le restó importancia al asunto.

Kay descubrió que la conclusión sobre los supuestos intentos de Irak por reiniciar su programa nuclear se basaba solamente en una pieza de evidencia física –Powell le había dicho a la ONU que Saddam seguía intentando conseguir "tubos de aluminio de alta especificación"–. "La mayoría de expertos estadounidenses piensan que estos tubos van a ser usados como rotores en centrifugadoras para enriquecer uranio", dijo Powell.

El archivo de la CIA sobre los tubos de aluminio tenía cientos de páginas y contenía información de fuentes extranjeras que sugerían que Irak había tratado de comprar 60.000 de estos tubos para usarlos como obuses. Kay estuvo de acuerdo en que, desde cualquier punto de vista, era una cantidad demasiado grande. Pero en los 90 había aprendido que los iraquíes gastaban y compraban mucho más de lo que pensaban que necesitarían. En el régimen de Saddam se consideraba una falta mucho más seria, para alguien del gobierno, no conseguir lo suficiente que comprar demasiado.

Después de varios días, la letra de una vieja canción de Peggy Lee empezó a rondar en la cabeza de Kay: *Is that all there is?*(¿Y eso es todo?). Más tarde declaró: "Entre más miras, menos encuentras. Fue una experiencia esclarecedora. Pero es necesario considerar que (a) yo seguía creyendo que las armas estaban en algún lado, y (b) que pensaba que la respuesta no la encontraríamos en Washington o en Doha; la íbamos a encontrar en Bagdad, en Irak. Así que estaba ansioso por ir allá y ver lo que podía hacer".

Luego de una semana del curso relámpago que tomara Kay sobre ADM, Tenet organizó un almuerzo de ellos dos con Rumsfeld en la oficina del secretario, en el Pentágono. Los generales Myers y Franks estaban allí, junto con Steve Cambone.

Tenet propuso compartir la responsabilidad de Kay y pedirle a éste que se reportara a Rumsfeld y a él.

"De ninguna manera", dijo Rumsfeld. Ahora era la responsabilidad de Tenet.

Kay entendió por qué Rumsfeld merecía ser reconocido como uno de los mejores luchadores burocráticos de todos los tiempos. Si Kay encontraba las ADM, eso confirmaría los estimados de la CIA. Si no las encontraba, no sería nada bueno estar asociado con una búsqueda infructuosa. No era una propuesta que le pudiera reportar algún beneficio, así que Rumsfeld la rechazó.

Franks todavía estaba en su vuelta de la victoria. Se retiraría el mes siguiente y su reemplazo, el general Abizaid, ya había sido anunciado.

"Quiero estar seguro de que usted y Keith Dayton se lleven bien", dijo Rumsfeld, "y que no discutan por esto".

"No tiene de qué preocuparse", prometió Kay, "porque si no nos llevamos bien, se lo aseguro, estaremos allí más tiempo de lo que los dos quisiéramos".

"Me gusta esa actitud", dijo Franks, riendo.

"Entiendo esa actitud", añadió Rumsfeld.

Antes de salir para Bagdad, Kay le expresó una última preocupación a Tenet. "No tengo base en la CIA", dijo Kay. "No quiero tener que discutir con la gente por recursos cuando esté allá".

"No se preocupe", dijo Tenet. "Tendrá lo que quiera. Si se le presenta algún problema, John y yo nos encargaremos". Tenet rodeó con sus manos a Kay en un gran abrazo y le dijo: "No metas la pata".

Era su despedida habitual para quienes iban a la zona de combate.

EL 12 DE JUNIO DE 2003, en la portada de *The Washington Post* apareció un artículo de Walter Pincus, en el que se reportaba que un "embajador retirado de los Estados Unidos" anónimo había sido enviado a África en el 2002 para verificar si Irak había intentado comprar uranio a Nigeria. El embajador retirado ponía en duda que hubiese alguna evidencia de un trato. La declaración contradecía lo que había afirmado el presidente Bush en su discurso del Estado de la Unión, antes de la guerra, 16 palabras que se volverían famosas: "El gobierno británico ha sabido que Saddam Hussein buscó recientemente cantidades significativas de uranio en África".

Al día siguiente, un viernes, entrevisté a un alto funcionario de la administración, alguien que no trabajaba en la Casa Blanca, para mi libro *Plan of Attack*. Después de casi hora y media de entrevista, nuestra conversación derivó en una charla informal, algo usual después de una discusión larga y trascendental. Mencioné que estaba enterado de que el "embajador estadounidense retirado" que estaba en una misión de la CIA era Joseph C. Wilson, quien había sido embajador en el país africano de Gabón, durante el gobierno de George Bush padre, y que había trabajado en el Consejo Nacional de Seguridad de Clinton.

"Su esposa trabaja en la agencia", dijo el oficial. "Es una analista de ADM".

Explicó que su esposa lo había propuesto para la misión porque Wilson conocía África. Pasamos a otro tema.

Después de la entrevista, le dije a Pincus lo que había oído sobre la esposa de Wilson y su trabajo como analista de ADM en la CIA, sin revelar el nombre de la fuente. Pincus expresó luego que no recordaba nuestra conversación.

Unas semanas después, el 6 de julio, Wilson escribió una columna en *The New York Times* y dijo que era "muy dudoso" que Irak y Nigeria hubieran tenido un trato. Ocho días más tarde, el columnista, Robert Novak escribió que "dos altos funcionarios de la administración" le habían revelado que la esposa de Wilson, Valerie Plame, era una "experta en armas de destrucción masiva" de la CIA y que había sido clave en su viaje a África. El Departamento de Justicia lanzó una investigación criminal para determinar cómo se había filtrado a la prensa la relación entre Wilson y su esposa, y si eso significaba que un agente encubierto la había revelado. Pronto, se nombró un fiscal especial para que se encargara de la investigación, Patrick Fitzgerald, de Chicago.

JAY GARNER prácticamente se escondió por un par de semanas cuando regresó a los Estados Unidos, a principios de junio. No quería ver a nadie del Pentágono ni hablar de su experiencia en Irak. Larry DiRita lo llamó varias veces. "Tienes que venir aquí y hablar con Rumsfeld", le imploró. Finalmente, Garner accedió a ir el miércoles 18 de junio.

Cuando estuvo a solas con Rumsfeld, sentado en la mesa de la famosa oficina del secretario, donde se habían reunido en enero, Garner sintió que tenía la obligación de expresar la magnitud de sus preocupaciones.

"Hemos tomado tres decisiones trágicas", confesó Garner.

"¿En verdad?", preguntó Rumsfeld.

"Tres equivocaciones terribles", dijo Garner, y resumió en pocas palabras lo que había omitido en el memorando del 27 de mayo al presidente. Se refirió a la magnitud de la *desbaathificación*, a la disolución del ejército y a la apresurada eliminación del grupo de liderazgo iraquí. Disolver el ejército había sido el mayor error. Ahora había cientos de miles de iraquíes desorganizados, desempleados y armados yendo de un lado a otro. Tomaría años volver a conformar un ejército. Habían tomado 30.000 o 50.000 baathistas y los habían enviado a la clandestinidad, le explicó Garner a Rumsfeld. Y habían eliminado el grupo de liderazgo iraquí. "Jerry Bremer no puede ser la cara del gobierno para la gente de Irak. Tienen que poner un rostro iraquí para el pueblo iraquí".

Garner hizo un señalamiento final: "Aún hay tiempo de rectificar esto. Todavía hay tiempo de darle la vuelta".

Rumsfeld miró a Garner por un momento con su mirada penetrante. "Pues, no creo que haya nada que podamos hacer, porque estamos aquí".

Él cree que estoy fuera de mis cabales, pensó Garner. Cree que estoy completamente equivocado. Garner no quería ser aguafiestas, pero hechos eran hechos. "Todos los errores son reversibles", reiteró Garner.

"No vamos a echarnos para atrás", dijo Rumsfeld de manera enfática. Discusión terminada. "Venga. Vamos a la otra sala".

En el 2006, le pregunté a Rumsfeld si recordaba la advertencia de Garner sobre los tres errores.

"Vagamente", respondió Rumsfeld. "Recuerdo haber tenido una muy buena discusión con él. Sentía que no lo estaban reconociendo como se merecía por lo que había hecho. Creo que es un excelente oficial retirado y un tipo muy talentoso que se preocupa mucho por Irak".

Después de su discusión, Rumsfeld y Garner entraron en la gran sala de conferencias donde estaba casi toda la gente importante de Rumsfeld: Wolfowitz, Feith, Ryan Henry, DiRita y Torie Clarke, el general Pace y el general Casey.

En una pequeña ceremonia, Rumsfeld impuso la medalla del Departamento de Defensa por servicio público distinguido a Garner, quien no quería recibirla.

Más tarde, Rumsfeld y Garner dieron una conferencia de prensa.

"Quiero agradecer a Jay por el espléndido trabajo que ha hecho", dijo el secretario, "al sentar las bases para que el pueblo iraquí empiece este proceso de reconstrucción, a partir de los escombros de décadas de tiranía de Saddam Hussein, y para que se encaminen en el sendero de un gobierno autónomo y democrático".

Rumsfeld informó a los periodistas que el sistema de agua en Irak estaba operando en un 80% del nivel anterior a la guerra y que cerca de 2 millones de servidores civiles iraquíes estaban recibiendo pago. Leyó una lista impresionante de estadísticas: Basora tenía electricidad las 24 horas del día, y Bagdad gozaba del servicio por unas 19 o 20 horas diarias. Las filas para comprar gasolina estaban despareciendo, no había crisis de salud y los niños iraquíes estaban regresando a estudiar. Había 8.000 oficiales de policía patrullando de nuevo. En cuanto a la situación de seguridad, Rumsfeld afirmó: "En aquellas regiones donde intentan reagruparse focos de marginales, el general Franks y su equipo los están erradicando. En pocas palabras, la coalición está haciendo grandes progresos. Todo esto fue posible gracias al excelente plan militar del general Franks y al fabuloso liderazgo de los esfuerzos de estabilización del señor Jay Garner y su equipo.

Cuando Garner finalmente tuvo la oportunidad de hablar, fue más sobrio. "A todos ustedes simplemente quisiera decirles algo. Hay problemas en Irak y los habrá por un tiempo. Siempre hay problemas cuando la gente ha recibido un trato brutal durante treinta años y es trasladada de la oscuridad absoluta a la luz. Así que pienso que hay más cosas buenas que malas, y, definitivamente, el vaso está medio lleno.

Al final de sus comentarios, Garner contradijo completamente lo que le había dicho en privado a Rumsfeld sobre Bremen: "Estoy convencido de que todas las cosas que está haciendo son las correctas".

A CONTINUACIÓN, Rumsfeld y Garner fueron a la Casa Blanca a ver a Bush. Era la segunda vez de Garner con el presidente.

"Señor secretario, ¿quién es ese famoso hombre que está con usted?", exclamó el Presidente mientras salía por la puerta del Salón Oval. Estiró su mano. "Hola, Jay".

"Señor presidente", dijo Garner, "usted tiene cosas más importantes que hacer hoy por esta nación que sacar tiempo para hablar conmigo, así que lo único que quiero es estrechar su mano y agradecerle por darme la oportunidad de servir".

Bush tomó la mano de Garner y, utilizando uno de sus personalísimos movimientos, lo acercó hacia sí.

"Claro que tengo tiempo para usted", dijo Bush, "y voy a sacar tiempo. Quiero hablar con usted". Bush rodeó a Garner con su brazo y lo condujo al Salón Oval; se detuvo en una de las ventanas. "Mire hacia fuera, Jay, allá en la grama. Si no estuviera con usted, probablemente estaría afuera besándole el trasero a los periodistas o a alguien más. O tal vez estaría en el Capitolio besándole el trasero a un puñado de congresistas".

Bush condujo a Garner al par de sillas principales del Salón Oval. "Siéntese ahí y yo me sentaré aquí", señaló el presidente, ocupando su posición habitual y ofreciendo la otra silla a Garner. "¿Por qué no querría estar en esta cómoda oficina, con estas dos hermosas sillas, sentado aquí con usted y besando su trasero?"

Cheney y Rice se les unieron.

"Señor presidente, permítame contarle un par de historias", dijo Garner. Era su turno.

Garner tenía un historia muy larga que contarle a Bush y recuerda haberlo hecho de esta manera: Buck Walters, un general de una estrella retirado de la Fuerza Aérea, quien era el hombre de Garner encargado de la región sur de Irak, lo llamó un día mientras visitaba Hillah, cerca de Babilonia. Allí estaban Malcolm MacPherson, un reportero de la revista *Time*, y Mike Gfoeller, un funcionario del Departamento de Estado que tenía reputación de hablar mejor árabe que, incluso, la mayoría de los iraquíes. "Antes de marcharse", dijo Walters, "tengo que llevarlo a hablar con Darth Vader".

"¿Quién es ese?", preguntó Garner.

"Es el líder clerical de aquí".

"¿Por qué lo llaman Darth Vader?" preguntó Garner.

"Lo entenderá cuando lo vea".

Entonces Garner le contó a Bush y a los demás que fue a reunirse con el hombre. Ante él apareció un tipo gigante, un clérigo chiíta del tamaño de Shaquille O'Neal, vestido todo de negro. Turbante negro. Una gran barba negra. Le habían dicho que era descendiente directo del profeta Mahoma. Todo el mundo se sentó. Su inglés era bueno.

"Su excelencia", empezó Garner, "como sabe, hemos estado aquí durante varias semanas y hemos hecho algunas cosas buenas y algunas cosas no tan buenas. Y muchas cosas no las hemos hecho porque no sabíamos cómo. Entonces, lo que me gustaría es su apreciación sobre lo que hemos hecho bien y lo que hemos hecho mal, y luego quisiera su orientación sobre nuestro próximo paso".

"Bien", dijo Darth Vader. "He pensado en eso durante un tiempo. Déjeme decirle algo. ¿Le molesta si hablo en árabe? ¿Tiene traductor?".

Garner les aseguró a Bush y a los demás: "Tenía el mejor traductor de los Estados Unidos conmigo". Así que Darth Vader habló en árabe durante la siguiente hora.

"Me he extendido mucho y me disculpo por eso", terminó Darth Vader (identificado más tarde como el jeque Farqat al-Qizwini), hablando nuevamente en inglés. "No debería haber ocupado tanto de su tiempo".

"No, ha sido maravilloso", recordó haber exclamado Garner. "Voy a regresar y vamos a trabajar en las cosas que usted mencionó".

Pero Darth Vader lo interrumpió: "Déjeme resumir. Lo que necesitamos hacer ahora es conseguir un gobierno que funcione. Pero un gobierno que funcione tiene que estar basado en una Constitución. Esa Constitución tiene que ser escrita por todo el pueblo de Irak. Tiene que estar fundamentada en principios democráticos, y debe proteger a todos sin distingos de religión o raza. Una vez que logremos eso, entonces podremos tener un gobierno iraquí.

Podremos empezar a ser un Estado democrático. Podremos ser un faro de luz en el Medio Oriente".

Darth Vader empezó a levantar la voz. "Entonces, debemos seguir estos principios y debemos organizar una democracia y tenemos que escribir una Constitución basada en los principios de Jesucristo".

A Bush y a los demás les encantó.

Garner continuó citando al clérigo: "Lograremos un gobierno así. Una vez lo tengamos, ustedes nos acogerán como su estado número 51".

De acuerdo con el recuento de Garner, él le respondió así: "Su excelencia, esa es una idea magnífica. Va a llevarme un poco más de tiempo trabajar en esta sugerencia que en las otras cosas, pero lo volveré a visitar y hablaremos de ella".

Garner narra que después de la sesión, él y el reportero de *Time* entraron al auto y se marcharon.

"¡Increíble!", exclamó el reportero. "¿Qué va a hacer con esto?".

"¡Oiga! Ese no es mi problema. La pregunta es qué va a hacer usted con esto, porque nadie va a creerlo cuando lo publique en *Time*".

"¡Por Dios santo! Nunca publicaré esto en *Time*. Nadie lo creería".

Es una historia verdadera, aseguró Garner. Estaba eufórico.

Cada tres días, aproximadamente, Garner le relató a Bush, trataba de ir al mercado, porque era ahí donde los iraquíes lo reconocían y se acercaban a hablar con él. Durante los primeros 20 o 25 minutos, la gente maldecía y rezongaba contra él, pero luego empezaban a calmarse y Garner tenía un minuto aproximadamente para dar un discurso corto y convincente y recitar de un tirón todos sus logros. "Ahora tienen x cantidad de megavoltios de electricidad y proyectamos tener más para la próxima semana. Próximamente abriremos escuelas y tal vez podamos tener elecciones provinciales. Empezaremos a escribir la constitución. Tienen x cantidad de agua que estamos trayendo. Sé que la crisis del combustible es grave, así que traeremos x cantidad de camiones cisterna todos los días. Vamos a empezar a comprar la cosecha la próxima semana".

Si venían con problemas específicos, decía Garner, les prometía que al siguiente día a las 10 a.m. enviaría a algún general para ayudar a solucionarlos. Y cuando estaba listo para marcharse, agradecía a la multitud por su tiempo.

"Me preparaba para salir de allí" dijo Garner, "y, esto es cierto, mientras me alejaba no veía más que pulgares levantados y gente diciendo, 'Díos bendiga al señor George Bush y al señor Tony Blair. Gracias por alejar a Saddam Hussein'. Lo mismo ocurrió en 70 encuentros. Esa era siempre la respuesta final de la gente".

"Eso está muy bien", dijo, satisfecho, Bush.

Garner le contó sobre como los baathistas intentaron controlar las primeras elecciones después de Saddam en la Universidad de Bagdad. Eso había provocado algo de mala prensa. Los norteamericanos se habían visto forzados a permitir las elecciones de modo que hubiera alguien allí y el año académico pudiera terminar a tiempo. Pero los baathistas del campus, si bien eran impopulares, estaban más organizados que cualquier otro grupo, y ganaron. La universidad se había sumergido en el caos.

"Eso fue muy malo", comentó Bush, indicando que lo sabía.

"Señor presidente, sólo le diré una cosa; he tenido tres semanas para trabajar con el embajador Bremer y él es uno de los hombres más trabajadores que he visto. Es un tipo muy brillante. Es elocuente y fluido y hará bien el trabajo. Hizo una buena elección".

"Yo no lo escogí", dijo Bush. "Rumsfeld lo escogió, tal como lo escogió a usted".

Garner miró a Rumsfeld. El secretario de Defensa le había dicho explícitamente a finales de abril que Bush había elegido a Bremer, y había agregado más tarde que ni la época de llegada de Bremer era su decisión. Pero ahora, Rumsfeld no dijo una sola palabra.

Cuando Garner se incorporó para salir, Rice lo detuvo y le extendió la mano. "Jay, tiene que seguir en contacto con nosotros", le dijo ella.

"Me gustaría hacerlo", dijo Garner, pensando para sí: ¿Cómo diablos voy a hacer eso? Después de todo, él solamente hablaba con Rumsfeld.

Mientras salía, Bush palmoteó a Garner en la espalda. "Jay, ¿te gustaría ocuparte de Irán?".

"Señor, los muchachos y yo hablamos sobre eso y queremos ofrecernos para Cuba. Pensamos que el ron y los tabacos son un poco mejor... las mujeres son más bonitas".

Bush rió. "Es tuyo. Cuenta con Cuba".

POR SUPUESTO, con todas las historias, la jocosidad, la charla de camaradería, la fanfarronada y la seguridad en sí mismo que había mostrado en el Salón Oval, Garner había dejado por fuera lo más importante. No había mencionado, ni siquiera aludido, los problemas que vio. No le contó a Bush sobre los tres errores trágicos que creía que Bremer, apoyado por Rumsfeld, había cometido: la *desbaathificación*, la disolución del ejército y la desintegración del grupo de gobierno iraquí. En cambio, había manifestado que Bremer era fenomenal y había hecho un retrato de un Irak donde un clérigo chiíta visualizaba su país regido por los principios de Jesucristo y acogiéndose a la

Unión como el Estado 51. Encima de todo, le contó a Bush que todos en las calles de Irak lo amaban. Una vez más, el aura de la presidencia había dejado por fuera las noticias más importantes, las malas noticias.

Más tarde, le pregunté a Rumsfeld sobre la obligación de asegurarse de que la persona en el cargo más alto estuviera al tanto de las malas noticias. "Creo que el presidente sabía que había una gran controversia por la *desbaathificación*. Y grandes desacuerdos sobre el ejército. No hay duda de que el presidente era consciente de esos problemas".

Pero no logré encontrar evidencia de que ese fuera el caso.

El 16 de octubre de 2005, durante una entrevista de cuatro horas en la casa de Garner, en un lago a las afueras de Orlando, Florida, le pregunté sobre su decisión de no mencionar los tres errores trágicos.

"¿No le debía eso al presidente?".

"Yo no trabajaba para el presidente", respondió Garner. "Yo trabajaba para Rumsfeld. Soy un tipo del ejército".

Le recordé mi época como oficial subalterno en la Armada. "Yo me reportaba al oficial de operaciones del barco en el que estaba. Y si creía que estábamos cometiendo aunque fuera medio error de trascendencia, se lo decía a mi jefe, pero me aseguraba de que el capitán se enterara".

"No", dijo Garner.

Tal vez por eso, concluí yo, no me había ido muy bien en la Marina.

"No", repitió Garner, "en mi opinión yo hice mi trabajo. Le hablé a mi jefe, en términos, según mi criterio, muy rigurosos sobre los errores que habíamos cometido".

"Ahora, suponga que usted dijera: 'Señor presidente, le acabo de reportar al secretario lo siguiente y quiero que usted lo oiga de mí, porque cuando él se lo cuente a usted quiero que sea…'".

Garner interrumpió. "No tengo idea de cómo habría reaccionado el presidente, pero creo que habría dicho, 'Bien, ya sabes, Rummy está a cargo de eso', o algo parecido".

"Tres errores trágicos", recalqué.

"Sí", dijo Garner en voz baja mientras dejaba escapar un suspiro.

"Porque con esos tres errores trágicos estamos viviendo más de dos años después. ¿Se da cuenta de eso?".

"Por supuesto", contestó Garner.

"Usted ve noticias".

"Sí", respondió.

"No siente que debería haber, particularmente en los niveles más altos…".

"Creo que Rumsfeld es el nivel más alto. No, si tuviera que hacerlo todo de nuevo, creo que tal vez lo volvería a hacer todo igual". Dijo no saber de cualquier cosa que Rumsfeld hubiera hecho y que el presidente hubiera rebatido. "No soy el único que pensaba eso", agregó.

"Si se lo hubiera dicho al presidente, y hubiera podido salvar una vida…". Me detuve, dejando la segunda parte de mi pregunta sin terminar. "Porque usted es un tipo muy inteligente, ha estado en el ruedo…".

"Sí. Usted lo pone como si…". Garner empezó pero no terminó la frase. "Pero recuerde, no lo veía de esa manera, para mí, Jay Garner, eso no era lo correcto. Yo, Jay Garner, le dije eso al hombre que estaba a cargo, se lo dije al hombre para quien trabajo. Eso lo hice. Ni si quiera se me pasó mencionarle eso al presidente Bush".

Dos meses después, el 3 de diciembre del 2005, durante un extenso desayuno en mi casa, en Washington D. C., volví a mencionar el asunto de lo que no le había contado al presidente.

"Ese fue más un encuentro de amigos que una reunión de trabajo", aseguró Garner.

Le pregunté: "Desearía haber dicho: 'Señor presidente, como le acabo de decir al secretario de Defensa, en mi opinión, yo he estado allí y necesito asegurarme de que usted entienda lo que creo que entiendo. Hemos cometido tres errores trágicos': este, este y este".

"No lo sé, si tuviera la oportunidad de volver a vivir ese momento no sé si haría algo así. Pero si lo hubiera hecho —y, honestamente, no habría tenido ningún reparo— en mi opinión la puerta estaba cerrada. Es decir que no hay nada que yo pueda hacer para volver a abrir esa alternativa. Y creo que si yo hubiera dicho eso frente a Cheney, Condoleezza Rice y Rumsfeld, el presidente los habría mirado y ellos habrían volteado los ojos y él habría pensado, Dios, me pregunto por qué no nos deshicimos de este tipo antes".

Me reí y comencé a hacer otra pregunta.

"No se lo esperaban", agregó Garner. "Como decían las tropas, ellos se tomaron el Kool-Aid"[11].

Este es solamente uno de los ejemplos en los que un visitante del Salón Oval no le contaba al presidente la historia completa o la verdad. De igual manera, en esos momentos en que Bush tenía a alguien que había estado en

---

11. Aceptar un argumento ciegamente. La expresión completa es "drink the Kool-Aid". Su uso se popularizó después de la masacre de Jonestown, en la que centenares de miembros de un culto se suicidaron con Kool-Aid mezclado con cianuro de potasio. (N. del E.)

la zona, tampoco presionaba, no intentaba abrir la puerta por sí mismo y preguntar lo que el visitante había visto y lo que opinaba. Muy a menudo toda la atmósfera tenía la apariencia de una corte real, con Cheney y Rice presentes, algunas historias optimistas, buenas noticias infladas y todos pasándola muy bien.

1. El vicepresidente Dick Cheney, el juez de la Corte Federal de Apelaciones Laurence Silberman, el presidente Bush, Joyce Rumsfeld, y Donald H. Rumsfeld, reunidos el 26 de enero de 2001. Rumsfeld jura como secretario del Departamento de Defensa, cargo que había ocupado por primera vez en 1970 durante la administración Ford. "Esta vez, hazlo bien", le dijo Cheney a Rumsfeld, su viejo amigo y mentor.

2. El vicepresidente Cheney, el príncipe Bandar, embajador de Arabia Saudita, la Consejera Nacional de Seguridad Condolezza Rice y el presidente Bush se reunen en el Balcón Truman de la Casa Blanca, varios días antes de los ataques terroristas del 11 de septiembre de 2001. "Si capturamos a alguien y no logramos que coopere, se lo entregaremos a ustedes", le dijo Bush a Bandar acerca de sus planes para manejar posibles terroristas.

© Sean Gallup (Getty)

© Cortesía de la Marina de los Estados Unidos

3. (*Izquierda*) Steve Herbits, anterior asistente especial y viejo amigo de Rumsfeld, fue contratado nuevamente como consultor durante la segunda administración de Rumsfeld como secretario de Defensa. "En los meses siguientes al cese de los bombardeos, es esencial que no haya una guerra civil", le escribió en un memo a Rumsfeld el 10 de abril de 2003. "Las guerras civiles, justificadas o injustificadas, recuerdan a Vietnam. La estrategia del presidente se iría al piso si se llegara a hacer tal comparación".

4. (*Derecha*) Almirante Vernon Clark, jefe de las operaciones de la Marina. "Si me escogen a mí como jefe", le dijo Clark a Rumsfeld en una reunión privada, "asumiré en propiedad la responsabilidad de ser el consejero militar del presidente".

© R. D. Ward (Departamento de Defensa)

5. Paul Wolfowitz, subsecretario de defensa (derecha), y el general Peter Pace, vicepresidente y posterior presidente del Comando Conjunto de Operaciones. A medida que la violencia se agravó en el otoño del 2003, Wolfowitz, uno de los primeros defensores de la guerra en Irak, se sintió marginado por Rumsfeld y concluyó que éste estaba bloqueando los primeros esfuerzos para entrenar los servicios de seguridad irquíes. Pace, veterano de Vietnam, aborrecía los conteos de cuerpos enemigos y advirtió el peligro de usarlos, pero el presidente Bush con frecuencia pedía cifras, y así los reportaban públicamente los militares.

6. L. Paul "Jerry" Bremer, III, (en el centro) reemplazó al teniente general Jay Garner (derecha) como cabeza de las operaciones de posguerra en Irak, apenas unas semanas después de la ocupación. Mientras Bremer vestía un traje formal y una corbata, con sus botas Timberland, algunos de su equipo ridiculizaban a Garner por su aspecto casual. Garner le dijo a Rumsfeld que Bremer cometió "tres equivocaciones trágicas" en los días de su llegada, dejando a la deriva a centenas de miles de iraquíes desordenados, desempleados y armados. Pero Rumsfeld nunca se lo dijo al presidente.

7. El presidente del Comando Conjunto, general Richard B. Myers, Rumsfeld, Bush y Bremer (de izquierda a derecha). "No era ni el hombre de Rumsfeld, ni el de Powell. Era el hombre del presidente", escribió Bremer refiriéndose a su autoridad en Irak.

8. Dr. David Kay, director del Grupo de Reconocimiento de Irak que asumió la búsqueda de armas de destrucción masiva en el verano del 2003. Luego de concluir que no encontrarían armas de destrucción masiva, Kay se reunió con Bush, quien le preguntó por qué la CIA se había equivocado tanto. "Uno de los problemas para un director", dijo Kay refiriéndose al director de la CIA, George Tenet, "es que si se encuentra en medio de un proceso político, pierde balance. Por ejemplo, George viene a diario por instrucciones y eso le da una sensación a las personas de la agencia de un proceso político... eso tiene un precio. Ahora, por favor no le diga a George que se lo he dicho".

© Luis Acosta (Getty)

9. El subsecretario de políticas de defensa, Doug Feith (*izquierda*). Una de las figuras más controversiales que surgieron de la guerra en Irak. Feith estaba a cargo de las partes clave de la planeación de la posguerra. En una evaluación escrita, el consejero de Rumsfeld, Steve Herbits, dijo que la labor de Feith era "ampliamente reconocida como una seria falla". Sin embargo, Rumsfeld, Wolfowitz, el general Pace y Steve Hadley, el primer subsecretario de seguridad nacional, defendían con vehemencia las actuaciones de Feith.

10. Frank Miller (*derecha*), secretario principal de defensa del Consejo Nacional de Seguridad, quien había ocupado varios altos cargos en el Pentágono para siete secretarios de defensa. "Arréglalo", le decía con frecuencia Rice a Miller, quien presionaba para que Rumsfeld o el Pentágono asumieran asuntos de apoyo a las tropas de Estados Unidos en Irak.

© Cortesía del Grupo Cohen

© Cortesía de James Spider Marks

11. El mayor general *Spider* Marks, encargado de las tareas de inteligencia militar para las tropas en tierra que invadieron Irak, creía en la existencia de las armas de destrucción masiva, pero estaba impresionado porque la lista con los 946 sitios donde podrían estar, no ofrecía evidencia alguna. Era consciente de que no podía afirmar que había armas de destrucción masiva en ninguno de los lugares señalados.

12. El general John Abizaid, jefe del Comando Central responsable del Medio Oriente, junto con el asistente especial y vocero de Rumsfeld, Larry DiRita. En una reunión privada en 2006 con el congresista de Pennsylvania Jack Murtha, quien pedía el retiro de las tropas, Abizaid levantó su mano y mostró su pulgar a una distancia de un cuarto de pulgada de su dedo índice y dijo "estamos así de cerca".

13. John Negroponte, el primer embajador estadounidense en Irak después de la invasión, con Jim Jeffrey. Jeffrey le mostró un mapa de Bagdad que mostraba un centenar de ataques insurgentes. El asunto principal era la seguridad, decía Jeffrey. "No la tenemos". Negroponte fue nombrado posteriormente como el primer director nacional de inteligencia y en junio de 2006 concluyó que la política de Estados Unidos en Irak estaba en problemas.

14. El secretario de Estado, Colin Powell, Cheney, Bush, Rumsfeld, y los generales Myers y Pace (de izquierda a derecha). Rumsfeld ofreció su renuncia cuando se destapó el escándalo de torturas a los prisioneros de Abu Ghraib, pero Bush no la aceptó. El presidente, en cambio, reunió a muchos de sus colaboradores en seguridad nacional para una singular reunión en el Pentágono donde se llevó a cabo una muestra pública de unidad.

15. Richard Armitage, subsecretario de Estado, Bush y el secretario de Estado Powell (de izquierda a derecha) se reunieron en el rancho de Bush en el 2003. Luego de que él y Powell renunciaron el año siguiente, le preguntaron a Armitage si aceptaría un cargo en la segunda adminsitración de Bush. "No sé cómo podría trabajar en una adminstración que permite que se vaya el secretario Powell, mientras que mantiene al señor Rumsfeld", respondió.

16. Los consejeros presidenciales Karl Rove, Karen Hughes, Bob Blackwill, uno de los subconsejeros de seguridad nacional, y el jefe del equipo, Andy Card (de izquierda a derecha) viajaron con el presidente en la campaña del 2004. Blackwill, que había pasado varias semanas en Irak y probablemente sabía tanto de la guerra como cualquier persona de la Casa Blanca, viajó regularmente con Bush en los últimos meses de la campaña presidencial. Se sorprendía de que cualquier discusión sobre Irak se sostenía en torno a la campaña, en torno a lo que el senador John Kerry hubiera dicho, o en torno al impacto que los eventos en Irak hubieran tenido en los intentos del presidente por obtener la reelección. En ningún momento Bush le preguntó a Blackwill cómo eran las cosas en Irak, qué había visto o qué debería hacerse.

17. George Tenet, el general retirado Tommy Franks, y Jerry Bremer recibieron la Medalla de la Libertad el 14 de diciembre de 2004. Los tres habían sido criticados por sus roles en la guerra, pero Bush los apoyó y los eligió para otorgarles la más alta distinción civil.

18. El juez Silberman (derecha) y el ex senador Chuck Robb, copresidente de la comisión que conformó Bush para investigar la inteligencia que buscó las armas de destrucción masiva. "Era claro y se había comprendido que no nos habían pedido evaluar el uso que la administración daba a la inteligencia", afirmó Silberman. Entre las figuras que la comisión no llamó a indagatoria estaban los generales Abizaid, McKiernan y Marks.

19. El presidente George H. W. Bush durante la segunda posesión de su hijo el 20 de enero de 2005. En un discurso pronunciado en 1999, Bush padre explicó por qué había decidido no extender la primera Guerra del Golfo y por qué no había intentado deponer a Saddam Hussein. "Hubiéramos sido una potencia invasora, sin aliados en el exterior. Eso hubiera sido desastrozo". En ocasiones comentaba en privado al príncipe Bandar y a otros amigos las políticas que estaba ejecutando su hijo. "¿Por qué no le aconsejas?", le preguntó Bandar una vez. "Tuve mi oportunidad. Ahora es su turno", replicó el ex presidente.

20. Rice y Rumsfeld contestaron las preguntas de la prensa en Bagdad en abril del 2006. Rumsfeld le sugirió al recién nombrado primer ministro iraquí Nouri al-Maliki que discutieran el papel de las tropas de los Estados Unidos. No utilizó las palabras "retiro" o "disminución", pero todos sabían a lo que se refería. Maliki miró al secretario de Defensa estadounidense como si estuviera loco. "Es aún muy pronto para hablar de eso", dijo.

21. Phlip Zelikow, ex director ejecutivo de la comisión que investigó los atentados del 9/11, quien se convirtió en consejero del Departamento de Estado y en uno de los colaboradores más cercanos de Rice. En septiembre de 2005, Rice lo envió a Irak. "Si presionan, las probabilidades de conseguir resultados exitosos es de, digamos, un 70 por ciento", le reportó a ella. "Eso quiere decir que hay un 30 por ciento de probabilidades de fallar, y es un riesgo significativo de un desastre catastrófico. Incluso, siendo optimistas, podríamos decir que hemos hecho apenas los esfuerzos suficientes para tener éxito. No es mucho, pero con suerte será apenas suficiente".

22. Bush con el saliente Andy Card en abril del 2006. "La mejor manera de mostrar que habla en serio en el momento de hacer cambios, es cambiar a la cabeza del equipo", le dijo Card al presidente después de las elecciones de 2004; dio infructuosamente una batalla de 18 meses para que reemplazaran también a Rumsfeld. Card le dijo a su sucesor, Joshua Bolten, que su trabajo sería "Irak, Irak, Irak".

23. Cheney, Bush y Rumsfeld en agosto de 2006. "No tenían sentido las versiones de que Cheney controlara a Bush. No asume posiciones fuertes cuando el presidente está presente y que puedan ponerlo en contra de él", dijo Rumsfeld. "No confronta al presidente ni muestra oposición alguna".

24. El ex secretario de Estado, Dr. Henry Kissinger. "De las personas externas con las que hablo en este trabajo, tal vez hablo más con Henry Kissinger que con cualquier otra persona", dijo Cheney en 2005, y agregó que Bush era un gran "admirador" de Kissinger. Bush se reunía en privado cada par de meses, convirtiendo al ex secretario en su consejero externo más frecuente en asuntos internacionales.

25. El senador Chuck Hagel, partido republicano de Nebraska, se convirtió en uno de los opositores a la manera como se manejaban las cosas en Irak después de la guerra. En junio de 2005 le dijo en privado al presidente Bush, "creo que acá en la Casa Blanca se están entusiasmando demasiado con Irak".

26. El senador Carl Levin de Michigan, partido demócrata del Comité de Servicios Armados del Senado. Levin creía en el 2003 que el entonces secretario de Estado Colin Powell tenía el poder y la influencia con Bush para detener la guerra en Irak. "No creo que él se haya dado cuenta alguna vez del poder que tiene en sus manos y eso es una abdicación", afirmó Levin. "¿Pueden imaginar el poder de esa sola persona para cambiar el curso de las cosas? Él lo tenía".

27. Condolezza Rice y el presidente Bush. Rice hacía frecuentes visitas –aunque no publici-tadas– a los hospitales militares donde estaban los combatientes heridos en Irak. "Debo ser capaz de mirar a estos soldados y preguntarme honestamente si de verdad creo que valió la pena todo por lo que pasaron y si estamos haciendo que valga la pena", dijo. "Estos no son soldados de juguete que alguien envió, sabes, como soldaditos. Estos son reales, son seres humanos vivos".

28. Steve Hadley con el presidente Bush en su rancho de Crawford, Texas. Cuando Hadley fue nombrado consejero nacional de seguridad, dijo del primer período, cuando era el segundo después de Rice: "califico con una B menos las políticas de desarrollo y con una D menos la ejecución de las políticas".

29. El 24 de abril de 2003, un mes después de la invasión, el presidente Bush habló en la planta de tanques del Ejército en Lima, Ohio, donde elogió los esfuerzos de posguerra del teniente general en retiro Jay Garner. "Hemos trabajado con un equipo de gente, liderado por Garner, quien tiene encomendada una meta preponderante: dejar una nación libre en las manos de un pueblo libre".

22

David Kay salió de Washington hacia Qatar el 18 de junio, el mismo día que Garner se reunió con Bush. No tardó mucho en darse cuenta de que su Grupo de Inspección de Irak era una organización militar bastante convencional. Había 1.400 personas asignadas, pero ese número incluía mucho personal de apoyo, incluso un capellán militar y otros a cargo de la recreación y animación del personal. Se contaban 25 personas clave y 40 funcionarios operativos de la CIA, al igual que algunos analistas y otra gente de la AID y de otras agencias de inteligencia. Su equipo experto en misiles estaba conformado por 12 o 15 personas y había cerca de media docena de expertos en armas biológicas. Además, había varios centenares de traductores de distintos niveles de habilidad.

Kay dio la orden de interrumpir los viajes diarios a los sitios sospechosos. "Vamos a manejar esto como una operación de inteligencia", le dijo a Dayton y a los otros; "eso significa que es necesario saber algo sobre lo que se está haciendo. Así que dividiremos los equipos en expertos en armas químicas y biológicas, en misiles y en armas nucleares, y conformaremos un equipo de aprovisionamiento".

El contrato firmado con la compañía que proporcionaba los traductores estipulaba que éstos no podían ser enviados a la zona de combate, de modo que los documentos encontrados en Irak debían ser enviados a Qatar para su traducción. Los traductores habían hecho una lista de varios cientos de palabras y términos en árabe, como "armas nucleares", "armas biológicas", "ántrax" o "toxina botulínica"; si, luego de hacer una rápida revisión de los documentos incautados, encontraban alguna de estas palabras o términos, aquéllos eran clasificados como prioritarios y revisados minuciosamente.

Pero tomaba demasiado tiempo tener de vuelta los documentos y, además, Kay no encontraba nada nuevo en ellos, con una excepción importante: el directorio de personal de la Comisión Militar e Industrial.

"No tenemos ningún interés en el registro del personal de un ministerio", dijo uno de los funcionarios del Grupo de Inspección de Irak.

"De hecho, sí lo tienen". El directorio conduciría a las personas, y las personas eran la clave.

Algunos de los miembros de su equipo se negaban a ir a Irak mientras no tuvieran instalaciones apropiadas para comer, dormir y vivir.

"No", repitió Kay. "Podemos comer raciones militares de campaña y dormir en tiendas o en lo que sea, pero vamos a continuar, porque no van a encontrar las armas en Doha".

"Detengan la búsqueda", ordenó Kay cuando llegaron a Bagdad. Olvídense de la Lista Maestra repitió. "Empiecen a pensar en las personas y a encontrarlas".

Las condiciones de vida habían mejorado desde la época de Garner. Kay dormía en un contenedor con aire acondicionado, en el aeropuerto, y podían desplazarse por la ciudad y comer en restaurantes. En vista de que no tenían nada más que hacer, trabajaban hasta tarde la mayoría de las noches.

Inicialmente Kay ordenó a su equipo analizar minuciosamente el discurso que Powell había pronunciado el 5 de febrero ante la ONU, con el fin de asegurarse de que estuvieran trabajando en todas las acusaciones que Powell había hecho. Supuestamente, se trataba de la mejor información de inteligencia y Kay quería estar seguro de que nadie pudiera decir luego, "Powell dijo esto y ustedes lo ignoraron". El grupo tenía en su poder una lista de los iraquíes que habían participado en programas de ADM, y que habían sido entrevistados extensamente por la miríada de equipos de inspección de la ONU en los años 90. Luego de tres semanas habían rastreado de 50 a 60 nombres, entre los que se contaban científicos, técnicos y funcionarios de alto rango. Los interrogaron, fueron a sus oficinas y buscaron en sus documentos. Un cuadro medianamente consistente empezó a surgir.

"La historia de las armas nucleares empezó a desmoronarse", recordaría Kay. "Comenzamos a tener una imagen muy clara de cuál era su capacidad nuclear y, francamente, era peor, mucho peor que en 1991, a principios de la primera Guerra del Golfo".

Aun más interesante era el estado del programa de armas químicas y biológicas. No había nada que respaldara la idea de que había depósitos de este tipo de armas. No encontraron a nadie que las hubiera producido, vigilado o transportado, o que supiera algo de ellas.

EL DOMINGO 22 DE JUNIO, cerca de 2.000 chiítas protestaban afuera de las oficinas de Bremer, diciendo que querían elecciones para formar un gobierno nacional. "Nada de americanos, nada de Saddam, toda la gente está con el Islam", repetían. Los manifestantes tenían un fuerte apoyo del Gran Ayatollah Ali Sistani, el reverenciado e infalible líder y guía espiritual de millones de chiítas en Irak. Sistani se negaba a reunirse directamente con Bremer, al parecer porque él no se reunía con infieles. Sistani, quien en ese entonces tenía

73 años, era para los chiítas lo que el papa es para los católicos. Insistía en la organización de elecciones antes de redactar el borrador de una Constitución. ¿Cómo podía escribir la Constitución gente que no había sido elegida?

En Washington, durante la reunión del CNS del día siguiente, el presidente estaba molesto.

"¿Cómo llegamos a la pregunta equivocada de si los iraquíes deben, o no, tener elecciones?", preguntó. En este punto es donde Estados Unidos, esta gran democracia, está equivocado. Tal vez las elecciones deban tener lugar primero, antes de que ellos intenten escribir una Constitución y organizar una nueva sociedad iraquí".

Para Rice, eso cristalizaba el problema. La mayoría de los chiítas sostenía que solamente un gobierno legítimo que tuviera la bendición del pueblo podía escribir una Constitución. Luego de décadas de gobierno de una minoría sunita, los chiítas no querían que gente designada —Saddam siempre estaba designando gente— escribiera la Constitución. A Rice eso le parecía razonable. Pero eran otros los que estaban a cargo, es decir, Rumsfeld y Bremer. Sistani agregó otra dimensión al problema. El 28 de junio, emitió una *fatwa* —un decreto islámico— rechazando cualquier consejo constitucional elegido por Estados Unidos, y declaró que el pueblo de Irak debía elegir a sus legisladores.

BUSH APARECIÓ en la Sala Roosevelt de la Casa Blanca el 2 de junio de 2003, para discutir una iniciativa de 15 millones de dólares para combatir el sida en el extranjero. Cuando, más tarde, accedió a contestar algunas preguntas de la prensa, Irak fue el asunto número uno.

Un reportero señaló que los ataques a fuerzas estadounidenses y bajas iban en aumento.

"Hay algunos que piensan que si nos atacan tal vez decidamos marcharnos antes", respondió el presidente, negando con la cabeza. "No tienen idea de lo que dicen, si ese es el caso".

Uno de los reporteros empezó a interrumpir.

"Déjeme terminar", dijo Bush. "Hay algunos que piensan que por las condiciones que tenemos allí, pueden atacarnos". Balanceó el brazo por delante del pecho en un gesto enfático. "Mi respuesta es: '¡Que lo hagan, si se atreven!' Tenemos las fuerzas necesarias para afrontar los problemas de seguridad".

Era un comentario desafortunado y provocador, que enviaba un mensaje errado al enemigo, casi incitándolo a atacar, y que reflejaba poco conocimiento de la guerra de guerrillas[12].

12. Tres años después, durante una conferencia de prensa en la Casa Blanca, el 25 de mayo de 2006, un reportero le pidió a Bush mencionar "los tropiezos y equivocaciones que más lamentaba". Bush respondió: "Me suena familiar la expresión 'pónganla como

ARMITAGE PARTICIPABA en una reunión informativa para el presidente en la Casa Blanca, cuando Hadley lo llamó aparte.

"Alguna gente dice que su lenguaje corporal es muy malo en las reuniones".

"¿Que mi lenguaje corporal es muy malo?", repitió Armitage.

"Está dejando ver su malestar", concluyó Hadley. "Se le percibe muy tenso".

"Steve, no me gusta lo que le han dicho al presidente", dijo Armitage. "Pues, sí, no me siento nada bien. No me siento mal con el presidente. Me siento mal por las asignaciones que estamos recibiendo. Son trabajos infantiles".

"Pensé que se trataba de eso", dijo Hadley. Indicó que el trabajo de verdad lo estaban haciendo allá arriba, en el Salón Oval, Cheney y Rumsfeld con el presidente.

¿Se suponía que eso lo tranquilizaría? Armitage entendió una vez más que él y Powell eran objetos decorativos, con tanta influencia como un par de plantas sembradas en macetas. En las reuniones de allá arriba lo que primaba era el tono optimista de Rumsfeld, porque no había nadie que lo cuestionara y las otras agencias no intervenían para revisar sus valoraciones.

EN EL IRAK DE SADDAM, tener una antena de televisión que diera acceso ilimitado a noticias sin censura se castigaba con seis meses de prisión y multa de 300 dólares. Una vez derrocado el régimen, las antenas satelitales se esparcieron como maleza por todo el país, incluso en las áreas más pobres. Las chozas y casuchas, carentes de agua potable o alcantarillado, tenían antenas de televisión satelital en los techos o en los patios. Fue muy repentino, y Estados Unidos intentó moverse con rapidez para que el mensaje de la coalición pudiera salir al aire y, por lo menos, competir con toda la televisión árabe que, repentinamente, estaba siendo transmitida y era vista con entusiasmo en Irak.

SAIC, la empresa contratista del Departamento de Defensa, había firmado un contrato de asignación directa por 82 millones de dólares para construir cadenas de radio y televisión en Irak. Rice era escéptica al respecto: "SAIC no sabe cómo hacer ese tipo de cosas", repuso, y envió un equipo a supervisar.

---

quieran', palabras duras que enviaron el mensaje equivocado a la gente. Aprendí algunas lecciones sobre la necesidad de expresarme de manera algo más sofisticada como 'vivo o muerto', ese tipo de expresiones. Creo que en ciertas partes del mundo eso fue malinterpretado, y también aprendí de eso".

Eventualmente, se instaló una cadena de televisión financiada por los Estados Unidos. Para llenar la programación, la cadena pasaba repeticiones de programas en árabe de otros lugares del Medio Oriente. Por eso algunos iraquíes lo llamaban el "canal de cocina libanés", especialmente después de un día en el que la mayoría de las cadenas más grandes, como Al Jazeera, cubrieron en vivo un importante evento mientras la cadena estadounidense pasaba un programa extranjero sobre cómo preparar conejo.

En la Zona Verde, un área muy bien fortificada de unos 10 kilómetros cuadrados donde estaba ubicada la APC, un grupo de consultores intentaba entender qué tipo de programas de televisión querían ver los iraquíes. Hablaban de capturar el segmento de mercado de amas de casa, con algún tipo de versión iraquí del show de Oprah Winfrey.

"Podríamos ir a Hollywood", le sugirió luego Bush a Rice. "Conozco gente de Hollywood. Podemos ir a Disney. Podemos dar participación a gente que sepa hacer este tipo de cosas".

"Entendemos, señor presidente", respondió Rice. "Entendemos".

El presidente la amonestó: "Haz algo al respecto".

Para el verano del 2003, Bush se dio cuenta de que la estrategia de comunicación iba mal. Le dijo a Tony Blair: "Estamos haciendo un trabajo muy deficiente en este aspecto. Si no he resuelto esto en diciembre, se lo voy a ceder al Reino Unido". Seguramente no hablaba en serio, pero eso expresaba su frustración.

La controversia sobre las declaraciones del Presidente, respecto al desmentido acuerdo comercial para la adquisición de uranio entre Irak y Nigeria, estaba cada vez más candente y se estaba convirtiendo rápidamente en el símbolo de la incapacidad de encontrar ADM y de la sospecha de que el presidente había hecho una elección selectiva de la información de inteligencia para justificar la guerra.

El sábado, 5 de julio, Tenet habló con la vocero del CNS, Anna Pérez. En lo que a ella concernía, el hecho de que las 16 palabras sobre el uranio se hubieran colado en el discurso del Estado de la Unión era el resultado de fallas, tanto del personal del CNS como de la CIA. "Ambos vamos a tener que compartir la responsabilidad de esto", aseguró Pérez. Debían hacer algo para rectificar el registro de lo que había dicho el presidente en su discurso.

Tenet había hecho suprimir la acusación del discurso de Bush en Cincinnati, en octubre, pero, al parecer, Hadley, quien había revisado la versión final del discurso de la Unión, había olvidado esa advertencia inicial. Tenet no revisó la versión final del discurso, como se suponía que debía hacerlo.

Tenet estuvo de acuerdo con Pérez en que todos compartirían la culpa. El plan era trabajar durante el fin de semana en una declaración conjunta que entregarían el lunes. Rice y Tenet hablaron al día siguiente y acordaron que debían tener listo el texto para imprimirlo. Rice se encontraba con el presidente, de viaje por África. Hadley y algunos funcionarios del CNS trabajaron en el borrador pero no lograron llegar a un acuerdo.

Tenet dijo que emitiría una declaración. Sin embargo, el martes 8 de julio, luego de que la columna del embajador Joseph Wilson en el *New York Times* arrojara dudas sobre la afirmación del presidente, la Casa Blanca lanzó una declaración que decía: "Después de conocer todo lo que conocemos en este momento, la alusión al intento de compra de uranio por parte de Irak en África no debió haberse incluido en el discurso del Estado de la Unión".

Los demócratas empezaron a pedir una investigación.

"¿De qué otra cosa no nos hemos enterado?", preguntó el senador de Florida, Bob Graham, ex presidente del Comité de Inteligencia del Senado, en un comentario público.

El viernes 11 de julio, Bush y Rice estaban en su cuarto día de viaje por África. En la parte trasera del Air Force One, Rice involucró a los reporteros en una discusión de aproximadamente una hora sobre el asunto. "Les puedo asegurar que si la CIA, el director de la inteligencia central, hubiera dicho 'eliminen esto del discurso', se habría removido sin ninguna objeción", aseguró. "Si había alguna preocupación sobre la información de inteligencia, el presidente no estaba al tanto de dicha preocupación, como lo estaba yo". Más tarde lo expresó de una manera más dura, culpando directamente a la CIA. "La agencia autorizó el discurso en su totalidad", remarcó.

Bush adoptó la línea de Rice. "Di un discurso a la nación que había sido autorizado por los servicios de inteligencia", declaró.

"Condi clavó la culpa en mi trasero", le dijo Tenet a un colega. Tenían un acuerdo y habían estado dos días trabajando en una declaración conjunta. Ahora Rice lo había vendido, al culpar solamente a la CIA. El problema era clásico. En la CIA había dos opiniones sobre el asunto del uranio en Nigeria. En el nivel inferior creían que era posible que hubiera una conexión. Pero Tenet tenía acceso a la inteligencia de más alto nivel, la más delicada, proveniente de un servicio de inteligencia extranjero con un agente infiltrado en el gobierno de Saddam que había desvirtuado la historia del uranio.

Tenet decidió enterrarse su espada. La declaración había sido actualizada, así que asumiría toda la responsabilidad. Lo publicó esa misma noche para evitar otra historia.

Una parte de su extensa declaración decía: "En primer lugar, la CIA aprobó el discurso del estado de la Unión antes de que fuera pronunciado. En segundo lugar, en mi agencia yo soy el responsable del proceso de aprobación. Y, tercero, el presidente tenía toda la razón para creer que el texto que se le presentó no tenía problemas. Estas 16 palabras nunca debieron haber sido incluidas en el texto escrito para el presidente".

A la mañana siguiente, el titular de la primera página de *The Washington Post* decía: "Bush y Rice culpan a la CIA por error en Irak; Tenet acepta responsabilidad por revisión de la declaración sobre armas nucleares en discurso de enero".

Era una tremenda humillación pública y, en privado, Tenet estaba furioso. Hizo que el personal de la CIA buscara en todos sus registros para ver lo que habían pasado por escrito a la Casa Blanca. Encontraron dos memorandos, enviados justo antes del discurso de Cincinnati, en octubre de 2002, en los que advertían de sus dudas sobre la información de inteligencia según la cual Irak estaba tratando de comprar uranio en África.

En lugar de llevar los memorandos a Rice o Hadley, Tenet los entregó a Andy Card para pasar la culpa a la consejera de seguridad nacional del presidente y a su asistente. Card escuchó a Tenet.

"No me dijeron la verdad", dijo Card desconsolado. Ordenó que la Casa Blanca investigara.

Ahora la Casa Blanca y la CIA estaban en guerra.

Once días después de que Tenet aceptara su responsabilidad, Hadley habló con la prensa.

"Debí haber recordado, en la época del discurso del estado de la Unión, que había controversia sobre el asunto del uranio".

Para el meticuloso y cuidadoso Hadley fue una declaración dolorosa. Estaba visiblemente conmovido. "Soy el funcionario de más alto rango del CNS y el directamente responsable de revisar exhaustivamente y autorizar los discursos presidenciales", admitió. "Fallé en esa labor al permitir la inclusión de esas 16 palabras".

No obstante, durante un largo y agotador informe que concedieron a la prensa, Hadley y Dan Barlett, el director de comunicaciones del presidente, declararon que, aunque la afirmación sobre el uranio no cumplía los estándares para ser incluida en un discurso presidencial, era precisa, ya que dicha declaración había sido atribuida, en el discurso del presidente, a los británicos".

"El verdadero error", recalcó Hadley, "es que hayamos entablado una discusión de proporciones nacionales sobre 16 palabras y que nos hayamos alejado del hecho de que los argumentos que apoyaban las preocupaciones sobre ADM en Irak eran abrumadores... tan fuertes como puede ser un argumento en estos asuntos".

Era su jugada maestra.

"Estas 16 palabras no afectan un ápice la decisión tomada por el presidente y que se basó en un caso de inteligencia", aseguró Hadley.

Armitage estaba convencido de que Hadley le había lanzado un dardo, no tanto al presidente, sino al vicepresidente. Fue Cheney quien con más fuerza sostuvo que Saddam estaba armando de nuevo su programa nuclear.

En privado, Tenet le manifestó a Armitage que pensaba que Hadley era un "agente dormido" de Cheney y Rumsfeld, término de inteligencia referido a un agente encubierto que merodea inactivo, sin una misión durante años, pero que puede ser despertado para hacer la voluntad de quienes lo manejan. Más allá de que fuese exagerada, la declaración reflejaba los ánimos, cada vez más exaltados, entre la CIA y el CNS.

Primero, Tenet y, ahora, Hadley habían asumido la culpa por el presidente. La discusión pública abrió viejas heridas, como la hostilidad entre Tenet y Rice y las acusaciones de incompetencia de la CIA.

En julio del 2003 Bremer aprobó un consejo de gobierno iraquí conformado por 25 miembros. El grupo estuvo reunido durante varios días tratando de decidir quién sería su líder, lo que reflejaba las profundas divisiones entre chiítas, sunitas y kurdos. Finalmente llegaron a un acuerdo: rotarían la presidencia del consejo entre nueve miembros, cada uno de los cuales sería presidente durante un mes. Además, cada uno de los nueve designados para presidir era exiliados que había regresado a Irak después de la invasión estadounidense.

Cuando la noticia llegó a la Casa Blanca, ni siquiera Hadley, con su temperamento contenido, lo podía creer.

"Irak ha sido un hijo abusado durante treinta años", afirmó. Saddam Hussein había asesinado a muchas de las personas más importantes de Irak y la mayoría de los sobrevivientes habían abandonado el país para vivir en el exilio. Ahora los exiliados habían regresado, pero el país estaba tan dividido que nadie lograba ponerse de acuerdo sobre gran cosa. Durante una reunión, Hadley expresó con sarcasmo: "Nosotros les decimos, 'escojan su presidente' y ellos dicen: 'El primer mes este tipo será el presidente. El segundo mes, este otro tipo será el presidente. El tercer mes, este tipo de allí será el presidente. El cuarto mes, este tipo de allá será el presidente'. Y, entonces, uno piensa: 'Esta gente aún no está lista para el gran *show*'. ¿Quién va a dirigir este país?". Eso es lo que el presidente quiere saber ¿Quién va a gobernar este país?".

Por el momento, era Bremer.

DAVID KAY ESTABA EN CONTACTO casi a diario con Tenet, a través de videoconferencias, pero funcionarios de otras agencias de inteligencia y del Pentágono –incluido Cambone, quien estaba en contra de la participación misma de Kay– intervenían en las discusiones. Kay, entonces, les escribía directamente a Tenet y a McLaughlin una vez a la semana, informándoles sobre sus conclusiones más importantes y confidenciales.

En lo que respecta a las armas químicas y biológicas, escribió Kay en un correo confidencial, empezaba a tomar forma la teoría de que los iraquíes habían adoptado algo similar a lo que los soviéticos llamaban "capacidad de respuesta ante la demanda inesperada". Significaba que seguían teniendo capacidad para producir armas biológicas y químicas, pero que sólo las fabricarían y guardarían cuando las necesitaran. "Las piezas del rompecabezas pueden encajar si uno las mira de esa manera", escribió Kay.

McLaughlin ordenó a Kay: "No le hable de esto a nadie. Podría causar problemas. Sea cuidadoso. No podemos dejar que esto salga a la luz hasta estar seguros".

Aproximadamente a las de la madrugada, mientras Kay dormía en su contenedor, un subalterno del equipo de comunicaciones golpeó su puerta. "Es de la oficina del vicepresidente; está al teléfono".

Kay se apresuró a contestar el teléfono confidencial, pero resultó que no era Cheney sino un funcionario de la oficina de éste. "El vicepresidente quiere saber si usted ya vio esta comunicación interceptada", preguntó el funcionario, y procedió a describir información que la Agencia de Seguridad Nacional había obtenido de Siria y que supuestamente contenía la ubicación de algunas armas químicas. Era una intercepción de señales ejecutivas altamente clasificada que solamente circularía entre los oficiales de más alto rango y que normalmente no era compartida con los soldados rasos.

"Honestamente, no la he revisado, pero lo haré", respondió Kay.

Más tarde ubicó al representante de la Agencia Nacional de Seguridad de su equipo, quien desenterró la intercepción. Era inocua –especialmente a las 3 de la madrugada, pensó Kay– y nada concluyente. Le sorprendió que Cheney o su gente se concentraran en detalles así. Kay no pensaba que las intercepciones fueran a conducirlos a las ADM, porque las conversaciones eran casi siempre vagas. Pocas veces era claro quién hablaba o sobre qué estaban discutiendo.

A FINALES DE JULIO, Bremer regresó a Washington. Allí se reunió con George Tenet y mencionó un asunto que había planteado en un cable que había enviado al Pentágono para que lo reenviaran a los otros directores del CNS. Tenet no tenía idea de lo que decía allí Bremer y aseguró que jamás había visto el cable.

Bremer había hecho las cosas al revés. Había estado enviando todos sus reportes a Rumsfeld a través de canales militares, y contaba con que éste o el Pentágono los haría llegar a las otras instancias del CNS. Pero era evidente que Rumsfeld no lo había hecho y que estaba guardando los reportes para sí mismo. Rumsfeld era tan exasperante. Las preguntas estaban por doquier y aquí él ni siquiera mantenía informados a los demás.

"Es imposible tratar con Rumsfeld" se desahogó Bremer con un colega. Estaba realmente furioso. Era un completo desastre. Rumsfeld estaba abusando de su poder y los otros miembros del CNS eran demasiado débiles para hacer algo al respecto. Todo el proceso interinstitucional estaba hecho un caos. ¿Dónde estaba Rice? Bremer siguió con su enojo y pidió el sistema de cables diplomáticos que los embajadores normalmente usan para enviar mensajes a Washington. Encárguese, le ordenó a McManaway.

Pocos días después, cuando regresó a Bagdad, Bremer llamó a su vocero y asistente personal, Dan Senor, joven funcionario de alta estatura que trabajó durante algún tiempo en la Casa Blanca y había sido miembro del equipo republicano en el congreso. Bremer recitó una lista de 48 asuntos pendientes que debían ser atendidos inmediatamente después de su regreso. La lista incluía asuntos relacionados con la salud, la economía, su equipo político, los bancos, los teléfonos móviles, las votaciones, los interrogatorios, la corrupción, los mercenarios, los museos, una visita al orfanato, nuevas leyes y varios presupuestos: un abrumador volumen de detalles.

KAY REGRESÓ A WASHINGTON el 26 de julio. Empezaba a concluir que tal vez no encontrarían depósitos de ADM en ningún lugar de Irak, y quería que Tenet consultara con las estaciones de la CIA en la región para ver si Saddam pudo haber camuflado y sacado ADM de Irak antes de la guerra. *Spider* Marks y su equipo habían visto camiones que se dirigían a la frontera de Siria pero aún no podían contradecir la afirmación de Marks de que los camiones podían, por todo lo que sabían, contener bicicletas de la juguetería Toys 'R' Us.

"Mire, es posible que las cosas hayan cruzado la frontera, pero usted va a tener que mover la comunidad internacional de inteligencia para averiguar lo que hay en esos países , porque nosotros no podemos hacerlo", le dijo Kay a Tenet. Su grupo no podía operar por fuera de Irak. "Lo único que podemos reportar es evidencia de movimiento hacia las fronteras".

"Quiero que venga conmigo a la Casa Blanca, mañana en la mañana, para el informe diario del presidente", manifestó Tenet. "Venga temprano y podrá llegar con la relatora de la sesión". El informe presidencial diario (President's Daily Brief, PDB) era un reporte altamente clasificado sobre la información de inteligencia más delicada y supuestamente importante que era transmitida solamente a Bush, Cheney, Powell, Rumsfeld, Rice y otros pocos.

A la mañana siguiente, Kay llegó a las oficinas centrales de la CIA a las 5:30 a.m. La encargada del PDB le dijo: "Nos complace que usted se encargue del informe esta mañana, porque eso significa que podremos volver a utilizar este material. Nos estamos quedando cortos y lo podemos reutilizar".

A Kay le sorprendió escuchar que la información de inteligencia del PDB no era tan urgente o relevante como para ser utilizada inmediatamente. Le sorprendió aun más el rol que él tendría que desempeñar esa mañana.

"¿Yo voy a presentar?", preguntó Kay.

Sí, respondió ella.

Tenet esperaba en la Casa Blanca, acompañado de Rumsfeld y Andy Card. Kay y la relatora fueron al Salón Oval donde los esperaban Bush y Cheney. La funcionaria enunció las secciones de la presentación y luego le pidieron a Kay su reporte.

"El error más grande que cometimos fue dejar que estallaran los saqueos y la anarquía", concluyó Kay. Irak era un desastre y eso hacía su trabajo muchísimo más difícil. "Parte de la evidencia recogida empieza a sugerir que tal vez tenían la política de fabricar justo en el momento necesario", dijo, y explicó la teoría de la capacidad de respuesta soviética. Tal vez tuvieran el equipo, las instalaciones y el material para fabricar ADM en un período de tiempo corto, pero probablemente no hubieran producido ninguna.

"No hemos encontrado grandes depósitos", reportó Kay. "No podemos descartarlos, no hemos llegado a la conclusión de que no existan, pero es obvio que no los tienen en ningún lugar visible. Hay mucho más por buscar y examinar".

"Sigue buscando", ordenó Bush. "Es necesario que entiendas que debes encontrar la verdad sobre el programa. David, ¿qué necesitas que hagamos por ti?".

"Señor, lo único que necesitamos ahora es tiempo y paciencia", fue la respuesta de Kay.

"Usted tiene el tiempo", aseguró Bush; "yo tengo la paciencia".

Kay se marchó de la reunión casi conmocionado por la falta de iniciativa de Bush para indagar. Kay tenía un doctorado y había enseñado en niveles superiores. Estaba acostumbrado a enfrentar preguntas desafiantes y agresivas. Gran parte del trauma que implicaba recibir un título era sobrevivir al ambiente de duda, escepticismo y desafío.

"Él confiaba más en mí que yo mismo", recordaría más tarde Kay. "Si yo hubiera estado en su cargo, aunque esto simplemente es un asunto de estilos, creo que habría investigado. Habría hecho preguntas. Habría dicho: '¿Qué has hecho? ¿Qué no has hecho?' '¿Por qué no lo has hecho?' '¿Tienes el apoyo necesario del Departamento de Defensa?'. Todos los puntos débiles. Él no lo hizo".

Cheney había estado muy callado en la reunión, pero al final de la misma él y Scooter Libby llevaron aparte a Kay. Ahora Cheney se mostraba tan inquisitivo como Bush había estado pasivo. Estaba especialmente preocupado por la posible conexión de Siria con las ADM. ¿Qué pensaba Kay?, le preguntó Cheney. ¿Había evidencia? ¿Era posible que las armas hubieran ido a Siria?

"Si algo ha cruzado la frontera", respondió Kay, "nosotros no podemos ir más allá de ella". Le había advertido a Tenet sobre ese problema, agregó.

Cheney preguntó sobre la posibilidad de que las ADM pudieran haber sido camufladas y llevadas al valle de Bekaa, en el Líbano, un área controlada por Hezbollah, el grupo apoyado por Irán que tenía fuertes nexos con el terrorismo.

De nuevo, dijo Kay, cualquier apreciación o acción significativa tendría que involucrar a las estaciones de la CIA.

Cheney presionó. Parecía tener la convicción de que algo había ido a parar al valle de Bekaa.

¿Líbano?, pensó Kay para sí. Los israelíes y su inteligencia eran los que más sabían de Bekaa. Pensó en decir, "No me pregunte a mí, pregúntele a los israelíes", pero no dijo nada.

Libby tenía un pequeño fajo de reportes de inteligencia, entre los cuales se encontraban delicadas comunicaciones interceptadas por la Agencia de Seguridad Nacional que aún no habían sido analizadas. Kay no las había revisado porque, al igual que la grabación por la que lo habían despertado a las 3 de la madrugada en Bagdad, se trataba de señales ejecutivas que contenían o conversaciones aisladas o fragmentos de información. La CIA tenía analistas cuyo trabajo era tomar docenas de estas grabaciones y escudriñarlas para extraer conclusiones. Al igual que muchas otras grabaciones, eran extremadamente vagas. Contenían fragmentos interesantes y, algunas veces, hasta menciones de lugares, pero eran tan claras como el humo.

Kay estaba asombrado de que el vicepresidente de los Estados Unidos estuviera usando ese tipo de inteligencia. En ese caso, Cheney y Libby estaban actuando como un par de analistas inexpertos, estudiando los fragmentos detenidamente como si intentaran descifrar el código Da Vinci. Ojalá el mundo se pudiera entender de esa manera.

Más tarde, Kay declaró: "Cheney tenía un montón de interpretaciones y hechos que él creía que probaban algo, y quería asegurarse de que los examináramos. Eran preguntas puntillosas, detalladas y evidentes, que se concentraban no en lo que yo había dicho, sino en lo que él sabía, y acerca de lo cual quería saber un poco más. Fue casi como un examen de doctorado, donde uno está preocupado por una persona que está intentando hacerlo equivocar. '¿Ya leyó esta fuente?'".

Tiempo después, Kay recibió una llamada de Colin Powell; le pedía que fuera al Departamento de Defensa. Había conocido a Powell en 1991, cuando trabajaba como jefe de inspecciones nucleares de la ONU y Powell era el jefe del Estado Mayor Conjunto. Powell no había sido llamado para la reunión informativa de la Casa Blanca, y quería oír sobre los hallazgos de Kay. Por ser la cara pública de la declaración estadounidense ante la ONU de que Saddam tenía ADM, Powell tenía casi tanto en juego como Bush.

En esencia, Kay le dio a Powell el mismo informe que le había dado a Bush: un reporte inconcluso pero básicamente neutral, con visos negativos.

"Este es mi correo personal", dijo Powell al entregarle a Kay una tarjeta mientras se disponía a salir. "Escríbame si tiene alguna preocupación o pregunta".

Kay miró la tarjeta cuando regresó a Langley y casi se destornilla de la risa. Powell le había dado una dirección de correo electrónico comercial, común y corriente, de American Online, un método de comunicación casi tan seguro y confidencial como un graffiti en el paso de mayor tráfico de una autopista.

"Aquí estoy, sentado en las oficinas centrales de la CIA", pensó Kay. "¿Y se supone que envíe algo a una cuenta de AOL?".

KAY FUE AL CONGRESO el 31 de julio para testificar durante una sesión cerrada ante los comités de servicios armados y de inteligencia. Entre sesión y sesión habló brevemente con los reporteros. No habían encontrado rastros de armas, declaró Kay, pero añadió, "Al pueblo norteamericano no deberían sorprenderlo las sorpresas. Estamos resueltos a tomar esto de manera especial, y cada día, debo decirlo, nos sorprendemos con los avances que estamos haciendo".

23

RUMSFELD, SIMPLEMENTE, no estaba haciendo caso. Esa fue la conclusión a la que llegaron Rice y Hadley en agosto de 2003. No mostraba tanto interés en la posguerra en Irak como lo había hecho con los planes de invasión. La única opción era que el CNS interviniera y se encargara directamente de Bremer.

Rice necesitaba alguien que se dedicara a esa labor y pensó en el hombre que había sido su jefe en el CNS bajo la administración de George Bush padre, Robert D. Blackwill, de 63 años, quien había renunciado recientemente a su cargo de embajador en India para enseñar en Harvard.

Blackwill había servido durante 22 años en el servicio diplomático y trabajado en los más altos niveles del Departamento de Estado, incluido un período como asesor de Henry Kissinger. Con su 1,90 de estatura, su contextura gruesa y su cabello cano, parecía Papá Noel cuando sonreía. Sin embargo, era un jefe demandante e irritable que a menudo se refería a sí mismo como Godzilla. En India, había enturbiado las relaciones entre el personal de la embajada. Dos informes de control interno del Departamento de Estado criticaban su estilo de administración.

Hadley, el consumado funcionario público, empezó a sondear la opinión de las personas que habían trabajado con Blackwill. El informe general concluía: "No lo traigan. Será problemático. Tiene una reputación terrible. Nadie quiere trabajar con él. Él está detrás de tu puesto y hasta ha expresado su deseo de ser el segundo al mando de Condi". La popular columna de Al Kamen en *The Washington Post*, "In the Loop", había citado en julio a funcionarios anónimos, "revoltosos", según Kamen, que sugerían que Hadley podría haberse ido al Pentágono para abrirle campo a Blackwill.

Pero Rice quería contar con la lucidez de éste, así que Hadley y ella lo citaron a la Casa Blanca. Le manifestaron sus reservas hacia él y le advirtieron que, si ingresaba al personal del CNS, habría nuevas reglas de civilidad y compañerismo.

"Entiendo", dijo Blackwill. "Comprendo exactamente a lo que se refieren y les puedo asegurar que no tendrán de qué preocuparse".

Más adelante, en una difícil segunda sesión, Rice le preguntó a Blackwill si tendría algún problema en trabajar para ella, quien había sido su subordinada, o para Hadley. Respondió que no.

Blackwill recibió el pomposo título de coordinador de planeación estratégica para el personal del CNS. Poco después, Rice lo puso al frente de la situación en Irak.

Algunas semanas después, Blackwill habló con Rice y Hadley y les dijo: "Estamos perdiendo. Absolutamente nada funciona aquí. La opinión pública se nos viene encima. Esto es terrible. Estamos perdiendo la batalla por ganar el alma y el corazón de Irak".

La preocupación inmediata de Rice no era la situación local en Irak. El problema, según le expresó a Blackwill, era el "gobierno disfuncional de los Estados Unidos". Él entendió al instante a lo que se refería. Había asistido a las reuniones del Comité de adjuntos en las que Armitage y Doug Feith solían sentarse uno frente al otro en la Sala de Situaciones. La hostilidad entre ambos era enorme, y Blackwill veía cómo Armitage, un hombre imponente, le gruñía a Feith. Era casi como si Armitage quisiera brincar por encima de la mesa y destrozarle el cuello con las manos. Incluso, los nudillos se le ponían blancos.

Las reuniones de directores o reuniones del CNS con Powell y Rumsfeld no eran tan ásperas pero tenían ese mismo rasgo surrealista; rara vez se ventilaban los verdaderos problemas. Blackwill, veterano de la escuela de Kissinger, estaba escandalizado. Rumsfeld hacía su exposición mirando al presidente, mientras que Powell miraba siempre al frente. Luego Powell hacía la suya, también dirigiéndose al presidente, y esta vez era Rumsfeld quien mantenía la mirada al frente. Ninguno de los dos comentaba siquiera las afirmaciones o las opiniones del otro. Así que Bush nunca tenía el beneficio de una discusión seria y sustancial entre sus asesores más importantes. Y el presidente, cuyas piernas se agitaban constantemente bajo la mesa, tampoco exigía tal discusión.

Blackwill veía cómo Rice trataba de intervenir sin éxito. Nunca surgían comentarios o preguntas de gran trascendencia –particularmente sobre la estrategia militar–. Blackwill compadecía a Rice. Esta jovencita, pensaba, tenía que lidiar con tres de los titanes de la seguridad nacional –Cheney, Rumsfeld y Powell– quienes acumulaban años y años de experiencia, prestigio y puntos de vista inamovibles. En la mente de Blackwill quedó grabada la imagen de una Rice diligente, bien informada y cortés, de un lado de la mesa, y del presidente inexperto, del otro, con las piernas bailándole, mientras que los toros marcaban su territorio, casi resoplando desafiantes, con sus cascos rasgando la mesa, proponiendo un desafío que nunca llegó.

La gente de David Kay planteó una explicación de por qué el régimen de Saddam se había empeñado tanto en adquirir 60.000 tubos de aluminio. Powell le había dicho a la ONU que los tubos eran para un sistema centrífugo que se usaría para el programa de armas nucleares de Saddam. La evidencia ahora demostraba que los tubos estaban destinados a la fabricación de proyectiles de artillería convencional, iguales a los que los iraquíes tenían antes de la guerra. El combustible propulsor para los cohetes era producido por una compañía iraquí dirigida por un amigo cercano de Qusay, el hijo de Saddam. El combustible era de mala calidad, pero ningún militar iraquí tenía las agallas para decirle a un amigo de Qusay que mejorara sus productos o perdería el contrato. Así que los científicos de artillería ingeniaron una solución alternativa: hacer más estrictas las especificaciones para los tubos de aluminio, haciéndolos más pequeños y livianos, para que el propulsor, con su poca potencia, funcionara.

Uno de los prisioneros que los Estados Unidos mantenía bajo custodia e interrogatorio era el antiguo jefe del cuerpo de aprovisionamiento del ejército iraquí. "Compramos esos tubos porque teníamos un contrato", declaró en el interrogatorio, y explicó el proceso burocrático, y cómo se les había ocurrido que hacer más estrictas las especificaciones fuera la única opción. El grupo de Kay rastreó a algunos de los funcionarios militares involucrados en el programa de cohetes, y ellos confirmaron la historia. "Nunca quisimos esos cohetes", declaró uno de ellos. "Seguimos intentando cancelar el contrato pero nos decían que teníamos que respetarlo".

Para Kay, sonaba casi como un escándalo de contratación en Washington o el Pentágono: sanitarios de 500 dólares y martillos de 1.000 dólares la unidad.

El equipo de Kay descubrió evidencia que mostraba la manera como Saddam había espiado y rastreado los programas de inspección de la ONU. En cierto momento encontraron una gran cantidad de facsímiles de documentos que los inspectores habían intercambiado entre Bagdad, Nueva York y Viena, sede de la Agencia Internacional de Energía Atómica, que antes de la guerra había practicado las inspecciones en busca de armas de destrucción masiva en Irak. No se trataba de intercepciones electrónicas, sino de los faxes mismos, lo que significaba que los iraquíes tenían espías o agentes de alguna clase que podían tener acceso físico a las oficinas de la AIEA. Una vez, incluso, Kay vio que uno de los facsímiles que los iraquíes habían tomado era original, con notas escritas a mano por un miembro de su equipo de inspección, hechas en el documento años antes.

Kay tenía extraordinarios incentivos para ofrecer a los iraquíes a cambio de pruebas sobre la existencia de ADM, incluidos diez millones de dólares de un fondo secreto de la CIA que él podía usar para pagar a los informantes. También podía entregar permisos de residencia a los iraquíes que cooperaran y quisieran vivir y trabajar en los Estados Unidos. Su equipo podía sacar gente de Irak y reubicarla en otros países. Difundieron el rumor sobre el programa en las calles, esperando atraer informantes auténticos, y aparecieron unas cien personas con información que ameritaba ser investigada, pero prácticamente nada se pudo encontrar, y Kay terminó trasladando sólo a una persona a los Estados Unidos. Lo único que oía era: "Yo no vi, pero mi vecino sí". Otros se acercaban con pedazos de equipos, inventando historias y diciendo que provenían de armas químicas. Había toda clase de falsas alarmas.

En otra ocasión, los equipos de comunicación de Kay lograron interceptar una conversación entre un científico iraquí y su esposa, mientras discutían. Estaban desesperados, y ella le imploraba que fuera con los estadounidenses y les contara cualquier cosa para poder cobrar alguna recompensa y abandonar el país.

"No sé nada", decía el científico. "Nosotros no teníamos nada, no tengo nada que darles. No teníamos nada".

Kay mandó a interrogar a todos los oficiales iraquíes de alto rango que se encontraban bajo custodia de los Estados Unidos. Era increíble. Ninguno de los iraquíes había visto realmente ninguna ADM, pero todos creían que tales armas no convencionales existían en algún lugar, en el arsenal de Saddam. Uno de ellos afirmó que todos asumían que Saddam Hussein hacía mucho alarde de la destrucción de sus depósitos de armas después de la guerra del golfo de 1991 por el bien del resto del mundo, pero que nunca habría sido tan estúpido como para cumplir realmente su palabra. Sin embargo, cada vez más parecía que era eso precisamente lo que había hecho.

Hacia finales de septiembre, el equipo de Kay hizo muchos descubrimientos ambiguos: instalaciones de producción de químicos de "doble uso", que se podía utilizar para la fabricación de armas, o de productos que no eran ADM. El cloro, por ejemplo, podía ser usado para fabricar armas químicas o para purificar el agua de las piscinas. Kay nunca pudo pronunciar un ¡Eureka!, pero poco a poco fue concluyendo que la razón por la que no encontraban los depósitos de ADM era porque, sencillamente, no existían.

El general John Abizaid se había posesionado como jefe del Comando Central en julio. Kay empezó a intuir que él y Rumsfeld querían reasignar su grupo de inspección en Irak a misiones adicionales, como las de contraterrorismo. Entonces llamó a Tenet. "George, eso no va a ocurrir", le aseguró. "Tú sabes que teníamos un acuerdo para centrarnos en las ADM; por lo menos eso creía yo. He estado el tiempo suficiente en Washington como para saber que cuando hay varios objetivos, normalmente no se logra ninguno".

"Por supuesto", contestó Tenet. "Tienes razón. Voy a hablar con Rumsfeld".

Al poco tiempo tuvieron otra conversación.

Esta vez Tenet dijo: "Le hice saber a Rumsfeld que tú renunciarías si él hacía eso".

ENTRE JUNIO Y AGOSTO DE 2003 cambió la naturaleza de los incidentes violentos en Irak. En junio se presentaron un promedio de 35 a 38 incidentes violentos diarios, la mitad de los cuales podían haber sido iniciados por las fuerzas estadounidenses. En contraste, en un solo día de agosto, los insurgentes dieron pie a 28 de 33 incidentes. Armitage se dio cuenta de que ahora, y de manera sistemática, los insurgentes estaban tomando la iniciativa en las dos terceras partes de los encuentros violentos. Para él, eso significaba que la población general de Irak se mantenía neutral, a la expectativa de un vencedor y preguntándose si las fuerzas de los Estados Unidos se quedarían. Era posible que los iraquíes supieran quiénes eran y dónde estaban algunos de los insurgentes, pero no se lo informaban con anticipación ni a los estadounidenses ni a las demás fuerzas de la coalición.

En su oficina del Departamento de Estado, Armitage revisó los datos. Sentía que ya había visto esta película durante sus tres estadías en Vietnam, y no le gustaba el final.

El 4 de agosto de 2003, en medio de la monotonía del verano, cuando escaseaban las noticias, *The Washington Post* publicó en primera página una historia que afirmaba que Powell y Armitage se apartarían del gobierno aun si Bush era reelegido. Era algo que ambos habían afirmado en privado, y que confirmaba una actitud fluctuante, profundamente esquizofrénica, frente a su participación como funcionarios de alto rango en el gobierno de Bush.

En vista de la escalada de la violencia en Irak, Bush no quería perder a su dubitativo guerrero ni dejar la impresión de que Powell y él estaban distanciados. Sabía que Powell y Armitage trabajaban siempre en equipo y eran inseparables, así que los invitó a su rancho de Crawford.

La tarde que llegaron, Powell y Armitage se vistieron de manera informal y fueron a reunirse con el presidente.

"¿Quieren tomar algo?", ofreció Bush.

"Un martini doble", respondió Armitage.

Bush, el antiguo bebedor empedernido, lo miró con cierta sorpresa.

"No, no", se retractó Armitage. "De hecho, prefiero una cerveza sin alcohol".

Bush se rio.

Después fumaron unos tabacos y Bush les guió en el recorrido habitual por el rancho.

Los tres tuvieron una agradable cena con Laura Bush, Rice y Alma, la esposa de Powell. Al día siguiente se dedicaron a hablar de política exterior durante tres horas.

"Vamos a aclarar algo de una vez, para que después podamos decir con toda honestidad que el tema nunca se trató", empezó a decir Powell. "No vamos a hablar de ese rumor de la prensa sobre la renuncia de Rich y la mía".

Bush sacudió su mano en el aire como queriendo dar el asunto por terminado, y continuaron con una conversación intrascendente sobre la política exterior.

En una breve sesión con la prensa, el 6 de agosto, Bush afirmó que Powell "había hecho un trabajo fabuloso", y añadió: "El hecho de que él esté aquí en Crawford, Texas, hablando de asuntos importantes, debe ser una prueba contundente para el pueblo norteamericano de que está totalmente comprometido y cumpliendo con su deber, que es servir como un gran secretario de Estado".

A lo que Powell añadió diligentemente: "Yo no tengo un período fijo. Trabajo a las órdenes del presidente". Lo que llamaban "campaña entre susurros" contra ellos se había aplacado, sólo para centrarse de nuevo en Tenet.

El ex presidente de la Cámara, Newt Gingrich mantenía contacto frecuente con la Casa Blanca, especialmente con Cheney y Rove. Había una explicación sencilla de por qué Bush se rehusaba a dejar ir a Powell, según él. "¿Por qué ir a elecciones generales deshaciéndose del tipo que tenía la mayor aceptación en el país?".

EL 19 DE AGOSTO DE 2003, Rice se encontraba en el Greenbrier Resort, en West Virginia, jugando tenis; era el último día de sus vacaciones en uno de esos escasos períodos de cuatro días en los que no pasaba gran cosa, cuando el operador a cargo de sus comunicaciones confidenciales apareció corriendo: "Tengo algo que decirle".

Un enorme camión-bomba había estallado en las oficinas centrales de la ONU, en Bagdad. Los informes no eran completos, pero se sabía que había muchos muertos y heridos. Sergio Vieira de Mello, jefe de la delegación, había sido herido y, al parecer, estaba atrapado bajo los escombros, pero era capaz de hablar con quienes iban a rescatarlo. Rice reunió a sus equipos de seguridad y comunicaciones y se dirigió inmediatamente a Washington.

El funcionario a cargo de la vigilancia en la Sala de Situaciones la llamó y le informó que Vieira de Mello había muerto.

Rice sintió como si le dieran un golpe en el estómago. Ella le había pedido personalmente a Vieira de Mello, un diplomático muy respetado que había trabajado con la ONU durante 34 años, que fuera a Irak.

Es indignante, le dijo Bush cuando hablaron más tarde, que los terroristas ataquen ahora a la ONU.

Ella dijo que, aparentemente, este era el primer ataque de tal magnitud contra unas oficinas centrales de la ONU. El número total de muertos era de 22, y muchas más personas habían resultado heridas. Ya antes había habido ataques sorpresivos, pero, ¿una barbaridad a tal escala? Para Rice, todo ello significaba que algo más estaba pasando. Era devastador y simbólico a la vez. ¿Qué estaba ocurriendo? Estaba confundida.

Al día siguiente, 20 de agosto, Bush se reunió con el Consejo Nacional de Seguridad. "Esta es una fecha terrible para la libertad, pero debe fortalecer nuestra determinación de hacer todo lo que sea necesario por ella," afirmó. "Estamos en guerra. Es un tipo de guerra diferente, pero, al fin y al cabo, es una guerra, y la vamos a ganar. Los terroristas quieren que nos retiremos, y no podemos hacerlo. Necesitamos redoblar nuestros esfuerzos contra el terror".

Después de dejar claro el tono de su discurso, el presidente procedió a hablar de cuestiones operativas. "Necesitamos evaluar cuáles son los objetivos más vulnerables en Irak y cómo los vamos a reforzar. Miren, tenemos que analizar de nuevo al enemigo. ¿Cuál es su estrategia? Tenemos que revisar continuamente nuestro plan ofensivo, teniendo en cuenta los cambios que se nos presenten". Luego añadió: "Nos enfrentamos a un enemigo inteligente y cambiante; de la misma manera, debemos cambiar nosotros. El ataque a la ONU fue un cambio. Entonces, ¿qué es lo que nos quiere decir este enemigo?".

Se enfrentaban a una infinidad de nuevas preguntas, y Bush recitó algunas: "¿Qué vamos a hacer con los chicos malos que llegan desde Irán y Siria? Tenemos que luchar contra ellos. Tenemos que mejorar nuestra inteligencia y nuestra capacidad militar para enfrentar a estos tipos". Pero rápidamente eludió los asuntos más específicos que se debía abordar. "Los grupos que responden retirándose de Irak simplemente están rindiéndose ante los asesinos y recompensándolos", dijo de nuevo, volviendo al tono solemne del principio.

Bremer, que participaba en la reunión a través de una teleconferencia confidencial, manifestó que el ataque a la ONU debía ser un llamado de alerta a los iraquíes, y que el Consejo de Gobierno temporal en Irak tenía que reaccionar. Tienen que dar la cara, repuso Bremer, no sólo al resto del mundo, sino también a su propio pueblo. Necesitamos movilizar al pueblo de Irak para que ellos movilicen a la comunidad internacional. Él quería que el Consejo de Gobierno le pidiera al pueblo apoyar a la policía y al ejército.

"¿Tenemos una estrategia de comunicaciones que pueda competir con Al Jazeera?", preguntó Bush.

"Tenemos una cadena, y la estamos usando", dijo alguien.

"Debemos… ¿Tenemos la red de comunicaciones?", volvió a preguntar Bush.

"Sí", contestó alguien de nuevo. "Tenemos nuestra propia cadena, y además estamos tratando de usar a Al Jazeera y Al Arabiya tanto como podamos".

"Nuestro mensaje debe ser que los iraquíes no pueden permitir que vengan extranjeros a pelear a Irak", afirmó el presidente. "Necesitamos apelar a algún tipo de nacionalismo que motive a los iraquíes a cooperar con nosotros para dejar por fuera a los extranjeros".

Nadie pareció percatarse de la ironía de que el comandante en jefe de una fuerza de ocupación de aproximadamente 130.000 soldados extranjeros fuertemente armados dijera que deberían apelar al nacionalismo y convencer al pueblo de Irak de "expulsar a los extranjeros".

"Tenemos que estar atentos a todas las posibles fuentes de ataques provenientes de cualquier grupo", enfatizó Bush. "¿Quién hizo esto y de quién debemos cuidarnos? Hemos aprendido algo. Tenemos que revaluar quién es nuestro enemigo, cuáles son sus tácticas y cómo adaptarnos a ellas".

Fue un llamado de alerta para Bush y su gabinete de guerra, pero el presidente evitó mencionarlo públicamente. Viajó al Pacífico noroeste a dar discursos sobre el medio ambiente. Dos días después de la reunión de CNS, un reportero le preguntó si el conflicto en Irak estaba convirtiéndose en una guerra de guerrillas contra Occidente.

"Como yo lo veo, Irak está resultando ser una batalla constante en la guerra contra el terror", respondió Bush. "Ustedes saben que una cosa es derrocar el régimen de Saddam Hussein para proteger a los Estados Unidos y a nuestros amigos y aliados, lo que ya hicimos, y otra es la resistencia que hemos encontrado de parte de algunos antiguos funcionarios baathistas. Esta gente decidió que ya que no iba a estar más en el poder, que prefería combatir en vez de trabajar por una reconstrucción pacífica del país. También me parece que hay un elemento extranjero que está acudiendo a Irak, y que son militantes como los de Al Qaeda. Quieren combatirnos porque no aceptan la idea de una sociedad libre en el Medio Oriente. Odian la libertad; odian la idea del surgimiento de una democracia, y, en consecuencia, desean evitar violentamente que eso pase".

En una alocución radial del 23 de agosto añadió que todo iba bien en Irak, a pesar del ataque a la ONU. "Hay un avance constante hacia la reconstrucción, y hacia una sociedad estable capaz de autogobernarse. Tal progreso desespera aun más a los terroristas y los hace arremeter contra los símbolos del orden y la esperanza, como el personal de las fuerzas de la coalición de la ONU. El mundo no se dejará intimidar. Unos cuantos violentos no decidirán el futuro de Irak, y no habrá un regreso a los tiempos de las cámaras de tortura y de las fosas comunes de Saddam Hussein".

RUMSFELD ESTABA DE REGRESO en Bagdad el 4 de septiembre. Quería ver si era posible reducir el número de efectivos estadounidenses. El plan inicial era que los Estados Unidos tuvieran en Irak únicamente 25.000 o 30.000 soldados, 60.000, como máximo, por aquella época. Dicha reducción era imposible debido a la violencia, y aún había unos 130.000. Aunque nadie lo publicaba, habían ocurrido cerca de 500 ataques contra las fuerzas estadounidenses y las de la coalición en julio, y más de 500 en agosto. En una cena privada con Bremer y su personal de alto rango, aquella noche, Rumsfeld dijo: "Me pregunto si todos ustedes, los que trabajan aquí, están verdaderamente comprometidos". Bremer, quien trabajaba día y noche, quedó estupefacto y se sintió indignado. Le insistió a Rumsfeld que el problema era la seguridad.

David Kay estuvo con el secretario de Defensa durante una media hora. Si existía alguna duda de que Rumsfeld pensaba que había logrado delegar a la CIA la responsabilidad de los militares de encontrar las ADM, dejó claras las cosas de manera cortés al contarle a los reporteros que él no le había pedido a Kay ningún reporte sobre la búsqueda de ADM. "Tengo tantas cosas por hacer en el Departamento de Defensa, que he tomado la decisión de que no necesito recibir informes cada quince minutos sobre el asunto. Ni siquiera pregunté… asumo que él me pondrá al tanto tan pronto haya algo que debamos saber".

BREMER DEJABA EN CLARO que, en lo que a él concernía, no había duda de que los Estados Unidos estarían en Irak por muchos años. El 8 de septiembre, 4 días después de su cena con Rumsfeld, publicó una columna de opinión en *The Washington Post* titulada "El camino de Irak hacia la soberanía". En ella usó de nuevo la palabra "ocupación", sin entender aparentemente que para los iraquíes la palabra ocupación –*ihtilal,* en árabe– implica humillación por parte de los extranjeros. Además, en el Medio Oriente, "ocupación" remite a la ocupación de los israelíes de territorios palestinos. Muy seguramente la mayoría de los iraquíes no pensaba en las ocupaciones de Alemania y Japón por parte de los Estados Unidos después de la Segunda Guerra Mundial. Tampoco en las grandes inversiones de capital norteamericano y la reconstrucción de esas sociedades como democracias y potencias económicas, evidencia que los Estados Unidos continuamente utilizaba para demostrar sus éxitos anteriores como fuerza ocupadora.

Bremer esbozó 7 pasos que era necesario seguir antes de devolver la soberanía a los iraquíes, incluida la redacción de un borrador para una nueva Constitución, su ratificación y, más adelante, las elecciones.

Rice no tenía idea de que Bremer iba a publicar una declaración tan imprudente. "No te voy a perder de vista", le dijo ella después. Pero ya lo había perdido. A Bremer le gustaba llevar las riendas. "Está obsesionado por tener el control de todo", comenzó a decir Bush en privado. Rice estuvo de acuerdo en que Bremer se ocupaba demasiado de los detalles. Pero nadie hizo nada al respecto. Seis meses antes, el CNS había acordado que la meta sería poner iraquíes al frente del gobierno tan pronto como fuese posible. Ahora era Bremer quien estaba al frente, usando el modelo de ocupación de MacArthur en Japón. Fue una redefinición desmesurada que no involucraba al Consejo. Era un cambio unilateral de política.

Bremer estaba dejándoles claro a los iraquíes que la coalición era la que por el momento mantenía la soberanía en Irak. En su libro relata cómo les dijo a un grupo de nuevos ministros iraquíes el 16 de septiembre: "Gústeles o no —y no es agradable estar bajo una ocupación, o ser quien ocupa, según aclaró— la coalición todavía es la fuerza soberana aquí". No intentó siquiera disimular su desdén por los iraquíes. "Esos no podrían ni organizar un desfile, mucho menos gobernar un país", le dijo a Wolfowitz.

EL 24 DE SEPTIEMBRE, Bremer estaba de regreso en Washington, donde él y su esposa Francie tuvieron una cena privada con el presidente y la primera dama. Bremer relata cómo le dijo al presidente que era optimista respecto a Irak pero que le preocupaba la creciente y sofisticada insurgencia. Bush no respondió, escribió Bremer.

El mismo Bremer se quejó del Congreso, de la cantidad de tropas estadounidenses, de la calidad de la inteligencia, de los nuevos soldados iraquíes en entrenamiento y de lo que él llamó "telarañas burocráticas". En su libro relata, además, cómo le dijo a Bush que era engañoso contar a todos los uniformados iraquíes como si fueran equivalentes a las tropas de los Estados Unidos. Durante la cena rezaron por uno de los iraquíes favoritos de Bremer que había muerto, pero nunca se habló de la soberanía en Irak.

Algo que Bremer no mencionó en su libro sobre su encuentro con el presidente fue la reacción de Bush a su organigrama, que mostraba a cerca de veinte personas directamente bajo su mando.

El presidente le dijo: "Mira, yo sé que estudiaste negocios en la universidad, pero yo también. Recibes demasiados reportes directos".

"Ya lo sé", respondió Bremer. "Es una locura, y voy a empezar el proceso de reorganización".

Más adelante reorganizó algunas cosas, pero aún casi todo tenía que pasar por él.

Bremer tampoco mencionó una de sus conclusiones, resultado de haber participado en 8 gobiernos. Él creía que los presidentes, en realidad, no tienen mucho poder. Aparte de empezar una guerra, pensaba Bremer, los presidentes sólo pueden fijar un norte y escoger a las personas adecuadas. En Irak era él, la Autoridad Provisional de la Coalición, quien tenía el poder.

Steve Herbits, que aún era los ojos y oídos de Rumsfeld en el Pentágono, entraba y salía constantemente de Washington. Era un partidario de la línea dura, un ferviente creyente de que la invasión había sido la decisión correcta. A pesar de ello, opinaba que Bremer no estaba dando resultados. Herbits no creía siquiera que sirviera de algo acudir a Rumsfeld para tratar la situación, porque sabía que el secretario no escuchaba razones. No obstante, pensaba que tal vez las escucharía si por lo menos él pudiera hacer que se ejerciera presión desde el interior del Pentágono y desde los círculos conservadores de Washington. Preocupado por la situación, acudió a dos de los conservadores más influyentes que conocía en Washington: Paul Wolfowitz y Newt Gingrich. Él los conocía a ambos desde hacía años, pero Wolfowitz y Gingrich no se conocían entre ellos muy bien. "Tenemos que reunirnos los tres para cenar y conversar", les dijo Herbits.

Entonces reservó un salón privado en Les Halles, un costoso restaurante francés en Pensilvannia Avenue, a cuatro cuadras de la Casa Blanca, para el martes 30 de septiembre de 2003. Wolfowitz y Gingrich llegaron cumplidamente.

Los tres conversaron informalmente durante un corto tiempo, y luego Herbits fue al grano: "Esta es la premisa de la reunión. El presidente está preocupado; a menos que esto se arregle, no lo van a reelegir. Hay dos cosas que tiene que hacer, y las tiene que hacer de inmediato, o va a perder. Esta es la premisa, y ustedes, señores, deben discutirla", dijo Herbits. "En primer lugar, tenemos que fijar una fecha para entregarle el gobierno a los iraquíes, y tenemos que fijarla ahora mismo. Yo propongo el 30 de junio de 2004".

Era una fecha arbitraria, reconoció Herbits, pero necesitaban que fuera antes de las elecciones presidenciales. El 30 de junio de 2004 parecía bien, ya que todavía faltaban nueve meses y era cuatro meses antes de las elecciones de noviembre.

"La razón por la que tenemos que hacer esto es que nadie se afanará por terminar el trabajo a menos que exista un plazo". Herbits era una persona de procesos, y aquí no había ninguno. Sabía cómo operaban las burocracias y también por qué no funcionaban. La gente no se mueve a menos que haya una fecha límite. Una ocupación larga e indefinida sería un desastre. "El pueblo estadounidense no lo toleraría, y mucho menos los iraquíes; nos echarían antes, si no tenemos una fecha".

"Lo segundo que propongo es la necesidad de uniformar a los iraquíes." Bremer y el Pentágono habían anunciado ese mes que planeaban contar con un ejército iraquí de 40.000 soldados en 2005 o después, y con 146.000 personas más en la policía, la guardia fronteriza y otras fuerzas de seguridad. Hasta ese momento, había apenas mil aspirantes a soldados en entrenamiento para el nuevo ejército iraquí.

"Mi idea es tener 300.000 en junio de 2004", dijo Herbits, haciendo una pausa teatral. "Así que, caballeros, a discutir".

"Estás completamente equivocado", comentó Gingrich. "Las elecciones van a girar en torno a la economía estadounidense".

"No", dijo Herbits. "La economía va a estar bien. Y aun si no lo estuviera, no hay mucho que Bush pudiera hacer al respecto". Sin embargo, Irak era importante y era algo en lo que se podía trabajar. "Es el proceso el que me preocupa", dijo, "y va muy mal".

Wolfowitz estuvo de acuerdo en que la ocupación era un enfoque errado, y empezó a explicarle a Herbits por qué.

"No se trata de convencerme a mí", insistió Herbits. "Se trata de que ustedes dos lo discutan".

Wolfowitz, un defensor de vieja data de la disolución del ejército iraquí como factor clave para deshacerse del legado de Saddam Hussein, les recordó que el ejército había desaparecido, que se había desvanecido por completo.

Herbits estuvo de acuerdo en que la disolución del ejército no había sido decisión de los Estados Unidos, pero que sí había sido resolución de los Estados Unidos y de Bremer el hecho de mantenerlo disuelto, y ese era el error que debía enmendarse. Era imprescindible que Irak tuviera un ejército iraquí.

El argumento final de Herbits era la necesidad política. "Escuchen, si ustedes no arreglan esto, a este presidente le van a dar una paliza".

Durante más de dos horas, Wolfowitz y Gingrich se ocuparon de ello, citando poesía, estudios, historiadores, los griegos, los modernos. Pero al final estuvieron de acuerdo con los dos puntos principales de Herbits: fechas límite y su conveniencia, así como con que debía hacerse algo respecto al ejército iraquí.

Al final de la cena, ambos se comprometieron a ayudar. Wolfowitz hablaría con Rumsfeld y Hadley. Gingrich era miembro de la Junta Asesora sobre Políticas de Defensa, un grupo externo que periódicamente aconsejaba a Rumsfeld, pero cuyo verdadero contacto era Cheney. Ambos habían sido elegidos para el Congreso por primera vez en 1978, y eran amigos hacía casi 25 años. Gingrich afirmó que hablaría con Cheney y *Scooter* Libby.

GINGRICH RECORDARÍA después a la perfección cada detalle de la cena.

"Fue el primer momento que recuerdo en que nos sentamos e intercambiamos opiniones sobre lo mal que iba todo, y acerca del grado hasta el cual Bremer estaba por fuera de la cadena de mando", expresó. Según él, a Washington "se le estaba desinformando sistemáticamente".

Con respecto a lo económico, Gingrich creía que "el modelo de Bremer era totalmente equivocado. Totalmente. Su modelo era el de los tiempos de paz, contratando con grandes multinacionales. Se podría planear todo desde Denver, y en dos o tres años, las cosas empezarían a suceder". Para él, la pugna interna en el Consejo Nacional de Seguridad seguía siendo intensa. "Los de arriba estaban tan cansados de pelear unos con otros que todos terminaron por decir: 'Ojalá Bremer lo resuelva'. Y cuando uno iba y les contaba que las cosas iban mal, su respuesta era que había que 'darle tiempo a Bremer'".

Pero Gingrich pensaba que no había manera de que Bremer solucionara los problemas. "Bremer es lo más desastroso que le ha pasado a la política exterior de los Estados Unidos en los tiempos modernos", declararía más adelante el ex presidente de la Cámara.

"Lo más peligroso del mundo es una persona inteligente y segura de sí misma tratando de implementar el modelo equivocado, pues pone un gran empeño insistiendo en algo que no sirve. Bremer viene aquí creyéndose MacArthur en Japón y diciendo que debemos tener un modelo centrado en los Estados Unidos".

Afirmaba que si se les preguntara a grandes hombres de negocios o empresarios estadounidenses cuál había sido el error más grande de sus carreras, su respuesta sería: "No haber despedido a alguien a tiempo".

"Está bien", estuvo de acuerdo Gingrich. "Bremer debe ser relevado antes de septiembre". Pero añadió que Wolfowitz y él se habían dado cuenta de que no podían despedir a Bremer. El mismo Bush lo había nombrado, y ya habían despedido a Jay Garner. Simplemente no era posible deshacerse de dos en un solo año.

"Hay que tratar de solucionar problemas concretos", opinó. En palabras de Gingrich, más que la fecha de entrega del poder en Irak o el restablecimiento del ejército iraquí, lo que le molestaba era que los militares no pudieran conseguir el dinero que necesitaban con urgencia para proyectos pequeños.

La Casa Blanca indicó que el dinero sí se había entregado, pero algunos oficiales que Gingrich conocía desde años atrás afirmaban que no era así. Finalmente, Gingrich dice haber llamado a Cheney.

Gingrich sostiene haberle dicho al vicepresidente que tanto a él como a "Condi" les estaban mintiendo.

"Me encargaré de eso", fue la respuesta de Cheney.

Aun así, transcurrieron 60 días de órdenes directas antes de que se obtuviera el dinero.

Gingrich cuenta que fue a ver a Rove y a Hadley y les entregó un memorando que advertía: "Bremer puede costarles las elecciones". Y continuó: "Vengo a informarles que las cosas van muy mal". A Gingrich le parecía que había que involucrar a Rice y a Cheney. "Van a tener que tomar miles de decisiones, y no es simple cuestión de decidir, sino de considerar lo que está en juego en cada una de ellas".

"En resumidas cuentas", concluyó Gingrich, "no es bueno perder una guerra".

24

En septiembre de 2003, la cúpula de la CIA se reunió con Condoleezza Rice para exponerle la conveniencia de que Estados Unidos desarrollara un nuevo servicio nacional de inteligencia iraquí. Tenet y McLaughlin ingresaron a la oficina de Rice en la Casa Blanca, seguidos por el subdirector de operaciones, Stephen R. Kappes, el jefe de la división del Cercano Oriente, Bob Richer, y el jefe de antiterrorismo, que seguía encubierto.

Tenet se sentó en la parte de atrás del recinto, masticando uno de sus medios cigarros. Era una reunión importante, pero él prefería dejar hablar a los demás. Su distanciamiento con Rice estaba alcanzando su punto más alto.

Ni el Departamento de Estado ni el Departamento de Defensa estaban de acuerdo con la idea. El servicio de inteligencia de Saddam había sido un símbolo de su brutal despotismo. Con su disolución, en mayo, se había dado un paso importante. Temían que cualquier intento de conformar un nuevo servicio de espionaje sería recibido con tal temor y odio por los iraquíes que eso contrarrestaría cualquier beneficio.

Kappes expuso el problema. Irak era el único país del mundo donde Estados Unidos estaba combatiendo el terrorismo sin la ayuda de un servicio de inteligencia local, lo cual implicaba una desventaja potencialmente catastrófica. Necesitaban un socio interno que pudiera suministrarle información a la CIA.

En Irak está hoy en día la más grande división de la CIA, dijo Kappes, porque allá es donde afrontamos la principal amenaza terrorista.

Además, la idea de que la creación de un nuevo servicio de espionaje podría enviar una señal equivocada y propiciar un retorno a las antiguas tácticas de policía secreta, al estilo Saddam, era sencillamente errónea. El nuevo servicio podía ser cuidadosamente reclutado y supervisado. McLaughlin dijo que, de acuerdo con su experiencia, después de la caída del Muro de Berlín y el desplome del comunismo, los servicios de inteligencia en Europa Oriental dieron un giro y se mostraron dispuestos a trabajar con la CIA. En 1990 había viajado a Hungría, donde el personal de inteligencia dijo al respecto: "Muy bien, antes trabajábamos para los soviéticos, ahora vamos a trabajar con ustedes". Los funcionarios de inteligencia en otros países podían ser comprados.

Necesitamos un mejor servicio de inteligencia en el terreno, adujeron. Se podía subsidiar y cooptar un servicio local. "Nosotros creamos el servicio de inteligencia jordano y ahora somos sus dueños", dijo Tenet.

"¿Cómo saben que no terminaremos creando otra KGB?", preguntó Rice, refiriéndose al antiguo servicio de inteligencia soviético.

La KGB original no fue creación de la CIA, dijo Kappes.

Tenet meneó la cabeza, sin pronunciar palabra, disimulando apenas su disgusto. La CIA obtenía parte de su mejor información de inteligencia de los servicios extranjeros. Era absurdo que alguien los quisiera ciegos en Irak.

McLaughlin consideraba que Hadley y Wolfowitz eran ingenuos y durante los meses siguientes presionó al comité de adjuntos para que se aprobara la creación de un servicio iraquí. En una reunión le dijo al grupo, en el que se hallaban Wolfowitz y Armitage: "He estado en el comité de adjuntos desde hace cuatro años y nunca había estado en tan profundo desacuerdo con mis colegas".

Por su parte, Wolfowitz no le otorgaba ninguna confianza a la idea. La CIA va a respaldar a la gente equivocada, pensó. Hasta el momento, la CIA había estado enviando a Irak, en misiones de 90 días, a gente que ni siquiera hablaba árabe. Los militares estaban realizando una labor de inteligencia mucho mejor.

Tras nueve meses de discusiones y presiones por parte de Tenet y McLaughlin, en julio de 2004, la CIA finalmente obtuvo autorización para reclutar a 1.000 funcionarios de inteligencia iraquíes.

UNA DE LAS FUNCIONES DE BLACKWILL era servir de coordinador de planeación estratégica del CNS, y Rice le pidió que hiciera algo de planeación entre organismos en relación con Pakistán. Después de que Blackwill se reunió varias veces con funcionarios de rango medio, Powell llamó a Rice.

"No voy a participar en ningún proyecto innecesario sobre Pakistán", dijo. "Nuestra política en Irak afronta cada vez más problemas. Encomiéndele a Blackwill la política iraquí. Debería asignarlo de tiempo completo a Irak. La política iraquí es un problema terrible".

Sin consultar a Blackwill, Rice lo asignó a Irak. Era obvio que Powell quería que Godzilla interviniera en un terreno que le pertenecía al Pentágono.

Blackwill se puso a trabajar, leyó los archivos y los informes del Pentágono, hizo las rondas y escribió un largo memorando para Rice a fines de septiembre. La conclusión: necesitamos más tropas terrestres en Irak, unas dos divisiones más, o 40.000 hombres.

Rice no dijo ni sí, ni no.

Como Blackwill era amigo de Bremer desde hacía muchos años y ambos habían sido funcionarios del servicio exterior, Rice envió a Blackwill a Bagdad para que le ayudara a Bremer. Se fueron convenciendo cada vez más de la necesidad de persuadir con dramatismo a Rice. Solicitaron una videoconferencia segura con Rice y Hadley, en la que no hubiera ninguna otra persona presente. Para enfatizar la importancia de la conferencia, pidieron que todo el personal técnico y de comunicaciones que había participado en el video seguro abandonara los recintos tanto en Washington como en Bagdad.

Desde donde estaban, Bremer y Blackwill sólo podían ver a Rice y a Hadley. Hicieron una presentación metódica sobre la geografía de Irak, el nivel de violencia y la manera como los comandantes militares afrontaban los ataques en un área, o en lugares donde se concentraban presuntos insurgentes, y luego se marchaban. Al cabo de un tiempo, los insurgentes simplemente retomaban sus antiguas zonas. Habiendo sido los dos protegidos de Kissinger, la presentación fue "completamente Kissinger". En sus mentes, era irrefutable que se necesitaba, por lo menos, dos divisiones más. Hadley tomaba notas afanosamente.

Debido al intervalo de tiempo en el video de seguridad, parecía como si Rice y Hadley no hubieran reaccionado.

"Muy bien, Jerry, Bob", dijo finalmente Rice, "muchas gracias por estas ideas. Vamos a reflexionar sobre ellas".

Y enseguida la pantalla quedó negra.

Bremer miró a Blackwill y dijo, "bamboleo y tiro errado".

"Un lanzamiento espacial profundo", contestó Blackwill, vaticinando que su propuesta se dirigía ahora hacia Marte para luego traspasar las galaxias externas y los sistemas estelares por toda la eternidad.

EN DOS ENTREVISTAS efectuadas en julio de 2006, le pregunté a Rumsfeld sobre los niveles de fuerzas, un tema crucial que, además, era objeto de controversia. Los documentos indicaban que el plan para invadir a Irak tenía un tope de 275.000 hombres de combate terrestres, incluidos cerca de 90.000 soldados que debían desplazarse en avión hasta Irak en las semanas y los meses posteriores al 19 de marzo de 2003, cuando empezó la guerra. Rumsfeld dijo que uno de los principales "rumores falsos" que circulaban era que él había decidido o influido indebidamente en la decisión de no enviar los 90.000 soldados. La recomendación había sido del general Franks. "Juzgó que ya tenía los que necesitaba, o que los tendría a medida que se desarrollaban los sucesos, y que no iba a requerir las tropas adicionales que aguardaban... Él hizo esa recomendación y yo le recomendé eso al presidente, y estuvimos de acuerdo". De modo que no se enviaron los 90.000 efectivos terrestres adicionales para la guerra o la estabilización.

Los críticos u "opinadores", como los llamaba Rumsfeld, "las personas que no tienen responsabilidad en la toma de decisiones", no entienden. "Muchos de ellos dicen, 'ah, es Rumsfeld', como si yo estuviera sentado con una caja negra ideando todo esto. Y cualquiera que me conozca o que me haya visto hacer cualquier cosa sabe que así no es como yo actúo. Yo asumí este trabajo a sabiendas de que no hay nadie lo bastante inteligente como para hacerlo". Por lo tanto, dijo, confiaba en "gente lista" y acogía "consejos de múltiples fuentes".

Sin embargo, media docena de generales y civiles que trabajaban estrechamente con Rumsfeld dejaron en claro en las entrevistas que era él quien conducía el tren.

En el verano de 2006, Rumsfeld había suavizado su posición con respecto al tema de si había suficientes soldados en Irak.

"Es perfectamente posible que hubiera demasiados en un momento dado, o muy pocos en otro momento, porque nadie es perfecto", dijo. "Todos los que nos esforzábamos al máximo por tomar estas decisiones lo hacíamos procurando que hubiera suficientes [soldados] para hacer el trabajo y permitir que avanzara el proceso político y económico, pero no un número excesivamente alto que hiciera pensar a la gente que estábamos allí para robarles su petróleo y ocupar su país, y perturbar y causar disturbios en los países vecinos que provocaran el derrocamiento de algunos de esos otros regímenes. De manera que nuestro juicio fue el mejor posible. En retrospectiva, no he visto o escuchado nada por parte de aquellos opinadores que me haga pensar que tienen algún motivo para creer que ellos tenían razón y nosotros estábamos equivocados. Tampoco puedo probar que nosotros teníamos razón y ellos estaban equivocados. Lo único que puedo decir es que parece que ellos tenían mucha más certeza de la que mi evaluación de los hechos me permitiría tener a mí".

DAVID KAY VOLVIÓ a Washington a tiempo para presentarle un informe inicial al Congreso el 2 de octubre de 2003. "No se lo vamos a presentar a la Casa Blanca sino en la mañana en que usted vaya a testificar", le dijo Tenet a Kay. Si la Casa Blanca no veía el testimonio de antemano, le sería más difícil presionar a Kay para que adaptara lo que iba a decir.

"Todavía no hemos encontrado arsenales", dijo Kay en el testimonio que había preparado, "pero aún no hemos llegado al punto en que podamos decir definitivamente que esos arsenales no existen ni existían antes de la guerra; nuestra única tarea es averiguar en dónde están". El nuevo giro que

Kay le dio a su trabajo fue decir que habían hallado "docenas de actividades de programas relacionados con ADM". En esencia, Kay estaba tratando de acertar de ambas maneras: no se había encontrado arsenales, pero era posible que algún día fueran encontrados.

Las noticias sobre el testimonio de Kay se concentraron casi con exclusividad en su admisión de que no se había hallado armas. Esa noche Kay fue entrevistado por Jim Lehrer, presentador de noticias PBS. "Encontramos bastante actividad en el área de armas, pero no hemos, nuevamente, no hemos... no hemos encontrado las armas".

Powell, quien tenía mucho que perder, llamó a Tenet, indignado de que el gobierno hubiera hecho una labor tan deficiente en la divulgación del informe. Ante la escalada de críticas, Bush trató de controlar la situación él mismo al día siguiente, diciendo que el informe de Kay "afirma que el régimen de Saddam Hussein tenía una red clandestina de laboratorios biológicos, un cepa viva del agente mortífero *botulinum*, dispositivos de ocultamiento sofisticados y un trabajo de diseño avanzado en misiles de largo alcance prohibidos". El *botulinum* no estaba en un arma o cerca de alguna, aunque el presidente pareció implicar que estaba a punto de ser introducido en un misil.

Un memorando que creaba el Grupo de Estabilización de Irak, adscrito a Rice –el nuevo intento del CNS de coordinar a Bremer que iba a ser dirigido por Blackwill–, cayó en manos de David Sanger, el recursivo periodista de *The New York Times* que cubría la Casa Blanca. El 6 de octubre, el *Times* publicó un artículo de primera plana titulado "Casa Blanca revisará misiones en Irak y Afganistán".

Bremer leyó el artículo en línea en Bagdad. Era la primera vez que escuchaba hablar sobre el Grupo de Estabilización de Irak, y fue así como se enteró de que Rice iba a asumir una función más amplia.

Cuando Rice y Bremer conversaron, Rice le dijo que la reorganización no era en realidad una reorganización. No significaba que estuvieran descontentos con él, le dijo, y añadió que el grupo se había diseñado únicamente para movilizar la burocracia.

En una rueda de prensa al día siguiente, a Rumsfeld se le vio claramente irritado.

"Creo que tendría que hacerle esa pregunta a Condi", dijo, cuando un periodista le preguntó acerca del Grupo de Estabilización de Irak, e insistió en que no había escuchado nada sobre la reorganización antes de que la información se filtrara a la prensa.

Un periodista hizo otra pregunta a ese mismo respecto.

"Dije que no sé. ¿No quedó claro? ¿Acaso no entiende inglés?", dijo Rumsfeld. "No estaba presente cuando se habló sobre eso".

Rumsfeld consideró indignante que Rice declarara que ella estaba a cargo. En los días siguientes, observó con cierta satisfacción que ella empezó a echarse para atrás.

Al secretario de Defensa le preocupaba que los artículos dieran la impresión de que había una estrategia nueva y que de alguna manera el asesor nacional de seguridad, los miembros del CNS y la gente del presidente tenían ahora bajo su responsabilidad los 130.000 soldados estadounidenses en Irak, y no él. ¿Cuántas veces tenía que recordárselo a todo el mundo? El Consejo Nacional de Seguridad no formaba parte de la cadena de mando. El problema no era que pudiera haber una nueva estrategia. El problema era que no había mucha estrategia, fuera de dejar a Bremer a cargo.

En Irak, David Kay recibió una llamada telefónica de *Scooter* Libby.

"El vicepresidente quiere saber si ha examinado esta área", dijo Libby. "Tenemos indicios –y aquí están las geocoordenadas– de que hay algo enterrado allí".

Kay recurrió a los expertos en mapas e imágenes de su equipo. Miraron las fotografías satelitales y otras fotos de monitoreo del lugar. Estaba en el centro de Líbano.

"Allá iremos luego", bromeó uno de los expertos en imágenes.

En otra ocasión, Kay recibió un cable de la CIA en el que se le informaba que el vicepresidente quería que él enviara a alguien a Suiza para reunirse con un iraní llamado Manucher Ghorbanifar.

"A ése lo reconozco", dijo Kay cuando vio el cable. "Esto no lo voy a hacer".

Ghorbanifar había sido el intermediario iraní en las desastrosas negociaciones secretas de armas a cambio de rehenes, en el escándalo *Irán-contras*, durante el gobierno de Reagan. Aunque había sido una fuente de la CIA en los años setenta, la organización había terminado sus contactos con él en 1983 y el año siguiente había expedido una nota formal advirtiendo que se trataba de una fuente "quemada", y que este personaje era un "fabulador talentoso".

Esta vez, según leyó Kay, Ghorbanifar aseguraba tener una fuente iraní que sabía todo acerca de las armas nucleares iraquíes, pero exigía US $2 millones por anticipado y no quería hablar directamente con Estados Unidos, sino sólo a través del propio Ghorbanifar.

Kay descubrió que la última hazaña de Ghorbanifar implicaba a Michael Ledeen, del American Enterprise Institute, un ex colega de Oliver North en el

CNS que había estado involucrado con Ghorbanifar en la época del asunto *Irán-contras*.

Kay envió a la CIA un cable en el que decía: "A menos que me den instrucciones directas de hablar con él, no permitiré que ningún miembro del Grupo de Inspección de Irak hable con ese tipo. El tipo es un fabulador-propagador reconocido, y eso perjudicará a alguien. Si el director de Inteligencia Central quiere enviarme instrucciones directas para que lo haga, desde luego lo haré. Pero tiene que ser directo".

La idea no prosperó. Cheney estaba actuando como una especie de súper investigador, intentando descubrir las esquivas ADM, concluyó Kay. Pero siempre había cabos sueltos en inteligencia, trozos dispersos de información que podían llevar a todo tipo de conclusiones aventuradas. Si se concentraban únicamente en unos temas y les asignaban una importancia desmesurada, podían terminar con un panorama sesgado. Esto le recordaba a Kay la exitosa novela *El código Da Vinci*, en la que un profesor de Harvard y una agente de policía francesa unen pistas extraídas de la Biblia y de obras maestras del arte, y mitos que supuestamente revelan una gigantesca conspiración para ocultar la verdadera naturaleza y vida de Jesucristo.

Kay iba a limitarse a lo básico: fuentes humanas, personas que quizás realmente supieran algo.

BREMER VIAJÓ VARIAS VECES entre Bagdad y Estados Unidos, tratando de hacer que las cosas avanzaran y afrontando lo que llamaba el destornillador de 8.000 kilómetros que apretaban los funcionarios y burócratas de Washington.

El 27 de octubre de 2003, fue a la Casa Blanca para hablar con Bush. Rice, Card, Rumsfeld y Myers también estaban presentes.

En una pantalla de video, el general Abizaid insistía en que necesitaban reclutar oficiales del ejército de Saddam.

"Eso plantea algunos riesgos", dijo Bremer, una de cuyas primeras actuaciones en Irak había sido firmar la Orden Número 2 de la APC, que desmantelaba formalmente el ejército. "Debemos proceder con sumo cuidado para no dar la impresión de estar reconstituyendo el antiguo régimen".

"Bueno, hay algo claro", dijo el presidente, según el libro de Bremer. "Mantendremos nuestro curso en Irak. No vamos a demostrar debilidad a la luz de estos nuevos ataques. No menguará nuestra determinación".

La duda era corrosiva y sólo llevaría a estrujamientos de manos nerviosos. El presidente había sido el principal animador del equipo de fútbol americano en la secundaria. Hay poca o ninguna evidencia de que hubiera participado en debates sobre políticas sustanciales en las reuniones del gabinete de guerra por esta época. Su función era manifestar confianza y entusiasmo.

En el Pentágono, Rumsfeld le presentó a Bremer lo que había dado en llamarse la "Opción Wolfowitz-Feith", un plan para devolver la soberanía desde el 9 de abril de 2004, fecha del primer aniversario de la caída de Saddam.

Demasiado pronto, contestó Bremer. "Correríamos el riesgo de que Irak sucumba a disturbios o guerra civil". Quería esperar a que hubiera un gobierno elegido y una Constitución. Era imposible lograr eso para abril.

Rumsfeld presionó. Al día siguiente, en una reunión de jefes, dijo que tenían que devolver la soberanía para quitarse el rótulo de que Estados Unidos era "ocupador". El general Pace, vicepresidente del Estado Mayor Conjunto, le enfatizó eso mismo a Bremer.

"La estrategia militar más importante es acelerar el camino de la gobernabilidad", dijo Pace. De modo que los generales, responsables de la seguridad y la estrategia militar, estaban buscando la pronta soberanía y la política como solución.

Pace luego dijo que se trató de un comentario que Bremer podría haber sacado de contexto. "Pueden matar gente durante los siguientes 27 años", dijo el general, "y no van a tener un mejor entorno. Lo que tienen que hacer es proveer suficiente seguridad como para permitir la gobernabilidad, y por eso es tan importante la pieza de la gobernabilidad: está entremezclada con la seguridad".

Powell le insistió en repetidas ocasiones a Bush que todo ese discurso sobre reconstrucción y proceso político, exploración petrolera y generación de electricidad, desarrollo económico y privatización era excelente, pero que lo más importante era la seguridad.

"Todo esto es fabuloso, pero sólo hay un problema", le dijo Powell a Bush en una ocasión. "Y si lo soluciona, esto va a parecer lo más grandioso que alguien haya jamás pensado. Se trata de la seguridad. Si no hay seguridad, no se podrá lograr nada más. Todo tiene que concentrarse en la seguridad, más que en el petróleo o la electricidad o el agua o cualquier otra cosa".

"Sí", dijo Bush. "Entiendo".

"Nada se podrá hacer si no se soluciona la situación de seguridad", dijo Powell.

Los informes confidenciales indicaban que los ataques de los insurgentes habían aumentado a 1.000 en el mes de octubre, más de 30 diarios. Muchos fracasaban, pero era un nivel de violencia impresionante. Las cifras se mantuvieron en secreto.

En un intento por responder las preguntas que había formulado el presidente después del ataque contra la sede de la ONU, John McLaughlin elaboró un documento informativo titulado "¿Quién es el enemigo?" y lo distribuyó entre los adjuntos y los jefes. Identificó a cuatro grupos: antiguos baathistas, con un proyecto de restauración para restituir a Saddam; combatientes extranjeros; nacionalistas iraquíes que odiaban la ocupación, y miembros tribales furiosos por la muerte de familiares y la dura presión ejercida por los militares de la coalición.

En las reuniones plenarias del CNS, Bremer presentó las opciones en lo referente a soberanía. Se retractó un poco de su posición y ahora estaba dispuesto a entregar la soberanía a fines del 2004; faltaba todavía más de un año y sería después de las elecciones presidenciales de Estados Unidos.

Bush seguía animándolos, según Bremer, quien dijo que el presidente terminó la reunión repitiendo más o menos su libreto público. "Vamos a triunfar en Irak a pesar de las épocas difíciles por las que estamos atravesando. Nadie debe abrigar ninguna duda. Haremos lo correcto, independientemente de lo que digan la prensa o los opositores políticos. El éxito en Irak cambiará el mundo. El pueblo estadounidense no debe tener duda alguna de que confiamos en el resultado. Es posible que todavía no hayamos triunfado en el momento de las elecciones. Que así sea".

Después, Bush invitó a Bremer a hacer ejercicio en el gimnasio privado de la Casa Blanca, en el tercer piso. Bush le preguntó a Bremer acerca de Rumsfeld.

"¿Qué tipo de persona es, cómo es trabajar con él? ¿Es verdad que microadministra?"

"Yo aprecio a Don, señor presidente. Lo conozco desde hace 30 años, lo admiro, lo considero sumamente inteligente. Pero sí microadministra".

Bush pareció sorprendido, según el recuento de Bremer.

"Don aterroriza a sus subordinados civiles, por lo cual casi nunca logro que alguien distinto de él tome alguna decisión. Eso funciona bien, pero no es lo ideal".

Bush no ofreció ninguna conclusión firme sobre el tema de la soberanía, pero su determinación era obvia. "No vamos a fracasar en Irak", dijo nuevamente el presidente.

Bremer regresó a Irak el 31 de octubre. Estaba razonablemente seguro de que contaba con el respaldo de Bush para demorar la transferencia temprana de la soberanía.

Rice le planteó a Andy Card su preocupación acerca de las reuniones privadas entre Bush y Bremer. ¿De qué temas hablaban? ¿Se tomaba decisiones o se daba instrucciones? Un encuentro tan privado le daba a Bremer una increíble libertad para operar. Ahora podía invocar la autoridad presidencial para casi cualquier cosa que hiciera, o como mínimo podía respaldar sus actuaciones diciendo que así había interpretado las palabras del presidente.

Card le contestó que el cargo de enviado era tan importante que el presidente y Bremer necesitaban conocerse bien.

Rumsfeld estaba furioso y se quejó ante Card sobre el hecho de haber sido excluido de una reunión celebrada por uno de sus subordinados con el presidente.

"¡Él trabaja para mí!", bramó Rumsfeld.

"Es el enviado presidencial", respondió Card.

En otra reunión del CNS con el presidente, surgió el tema del ejército iraquí.

Powell quería utilizar a algunos líderes de rango medio del antiguo ejército para crear el nuevo. "Escuchen", dijo, "por qué no aprovechamos a estos comandantes de batallón y, como necesitamos reconstituir una fuerza, les damos dinero y les decimos que recreen sus batallones. Esta gente necesita dinero".

Rumsfeld contestó que ya estaban reclutando y entrenando policías y un nuevo ejército. Se habló de cifras. Primero se dijo que 54.000 y luego el doble de eso, y en un momento dado se llegó hasta 200.000.

Bremer se preguntó de dónde diablos salían las cifras. En el video seguro que se había instalado en la Sala de Situaciones de la Casa Blanca, se podía ver a Bremer meneando la cabeza en señal de desacuerdo cuando se mencionó la última cifra. ¿200.000? Era primera noticia para él. En otros instantes se le veía anotando sus observaciones en una pila de "papel de trabajo" de la APC que tenía frente a él.

BUSH Y RICE querían acortar el tiempo de ocupación, pero ahora estaban atrapados en el largo proceso político de Bremer. "Nadie quiere que su país esté ocupado. A nosotros no nos gustaría estar ocupados", repetía Bush una y otra vez. La pregunta era cómo salir de la ocupación.

En Bagdad, Meghan O'Sullivan y Roman Martínez luchaban con el complejo proceso electoral de tres pasos que Bremer y la ONU habían estructurado. Durante algunos días, les había preocupado la posibilidad de que la objeción de Bremer a que se celebrara elecciones directas para escoger al grupo de personas encargadas de redactar la Constitución pudiera provocar una crisis de gobernabilidad imposible de capotear. Parecía como si Bremer fuera a empantanar la situación, lo cual fomentaría un distanciamiento por parte de Sistani. Personas cercanas a Sistani le dijeron a O'Sullivan que el líder religioso había expedido el *fatwa* del 28 de junio donde insistía en que la Constitución fuera redactada por iraquíes elegidos de modo apropiado, porque temía que Irak terminara pareciéndose al Japón ocupado por los estadounidenses después de la Segunda Guerra Mundial. La gente de MacArthur había redactado la mayor parte de la Constitución nacional de la posguerra, y Japón, que se había rendido incondicionalmente, la había adoptado tras hacerle apenas unos cambios menores. Sistani quería elecciones plenas, pero eso tomaría otros seis a nueve meses, lo cual probablemente doblaría el tiempo en que Estados Unidos estaría ocupando Irak.

Otra crisis posible era que el Consejo de Gobierno interino de 25 miembros se rebelara o se disolviera en torno al tema. Estar del lado equivocado de Sistani o perder el Consejo de Gobierno sería un duro golpe que los dejaría sin alternativas viables.

En una reunión del CNS celebrada en el otoño del 2003, la discusión giró en torno al papel del Gran Ayatollah Sistani. Bremer se conectó mediante la red de video seguro.

"¿Vamos a permitir que un clérigo de 75 años decida cuál va a ser nuestra política en Irak?", preguntó.

"Jerry", dijo el vicepresidente Cheney, "quizás haya otra manera de mirar esto. Empiezo a pensar que tenemos que tratar a Sistani como se trata en el Congreso a un malhumorado presidente de comisión, si uno pertenece a la rama ejecutiva. Tal vez a uno no le caiga bien, tal vez no esté de acuerdo con él, pero hay que cultivarlo porque le puede hacer a uno mucho daño".

Desde ese momento, Sistani fue el clérigo certificado por el gobierno de Bush. Malhumorado, iraní o bienamado, una cosa era segura: tenía poder sobre millones de personas en Irak.

O'Sullivan y Martínez redactaron dos memorandos con fecha 4 de noviembre en los que se diseñaba un plan alternativo, e informaron a Bremer al respecto en un refugio antibombas durante un ataque con morteros. La idea era crear una Constitución interina sin llamarla así, pues Saddam había regido el país bajo una Constitución interina y la sola idea tenía una connotación muy negativa para los iraquíes. En vez de eso la llamarían la Ley Administrativa de Transición (TAL). Aunque sería redactada e impuesta a Irak en gran parte por estadounidenses, incluiría cláusulas que estipulaban la celebración de elecciones y la redacción de una Constitución nueva y permanente en un plazo determinado.

Se envió a alguien a Najaf para que le planteara la idea a Sistani. Él la aprobó.

Hadley y Blackwill le dijeron a Rice que quizás podrían celebrar elecciones interinas en Irak y luego transferir la soberanía. Rice llamó a Bremer.

"Tenemos una nueva propuesta, creo, un consenso emergente", le dijo Bremer, y se lo esbozó.

"¿No le parece que debería venir para que todos hablemos sobre esto primero? Porque en realidad se trata de una decisión de nivel presidencial".

"Claro. Tomaré un avión mañana".

Hadley suspiró con alivio. "Aleluya", le dijo a Rice. "Acabamos de lograr algo importante".

"Le dije a Jerry Bremer que tiene que venir", le comentó Rice al presidente.

"¿Y por qué hizo eso?", quiso saber Bush.

"Porque creo que es mejor que discutamos esto aquí".

"No tenemos una estrategia militar para ganar en Irak", se quejó Bremer a Cheney en una llamada telefónica segura varios días después.

"He estado haciendo esa misma pregunta", dijo Cheney. "¿Cuál es nuestra estrategia para ganar? Tengo la impresión de que el Pentágono está pensando que la guerra ya terminó y que ahora están en la fase de 'recoger y limpiar'. No ven que estamos librando una gran batalla contra los terroristas en Irak y en todas partes".

Prometió plantear estos temas personalmente en la Casa Blanca.

El 7 de noviembre, Bremer se reunió con el general Abizaid. Había sido un mal día, pues por segunda vez en esa semana habían derribado un helicóptero norteamericano y habían muerto cuatro soldados estadounidenses.

"Me preocupa que la gente en Washington intente abrir una brecha entre nosotros", dijo Abizaid. Pero mientras hablaban era claro que la brecha ya existía. Abizaid dijo que necesitaba volver a contratar en el ejército a oficiales sunitas con experiencia que habían servido en el antiguo ejército de Saddam. Estaba hastiado de que Walt Slocombe, uno de los altos subalternos de Bremer, criticara públicamente la idea. "Yo siempre le he dicho a usted que no estoy de acuerdo con el desmantelamiento del ejército, pero nunca le he dicho a la prensa lo que opino".

"Reconstituir el ejército de Saddam habría detonado una guerra civil", contestó Bremer. "Si cree que ahora tenemos problemas, imagínese cómo *hubieran* podido llegar a ser los problemas".

EL 11 DE NOVIEMBRE DE 2003, Día de los Veteranos, Bush pronunció un discurso de corte conservador a la hora del almuerzo en la Fundación Heritage. La guerra en Irak se parecía mucho a los esfuerzos realizados por los presidentes Truman y Reagan para contener el comunismo, le dijo al público.

"La voluntad y la determinación de Estados Unidos se están poniendo a prueba en Afganistán y en Irak. No estamos únicamente conteniendo la amenaza terrorista, la estamos obligando a retroceder".

Esta afirmación iba en contra de los hechos que sucedían en Irak. No había ningún retroceso. Los informes confidenciales indicaban que en septiembre había habido cerca de 750 ataques iniciados por enemigos en Irak, y la cifra se volvió a elevar a unos 1.000 en octubre. Eso seguía significando más de 30 ataques diarios.

Aproximadamente una hora después de su discurso, Bush estaba de regreso en la Casa Blanca, donde se reunió con su Consejo Nacional de Seguridad.

"Muy bien", dijo Bush. "Veamos cómo van las cosas en Irak".

Rob Richer, quien llevaba un año dirigiendo la División del Cercano Oriente de la CIA, empezó con el informe de inteligencia.

"Estamos viendo el establecimiento de una insurgencia en Irak", dijo.

Rumsfeld interrumpió al hombre de la CIA. "Esa es una palabra fuerte. ¿Qué quiere decir? ¿Cómo define insurgencia?"

"Señor", contestó Richer, "según las propias publicaciones del Departamento de Defensa, una insurgencia tiene tres características". Procedió a enumerarlas: apoyo popular, sabotaje o ataques armados sostenidos y la capacidad de actuar a voluntad y moverse con independencia.

"Quizás no esté de acuerdo con usted", dijo Rumsfeld, recostándose en la silla y dejando el asunto así. Era la actitud típica de Rumsfeld. Quizás sí. Quizás no.

Richer entendió por qué Rumsfeld podría objetar el uso de la palabra "insurgencia". Significaba claramente que los del otro lado eran una fuerza perdurable, organizada y quizás catastrófica. Pero, en opinión de Richer, esa era la realidad, y había que afrontarla. A juicio de la CIA, Irak era ahora un escenario clásico de guerra de guerrillas y los militares estaban teniendo que afrontar el problema no sólo de proteger a sus propias tropas sino de proteger a la población iraquí. Los hombres jóvenes en Irak estaban tomando decisiones prácticas. ¿Debían unirse a la nueva fuerza policial iraquí o a la insurgencia?

Bush se dirigió a Bremer.

"¿Así es como usted lo ve?", preguntó el presidente.

Bremer asintió.

Richer, que había ido a Irak para visitar las siete bases principales de la CIA dos meses antes, había descubierto que Bremer se mostraba de acuerdo en el campo, pero no se comprometía en el debate en Washington. Nunca iba a ser franco frente a Rumsfeld.

Richer abordó directamente al presidente, planteando la necesidad de conformar un nuevo servicio de inteligencia iraquí. Los esfuerzos de recopilación de inteligencia de la CIA eran limitados en Irak porque no había un servicio de inteligencia iraquí que les ayudara a obtener información. La CIA tenía unos 200 funcionarios en Irak, y Tenet planeaba expandir la presencia de la agencia.

"Necesito más información", dijo Bush. "No quiero leer en *The New York Times* que estamos afrontando una insurgencia. No quiero que nadie en el gabinete diga que es una insurgencia. No creo que estemos en eso todavía".

El general Myers mencionó varios éxitos y describió un panorama favorable.

"No voy a escuchar eso", interpuso Tenet. Quería que su jefe de estación en Irak se vinculara al video seguro para que expresara sus puntos de vista.

"Creo que los generales son quienes mejor nos pueden informar", dijo Rumsfeld.

"Está bien", dijo Tenet, levantando las manos en un gesto de resignación. No sólo parecía estar cediendo, sino renunciando.

"Quiero claridad", dijo Bush, pero no le resolvieron las contradicciones, y el presidente no insistió.

Más tarde, dijo Rumsfeld, él buscó "insurgencia" y otras palabras relacionadas en un diccionario militar. "No estaba convencido de que fuera yo quien debería utilizar la palabra, decir cómo lo deberíamos llamar en un momento determinado".

Armitage había concluido que su amigo Tenet llevaba demasiado tiempo como director de la CIA. Creía que Tenet habría hecho bien en irse en el 2002, después de la exitosa guerra en Afganistán, o más recientemente, en el verano, cuando se había matado a los brutales hijos de Saddam, Uday y Qusay, el 22 de julio de 2003. Solía decir que dejar un alto cargo en el gobierno no era tan traumático como temían muchas personas. "Cuando uno deja el gobierno, su cociente intelectual sube 30 puntos", afirmaba. Las personas tendían a pensar incorrectamente que eran indispensables. Convenía recordar que cuando uno retira el puño de un balde con agua no queda un agujero.

Pero el enorme problema que afrontaban ahora era el estado mental del presidente, pensó Armitage. Bush persistía en negar la evidencia con respecto a Irak.

25

En otro momento, durante la reunión del CNS, Rumsfeld argumentó que era importante devolverles a los iraquíes el mando sobre ciertas cosas, para que demostraran que ellos podían dirigir el país.

"Debemos aceptar la realidad de que no podemos tener una Constitución permanente de inmediato", dijo el presidente. Le preguntó a Bremer: "¿Los *caucuses*[13] permitirían una mejor seguridad? Es decir que así no se daría el espectáculo de las filas en las urnas, sometidas a bombas o disparos".

El presidente terminó la reunión diciendo: "Es importante que todos sepan que vamos a seguir nuestro curso y que estoy decidido a triunfar". Más tarde, cuando se reunió con Bremer en el Salón Oval, preguntó: "¿Cuál es la situación real en el terreno?".

"La inteligencia no es buena", contestó Bremer. "Y personalmente no estoy convencido de que los militares tengan una estrategia para triunfar".

La charla se prolongó otro rato. Al final, Bush le dijo a su enviado especial: "Está realizando un excelente trabajo. Siga así".

Confrontado por los informes desalentadores de su hombre principal en Irak, Bush parecía querer cambiar la situación en el terreno de Irak únicamente con su voluntad. Sus comentarios en público por esta época denotaban una pasión y un optimismo similares.

"El fracaso de la democracia iraquí podría envalentonar a los terroristas en todo el mundo, incrementar el peligro para el pueblo estadounidense y extinguir las esperanzas de millones en la región", dijo Bush en un discurso pronunciado el 6 de noviembre. "La democracia iraquí triunfará y ese triunfo propagará la noticia, desde Damasco hasta Teherán, de que la libertad puede ser el futuro de toda nación".

Pero si el éxito era en verdad tan importante, ¿dónde estaba la urgencia para desarrollar una estrategia de triunfo? Y si no había tal estrategia, como creía Bremer, ¿qué sustentaba el optimismo?

---

13. Reunión de los miembros locales de un partido político para nominar candidatos o elegir delegados a una convención.

A BREMER LE PREOCUPABA que todo el mundo se estaba contagiando de lo que llamaba en privado "fiebre de retirada". Aunque seguía insistiendo en que la soberanía temprana –que pondría fin a su trabajo en la APC– era una "mala idea", la idea seguía surgiendo.

Bremer podía leer un calendario. El presidente iba a presentarse para la reelección en el 2004, y las campañas de reelección absorbían toda la atención de la Casa Blanca. Nadie le dijo nunca explícitamente a Bremer algo como: "Tiene que salir de allá antes de las elecciones presidenciales". Sin embargo, ese triunfo sería lo más importante en la vida de Bush. Estaría en campaña casi todos los días. Irak era importante, pero el gran premio era la reelección.

Bremer habló con Andy Card a fines de octubre de 2003, y le insistió en que tenían que hacer lo correcto para la historia y para Irak. "Esto podría complicarle más la vida al presidente el año próximo. Incluso le podría costar la elección".

Card urgió a Bremer hablar con el presidente.

"Haga lo correcto", dijo Bush. "Incluso, si no logramos arreglar ese asunto antes de las elecciones".

Más tarde, Bremer dijo: "Esta presión, esta presión a favor de la soberanía temprana, creo que parte de ella era política... aunque nadie me lo dijo con esas palabras. Yo me di cuenta".

Los militares pronto empezaron a argumentar que, si se ponía fin a la ocupación, mejoraría la situación de la seguridad, porque a los iraquíes no les gustaba la ocupación. En una reunión, Bremer dijo: "Terminar la ocupación es una buena idea. Pero nos estaremos engañando si pensamos que es la bala de plata que va a poner fin a la oposición. No será así, porque el iraquí corriente va a salir de su casa y, de todas maneras, va a haber un tanque Bradley estacionado allí, aun cuando ya no seamos la ocupación".

El 12 de noviembre, el presidente finalmente decidió que debían proceder con la soberanía temprana.

Bremer recuerda en su libro que insistió en que la decisión que acababan de tomar, sobre entregar la soberanía, debía mostrarse como algo que habían ideado los iraquíes, no los estadounidenses.

Bush rio. "Estoy de acuerdo. Y ojalá esta sea la única reunión en la historia en que no sale todo el mundo a decirle a la prensa lo que decidimos".

Funcionó. El titular de primera página de *The Washington Post* del 15 de noviembre decía: "Los iraquíes dicen que Estados Unidos cederá el poder en el verano; reuniones urbanas para iniciar el proceso", mientras que *The New York Times* tituló: "Estados Unidos devolverá el poder a los iraquíes desde junio". Tal como se había acordado en la Casa Blanca, en el *Times* y en los demás medios se presentó la idea como un plan "planteado por líderes iraquíes", transmitido a Washington por Bremer y luego "ampliamente aceptado" por Bush.

Dos DÍAS DESPUÉS del anuncio de que la soberanía sería devuelta a los iraquíes, un grupo de 17 mujeres iraquíes visitó la Casa Blanca. Dina Powell, la asistente especial de Bush para asuntos de personal, oriunda de Egipto y conocedora del árabe, hacía las veces de guía.

Alguien le informó a Bush sobre la visita y él aceptó recibirlas. Muchas de las mujeres tenían historias de horror sobre la brutalidad del régimen de Saddam. Una de ellas había visto a su hijo mientras lo torturaban hasta morir. Otras habían sido violadas. Varias de las mujeres prefirieron no entrar al Salón Oval a hablar con Bush, pero cinco ingresaron para una reunión privada.

"*Muharrir*", le dijo una mujer en árabe al presidente, tan pronto ingresó al Salón Oval.

¿Qué quiere decir?, le preguntó Bush a Dina Powell.

"Libertador", tradujo ella.

El presidente no pudo contener las lágrimas.

DAN SENOR, EL CONSULTOR POLÍTICO republicano que actuaba como vocero de Bremer, pensó que las mejores evaluaciones de la situación de este último eran las de Hume Horan, quien había sido embajador de Estados Unidos en cinco países: Camerún, Guinea Ecuatorial, Sudán, Arabia Saudita y Costa de Marfil. Con un buen dominio del árabe y considerado por muchos como el mejor conocedor del Medio Oriente, Horan, de 68 años, cuyo primer cargo en el servicio exterior había sido en Bagdad en los años sesenta, era uno de los primeros especialistas en temas árabes que Bremer había reclutado para la autoridad provisional. En un largo viaje por carretera, saliendo de Bagdad, Horan le dijo a Senor que ahora estaban dedicados a la construcción de nación, y que calculaba que las posibilidades de construir una democracia en Irak eran apenas del 30%.

"Esa es la probabilidad más alta que hemos tenido o tendremos en esto", dijo Horan, refiriéndose a todo el Medio Oriente. Pero, incluso, con un 30%, debían intentarlo. "Vale la pena hacerlo", señaló.

En noviembre, justo antes de que Horan dejara la APC, Senor cenó con él en el Café Ranana, un restaurante del hotel Al Rashid de Bagdad. Fue una noche grata, y Horan se mostró reflexivo.

Cuando había sido embajador en Arabia Saudita o había ejercido otro cargo importante, dijo, todos los años afrontaba una decisión lo bastante crucial y difícil como para desvelarlo. "Una decisión al año, que constituía una presión enorme, en la que no se podía cometer errores, de gran intensidad y alto nivel de estrés", dijo. Bremer, por el contrario, estaba tomando entre 10 y 100 decisiones de esa magnitud todos los días. "Ningún diplomático puede apreciar cabalmente a qué se enfrenta Bremer", dijo Horan.

UNO DE LOS INTERROGADORES de David Kay en Bagdad fue a visitar al ex jefe de la comisión iraquí de adquisiciones militares. Ahora que había cooperado con los estadounidenses, le preguntaron al iraquí qué esperanzas abrigaba para su futuro.

"Mientras estén aquí, quiero seguir en confinamiento", contestó el iraquí. "Es seguro".

Kay consideró que era una prueba perturbadora de lo que los iraquíes pensaban sobre la situación de la seguridad en su país.

Justo antes del Día de Acción de Gracias, el general Abizaid mandó a decir que se quería reunir con Kay. "Solo", dijeron en la oficina de Abizaid, lo cual significaba que Kay no debía llevar al general Dayton.

"Necesito su ayuda", le dijo Abizaid a Kay. Estaba tratando desesperadamente de obtener mejor inteligencia para ayudarles a sus fuerzas a combatir la insurgencia. El Grupo de Inspección de Irak de Kay era, quizás, la más grande y mejor red de inteligencia que existía en ese momento en Irak. "Necesito estos recursos. Ustedes tienen traductores. Ustedes tienen analistas".

Kay objetó. "Tengo analistas que son expertos en ADM. No le van a ayudar a nadie en asuntos de contrainsurgencia. No saben de eso. Tengo exactamente dos oficiales operacionales que hablan árabe con fluidez". Si se los quitaban, más le valdría cerrar e irse. No iba a poder entrevistar a ningún iraquí que no estuviera en custodia.

Abizaid negoció. Estaba dispuesto a tomar sólo una docena de los aproximadamente 60 analistas de Kay. La cifra luego se redujo a 6 o 7.

"No, no puedo hacerlo porque me asignaron esta misión. No tengo ningún problema con que usted vaya a Washington y que Washington decida en este momento que la contrainsurgencia es más importante que las ADM", dijo Kay. "Escúcheme. Yo vivo aquí. Recorro la autopista BIAP cuatro veces al día. Han atacado a mi gente. Si usted dice eso y Washington dice que eso es importante, lo entenderé. Pero la decisión no depende de mí".

"No. No quiero volver a Washington. No quiero pedir. Sólo quiero que nosotros nos pongamos de acuerdo", contestó Abizaid.

Kay no cedía ni un milímetro y Abizaid hizo entrar a su personal de inteligencia al recinto. Repitió la solicitud, dejando que Kay concluyera que Abizaid pensaba que no iba a querer enfrentarlo frente a su personal, o, quizás, que el general simplemente quería demostrar que lo había intentado. El personal estaba en una posición incómoda, pensó Kay, porque él estaba haciendo algo que ninguno de ellos soñaría siquiera hacer: le estaba diciendo "no" a un general de cuatro estrellas.

EN DICIEMBRE, TENET LLAMÓ a Kay para decirle que había perdido su prueba de fuerza con los militares. El Grupo de Inspección de Irak de Kay iba a tener que encargarse de otras misiones, además de las ADM. Kay regresó a Washington para recordarle a Tenet que parte del trato para que asumiera la labor era que su grupo se enfocaría exclusivamente en la cacería de ADM.

"Es hora de irme", dijo Kay.

Tenet no se interpuso en el camino de Kay, aunque le preocupaba lo que pudiera decir Kay después. No quería que se pusiera a despotricar contra la CIA.

"No, no tengo esa intención", dijo Kay.

¿Acaso planeaba escribir un libro?

"Yo no hago eso. Nunca lo he hecho. No lo hice después de la primera Guerra del Golfo". Además, quizás un libro sobre su exitosa búsqueda de ADM después de la Guerra del Golfo habría sido más comercial que un libro sobre la búsqueda de ADM en el 2003, que no estaba conduciendo a ninguna parte.

Tenet le propuso a Kay que permaneciera en la nómina de la CIA como consultor. Kay aceptó, aunque se dio cuenta de que si se quedaba y se mantenían sus certificaciones de seguridad, Tenet podría pensar que eso le impediría hablar. Había venido a ver a Tenet como relacionista, como alguien que creía que podía manejar cualquier cosa o a cualquier persona.

No mucho después, Kay se reunió con Charles Allen, el subdirector de inteligencia central para recopilación de información, quien le habló a Kay de una operación ultra encubierta para recopilar inteligencia sobre ADM, unos 8 meses antes de la guerra, tan secreta que ni siquiera figuraba en los archivos. Era algo parecido al denominado Programa de Almas Muertas que se lanzó tras el desplome de la Unión Soviética, para ubicar y pagar a científicos soviéticos especializados en armas, que vivían fuera del país, con el fin de averiguar qué había estado ocurriendo de puertas para adentro.

En lo que respecta a Irak, la CIA había dirigido un programa clandestino de dos partes para tratar de desarrollar inteligencia confiable de fuentes humanas sobre las ADM. Durante los días de inspección de las Naciones Unidas en la década de los 90, la CIA se había hecho a una muy buena lista de los científicos iraquíes involucrados en investigación y producción de ADM. La primera parte de la operación implicaba contratar a científicos iraquíes que vivían fuera de Irak y pagarles, para establecer si conocían algo sobre programas de ADM. La segunda parte, que era más peligrosa, implicaba pagarles a iraquíes en Europa o Asia para que regresaran a Irak y hablaran con parientes que hubieran participado en programas de ADM en el pasado.

No se había conseguido pruebas sobre la existencia de ADM, pero la CIA estaba tan convencida de que Irak tenía estas armas, que la ausencia de pruebas se tomó como evidencia de que el programa estilo Almas Muertas no estaba funcionando. Después de haber hecho cerca de 120 contactos sin mayores avances, se puso fin al programa.

Cuando escuchó esto, Kay se molestó, porque las pruebas en contra no habían sido reportadas ni incluidas en el extenso expediente de inteligencia que le habían mostrado antes de iniciar su misión ese verano. "No creo que le informaran al presidente", dijo más tarde Kay. "No creo que le hayan informado a Powell. No creo que Condi haya preguntado ni que le hayan dicho nada"[14].

El 6 de diciembre de 2003, Rumsfeld andaba en uno de sus viajes relámpago por el Medio Oriente. Se detuvo en Bagdad, en cuyo aeropuerto se reunió con Bremer.

"Veamos", dijo Rumsfeld, "para mí es claro que su canal de reportes es ahora directo con el presidente y no a través de mí. Condi ha asumido el control de los asuntos políticos. Creo que es un error. La última vez que el CNS se inmiscuyó en temas operacionales, tuvimos el [caso] Irán-contras. Pero ella parece haberse metido en esto con ambos pies".

Se trataba de una acusación extraordinaria. El caso Irán-contras había sido el escándalo surgido en el gobierno de Reagan en torno a la venta secreta de armas a Irán y el desvío ilegal de millones de dólares de utilidades para ayudarles a los contrarrevolucionarios anticomunistas en Nicaragua. Las diversas investigaciones sobre el caso Irán-contras concluyeron unánimemente que el Consejo Nacional de Seguridad sólo debía participar en asuntos de política y coordinación, no en operaciones, y criticaron el trabajo encubierto.

Según Bremer, Rumsfeld agregó con una sonrisa tensa: "Me voy a marginar del proceso político. Que Condi y el CNS manejen las cosas. Eso podría hacerle a usted la vida un poco más fácil".

Por esta misma época, al salir un día de la Sala de Situaciones, Rice le pidió a Rumsfeld que llamara a Bremer para que se ocupara de algunos asuntos de rutina.

"No", dijo Rumsfeld. "Él no trabaja para mí".

"¿Entonces para quién trabaja?", preguntó Rice.

---

14. McLaughlin no creía que el programa fuera de gran alcance y consideraba que, ciertamente, no era concluyente. En su opinión, era ridículo pensar que se hubiera suprimido algo.

"Trabaja para usted", dijo Rumsfeld.

Rumsfeld me confirmó después, en una entrevista, que él percibía que Bremer sólo le reportaba a él "técnicamente, pero no en verdad".

"No llamaba mucho", dijo Rumsfeld refiriéndose a Bremer. "Estaba allá, en un entorno difícil, tomando muchas decisiones; su labor era difícil".

"¿Y percibía que era el hombre del presidente?", le pregunté, con las palabras mismas que Bremer había utilizado en su libro.

"Claro que sí. Y lo era. No era cuestión de percibir. Lo era".

A COMIENZOS DE DICIEMBRE, Newt Gingrich decidió crear cierta presión pública con sus quejas sobre Bremer. "Estaba lanzando una advertencia porque las cosas que habían empezado en septiembre no estaban sucediendo con suficiente rapidez", explicó después. Dio una entrevista a la revista *Newsweek* en la que dijo que Estados Unidos se estaba "despeñando por un precipicio" en Irak.

"Me dicen allá que CPA (la sigla en inglés de la ACP) significa 'Can't Produce Anything' (no podemos producir nada)", le dijo Gingrich a la revista. No criticó a Bremer personalmente, pero su argumento central era que se debía haber trasladado el gobierno a manos de los iraquíes mucho antes. Gingrich luego habló en *Meet the Press* el domingo 7 de diciembre de 2003, y dijo que el modelo de posguerra debería haber sido el que Estados Unidos había aplicado en Afganistán, donde instaló rápidamente a Hamid Karzai.

Los iraquíes querían su propio gobierno, dijo Gingrich. "Cuanto más tiempo mantengamos a los estadounidenses al frente y en el centro, mayor será el peligro de que los nacionalistas iraquíes decidan que deben ser antinorteamericanos".

Al día siguiente, Bremer llamó a Gingrich. "Usted no entiende", le dijo Bremer. No nos estamos despeñando por ningún precipicio. Aseguró que tenía las cosas bajo control. "¿Por qué no viene a ver?"

"Iré una semana", dijo Gingrich. Pero, como había estado en un sinnúmero de sesiones de información apresuradas, en su calidad de congresista visitante criticón, agregó: "No voy a ir para que me monten un espectáculo de mostrar durante un día".

Bremer estuvo de acuerdo y Rumsfeld y Abizaid lo aprobaron.

Sin embargo, una semana antes del viaje programado de Gingrich, Bremer le mandó decir con un asistente: "Estamos demasiado ocupados. No puede venir".

"Rumsfeld no estaba dispuesto a desautorizar a Bremer", dijo Gingrich después. "No estaban dispuestos a traerlo a casa de una manera que lo instara a convertirse en enemigo abierto del presidente". Por consiguiente, se sentían angustiados por "saber que no está funcionando y no ser capaces de idear la manera de cambiar la situación".

En opinión de Rumsfeld, la pregunta era por qué no podían hacer en Irak lo mismo que habían hecho en Afganistán. Sin duda, necesitaban alguna versión de Karzai, alguien a quienes los iraquíes pudieran reconocer como líder.

EL 13 DE DICIEMBRE, los militares estadounidenses capturaron a Saddam Hussein. El ex dictador estaba oculto en una caleta cerca de una granja en las afueras de Tikrit, 90 kilómetros al norte de Bagdad, donde había nacido en 1937.

"Damas y caballeros, ¡lo atrapamos!", anunció Bremer por televisión. Esto les enfatizó a los iraquíes que se trataba de un espectáculo estadounidense.

"Tenemos que aprovechar este triunfo", le dijo Bremer a su segundo al mando. "Podría ser el factor decisivo".

Más tarde le dijo a uno de sus asistentes: "Quizás ahora los sunitas moderados entiendan que el baathismo finalmente murió".

Pero no fue así. La violencia continuó, aunque los ataques se redujeron a cerca de 800 en diciembre.

EL GENERAL MYERS PENSABA que los primeros ocho meses de la ocupación de Irak habían sido relativamente tranquilos. Eso sólo probaba que él no estaba estacionado allí. En enero de 2004, él y Rumsfeld fueron a la Casa Blanca a informar a Bush sobre una serie de temas.

"A propósito", dijo Rumsfeld, "se presentó un incidente". Había acusaciones de abusos de la policía militar contra los prisioneros en Abu Ghraib, la antigua prisión fortaleza de Saddam. "Parece que hay fotos". Dijo que se estaba investigando el asunto. "Estamos en eso".

El 16 de enero, el teniente general Ricardo S. Sánchez emitió un comunicado de prensa en el que se anunciaba una investigación sobre "abuso contra internos en un centro de detención de las fuerzas de coalición". Los detalles específicos podrían obstaculizar la investigación, decía el comunicado.

LA FRUSTRACIÓN QUE DESPERTABA Rumsfeld en Rice iba en aumento, aunque ella hacía todo lo posible por disimularla. En un momento dado, el presidente había decidido que los cientos de sospechosos de terrorismo detenidos en la base estadounidense de Guantánamo, en Cuba, eran combatientes al margen de la ley que podían ser juzgados por un tribunal militar, sin acceso al sistema de cortes federales de Estados Unidos. Esto significaba que habían sido entregados al Departamento de Defensa, pero Rumsfeld no iba a iniciar el proceso del tribunal. El secretario de Defensa se mostraba reacio. Rice había supervisado una compleja revisión de los organismos, que había tardado varias semanas y había implicado a los principales abogados del gobierno. Su objetivo era hacer que el presidente le ordenara a Rumsfeld que iniciara el proceso del tribunal.

El fiscal general John Ashcroft se había convertido en un fuerte defensor interno del inicio del proceso del tribunal. De una u otra forma, los casos de los detenidos iban a terminar siendo revisados por las cortes federales. Si no tenían un proceso de tribunal verosímil en funcionamiento, dijo Ashcroft, el Departamento de Justicia se vería en serios aprietos cuando trataran de defender el sistema en las cortes de apelación federales.

En una reunión del CNS con el presidente, Rice empezó a revisar un largo documento sobre los temas que todos deberían haber leído y entendido.

Rumsfeld se recostó en el asiento y dejó ver que no estaba prestando mucha atención. El presidente también parecía aburrido. Pero Rice siguió.

"Don, ¿qué opina sobre esto?", preguntó Bush, interrumpiendo a Rice.

"Son tipos malos", contestó Rumsfeld. Creía que los estadounidenses se inclinaban a pensar automáticamente en los derechos de los acusados o los encarcelados. El problema era mantener a los terroristas arrestados por fuera del campo de batalla y luego interrogarlos para obtener información de inteligencia útil. El gobierno tenía que buscar la manera de hacer que la opinión pública entendiera esto.

Bush estuvo de acuerdo. ¿Cómo? ¿Cuándo?

"No soy abogado", les recordó Rumsfeld. No lo podía hacer y no lo iba a hacer.

La discusión se fue diluyendo y la decisión quedó pendiente. Algunos de los asistentes a la reunión del CNS se sorprendieron al ver la deferencia con que el presidente trató a Rumsfeld. Era como si Rice y el CNS tuvieran un proceso serio y formal en marcha mientras el presidente y Rumsfeld tenían otro, informal y dominante.

EN ENERO DE 2004 el general Abuzaid se quejó ante Tenet y Bob Richer sobre Rumsfeld y Steve Cambone, el jefe de inteligencia del Pentágono. "El mundo no es tan color de rosa como dicen Cambone y el secretario de Defensa", señaló; "tienen que dejarme dirigir la guerra". La política draconiana de *desbaathificación* era absurda y de autoderrota. "Tenemos que cortarle la cabeza a la hidra pero no el cuerpo". En cuanto a Bremer, Abizaid agregó: "No puedo hablar con él".

En otro momento, Abizaid les dijo a altos funcionarios de la CIA que dirigir la guerra contra los sunitas, que estaban liderando la insurgencia en Irak, no iba a funcionar. "No se puede matar a todos los sunitas en el interior".

El rey Abdullah de Jordania visitó al presidente de Estados Unidos en enero de 2004. Jordania sólo compartía una frontera de 80 kilómetros con Irak, dijo Abdullah, pero "me preocupa mucho tener una insurgencia del otro lado".

"Entiendo", dijo Bush, "pero mis generales me dicen que el 85% del país está en perfecta calma. Sólo el 15% tiene algunos problemas, y éstos son de bajo nivel".

Los informes confidenciales indicaban que había habido cerca de 800 ataques iniciados por el enemigo en ese mes de enero, más o menos la misma cifra que en diciembre.

Tenet le pidió a David Kay que se abstuviera de anunciar su renuncia del Grupo de Inspección de Irak hasta después del discurso presidencial del Estado de la Unión, el 20 de enero. Kay aceptó. En ese discurso, el presidente repitió cuidadosamente las palabras que Kay había pronunciado ante el Congreso en octubre, distanciándose notoriamente de las acusaciones que había hecho el año anterior sobre el estado de los programas de armas de Irak. Se refirió, no a las ADM, sino a las "actividades de programas relacionados con armas de destrucción masiva".

Kay se reunió en privado con algunos senadores y representantes republicanos, para instarlos a imitar al presidente. No sigan hablando de las ADM, les dijo. "Tengan mucho cuidado, porque no van a encontrarlas. Eso no quiere decir que aquel régimen no debería haber sido reemplazado, que a ese régimen no se le pueda montar un caso sobre ADM en la ONU; pero no se podría hacerlo sobre las armas de verdad".

El 23 de enero de 2004, Kay presentó su renuncia oficial. Esa noche un periodista de la agencia noticiosa Reuters averiguó el número telefónico de su casa y lo llamó.

"Creo que no existían", dijo Kay cuando le preguntaron sobre las ADM. "Todo el mundo hablaba de un arsenal producido después de que finalizó la última Guerra del Golfo, y no creo que hubiera un programa de producción a gran escala en los años 90".

Bill Harlow, el vocero de Tenet en la CIA, llamó a Kay. Estaba iracundo. Se suponía que Kay iba a seguir vinculado a la organización como consultor y asesor *senior*. El mensaje era que debía mantener la reserva. Tenet llegó hasta decirle a Powell que la CIA "lo mantendría en la granja".

Kay testificó públicamente ante la Comisión de Servicios Armados del Senado algunos días después, el 28 de enero, y dijo lo que sería el titular principal y la cubierta de *Newsweek*. "Casi todos estábamos equivocados, y, desde luego, me incluyo también". Kay dijo que el 85% del trabajo ya estaba hecho y que no tenía razón alguna para creer que fueran a encontrar arsenales de ADM en Irak. "Es importante reconocer el fracaso", dijo Kay, y añadió que se requería una investigación externa.

El día siguiente, aproximadamente a las 10:30 de la mañana, Kay estaba en su casa de Virginia cuando lo llamó Rice para invitarlo a almorzar con el presidente. Kay disponía de cerca de hora y media, de modo que se apresuró a ducharse, vestirse y conducir hasta la ciudad, a 48 kilómetros de distancia.

El almuerzo era con Bush, Cheney, Rice y Andy Card, en un pequeño comedor ubicado en el Salón Oval.

¿Cómo llegó a esa conclusión?, quiso saber Bush. ¿Y por qué la inteligencia estadounidense no se había dado cuenta?

"No nos dimos cuenta, porque los iraquíes se comportaban como si tuvieran armas", dijo Kay. "Y no fuimos lo bastante listos como para entender que lo más difícil en materia de inteligencia se presenta cuando el comportamiento sigue siendo consistente pero las razones subyacentes cambian". Saddam no tenía ADM pero quería aparentar que sí las tenía. Su objetivo era engañar. Kay dijo que creía que Saddam había decidido deshacerse de sus ADM porque eran demasiado fáciles de descubrir.

Tomemos los tubos de aluminio, dijo. El alto costo, el secreto, las especificaciones más estrictas y alguna información de inteligencia, en el sentido de que el propio Saddam había supervisado la compra de los tubos, habían llevado a la conclusión de que su destino era un programa nuclear.

Pero Kay y los inspectores habían entrevistado ingenieros, revisado los archivos y hallado los contratos. Los tubos eran para artillería convencional, una adaptación de un sistema de misiles italiano. Explicó que el propergol no era lo suficientemente potente, pero el contrato para comprarlo no se podía modificar, porque el hombre que dirigía la fábrica de propergol era cercano al hijo de Saddam. Trataron de hacer tubos más delgados –lo cual requería especificaciones más exigentes– para que funcionara el propergol. Todos los involucrados dijeron que eso era bueno, porque las especificaciones más exigentes subían el precio de los tubos. Los involucrados ganaban dinero mediante comisiones, de modo que, cuanto más costosos, mejor. Los contratos eran de costos más honorarios, a semejanza de los contratos de muchos sistemas de armas estadounidenses.

Kay les dijo que se había hecho todo tipo de compras a través de canales clandestinos y el mercado negro, y no mediante el mecanismo de control de exportaciones de la ONU. Los analistas de inteligencia supusieron que debía haber una razón, y que la razón era que esos elementos eran para programas de armas prohibidas.

"El problema es que intentaban conseguir casi todo clandestinamente", dijo Kay. "Lo podían hacer porque la familia recibía una tajada. El mercado negro estaba esencialmente dirigido por Uday Hussein y sus amigos".

Más importante aun, la CIA no había entendido cuán corrupto era el sistema ni el deterioro de la sociedad iraquí, dijo Kay. Las cosas habían empeorado hasta el punto de que el régimen mismo no era capaz de desarrollar de manera útil programas de ADM. El grupo de Kay les preguntaba a los iraquíes durante las investigaciones: "¿Cómo pudieron hacer esto? ¿Por qué mintieron?", y la respuesta era: "¡Todo el mundo mentía! Todo el mundo iba por su cuenta". La corrupción era tan severa y generalizada que, simplemente, afectaba la capacidad del gobierno de funcionar.

Bush quiso saber por qué creía Kay que Saddam no había, simplemente, demostrado que no tenía ADM desde hacía mucho tiempo. ¿Por qué había arriesgado su vida entera, su gobierno, en vez de limitarse a abrir las puertas?

Kay dijo que pensaba que Saddam nunca había creído que Estados Unidos en verdad invadiría su país. Más importante aun, temía a los chiítas y kurdos que vivían en Irak más de lo que temía a Estados Unidos. Sabía que aquellos también lo temían a él porque pensaban que tenía ADM.

"Como es preciso reconocer, los regímenes totalitarios, por lo general, terminan temiendo a su propia gente más de lo que temen las amenazas externas. Ésa es la historia de los regímenes totalitarios", dijo Kay. "No nos dimos cuenta de eso". Además, agregó, era muy fácil que no se dieran cuenta porque tenían muy poca inteligencia humana y dependían más bien de la recopilación técnica de información.

Cheney guardó silencio mientras Bush hababa. Quería saber más acerca de lo que Kay pensaba sobre el proceso de inteligencia de Estados Unidos.

"La enfermedad de la comunidad de inteligencia es el énfasis excesivo en la inteligencia de actualidad", es decir, en lo que estaba ocurriendo durante ese día o esa semana, en comparación con una inteligencia estratégica de más largo plazo. "El análisis de actualidad es mejor si uno se conecta con CNN o lee la prensa", dijo. "Francamente hablando, la prensa hace un mejor trabajo".

"Un buen ejemplo de esto es el PDB", el *President's Daily Brief* (Informe diario del presidente). "¿Comprende que, si responde positivamente a cualquier tema, sólo recibirá información sobre ese tema durante el siguiente mes, más o menos?" El hecho de que el presidente manifieste interés le asigna prioridad al tema en la comunidad de inteligencia. "George lo retoma y lo impulsa, y seguirá figurando. Responde al tema. Si responde a un ítem del PDB, se va a quedar ahí durante mucho tiempo con más y más información".

El interés del presidente sugiere que es importante, y el flujo de inteligencia simplemente se sale de control.

Bush se dirigió a Cheney. "Por eso me siguen contando sobre ese HP de Mozambique", dijo. "Una vez tuve que hacer una pregunta sobre eso, y me siguen dando información".

Bush se preguntó cómo la CIA y la inteligencia estadounidense pudieron haberse equivocado tanto.

"Uno de los problemas de un director es que, si está dentro del proceso político, pierde el equilibrio", contestó Kay. "Por ejemplo, George viene aquí todos los días para la sesión informativa, e inevitablemente eso transmite una sensación del proceso político a la gente en la agencia".

"¿Cree que no debo llamar a George aquí todos los días?", preguntó Bush.

Kay pensó que quizás se estaba excediendo. "No, pero hay un costo", dijo. "Por favor, no le diga a George que yo le dije esto. Reconozca que el problema es la inteligencia de actualidad. Cuando usted expresa interés en asuntos de actualidad, impulsa a la comunidad de la inteligencia".

Las preguntas seguían fluyendo. Kay casi no pudo tocar su almuerzo. Card preguntó: "Usted nos habló sobre el servicio de inteligencia de Estados Unidos. ¿Quién, según piensa usted, tiene un servicio de inteligencia realmente bueno?"

"De acuerdo con mi experiencia, no son los británicos ni los israelíes, pese a su reputación", dijo Kay. El M16 y el Mossad eran leyendas en el mundo de los servicios de inteligencia, pero Kay dijo que no siempre se había impresionado con la utilidad de sus productos. "A mi juicio, el mejor es el chino".

"Sí, siempre están tratando de robarnos nuestros secretos técnicos", dijo Bush.

DESPUÉS, KAY REFLEXIONÓ sobre lo que no había dicho. Creía que el presidente afrontaba un problema más grande que el simple fracaso de la inteligencia en Irak. Quedaba con un servicio de inteligencia en el que no podía ni debía confiar para gran cosa.

Al día siguiente, Rice le pidió a Kay que volviera a la Casa Blanca.

"Hubo algo que le dijo al presidente que realmente me tocó un nervio", le dijo ella. Le había impresionado lo que había dicho sobre cómo una de las cosas más difíciles de hacer en materia de inteligencia era distinguir un cambio real, entender por qué alguien sigue haciendo la misma cosa pero por razones diferentes.

"He debido ser más lista", dijo Rice. "Cuando lo escuché decir eso, comprendí que era exactamente lo mismo que había sucedido en la RDA", la

República Democrática Alemana, o Alemania Oriental, que colapsó en 1988. "He debido darme cuenta por eso".

"Sí", respondió Kay. "Tengo un amigo alemán que me dijo, 'no se sientan mal por lo que no vieron en Irak, porque nosotros ni siquiera pudimos saber que la RDA no podía recoger su propia basura, sino después de que cayó'". Los servicios de inteligencia, dijo, no hacen un buen trabajo al tratar de entender el lado suave de las sociedades: cuán bien está funcionando el gobierno y las actitudes fundamentales de la gente.

POWELL FUE A *The Washington Post* el 2 de febrero de 2004 para una entrevista con un grupo de periodistas y editores, entre quienes no me incluía yo. Le preguntaron cuál habría sido su postura con respecto a la guerra, si hubiera sabido que no había arsenales de ADM.

"La ausencia de arsenales cambia el cálculo político", dijo Powell. "Cambia la respuesta que se obtiene".

Sus palabras fueron el artículo principal del *Post* al día siguiente, bajo el titular: "Powell dice que nuevos datos podrían haber afectado la decisión de guerra".

Temprano, esa mañana, en el Salón Oval, Bush se desahogó con Rice y otros colaboradores. El presidente decía en público que no leía la prensa, pero esa mañana sí lo había hecho. "Esta mañana me desperté y leí la prensa y descubrí que soy la única persona en Washington dispuesta a defenderme", dijo.

Rice llamó a Powell. Ella y el presidente estaban "furiosos", dijo. Powell "les había dado a los demócratas una herramienta excelente". Sus comentarios ocupaban los titulares de prensa en el mundo entero. La posición pública de Bush era que aún no se sabía nada concreto sobre las ADM. De modo que Powell tenía que volver a hablar en público y retractarse de lo que había dicho, y decir cinco veces que la decisión de ir a la guerra había sido "correcta".

MESES DESPUÉS, Kay se encontró con Tenet en una conferencia, en Aspen, Colorado. Era evidente que Tenet sabía lo que Kay les había dicho a Bush y a Rice. Kay trató de explicarle que sólo había expresado su opinión profesional sobre el tema de la inteligencia. No se había propuesto criticar a la CIA.

"George, yo en verdad lo estimo", dijo Kay.

"Pues yo también lo estimo, David", contestó Tenet. "Pero parte de esto se ha vuelto un poco personal".

KAY CONSIDERABA que, con respecto a los fracasos en materia de inteligencia, había culpas suficientes como para distribuir entre varios. Parte de la culpa, sin duda, recaía en los hombros de Rice. Su función había sido proteger la espalda del presidente, y no lo había hecho.

Tenet también era culpable. Había sido enganchado, no como un profesional de inteligencia, sino como una especie de líder del cuadro más grande, alguien que mejorara la moral y reconstruyera el servicio clandestino. Había sido víctima de su mayor debilidad, según creía Kay, que era la falta de afinidad con el monótono y detallado análisis de inteligencia.

Pero el verdadero villano de la CIA, en opinión de Kay, era McLaughlin. Tenet se había abierto camino en el lado político del mundo de la inteligencia, pero McLaughlin llevaba más de 30 años en la agencia. Era el profesional, y Kay consideraba que también había sido quien con más obstinación se había aferrado a la creencia de que Irak tenía laboratorios móviles de armas biológicas. También recordó que, en cierto momento, McLaughlin le había dicho que no importaba lo que Kay dijera o encontrara, pues él siempre iba a creer que los tubos de aluminio habían sido parte de un programa nuclear. McLaughlin había tomado la información sobre los tubos de aluminio y la había convertido en algo propio; grave error, en alguien que ocupa un cargo tan alto como el de subdirector.

McLaughlin reconocía que los no conocedores quizás pudieran pensar que había tomado como propio el recuento de los tubos de aluminio. Pero era porque estaba comprometido. Creía que los subalternos en quienes confiaba no habían sido lo suficientemente agresivos al expresar sus dudas. Sean cuales fueren las excusas por la inteligencia con respecto a las ADM, él, Tenet y la CIA habían fallado. Tenet más tarde reconocería en privado que la CIA no había tenido nada en qué basarse.

26

En el piso superior de la Corte Federal, en la Pennsylvania Avenue de Washington, uno de los legados perdurables de la Revolución de Reagan caminaba en sus amplias oficinas. El juez superior Laurence H. Silberman, de la Corte de Apelaciones de Estados Unidos para el Distrito de Columbia, seguía de cerca la controversia sobre las ADM en la prensa. Silberman, de 68 años, trabajaba en la segunda corte más importante y prestigiosa de Estados Unidos, después de la Corte Suprema. La corte había sido un bastión liberal hasta que Reagan hizo una serie de nombramientos conservadores en el circuito del D. C.: Antonin Scalia, quien había pasado a la Corte Suprema; Robert Bork, cuyo nombramiento en la Corte Suprema fue rechazado por el Senado; Kenneth Starr, quien más tarde fue el abogado independiente que investigó la relación del presidente Clinton con Mónica Lewinsky, y Silberman, en 1985.

Todavía estaba allí, casi dos decenios después, en calidad *senior*, lo que significaba que sólo tenía que trabajar durante tres meses al año.

Silberman consideraba tanto a Cheney como a Rumsfeld amigos personales cercanos. Había sido vicefiscal general durante los últimos meses del gobierno de Nixon y fiscal general encargado durante parte del gobierno de Ford, y había trabajado de cerca con los actuales vicepresidente y secretario de Defensa.

Silberman sabía un poco sobre inteligencia. En la pared de uno de los recintos de su oficina había una fotografía suya con el presidente Ford y Rumsfeld. En esa época, Rumsfeld, que se desempeñaba como jefe de gabinete de la Casa Blanca, había tratado de persuadir a Silberman, entonces fiscal general encargado, de vincularse a la Casa Blanca como zar de inteligencia. Cuando Rumsfeld mencionó vagamente la posibilidad de nombrarlo director de la CIA, seis meses después de tomar posesión de su cargo en la Casa Blanca, Silberman rechazó el ofrecimiento. No creía que fuera posible dirigir la inteligencia desde la Casa Blanca ni siquiera durante seis meses. Más de un cuarto de siglo después, fue Silberman quien le tomó el juramento a Rumsfeld como secretario de Defensa, en el Salón Oval, el sexto día de la presidencia de Bush, el 26 de enero de 2001.

Silberman no se sorprendió, pocos días después del testimonio "estábamos casi todos equivocados" de David Kay ante el Congreso, cuando lo llamó por teléfono el vicepresidente. En una entrevista, Silberman recordó la conversación.

"Queremos una comisión que examine la comunidad de inteligencia", le dijo Cheney a Silberman, "con el fin de determinar si la comunidad de inteligencia evaluó apropiadamente el asunto de las armas de destrucción masiva en Irak". Quería que Silberman fuera copresidente de la comisión.

Silberman tenía la confianza suficiente para dirigirse al vicepresidente de Estados Unidos por su nombre de pila. "Creo que eso significa, Dick, que tendría que renunciar a la corte".

Cheney dijo que eso creía.

"Déjeme pensarlo y conversar sobre el asunto con Ricky", dijo Silberman. Ricky, su esposa, que también era abogada, había trabajado con la esposa del vicepresidente, Lynne Cheney, en el Foro Independiente de Mujeres, un grupo de mujeres conservadoras que había apoyado el nombramiento de Clarence Thomas en la Corte Suprema.

A Silberman le gustaba su cargo, pero consideró, dijo, que en tiempos de guerra debía acatar el llamado del vicepresidente. La mañana siguiente, llamó a Cheney y le dijo que asumiría el cargo. Un día después, según dijo, se reunió con el asesor jurídico de la Casa Blanca, Alberto Gonzáles, y con otros abogados de la Casa Blanca y del Departamento de Justicia. Le tenían una noticia grata: un juez *senior* no tenía vedado aceptar un nombramiento en este tipo de comisiones presidenciales.

"Eso lo hace bastante fácil, pues estaba dispuesto a renunciar", dijo Silberman.

El presidente Bush llamó a Tom Foley, el ex presidente demócrata de la Cámara de Representantes, quien ejercía ahora como abogado en Washington. Necesitaba a un demócrata para presidir conjuntamente con Silberman la comisión, para que esta fuera bipartidista. Foley aceptó.

El 5 de febrero, Silberman fue a la Casa Blanca para reunirse con Card y hablar sobre los detalles del cargo.

"Acabo de recibir la llamada telefónica más extraña de Tom Foley; me expresó que no podía aceptar el cargo", dijo Card. La noticia sobre la participación de aquél en la comisión se había filtrado a la prensa y Foley había sido presionado por los demócratas en el Congreso para que no participara. La líder de minorías en la Cámara, Nancy Pelosi, demócrata de San Francisco, había convencido a Foley de que se retractara de su aceptación, dijo Card, argumentando que la comisión presidencial estaba diseñada para cubrir políticamente a Bush por el hecho de no haber hallado ADM casi un año después de la invasión de Irak.

"Una comisión nombrada y controlada por la Casa Blanca no tendrá la independencia o la credibilidad necesarias para investigar estos temas", escribieron Pelosi y dos demócratas veteranos del Senado, el líder de minorías Tom Daschle y el senador John D. Rockefeller IV, el principal demócrata en la Comisión de Inteligencia del Senado, en una carta dirigida a Bush. "Incluso, algunos de sus propios pronunciamientos, y también los del vicepresidente Cheney, necesitan un escrutinio independiente".

En privado, habían convencido a Foley de no prestar su nombre para eso. Card dijo que el presidente estaba decepcionado.

Bush y Cheney fueron a la oficina de Card.

"¿Qué piensa, Larry?", preguntó el presidente. "¿Quiere ser el único presidente?".

"No creo que eso sea conveniente", contestó Silberman. "Me nombraron como republicano. Seré percibido como republicano. Creo que debe haber un copresidente".

"Yo también lo creo", dijo Bush.

Bush, Cheney, Card y Silberman se dedicaron a pensar en quién podría presidir conjuntamente la comisión, alguien que pudiera ofrecerle algo de equilibrio político y cubrirlos a ellos políticamente.

¿Qué tal Chuck Robb?, sugirió Bush. Charles S. Robb era un ex gobernador y senador demócrata de Virginia, yerno de Lyndon Johnson. Robb había sido capitán de Marina en Vietnam y, como senador durante 12 años, entre 1989 y 2001, había formado parte de las principales comisiones relacionadas con seguridad nacional: relaciones exteriores, fuerzas armadas e inteligencia.

A Robb se le consideraba demócrata moderado, y hasta conservador. En Virginia se le tenía como casi republicano. Había apoyado la Guerra del Golfo Pérsico en 1991 y había criticado la decisión del presidente Clinton de no utilizar tropas terrestres en Kosovo en 1999.

El presidente llamó a Robb, quien aceptó el cargo.

Bush, Cheney, Card y Silberman examinaron algunas listas de nombres para conformar la comisión. Silberman sabía que iban a necesitar por lo menos un demócrata verdaderamente liberal, y sugirió a la juez Patricia Wald, que había sido nombrada por Carter y con quien él había trabajado en la corte de apelaciones federal. Ambos se ubicaban en extremos opuestos del espectro ideológico, pero Silberman dijo que sentía un gran respeto por ella.

"Celo, inteligencia, coraje e integridad", dijo.

"Pues, usted decide", respondió Card.

Más tarde, cuando Karl Rove supo sobre los demócratas que integrarían la comisión, se sorprendió muchísimo.

"¿Pat Wald?", le preguntó Rove a Bush con incredulidad. "¿No recuerda, señor Presidente? En la era antediluviana ella era comunista".

Bush le dijo a Rice que no quería una investigación del Congreso que se pareciera a las comisiones de Church y Pike después de Watergate, en 1975-1976, que expusieron el espionaje de la CIA y la Agencia de Seguridad Nacional a ciudadanos de Estados Unidos, las pruebas de dopaje y los complots para asesinar líderes extranjeros, entre ellos el cubano Fidel Castro. El presidente creía que esas investigaciones habían sido cacerías de brujas. Habían desmoralizado a la CIA y habían terminado por limitar el poder presidencial.

Los líderes demócratas de la Cámara y el Senado querían moldear la investigación sobre las ADM en forma similar a la Comisión del 9/11, creada por ley, para la cual el presidente y el Congreso nombraban, cada uno, a la mitad de sus miembros. El senador por Massachusetts John F. Kerry, quien estaba surgiendo como líder en la contienda por la nominación demócrata para la presidencia, pidió una investigación privada sobre la inteligencia referida a las ADM.

"Esto va al meollo de por qué la nación entró en guerra", dijo. "Si hay esa clase de falla, esa clase de separación entre la verdad que la CIA le dice a la Casa Blanca y lo que realmente sucede, entonces tenemos que independizar esa investigación de la Casa Blanca para que el pueblo estadounidense sepa la verdad".

El presidente no estaba dispuesto a ceder el control sobre la investigación. A la 1:30 de la tarde del viernes 6 de febrero, subió al podio en la sala de prensa de la Casa Blanca y anunció su intención de firmar una orden ejecutiva que nombraba a nueve personas en la Comisión Silberman-Robb. Tendrían amplias facultades para examinar no sólo la inteligencia sobre ADM en Irak, sino para estudiar la inteligencia sobre ADM en el mundo entero y examinar todas las capacidades y organizaciones de inteligencia de Estados Unidos.

En seguida, Bush agregó: "Los miembros de la comisión presentarán su informe el 31 de marzo de 2005". Eso sería cinco meses después de las elecciones presidenciales.

"Se entendía claramente que no se nos iba a pedir que evaluáramos el uso que había hecho el gobierno de la información de inteligencia", recordó después Silberman. "Y, francamente, si esa hubiera sido la misión, yo no habría querido aceptar el cargo. Era demasiado político. Todo el mundo sabía lo que el presidente y el vicepresidente habían dicho sobre la inteligencia. Pueden hacer sus propios juicios sobre si eso fue apropiado o justo o lo que sea".

Unos pocos demócratas manifestaron su indignación por la restricción. El representante Henry Waxman, demócrata de California y veterano con 29 años de ejercicio en la Cámara, dijo que a la comisión "le han dicho que haga caso omiso del elefante que está en medio de la habitación, que es la manera como el presidente Bush, el vicepresidente Dick Cheney y otros altos funcionarios del gobierno utilizaron y maltrataron la inteligencia". El senador Harry Reid, el demócrata número dos, dijo que la comisión había sido nombrada "para proteger al presidente".

EL PRÍNCIPE BANDAR REGRESÓ al Salón Oval el viernes 20 de febrero de 2004, con el fin de reunirse con Bush, Rice y Card. Los sauditas habían recibido un mensaje de la esposa de Saddam, que estaba en Jordania, en el que se solicitaba permiso para que ella y sus hijas pudieran visitar el lugar sagrado de La Meca en el Reino Saudí. Lo iban a aprobar, pero la visita sería secreta.

Luego Bandar informó que el príncipe heredero estaba comprometido con sus reformas políticas y económicas. Iba a ampliar la participación a todos los sauditas. "Pero estamos pidiendo que Estados Unidos mengüe su continua retórica sobre este tema para que los individuos sauditas no crean que lo estamos haciendo debido a la presión ejercida por Estados Unidos", dijo Bandar.

Bush repitió su aprecio por las ideas del príncipe heredero y por sus esfuerzos de reforma democrática. "Quizás la rapidez de este proceso se podría acelerar un poco", dijo Bush, conviniendo en que las reformas tenían que ser internas. Luego agradeció a Bandar por lo que estaban haciendo los sauditas con el petróleo: esencialmente, inundar el mercado y tratar de mantener el precio lo más bajo posible. Manifestó su aprecio por esta política y por el impacto que podría tener durante el año electoral.

Sobre un nuevo e importante tema, Bush dijo que Estados Unidos tenía un programa de US $3.000 millones de ayuda para Pakistán. El general Pervez Musharraf, presidente de Pakistán, estaba en una posición precaria. El 11 de diciembre, y de nuevo el 25 del mismo mes, Musharraf se había salvado de ser asesinado.

"Pakistán necesita desesperadamente 26 helicópteros que cuestan cerca de US $250 millones", dijo Bush. "Como presentar el programa ante el Congreso tomaría mucho tiempo", preguntó si su amigo, "el príncipe heredero, podría pagar por estos helicópteros".

Los helicópteros Bell modelo 412EP, compatibles con NVG, son aeronaves para operaciones especiales, ideales para rastrear terroristas y asesinos en potencia; en otras palabras, a Osama bin Laden y los violentos opositores de Musharraf. Son helicópteros de buen desempeño, que han sido utilizados por las fuerzas armadas británicas y canadienses.

Bandar dijo que tendría que transmitirle la solicitud al príncipe heredero.

Cuatro días después, el Pentágono le rindió a Bandar un informe detallado sobre la flota de helicópteros. El informe escrito convenció a Bandar. "Estas aeronaves prestarán servicio y apoyo operacional para promover los intereses estratégicos de Estados Unidos y sus aliados en la región". El príncipe heredero pronto aceptó y Arabia Saudita pagó US $235 millones por 24 helicópteros Bell para el ejército paquistaní, en un contrato que incluía un programa de capacitación y mantenimiento, así como representantes técnicos y piezas de repuesto, según consta en archivos sauditas.

Los sauditas ya antes habían satisfecho peticiones especiales de presidentes estadounidenses. En los años 80, el asesor nacional de seguridad de Reagan le había pedido a Bandar que organizara la entrega de cerca de US $22 millones de financiación encubierta con destino a los *contras* nicaragüenses, los "luchadores de la libertad" favoritos de Reagan, después de que el Congreso suspendió la ayuda para la contrarrevolución. En esta ocasión la petición no era, al menos en este caso, de dineros encubiertos, pero el precio de la amistad y de los negocios conjuntos era mayor, diez veces mayor.

Para febrero de 2004, Bremer ya se había plegado en el tema del antiguo ejército de Saddam. Le dijo a un dirigente iraquí: "La coalición no tiene una objeción de principio contra el antiguo personal del ejército. Cerca del 80% del nuevo ejército iraquí y del cuerpo de defensa civil está compuesto por antiguos soldados. Todos los oficiales y suboficiales lo son". Los oficiales y los suboficiales eran los que inquietaban a Bremer y Slocombe. Se creía que tenían conexiones baathistas. Ahora *toda* la dirigencia del nuevo ejército provenía del antiguo ejército.

Ese mismo mes, el general Abizaid propuso en una reunión del CNS empezar a introducir fuerzas estadounidenses en unidades militares iraquíes. Las tropas de Estados Unidos podían proveer liderazgo, inteligencia y comunicaciones.

"Don, eso es estupendo", dijo el presidente, dirigiéndose a Rumsfeld. Bush dijo que debían darle mucha publicidad al asunto porque eso demostraría que estaban trasladando la carga de la guerra a los iraquíes, que era exactamente el tema que quería enfatizar. "Es magnífico". Enseguida, Bush se dirigió a Dan Bartlett: "Bartlett, quiero un…".

"Pero, señor presidente, todavía no he aprobado esto", interrumpió Rumsfeld. Consideraba de suma importancia investigar las unidades iraquíes que iban a recibir tropas estadounidenses. En otras guerras, oficiales norteamericanos habían sido asesinados por sus propios soldados. ¿Qué tipo de salvaguardas podían utilizar para impedir que las fuerzas estadounidenses fueran asesinadas por insurgentes u otros enemigos en unidades iraquíes? "Es una recomendación para mí, y cuando yo me sienta satisfecho con ella se la transmitiré, señor presidente".

"Muy bien", dijo Bush. "Lo entiendo, pero cuando la apruebe, si la aprueba, hágamelo saber para que la podamos aprovechar debidamente".

Frank Miller, del equipo del CNS, había asistido a la reunión, y luego buscó a Hadley.

"Steve", dijo, "estamos introduciendo gente en unidades iraquíes". Estaba en contacto con oficiales que se hallaban en Irak, y eso ya se estaba haciendo, incluso si no era un programa oficial del Pentágono.

"No", dijo Hadley, con la esperanza de que no fuera cierto.

"Steve, confíe en mí. Soy Frank. Estoy hablando con gente que sabe lo que está sucediendo. Estamos haciéndolo".

"Está bien", dijo Hadley. "Gracias".

Más tarde, Miller conversó con uno de los generales de cuatro estrellas del Pentágono. "¿Por qué no aprueba esto Rumsfeld?", preguntó el general. "¿El presidente está interviniendo y diciendo 'no lo hagan'?".

"No, todo lo contrario", dijo Miller. "El presidente quiere hacerlo. El presidente quiere aprovechar esto".

Rumsfeld finalmente aprobó, bien que mal, la introducción de fuerzas, sin decir mucho. Más tarde, esto se convirtió en el principal método utilizado por Estados Unidos para mejorar la capacidad de combate de las tropas iraquíes. La noticia se fue publicando poco a poco en algunos artículos de prensa, pero no recibió gran publicidad como, había querido Bush.

RICE ESTABA ANSIOSA de información e inteligencia. Quería saber qué estaba pasando realmente "allá". Cada rato le decía a Frank Miller: "Consígame más. Tráigame más".

En marzo de 2004, envió a Miller a Irak para que averiguara qué estaba pasando realmente. Él viajó como representante de ella, pero trató de minimizar su papel en el CNS. Eso no le sería útil, pensó. Quería evitar presentaciones maquilladas, calibradas para impresionar, y quizás engañar, a visitantes de Washington. No pidió reunirse con Bremer. No creía que le sería de ayuda, pero tampoco quería arriesgarse a que no lo recibiera. Tal era la independencia percibida de Bremen con respecto a la supervisión del CNS.

A Miller le sorprendió cómo la Autoridad Provisional de Coalición se había convertido en una ciudad ermitaña, instalada en la Zona Verde. Le explicó a uno de los oficiales de la Autoridad que planeaba viajar en avión por el país para visitar a los comandantes de las divisiones militares estadounidenses que estaban al mando de las decenas de miles de soldados de Estados Unidos.

"Caramba", dijo el oficial de la Autoridad. "Ojalá nosotros pudiéramos hacer eso. Ojalá pudiéramos ver el país".

Eso era diciente, pensó Miller. Había una sensación de letargo; parecían un grupo de basquetbolistas pasándose la pelota, una y otra vez, todos renuentes a encestarla. Era marzo y la entrega estaba programada para junio, pensó. No era el momento para seguir haciendo pases sino para encestar.

Miller y las dos personas que había llevado consigo –el coronel retirado del ejército Jeff Jones, del CNS, y un coronel del ejército en servicio activo, del Estado Mayor Conjunto– se conectaron con la 1ª División Acorazada, establecida en Bagdad, cuyo subcomandante, un general de una estrella de nombre Mark Hertling, era un viejo amigo de Miller desde su época en el Pentágono. El grupo se unió a una patrulla Humvee en un área justo al sur del famoso tugurio chiíta de Bagdad, Ciudad Sadr. Pobreza a gritos, pensó Miller; sin agua potable, con pocas alcantarillas en funcionamiento. La gente vivía en covachas y arrojaba basura y excrementos humanos en sus jardines del frente.

Los soldados estadounidenses ahora parecían estar actuando tanto como ingenieros que como militares en Ciudad Sadr y otros lugares, organizando puntos de distribución de agua y mejorando algunas carreteras. Pero el único dinero para financiar estos proyectos *ad hoc* provenía de los fondos de emergencia de los militares, denominados Programa de Respuesta de Emergencia del Comandante (CERP es su sigla en inglés). Miller tomó nota de que iban a tener que aumentar y agilizar estos fondos CERP –dinero disponible para los comandantes de batallón y brigada–, pues eran los únicos gastos que parecían tener un impacto visible en la población.

Era asombroso, pensó Miller, que los iraquíes que veía parecieran, en general, amigables o, por lo menos, no antagónicos. Salían chiquillos sonrientes que saludaban y levantaban el pulgar mientras ellas pasaban. No era el dedo del medio, observó, sin darse cuenta de que en Irak mostrar el pulgar no era señal de aprobación, sino el equivalente del gesto norteamericano que se hace con el dedo del medio.

Miller se dirigió luego a Tikrit, donde operaba la 4ª División de Infantería y donde Saddam Hussein había sido capturado tres meses antes. Los altos oficiales de la división dijeron que creían haber quebrantado o capturado a gran parte del liderazgo mayor de la insurgencia. El sólo hecho de que los iraquíes estuvieran hablando a los estadounidenses era un indicio prometedor, y estaban obteniendo mejor información de inteligencia de los iraquíes, de muchas personas que llegaban con buenos datos. Nadie parecía querer regresar a las épocas de Saddam. Las divisiones estaban estableciendo el Cuerpo de Defensa Civil Iraquí, utilizando sus fondos de emergencia –nuevamente el dinero CERP, observó Miller– para comprar armas y uniformes.

En todas partes, Miller encontró que las unidades iraquíes sufrían de una grave escasez de vehículos y equipos de comunicaciones. Y las unidades del Cuerpo de Defensa Civil –cuya primera misión era proteger infraestructura valiosa, como bancos y otros edificios, liberando así a fuerzas mejor entrenadas para realizar tareas más difíciles– eran criaturas engendradas por las divisiones militares individuales de Estados Unidos. Una unidad tenía un programa de entrenamiento de una semana, otra, un programa de dos semanas, y una tercera lo había ampliado a tres semanas. Era ridículo. Un poco antes, ese mismo año, se enteró Miller, un general de dos estrellas había enviado un informe al Departamento de Defensa, en el que prácticamente rogaba que se impusiera un estándar nacional para los nuevos cuerpos iraquíes, pero sin resultado.

Miller registró en sus notas el comentario de un comandante de división: "¿Qué le pasa a Bagdad?", dijo el comandante, refiriéndose a la Autoridad Provisional de Coalición de Bremer. "¿Por qué no nos dan dinero para hacer esto, y para realizar los proyectos de reconstrucción que es preciso emprender?". Construir unidades iraquíes, tanto de policía como militares, y reconstruir la infraestructura del país eran prerrequisitos de una estrategia de salida para Estados Unidos. Pero había muy poco dinero, y muy poca coordinación para llevar a cabo correctamente la tarea.

Irak se veía y se percibía como una zona de guerra. Los ataques habían vuelto a aumentar, a cerca de 1.000 por mes. Todos los soldados que Miller vio llevaban un arma. Un comedor donde estaba comiendo Miller fue atacado con morteros. Cuando volaba en helicópteros, los artilleros de las puertas mantenían sus armas apuntando hacia abajo, contra blancos potenciales. Miller llevaba puesta una chaqueta blindada, y él y sus dos asistentes viajaban bajo la mirada vigilante de un diligente teniente joven de artillería de campo, de Kansas, a quien asignaron como escolta. Cuando se desplazaban por tierra, era en caravanas con Humvees y grandes vehículos de pasajeros, un artillero con ametralladora encima de los Humvees y el escolta con su M-16 apuntada desde la ventana. Era bueno por una parte –Miller se sentía bastante seguro–, pero, por otro, lado pensaba: "No nos estamos ganando ni los corazones ni las mentes de esta manera".

Desde Tikrit, Miller voló a Kirkuk, donde se conectó con una brigada de la 25ª División de Infantería, proveniente de Hawai. Fue a una estación de policía iraquí, donde el ejército de Estados Unidos estaba tratando de entrenar a los iraquíes para convertirlos en verdaderos agentes de policía. Bastante impresionante, pensó Miller, pero también escuchó acerca de los miles de maestros iraquíes que habían sido despedidos por orden de la *desbaathificación*. Era un verdadero dilema, porque en el Irak de Saddam se había exigido a todos los maestros que se unieran al partido Baath.

Miller se dirigió a la ciudad de Basora, en el extremo suroriental de Irak, que estaba bajo control británico. Un general de dos estrellas y un teniente general británicos le dieron lo que consideró un informe optimista sobre el gran éxito obtenido enseñando a la policía iraquí local a patrullar. Los agentes de policía locales no podían leer los mapas en inglés que les habían dado los británicos, dijeron, de modo que memorizaron sus rutas de patrullaje: salga de la estación y gire a la derecha, camine 10 cuadras hasta la plaza de mercado, gire a la derecha, camine 15 cuadras hacia la mezquita, gire a la derecha, y ese tipo de cosas.

Los oficiales británicos llevaron a Miller a la estación de policía iraquí para que recibiera información de un capitán británico.

"Cuénteme", le dijo Miller a un brigadier de policía iraquí, ya mayor y con sobrepeso, "¿qué hacen sus hombres cuando llegan a trabajar por la mañana?".

El iraquí dijo: "Bueno, ellos entran y se toman un café y aguardan aquí hasta que los envío a arrestar a alguien".

Miller miró duramente al general de dos estrellas y al teniente coronel británicos. "Muchachos, eso es lo que Saddam hacía", les dijo. "Me cuentan toda esta mierda sobre cómo han reformado a la policía. No han hecho absolutamente nada".

Miller luego se reunió con el comandante polaco de la División Multinacional, conformada por soldados de 23 naciones. Esta era la parte más débil de la coalición, pero era importante, en el sentido de que sugería que la guerra era un esfuerzo internacional amplio.

El comandante polaco de la división le dijo a Miller: "Tengo 23 unidades nacionales independientes. Tienen 23 reglas de participación independientes. Tomo el teléfono, le dijo al coronel al mando de la Brigada Española qué hacer. Él toma el teléfono, llama a Madrid y dice: 'Me dijeron que hiciera esto. ¿Está bien?'".

Miller entendió que esto significaba que la División Multinacional tenía poca o ninguna capacidad de combate.

En la Zona Verde, antes de salir del país, Miller trató de identificar los cuellos de botella de la APC. Uno de los principales problemas era que Bremer y el teniente general Ricardo Sánchez, el comandante de las fuerzas terrestres que había reemplazado al general McKiernan, no se hablaban. Bremer estaba tratando de abordar el esfuerzo interno de política y reconstrucción iraquí, en tanto que Sánchez debía tratar los asuntos de seguridad y violencia. Bremer decía cada rato que el problema central era la falta de seguridad, que era función de Sánchez.

Sánchez pidió ver a Miller en la cena.

Hay un gran problema de comunicación, le dijo Miller a Sánchez. Pasé una semana con sus comandantes de división y ellos no entienden lo mismo sobre qué facultades tienen. Uno de ellos pensaba que podía despedir a los agentes de policía malos. Otro pensaba que tenía autoridad para dirigir sus propias operaciones psicológicas. Otro pensaba que tenía que consultar todo con Bagdad. Con todas estas nuevas divisiones, sugirió Miller, "quizás sería útil que promulgaran de nuevo sus órdenes vigentes para beneficio de los nuevos".

Sánchez dijo que les estaba costando trabajo obtener el dinero que el Congreso había autorizado para proyectos de reconstrucción en Irak: miles de millones de dólares. Se volvió al coronel Jeff Jones, quien acompañaba a Miller y dijo que todo lo que se decía en Washington tenía muy poco seguimiento. "Pruébeme que Irak es la principal prioridad, porque no lo percibo desde aquí", dijo Sánchez.

En una semana en Irak, Miller consideró que había visto más del país y tenía una mejor idea sobre qué estaba sucediendo, que la mayor parte de la gente de la APC que llevaba meses allí.

27

Miller informó a Rice y a Hadley. "Hay mucha urgencia fuera de la Zona Verde, pero no encontré conciencia de esa urgencia dentro de la zona. Todo era lento, sin respuesta, inefectivo". Leyó de sus notas: "Bremer no delega, y no tiene tiempo para hacer todo". Un general había resumido muy bien el asunto, dijo Miller: "La burocracia mata".

Citó lo que le había dicho un comandante sobre el Programa de Respuesta de Emergencia del Comandante (CERP): "Si no lo hago con el CERP, no se hace", y agregó que era de vital importancia mantener funcionando este programa después de haber entregado la soberanía.

Aunque Bremer trataba de controlar todo, según Miller, en muchos asuntos el personal de la APC estaba jugando a dejar pasar el tiempo. Se la pasaban difiriendo el Consejo de Gobierno iraquí, que era lento o estancado en la toma de decisiones sobre comunicaciones, política reglamentaria, código policivo de conducta, contratación de ex oficiales, despido de los maestros de Kirkuk. Siempre era la misma historia. La gente de la APC estaba cansada y se sentía amargada y derrotista. Había pocas personas que solucionaran problemas, y los ministerios iraquíes no ayudaban mucho.

"Necesitamos escoger nuestros 10 temas más importantes", aconsejó, cosas que había que hacer antes de la entrega de la soberanía.

Dio cinco consejos adicionales. Ante todo, no debían subestimar la cantidad de iraquíes que veían Al Jazeera en la televisión satelital. La electricidad es un problema, agregó, no sólo porque no tienen suficiente, sino porque los iraquíes la han visto como algo que debía ser gratuito.

En segundo lugar, Sánchez y Bremer no se hablaban. Y Sánchez y sus comandantes de división no se comunicaban con suficiente efectividad.

Tercero, la APC nunca sale de la Zona Verde. Sus oficinas regionales en las 18 provincias fuera de Bagdad valían su peso en oro, pero la gente de la Zona Verde no estaba haciendo nada.

Cuarto, la *desbaathificación* es un enredo. Hay personas buenas con conexiones baathistas muy tenues a quienes no se les permite ingresar, dijo Miller. No estaba seguro de si el responsable era la APC o el grupo de *desbaathificación* dirigido por el sobrino de Ahmed Chalabi, pero Chalabi tenía guardados los archivos del antiguo servicio de inteligencia iraquí –una fuente esencial de información sobre quién había sido un verdadero baathista bajo Saddam–, lo cual impedía determinar los niveles de participación.

Por último, necesitaban hacer los contratos con base en el cronograma de guerra. La APC estaba pidiendo propuestas con fechas límite de 90 días. Eso no tenía sentido, no era más que tramitología burocrática. En 90 días, la APC prácticamente no existiría.

Miller repitió su informe a la mayor parte de los miembros del CNS, incluidos Armitage y Pace. Habló con *Scooter* Libby, con la esperanza de que sus observaciones más relevantes le llegaran al vicepresidente.

En la sesión informativa del Pentágono para Wolfowitz, estaban todos de pie, con mucha gente del grupo de políticas de Feith y el enlace APC-Washington. Ninguna persona en este recinto hará nada acerca de lo que yo informe, pensó Miller, incluso si lo creen. El problema, como siempre, era la implementación.

Empezó a incluir estos temas en las agendas de los comités de adjuntos. ¿Cómo podemos reducir el tiempo de contratación? ¿Cómo obtenemos más fondos CERP para los comandantes militares? ¿No podemos estandarizar la capacitación para el Cuerpo de Defensa Civil iraquí? ¿Cómo sacamos las manzanas podridas, para tener un proceso de *desbaathificación* mejor, más sensato y más rápido?

"Yo me encargo", le dijo Rice a Miller. Llamó a Bremer. "Déles a los comandantes de división más dinero". Los comandantes de división obtuvieron otros mil millones de dólares en fondos CERP.

RICE VEÍA que tenían que volver a comprometer a las Naciones Unidas en Irak. Anteriormente se había opuesto a la insistencia de Jay Garner de internacionalizar la fase de posguerra, pero ahora comprendía que era necesario hacerlo. La ONU prácticamente se había retirado de Irak después del ataque terrorista contra su sede, que causó 22 muertos, incluido su principal enviado, Sergio Vieira de Mello.

A Bob Blackwill le asignaron la tarea de la ONU. Como no era de sorprender, descubrió que ni Cheney ni Rumsfeld acogían la idea con entusiasmo. "Si metemos a la ONU", le advirtió Rumsfeld a Blackwill, "perdemos el control".

"Sí, pero creo que lo podemos manejar", insistió Blackwill, y se dio a la tarea de reclutar gente. Buscó a Lakhdar Brahimi, ex ministro de Relaciones Exteriores argelino que había dirigido la misión de la ONU en Afganistán durante dos años. En opinión de Blackwill, Brahimi, un sunita seglar de 70 años, era un excelente diplomático, el tipo de persona que podía realmente ayudar en toda clase de asuntos, desde financiación hasta estabilidad y elecciones.

"De ninguna manera", dijo Brahimi, cuando Blackwill le pidió su ayuda. Brahimi detestaba el enfoque norteamericano y no quería convertirse en facilitador o vocero de la política iraquí de Estados Unidos.

Aun así, Blackwill siguió insistiendo diplomáticamente. En enero, Brahimi fue nombrado asesor principal del secretario general de la ONU, Kofi Annan, para asuntos de paz y seguridad. Aunque en su nuevo cargo se opuso a concentrarse principalmente en Irak, Blackwill y Rice lo invitaron a la Casa Blanca a fin de presionarlo para que ayudara en lo de Irak. Powell participó un rato en la visita y Bush sacó tiempo para conversar con Brahimi también.

El cortejo funcionó y Brahimi y Blackwill viajaron a Irak. Los dos hombres prácticamente vivieron juntos allí durante tres meses. Como la soberanía estaba próxima a ser transferida, Brahimi le advirtió a Blackwill que había que hacer algo por los sunitas, quienes habían dirigido todo bajo Saddam. Estaban acostumbrados a sus privilegios: el primer grupo de cargos en la academia militar, las facultades médicas y casi cualquier otra cosa. "Si te ganaste a todos estos exiliados", dijo Brahimi, refiriéndose a los chiítas que seguramente iban a gobernar, "ninguno de los cuales tiene verdaderas raíces políticas en este país, esto se va a convertir en un enredo terrible".

Blackwill trató de comunicarse con los sunitas, que constituían apenas una quinta parte de la población, y de mantenerlos involucrados. En una reunión con un líder sunita clave, dijo: "Quiero garantizarle que nuestra intención es que los sunitas, en este nuevo Irak, tengan en cada dimensión posiciones y privilegios consistentes con su papel y número dentro de la sociedad iraquí".

"Señor embajador", dijo el sunita, dirigiéndose formalmente al ex enviado a India, "usted no entiende. Queremos gobernar a Irak".

Fue un momento de temor para Blackwill, quien percibió que se requerirían una o dos generaciones para que los sunitas se adaptaran al gobierno de la mayoría chiíta.

EL MIÉRCOLES 31 DE MARZO DE 2004, en la ciudad de Fallujah, insurgentes atacaron un pequeño convoy de vehículos de pasajeros, y mataron a cuatro guardias de seguridad de Blackwater, que trabajaban como contratistas independientes de Estados Unidos. Los cadáveres grotescamente desfigurados y ennegrecidos de dos de los norteamericanos muertos fueron colgados de las vigas de acero del puente principal sobre el Éufrates, que las tropas estadounidenses apodaban el puente de Brooklyn. Las imágenes, ampliamente difundidas, con multitudes de iraquíes celebrando jubilosos en el trasfondo, se convirtieron en uno de los símbolos más feos de la guerra, de sus horrores y de la impotencia de Estados Unidos.

"Todavía afrontamos matones y terroristas, en Irak, que prefieren seguir asesinando a los inocentes en vez de aceptar al avance de la libertad", dijo Bush en el discurso que pronunció en la reunión de recaudación de fondos para Bush-Cheney, en el Marriott Wardman Park Hotel de Washington, ese día a las 6:30 de la tarde. Y agregó: "Este grupo de matones está tratando de hacer tambalear nuestra voluntad. Estados Unidos nunca se dejará intimidar por matones y asesinos. Estamos atacando agresivamente a los terroristas en Irak".

"Sus muertes no quedarán impunes", prometió Bremer. Fallujah, una ciudad de cerca de 250.000 habitantes sobre el río Éufrates, a unos 80 kilómetros al oeste de Bagdad, era el corazón del territorio al margen de la ley, un lugar tan rudo que ni siquiera Saddam se había tomado el trabajo de domesticarlo. La ciudad era ahora el epicentro de la insurgencia sunita. Si las fuerzas estadounidenses lograban tomarse la ciudad, significaría un serio revés para los insurgentes. Bush le dijo al general Abizaid: "Prepárese para entrar", y añadió: "Si esto no se ha resuelto en 48 horas, usted entra".

A su vez, Abizaid le transmitió la orden al general Sánchez, el comandante de las fuerzas terrestres estadounidenses en Irak. Las unidades de *marines* de Estados Unidos que se hallaban alrededor de Fallujah debía iniciar un asalto completo a la ciudad.

Bremer no tenía mucha claridad sobre lo que estaba sucediendo. No vio los mensajes operacionales de los militares estadounidenses. Peor aun, existía un distanciamiento personal y una ruptura real de la comunicación entre él y Sánchez. Los dos provenían de mundos diferentes. Sánchez creció en el seno de una familia pobre, en Río Grande, una pequeña ciudad tejana de la frontera con México. Él y sus cinco hermanos y hermanas vivían en una casa de una sola habitación desprovista de agua corriente, situada al final de una calle sin pavimentar. Muchas veces, el único alimento del día consistía en fríjoles y arroz. Pero Sánchez progresó por sí mismo; obtuvo un título de matemático en Texas A&I y sobresalió en el ejército.

Bremer, criado en la elegante New Canaan, Connecticut, y egresado de Yale y de la facultad de administración de Harvard, provenía de un trasfondo social completamente diferente. Ya fuere intencional o no, "el elitismo condescendiente de Jerry", como lo llamó una persona de su entorno, era palpable en su trato con Sánchez.

Sánchez era un general *junior* de tres estrellas del ejército. Le habían asignado el comando terrestre más importante de Estados Unidos y contaba con una nómina pequeña y sin experiencia. En el 2006, Rumsfeld reconoció, en una entrevista, que no había tenido nada que ver con el hecho de que a un general *junior* de tres estrellas le hubieran asignado el crucial comando terrestre en Irak, y dijo que ni siquiera lo había sabido. "Le he dicho a la gente que reflexionemos sobre eso para no repetir el error", dijo Rumsfeld. Durante unos seis meses después de finalizado el importante combate del 1 de mayo de 2003, dijo Rumsfeld, fueron tomadas decisiones –incluido el nombramiento de Sánchez– de las que él no se había enterado. "Me sentí mal un año después, cuando empecé a examinar todas esas cosas que habían sucedido tan rápidamente sin mi conocimiento, y, honestamente, lo lamenté por el general Sánchez. Creo que terminó en una posición complicada".

Mientras los militares se preparaban para un asalto a gran escala sobre Fallujah, Brahimi expresó espantosas advertencias a Blackwill, amenazando con sacar la misión de la ONU si atacaban aquella ciudad árabe sunita. Brahimi estaba ayudando a organizar un gobierno soberano que pudiera asumir el gobierno. Un ataque contra Fallujah, dijo, acabaría con cualquier posibilidad en ese sentido, porque tanto las Naciones Unidas como el Consejo de Gobierno iraquí interino estaban en contra. Perder a la ONU y al Consejo de Gobierno significaría perder el país.

Rice entendió las implicaciones. Si no había gobierno, significaría que podían perder la guerra. El problema de seguridad y los problemas políticos finalmente habían convergido. Bremer también manifestó incertidumbre. No podía juzgar si un ataque echaría al traste el proceso político, pero la dirigencia sunita había dejado en claro que se irían, y, si eso sucedía, estarían transfiriendo la soberanía únicamente a los chiítas. Era un desagradable dilema.

Bremer y Blackwill vieron al general Abizaid, que era el jefe de Sánchez, en las videoconferencias seguras mientras discutían allá y acá sobre si se debía proseguir el plan de ataque pleno.

"Tenemos que hacer esto ahora en grande", dijo Abizaid en un momento dado, "y terminar de una vez por todas, porque mis muchachos son blancos perfectos allí afuera". Perderían la guerra si no limpiaban Fallujah, dijo. "Olviden la política. Tenemos que hacer esto. Estamos sufriendo bajas". Luego, en la siguiente videoconferencia segura, cambió de opinión: "Si limpiamos Fallujah vamos a tener una revuelta árabe que se extenderá mucho más allá de Irak".

A Blackwill le sorprendió lo errático y emocional del comandante de combate, totalmente esquizofrénico.

También en el CNS, Frank Miller observó que Abizaid de repente ya no parecía el comandante de campo. "Tal vez no deba estar listo", le dijo Abizaid a Miller. "Tal vez no debamos asaltar el lugar".

A Miller le preocupaba hasta tal punto la posibilidad de que Abizaid perdiera el coraje, que recurrió a su antigua amistad con Colin Powell.

"Tiene que hablar con John Abizaid", le dijo a Miller por el teléfono seguro. "Tiene que levantarle el ánimo". Recuérdele que es un soldado que libra una guerra, le recomendó Miller, y que sería un terrible error echarse para atrás en Fallujah. No se sabe a ciencia cierta si Powell llamó a Abizaid.

En Bagdad, el Consejo de Gobierno interino de Bremer se empezó a desintegrar. "Vamos a dejar el Consejo de Gobierno para siempre", le dijo a Blackwill Adnan Pachachi, un líder sunita. Brahimi le volvió a advertir a Blackwill que él se marcharía también y se llevaría la misión de la ONU.

Bremer y Blackwill se comunicaron mediante el video seguro con Washington y alertaron al presidente. "Tenemos que detenernos", dijo Blackwill. No podían mantener unido al Consejo de Gobierno. Se desintegraría. Se suponía que la soberanía se iba a transferir al consejo. Sin el consejo, no podía haber transferencia.

Bush empezó a dar marcha atrás. Un ataque podría ser riesgoso, dijo. Empezó a hacer una gran cantidad de preguntas, algo inusual en el usualmente seguro Bush. ¿Por qué atacar ahora? ¿Por qué no dejar que la situación política evolucione? ¿Y si había una retaliación más fuerte contra Estados Unidos en otro lugar de Irak? Bush nunca dijo: "No ataquen Fallujah ahora", pero quienes lo acompañaban en el recinto podían leer el lenguaje corporal del presidente, así como su nueva cautela. Un presidente puede matar una operación a punta de preguntas, se dijo Bremer, y las preguntas de Bush eran, en efecto, una orden de no atacar.

Blackwill estaba bastante seguro de que Bush estaba calculando el impacto potencial sobre las elecciones presidenciales. Uno de los pilares de su política iraquí era la transferencia de la soberanía. La fecha de transferencia del 30 de junio se había anunciado como indicio de un gran progreso. Si no había nadie que pudiera asumir las riendas del gobierno, la política de Bush afrontaría aun más problemas.

El ataque se suspendió, pero se ordenó a los *marines* permanecer alrededor de la ciudad, sitiándola, con la esperanza de atrapar a los insurgentes adentro.

"No podemos simplemente permitir que se ablanden y abandonen Fallujah", dijo el presidente. "Por lo menos están allá adentro". Se convirtió casi en una preocupación personal de Bush.

En la Casa Blanca, Frank Miller examinó la situación con Blackwill, quien le dijo que iban a mantener a los *marines* en el lugar.

"Tenemos heridos", objetó Miller. "Nos están matando gente. No se puede mantener la moral de una unidad diciendo que vamos a rodear la ciudad y recibir los disparos. Eso no se puede hacer, Bob".

"Pues enséñeme las cifras de muertos y heridos", dijo Blackwill. Se mostraba muy escéptico de que las bajas fueran altas.

"Bob, usted no ha prestado servicio", dijo Miller horrorizado. "Yo fui oficial naval. No he prestado servicio terrestre, pero conozco a estos tipos. No puede esperar que vivan en medio del polvo sin ducharse durante semanas enteras, y sin nada que hacer, excepto pensar 'soy un blanco'".

Blackwill se refirió por su nombre a algunos de los generales. "No saben lo que están haciendo", se quejó en un momento dado. "¿Por qué estamos perdiendo soldados debido a los AEI?". Los artefactos explosivos improvisados, o AEI, eran bombas de fabricación casera hechas de municiones viejas, proyectiles u otros explosivos. Eran el arma terrorista por excelencia. Los insurgentes los camuflaban ingeniosamente y los ocultaban en carreteras, entre pilas de basura y hasta en cuerpos de animales muertos. Eran los principales asesinos de personal estadounidense. "¿Por qué estamos conduciendo por todas partes?", preguntó Blackwill. "Debemos salir de las carreteras. ¿Qué misiones se les han asignado a estas personas para que estén en las carreteras, donde terminan volados en pedazos? ¿Van simplemente de un lugar a otro?".

"Bob, tenemos una fuerza aquí, una fuerza allá, y una base de logística aquí", dijo Miller. "Hay que reabastecer los puestos".

"Hagámoslo todo por aire", sugirió Blackwill.

Miller consideró que esa sugerencia denotaba una falta total de comprensión de lo que requerían las tropas y lo que era vivir en un país extranjero violento. Cien versiones mínimas del puente aéreo de Berlín, en las zonas rurales hostiles de Irak, serían sumamente imprácticos.

En un momento dado, Blackwill y Bremer fueron a la región de Fallujah. Para ellos la situación era un ejemplo vívido –el ejemplo más dramático– que demostraba que Estados Unidos simplemente no tenía suficientes tropas en Irak. Con más tropas, se podría tomar Fallujah con relativa rapidez, pensaban, lo bastante rápido como para haber mantenido unido el Consejo de Gobierno hasta que terminara.

POR ESA MISMA ÉPOCA, la CIA optó por seguir lo que parecía ser un curso intermedio. Un general baathista de dos estrellas, renegado, que había servido en la Guardia Republicana, dijo que podía conformar una brigada de iraquíes en Fallujah y limpiar la ciudad. El general, Jassim Mohammed Saleh, apareció en la televisión con uniforme y boina de color verde oscuro. Cuando Rice vio su imagen, gritó: "Dios santo. ¡Se parece a Saddam Hussein! ¿No pueden escoger a alguien que no se parezca a Saddam?"

La inefectiva brigada iraquí de Fallujah terminó por plegarse. Al cabo de unos cuantos meses, la mayor parte de sus miembros se pasó al bando insurgente.

BLACKWILL SE MANTENÍA en estrecho contacto con los kurdos en el norte. Massoud Barzani, uno de los dos principales líderes kurdos, le dijo que Estados Unidos había cometido un terrible error al intentar incluir a los sunitas en el proceso político. Los sunitas, tan habituados a gobernar en Irak, tenían que ser derrotados y aplastados. Se les tenía que decir que iban a pagar un precio por su brutalidad contra los demás: los kurdos y los chiítas. Sólo cuando los sunitas fueran totalmente derrotados y aislados, podría Estados Unidos darse el lujo de mostrarse magnánimo, dijo Barzani.

El retiro de Fallujah constituía un serio fracaso estratégico, afirmó Barzani. "Fue un desastre, porque le comunicaron a todo insurgente sunita potencial que ellos pueden ganar en la espera, que si les causan a ustedes suficientes bajas, ustedes se detendrán. Esto tenía una respuesta".

"Massoud, ¿cuál era la respuesta?", quiso saber Blackwill.

"El *pesh merga*", contestó, refiriéndose a la formidable milicia kurda de unos 50.000 o más combatientes. "Han debido, simplemente, pedirnos que enviáramos 30.000 *pesh merga* a Fallujah. Si sus *marines* no podían hacerlo, debían dejar que lo hicieran los *pesh*".

Entre el norte kurdo y Fallujah sólo había unos cientos de kilómetros.

"Pues a mí me parece como una receta para la guerra civil", replicó Blackwill, "que los kurdos limpien la Fallujah sunita".

"En el corto plazo eso podría ser un problema", convino Barzani, "pero no es tan serio como el largo plazo: la lección que les están enseñando a los sunitas, esto es, que los pueden derrotar a ustedes".

Blackwill llegó a creer que el bajo nivel de tropas tenía otra consecuencia. Los oficiales iraquíes profesionales –los mayores y tenientes coroneles sunitas cercanos a los cuarenta años– habían quedado sorprendidos por su derrota y completamente intimidados por el *blitzkrieg* estadounidense. El golpe bélico rápido y contundente de Rumsfeld había funcionado. Pero Blackwill creía que Estados Unidos no había matado suficientes miembros del cuerpo de oficiales iraquí. Los norteamericanos se habían mantenido al margen de la insurgencia inicial, pero Fallujah y el crecimiento estable de la violencia y los ataques los habían instado a pensar que esta insurgencia podría tener piernas y los podría volver a poner en aprietos. Ahora quienes antes se habían quedado a un lado estaban ayudando a la insurgencia o uniéndose a ella.

"A menos que esto termine pronto", le dijo Bremer a Blackwill, "no vamos a poder terminarlo".

De regreso a la Casa Blanca y al CNS, Blackwill les dijo a Rice y a Hadley que el CNS debía revisar su actuación militar. ¿Cuál era la estrategia militar? ¿Cuáles eran los emplazamientos militares y los niveles de tropa?

Rice estuvo de acuerdo y expresó su gran frustración respecto a Rumsfeld y el Pentágono, pero nunca dijo que forzaría el tema. Blackwill, que todavía solía referirse a sí mismo como Godzilla, no se dejó amilanar. Como ex jefe de Rice en el CNS de Bush padre, tenía la oportunidad de presionar. Pero no quería ser tan burdo como para preguntar: "¿Entonces, qué piensa hacer al respecto?". Rice había interpuesto una barrera ligera, y Blackwill no quería que pensaran que él estaba tratando de penetrar la relación de Rice con el presidente.

Blackwill también presionó a Hadley con respecto a la estrategia militar. "Si tenemos una estrategia militar, no la puedo identificar", dijo el subconsejero nacional de seguridad. "No sé qué es peor: que tengan una y no nos informen, o que no tengan ninguna".

Y TAMBIÉN ESTABA el pobre Frank Miller, pensó Blackwill, tratando de encontrar soluciones. Miller era infatigable y trataba de ayudarles a las tropas que transportaban generadores eléctricos o protegían oleoductos o aseguraban rutas de transporte en Irak. Blackwill pensó que no le estaban pagando lo suficiente para asistir alguna vez a una de las reuniones de Miller. Eran ejercicios frustrantes e inútiles.

Blackwill había tomado algún tiempo para comprender cuál era en realidad el problema, pero ahora creía entenderlo bien. No había forma de que Rice, Hadley, Miller o él pudieran arreglar a Irak, porque no ejercían ningún control sobre el problema real: no había suficientes tropas. Cada persona era desviada, tratando de solucionar los derivados del problema real. Pero no se podía solucionar esos problemas sino cuando alguien resolviera el problema verdadero de no tener suficientes tropas terrestres.

En vez de la lista de las 10 tareas principales que había querido hacer cuando regresó de Irak en marzo, el Grupo Directivo Ejecutivo reconstituido de Miller tenía ahora una lista de 90 cosas que se suponía que había que completar antes del 30 de junio, apenas en unos meses, para cuando se tenía programada la transferencia de la soberanía. Eso es inútil, volvió a decir. Necesitamos escoger las 10 tareas más importantes. Presidir el Grupo Directivo Ejecutivo era frustrante. El Departamento de Defensa cada vez desempeñaba un rol menos importante. Feith enviaba a una persona diferente de su personal de política cada vez. Cuando iba Feith, se negaba a discutir los temas, diciendo que no había hablado sobre ellos con Rumsfeld, por lo que no se podía comprometer. Luego volvía con la posición inflexible de Rumsfeld.

Miller pensó que nunca había visto un grupo de personas menos capaces de promover sus propios intereses. En el campo, los comandantes de división sabían qué había que hacer, pero no estaban obteniendo apoyo. ¿En dónde está el presidente del Estado Mayor Conjunto, Dick Myers?, se preguntó Miller. ¿Por qué Myers no estaba golpeando la mesa, diciendo: "¿Por qué no se está dando apoyo a mis soldados?".

MILLER OBSERVÓ QUE RUMSFELD tenía espacios cortos de atención en las reuniones de la Casa Blanca. Alguien se detenía en un tema, lo analizaba a cabalidad, pero luego Rumsfeld sugería que hablaran sobre ese mismo tema.

"Es un bravucón", le dijo Miller a Rice un día.

"No, no lo es".

"Vamos, Condi. Soy yo".

"Don es Don. Sabremos tratarlo", dijo en una ocasión. A Miller le quedó claro que a ella le era imposible impugnar a Rumsfeld.

EN ABRIL DE 2004, se publicó mi libro *Plan of Attack*. Decía que, tres meses antes de la guerra, Tenet le había dicho dos veces al presidente, en una reunión en el Salón Oval, que el caso de inteligencia sobre las ADM de Irak era un *"slam dunk"*.[15] La pintoresca escena del director de la CIA levantando los brazos para imitar la pelota de baloncesto pasando por el aro llamó mucho la atención. Yo había citado al presidente en el libro confirmando oficialmente que Tenet había hecho esa afirmación.

Tenet llamó a Andy Card y se quejó amargamente de que conversaciones delicadas sostenidas en el Salón Oval estaban siendo citadas por un periodista.

Tenet compartió su ira con Armitage.

"George", le dijo Armitage, "se acabó. Terminó. Alguien lo informa; es lo último que le debe preocupar".

"George, soy su amigo", continuó Armitage. "No lo estoy criticando. Pero esto es Washington. Un solo 'maldición' borra diez 'muy bien, muchachos'. Punto". Era feo, mezquino, injusto, pero cierto, y no era algo sobre lo cual había que preocuparse mucho.

A Tenet sí le preocupaba. La confianza se había perdido.

Tenet dijo luego que no recordaba haber dicho *"slam dunk"*, aunque no lo negó. Afirmó que la reunión tenía como propósito determinar cuál inte-

---

15. Término del baloncesto que se refiere a las "clavadas".

ligencia podía divulgarse públicamente para "comercializar" la guerra. Eso es correcto, según informé en *Plan of Attack*. Pero una defensa pública de la guerra difícilmente podía ser una "clavada" si el director de la CIA no creía que la inteligencia subyacente también era una "clavada". Obviamente, Tenet había creído que lo era. Desde que la Estimación Nacional de Inteligencia de hacía tres meses había afirmado claramente que Irak poseía armas químicas y biológicas, no sorprendía que Tenet lo creyera. Tiene bastante razón cuando afirma que su frase con la expresión "clavada" no hizo que el presidente se decidiera por la guerra. Tenet cree que Bush ya había tomado la decisión.

Un año después de la publicación de *Plan of Attack*, asistí a un foro público en Los Ángeles, en el que le preguntaron a Tenet frente a unos 5.000 asistentes acerca del comentario del "*slam dunk*".

"Han sido las dos palabras más tontas que he pronunciado en mi vida", contestó.

28

A FINES DE ABRIL, *60 Minutes II* mostró fotografías de reclusos desnudos, encapuchados e, incluso, atados, que eran apilados o bruscamente interrogados en la prisión de Abu Ghraib, en Irak, mientras guardias militares estadounidenses observaban sonriendo. Seymour Hersh, de *The New Yorker*, publicó detalles de una investigación secreta del ejército que documentaba el abuso contra los detenidos. Docenas de fotografías desquiciadas e infames de prisioneros inundaron las pantallas de televisión, los periódicos y el Internet.

Rumsfeld y el general Myers desestimaron su importancia. Rumsfeld dijo públicamente que no había visto las fotografías. "Creo que sí pregunté por las fotos y me dijeron que no teníamos copias", afirmó. En un programa de televisión del domingo, a Myers le preguntaron si había visto la investigación del ejército sobre Abu Ghraib. "No he visto ese informe", contestó.

"Bush reprende a Rumsfeld en privado", fue el titular de primera página de *The Washington Post* el 6 de mayo de 2004. El artículo relataba que el presidente había reprendido a Rumsfeld por el escándalo de Abu Ghraib y que se sentía insatisfecho y descontento por la manera como el secretario de Defensa había manejado el asunto.

Rumsfeld se preguntó frente a su gente cómo diablos alguien en la Casa Blanca podía pensar que al presidente le ayudaría tener este tipo de campaña de chismes y rumores. Siempre había alguien en la Casa Blanca que consideraba como un elevado arte político que el presidente demostrara que era severo con los miembros de su gabinete y que los podía maltratar. ¿Cómo podía ayudarle a un presidente en guerra el hecho de que su secretario de Defensa fuera percibido como un funcionario en problemas o debilitado, de alguna manera sospechoso, sin contar con la "confianza presidencial plena"? El presidente y todos los demás requerían claridad. Si era hora de que él se marchara, lo haría, dijo Rumsfeld. Decidió forzar esa claridad.

El día siguiente, 7 de mayo, el secretario de Defensa testificó en público ante el Congreso. Cuando le preguntaron si iba a renunciar, contestó: "Es una pregunta pertinente. Desde que empezó la tormenta, he reflexionado mucho sobre eso". También le dijo a la Comisión de Servicios Armados de la

Cámara: "Si pensara que no podía ser efectivo, ciertamente no querría servir. Y tengo que tener eso en cuenta".

La evasiva sugerencia de que aún no había tomado una decisión produjo una serie de llamadas a los subalternos de Rumsfeld desde la Casa Blanca, casi desde que salieron las palabras de su boca.

Al día siguiente *The New York Times* informó en su artículo de primera plana que Rice quizás no se sentiría descontenta si Rumsfeld renunciaba. Se citó a una persona no identificada cercana a Rice diciendo que Rumsfeld "parece haberse convertido en un lastre para el presidente, y ha complicado la misión en Irak".

Dos días después, el lunes 10 de mayo, Bush fue al Pentágono y se reunió con Rumsfeld, quien ofreció renunciar.

Poco antes del mediodía, Bush apareció en público con Cheney, Powell, Rumsfeld y el general Myers.

Mirando a Rumsfeld, dijo: "Usted está haciendo una excelente labor. Es un secretario de Defensa fuerte y nuestra nación tiene con usted una deuda de gratitud".

"Presenté mi renuncia por escrito dos veces", recordó Rumsfeld en una entrevista. "Él me devolvió la primera y dijo 'no'. La segunda me la devolvió y yo se la di de nuevo y le dije, 'debería guardar esta'. Y él dijo 'no'. Él no quería que yo me fuera. Y lo dice públicamente".

Le pregunté a Rumsfeld qué decían las dos cartas. "Una era una carta relativamente corta y la otra era una carta relativamente larga". No quiso decir más.

ANTE LA INMINENTE TRANSFERENCIA de la soberanía a los iraquíes, Powell enfocó su atención en la apertura de una embajada en Bagdad. Era una oportunidad; una oportunidad traicionera. En circunstancias normales, una embajada de Estados Unidos significa que el Departamento de Estado es el organismo principal. Pero las circunstancias no se acercaban a la normalidad. Era difícil saber qué podría ocurrir y Powell quería estar preparado. Algunos meses antes había convocado a Armitage y a Frank Ricciardone, el embajador de Estados Unidos en Filipinas, quien llevaba 26 años en el servicio exterior.

"Esto tiene que ser una gran ofensiva", había ordenado Powell, "y un esfuerzo muy organizado, porque estos tipos están dejando un enredo, y nos lo dejan a nosotros. Y tenemos que estar preparados en el verano para asumir esto y no meter la pata".

¿Quién sería el nuevo embajador de Estados Unidos? La Casa Blanca, el Pentágono y Powell empezaron a hacer sus listas.

John Negroponte, de 64 años, embajador de Estados Unidos ante las Naciones Unidas, decidió que él quería el cargo. Negroponte provenía de la vieja escuela de servicio exterior. Sus modelos de rol eran Ellsworth Bunker y Henry Cabot Lodge, los embajadores estadounidenses en Vietnam que se habían batido en circunstancias difíciles, combatiendo una insurgencia y una guerra civil. De joven, Negroponte había trabajado en la embajada de Estados Unidos en Saigón, entre 1964 y 1968, y creía que los embajadores eran los ejecutores de programas y políticas formulados por otros. Había sido el segundo de Powell cuando este fue asesor de seguridad nacional de Reagan, casi dos decenios atrás. La mayor parte de su carrera de 40 años la había pasado en el tercer mundo. Había sido embajador en Honduras, México y Filipinas. Estaba acostumbrado a gobiernos malos e inefectivos. Pensaba que Garner y Bremer habían sido un poco ilusos al creer que podían reconstruir rápidamente el país. La primera orden de negocios tendría que ser el restablecimiento de la autoridad central en el gobierno iraquí.

Llamó a Powell. "Diana y yo hemos estado conversando sobre esto", dijo Negroponte, refiriéndose a su esposa. "Sé que está buscando nombres y yo lo haría si me lo pidiera".

¡Un voluntario! Una de las reglas implícitas en el ejército en que Powell había servido durante 35 años era nunca ofrecerse como voluntario. Pero consideraba que Negroponte era un diplomático experto. Ser embajador ante las Naciones Unidos era un cargo complicado en el gobierno de Bush. Powell pensaba que Negroponte lo había hecho muy bien, trabajando dentro del sistema de la ONU y atendiendo las instrucciones de Powell. Cuando a Rice le pareció que Powell y el embajador ante la ONU se estaban volviendo demasiado internacionales, envió a Elliott Abrams a vigilar a Negroponte. Powell pensaba que Rice quería fortalecer a la gente del Departamento de Estado.

"No soporto esto", le dijo Negroponte a Powell en una ocasión. "no lo quiero".

"John", le había contestado Powell en tono tranquilizante, "deje que vaya. Va a comprobar que usted está cumpliendo con su trabajo. Será una molestia ocasional. Pero con eso evitamos que nos estén chequeando todo el día, lo cual sucedería si él no estuviera allá". Negroponte sobrevivió a Elliott Abrams.

Cuando Powell mencionó el nombre de Negroponte en la Casa Blanca, no fue aclamado de inmediato. Pero había hecho una buena labor en sus más de dos años en la ONU, y su prestigio en la Casa Blanca había mejorado. El consenso fue que no tenían a nadie mejor que él, además de que se había ofrecido como voluntario.

El presidente tenía una pregunta para Negroponte: "¿Cree que la democracia es posible en Irak?".

El embajador contestó diplomáticamente: "No creo que trascienda las posibilidades del hombre".

POWELL Y NEGROPONTE pensaron en James F. Jeffrey, el embajador de Estados Unidos en Albania, para ejercer el segundo cargo en la nueva embajada –subjefe de misión– en Bagdad. Jeffrey había sido el segundo al mando en las embajadas estadounidenses en Turquía y Kuwait. Funcionario de carrera en el servicio exterior, había estado en el ejército ocho años, parte de ellos en Vietnam. Oriundo de Boston y de casi 1,90 metros de estatura, con cabello blanco ralo y un paso amable y pesado, Jeffrey hablaba directamente y con rapidez. No le gustaba la lentitud de la burocracia gubernamental.

Jeffrey viajó a Bagdad pronto, para coincidir con Bremer durante unas seis semanas antes del arribo de Negroponte. Su reporte fue: "Estamos montando una embajada para esta maldita y absurda APC en medio de este palacio burlesco, mientras somos bombardeados todos los días… una pesadilla terrible".

Se dio cuenta de inmediato de que Bremer tenía una relación áspera con el general Sánchez, quien no quería jugar de defensa ante la insurgencia. El general se oponía a asegurar la ruta hasta el aeropuerto y no quería establecer defensas de perímetro. Jeffrey entendía que el ejército de Estados Unidos era un organismo muy orientado a la ofensiva que detestaba la acción civil de mantenimiento de la paz, en este caso, entrenar a otras fuerzas y jugar de defensa.

Jeffrey también comprendió que la idea de un ejército iraquí era una farsa. Wolfowitz viajó a Irak para supervisar el entrenamiento del ejército iraquí. Estados Unidos había comprado equipos para docenas de batallones iraquíes –ametralladoras, camiones, blindaje corporal– pero el contrato había sido impugnado en una corte de Estados Unidos y detenido durante seis meses. No había un ejército iraquí.

Bremer y Sánchez estaban de salida. Después de más de un año de conversaciones, Rumsfeld finalmente había decidido poner a un general de cuatro estrellas al mando en Irak, y para ello había escogido al general George Casey, ex jefe del Estado Mayor Conjunto.

EN LA PRIMAVERA DEL 2004, Wolfowitz se sentía frustrado. Como, quizás, principal arquitecto intelectual neoconservador de la guerra, había emprendido una cruzada de un año de duración para lograr que Rumsfeld tomara en serio el entrenamiento de las fuerzas de seguridad iraquíes. La oposición del secretario de Defensa era enloquecedora.

Rumsfeld dijo, en una entrevista posterior, que en el Pentágono demasiadas personas pensaban que sólo las fuerzas especiales podían ocuparse del entrenamiento. "Cada vez que daba media vuelta", dijo, la fuerza elite estaba siendo despachada a misiones de entrenamiento. "No hay razón alguna para que los *marines* o los militares del ejército no entrenen gente", agregó. "Luego dije, 'consigamos contratistas para que se encarguen de una parte'". Había insistido en que no debían tratar de lograr que los iraquíes fueran tan buenos como las tropas estadounidenses. "No se trata de que se ganen el premio de soldado del año en Fort Bragg. Tenemos muy poco tiempo y demasiada gente con la que hay que tratar, una rotación muy rápida".

En una ocasión, Wolfowitz le había dicho en privado a Rumsfeld que creía que la invasión sólo tomaría siete días. Pero había sospechado que los antiguos saddamistas y baathistas lanzarían una guerra de guerrillas prolongada. En su opinión, el antiguo régimen era maldad pura, una forma de fascismo del Medio Oriente.

Wolfowitz viajó por primera vez a Irak en julio de 2003, y encontró que la seguridad era mucho peor de lo que había anticipado. La policía necesitaba una reestructuración total. Se reunió con el general Sánchez, quien era entonces el recién nombrado comandante de las fuerzas terrestres en Irak. Escuchó mientras Sánchez le recitó una lista de 10 problemas. El número 10 era reclutar el nuevo ejército iraquí. Wolfowitz consideró que eso era lo más importante. Estaba seguro de que el entrenamiento tomaría dos o tres años.

Pero Wolfowitz descubrió que no podía lograr que Rumsfeld se concentrara en el problema. A medida que la violencia se intensificaba en el otoño del 2003, presionó a Rumsfeld. "Enviemos una misión de estudio para que determine cuáles son los requerimientos reales para las fuerzas de seguridad iraquíes", sugirió. No sucedió nada. Wolfowitz pensaba que la policía iraquí era un problema tan serio como el ejército, pero no lograba que su jefe actuara. Pasó cerca de ocho semanas tratando de persuadir a Rumsfeld de que enviara la misión de estudio. Cuando finalmente aceptó, Wolfowitz sintió como si prácticamente hubiera tenido que sostener la mano de Rumsfeld cuando firmó la orden que enviaba al mayor general del ejército Karl W. Eikenberry, quien había ayudado a organizar el nuevo ejército en Afganistán, a Irak. En una entrevista, Rumsfeld negó esto. "Eso es tonto", comentó, agregando que la única discusión fue hasta qué nivel debían entrenar a los iraquíes. "Recuerdo que durante la guerra de Vietnam, cuando me di cuenta, estábamos entrenando a la gente para que fueran doctores en vez de paramédicos. En ese momento no necesitaban una atención hospitalaria del estilo de la de Estados Unidos".

La conclusión enfática de Eikenberry fue que había que establecer un comando unificado para la misión de entrenamiento en Irak. En abril de 2004, al mayor general del ejército David Petraeus fue enviado a Irak y pronto se le otorgó su tercera estrella como jefe de entrenamiento de las fuerzas iraquíes. Tuvo que empezar de cero, más de un año después de la invasión.

En mayo de 2004, Negroponte se reunió con Wolfowitz antes de viajar a Irak.

"Temo que quizás hayamos cometido el mismo error que cometimos en Vietnam, donde no iniciamos la vietnamización sino cuando ya era demasiado tarde", dijo Negroponte. La estrategia de vietnamización había sido diseñada para transferir la responsabilidad por los combates y la seguridad interna a los vietnamitas. El presidente Nixon la había adoptado ya bien entrada la guerra.

"Pues, indudablemente, ha dado en el clavo", respondió Wolfowitz. "No creo que sea demasiado tarde, pero ése es el problema".

Wolfowitz se estaba sintiendo cada vez más marginado por Rumsfeld, quien canceló varios de los viajes de su segundo a Irak. Las razones nunca fueron claras. Rumsfeld decía que había demasiado trabajo por hacer. Antes de uno de los viajes programados, Rumsfeld simplemente dijo: "No es necesario que vaya". Su subalterno se sintió más o menos solo. El Pentágono respondía al primero al mando, no al segundo, y eso era lo que el primero estaba disponiendo.

En una ocasión, después de que Rumsfeld cancelara un viaje, Wolfowitz organizó una gira virtual por Irak, y pidió que cada uno de los comandantes de las principales divisiones y su personal le rindieran informes de dos horas en una videoconferencia segura. Llegó un sábado a las 6:30 de la mañana y pasó todo el día escuchando y haciendo preguntas. El tema predominante era que los comandantes se sentían decepcionados por el desempeño de las fuerzas de seguridad iraquíes. El nuevo ejército, la policía y hasta las patrullas fronterizas necesitaban mejores equipos, mejor entrenamiento y mucho más dinero.

En un testimonio público que poco se tuvo en cuenta, Wolfowitz le dijo a la Comisión de Servicios Armados de la Cámara que el entrenamiento de los iraquíes había sido el tema central "incluso, antes de la guerra". En la lucha contra los insurgentes, agregó, "la clave para derrotarlos siempre ha sido entrenar y equipar a los iraquíes y capacitarlos para combatir lo más pronto posible".

Ninguno de los miembros de la comisión preguntó por qué habían tardado más de un año para llegar a esa conclusión. Wolfowitz les dijo a colaboradores cercanos que no se trataba únicamente de negligencia sino que Rumsfeld había bloqueado los esfuerzos por iniciar el entrenamiento antes.

"No lo puedo entender", le dijo Wolfowitz a un colaborador.

El personal de la comisión de inteligencia sobre las ADM presidida por el juez Silberman practicó cientos de entrevistas en la comunidad de inteligencia, y también se basó fuertemente en las entrevistas del Grupo de Inspección de Irak de David Kay. Silberman y Robb acordaron que sólo ellos podían ver algunos informes de inteligencia muy secretos. No los compartirían con nadie más en la comisión. En una entrevista efectuada en el 2005, le pregunté a Silberman si Rumsfeld fue una de las personas a quienes entrevistó la comisión.

"Tuvimos problemas para convencer a Don de que viniera a ser entrevistado por la comisión en pleno", dijo Silberman. Amenazó con enviarle una citación, pensando que Rumsfeld no sabría que la comisión no tenía ese poder, y Rumsfeld cedió. Rumsfeld se mostró "particularmente sensible acerca del hecho de que la DIA no se había cubierto precisamente de gloria", dijo.

Yo dije que algunos de los generales abrigaban dudas acerca de las ADM, y que se habían dado cuenta antes de la guerra de que no podían probar que hubiera armas de destrucción masiva en un lugar determinado.

Silberman preguntó quiénes.

Mencioné a los generales Abizaid, McKiernan y Marks.

"Interesante", dijo Silberman. "Es una lástima que no hayamos hablado con ellos".

Tenet fue entrevistado voluntariamente tres o cuatro veces, dijo Silberman. Concluyó que Tenet había confiado demasiado en un par de informes de inteligencia de los servicios exteriores. "Pobre George", dijo Silberman. "Quiero decir que le tomó mucho tiempo en este proceso tratar de entender qué diablos había salido mal, por qué estaban tan equivocados y cuán increíblemente estúpidas habían sido algunas de sus decisiones".

John McLaughlin, el subdirector de la CIA, insistió en que el fracaso de la comunidad de inteligencia en lo referente a las ADM era el resultado de "una tormenta perfecta"; que todo había salido mal al tiempo pero no se había podido anticipar. "Pensamos que era basura", dijo Silberman. "Hubo algunas fallas fundamentales. Lo peor de todo fue la cosa química". Los analistas habían visto fotos satelitales de grandes camiones cisternas en Irak y habían concluido que contenían armas químicas. "Fue una suposición, una deducción. No era una prueba contundente, pero uno podría decir que era un razonamiento lógico", dijo Silberman. Pero luego los analistas "concluyeron que estaban acelerando el proceso, porque vimos muchos camiones más. Nadie se tomó el trabajo de decirles a los analistas que veían muchos más camiones porque estábamos dirigiendo más el satélite sobre ellos. Eso fue casi como *Saturday Night Live*".

Mientras Bremer se preparaba para entregar la soberanía a los iraquíes, Powell y Rumsfeld se enzarzaron en otra pelea. La pregunta era una vez más ¿quién iba a estar al mando? Powell y Negroponte iban a establecer la primera embajada de Estados Unidos en Bagdad desde la Guerra del Golfo de 1991. Powell quería que el Departamento de Estado estuviera a cargo.

Rumsfeld argumentaba que con 130.000 hombres en Irak, no se trataba de una situación normal. Y así, una y otra vez. Un tema contencioso eran los US $18.400 millones que el Congreso había asignado para el Fondo de Alivio y Reconstrucción de Irak el año anterior. Era dinero destinado a la reconstrucción económica y de infraestructura clave. Rice y Hadley terminaron implicados en negociaciones ásperas entre Powell y Rumsfeld.

Rice insistía en que esto debía quedar muy claro. Durante los últimos ocho meses de estadía de Bremer en Irak, ella había sido su canal nominal de reportes, aunque sobre el papel se suponía que Rumsfeld y el Departamento de Defensa estaban a cargo. Ya no más. Ella no iba a dejar que la pregunta sobre quién estaba al mando quedara sujeta a los caprichos de Rumsfeld.

Después de una intervención directa del presidente, se redactó una orden de tres páginas. El 11 de mayo de 2004, Bush firmó la Directiva Presidencial de Seguridad Nacional NSPD-36. La directiva de tres páginas, clasificada como SECRETA, trasladó formalmente la responsabilidad de Irak, del Pentágono al Departamento de Estado, después de la terminación de la Autoridad Provisional de Coalición y la transferencia de la soberanía a los iraquíes.

"Bajo la orientación del secretario de Estado", empezaba la directiva de Bush, Estados Unidos estaría representado en Irak por un "Jefe de Misión" –un embajador– que sería "responsable de la dirección, coordinación y supervisión de los empleados del gobierno de Estados Unidos, sus políticas y sus actividades en el país, salvo las que se hallen bajo el mando de un comandante militar de área".

Aunque se trataba de un lenguaje bastante estándar, era un traslado claro y definido al Departamento de Estado, en medio de la zona de guerra. Si el modelo funcionaba, el nuevo embajador, Negroponte, y el comandante militar, Casey, tendrían que cooperar. Para enfatizar esto y cerciorarse de que hubiera alguna base para establecer esta relación, Bush invitó a los dos hombres y sus esposas a una pequeña cena en la Casa Blanca.

El gobierno iraquí interino estaba a punto de establecerse. Bremer y Blackwill estaban buscando un líder chiíta que lo pudiera dirigir. Los criterios incluían a alguien fuerte, que se llevara bien con los sunitas y que fuera aprobado por el Gran Ayatollah Sistani. Blackwill se inclinaba por Ayad Allawi, un médico de 58 años, hijo de una de las principales familias chiítas, cuyo abuelo había ayudado a negociar la independencia de Irak del Reino Unido en 1932. Vivía exiliado en Gran Bretaña desde 1971, y había sobrevivido a un intento de asesinato en Inglaterra cuando tenía un poco más de treinta años, atentado que, según se afirmaba, había sido ordenado por Saddam Hussein. Tenía nexos fuertes con la CIA.

Blackwill-*Godzilla* se convirtió en gerente de campaña de Allawi.

"¿El primer ministro de este nuevo Irak va a ser una persona que fue agente de la CIA durante una docena de años?", le preguntó Brahami a Blackwill con incredulidad.

"Sí", contestó Blackwill. "¿Preferiría que fuera un agente de inteligencia iraní?".

A Wolfowitz no le gustaba Allawi, pues era el principal rival de Chalabi, pero Bremer lo apoyaba, e insistió. "Es el tipo apropiado para Irak", le dijo Bremer a Jeffrey, "pero ojo. Este tipo no es un demócrata". El Allawi seglar era básicamente un baathista reformado y no le gustaban lo que denominaba "los turbantes", es decir, los líderes religiosos. De modo que el nuevo líder de Irak iba a ser un hombre de la CIA, de actitud escéptica frente a la democracia, que tenía poca influencia sobre Sistani y los clérigos, que eran quienes detentaban la mayor parte del poder.

LA TRANSFERENCIA DE LA SOBERANÍA estaba programada para el 30 de junio, y se creía que los insurgentes estaban planeando una ola de violencia para marcar la ocasión. A Bremer le preocupaba sobre todo la información de que los ataques incluirían el sabotaje de los oleoductos y refinerías de Irak. El 1 de junio, Scott Carpener, uno de un puñado de funcionarios de la Autoridad Provisional de Coalición que habían permanecido con Bremer en Irak durante todos los 14 meses, propuso una idea novedosa: ¿Qué tanto iban en verdad a lograr en las próximas semanas, por lo que valía la pena arriesgar todo el terror y la violencia que se anticipaba para el 30 de junio? ¿Por qué no transferir la soberanía de inmediato y tomar por sorpresa a los insurgentes?

A Bremer le gustó la idea, pero los abogados de la APC y del Pentágono advirtieron que existían problemas legales. De conformidad con el derecho internacional, una potencia de ocupación no podía simplemente empacar y marcharse. Además, había todo tipo de eventos oficiales planeados para el 30 de junio.

El 17 de junio, Rice llamó a Bremer para decirle que el presidente quería proceder a la entrega temprana. Pero la violencia estaba en cerca de 60 ataques diarios, y nunca tenían la plena seguridad de que eso sería posible. El 27 de junio, Bremer presionó bastante para que la transferencia se efectuara el día siguiente, es decir dos días antes de lo planeado, tiempo suficiente para tomar por sorpresa a los insurgentes. Llamó al presidente, quien se encontraba en Estambul con Blair y Powell para una reunión cumbre de la OTAN.

"A mí me parece bien. Preguntémosle a Tony", le dijo Bush a Bremer, y enseguida se dirigió a Blair. "Tony, ¿a usted cómo le parece?" Bush no tardó mucho. "Sí, parece bien. Adelante".

Bremer y el primer ministro Allawi hicieron la transferencia oficial poco después de las 10 de la mañana del 28 de junio, en una ceremonia sencilla en la oficina de Allawi. Para el mediodía, Bremer ya había salido del país en un avión camuflado de cuatro motores C-130 de la Guardia Nacional Aérea. El secreto se había mantenido. Casi ningún miembro del personal de la APC —muchos de los cuales se iban a quedar en el país en la nómina de la nueva embajada de Estados Unidos— supo sobre la transferencia temprana antes de que sucediera.

29

NEGROPONTE LLEGÓ A BAGDAD ese mismo día. Iba a ejercer su cargo bajo el supuesto de que la tarea de instaurar la democracia era factible y que tenían más de un 50% de posibilidades de derrotar a la insurgencia sunita. Jeffrey le pidió a los militares que hicieran una transparencia con un mapa de Bagdad, ubicando con precisión los ataques insurgentes de una semana entera: puntos rojos para ataques con granadas propulsadas por cohetes (RPG), puntos amarillos para indicar fuego indirecto, puntos verdes que representaran los ataques terrestres. Había más de 100 puntos en el mapa… sólo en Bagdad.

"John, estas son las instalaciones de su embajada", le dijo Jeffrey a Negroponte, entregándole la transparencia cuando llegó. El problema principal era la seguridad. "No la tenemos".

Powell y Rice le habían dado instrucciones a Negroponte de que tratara con cuidado a los iraquíes. Ellos tenían la soberanía. No debía asumir el rol proconsular de Jerry Bremer. Negroponte estuvo de acuerdo y asumió su cargo como una misión extranjera tradicional: relaciones diplomáticas con un país soberano. Pero pronto se dio cuenta de que, pese a que Irak tenía los símbolos de un gobierno y una sociedad modernos, casi nada funcionaba. El transporte era un caos. Todo lo básico estaba corroído. Era una aldea Potemkin. La agricultura había colapsado por completo y el sistema de racionamiento de alimentos, que dependía de las importaciones, era caótico. La embajada de Estados Unidos tenía que rastrear cartas de crédito y cuentas de granos de soya en los bancos libaneses y turcos, pues, si no lo hacía, la gente no tendría alimentos.

Una de las primeras actuaciones de Negroponte fue trasladar cerca de US $3.300 millones, de sus fondos de proyectos de electricidad y agua a largo plazo, a necesidades más apremiantes. Le dio al general Casey US $2.000 millones para seguridad y cerca de US $200 millones en fondos CERP, lo cual tuvo un impacto inmediato, porque así los oficiales estadounidenses podían contratar iraquíes sin más problemas.

El cambio fue de gran ayuda para Casey y Petraeus. El dinero disponible también ayudó a consolidar la relación entre Negroponte y Casey. Casey decidió tener dos oficinas: una en Camp Victory, en el aeropuerto, y la otra en la embajada, casi enfrente de la de Negroponte. Ambos estaban decididos a evitar un conflicto, como lo que el personal antiguo llamaba el "Show de Jerry y Rick", Bremer y Sánchez.

La disponibilidad de electricidad era uno de los indicadores más visibles de progreso en Irak, de modo que, durante ese verano de la campaña presidencial estadounidense, se concentró la atención en el frágil sistema eléctrico. La disponibilidad aumentó establemente según algunas mediciones. Rice descubrió que pronto se estaba convirtiendo en experta en electricidad iraquí. Preferiblemente se hubiera utilizado gas natural limpio en los generadores. Pero los gasoductos de gas natural existentes habían sido atacados por los insurgentes. El diesel era el combustible de respaldo, y había escasez de suministros porque las refinerías producían menos del requerido. De modo que los nuevos generadores funcionaban con *fuel oil*, pero eso exigía que se desactivaran cada tantas semanas para hacerles mantenimiento. En el otoño el sistema prácticamente colapsaría; un día perdió la mitad de su capacidad.

El 15 DE JULIO DE 2004, Steve Herbits, asesor político de Rumsfeld, se sentó frente a su computador y escribió un mordaz informe de siete páginas titulado "Resumen de los problemas de planeación y ejecución *post-Irak*". Aunque discutía la planeación y las políticas de posguerra, y también a Bremer, su verdadero blanco era su amigo desde hacía 37 años, Don Rumsfeld. El memorando incluía una serie de preguntas difíciles:

- "¿Por qué Rumsfeld no lo supervisaba a él [Bremer] como supervisaba a Franks?".
- "¿Quién tomó la decisión y por qué no reconstituimos el ejército iraquí?".
- "¿No se dio cuenta nadie de que íbamos a necesitar fuerzas de seguridad iraquíes?".
- "¿Nadie anticipó la importancia de la estabilización y la mejor manera de lograrla?".
- "¿Por qué la *desbaathificación* era tan amplia y tan profunda?".

"El estilo de operación de Rumsfeld", escribió Herbits, era el "modelo Haldeman, arrogante", en referencia al jefe de gabinete de la Casa Blanca durante el gobierno de Nixon, H. R. *Bob* Haldeman.

"Indeciso, contrario a la imagen popular", escribió Herbits sobre Rumsfeld, "no acepta que algunas personas en ciertas áreas sean más inteligentes que él... Confía en muy poca gente. Muy, muy cauteloso. Síndrome del guante de caucho": la tendencia a no dejar huellas de sus decisiones.

Rumsfeld era "a menudo abusivo" en las reuniones. "Menospreciaba a personas importantes frente a otras".

"Tenía el estilo de interrogatorio de un fiscal. Cuando estaba tratando de mejorar el producto –y sus cuestionamientos casi siempre buscaban eso–, su estilo se volvía contraproducente… Resumen: ¿Se equivocó Rumsfeld en el cálculo político fundamental de este gobierno, al no lograrse correctamente el proceso de reconstrucción *post-Irak* en el término de 18 meses?".

A COMIENZOS DE JUNIO, Tenet fue a ver a Bush solo. Tenía que renunciar. Su médico le había dicho que estaba poniendo en riesgo su salud. Ya había sufrido un infarto hacía algunos años, cuando formaba parte del CNS en el gobierno de Clinton.

Bush le dijo que no quería que ningún miembro de su gabinete de guerra renunciara ahora, en el año electoral.

Tenet sabía que él y la CIA eran blancos desde varios ángulos. La Comisión de Inteligencia del Senado estaba investigando el asunto de las ADM en Irak, Silberman y Robb estaban investigando. El informe de la Comisión 9/11 se iba a presentar pronto. Tenet insistió en que se tenía que ir.

El presidente no tenía otra opción que aceptar.

El 4 de junio, el titular de primera página del *Washington Post* decía: "Tenet renuncia como director de la CIA; jefe de inteligencia elogiado por Bush, pero críticos citan fallas en guerra de Irak". Tenet había pronunciado un discurso lloroso en la sede de la CIA, en Langley, Virginia, el día anterior, en el que dijo que renunciaba porque quería pasar más tiempo con su esposa y su hijo adolescente, el cual se marcharía el año siguiente para estudiar en la universidad. Había ocupado el cargo de director siete años, bajo dos presidentes, y había marcado el curso de la agencia, para bien o para mal, tanto en lo referente a los ataques del 9/11 como durante las guerras de Irak y Afganistán. El 11 de julio dejó oficialmente el cargo.

11 días después, la Comisión 9/11 presentó su informe. Entre sus numerosas recomendaciones estaba la creación del cargo de director de inteligencia nacional, quien supervisaría a toda la comunidad de inteligencia, incluida la CIA.

EL JUEZ SILBERMAN y algunos de los otros miembros de la comisión sobre ADM sintieron que la Comisión 9/11 se les había adelantado. ¿Cuál era su propósito ahora? Pero si la comisión se cancelaba, la Casa Blanca perdería su influencia política respecto al tema de la inteligencia sobre las ADM en Irak, apenas unos meses antes de las elecciones presidenciales.

Card llamó a Silberman. "El presidente quiere que sepa que, sólo porque la Comisión 9/11 presentó su informe, no quiere que ustedes se detengan". Además, sugirió: "¿Nos podrían dar algún tipo de análisis estructural sobre el informe 9/11, sobre sus recomendaciones estructurales?"

Silberman y Robb escribieron un memorando dirigido a los demás miembros de su comisión sobre las recomendaciones de la Comisión 9/11 y se lo enviaron a Card. Poco después, Silberman y su esposa fueron al oeste de Estados Unidos. En Jackson Hole, Wyoming, estuvieron cenando en la casa de Cheney. "De enorme utilidad", dijo Cheney, refiriéndose al memorando.

"Nosotros no implementamos", le repetía con frecuencia Hadley a Frank Miller. La implementación era función de diversos departamentos y organismos como el Pentágono y el Departamento de Estado. La función del Consejo Nacional de Seguridad era coordinar. Si Miller no podía hacer que la gente implementara una solución para algún problema, le ordenó Hadley: "Dígamelo y yo haré que lo hagan por medio de adjuntos", refiriéndose al comité de adjuntos. Miller se dijo que había algo de farsa en eso. Nada se hacía nunca a nivel de adjuntos.

La recomendación de Rice era completamente diferente. Si las cosas no se estaban haciendo a través de los canales normales, le dijo a Miller, "ya sabe qué debe hacer. Hacer que se hagan".

Era una de las múltiples contradicciones de la vida cotidiana de Miller en la Casa Blanca de Bush.

Uno de los ejemplos más inexcusables de cosas que no se hacían, creía Miller, tenía que ver con la confidencial *Secret Internet Protocol Router Network* (SIPRNET), que se utilizaba para guardar y comunicar información sobre inteligencia, órdenes de operaciones y otros datos técnicos. La información confidencial en la SIPRNET tenía una salvedad –"NOFORN"–, que significaba que no se permitía el acceso a ningún extranjero, restricción que incluía también a las tropas británicas y australianas que estaban combatiendo junto con los estadounidenses en Irak.

A veces la situación rayaba en lo absurdo. A los pilotos británicos que volaban aviones de guerra estadounidenses, los F-117 y F-15E, no se les permitía leer partes de los manuales confidenciales de pilotaje y mantenimiento porque estaban marcados NOFORN. En otro caso, los informes de inteligencia en bruto recopilados en operativos británicos en Irak se entregaban al centro estadounidense de fusión de inteligencia, que se suponía debía unir la inteligencia de todas las fuentes en un solo producto. Se hacía el informe pero los británicos no lo podían ver, y mucho menos conseguir un ejemplar, porque estaba marcado NOFORN.

El primer ministro británico Blair y el primer ministro australiano John Howard se quejaron directamente al presidente sobre este tema varias veces. En julio de 2004, Bush firmó una directiva, con el apoyo de Rumsfeld y John McLaughlin como director encargado de Inteligencia Central, que decía que NOFORN ya no se aplicaría a los británicos y los australianos cuando estuvieran formulando planes para operaciones de combate, entrenando con los estadounidenses o participando en actividades antiterroristas. Bush les informó a Blair y a Howard sobre la directiva, diciendo "acabo de firmar algo". Problema resuelto.

Pero Miller pronto descubrió que, en vez de dar acceso a los británicos y a los australianos, el Pentágono empezó a crear un SIPRNET nuevo e independiente para ellos. El SIPRNET contenía años de información y los militares estadounidenses no querían mostrársela a los británicos y australianos. Se requeriría años para clasificar y analizar toda esa información. Las órdenes del presidente habían sido dar a los británicos y los australianos acceso a la verdadera SIPRNET, no crear una nueva versión para ellos.

El problema persistió. Meses después, aún no se había solucionado.

"TENEMOS UNA SITUACIÓN realmente mala aquí", le dijo el general Abizaid a Armitage, muy frustrado, un día del verano de 2004. "No se puede ganar militarmente".

Armitage le dijo esto a Powell. Más tarde, Powell regresó de una videoconferencia que incluyó al presidente y a Abizaid.

"No lo dijo allí, eso que le dijo a usted", le comentó Powell a Armitage.

"Ya lo sé", contestó Armitage. Peor aun. Cuando asistía a las reuniones del CNS, los jefes ahora hablaban sobre conteo de muertos. El número de insurgentes muertos era una parte habitual de las sesiones informativas. O bien Bush preguntaba, o bien los militares le contaban. A Armitage y los otros veteranos de Vietnam presentes en las reuniones esto les sonaba mal y además familiar.

Abizaid le había dicho antes al presidente que había cerca de 5.000 insurgentes violentos. "Señor presidente, hemos matado a montones de ellos aquí, pero sé que le dije en un momento dado que había 5.000 enemigos", dijo Abizaid más tarde, y agregó: "Hemos matado a más de 5.000 y todavía hay muchos". En otro momento, Abizaid afirmó que habían matado tres veces 5.000.

Cuando había una batalla grande cerca de la frontera con Siria, el presidente, atento a cualquier indicio de progreso, preguntaba: "¿A cuántos matamos?"

En su deseo de demostrar progreso, Abizaid daba la cifra.

En el 2003, aproximadamente un año antes de estas reuniones, entrevisté al general Pace, subjefe del Estado Mayor Conjunto, en varias ocasiones. Lo que se destacó en las diversas sesiones fueron sus denuncias enfáticas del conteo de muertos. "Ni una sola vez en este edificio hemos reportado una cifra", dijo. "Probablemente porque gente como yo, de Vietnam, sabe lo que sucede cuando uno empieza a contar. Se propicia un sesgo completo en la manera como la gente piensa, en la manera como operan las fuerzas terrestres. Queremos que el personal terrestre entienda que queremos que se haga el trabajo con el mínimo posible de muertos, pero que hay que hacer lo necesario para proteger a nuestros muchachos".

Las cifras de muertos se siguieron reportando y utilizando a manera de medición del progreso.

EN AGOSTO DE 2004, Frank Miller regresó a Irak, esta vez con Pace, quien era uno de los predilectos de Rumsfeld.

Miller consideraba que Pace era una excelente persona y un excelente oficial, pero se dio cuenta de que no era capaz de enfrentársele a Rumsfeld. Durante cuatro días, los dos hombres visitaron las principales ciudades de Irak y las zonas de combate. El 5 de agosto se detuvieron en el campamento Fallujah, donde Pace condecoró con medallas Corazón Púrpura a siete *marines* heridos en el, al parecer, interminable sitio. Miller les hacía a los comandantes de las fuerzas terrestres de todos los rangos la misma pregunta: ¿qué necesitan?

Los comandantes de división de entre 10.000 y 20.000 hombres y mujeres decían: traductores. Los comandantes de brigada de varios miles de personas decían: traductores. Los comandantes de batallón de entre 600 y 800 soldados decían: traductores. Se estaba enviando pequeños grupos o pelotones para requisar casas, aislar áreas y golpear y derribar puertas, sin traductores que supieran árabe.

La escasez era desmesurada, pensó Miller. Si las tropas estadounidenses y los iraquíes no podían hablar unos con otros, las posibilidades de malentendidos se multiplicaban. Se estaban presentando enormes fallas de comunicación todos los días. A veces, las tropas en misiones de patrullaje bien podrían haber sido ciegas. Nada consolidaría mejor la imagen de los estadounidenses como ocupantes imperiales que los grupos de soldados fuertemente armados con cascos y chaquetas blindadas recorriendo palmo a palmo el país, incapaces de comunicarse y sin que, al parecer, les interesara lo que los iraquíes pensaban, sentían o querían.

Una vez más, Miller recordó el valor de la verdad en el terreno. Cuando regresaron a Washington, observó a Pace, quien también había entendido el mensaje, esperando que él pudiera echar a rodar la bola. No sucedió nada. Miller llamó al teniente general Walter L. *Skip* Sharp, director de Planes y Política Estratégicos, el J-5, en el Estado Mayor Conjunto.

"Traductores", dijo Miller. "Necesitan traductores".

"No", dijo Sharp. "Necesitamos interrogadores". Él estaba pensando en lingüistas con otro tipo de destrezas, que no sólo hablaran árabe sino que también supieran cómo extraer información de inteligencia de los iraquíes capturados.

"Muy bien, necesitan interrogadores", dijo Miller, pero agregó que también necesitaban más traductores básicos.

"Hablaré con mi gente", prometió Sharp. Más tarde informó que había hablado sobre eso con algunos comandantes de brigada. "Estamos bien", dijo.

"Maldición", dijo Miller, "no están bien".

Finalmente, el Estado Mayor Conjunto envió a un brigadier general a Mosul para examinar la situación antes de la fecha en que debía asumir como segundo al mando de los militares estadounidenses en esa región.

"Le debo una disculpa", le dijo más tarde el general a Miller.

"Qué bien. ¿Por qué?"

"Necesitamos traductores".

Miller se preguntó por qué un viejo burócrata civil, como él, que formaba parte del CNS, tenía que decirles a los militares que necesitaban traductores a nivel de las unidades. Estaban muriendo niños debido a esta escasez. Planteó el asunto al comandante del cuerpo de *marines* y al jefe del Estado Mayor del Ejército, y finalmente habló con Rice.

"Solucione eso", dijo Rice. Miller debía recurrir a su autoridad, aunque a veces se preguntaba en qué consistía exactamente su autoridad. Era difícil conseguir traductores; podrían tardar años capacitándolos, años con los que no contaban. Decidió que la solución era hacer que el Departamento de Estado hiciera una convocatoria internacional de traductores. No tenía que ser en Irak. Podían ir a Argelia o Marruecos. Los traductores no necesitaban chequeos de seguridad; sólo necesitaban personas que hablaran tanto inglés como árabe. Había que enviarlos a Irak, pensó Miller, aislarlos por la noche en unas instalaciones seguras, quitarles los teléfonos celulares. Los emplearían durante seis meses y luego los enviarían de vuelta a casa con un cheque abultado. El dinero convencía.

Meses después, el problema aún no se había solucionado. Ahora era peor que un escándalo, creía Miller. "Creo que lo arruinamos", dijo después, con desesperación creciente. Más tarde aun, a fines del 2005, el "nosotros" se convirtió en "yo", y se culpó a sí mismo. "Fracasé, y no lo logré hacer", dijo.

En agosto de 2004, Moqtada al-Sadr, el joven clérigo chiíta militante, decidió enfrentar a Estados Unidos. El Gran Ayatollah Sistani, el verdadero centro de poder chiíta en Irak, había viajado a Londres para someterse a un tratamiento médico, y Moqtada había infiltrado a su gente en la ciudad de Najaf y, finalmente, en el santuario más sagrado de los chiítas, la mezquita del imán Alí.

Moqtada siempre había sido un buscapleitos, en opinión de Estados Unidos, y cerca de 4.000 *marines* y soldados estadounidenses rodearon el área y empezaron a acercarse al santuario de Alí.

Líderes árabes y musulmanes llamaron a la Casa Blanca y enviaron mensajes que decían: "Hagan lo que hagan, no ataquen la mezquita sagrada de Alí". Rice comprendió que un ataque contra el santuario crearía un problema tan grande con los chiítas, que Estados Unidos nunca iba a poder entregar un Irak unificado. Tenía el corazón en la boca. Si eso salía mal, posiblemente no iban a poder ganar.

Diversas órdenes de Washington –de la Casa Blanca, del Pentágono y del Departamento de Estado– llegaron pronto a Bagdad. Negroponte estaba de licencia, de modo que el general Casey y Jim Jeffrey intentaron discernir los mensajes contradictorios, que eran variaciones de: "Afronten al tipo". "No enfurezcan a los chiítas". "Manéjenlo; para eso tenemos embajadas y generales".

Jeffrey se reunía todas las noches con el primer ministro encargado Allawi. El seglar Allawi, a quien no le gustaban los *turbantes*, no quería dejar que Sistani volviera al país. Incluso, si eso significaba tomarse la mezquita por la fuerza, Allawi quería solucionar el problema sin Sistani. "Tenemos que aplastarlos", le dijo Allawi a Blackwill.

Con la previa autorización de Washington, Jeffrey le dijo a Allawi: "No puede hacer eso". Sistani, el líder de millones de chiítas iraquíes, tenía que poder regresar a Irak. Punto. ¿Por favor?

Allawi cedió. Su asesor de seguridad, Qasim Dawood, que tenía mejores relaciones con Sistani, se reunió con el ayatollah cuando ingresó al país por Basora, en el Sur.

Casey ordenó que prácticamente todos los grupos de francotiradores estadounidenses en el país se desplazaran a Najaf: las fuerzas especiales, los SEAL de la fuerza naval. Estaban disparando contra docenas de hombres de Moqtada en las instalaciones, semejantes a una ciudad, alrededor de la mezquita.

"¿Dónde diablos está John Negroponte?", preguntó Jeffrey, quien se dio cuenta de que esto podía ser la partida definitoria. Negroponte, que se había ido de vacaciones al Mar Egeo, estaba tratando de regresar. Allawi envió un ultimátum suave a Moqtada, que, en opinión de Jeffrey, era esencialmente una propuesta de "ellos ganan, nosotros perdemos". Sólo su nerviosismo superaba su ira.

Sistani ordenó entonces una marcha a Najaf y el sitio del Santuario de Alí.

"¿Qué están haciendo allá?", preguntaron la Casa Blanca, el Pentágono y el Departamento de Estado.

"Estamos más o menos mandando desde afuera", contestó Jeffrey, "y creemos que todo va a salir bien. Tenemos que confiar en estos tipos".

En Washington les costaba trabajo confiar.

Miles de personas bajaron pacíficamente hasta Najaf. Sistani convenció a Moqtada de que fuera a hablar con él y finalmente negociaron el retiro del Santuario de Alí. Jeffrey y Casey sólo tuvieron que prometer que no dispararían contra las fuerzas de Moqtada mientras salían de la mezquita. A Jeffrey esto le pareció un triunfo y reconoció una vez más el poder de Sistani. "Mientras logre urgir políticas que nos mantengan cerca de Sistani, estaré bien", dijo Jeffrey medio en broma. El presidente captó el mensaje. "¿Qué opina Sistani sobre esto?", se convirtió en una pregunta habitual. "Necesitamos saberlo. Averígüenlo".

Moqtada se replegó por el momento a su centro de poder en Ciudad Sadr, en el cuadrante nororiental de Bagdad, con sus 2 millones de seguidores.

FRANCES FRAGOS TOWNSEND, una ex fiscal federal de Nueva York de 42 años, fue nombrada jefe del Consejo de Seguridad Interna a mediados del 2004, lo que la convirtió en la principal asesora de Bush en materia de antiterrorismo en la Casa Blanca. Organizó varias reuniones con los jefes para abordar diversas propuestas delicadas de antiterrorismo. Rumsfeld envió a una persona de segundo o tercer nivel. Townsend, que había trabajado 13 años en el Departamento de Justicia, había aprendido que para sobrevivir era preciso evitar peleas burocráticas innecesarias. Decidió no objetar y prosiguió con las reuniones. Unas tres semanas después de asumir su cargo, tuvo una reunión del consejo con el presidente, en la que Rumsfeld la emprendió contra ella. Todas estas decisiones se estaban tomando sin su participación, dijo. Aseguró que nunca había recibido notificación de las reuniones. Townsend lo corrigió, diciendo que las notificaciones se habían hecho a través de la persona de su oficina encargada de recibir ese tipo de notificaciones, y citó el nombre y la información de contacto.

Poco después, Townsend recibió una invitación a un coctel en casa de Rumsfeld. Le preguntó a Rice si a ella la habían invitado; Rice contestó que no. Las dos mujeres rieron y bromearon sobre la necesidad de ir mano a mano con Rumsfeld.

Townsend tenía un asunto de antiterrorismo más delicado en su agenda. A lo largo de los años, Tenet había negociado acuerdos con entidades financieras y de telecomunicaciones para obtener acceso a ciertos registros telefónicos, financieros y de Internet relacionados con operaciones de inteligencia "negras". Tenet se encargó personalmente de casi todos estos acuerdos con los diversos directores ejecutivos de las empresas. Eran muy secretos y sumamente delicados; se basaban en gran parte en entendimientos informales. Tenet lo había hecho con gran pericia, jugando la carta del patriotismo y pidiendo a los directores ejecutivos que colaboraran en asuntos de seguridad nacional.

Después del 9/11, a medida que el FBI se fue involucrando cada vez más en operaciones antiterroristas en Estados Unidos, sus agentes a menudo iban a las corporaciones con requerimientos para obtener los mismos o similares registros telefónicos, financieros o de Internet. Además, el nuevo Departamento de Seguridad Interna, que se creó a fines del 2002 para reunir a 22 organismos federales tan disímiles como Aduanas, la Guardia Costera y el Servicio Secreto, quería hacer esto también.

Los directores ejecutivos empezaron a decir, muy bien, lo haremos una vez, pero no tres veces. Los requerimientos formales del FBI tendieron a prevalecer sobre los demás intentos.

El principal conflicto era entre el FBI y la CIA. Parte del acuerdo que había pactado Tenet implicaba a la División de Recursos Nacionales de la CIA, que tenía personal emplazado en una docena de ciudades importantes de Estados Unidos, para que la agencia pudiera entrevistar y reclutar a extranjeros que visitaban Estados Unidos. Los NR, como se les llamaba, aparentemente hacían arreglos de modo que otros organismos de inteligencia, como la Agencia Nacional de Seguridad, pudieran tener acceso a la información y los registros que los directores ejecutivos de las empresas habían aceptado suministrar.

El conflicto se volvió tan intenso que Townsend les pidió al director del FBI, Robert Mueller, y al director encargado de la CIA, John McLaughlin, que se reunieran con ella en la Casa Blanca, y les dijo que tenían que solucionar sus diferencias. Luego se reunió periódicamente con ellos hasta que cada uno nombró a un alto funcionario encargado de la coordinación, para que las empresas no se vieran bombardeadas con múltiples solicitudes.

Esto planteó una serie de interrogantes legales serios. A la CIA le estaba prohibido por ley recopilar inteligencia en Estados Unidos. Un funcionario, con quien conversé, dijo que los acuerdos que pactó Tenet sólo daban acceso a bancos de datos pasivos de las entidades financieras y de telecomunicaciones estadounidenses. Para obtener información específica sobre individuos específicos se necesitaba ya fueran requerimientos, órdenes FISA[16] (Ley de Vigilancia de Inteligencia Extranjera) autorizadas por la corte, o, bien, operaciones bajo la controvertida orden ejecutiva firmada por el presidente Bush después del 9/11, denominada Programa de Vigilancia de Terroristas[17], que facultaba a la Agencia Nacional de Seguridad para interceptar comunicaciones telefónicas o por Internet internacionales hacia o desde operativos sospechosos de Al Qaeda y sus partidarios.

No obstante, los acuerdos de Tenet eran una parte del turbio mundo de recopilación de inteligencia en el siglo XXI, que planteaba serios interrogantes sobre las libertades civiles y también demostraba que las leyes no habían avanzado al ritmo de la tecnología.

POWELL Y ARMITAGE conversaban en privado acerca de Bush, Cheney, la Casa Blanca y lo que en realidad estaba ocurriendo. Ambos querían que Bush triunfara y creían que la guerra de Irak se tenía que ganar, en aras de la estabilidad del Medio Oriente. Si se daba un retiro precipitado de Estados Unidos, sobrevendría el caos. Pero, ¿acaso no se podía ajustar la política?, se preguntaban. ¿No deberíamos ser todos más realistas?

"¿No los asaltarán dudas en algunos momentos?", le preguntó Armitage a Powell un día. ¿Acaso Bush no se preguntaba en lo más íntimo de su ser si todo esto era correcto?

Powell dijo que él se preguntaba lo mismo. Siempre estaban dudando. Vivían con la duda, se la inyectaban a sí mismos. Si uno no hacía esto, decía Powell, si no se levantaba por la mañana preguntándose si estaba haciendo bien las cosas o si todavía podía hacer algo mejor, no valía mucho.

"No vale nada", dijo Armitage.

La duda nunca se filtraba en la retórica pública del presidente. Y, según lo que veían Powell y Armitage, tampoco en privado.

Powell decía que Bush y Cheney no se atrevían a expresar reservas. Armitage se mostraba de acuerdo. "No pueden abrigar ninguna duda sobre lo correcto de la política porque eso suscitaría demasiadas preguntas en sus mentes".

Pero el presidente era el epicentro. Armitage estaba desconcertado. "¿Ha pensado detenidamente en esto?", le preguntó a Powell. "Lo que el presidente dice, en efecto, es que tenemos que seguir adelante para honrar la memoria de quienes han caído. Otra manera de decir esto es que más hombres tienen que caer con el fin de honrar la memoria de quienes ya han caído".

---

16. Foreign Intelligence Surveillance Act.
17. Terrorist Surveillance Program, TSP.

Yo HABÍA EXPLORADO el tema de la duda con Bush en varias entrevistas. En diciembre de 2001, tres meses después del 9/11 y varias semanas después del aparente éxito de la primera parte de la guerra en Afganistán, dijo lo siguiente cuando finalizaba una entrevista: "Sé que le es difícil creerlo, pero no he tenido dudas sobre lo que estamos haciendo. No he tenido dudas sobre lo que estamos haciendo... No existe ninguna duda en mi mente en cuanto a que estamos haciendo lo correcto".

Rice y otros habían dicho que la duda es un ingrediente esencial en la toma de decisiones, porque obliga a reconsiderar y reajustar los planes con cuidado. Insistí sobre este asunto con Bush en una entrevista que le hice en agosto de 2002 en su rancho de Crawford. El tema era la guerra de Afganistán, pero el presidente estaba, por supuesto, muy implicado en la planeación secreta de la guerra contra Irak, que iniciaría siete meses después.

"Primero que todo", dijo, "un presidente tiene que ser el calcio de la espina dorsal. Si yo me debilito, todo el equipo se debilita. Si tengo dudas, le aseguro que habrá muchas dudas. Si mi nivel de confianza en nuestra capacidad disminuye, se sentirán las ondas en toda la organización. Es decir que es esencial que nos mostremos confiados y decididos y unidos.

"No necesito a mi lado gente inestable... Y si hay una actitud de estrujarse las manos en tiempos difíciles, no me gusta".

Los tiempos difíciles iniciales en la guerra de Afganistán, en realidad, sólo duraron un rato. Fue el breve lapso entre la discusión pública sobre un empantanamiento y el rápido colapso de los talibanes. En Irak, sin embargo, los tiempos difíciles –la violencia, las muertes, la incertidumbre y todos los indicios de un empantanamiento– habían durado años y persistían.

EN LOS ESCASOS MOMENTOS en que Rice tenía algo de tiempo para leer, le gustaba hacerlo sobre los padres fundadores para recordar que los Estados Unidos de América nunca han debido nacer. En particular, le impresionaba el libro *1776*, de David McCullough, sobre la época más oscura de la revolución estadounidense. El general George Washington le escribió una carta privada a su hermano, en la que reflexionaba sobre el contraste entre su comportamiento público y su conocimiento de tantas circunstancias funestas. "Muchas de mis dificultades y aflicciones eran de unas características tan peculiares que, con el fin de ocultarlas al enemigo, me veía forzado a ocultarlas a mis amigos, incluso a mi propio ejército", escribió Washington, "con lo cual sometía mi conducta a interpretaciones que en poco favorecían mi carácter".

Rice sostenía ante sus colegas que ni ella ni el presidente sentían una aflicción similar. "Asunto difícil", decía, pero Bush le había dicho, "veo el camino en Irak".

A menudo Rice utilizaba analogías del fútbol americano en su círculo interno. "Van a ser sacados de vez en cuando", dijo en una ocasión. "De vez en cuando quizás metan la pata. Pero no quiere decir que sintamos que hemos perdido 25 puntos sin tiempos y quedándonos un minuto y 34 segundos para actuar".

PERO LA REALIDAD EN IRAK era la violencia en aumento. Los ataques iniciados por enemigos contra la coalición y los iraquíes habían sumado cerca de 200 en junio de 2003. En el verano de 2004 ascendían a cerca de 1.750 mensuales, un incremento de casi nueve veces, según los resúmenes confidenciales que se entregaban a los altos funcionarios. Esta información no necesariamente se le ocultaba a la opinión pública, pero se procuraba no destacarla, y no se informaba con regularidad. Los informes noticiosos en la televisión y la prensa tendían a concentrarse en los ataques espectaculares que mataban a docenas de personas o más. Pero la perturbadora verdad era que Irak se había convertido en un país en donde lo normal eran casi 60 ataques diarios.

30

Poco después de la renuncia de Tenet, Andy Card llamó a Armitage y le preguntó si le interesaba el cargo de director de la CIA.

No, contestó Armitage enfáticamente.

"¿Puedo saber la razón? Nos decepciona".

Armitage contestó que podía decirle la razón pero que preferiría no hacerlo porque podría herirle los sentimientos.

Card sabía que el problema de Armitage eran Cheney y Rumsfeld. No obstante, le preguntó a Powell si habría alguna manera de persuadir a Armitage.

"Le puede preguntar nuevamente", contestó Powell, "pero él no se anda con rodeos". Un no de Armitage es un no. "Yo creo que no aceptará".

En opinión de Armitage, la segunda mejor respuesta, después de "sí", que alguien podía dar, era "no". Era una respuesta contundente. Permitía avanzar. Según creía, en Washington se tentaba la suerte si uno se quedaba mucho tiempo. El momento para marcharse era cuando uno estaba en la cima, cuando todo el mundo decía "usted es el hombre". Según ese estándar, Powell y él ya se habían quedado demasiado tiempo.

Armitage concluyó que la sanción por estar en desacuerdo en la Casa Blanca de Bush era una acusación implícita o explícita de no formar parte del equipo. Si él o Powell decían que algo podría ser más difícil de lo que parecía, Rice o Hadley consideraban que no formaban parte del equipo. Si decían, como lo habían hecho, "quizás a los iraquíes no les guste que ocupemos su país mucho tiempo", eso significaba que no eran del equipo.

Powell estaba logrando hablar con Bush durante unos 20 minutos a la semana. En teoría, se suponía que debían reunirse solos, pero Cheney muchas veces estaba presente. El vicepresidente no decía nada, pero después, según creía firmemente Powell, Cheney le presentaba a Bush una u otra versión de aquél "no está en el equipo".

Powell y Armitage entendían que la Casa Blanca percibiera al Departamento de Estado y sus diplomáticos como apaciguadores. Cheney, Rumsfeld y, hasta cierto punto, Rice no permitían que el Departamento de Estado participara en diplomacia porque consideraban la diplomacia como una debilidad.

"La idea que tienen de la diplomacia", le dijo Armitage a Powell en una ocasión, "es que consiste en decir 'escuche, cabrón, haga lo que nosotros queremos'".

No obstante, como Irak había consumido tanta atención, dinero, fuerza militar y esfuerzo político –absorbiendo el oxígeno de todo lo demás, como le había advertido Powell a Bush seis meses antes de la guerra–, el resultado era que Estados Unidos no tenía una opción distinta de comprometerse en la diplomacia. Era, por ejemplo, la única herramienta que les quedaba para tratar con Corea del Norte e Irán.

EL 11 DE AGOSTO, EL PRESIDENTE BUSH nombró a Porter Goss, de 65 años, veterano de ocho períodos en el Congreso por el estado de Florida y presidente de la Comisión de Inteligencia de la Cámara, nuevo director de la CIA. Armitage se topó con él poco después. Pobre Porter, pensó.

"¿Qué hace un tipo buena gente como usted en un cargo como éste?", le preguntó Armitage.

"Pensé que usted iba a asumir el cargo y que yo lo podría evitar", contestó Goss.

"Por ningún motivo", dijo Armitage. "He estado adentro demasiado tiempo. Porter, uno nunca debe aceptar un cargo si no sabe quién va a ser su jefe".

De conformidad con la nueva legislación sobre inteligencia, el director nacional de inteligencia tendría un rango superior al del director de la CIA. Goss y sus sucesores tendrían que reportarle al DNI, fuera quien fuese.

EL 18 DE AGOSTO, DAVID KAY testificó ante el Congreso acerca de la inteligencia sobre las ADM en Irak. Había muchas culpas por repartir, dijo, pero su crítica más específica se dirigió al CNS y, por implicación, a Rice.

"Muy francamente, en mi opinión, el perro que no ladró en el caso del programa de ADM de Irak es el Consejo Nacional de Seguridad", testificó Kay.

Al día siguiente, el testimonio de Kay apareció en la prensa. Kay acababa de leer el artículo cuando recibió una llamada de Robert Joseph, el funcionario del CNS encargado de proliferación de armas, quien trabajaba para Rice. Lo invitó a almorzar. Kay y Joseph se conocían desde hacía 15 años.

"Esta conversación nunca tuvo lugar", le dijo Joseph tan pronto se sentaron. La emprendió contra Kay. ¿Cómo pudo testificar sobre Rice de semejante manera? Ella era la mejor consejera nacional de seguridad en la historia de Estados Unidos.

"Pues podría haber dejado de tratar de ser la mejor amiga del presidente, para ser más bien la mejor consejera, y haberse dado cuenta de que su función es de escrutinio", dijo Kay. Cuando Tenet insistió en que el caso de las ADM era una "clavada", ella ha debido adoptar una actitud agresiva y exigir que se reexaminara en profundidad hasta la última prueba de la "clavada".

Joseph fue categórico. Rice había hecho lo más posible. La comunidad de inteligencia y la CIA la habían ofuscado, dijo.

Kay concluyó que Joseph había sido enviado por Rice a hablar con él, y que no ganaba nada con matar al mensajero. Le sorprendió lo susceptible que era.

No se dejó conmover. "Probablemente ha sido la peor asesora nacional de seguridad en tiempos modernos desde que se creó la oficina", dijo Kay.

MEGHAN O'SULLIVAN, la joven Ph. D. de Oxford que había sido temporalmente retirada del equipo de Jay Garner por recomendación de la vicepresidencia, resultó siendo una sobreviviente tanto de Bagdad como de Washington. Después de su experiencia de inclusión, exclusión e inclusión en el grupo de Garner, había llegado a Irak. Ella, Scott Carpenter y Roman Martínez eran unos de los subalternos de más confianza de Bremer, y unos de los pocos que habían trabajado con él en Irak durante la toda la vigencia de la Autoridad Provisional de Coalición. Después del traslado de la soberanía, volvió a la Casa Blanca con Blackwill para trabajar con el equipo del CNS.

"Entonces", le dijo a Miller cuando llegó, "según entiendo, se supone que yo voy a asumir todo Irak en algún momento".

"Tal vez", respondió Miller, un tanto irritado. "Pero yo todavía estoy aquí".

Miller empezó a recibir quejas de algunos de sus contactos en el Pentágono, fuentes que había cultivado durante sus tres decenios en el gobierno. Confrontó a O'Sullivan. El Departamento de Defensa era su territorio. "Yo no me meto en sus asuntos", le dijo Miller. "No se meta usted en los míos". Pronto concluyó que O'Sullivan era muy brillante, pero que sabía muy poco sobre seguridad, reconstrucción o la manera como los militares libran guerras. Era del área de políticas, pensó. Con el surgimiento de las milicias iraquíes, los grupos sectarios armados privados, a ella se le ocurrió una idea: "Reclutemos a los milicianos en el ejército iraquí", propuso.

"Meghan, esa es una idea muy mala", le dijo Miller. Las milicias no eran controlables. Trabajaban para líderes o clérigos sectarios como Moqtada al-Sadr.

Todas las noches, Miller y O'Sullivan elaboraban el informe para Bush sobre la situación en Irak. Era corto —una o dos páginas, quizás, nunca más de cuatro– y se limitaba a referir los desarrollos clave en materia de política, reconstrucción y asuntos militares, y siempre incluía las cifras de muertos más recientes. O'Sullivan tenía contactos personales con muchos líderes iraquíes debido al tiempo que pasó con Bremer, y solía conversar largamente por teléfono con algunos de ellos. Miller observó que incluía en los informes para el presidente lo que les había escuchado.

Estos viejos y astutos jeques le están sacando partido, y lo que le dicen le llega directamente y sin filtros al presidente, pensó Miller. Decidió hablar con Hadley, quien, al parecer, entendió su inquietud. Es muy brillante pero tiene algunas fallas significativas y necesita que la supervisen, convino Hadley. Dijo que buscaría la manera de asignarle un superior para que la mantuviera a raya. Pero eso no sucedió. Pronto ella fue su propia jefa y la encargada de Irak en el CNS. Miller estaba asombrado.

En agosto de 2004, la cifra de ataques iniciados por enemigos aumentó en 1.000, en comparación con el mes anterior, y llegó a 3.000, según los informes confidenciales. Rice odiaba levantarse por la mañana a leer el periódico. Había siempre artículos negativos, y las elecciones presidenciales de Estados Unidos tendrían lugar en pocos meses.

"Me siento como un personaje del Correcaminos", le dijo a su gente, "aferrándose a una rama y moviendo rápidamente los pies, mientras ciertos artículos de periódico llegan y cortan la rama".

A comienzos de septiembre, el director de comunicaciones de la Casa Blanca, Dan Bartlett, convocó una reunión de expertos de los diversos departamentos y organismos, con el fin de establecer qué se podía hacer para mejorar el mensaje sobre Irak.

Varias personas sugirieron que el presidente debía reconocer con cautela algunos de los errores cometidos en Irak, aduciendo que es humano y poderoso admitir una equivocación.

No, dijo Bartlett, cerrando la puerta, con lo que dejó en claro que el presidente no iba a referirse a ningún error.

"¿Quiere que inspire o que informe?", preguntó uno de los generales presentes en la reunión.

Las dos cosas, dijo Bartlett.

"Es probable que no se pueda hacer ambas cosas", dijo el general. Informar a la gente a veces es aburrido, y un mensaje que inspire suele ser más retórico y no basarse en los hechos. Citó al ex presidente Reagan, a quien llamaban el Gran Comunicador, que rehuía los hechos pero podía pronunciar discursos alentadores.

"Gracias", dijo Bartlett.

Bush no tuvo que reelaborar su mensaje. Aunque era su guerra, el foco de las comunicaciones alumbraba a su oponente, el senador John Kerry, candidato demócrata, por su servicio en Vietnam como comandante de Lanchas Rápidas de la Armada, y también por sus votos en el Senado autorizando la guerra, y por haber votado en contra de la asignación de US $87.000 millones para financiación bélica.

El presidente no tenía que inspirar o informar. Podía ocultarse en la bruma creada por el mal manejo del mensaje de Kerry. El senador se enfocó en el pasado para defender su servicio en Vietnam y en el Senado pero nunca explicó cómo utilizaría el poder presidencial. Bush lo había dejado muy en claro. Había utilizado el poder para lanzar una guerra, y no se iba a echar para atrás.

NEWT GINGRICH llegó a la Casa Blanca a comienzos del otoño del 2004 para hablar con el equipo del CNS sobre Irak. Esto es lo que anda mal, dijo, soltando con gran seguridad su letanía. Los administradores no tienen flexibilidad. No estamos abordando las causas profundas de las inquietudes de la gente. No nos hemos acercado lo suficiente a las poblaciones locales. No tenemos traductores.

Traductores, pensó Frank Miller. Otra vez ese tema.

Más tarde, Gingrich habló con Miller. "¿No le interesó lo que yo estaba diciendo, o ya lo sabía? Porque, por lo general, cuando digo estas cosas la gente se sorprende y reacciona".

"No", dijo Miller. "He ido dos veces. He estado haciendo esto desde hace dieciocho meses. No me está contando nada que no sepa".

CARD EMPEZÓ A ESCUCHAR que las cosas no marchaban bien en Langley bajo la dirección de Porter Goss. Goss seguía con demasiada frecuencia un cronograma de tipo parlamentario: salía de Washington el jueves por la noche y regresaba el lunes. Había presidido la Comisión de Inteligencia de la Cámara durante siete años y había nombrado a su director de personal en la comisión, Pat Murray, nuevo jefe de gabinete de la CIA. Murray estaba tratando a muchas personas con experiencia en la agencia de una manera equivocada. De modo que Card tomó la muy inusual decisión de pedir una cita para conversar con Goss en la sede de la CIA.

"El presidente lo escogió a usted para dirigir la CIA", le dijo Card a Goss. "No escogió a Pat Murray".

"Sólo me está ayudando", dijo Goss.

Porter, le dijo Card, usted está aislado en el edificio. Todo parecía estar pasando a través de Pat Murray. Salga de esta oficina del séptimo piso, desplácese e interactúe con la gente en el edificio, coma en la cafetería, agite la bandera, levante la moral, dé golpecitos en las espaldas, recorra las oficinas.

Buenas sugerencias, dijo Goss.

Hable con los ex directores de la CIA, con Bob Gates, incluso con el ex presidente Bush. Y converse con otras personas como el almirante William Studeman, quien fue director de la ANS y subdirector de la CIA. "Todos están hablando", le advirtió Card. "Llámelos. Invítelos a que vengan y pregúnteles". Card consideró que simplemente le estaba dando a Goss unos consejos básicos sobre liderazgo. Trabaje en estrecho contacto con Bob Mueller, el director del FBI, y establezca relaciones con la gente de Seguridad Interna y del Departamento de Defensa.

Card le dijo al presidente que había ido a la CIA para darle a Goss un poco de capacitación gerencial.

"Bien, bien, bien", dijo Bush. "Me alegra que haya hecho eso".

En octubre de 2004, el primer ministro interino Allawi le escribió al presidente Bush. Por donde quiera que viajara en Irak, estaba siendo transportado en un avión militar de gran tamaño que decía "U. S. AIR FORCE" en el costado, dijo Allawi. No era precisamente la imagen de un Irak libre y soberano que él o Estados Unidos querían proyectar. ¿Podría disponer de un avión propio?

El tema se trató en una reunión del CNS, y Bush dejó claro que quería que Allawi tuviera aviones propios. Después, Frank Miller salió con el jefe y el subjefe del Estado Mayor Conjunto.

"Hágalo", le dijo Myers a Pace.

Pasaron varias semanas y Miller no supo nada más, de modo que llamó a algunos de sus contactos en el Estado Mayor Conjunto.

"Ya está solucionado", fue la respuesta. "Los británicos los están transportando ahora".

Esto no es posible, se dijo Miller. "No, ese no es el punto", dijo. "Lo importante no es la Real Fuerza Aérea en vez de la Fuerza Aérea de Estados Unidos". Lo importante era que el avión de Allawi fuera iraquí.

"Ah, ya entiendo".

Transcurrieron otras semanas. Ahora el plan había sido frenado por el Departamento de Estado, al que le preocupaba transferir tecnología militar estadounidense sensible a un gobierno extranjero. Finalmente, a fines de diciembre pintaron tres C-130 con banderas iraquíes en la cola.

Myers pensó que no estaba mal, en lo que a tiempo se refería. Tres meses era un logro. Pero Miller consideró ridículo que se requiriera tanto esfuerzo para lograr el cumplimiento de una sencilla orden presidencial, en el espíritu en que se había dado. El ritmo de caracol no se debía a que a nadie le importara, aunque Miller pensaba que a veces eso era lo que parecía. Se debía a que con mucha frecuencia no se asignaba la responsabilidad a una persona específica que tuviera que rendir cuentas por su función.

Las quejas de Miller finalmente fueron atendidas, hasta cierto punto, por el Pentágono.

Myers llamó para decir: "Tenemos un plan maestro".

Hadley fue al Pentágono para que le informaran, y llevó a Miller y a O'Sullivan consigo. Skip Sharp, quien presidía la dirección de planes y política, les hizo una presentación con 60 o 70 asuntos que, según dijo, había que lograr en Irak. Era otra pesada lista de temas básicos de infraestructura y seguridad. Cada elemento estaba marcado con los usuales rojo, amarillo o verde, que indicaban el supuesto progreso.

Al finalizar la reunión del Pentágono, Hadley le dijo a Miller: "Tome, Frank, llévesela. Guardián de las listas. Llévesela".

Miller sabía que el Departamento de Estado tenía una lista muy similar. Una gran parte coincidía: objetivos encomiables, como poner a funcionar la electricidad, construir redes de alcantarillado y dar nuevamente empleo a los iraquíes. Había que cerciorarse de que hubiera representantes de la embajada con cada comandante militar, decía la lista del Departamento de Estado, y de que cada representante de la embajada estuviera acompañado por alguien de USAID. Pero la lista nunca se redujo a ocho o diez objetivos prioritarios.

El príncipe Bandar y su asistente, Rihab Massoud, se reunieron media docena de veces con el presidente Bush en el 2004. Las profundas convicciones religiosas de Bush afloraron en repetidas ocasiones, mientras hablaba sobre su fe y su relación con Dios. El presidente dejó claro que no abrigaba duda alguna de que una autoridad superior lo estaba cuidando y guiando. "Obtengo la guía de Dios en la oración", dijo, y se refirió a varias ocasiones en las que había orado para recibir esta guía y la había obtenido.

El Señor había desempeñado una función importante en su vida, dijo Bush, y la oración era un elemento significativo de su rutina diaria. Le ayudaba, afirmó, y le brindaba consuelo. Afirmó que sentía las cargas que Dios le había puesto sobre los hombros como presidente. Bush dijo que confiaba en su fe para seguir adelante.

Cada vez que Bush veía o hablaba con el príncipe heredero, se refería a la creencia profunda en Dios que ambos compartían. El príncipe le mandó a Bush una oración, y el presidente le dijo a Bandar que la utilizaba.

"Es la cosa más preciosa que he recibido en mi vida", dijo el presidente.

En los dos meses anteriores a las elecciones presidenciales, Bush anduvo incesantemente en campaña. Rice decidió que ella, Hadley o Bob Blackwill debían viajar con el presidente a donde quiera que él fuera.

Como Rice estaba pronunciando discursos propios en todo el país –una función controvertida para un asesor nacional de seguridad– y Hadley era más una especie de gerente práctico del CNS, los viajes de campaña con frecuencia le tocaron a Blackwill. Se levantaba a las 4:30 todas las mañanas, para revisar el Informe Diario para el presidente con la CIA, antes de que lo recibiera Bush. Blackwill concentraba su atención en si algo en el informe diario podría causar dificultades en la campaña. ¿Qué podía estar sucediendo, que de repente pudiera surgir como tema electoral? Prestaba especial atención a los informes de inteligencia sobre posibles ataques terroristas en Estados Unidos.

La rutina diaria de campaña empezaba después de que Bush escuchaba el Informe Diario, lo cual tomaba entre 20 y 25 minutos antes de las 7 de la mañana. Luego él y su séquito se dirigían a la Base Andrews de la Fuerza Aérea. Por lo general había 6 o 7 eventos programados, quizás en tres Estados, y Bush viajaba en helicóptero para desplazarse entre uno y otro. Las paradas muchas veces duraban una hora o menos. Bush aterrizaba, pronunciaba su discurso y enseguida volvía a estar en el aire.

Karen Hughes, asistente y asesora de comunicaciones de Bush desde hacía bastante tiempo, dedicaba las horas de viaje a escribir las palabras que pronunciaría Bush y a reelaborar su discurso de base. Karl Rove se encargaba de informar al presidente sobre la estrategia de campaña, calibrando el impacto de las visitas presidenciales en los Estados clave.

"Si se detiene aquí en Ohio, puede llegarle al extremo de West Virginia", le dijo Rove a Bush en un momento dado.

Blackwill se sorprendía de que no hubiera en realidad tiempo para hablar sobre políticas. Entre parada y parada o mientras volaban, cada vez que surgía el tema de Irak siempre era a través del prisma de la campaña. ¿Qué había dicho el candidato demócrata, el senador de Massachusetts John Kerry, ese día sobre Irak? ¿Qué había sucedido en Irak que pudiera tener algún impacto en la reelección del presidente? Como coordinador del CNS para Irak, Blackwill probablemente sabía tanto sobre la guerra como cualquier persona en la Casa Blanca. Había pasado meses en Irak con Bremer. Pero estaba con la campaña únicamente como parte de la política de reelección. Ni una sola vez le preguntó Bush a Blackwill cómo eran las cosas en Irak, qué había visto o qué se debería hacer. A Blackwill le sorprendía la concentración exclusiva y permanente en ganar las elecciones. Nada más parecía importar.

En los días y semanas anteriores al día de los comicios, se incrementó la violencia en Irak. Las cifras confidenciales indicaban que el número de ataques insurgentes había aumentado fuertemente en el verano, pasando de aproximadamente 1.750 en junio y julio a más de 3.000 en agosto. En septiembre había surgido algo de esperanza, pues el número de ataques se redujo a poco más de 2.000, pero en octubre otra vez habían aumentado a cerca de 2.500.

La violencia era ahora 10 veces peor que cuando Bush había aterrizado en el portaaviones, en mayo de 2003 y había declarado que el principal combate había terminado. Las nuevas unidades del ejército y la policía iraquíes, recién entrenados, estaban siendo masacradas. Los insurgentes estaban obteniendo inteligencia confiable y actuando de conformidad con ella. En la provincia de Diyala, unos 100 kilómetros al nororiente de Bagdad, insurgentes disfrazados de policías iraquíes montaron un retén falso el 23 de octubre. Sacaron a 49 nuevos soldados iraquíes de un bus, los forzaron a acostarse sobre el piso y los ejecutaron con disparos en la cabeza. Entre el 30% y el 50% de las unidades iraquíes entrenadas se desintegraron y sus miembros regresaron a sus casas.

Para Blackwill era claro que las cosas no marchaban bien. Durante más de un año lo había desconcertado el hecho de que no hubiera ninguna estrategia militar. Una y otra vez, Bush se refería a su estrategia en Irak en sus discursos de campaña, pero nunca daba detalles específicos. Mencionaba metas, expresaba su optimismo y su determinación y daba charlas animosas. "Tenemos una estrategia que les dice a nuestros comandantes que se adapten a los usos en el terreno", dijo Bush en un discurso pronunciado el 23 de septiembre en Bangor, Maine. "El camino para prevalecer, el camino hacia la conclusión exitosa que todos queremos, el camino para asegurar a Irak y traer a nuestros soldados de regreso es no languidecer ni flaquear, y no enviar señales mixtas al enemigo. Podemos entristecernos, pero no vamos a flaquear".

Blackwill había enseñado estrategia en Harvard. La estrategia implica una serie de acciones para alcanzar una meta y exige contestar preguntas como ¿qué se va a hacer?, ¿quién lo va a hacer?, ¿cuándo?, ¿dónde?, ¿cómo? El presidente, a quien Blackwill admiraba y respetaba como líder político, hablaba más bien sobre victorias y metas. Pero como solía enseñar Blackwill en sus clases, "las aspiraciones no son estrategia". El gobierno no tenía una estrategia real, concluyó.

Rice había dejado en claro que su autoridad no se extendía a Rumsfeld o a los militares, de modo que Blackwill nunca forzó el tema con ella. Sin embargo, se preguntaba por qué el presidente nunca impugnaba a los militares. ¿Por qué no le decía al general Abizaid, al finalizar alguna de sus sesiones informativas por video seguro, "John, hagamos otra de estas el jueves; lo que en realidad quiero de usted es que, por favor, me explique, digamos en una hora y media, su estrategia militar para ganar".

La ausencia de estrategia en Irak y la situación cada vez peor en el terreno eran temas que nunca se discutían en la campaña. En parte, eso obedeció a la destreza política. La opinión pública se enteraba de los actos de violencia espectaculares específicos por las noticias que transmitían los medios. Pero la evidencia real de cuán mal marchaban las cosas –los datos y tendencias de la violencia, la cantidad y efectividad de los ataques iniciados por enemigos– se mantenía como información confidencial, oculta a los votantes.

31

El 2 de noviembre de 2004 fue uno de los días más importantes en la vida de Bush. Sus comentarios, interacciones y comportamiento el día de las elecciones fueron bien documentados internamente en la Casa Blanca por sus subalternos, amigos y tomadores de notas. El día muestra cómo Bush procesaba la información, tomaba decisiones y reaccionaba, tanto ante las malas noticias como ante las buenas.

Bush votó temprano ese día en la estación de bomberos de Crawford, en el distrito electoral 80, cerca de su rancho de Texas. Tomó un teléfono móvil para llamar a su principal estratega y encuestador, Matthew Dowd.

"Matty, ¿qué cree que va a suceder?".

"Señor Presidente, creo que va a ganar por dos o tres puntos porcentuales".

"¿Sí?", dijo Bush. "Como sabe, soy un hombre de cinco puntos". El último sondeo daba a Bush y al candidato demócrata, el senador Kerry, un empate: 48% para cada uno. Pero Bush había estado diciendo que quería ganar por un 5%. Eso le decían sus entrañas.

"Sí, lo sé", dijo Dowd. "Me agrada su optimismo, pero no creo que eso vaya a suceder".

"Ya lo veremos", dijo Bush, poniendo fin a la llamada.

A primera vista, John Kerry había parecido un contendor formidable. Senador por Massachusetts durante cuatro períodos del Congreso y dos años mayor que Bush, se había ganado la Estrella de Plata y tres Corazones Púrpura en combate, al mando de una Lancha Rápida de la Armada, en Vietnam en 1968 y 1969. Pero el grupo denominado Veteranos de Lanchas Rápidas por la Verdad había impugnado el heroísmo de Kerry y publicado un libro, *Unfit for Command*, que de inmediato se convirtió en el más vendido en las listas de *best-sellers*. Kerry y su campaña no habían respondido con suficiente fuerza. Como senador, Kerry había votado para autorizar la guerra en Irak, y durante la campaña no había encontrado una manera de criticarla efectivamente. En términos generales Kerry, parecía inseguro y dudoso, mientras que Bush logró proyectarse en la campaña como consistente y decidido.

El día de las elecciones, después de votar en Crawford, Bush hizo una última parada en Ohio, antes de regresar en el Air Force One, el avión presidencial, a Washington a media tarde. Karl Rove recibió una llamada de Dowd cerca de las 3 de la tarde, mientras el avión descendía en medio de las nubes para aterrizar en la Base Andrews de la Fuerza Aérea, en Maryland. La conexión se cortó, pero pronto se reestableció en el teléfono móvil de Rove.

"No se ve bien", le dijo Dowd a Rove, recitando cifras del primer conteo de votos en boca de urna, un muestreo de los votantes de los distritos electorales clave. Rove sostuvo el teléfono contra el cuello y trató de escribir en una hoja de papel sobre la rodilla.

En Mississippi, un bastión del sólido sur republicano, Bush sólo llevaba un punto porcentual de ventaja, según las encuestas en boca de urna. Los resultados en Pennsylvania y en New Hampshire eran todavía peores. Bush estaba por debajo 17 y 19 puntos, respectivamente, pese a que los sondeos preelectorales habían indicado sólo uno o dos puntos por debajo. Otras cifras le daban a Bush un solo punto de ventaja en el Estado de Virginia, notoriamente republicano, e indicaban que en Colorado y Nevada la contienda estaba demasiado reñida.

"Maldición", dijo Rove. "¿Cómo puede estar sucediendo esto?".

Dowd también intentaba encontrar una respuesta para esa pregunta. "Es una de dos", dijo, "o estas cifras están completamente equivocadas, o entendimos completamente mal al electorado, y no quiero pensar que se trata del segundo caso, porque eso significaría que en realidad no sabíamos lo que estábamos haciendo". Se convertirían en leyenda, culpables de mal desempeño en campaña.

Rice, que había acompañado a Bush en sus viajes durante los últimos cuatro días de campaña, vio que las encuestas indicaban que en su Estado natal, Alabama, Bush iba "+ 1%". ¿En Alabama, uno de los Estados republicanos más confiables, Bush sólo llevaba un punto de ventaja? Según los sondeos preelectorales, en ese Estado iba a obtener un cómodo margen de doble dígito. Salió de la cabina de Bush para no tener que verle la cara al presidente y se dirigió a la parte de atrás del avión.

"No quería estar en el mismo recinto con el presidente en ese momento", les dijo luego a sus colegas. "Simplemente no quería".

Rove caminó en dirección contraria, hacia la cabina de adelante, mientras el Air Force One tocaba tierra.

"Tengo las cifras", le dijo a Bush, "y no parecen muy alentadoras". Se las leyó. Se limitó cuidadosamente a los hechos, pero luego agregó con desconcierto: "Algunas simplemente no tienen sentido".

"No lo puedo creer", dijo Bush. "¿Usted qué piensa?", preguntó cuando recuperó el aliento.

"No lo sé", contestó Rove, y añadió que no había revisado los datos de las encuestas en boca de urna en detalle. "Tengo que esperar hasta que lleguemos a la Casa Blanca y examine las cifras. Es la primera ola. Por lo general, son poco confiables pero algo… o nos van a ganar o hay algún problema grande con estos números".

"Bueno", dijo Bush con tranquilidad, "esperemos a ver qué pasa. Ya hemos pasado por esto antes". No tuvo que mencionar los 36 días de agitación después de la campaña del 2000, antes de que la Corte Suprema definiera la elección a favor suyo. Ese año, el triunfo en la Florida había sido por apenas 537 de los 6.138.765 votos. "Les voy a contar a Laura y a las chicas", dijo el presidente.

Una de sus hijas mellizas estalló en lágrimas cuando él dio la noticia.

"Escuchen, quiero que tengan fe", le dijo el presidente a su familia. "Quiero ver una sonrisa en todas las caras. La noche no ha terminado".

Mientras volaban en helicóptero desde la base Andrews hasta la Casa Blanca, Bush cayó en cuenta de que los medios habían visto las mismas cifras de las encuestas en boca de urna. Las cámaras iban a estar a la caza de rostros de angustia o derrota: la fotografía o filmación mortal que revelara la cruda emoción de las malas noticias.

"Todos, a poner buena cara", ordenó el presidente.

EN LA CASA BLANCA, el jefe de gabinete Card también había visto las mismas cifras de los sondeos en boca de urna, y él y algunos otros miembros del personal estaban aguardando para saludar al presidente cuando descendió del helicóptero.

"Todos sonriendo", les dijo Card a los demás tan pronto salieron.

"Me alegra mucho verlo", le dijo Card al presidente, exhibiendo una sonrisa de oreja a oreja. "Excelente día. ¡Qué día tan maravilloso!".

"¿Vio las cifras?", preguntó Bush mientras entraban.

"Sí", contestó. "Vi las cifras. No creo en esas cifras. Y no sólo eso, usted no cree en esas cifras. Entonces estamos en una buena posición.

"¿Qué está pasando?", preguntó Bush. "¿Qué está pasando?".

Card y Rove se apartaron para conferenciar y el presidente se fue detrás de ellos. Card dijo que no creía que las cifras fueran verosímiles.

"No se preocupe", le dijo a Bush. Iban a tratar de obtener más información. "No se obsesione con eso. Todo va a salir bien".

El presidente dijo que no quería estar rodeado de gente. "Voy a subir", dijo, refiriéndose a su residencia en la Casa Blanca. Él y Laura habían invitado a una docena de amigos y familiares a pasar la noche allí. La Casa Blair, la casa de huéspedes auxiliar, al otro lado de Pennsylvania Avenue, también estaba llena de amigos. Los hoteles locales estaban repletos. El presidente no quería ver a toda esa gente todavía. "No estoy listo", dijo. "No estoy listo".

RICE SE ENCAMINÓ directamente desde el helicóptero a sus oficinas en el Ala Oeste. A Hadley le sorprendió su aspecto. La había visto unas 20 veces al día, casi a diario durante cuatro años, en medio de la crisis del 9/11, la guerra de Afganistán, la guerra de Irak. En las buenas y en las malas, siempre había sido fiel al apodo que su gente le había puesto –la Princesa Guerrera– y siempre había parecido en perfecto control de sus emociones. Pero ahora Rice se veía mal. Incluso, había relajado ligeramente su pose, por lo general, casi perfecta. Hadley, quien vivía ajeno al mundo político de Washington y tenía pocos contactos en los medios de comunicación, no se había enterado de los resultados de las encuestas en boca de urna. Siguió a Rice hasta su oficina y cerró la puerta.

"Condi, ¿qué pasa?", espetó.

"Acabamos de ver las encuestas iniciales, y no son buenas", dijo ella. De hecho, eran bastante alarmantes pues vaticinaban un triunfo apabullante del senador Kerry.

LOS PADRES DEL MANDATARIO, el ex presidente Bush y la primera dama Bárbara Bush, se contaban entre quienes iban a pasar la noche en la Casa Blanca. Uno de los amigos de larga data de la familia Bush se acercó a Bárbara Bush.

"Nos sentimos muy emocionados de estar aquí", dijo, "pero sé que esta noche está llena de tensiones. Necesitan privacidad".

Bárbara Bush se mostró de acuerdo. Informó que su esposo, el ex presidente, ya de 80 años, estaba tan nervioso que el estómago le estaba molestando.

A las 5:10 de la tarde, Bush padre fue a ver a Rove. ¿Qué estaba sucediendo?, quiso saber.

Rove dijo que las encuestas en boca de urna no parecían acertadas. Las firmas que hacían estos sondeos estaban encuestando a un porcentaje de mujeres mayor del que en realidad estaba votando, dijo, y estaban calculando más votantes tardíos de los que en realidad había. A las 5:18 el presidente llamó a Rove e interrumpió esta conversación.

Rove repitió sus conclusiones.

"Bueno", dijo Bush, "pronto sabremos".

No, no, no, pensó Rove. Todos sus argumentos y análisis le indicaban que las cifras tenían que estar erradas, bastante erradas. Pero, por metódicos que fueran sus pensamientos, no podía sacudirse de encima la duda. Le parecía que no tenía sentido, ¿pero quién iba a saber? Existía la posibilidad de que las cifras fueran correctas. Pensó que si en algún momento de su vida iba a sufrir un infarto, probablemente sería en las próximas horas.

A las 5:20 de la tarde, Bush padre lo dejó y se fue a recorrer su antigua residencia y sus antiguas oficinas. Seis minutos más tarde entró Rice.

"¡Malo, malo, malo!", exclamó Rove. "Estoy tan asustado que no logro ver con claridad".

A LAS 6:30 DE LA TARDE, MICHAEL GERSON, el hombre que escribía los discursos del presidente, se puso a enviar correos electrónicos a algunos de los principales funcionarios de la campaña de Bush, preguntándoles qué había sucedido. Gerson, un cristiano evangélico de 40 años, titulado en teología por el *alma mater* del evangelista Billy Graham, el Wheaton College, de Wheaton, Illinois, había escrito todos los discursos memorables de Bush después del 9/11, incluido el que pronunció en la Catedral Nacional de Washington el 14 de septiembre de 2001: "Este conflicto comenzó de acuerdo con el cronograma y las condiciones de otros. Terminará de la manera y a la hora que nosotros escojamos". También fue autor de las palabras que dijo el presidente ante una sesión conjunta del Congreso el 20 de septiembre de 2001: "Los estadounidenses no deben esperar una sola batalla sino una campaña prolongada". Gerson había escrito el discurso sobre el Estado de la Unión en el 2002, en el que Bush identificó a Irak, Irán y Corea del Norte como un "eje del mal" que conectaba el terrorismo con las armas de destrucción masiva, y también había ideado las raíces intelectuales e históricas del discurso doctrinario *preventivo* que pronunció el presidente en West Point en junio de 2002: "La guerra contra el terrorismo no se ganará a la defensiva". Sabía que su deber no era únicamente tener listo el discurso de victoria de Bush, sino también el que denominaba "segundo discurso". Se suponía que iba a ser graciosa la admisión contingente del triunfo de John Kerry. Gerson se sentía muy orgulloso del primer renglón de su borrador. Bush diría: "Acabo de recibir una llamada de mi contendor, que ya no es mi contendor. Es el presidente electo de los Estados Unidos".

A LAS 7:35 DE LA TARDE, cuando empezaban a cerrarse las urnas en el este, Rove se trasladó a la Sala de Guerra , dotada de la más alta tecnología de campaña, que se había montado en el antiguo comedor de la primera planta de la residencia de la Casa Blanca. Cinco grandes pantallas planas de televisión dominaban una de las paredes. Rove se instaló en el extremo de una mesa amplia, en el centro de la habitación. Tenía un mapa grande de los Estados Unidos en la pantalla de su computador. Con sólo hacer clic sobre un Estado, aparecían las cifras más recientes de Bush y Kerry. Luego aparecía un mapa de ese Estado. Podía buscar cualquier condado del Estado y ver las cifras que fluían de los asistentes de la campaña a los funcionarios republicanos locales, en los tribunales de condado y los centros electorales de todo el país.

Bush padre entró a la Sala de Guerra a las 9:14 de la noche. Estaba nervioso.

Vamos ganando en Ohio y la Florida, informó Rove. Acababa de hablar por teléfono con el gobernador de la Florida, Jeb Bush, quien le informó que en su Estado estaban superando las metas. Con las urnas ya cerradas en todos, salvo seis Estados del Oeste, Rove navegó en su computador, examinando las cifras de los condados clave alrededor de las principales ciudades. Rice también estaba allí, trabajando como una especie de secretaria, consultando el libro de metas de Rove y el desempeño en el 2000 en los condados que él llamaba a la pantalla.

"Hora de actuar", declaró Rove. Llamó a varios periodistas clave de televisión y preguntó por Ohio. "Estamos por encima del porcentaje de votación en todas las ciudades, en comparación con el 2000, y ellos están por debajo", dijo Rove.

El presidente bajó y Rove le mostró las cifras de los principales condados, que indicaban que iba ganando en Ohio. Bush se marchó, pero a las 9:50 de la noche Rove lo volvió a llamar.

"Vamos a ganar en Ohio", le dijo Rove con gran seguridad.

"Siga mirando", le ordenó Bush.

Aproximadamente una hora más tarde, justo antes de las 11, Card telefoneó a la gerente de campaña de Kerry, Mary Beth Cahill, con la idea de darle un preaviso a la campaña de Kerry.

"No sé qué indican sus cifras, pero nuestras cifras indican que vamos a ganar. Y si sus cifras muestran eso también, probablemente deberíamos programar una llamada telefónica. ¿Sus cifras indican eso?".

"No", contestó Cahill cortésmente. Dejó en claro que las cifras de la campaña de Kerry no indicaban eso.

"Está bien, no estoy presionando", dijo Card. "No estoy presionando. Eso es todo".

A las 11:29, el presidente, vestido de pantalones deportivos y camisa sin corbata, volvió a la Sala de Guerra.

"Las elecciones que no terminarán nunca", dijo Bush. Manifestó que estaba "muy cansado", y así se veía. La noche no le proporcionaba una claridad contundente de datos, como deseaba. El desempeño de las cadenas de noticias era especialmente indignante, dijo. Nadie había proclamado su victoria en la Florida, incluso cuando el 95% de los distritos electorales ya habían reportado sus cifras. Era casi increíble.

A las 11:40 de la noche, ABC News proclamó la victoria de Bush en la Florida. La Sala de Guerra de Rove estalló en vítores.

Pasada la media noche, a las 12:29, la ansiedad de Bush era visible. "¿Cuándo terminará?", le preguntó a Rove. Quería ir al Edificio Reagan, donde estaban reunidos sus partidarios, y proclamar su triunfo. ¿Cuándo podría ir?

"Tal vez dentro de una hora", dijo Rove. Menos de 10 minutos después, dijo que Ohio ya estaba asegurado. Pero las redes de televisión todavía no lo estaban proclamando.

A las 12:51, Card decidió que las cifras eran lo suficientemente claras y contundentes. "Felicitaciones", le dijo a Rove, "acabamos de ganar las elecciones". Él y Rove se abrazaron. Rice y Rove también se abrazaron.

Después de la 1 de la madrugada, Card volvió a llamar a Cahill.

Cahill dijo que la campaña de Kerry se sentía confiada.

Card quedó un poco desconcertado. "Muy bien. ¿Cree que vamos a hacer... va a haber una llamada telefónica?". Se refería a una llamada de Kerry concediéndole el triunfo a Bush.

"Nosotros no los vamos a llamar", contestó Cahill. Parecía estar en cierto modo preguntando si Bush pensaba llamar a Kerry para concederle a él la victoria.

Entre los amigos cercanos de Bush en la Casa Blanca estaba Mary Matalin, de 51 años, republicana experta en frases políticas contundentes y asesora en materia de comunicaciones para los Bush desde hacía casi dos decenios. Más recientemente había sido directora de comunicaciones del vicepresidente Cheney durante varios años. Tanto el ex presidente como el presidente en ejercicio la abrazaron y la saludaron de beso cuando llegó.

Matalin está casada con James Carville, un demócrata que fue el principal estratega político de Bill Clinton en 1992. No había participado directamente en la campaña de Kerry, pero estaba muy en contacto con ella. Su esposa lo llamó.

"Sé que esto es difícil para ti", le dijo comprensivamente.

Carville le contó que le tenía una noticia. La campaña de Kerry iba a impugnar las papeletas provisionales en Ohio; quizás hasta 250.000. "Yo no estoy de acuerdo", le dijo Carville. "Sólo te cuento que eso es lo que están diciendo".

Matalin fue a donde Cheney para informarle.

¿Cómo?, preguntó el vicepresidente. La legislación federal requería que se diera papeletas provisionales a las personas que llegaran a votar y cuyos nombres no aparecieran registrados en las listas. Se podía revisarlas más tarde en una elección cerrada. Si en verdad había 250.000 votos provisionales, eso podría cambiar los resultados en Ohio o, por lo menos, demorar los resultados durante varios días.

"Es mejor que le informe al presidente", le dijo Cheney.

Matalin y Cheney ubicaron a Bush y los tres se sentaron en una esquina.

"Lo van a impugnar", dijo Matalin.

"¿Eso qué significa?", preguntó el presidente. Tenía sus tarjetas con anotaciones a la mano, listo para ir al Edificio Reagan a proclamar el triunfo.

Matalin dijo que alguien con autoridad tenía que ponerse en contacto con J. Kenneth Blackwell, el secretario de Estado republicano de Ohio, quien estaría a cargo de cualquier impugnación de los votos provisionales.

A la 1:30 a.m., Mary Beth Cahill hizo una declaración. "El conteo de votos de Ohio aún no se ha completado. Hay más de 250.000 votos que todavía hay que contar", dijo, refiriéndose a las papeletas provisionales. "Creemos que cuando se cuenten, John Kerry ganará en Ohio".

En la Casa Blanca pensaron que, en efecto, Carville le había dado a Matalin una información acertada. Aunque las dos principales cadenas, NBC y Fox, habían proclamado el triunfo de Bush en Ohio, la implicación obvia era que allí todavía no habían terminado.

A la 1:49, Rove habló por teléfono móvil con la oficina del secretario de Estado de Nevada. En 20 minutos se anunciaría el triunfo de Bush en ese Estado. Salvo por una impugnación en Ohio, Nevada le daría la victoria a Bush.

Rice estaba escuchando. El triunfo de Bush parecía muy seguro. "Felicitaciones", le dijo a Rove, "después de todo lo que hicimos por arruinarlo".

Aproximadamente a las 2 de la madrugada, Jim Francis, que había sido director de las dos exitosas campañas de Bush para la gobernación de Texas, estaba solo con el presidente en un rincón del segundo piso de la residencia de la Casa Blanca. Habían sido amigos durante 34 años, desde 1970, cuando Francis, entonces de 21 años, había sido coordinador de programas del congresista George H. W. Bush en su infructuosa campaña para el Senado por Texas.

"George", le dijo Francis al presidente, "tengo que decirle que usted es el hijo de puta más resistente que he visto en mi vida. Ningún presidente ha tenido nunca tantas armas apuntadas contra él. Los 527 –las organizaciones de campaña independientes que financiaban publicidad masiva por televisión–, la prensa nacional, el cuerpo diplomático, todos los grupos de interés demócratas, además del Comité Demócrata Nacional y la campaña de Kerry. El mundo entero estaba tratando de desbancarlo. Y usted les ganó a todos".

Bush murmuró las gracias. Con ojos aguados, le dio un gran abrazo de oso a Francis. Francis comprendió que así era como George W. Bush se percibía a sí mismo: resistente y decidido, firme contra el mundo.

Bush habló nuevamente por teléfono con Rove. A Rove le parecía que el presidente ahora lo estaba llamando cada dos o tres minutos. Si era verdad que había ganado, quería saber Bush, ¿por qué el resto del mundo –la televisión, Kerry– no aceptaba la realidad?

Rove prometió comunicarse nuevamente con el presidente luego de confrontar más datos con las expectativas de condados y estados clave. "Se está enloqueciendo", le dijo Rove a Susan Ralston, su asistente, quien anotó diligentemente el comentario en sus notas a las 2:16 a.m.

Bartlett habló con uno de los vicepresidentes de Fox News Channel, el canal de televisión por cable conservador cuyos *ratings* se estaban disparando y cuyo director ejecutivo, Roger Ailes, había sido consultor de medios de Bush padre. Esa noche, Ailes se estaba cuidando de no hablar directamente con la Casa Blanca. Pero el funcionario de la cadena con quien Bartlett conversó le transmitió un mensaje de Ailes para Rove. En el 2000, Fox había sido la primera cadena en proclamar el triunfo de Bush en el Estado impugnado de la Florida y, por ende, su victoria electoral. Esta vez, el mensaje de Ailes era: "A usted no le conviene que yo sea el primero en proclamarlo".

Matalin y Scooter Libby estaban hablando sobre mandar a Cheney con Bush al Edificio Reagan, donde estaban reunidos sus partidarios, para la fiesta de la victoria. Tendría que estar alerta y preparado para hablar.

"Consígale un sitio donde pueda dormir", dijo. "No lo mande para la casa".

Cheney se metió a su oficina a dormir, mientras su esposa, Lynne, se fue a descansar al despacho del médico de la Casa Blanca.

"Manténgame al tanto", le pidió Libby a Matalin, cuando esta ingresó a la Sala de Guerra.

"Baje y usted mismo se pone al tanto", contestó Matalin. "Porque esto tiene muchas piezas en movimiento".

Bush volvió a la Sala de Guerra, donde caminó de arriba abajo, aguardando. A las 2:35 de la madrugada estaba viendo a Dan Rather en CBS. En septiembre, Rather había informado en un segmento de *60 Minutes II* que unos documentos de la Guardia Nacional de Texas indicaban que Bush había recibido un tratamiento preferencial cuando ingresó, en 1968. Al parecer, los documentos terminaron siendo falsos.

"CBS es horrible", dijo Bush.

A las 2:43 alguien señaló que Bush llevaba una ventaja de 3,8 millones en la votación popular a nivel nacional.

"Si la votación popular lo definiera", le dijo Bush maliciosamente a Rove, "yo no estaría aquí".

"Vamos adelante en el voto electoral", le recordó Rove.

Bush contestó una llamada del primer ministro británico Tony Blair. En Londres ya era de mañana, y Blair se había acostado pensando que Bush iba a perder. Estaba francamente sorprendido de que Bush siguiera en la contienda, y ni qué decir de que fuera el probable ganador.

"No había trasnochado tanto desde la universidad", le dijo Bush a Blair. "Necesito un Estado más".

Rove informó que tendrían una propuesta de declaración de Blackwell, en Ohio, en la siguiente media hora. Blackwell, un ex líder estudiantil defensor del poder negro, que se había pasado al partido republicano, era un llanero solitario que eludía la disciplina partidista.

"Soy el presidente de los Estados Unidos", dijo Bush furioso, "esperando a un secretario de Estado chiflado".

Caminó por la sala con las manos en los bolsillos, mordisqueando nerviosamente si cigarro. Rove dijo que la Associated Press iba a proclamar el triunfo de Bush en Nevada.

"¿Puedo ir por mi abrigo?", preguntó Bush con sarcasmo.

En Ohio, Blackwell informó que probablemente no había más de 175.000 papeletas provisionales, lo cual casi imposibilitaba que Kerry superara la ventaja de Bush, que era de unos 140.000 votos. Pero aun así, Blackwell no proclamaba el triunfo.

Llegó información de que las cadenas pensaban salir del aire sin proclamar la victoria de uno de los candidatos.

Rove gritó: "¡No pueden salir del aire!".

A las 3:36 a.m., una comunicación muy sensible de la campaña de Kerry les llegó a Rove y Bartlett en la Casa Blanca. Mike McCurry, el ex secretario de prensa de Clinton en la Casa Blanca y una adición de último minuto a la campaña de Kerry, le había enviado por correo electrónico a Nicole Devenish, la directora de comunicaciones de la campaña de Bush, sus felicitaciones *off-the-record*, advirtiéndole que el equipo de Bush no debía tratar de forzar una resolución ahora. No presionen a Kerry, había dicho McCurry. Creía que, finalmente, Kerry haría lo correcto.

Bartlett y los demás le contaron a Bush sobre el correo electrónico, resumiendo el mensaje como "haremos lo correcto en el momento correcto". Podían confiar en que McCurry estaba en una posición en la que podía saber lo que pensaba la campaña de Kerry, dijo Bartlett, pero tenían que tener cuidado de no depender mucho de eso. Por lo menos sabemos que hay personas en la campaña de Kerry que están dando consejos racionales, dijo Bartlett.

Bush dijo nuevamente que estaba cansado. "No me voy a quedar despierto toda la noche", dijo. "Despiértenme cuando sepan qué está pasando".

"¿Qué debemos hacer?", le preguntó Rove a Card a las 4:24. "Las cadenas no van a anunciar".

Card opinó que debían proclamar el triunfo. Le preocupaba un posible vacío, otro Florida. Esta batalla se estaba librando en muchos frentes, y la segunda en importancia, después de la de las cifras, era la batalla de las percepciones. "Sabemos que ganamos. Deberíamos proclamarlo".

Despertaron al presidente y lo comunicaron mediante un teléfono con altoparlante con la Sala de Guerra.

CARD Y JIM FRANCIS dejaron en claro que creían que el presidente debía ir al Edificio Reagan y pronunciar su discurso de victoria. Sería como una especie de golpe preventivo. De lo contrario, los medios no dejarían de hablar de la situación. Tenían que llenar el vacío. Suministrar los titulares: "¡Bush proclama victoria!". La declaración se convertiría en realidad.

Francis fue bastante insistente. "Los demócratas van a tratar de convertir Ohio en la Florida y a actuar como si se tratara de una diferencia de 500 votos en vez de 150.000". No podían dejar que la votación terminara en el limbo: litigio, reconteo, peleas en la corte. El margen de entre 140.000 y 150.000 votos en Ohio no representaba un triunfo apabullante, pero era bastante más que los 537 que habían definido el resultado de la Florida en el 2000.

Anteriormente Rover había estado a favor de pronunciar el discurso de la victoria, pero ahora, a las 4:30 a.m., reconsideró la idea. ¿Para qué? ¿Qué público tendrían? ¿La gente en el Edificio Reagan? Todos los demás dormían.

Matalin, quien había estado durmiendo en el piso del la Sala de Guerra, se despertó aproximadamente a las 4:40. A los cincos minutos estaba participando en el debate.

"¿Qué ha cambiado?", preguntó. Si Bush salía ahora y proclamaba la victoria, la prensa se preguntaría qué había cambiado en el último par de horas. Preguntaría "¿por qué en este momento y no hace una hora?" Los medios de comunicación podrían aprovechar la coyuntura. La ausencia de una razón podría convertirse en parte de la historia. ¿Qué dirían?

Steve Hadley había sido llamado a la Sala de Guerra desde el Salón Roosevelt, donde había estado aguardando y observando, yendo de cuando en cuando a la oficina de Rove para ver qué pasaba. Por lo general un modelo de cautela, Hadley en esta ocasión insistió. Una declaración de victoria preventiva sería lo peor que el presidente podría hacer, dijo. No arrinconen a Kerry. No lo presionen. En las siguientes dos o tres horas, las cifras que Rove había visto serían claras para Kerry. Los márgenes de Ohio bastaban, incluso, eran amplios. "Si lo arrinconan, los abogados intervendrán y se armará un enredo".

Bartlett estuvo de acuerdo. Era exactamente el mismo consejo que habían recibido de McCurry. El presidente debía quedarse callado. La validación del triunfo debía provenir ya fuese de los medios, preferiblemente la televisión, o, mejor aún, de la admisión de Kerry. Bartlett agitó entonces una gigantesca bandera de precaución.

"Durante unas siete horas, John Kerry fue en su mente presidente de los Estados Unidos", dijo Bartlett, "y estoy seguro de que así lo trataron y así actuó".

"No lo arrinconen", repitió Hadley.

"Tiene razón", interpuso Matalin. "Tiene toda la razón".

Jim Francis siguió presionando apasionadamente para que Bush proclamara de inmediato su victoria. Tenían que aprovechar la ventaja de los 150.000 votos. Dos cadenas de televisión la consideraban suficiente. Había que evitar otro infierno legal. ¿No arrinconar a Kerry? Eso era precisamente lo que debían hacer. Lo habían hecho durante la campaña; ¿por qué detenerse ahora? El hecho de que el presidente de los Estados Unidos proclamara la victoria tendría peso propio, y eso le dificultaría más las cosas a Kerry.

Pronto Francis y Bartlett estaban trenzados en un acalorado debate.

"Hay un recuadro en la esquina de cada televisor de Estados Unidos", dijo Bartlett, "que no indica el número exigido de votos electorales". El presidente necesitaba 270 para ganar, y las cadenas sólo mostraban 269. "La gente va a pensar que es presuntuoso de nuestra parte hacer esto". Sugirió que todos se consolaran con la certeza de que habían ganado. No había ninguna discusión a ese respecto. "Lo sabemos. Tengamos paciencia".

No, repitió Francis, la realidad era el precedente de la Florida, la perspectiva de batallas legales, pleitos una vez más. Tenían que hacer lo que fuera necesario para evitar eso. "Van a tener abogados en la televisión a las 7 de la mañana hablando sobre cómo van a a aprovechar esto, detener el reloj, y van a controlar el espectáculo. ¡Y nos lo van a quitar a nosotros!".

Bush murmuraba por el teléfono con altoparlante, aparentemente de acuerdo. Bartlett sabía muy bien que la sugerencia de que alguien le iba a quitar algo a Bush instaría al luchador a actuar.

Varios en la Sala de Guerra se dijeron que casi podían escuchar a Bush poniéndose el abrigo.

Bartlett utilizó la munición más poderosa que se le ocurrió. "No puede salir y coronarse a sí mismo", resumió finalmente. "Es algo que simplemente no puede hacer".

Hubo un par de segundos de silencio.

"Laura piensa lo mismo", contestó Bush por el teléfono con altoparlante. "Laura tampoco cree que deba salir".

A las 4:59, Card seguía presionando.

"Hagámoslo mañana", dijo Bush finalmente.

Hadley consideró que detener la cascada había sido la mejor actuación de Bartlett. Si Bush hubiera salido podría haber forzado una confrontación con legiones de abogados y un enorme enredo.

En cuanto a su propio pequeño papel en la argumentación contra la ida al Edificio Reagan, Hadley más tarde bromeó con un colega: "Eso quizás fue lo más útil que hice en esos cuatro años".

SI BUSH NO IBA A PROCLAMAR LA VICTORIA, Card consideraba que alguien debía, por lo menos, ir a decir algo, sobre todo a la gente que aguardaba en el Edificio Reagan. La tarea recayó sobre él. Llegó al Edificio Reagan aproximadamente a las 5:30 de la mañana.

"Estamos convencidos de que el presidente Bush ganó la reelección con, por lo menos, 286 votos colegiados electorales", dijo Card a las personas que aún seguían aguardando. "Y también tiene un margen de más de 3,5 millones de votos populares".

Tendió cuidadosa y deliberadamente una rama de oliva. "El presidente Bush decidió concederle respetuosamente al senador Kerry más tiempo para reflexionar sobre los resultados de las elecciones. El presidente hará una declaración más tarde en el día de hoy".

KERRY ESTABA DE PIE a las 7 de la mañana, conversando con tres de sus principales colaboradores de campaña. Tenía que tomar decisiones.

En primer lugar, podía optar por una impugnación en Ohio con base en las papeletas provisionales. Pero el número de provisionales equivalía más o menos a la ventaja de Bush en ese Estado, de modo que Kerry tendría que ganar con prácticamente todas aquellas papeletas.

La segunda posibilidad era impugnar los resultados de Ohio con base en acusaciones de irregularidades en la votación.

La tercera opción que Kerry debía considerar era la más dramática. Su campaña tenía un expediente que mostraba cómo ciertas personas, en distritos electorales demócratas en Ohio, habían esperado tres, cuatro, cinco y siete horas para votar. En los distritos electorales republicanos no había filas, según parecía, y los electores votaban en cinco minutos, quizás hasta en tres. Ocho máquinas de votación en algunos distritos electorales republicanos y sólo una o dos en los distritos electorales demócratas, ese tipo de cosas. Había una disparidad real.

Podría ser algo muy poderoso, pensó Kerry. Podía volar a Ohio con su equipo de prensa y aliarse con todo un grupo de gente cuyos derechos no habían sido respetados. Podía, literalmente, acampar en Akron, quizás, con su fórmula vicepresidencial, el senador John Edwards, en Columbus. Dirían: "Estas elecciones fueron fraudulentas en Ohio y los Estados Unidos de América merecen un presidente que haya sido correctamente elegido. Y vamos a ir a la corte para impugnar, bajo la cláusula de debido proceso de la Constitución. El derecho de la gente al voto no les fue acordado. Y queremos que, dentro de una semana a partir de hoy Ohio vote para presidente".

Bush, la Casa Blanca y los republicanos podrían terminar enredados en un lodazal moral, creía Kerry. ¿Qué haría Bush? ¿Pelear contra unas elecciones justas para presidente?

Pero lo que más impacto ejercía en Kerry era el número de votos provisionales. Lo cierto es que no había suficientes provisionales como para que él superara las cifras.

Kerry comprendió que una pelea dejaría al país en una situación confusa tras las elecciones presidenciales, por segunda vez consecutiva. Era una decisión que él tendría que tomar solo. Decidió aceptar el resultado. "Haber hecho lo contrario", dijo después en una entrevista, "habría sido algo personal. Habría sido venal. Habría significado hacer justamente lo que no se debe hacer cuando uno se presenta como candidato a la presidencia de los Estados Unidos. Eso fue lo que me dijeron mis entrañas. Me dijeron 'se trata de la presidencia'. Y por mucho que luché por ella y por mucho que nos importa aquello por lo que luchamos, hay intereses más amplios en los que hay que pensar". Irónicamente, aunque no iba a ser presidente, dijo: "Fue un poco como una instancia presidencial, si se quiere, y consideré que lo correcto en ese momento era no prolongar la agonía y no hacer pasar al país por eso, sin importar cuán personalmente estábamos todos comprometidos".

Agregó: "Con base en las cifras que teníamos, habríamos tenido que impugnar la base subyacente de las elecciones. Y por mucho que considerara yo que había una falla, una falla profunda, tomé justamente la decisión fundamental de que hacer aquello era incorrecto".

CERCA DE LAS 10:30 de la mañana del 3 de noviembre, Kerry llamó a Cahill para decirle que no pensaba impugnar las elecciones en Ohio ni en ningún otro lugar. Iba a llamar a Bush y le concedería el triunfo. "¿Cuál es el número telefónico?", le preguntó.

Un asistente de la Casa Blanca comunicó a Kerry con Bush. Rove, Card, Hughes, Bartlett y Gerson estaban en el Salón Oval.

"Felicitaciones, señor Presidente", dijo Kerry.

"Usted fue un contendor muy, muy fuerte", respondió Bush. "Realmente nos puso a correr. Espero que esté orgulloso de su esfuerzo. Debe estarlo".

"Señor Presidente, este es, en realidad, un momento en el que la nación debe estar unida. Es lo que la gente anhela. Y espero que usted aproveche esto para hablarle a la nación y unir a la gente y, en verdad, extender la mano. Estoy dispuesto a colaborar con usted para tratar de hacer las cosas que necesitamos hacer".

Bush dijo que Laura y él les deseaban lo mejor a Kerry, su esposa y su familia. Los dos hicieron unos cuantos comentarios benignos pero cálidos y luego se despidieron.

El presidente colgó el auricular y se echó a llorar, profunda y convulsivamente. Mientras procuraba recobrar la compostura, caminó por el recinto y abrazó a cada una de las personas que lo acompañaban: Rove, Hughes, Bartlett, Card y Gerson.

"Felicitaciones", murmuró Rove. Se le aguaron los ojos y no pudo decir nada más. Gerson también lloró.

"Le ha dado un maravilloso obsequio a su papá", le dijo Card al presidente.

Bush salió con ellos del Salón Oval y todos caminaron por el corredor hasta la oficina de Cheney. Pero el vicepresidente estaba en la Sala de Situaciones, de modo que Gerson lo llamó para decirle que el presidente tenía noticias.

Cheney subió y se encontraron en el corredor, donde Bush le contó sobre la llamada de Kerry.

"Sé que no le gustan los abrazos", dijo Bush. Le dio la mano a su vicepresidente.

32

Bush se reunió con su gabinete a la mañana siguiente, el jueves 4 de noviembre.

"Estas elecciones no las ganaron republicanos de club campestre", dijo. "No sé si existan. Sólo hay demócratas de club campestre. Estas elecciones las ganaron personas que llevan a sus trabajos portacomidas con el almuerzo. Creo que si sólo hubieran votado policías y bomberos en estas elecciones, habría ganado la mayor parte... ya saben, el 90% de los votos".

Bush había atraído a un nuevo grupo de votantes de clase baja y media, a quienes les inquietaba la seguridad. Después del 9/11, creía, a muchas más personas les preocupaba esencialmente el terrorismo, temerosos de un próximo ataque. Antes de la invasión de Irak, Bush había utilizado el temor al máximo, insinuando que Irak podría lanzar un ataque nuclear. "No podemos esperar la prueba definitiva –el arma humeante–, que podría llegar como una nube en forma de champiñón", había advertido. En otras instancias se había referido a un ataque de Irak que podría "matar a miles" y "producir un día de horror como jamás hemos visto".

En la campaña, el equipo de reelección de Bush había presentado dramáticamente los temas de forma que el temor que los votantes sentían por el terrorismo fuera lo más palpable posible. La insinuación más cruda y directa de que la reelección de Bush salvaría a Estados Unidos, mientras que la elección de Kerry podría ocasionar la extinción del país, provino de Cheney, el 7 de septiembre. "Es absolutamente esencial que dentro de ocho días, el 2 de noviembre, elijamos correctamente", advirtió Cheney, "porque si elegimos mal, el peligro será que nos ataquen de nuevo, que nos ataquen de una manera que será devastadora desde el punto de vista de los Estados Unidos".

La campaña de Bush había utilizado deliberadamente la generación de temor, y los registros así lo indican. Los resultados de las elecciones demostraron que la táctica había funcionado.

Dos días después de las elecciones, Bush y la primera dama viajaron a Camp David. Card, su esposa Kathi y Rice los acompañaron.

Como jefe de gabinete de un presidente recién reelegido, parte de la gloria del triunfo le correspondía a Card. Estaba en una posición poderosa. Al fin y al cabo, algo había salido bien.

Pero Card sabía que otras cosas habían salido mal, extremadamente mal. La información de inteligencia que indicaba que Saddam Hussein tenía arsenales de armas de destrucción masiva había resultado completamente errada. Card había estado en el Salón Oval tres meses antes de la invasión y había escuchado la presentación de la CIA sobre las ADM iraquíes. Era débil y poco convincente, y a él le había preocupado la posibilidad de que no hubiera nada "allá". Pero luego se había tranquilizado con la afirmación de Tenet de que el caso de las ADM era una "clavada". Card se preguntó si había hecho lo suficiente. Se enorgullecía por la calidad del flujo de información que le llegaba al presidente, pero esta información había sido absolutamente errada.

El presidente ya le había hablado a Card sobre los muchos cambios que pensaba hacer para el segundo período: varias caras nuevas en el gabinete, algunos altos funcionarios nuevos en la Casa Blanca. El cambio era positivo, había dicho Bush, aunque Card sabía que el cambio iba en contra de los gustos de Bush. El presidente prefería la comodidad de los zapatos viejos. Su equipo se le había convertido en unos zapatos cómodos.

Bush y Card entraron a la oficina del presidente en Camp David.

"Usted quiere hacer muchos cambios", empezó Card. "La mejor manera de demostrar que en verdad piensa hacer cambios, es cambiar a su jefe de gabinete. Si no cambia a su jefe de gabinete, todos los demás supondrán que no hay ningún cambio".

"¿Piensa renunciar?", preguntó el presidente.

"Esa pregunta es incorrecta", contestó Card. "No es la pregunta apropiada. La pregunta es, ¿qué necesita para lograr lo que tiene que lograr en el segundo mandato? Y tal vez yo no sea lo que usted necesita".

Card sabía, mejor que muchos, que ese tipo de ofertas de renuncia casi siempre eran poco sinceras. La oferta era a menudo una forma de preguntar ¿todavía me quiere? Dado todo lo que estaba en juego, Card sintió que tenía que trascender lo personal.

"Cuando se casó con Laura", agregó Card, "fue para bien y para mal. Conmigo es sólo para bien. Si no hay bien, yo me voy".

"Quiero que se quede", dijo Bush.

"No debería", contestó Card. "No me debería pedir que me quede. Es un error pedirme que me quede".

El presidente le restó importancia al asunto. Dijo que quería terminar pronto y también descansar y divertirse un poco. Card sintió que la campaña de reelección había sido una "carga emocional" para Bush.

"Por favor escúcheme", dijo Card. "Hay muchas opciones buenas. Y no debería existir el supuesto de que yo me quede, sobre todo si habla de su deseo de hacer cambios".

Card sacó una libreta de espiral tamaño carta, de un centímetro de grosor y tapa azul. La llamaba su libreta "*hit-by-the-bus*". En páginas separadas tenía listas de posibles reemplazos para todos los principales cargos administrativos, el suyo incluido. Los nombres figuraban sin un orden particular. Card mantenía su libreta de posibles reemplazos en su escritorio en la Casa Blanca y periódicamente agregaba o suprimía nombres. Utilizaba adrede una libreta escolar, algo que había comprado él mismo, para que no fuera considerara un documento gubernamental o un registro presidencial que algún día podría ser abierto para la historia. Era algo privado y personal.

Tenía una lista de 54 reemplazos para sí mismo como jefe de gabinete de la Casa Blanca, divididos en tres categorías que reflejaban diferentes estilos y enfoques.

Bush hizo ademán de ponerse de pie.

"No, no, no, siéntese", dijo Card quedamente. Sabía que esta podía ser una conversación diseñada más para satisfacerse a sí mismo, no a Bush. "Por favor, escuche mientras leo estas categorías y estos nombres".

El primer tipo de jefe de gabinete de la Casa Blanca era el microgerente: control severo, alguien que determinaba que ninguna persona y ningún documento podían llegarle al presidente sin el conocimiento y la aprobación del jefe. Ambos sabían que el modelo de este tipo era el ex gobernador de New Hampshire, John Sununu, el famoso jefe de gabinete imperial y tempestuoso de los primeros tres años de gobierno de Bush padre.

El segundo tipo se asemejaba más a un primer ministro: un conocedor de Capitol Hill, experto en acuerdos, negociaciones y política, con habilidad para manejar el Congreso, los medios de comunicación y el mundo.

El tercero y último tipo era el facilitador: una persona que hacía lo que el presidente quería y que mantenía al gabinete y al personal concentrados en la agenda presidencial. Ese era el tipo al que pertenecía Card.

Bush realmente no quería hacer el ejercicio.

"Josh Bolten", continuó Card. Bolten, soltero de 49 años, una persona de organización, había sido el segundo de Card durante los primeros años del gobierno de Bush. Ahora era director de la Oficina de Administración y Presupuesto. Había impresionado a todos con su capacidad para el trabajo arduo.

Bolten era una opción posible, dijo Bush.

"Don Evans", leyó Card.

No, dijo Bush. El secretario de Comercio Evans era el mejor amigo tejano de Bush en Washington. Card convino en que el presidente no debía escoger a su mejor amigo.

"Al Gonzáles", leyó Card, el asesor jurídico de la Casa Blanca.

Bush parecía tener otros planes para Gonzáles.

Card siguió leyendo, sin notar en Bush ninguna reacción particular: Harriet Miers, la segunda asesora jurídica de la Casa Blanca, una de los funcionarios favoritos de Bush, y Scooter Libby, jefe de gabinete de Cheney.

"Larry Thompson", sugirió Card. Thompson había sido vicefiscal general y había renunciado en agosto de 2003. A Bush pareció interesarle esa posibilidad.

¿Qué tal Ronald Betts?, preguntó Card. Betts había sido compañero de Bush en Yale; era un importante inversionista de Nueva York que formó parte del grupo de Bush que fue dueño del equipo de béisbol Texas Rangers.

"No".

"Jim Francis", sugirió Card.

"No".

"Ed Gillespie", leyó Card. Gillespie era el presidente del Comité Nacional Republicano.

También su nombre llamó la atención de Bush, pero hasta el momento nadie le había generado mucho entusiasmo. Parecía gustarle la idea de escoger un gobernador o un ex gobernador republicanos. Entre los nombres que sugirió Card figuraban George Pataki, gobernador de Nueva York; Frank Keating, ex gobernador de Oklahoma, y John Engler, ex gobernador de Michigan.

"Karen Hughes", aventuró Card.

Imposible, indicó Bush.

"Karl Rove".

"No podría ser jefe de Gabinete".

"Condi Rice".

Bush tenía otros planes para ella.

Card leyó los nombres de algunos ex congresistas: Chris Cox, de California; Vin Weber, Bill Paxon. También propuso al ex senador Fred Thompson, de Tennessee, que por entonces actuaba en la serie de televisión *Law & Order*.

"¿Usted se quedaría?", preguntó Bush.

"Un presidente en su segundo período sí termina por perder poder", dijo Card. "La pregunta es cuándo, y cuáles son las consecuencias". Bush tenía que cerciorarse de controlar eso lo mejor posible.

El presidente estaba decidido a tener una agenda ambiciosa para su segundo mandato.

Reconozca que importará menos su perspectiva, porque ya no será tan relevante, dijo Card. Los medios de comunicación tendrían una perspectiva, pero esa también sería menos relevante. Tenía más que ver con los grupos que tendrían que responder a su llamado: el Congreso, la opinión pública y sus partidarios, su base. El jefe de gabinete tendría que asegurarse de que esos grupos respondieran. Había algo de espacio para maniobrar, dijo Card. Ya reelegido, y sin posibilidades de buscar nuevamente la reelección, sería definido como estadista durante un tiempo imposible de determinar.

Eran cerca de las 5 de la tarde cuando terminaron de hablar. Pronto la gente se congregó para la cena. Bush se llevó a Kathi Card a un lado. Después, el presidente se dirigió a su jefe de gabinete.

"Kathi se siente a gusto", dijo.

Confiar, pero verificar. Card habló con su esposa.

"Si esto es lo que quieres hacer", dijo ella, "y el presidente quiere que lo hagas, está bien".

De modo que ella se sentía "a gusto" y "bien", lo que no era precisamente un apoyo.

Bush había observado que los Card estaban hablando. Cuando su jefe de gabinete ingresó al comedor, el presidente lo aguardaba en el umbral.

"Lo haremos", dijo el presidente, dándole a Card un golpe en la espalda. "¡Lo haremos!".

CARD PRONTO SE PREGUNTÓ si miraría en retrospectiva ese día en Camp David y concluiría que pedirle que se quedara, que aceptara, quizás podría haber sido un error del presidente mucho mayor de lo que imaginó inicialmente. ¿Podía un jefe de gabinete que venía del gobierno anterior ser un agente de cambio? No transcurrió mucho tiempo antes de que Card le hiciera estas preguntas directamente al presidente. ¿Cuánto cambio se necesitaba? No sólo cambios en el personal, sino también en las políticas, y la pregunta más amplia de hacia donde se dirigía la presidencia de Bush. ¿Qué decisiones había que revaluar? ¿Formaba Card una parte demasiado importante del pasado como para ser parte de un futuro de cambio? Desde luego, la parte más importante de ese pasado era la guerra de Irak, los 18 meses de decisiones relacionadas con ella. ¿Quién más podría estar demasiado relacionado con esas decisiones anteriores como para ser parte de un futuro de cambio?

AL DÍA SIGUIENTE, un viernes, Bush se reunió con Rice por la tarde. Le dijo que había reflexionado mucho acerca de su segundo período de gobierno y que quería que ella reemplazara a Powell como secretaria de Estado.

"Me siento honrada de que piense en mí de esa manera", contestó Rice, y agregó algunas frases apropiadas sobre la importancia que revestía su voto de confianza. Luego pasó a lo que tenía en mente. "Señor presidente, en verdad creo que debería marcharme".

No, dijo Bush. Necesitaban hacer muchas cosas. La cantidad de asuntos sin terminar era abrumadora.

Irak: su guerra. La paz en el Medio Oriente: su esperanza.

"¿Quiere decir", dijo ella, "que su compromiso es tratar de propiciar un Estado palestino en este período?" Era uno de sus temas favoritos.

Bush dijo que era uno de sus compromisos, y enseguida la introdujo en una discusión a fondo sobre otras inquietudes y oportunidades.

Caía la tarde y el sol se ponía sobre las montañas Catoctin. Rice no había planeado una conversación como esa y todavía se sentía exhausta por la campaña. Independientemente de lo que ella decidiera hacer, dijo, consideraba que Steve Hadley era su sucesor natural como asesor nacional de seguridad.

Bush no dijo si estaba de acuerdo.

"No conozco a nadie más equilibrado, consagrado e inteligente, y que solucione más problemas que Steve", prosiguió Rice. Comentó que era obvio que el presidente confiaba en Hadley, y que, sin esa confianza, a Bush podría pasarle lo que le sucedió a Reagan: seis asesores nacionales de seguridad en dos períodos de gobierno.

"Sabe, señor presidente, es probable que necesite gente nueva", siguió diciendo Rice. "Y no sólo se trata de cambiar a ciertas personas de cargos. Necesita nueva gente porque hemos sufrido un ataque terrorista, el peor en la historia de los Estados Unidos. Hemos estado en dos guerras. Quizás necesite un nuevo equipo que le ayude".

"No me diga lo que necesito", contestó Bush.

"Señor Presidente, el tema crucial para mí es si me quedo o no". Muchas personas estaban diciendo que ella quería el cargo de Rumsfeld en el Departamento de Defensa. "No se trata del cargo que me ofrezca. Se trata de si me quedo o no".

Hablaron durante otra media hora. Bush trató de dirigir la conversación nuevamente a lo que podían hacer en el segundo mandato. Él siempre había dominado la relación entre ambos, y Rice casi siempre había hecho lo que el presidente quería. Pero esta vez no lograba convencerla de que aceptara.

"Señor presidente", dijo ella finalmente, "tengo que pensarlo".

"Por supuesto que tiene que pensarlo".

Al terminar el fin de semana, Rice le dijo a Bush: "Sabe, todavía lo estoy pensando". Pero sentía en su propio movimiento corporal que ya se inclinaba a aceptar. Al día siguiente la embargó la emoción ante la perspectiva de ser secretaria de Estado.

Le dijo a Bush que aceptaba su ofrecimiento. "Sí", dijo, "si eso es lo que usted quiere que yo haga".

En Irak, la guerra continuaba. Fallujah se había convertido en el epicentro del terrorismo y exportaba carros bomba a Bagdad y al resto del país. El general Casey movilizó una fuerza numerosa de seis batallones de asalto estadounidenses, con respaldo de otros tantos batallones de soldados iraquíes, y acordonaron la ciudad. Casi toda la población civil salió de la ciudad, mientras que el severo cordón mantenía a los sospechosos de terrorismo atrapados adentro. El mensaje era que Casey finalmente iba a ocuparse de Fallujah.

Una delegación sunita tras otra fue a ver al primer ministro interino Allawi para transmitirle el mismo mensaje: "No ataquen Fallujah". El mensaje que enviaba Washington era básicamente "por favor, hagan otro Najaf", con una resolución pacífica.

Pero no había resolución. Pasadas ya las elecciones presidenciales en Estados Unidos y faltando dos meses para las primeras elecciones nacionales iraquíes, Casey y Negroponte transmitieron su opinión al CNS y al presidente. Según un funcionario, el mensaje escueto era: "No hay forma de que este país celebre elecciones, ni desde el punto de vista de la seguridad ni desde el punto de vista de convicción política de lo que representa este esfuerzo, si no atacan Fallujah y no afrontan a Moqtada. Y tienen que afrontar eso o, de lo contrario, el país se va a desintegrar".

Bush le dio a Casey el visto bueno para ordenar el ataque. La gente de Fallujah resistió y peleó. Los militares estadounidenses consideraban que la ciudad era un polígono perfecto y mataron a entre 1.000 y 2.000 presuntos insurgentes violentos. Estados Unidos perdió 70 soldados: aproximadamente un soldado o *marine* por pelotón. Los batallones iraquíes perdieron entre 20 y 30 de cada uno. Aunque su función no era muy importante, lo significativo era que los iraquíes no habían salido huyendo. Casi todos sus batallones fueron emboscados cuando salían, pero siguieron combatiendo.

En medio de la batalla, la atención de los árabes y del resto del mundo se desvió a París, donde Yasser Arafat, el líder palestino e ídolo de la denominada Calle Árabe, estaba agonizando. Como casi todo lo que tenía que ver con Arafat, fue un drama prolongado y orquestado con tratamiento médico divulgado a los medios, controversia sobre la causa de su eventual muerte, ocurrida el 11 de noviembre, y el envío de sus despojos mortales a Palestina. El drama Arafat copaba a Al Jazeera y a los demás medios árabes, pese a los combates y las muertes en Fallujah, con lo cual la historia a veces se limitaba a poco más de "mientras tanto, en Fallujah…".

Bush, Rice y Powell trataron de explicarles a los diversos líderes árabes por qué Estados Unidos creía que el ataque contra Fallujah era necesario, y les rogaron que los apoyaran. No podría decirse que los líderes árabes les brindaron apoyo, pero no asumieron posiciones severas contra los estadounidenses.

EN LA CASA BLANCA, el principal interrogante seguía siendo Rumsfeld. ¿Debía quedarse? Card tuvo que abordar el tema con delicadeza. Rumsfeld le había dificultado el trabajo a Card. Rice y Card no formaban parte de la cadena de mando –y todo el mundo sabía quién formaba parte–, pero la función de Card era ayudarle a Bush. Ahora Irak era el centro de todo, y Rumsfeld había sido, efectivamente, reemplazado como la persona a cargo, primero por Rice en el otoño de 2003, cuando se encargó de los asuntos de Bremer, y luego en el 2004, cuando la NSPD-36 había convertido al Departamento de Estado en la entidad principal en lo referente a Irak. No obstante, en Irak el tema era, sobre todo, la violencia y los 130.000 soldados estadounidenses, y eso indudablemente le competía a Rumsfeld.

Era claro que el presidente no quería hacer nada que perturbara el esfuerzo de guerra, y el efecto que podría tener el reemplazo de Rumsfeld era bastante incierto. Si Rumsfeld se iba, ¿qué impacto tendría eso en la fortaleza general y en la moral de quienes estaban peleando? Desde luego, como Rumsfeld ejercía un virtual monopolio sobre los contactos del Departamento de Defensa con el presidente, no había forma de que Bush obtuviera información independiente que le permitiera contestar ese tipo de preguntas.

El principal abanderado del cambio era Powell. En una conversación, Powell le había dicho a Card: "Si yo me voy, Don se debería ir". Pero ahora que Bush había decidido reemplazar a Powell y nombrar a Rice en su lugar, no se sabía a quién quería como secretario de Defensa.

Había otros partidarios más sutiles del cambio en el Departamento de Defensa, como Rice, Hadley y, bajo circunstancias apropiadas, el mismo Card. La primera y mejor manera de plantearle el asunto a Bush era argumentar que necesitaba todo un equipo nacional de seguridad nuevo. Pero Rice ya había fracasado cuando esgrimió el argumento del nuevo equipo, y luego había aceptado el cargo de secretaria de Estado, con lo cual menoscababa su propia sugerencia.

Sin embargo, Card decidió proceder. Como había propuesto varias docenas de alternativas para su propio cargo como jefe de gabinete, pensó que podría hacer lo mismo en lo concerniente a Rumsfeld. Sacó su libreta de posibles reemplazos.

La lista de posibles reemplazos de Rumsfeld incluía algunos nombres conocidos, como el ex senador Dan Coats de Indiana, que no había sido mencionado la primera vez; Fred Smith, el director ejecutivo de FedEx, que había pertenecido a la misma fraternidad de Bush pero quien, al parecer, no quería aceptar un cargo en el gobierno; el subsecretario de Defensa Wolfowitz; y el subsecretario de Estado Armitage. Card sabía que la mención de Armitage en el Pentágono no le gustaría a Cheney, de modo que probablemente no era una opción realista. Mencionó al senador John Warner, el republicano de Virginia que presidía la Comisión de Servicios Armados del Senado; el senador Joe Lieberman, demócrata de Connecticut que había sido la fórmula vicepresidencial de Gore en su campaña para la presidencia y era un firme defensor de la guerra de Irak; el gobernador Pataki, y el ex alcalde de Nueva York, Rudy Giuliani. Otras posibilidades eran el senador John McCain de Arizona y el ex gobernador de California Pete Wilson.

Pero a Card se le ocurrió lo que consideró una excelente idea: un "candidato durmiente". El mejor reemplazo de Rumsfeld sería James A. Baker III, quien había sido jefe de gabinete y secretario del Tesoro de Reagan, y también secretario de Estado y principal asesor político de Bush padre.

Card le mencionó todos estos nombres a Bush a lo largo de varias semanas, insistiendo todo el tiempo en las ventajas del cambio. Pero su punto focal era Baker.

"Todo el mundo respiraría aliviado", dijo Card. "Sin curva de aprendizaje. Excelente. Interesante". Baker tenía 74 años, apenas dos más que Rumsfeld. Había estado en el cuerpo de *marines*. Había sido el mejor jefe de gabinete en la historia moderna de la Casa Blanca, pensaba Card. En el 2000, había manejado exitosamente el recuento de votos de la Florida para Bush. Señor presidente, éste es mi consejo íntimo, dijo Card. Nombre a un diplomático en el Departamento de Defensa.

El presidente parecía genuinamente interesado.

No tiene que apresurarse para tomar una decisión, le advirtió Card.

Card habló con Rumsfeld, quien aparentemente presumía que no iba a haber ningún cambio. Card tenía fuentes en el Pentágono, incluso dentro del círculo de allegados de Rumsfeld, y conversó con ellos. ¿Qué pensaban? Una fuente dijo que Rumsfeld creía que, si se iba a dar un cambio, eso sería después, quizás dentro de cuatro o cinco meses. Tal vez en marzo. Luego

Card escuchó que Rumsfeld quería permanecer en el cargo hasta que se aprobara el presupuesto. Otra persona dijo entonces que esperaba quedarse hasta junio. Finalmente, uno de los subalternos de Rumsfeld le dijo a Card: "Nada pasará hasta que termine la guerra".

Rumsfeld se quería quedar. Siempre había algo en el horizonte de Irak: las elecciones programadas para el 30 de enero de 2005, el programa de reconstitución de las fuerzas de seguridad iraquíes, una nueva oleada de violencia. ¿Acaso querían un cambio en momentos tan críticos?

Karl Rove también intervino. Se aproximaba una sesión contenciosa con el Congreso. En su opinión, los demócratas no estaban de humor para una luna de miel. Con la audiencia de confirmación de Rice y con el esperado nombramiento del consejero jurídico de la Casa Blanca, Alberto Gonzáles, como fiscal general, ¿podría otra confirmación del Senado sobrecargar el sistema?

"Powell se va. Voy a tener que reemplazar a Condi", le dijo el presidente a Rove. "¿He de tener algo de continuidad en todo esto? Me siento más seguro con el cambio de secretario de Estado porque tengo a Condi, en quien confío. ¿En quién puedo confiar hasta ese grado en el Departamento de Defensa, sobre todo en medio de una guerra?". Y, sin duda, el curso de la guerra en Irak sería el tema de las audiencias de confirmación para cualquier persona a quien Bush nombrara como nuevo secretario de Defensa.

Rove estuvo de acuerdo en que no convenía hacer nada que promoviera audiencias sobre la guerra. Por Dios, no.

"Si necesitamos hacer eso, es preciso hacerlo. Pero si no es necesario, sabe...", dijo Bush, sin tomar una decisión pero dando la impresión de que no quería un cambio.

Bush conversó con Cheney. Luego volvió a hablar con Card y le hizo algunas preguntas, especulando sobre el impacto que podrían tener algunos de los nombres de la lista de Card, especialmente Baker. Pero la gran decisión seguía sin ser tomada.

MICHAEL GERSON TAMBIÉN HABLÓ con el presidente sobre la conveniencia de un cambio en el Pentágono. Como símbolo del cambio, dijo Gerson, convendría reemplazar a Rumsfeld. Sí, se había hecho o se estaba haciendo algunos ajustes en la política sobre Irak, y Rumsfeld había contribuido a ese cambio, y tal vez era injusto reemplazarlo en este momento, pese a los errores que pudo haber cometido. Pero era necesario definir los elementos de una estrategia mucho más efectiva en Irak. El presidente debía proponerle a Lieberman que ocupara el cargo de Rumsfeld, recomendó Gerson. ¿Qué mejor símbolo de cambio que nombrar al compañero de fórmula de Al Gore?

Bush dijo que le seguían impresionando los esfuerzos de transformación de Rumsfeld, así como su capacidad para afrontar los arraigados intereses militares.

Eso no menoscababa el argumento a favor de un liderazgo diferente, dijo Gerson. Consciente de la importancia que revestía para Bush la lealtad, le dijo: "Señor presidente, no es desleal tener a alguien durante cuatro años, cuatro años y medio, en un cargo como este, y luego, por diversas razones, muchas que no son responsabilidad de esa persona, decir que conviene efectuar un cambio".

Interesante esa idea, dijo Bush.

Card sabía que Gerson iba a conversar con el presidente acerca de Rumsfeld y lo había alentado. Era parte de su plan de campaña.

OTRO PROBLEMA ERA LA CIA. El jefe de gabinete de Porter Goss, Pat Murray, tuvo un fuerte enfrentamiento con el subdirector de operaciones Stephen Kappes y con el subalterno de éste, Michael Sulick, en noviembre de 2004. Kappes y Sulick dirigían las operaciones clandestinas y encubiertas de la agencia en los esfuerzos antiterroristas. Ambos renunciaron, lo cual causó una tormenta interna.

Card concertó otra cita para reunirse con Goss en Langley. No todo lo que escuchaba Card era negativo, pero las perturbaciones eran preocupantes. Era precisamente el tipo de sacudón que no le convenía a una institución que necesitaba concentrarse en su trabajo.

Goss insistió en que había hecho lo correcto con Kappes y Sulick.

Card dedicó medio día a recopilar información, hacer preguntas y recorrer toda la sede, con la esperanza de mejorar la moral. Procuró demostrar su aprecio y su respeto por quienes estaban en la línea del frente, en la guerra contra el terror. Pero se marchó sin saber a ciencia cierta si su visita había sido útil o perjudicial.

HADLEY, QUIEN A LA SAZÓN TENÍA 57 AÑOS, también estaba pensando en un cambio. Se quería ir. Poco antes de que terminara el primer período de gobierno, conversó un par de veces con Armitage sobre las virtudes de su renuncia.

Lo peor de todo, dijo Armitage, sería que un adjunto fuera ascendido al cargo titular. "No lo haga", advirtió Armitage.

Hadley dijo que él estaba de acuerdo. Los cargos número uno y número dos eran diferentes, y requerían capacidades diferentes. También pensaba que era importante para un presidente en su segundo mandato demostrar que era fuerte y poderoso, que podía nombrar personas, incluso, más calificadas para los cargos principales, que quienes dejaban los puestos. Esto lo llamaba el factor "oh, ¡vaya!". El hecho de nombrar nuevos y verdaderos pesos pesados en los principales cargos generaría su propio fortalecimiento y credibilidad.

Hadley también convenía en que el presidente debía reemplazar a la mayor parte de su equipo nacional de seguridad. Tenían mucho bagaje encima, sobre todo la guerra de Irak. Bush necesitaba un nuevo inicio. En el primer período de gobierno no había integrado bien en su agenda la diplomacia del país, creía Hadley, y Powell sólo había llevado a efecto una versión modificada de la agenda de Bush. A menudo había sido demasiado Powell y no suficiente Bush. Powell era demasiado independiente en su modo de pensar. De modo que tenía sentido nombrar a Rice secretaria de Estado.

Pero Rumsfeld era un llanero solitario, tanto en el ámbito administrativo como burocrático. Nadie diría que Rumsfeld era un jugador de equipo, y no iba a cambiar. Seguía menospreciando al CNS y la colaboración entre organismos, tanto en los asuntos grandes como en los pequeños. Se sabía que Hadley se refería sarcásticamente en privado al "gran Don Rumsfeld".

Hadley se unió al desfile de personas que le dijeron a Bush que necesitaba un nuevo equipo nacional de seguridad. Pero Bush tenía otras ideas y le pidió a Hadley que reemplazara a Rice como asesor nacional de seguridad. "Necesito que haga esto", dijo el presidente.

La petición –y oportunidad– de trabajar para el presidente a este nivel no era algo que se pudiera rechazar; por lo menos, Hadley no podía rechazarla.

"Entonces, es irónico, ¿no le parece?, que esté en este cargo", le dijo más tarde Hadley a Armitage.

"Sí", dijo Armitage. "No sé si felicitarlo o darle el pésame".

Hadley comentó que tampoco él estaba muy seguro.

La DIFÍCIL TAREA de informarle a Colin Powell que iba a ser reemplazado le correspondió a Card. Telefoneó a Powell y lo invitó a su oficina en el Ala Oeste.

"El presidente quiere un cambio", dijo Card, pronunciando las palabras clásicas.

"Muy bien. Ya habíamos hablado sobre eso", contestó Powell.

"Es probable que el presiente nombre a Condi. Estoy casi seguro que va a ser Condi. Obviamente algo podría suceder entre ahora y el momento en que la nombre, pero creo que así será, y es bueno que usted haga los planes correspondientes".

"Muy bien", dijo Powell. "¿Cuándo quiere mi carta?".

"Si me da la carta a mí, yo la guardaré. Nadie sabrá que la tengo". La divulgarían únicamente en un momento previamente acordado entre los dos.

"Hay muchas cosas pendientes en este momento", dijo Powell, "Tenemos todas las reuniones en diciembre, todas las reuniones ministeriales, y muchas otras cosas". Estaban las conferencias de la OTAN, una cumbre anual en Chile, una reunión de líderes árabes en Marruecos en diciembre. El 30 de enero se iban a celebrar las elecciones en Irak. "¿Quiere esperar a que yo me encargue de todo eso?".

"No", contestó Card, y dijo que también iba a haber otros cambios en el gabinete. "El presidente cree que si vamos a hacer este cambio y vamos a hacer todos los demás cambios, es mejor que los hagamos todos de una vez".

"¿Habrá cambio en el Departamento de Defensa?", preguntó Powell.

"No he visto indicio de eso por el momento", contestó Card. Powell entendió. Si todos los cambios en el gabinete iban a ser anunciados al tiempo, y todavía no había indicios de cambio en Defensa, significaba esto que lo más probable era que Rumsfeld permaneciera en el cargo. Claramente decepcionado, Powell adoptó una actitud mucho más emotiva de lo que había esperado Card.

De repente, el asunto también se volvió emotivo para Card. La reunión se tornó triste. Nadie podría haber sido un mejor secretario de Estado durante los primeros cuatro años de gobierno de Bush, pensó Card. Bush había llegado sin experiencia o interés en la política exterior, y había escogido a Powell, quien era conocido y respetado en Estados Unidos y en el mundo. Powell no era un tejano cualquiera. Había sido exitoso asesor nacional de seguridad y jefe del Estado Mayor Conjunto durante el gobierno de Reagan. En el 2001, Powell ya era considerado como un estadista, y le había ayudado a Bush a superar muchos obstáculos. Pero Card no creía que Powell fuera la persona adecuada para el segundo mandato. A lo mejor lo nombraban secretario general de las Naciones Unidas.

Powell era una figura imponente, y Card quería que se marchara en la cumbre de su carrera, pero pensaba que el secretario de Estado era como una especie de beisbolista, listo para ingresar al Salón de la Fama, que quiere una última oportunidad de batear. Era triste, pero no todos podían ser como Ted Williams y culminar su carrera con un *home run*.

"Usted ha hecho excelentes contribuciones", le dijo Card, procurando brindarle algún consuelo, "pero ahora entramos en otra fase".

Después, Card le rindió un informe completo al presidente y le manifestó su sentimiento de tristeza y su reflexión de que Colin Powell no era Ted Williams.

Como de costumbre, Bush se mostró impaciente. Había escogido a Rice y ella había aceptado. Quería anunciar el nombramiento. ¿Dónde estaba la carta de renuncia de Powell?

Card esperó varios días pero la carta no llegó. Llamó a Powell a su casa. Fue una conversación cortés pero seca. ¿Qué pasó con la carta?

"Va en camino", dijo Powell.

La carta llegó el domingo 14 de noviembre. Dos días después, Bush anunció el nombramiento de Rice. Elogió a Powell y, en un solo párrafo, anunció que Hadley iba a ser su nuevo asesor nacional de seguridad.

33

CARD SEGUÍA INSISTIENDO con respecto a Rumsfeld. Con Rice a cargo del Departamento de Estado y Hadley como asesor nacional de seguridad, la falta de voluntad de Rumsfeld de comprometerse en el proceso de colaboración entre organismos los iba a enloquecer. Card había tenido que mediar constantemente. En una ocasión dijo: "A menudo yo era la persona que trataba de retirar la arena de la ropa interior de la gente, que es una tarea muy difícil, si no es la ropa interior de uno mismo".

En un momento dado, Card habló con Cheney sobre un posible cambio en el Pentágono.

No, dijo Cheney; su recomendación era que el presidente dejara a Rumsfeld donde estaba. Su postura no era una sorpresa.

Bush y Cheney conversaban en privado. Según Cheney, las presiones sobre el sistema político de Washington eran bien conocidas. La salida de Rumsfeld, independientemente de cómo se presentara, sólo se percibiría como un indicio de duda y vacilación frente a la guerra. Les daría a los críticos de la guerra mucho ánimo y fuerza, le confió a uno de sus subalternos; pronto enfilarían sus críticas contra él y luego contra el presidente mismo. Prácticamente insistió en que Rumsfeld se quedara.

Card no podía saber a ciencia cierta lo que estaba pasando, y lo único que supo fue que ahora Rumsfeld quería efectuar algunos cambios propios en el Departamento de Defensa. Iba a reemplazar a Wolfowitz y a Feith. Bush estaba de acuerdo en que esos cargos no eran propios para ellos. Rumsfeld recomendó que el cronograma para dichos cambios se ampliara.

Bush se la pasaba hablando con Cheney. Lo importante, decía Cheney, era que en medio de la guerra el presidente no podía cambiar a su secretario de Defensa sin suscitar todo tipo de interrogantes.

A mediados de diciembre, el presidente tomó su decisión definitiva. Rumsfeld se quedaría, les dijo a Cheney y a Card. No podía cambiar a Rumsfeld.

"Eso no significaba que no quisiera hacerlo", dijo más tarde Card.

EN EL 2006, LE DIJE A RUMSFELD durante una entrevista que Powell, Card, Rice y Hadley le habían recomendado, todos, a Bush que nombrara un nuevo equipo nacional de seguridad.

"No me comprometí con esas personas para recomendarle al presidente que debía despedir a alguien", dijo Rumsfeld.

"¿Cuándo le pidió el presidente que se quedara?", pregunté.

"No recuerdo que lo haya hecho. No me acuerdo de que me hubiera pedido que me quedara".

"¿Usted quería quedarse?".

"Aquí estoy", respondió.

"Ya me he dado cuenta".

"En verdad quería, y sigo queriendo, lo mejor para el país, y lo que el presidente considere apropiado. Tiene un trabajo muy exigente y debe hacerlo a su manera".

"¿Pero nunca hubo un momento o una reunión en que le dijera, 'quiero que se quede'?".

"No recuerdo que haya habido algo así", dijo. "Pero, por otra parte", agregó riendo, "estoy muy seguro de que nunca hubo un momento en el que dijera, 'quiero que se vaya'".

UNO DE LOS ARGUMENTOS del gobierno era que 14 de las 18 provincias de Irak eran relativamente tranquilas o estables, y que la violencia y los problemas en realidad se limitaban a cuatro provincias. Rumsfeld personalmente lo había dicho el 8 de noviembre.

"Eso es verdad", le dijo Wolfowitz a Rumsfeld, "pero las que son relativamente estables no se están volviendo más estables. Se están volviendo menos estables". Era el pequeño secreto sucio que no divulgaban y que pondría las cosas en contexto: los ataques estaban aumentando en todas partes. En total, los ataques habían vuelto a subir a casi 3.000 en noviembre, lo que se acercaba a un récord, según los informes confidenciales. "¿Por qué no nos concentramos más en lograr que los 14 sean realmente estables para que se conviertan en modelos para el resto del país?".

A Rumsfeld pareció gustarle la idea.

Wolfowitz preparó unos gráficos y unos mapas que mostraban con los tres colores de semáforo estándar –rojo, amarillo y verde– un plan para evitar entregar parte del país y para aislar y, finalmente, cercar a los insurgentes en las cuatro provincias más violentas.

Por solicitud de Rumsfeld, Wolfowitz preparó varios borradores. Siguió insistiendo, y en una ocasión habló con Cheney y le mostró los mapas, pero su plan nunca fue aceptado. Casi como para enfatizar la falta de interés y la pérdida de influencia de Wolfowitz, Bush volvió a insistir en los viejos argumentos en un foro público de preguntas y respuestas.

"14 de las 18 provincias parecen relativamente tranquilas", dijo.

CARD LANZÓ OTRAS DOS BÚSQUEDAS de personal. Tenía que encontrar a alguien para inaugurar el cargo de director nacional de inteligencia, y a alguien para reemplazar al secretario de Seguridad Interna, Tom Ridge. Seguridad Interna había bajado la "alerta de terror" de naranja a amarillo el 10 de noviembre, ocho días después de las elecciones, y poco después Ridge le dijo a Bush que quería renunciar.

Card sacó su libreta de posibles reemplazos. Sus listas incluían muchos de los nombres usuales: el ex senador Coats, el senador Lieberman, Rudy Giuliani y Armitage.

Telefoneó nuevamente a Armitage para preguntarle si le interesaba Seguridad Interna.

"No, gracias", contestó Armitage. "El secretario y yo estamos más o menos en que entramos juntos, salimos juntos".

"Pero podría salir con él un día y volver a entrar por otra puerta el día siguiente", le propuso Card.

"No lo creo", dijo Armitage.

Más tarde Hadley llamó a Armitage para saber qué le había dicho Card.

"¿También le preguntó sobre el cargo de director nacional de inteligencia?", preguntó Hadley.

No.

"Pues se suponía que debía hacerlo. ¿Representaría eso una diferencia?".

Armitage dijo que no, y luego le comentó francamente: "No sé cómo podría trabajar en un gobierno que deja que se vaya el secretario Powell y mantiene al señor Rumsfeld".

MOSUL, UNA CIUDAD de 1,8 millones de habitantes, hizo erupción. Los insurgentes asaltaron la estación de policía, robaron las armas y sembraron el caos. El 14 de noviembre sacaron a un agente de policía herido del hospital y lo desmembraron. Por lo menos la mitad de los agentes de policía de la ciudad abandonaron sus cargos. Los insurgentes impactaron a dos C-130 con misiles tierra-aire, y tropas estadounidenses en sus vehículos blindados ingresaron a la ciudad. Negroponte viajó hasta allá para ver qué estaba sucediendo, pero no dejaron acercar el avión. Estaba iracundo y profirió todo tipo de maldiciones mientras volaban los 200 kilómetros de regreso a Bagdad.

El general Casey y Jim Jeffrey viajaron a Mosul por la noche. Le dispararon al avión tan pronto aterrizó. Hacia fines de noviembre, apenas 60 días antes de las elecciones programadas para el 30 de enero, había problemas logísticos masivos. Lo de menos era la seguridad en las urnas, ya de por sí precaria; el caso era que los iraquíes planeaban importar millones de papeletas en docenas de aviones de cabina ancha. Aunque contaban con la ayuda de las Naciones Unidas, Jeffrey se preguntaba cómo iban a lograr todo eso. En general, concluyó, Irak estaba "en la más profunda mierda".

Lakhdar Brahimi, de la ONU, le estaba enviando mensajes a Bush, rogándole que aplazara las elecciones iraquíes. Las minorías sunitas estaban dejando en claro que se opondrían a las elecciones y que hasta las boicotearían, y Brahimi quería más tiempo para convencerlos de que reconsideraran y participaran activamente en el proceso electoral. En la década de 1920, los chiítas se habían negado a participar en el proceso político. Se decía que eso había ocasionado la exclusión chiíta durante varios decenios. Ahora se temía que los sunitas terminaran atrapados en un ciclo similar de aislamiento y pérdida de derechos, excluidos del nuevo gobierno iraquí durante mucho tiempo.

El primer ministro Allawi y otros estaban enviando el mismo mensaje sobre aplazamiento. Una buena parte de los medios de comunicación iraquíes decían que las elecciones fomentarían la violencia indefinidamente. La adhesión ciega a una fecha arbitraria no tenía sentido.

La única voz iraquí a favor de proseguir con las elecciones era la del líder chiíta, el Gran Ayatollah Sistani. Los chiítas habían esperado ya bastante tiempo. Querían democracia. Querían probar su músculo político.

"Es muy importante que se celebren las elecciones el 30 de enero", dijo el presidente en una reunión del CNS el 29 de noviembre. Algunos de los miembros principales del CNS estaban vacilando y se les habría podido convencer sobre el aplazamiento, entre ellos Hadley. Pero Bush nunca le pidió a nadie que diera razones para posponerlas.

"Todos están a favor de proseguir, ¿verdad?", dijo el presidente. En realidad no era una pregunta.

Todos guardaron silencio.

"Gracias por ser firmes", continuó, prosiguiendo como si el silencio significara consenso. "No ganamos nada con el aplazamiento. Sistani tiene razón. Esta es la situación en que me encuentro. La mayoría de la población quiere elecciones, ¿y se supone que yo deba decir que no?".

También dijo: "No vamos a escoger ganadores". Ni la embajada ni la CIA iban a ayudar. "Que las fichas caigan donde sea".

Era una orden difícil de obedecer, tanto para los diplomáticos, que estaban habituados a apoyar a los candidatos cercanos a los Estados Unidos, como para la CIA, que favorecía al primer ministro interino Allawi. Sin embargo, Tony Blair había enviado dos operativos británicos para ayudarle a Allawi. Le dijo a Bush que los británicos se encargarían.

Las elecciones fueron otro asunto en el que el general Myers, jefe del Estado Mayor Conjunto, no obtuvo un voto. De hecho, nadie más lo recibió. Myers sentía que cuando empezaba a surgir cualquier duda en la Sala de Situaciones, un cuarto pequeño sin ventanas, el presidente casi la eliminaba a la fuerza. Ya fueren bajas alarmantes, malas noticias, la decisión actual sobre el cronograma de las elecciones iraquíes, algún otro problema o, simplemente, el menor indicio de una de las incertidumbres que vienen con la guerra, el presidente trataba de eliminarlas todas.

"Un momento", dijo Bush en una ocasión. "Sabemos que estamos haciendo lo correcto. Estamos en el camino correcto. Estamos haciendo lo correcto para nosotros, para nuestro propio interés y para el mundo. Y no lo olviden. Adelante, muchachos".

Bush abrigaba ambiciones más profundas, grandiosas, incluso. En la mañana del viernes 3 de diciembre de 2004, llamó a su principal redactor de discursos, Michael Gerson. La meta de Bush en ese momento era cambiar radicalmente la concepción de la política exterior estadounidense, tanto como había cambiado al comienzo de la Guerra Fría, a fines de los años cuarenta, con políticas de contención y disuasión. El discurso de Bush en West Point en junio de 2002 había sentado las bases y la justificación para la invasión de Irak. El historiador Arthur Schlesinger Jr., quien despreciaba a Bush, se maravilló de que pudiera cambiar la política exterior estadounidense de manera tan significativa, convirtiéndola en una doctrina que se resumía en una "guerra preventiva": una guerra para detener una guerra. "Lograr esto sin iniciar un debate nacional denota unas increíbles dotes de liderazgo", señaló Schlesinger.

Cuando Gerson llegó ese viernes por la mañana, el presidente le dijo que quería que el segundo discurso de posesión, que debía pronunciar en poco tiempo, dejara una idea muy en claro: "El futuro de Estados Unidos y la seguridad de Estados Unidos dependen de la propagación de la libertad". Eso era todo. Quería un discurso de posesión que versara sobre la libertad. Quería que Gerson encontrara la manera más memorable y escueta posible de decir esto de una vez por todas, palabras que definieran su política en relación con el nuevo mundo que estaban afrontando. El terrorista Abu Musad al-Zarqawi y los jihadistas internacionales habían escogido pelear en Irak, por una buena razón, dijo Bush. Sabían que un fracaso de Estados Unidos en Irak tendría consecuencias de amplio alcance en el Medio Oriente.

"Ellos entienden lo que está en juego, y también nosotros lo debemos entender", dijo Bush.

Rara vez había tenido un redactor de discursos semejante oportunidad de definir una era. Era la ocasión para quebrar un poco más las barreras tradicionales entre realismo e idealismo en la política exterior estadounidense. Los intereses realistas de Estados Unidos serían ahora defendidos mediante la fidelidad a los ideales norteamericanos, en especial, la democracia. Como de costumbre, Gerson había leído muchos discursos viejos, sobre todo los discursos de posesión en los que Harry Truman había definido las doctrinas de la Guerra Fría y John Kennedy las había ampliado.

Pero, en opinión de Gerson, la retórica de Kennedy se había excedido y había sido exageradamente grandiosa. "Pagar cualquier precio, soportar cualquier carga, enfrentar cualquier dificultad, apoyar a cualquier amigo, oponerse a cualquier enemigo para garantizar la supervivencia y el éxito de la libertad", había dicho en su discurso de posesión en 1961. Esa mentalidad había llevado a Vietnam. Gerson no quería algo que sugiriera un compromiso excesivamente entusiasta e ilimitado con la democracia plena en todo el mundo. La caída del gobierno no democrático pero amistoso de Hosni Mubarak en Egipto, por ejemplo, difícilmente favorecería los intereses inmediatos de Estados Unidos.

Gerson quería que el discurso definiera elementos realistas de reforma democrática: no sólo elecciones, sino el desarrollo de culturas democráticas en Egipto, Arabia Saudita y Jordania. Eso incluiría los derechos de las mujeres y las minorías, libertad religiosa, más comercio y reformas jurídicas.

"Vamos a definir un rango serio de opciones de política que se ubiquen entre la indiferencia frente a la suerte de otros y la guerra constante", le dijo Gerson a un colega. Por ejemplo, en Irán había una opción, en algún punto, entre los extremos de una invasión directa o no hacer nada. Gerson esperaba presentar el proyecto para una estrategia de largo plazo que no fuera desestabilizador y de confrontación, sino más bien firme y moral.

El discurso podía unir temáticamente todo lo que Bush había hecho desde el 9/11. Para Bush, el 9/11 representaba la línea de demarcación entre el nuevo siglo y los años 90, cuando Clinton no había respondido con suficiente agresividad una serie de ataques. Los ataques del 9/11 eran una advertencia sobre el tipo de circunstancias estratégicas que todo presidente tendría que afrontar en los próximos 50 años.

Hadley tenía varias encuestas de iraquíes que supuestamente indicaban un cambio importante en la opinión pública en los últimos meses. Las encuestas revelaban un profundo resentimiento por la ocupación estadounidense, pero no indicaban desconfianza con respecto a las instituciones democráticas. Por eso, elogiar la democracia en el discurso sobre el estado de la Unión podría gustarles a los iraquíes.

Gerson sabía muy bien que la política exterior de Bush no era del tipo que acogían los conservadores tradicionales, quienes, como escribió William F. Buckley, "se paran en contravía de la historia gritando '¡deténganse!'". Bush estaba diciendo claramente "adelante", y Gerson creía que el presidente estaba actuando más dentro de la tradición de Franklin D. Roosevelt al utilizar el gobierno para expandir la libertad.

Gerson estaba muy entusiasmado, esperando algo equivalente, en política exterior, a la teoría del campo unificado del universo de Einstein. Estaba tan acelerado, que sufrió un infarto a mediados de diciembre. Los médicos le dijeron que no se debía a exceso de trabajo. Era una combinación de genes y estrés.

Bush llamó a Gerson al hospital de Alexandria, donde estaba registrado bajo el seudónimo John Alexandria.

"No lo estoy llamando para ver cómo va el discurso de posesión", le dijo Bush. "Estoy llamando para ver cómo está el tipo que está escribiendo el discurso".

Gerson se recuperó. Al cabo de algunas semanas había regresado al trabajo, con un horario reducido y concentrado en el discurso.

Armitage viajó a Irak a fines del 2004.

"¿Qué vio?", le preguntó el presidente tan pronto regresó.

"No estamos ganando", dijo Armitage, y añadió con cautela: "No estamos perdiendo. No perder durante un largo período de tiempo funciona para los insurgentes". Dijo que los insurgentes estaban haciendo una increíble campaña de intimidación.

Bush no lo rebatió. Después, Armitage llamó tanto a Negroponte como a Casey para informarles sobre lo que le había dicho al presidente, porque no quería que los tomara por sorpresa. Lo que resultó sorprendente fue que ninguno de los dos lo contradijo. Era un enredo terrible. También descubrió que los análisis de la CIA y la DIA coincidían con el suyo. El enemigo es, en su mayor parte, interno. Las fuerzas externas, Siria e Irán, son importantes pero no cruciales para la insurgencia.

Hadley escuchó la versión de Armitage de "no estamos ganando, no estamos perdiendo", y consideró que se trataba de un problema de ejecución e instrumentación. Lo que sucedía era que no lo estaban haciendo bien.

Después de los violentos ataques contra estaciones de policía iraquíes, Frank Miller volvió a expresar su inquietud acerca de la manera como los militares estadounidenses estaban entrenando a la policía. Diversas estimaciones indicaban que se había entrenado a 60.000 personas, pero era difícil saber qué representaba esa cifra. Otra estimación indicaba que sólo la mitad de dicha cifra estaba realmente prestando servicio. En todo caso, no iban a poder derrotar a la insurgencia con la policía. Esto era una guerra. Tenían que concentrarse más en combate de elite y poderío paramilitar.

"Hay algo que no funciona en todo esto", le dijo a Rice. "Estamos formando policías de ronda. Además del hecho de que van a trabajar con coroneles de la época de Saddam. No hay una sola estación en el mundo, no importa si es en Los Ángeles o en Nueva York, que vaya a aguantar un ataque con RPG y ametralladoras pesadas".

Miller había insistido infructuosamente en las reuniones del comité de adjuntos en que la embajada de Estados Unidos en Irak debía tener "puestos de avanzada" en todo el país. Esa había sido una de las pocas cosas positivas durante la era de Bremer, pensó. En esa época tenían 18 administradores regionales que estaban realmente conectados con lo que sucedía en el país. Pero su idea no prosperó. La presencia de la embajada de Estados Unidos se limitaba a la Zona Verde.

Había soluciones sencillas que, en opinión de Miller, la embajada en Bagdad debía estar promoviendo. Por ejemplo, los ataques insurgentes estaban causando el cierre de los oleoductos iraquíes, y Miller ordenó un estudio que reveló que casi todos los ataques estaban dirigidos contra secciones pequeñas y vulnerables de los oleoductos; les sugirió a los militares que enterraran estas secciones entre arena y tierra, pero no lo hicieron. También fracasó en su intento de lograr que los militares elevaran su meta en cuanto a asegurar la disponibilidad eléctrica.

"¿Cómo logro que la embajada en Bagdad siga las órdenes del gobierno?", le preguntó Rice a Miller en diciembre de 2004. A los seis meses de haber llegado, Negroponte quiso regresar a Estados Unidos, y tenían que decidir quién iba a ser su reemplazo. Rice y Miller empezaron a hablar sobre Zalmay Khalilzad, el norteamericano afgano que había sido el hombre clave del CNS en relación con la oposición iraquí y luego había sido nombrado embajador en Afganistán. "Zal ha convertido la embajada en Kabul en una embajada de tiempos de guerra", dijo Rice. "Logra que las cosas se hagan".

Era el tipo de chisme que no se podía mantener en secreto durante mucho tiempo en Washington; a comienzos de enero, la columna "In the Loop" de Al Kamen en *The Washington Post* informó que Khalilzad iba a reemplazar a Negroponte.

Sin embargo, surgió un inconveniente. Informes de inteligencia revelaron conversaciones en las que Khalilzad le decía a Lakhdar Brahimi, de la

ONU, que no se preocupara por la fecha del 30 de enero para las elecciones iraquíes, porque podía no cumplirse. Resultaba extraordinario que uno de los embajadores de Bush le dijera a un funcionario extranjero que no debía preocuparse por la política oficial de Estados Unidos.

Armitage llamó a Miller. "Tiene que ver esto", le dijo.

Miller fue a la Sala de Situaciones de la Casa Blanca y pidió ver los cables, pero no estaban allí. Llamó a Armitage.

"Rich, no los encuentro. En la Sala de Situaciones no los encuentran".

"Sí, lo sé", dijo Armitage. "Los incautaron todos".

Eso es, pensó Miller.

"Zal, metió la pata en serio", le dijo Hadley a Khalilzad por teléfono. "Dudo que el presidente lo pueda nombrar en algún momento embajador en Irak; en todo caso, ahora no. Tendrá que pasar un intervalo decente de mínimo varios meses antes de que lo pueda hacer. Pero quizás ni siquiera entonces se pueda".

EL 3 DE ENERO DE 2005 Bush ofreció una recepción en la Casa Blanca para los congresistas recién elegidos y sus cónyuges. "Laura y yo sabemos cuán difícil es para una familia estar en la política", dijo. "Es el sacrificio máximo, en verdad; se sacrifica la privacidad, se sacrifica el tiempo con los hijos".

El comentario era extremadamente inapropiado, si se tenía en cuenta que 1.333 estadounidenses y miles de iraquíes habían hecho el verdadero sacrificio máximo. Bush estaba en una burbuja postelectoral.

El presidente sólo hizo una ligera referencia a Irak. "Tenemos que cerciorarnos de ganar la guerra. Tenemos que cerciorarnos de apoyar a nuestras tropas".

Dos días después, en una reunión del CNS, hubo una prolongada discusión sobre cómo aumentar la participación sunita en las elecciones que se avecinaban.

"Utilicemos la creatividad para explorar ideas sobre cómo podemos permitir la participación sunita a pesar de la violencia", dijo el presidente. "¿Qué tal una votación telefónica? ¿Qué tal enviar las papeletas por correo? ¿Qué tal enviar embajadores a los países árabes e instar a esos países árabes a establecer contacto con los sunitas y alentarlos para que participen en el proceso?".

Jeffrey veía sorprendido a Bush desde Bagdad en el video seguro. Pocas veces un comandante en jefe les daba a los diplomáticos o a los militares en el campo directrices tan específicas y claras: "Ustedes lo lograrán". Las ideas de Bush sobre votar por correo y por teléfono no eran prácticas, pero había algo en el entusiasmo y la convicción del presidente. Bush estaba diciendo, en efecto: "En realidad no tienen opción en este caso. Esto es algo que no pueden hacer mal". A medida que se aproximaban las elecciones, Jeffrey sintió una mezcla de temor y esperanza.

En la Casa Blanca, Hadley observaba con asombro cómo la CIA iba con regularidad a informar al presidente sobre sus pronósticos pesimistas de guerra civil. Las elecciones no disminuirían la violencia; probablemente, empeorarían la situación, decía la CIA.

"Vamos a celebrar las elecciones el 30 de enero", contestaba Bush. Las fechas programadas eran cruciales para avanzar en el proceso. Si no había una fecha programada, no habría progreso y nada sucedería.

La CIA –tanto verbalmente como en informes confidenciales escritos– repetía su mensaje. La fecha del 30 de enero equivalía a convertir en blanco a todo Irak; sería día propicio para los ataques, sobre todo en los sitios de votación. Como la minoría sunita sabía que iba a perder en las elecciones, se iba a generar violencia sectaria entre sunitas y chiítas. La agencia volvió a recomendar el aplazamiento de las elecciones.

Hadley se enfrentó con el director de la CIA, Porter Goss, y algunos de sus analistas y personal operativo. Quería que se comprometieran en operaciones de propaganda para apoyar las elecciones. Pero la idea que tenía la CIA de las operaciones informativas era que estas consistirían en propagar mentiras, pensó.

"¿Para qué propagar mentiras?", preguntó Hadley. "Propaguen la verdad. Es mucho más poderosa. Ustedes no lo entienden. Hay que buscar maneras de decir la verdad de modo que no quede instantáneamente desacreditada porque proviene de nosotros".

Estados Unidos tenía la voz más potente del mundo con su cine, su música y su televisión. Pero, se lamentó Hadley, todos los días su país era derrotado por los mensajes de los terroristas y Al Jazeera.

En una reunión del CNS, el 10 de enero de 2005, Bush reafirmó que respetarían la fecha de las elecciones en Irak, que sería dentro de 20 días. "Tenemos que reflexionar sobre la estrategia postelectoral", dijo. El éxito dependía en parte de si la minoría sunita llegaba a percibir que sería parte del nuevo gobierno. "Tenemos que influir en los triunfadores chiítas para que dejen en claro que los sunitas serán incluidos. Lo importante no es tanto la votación, sino cómo será el gobierno que surja de la votación".

¿Pero, cuáles sunitas? ¿Quiénes tenían poder entre la minoría? La invasión estadounidense había expulsado a los sunitas; entonces ¿cómo se podría percibir a Estados Unidos como un agente honesto y, mucho menos, como un forastero atento a los intereses sunitas? Esas preguntas no fueron hechas, y, por lo tanto, no fueron contestadas.

Hadley se estaba poniendo nervioso. Tal vez debían aplazar los comicios.

"Seguimos con las elecciones", repitió Bush. En privado criticaba la ausencia de un liderazgo fuerte en Irak. ¿Dónde estaban los líderes? ¿Por qué no salían a la palestra? "¿Por qué no se hacen cargo de su propio destino?".

34

El 18 DE ENERO, Rice compareció ante la Comisión de Relaciones Exteriores del Senado para sus audiencias de confirmación. Los demócratas llegaron atacando. "Su lealtad a la misión que se le asignó, vender esta guerra, sobrepasó su respeto por la verdad", fue la acusación de la senadora Bárbara Boxer, de California, antes de lanzarse con una letanía sobre los juicios de Rice acerca de las armas de destrucción masiva antes de la invasión.

Mientras respondía, era evidente que Rice había sido tomada por sorpresa. "Senadora, debo decir que nunca he perdido el respeto por la verdad en función de nada", dijo. Pero de regreso en la Casa Blanca estaba claramente abatida.

"Anímese", le dijo Rove. Los republicanos controlaban el Senado, por lo que podría salir magullada tras su confirmación, pero solo sería una formalidad. Era el costo de estar en el negocio de la política en Washington. Los ganadores salían heridos, pero podían sobrevivir y hasta tener éxito. "Usted va a estar bien. Está ganando".

Una semana después el senado votó 85 a 13 para confirmarla.

PARA EL DÍA DE LA POSESIÓN, el 20 de enero, Bush había practicado su alocución varias veces. "No puedo esperar a dar este discurso", le comentó a Gerson. Aunque tenía aportes de otros, se trataba de un discurso y de una política que esencialmente habían sido trabajados por Bush y su escritor de discursos. Después de leer un borrador final, Andy Carf dijo medio en broma "Este no es un discurso que daría Dick Cheney".

Después de que Bush hizo el juramento oficial sobre las gradas del Capitolio, ascendió al podio y presentó su alocución de 2.000 palabras en 17 minutos. En términos expresivos, fue una de sus mejores presentaciones. Habló de manera vigorosa, sin un solo tropiezo, sin un solo momento de vacilación o de duda.

"La política de Estados Unidos es buscar y apoyar el crecimiento de movimientos e instituciones democráticos en todas las naciones y culturas, con la meta final de hacer cesar la tiranía en nuestro mundo", declaró Bush.

Utilizó la palabra "libertad" –o variaciones como "libre" o "liberador"– en 44 ocasiones, nueve de ellas en los dos últimos párrafos.

Gerson usualmente veía los discursos de Bush en la televisión, como los veían las personas promedio, y así podía entender mejor las reacciones. Pero, en esta ocasión, se encontraba en la plataforma de la posesión. Nunca antes había tenido la sensación palpable de estar haciendo parte de una importante empresa histórica. Todo futuro presidente, desde el punto de vista de Gerson, tendría que tomar en serio la doctrina de Bush. Señalaría un camino para las décadas venideras.

"Algo grande ha sucedido", informó Hadley después de recoger algunas reacciones internacionales.

Para muchos conservadores, el discurso fue un gran error. Peggy Noonan, la escritora de discursos de Bush padre, atacó el discurso en *The Wall Street Journal*, poniendo el dedo en la llaga de su principio central. "Fue un revés presentar una agenda tan vasta, tanto así que un observador apuntó burlonamente que no se habría sorprendido si al final el presidente hubiera anunciado que íbamos a colonizar Marte".

"Parecía un documento producido por la Casa Blanca para una misión. Estados Unidos, según el discurso, había alertado al mundo". Ella dijo que la ambición de acabar con la tiranía era loable, pero "Esto es –¿cómo decirlo?– algo excesivo", y agregó: "Los discursos más movilizadores son los que nos invitan a hacer parte de una causa realmente posible".

Al conocer la reacción de la escritora de discursos preferida de su padre, Bush la ignoró.

Rice pensó que el discurso fue exaltador, uno de los mejores que hubiera oído. Pero mientras estaba allí sentada escuchando, pensaba "Bien, ¿y cómo vamos a hacer esto?". Se dio cuenta de que tomaría años. La pregunta que le hizo a su equipo fue: "Si la gente dentro de 30 años mira hacia atrás y lee el discurso de la segunda posesión presidencial de Bush ¿dirán que la política estadounidense contribuyó a hacerlo posible, o a dejar los cimientos para lograrlo?". En cuanto a las críticas, comentó "Si el presidente de Estados Unidos no puede levantarse y decir durante su posesión que deberíamos aspirar a que un día cese la tiranía y todos vivamos en libertad, entonces, ¿cuándo se puede decir? Este es el momento para tener un sueño temerario".

Steve Hadley se había dado cuenta de que en los últimos cuatro años algunos de los jefes se quejaban de los problemas, en lugar de solucionarlos. El general Myers alguna vez le dijo a Hadley que tenía un problema de coordinación de asuntos militares con los sauditas.

"Ya lo solucioné", respondió Hadley.

"Grandioso", replicó Myers. "Es un buen ejemplo, pero tengo otros nueve problemas".

"Envíeme su lista, Dick", le dijo Hadley, "y los revisaré uno por uno".

En la noche del 22 de enero de 2005, Rumsfeld y Myers arrinconaron a Hadley en la cena anual del Club Alfalfa, en Washington.

"La coordinación entre agencias no está funcionando", dijo Rumsfeld, dirigiéndose a Hadley. La coordinación entre agencias era el trabajo de este. "Dick Myers tiene una lista larga. Todos los días viene a fastidiarme diciendo que la coordinación entre agencias no funciona. Tiene una larga lista de cosas que quiere que se hagan".

"Don", respondió Hadley, "le dije a Dick Myers que necesitábamos hacer esto hace cuatro meses. Envíemela e intentaré evacuarla lo antes posible, como si fuera la lista de reparaciones para la compra de una casa".

Dos semanas después Hadley aún esperaba la lista.

RUMSFELD CONFIRMÓ DESPUÉS, en una entrevista, que creía que el proceso entre agencias no funcionaba. "En pleno siglo XXI", dijo, "en la era de la información, estamos funcionando todavía con un proceso entre agencias y una estructura gubernamental que datan de la era industrial del siglo pasado. Es como si el Departamento de Estado tratara de funcionar hoy sin la reforma Goldwater-Nichols del Estado Mayor Conjunto, como en el pasado, cuando cada servicio se iba a luchar la guerra de la Armada, la guerra del Ejército, la guerra de la Fuerza Aérea. Eso ya no funciona en este mundo en que vivimos. Mi comentario, acerca de que la coordinación entre agencias no funciona, de ninguna manera pretende describir a las personas que se encuentran en ellas ni la estructura que controlan. Es una reflexión sobre el hecho de que la estructura del gobierno es un rezago de una era pasada. Y es algo que creo que todos sentimos de vez en cuando".

"¿Le ha comentado esto al presidente?", le pregunté.

"Claro".

"¿Qué dice él?".

"No voy a decir lo que él dice".

"Pero eso es algo que valdría la pena arreglar, ¿no es así?".

"Por supuesto", dijo Rumsfeld. Sobre la pared de su despacho, justo al frente de su gran escritorio, colgaba una copia del viejo afiche de reclutamiento de la Primera Guerra Mundial donde el Tío Sam dice: "I WANT YOU" (Te busco a ti). El lema de aquel afiche de Rumsfeld decía: "Estamos en guerra. ¿Estás haciendo todo lo que puedes?". Él dijo que no creía que el resto del gobierno estuviera haciendo todo lo que podía.

"Este departamento está para la guerra", dijo Rumsfeld. "Los demás departamentos no están para eso. Se les está exigiendo que hagan algo para lo que no están organizados, entrenados o equipados. Y eso toma tiempo y es difícil, y hay resistencia en el Congreso. Las personas se sienten atraídas por diferentes organizaciones, según sus inclinaciones, y quienes llegan atraídos aquí son gente que está lista para ser desplegada y para ir a las zonas de peligro. Y la gente atraída por otros departamentos puede, o no, estar lista. Y si se les exige, dirán que no se enrolaron para eso, y puede que esto no les sirva para avanzar en sus carreras".

Rumsfeld citó un ejemplo del año 2001, cuando dijo que no había sido capaz de conseguir fondos para entrenar soldados en Afganistán. "¿Por qué no pudimos? Bueno, porque el Departamento de Estado tenía los fondos para el entrenamiento, y estos son programados con dos o tres años de anticipación".

Le dije que, entre los militares, muchos sentían que el resto del gobierno de Estados Unidos no se había hecho presente para la guerra y que no estaba cumpliendo con su parte.

"¿Comparte la preocupación de los militares?", le pregunté.

"¡Claro que la comparto! ¡Por Dios! ¿Que si la comparto? ¡Estoy aquí!".

"¿Puede usted movilizar al resto del gobierno?".

"Lo hemos intentado una y otra vez", dijo Rumsfeld.

MILLER AÚN SE ENCONTRABA en su misión para implementar la orden del presidente, de permitir que los británicos y los australianos tuvieran acceso a la red militar secreta SIPRNET completa. Asistió a una reunión en el Pentágono con algunos de los civiles y oficiales claves del Estado Mayor Conjunto involucrados en este asunto. Le leyó al grupo las instrucciones de Rumsfeld y del presidente.

"No querrá decir acceso irrestricto…", dijo uno de los generales de tres estrellas del Estado Mayor Conjunto.

"Si el presidente o el secretario de Defensa hubieran querido decir que se les diera acceso de acuerdo con determinadas limitaciones, lo habrían dicho", replicó Miller, mirando fijamente al general. "Este es un documento para uso libre entre agencias. Su gente firmó esto. Acceso significa acceso. ¿Qué parte de la palabra 'acceso' no entiende?".

Miller preparó algo para que Hadley se lo enviara a Rumsfeld en nombre del presidente, solicitándole que solucionara lo del acceso a SIPRNET.

"Verá", respondió Hadley en tono amigable, "personalmente tengo dos tareas difíciles para mí. Tengo que establecer mi propia relación con el presidente, y tengo que hacer que mi relación con Rumsfeld cambie de ser la de un delegado a ser la de un igual. Y en mi primera salida no puedo decirle "Don, su gente lo está estropeando. Soluciónelo".

Miller reconoció que tenía lógica. Tenían que trabajar en muchas otras cosas además del asunto de compartir información. Pero esto significaba que tendrían que trabajar aun más duro en el canal de respaldo para que la orden del presidente se instrumentara. Miller estaba sorprendido de que todos los funcionarios de alto nivel –el presidente, Rumsfeld, Rice y Hadley– parecieran aceptar la laxitud y las provocaciones en el sistema.

Arriba en su oficina en el segundo piso del ala oeste, Karl Rove se encontraba en una posición inestable, casi con un pie en la calle, cuatro días después de la segunda posesión de Bush. Su trabajo real, conseguir la reelección de Bush, había terminado. ¿Qué iba a hacer ahora, a los 54 años?

"Hasta aquí llegué, *bubba*", trató de bromear con un colega. "No sé lo que digo. Me gusta mi trabajo y seguiré por aquí por un tiempo". Como consejero de Bush padre, tendría un papel importante en la política económica y otras políticas. "Mi trabajo es ser un buen colega. Agito las cosas sin pisarle los callos a nadie".

Pero Rove estaba aburrido. Jugaba con una bocina de payaso de baterías que le había mostrado al presidente. Al oprimir un botón de esta novedad plástica de 25 centímetros cuadrados, que podía ser instalada en el tablero de un auto, profería una serie de groserías e improperios grabados con un encolerizado acento sureño. "¡Más lento imbécil! Wal-Mart está abierto toda la noche", tronaba el juguete rojo cuando Rove oprimía el botón. Y de nuevo: "¿Licencia de conducción? ¡Eres tú el que debe conseguir una, estúpido!"[18].

La CIA continuó con su flujo permanente de advertencias acerca del ejercicio democrático por venir en Irak. Advertía que se excluiría a los sunitas y la violencia aumentaría. Los informes clasificados alarmistas no cesaban, y aumentaron en los días anteriores al 30 de enero. En Bagdad, Negroponte estaba en desacuerdo con el punto de vista de la CIA, y la embajada animaba a la ONU y a los iraquíes para que siguieran adelante. Públicamente afirmó que la seguridad era adecuada.

Después de que un informante de la CIA presentara otra advertencia, Bush intervino: "¿Esto es Bob Bagdad?", refiriéndose al propagandista de

---

18. El juguete tenía otras ocho grabaciones: "Oye, estúpido, ¿quién te enseñó a conducir?", "¿Qué demonios fue esa maniobra?", "¿En qué carrera estás, cabeza hueca?", "Hijo de perra", "Apártate de mi camino", "¿Acaso estás ciego?", "¡Deja ya de hablar por teléfono, imbécil!", y finalmente, "¡Eres un maldito cretino!".

Saddam. Fue un tremendo insulto. "Solo he escuchado este tipo de cosas de la CIA", dijo Bush. "Aunque me demore más, no hay evidencia de que la seguridad vaya a mejorar. Dependo de la perspectiva de las elecciones y de un gobierno electo para reducir a la insurgencia y mejorar la seguridad".

Las elecciones serían para una Asamblea Nacional provisional que designaría a un gobierno interino y redactaría el borrador de una Constitución permanente. Luego la Constitución sería sometida a votación del pueblo iraquí en un referendo, en el otoño, dentro de nueve meses. Si se aprobaba, se haría una segunda elección nacional a los dos meses para escoger un gobierno permanente, bajo la nueva Constitución. Era un proceso largo y tedioso de tres etapas. Pero había sido aprobado por las Naciones Unidas y todos estaban de acuerdo. Bush de nuevo dijo que no veía la utilidad de la espera.

Finalmente, durante la presentación de un informe en el Salón Oval, justo antes del día de las elecciones en Irak, tras escuchar las últimas terribles predicciones de la CIA, el presidente golpeó sus manos sonoramente, como un disparo de rifle, y cerró de un golpe su libro de informes.

"Bueno", dijo, "veremos quien tiene la razón".

A MEDIDA QUE SE ACERCABA la fecha, surgía la violencia. "Espero que suceda algo espectacular" el día de la elección o justo antes, advirtió en Bagdad el mayor general Peter Chiarelli, quien se desempeñaba como comandante de la 1ª División de Caballería por un año. En enero 26, un helicóptero Super Stallion de la Infantería de Marina se había desplomado en el occidente del país, con un saldo de 31 estadounidenses muertos. Fue el incidente aislado que causó más muertes entre las fuerzas de Estados Unidos desde la invasión.

En su alocución por radio del sábado, el día anterior a las elecciones en Irak, el presidente fue más temerario, si eso era todavía posible. "Mañana el mundo será testigo de un viraje en la historia de Irak", dijo. Señaló que el terrorista Zarqawi, de Al Qaeda, quien estaba detrás de muchos de los carros bomba y las decapitaciones en Irak, recientemente se había referido a la democracia como un "principio maligno".

Rice despertó la mañana del domingo 30 de enero y sintonizó a CNN. Oyó primero el sonido antes de que la imagen estuviera clara en su televisor.

"…un día extraordinario para los iraquíes", escuchó.

La imagen apareció, y se veían largas filas de iraquíes esperando para votar. Rice llamó al presidente.

"Tiene que encender la televisión", dijo Rice. "Tiene que ver esto".

"¿Es algo bueno? ¿Es un buen resultado?", preguntó Bush.

"Es asombroso. Es asombroso ver lo que están haciendo estos iraquíes".

Unos 8 millones de iraquíes fueron a las urnas. Muchos agitaban en el aire sus dedos teñidos de púrpura para demostrar que habían votado. Era un giro sorprendente, con un mínimo de violencia.

Bush pensó que se trataba de una reivindicación, no solo de su política sobre Irak, sino de su agenda de la libertad. Los iraquíes estaban apropiándose del momento y tomaban el control de su futuro. Bush hizo una breve alocución televisada a la nación.

"El mundo está escuchando la voz de la libertad proveniente del centro del Medio Oriente", dijo, y los iraquíes "han tomado legítimo control del destino de su país".

Gerson sintió que los ánimos y la atmósfera en la Casa Blanca se transformaban; era como si se hubiera doblado una esquina. Pero la minoría sunita, efectivamente, había boicoteado la elección, dejando por fuera a un 20% de la población, un segmento crítico conformado por los privilegiados del régimen Sadam. Los sunitas eran la columna vertebral de la insurgencia.

En Bagdad, durante enero de 2005, la estación de la CIA recopiló un AARD-WOLF, nombre dado a una evaluación general del jefe de de la estación. Era un documento importante donde se decía que la insurgencia se estaba fortaleciendo y que Irak estaba al borde de la guerra civil. A pesar de la emoción debida a las elecciones, los ataques iniciados por el enemigo habían pasado de 2.000, en diciembre, a 3.000 en enero. Negroponte revisó la AARDWOLF, y les dijo al jefe de división de la CIA Rob Richer y al jefe de la estación de la CIA en Bagdad que hablaran con Bush.

"Coincidimos en lo mismo", le dijo al jefe de la estación.

Negroponte simplemente le dijo a Bush, "tenemos algunos altibajos".

Richer sintió que había sido un caso típico de endulzamiento de la verdad. Más tarde confrontó a Negroponte por no haber respaldado al jefe de la estación como lo había prometido.

"Comprendo el mensaje", dijo Negroponte.

Cuando Hadley se posesionaba como asesor para la seguridad nacional, Bush le dio una instrucción básica: "Confío en que usted asegure que haya un proceso del que yo me entere a través de mis secretarios del gabinete". El presidente creía que había que permitir que cada uno manejara su departamento. "Puede tener sus propias opiniones", le dijo Bush, "y me las dirá si se las pido".

A partir de su experiencia como delegado de Rice, Hadley sabía que pasaría bastante tiempo trabajando junto al presidente. Ya habría manera de hacerle llegar sus ideas. Pero Hadley creía firmemente que él y el personal del Comité para la Seguridad Nacional tenían un papel limitado. No eran elegidos ni confirmados por el Senado. Se debía evitar la ejecución de programas del comité porque nadie era responsable.

El éxito sería para el presidente o los secretarios del gabinete, concluyó Hadley. El fracaso, en parte, sería de él. Su trabajo era importante pero, finalmente, ingrato. Era impensable que intentara ser un asesor para la seguridad al estilo viajero y altamente visible de un Henry Kissinger, quien competía y finalmente dominaba a los secretarios del gabinete. Ni siquiera deseaba ser tan visible como lo había sido Rice. Hadley esperaba ser como Brent Scowcroft, el asesor para la seguridad nacional de Bush padre, quien era de bajo perfil y operaba principalmente tras bambalinas.

Como delegado de Rice, Hadley había sido el que lo arreglaba todo, el que llamaba a Armitage o a Wolfowitz o a alguien de la CIA para solucionar un problema inmediato. Ahora el presidente le decía que ya no podría ser el señor Arréglalo Todo. "Hadley", dijo Bush, "debe conseguirse un buen adjunto porque usted tiene que ayudarme a pensar cuál es nuestra estrategia general, y si estamos bien organizados, y cómo realizarlo todo". Al mismo tiempo, como Hadley lo sabía muy bien, la emoción predominante del presidente, a menudo, era la impaciencia. Si quería que algo se arreglara, generalmente se lo asignaría a la persona más cercana. Generalmente este era el propósito de Rice o Handey. Así que, en cierto modo, Hadley conservaría su antiguo trabajo, y también se ganaría uno nuevo.

Hizo una evaluación de los problemas desde el primer aspecto.

"En desarrollo de políticas, obtendríamos una B menos", le comentó a un colega el sábado 5 de febrero, "y una D menos en ejecución de políticas".

Hadley sabía que, casi dos años después de la invasión, los problemas básicos de Irak no habían sido solucionados: seguridad, infraestructura y gobernabilidad. Su evaluación era bastante interesante porque continuamente insistía en que el Comité para la Seguridad Nacional no tenía ningún papel en la ejecución de políticas. Por lo que la D menos aparentemente no se aplicaría a él. Se debía al trabajo realizado por personas como Powell y Rumsfeld.

¿Qué pensaba Rumsfeld de esa percepción?

"Si quisiera podría darle vuelta", me dijo Rumsfeld después, en una entrevista, cuando traje a colación la evaluación de Hadley. El problema no era la ejecución; era el desarrollo de políticas. "Creo que ha habido ejecuciones, en varios aspectos, que han funcionado bastante bien", añadió.

En otras palabras, el problema era el trabajo entre agencias, no él.

35

BANDAR LLEGÓ A LA CASA BLANCA el 5 de febrero para ver a Bush. Un afgano recientemente había pasado por la embajada saudita en Islamabad, Pakistán, y había dicho que sabía dónde se escondía Osama bin Laden. Decía que podría señalar su ubicación si le daban un mapa. Como él y su familia se estaban arriesgando, quería que los sauditas les prometieran que los llevarían al Reino y los dejarían vivir allí por el resto de sus vidas.

Los sauditas hicieron algunas evaluaciones preliminares y el informante casual les pareció interesante, por lo que le prometieron asilo. Él había señalado un punto en el mapa que parecía posible.

Bandar dijo que los sauditas planeaban enviar una unidad militar o de inteligencia a dicho punto y capturar a bin Laden. "No vamos a pasar por un juicio", explicó Bandar. "Lo capturamos, lo matamos y dejamos todo atrás".

"Adelante", dijo el presidente. "No me interesa en absoluto".

Bandar preguntó si la CIA podía apoyarlos en la evaluación de la fuente, y Bush dio su aprobación.

Bandar no había tenido éxito con Porter Gross, y por eso, antes de dejar la Casa Blanca, llamó a Rob Richer, el jefe de la división para el Oriente Cercano y el Sur de Asia de la CIA.

"Vamos a ir a Pakistán", dijo Bandar.

"No puedo seguir órdenes suyas", le objetó Richer.

Pero, casi instantáneamente, Richer recibió sus órdenes a través de los canales regulares. Fue a la mansión de Bandar, y rápidamente ellos y otro experto de la CIA volaban en el avión de Bandar.

Una vez llegaron a Pakistán, empezaron a hacer la evaluación del informante. Sucedió que los hombres de la CIA pronto se dieron cuenta de que el informante era un colaborador conocido de la CIA y del servicio de inteligencia británico MI6, que ya había intentado engañar antes.

¿Por qué los sauditas y la CIA no se habían dado cuenta de eso antes de informarle al presidente y de que se enviara una misión a Pakistán? "Porque nadie comparte nunca sus fuentes", dijo uno de los involucrados. "Es el *modus operandi* usual. Se trataba de un embustero que básicamente buscaba dinero.

El mensaje fue transmitido a Bush: no se ubicó a bin Laden.

A COMIENZOS DE 2005, Rumsfeld envió al general retirado Gary E. Luck a Irak para una inspección general. Luck, anteriormente líder de las fuerzas estadounidenses en Corea del Sur, fue asesor del general Franks durante la invasión a Irak de 2003.

Luck, quien tenía un doctorado en matemáticas, debería examinar la estrategia, el nivel de las tropas y los programas de entrenamiento. Encontró que el entrenamiento del nuevo ejército iraquí era un completo desastre. En muchos casos, solo consistía en entregarle un rifle al recluta, darle tres días de entrenamiento y llamarlo miembro del nuevo ejército iraquí.

Luck le dijo al general Myers: "Hemos subestimado el efecto que Saddam Hussein y su régimen tuvieron sobre el espíritu del pueblo iraquí. Nunca se reconoció a nadie por mostrar algo de iniciativa, bajo Saddam Hussein. Ahora les pedimos que dejen salir toda esa iniciativa, pero ellos no saben cómo hacerlo".

Rice no necesitaba el informe de Luck para saber que el entrenamiento del ejército iraquí era un desastre. Pero el informe señalaba algo valioso: no podían entrenar soldados individualmente, sino unidades completas.

Rice contrató a Philip Zelikow, un viejo amigo, como consultor para el Departamento de Estado, un alto cargo desconocido pero con poder que le permitiría a llevar a cabo tareas especiales para ella.

Zelikow, un abogado de 50 años doctorado en historia, dirigía el Centro Miller en la Universidad de Virginia, dedicado al estudio de las presidencias modernas. Fue coautor, junto con Rice, del libro de 1995 *La unificación de Alemania y la transformación de Europa*, el único libro que el expresidente Bush y Brent Scowcroft dijeron haber utilizado para escribir sus memorias. El fin de la Guerra Fría y el colapso de la Unión Soviética habían dejado optimistas a Rice y Zelikow. Era posible enderezar la política exterior.

Zelikow, quien habría podido pasar por un banquero de aspecto impecable, también era autor de libros acerca de la crisis de los misiles con Cuba, y trabajó en el Comité Consultivo para la Política Exterior del presidente. Más recientemente, había sido el director ejecutivo de la Comisión del 9/11, que forzó a Rice a testificar en público e hizo serios cuestionamientos acerca de la respuesta de la administración frente a Al Qaeda antes del 9/11. También supervisó la escritura y edición del informe final de la Comisión del 9/11, un *best-seller* ampliamente elogiado que contiene detalles exhaustivos y reveladores sobre los orígenes, planeación y ejecución de los ataques.

Rice envió a Zelikow y un pequeño equipo a Irak. Necesitaba tener verdades de primera mano, un informe detallado de alguien en quien ella confiara. Zelikow tenía autorización para ir a cualquier parte y hacer cualquier pregunta.

El 10 de febrero, el decimocuarto día de Rice como secretaria, Zelikow presentó un memorando para la secretaria de Estado, de 15 páginas a espacio sencillo. El informe estaba clasificado como SECRETO/NODIS, es decir que no se podía distribuir a nadie más.

Las elecciones de enero, que habían mantenido a flote a la Casa Blanca, han sido un hito exitoso, leyó Rice, "pero aún debemos seguir en alerta".

"En este punto Irak sigue siendo un Estado fallido ensombrecido por la violencia constante en medio de un cambio político revolucionario", leyó Rice. Esta idea era impactante: "un Estado fallido", después de dos años, miles de vidas y cientos de miles de millones de dólares. "Estado fallido" era lo más bajo a que se podía llegar en geopolítica, y Rice querría poder recordarlo diferente más adelante, como si Zelikow hubiera dicho que existía el riesgo de que se convirtiera en un Estado fallido. Pero él había dicho que eso ya era una realidad.

Era horrible. La insurgencia "era contenida militarmente" pero seguía "bastante activa", por lo que los civiles iraquíes se sentían "muy inseguros", decía Zelikow.

Las condiciones para los oficiales estadounidenses recordaban las de la era Bremen, confinados en la Zona Verde. "La movilidad de los oficiales de la coalición es extremadamente limitada; la actividad productiva del gobierno está restringida".

Como los chiítas y los kurdos habían dominado las elecciones, existía "el riesgo de que los sunitas descontentos reaccionen", leía.

La evidencia de esta reacción podía verse a diario. Dos días antes, por ejemplo, un hombre se había acercado caminado a una multitud de reclutas del ejército iraquí, en Bagdad, y se había hecho estallar; había dado muerte a 21 reclutas y herido a otros 27. Los insurgentes asesinaron a 168 iraquíes en los 10 días siguientes a las elecciones del 30 de enero. El hecho sorprendente es que se habían presentado 3.000 ataques en enero –aproximadamente dos terceras partes sobre las fuerzas de la coalición, y el resto sobre las fuerzas de seguridad y civiles iraquíes– pero esa información permanecía clasificada.

Zelikow criticaba la centralización de los esfuerzos en Bagdad, y señalaba que "ciertamente puede perderse la guerra en Bagdad, pero sólo puede ganarse en las ciudades y provincias alejadas de Bagdad". Instaba a la coalición para que habilitara a las autoridades provinciales y locales para mejorar la seguridad y la inteligencia, y proponía la creación de Equipos de Seguridad Regional, compuestos por militares y civiles de la coalición. Así se reemplazaría la colcha de retazos conformada por personal de los cuarteles generales militares, las oficinas regionales de la embajada y los equipos del Departamento de Estado.

Leyó que Zelikow había quedado impresionado con el mayor general Peter Chiarelli, comandante de la 1ª División de Caballería del Ejército, quien fue uno de los proponentes de lo que los militares denominaban "operaciones de espectro completo", lo que significaba que sus soldados no se limitaban a las tareas típicas de infantería, como eliminar insurgentes, sino que también realizaban proyectos civiles que ayudaban a la población local. Chiarelli tenía a sus soldados de infantería afuera, conectando las casas a las redes locales de alcantarillado. Zelikow comentó que era uno de los mejores informes que había recibido de parte de un general.

"Todos nos insistieron en que la participación en esta dimensión civil de la gobernabilidad era clave para resolver su problema militar. Recomendamos que Estados Unidos lidere el establecimiento de objetivos sólidos para una mejor distribución de electricidad y combustible a lo largo del país, dentro de los próximos seis meses". En los últimos seis meses había disminuido el abastecimiento de electricidad y combustible.

El memorando también señalaba que sería difícil obtener más dinero para la reconstrucción, que el entrenamiento policial se estaba quedando rezagado, que la ciudad kurda de Kirkuk, ubicada cerca de los principales campos petroleros, a unos 320 kilómetros al norte de Bagdad, era un polvorín, que el sistema bancario era un desastre, que el sistema agrícola era una reliquia soviética, que se necesitaba un verdadero sistema de justicia iraquí para que los prisioneros valiosos pudieran ser juzgados justamente.

Sobre todo, leía Rice, el problema del esfuerzo de Estados Unidos es que carecía de una política general articulada y unificada.

El memorando de Zelikow era deprimente, pero Rice no era de las que se amilanan.

"He trabajado en esto por años", dijo Rice. Sentía una fuerte responsabilidad, y no solamente por su posición en el gobierno. Había estado en la Casa Blanca cuando Bush decidió invadir, y fue una de las dos únicas personas a las que él les pidió su opinión antes. "Irak me pertenece", dijo ella. "Tengo que operar de esa forma. Fui parte del equipo que tomó la decisión". Claramente, el esfuerzo del Departamento de Estado era insuficiente. No se había prestado suficiente atención al aspecto político de la lucha de contrainsurgencia. Tenían que hacer un esfuerzo concertado para ganar los corazones y las mentes en el nivel local en Irak.

Rice sólo había visitado Irak una vez, muy brevemente, cuando acompañó a Bush en su viaje sorpresa para Acción de Gracias en 2003. Fue sólo una oportunidad para tomarse una foto. Estaba ansiosa de una visita de verdad.

"No es el momento apropiado", le dijo Jim Jeffrey, pero ella insistió y organizó un viaje para el 1 de mayo. Su asistente personal, Jim Wilkinson, les hizo una confidencia acerca del viaje a los periodistas que cubrían el Departamento de Estado. "No pueden informar sobre esto. Sólo es para efectos de planeación", dijo. Wilkinson, de 35 años, había sido director de comunicaciones estratégicas para Rice en el Comité para la Seguridad Nacional de la Casa Blanca, y luego para el general Tommy Franks durante la reconstrucción e invasión de Irak. En sus memorias, Franks escribió que el joven de las relaciones públicas "tenía un aire a Tom Sawyer, sin la caña de pescar".

A pesar de las advertencias de Wilkinson, los correos electrónicos empezaron a circular. Rice era la estrella de la administración Bush, la cara de una nueva diplomacia activa. "El uniforme de combate de Condolezza Rice" era el titular de la sección de moda del *Washington Post* a finales de febrero, que se centraba en sus "sensuales" botas arriba de la rodilla. Pronto aparecieron noticias en la prensa acerca de su viaje pendiente a Irak.

Rice recibió amenazas de muerte todas las semanas, provenientes de extremistas de todo el espectro político, desde racistas blancos de derecha hasta izquierdistas que la acusaban de traicionar a los afroamericanos. Wilkinson y el jefe de seguridad de Rice se dieron cuenta de que la muerte de Rice sería un golpe sensacional para los insurgentes iraquíes. Una visita sorpresa rápida sería lo más apropiado. Pero eso era imposible ahora. Era demasiado peligroso. Le dijeron que no podía ir, y se puso furiosa. "¿Cómo sucedió esto?".

"Francamente", le dijo Wilkinson a los cuerpos de prensa del Departamento de Estado, "la próxima vez que ella viaje ustedes no van a enterarse. Cuando se levanten en la mañana, Condi Rice ya estará en Bagdad. Lo siento".

BUSH ESTABA TRATANDO de encontrar un director de inteligencia nacional. Quería a alguien que llevara la perspectiva de un presidente a ese cargo, alguien que hubiera hecho uso de la información de inteligencia, que conociera la importancia de producir información de inteligencia para que los diseñadores de políticas tomen decisiones. Quería a alguien que se preguntara cuál sería la mejor manera de hacer llegar la información de inteligencia al presidente. Y necesitaba a alguien que no fuera capturado por la burocracia de los departamentos de Estado o Defensa o de alguna de las agencias de inteligencia. Aun más importante, tenían que encontrar a alguien que asegurara, a cualquier costo, que no habría más fiascos de inteligencia como el de las armas de destrucción masiva.

Card llamó a Negroponte a Irak. Negroponte dijo que estaba interesado, y que viajaría a la Casa Blanca para conversar sobre eso. En el avión desde Bagdad, leyó la nueva ley de 262 páginas.

"¿De qué se trata este cargo?", le preguntó a Card cuando se encontraron. El director de inteligencia nacional tendría alguna autoridad sobre las agencias de inteligencia del Pentágono pero, en realidad, no las manejaría ni tendría control completo sobre el personal. Existían muchos casos de doble rendición de cuentas, por ejemplo, el director de la agencia nacional de seguridad debía informar tanto a Rumsfeld como al nuevo director de inteligencia nacional. El FBI seguiría como parte del Departamento de Justicia. Estaba fuera del control del Director de Inteligencia Nacional, aunque era una agencia de inteligencia de contraterrorismo clave.

"Es algo nuevo", respondió Card. Era muy buena pregunta, y él no tenía la respuesta. Usted llega para inventarlo, le dijo. "¿No es mejor así? Lo que usted defina, probablemente, será lo que tendrá que hacer el director dentro de 15 o 20 años ¿Cuántas oportunidades hay en el gobierno de Estados Unidos para construir una institución?".

Negroponte se reunió con el presidente. "Esta será la cúspide de su carrera", le dijo Bush.

No había muchos candidatos para el cargo, y Negroponte quería irse de Bagdad. Bush necesitaba a alguien rudo, pero, en vez de un ángel de la muerte, iba a conseguir a uno de los diplomáticos más suaves y menos conflictivos de la vieja escuela.

Bush anunció el nombramiento de Negroponte el 17 de febrero de 2005. El problema ahora sería reemplazarlo. La única opción real era Khalilzad, y tanto Rice como Hadley estaban ansiosos de que llegara a Bagdad, pero antes tuvieron que prevenirlo de que no contradijera al presidente acerca de la fecha para las elecciones en Irak. Por ello no lo pudieron nombrar inmediatamente. Pasaron más de dos meses para que Negroponte regresara y Khalilzad se posesionara en Irak.

No era un momento fácil para el vicepresidente Cheney. Había sido el vicepresidente más activo e influyente de la historia. Pero el centro de gravedad de Irak se había desplazado hacia afuera de la Casa Blanca: primero al Departamento de Defensa y luego al de Estado.

Sentía que estaba siendo apartado de la toma de decisiones sobre Irak. "¿Quiénes creen que son?", le dijo Cheney al príncipe Bandar el 28 de febrero. "Yo también fui reelegido".

Rice estaba decidida a comprometerse activamente con el manejo de Irak a diario. El enfoque de "que los oficiales de alto nivel no intervengan; que Bagdad sea el que lo maneje", había terminado. La Directiva Presidencial sobre Seguridad Nacional 36 (NSPD-36) puso al Departamento de Estado a cargo.

El principal candidato para convertirse en el primer ministro interino, después de las elecciones del 30 de enero, era Ibrahim al–Jafari, un chiíta que había sido parte del Consejo de Gobierno iraquí en la era Bremen y del gobierno provisional después de la transferencia de la soberanía. Para Negroponte era una persona extremadamente difícil, tal vez la única persona que conocía que podía hablar durante una hora para desarrollar una sola idea. En una de esas conversaciones de una hora, Jafari dijo que Talabani, un kurdo, no debería ocupar el cargo esencialmente simbólico de presidente. Él estaba tratando de llegarles a los sunitas, y sería terrible tener a un kurdo. Luego, en los dos minutos finales, Jafari dijo que, si era necesario, podría aceptar a Talabani.

Después de que Negroponte salió de Bagdad hacia Washington, para iniciar sus audiencias de confirmación como el primer director de inteligencia nacional, Jeffrey se convirtió en la cabeza de la embajada, como encargado de negocios. Rice empezó a bombardearlo con llamadas en las que decía que ya se dirigía a Irak.

"No", le aconsejaba de nuevo. "No es el momento indicado".

"Muy bien", dijo Rice. Después de las elecciones del 30 de enero, la conformación del nuevo gobierno iba muy lenta. "¿A quién llamamos?".

Jeffrey sintió temor de su solicitud. Primero, creía que él podía manejar a los iraquíes. Segundo, Rice –y Bush, Cheney y Hadley, por lo tanto– sólo tenían una comprensión general de la situación sobre el terreno y de las personas involucradas. Los funcionarios de Washington no podían competir con los astutos iraquíes.

Talabani asumió como presidente de Irak el 7 de abril. Minutos después, Jafari fue nombrado primer ministro. La siguiente tarea era escoger otros funcionarios para completar el gobierno.

Rice deseaba participar presionando la instalación del gobierno. Insistió en llamar a Talabani, quien había estado comprometido con la supervivencia de las negociaciones durante décadas.

"¿Cómo va todo, señor presidente?", le preguntó Rice a Talabani el 22 de abril en una llamada telefónica.

Él le respondió que todo estaba bien, incluso cuando le preguntó acerca de la necesidad de incluir sunitas en el nuevo gobierno. "Le digo eso a su hombre Jeffrey todos los días. Trabajo conjuntamente con él y creo que estamos avanzando".

Jeffrey observó que Rice no quería que nada saliera mal en ninguna llamada. Talabani estaba diciendo cosas buenas, no discutía, y Rice no quería interferir con las buenas vibraciones. Jeffrey temía que Talabani sugiriera alguna idea o solución que hubiera sido rechazada anteriormente, y que Rice le dijera que parecía alentador o que le ordenara a Jeffrey que procediera con eso. Jeffrey quedó aliviado al ver que la llamada no había estropeado nada. Vió que Rice afrontaba todos los problemas. Ella no iba a retroceder; entonces cambio de estrategia y la animó a que viajara a Irak para discusiones importantes. De ese modo, él podría sentarse a su lado cuando ella se reuniera con los líderes iraquíes, y susurrar en su oído: "Ese es el plan C, que usted canceló en una reunión del Comité para la Seguridad Nacional hace tres semanas".

Jeffrey asistía a las reuniones del Comité para la Seguridad Nacional a través del video seguro, y se le hizo muy evidente un patrón. Hadley decía que Irak era como un "niño víctima de abuso" y que Estados Unidos tendría que seguir actuando como un cuidador. Rumsfeld repetía con fuerza que los iraquíes necesitaban tener la oportunidad de equivocarse y caer de bruces, y que sólo hasta entonces podrían levantarse, sacudirse el polvo y encontrar soluciones. Utilizó la analogía de un padre tratando de enseñar a su hijo a montar en bicicleta. Debían retirar las ruedas de entrenamiento y quitar su mano del asiento, o terminarían con un hijo de 40 años que no sabe montar en bicicleta. Rice estaba entre Hadley y Rumsfeld, y una vez comentó: "Permitamos que intenten pedalear por sí mismos, pero es mejor que permanezcamos cerca para recogerlos si caen".

Cuando Card oyó esto, pensó que aparentemente la bicicleta se movía hacia delante en línea recta y estaba momentáneamente estable. Pero él sabía que no tenía pedales.

36

A COMIENZOS DE MAYO, Jeffrey destapó champaña y whisky en Bagdad. Había estado presionando sin descanso a los chiítas para que incluyeran a más sunitas en el proceso del nuevo gobierno. Eran estos quienes hacían insurgencia, les había dicho. Los líderes chiítas finalmente accedieron, y añadieron nueve sunitas al proceso del gobierno.

Luego, 36 horas antes de que Rice llegara a Irak para su largamente anticipada, aunque secreta, visita, todo se vino abajo.

Jeffrey se dio cuenta de que no había convencido a los chiítas de nada. No captaron los puntos fundamentales sobre reconciliación, superación e inclusión. Inicialmente habían sido complacientes porque él estaba en frente diciéndoles: "Deben hacer esto".

Habían retrocedido al mismo punto en el que habían estado dos meses atrás, cuando Negroponte se había marchado. Rice llegaría el 15 de mayo. Jeffrey estaba furioso.

Rice viajó en el avión del general Abizaid, en una cabina privada de la parte de atrás. Desde el punto de vista de la seguridad, tal vez era la aeronave más indicada para evitar llamar la atención, porque salía desde y hacia Irak todo el tiempo. Primero voló a Irbil, a 320 kilómetros al norte de Bagdad dentro de territorio kurdo, para reunirse con el líder kurdo Massoud Barzani. Para el primer ministro Jafari fue casi un insulto que la primera reunión no fuera con el jefe del gobierno, pero los kurdos eran claves para la reconciliación.

Rice le comentó a Barzani lo importante que era para el presidente Bush que todo el mundo asumiera compromisos. Se debía incluir a los sunitas. Le expresó su preocupación por la intromisión de los sirios y, especialmente, de los iraníes en Irak.

Los dos son enemigos, le dijo Barzani. Siria es el enemigo torpe, e Irán, el enemigo astuto, que, además, es el problema a largo plazo.

Rice coincidió.

El vuelo a Bagdad duró 45 minutos. En su siguiente reunión con Jafari, ella endureció su posición.

"Usted no comprende", le dijo Rice al primer ministro. "Todo esto es un asunto de inclusión". Ella reconoció que los sunitas no habían participado en las elecciones del 30 de enero, ya fuera por haber sido intimidados o porque decidieron boicotearlas. "Ahora le pedimos que deje todo eso atrás y los acompañe efectivamente para que hagan parte del proceso político". Puede ser lo más difícil, añadió, "pero debe hacerlo, porque si no son parte del proceso político, pueden minar su capacidad de gobernar".

Todos los demás miembros del grupo de Rice estaban cabeceando después de 20 horas de viaje. Ella realmente asombraba a algunos de sus acompañantes, porque seguía allí sentada, sin un cabello fuera de sitio, pendiente de cada palabra, como una máquina.

Jafari era su propia máquina, una máquina de humo. Era muy deprimente, pero Rice puso su mejor cara pública acerca de ello más adelante, y concedió entrevistas de siete minutos para cuatro medios de comunicación de Estados Unidos y dos de Arabia. Su mensaje era la persistencia. "Si ustedes lo piensan, este gobierno ha estado muy poco tiempo en el poder" le dijo Rice a un reportero de la NBC. "De hecho, ha pasado menos de un año desde que se le transfirió la soberanía al pueblo iraquí. Y por lo tanto habrá altibajos. Las cosas no sucederán de la noche a la mañana".

Posteriormente Rice asistió a una visita no publicitada al hospital militar de combate en Bagdad. Algunos soldados tenían cámaras digitales y pedían tomarse una foto con Rice.

Después de conversar con los doctores y las enfermeras, visitó a una joven iraquí de 19 años que había hecho parte del destacamento de seguridad de Jafari. Se había lanzado sobre una bomba como escudo humano. La bomba había explotado parcialmente y la adolescente iraquí había perdido una pierna.

"Usted es una joven muy valiente", le dijo Rice. "Es una de las personas que ya está sacrificándose por su nueva democracia".

La mujer iraquí le agradeció suavemente. Fue una de las primeras veces en que Rice encontró un sentido personal en los sacrificios que los iraquíes estaban haciendo.

Intentando ser lo menos visible y entrometida en su visita, Rice avanzó por un corredor hasta llegar a una habitación donde había un solo paciente. Era un soldado estadounidense en terribles condiciones, con la cara vendada y soporte vital, que apenas seguía con vida.

Rice estaba presenciando de primera mano el costo humano: los costos verdaderos y personales de la guerra, una guerra que ella le aconsejó al presidente emprender.

MÁS ADELANTE RICE le dijo a varios miembros de su personal: "Debo poder mirar a estos jóvenes soldados y preguntarme con sinceridad si creo que vale la pena esto por lo que están pasando. Y no se trata de soldados de juguete que alguien envía allá. Son seres de verdad, seres humanos de carne y hueso.

"Si existiera una forma de ganar guerras y dar seguridad a los países sin enviar jóvenes a afrontar circunstancias en las que pueden perder la vida o quedar mutilados, lo haríamos.

"Pero las guerras tienen un precio. Y nada me enfurece más que oír a la gente que dice 'George Bush quería ir a la guerra. Estaba buscando una razón para ir a la guerra'. Conociendo a este o a cualquier otro presidente, lo que ellos ven y sienten cuando saben las implicaciones de sus acciones, es imposible creer que puedan estar ansiosos por ir a la guerra. Creo que esa es una afirmación completamente ofensiva".

JEFFREY FUE A TRABAJAR en el asunto de los sunitas. Ellos querían 30 representantes en el Comité Constitucional, la siguiente etapa del camino hacia la democracia ¿Por qué 30?, les preguntó. El argumento era que los sunitas eran al menos el 30%, probablemente, el 40% de la población.

"Bueno, en realidad no", replicó Jeffrey, "son el 20% de la población".

Y seguía el ir y venir. Los sunitas sólo habían obtenido dos de los 55 asientos del comité. Diez días después de la visita de Rice, los chiítas accedieron a ampliar el Comité Constitucional para incluir más sunitas; tras varias semanas de negociaciones se estableció un número de 15 miembros permanentes y 10 asesores sunitas.

ZELIKOW REGRESÓ A IRAK por Rice en mayo de 2005, para concentrarse en la manera como Estados Unidos estaba entrenando a la policía iraquí: la solución local al problema de seguridad. Ella había relevado al jefe de la oficina del Departamento de Estado que se encargaba de dicho entrenamiento. En resumen, no había funcionado. Él había viajado fuera de Bagdad a lugares como Mosul. Estados Unidos había establecido una academia de entrenamiento policial iraquí y hasta la había dotado de personal. Algo de entrenamiento, un uniforme, una pistola y el mensaje "Decídete y conviértete en policía". Era la misma vieja historia. La única medida del progreso era el número de personas entrenadas. Zelikow encontró que nadie sabía si los policías recién formados se presentaban para cumplir sus asignaciones. No había un seguimiento al entrenamiento en el terreno, igual de crítico tanto para el entrenamiento político como para el militar.

Se contrataron varios cientos de oficiales de enlace policial internacionales, sobre todo de Estados Unidos, para hacer entrenamiento de campo, pero no se esperaba que tuvieran que trabajar en zonas de combate. Visitaron las estaciones de policía iraquíes, hicieron inventarios de las armas e inspecciones de rutina, más que entrenamiento como tal. No se instalaron en las unidades de policía iraquíes, donde Zelikow creía que, con seguridad, podrían ser más efectivos.

Él también descubrió el estrecho vínculo que existía entre los problemas policiales y los de inteligencia, entre ellos la calidad de la inteligencia y la posibilidad real de que alguien pudiera estar informado acerca de la insurgencia y sus planes.

Zelikow encontró que la CIA estaba concentrada en Al Qaeda y utilizaba de manera efectiva el aspecto técnico de la inteligencia –intercepciones a las comunicaciones e imágenes aéreas– pero, en realidad, no estaba involucrada en los aspectos principales de la inteligencia de contrainsurgencia en el nivel local.

Aunque más específicos, estos hallazgos coincidían con el fracaso para comprometer a la policía local iraquí que Frank Miller, del equipo del Comité para la Seguridad Nacional, ya le había señalado a Rice hacía más de un año, después de que hizo el viaje de inspección a Irak para ella. A medida que Zelikow seguía escudriñando, se hacía más obvio que estos oficiales de enlace debían estar instalados, viviendo, en las bases de operaciones, e interactuando más con la policía iraquí.

Pero el entrenamiento policial del Departamento de Estado sólo era una tercera parte del esfuerzo. Al general Petraeus le correspondía otra tercera parte del entrenamiento de la policía. El tercio restante era responsabilidad de las divisiones militares básicas de Estados Unidos, quienes tenían policía militar en su espacio de batalla o en áreas específicas de las provincias o ciudades.

Zelikow recomendó que los tres debían combinarse y dejar a los batallones y brigadas de Estados Unidos el manejo de las operaciones militares y de las patrullas a pie en regiones específicas. Había estudiado la insurgencia, y se dio cuenta de que estaban descubriendo las lecciones que ya otros habían aprendido: La política es local, incluso durante una insurrección. También se trataba del problema de siempre: unidad de mando. Con tantos responsables, finalmente la responsabilidad no era de nadie.

CHENEY APARECIÓ en el programa de CNN *Larry King Live* el 30 de mayo. "Creo que la insurgencia está en las últimas, por así decirlo". Era una absoluta negación de la realidad y de las perspectivas. En abril hubo en total 1.700 ataques de la insurgencia, con 52 estadounidenses muertos. En mayo, los ataques aumentaron a 2.000, y 82 estadounidenses murieron.

EL SENADOR CHUCK HAGEL, un serio republicano de Nebraska, bajo de estatura, de 58 años, no recibía muchas invitaciones de la Casa Blanca de

Bush. Aunque había votado la resolución que autorizaba la guerra, se había convertido en un abierto crítico del manejo de la fase de posguerra. La Casa Blanca tuvo que incluirlo en la invitación dirigida a todos los senadores republicanos para el almuerzo de política semanal de los martes en la Casa Blanca, el 21 de junio de 2005.

Hagel había sido sargento del Ejército; fue condecorado durante la Guerra de Vietnam, y entendía que el uso de la fuerza militar era la decisión más importante para un presidente y para una nación. Meses antes de la invasión a Irak, públicamente formuló preguntas como: "¿Quién va a gobernar después de Saddam?" y "¿Hemos medido las consecuencias?". En su discurso del 9 de octubre de 2002, en el que favorecía la resolución de guerra, dijo que reconocía el solemne deber que esto implicaba, y añadió "No lo podemos hacer solos... ¿Cuántos de nosotros conocemos y comprendemos realmente a Irak, al país, su historia, su gente y su papel en el mundo árabe? Asumo el tema del Irak después de Saddam, y del futuro de la democracia y la estabilidad de Medio Oriente, con mayor precaución, realismo y humildad". Un mes antes de la guerra dijo: "En primer lugar, una transición después de Saddam debe centrarse en la seguridad, la estabilidad económica y la creación de las condiciones para el cambio democrático. Debemos dejar a un lado la ilusión errada de que la democracia se encuentra a la vuelta de la esquina".

Los senadores llegaron en autobús a la Casa Blanca antes del almuerzo del 21 de junio, se dirigieron a la fila para el bufé hacia el medio día, y Bush llegó a las 12:30.

El presidente habló durante unos 25 minutos sobre seguridad social, gastos, déficit..., de todo menos del gran elefante metido en el salón.

El senador John Warner, presidente de la Comisión de Servicios Armados, tomó la palabra, dijo algunas cosas amables de Bush y luego abordó lo del elefante. "Estuve cenando con mi anterior jefe, de cuando era secretario de la Armada", dijo Warner, refiriéndose al ex secretario de Defensa James Schlesinger. "Mi ex jefe estaba muy preocupado por Irak, porque ve que están surgiendo unos paralelos inquietantes con Vietnam".

Bush empezó a defenderse inmediatamente: el 9/11, la continua amenaza del terrorismo, su convicción de que Saddam era una amenaza. Nada nuevo.

El senador Ted Stevens, presidente del Comité de Apropiación Presupuestal, entonces dijo: "Quiero secundar parte de lo que John Warner acaba de decir. Creo que aquí hay unos problemas graves".

Bush regresó a su retórica florida de que era lo correcto, que tenían que persistir.

Después del almuerzo, Hagel salió con Bush y se apartaron a un rincón. "Señor presidente", dijo Hagel, "permítame hacerle una pregunta. Creo que aquí en la Casa Blanca usted está bastante desconectado de Irak ¿Alguna vez recurre a alguien fuera de su círculo más cercano, fuera de su consejo de seguridad nacional?". Luego trató de suavizar como correspondía: "De ninguna manera trato de sugerir incompetencia. Ese no es mi punto. Creo que es importante que los presidentes, sobre todo en tiempo de guerra, escuchen otras opiniones, de personas que puedan no estar de acuerdo con usted, o usted no estar de acuerdo con ellas. Llámelas, reúnase con ellas y escúchelas ¿Alguna vez lo ha hecho?".

"Digamos que se lo dejo a Hadley".

"Sé que su asesor para la seguridad nacional conversa con la gente, pero ¿usted lo hace?".

"Tal vez yo debería conversar con Hadley sobre eso".

"Señor presidente, creo que es muy importante que usted escuche otras opiniones externas. Sólo para poner a prueba sus teorías y ver como están funcionando".

Hagel mencionó temas de relatos y biografías que había leído. "Con una nación en guerra, el presidente está bajo una enorme presión. Usted se encierra en ese búnker, y no creo que eso sea bueno para usted". Finalmente se lo había dicho.

"Es un buen consejo", dijo Bush.

Hagel regresó al Senado. Dos horas después recibió una llamada de Hadley. "El presidente me contó acerca de la conversación", dijo Hadley. "¿Quisiera venir a hablar conmigo?".

"No se trató de eso la conversación, Steve", dijo Hagel. El problema eran las voces nuevas o que disentían. "Usted sabe a qué me refiero".

"Ya se a qué se refiere", dijo Hadley.

Hagel ofreció entregarle listas de personas con las que el presidente debería hablar, y le aclaró que no estaba obligado a incluirlo a él. No obstante, Hadley lo invitó a la Casa Blanca varios días después. Hagel, un dedicado estudioso de la política exterior, le envió a Hadley copias de varios memorandos extensos que le había entregado a Rice. Cuando llegó a la oficina de Hadley, ésta se veía atestada de personal del Comité para la Seguridad Nacional. "¿En realidad, es necesario que todos estén aquí?", preguntó Hagel. Aparentemente así era. Durante una hora Hagel afirmó que Irak era un desastre mucho mayor de lo que ellos reconocían, y que la administración debía hacer más por la seguridad, el entrenamiento, la gobernabilidad y la infraestructura.

Se marchó insatisfecho y le concedió una entrevista a *U.S. News & World Report* en la que afirmó: "Las cosas no están mejorando; están empeorando. La Casa Blanca está completamente desconectada de la realidad".

Hadley y otros en la Casa Blanca estaban furiosos, pero Hagel consideraba que era una de las cosas más claras que alguna vez hubiera dicho. Su evaluación privada era peor: en la administración no había un pensador estratégico. Rice era débil. Los militares estaban siendo emasculados y seriamente dañados por parásitos en uniforme.

EL 21 DE JUNIO, Zal Khalilzad se posesionó como embajador en Irak, y Jim Jeffrey regresó a Washington para convertirse en el principal asesor de Rice, con el título de coordinador para la política de Irak. Trabajaría junto a ella en el tema crucial.

En julio de 2005, los temas que encabezaban las agendas de muchas de las reuniones de los delegados y jefes de comisiones tenían que ver con la "seguridad de la infraestructura", e incluían debates sobre la seguridad de los oleoductos y las centrales eléctricas. Hablaban acerca de problemas de los servicios públicos como si se tratara de una comisión de obras públicas del gobierno local. Un día Bagdad sólo tuvo seis horas de electricidad.

"¿No estábamos en ese punto hace 15 meses?", preguntó Hadley.

Rumsfeld, el general Casey y los militares no quería gastar recursos en vigilancia permanente para los oleoductos o las centrales eléctricas, y se rehusaron. Se acordó finalmente que el nuevo embajador, Zal Khalilzad sería el responsable de abordar el asunto de la seguridad de la infraestructura, incluida la protección de miles de kilómetros de tuberías superficiales. Pero, por supuesto, no contaba con los recursos de seguridad, por lo que sería algo casi imposible de hacer.

EL 7 DE JULIO DE 2005, cuatro bombas suicidas destrozaron autobuses y trenes en Londres, y 52 personas murieron. Fue el bombardeo más mortífero en Londres desde la Segunda Guerra Mundial.

En Washington, dos días antes, Rihab Massoud, el asistente del príncipe Bandar, embajador saudita, recibió una llamad de Riad en la que se le pedía que revisara los archivos y buscara un memorando de inteligencia de fecha 14 de diciembre de 2004, que había sido compartido con la CIA y la inteligencia británica.

Cuando Massoud encontró el memorando interrogativo de cuatro páginas, tuvo que leerlo dos veces. En diciembre, el gobierno saudita había capturado a uno de sus nacionales en el aeropuerto en Burayda, al norte de Arabia central. Este hombre, cuyo nombre de pila era Adel, había ingresado al país desde Irán o los Emiratos Árabes Unidos con un pasaporte falso. Quedó en custodia, y durante el interrogatorio reveló que en seis meses habría una operación en múltiples fases en Londres, en la que utilizarían explosivos de Bosnia, y dijo que ocurriría específicamente en un área de las inmediaciones de Edgewood Road. Massoud sabía que uno de los cuatros hombres bomba suicidas de Londres había detonado sus explosivos en un tren, en la estación del subterráneo de Edgware Road.

"Dentro de seis meses…", Massoud leyó de nuevo. Supuestamente Adel conocía a Abu Musab al-Zarqawi, el líder jordano de Al Qaeda en Irak. En ese punto afirmaba que aún faltaban US $500.000 para financiar la operación de Londres. Cuatro personas la llevarían a cabo. No sabía sus nombres, pero suministró sus edades y estaturas aproximadas, sus descripciones, y, además, dijo que uno de ellos tenía tatuajes en sus dedos. También dijo que el coordinador del grupo era un empresario libanés que estaba en Londres, que debía ayudarlos a moverse y encontrar alojamientos seguros y automóviles.

Después de conseguir los US $500.000, Adel debía llamar a un número telefónico en Siria para recibir nuevas instrucciones. En febrero de 2005, leyó Massoud, los sauditas le enviaron un nuevo informe a la inteligencia británica y estadounidense, con mejores descripciones de los individuos que iban a ejecutar el plan. Además de los cuatro, Adel mencionó que había otro "británico británico" y otro "alemán alemán", es decir, caucásicos de apariencia europea, diferentes de los árabes. En el informe de febrero, los sauditas habían dicho que Adel afirmó que los cuatro vendrían de diferentes países.

Después de los ataques del 7 de julio, los británicos solicitaron inmediatamente entrevistar ellos mismos a Adel. Los sauditas aceptaron. El 11 de julio, Massoud se reportó a la CIA, donde le dijeron que habían recibido el memorando de los sauditas pero no habían encontrado nada que lo respaldara. Habían revisado el número telefónico en Siria pero sin ningún resultado.

Luego Massoud llamó a Fran Townsend, asesora para la seguridad nacional delegada del presidente para la seguridad interna, y le contó acerca del memorando.

"El presidente debe saber esto", le dijo Massoud. Bandar estaba fuera del país.

"Creo que usted debería venir", dijo Townsend.

Massoud fue a la Casa Blanca y Townsend lo llevó para que viera a Bush.

"Señor presidente, esta es una copia del memorando", le dijo sosteniendo en su mano el documento saudita escrito en árabe pero leyendo una traducción al inglés.

Bush quería todos los detalles. La CIA y la inteligencia británica investigaron hasta donde les fue posible. Pronto pareció como si fuera otro embaucador que debían manejar en un nivel mucho más bajo. Pero el presidente Bush, todavía perturbado por Al Qaeda, se había convertido en su propio coordinador de inteligencia.

BUSH TODAVÍA SE DIVERTÍA con las bromas de universitarios. En julio de 2005, Ben S. Bernanke, presidente del Consejo de Asesores Económicos de Bush, que pronto sucedería a Alan Greenspan como director de la Reserva Federal, usó unos calcetines de color marrón en una reunión con el presidente. Los calcetines resaltaban entre un mar de conservadores calcetines de color oscuro, y el presidente lo hizo notar. Días después, el presidente tuvo otra reunión económica, y todos los demás, incluido Cheney, aparecieron usando calcetines marrón. Todos rieron de buena gana.

Bush y Rove insistían particularmente en las "flatulencias" –dejar escapar gases– y compartían un buen número de bromas sobre ventosidades. El hijo de uno de los funcionarios de alto nivel de la Casa Blanca tenía un pequeño juguete de control remoto que producía el sonido de una ventosidad. El funcionario lo llevó a la Casa Blanca y lo colocó bajo la silla de Rove en la reunión matinal del personal de alto nivel del 7 de julio. Pero cuando se supo de las bombas terroristas del metro y los autobuses de Londres de esa mañana, la broma se pospuso.

Varias semanas después, el 20 de julio, se colocó aquel dispositivo bajo la silla de Rove y fue activado durante la reunión del personal de alto nivel. Se activó varias veces y Rove demoró varios minutos en ubicar el juguete. Todos reían. El humor era necesario, recordó uno de los principales asesores de Bush.

37

Por esta época, el general Jim Jones, comandante de la OTAN, hizo una llamada a su viejo amigo, el general Pete Pace, subjefe del Estado Mayor Conjunto. Era virtualmente un hecho que Pace iba a ser ascendido para reemplazar a Myers como jefe.

No podría haber dos personas, dos generales de la infantería de marina, tan parecidos y al mismo tiempo tan diferentes. Habían estado en Vietnam aproximadamente al mismo tiempo, experiencia que los curtió y formó, y luego sirvieron juntos como tenientes en 1970 en las barracas de la infantería de marina al sureste de Washington.

Pace, un delgado y atento graduado de la Academia Naval en 1967, pasó cuatro años como subjefe, segundo oficial en importancia entre los militares de Estados Unidos. Jones, un espigado graduado del servicio exterior de Georgetown, hablaba francés con fluidez y había vivido en las barracas como comandante de 1999 a 2003, antes de que Rumsfeld lo trasladara a la OTAN.

Era una amistad profesional que había durado hasta donde era posible entre militares estadounidenses en servicio activo, más de tres décadas.

Jones expresó malestar por el hecho de que Pace estuviera considerando ser el jefe de Estado Mayor Conjunto. "Vas a enfrentar una debacle y vas a ser parte de ella en Irak", le dijo. El prestigio mundial de Estados Unidos había descendido en un 50% o 75%. Le dijo que estaba tan preocupado por Irak y la manera como Rumsfeld manejaba las cosas, que se preguntaba si él mismo no debería renunciar. "¿Cómo puedes tener el aguante para pasar ocho años en el Pentágono?", preguntó finalmente.

Pace le contestó que alguien tenía que ser el jefe. ¿Quién más lo haría?

Jones no tenía la respuesta. "La opinión de los militares está siendo influida en el nivel político", dijo. El Estado Mayor Conjunto se había "rendido" de manera inapropiada a Rumsfeld. "No puedes ser un loro en el hombro del secretario".

Su preocupación era completa. Cuando los senadores John Warner y Carl Levin, el presidente y uno de los demócratas insignes de la Comisión de Servicios Armados del Senado, lo visitaron en su cuartel general en Bélgica,

Jones les habló acerca de todos los problemas. Les dijo que se necesitaba una nueva legislación, algo como una segunda Goldwater-Nichols, para volver a facultar a los jefes de servicio o darle algún sentido a este sistema de locos.

"Rumsfeld ha emasculado sistemáticamente a los jefes de Estado Mayor", dijo Jones.

Pace comentó después que él y Jones habían tenido muchas discusiones acerca de los problemas del proceso de trabajo entre agencias. La coordinación es inadecuada, dijo, "porque nadie por debajo del presidente tiene autoridad para decirle a la gente lo que debe hacer". Negó de plano que Jones le hubiera dicho que Irak era una debacle, o que Rumsfeld hubiera emasculado sistemáticamente a los jefes de Estado Mayor. "Él es un buen amigo. Estuvo en mi boda", dijo Pace, señalando que se conocían desde hacía 36 años. "Si Jim pensara eso, me lo diría".

DESPUÉS DE QUE PACE FUERA CONFIRMADO como jefe, le pidió al admirante Vern Clark, quien acababa de retirarse como jefe de operaciones navales, que se reunieran.

"Vern, déme luces sobre esto", le pidió.

"Está bien", dijo Clark. "Le entregará cinco años de su vida al país y a este trabajo. ¿Qué le gustaría que dijeran de su paso por aquí cuando se haya retirado? Lo reto a que resuma en dos frases los logros de los jefes anteriores. Nómbreme uno. Recuerde y escoja uno".

Pace quedó en silencio.

"Se lo voy a poner fácil", continuó Clark. "Empiece con Collin Powell, un tipo como ese. ¿Qué logró como jefe?".

Pace continuó en silencio.

"Démosle crédito por traer la política de la aplicación avasalladora de la fuerza".

La ironía era obvia. Rumsfeld había desechado la doctrina de la fuerza avasalladora de Powell en la invasión a Irak.

"Pasemos a Hugh Shelton", dijo Clark. "Resuma todos los logros de Hugh Shelton aquí. Descríbalos en dos frases".

Pace no respondió.

"Le reconozco algo", dijo Clark. "En realidad, creó una conciencia acerca de la importancia de prestarle mas atención a las Fuerzas Especiales". Shelton había sido el comandante de las Fuerzas Especiales antes de llegar a ser jefe de Estado Mayor Conjunto.

"¿Shalikashvili?". El general del ejército John Shalikashvili había sido jefe de 1993 a 1997. Clark esperó que Pace respondiera. "Tampoco se me ocurre nada". Dijo que no sería tan poco elegante como para pedirle a Pace que resumiera lo que Dick Myers había hecho. "Usted lo debe saber, pues estuvo aquí con él".

Clark le dijo que creía que en sus cinco años como jefe de operaciones navales había introducido cambios radicales en la Armada. "Esta pregunta es para usted, Pete: ¿Qué quisiera que dijeran acerca de su trabajo como jefe de Estado Mayor Conjunto?".

"Fundamentalmente", continuó Clark "el papeleo de todos los días en este trabajo se lo va a comer vivo, y este trabajo merece algo mejor". La descripción del cargo tenía que ir más allá de lo que Rumsfeld decretara o deseara. Rumsfeld había dejado inoperantes las pocas facultades que la ley le otorga al jefe de Estado Mayor Conjunto, incluida la disposición de que la evaluación del programa del jefe de Estado Mayor Conjunto fuera enviada directamente al Congreso. Aunque sólo se tratara de un informe, era algo simbólico. Rumsfeld no había permitido que llegara al Congreso por un año.

Clark le dijo a Pace que debería reafirmar su responsabilidad legal como jefe. "Debe tener algo que decir acerca de ella cuando el tipo que esté un nivel más arriba se niegue a enviar su evaluación al Congreso durante 13 meses. Esta no es sólo una falla del sistema. Es un acto de mala fe".

Pace le agradeció, y Clark se marchó.

Más adelante Pace dijo que recordaba la reunión con Clark y su pregunta: "¿Qué le gustaría que dijeran de su paso por aquí cuando se haya retirado?".

"Era una gran pregunta", dijo Pace. Parecía que "tenía sentido", dijo, que Rumsfeld se había sentado sobre la evaluación del programa del jefe de Estado Mayor Conjunto durante 13 meses. "No que yo sepa", dijo acerca de si Clark había afirmado que la demora era un asunto de mala fe. "La conversación que tuve con Vern Clark fue bastante relajada, sin rabia ni resentimiento".

En el verano de 2005, Dan Bartlett ejercía cada vez más presión de modo constante, dentro de la Casa Blanca y sobre el presidente; y urgía sobre la necesidad de cambiar su estrategia de comunicaciones sobre Irak. El lenguaje de resolución no estaba funcionando. Estaban perdiendo cada vez más credibilidad, y la única manera de recuperarla era reconocer que se había cometido errores en el camino. Reconocer los errores era algo muy poderoso. Convencería a la gente de que estaban dispuestos a ajustar y modificar su política, al admitir, en primer lugar, que había que cambiar algunas cosas. Esto era consistente con su meta de comunicar que el presidente tenía una estrategia flexible.

El otro punto que señaló Bartlett al presidente era la necesidad de mostrar que él escuchaba a sus críticos. Recomendó que, en caso de que creyera que sus intenciones eran buenas, el presidente debería decirlo. La resolución y la determinación estaban siendo percibidas como terquedad.

Todo esto ponía aprueba las tendencias naturales de Bush. Su mensaje básico para los estadounidenses y los iraquíes debería ser que él no temblaría. Los sunitas, en particular, jugaban en ambos bandos. El presidente creía que la firmeza de Estados Unidos los animaría a participar. Cualquier retroceso de los estadounidenses alimentaría la insurgencia sunita, y la dejaría optimistas con respecto al futuro después de Estados Unidos, cuando podría haber una guerra sectaria final que le permitiría arrebatar de nuevo el control del país.

Bush no estaba en total desacuerdo con Bartlett en cuanto a que se debería ajustar el mensaje. Pero tomaría tiempo lograr que el presidente dejara atrás sus proclamaciones libres de errores.

EL EX SECRETARIO DE ESTADO HENRY KISSINGER tenía una poco visible pero poderosa influencia sobre la política exterior de la administración Bush.

"Entre las personas externas con las que hablo en este trabajo", me comentó el vicepresidente Cheney en el verano de 2005, "tal vez hablo más con Henry Kissinger que con cualquier otra. Él simplemente pasa por aquí, y creo que al menos una vez al mes *Scooter* y yo nos sentamos a hablar con él".

Cheney había trabajado estrechamente con Kissinger durante la administración Ford, cuando Cheney fue delegado y, más adelante, jefe de Estado Mayor. Kissinger había sido secretario de Estado y asesor para la seguridad nacional; era una combinación que todo secretario de Estado subsiguiente había envidiado. El ego de Kissinger era monumental, pero Cheney consideraba que su asesoría de línea dura era útil después del 9/11. Compartían la visión de que las relaciones internacionales eran una cuestión de poder militar y político. El poder diplomático se derivaba de la amenaza de hacer uso y de usar efectivamente ese poder. En su forma más elemental, el uso del poder militar le enviaba un mensaje útil al mundo: es peligroso ser enemigo de Estados Unidos.

El presidente también se reunía en privado con Kissinger cada dos meses, por lo que el ex secretario era el asesor externo más frecuente y regular de Bush en asuntos exteriores. Según Cheney, Bush era un "gran admirador" de Kissinger. Acerca de las reuniones de Bush y Kissinger, Rumsfeld dijo: "Ayudé a arreglarlas". El presidente, que generalmente daba poca importancia a los asesores externos, consideraba que sus reuniones con Kissinger eran importantes, según Cheney, Rumsfeld y otros en la Casa Blanca.

Card y el equipo de la oficina personal del presidente sabían que Kissinger era una de las pocas personas externas, además de la familia, que podía llamar cada vez que viniera a Washington y ver si el presidente estaba disponible. Según los cálculos de Card, cerca de la mitad de las reuniones eran a solas entre Kissinger y el presidente. Él o Rice asistían a la otra mitad.

Nadie era tan controversial en el medio de la política exterior estadounidense o tenía más historia a cuestas que Kissinger, de 82 años en ese entonces.

Vietnam era como un lastre alrededor de su cuello, y el prisma a través del cual observaba el mundo. Después de Lyndon Johnson, Richard Nixon y Robert McNamara, probablemente no se asociaba tanto a nadie con la guerra. Había sido el arquitecto, primero, junto a Nixon, y luego, con Ford, de la política exterior de Estados Unidos entre 1969 y 1975. En sus escritos, discursos y comentarios privados, Kissinger afirmaba que Estados Unidos esencialmente había ganado la guerra en 1972, para perderla debido a una capacidad de resolución debilitada por la opinión pública y el Congreso.

Cuando Kissinger sentía que tenía algo que decir generalmente lo escribía, a menudo en la sección de opinión de *The Washington Post*. Tenía muchas ideas acerca de Irak y de Bush. Él apoyaba la guerra. Aunque no tenía mayores objeciones sobre el apremio para difundir la democracia y cesar la tiranía, expresado en el discurso de la segunda posesión de Bush, Kissinger habría sido más moderado a la hora de ponerlo en práctica. "No podemos abandonar la seguridad nacional por ir en pos de la virtud", había escrito en su libro de 1999, *Años de renovación,* sobre la presidencia de Ford. Estados Unidos "debe moderar su espíritu misionero con un sentido de interés nacional y hacer depender la definición de su deber con el mundo de su cabeza tanto como de su corazón".

En un sentido práctico, Kissinger no tenía certeza de que Irak estuviera listo para la democracia, y tenía sus reservas acerca del uso de las tropas de combate estadounidenses en esfuerzos a gran escala para entrenar a militares extranjeros. Además, como la mayoría de iraquíes se identificaban, en primer lugar, por su origen sectario tribal o religioso –sunita, chiíta o kurdo–, la pregunta era cómo impulsar el desarrollo de una identidad nacional iraquí. Estrechamente relacionada estaba la pregunta crucial de para quién pelearía el ejército iraquí.

Kissinger estimaba a Bush en lo personal, aunque les había dicho a algunos colegas que no tenía claro si el presidente en realidad sabía cómo gobernar. Observaba que uno de los grandes problemas era que Bush no tenía el personal o el sistema de toma de decisiones de seguridad nacional que aseguraran una evaluación cuidadosa de las desventajas de las principales decisiones.

Kissinger percibía titubeos por donde quiera en Irak, y cada vez veía más esto a través del prisma de Vietnam. Para Kissinger, la principal lección que dejó Vietnam fue la de persistir.

El título de su columna del 12 de agosto de 2005 en el *Post* fue "Lecciones para una estrategia de salida válida". Fue como un segundo discurso de posesión de Bush. La línea clave del texto decía: "La victoria sobre la insurgencia es la única estrategia de salida válida". Luego tuvo sus encuentros en la Casa Blanca con Bush, Cheney y Hadley. La victoria tenía que ser la meta, les dijo a todos. No permitan que suceda de nuevo. No cedan ni una pulgada, o los medios de comunicación, el Congreso o la cultura estadounidense de evitar las penalidades los harán retroceder. También dijo que el resultado eventual en Irak sería más importante que el de Vietnam. Un estilo de gobierno radical islámico o talibán en Irak sería un modelo que podría desafiar la estabilidad interna de los países clave en el Medio Oriente y otras regiones.

Kissinger le dijo a Rice que en Vietnam no hubo tiempo, orientación, energía o apoyo interno para que las políticas funcionaran. Por eso todo había colapsado como un castillo de naipes. Instó a la administración de Bush a que arreglara la política tanto en Irak como en el frente doméstico. El retiro parcial de las tropas tenía sus propios peligros. Incluso, contemplar la idea de retirar las topas podría crear el ambiente para una salida que era menos que victoriosa.

Rice entendió que el mensaje de Kissinger reforzaba una convicción que ya tenía el presidente.

A COMIENZOS DE SEPTIEMBRE DE 2005, Mike Gerson quería encontrarse con Kissinger en la ciudad de Nueva York.

"¿Por qué apoya la Guerra de Irak?", le preguntó Gerson.

"Porque Afganistán no fue suficiente", respondió Kissinger. En el conflicto con el islamismo radical, dijo, ellos querían humillarnos. "Y nosotros necesitamos humillarlos a ellos". La respuesta estadounidense al 9/11 tenía que ser esencialmente más que proporcionada, a una escala mayor que la simple invasión a Afganistán y el derrocamiento de los talibanes. Se necesitaba algo más. La Guerra de Irak era esencial para enviar un mensaje mayor, "para sentar la posición de que no vamos a vivir en el mundo que ellos quieran para nosotros". Dijo que desde entonces él había estado defendiendo la guerra. En Manhattan, esta posición le ocasionó problemas, sobre todo en cocteles, señaló con una sonrisa.

Gerson comprendió que Kissinger veía a Irak puramente dentro del contexto de la política del poder. No era idealismo. No parecía conectarse con la meta de Bush de promover la democracia. "¿Qué pensó del discurso de la segunda posesión?", le preguntó Gerson.

"Al principio quedé aterrado", dijo Kissinger, cuidándose de cubrirse, porque eso era lo que les había dicho a otros, y siguió hablando en privado. Afirmó que, después de reflexionar, ahora creía que el discurso cumplió su propósito y fue una movida muy astuta que ubicó la guerra contra el terror y la política exterior de Estados Unidos en el contexto de los valores estadounidenses. Eso ayudaría a sostener una larga campaña.

Sobre Irán, Kissinger dijo que era absolutamente crítico impedir que Irán ganara capacidad nuclear y armas nucleares. Si lo hace, dijo, todas las potencias en la región –Turquía, Egipto, Arabia Saudita y los demás– se volverían nucleares. "Esa sería una de las peores pesadillas estratégicas que Estados Unidos pudiera concebir", dijo. A su lado las incertidumbres de la Guerra Fría lucirían pequeñas.

Volviendo a Irak, Kissinger le comentó a Gerson que Bush debía resistir la presión para retirar las tropas estadounidenses, repitiendo su axioma de que la única estrategia válida de salida era la victoria. "El presidente no puede hablar de reducción de tropas como algo central", dijo Kissinger. "Puede pensarse en reducir las tropas". Pero no debería ser un objetivo. "No es ahí donde hay que hacer el énfasis".

Luego le dio a Gerson una copia de su memorando llamado del "maní salado", escrito durante el primer año de la administración Nixon. En ese memorando al presidente Nixon, de fecha 10 de septiembre de 1969, Kissinger advertía: "El retiro de las tropas de Estados Unidos será como maní salado para la opinión pública estadounidense; entre más tropas envíen a su hogar, más le exigirán después". Kissinger escribió que la política de la "vietnamización", que les trasladó la lucha a los militares de Vietnam del Sur, podía incrementar la presión para terminar la guerra, porque la opinión pública estadounidense quería una solución rápida. El retiro de las tropas sólo alentaría al enemigo. "Cada vez será más difícil mantener la moral de los que se queden, sin hablar de la de sus madres".

Para Kissinger, Irak era la secuela de Vietnam. Le repitió a Gerson su versión del fin de la Guerra de Vietnam. La opinión pública, el Congreso, el Departamento de Defensa y los militares habían perdido su determinación. En algún punto, él le propuso al presidente Nixon que enviara un gran ultimátum a Vietnam del Norte, advirtiendo consecuencias terribles si no negociaba la paz. Pero eso no ocurrió, dijo melancólicamente el ex asesor de seguridad nacional. "Yo no tenía suficiente poder".

YA EN WASHINGTON, como coordinador de la política para Irak, Jim Jeffrey le dijo a Rice que veía algunos problemas graves con el "Plan de Campaña" del general Casey, el esquema clasificado de las metas para Estados Unidos y otras fuerzas de la coalición en Irak.

En síntesis, el voluminoso documento decía que la fuerza multinacional de Irak, que comandaba Casey, tenía dos objetivos: primero, derrotar a los terroristas, lo que significaba asesinar a Zarqawi y neutralizar la insurgencia, y, segundo, restablecer, entrenar y equipar las fuerzas armadas iraquíes. Había también otras seis misiones llamadas "líneas de operaciones"[19].

La guerra ya no consistía en aplicar el poder letal de las armas, la artillería y las bombas. La tarea mayor y más constante era el esfuerzo concertado para ganar los corazones, las mentes y el apoyo del pueblo de Irak. Esto no sólo implicaba solucionar el inmenso problema de seguridad. Quería decir mejorar la vida diaria de los iraquíes del común. Significaba que se requeriría mucho más que seguridad física para ganar la guerra, y que las condiciones políticas y económicas serían decisivas para conseguir la paz.

El problema era de ejecución. Zarqawi aún estaba vivo y no se había neutralizado a la insurgencia. Ya se le había señalado eso a Casey en informes clasificados. "Están conteniendo a la insurgencia", dijo Jeffrey. Era el mismo tipo de "contención" de la Unión Soviética durante la Guerra Fría. La Unión Soviética continuó siendo una amenaza poderosa y nunca llegó a ser neutralizada hasta su colapso.

La insurgencia de Irak representaba una amenaza devastadora similar. "Los ataques han escalado a lo largo de los dos últimos años", dijo Jeffrey. Aunque la tasa de bajas estadounidenses seguía siendo la misma, las fuerzas de seguridad iraquíes cada vez resultaban más afectadas. "Están perdiendo a dos por cada uno de los nuestros", dijo Jeffrey. "Y así los efectos sobre la insurgencia son casi los mismos o ligeramente mayores. No vamos a ningún lado.

"Aún nos pueden volver un lío con lo de la electricidad", dijo Jeffrey, "matar muchas personas, hacer estallar la violencia sectaria y, en general, ser toda una pesadilla. No van a tomarse el país, pero tampoco se van a marchar, y no permitirán que se les neutralice".

Rice comprendió que necesitaba salir un poco de su ruta y meterse más en la de Rumsfeld. Esto estaba creando notables roces con el secretario de Defensa.

Rumsfeld reaccionó, subrayando con frecuencia que la falta de progreso en el frente político y económico, las áreas de Rice, tenía un impacto negativo

---

19. Las líneas de operaciones incluían: Asistir a los iraquíes en el gobierno y en el desarrollo de la democracia; ayudar a la prestación de servicios esenciales como electricidad, agua, salud y escuelas; ayudar a fortalecer la economía; apoyar el fortalecimiento de la legalidad y los derechos humanos; aumentar el apoyo internacional, y comunicar y promover "medios de comunicación libres, independientes y responsables".

sobre la seguridad. Públicamente insistía en que era necesario progresar en los tres frentes.

El conflicto entre Rice y Rumsfeld pronto se concentró en la economía iraquí. La "Estrategia Nacional para el Apoyo a Irak", un voluminoso documento clasificado de 500 páginas, lleno de gráficos con códigos de color, describía cómo se invertirían unos US $21.000 millones en ayudas de Estados Unidos para Irak, en restauración de escuelas, construcción de gigantescas plantas de energía eléctrica y reconstrucción de la infraestructura petrolera. La mayor parte del dinero y personal de campo del Departamento de Estado estaba destinado para esto, como lo estaba gran parte del esfuerzo militar de Estados Unidos.

Pero no funcionaba, y la razón tenía que ver con los mismos problemas de seguridad de la infraestructura que Frank Miller, desde el equipo de Rice del Comité para la Seguridad Nacional, y otros ya habían identificado para ella años antes.

BANDAR HABÍA ESTADO ENFERMO y en comisión por meses; incluso, estuvo en el hospital por un tiempo. Ahora se iba a marchar de Estados Unidos, después de 22 años como embajador. El rey saudita iba a crear un Consejo de Seguridad Nacional inspirado en la versión estadounidense, y Bandar iba a ser secretario general de ese consejo, un equivalente del asesor para la seguridad nacional estadounidense.

Pasó a despedirse del presidente Bush el 8 de septiembre de 2005. No se discutió nada acerca de política. Bandar le entregó un medallón de plata grabado con una paloma y las iniciales suyas y de su esposa, la princesa Haifa. En una foto con Bush, Bandar lucía agotado y distante.

38

Zelikow regresó a Irak en septiembre de 2005 para otra gira de inspección, esta vez durante nueve días. Viajó muy ligero con seis personas, un asistente de su equipo, un coronel bajo el mando del general Casey, un funcionario de seguridad del Departamento de Estado y tres soldados. Visitó cuatro ciudades y Bagdad dos veces. Al regresar escribió un memorando SECRETO/NODIS para Rice con fecha 26 de septiembre de 2005.

En primer lugar, señaló que la seguridad había progresado significativamente durante el último año, pero que la insurgencia se había adaptado. Habían mejorado sus tácticas y ahora estaban empleando artefactos explosivos hechizos más efectivos. Su elección de los objetivos y la manera de alcanzarlos era bastante inquietante, teniendo en cuenta que ahora contaban con más armas letales. La dura realidad era que los insurgentes podían operar con libertad en muchas partes del país, y las fuerzas de Estados Unidos estaban demasiado dispersas.

La emoción después de las elecciones del 30 de enero ya se había disipado sustancialmente, informaba Zelikow, y el gobierno de transición de Jafari, en términos generales, iba a media marcha. Uno de los hallazgos más dramáticos era que el ministro del Interior iraquí, que supervisaba las fuerzas policiales, estaba manejando un "oscuro sistema de detenciones y ejecuciones extrajudiciales".

Acerca de los otros dos pilares de la posguerra en Irak —desarrollo económico y gobernabilidad, los dos, responsabilidad del Departamento de Estado—, el informe era terrible: "No se ha avanzado visiblemente, y en algunas áreas se ha retrocedido". En las áreas de electricidad, petróleo y agua, Estados Unidos estaba haciendo un enorme esfuerzo sólo para permanecer en el mismo punto. Luego venía la frase devastadora: "Los iraquíes tienen expectativas exageradas acerca de lo que podemos hacer en su país, y el fracaso general con los servicios públicos los ha desilusionado profundamente de Estados Unidos".

Zelikow formulaba la última pregunta: "¿Estamos en el camino indicado? Es difícil definir el éxito en Irak si se dejan a un lado los lugares comunes ¿Qué significa éxito?".

Proponía algunas metas medibles o aspectos que podrían interpretarse como éxito:

Primero: "Una insurgencia lo suficientemente debilitada y neutralizada como para que el gobierno iraquí pueda contenerla sin necesidad de la ayuda a gran escala de Estados Unidos. En otras palabras, Estados Unidos no tendría que seguir comprometiendo sus fuerzas terrestres, quizás, más allá del 2008". Eso quería decir que en Irak no permanecerían más de 40.000 o 50.000 miembros de las tropas estadounidenses en el último año del periodo presidencial de Bush.

Segundo: "Un gobierno iraquí independiente, capaz de mantener el orden público de manera que Irak no sea una base importante para el terrorismo islámico contra Estados Unidos, ni un campo abierto para la violenta subversión iraní, y que no haya interferencias para el suministro mundial de petróleo".

Tercero: "Un gobierno iraquí que muestre un potencial positivo para procesos democráticos dentro del mundo árabe y musulmán".

Cuarto: "Un gobierno iraquí que salga adelante fiscal y económicamente, a tal punto que exista un sentimiento de esperanza en la economía y un camino visible hacia la autosuficiencia financiera".

Zelikow concluía: "Fracaso sería una situación en la que no se haya conseguido lo anterior en el momento en que esta administración concluya su periodo" –enero del 2009–. Se podría hablar de "fracaso catastrófico si el centro no se mantiene en pie y el experimento iraquí de un gobierno verdaderamente nacional colapsa".

A pesar de los detalles, Zelikow se daba cuenta de que todos en Washington querían que él les respondiera una pregunta básica: "¿Cómo va todo?". Responderla era extremadamente difícil. Él era abogado, y sentía que estaba en un punto en el que podía justificar con fluidez la versión optimista, tan fácil y convincentemente como la pesimista.

"No estoy seguro", concluía Zelikow. Esa era la última línea. Pero, escribió, "en el mejor caso, en un buen día, podría decirle al presidente: 'Creemos que nuestro esfuerzo en Bagdad probablemente tendrá éxito'". Utilizó con cuidado la palabra "probablemente". "De hecho, forzándolas, las probabilidades de éxito llegan a un 70%. Eso significa, al menos, un 30% de riesgo de fracasar, y un riesgo significativo de fracaso catastrófico".

Zelikow señalaba que no había encontrado a nadie que creyera que la probabilidad de éxito fuera mayor del 70%. "Incluso, con una evaluación optimista", continuaba, "podemos creer que nuestros esfuerzos son apenas suficientes para tener éxito".

Por supuesto, "apenas suficientes" en realidad significaba "ni remotamente cerca". El presidente había dicho que el fracaso en Irak no era una opción. Zelikow coincidía, y eso quería decir que el riesgo en el momento era inaceptablemente alto. Necesitaban un plan y una estrategia que fueran más que suficientes para tener éxito. Tenían que "ganar sobre la marcha", escribió. Como el informe estaba dirigido a Rice, la entusiasta fanática del fútbol de la NFL, describió la meta en de que era necesario ganar por dos o tres anotaciones.

En el informe había demasiadas referencias a lidiar escasamente, sobrevivir apenas y mejoras en aumento. Se necesitaba un mayor esfuerzo para vencer. Aparte de algunos aspectos militares y del Departamento de Defensa, eran pocos los que estaban marchando.

"Tenemos que intentar que el año 2006 sea un punto de giro, en el que dirijamos por una ruta positiva al nuevo gobierno que va a ganar o perder la guerra".

Sobre el "tamaño de las fuerzas de Estados Unidos y la protección de la infraestructura crítica", decía que las fuerzas estaban muy dispersas, pero no era partidario de un envío masivo de tropas de Estados Unidos. El general Casey debía aceptar que una de sus misiones centrales era la protección de la infraestructura. Los batallones de infraestructura iraquíes eran un desastre, y mucha gente estaba siendo asesinada por la falta de seguridad. "Tenemos que tratar los oleoductos claves y las redes eléctricas con la misma consideración con la que tratamos las principales rutas de suministro de la fuerza multinacional" –el término militar para las carreteras– "e ingeniar un plan de seguridad de acuerdo con una combinación de fuerzas iraquíes y de la coalición".

De nuevo, señaló que la mayor utilización de artefactos explosivos hechizos letales por parte de los insurgentes, que ocasionaban la mayor parte de las muertes de militares estadounidenses, era especialmente problemática. Existía una fuerte evidencia de que, desde mediados de 2005, existía un flujo de componentes avanzados para artefactos explosivos hechizos que llegaba a Irak desde Irán. Los diseños no eran revolucionarios, pero al ajustar la carga y conseguir una trayectoria en línea recta de los explosivos y proyectiles, a diferencia de las explosiones grandes y no dirigidas, los nuevos artefactos explosivos hechizos concentraban su fuerza y podían penetrar el blindaje. Eran muy letales –al menos cuatro veces más letales que los que podían ser producidos por los iraquíes– y capaces de matar a todos los que estuvieran dentro de un Humvee blindado.

El Pentágono tenía un plan de US $3.300 millones para obtener defensas efectivas contra los artefactos explosivos hechizos. Pero en realidad se trataba de un problema de varias caras. La letalidad de las armas ya no era lo único importante, sino el hecho de que estuvieran llegando de Irán.

Algunas evidencias indicaban que el grupo terrorista Hezbolá, apoyado por Irán, estaba entrenando insurgentes para construir y usar los artefactos explosivos hechizos ensamblados, con la anuencia de la Guardia Revolucionaria Iraní. Se podía argüir que se trataba de un acto de guerra de Irán contra de Estados Unidos. Zelikow pensaba que si se daba a conocer todo lo que se sabía acerca de estos asuntos, la administración iniciaría una conflagración que no podría apagar.

Rice reconocía el modelo académico estándar que Zelikow utilizó para evaluar los riesgos, y se dio cuenta de que se preguntaba si estaban dejando suficiente margen para la victoria, dados los enormes riesgos. Pero ella tenía que ser práctica. En términos generales, el cálculo de Zelikow de un 70% de probabilidad de éxito podía llevar a la conclusión de que se requería la fuerza avasalladora porque, según la doctrina de Collin Powell, había que garantizar el éxito. Pero, más en detalle, no era claro que la fuerza militar avasalladora era la manera de vencer la insurgencia. Rice creía que no se le vencería solamente en el aspecto militar. Debía ser vencida políticamente. Por eso, debía concentrarse en el papel del Departamento de Estado. ¿Era necesario cambiar la manera como ella utilizaba a su gente? ¿Cómo podía lograr que la mejor gente fuera a Irak? ¿Qué incentivos podía ofrecer para que las personas adecuadas fueran allá? ¿Cómo podía hacer que su departamento estuviera más en pie de guerra?

Era consciente de que Rumsfeld había insistido en reducir la dependencia iraquí de la asistencia de Estados Unidos y que ya era tiempo de retirar las manos estadounidenses del asiento de la bicicleta.

"Creo que es cierto que la gente seguirá aferrada a la asistencia, tanto como les sea posible", dijo Rice. "Pero también es cierto que si uno retira la mano de la bicicleta y esa gente se va a una zanja, no es algo bueno. Es una cuestión de equilibrio ¿Cómo saber que ya son capaces de soltarse? Creo que mediante un proceso gradual".

EL 29 DE SEPTIEMBRE DE 2005, fui al Senado para desayunar con el senador de Michigan Carl Levin, de 71 años, un veterano de 26 años en el Senado y demócrata insigne de la Comisión de Servicios Armados. A menudo descrito apropiadamente como "arrugado", Levin atisbaba teatralmente sobre sus gafas diminutas. En el Pentágono de Rumsfeld frecuentemente se referían a Levin como "el perseguidor", porque siempre estaba encima de ellos. Antes de la guerra, él había creído que Saddam tenía armas de destrucción masiva, pero no creyó que fuera una buena razón para invadirlo.

Levin votó en contra de la guerra y había atacado fuertemente a la CIA, convencido de que no había compartido todos los sitios en los que se sospechaba la presencia de armas de destrucción masiva con los inspectores de la ONU. Es decir, que no todos los sitios habían sido inspeccionados antes de que Bush ordenara la invasión. Pero esta información de la Lista Maestra era clasificada.

"Intenté de diez maneras diferentes que la desclasificaran", dijo Levin, "porque si antes de atacar se hubiera sabido que no habíamos compartido con la ONU todos los sitios de los que teníamos sospechas, la decisión de ir a la guerra se habría enfriado".

Le señalé que la Lista Maestra se basaba en datos de inteligencia de más de cinco años de antigüedad, y que el personal de inteligencia militar no confiaba mucho en ella.

Levin dijo que el proceso de inspección fue incompleto, que no fue exhaustivo. Podría haber retrasado la guerra, pero no detenerla. Se quejó de "todas las faltas de claridad y exageraciones" acerca de las armas de destrucción masiva de parte de Bush y Cheney, y dijo que se trató del "intento más deliberado" para producir decepción.

"Nunca he creído que Bush sea un tonto", dijo Levin, golpeando suavemente la mesa para enfatizar. "Pero pienso que es perezoso intelectualmente, y que quiere que la gente que lo rodea no lo desafíe pero le dé todo el apoyo que necesita o desea para alcanzar una meta más general".

Le dije que creía que Powell estaba angustiado por lo que había sucedido en Irak, por los 130.000 estadounidenses que seguían varados allá, enfrentando una insurgencia que no dejaba de crecer.

"No me interesa su angustia", dijo Levin, casi estallando de ira. "No soporto oír acerca de su angustia. Él es tan astuto y sus instintos son tan buenos, que no puedo aceptar su angustia. Quiero algo más que angustia. Esperaba más que angustia".

"¿Qué era lo que quería?", le pregunte. "¿Una disculpa?".

"Honestidad. Quería honestidad. No quiero leer uno o dos años después que fue el peor momento de su vida o algo así. El tuvo problemas con esto todo el tiempo. Yo había esperado algo del estilo de George Marshall". En la Segunda Guerra Mundial, el general George Marshall se mantuvo a distancia del presidente Roosevelt, y en algún momento le dijo: "Señor presidente, no me llame George".

"Powell tenía el poder de cambiar el curso de esto", continuó Levin. "Era el único que tenía la capacidad de hacerlo".

¿Cómo podría haberlo hecho?, le pregunté.

"Si le hubiera dicho al presidente que ese era el camino equivocado", dijo Levin. "Creo que nunca se dio cuenta del poder que tenía en sus manos, y eso es renunciar. Creo que Powell tiene un poder tremendo". Dijo que hubo varias cosas que Powell podía haber hecho para retrasar la guerra, si no era posible detenerla. Pudo haber amenazado con renunciar, o haber insistido en que se les permitiera a los inspectores de la ONU continuar, dijo Levin. Cuando Bush le preguntó a Powell, en enero de 2003, si lo acompañaría en la guerra, Powell estaba en el punto máximo de su influencia, dijo Levin.

"¿Se imagina lo que habría pasado si el hubiera dicho 'Tengo que pensarlo'? ¿Puede imaginase el poder de esa persona para cambiar las cosas? Él lo tenía".

Bush asistió a las llamadas cinco grandes reuniones con los líderes máximos del Congreso: los líderes de la mayoría y la minoría en el Senado y la Cámara de Representantes, y el vocero de la Cámara. Las reuniones generalmente comenzaban puntualmente a las 8 de la mañana, y Bush hacía un monólogo de 45 minutos sobre política exterior, principalmente. Seguían 10 o 15 minutos para preguntas y comentarios, y las reuniones siempre terminaban a las 9:00. Nunca había nada tan importante como para extenderlas.

Al senador Harry Reid de Nevada, líder de la minoría demócrata del Senado, un ex boxeador de 65 años que había sido presidente de la Comisión de Apuestas de Nevada, le pareció que Bush era agradable, incluso, amigable, en estas reuniones. Pero la división de partido era tan grande que Reid le dijo a su equipo "No lo soporto". Le parecían insufribles la mayoría de los discursos del presidente que se transmitían por la televisión nacional. Por eso, los miembros de su equipo los veían y luego le hacían un resumen de lo que había dicho Bush.

Acerca de Irak, los dos partidos tenían muy poco en común. La verdadera comunicación se había perdido.

La Comisión de Asuntos Exteriores del Senado, donde alguna vez se generaban los debates sobre la política exterior nacional, había estado reclamando el testimonio de Rice sobre Irak. Sus evasivas resultaban humillantes para los senadores, quienes en su mayoría pensaban que ella quería evitar que la prolongada guerra la salpicara. Finamente, aceptó presentar su testimonio en el otoño.

Rice consultó con Zelikow y otros miembros de su equipo, esperando que saliera una definición de éxito para su testimonio. Revisó el memorando de Zelikow de septiembre, en el que decía que el éxito incluiría vencer y neutralizar a la insurgencia, para evitar que Irak se convirtiera en una base importante para el terrorismo, demostrar un proceso democrático y salir adelante financiera y económicamente. Ella decidió incorporar estos puntos casi al pie de la letra. Pero el testimonio que planeó carecía de un resumen inicial llamativo, coherente y comprensible.

Zelikow había estado leyendo *A Better War*, un libro de 1999 de Lewis Sorley, acerca de una estrategia de "despejar y conservar" que había producido algo de éxito en la Guerra de Vietnam, según Sorley, después de descartar la estrategia de "buscar y destruir".

Para Zelikow, "despejar y conservar" no era suficiente. Se necesitaba otro pilar positivo, más afirmativo. Conservar era algo muy pasivo. Ideó el concepto de "despejar, conservar y… construir".

Rice lo convirtió en la pieza central de su testimonio ante la comisión del Senado, el miércoles 19 de octubre. Era la primera vez que un funcionario de alto nivel de la administración había venido a la comisión en más de año y medio para hablar específicamente de Irak. Les dijo a los senadores: "Nuestra estrategia política y militar debe ser la de despejar, conservar y construir: despejar áreas del control de los insurgentes, conservarlas con seguridad y construir instituciones iraquíes durables".

Gran parte de esto era una misión militar, y Rumsfeld estaba furioso. Hasta donde él sabía, no daba a entender lo que estaban haciendo o lo que deberían hacer: que los iraquíes llevaran algo más de la carga. Era un error decir que "la estrategia política y militar" de Estados Unidos sólo tenía que ver con lo que haría Estados Unidos y no con lo que harían los iraquíes. Tenían que retirar sus manos del asiento de la bicicleta y las ruedas de entrenamiento.

Según Rumsfeld, Rice creía que lo que se necesitaba para explicar lo que estaba haciendo el Departamento de Estado en Irak era "un lema para golpear en la defensa el auto".

"Yo no la necesito", me dijo después en una entrevista. "Tenemos un trabajo que hacer y lo estamos haciendo. Tienen que diseñar algo así y tienen razón. Si uno va a comunicarse con diferentes audiencias, incluyéndonos –nuestro Congreso, nuestra opinión pública–, el pueblo iraquí, luego querrán saber '¿Qué están haciendo? ¿Tienen una estrategia? ¿Tienen un plan?' La respuesta es que tenemos un plan".

"Pero, ¿sí tenemos fuerzas de seguridad iraquíes con 263.000 hombres? Yo los quería librando y conservando áreas. No me gustaba la idea de que sólo íbamos a estar nosotros. Y esa era mi preocupación, porque eso sería aferrarse al asiento de la bicicleta y quedarse ahí por el resto de la vida".

EL VIERNES 28 DE OCTUBRE DE 2005, *Scooter* Libby fue acusado de perjurio, obstrucción a la justicia y declaraciones falsas al FBI en el caso de la filtración de la CIA. Renunció ese mismo día. Los funcionarios de seguridad de la Casa Blanca entraron a su oficina, le quitaron sus pases y le dijeron que tenía que marcharse inmediatamente. Libby se había fracturado un hueso del pie y no tenía auto. Literalmente fue puesto en la calle, mientras cojeaba con sus muletas. Después, cuando vio una copia de su sumario, *Estados Unidos de América contra I. Lewis "Scooter" Libby*, no pudo evitar el llanto. Después les comentaría a sus amigos que estaba leyendo a Kafka.

UNA NOCHE EN ESE OTOÑO, Brent Scowcroft se sentó junto al senador McCain en una cena. McCain, quien había hecho una intensa campaña junto a Bush el año anterior para la reelección presidencial, dijo que Bush le estaba empezando a agradar.

"¿Alguna vez le pide su opinión?", preguntó Scowcroft.

"No me parece que sea necesario dar mi opinión cuando estoy haciendo campaña para él", respondió McCain. "Hay algunos que apenas llegan y están dos minutos con el presidente ya pretenden decirle cómo manejar el país. Yo no".

"No es eso lo que pregunto", dijo Scowcroft. "Alguna vez le ha dicho: '¿John, que piensa sobre…?'".

"No lo ha hecho", dijo McCain. "En realidad no es intelectualmente curioso. Pero alguna vez dijo: 'No quiero ser como mi padre. Quiero ser como Ronald Reagan'".

Eso consumió a Scowcroft, que se sentía cada vez más desesperanzado. Concluyó que la administración estaba haciendo lo impensable, repitiendo los errores de Vietnam. Pocos sabían más sobre Vietnam que Scowcroft, quien trabajó allí para los presidentes Nixon y Ford. Pensaba que las probabilidades de construir un ejército iraquí que pudiera luchar eran aun menores que tres décadas atrás, cuando trataron de reconstruir el ejército de Vietnam del Sur, que ya había sido una fuerza poderosa y casi autónoma en Vietnam. En Irak, todos los ejércitos estaban conectados de alguna manera con los chiítas, los sunitas o los kurdos. Era una catástrofe política.

La decepción de Scowcroft aumentaba respecto al desempeño de aquellos con quienes había trabajado o a quienes había guiado. Consideraba a Hadley, quien había estado en su equipo del Comité para la Seguridad Nacional a comienzos de los años setenta, un amigo entrañable. Pero Hadley no se enfrentaría con nadie; no con Cheney o Rice, y seguramente tampoco con Rumsfeld. No defendería ni sus propias opiniones.

Hasta el padre del presidente había comentado que estaba descontento con Rice. "Condi es una decepción, ¿no es así?", dijo el ex presidente y añadió "No da la talla para el cargo".

Entre sus contactos militares, hasta donde Scowcroft podía decir, el general Myers, el jefe saliente del Estado Mayor Conjunto, era un hombre domado, un cachorro. El general Pace era peor. Pace había visto a Myers con Rumsfeld durante cuatro años, sabía exactamente en qué se metía y aceptó de todos modos.

Cheney era el peor, creía Scowcroft. "¿Qué le ocurrió a Dick Cheney?", le comentaban todos los que lo habían conocido por años. "Esto es un coro. 'No reconocemos a este Dick Cheney'".

Rumsfeld se comportaba como siempre, de regreso a la administración Ford: "enigmático, obstructivo, errático, siempre ignorando cuál es su juego". Para Scowcroft, Rumsfeld era una fuerza completamente negativa.

Aun peor, Scowcroft pensaba que la administración había creído que Saddam dirigía un estado moderno y eficiente, y que cuando lo derrocaran dejaría atrás una sociedad operante. No vieron que todo colapsaría y que tendrían que comenzar a partir de cero. No vieron la necesidad de la seguridad, o que probablemente el 90% del ejército iraquí podría haber sido salvado y aprovechado. Ahora los iraquíes se sentían abrumadoramente inseguros. Sin seguridad, había pocas oportunidades para que la gente le apostara a su sociedad y mantuvieran una actitud positiva. A Scowcroft le parecía que los iraquíes estaban desesperados.

Pero la administración no reexaminaría ni revaluaría su política. Como decía él a menudo, "no sé como puede funcionar sin desafiar continuamente sus suposiciones". Para Scowcroft resultaba aun más acongojante ver la zozobra de su viejo amigo Bush padre, "41", como lo llamaba Scowcroft, en "zozobra", "angustia" y "tormento" por la guerra y lo que había sucedido después. Era terrible. El padre aún deseaba que su hijo tuviera éxito ¡Pero, que relación tan confusa! En sus años de juventud, pensaba Scowcroft, George W. no podía decidir si iba a rebelarse contra su padre o si iba a intentar vencerlo en su propio campo. Trató de vencerlo, y fue un desastre. Scowcroft estaba seguro de que 41 nunca se habría comportado así "ni en un millón de años".

39

Las agencias de inteligencia de Estados Unidos estaban practicando encuestas en Irak para medir los niveles de favorabilidad de algunos líderes y figuras iraquíes.

La persona ubicada en la primera posición entre el 11 y el 18 de enero era Sistani, con 61% de favorabilidad y 39% de desfavorabilidad.

El ex primer ministro Allawi se le acercaba, con 59,7% de favorabilidad y 40,3% de desfavorabilidad[20].

Rice quería que el Departamento de Estado hiciera presencia de una manera concreta en Irak, fuera de la Zona Verde. Tomó seriamente las críticas de Zelikow acerca de que las agencias civiles no estaban distribuidas más allá de Bagdad, y quería crear Equipos Provinciales de Reconstrucción con expertos políticos y económicos, trabajadores de asistencia e ingenieros, que irían a las 18 provincias, establecerían puestos de avanzada y colaborarían en la reconstrucción. Khalilzad había establecido Equipos Provinciales de Reconstrucción similares en Afganistán durante su paso como embajador. Rice y Rumsfeld se enfrascaron en otra disputa porque él quería que el Departamento de Estado empleara contratistas privados para prestar seguridad a los equipos, con un costo de cientos de millones de dólares. Rice, por supuesto, quería que los militares lo hicieran. Seguía el tire y afloje.

El 11 de noviembre, Rice hizo su segundo viaje a Irak, y llegó a la ciudad de Mosul, la principal ciudad kurda ubicada unos 360 kilómetros al noroeste de Bagdad, para anunciar la inauguración del primer Equipo Provincial de Reconstrucción. Se establecieron otros tres, que para ella valían su peso en oro, en igual número de ciudades iraquíes. Pero los asuntos de financiación, búsqueda de personal y seguridad retrasaron algunos de los demás equipos, y unos cientos de personas en el campo no iban a hacer una diferencia significativa en un país de 25 millones de personas.

---

20. Otros en las encuestas de Irak tenían alta desfavorabilidad. Chalabi tenía un 34% de favorabilidad y 66% de desfavorabilidad. Saddam Hussein, 22% favorable, 78% desfavorable. El puntaje más bajo fue el de Izzat al-Duri, el vicepresidente de Saddam que Estados Unidos no pudo capturar, con un 20% favorable y 80% desfavorable.

LOS ATAQUES INICIADOS por el enemigo eran responsables de la muerte de 3.000 personas en octubre, la cifra más elevada hasta entonces según los informes clasificados.

Estaba programado que Bush diera el Día de los Veteranos un discurso en el Almacén de Suministros del Ejército, en Tobyhanna, Pensilvania, gigantescas instalaciones militares para reparaciones y mantenimiento. Se hizo circular un borrador del discurso entre los altos funcionarios, y Rumsfeld notó que el presidente planeaba apropiarse del lenguaje de "despejar, conservar y construir", de Rice, como "nuestra estrategia".

Rumsfeld llamó a Card una hora y media antes de la hora programada para el discurso del presidente.

"Elimine eso", dijo Rumsfeld.

"Es el centro del discurso", contestó Card. Aun más, era el centro de toda su estrategia.

"Recomiendo que se elimine", insistió Rumsfeld, señalando que "despejar, conservar y construir" no era lo que estaba sucediendo. La parte de "despejar" iba bien, dijo. "Despejar es lo que estamos haciendo", refiriéndose a los militares. "A los iraquíes les corresponde conservar. Y el Departamento de Estado trabajará con otros para construir".

Rumsfeld me confirmó en una entrevista que había solicitado que se removiera la frase. Podía sonar bien al principio, pero podía volverse en su contra después. "No somos sólo nosotros los que hacemos el despeje; es la coalición. Y la conservación es cada vez más de ellos que de nosotros. Y en cuanto a la construcción, queremos colaborar en la creación de un ambiente que les permita a ellos reconstruir su propio país".

Rumsfeld perdió esa batalla. El presidente dijo: "Nuestra estrategia es despejar, conservar y construir".Gerson no comprendía las objeciones de Rumsfeld. Era el único lema efectivo para explicar su estrategia de contra-insurgencia.

El otro gran mensaje del discurso de Bush, sin embargo, era que la Casa Blanca iba a sacudir a todo aquel que afirmara que Bush y Cheney habían engañado al país antes de la guerra. Así, criticar sería sinónimo de quebrantar el ánimo de las tropas.

"Aunque sea perfectamente legítimo criticar mi decisión o el curso de la guerra, es profundamente irresponsable tratar de reescribir la historia de cómo comenzó la guerra", dijo Bush, y arrancó aplausos de la audiencia de combatientes y veteranos. "Los riesgos de la guerra global contra el terror son muy altos, y el interés nacional es muy importante como para que los políticos lancen acusaciones falsas", añadió, y hubo más aplausos. "Estos ataques sin fundamento envían una señal errada a nuestras tropas y a un enemigo que cuestiona la voluntad de Estados Unidos".

EL 16 DE NOVIEMBRE, Cheney hizo una alocución para una organización conservadora llamada Instituto Fronteras de Libertad, e hizo eco del desafío de Bush. La acusación de que ellos habían mentido era "uno de los señalamientos más deshonestos y censurables que alguna vez se haya hecho en esta ciudad", dijo, y añadió: "Lo más triste es que nuestros uniformados han sido objeto de estas falsedades cínicas y perniciosas día tras día. Los soldados y *marines* están allá afuera todos los días en condiciones peligrosas y soportando las temperaturas del desierto –haciendo incursiones, entrenando las fuerzas iraquíes, repeliendo ataques, incautando armas y capturando asesinos– ,mientras aquí unos pocos oportunistas sugieren que ellos fueron enviados a la batalla con base en una mentira. El presidente y yo no podemos evitar que ciertos políticos pierdan la memoria o su firmeza, pero no nos vamos a quedar viendo como reescriben la historia".

Ese día, la Casa Blanca publicó un documento de 5.000 palabras que refutaba punto por punto un editorial de 913 palabras del *New York Times*, en el que se criticaba agudamente la retórica de Bush sobre armas de destrucción masiva antes de la guerra, y las más recientes "declaraciones de la administración, según las cuales cuestionar sus acciones de hace tres años es una traición para las tropas que están en el campo de batalla hoy".

EL DÍA SIGUIENTE, el congresista Jack Murtha, demócrata de Pensilvania, introdujo una resolución en el Congreso que pedía el "repliegue" –término militar para hacer regresar a las tropas a sus bases en el país– de las tropas estadounidenses que se hallaban en Irak "en la fecha más cercana posible". Murtha, ex instructor de ejercicios militares del Cuerpo de Infantería de Marina y primer veterano de Vietnam elegido al Congreso, tenía excelentes fuentes entre las Fuerzas Armadas. Nadie tenía mejor trayectoria como defensor de los militares que este hombre de 73 años. Murtha había votado afirmativamente la resolución de octubre de 2002 que autorizaba al presidente a utilizar la fuerza militar en Irak. Visitante de Irak en cuatro ocasiones, Murtha hacía viajes semanales a los hospitales militares para visitar a los veteranos de Irak heridos.

"La guerra en Irak no va como se había anunciado", dijo Murtha. "Es una política defectuosa oculta por un espejismo". Los militares están sufriendo, afirmó en la Cámara de Representantes. Conteniendo las lágrimas, añadió: "Nuestros militares han hecho todo lo que se esperaba de ellos. Ya es tiempo de traerlos a casa". Muchas de las tropas estaban desmoralizadas y mal equipadas. Dos años después de la guerra, su presencia en Irak estaba siendo un obstáculo para que ese país progresara hacia la estabilidad y el autogobierno.

Esto era espantoso, y los representantes republicanos sabían que había que enfrentarlo. Al día siguiente, la Cámara de Representantes tuvo uno de sus debates más emotivos y profundos. El vocero Dennis Hastert afirmó que Murtha y otros demócratas habían "adoptado la política de cortar y correr. Preferirían que Estados Unidos se rindiera a los terroristas que harían daño a ciudadanos estadounidenses inocentes".

El presidente del Comité de Servicios Armados de la Cámara de Representantes, Duncan Hunter, republicano de California, introdujo una resolución que tergiversaba cínicamente la propuesta de Murtha de salir "en la fecha más cercana posible". La resolución de Hunter pedía una salida inmediata de las tropas. El mismo Murtha no podía votar, y de hecho no votó, a favor de ella. Fue derrotada por 403 a 3.

Más tarde, ese día, el secretario de prensa del presidente, Scott McClellan, hizo una declaración. "El congresista Murtha es un veterano y un político respetado que siempre ha defendido decididamente a Estados Unidos. Por ello es frustrante que se identifique con las posiciones políticas de Michael Moore[21] y el ala liberal extremista del partido demócrata. La víspera de una histórica elección en Irak no es el momento para rendirse a los terroristas. Después de conocer su afirmación, seguimos contrariados. Él no explica cómo el retiro de Irak le dará más seguridad a Estados Unidos". La elección del 15 de diciembre, a la que se refería McClellan, era para una asamblea permanente que seleccionaría a un primer ministro que ejercería por cuatro años.

Murtha era la voz del alma y la conciencia de los militares estadounidenses. Los militares que estaban informados sabían que él hablaba por muchos otros.

CARD TRATABA DE TENER una reunión privada y sencilla con Laura Bush cada seis semanas, para oír sus preocupaciones. Reservaba una hora y media para cada reunión. A veces tardaba 30 minutos, a veces toda la hora y media, y, en ocasiones, dos horas.

La primera dama estaba angustiada por la guerra, aunque Card sabía que ella no estaba al tanto de la información de inteligencia clasificada sobre Irak. No obstante, ella lo presionaba a menudo pidiéndole información.

"No puedo hablar sobre eso", decía Card.

---

21. Moore realizó el controversial documental anti Bush *Fahrenheit 9/11*.

"Bueno, él tampoco me lo va a contar".

La primera dama estaba preocupada de que Rumsfeld estuviera haciéndole daño a su esposo, y su punto de vista parecía coincidir con el de Rice acerca del estilo despótico y la tendencia dominante de Rumsfeld. Card sabía que la primera dama y Rice a menudo hacían largas caminatas durante los fines de semana en Camp David.

"Estoy de acuerdo con usted", decía Card. Por un lado estaba tratando de educar y explicar, pero por otro estaba haciendo *lobby*. Él resumió sus problemas con Rumsfeld y por qué creía que era tiempo de un cambio.

"¿Y el presidente sabe acerca de esto?", preguntó ella. ¿Estaba siendo Card sincero con su esposo?

Card dijo que así era. "Por eso es que he estado discutiendo", dijo. Sin embargo su opinión acerca de la situación con Rumsfeld había sido ignorada.

"Él está a gusto con esto", dijo la primera dama, "pero yo no". En otra ocasión dijo: "No entiendo por qué no está contrariado con esto".

Durante gran parte del año el presidente había estado buscando la manera de explicar la estrategia para ganar en Irak. El 4 de febrero de 2005, en Nebraska, dijo: "Nuestra estrategia es clara. Vamos a ayudar a los iraquíes para que se defiendan por sí mismos. Aceleraremos el entrenamiento… Les ayudaremos a establecer unas fuerzas de seguridad de alta calidad. Y cuando se complete esa misión e Irak sea democrático y capaz de defenderse por sí mismo, nuestras tropas regresarán a casa con el honor que merecen".

El problema era que entrenar iraquíes y construir las defensas de Irak no era la estrategia para una victoria militar clásica, es decir, la dinámica del bombardeo y los enfrentamientos con otras fuerzas militares. Los generales Abizaid y Casey se daban cuenta de que la meta de "neutralizar" a los insurgentes, que se delineaba en el "Plan de Campaña" clasificado, no se había alcanzado. En un sentido práctico, los militares habían adoptado una estrategia de transición para trasladar el problema a los iraquíes, lo que es opuesto a una estrategia para ganar. "Neutralizar" o, incluso, derrotar a la insurgencia era demasiado difícil. El plan era entrenar a las fuerzas de seguridad iraquíes para que lo hicieran.

La clave era hacer ver la estrategia de transición como un progreso. En una alocución a la nación desde Fort Bragg, Carolina del Norte, el 28 de junio de 2005, el presidente dijo: "Se puede resumir nuestra estrategia así: en la medida en que los iraquíes avancen, nosotros nos retiraremos".

Abizaid asistió al Congreso y luego apareció en televisión el sábado 2 de octubre de 2005. "Tenemos una fuerza de seguridad de alrededor de 200.000

iraquíes en el campo; hemos avanzado un largo trecho", le dijo a Tim Russert, de la NBC. "Estoy optimista".

Ciertamente, el tamaño de las fuerzas de seguridad iraquíes había aumentado de manera estable mientras que las estadounidenses seguían constantes. Pero los informes clasificados mostraban que, en los ocho meses anteriores, los ataques iniciados por el enemigo habían aumentado hasta llegar a 2.500 en el mes de septiembre de 2005.

Abizaid se mantenía en contacto con un puñado de viejos camaradas del ejército, muchos de West Point y retirados, entre ellos el general retirado del ejército Wayne Downing, y Jim Kinsey, uno de los fundadores de America Online. Les preocupaba que el caso de Irak se estuviera convirtiendo lentamente en un Vietnam, que iba a debilitarse prematuramente o a convertirse en una guerra que no podía ser ganada.

Algunos de ellos visitaron a Abizaid en su cuartel general de Doha y luego en Irak. Abizaid se aferraba a la posición de que ahora la guerra era cuestión de los iraquíes. Debían ganar la guerra ahora. Los militares de Estados Unidos hicieron lo que pudieron. Señalaba que era prioritario reducir la presencia de tropas estadounidenses. Aún existía la percepción de una ocupación de fuerzas estadounidenses patrullando, derribando puertas, mirando a las mujeres iraquíes, lo que enfurecía a los hombres iraquíes.

"Debemos largarnos", decía.

Los viejos amigos de Abizaid estaban muy preocupados de que el final del ejército voluntario fuera otro Vietnam o algo parecido.

¿Cuál es la estrategia para ganar?, lo presionaban.

"Ese no es mi trabajo", insistía Abizaid.

Sí es parte de tu trabajo, le insistieron. Abizaid era el que tenía las cosas claras. Podía hablar durante horas y sonar muy bien, mejor que nadie.

No, decía Abizaid. Les corresponde a otros articular la estrategia.

¿A quién?

"Al presidente y a Condi Rice, porque Rumsfeld ya no tiene ninguna credibilidad", dijo.

HADLEY ESCUCHÓ QUEJAS similares acerca de que no había una estrategia. Quería lanzar una ofensiva de relaciones públicas. Le asignó a su directora del Comité para la Seguridad Nacional para Irak, Meghan O'Sullivan, escudriñar entre los documentos clasificados que él creía que resumían su estrategia, y ver qué se podía hacer público.

En junio de 2005, Hadley había contratado a Peter Feaver, profesor de ciencias políticas de la Universidad de Duke y oficial de la reserva de la Armada de 43 años, que había trabajado para el Comité para la Seguridad

Nacional de Clinton. Feaver había estudiado el impacto de la guerra sobre la opinión pública y concluyó que ésta era más tolerante ante las derrotas en combate que los políticos o los altos oficiales militares. Él sentía que Clinton llegó casi al punto de cuestionar su autoridad como comandante supremo antes de ordenar la muerte de alguien. Esto derivó en que los líderes militares y políticos, durante su presidencia, prácticamente, no tuvieran ninguna tolerancia ante las bajas.

El trabajo de Feaver sugería que la opinión pública toleraría las bajas si creía que la política de guerra era razonable, dirigida a ganar. O`Sullivan y Feaver trabajaron en un documento de estrategia que trazaría un camino razonable hacia la victoria. Feaver creía que el documento resultante mostraba variados progresos, y no planteaba de manera descuidada la necesidad de mantener el actual curso.

Hadley envió el documento a los altos funcionarios. Rumsfeld hizo numerosos comentarios, cuidadosamente defensivos. El documento final decía: "Esperamos, pero no podemos garantizar, que la posición de nuestra fuerza cambie a lo largo del año". En otras palabras, no había un cronograma para el retiro de las fuerzas.

El título del documento era "Estrategia nacional para la victoria en Irak". Seguía el libreto de Kissinger: la única estrategia de salida válida sería la victoria.

Bush le dio su aprobación y el plan iba a salir a la luz en un documento de 35 páginas titulado "Estrategia para la victoria", en septiembre. Pero el 29 de agosto el huracán Katrina devastó Nueva Orleans y la costa del Golfo, y tomó desprevenida a la administración de Bush. La presentación debió aplazarse.

La relación de Card con Rumsfeld siempre fue difícil. En muchas ocasiones, Rumsfeld aceptaba cuando Card le decía que el presidente quería que se hiciera algo, y le daba al jefe del equipo el beneficio de la duda cuando le transmitía una orden. Pero a veces Rumsfeld ponía obstáculos.

En los días siguientes al Katrina, Bush decidió que necesitaba más tropa de la Guardia Nacional, y le pidió a Card que le transmitiera el mensaje a Rumsfeld.

"Yo no tengo que rendirle cuentas a usted", dijo Rumsfeld.

"Ya sé que usted no me rinde cuentas", respondió Card. "Usted le rinde cuentas al presidente. Pero créame, él quiere que usted haga esto".

"No lo voy a hacer hasta que él me lo diga", le respondió Rumsfeld. Se estaban manifestando muchas tensiones y obligaciones de entrada.

Card reclamó que él acababa de hablar con el presidente, quien había tomado esa decisión final.

"Pues, entonces, él va a tener que decírmelo", dijo Rumsfeld.

"Oye", le dijo luego el presidente a Card, "Rumsfeld me llamó. Pensé que te ibas a encargar de eso".

"Lo hice", dijo Card fríamente "pero supongo que él quería oírlo de usted".

Después del Día de Acción de Gracias, Card hizo otro esfuerzo para que el presidente reemplazara a Rumsfeld. No quería que el presidente tuviera tapaojos. El ataque de Rumsfeld a "despejar, conservar y construir" era sólo un ejemplo. Muchos de los líderes republicanos y demócratas ya le habían comentado a Card que no soportaban a Rumsfeld. Era más arrogante y despectivo que nunca. También estaba enterado de que algunos del antiguo círculo de la política exterior vinculados con el padre del presidente, a los que llamaba "Barbas Grises", se quejaban cada vez más. La causa era Rumsfeld.

"¿Y quién va a hacer su trabajo?", le preguntó el presidente a Card.

Card mencionó de nuevo a Jim Baker. "¿Cómo hacemos que Roger Clemens regrese al juego?", preguntó Card, comparando a Baker con uno de los lanzadores más grandes de todos los tiempos. Clemens se había retirado de los Yankees de Nueva York en 2003, para regresar a jugar durante un año con el equipo de su tierra natal, los Astros de Houston. "Todavía puede lanzar", decía Card acerca de Baker.

Bush le recordó que estaban en medio de la guerra. Rumsfeld estaba transformando el ejército, no se había insubordinado y era importante que el nuevo presupuesto del Pentágono fuera aprobado. Reemplazarlo ahora podría interferir con las elecciones del 15 de diciembre en Irak. "Interesante", sin embargo, dijo el presidente. "Interesante".

Card pudo ver que el tema quedó dando vueltas en la cabeza de Bush. Podría resultar. Pero aun así el presidente no autorizaría a Card para que empezara a tantear o discutir algo con Baker.

EL DOCUMENTO DE 25 PÁGINAS "Estrategia nacional para la victoria en Irak" finalmente se hizo público el 30 de noviembre de 2005. "Ninguna guerra ha sido ganada siguiendo un cronograma y esta tampoco lo será", decía el resumen ejecutivo. Las fuerzas de Estados Unidos serán retiradas "a medida que el proceso político avance y las fuerzas de seguridad iraquíes crezcan y ganen experiencia. Aunque nuestra presencia militar puede hacerse menos visible, seguirá siendo letal y decisiva, capaz de confrontar al enemigo donde quiera que se organice. Nuestra misión en Irak es ganar la guerra. Nuestras tropas regresarán a casa cuando se complete la misión".

Parte del plan era que Bush diera cuatro discursos sobre Irak, empezando con uno en el día de la Academia Naval de Anápolis, Maryland. Se podía ver docenas de grandes símbolos del "Plan de la Victoria" colgados al fondo. Bush utilizó la palabra "victoria" en 15 ocasiones, insistió en que no transigiría y mantuvo su tono optimista. Admitió algunos errores, diciendo por ejemplo que el entrenamiento de las fuerzas de seguridad iraquíes no había sido fácil siempre, pero dijo que se había aprendido algunas lecciones. "Cambiamos la manera como se entrena la policía iraquí. Ahora, los policías reclutados pasan más tiempo fuera del salón de clases, con entrenamiento práctico en operaciones de antiterrorismo y habilidades de supervivencia en el mundo real".

LA POLÍTICA DE GUERRA de Bush no había cambiado, pero las noticias sugerían que ahora era más explícito y comprensible. Desde Irak, *The Washington Post* informaba que la violencia no era sólo un concepto. "En las calles de Bagdad, dicha retórica optimista contrasta tajantemente con el tronar de las bombas suicidas, el sonido de las sirenas de las ambulancias, el rugido de los autos de la policía que transportan hombres enmascarados y ametralladoras, y los espantosos informes diarios sobre masacres, asesinatos y tomas de rehenes.

"El mismo día del discurso de Bush, nueve trabajadores de una granja fueron asesinados por pistoleros que abrieron fuego cerca de Bakuba, francotiradores dispararon sobre la oficina de un miembro de la Asamblea Nacional en la capital, y tres oficiales del ejército iraquí resultaron heridos cuando una bomba estalló cerca de su patrulla. En Faluya, 20.000 personas marchaban en el funeral de un clérigo sunita, a quien le dispararon mientras hacía sus oraciones".

Sobre el terreno la violencia no había cambiado. Pero un despacho de dos respetados corresponsales del *New York Times*, John F. Burns y Dexter Filkins, desde Bagdad, fue más allá, al señalar un cambio en el presidente. Bajo el título "Por primera vez, el presidente y sus generales ven la misma guerra", denominaron el discurso de Bush "decisivo", porque reconocía las inmensas dificultades de entrenar a los iraquíes y llevar a los batallones de policía y al ejército de Irak a un punto donde pudieran enfrentarse solos a la insurgencia.

EL 7 DE DICIEMBRE, el presidente viajó a la ciudad de Nueva York para dirigirse al Consejo de Relaciones Exteriores, en el segundo de los cuatro discursos planeados sobre Irak.

"Hoy recordamos el aniversario de un día funesto en la historia estadounidense", dijo, y comparó a Pearl Harbor con el 9/11. Seguía siendo su tema principal.

Más adelante, es misma tarde, en Washington, Bush invitó a la Casa Blanca a los líderes republicanos de la Cámara de Representantes, entre ellos 15 diputados que eran el grupo principal de ese partido en la Cámara de Representantes. Estos eran los ambiciosos republicanos que Bush quería tener a su lado. Cheney, Rove, Card y Bartlett asistieron a la reunión en el Salón Oval de la Casa Blanca.

El presidente reconoció que había estado alejado de sus asuntos desde el huracán Katrina. Sin duda, había un respiro en el ambiente político, dijo. Pero ahora se estaban haciendo las cosas de manera diferente en Irak, en comparación a como se hacían dos años antes. No retiraría las tropas hasta que las condiciones no fueran las adecuadas.

"No nos retiraremos, aunque Laura y Barney[22] sean los únicos que me apoyen", dijo Bush.

El representante Roy Blunt, republicano de Missouri y líder de la mayoría, dijo que cuando el demócrata Murtha propuso salir de Irak, la gente se dio cuenta de que la única alternativa aceptable era lo que estaba haciendo Bush. Todos coincidieron en que forzar a que se votara el asunto en la Cámara de Representantes había sido una gran victoria táctica.

"Sé que hago discursos largos y aburridos, pero mis asesores me dicen que es necesario", dijo Bush.

Varios congresistas animaron al presidente y le dijeron que debía hacer discursos largos y concentrados en un solo tema, porque eso obligaba a los medios noticiosos a cubrirlos ¿Qué importaba si los medios se fastidiaban? Era cuestión de tratar de controlar su cubrimiento.

---

22. Barney es el terrier escocés de Laura y George W. Bush.

40

Al día siguiente, el 8 de diciembre de 2005, Bush y Cheney tuvieron una videoconferencia con el embajador Khalilzad y el general Casey.

¿Cuánto tiempo sería necesario para instalar el nuevo gobierno permanente, después de las elecciones de la Asamblea Nacional que escogería un primer ministro?, preguntó Bush.

La última vez se tardó 90 días, dijo Khalilzad, pero esta vez esperaba que tomara la mitad de tiempo, seis semanas después de las próximas elecciones del 15 de diciembre.

Bush dio su tercer discurso sobre Irak, en Filadelfia, el 12 de Diciembre. Esta vez respondió preguntas de la audiencia, de personas comunes que no habían sido previamente seleccionadas.

Se le formuló la primera pregunta: "Me gustaría saber el total aproximado de iraquíes que han muerto desde el inicio de la guerra. Me refiero a civiles, militares, policías, insurgentes y traductores".

"¿Cuántos ciudadanos iraquíes han muerto en esta guerra?", respondió el presidente. "Diría que 30.000, más o menos, han muerto como resultado de la incursión inicial y la violencia actual contra los iraquíes. Hemos perdido unos 2.140 miembros de nuestras tropas en Irak". Los números eran sorprendentes, como lo era el hecho de que Bush tuviera la cifra casi exacta de los estadounidenses, 2.144, justo en la punta de la lengua.

El Comité Consultivo de Política de Defensa, el grupo externo de alto nivel asesor de Rumsfeld, que incluía a Kissinger, Newt Gingrich y Ken Adelman, se reunió en el Pentágono durante dos días para presentar sus informes a puerta cerrada. El primer día, Ryan Henry, un alto delegado de Rumsfeld, presentó la Revisión de Defensa Cuadrienal, una estrategia detallada para los militares de Estados Unidos que cubriría los próximos 20 años. Rumsfeld pensaba que era uno de sus mayores logros: un plan para el futuro. A la mitad de una larga presentación de PowerPoint con diapositivas y gráficos, Henry hizo una pausa. "La buena noticia es que no tendremos que hacer recortes en el programa de defensa", dijo.

"¿Y por qué es una buena noticia?", interrumpió Adelman. Las interrupciones no eran habituales. "Después de revisar los cuatro años siguientes al inicio de la guerra al terrorismo, después del 9/11, después de que el mundo ha cambiado, ¿no hay ni un solo programa que se pueda eliminar?".

Henry dijo que todos en el Departamento de Defensa, los civiles y los uniformados, habían decidido que no había que eliminar nada.

"Perdón por la interrupción", dijo Adelman, "pero me cuesta trabajo creerlo".

Al día siguiente el comité se reunió con Rumsfeld, que estaba orgulloso de la profunda revisión, que incluía planes para aumentar en un 15% las Fuerzas de Operaciones Especiales y añadir sofisticados programas para la lucha contra el terrorismo y el manejo del tema de las armas de destrucción masiva.

"Creo que Ken tiene una visión diferente", dijo Chris Williams, un contratista de defensa y cabildero que, además, era el presidente del comité. Disentir no era algo usual.

"¿Cómo?", le preguntó agriamente Rumsfeld al hombre que había querido manejar su campaña presidencial 20 años atrás.

Adelman, exasperado, dijo que después de cuatro años de trabajo, después del 9/11, y de todos los esfuerzos para hacer una transformación, y una vez que Rumsfeld había dedicando casi la cuarta parte de su tiempo a la Revisión de Defensa Cuadrienal, y el delegado casi la mitad de su tiempo, le parecía "increíble que no se vaya a eliminar nada".

"¿Quién le dijo eso?".

Al principio Adelman no quería señalar a Ryan Henry, y dijo que seguramente no había entendido bien.

"¿Quién dijo eso?", presionó Rumsfeld.

"Ryan Henry, sentado justo allí, nos lo dijo", dijo Adelman, señalando a Henry, que estaba sentado en la parte de atrás.

"La revisión no ha terminado", dijo Rumsfeld.

"Discúlpeme, pensé que ya estaba lista para imprimir".

"Bueno, el presidente no le ha dado el visto bueno".

"Si va a imprimirse", dijo Adelman, "ya sea que el presidente la apruebe o no, aún falta bastante para eso".

"Muy bien", lo desafió Rumsfeld. "Asumiendo que no se eliminará nada".

"Creo que es asombroso", dijo Adelman. "El mundo ha cambiado por completo. Se suponía que esto iba a ser el nuevo Pentágono".

Rumsfeld contemplaba a Adelman, evidentemente furioso. Decía que todos en el Departamento habían estado de acuerdo. "Todos coincidimos", añadió. "A veces no es necesario eliminar nada".

Una hora después, el comité de política conversaba acerca de los informes que había recibido de Abizaid y Casey. Los dos decían que estaban progresando en Irak y que las cosas parecían ir bien.

"De nuevo creo que Ken tiene una opinión diferente", dijo William.

"¿Cómo?", preguntó Rumsfeld.

Adelman dijo que Casey informaba que al personal militar, oficiales y soldados, se le rotaba fuera de Irak cada nueve meses o menos, en promedio. "En la historia, no conozco una guerra de contrainsurgencia que haya sido ganada por un país que rote su gente cada seis o nueve meses".

"No estamos rotando a toda nuestra gente", dijo Rumsfeld. "Tenemos a Casey allá".

"No me refiero a eso", dijo Adelman. "Hablo sobre la gente".

"Permítame explicarle la razón de eso", respondió Rumsfeld, y describió los procesos de reclutamiento y promoción del Ejército y la Armada.

"No me refiero a lo que quieren hacer el Ejército y los *marines*", dijo Adelman. "De lo que hablo es de ganar la guerra. No conozco ninguna guerra de contrainsurgencia que pueda ganarse con una estrategia como esa".

"Bueno, creo que está equivocado, porque muchos de los soldados regresan al teatro para una segunda ronda", le dijo Rumsfeld.

"¿Qué quiere decir con teatro?", le preguntó Adelman.

"El teatro CENTCOM".

"Ah, entonces, regresan a Afganistán. No es a eso a lo que me refiero".

"Bueno, algunos regresan a Irak".

"Muy bien. ¿Pero alguno de ellos regresa al vecindario donde estuvo antes?".

"Casi nunca", respondió con sinceridad el secretario.

"Bueno, ese es mi punto".

"¿Cuál es su punto?".

"Tienen que saber con quién van a desquitarse", dijo Adelman. "Deben saber con quién van a tratar, a quién van a manipular, es un camino difícil. Eso toma tiempo. En seis meses no saben nada. ¿En nueve meses?".

Rumsfeld retorció la cara. Citó un estudio reciente que mostraba que la mayoría de las bajas ocurrían en los primeros meses.

"Eso refuerza mi punto", dijo Adelman.

"Es cierto", admitió Rumsfeld.

GINGRICH DIJO que aunque se había invertido una fortuna en personal ejecutivo para la estrategia de la Revisión de Defensa Cuadrienal, "nada de eso importaba".

Rumsfeld lo miró incómodo.

"Lo único que importa es Irak", continuó el ex vocero. Dijo que la medida de la seriedad fueron los 132 días necesarios para pasar del embajador Negroponte al embajador Khalilzad. Irak sólo era "el país más importante en el mundo, alrededor del cual gira toda la política exterior de Estados Unidos", añadió sarcásticamente.

Después de la reunión, Adelman se encontró con Rumsfeld en el vestíbulo del Pentágono. Rumsfeld le indicó que quería conversar con él más detenidamente.

"Nos vemos", le dijo Adelman.

ENTRE BASTIDORES, el 13 de diciembre, los altos funcionarios del Comité para la Seguridad Nacional aprobaron un documento clasificado de 10 reglas y principios guía para aplicar en la formación del nuevo gobierno iraquí. Los ministros del nuevo gobierno no deberían tener ningún tipo de relación con las milicias o con potencias extranjeras como Irán o Siria. Los nuevos ministros deberían tener hojas de vida impecables. El nuevo gobierno debía formarse rápidamente pero no a expensas de la calidad; el ministro del petróleo, por ejemplo, debería tener una trayectoria en esa industria.

En otras palabras, Estados Unidos seguiría decidiendo acerca del soberano gobierno de Irak.

En su cuarto discurso sobre Irak, al día siguiente, 14 de diciembre, en el Centro Woodrow Wilson en Washington, Bush dijo: "Cuando se escriba la historia de estos días, ella dirá cómo Estados Unidos defendió una vez más su propia libertad transformando amargos adversarios en fuertes aliados por medio de la libertad".

EL DÍA DE LAS ELECCIONES en Irak, el 15 de diciembre, unos 11 millones de personas votaron para elegir a los miembros de la Asamblea Nacional, que ejercería por un periodo de cuatro años. Era un incremento del 70%, mucho mayor que en la mayoría de las democracias occidentales.

"Hay un gran júbilo", dijo el presidente.

Al día siguiente el titular de la primera página de *The New York Times* fue: "Los iraquíes, incluso sunitas, votan en grandes cantidades en un día tranquilo". Bush estaba emocionado. Durante una reunión con el embajador iraquí para las Naciones Unidas, el embajador afirmó, "Creo que fue un momento decisivo", y añadió exageradamente, "y el comienzo del fin del terrorismo en Irak".

Pero la violencia continuó, con más de 2.500 ataques de los insurgentes durante diciembre, de acuerdo con los informes clasificados.

En una reunión en la Sala de Situaciones, Rumsfeld señaló, "Ya no tendremos más elecciones".

TRES DÍAS DESPUÉS de las elecciones, el 18 de diciembre, el presidente pronunció un discurso por televisión, en horario, estelar desde el Salón Oval. Después de resaltar el éxito aparente de las elecciones, rescató su historia de la guerra, empezando por la decisión de invadir, el derrocamiento de Saddam, y el tema de las armas de destrucción masiva; admitió que "no encontramos esas armas".

Mientras la guerra continuaba, reconocía que muchas personas argumentaban que Estados Unidos estaba "creando más problemas de los que podía resolver" al quedarse en Irak. Negó este punto de vista. "El derrotismo puede tener sus partidarios, pero los hechos no lo justifican", dijo Bush y añadió: "Retirarse antes de la victoria sería un acto de imprudencia y deshonor que no voy a permitir".

Hacia el final de su discurso, Bush agregó un mensaje dirigido a "aquellos de ustedes que no apoyan mi decisión de enviar tropas a Irak: He oído su inconformidad, y sé lo profunda que es. Sin embargo, sólo hay dos opciones para nuestro país: la victoria o la derrota. Y la necesidad de victoria es más grande que cualquier presidente o partido político, porque está en juego la seguridad de nuestro pueblo. No espero que apoyen todo lo que yo hago, pero esta noche les pido algo: No pierdan la esperanza y no se rindan en esta lucha por la libertad.

"De igual modo, los estadounidenses pueden esperar algunas cosas de parte mía. Mi responsabilidad más seria es la de proteger nuestra nación, y eso requiere que yo tome algunas decisiones difíciles. Veo las consecuencias de esas decisiones cuando miro a hombres y mujeres que nos sirven, que no pueden dejar sus camas de hospital, pero sacan fuerzas para mirarme a los ojos y decirme que lo volverían a hacer. Veo las consecuencias, cuando hablo con los padres que extrañan tanto a un hijo, pero me dicen que él amaba ser soldado, que creía en su misión y que debo terminar el trabajo.

"Sé que algunas de mis decisiones han ocasionado pérdidas terribles, pero ninguna de esas decisiones ha sido tomada a la ligera. Sé que esta guerra es controversial, pero ser su presidente implica hacer lo que creo que es correcto, y aceptar las consecuencias. Y nunca he estado más convencido que las acciones de Estados Unidos en Irak son esenciales para la seguridad de nuestros ciudadanos, y que establecerán los cimientos para la paz de nuestros hijos y nietos".

Raramente había sonado tan sombrío.

En la reunión del CNS del 21 de diciembre de 2005, se presentó al presidente el documento con las reglas para la formación del nuevo gobierno. "Una cosa es influir en los votantes durante una elección", dijo Bush, refiriéndose a su clara decisión de tratar de no influir en los resultados de la elección del 15 de diciembre, "y otra cosa es influir sobre la formación del gobierno". Dejó claro que quería ser parte de ello, y miró al embajador Khalilzad, que participaba a través de video desde Irak. "Zal, tenemos que trabajar con los británicos, no para imponer resultados o escoger nombres, sino para dar forma a los resultados". Esos resultados debían ser consistentes con los principios. Era una diferencia sutil: dar forma a un resultado pero no imponerlo. Después de más de dos años y medio en guerra, era claro que Bush y los demás no iban a permitir que el poder en Irak cayera en manos de alguien inaceptable para ellos.

La discusión se trasladó al calibre de las personas que estarían disponibles en Irak, y de nuevo se expresó la frustración general acerca de la ausencia de un Washington o un Jefferson, sin hablar de un John Adams o figuras menos notables. Había demasiada corrupción. Eso era un gran obstáculo. Coincidieron en que la ausencia de corrupción debía quedar incluida en su lista de reglas para Irak. Debían encontrar ministros que no tuvieran antecedentes de corrupción.

"Muy bien", dijo Bush, "agreguen la corrupción a esta lista de principios y luego, Zal, utiliza tu influencia para que sea una realidad".

El problema quedaba completamente sobre los hombros del embajador. El presidente sería su supervisor.

"Tienes que ser astuto con esto, Zal", continuó Bush. "Tienes que darte cuenta de las cosas que los sunitas consideran suficientes para declarar exitoso el proceso, sin hacérselo demasiado difícil a los kurdos y a los chiítas como para que el proceso se fracture".

Era otra orden sonora. Bush quería negociaciones contundentes. Zal podía amenazar con eliminar la ayuda de Estados Unidos, o lo con lo que fuera necesario. Sólo debía solucionarlo.

El equipo del CNS de Hadley preparaba un informe de la situación para el presidente todas las mañanas; invariablemente, el primer asunto era Irak y las bajas. En noviembre, 88 miembros de las tropas estadounidenses fueron asesinados; en diciembre lo fueron 67. También había un informe de la situación, disponible al medio día y en la noche.

Pero el sube y baja de la tasa de ataques, probablemente la mejor medida del nivel de violencia y amenaza, era difícil de predecir. En octubre había sido de 3.000, bajó a 2.100 en noviembre y luego se disparó de nuevo a 2.500 en diciembre.

EL 1 DE ENERO DE 2006, Bush visitó el Centro Médico Brook del Ejército, en San Antonio, Texas, donde los doctores y las enfermeras habían tratado a 2.300 caídos en Afganistán e Irak. Era la trigésimocuarta ocasión en que Bush iba a visitar a los heridos.

Encontró un joven soldado que tenía el 99% de su cuerpo quemado, y permaneció sin habla por unos 30 segundos. Después Bush les dijo a sus asistentes, "Nunca creí que fuera posible que, como el hombre más poderoso del mundo, yo no tuviera nada que pudiera decir". Luego se sentó a orar con la familia del soldado, les agradeció por su servicio y se marchó, asombrado por la entereza de la familia.

Después habló con un grupo de periodistas. Tenía una herida menor en su frente, después de podar árboles en su rancho, y de manera inapropiada dirigió la atención hacia su herida.

"Como podrán ver, me lastimé, no en el hospital sino durante el combate con un cedro. Eventualmente gané. El cedro me causó un pequeño rasguño". Un médico militar le preguntó si necesitaba primeros auxilios, y Bush le dijo: "He sido capaz de evitar cualquier cirugía mayor aquí".

La oficina del médico de cabecera de la Casa Blanca, el Dr. Richard J. Tubb, general de una estrella en los cuerpos médicos de la Fuerza Aérea, le hizo seguimiento a los heridos que el presidente había conocido, para enviarles notas personales o llamarlos por teléfono. Poco después, Tubb le avisó a Bush que el soldado que había visto en el hospital de San Antonio había muerto.

Fue un duro golpe para el presidente. Dan Bartlett, su director de comunicaciones, pudo notar la angustia de Bush. Pero Bush y los demás en la Casa Blanca evitaban tener que admitir públicamente que el presidente se sentía atormentado de alguna manera. Creían que una revelación como esa sugeriría que él tenía dudas.

Sin embargo, durante las visitas a los heridos, en varias ocasiones los familiares confrontaban al presidente.

"¿Lo ve?", dijo un familiar, señalando a un soldado mutilado en la cama de un hospital. "No vale la pena".

"Usted puede detener esto", le dijo otro.

"Sólo usted puede detener esto", le dijo alguien en una tercera ocasión.

"Comprendo por qué se sienten así".

"UNO NO PUEDE AYUDAR pero sale sintiéndose...", dijo Rumsfeld en una entrevista, recordando sus visitas a los hospitales militares, "se lo voy a poner en orden de prioridad: inspirado, fortalecido. Y uno se siente así porque los heridos están, en su mayoría lo están, ansiosos por regresar a sus unidades, orgullosos de lo que han hecho, confiados en que podrán sobrevivir a las lesiones de una manera u otra. En el caso de la pérdida de una pierna, es como regresar a la escuela de saltos, obtener el primer lugar de la clase y regresar a Irak. Entonces, uno sale inspirado y fortalecido, con seguridad. Uno no puede ayudarles, pero ve estos maravillosos seres humanos y el daño inflingido a sus cuerpos, y puede no entender la dificultad para atar una corbata o ponerse una camisa o hacer las cosas más simples".

"¿Entonces, se siente angustiado?", le pregunté.

"Claro que sí".

"¿En esos momentos?".

"Por supuesto. Por Dios. Nadie puede no sentirse así, es lo que pienso", respondió. "Uno sale de allí, se sube al auto y habla acerca de conocer a esas personas, los soldados, marineros y *marines*, sus familias, y de lo inspiradores que son, y sobre lo diferentes que son, y, aun así, lo casi predecible que es su orgullo por el servicio. Somos muy afortunados de tener personas así".

Le pregunté si alguna vez los heridos o sus familias lo habían encarado.

"Claro, claro".

"¿Qué le dijeron?".

"No voy a discutir las conversaciones privadas", dijo Rumsfeld. "Pero señalaron su desacuerdo con el conflicto en Afganistán o en Irak. Descontento personal".

¿Qué les responde?, pregunté.

"Cielos. Están pasando por un momento de sus vidas en el que algo que han amado y cuidado es destruido, de una manera que no habrían podido anticipar. Uno puede entender que cualquier persona en esas circunstancias estará agitada emocionalmente, y depende de cómo se acerque uno a ellos".

"¿Y eso no le hace preguntarse por qué sigue haciendo este trabajo?", pregunté.

"No", dijo Rumsfeld. "Hay cosas que me hacen cuestionarme, pero no a tal punto".

"¿Cuáles son esas cosas?", le pregunté.

"No voy a hablar sobre eso", dijo con incomodidad.

Dijo que visitar a los heridos en los hospitales militares es parte de trabajo del secretario de Defensa. "Así ha sido históricamente. Lo entendí desde mi anterior trabajo aquí. Lo entiendo hoy. Entonces, no pienso que sea algo por lo que deba tirar la toalla o algo así".

41

El 23 se diciembre de 2005, el Fondo Monetario Internacional aprobó US $685 millones para Irak. Casi tan importante como el dinero era el hecho de que el FMI hubiera determinado que la tasa de cambio iraquí era estable, que la inflación era baja, que estimara el crecimiento económico en 2,6%, y que sus perspectivas en el mediano plazo fueran "favorables". Eran excelentes noticias, aunque el FMI exigía que Irak alcanzara cierto nivel de ingresos y otros temas.

No obstante, poco después, en enero de 2006, Bush y el CNS enfrentaron una nueva crisis. Las exportaciones de petróleo de Irak, el salvavidas económico del país, cayeron alrededor de un 20% con respecto al año anterior. La caída significaba que el gobierno iraquí se enfrentaba a una reducción de 2.000 a 3.000 millones de dólares para el primer trimestre, incluso con los precios del petróleo en alza. La reducción pondría inmediatamente en riesgo su situación frente al FMI, e iniciaría potencialmente una reacción en cadena. En el equipo del CSN, Meghan O'Sullivan examinaba las cifras detalladamente. Eran tan malas que se pondría en entredicho la viabilidad misma del gobierno. Irak no sólo estaba perdiendo los ingresos del petróleo que no estaba exportando, sino que, además, tenía que importar combustible para cubrir el faltante. Era como importar arena al desierto. El petróleo era la gallina de los huevos de oro de Irak, pero los ataques de los insurgentes y el deterioro de la infraestructura puso al país al borde de un ciclo económico increíblemente negativo. A pesar de todo lo que se había dicho antes acerca de "momentos decisivos", estaban en un verdadero momento crítico. Todo podía colapsar.

O'Sullivan y el grupo de iniciativas para Irak de Jeffery se reunieron, al igual que los delegados del comité. Finalmente, Andy Card se unió a la discusión en una reunión de altos funcionarios. Las causas de la caída de las exportaciones de petróleo incluían el mantenimiento irregular de las refinerías, el mal clima en el sur, la inadecuada capacidad de almacenamiento, los ataques de los insurgentes y las redes de delincuentes dentro de los ministerios iraquíes.

Los iraquíes debían asumir seriamente la responsabilidad, afirmaba Rumsfeld. Si lo hacemos por ellos, nos lo permitirán, y de nuevo aumentará nuestra misión. El plan era darles más responsabilidad a los iraquíes. ¿Cómo podrían los militares de Estados Unidos proteger miles de kilómetros de tuberías?

Rice estaba en desacuerdo. Dijo que una parte clave de la estrategia de contrainsurgencia incluía proteger el salvavidas económico de Irak, el flujo de petróleo. Esto, a su vez, afectaba la electricidad. Ahora en Bagdad, a menudo, tenían sólo dos o tres horas diarias de electricidad.

También había corrupción. El petróleo estaba siendo robado. El ministro iraquí de petróleo pagaba varias veces lo que debería pagarse por las bombas y otros equipos petroleros, y se estaban robando la diferencia. A ello había que agregar los ataques de los insurgentes contra los oleoductos y otras instalaciones, más la decrépita condición de la infraestructura, con sus tuberías goteantes y bombas dañadas, y era un desastre. Al menos en un caso, parecía ser que los mismos iraquíes que vigilaban un oleoducto lo habían atacado, o al menos permitieron que otros lo atacaran, para conseguir un contrato de vigilancia más grande.

El teniente general Gene Renuart, ahora director de la división de planes y políticas del Estado Mayor Conjunto, dijo: "Si uno necesita las líneas y las plantas eléctricas, allí hay corrupción. ¡Ese es el problema: hay demasiada corrupción!".

Rice arreció. "Usted sabe que ese país ha visto corrupción por miles de años", dijo. "Probablemente seguirá viendo corrupción por miles de años más. No puedo solucionar lo de la corrupción, pero usted sí puede solucionar en parte lo de la seguridad".

Hubo un silencio mortal. Este tema había quedado sobre la mesa. ¿Dónde estaba la seguridad? ¿Qué tipo de país estaban tratando de arreglar?

Los militares estaban invadiendo agresivamente los escondrijos de los insurgentes, y tenían unos 15.000 detenidos. Los altos funcionarios discutían si, en realidad, se estaba logrando algo con las incursiones. No hubo conclusiones después de un largo debate.

Card se sentía tocado por la tensión entre Rice y Rumsfeld. No era algo nuevo, pero tenía un lado más agudo. Se inclinaba a coincidir con Rice. Era cierto que había que ayudar a los iraquíes a superarse tanto como fuera posible, pero no podían permitir que el salvavidas económico fuera puesto en riesgo. No se podía despilfarrar los recursos del petróleo.

Como siempre, el debate se dirigió a las preguntas que permanecían sin respuesta:

¿Cuál es el papel de Estados Unidos en Irak? ¿Cuánto les estamos dejando a los iraquíes? ¿Cuánto los estamos ayudando? ¿Hasta dónde llega nuestra responsabilidad? El presidente nunca había tomado una decisión, a pesar de que el debate había estado endureciéndose durante tres años. ¿Qué modelo era aplicable a Irak y a la misión de Estados Unidos? ¿El del niño víctima de abuso de Hadley? ¿O el modelo darwiniano de libre empresa de Rumsfeld, de dejar fracasar a los iraquíes? ¿Vencería la visión intermedia de Rice? ¿En realidad, había una estrategia?

Bush asistió a una reunión del CNS sobre el asunto de las exportaciones iraquíes de petróleo. Rumsfeld de nuevo argumentó que eso era trabajo de los iraquíes. Lo podían hacer, dijo. Sólo hay que decirles que lo hagan. Pero no había entrenamiento específico para dar seguridad a los oleoductos y el resto de la infraestructura petrolera, por lo que tomaría meses que los iraquíes quedaran listos para tomar el control de la seguridad de la misma.

Rice dijo que no había tiempo que perder. La seguridad era tan crucial para todo lo que pretendían hacer en Irak, que debía ser un componente explícito de la misión militar estadounidense.

Bush expresó posteriormente a Card su frustración por estar siendo absorbido por los detalles de este asunto.

Rumsfeld estaba completamente de acuerdo. "Esto no es un asunto presidencial", le dijo a Card. "No se le debe quitar tanto tiempo con esta cuestión. Nosotros podemos solucionarlo".

Rice seguía presionando. Ella se había quedado sola en esto, y quería al presidente a su lado. Era allí donde tenía que estar. Además, si Bush no se involucraba, le daba carta blanca a Rumsfeld.

El presidente asistió a otra reunión del CNS, para la presentación de un informe sobre la seguridad de la infraestructura petrolera de Irak, de la que participaban el general Casey y Khalilzad. Al final, el presidente se dirigió a Khalilzad en la pantalla de video. "Mira, todos tenemos que coincidir en que esto es inaceptable".

Era lo único en lo que todos estaban de acuerdo.

"Zal", continuó el presidente, "necesito que hagas un plan para que los iraquíes arreglen el problema. No se cuáles sean las respuestas, pero necesito que pienses de otra manera. Tenemos que arreglar esto".

Khalilzad y el general Casey dijeron que asumirían la responsabilidad del nuevo plan.

Hadley y O'Sullivan tomaron en serio la orden del presidente. También tenían que "pensar de otra manera". Lo que habían estado haciendo no funcionaba. Pero no había funcionado por casi tres años, y nunca se había prohibido el pensamiento creativo. En cambio, para ese momento de febrero de 2006, todos entraron en crisis. Se preparó una serie de conferencias para que Hadley pudiera conversar extensamente con Bagdad, con la embajada y el comando del general Casey. Entraba en tantos detalles, profundizaba tanto y solicitaba tanta información, que, a menudo, las conferencias no eran con Casey y Khalilzad sino con sus delegados. El asesor para la seguridad nacional de Irak se convirtió, en efecto, en el gerente de la producción de petróleo en Irak.

Card notó lo incómodo que era para Hadley tratar de conciliar las posiciones de Rice y Rumsfeld. No estaba seguro de que Hadley lo pudiera lograr. Después de semanas de trabajo, Hadley presentó un plan que, al menos sobre el papel, parecía integrar las seis partes principales. Un nuevo componente era la propuesta de crear elementos de reparación rápida que pudieran arreglar con prontitud casi cualquier daño ocasionado por los insurgentes, una idea que el gobierno de Colombia había utilizado en su lucha contra los insurgentes de las FARC.

Estas unidades de reparación se denominarían Batallones de Infraestructura Estratégica y estarían conformados principalmente por fuerzas tribales iraquíes que vivían cerca de los oleoductos. Como existía evidencia de que estos batallones habían tenido complicidad en los ataques, se llevaría a cabo un nuevo esfuerzo de reentrenamiento y evaluación. Además, las fuerzas de Estados Unidos y las fuerzas regulares de Irak estarían instaladas o asociadas con las unidades tribales para aumentar su efectividad y hacerles seguimiento.

Los otros componentes incluían: reforzar físicamente los oleoductos; hacer que los oleoductos tuvieran capacidad de recuperación y que fueran redundantes, con algunas tuberías secundarias que correrían a lo largo de las principales; erradicar la corrupción de los ministerios de petróleos y energía eléctrica, y mejorar la coordinación de la inteligencia. Solicitarían una adición presupuestal de US $250 millones para financiar este plan.

Hadley pidió que Rumsfeld y Rice presentaran su informe por separado. El plan se presentó como lo que un funcionario denominó "una estrategia totalmente coordinada, integrada, revisada, y con múltiples herramientas para ayudar a los iraquíes a que solucionen este problema".

Rumsfeld parecía satisfecho porque el plan incluía apoyo a los iraquíes para encontrar una solución propia. "No podemos resolver esto por ellos, pero podemos ayudar a que ellos lo hagan".

Casi tres años después de la invasión y dos años después de la transferencia de soberanía, la administración seguía trabajando en los mismos asuntos.

El general Chiarelli, comandante de la 1ª División de Caballería del Ejército, de 2004 a 2005, que había impresionado al consejero de Rice en el Departamento de Estado, Philip Zelikow, se había convertido en el principal defensor uniformado de la reducción del uso de la denominada estrategia militar coercitiva, con equipo y tropas armados hasta los dientes.

En un artículo publicado en el verano de 2005 en *Military Review*, una revista especializada de las Fuerzas Armadas, Chiarelli dijo que, durante tres décadas en el Ejército, se había formado para manejar tropas numerosas y unidades blindadas con el fin de encontrar el "punto de penetración" en las líneas enemigas. Ahora en Irak, decía, "el punto de penetración" consistía en que sus tropas conectaran una red de drenaje, construyeran una escuela o supervisaran unas elecciones democráticas de ese país. Él avizoró una presencia más amable y moderada, disparando y arrestando a unos pocos iraquíes, y derribando algunas puertas. A veces sonaba como si sus soldados actuaran como trabajadores de los Cuerpos de Paz.

Chiarelli recibió su tercera estrella y en enero de 2006 se convirtió en comandante de todas las fuerzas de tierra de Estados Unidos en Irak. Afirmó con convicción que Irak tenía una cultura de venganza y honor. Las desvergonzadas matanzas y capturas de insurgentes o sospechosos de insurgencia habían enajenado a los iraquíes, que luego se unieron a la insurgencia o la apoyaban. Como dijo Thomas E. Ricks, un colega del *Post* que había estudiado al Ejército y la contrainsurgencia, en su libro *Fiasco*, "La gente es la recompensa". Los militares estadounidenses se iban a dar cuenta de eso, por lo menos sobre el papel.

La mañana del miércoles 22 de febrero de 2006, las bombas derribaron y dejaron en ruinas la cúpula dorada de la mezquita de Askariya en Samarra, unos 100 kilómetros al norte de Bagdad. El ataque de uno de los lugares santos más sagrados para los chiítas había sido planeado cuidadosamente. Las milicias chiítas, especialmente las que estaban alineadas con Moqtada al-Sadr, se volcaron a las calles, lanzaron granadas y dispararon ametralladoras sobre, al menos, dos docenas de mezquitas sunitas en Bagdad, como retaliación. Tres imanes sunitas fueron asesinados y un cuarto secuestrado. Decenas de miles se alzaron. Se impuso un toque de queda diurno en Bagdad. El primer ministro Jafari condenó la violencia pero no criticó públicamente a Moqtada, quien lo había apoyado desde sus comienzos.

Bush apeló a la calma.

La inteligencia indicaba que Zarqawi era responsable. El general Casey tenía un problema adicional. Rumsfeld tenía una lista de cosas que podrían salir mal, y Casey, con ayuda de la embajada, había reunido una lista de eventos potencialmente catastróficos. Incluía una invasión de Irán o Siria, una interrupción de las exportaciones de petróleo y el asesinato de Sistani. La lista incluía santuarios religiosos, pero no aparecía la mezquita de Askariya. Significaba que no había sido vigilada. La bomba casi fue el punto de quiebre para los chiítas y su líder más prominente, Sistani. Rice pensaba que era improbable que Irak pudiera resistir otro ataque como ese.

Esto le planteaba de nuevo a Card la pregunta sobre Rumsfeld. No era claro hasta qué punto el Departamento de Defensa había planeado brindar protección frente a la violencia sectaria, de la que éste era un típico caso. Irak parecía estar al borde de una guerra civil.

En marzo de 2006, Rumsfeld invitó a seis asesores externos del Pentágono para que recibieran el informe del general Richard A. Cody, subjefe del Estado Mayor del Ejército, que acababa de regresar de Irak. Después del informe, los seis se reunirían con Rumsfeld. Entre los seis estaba Ken Adelman, cuya relación con Rumsfeld casi había terminado, y James Dobbins, de RAND Corporation.

Adelman le preguntó a Cody, un recio graduado de West Point en 1972 y experto aviador con 5.000 horas de vuelo, qué estaban midiendo para saber cómo iba la guerra. "¿Qué aspectos hay que medir para saber si estamos ganando o perdiendo?".

"Yo diría que tres", respondió Cody. "El primero es el número de civiles iraquíes asesinados en estos ataques de los insurgentes. El segundo es el número de unidades de información utilizable que obtenemos de los iraquíes, la inteligencia procesable. Y el tercero es el número de policías y militares iraquíes competentes". No tocó el conteo de cadáveres ni el número de ataques iniciados por el enemigo.

Poco después, Rumsfeld intervino. "Respondamos algunas preguntas", dijo. Adelman le hizo la misma pregunta que le hizo a Cody. "¿Qué indicador usaría para medir el éxito en Irak, para ganar la guerra?".

"Hay cientos", respondió Rumsfeld. "Es complicado que haya tantos".

Dobbins presionó a Rumsfeld para que diera el número de bajas de civiles iraquíes.

Rumsfeld dijo que no creía que los números fueran relevantes. "El país no se encuentra en guerra civil", dijo. "Si fuera una guerra civil, habría un gran número de refugiados".

Dobbins citó la afirmación del presidente de que 300.000 iraquíes habían muerto en los últimos tres años. Parecía consistente con las cifras clasificadas que todos habían visto. Eso era como 200 a la semana.

"Considerando que Irak es 15 veces más pequeño que Estados Unidos", dijo Dobbins, "los iraquíes han sufrido en los primeros tres años el equivalente al ataque del 9/11 todas las semanas. Usted puede imaginar el efecto traumático que tendría la repetición del ataque del 9/11 cada semana sobre la sociedad estadounidense ¿No cree que está teniendo un efecto similar sobre la sociedad iraquí?".

Rumsfeld rechazó esa perspectiva.

"Un momento", insistió Adelman. "Un antiguo jefe me dijo alguna vez que había que identificar tres o cuatro cosas, luego averiguar sobre ellas, y medirlas; de lo contrario, no se haría ningún progreso". El antiguo jefe era el mismo Rumsfeld, quien le había dado el consejo a Adelman 35 años antes, cuando trabajaba para él en la Oficina de Oportunidades Económicas. Adelman insistió ¿Cuáles son esas cosas?

Rumsfeld dijo que era tan complicado que no podría hacer una lista.

Adelman creía que eso significaba una completa falta de compromiso. Si Rumsfeld no aceptaba ningún criterio, no era posible señalar su fracaso con base en ninguna de tales cosas.

"Cientos", insistió Rumsfeld.

"Entonces, no tiene nada", dijo Adelman. Se fue tan disgustado como siempre. No había compromiso. Cuando él había sido asistente civil de Rumsfeld en la administración de Ford, lo único que éste tenía que hacer para ser una excelente secretario de Defensa era quejarse de Kissinger. Se convirtió en su principal ocupación, además de aplastar a la Unión Soviética y detener el SALT III, el tratado para la limitación de armas estratégicas.

Ahora, la tarea de Rumsfeld tenía un significado estratégico e histórico mucho mayor. El Pentágono, Rumsfeld y Bush, para no decir nada de la época en que vivieron, serían recordados bien fuera por haber ganado la Guerra de Irak, o por haberla perdido.

EL PRESIDENTE hacía seguimiento de los esfuerzos de Khalilzad para armar un nuevo gobierno. Era algo lento y tedioso. Reiteradamente Bush le recordaba a su embajador la gran frustración que había en Estados Unidos. La gente quería ver progresos en Irak, le dijo a Khalilzad, y era difícil mostrar progreso cuando había tantas disputas políticas alrededor de este nuevo gobierno.

Los iraníes empezaron a afirmar abierta y enfáticamente que Jafari era su candidato. Para Washington, el apoyo de Irán a Jafari era motivo suficiente para descartarlo. Además, nadie en el CNS podía recodar una ocasión en que Jafari hubiera asumido una posición decisiva acerca de algo.

Además, Jafari se apoyaba en Moqtada al-Sadr, quien lo había respaldado desde el inicio del proceso.

La irritación de Bush crecía. Le repetía a Card su *mantra*: "¿Dónde está el líder? ¿Dónde está George Washington? ¿Dónde está Thomas Jefferson? ¿Dónde está John Adams para hacerse sentir? Él ni siquiera tiene mucha personalidad".

En retrospectiva, Card quería que ampliaran su búsqueda entre los líderes de provincia o de las tribus, para ver si un Thomas Jefferson andaba por ahí. Ahora parecía que la mayor parte de los líderes iraquíes que habían favorecido la invasión no eran tan iraquíes, sino más bien exiliados que habían estado viviendo por largo tiempo en Europa o Estados Unidos. ¿Dónde estaban las historias sobre políticos de base exitosos?, se preguntaba Card.

A finales de marzo, el presidente Bush envió en secreto una carta personal al ayatolah Sistani, la primera que escribía directamente al líder chiíta. Sin referirse personalmente a Jafari, Bush decía que Estados Unidos quería trabajar con alguien que tuviera el apoyo de todos los iraquíes. La situación actual no cumplía esa condición. Bush decía que Estados Unidos quería trabajar con Sistani, quien hacía una excelente labor como conciliador. Normalmente, las cartas presidenciales eran escritas en inglés, para que el receptor las tradujera, pero la Casa Blanca la tradujo y envió el original en árabe para evitar ambigüedades y mostrar respeto. Sistani agradeció la carta y su contenido.

Dada la reacción de Sistani, Hadley y Rice concluyeron que Irán se había apresurado al apoyar a Jafari.

EL MIÉRCOLES 8 DE MARZO, antes de las 7 de la mañana, Andy Card caminó los cerca de 35 pasos que había entre su oficina de la esquina del ala oeste y el Salón Oval, para lo que sería una de las conversaciones más difíciles de su vida. Planeaba hablar sobre su salida voluntaria de su cargo.

La situación de la presidencia de Bush no era buena. Irak era un desastre. La plataforma política del presidente se estaba hundiendo, con su índice de aprobación por debajo del 40%, y cayendo. Diecisiete meses antes, en el fin de semana después de la reelección de Bush, Card había solicitado, sin éxito, más cambios en el equipo y el gabinete, incluida su propia renuncia. Desde entonces, se había concentrado en hacer que el presidente reemplazara a Rumsfeld, otra misión fallida.

El segundo aspecto estaba lleno de reveses. Un plan para reformar la seguridad social ni siquiera había visto la luz. El huracán Katrina había destruido Nueva Orleans, y el manejo presidencial de la crisis se había convertido en sinónimo de ineptitud. La nominación de la consejera de la Casa Blanca, Harriet Miers, a la Corte Suprema tuvo que ser retirada cuando los conservadores se rebelaron. *Scooter* Libby había sido acusado de perjurio en la investigación por filtraciones de la CIA.

El mes anterior, Cheney había protagonizado un escándalo al disparar accidentalmente en la cara a un amigo durante una expedición de caza en Texas, aventura que llevó la imagen del vicepresidente cargando una escopeta a las portadas de *Time* y *Newsweek*. La Casa Blanca también tuvo que dar explicaciones acerca de un trato controversial dado a una empresa de Dubai para que manejara varios puertos de Estados Unidos. Lo único positivo para Bush era que dos de sus candidatos conservadores para la Corte Suprema habían sido confirmados y se habían posesionado: el presidente de la Corte John Roberts y el magistrado Samuel Alito.

"El clamor por cambios no va a detenerse", le dijo Card al presidente mientras conversaban en el Salón Oval esa mañana, "y no debe temer cambiarme". La acumulación de problemas exigía una acción decisiva y visible del presidente.

"No, es algo estúpido", respondió el presidente. "Esa no es la forma".

"Bien, debería pensarlo", dijo Card. "Tiene que pensarlo". Era necesario un gran movimiento de personal. "Sólo hay unas cinco personas cuyos cambios le darían buena imagen. Don Rumsfeld, Karl Rove, Andy Card, Condi Rice, Dan Bartlett". El presidente no recibiría mucha aprobación por reemplazar a Bartlett, pues, muchas personas no sabían quien era. "Recibirá algo de aprobación si cambia a John Snow". Snow era el secretario del Tesoro, que recibía calificaciones tibias de casi todo el mundo. "No ganará aprobación por retirarlo, sino por poner a alguien más allí".

A Karl probablemente no lo podría tocar", dijo Card. Rove estaba siendo investigado por una discusión con un periodista de la revista *Time* en el caso de la filtración de la CIA, y nadie sabía si iba a ser acusado. "Hay una nube sobre él", continuó Card, "y como no se sabe hacia dónde soplará el viento, probablemente no podrá cambiar a Karl".

"Cambiar al secretario de Defensa es algo diferente". Los dos eran conscientes de los esfuerzos de Card en este frente. "No puede cambiar a Condi. Es la estrella de la administración". Pero, añadió, "me puede cambiar a mí". Habló con tristeza. "No habría una audiencia ante el Senado. El cambio se puede hacer durante la noche. No se necesita una confirmación. Nadie sería cuestionado por políticas anteriores o acciones futuras. Y Dan Bartlett es un consejero valioso, por lo que no sería aceptable que usted lo cambiara. Lo de Snow es como es, pero no representaría un verdadero cambio". El jefe de gabinete de la Casa Blanca sería un cambio de verdad.

"No, es absurdo. No", dijo Bush, despachando a Card. Se dirigió a Nueva Orleans para su décimo viaje desde el paso del huracán Katrina.

Dos días después, el viernes 10 de mayo, Card se dirigió de nuevo a Bush. "¿Ya lo pensó?, porque es lo correcto". Bush de nuevo lo alejó. Esa tarde la revista en línea *Slate* informó que Claude A. Allen, que había sido el principal asesor en política interna de Bush hasta cuando renunció el mes anterior, había sido arrestado por la policía en los suburbios de Maryland, por cargos en un extraño caso de defraudación a tiendas locales por más de US $5.000.

Bush llamó a Card a su casa a las 9:30 de la noche; tarde para el presidente. Quería una explicación detallada de lo que había ocurrido con Allen, de 45 años, uno de los favoritos del equipo, abogado y recientemente convertido al cristianismo. Allen era el asesor afroamericano de Bush de más alto rango en la Casa Blanca, y con frecuencia viajaba con el presidente. Card le contó que cuando Allen renunció el mes anterior les había dicho a él y a Harriet Miers que había un malentendido. Bush dijo que creía que la Casa Blanca había hecho lo correcto, que había manejado todo adecuadamente, pero se preguntaba cómo era posible que un alto funcionario de la Casa Blanca pudiera ser arrestado sin que el jefe de gabinete se diera cuenta.

"Bien, señor presidente, si esto le incomoda, es el momento perfecto para que me lo achaque. Acháquemelo todo a mí. Es perfecto".

"¡No! Eso es…". Bush ni siquiera terminó la oración. Estaba fuera de discusión.

A la mañana siguiente, el sábado 11, Card fue temprano a la Casa Blanca. Bush recibió su informe diario de inteligencia y después se reunió con Rumsfeld y el general retirado Montgomery C. Meigs, director de un programa del Departamento de Defensa de US $3.300 millones para derrotar los nuevos artefactos explosivos de fabricación casera cada vez más letales y avanzados de Irak. Los componentes y el entrenamiento para usarlos apuntaban cada vez más a Irán, uno de los giros más problemáticos en la guerra.

Después, Bush y Card conversaron de nuevo. El presidente dijo que estaba contrariado por la conversación de la noche anterior sobre Claude Allen, y con el comentario de Card.

"No se preocupe por eso", respondió Card. "En realidad, ese es el trabajo del jefe de gabinete. Si el asunto no se manejó como usted o el mundo creen que debió haberse manejado, eso es responsabilidad del jefe de gabinete. Entonces es perfectamente apropiado".

Esa noche, Bush y Card asistieron a la cena de Gridiron. En un discurso satírico, Bush se burló de que los medios hubieran sacado de proporciones el accidente de caza de Cheney. "Por Dios, cualquiera pensaría que le disparó a alguien o a algo".

Dos DÍAS DESPUÉS, el 13 de marzo, Card estaba de nuevo a solas con el presidente. "¿Ya pensó sobre este asunto?", le preguntó.

"No sé qué hacer", dijo el presidente.

"Bueno, el clamor sigue allá afuera", dijo Card.

"¿Hay algo nuevo sobre Karl?", preguntó con impaciencia Bush.

No había nada nuevo. Por razones prácticas y legales no podían averiguar mucho. Había preguntas que nadie de la Casa Blanca o la administración podían expresar de manera apropiada al fiscal, al Departamento de Justicia o, incluso, a Rove. El 15 de marzo, Card seguía presionando.

"¿Ya lo pensó?".

"Sí, he estado pensando en eso", respondió el presidente. "¿Qué piensa?".

"Bueno, en primer lugar no debería pedir mi asesoría acerca de esto. Debe hablar con alguien que lo aconseje sabiamente".

"Muy bien, ¿a quién sugiere?".

"Usted lo debe saber mejor que yo, pero va reunirse con Jim Baker más tarde hoy. Yo escucharía su consejo".

"Sí, él me dirá lo que piensa".

"Sí lo hará" dijo Card. "Creo que le dirá justo lo que piensa. Pregúntele a Jim".

"Lo haré, lo haré".

Normalmente, cuando Bush se reunía con Jim Baker o Henry Kissinger o uno de los viejos zorros, siempre tenía a Card a su lado o le resumía después lo que había sucedido. Pero esta vez no habría recapitulación.

Más tarde, esa noche, en su casa en Arlington, Virginia, Card le dijo a su esposa Kathi lo que había sucedido.

"Creo que el presidente tomó la difícil decisión pero aún no lo sabe", dijo.

EL 16 DE MARZO, el general Abizaid estaba en Washington para testificar ante la Comisión de Servicios Armados del Senado. Hizo un retrato cuidadoso pero optimista de la situación en Irak.

La senadora Elizabeth Dole, republicana de Carolina del Norte, atribuía a los medios noticiosos la idea de que Irak era un desastre. "Ahora, al conocer el gran progreso que se ha hecho y que continúa haciéndose, y todos los logros en Irak, es frustrante escuchar las notas de nuestros medios que a veces no ofrecen sino negatividad y pesimismo".

Abizaid era discreto, pero dijo que no creía que los medios de comunicación tuvieran ningún impacto negativo sobre la moral.

Después, fue a ver al congresista Murtha en el edificio de oficinas Rayburn. Sentado en la mesa redonda de madera oscura de la oficina de Murtha,

Abizaid, el comandante delegado de CENTCOM durante la invasión y principal general para la región desde el año 2003 —el único comandante militar que seguía íntimamente involucrado en Irak, desde el principio— le indicó que quería hablar con franqueza. Según Murtha, Abizaid levantó su mano y mostró su pulgar a una distancia de un cuarto de pulgada de su dedo índice y dijo "estamos así de cerca".

42

RICE QUERÍA QUE ZELIKOW regresara a Irak de nuevo en febrero de 2006, pero el bombardeo a la mezquita de Askariya y la crisis posterior hicieron que la gira se aplazara. Finalmente pudo viajar y le escribió a Rice un memorando SECRETO/NODIS de nueve páginas fechado el 18 de marzo.

Informaba que Irak se mantenía en un equilibrio precario. "Se ha reconstruido el ejército iraquí y la insurgencia ha sido contenida, pero el ritmo subyacente y la escala de los ataques de la insurgencia se han mantenido notablemente estables durante más de un año. Ninguno de los lados ha hecho un avance decisivo. El resultado es un prolongado equilibrio inestable". Todo el buen ambiente que se había logrado generar con las elecciones de diciembre de 2005 comenzaba a disiparse, y todos estaban preocupados de que el centro no pudiera seguir manteniéndose.

Zelikow argumentaba que los iraquíes tendrían que superar tres grandes pruebas en los meses siguientes: "establecer un gobierno verdaderamente nacional, contrarrestar la violencia en la comunidad y desarrollar un pacto de seguridad que permitiera a los chiítas y a los sunitas permanecer moderados, y permitir que el nuevo gobierno avance hacia un comienzo visiblemente prometedor".

Zelikow se preguntaba si Estados Unidos podría vivir con Jafari. Aunque no era la primera opción para nadie, Zelikow temía que pudieran llegar a verlo como una segunda opción aceptable. Hasta donde Zelikow sabía, Jafari era un incompetente. Pero era un político de pasillos, astuto y tenaz, que estaba dilatando de manera sorprendente los intentos de formar un nuevo gobierno. "Podríamos decir que hemos perdido confianza en la capacidad de Jafari para sacar al país de esta crisis actual, y que si continúa como primer ministro tendremos que revaluar, ante todo, nuestra posición y nuestra estrategia en Irak, porque ya no tendremos la confianza suficiente en que nuestras estrategias puedan tener éxito".

En otras palabras, había que echar a Jafari. Sería algo temerario y audaz. Era peligroso no igualar la apuesta en la política iraquí.

CARD AÚN INTENTABA que lo reemplazaran, cuando acompañó al presidente y a la primera dama a pasar un fin de semana en Camp David. Estaba el gentío usual formado por la familia y los amigos de Bush. Card trató sin éxito de hablar a solas con el presidente. No era que Bush tratara de evitar a Card; estaba evitando estar a solas con él. Siempre había alguien alrededor. Bush seguía diciendo "vamos a hablar", pero cada vez que Card trataba de hablar con Bush, alguien se sentaba cerca de ellos.

El domingo, Card se marchó de Camp David a las 5:30 de la mañana para poder asistir al servicio eclesiástico con su esposa.

"Me siento terrible", le dijo a su esposa en una llamada desde el auto. "No voy a poder ir a la iglesia. Me voy derecho a casa para meterme en la cama". Así lo hizo, y el lunes amaneció terriblemente enfermo. Sin embargo, llegó a la Casa Blanca a las 5:30 de la mañana. Hacia las 6:15, el doctor Tubb, médico de la Casa Blanca, le hacía un examen rápido a Card en su oficina.

"Tiene una gripe altamente contagiosa". Tubb dijo que era influenza B.

"Entonces me voy de aquí. Voy a casa. No quiero ver a nadie. No quiero ver al presidente. No quiero ver a nadie". Card reunió algunos papeles y se marchó a casa. Permaneció tres días allí.

"NUESTRA ESTRATEGIA ES OBTENER RESULTADOS", dijo Bush en su alocución del 18 de marzo desde Camp David. "Las evidencias de verdadero progreso" se perdían entre los informes noticiosos y las imágenes de violencia. "En los tres últimos años, los iraquíes han pasado de vivir bajo una tiranía brutal a tener libertad, soberanía, elecciones libres, un referendo constitucional, y en el mes de diciembre, elecciones para un gobierno completamente constitucional". Ninguno de estos avances había resuelto por sí mismo el problema de la seguridad ni los problemas básicos de política e infraestructura.

En una conferencia de prensa, el 21 de marzo, se le preguntó a Bush acerca de la declaración del ex primer ministro Allawi acerca de que todos los días estaban muriendo entre 50 y 60 iraquíes. "Si esto no es guerra civil, Dios sabrá lo que es una guerra civil", había dicho Allawi.

Bush dijo que no estaba de acuerdo. Otras voces, el líder kurdo Talabani, el general Casey, Khalilzad, lo veían de otro modo, señaló. "Los iraquíes lo pensaron y decidieron no ir a la guerra civil".

Esa mañana, en una población al norte de Bagdad, unos hombres armados se tomaron una estación de policía y un edificio de juzgados, asesinaron a 17 policías y liberaron, al menos, 20 prisioneros ¿Cuál fue su reacción?, le preguntaron a Bush. "Tenemos un plan para la victoria", respondió. "Soy optimista en cuanto a nuestra capacidad para conseguir la victoria".

¿Y qué pasaba con el mayor general retirado del Ejército Paul D. Eaton, quien había dirigido el entrenamiento de los militares iraquíes durante el primer año y del artículo de opinión publicado ese fin de semana en *The New York Times*, que llamó a Rumsfeld "incompetente estratégica, operacional y tácticamente" y pedía su renuncia?

"No", respondió Bush, "no creo que deba renunciar. Creo que está haciendo un buen trabajo". La instalación de tropas de Estados Unidos entre las iraquíes ha "sido un éxito".

Y así continuó, 7.484 palabras según la transcripción.

Card estaba de regreso en la Casa Blanca el jueves 23 de marzo, pero no fue sino hasta el final del día cuando encontró al presidente solo. Los dos hombres salieron caminando del Salón Oval hacia el Rose Garden. El día estaba nublado y fresco. "Señor presidente", le dijo, "la cuerda ya se acabó. Usted y yo lo sabemos". En una de sus síntesis menos elegantes, añadió "y en este momento la cuerda esta agitándose".

"¿Por qué? ¿Por qué dice eso?".

"Lo sé".

"No. No sé por qué lo dice".

"Bueno, la cuerda ya se acabó".

EL VIERNES 24 DE MARZO, Card acompañó de nuevo al presidente a Camp David. Finalmente Bush dijo lo que Card ya sabía. Probablemente había llegado el momento.

Fue triste. El fin de una era para los dos.

"No se preocupe", dijo Card, al darse cuenta de que era un momento emotivo para el presidente. "Esto es lo correcto. No se preocupe. Es el momento indicado", le dijo casi como un padre consolador. "No lo piense más. Es lo correcto, y puede hacerse con facilidad". Él también estaba muy conmovido. "Yo no habría escrito el libreto de esta forma, pero no era yo quien debía escribirlo".

Tomada la decisión, como si ya lo hubieran hecho antes, pasaron a preguntarse quiénes deberían saberla, en qué orden, y cuándo y cómo darla a conocer.

No iban a discutir el porqué. Como muchas de las decisiones de Bush, como la de invadir a Irak, había un momento culminante cuando los pasos grandes y pequeños convergían repentinamente. La renuncia de Card le daba a Bush un poco de tiempo. Necesitaba una nueva dirección.

El presidente dijo que Josh Bolten, director de la Oficina de Gestión y Presupuesto, había aceptado ocupar el lugar de Card. Aunque Card era el que había estado presionando, fue una sorpresa saber que Bush iba un paso adelante de él. Bolten, que había sido delegado de Card durante dos años, antes de ir a la oficina de presupuesto, tenía un título de Stanford en leyes y había trabajado para Goldman Sachs antes de unirse a la campaña de Bush en 1999 como director de políticas.

"Quisiera hacer el anuncio lo antes posible", dijo Card. "Por cortesía, quisiera decírselo a mis hijos, mis hermanos y tres amigos muy cercanos".

El martes en la tarde, Card voló a Cincinatti para dar un discurso largamente preparado en la cena del Día de Lincoln.

Ante casi 600 personas, Card se concentró principalmente en lo que había ocurrido el 14 de septiembre de 2001, tres días después de los ataques terroristas del 9/11, cuando Bush ordenó un cambio de dirección para el FBI, visitó la Zona Cero en Manhattan y estuvo con las familias de quienes murieron en los ataques.

La siguiente mañana, el martes 28 de Marzo a las 8:30, el presidente, Card y Bolten ingresaron al Salón Oval y anunciaron los cambios.

CARD TENÍA UN SENTIMIENTO de alivio mezclado con la sensación que le generaba saber que dejaba asuntos pendientes. Una de sus grandes preocupaciones era que se comparara a Irak con Vietnam. Había 58.249 nombres en el Monumento a los Veteranos de Vietnam, en Washington. Una de las críticas privadas de Henry Kissinger a Bush era que no tenía ningún mecanismo, ni siquiera la inclinación, para considerar las desventajas de las decisiones inminentes. Rara vez se consideraba las alternativas. Lo más cercano que Card podía recordar eran algunas discusiones informales e inocentes, en la línea de: "¿Qué cosas podríamos hacer de otra forma?". Pero nunca hubo sesiones formales para evaluar alternativas a la estadía en Irak. Hasta donde sabía, no hubo memorandos angustiosos con los nombres de Cheney, Rice, Hadley, Rumsfeld, la CIA, el mismo Card u otro, pidiendo que se examinaran alternativas, como se hizo después de la era de Vietnam.

Card le atribuyó la responsabilidad a los generales: Myers y Pace en el pentágono, y Abizaid y Casey en Irak. Si le hubieran dicho al presidente: "No vale la pena", o "No se puede cumplir la misión", tenía la certeza de que el presidente habría dicho, "No voy a pedir que se sacrifique a otro muchacho por esto".

Card era suficientemente realista para ver que existían dos aspectos negativos en la imagen pública de Bush, que habían llegado a definir su presidencia: incompetencia y arrogancia. Card no creía que Bush fuera incompetente. Tampoco creía que fuera arrogante. Pero la personalidad y presentación, el *marketing*, de Bush lo hacían ver arrogante. Tal vez era injusto y sin fundamentos, en opinión de Card, pero así era. Él se marchaba.

Y Rumsfeld, el mayor responsable de los problemas de la posguerra, el que debería marcharse, se quedaba.

"Es Irak, Irak, Irak", le dijo Card a Bolten. "Después está la economía". Como director de presupuesto y anterior delegado de Card, Bolten no se había involucrado con Irak. "Ya no se podrá dar ese lujo".

"Puedo contar con Steve", dijo Bolten.

"No puede hacer eso. No es justo con el presidente. Debe tomarse el tiempo necesario para estar informado. Y yo no lo podré mantener informado. Debe ser una nueva mirada. Ya he estado involucrado y tengo mis sesgos, pero usted deberá darle una nueva mirada porque el presidente necesita a alguien que le dé una nueva perspectiva".

"No quiero tener que ver con eso", dijo Bolten.

"No tiene opción".

En sus primeros días como jefe de gabinete, Bolten llamó a algunos de los altos funcionarios del gobierno de Estados Unidos que conocían Irak.

"¿En dónde estará Irak dentro de seis meses?", le preguntó a uno.

"Más o menos donde está hoy".

Desde el año 2005, hasta donde podían decir los asistentes de Rice y Rumsfeld, el vicepresidente Cheney ya no tenía un papel visible en el manejo de Irak. En el CNS y otras reuniones y discusiones, él tenía un mensaje para Rice: "Hay que ganar". Una vez le dijo: "Haga todo lo que pueda con todos los recursos de que dispone, para ganar. Es demasiado importante para la guerra contra el terrorismo. Es demasiado importante para nuestras políticas alrededor del mundo. No es algo que se pueda conseguir sin el máximo esfuerzo". Rice empezó a llamarlo "señor 100 por ciento". Había que esforzarse un 100% en Irak. Ella y Cheney estaban completamente de acuerdo.

Pero Cheney estaba perdido sin Libby; así lo creían muchos de los compañeros cercanos al vicepresidente. Libby hizo gran parte de la preparación para las reuniones y eventos del vicepresidente, y gran parte del trabajo duro. Había sido casi una parte del cerebro de Cheney.

A medida que las críticas al manejo que la administración le daba a Irak aumentaban, y la duda embargaba a muchos colaboradores débiles, Cheney le dijo a sus compañeros que eso sería una verdadera prueba para el liderazgo de Bush. Cheney dijo que había pocos políticos, incluso grandes líderes, que pudieran soportar la presión política. La mayoría sucumbía, pero Bush no lo había hecho, y Cheney decía que eso lo maravillaba.

Cheney confiaba más en los consejos de su esposa Lynne y su hija Liz. Ellas reforzaban su convicción de que estaba haciendo las cosas bien, y algunos de sus amigos más cercanos pensaban que Cheney cada vez estaba más ajeno a la realidad. Incluso, estaba convencido de que los dos traspiés de la administración, universalmente aceptados –el manejo del huracán Katrina y la nominación abortada de la consejera de la Casa Blanca Harriet Miers para la Corte Suprema de Justicia–, terminarían convirtiéndose en resultados positivos para Bush.

A Tony Blair, la Guerra de Irak cada vez lo afectaba más y le causaba problemas políticos graves. Le propuso a Bush que sus funcionarios más altos de política exterior viajaran juntos a Irak para presionar la formación del nuevo gobierno.

Bush compartía la impaciencia de Blair. ¿Qué estaba sucediendo? ¿Por qué estaban tardándose meses? Le comentó a Rice la idea de Blair, de que ella y el ministro británico de relaciones exteriores, Jack Straw, viajaran.

"Es demasiado", le dijo ella al presidente. "No me parece una buena idea". Fácilmente podía llegar a percibirse como intentar hacer una anotación de campo de 63 yardas en los segundos finales, algo desesperado.

Bueno, ellos estaban desesperados. Bush dijo que enviaría un mensaje fuerte. Y alguien tenía que ir a conversar sobre su creciente impaciencia.

Rice llegó a Inglaterra el 2 de abril para viajar secretamente a Irak en su avión con Straw. Él estaba enfermo, por lo que ella le cedió la única cama plegable y se acomodó en el piso, cerca de las bolsas para información clasificada, y durmió durante el viaje nocturno. Había una lluvia torrencial cuando llegaron, por lo que no pudieron ir en helicóptero a la Zona Verde. El equipo de Rice y la prensa se apretujaron dentro de grandes Rhinos, un tipo de vehículo Death Star blindado que parece un cruce entre autobús y tanque. Era un poco espeluznante saber que iban a viajar por la carretera BIAP –la llamada carretera de la muerte– hacia la ciudad.

"No se preocupen", bromeaba sarcásticamente Jim Wilkinson, recordando la famosa expresión de Cheney "nos darán la bienvenida con flores y dulces".

Rice y Straw iban en una camioneta blindada. Pronto quedaron atascados en el tráfico durante media hora en un punto de control, y el corazón del jefe de seguridad se aceleró. A medida que avanzaban, Rice y Straw trataban de descubrir lo que pasaba por la cabeza de Jafari. Iban a presionarlo. Durante el último año había estado a la deriva. Tenían que sacarlo. Los chiítas en la Asamblea Nacional lo habían apoyado por un solo voto, 64 a 63, y no contaba con ningún otro apoyo. Los kurdos, en particular, querían deshacerse de él.

Después, esa tarde, se encontraron a solas con Jafari. Querían un encuentro privado. Iba a ser una reunión tan difícil como la que diplomáticos extranjeros podrían tener con el líder de un gobierno soberano. Rice tenía algunas caricaturas iraquíes publicadas en la prensa de Irak que ridiculizaban y se burlaban del fracaso en la conformación del gobierno. Rice dijo que los iraquíes estaban muy frustrados. Los estadounidenses y el presidente Bush estaban muy frustrados e impacientes.

"Es tiempo de dar un paso al costado", le dijo ella a Jafari lisa y llanamente. Straw lo repitió. Señaló que los británicos también tenían un sistema parlamentario y explicó la importancia de conformar los nuevos gobiernos con rapidez, o, de lo contrario, la opinión pública se frustra ¿Tenían un gobierno? ¿Tenían líderes?

Jafari no se entregaría.

Después, en la presentación de un informe a la prensa, un periodista le preguntó a Rice lo que ella haría si no veía que un nuevo gobierno tomaba forma en cinco semanas.

"Le puedo asegurar que no voy a esperar cinco semanas", respondió.

MEGHAN O'SULLIVAN, la jefe de Hadley en Irak, acompañó a Rice en el viaje y se quedó después de que Rice y Straw se marcharon. Después, ella y Khalilzad pasaron tres horas con Jafari. Su mensaje era simple: de acuerdo con la Constitución iraquí, tiene que conformar un gobierno con el apoyo de otras comunidades –sunitas y kurdos–. No parecía contar con ese apoyo, entonces ¿cuál era su plan para avanzar?

Jafari dijo que creía que él tenía más apoyo que el que de las expresiones públicas en declaraciones y cartas.

El problema para Estados Unidos y el Reino Unido era que el apoyo de Jafari venía de los iraníes y del abominado Moqtada al-Sadr. Después del bombardeo de Samarra, del 22 de febrero, Jafari no fue lo suficientemente astuto para exigirle cuentas a Moqtada por sus ataques a los sunitas, que habían sido espantosos, sobre todo en Bagdad. La preocupación era que, si Jafari era elegido como primer ministro para cuatro años, se convertiría en el peón de Moqtada.

Después de tantos años de esfuerzo, un resultado como ese, un primer ministro comprometido con un señor de la guerra como Moqtada, era algo impensable.

NO IMPORTABA cuán malas fueran las noticias, había pocos tan buenos para reacomodar las cosas como Rumsfeld. En abril de 2006, seis generales retirados pidieron públicamente su renuncia, con base en sus equivocaciones sobre Irak, especialmente el fracaso para conseguir suficientes tropas. El martes 18 de abril de 2006, Rumsfeld apareció con el general Pace en unas de sus conferencias de prensa periódicas. Había mucha expectativa sobre su respuesta a la muy pública crítica, que había sido llamada "la revuelta de los generales".

"Buenas tardes amigos", comenzó Rumsfeld. "Una de las cosas interesantes de esta ciudad es que, hay tantas distracciones, que la gente a veces no se da cuenta de lo afortunados que somos".

"Hoy hace 64 años, Jimmy Doolittle llevó a cabo, contra todas las probabilidades, una incursión hostil sobre Tokio en los primeros días de la Segunda Guerra Mundial", dijo, y añadió que "también, hoy hace cien años, San Francisco quedó casi destruida por un terremoto".

Después de cinco minutos de esto, un reportero preguntó acerca de los generales retirados que habían dicho "que usted ha sido desatento y hasta desdeñoso de los consejos ofrecidos por los altos oficiales militares".

"Prefiero dejar pasar un tiempo antes de abordar eso", dijo Rumsfeld y añadió, como si los comentarios acerca de él fueran el problema de ellos, "No me inclino a emitir un juicio inmediatamente sobre eso".

"Señor secretario", intentó un periodista.

"Viniendo hoy al trabajo", continuó Rumsfeld con su lección de historia, "pensé en algo que ocurrió hace 30 años, creo que en este mes. Yo era secretario de Defensa". Describió en detalle cómo ignoró la recomendación del Ejército acerca de las armas y el motor del tanque M1.

"Bueno, parecía que el mundo se iba a acabar", continuó. "El cielo se iba a caer ¿Se imaginan lo que fue tomar esa decisión y romper una tradición de décadas en este país? ¿Pueden imaginar echar abajo lo que el servicio había propuesto para un tanque de guerra importante? Bueno, aparecía una y otra vez en la prensa, y fue toda una tempestad".

"Los involucrados eran buenas personas", añadió, "y habíandiferentes puntos de vista, y alguien tenía que tomar la decisión". Durante otros cinco minutos listó todos los cambios que había hecho en años recientes. Muchas de sus movidas personales habían levantado ampolla, dijo, como hacer comandante de la OTAN a un *marine* como el general Jones, o jefe de Estado Mayor Conjunto al general Pace. "Imaginen, un *marine* como jefe de Estado Mayor Conjunto, por primera vez en la historia ¡Hacer eso era algo sorprendente!", dijo Rumsfeld.

Un periodista trató de interrumpirlo con una pregunta.

"¡Me hicieron una pregunta y voy a tomarme todo el tiempo que quiera!", dijo Rumsfeld. Hubo risas.

"Pero creo que es importante reconocer que están sucediendo muchos cambios; esto es desafiante y difícil para la gente". Cuando se le volvió a preguntar acerca de las preocupaciones de los seis generales retirados, anotó:

"Tenemos unos 6.000 o 7.000 almirantes y generales… ¿Cómo puede esperarse que todos estén de acuerdo en algo?".

En otras palabras, era muy difícil ser secretario de Defensa con tantas fuerzas retardatarias apuntando en su contra. Después de la conferencia de prensa se reunió en privado con una docena de generales retirados, ninguno de los cuales había pedido su renuncia, y otros asesores externos. Se trataba de una reunión informal, no oficial.

Le preguntaron su opinión sobre el tamaño de las tropas utilizadas en el plan de guerra de Irak.

"El plan final de guerra requería que se aumentaran a 400.000 hombres", dijo Rumsfeld desde un extremo de la mesa. "Es correcto, ¿cierto Pete?".

"Sí, señor", respondió el general Pace desde el otro extremo.

"Entonces, el general Franks me llamó", relató Rumsfeld, "y dijo que detuviera el flujo de fuerza. Ya no necesitaba más". Franks era el comandante que combatía sobre el terreno, por lo que, dijo Rumsfeld, él había seguido las recomendaciones de sus generales.

Muy conveniente, pensó uno de los militares retirados, el mayor general William L. Nash, miembro del Consejo de Relaciones Exteriores. En la conferencia de prensa, Rumsfeld se había presentado a sí mismo como el agente de cambio audaz y decisivo. Pero al tratarse de una de las decisiones más importantes durante la guerra, Rumsfeld simplemente se sometió a la voluntad del general Franks.

43

Jafari finalmente dejó el camino libre el 20 de abril, y al día siguiente, el parlamento iraquí eligió por primera vez a su primer ministro permanente —un chiíta duro pero cerebral de 56 años llamado Jawad al-Maliki. La inteligencia de Estados Unidos sabía poco acerca de él. Había estado en el exilio durante 23 años, aparentemente yendo y viniendo entre Siria e Irán, como vocero del partido chiíta Al Dawa (La Llamada), y parecía que decía siempre lo correcto. Pero para los ojos occidentales, básicamente era un personaje anónimo del Dawa.

El presidente habló con Rice. Estaba consciente de la tensión entre Rice y Rumsfeld. Estaban saliendo de sus sendas: ella estaba mirando lo militar, y él lo político. "Creo que sería muy bueno si tú y Don lo aceptaran", dijo Bush. "Mostraría que tenemos lo militar y lo político realmente unido. Y yo podría escucharlo de ustedes dos. Si los dos se ocupan de las dos cosas podré enterarme simultáneamente".

Cuatro días antes, Rice y Rumsfeld estuvieron en Bagdad. Visitaron a Khalilzad en su residencia y se reunieron con Maliki a las 4 de la tarde del el miércoles 26 de abril. Maliki no saludaba de mano a las mujeres; cruzó el brazo extendido sobre su pecho y su corazón, el gesto común entre de los árabes. Maliki era un hombre de corta estatura, cuya calvicie le dejaba un característico mechón sobre la frente; no perdía el tiempo con palabrerías. Entendía el inglés, pero hablaba en árabe y tenía un traductor.

Su primer reto, de acuerdo con las notas de un estadounidense, era abordar la desconfianza sectaria entre chiítas, sunitas y kurdos. Su segundo gran desafío, dijo, era el terrorismo. "Si tengo éxito con el primero", dijo, "será un avance para lo del terrorismo".

Maliki dijo que en los tres primeros meses iba a tener que demostrar mejoras en los servicios. "La gente necesita energía", dijo refiriéndose a la energía eléctrica.

Acerca del tema de la seguridad, Maliki dijo: "Si me encuentro en la carretera, no me agrada ver a la policía". El no confiaba en la policía, y hasta indicó que procuraba pasar desapercibido por ella.

Rice dijo que lo entendía personalmente. Creció como una niña negra en la ciudad racialmente fragmentada de Birmingham, Alabama, a comienzos de los años sesenta, dijo. "Si la policía llegaba a mi vecindario, no nos sentíamos cómodos. Sentíamos temor". Durante los años sesenta, el comisionado para la seguridad pública de la ciudad era Bull Connor, un notable segregacionista que ordenaba atacar con chorros de agua y perros a quienes marchaban por los derechos civiles. "Una de las cosas más notables para mí fue regresar a Birmingham el año pasado y conocer a la mujer negra sucesora de Bull Connor. Estas cosas pueden cambiar". Ella no mencionó que en Alabama eso tardó décadas.

Maliki pareció conmoverse con esa imagen, y dijo que iba a tratar de restablecer el Ministerio del Interior, encargado de supervisar a la policía. "Hay muchos de ellos que no son malas personas", dijo. "Es que no están entrenados para el trabajo, y debemos ocuparnos de eso". Esperaba tener un plan de seguridad al que iba a llamar "Recuperación de Bagdad". Si el nuevo gobierno podía asegurar la capital, indicó, seguiría el resto del país. Dijo que como él se encargaría de seleccionar a los ministros, estos "serían ministros para Irak, no para un partido político".

Khalilzad estaba repasando enérgicamente su rosario, y Maliki lo notó y empezó a buscar el suyo. Lo encontró, lo sacó y pronto empezó a agitarlo.

En algún punto, dijo Rumsfeld, tendrían que hablar de las fuerzas de Estados Unidos. Fue en el contexto de la patrullas. No utilizó las palabras "partida" o "retirada", pero todos, incluso Malik, sabían lo que él quería decir.

El primer ministro designado miró al secretario de Defensa estadounidense como si estuviera loco. "Es demasiado prematuro hablar sobre eso", le dijo.

En una cena, esa noche, con los personajes iraquíes y estadounidenses clave, Maliki miró alrededor y dijo: "Este es el equipo que lleva sobre sus hombros la responsabilidad de nuestro país. Este equipo representa todos los elementos de la sociedad iraquí. Creemos en la unidad de Irak y vamos a trabajar en nuestra seguridad nacional".

"El éxito depende de ser competentes", le dijo a Rice. Durante la excesivamente larga discusión acerca del mensaje que querían enviar, dijo. "El mundo tiene los ojos sobre Irak", refiriéndose a la violencia en televisión y las grandes expectativas.

Posteriormente, Rice tuvo una reunión privada con Maliki. "Los iraquíes ya han tenido suficiente", le dijo Maliki, "y si no les podemos demostrar que podemos gobernar, no lo vamos a lograr. Todo se perderá si no podemos demostrar que podemos gobernar".

Rice se sorprendió. Era la primera vez que conocía a un líder iraquí que asumía el asunto como algo suyo y no se limitaba a preguntar qué iba a hacer Estados Unidos Ella comentó que hubo una época en la que la confianza del pueblo estadounidense había desaparecido como consecuencia de la Gran Depresión de los años treinta. El *New Deal* de Franklin Roosevelt había creado la impresión de que algo iba a ser diferente. El *New Deal* no mejoró las vidas de la gente de la noche a la mañana. Pero sentían que alguien se preocupaba. Sentían que había alguien completamente comprometido tratando de hacer lo necesario y trabajar con ellos. Fue un mensaje esperanzador de que alguien estaba a cargo y que la vida iba a ser diferente.

¿Qué sería la primera cosa que él podría hacer?, preguntó Maliki. ¿Sería llevar la electricidad? ¿O tratar de darle a la gente la sensación de que las cosas serían diferentes?

Rice estaba impresionada. Lo llevó a que viera a Jim Wilkinson, su asesor de comunicaciones.

"Este es el hombre del que le hablé", le dijo Rice a Maliki. "Este es Jim; voy a dejarlo con usted para que le ayude". Wilkinson había encabezado transiciones de gobiernos, incluida la de Rice al Departamento de Estado, y en sitios como Mongolia y Palestina. Rice dijo que él había estudiado árabe durante un año después del 9/11, y que sabía cómo ayudarle, desde los aspectos gerenciales y estructurales del nuevo cargo hasta los asuntos logísticos relacionados con espacio y líneas telefónicas. "Se ve muy joven pero tiene mucha experiencia en gestión y política, y puede ayudarle bastante. Voy a dejarlo aquí con usted tanto tiempo como lo necesite".

Esto tomó por sorpresa a Wilkinson, que no había sido advertido y solo había traído ropa para unos pocos días.

"Usted es el profesor, yo su alumno", le dijo a Maliki en árabe. Maliki rió y le dio un abrazo a su nuevo asesor.

RICE Y RUMSFELD se reunieron con los periodistas estadounidenses.

"Tendrán que viajar en secreto", dijo un reportero de Bloomberg News.

"¿Qué dice eso acerca de las perspectivas de restaurar la seguridad y la estabilidad, y sobre el verdadero estado de la situación de seguridad?".

Ese era uno de los puntos de desacuerdo entre Rice y Rumsfeld. La seguridad era asunto de él. Hubo diez minutos de silencio antes de que Rumsfeld respondiera, mirando fijamente al reportero.

"No creo que diga nada acerca de eso", respondió secamente. Dijo que estaba allí para reunirse con sus generales. "Pero no veo ninguna relación de su pregunta con esto".

Rice intervino: "Obviamente, seguiremos dirigiendo nuestra atención a la situación de seguridad, lo mismo que los iraquíes. Pero siempre hemos dicho, y ahora estoy aun más convencida, que los terroristas finalmente serán derrotados mediante un proceso político".

La siguiente pregunta fue acerca de cómo disminuir la influencia sectaria sobre los militares, la policía y las milicias. "¿Exactamente, cómo cumplir ese objetivo?".

"Creo que lo primero que tengo que decir es: Este es un país soberano. No es un gobierno interino o de transición. Otros países han tenido que solucionar problemas similares; lo han hecho de una manera razonablemente ordenada y a lo largo del tiempo, en muchos casos, sin demasiada violencia. Es posible que esto sea una realidad".

Rumsfeld escribía o garabateaba con su bolígrafo, o miraba el cielo raso mientras Rice se hacía cargo de la conferencia de prensa.

Rice ahora sabía que sería inevitable que su legado también llegara a ser juzgado por lo que sucedía en Irak. A su regreso, le presentó a Bush un informe acerca de su reunión con Maliki, y le dijo que estaba animada. Le dijo que era el primer líder iraquí en decir, "Este es mi trabajo".

WILKINSON FUE A LA OFICINA de Maliki en el centro internacional de prensa. No tenía aire acondicionado y el calor era sofocante. La primera orden, sin embargo, estuvo relacionada con la seguridad personal de Maliki. Después de los tres años de lucha para llevar la seguridad a Irak, el poder simbólico del asesinato del nuevo primer ministro iraquí sería algo demasiado difícil de manejar. Wilkinson presentó a Maliki el equipo SEAL de la Armada que le sería asignado para vigilarlo a toda hora.

"Escoja su propio modelo de gestión", sugirió Wilkinson. "Están el estilo iraquí, el estilo de Estados Unidos y Occidente, y está el estilo Maliki de hacer las cosas. Lo invito a que aplique el estilo Maliki".

Pasaron dos horas y media frente a tablas y gráficos computarizados –Maliki parecía saber bastante de tecnología– armando una configuración que les permitiera supervisar a los ministros del gabinete, la oficina personal y las oficinas para los medios de comunicación y los asesores de finanzas, protocolo y política. A solicitud de Maliki, Wilkinson escribió las funciones de cada uno de los cargos y presentó un plan por escrito para los primeros cinco días tras la posesión formal que tendría lugar el mes siguiente. Observó que Maliki tenía cinco teléfonos celulares.

Wilkinson necesitaba que Khalilzad se encargara de la seguridad de las oficinas de Maliki. Maliki había designado como vocero al doctor Salah Abdulrazak, quien vivía afuera de la Zona Verde con su esposa y dos niños pequeños. No era sorprendente que temiera por sus vidas. "¿Qué puedo hacer?", le preguntó el nuevo vocero a Wilkinson, que lo llevó al hotel Al Rashid.

"Tenemos que conseguirle una habitación a él y su familia para esta noche", dijo Wilkinson.

Bueno, eso demoraría un poco.

"Se muda aquí esta noche".

Lo hizo al día siguiente.

El jefe del gabinete y el vocero de Maliki necesitaban credenciales para ingresar a la Zona Verde.

"¿Puede conseguirles identificaciones?", le pidió Maliki a Wilkinson.

Claro, le dijeron a Wilkinson en su primera averiguación, pero demorarían de seis a ocho semanas. Wilkinson desfalleció y le pidió ayuda a Khalilzad. Los dos hombres de Maliki consiguieron pronto sus identificaciones permanentes.

Los siguientes días estuvieron dedicados a temas más mundanos. La oficina de Maliki no tenía computadoras. Wilkinson consiguió unas e hizo que las instalaran. "Necesitamos teléfonos", dijo Maliki. Entonces el equipo de la embajada instaló teléfonos. En algún momento, Wilkinson tuvo que enviar bolígrafos y papel.

Ante la proximidad de su posesión, Maliki dijo que sólo iba a poder invitar al 10% del parlamento porque no había aire acondicionado en el salón principal. "¿Podría encargarse de eso?", le pidió a Wilkinson. Pronto llegaron los nuevos equipos de aire acondicionado desde todo el Medio Oriente, y la embajada de Estados Unidos y los militares los instalaron en el salón principal.

Maliki no quería una posesión espectacular o elaborada. "¿Cómo puedo hacer algo así, mientras mueren tantos iraquíes?".

Wilkinson observó que Maliki seguía diciendo las cosas apropiadas, y sonaba casi como el embajador de Estados Unidos. Un miembro de la embajada le pidió a Wilkinson una evaluación preliminar.

"O es todo un fraude, o verdaderamente es lo que necesitamos", respondió Wilkinson. Hasta donde podía decir, parecía que Maliki tenía un grupo de unas siete personas que tomaban todas las decisiones personales y las demás decisiones críticas. Se daba cuenta de que había encontrado la manera de entrar al sistema de Maliki por el lado de la gestión, pero no por el de la política. Maliki mantenía ocultas sus cartas. Uno de los asesores británicos claves le preguntó a Maliki si querría ayuda para escribir su discurso de posesión.

Maliki respondió con el equivalente en árabe de "¡Alto ahí!". Era claro que había límites que él no quería que fueran rebasados. Cada vez que Wilkinson le preguntaba algo sobre política podía sentir la cortés pero impenetrable barrera que levantaba Maliki.

CUANDO WILKINSON CONVERSABA con los oficiales de alto y bajo rango, veía las contradicciones. Las fuerzas estaban recibiendo dos mensajes. Bush y Rice decían que Irak era lo más importante, que era central en la guerra contra el terrorismo y esencial para la estabilidad del Medio Oriente y el futuro de la civilización. Al mismo tiempo, la presión interna sobre los militares se dirigía a que había que salir de allí lo antes posible.

Al final, Wilkinson concluyó que esta era la última oportunidad. Si Maliki no lograba mostrarle a su pueblo por qué la democracia era mejor, hacer que su gobierno proporcionara los servicios públicos y más seguridad, no iba a funcionar.

"No estoy seguro de cuál sea el plan B", decía Wilkinson a menudo.

En ocasiones se preguntaba si la agenda para la democracia de George W. Bush realmente funcionaría. ¿Su retórica de alto nivel había tenido eco, o no? ¿No se habría destruido gran parte de la voluntad real o potencial de los iraquíes, de manera que ya no podrían creer que la democracia funcionaría para ellos? ¿Los estadounidenses, con todas sus ideas y promesas habían llevado al hombre a la Luna, pero no podían lograr que hubiera electricidad? Se preguntaba si Maliki iba a ser juzgado por los errores estadounidenses, y si, a su vez, Estados Unidos sería juzgado por esto ¿Y cómo se quebraría la espalda del fundamentalismo islámico militante?

¿Bush estaba siendo bien informado? A Bush le habían dicho ya muchas veces, por ejemplo, que la electricidad ya estaba lista o que faltaba poco para que estuviera lista. No lo estaba. Por mucho tiempo Wilkinson creyó que la electricidad era el centro de gravedad, porque era algo sobre lo que Rice y el Departamento de Estado podían influir.

Pero el verdadero problema era la seguridad. Vio *Bagdad ER*, el documental de una hora, altamente gráfico y escalofriante, de HBO, acerca del mismo hospital de combate situado en Bagdad que Rice había visitado el año anterior. El documental era una descripción llamativa y sangrienta de los horrores de la guerra, centrada en aquellos desgarrados, mutilados y asesinados por los artefactos explosivos hechizos, los proyectiles y los morteros. El protagonista era el cuerpo de los soldados. Las tomas dentro de la sala de emergencia mostraban piernas y brazos que habían sido volados o que debían ser amputados. Los soldaos llegaban con sus caras ensangrentadas y desgarradas por las granadas, y con metralla incrustada en sus miembros, pechos y ojos. Muchos de los sobrevivientes eran evacuados a hospitales de Alemania o al Centro Médico del Ejército Walter Reed. Se mostraba cómo ponían los numerosos muertos dentro de bolsas negras. La sangre era limpiada incesantemente de los pisos de la sala de operación.

"Odio esta estúpida guerra", decía uno de los trabajadores del hospital. "Creo que es lo más ridículo que he visto. No creo que sea más inteligente que cualquier otra guerra que se haya peleado".

Wilkinson quedó golpeado después de verlo. Su hermano se había enlistado como soldado para ir a Irak.

"¿Esto vale su vida?", se preguntaba Wilkinson.

Toda la situación de Irak era verdaderamente trágica. Él tenía la impresión de que Rice, que a veces parecía desmoralizada, comenzaba a sentir lo mismo.

Rice le comentó alguna vez: "No me gustan los extremistas".

¿Por qué no?

"Porque en algunos de estos asuntos no confío en alguien que se sienta tan seguro", dijo la secretaria de Estado.

El coordinador de la política para Irak de Rice, Jim Jeffrey, había escuchado el comentario repetitivo de que Maliki era la última oportunidad para Irak. Pensaba que era palabrería. La idea de una "última oportunidad" para Irak era simplemente impensable. Los ataques habían aumentado, pero habían tenido algo de éxito al conformar un gobierno. Creía que estaban progresando.

Jeffrey, sencillamente, no podía imaginar un escenario como Vietnam en 1975 o Somalia en 1993. En esos casos, el creía, Estados Unidos sencillamente decidió que era demasiado difícil y que no valía la pena.

Pensaba que, si se marchaban, Irak haría una de dos cosas. Se sumiría en un completo caos, o se convertiría en una nación dedicada a odiar al denominado Gran Satán, o sea Estados Unidos.

Además, el país estaba asentado encima de entre un tercio y la mitad de las reservas de petróleo del Medio Oriente, según el experto al que se escuchara. Bush reconocía que su presidencia dependía de su éxito allí. Por lo tanto, concluyó Jeffrey, Estados Unidos no se iba a marchar. Si Maliki no funcionaba, encontrarían un plan B, C o D, o lo que fuera necesario.

El presidente invitó a diez ex secretarios de Estado y de Defensa al Salón Roosevelt, el viernes 12 de mayo, para escuchar sus impresiones sobre Irak. Cinco meses antes, en enero, había tenido una sesión similar con, básicamente, el mismo grupo, pero le había dedicado poco tiempo y había estado muy a la defensiva.

Powell estaba sentado junto a Rice, quien estaba a la izquierda del presidente. Powell había seguido los informes de prensa acerca del nuevo primer ministro designado Maliki. De repente, todos, incluso Bush y Rice, lo estaban acogiendo ¿Quién era él?, se preguntaba Powell. Este nuevo personaje, al parecer, era un líder más efectivo que Jafari ¿Por qué? Tras haber servido durante cuatro años en la administración de Bush, sabía que había otra pregunta importante por hacer: "¿Es cierto?". ¿Qué sabemos acerca de él?". Después de un poco de lectura, investigación y presión sobre sus propios contactos que aún hacían parte del gobierno, Powell estaba sorprendido de que nadie en Estados Unidos, incluida Rice, lo hubiera conocido antes.

"¿Que destrezas ejecutivas justifican este voto de confianza?", se preguntaba Powell. Maliki estaba diciendo todas cosas que agradaban muchísimo a todos. Se estaba comprometiendo a controlar las milicias, reconstruir los oleoductos y ocuparse del agua.

El principal punto de Bush era el carácter de centro de Maliki.

La ex secretaria de Estado Madeleine K. Albright y el ex secretario de Defensa William Cohen pasaron a concentrarse en Irán. Albright también dijo que el presidente debía conversar con el primer ministro Badawi de Malasia.

Powell se había reunido con Badawi la semana anterior. Levantó su mano y Bush asintió.

"Pero mientras yo tenga la palabra", continuó Powell, "quisiera sugerirle cautela con el señor Maliki, porque francamente creo que ninguno de nosotros había oído o sabía algo de él, hasta cuando fue anunciado la semana pasada. Hicimos a un lado a Jafari, pero él es un delegado de Jafari fuera del partido Dawa. Y creo que hay que tener un poco de cautela con alguien que pasó los últimos veintitantos años en Irán y Siria.

"La diferencia significativa entre la reunión que tuvimos con usted en enero y esta reunión es que en enero teníamos una insurgencia furiosa y terrorismo. Creo que las cosas han empeorado. Aún tenemos una insurgencia furiosa. Aún tenemos terrorismo. Pero el bombardeo al sitio religioso en Samarra evidenció que además ahora tenemos violencia entre sectas, y eso es grave. Esta es una nueva guerra, y es una guerra en la que las tropas estadounidenses cada vez pueden hacer menos. Entiendo que los jefes de estación [de la CIA] tienen una visión aun más negativa".

Powell no pudo contenerse. Tenía la atención del presidente de una manera que rara vez la tuvo cuando fue secretario de Defensa. Intencionalmente, no deseaba contaminar la discusión diciendo que Irak estaba en guerra civil, pero quería subrayar lo que él consideraba como peor peligro. "Su estrategia es correcta en términos de reconstruir las fuerzas militares y policiales y el gobierno", dijo Powell, "porque si no existe un gobierno al que se puedan articular esas fuerzas, entonces, señor presidente, no se está construyendo fuerzas armadas sino milicias".

Bush asintió.

Cohen y Albright regresaron al tema de Irán.

"Señor presidente", dijo Powell, pidiendo la palabra de nuevo. "Me sumo a lo que Bill, Madeleine y otros han dicho sobre Irán. Pero lo principal es *Irak e Irak*. Irak es el que va a determinar todo. Es importante lo que hagamos con Irán, pero hay que dar un vistazo al lobo que nos está comiendo".

Más tarde, Hadley se acercó a Powell y le dijo que quería seguir conversando. Josh Bolten, el nuevo jefe de gabinete, le dijo lo mismo. "Cenemos juntos", le dijo Rice a Powell. Se pusieron de acuerdo, pero ella no pudo asistir. Había sido enviada inesperadamente a Europa para reunirse con los líderes de las negociaciones nucleares con Irán.

MALIKI SE POSESIONÓ en una ceremonia formal el sábado 20 de mayo. En un salón de alta seguridad dentro de la protegida Zona Verde, él presentó un programa de 33 puntos. Los tres principales desafíos, dijo, eran el terrorismo, la corrupción y la prestación de servicios públicos.

En un discurso pronunciado en Chicago dos días después, el 22 de mayo, Bush dijo que aumentaban los progresos en Irak pero también había algunos retrocesos. "Sin embargo, hemos llegado a un punto importante en la lucha entre la libertad y el terrorismo", dijo, derramando optimismo. Dijo que los iraquíes habían "demostrado que la democracia es la esperanza del Medio Oriente y el destino de toda la humanidad".

Bush, usualmente, evitaba hacer predicciones sobre la historia y sus juicios, pero este día finalizó diciendo: "Dentro de unos años, la gente recordará la formación de un gobierno de unidad en Irak como un momento decisivo en la historia de la libertad, un momento en que la libertad ganó un punto de apoyo firme en el Medio Oriente y en el que las fuerzas del terror iniciaron su larga retirada".

ESA SEMANA, RUMSFELD asistía a tres días de reuniones a puerta cerrada en el Pentágono, con los comandantes de combate y civiles más importantes del Departamento de Defensa. Antes de Rumsfeld, estas reuniones periódicas habían sido conducidas por el jefe de Estado Mayor Conjunto; ahora Rumsfeld las dirigía.

El general Jones, comandante de la OTAN, le dijo a Pace que creía que Rumsfeld controlaba tanto todo, hasta las primeras etapas, que no estaban prestando una asesoría militar independiente, como la que tenían obligación legal de hacer. Rumsfeld estaba conduciendo y afectando los debates y las decisiones "políticamente". Ellos, los militares uniformados, debían preocuparse por este "giro político", dijo. Propuso que Pace se reuniera a solas con los comandantes de combate y los jefes de servicio, sin Rumsfeld ni ningún civil del Departamento de Defensa. "Tengo algunos asuntos", dijo, que debían ser tratados y debatidos sin que Rumsfeld estuviera presente.

Pace accedió a tener una reunión de una hora esa semana sólo con los jefes de servicio y los comandantes de combate.

En esta reunión, Jones dijo que quería concentrarse en un asunto, en la importancia del establecimiento preventivo de bases. Los *marines*, el Ejército, la Armada y la Fuerza Aérea tenían bases por todo el mundo, de manera que podrían estar en cualquier punto problemático para prevenir los conflictos, asegurar las fronteras y capturar y derrotar a los terroristas. La idea de Rumsfeld era traer de regreso a Estados Unidos tantas fuerzas como fuera posible. Jones argumentaba que esto alteraba el concepto y premisa básicos de la presencia mundial estadounidense. Tenían la obligación de expresar sus opiniones y luchar contra esta nueva doctrina por que ella debilitaría la posición de Estados Unidos en el mundo. Muchos de los presentes estuvieron de acuerdo, en principio, pero ninguno parecía dispuesto a enfrentar al secretario de Defensa.

44

Al día siguiente, el miércoles 24 de mayo, la división de inteligencia del Estado Mayor Conjunto, la J-2, hizo circular una evaluación de inteligencia clasificada como SECRETA, donde se mostraba que las fuerzas del terrorismo en Irak no estaban en retirada. Era una refutación sorprendente de los pronósticos del presidente, hechos apenas dos días antes en Chicago. El informe fue enviado a la Casa Blanca, al Departamento de Estado y otras agencias de inteligencia.

Demostraba con cifras las tendencias que habían sido informadas a Bush a lo largo de todo el año. Los ataques terroristas habían estado aumentando de manera constante. La insurgencia estaba ganando.

En mayúsculas, la evaluación decía, "*LOS ATAQUES EN MAYO, PROBABLEMENTE, SUPERARÁN LOS NIVELES DE ABRIL, QUE FUERON LOS MÁS ALTOS QUE SE HAYA REGISTRADO. LA INSURGENCIA SUNITA ÁRABE ESTÁ FORTALECIÉNDOSE Y AUMENTANDO SU CAPACIDAD, A PESAR DEL AVANCE POLÍTICO Y EL DESARROLLO DE LAS FUERZAS DE SEGURIDAD IRAQUÍES*".

A esta afirmación seguía un gráfico de barras que mostraba el promedio de ataques diarios en los primeros cinco meses del año 2006. Se veía un aumento constante:

Enero	72
Febrero	87
Marzo	95
Abril	110
Mayo	113

Esto quería decir que ahora los ataques promediaban entre 600 y 700 por semana. Cada artefacto explosivo de fabricación casera descubierto –ya fuera que detonara causando daños y bajas o que fuera identificado y desarmado antes de que pudiera hacer cualquier daño– se contaba como un ataque.

Un gráfico que medía los ataques entre mayo de 2003 y mayo de 2006 mostraba algunos descensos significativos, pero el número actual de ataques era tan alto como siempre: más de 3.500 al mes.

**ATAQUES INICIADOS POR EL ENEMIGO EN CONTRA DE LA
COALICIÓN Y LOS IRAQUÍES CADA MES ENTRE MAYO DE 2003 Y MAYO DE 2006
SECRETO**

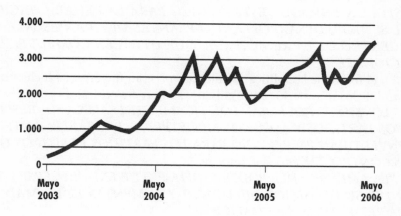

La evaluación también decía: *"LOS INSURGENTES Y LOS TERRORISTAS CONSERVAN SUS RECURSOS Y CAPACIDADES PARA SOSTENER Y HASTA AUMENTAR EL NIVEL ACTUAL DE VIOLENCIA DURANTE EL PRÓXIMO AÑO".*

El panorama no podía ser más desolador. Aunque Estados Unidos tenía ceca de 130.000 miembros de sus tropas –un 80% del máximo de 160.000–, los iraquíes habían aumentado de manera constante sus fuerzas de seguridad, y ahora tenían unos 263.000 militares y policías. Tal vez la mitad de ellos estaban en el frente, ejecutando operaciones de seguridad por todo Irak, y tenían asesores militares de Estados Unidos trabajando a su lado.

La evaluación SECRETA incluía un informe pesimista acerca de la producción de crudo. El gobierno Iraquí había fijado como meta 2,5 millones de barriles al día para junio de 2006. Era una meta alta y probablemente nada realista. Estaban produciendo en promedio 2.1 millones a día.

El informe SECRETO decía: *"EVALUACIÓN: LA SEGURIDAD PERMANENTE Y LOS SABOTAJES DESVÍAN LOS FONDOS PARA LA RECONSTRUCCIÓN HACIA REPARACIONES PROVISIONALES E IMPORTACIONES DE COMBUSTIBLE. ES IMPROBABLE QUE LA PRODUCCIÓN ALCANCE LAS METAS DEL MINISTERIO DEL PETRÓLEO*

PARA EL 2006, SIN UNA REHABILITACIÓN DE LA INFRAESTRUCTURA, AUMENTO DE LA SEGURIDAD Y UN INCREMENTO DE LA INVERSIÓN EXTRANJERA".

Acerca de la electricidad: *"EVALUACIÓN: A PESAR DE LA CAPACIDAD AUMENTADA, HA HABIDO POCAS GANANCIAS NETAS EN LA GENERACIÓN DESDE LA PRE-OLI [OPERACIÓN LIBERACIÓN DE IRAK]. ADEMÁS DE LA MEJORA EN LA SEGURIDAD, IRAK NECESITA UN ENFOQUE ESTRATÉGICO PARA LA REHABILITACIÓN DEL SECTOR, DESARROLLANDO PLANTAS DE GRAN ESCALA EN EL CENTRO DE LA REGIÓN SUR, QUE UTILICEN COMBUSTIBLES NACIONALES".*

En el frente de la política, las noticias no eran mejores. La lucha por el control de los ministerios entre chiítas y sunitas era crítica.

"LOS MINISTROS SERÁN POLÍTICAMENTE LEALES A SUS RESPECTIVOS PARTIDOS Y ALGUNOS MINISTERIOS, PROBABLEMENTE, SE CONVERTIRÁN EN REFUGIO PARA LOS PARTIDOS POLÍTICOS QUE LOS CONTROLEN", decía el informe.

"LA AMENAZA DEL PODER CHIÍTA PUEDE ENDURECERSE Y EXPANDIR SU OPOSICIÓN MILITANTE, Y AUMENTAR EL LLAMADO A UNA RETIRADA DE LA COALICIÓN".

Otra sección decía, *"LA INTEGRACIÓN DE LA MILICIA CHIÍTA PUEDE EXASPERAR A LOS SUNITAS ÁRABES, MUCHOS DE LOS CUALES VEN A LOS GRUPOS CHIÍTAS COMO CÓMPLICES EN LOS ASESINATOS EXTRAJUDICIALES".*

OTRA INFORMACIÓN de inteligencia se sumaba al desolador panorama: Artefactos de fabricación casera más avanzados, denominados explosivos para penetrar —configurados para penetrar Humvees, vehículos para transporte de personal, y hasta tanques, y explotar dentro de ellos —estaban siendo encontrados en Irak. Aunque habían aparecido un año antes, a mediados de 2005, para la primavera de 2006 se había detonado o desarmado unos 15 por mes, probablemente hasta 40 mensuales, según algunos cálculos. No eran de alta tecnología pero sí lo suficientemente sofisticados como para no ser de fabricación casera. La alta calidad de su maquinaria y sus dispositivos de activación apuntaban hacia Irán. Algunos se disparaban por medio de dispositivos infrarrojos pasivos que podían contrarrestar las defensas de Estados Unidos Los explosivos penetradores eran casi cuatro veces más letales que los artefactos explosivos hechizos convencionales. Un estudio estableció que mientras una persona moría por cada dos artefactos explosivos hechizos convencionales, cada explosivo penetrador mataba en promedio a 2,2 personas. Había ocurrido, por lo menos, un caso en que un explosivo penetrador había atravesado el grueso blindaje de un enorme tanque Abrams.

Según la inteligencia estadounidense, los Cuerpos de la Guardia Revolucionaria Iraní le habían pedido a Hezbolá, la organización terrorista, que entrenara a los iraquíes en el uso de explosivos penetradores.

Si todo esto se llegaba a hacer público, iniciaría un incendio que nadie podría apagar. Primero, surgirían preguntas inmediatas acerca de la calidad de la inteligencia. ¿Potencialmente, podría tratarse de otro fiasco como el de las armas de destrucción masiva? Segundo, si esto era cierto, significaba que los iraníes estaban matando soldados estadounidenses, es decir, efectuando un acto de guerra. La premisa principal de la política exterior republicana había sido la dureza: no más debilidad, no más Carter ni Clinton ni su negación patológica a hacer uso de la fuerza ¿A dónde llevaría eso a los republicanos, al tratar ahora con los iraníes?

Había un tercer problema. Los grupos chiítas estaban recibiendo explosivos penetradores en el Sur, y algunos en Bagdad, pero, comparativamente la cantidad de estos artefactos no era tan alta. ¿Y si los iraníes dedicaban sus esfuerzos a suministrar tecnología, conocimientos y equipos en gran cantidad a la insurgencia sunita árabe, al igual que a los chiítas? Esa sería una situación completamente diferente.

Las encuestas mostraban que casi un 50% de los sunitas tenían una actitud positiva frente a la insurgencia. Como los sunitas eran un 20% de la población, eso quería decir que al menos un 10% de la población iraquí –más de 2 millones de personas– tenía una actitud favorable hacia los insurgentes.

EN JULIO DE 2006, le comenté a Rumsfeld que estaba al tanto de que el número de ataques se estaba incrementando.

"Probablemente eso es cierto", dijo. "También es probable que nuestros datos sean mejores y que estemos clasificando más cosas como ataques. Un disparo involuntario puede ser un ataque suficiente para matar a 50 personas en algún lugar. Entonces se está mezclando diferentes cosas en un mismo frutero, bananas con manzanas y naranjas".

Quedé sin palabras. Incluso, con el uso más relajado y descuidado del lenguaje y la analogía, no entendía cómo el secretario de Defensa podía comparar ataques de los insurgentes con un "frutero", una metáfora que eliminaba toda la carga de urgencia y emotividad. Las categorías oficiales en los informes clasificados que Rumsfeld recibía regularmente eran de artefactos explosivos hechizos letales, ataques a distancia con morteros, y combates cercanos como las emboscadas: nada que ver con bananas, manzanas y naranjas.

"Los ataques están aumentando", confirmó el general Pace, jefe del Estado Mayor Conjunto, "porque esa gente quiere que el lugar sea ingobernable para que nosotros nos marchemos y, entonces, ellos puedan apoderarse". Luego añadió ofendido: "Entonces, lo que se puede esperar es que los ataques continúen, porque, cada vez que el primer ministro Maliki y su parlamento se reúnen y toman decisiones, es un mal día para quienes ejecutan estos ataques... Están contra las cuerdas... si este parlamento y este primer ministro siguen actuando".

"Muy bien", dije, "¿pero, están contra las cuerdas?".

"Expresión equivocada", dijo Pace.

"Usted va a sonar como Cheney", le dije. "¿Quiere retirar lo que dijo?".

"Sí", dijo, "quisiera retirar eso. Gracias. Le agradezco la cortesía".

Le pregunté acerca de la victoria y cómo podría lograrse, y dijo que esto requeriría más que seguridad en Irak. Se necesitaría autogobierno y reconstrucción física del país: todas las "líneas de operación" del plan de guerra de Casey.

"¿Vivirá para ver eso?", le pregunté.

"Así es. Bueno, eso espero. No lo sé", dijo. "Tengo que retirar esa frase. Viviré para verlo".

"¿Tiene alguna duda acerca de si la decisión de invadir a Irak fue correcta?".

"No tengo ninguna duda", dijo. "Ninguna. Cero".

"¿Sin embargo, no es con respecto al proceso que usted siempre ha tenido dudas?", le dije. "Yo vivo dudando".

"Lo siento por usted", dijo el general de los *marines*.

"No lo sienta", respondí. "Es un proceso maravilloso".

"No tengo dudas acerca de lo que hemos hecho", dijo. "Nosotros no hicimos esto. Cuando estábamos en nuestra casa ocupándonos de nuestros asuntos, recibimos el ataque del 9/11".

Ahí estaba: "Nosotros no hicimos esto". Existía un sentimiento muy profundo entre algunos altos funcionarios de la administración Bush, en el sentido de que, de alguna manera, nosotros no habíamos empezado la Guerra de Irak. Habíamos sido atacados. Bin Laden, Al Qaeda, los demás terroristas y las fuerzas antiestadounidenses –ya fueran grupos, países o filosofías– podían juntarse en uno solo. Era una sola guerra, la larga guerra, la guerra de dos generaciones que el grupo Bletchley II de Wolfowitz había descrito después del 9/11.

"¿Está seguro de que es la guerra correcta en el momento correcto?", le pregunté al general Pace.

"Sí".

"¿En el lugar correcto?".

"Sí, absolutamente", dijo Pace. "Fundamentalmente, sí. Lo dije antes de que comenzáramos. Y lo diré hoy. No le sorprenderá saber que creo que tenemos que estar luchando las batallas contra los enemigos de mi país en su campo de batalla. No tengo ninguna duda de que hemos hecho lo correcto para proteger a mi país, para cumplir el deber con mi país y para proteger a mis hijos y mis nietos y a sus hijos y sus nietos".

EL 26 DE MAYO, dos días después de la evaluación SECRETA de inteligencia, el Pentágono dio a conocer un informe público al Congreso, titulado "Medición de la estabilidad y la seguridad en Irak". Era el informe trimestral exigido por la ley. Aunque había un gráfico oculto en medio del documento de 65 páginas, que mostraba que el promedio semanal de ataques había subido a más de 600, el documento resaltaba de la manera más positiva la estabilidad y la seguridad.

La introducción, de cuatro páginas, no era más que palabras positivas. "Las fuerzas antiiraquíes –extremistas y terroristas– siguen fracasando en su campaña para descarrilar el proceso político… y para fomentar la guerra civil", decía el informe, evitando cualquier mención de que el panorama de seguridad era significativamente peor.

"Más del 80% de los ataques terroristas se concentraron en sólo cuatro de las 18 provincias de Irak", decía respecto a la disminución de la violencia. Estas cuatro provincias, incluida Bagdad, tenían el 37% de la población.

El informe definía como "Contradictores iraquíes" a quienes eran leales al anterior régimen, sadammistas y terroristas, incluida Al Qaeda. "La fuerza de los contradictores probablemente permanecerá estable a lo largo de 2006", decía el informe, que era consistente con la evaluación SECRETA de inteligencia. Pero el informe del Pentágono iba más allá, al afirmar que "la necesidad y la motivación para continuar con acciones violentas comenzarán a decaer a comienzos del 2007". El informe del Pentágono contradecía de plano su propia evaluación secreta de hacía dos días, que decía que los insurgentes y terroristas conservaban los recursos y capacidades para "mantener y hasta aumentar el nivel actual de violencia durante el próximo año".

JOHN NEGROPONTE había sido director de inteligencia nacional durante un año. Tenía acceso a todo, y veía al presidente casi a diario. Era uno de los pocos que sabía casi todo acerca de la participación de Estados Unidos en Irak. Creía que, desde el comienzo de la insurgencia en 2003, la administración había subestimado su tamaño y nivel de motivación. Lo peor era que seguía haciéndolo.

La violencia sectaria, en particular la de chiítas y sunitas, que se mataban entre sí, estaba descendiendo a la comunidad, hasta los vecindarios y manzanas. Este era un nuevo y alarmante fenómeno. En marzo, después del bombardeo a la mezquita de Samarra, hubo más de 450 incidentes sectarios violentos, con 1.800 bajas iraquíes. Al mes siguiente habían descendido a 330 incidentes con unas 1.300 bajas, cifras todavía increíblemente altas.

La clave era que Zarqawi, el asesino jordano que se convirtió en el líder de Al Qaeda en Irak, había tenido éxito en enfrentar a unos contra otros. De alguna manera, era como lanzar un puñetazo a alguien en un bar repleto de enemigos permanentes. Los ataques indiscriminados sobre los iraquíes, y la hostilidad sectaria largamente alimentada, fueron el combustible para una reacción en cadena. Irak era ahora un campo mucho más fértil para la violencia sectaria. Zarqawi había creado ese campo fértil.

Negroponte no estaba sorprendido de que el Pentágono diera a conocer informes optimistas. Era natural. Ya lo había visto en Vietnam. Los generales y civiles endulzarían las cosas, ensalzando a su gente e insistiendo que había una luz a final del túnel.

Pero endulzar la realidad no era su trabajo. Ahora había tanta violencia sectaria en Irak, que los militares de Estados Unidos o las agencias de inteligencia podrían no saber mucho de ella o no ser capaces de medirla, concluyó Negroponte. El verdadero problema era que la coalición, Estados Unidos y las agencias de inteligencias andaban a ciegas en Irak.

¿Quién es el enemigo? Negroponte preguntó, planteando la misma pregunta que el director delegado de la CIA John McLaughlin había formulado casi tres años atrás, cuando concluyó que era una mezcla de antiguos miembros del Baath, combatientes extranjeros como Zarqawi, nacionalistas iraquíes y miembros de las tribus ofendidos con la agresividad estadounidense. Negroponte llegó a las mismas respuestas: sadammistas, personajes problemáticos y Zarqawi, quien, obviamente, era el más importante. Pero no pudo llegar a ningún lado con esto. La razón era que el recurso humano que la CIA había reclutado era un reflejo de la polarización de Irak. Todos habían tomado partido, y era difícil encontrar fuentes iraquíes no sesgadas. Después de clasificar y analizar todo, se hizo más profundo el misterio para él.

Negroponte solía contar un chiste acerca de una admirante que le preguntaba a un científico cómo manejar el problema que representaban los submarinos. "Descubra cómo hacer hervir el océano", le dice el científico. "Eso resolverá el problema de los submarinos. La puesta en práctica se la dejo a usted".

En términos generales, concluyó, todo iba cuesta abajo en los seis primeros meses de 2006. Claramente, ahora, a comienzos de junio, podía ver que la política estadounidense para Irak estaba en problemas. Era el momento de enfrentar los hechos. Los chiítas ya eran los ganadores. Ellos vencerían. La única pregunta era cómo podía ayudar Estados Unidos a darle forma a las cosas –diferente a determinarlas–. Era el momento para que Estados Unidos retirara sus manos.

"Si tuviéramos 10 años, podríamos hacer las cosas de otra forma", dijo en privado Negroponte. "Ahora coincido con Rumsfeld en lo de las ruedas de entrenamiento. Ya vamos a tener que retirarlas".

RICE PENSABA que tenían que ser cuidadosos con la reducción de las fuerzas. Al mismo tiempo, ella quería ser flexible con una solución política que incluyera a la insurgencia y la involucrara en el nuevo gobierno. Pero eso no podía incluir compromisos o ningún tipo de acercamiento con aquellos que tenían sangre estadounidense en sus manos. Era algo que se hacía cada vez más difícil, a medida que la insurgencia se fortalecía y los ataques aumentaban. Era casi imposible.

Rice siempre había sido la gran realizadora que no se amilanaba ante los retos imposibles. "Nuestra obligación es arreglar esto", decía. La palabra "obligación" relucía a menudo en lo que ella decía. "Nuestra obligación es abrirnos camino a través de la maleza de problemas que existen aquí".

Con regularidad, se desafiaba a Rice en relación con las aseveraciones de progreso de la administración. "Lo más difícil de decir", comentaba, "lo que creo honestamente, era que el caos y el progreso estaban uno al lado del otro, ¿no es así? Y era difícil que la gente aceptara eso. Habrán pensado que estaba dando vueltas". Pero ella sentía sinceramente que era una mezcla de progreso y caos. Esa era la paradoja.

En el análisis de Rice, la invasión a Irak había desafiado la antigua estructura autoritaria y los cimientos del Medio Oriente. Ahora el viejo Medio Oriente estaba destruido, y tenían que establecer un nuevo orden allí. Recordaba a la gente que, no hace mucho, daba por sentado que Francia y Alemania siempre estarían peleándose entre sí. Nadie creería hoy que Francia y Alemania volverían a enfrentarse. Las dos guerras mundiales habían cambiado los pilares fundamentales. Esto también podría pasar en el Medio Oriente, pero tomaría tiempo. El presidente y su gabinete para la guerra tendrían que mostrar cómo iban a ser construidos los nuevos cimientos.

Una parte de ella parecía anhelar el día en que todo termine, cuando ya se encuentre fuera del gobierno.

"Estoy segura que en siete u ocho años iré a visitarlo en Crawford", le decía al presidente. "Y pensaremos: 'Debimos haber hecho esto o aquello'. O tal vez veamos las cosas muy bien en retrospectiva, como se ven a medida que nos hacemos viejos".

45

Los INFORMES CLASIFICADOS presentaban exactamente las mismas terribles predicciones que el informe de inteligencia del Estado Mayor Conjunto había expuesto en mayo: niveles aun más altos de ataques insurgentes en Irak. Durante una semana, en mayo de 2006, los ataques iniciados por el enemigo se elevaron a 900, una nueva marca. En junio, los ataques descendieron a 825 durante una semana pero luego se incrementaron de nuevo[23].

Era aun peor, si se consideraba que este nivel de violencia existía después de dos años de entrenar, equipar y financiar 263.000 soldados y policías iraquíes. Todo había costado US $10.000 millones, y los equipos estadounidenses habían estado instalados entre las unidades iraquíes durante un año. En un momento equivalente de 1971, después de varios años de vietnamización, la línea de tendencia de la violencia insurgente había descendido, no aumentado. La conclusión simple era que la estrategia de Irak no estaba funcionando, y que la insurgencia era fuerte y sostenible.

---

23. El informe clasificado acerca de los incidentes de seguridad semanales, correspondiente a la semana del 16 al 22 de junio de 2006, dividía los aproximadamente 825 ataques en cinco categorías:

    A) Artefactos explosivos de fabricación casera no detonados, descubiertos o desactivados, alrededor de 200.

    B) Minas, artefactos explosivos de fabricación casera, otros vehículos de artillería modificados y artefactos explosivos de fabricación casera montados en vehículos (carros bomba), más de 200.

    C) Enfrentamientos cercanos, fuego de armas pequeñas, emboscadas, tiroteos, francotiradores, granadas propulsadas por cohetes y granadas convencionales, alrededor de 175.

    D) Ataques a distancia, con mortero, artillería y barreras de lanzadores múltiples de cohetes, misiles tierra-tierra, misiles tierra-aire, alrededor de 100.

    E) Ataques a autoridades iraquíes, alrededor de 150.

Una nota, en un gráfico que mostraba la escalada de ataques violentos, decía que los incidentes no incluían las "reacciones de los insurgentes a las acciones iniciadas por la Coalición, tales como barridas, tomas de refugios, incautación de armas o capturas de objetivos valiosos".

Steve Herbits fue al Pentágono a comer un emparedado con Rumsfeld el miércoles 14 de julio.

El artículo de opinión más importante del año, le dijo Herbits, probablemente fue el que apareció en *The New York Times* el mes anterior, escrito por el senador Joseph R. Biden Jr., demócrata de Delaware y miembro insigne de la Comisión de Relaciones Exteriores del Senado, y Les Gelb, ex presidente del Consejo de Relaciones Exteriores.

Rumsfeld comenzó a tomar notas.

Biden y Gelb habían propuesto una opción intermedia entre mantener el mismo curso indefinidamente y traer de regreso las tropas estadounidense, siguiendo algún tipo de cronograma, anotó Herbits. Esto se realizaría estableciendo tres regiones ampliamente autónomas, una para los kurdos, una para los chiítas y otra para los sunitas, quienes harían sus propias leyes internas y serían responsables por la seguridad en sus regiones. El gobierno central de Bagdad controlaría la seguridad fronteriza, los asuntos exteriores y los ingresos del petróleo. Irak ya se dirigía hacia la desintegración y este federalismo laxo de tres Estados étnicos se estaba desarrollando por sí solo.

Herbits decía que el concepto común de una policía nacional integrada no estaba funcionando en absoluto, y que las milicias sectarias cada vez eran más poderosas y violentas. Decenas de miles de iraquíes ya estaban migrando por sus medios hacia sus regiones étnicas, dijo, y el voto a pie era más importante que cualquier elección altamente arreglada. Los hechos estaban llevando a Irak hacia esa dirección, y esto sería algo imposible de detener. La política estadounidense podría, efectivamente, aceptarlo. Dijo que esta era la conclusión de un próximo libro de Peter W. Galbraith, un conocedor que había acumulado dos décadas de experiencia en Irak, titulado *El fin de Irak*.

Rumsfeld seguía tomando nota, sin expresar aprobación o desaprobación.

Herbits le propuso armar un equipo A y un equipo B a su debido tiempo, y pedirle a cada uno que le presentara una argumentación de 30 minutos para familiarizarse con el lenguaje y los problemas de cada lado, ya que probablemente esto llegaría a convertirse en el centro del debate.

"Es una estrategia de salida", le dijo Herbits al secretario, y, francamente, la administración no tenía ninguna viable. "Es algo que esta administración podría adoptar en el nombre de la libertad y la autodeterminación. Y podrían llamarla victoria".

Estados Unidos aún seguía anotando el puntaje y dando a conocer el conteo de cuerpos. Dentro de Irak, la evidencia de la Gran Máquina Asesina

Estadounidense y el anuncio sonoro del conteo de cuerpos más reciente se convirtieron en herramientas de reclutamiento para los insurgentes. La realidad era que, desde que los insurgentes habían dejado de llevar uniforme y vivían entremezclados con la población civil, algunos de aquellos muertos, posiblemente un número significativo, eran civiles inocentes. El conteo de cuerpos también recordaba a los iraquíes que vivían en una ocupación. Los expertos en contrainsurgencia decían que el conteo de cuerpos eran una falsa medida del éxito, y citaban la Guerra de Vietnam, en la que los vietnamitas del Norte, el lado vencedor, perdieron casi un millón, en comparación con Estados Unidos, que tuvo 58.000 muertos, pero perdió la guerra.

Pero al presidente Bush le encantaba llevar tarjetas de puntos ganados. Las notas de las reuniones del Comité para la Seguridad Nacional en los días que siguieron a los ataques terroristas del 9/11 daban cuenta de que Bush pedía constantemente una "tarjeta de puntos" para medir la guerra contra el terrorismo. El 10 de octubre de 2001, Bush fue a los cuarteles generales del FBI y personalmente develó una lista de los "Terroristas más buscados", que incluía a Osama bin Laden. Tomó una versión clasificada de la lista, que tenía fotografías, breves biografías y perfiles de personalidad de los 22 terroristas y la guardó en una gaveta en el Salón Oval. Cuando alguno de la lista era dado de baja o capturado, personalmente dibujaba una gran "X" sobre la foto. Orgullosamente, Bush exhibió su tarjeta de puntos de terroristas durante una entrevista en el Salón Oval el 20 de diciembre de 2001. En una entrevista en su rancho de Crawford, el 20 de agosto de 2002, dijo: "La tarjeta de puntos es importante porque quiero que la gente sepa que hay avances".

Durante la Guerra de Irak, por lo tanto, era difícil que el presidente se contuviera. Rumsfeld, Rice y Card le advertían acerca del conteo de cuerpos, pero él quería saber, quería la hoja de cuentas para lo que veía como un conjunto de batallas aisladas. "Mataron a tres de los nuestros; ¿a cuántos de ellos matamos?"

Esto se mezclaba entre sus pronunciamientos públicos. Por ejemplo, en una intervención radial del 1 de octubre de 2005, el anotó que una señal de éxito era que cientos de insurgentes y terroristas habían sido abatidos.

Ignorando su propia recomendación, Rumsfeld tampoco podía evitarlo. El 11 de julio de 2006, en una conferencia de prensa con el presidente Karzai de Afganistán, el secretario de Defensa dijo: "Viendo el número de terroristas talibanes y de Al Qaeda que han muerto cada mes, sería difícil decir que las fuerzas de la coalición y las fuerzas de seguridad afganas estén perdiendo".

Nueve días después entrevisté al general Pace, el jefe del Estado Mayor Conjunto. Me confirmó que el conteo de cuerpos era una línea roja para él. Pero a pesar de su fuerte convicción de que los conteos de cuerpos eran una falsa medida del éxito, el presidente Bush seguía pidiéndolos. "En alguna ocasión el presidente pidió que lo pusieran al tanto de los enemigos muertos en el toma y dame", dijo Pace, y añadió que, en las videoconferencias, los generales Abizaid o Casey le "informaron el número correspondiente a esa batalla".

"El presidente quería saber si le estábamos haciendo daño al enemigo. Es así como funciona. Pero no es algo frecuente… No es inadecuado para el liderazgo saber en su debido momento que estamos causando más daño del que nos causan". Dijo que Abizaid estaba de acuerdo con él en que no se debía utilizar los conteos de cuerpos. "John y yo estamos completamente de acuerdo", dijo Pace. "Él es un buen soldado y ve las cosas exactamente de la misma forma".

Pero, ya avanzado el verano de 2006, el presidente seguía pidiéndolos. "Estoy satisfecho de que el presidente sepa exactamente cuál es mi posición acerca del conteo de cuerpos", dijo Pace.

Tres días después de mi entrevista con Pace, por ejemplo, los cuarteles generales de Casey presentaron un informe: "La coalición y las tropas iraquíes dan de baja a 15 terroristas". La cautela de Pace con el conteo de cuerpos era sólo otro ejemplo de una recomendación desechada. Era otra discusión que el militar número uno de Estados Unidos había perdido, a pesar de que se revivían los fantasmas y la angustia de Vietnam. Aparentemente, era más importante satisfacer las necesidades emocionales y políticas del presidente.

En julio de 2006, entrevisté a Rumsfeld en dos tardes sucesivas. Le pregunté acerca de la batalla contra la insurgencia iraquí, y dijo: "Puede tardar entre ocho y diez años. Las insurgencias tienen la tendencia a hacer eso". En términos generales, dijo, "nuestra estrategia de salida es hacer que el gobierno iraquí y las fuerzas de seguridad sean capaces de manejar una insurgencia de menor nivel y, finalmente, vencerla y contenerla en el tiempo. Pero puede ser un periodo en el que bien podríamos no tener una gran cantidad de gente allí".

Dije que tenía entendido que el general Casey había informado que la insurgencia no había sido neutralizada –un objetivo clave de su plan– sino contenida. Después de dar unas vueltas, pude preguntar directamente "¿Está de acuerdo en que no ha sido neutralizada?".

"Claramente, no", respondió Rumsfeld.

"¿Sólo contenida?".

"Sí", dijo, "hasta ahora".

Luego leí, en la evaluación de mayo de 2006, que "la insurgencia sunita árabe está fortaleciéndose y aumentando su capacidad". Le pregunté "¿Cómo le suena esto?".

Aquí estaba una de las preguntas centrales en cualquier guerra ¿El otro bando estaba "fortaleciéndose y aumentando su capacidad"? Casey, la inteligencia del Estado Mayor Conjunto y la CIA habían afirmado categóricamente que la insurgencia estaba ganando. Rumsfeld sabía eso con certeza. Yo había incluido la cita de la evaluación en la lista de 29 preguntas de muestra que le había enviado previamente, y sabía que él había pasado al menos un hora del día anterior preparándose para la entrevista.

"¿Cuándo fue eso?", preguntó Rumsfeld.

Le respondí que seis semanas antes. La pregunta que estaba sobre la mesa era si él estaba de acuerdo, o no, con la afirmación de que la insurgencia estaba ganando la Guerra de Irak. Yo estaba listo para un típico momento rumsfeldiano, y no quedé defraudado.

"Dios, no lo sé", respondió el secretario de Defensa. "No quiero hacer comentarios sobre eso. Leo tantos de esos informes de inteligencia" –yo nunca le mencioné que fuera un informe de inteligencia– "y todos son tan extensos. En un mismo día uno puede ver uno de una agencia y luego otro de otra, y luego le pregunto a Casey o a Abizaid lo que piensan de ellos, o a Pete Pace '¿Eso es lo que piensas?', e intento triangular y ver lo que la gente piensa. Pero cambia de un mes a otro. No puedo recordar y decir que estoy de acuerdo, o no, con algo así".

Tenía razón en que podía haber cambios de un mes a otro, pero, como él sabía, la evaluación general y la tendencia eran visibles, medibles y dramáticamente peores.

Luego cité un discurso que Rumsfeld había dado antes en la Biblioteca Presidencial Truman, en Independence, Missouri, cuando contó algunas historias acerca de Truman, quien fue un líder que se oponía al ministro de relaciones exteriores soviético ¿Podía recordar algún momento importante en el que Bush pareciera un líder en tiempos de guerra?

"Lo que yo intento hacer es ponerme en sus zapatos y decir: '¿Qué me gustaría saber?'", dijo Rumsfeld. Luego pasó a describirse a sí mismo –no a Bush– como un líder en tiempos de guerra, trabajando con el general Franks para mantener informado al presidente acerca de los factores necesarios para escoger los objetivos a bombardear en Irak. Aunque la pregunta era sobre Bush, Rumsfeld expuso cómo todo ese cuidado para seleccionar los objetivos haría sentir cómodo al presidente, y mostraba que Rumsfeld y Franks "tenían un enfoque que era tan racional y humano como era posible, pero tan efectivo como era posible en términos de salvar vidas estadounidenses".

Le pregunté si podía recordar algún momento de liderazgo de Bush en el periodo de posguerra.

Entonces pasó a relatar cómo él había enviado "tres o cuatro equipos de evaluación" –uno cada seis meses, o algo así– a Irak para "dar un vistazo de cómo nos estaba yendo".

"Me devuelvo a este punto", dije, "el presidente como un líder en tiempos de guerra, porque esa es la cuestión aquí".

"Él es uno bueno", dijo Rumsfeld. "Es uno muy bueno. Uno lo mira y no sabe cómo lo hace. En este departamento nos movemos en un espectro de 180 grados. Él se mueve 360 grados. Pasa de la investigación en células madre a la inmigración y a otros 15 asuntos en un solo día. Y lo que le llevamos regularmente es complicado. Es nuevo. Y tiene una técnica muy efectiva… Sigue lanzando una pregunta tras otra".

Estaba entendiendo la descripción del estilo Rumsfeld.

"Va conociendo a las personas y evaluándolas", continuaba Rumsfeld, "y viendo cómo manejan esas preguntas y cómo las responden, y cuánto saben y de quién dependen para responderlas. Y así termina aumentando el nivel de confianza, y desarrolla una habilidad para saber qué tanto debe soltarle la rienda a diferentes personas".

"¿Qué tan larga le dejó la rienda a usted?", le pregunté.

"Por Dios santo", respondió. "No me lo pregunte a mí".

"Se lo pregunto".

"No tengo idea", dijo.

Ciertamente, Rumsfeld sabía que Bush le dejaba la rienda bien suelta.

"¿A veces siente un tirón?".

Prefirió no responder.

¿Qué pasaba con la versión de que Cheney era un vicepresidente todo-poderoso que controlaba al presidente?

"No tiene sentido", dijo Rumsfeld. "Es claro que tienen una buena rela-ción. Se puede sentir en el ambiente. Pero el presidente es *el* presidente, y que no quede duda de eso. El vicepresidente no tiene la más ligera confusión en cuanto a eso. Su manejo de los asuntos, cuando el presidente se encuentra en el salón es, en mi opinión, perfecto en el sentido de que no asume posiciones fuertes que puedan ponerlo en contra de él… Hace buenas preguntas. Pero no confronta al presidente ni muestra posición alguna".

Era un comentario revelador. Me preguntaba cómo podrían las pregun-tas o comentarios de Cheney acorralar al presidente o quitarle sus opciones. Presumiblemente, si no tenía sentido que Cheney fuera todopoderoso, no estaría en posición de hacer ninguna de las dos cosas.

Rumsfeld dijo que creía que Cheney era completamente sincero con Bush en privado. "Sabe que una de las ventajas de la cercanía al presidente es la buena voluntad, la carga que viene con ella es la carga de tener que decirle la verdad".

LE PREGUNTÉ A RUMSFELD cuál era el mejor escenario, el más optimista, de un resultado positivo en Irak.

"El asunto está feo", respondió. "Es duro. No hay uno que sea mejor. Un largo y duro golpe, creo que escribí hace algunos años. Estamos enfrentando un conjunto de desafíos que son diferentes de lo que el país comprende… de lo que el Congreso entiende. Son diferentes de lo que nuestro gobierno, gran parte de él, probablemente entiende, y de aquello para cuyo enfrentamiento está entrenado o equipado. Estamos tratando con enemigos que pueden dar vuelta a nuestros círculos de decisión". Dijo que el enemigo podía moverse con rapidez. "Ellos no tienen parlamentos, burocracias y ni un Estado real para defender, interactuar o enfrentar. Pueden hacer lo que les plazca. No tienen que dar cuentas por mentir o por asesinar hombres, mujeres y niños inocentes".

"Hay algo en la política de Estados Unidos que hace aceptable que el enemigo asesine hombres, mujeres y niños inocentes y haga decapitaciones, pero intolerable que un soldado haga algo que no debiera".

"¿Es optimista?", le pregunté.

Rumsfeld me miró inquisitivamente y continuó. Tres de sus asistentes, que estaban sentados con nosotros en la mesa en su oficina, no pudieron evitar demostrar su sorpresa mientras Rumsfeld daba vueltas sin responder.

"Estamos luchando la primera guerra en la historia del nuevo siglo", continuó, "con todas estas nuevas realidades, con una organización de la era industrial, en medio de un ambiente que no se ha adaptado ni ajustado, un ambiente público que no se ha adaptado ni ajustado".

Entre otras cosas, Rumsfeld estaba claramente contrariado por la decisión de la Corte Suprema, de una semana antes, en el caso *Hamdan vs. Rumsfeld*, que disponía que la administración Bush, en efecto, debía respetar el derecho de los sospechosos de terrorismo recluidos en la bahía de Guantánamo, Cuba, a tener abogados y ser enjuiciados. Rumsfeld creía que debían ser interrogados y seguir detenidos para mantenerlos fuera del campo de batalla. La decisión de la Corte fue un gran revés para las ideas de la administración Bush acerca de cómo luchar la guerra contra el terrorismo. En la decisión de 5 contra 3, la alta corte dijo que la administración tenía que adherir al debido proceso.

Varios meses antes, el primero de mayo, Rumsfeld hizo circular un memorando secreto de 6 páginas titulado "Nuevas instituciones y enfoques ilustrativos del siglo XXI".

Casi era una versión más reciente de los memorandos "Cadena del ancla" que había escrito en sus primeros meses como secretario, en el año 2001: un clamor de su corazón burocrático y gerencial. El Departamento de Estado no era el único enredado en la cadena de su ancla; también lo estaban el resto del gobierno de Estados Unidos y el mundo.

Como Andy Card, Rumsfeld era sensible a la acusación de incompetencia. Afirmaba: "La acusación de incompetencia contra el gobierno de Estados Unidos sería fácilmente refutable si el pueblo estadounidense comprendiera cómo el actual sistema de gobierno lleva la idoneidad a niveles casi extremos".

AL FINAL DE LA SEGUNDA ENTREVISTA, cité al ex secretario de Defensa Robert McNamara: "Cualquier comandante militar que sea honesto le dirá que ha cometido errores que han costado vidas".

"Umm", dijo Rumsfeld.

"¿Eso es correcto?".

"No sé. Supongo que un comandante militar…".

"Como lo es usted", lo interrumpí.

"No, no lo soy", dijo el secretario de Defensa.

"Si, señor", le dije.

"No, no. Bueno…".

"Sí, sí", dije levantando mi mano para señalar la jerarquía. "Es comandante en jefe, secretario de Defensa, comandante de combate".

"Puedo ver a un comandante uniformado en medio de un conflicto obligado a tomar decisiones que determinarán la vida o la muerte de personas, y eso podría ser cierto. Y, ciertamente, si se asciende en la cadena por el lado civil hasta el presidente y hasta mí, indirectamente, eliminando dos o tres niveles, podría ser el caso".

¿Indirectamente? ¿Eliminando dos o tres niveles? Era inexplicable. Rumsfeld había insistido mucho acerca de la cadena de mando. Él tenía el control, no los jefes de estado mayor, ni los militares uniformados, ni el Comité para la Seguridad Nacional, ni los críticos, ni la opinión ¿Cómo era posible que no viera su papel y su responsabilidad?

No se me ocurría qué mas decir.

EL 11 DE DICIEMBRE DE 2003, entrevisté al presidente Bush y pude experimentar algo de su estilo y su hábito de negación. Fue ocho meses después de la invasión, y no se habían hallado las armas de destrucción masiva.

"Acerca de las armas de destrucción masiva", le pregunté.

"Seguro", dijo el presidente.

Uno de mis jefes en *The Washington Post* sugirió que le preguntara "¿El presidente fue engañado…".

"No", dijo Bush.

Continué con la pregunta, "…por la inteligencia, o él engañó al país?".

"No".

"No, muy bien", repetí su respuesta.

"La respuesta es absolutamente no".

"¿Qué sucedió?".

"¿Qué quiere decir con 'qué sucedió'?", preguntó Bush, como si no hubiera sido él quien dio todos aquellos discursos acerca de las ADM.

"En términos de armas de destrucción masiva", le expliqué. "Y el caso del 'pan comido'".

El presidente dijo que el informe inicial del inspector de armas David Kay justificaba la idea de que Saddam tenía programas bélicos. "Creo que aún es muy temprano para entender la historia completa. Esto es inteligencia", señaló.

"Ya entiendo", le dije. "No hechos".

"Era inteligencia, lo suficientemente sólida como para que las Naciones Unidas aprobaran varias resoluciones. Tan sólida como para que el presidente Clinton tomara una decisión militar con base en ella", al ordenar el bombardeo de los supuestos sitios de armas de destrucción masiva en Irak en 1998.

"Pero no encontramos ningún arma de destrucción masiva", dije.

"Encontramos programas bélicos que podrían reconstituirse".

"Podrían, estoy de acuerdo".

"Un arma puede salir muy rápido. Y por lo tanto, considerando eso, incluso, si es lo mínimo que se tiene, cómo no actuar, dada la naturaleza de Saddam Hussein", dijo Bush.

Mencioné que mientras viajaba por el país había conversado con estadounidenses que creían que después del 9/11 él había sido abanderado del realismo, al decir que había sido un ataque catastrófico, que los terroristas eran asesinos, y que Estados Unidos tenía en frente una larga batalla. Su renuncia a reconocer que no se había encontrado ninguna arma de destrucción masiva le hacía perder ese carácter de abanderado del realismo.

"No estoy de acuerdo con ese razonamiento", respondió Bush.

"Correcto".

"Saddam Hussein tenía armas, utilizó armas".

"Indudablemente".

"Y el ocultó armas. Ocultó sistemas. Tenía planes", siguió Bush. "Y por lo tanto, la voz del realismo se encuentra aquí mismo. Esa es una mirada realista".

"Y hay que agregar que todavía no las hemos encontrado", le dije.

Rio entre dientes. "Desde mi punto de vista, no quiero que la gente diga: 'Se lo advertimos'. Quiero que la gente sepa que hay un proceso que se desarrolla en una parte muy peligrosa del mundo. Y, francamente, nadie me ha dicho eso, pero usted se mueve en círculos diferentes de los míos. Mucho más selectos".

Le comenté que me refería a la gente de negocios.

"Realismo es ser capaz de entender la naturaleza de Saddam Hussein, su historia, su potencial para ser una amenaza para Estados Unidos".

"Obviamente, no encontramos pozos burbujeantes", dije.

"Bueno", el presidente soltó una risita.

"Pero el informe de la situación, durante los últimos seis o siete meses, es que no hemos encontrado armas. Eso es todo", presioné a Bush.

"Cierto, cierto, cierto".

Bush tardó cinco minutos y 18 segundos para reconocer, simplemente, el *hecho* de que no habían encontrado armas de destrucción masiva.

"La persona que quiere que el presidente se levante y declare eso públicamente es la misma persona que quiere decir que no se debería haber hecho eso", dijo Bush y añadió: "Probablemente, de repente, estoy sonando increíblemente a la defensiva".

Le dije que en mi libro, próximo a salir en el año 2004, abordaría lo que él dijo acerca de la decisión de invadir.

"¿Para qué necesita tratar ese tema en un libro?".

Dije que tenía que hacerlo porque era un asunto importante.

Después quiso estar seguro de que yo había entendido las condiciones de la entrevista, que sus comentarios eran para el libro y no para un artículo de *The Washington Post*. "En otras palabras, que no me vaya a encontrar con un titular que diga: 'Bush afirma que no hay armas'".

Le dije que yo esperaría.

RECORDABA VÍVIDAMENTE que él me había dicho en una entrevista anterior: "Un presidente debe ser el calcio de la columna vertebral". Su retórica de la posguerra en Irak salía directamente de ese libreto del "calcio de la columna vertebral". Su discurso permanentemente optimista –desde "Misión cumplida", pasando por "mantener el rumbo" y "cuando ellos avancen, nosotros nos retiraremos", sus afirmaciones de que seguiría el mismo camino aunque sólo lo apoyaran la primera dama y su perro, su discurso sobre puntos de giro y dar la vuelta a la esquina, y los dardos que sugerían que todo aquel que cuestionara su estrategia en Irak no apoyaba a las tropas y en cambio deseaba que Estados Unidos "atacara y huyera" o "se rindiera a los terroristas"– era lo mismo una y otra vez. Su estrategia era hacer declaraciones repetitivas de optimismo y evitar aceptar cualquier duda.

En la investigación y el reportaje para una serie periodística de *The Washington Post* y para mis dos libros anteriores, acerca de las decisiones de guerra de Bush, lo entrevisté cuatro veces: diciembre de 2001, agosto de 2002 y, finalmente, dos veces en diciembre de 2003. Las transcripciones de las siete horas y media de entrevistas ocupaban cientos de páginas.

Aquéllos eran los días en que Bush era un presidente popular, pasado el 9/11 y durante los nueve primeros meses siguientes a la invasión a Irak. A medida que la guerra se prolongaba, que continuaban muriendo estadounidenses e iraquíes, y los niveles de aprobación de Bush caían dramáticamente en 2005 y 2006, también lo hacían mis oportunidades de conseguir otra entrevista con él.

Pedí repetidamente una oportunidad para hablar con Bush. En febrero de 2006, Dan Bartlett me dijo que él y Hadley seguirían ayudándome pero que probablemente no entrevistaría al presidente. Entrevisté a miembros claves de la administración muchas veces y revisé miles de páginas de documentos. Hasta el verano de 2006, Rumsfeld había conversado conmigo oficialmente durante dos tardes, pero Bartlett y Hadley habían enmudecido y no devolvían mis llamadas.

Supe que, ya en 2005, Hadley se mostraba en contra de una mayor cooperación por parte de la Casa Blanca. Conocía los asuntos y eventos sobre los que yo estaba indagando y el tipo de preguntas que estaba haciendo: ¿Cuál es la estrategia para vencer en Irak? ¿Acaso nadie en la Casa Blanca se daba cuenta de que las acciones ejecutadas sobre el terreno en los meses siguientes a la invasión eran casi diametralmente opuestas al plan que había sido presentado a Bush? ¿Qué le estaba diciendo Rumsfeld a Bush? ¿Qué decidió Bush? ¿Qué descuidó? ¿Cuándo empezó a darse cuenta la administración de que estaba frente a una tarea monumental, y que los combates no habían terminado? ¿Cuándo se dieron cuanta de que probablemente nunca se encontraría arma alguna de destrucción masiva en Irak? ¿Las cosas en Irak, en realidad, son tan buenas como los altos funcionarios civiles y militares del gobierno de Estados Unidos continúan insistiendo públicamente?

"Lo que yo creo es que esto va a ser grandioso", le dijo sarcásticamente Hadley a un colega en octubre de 2005. Mi libro sobre la posguerra en Irak, dijo, sería publicado en 2006, después del libro de Jerry Bremen. "Veremos, entonces; esto va a ser un problema. Vamos a ir a las elecciones para Congreso de 2006 con un debate furibundo contra todo el que diga: 'Estuve con la administración. No habría ido a Irak, pero reconozco lo importante que fue. Y si la administración hubiera tenido un plan, y si hubiera sido mínimamente competente, yo habría seguido con ellos. Pero, obviamente, no la tenían. Esta es una administración incompetente. Irak es lo más importante. Yo apoyo a las tropas. Comprendo la importancia de la misión, pero dada la incompetencia de la administración, como lo demuestran los libros de Bremen y Woodward, no tenemos otra opción más que excluir a los republicanos y traer las tropas a casa'. Es decir, esto va a ser espantoso".

Hadley suspiró. Después retomó el tema, y le dijo a su colega: "Tengo que ayudar a este presidente a atravesar por lo que van a ser tres años verdaderamente borrascosos. Y si los demócratas se toman la Cámara de Representantes y el Senado, eso va a ser algo increíble después de 2006".

El asesor del presidente para la seguridad nacional, naturalmente, quería ganar las elecciones para el Congreso de 2006. Era claro que permitir que el presidente respondiera preguntas acerca de Irak no era compatible con esa meta. La estrategia era la negación.

Con todo su discurso optimista, Bush no le había dicho a la opinión pública de Estados Unidos la verdad acerca de aquello en lo que se había convertido Irak.

NOTA SOBRE LAS FUENTES

CASI TODA LA INFORMACIÓN de este libro proviene de entrevistas con el equipo de seguridad nacional del presidente Bush, sus secretarios y otros funcionarios de alto rango, protagonistas y responsables dentro de la administración de los asuntos militares, diplomáticos y de inteligencia en la Guerra de Irak. Oficiales de varios niveles que trabajan en la Casa Blanca, los departamentos de Estado y de Defensa y en la CIA, con conocimiento de primera mano de las reuniones, documentos y hechos, también fueron fuentes primordiales. La mayoría de estas entrevistas se hicieron bajo reserva, es decir que la información obtenida podía ser usada pero las fuentes no serían identificadas por su nombre a lo largo del libro.

Las entrevistas con varios funcionarios retirados y en ejercicio, como el secretario de Defensa Donald H. Rumsfeld, fueron registradas. El presidente Bush y el vicepresidente Cheney se negaron a ser entrevistados para este libro, por lo que recurrí a material de entrevistas pasadas.

Adicionalmente, recopilé información clave de documentos como memorandos, notas oficiales, notas personales, cartas, conversaciones, resúmenes, actas, correos electrónicos, cronologías y calendarios.

Varias fuentes fueron entrevistadas en diversas ocasiones, por mí o por mi asistente Hill Murió Jr. Entrevisté a varias fuentes media docena de veces. Casi todos nos permitieron grabar las entrevistas, de manera que la historia pudiera contarse de manera más completa y precisa, con el lenguaje exacto que usaron.

Cuando se atribuye un pensamiento, una conclusión o un sentimiento a un participante concreto, los he obtenido de esa persona directamente, de un registro escrito, o de algún colega a quien esa persona lo haya confiado.